CODE OF FEDERAL REGULATIONS

Title 25
Indians

Parts 1 to 299

Revised as of April 1, 2019

Containing a codification of documents of general applicability and future effect

As of April 1, 2019

Published by the Office of the Federal Register
National Archives and Records Administration
as a Special Edition of the Federal Register

Table of Contents

Cite this Code: CFR

To cite the regulations in this volume use title, part and section number. Thus, 25 CFR 1.2 *refers to title 25, part 1, section 2.*

Explanation

The Code of Federal Regulations is a codification of the general and permanent rules published in the Federal Register by the Executive departments and agencies of the Federal Government. The Code is divided into 50 titles which represent broad areas subject to Federal regulation. Each title is divided into chapters which usually bear the name of the issuing agency. Each chapter is further subdivided into parts covering specific regulatory areas.

Each volume of the Code is revised at least once each calendar year and issued on a quarterly basis approximately as follows:

Title 1 through Title 16..as of January 1
Title 17 through Title 27..as of April 1
Title 28 through Title 41..as of July 1
Title 42 through Title 50..as of October 1

The appropriate revision date is printed on the cover of each volume.

LEGAL STATUS

The contents of the Federal Register are required to be judicially noticed (44 U.S.C. 1507). The Code of Federal Regulations is prima facie evidence of the text of the original documents (44 U.S.C. 1510).

HOW TO USE THE CODE OF FEDERAL REGULATIONS

The Code of Federal Regulations is kept up to date by the individual issues of the Federal Register. These two publications must be used together to determine the latest version of any given rule.

To determine whether a Code volume has been amended since its revision date (in this case, April 1, 2019), consult the "List of CFR Sections Affected (LSA)," which is issued monthly, and the "Cumulative List of Parts Affected," which appears in the Reader Aids section of the daily Federal Register. These two lists will identify the Federal Register page number of the latest amendment of any given rule.

EFFECTIVE AND EXPIRATION DATES

Each volume of the Code contains amendments published in the Federal Register since the last revision of that volume of the Code. Source citations for the regulations are referred to by volume number and page number of the Federal Register and date of publication. Publication dates and effective dates are usually not the same and care must be exercised by the user in determining the actual effective date. In instances where the effective date is beyond the cut-off date for the Code a note has been inserted to reflect the future effective date. In those instances where a regulation published in the Federal Register states a date certain for expiration, an appropriate note will be inserted following the text.

OMB CONTROL NUMBERS

The Paperwork Reduction Act of 1980 (Pub. L. 96–511) requires Federal agencies to display an OMB control number with their information collection request.

Many agencies have begun publishing numerous OMB control numbers as amendments to existing regulations in the CFR. These OMB numbers are placed as close as possible to the applicable recordkeeping or reporting requirements.

PAST PROVISIONS OF THE CODE

Provisions of the Code that are no longer in force and effect as of the revision date stated on the cover of each volume are not carried. Code users may find the text of provisions in effect on any given date in the past by using the appropriate List of CFR Sections Affected (LSA). For the convenience of the reader, a "List of CFR Sections Affected" is published at the end of each CFR volume. For changes to the Code prior to the LSA listings at the end of the volume, consult previous annual editions of the LSA. For changes to the Code prior to 2001, consult the List of CFR Sections Affected compilations, published for 1949-1963, 1964-1972, 1973-1985, and 1986-2000.

"[RESERVED]" TERMINOLOGY

The term "[Reserved]" is used as a place holder within the Code of Federal Regulations. An agency may add regulatory information at a "[Reserved]" location at any time. Occasionally "[Reserved]" is used editorially to indicate that a portion of the CFR was left vacant and not accidentally dropped due to a printing or computer error.

INCORPORATION BY REFERENCE

What is incorporation by reference? Incorporation by reference was established by statute and allows Federal agencies to meet the requirement to publish regulations in the Federal Register by referring to materials already published elsewhere. For an incorporation to be valid, the Director of the Federal Register must approve it. The legal effect of incorporation by reference is that the material is treated as if it were published in full in the Federal Register (5 U.S.C. 552(a)). This material, like any other properly issued regulation, has the force of law.

What is a proper incorporation by reference? The Director of the Federal Register will approve an incorporation by reference only when the requirements of 1 CFR part 51 are met. Some of the elements on which approval is based are:

(a) The incorporation will substantially reduce the volume of material published in the Federal Register.

(b) The matter incorporated is in fact available to the extent necessary to afford fairness and uniformity in the administrative process.

(c) The incorporating document is drafted and submitted for publication in accordance with 1 CFR part 51.

What if the material incorporated by reference cannot be found? If you have any problem locating or obtaining a copy of material listed as an approved incorporation by reference, please contact the agency that issued the regulation containing that incorporation. If, after contacting the agency, you find the material is not available, please notify the Director of the Federal Register, National Archives and Records Administration, 8601 Adelphi Road, College Park, MD 20740-6001, or call 202-741-6010.

CFR INDEXES AND TABULAR GUIDES

A subject index to the Code of Federal Regulations is contained in a separate volume, revised annually as of January 1, entitled CFR INDEX AND FINDING AIDS. This volume contains the Parallel Table of Authorities and Rules. A list of CFR titles, chapters, subchapters, and parts and an alphabetical list of agencies publishing in the CFR are also included in this volume.

An index to the text of "Title 3—The President" is carried within that volume.

The Federal Register Index is issued monthly in cumulative form. This index is based on a consolidation of the "Contents" entries in the daily Federal Register.

A List of CFR Sections Affected (LSA) is published monthly, keyed to the revision dates of the 50 CFR titles.

REPUBLICATION OF MATERIAL

There are no restrictions on the republication of material appearing in the Code of Federal Regulations.

INQUIRIES

For a legal interpretation or explanation of any regulation in this volume, contact the issuing agency. The issuing agency's name appears at the top of odd-numbered pages.

For inquiries concerning CFR reference assistance, call 202–741–6000 or write to the Director, Office of the Federal Register, National Archives and Records Administration, 8601 Adelphi Road, College Park, MD 20740-6001 or e-mail *fedreg.info@nara.gov.*

SALES

The Government Publishing Office (GPO) processes all sales and distribution of the CFR. For payment by credit card, call toll-free, 866-512-1800, or DC area, 202-512-1800, M-F 8 a.m. to 4 p.m. e.s.t. or fax your order to 202-512-2104, 24 hours a day. For payment by check, write to: US Government Publishing Office – New Orders, P.O. Box 979050, St. Louis, MO 63197-9000.

ELECTRONIC SERVICES

The full text of the Code of Federal Regulations, the LSA (List of CFR Sections Affected), The United States Government Manual, the Federal Register, Public Laws, Public Papers of the Presidents of the United States, Compilation of Presidential Documents and the Privacy Act Compilation are available in electronic format via *www.govinfo.gov*. For more information, contact the GPO Customer Contact Center, U.S. Government Publishing Office. Phone 202-512-1800, or 866-512-1800 (toll-free). E-mail, *ContactCenter@gpo.gov.*

The Office of the Federal Register also offers a free service on the National Archives and Records Administration's (NARA) World Wide Web site for public law numbers, Federal Register finding aids, and related information. Connect to NARA's web site at *www.archives.gov/federal-register.*

The e-CFR is a regularly updated, unofficial editorial compilation of CFR material and Federal Register amendments, produced by the Office of the Federal Register and the Government Publishing Office. It is available at *www.ecfr.gov.*

OLIVER A. POTTS,
Director,
Office of the Federal Register
April 1, 2019.

THIS TITLE

Title 25—INDIANS is composed of two volumes. The parts in these volumes are arranged in the following order: Parts 1—299, and part 300 to end. The contents of these volumes represent all current regulations codified under this title of the CFR as of April 1, 2019.

For this volume, Stephen J. Frattini was Chief Editor. The Code of Federal Regulations publication program is under the direction of John Hyrum Martinez.

Title 25—Indians

(This book contains parts 1 to 299)

CHAPTER I—BUREAU OF INDIAN AFFAIRS, DEPARTMENT OF THE INTERIOR

SUBCHAPTER A—PROCEDURES AND PRACTICE

SUBCHAPTER B—LAW AND ORDER

SUBCHAPTER C—PROBATE

SUBCHAPTER D—HUMAN SERVICES

SUBCHAPTER E—EDUCATION

SUBCHAPTER A—PROCEDURES AND PRACTICE

PART 1—APPLICABILITY OF RULES OF THE BUREAU OF INDIAN AFFAIRS

AUTHORITY: 5 U.S.C. 301; R.S. 463, 25 U.S.C. 2.

§ 1.1 [Reserved]

§ 1.2 Applicability of regulations and reserved authority of the Secretary of the Interior.

The regulations in chapter I of title 25 of the Code of Federal Regulations are of general application. Notwithstanding any limitations contained in the regulations of this chapter, the Secretary retains the power to waive or make exceptions to his regulations as found in chapter I of title 25 CFR in all cases where permitted by law and the Secretary finds that such waiver or exception is in the best interest of the Indians.

[25 FR 3124, Apr. 12, 1960]

§ 1.3 Scope.

Chapters I and II of this title contain the bulk of the regulations of the Department of the Interior of general application relating to Indian affairs. Subtitle B, chapter I, title 43 of the Code or Federal Regulations contains rules relating to the relationship of Indians to public lands and townsites. Subtitle A of title 43 CFR has application to certain aspects of Indian affairs and, among other things, contains procedural rules for appellate and other administrative review and for practice before the Department of the Interior, of which the Bureau of Indian Affairs is a part. Indian health matters are covered in 42 CFR part 36. Title 30 CFR contains regulations on oil and gas and other mining operations, which, under certain circumstances, may be applicable to Indian resources.

[25 FR 3124, Apr. 12, 1960, as amended at 40 FR 20625, May 12, 1975; 48 FR 13414, Mar. 31, 1983]

§ 1.4 State and local regulation of the use of Indian property.

(a) Except as provided in paragraph (b) of this section, none of the laws, ordinances, codes, resolutions, rules or other regulations of any State or political subdivision thereof limiting, zoning or otherwise governing, regulating, or controlling the use or development of any real or personal property, including water rights, shall be applicable to any such property leased from or held or used under agreement with and belonging to any Indian or Indian tribe, band, or community that is held in trust by the United States or is subject to a restriction against alienation imposed by the United States.

(b) The Secretary of the Interior or his authorized representative may in specific cases or in specific geographic areas adopt or make applicable to Indian lands all or any part of such laws, ordinances, codes, resolutions, rules or other regulations referred to in paragraph (a) of this section as he shall determine to be in the best interest of the Indian owner or owners in achieving the highest and best use of such property. In determining whether, or to what extent, such laws, ordinances, codes, resolutions, rules or other regulations shall be adopted or made applicable, the Secretary or his authorized representative may consult with the Indian owner or owners and may consider the use of, and restrictions or limitations on the use of, other property in the vicinity, and such other factors as he shall deem appropriate.

[30 FR 7520, June 9, 1965]

§ 1.10 Availability of forms.

Forms upon which applications and related documents may be filed and upon which rights and privileges may be granted may be inspected and procured at the Bureau of Indian Affairs, Washington, DC, and at the office of any Area Director or Agency Superintendent.

[25 FR 3124, Apr. 12, 1960]

PART 2—APPEALS FROM ADMINISTRATIVE ACTIONS

Sec.

AUTHORITY: R.S. 463, 465; 5 U.S.C. 301, 25 U.S.C. 2, 9.

SOURCE: 54 FR 6480, Feb. 10, 1989, unless otherwise noted.

§ 2.1 Information collection.

In accordance with Office of Management and Budget regulations in 5 CFR 1320.3(c), approval of information collections contained in this regulation is not required.

§ 2.2 Definitions.

Appeal means a written request for review of an action or the inaction of an official of the Bureau of Indian Affairs that is claimed to adversely affect the interested party making the request.

Appellant means any interested party who files an appeal under this part.

Interested party means any person whose interests could be adversely affected by a decision in an appeal.

Legal holiday means a Federal holiday as designated by the President or the Congress of the United States.

Notice of appeal means the written document sent to the official designated in this part, indicating that a decision is being appealed (see § 2.9).

Person includes any Indian or non-Indian individual, corporation, tribe or other organization.

Statement of reasons means a written document submitted by the appellant explaining why the decision being appealed is in error (see § 2.10).

[54 FR 6480, Feb. 10, 1989; 54 FR 7666, Feb. 22, 1989]

§ 2.3 Applicability.

(a) Except as provided in paragraph (b) of this section, this part applies to all appeals from decisions made by officials of the Bureau of Indian Affairs by persons who may be adversely affected by such decisions.

(b) This part does not apply if any other regulation or Federal statute provides a different administrative appeal procedure applicable to a specific type of decision.

§ 2.4 Officials who may decide appeals.

The following officials may decide appeals:

(a) An Area Director, if the subject of appeal is a decision by a person under the authority of that Area Director.

(b) An Area Education Programs Administrator, Agency Superintendent for Education, President of a Post-Secondary School, or the Deputy to the Assistant Secretary—Indian Affairs/Director (Indian Education Programs), if the appeal is from a decision by an Office of Indian Education Programs (OIEP) official under his/her jurisdiction.

(c) The Assistant Secretary—Indian Affairs pursuant to the provisions of § 2.20 of this part.

(d) A Deputy to the Assistant Secretary—Indian Affairs pursuant to the provisions of § 2.20(c) of this part.

(e) The Interior Board of Indian Appeals, pursuant to the provisions of 43 CFR part 4, subpart D, if the appeal is from a decision made by an Area Director or a Deputy to the Assistant Secretary—Indian Affairs other than the Deputy to the Assistant Secretary—Indian Affairs/Director (Indian Education Programs).

§2.5 Appeal bond.

(a) If a person believes that he/she may suffer a measurable and substantial financial loss as a direct result of the delay caused by an appeal, that person may request that the official before whom the appeal is pending require the posting of a reasonable bond by the appellant adequate to protect against that financial loss.

(b) A person requesting that a bond be posted bears the burden of proving the likelihood that he/she may suffer a measurable and substantial financial loss as a direct result of the delay caused by the appeal.

(c) In those cases in which the official before whom an appeal is pending determines that a bond is necessary to protect the financial interests of an Indian or Indian tribe, that official may require the posting of a bond on his/her own initiative.

(d) Where the official before whom an appeal is pending requires a bond to be posted or denies a request that a bond be posted, he/she shall give notice of his/her decision pursuant to §2.7.

§2.6 Finality of decisions.

(a) No decision, which at the time of its rendition is subject to appeal to a superior authority in the Department, shall be considered final so as to constitute Departmental action subject to judicial review under 5 U.S.C. 704, unless when an appeal is filed, the official to whom the appeal is made determines that public safety, protection of trust resources, or other public exigency requires that the decision be made effective immediately.

(b) Decisions made by officials of the Bureau of Indian Affairs shall be effective when the time for filing a notice of appeal has expired and no notice of appeal has been filed.

(c) Decisions made by the Assistant Secretary—Indian Affairs shall be final for the Department and effective immediately unless the Assistant Secretary—Indian Affairs provides otherwise in the decision.

[54 FR 6480, Feb. 10, 1989; 54 FR 7666, Feb. 22, 1989]

§2.7 Notice of administrative decision or action.

(a) The official making a decision shall give all interested parties known to the decisionmaker written notice of the decision by personal delivery or mail.

(b) Failure to give such notice shall not affect the validity of the decision or action but the time to file a notice of appeal regarding such a decision shall not begin to run until notice has been given in accordance with paragraph (c) of this section.

(c) All written decisions, except decisions which are final for the Department pursuant to §2.6(c), shall include a statement that the decision may be appealed pursuant to this part, identify the official to whom it may be appealed and indicate the appeal procedures, including the 30-day time limit for filing a notice of appeal.

[54 FR 6480, Feb. 10, 1989; 54 FR 7666, Feb. 22, 1989]

§2.8 Appeal from inaction of official.

(a) A person or persons whose interests are adversely affected, or whose ability to protect such interests is impeded by the failure of an official to act on a request to the official, can make the official's inaction the subject of appeal, as follows:

(1) Request in writing that the official take the action originally asked of him/her;

(2) Describe the interest adversely affected by the official's inaction, including a description of the loss, impairment or impediment of such interest caused by the official's inaction;

(3) State that, unless the official involved either takes action on the merits of the written request within 10 days of receipt of such request by the official, or establishes a date by which action will be taken, an appeal shall be filed in accordance with this part.

(b) The official receiving a request as specified in paragraph (a) of this section must either make a decision on the merits of the initial request within 10 days from receipt of the request for a decision or establish a reasonable later date by which the decision shall be made, not to exceed 60 days from the date of request. If an official establishes a date by which a requested decision shall be made, this date shall be the date by which failure to make a decision shall be appealable under this part. If the official, within the 10-day period specified in paragraph (a) of this section, neither makes a decision on the merits of the initial request nor establishes a later date by which a decision shall be made, the official's inaction shall be appealable to the next official in the process established in this part.

[54 FR 6480, Feb. 10, 1989; 54 FR 7666, Feb. 22, 1989]

§2.9 Notice of an appeal.

(a) An appellant must file a written notice of appeal in the office of the official whose decision is being appealed. The appellant must also send a copy of the notice of appeal to the official who will decide the appeal and to all known interested parties. The notice of appeal must be filed in the office of the official whose decision is being appealed within 30 days of receipt by the appellant of the notice of administrative action described in §2.7. A notice of appeal that is filed by mail is considered filed on the date that it is postmarked. The burden of proof of timely filing is on the appellant. No extension of time shall be granted for filing a notice of appeal. Notices of appeal not filed in the specified time shall not be considered, and the decision involved shall be considered final for the Department and effective in accordance with §2.6(b).

(b) When the appellant is an Indian or Indian tribe not represented by counsel, the official who issued the decision appealed shall, upon request of the appellant, render such assistance as is appropriate in the preparation of the appeal.

(c) The notice of appeal shall:

(1) Include name, address, and phone number of appellant.

(2) Be clearly labeled or titled with the words "NOTICE OF APPEAL."

(3) Have on the face of any envelope in which the notice is mailed or delivered, in addition to the address, the clearly visible words "NOTICE OF APPEAL."

(4) Contain a statement of the decision being appealed that is sufficient to permit identification of the decision.

(5) If possible, attach either a copy of the notice of the administrative decision received under §2.7, or when an official has failed to make a decision or take any action, attach a copy of the appellant's request for a decision or action under §2.8 with a written statement that the official failed to make a decision or take any action or to establish a date by which a decision would be made upon the request.

(6) Certify that copies of the notice of appeal have been served on interested parties, as prescribed in §2.12(a).

§2.10 Statement of reasons.

(a) A statement of reasons shall be filed by the appellant in every appeal, and shall be accompanied by or otherwise incorporate all supporting documents.

(b) The statement of reasons may be included in or filed with the notice of appeal.

(c) If the statement of reasons is not filed with the notice of appeal, the appellant shall file a separate statement of reasons in the office of the official whose decision is being appealed within 30 days after the notice of appeal was filed in that office.

(d) The statement of reasons whether filed with the notice of appeal or filed separately should:

(1) Be clearly labeled "STATEMENT OF REASONS".

(2) Have on the face of any envelope in which the statement of reasons is mailed or delivered, in addition to the address, the clearly visible words "STATEMENT OF REASONS".

[54 FR 6480, Feb. 10, 1989; 54 FR 7666, Feb. 22, 1989]

§2.11 Answer of interested party.

(a) Any interested party wishing to participate in an appeal proceeding should file a written answer responding to the appellant's notice of appeal and statement of reasons. An answer should describe the party's interest.

(b) An answer shall state the party's position or response to the appeal in any manner the party deems appropriate and may be accompanied by or otherwise incorporate supporting documents.

(c) An answer must be filed within 30 days after receipt of the statement of reasons by the person filing an answer.

(d) An answer and any supporting documents shall be filed in the office of the official before whom the appeal is pending as specified in §2.13.

(e) An answer should:

(1) Be clearly labelled or titled with the words "ANSWER OF INTERESTED PARTY."

(2) Have on the face of any envelope in which the answer is mailed or delivered, in addition to the address, the clearly visible words "ANSWER OF INTERESTED PARTY," and

(3) Contain a statement of the decision being appealed that is sufficient to permit identification of the decision.

§2.12 Service of appeal documents.

(a) Persons filing documents in an appeal must serve copies of those documents on all other interested parties known to the person making the filing. A person serving a document either by mail or personal delivery must, at the time of filing the document, also file a written statement certifying service on each interested party, showing the document involved, the name and address of the party served, and the date of service.

(b) If an appeal is filed with the Interior Board of Indian Appeals, a copy of the notice of appeal shall also be sent to the Assistant Secretary—Indian Affairs. The notice of appeal sent to the Interior Board of Indian Appeals shall certify that a copy has been sent to the Assistant Secretary—Indian Affairs.

(c) If the appellant is an Indian or Indian tribe not represented by counsel, the official with whom the appeal is filed (i.e., official making the decision being appealed) shall, in the manner prescribed in this section, personally or by mail serve a copy of all appeal documents on the official who will decide the appeal and on each interested party known to the official making such service.

(d) Service of any document under this part shall be by personal delivery or by mail to the record address as specified in §2.14. Service on a tribe shall be to the principal or designated tribal official or to the governing body.

(e) In all cases where a party is represented by an attorney in an appeal, service of any document on the attorney is service on the party represented. Where a party is represented by more than one attorney, service on any one attorney is sufficient. The certificate of service on an attorney shall include the name of the party whom the attorney represents and indicate that service was made on the attorney representing that party.

(f) When an official deciding an appeal determines that there has not been service of a document affecting a person's interest, the official shall either serve the document on the person or direct the appropriate legal counsel to serve the document on the person and allow the person an opportunity to respond.

[54 FR 6480, Feb. 10, 1989; 54 FR 7666, Feb. 22, 1989]

§2.13 Filing documents.

(a) An appeal document is properly filed with an official of the Bureau of Indian Affairs:

(1) By personal delivery during regular business hours to the person designated to receive mail in the immediate office of the official, or

(2) By mail to the facility officially designated for receipt of mail addressed to the official; the document is considered filed by mail on the date that it is postmarked.

(b) Bureau of Indian Affairs offices receiving a misdirected appeal document shall forward the document to the proper office promptly. If a person delivers an appeal document to the wrong office or mails an appeal document to an incorrect address, no extension of time should be allowed because of the time necessary for a Bureau office to redirect the document to the correct address.

(c) Notwithstanding any other provision of this section, an official deciding an appeal shall allow late filing of a misdirected document, including a notice of appeal, where the official finds that the misdirection is the fault of the government.

§ 2.14 Record address.

(a) Every interested party who files a document in connection with an appeal shall, when he/she files the document, also indicate his/her address. Thereafter, any change of address shall be promptly reported to the official with whom the previous address was filed. The most current address on file under this subsection shall be deemed the proper address for all purposes under this part.

(b) The successors in interest of a party shall also promptly inform the official specified in paragraph (a) of this section of their interest in the appeal and their address.

(c) An appellant or interested party failing to file an address or change of address as specified in this section may not object to lack of notice or service attributable to his/her failure to indicate a new address.

§ 2.15 Computation of time.

In computing any period of time prescribed or allowed in this part, calendar days shall be used. Computation shall not include the day on which a decision being appealed was made, service or notice was received, a document was filed, or other event occurred causing time to begin to run. Computation shall include the last day of the period, unless it is a Saturday, a Sunday, or a legal holiday, in which event the period runs until the end of the next day which is not a Saturday, a Sunday, or a legal holiday.

§ 2.16 Extensions of time.

An official to whom an appeal is made may, upon a showing of good cause by a party and with notice to all other parties, extend the period for filing or serving any document; *provided*, however, that no extension will be granted for filing a notice of appeal under § 2.9 of this part or serve by itself to extend any period specified by law or regulation other than in this part.

§ 2.17 Summary dismissal.

(a) An appeal under this part will be dismissed if the notice of appeal is not filed within the time specified in § 2.9(a).

(b) An appeal under this part may be subject to summary dismissal for the following causes:

(1) If after the appellant is given an opportunity to amend them, the appeal documents do not state the reasons why the appellant believes the decision being appealed is in error, or the reasons for the appeal are not otherwise evident in the documents, or

(2) If the appellant has been required to post a bond and fails to do so.

§ 2.18 Consolidation of appeals.

Separate proceedings pending before one official under this part and involving common questions of law or fact may be consolidated by the official conducting such proceedings, pursuant to a motion by any party or on the initiative of the official.

§ 2.19 Action by Area Directors and Education Programs officials on appeal.

(a) Area Directors, Area Education Programs Administrators, Agency Superintendents for Education, Presidents of Post-Secondary Schools and the Deputy to the Assistant Secretary—Indian Affairs/Director (Indian Education Programs) shall render written decisions in all cases appealed to them within 60 days after all time for pleadings (including all extensions granted) has expired. The decision shall include a statement that the decision may be appealed pursuant to this part, identify the official to whom it may be appealed and indicate the appeal procedures, including the 30-day time limit for filing a notice of appeal.

(b) A copy of the decision shall be sent to the appellant and each known interested party by certified or registered mail, return receipt requested. Such receipts shall become a permanent part of the record.

§ 2.20 Action by the Assistant Secretary—Indian Affairs on appeal.

(a) When a decision is appealed to the Interior Board of Indian Appeals, a copy of the notice of appeal shall be sent to the Assistant Secretary—Indian Affairs.

(b) The notice of appeal sent to the Interior Board of Indian Appeals shall certify that a copy has been sent to the Assistant Secretary—Indian Affairs.

(c) In accordance with the provisions of §4.332(b) of title 43 of the Code of Federal Regulations, a notice of appeal to the Board of Indian Appeals shall not be effective until 20 days after receipt by the Board, during which time the Assistant Secretary—Indian Affairs shall have authority to decide to:

(1) Issue a decision in the appeal, or

(2) Assign responsibility to issue a decision in the appeal to a Deputy to the Assistant Secretary—Indian Affairs.

The Assistant Secretary—Indian Affairs will not consider petitions to exercise this authority. If the Assistant Secretary—Indian Affairs decides to issue a decision in the appeal or to assign responsibility to issue a decision in the appeal to a Deputy to the Assistant Secretary—Indian Affairs, he/she shall notify the Board of Indian Appeals, the deciding official, the appellant, and interested parties within 15 days of his/her receipt of a copy of the notice of appeal. Upon receipt of such notification, the Board of Indian Appeals shall transfer the appeal to the Assistant Secretary—Indian Affairs. The decision shall be signed by the Assistant Secretary—Indian Affairs or a Deputy to the Assistant Secretary—Indian Affairs within 60 days after all time for pleadings (including all extensions granted) has expired. If the decision is signed by the Assistant Secretary—Indian Affairs, it shall be final for the Department and effective immediately unless the Assistant Secretary—Indian Affairs provides otherwise in the decision. Except as otherwise provided in §2.20(g), if the decision is signed by a Deputy to the Assistant Secretary—Indian Affairs, it may be appealed to the Board of Indian Appeals pursuant to the provisions of 43 CFR part 4, subpart D.

(d) A copy of the decision shall be sent to the appellant and each known interested party by certified or registered mail, return receipt requested. Such receipts shall become a permanent part of the record.

(e) If the Assistant Secretary—Indian Affairs or the Deputy to the Assistant Secretary—Indian Affairs to whom the authority to issue a decision has been assigned pursuant to §2.20(c) does not make a decision within 60 days after all time for pleadings (including all extensions granted) has expired, any party may move the Board of Indian Appeals to assume jurisdiction subject to 43 CFR 4.337(b). A motion for Board decision under this section shall invest the Board with jurisdiction as of the date the motion is received by the Board.

(f) When the Board of Indian Appeals, in accordance with 43 CFR 4.337(b), refers an appeal containing one or more discretionary issues to the Assistant Secretary—Indian Affairs for further consideration, the Assistant Secretary—Indian Affairs shall take action on the appeal consistent with the procedures in this section.

(g) The Assistant Secretary—Indian Affairs shall render a written decision in an appeal from a decision of the Deputy to the Assistant Secretary—Indian Affairs/Director (Indian Education Programs) within 60 days after all time for pleadings (including all extensions granted) has expired. A copy of the decision shall be sent to the appellant and each known interested party by certified or registered mail, return receipt requested. Such receipts shall become a permanent part of the record. The decision shall be final for the Department and effective immediately unless the Assistant Secretary—Indian Affairs provides otherwise in the decision.

§2.21 Scope of review.

(a) When a decision has been appealed, any information available to the reviewing official may be used in reaching a decision whether part of the record or not.

(b) When the official deciding an appeal believes it appropriate to consider documents or information not contained in the record on appeal, the official shall notify all interested parties of the information and they shall be given not less than 10 days to comment on the information before the appeal is decided. The deciding official shall include in the record copies of documents or a description of the information used in arriving at the decision. Except where disclosure of the actual documents used may be prohibited by law, copies of the information shall be made available to the parties upon request and at their expense.

PART 5—PREFERENCE IN EMPLOYMENT

Sec.

AUTHORITY: 4 Stat. 737, 25 U.S.C. 43; 22 Stat. 88, 25 U.S.C. 46; 28 Stat. 313, 25 U.S.C. 44; 24 Stat. 389, 25 U.S.C. 348; and 48 Stat. 986, 25 U.S.C. 472 and 479.

§ 5.1 Definitions.

For purposes of making appointments to vacancies in all positions in the Bureau of Indian Affairs a preference will be extended to persons of Indian descent who are:

(a) Members of any recognized Indian tribe now under Federal Jurisdiction;

(b) Descendants of such members who were, on June 1, 1934, residing within the present boundaries of any Indian reservation;

(c) All others of one-half or more Indian blood of tribes indigenous to the United States;

(d) Eskimos and other aboriginal people of Alaska; and

(e) For one (1) year or until the Osage Tribe has formally organized, whichever comes first, effective January 5, 1989, a person of at least one-quarter degree Indian ancestry of the Osage Tribe of Indians, whose rolls were closed by an act of Congress.

[43 FR 2393, Jan. 17, 1978. Redesignated at 47 FR 13327, Mar. 30, 1982, as amended at 54 FR 283, Jan. 5, 1989]

§ 5.2 Appointment actions.

(a) Preference will be afforded a person meeting any one of the standards of § 5.1 whether the appointment involves initial hiring, reinstatement, transfer, reassignment or promotion.

(b) Preference eligibles may be given a Schedule A excepted appointment under Exception Number 213.3112(a)(7). However, if the individuals are within reach on a Civil Service Register, they may be given a competitive appointment.

[43 FR 2393, Jan. 17, 1978. Redesignated at 47 FR 13327, Mar. 30, 1982, as amended at 49 FR 12702, Mar. 30, 1984]

§ 5.3 Application procedure for preference eligibility.

(a) Proof of eligibility must be submitted with the person's application for a position.

(b) In order for a person to be considered a preference eligible according to the standards of § 5.1, they must submit proof of membership, descendancy or degree of Indian ancestry as indicated on rolls or records acceptable to the Secretary.

[43 FR 2393, Jan. 17, 1978. Redesignated at 47 FR 13327, Mar. 30, 1982]

§ 5.4 Information collection.

The Office of Management and Budget has informed the Department of the Interior that the information collection requirements contained in part 5 need not be reviewed by them under the Paperwork Reduction Act (44 U.S.C. 3501 *et seq.*).

[54 FR 283, Jan. 5, 1989]

SUBCHAPTER B—LAW AND ORDER

PART 10—INDIAN COUNTRY DETENTION FACILITIES AND PROGRAMS

AUTHORITY: 5 U.S.C. 301; 25 U.S.C. 2, 9, 13, 2417, 2453, and 2802.

SOURCE: 61 FR 34374, July 2, 1996, unless otherwise noted.

§ 10.1 Why are policies and standards needed for Indian country detention programs?

Policies and standards are required to ensure that all Bureau of Indian Affairs (BIA) and tribal entities that receive Federal funding for the operation, maintenance, design and construction or renovation of detention facilities, community residential, or holding facilities are supporting constitutional rights and are complying with the Indian Law Enforcement Reform Act of 1990. Self-governance tribes and tribes with limited jurisdiction are encouraged to follow the regulations in this part, and other BIA manuals and handbooks. The provision for funding tribes for detention programs under the Indian Alcohol and Substance Abuse Prevention and Treatment Act, Public Law 99–570, (25 U.S.C. 2453) requires standards and procedures for such facilities.

[61 FR 34374, July 2, 1996; 61 FR 65473, Dec. 13, 1996]

§ 10.2 Who is responsible for developing and maintaining the policies and standards for detention and holding facilities in Indian country?

The Director, Office of Law Enforcement Services who reports to the Deputy Commissioner of Indian Affairs, BIA, establishes policies, procedures, and standards for the operations, design, planning, maintenance, renovation, and construction of detention programs in the BIA and by tribal contract under Indian Self-Determination and Education Assistance Act, Public Law 93–638, as amended, 25 U.S.C. 450.

§ 10.3 Who must follow these policies and standards?

You must follow these minimum policies, standards, and guides if you are part of the BIA or tribal detention or rehabilitation program receiving Federal funding. Self-governance tribes and tribes with limited jurisdiction are encouraged to follow the regulations in this part, and other BIA manuals and handbooks. Detention officers, guards, cooks and other staff conducting business in the facilities must meet minimum standards of law enforcement personnel as prescribed in 25 CFR part 12, subpart D, "Qualifications and Training Requirements." Those tribal programs not receiving Federal funding under the Indian Self-Determination and Education Assistance Act (Public Law 93–638, as amended) who wish to be accredited are encouraged to use the policies and standards in that part since they have been modified and approved for Indian country.

§ 10.4 What happens if the policies and standards are not followed?

The risk for human and civil rights violations due to lack of common standards will subject the operation and/or facility to unnecessary exposure to liability. Lack of employee standards, particularly for training and background checks, will increase the risk of misconduct and vicarious liability of the tribes and the Federal government through tort claims. Funding sources for detention programs may become scarce to nonexistent because of contract noncompliance. The tribes' opportunity to receive funding from potential resource sharing agreements with other law enforcement agencies may be damaged because the facility may have to be closed for cause due to violation of the life safety codes.

§ 10.5 Where can I find the policies and standards for the administration, operation, services, and physical plant/construction of Indian country detention, community residential, and holding facilities?

The Bureau of Indian Affairs, Department of the Interior, maintains a manual of policies and procedures called the *Bureau of Indian Affairs Manual (BIAM).* The chapter 69 BIAM titled "Indian Country Detention Facilities and Programs," contains the BIA's policies, procedures, and standards for detention and holding programs in Indian country. The standards for the programs within the *BIAM* are in handbook format for easy field reference and use. Copies of the chapter 69 *BIAM* and handbooks may be obtained from the Director, Office of Law Enforcement Services.

[61 FR 34374, July 2, 1996; 61 FR 65473, Dec. 13, 1996]

§ 10.6 How is the BIA assured that the policies and standards are being applied uniformly and facilities are properly accredited?

The tribes and BIA programs will use a phased approach to meeting all non-mandatory detention standards and will document progress on uniform reporting. The BIA Office of Law Enforcement Services will conduct periodic operational evaluations for oversight.

§ 10.7 Where do I find help or receive technical assistance in complying with the policies and standards?

The BIA has a trained Detention Specialist on the staff of the Office of Law Enforcement Services, Albuquerque, New Mexico, who is available to conduct evaluations and provide technical assistance or guidance in all facets of Indian country detention programs.

§ 10.8 What minimum records must be kept and reports made at each detention, community residential, or holding facility in Indian country?

The Director, Office of Law Enforcement Services, BIA, will develop all necessary requirements for maintaining records, reporting data, and archiving information. These requirements will be published in 69 BIAM, "Indian Country Detention Facilities and Programs."

[61 FR 34374, July 2, 1996; 61 FR 65473, Dec. 13, 1996]

§ 10.9 If a person is detained or incarcerated in an Indian country detention, community residential, or holding facility, how would they know what their rights, privileges, safety, protection and expected behavior would be?

When an individual is incarcerated in an Indian country detention, community residential, or holding facility, he/she will be given, or in some cases notified of the availability of, an Inmate Handbook. This book of guidelines describes in detail the inmate's rights, privileges, protection and safety, cleanliness and sanitation, and general health and nutritional standards. The Inmate Handbook describes the emergency evacuation procedures, medical, counseling, rehabilitation services, visitation procedures, and other appropriate information. The Inmate Handbook is published by the Director, Office of Law Enforcement Services and maintained by the detention facility administrator at each facility location.

[61 FR 34374, July 2, 1996; 61 FR 65473, Dec. 13, 1996]

§ 10.10 What happens if I believe my civil rights have been violated while incarcerated in an Indian country detention or holding facility?

All allegations of civil rights violations must be reported immediately to the Internal Affairs Branch of the Office of Law Enforcement Services. This office will ensure that such allegations are immediately reported to the Civil Rights Division of the U.S. Department of Justice through established procedures. The BIA Internal Affairs Branch may also investigate alleged violations and make recommendations for additional action as necessary. Detailed instructions on the procedure to report violations can be found in the Inmate Handbook.

§ 10.11 How would someone detained or incarcerated, or their representative, get the BIA policies and standards?

At each detention, community residential, or holding facility located in a tribal jurisdiction where federal funds are used for operations or maintenance programs, the BIA's policies, standards, and procedures will be made available upon request. The Inmate Handbook will be made available to all persons at the time they are incarcerated or detained in a facility. There may be times when this may be delayed due to the physical or mental condition of the person at time of incarceration. In these cases, the Inmate Handbook will be made available when the person is deemed receptive and cognizant by the detention officer in charge. All policies, standards, procedures, and guidelines are available at each facility to the public or by writing to the Director, Office of Law Enforcement Services.

[61 FR 34374, July 2, 1996; 61 FR 65473, Dec. 13, 1996]

PART 11—COURTS OF INDIAN OFFENSES AND LAW AND ORDER CODE

Subpart A—Application; Jurisdiction

Sec.

Subpart B—Courts of Indian Offenses; Personnel; Administration

Subpart C—Criminal Procedure

Subpart D—Criminal Offenses

Subpart E—Civil Actions

Subpart F—Domestic Relations

Subpart G—Probate Proceedings

Subpart H—Appellate Proceedings

Subpart I—Children's Court

Subpart J—Juvenile Offender Procedure

Subpart K—Minor-in-Need-of-Care Procedure

Subpart L—Child protection and domestic violence procedures

AUTHORITY: 5 U.S.C. 301; R.S. 463, 25 U.S.C. 2; R.S. 465, 25 U.S.C. 9; 42 Stat. 208, 25 U.S.C. 13; 38 Stat. 586, 25 U.S.C. 200.

SOURCE: 58 FR 54411, Oct. 21, 1993, unless otherwise noted.

Subpart A—Application; Jurisdiction

SOURCE: 73 FR 39859, July 11, 2008, unless otherwise noted.

§11.100 Where are Courts of Indian Offenses established?

(a) Unless indicated otherwise in this title, these Courts of Indian Offenses are established and the regulations in this part apply to the Indian country (as defined in 18 U.S.C. 1151 and by Federal court precedent) occupied by the following tribes:

(1) Santa Fe Indian School Property, including the Santa Fe Indian Health Hospital, and the Albuquerque Indian School Property (land held in trust for the 19 Pueblos of New Mexico);

(2) Skull Valley Band of Goshutes Indians (Utah);

(3) Te-Moak Band of Western Shoshone Indians (Nevada);

(4) Tribes located in the former Oklahoma Territory (Oklahoma) that are listed in paragraph (b) of this section;

(5) Tribes located in the former Indian Territory (Oklahoma) that are listed in paragraph (c) of this section;

(6) Ute Mountain Ute Tribe (Colorado); and

(7) Winnemucca Indian Tribe.

(b) This part applies to the following tribes located in the former Oklahoma Territory (Oklahoma):

(1) Apache Tribe of Oklahoma;

(2) Caddo Nation of Oklahoma;

(3) Comanche Nation (except Comanche Children's Court);

(4) Delaware Nation;

(5) Fort Sill Apache Tribe of Oklahoma;

(6) Kiowa Indian Tribe of Oklahoma;

(7) Otoe-Missouria Tribe of Indians; and

(8) Wichita and Affiliated Tribe of Indians.

(c) This part applies to the following tribes located in the former Indian Territory (Oklahoma):

(1) Eastern Shawnee Tribe of Oklahoma;

(2) Modoc Tribe of Oklahoma;

(3) Ottawa Tribe of Oklahoma;

(4) Peoria Tribe of Indians of Oklahoma; and

(5) Seneca-Cayuga Tribe of Oklahoma.

(d) This part applies to the Indian country (as defined in 18 U.S.C. 1151 and by Federal precedent) within the exterior boundaries of the Wind River Reservation in Wyoming.

[78 FR 14020, Mar. 4, 2013, as amended at 81 FR 74677, Oct. 27, 2016]

§ 11.102 What is the purpose of this part?

It is the purpose of the regulations in this part to provide adequate machinery for the administration of justice for Indian tribes in those areas of Indian country where tribes retain jurisdiction over Indians that is exclusive of State jurisdiction but where tribal courts have not been established to exercise that jurisdiction.

§ 11.104 When does this part apply?

(a) The regulations in this part continue to apply to each tribe listed in § 11.100 until either:

(1) BIA and the tribe enter into a contract or compact for the tribe to provide judicial services; or

(2) The tribe has put into effect a law-and-order code that establishes a court system and that meets the requirements of paragraph (b) of this section.

(b) When a tribe adopts a legal code and establishes a judicial system, the tribe must notify the Assistant Secretary—Indian Affairs or his or her designee. The law-and-order code must be adopted by the tribe in accordance with its constitution and by-laws or other governing documents.

§ 11.106 Who is an Indian for purposes of this part?

For the purposes of the enforcement of the regulations in this part, an Indian is defined as a person who is a member of an Indian tribe which is recognized by the Federal Government as eligible for services from the BIA, and any other individual who is an "Indian" for the purposes of 18 U.S.C. 1152–1153.

§ 11.108 How are tribal ordinances affected by this part?

The governing body of each tribe occupying the Indian country over which a Court of Indian Offenses has jurisdiction may enact ordinances which, when approved by the Assistant Secretary—Indian Affairs or his or her designee:

(a) Are enforceable in the Court of Indian Offenses having jurisdiction over the Indian country occupied by that tribe; and

(b) Supersede any conflicting regulation in this part.

§ 11.110 How are tribal customs affected by this part?

Each Court of Indian Offenses shall apply the customs of the tribe occupying the Indian country over which it has jurisdiction to the extent that they are consistent with the regulations of this part.

§ 11.112 [Reserved]

§ 11.114 What is the criminal jurisdiction of the Court of Indian Offenses?

(a) Except as otherwise provided in this title, each Court of Indian Offenses has jurisdiction over any action by an Indian (hereafter referred to as person) that is made a criminal offense under this part and that occurred within the Indian country subject to the court's jurisdiction.

(b) No person may be prosecuted, tried or punished for any offense unless the complaint is filed within 5 years after the offense is committed.

§ 11.116 What is the civil jurisdiction of a Court of Indian Offenses?

(a) Except as otherwise provided in this title, each Court of Indian Offenses has jurisdiction over any civil action arising within the territorial jurisdiction of the court in which:

(1) The defendant is an Indian; or

(2) Other claims, provided at least one party is an Indian.

(b) Any civil action commenced in a Court of Indian Offenses is barred unless the complaint is filed within 3 years after the right of action first accrues.

§ 11.118 What are the jurisdictional limitations of the Court of Indian Offenses?

(a) A Court of Indian Offenses may exercise over a Federal or State official only the same jurisdiction that it could exercise if it were a tribal court. The jurisdiction of Courts of Indian Offenses does not extend to Federal or State employees acting within the scope of their employment.

(b) A Court of Indian Offenses may not adjudicate an election dispute, take jurisdiction over a suit against a tribe, or adjudicate any internal tribal government dispute, unless the relevant tribal governing body passes a resolution, ordinance, or referendum granting the court jurisdiction.

(c) In deciding who is a tribal official, BIA will give deference to a decision of the Court of Indian Offenses, acting as a tribal forum by resolution or ordinance of a tribal governing body under paragraph (b) of this section.

(d) A tribe may not be sued in a Court of Indian Offenses unless its tribal governing body explicitly waives its tribal immunity by tribal resolution or ordinance.

Subpart B—Courts of Indian Offenses; Personnel; Administration

§ 11.200 What is the composition of the Court of Indian Offenses?

(a) Each court shall be composed of a trial division and an appellate division.

(b) A chief magistrate will be appointed for each court who will, in addition to other judicial duties, be responsible for the administration of the court and the supervision of all court personnel.

(c) Appeals must be heard by a panel of magistrates who were not involved at the tribal/trial level.

(d) Decisions of the appellate division are final and are not subject to administrative appeals within the Department of the Interior.

[58 FR 54411, Oct. 21, 1993, as amended at 73 FR 39860, July 11, 2008]

§ 11.201 How are magistrates for the Court of Indian Offenses appointed?

(a) Each magistrate shall be appointed by the Assistant Secretary—Indian Affairs or his or her designee subject to confirmation by a majority vote of the tribal governing body of the tribe occupying the Indian country over which the court has jurisdiction, or, in the case of multi-tribal courts, confirmation by a majority of the tribal governing bodies of the tribes under the jurisdiction of a Court of Indian Offenses.

(b) Each magistrate shall hold office for a period of four years, unless sooner removed for cause or by reason of the abolition of the office, but is eligible for reappointment.

(c) No person is eligible to serve as a magistrate of a Court of Indian Offenses who has ever been convicted of a felony or, within one year of the date of service or application, of a misdemeanor.

(d) No magistrate shall be qualified to act as such wherein he or she has any direct conflicting interest, real or apparent.

(e) A tribal governing body may set forth such other qualifications for magistrates of the Court of Indian Offenses as it deems appropriate, subject to the approval of the Assistant Secretary—Indian Affairs, or his or her designee.

(f) A tribal governing body may also recommend requirements for the training of magistrates of the Court of Indian Offenses to the Assistant Secretary—Indian Affairs.

§ 11.202 How is a magistrate of the Court of Indian Offenses removed?

Any magistrate of a Court of Indian Offenses may be suspended, dismissed or removed by the Assistant Secretary—Indian Affairs, or his or her designee, for cause, upon the written recommendation of the tribal governing body, and, in the case of multi-tribal courts, upon the recommendation of a majority of the tribal governing bodies of the tribes under the jurisdiction of a Court of Indian Offenses, or pursuant to his or her own discretion.

§ 11.203 How are the clerks of the Court of Indian Offenses appointed and what are their duties?

(a) Except as may otherwise be provided in a contract with the tribe occupying the Indian country over which the court has jurisdiction, the chief magistrate shall appoint a clerk of court for the Court of Indian Offenses within his or her jurisdiction, subject to the superintendent's approval.

(b) The clerk shall render assistance to the court, to local law enforcement officers and to individual members of the tribe in the drafting of complaints, subpoenas, warrants, commitments, and other documents incidental to the functions of the court. The clerk shall also attend and keep a record of all proceedings of the court and manage all monies received by the court.

(c) The clerk of court shall forward any monies received on judgments due to the person, agency, or corporation to which entitled, within 30 days unless directed otherwise by a magistrate of the Court of Indian Offenses.

§ 11.204 Prosecutors.

Except as may otherwise be provided in a contract with the tribe occupying the Indian country over which the court has jurisdiction, the superintendent shall appoint a prosecutor for each Court of Indian Offenses within his or her jurisdiction.

§ 11.205 Are there standards for the appearance of attorneys and lay counselors?

(a) No defendant in a criminal proceeding shall be denied the right to counsel.

(b) The chief magistrate shall prescribe in writing standards governing the admission and practice in the Court of Indian Offenses of professional attorneys and lay counselors.

§ 11.206 Is the Court of Indian Offenses a court of record?

(a) Each Court of Indian Offenses shall keep a record of all proceedings of the court containing the title of the case, the names of the parties, the complaint, all pleadings, the names and addresses of all witnesses, the date of any hearing or trial, the name of any magistrate conducting such hearing or trial, the findings of the court or jury, the judgment and any other information the court determines is important to the case.

(b) The record in each case shall be available for inspection by the parties to the case.

(c) Except for cases in which a juvenile is a party or the subject of a proceeding, and for cases whose records have been sealed by the court, all case records shall be available for inspection by the public.

(d) Such court records are part of the records of the BIA agency having jurisdiction over the Indian country where the Court of Indian Offenses is located and shall be protected in accordance with 44 U.S.C. 3102.

§ 11.207 What are the responsibilities of Bureau of Indian Affairs employees?

(a) No employee of the BIA may obstruct, interfere with, or control the functions of any Court of Indian Offenses, or influence such functions in any manner except as permitted by Federal statutes or the regulations in this part or in response to a request for advice or information from the court.

(b) Employees of the BIA shall assist the court, upon its request, in the preparation and presentation of facts in the case and in the proper treatment of individual offenders.

§ 11.208 May Individual Indian Money accounts be used for payment of judgments?

(a) Any Court of Indian Offenses may make application to the superintendent who administers the individual Indian money account of a defendant who has failed to satisfy a money judgment from the court to obtain payment of the judgment from funds in the defendant's account. The court shall certify the record of the case to the superintendent. If the superintendent so directs, the disbursing agent shall pay over to the injured party the amount of the judgment or such lesser amount as may be specified by the superintendent.

(b) A judgment of a Court of Indian Offenses shall be considered a lawful debt in all proceedings held by the Department of the Interior or by a Court of Indian Offenses to distribute decedents' estates.

§ 11.209 How does the Court of Indian Offenses dispose of fines?

All money fines imposed for the commission of an offense shall be in the nature of an assessment for the payment of designated court expenses. The fines assessed shall be paid over by the clerk of the court to the disbursing agent of the reservation for deposit as a "special deposit, court funds" to the disbursing agent's official credit in the Treasury of the United States. The disbursing agent shall withdraw such funds, in accordance with existing regulations, upon order of the clerk of the court signed by a judge of the court for the payment of specified expenses. The disbursing agent and the clerk of the court shall keep an account of all such deposits and withdrawals available for public inspection.

Subpart C—Criminal Procedure

§11.300 Complaints.

(a) A complaint is a written statement of the essential facts charging that a named individual(s) has committed a particular offense. All criminal prosecutions shall be initiated by a complaint filed with the court by a law enforcement officer and sworn to by a person having personal knowledge of the offense.

(b) Complaints shall contain:

(1) The signature of the complaining witness, or witnesses, sworn before a magistrate, a court clerk, a prosecutor, or any law enforcement officer.

(2) A written statement by the complaining witness or witnesses having personal knowledge of the violation, describing in ordinary language the nature of the offense committed including the time and place as nearly as may be ascertained.

(3) The name or description of the person alleged to have committed the offense.

(4) A description of the offense charged and the section of the code allegedly violated.

(c) Complaints must be submitted without unnecessary delay by a law enforcement officer to the prosecutor and, if he or she approves, to a judge to determine whether an arrest warrant or summons should be issued.

(d) When an accused has been arrested without a warrant, a complaint shall be filed forthwith with the court for review as to whether probable cause exists to hold the accused, and in no instance shall a complaint be filed later than at the time of arraignment.

§11.301 Arrests.

(a) Arrest is the taking of a person into police custody in order that he or she may be held to answer for a criminal offense.

(b) No law enforcement officer shall arrest any person for a criminal offense except when:

(1) The officer shall have a warrant signed by a magistrate commanding the arrest of such person, or the officer knows for a certainty that such a warrant has been issued; or

(2) The offense shall occur in the presence of the arresting officer; or

(3) The officer shall have probable cause to believe that the person arrested has committed an offense.

§11.302 Arrest warrants.

(a) Each magistrate of a Court of Indian Offenses shall have the authority to issue warrants to apprehend any person the magistrate has probable cause to believe has committed a criminal offense in violation of the regulations under this part based on a written complaint filed with the court by a law enforcement officer and bearing the signature of the complainant.

(b) The arrest warrant shall contain the following information:

(1) Name or description and address, if known, of the person to be arrested.

(2) Date of issuance of the warrant.

(3) Description of the offense charged.

(4) Signature of the issuing magistrate.

(c) Such warrants may be served only by a BIA or tribal police officer or other officer commissioned to enforce the regulations of this part.

§11.303 Notification of rights prior to custodial interrogation.

Prior to custodial interrogation, the suspect shall be advised of the following rights:

(a) That he or she has the right to remain silent.

(b) That any statements made by him or her may be used against him or her in court.

(c) That he or she has the right to obtain counsel and, if indigent, to have counsel appointed for him/her.

§ 11.304 Summons in lieu of warrant.

(a) When otherwise authorized to arrest a suspect, a law enforcement officer or a magistrate may, in lieu of a warrant, issue a summons commanding the accused to appear before the Court of Indian Offenses at a stated time and place and answer to the charge.

(b) The summons shall contain the same information as a warrant, except that it may be signed by a police officer.

(c) The summons shall state that if a defendant fails to appear in response to a summons, a warrant for his or her arrest shall be issued.

(d) The summons, together with a copy of the complaint, shall be served upon the defendant by delivering a copy to the defendant personally or by leaving a copy at his or her usual residence or place of business with any person 18 years of age or older who also resides or works there. Service shall be made by an authorized law enforcement officer, who shall file with the record of the case a form indicating when the summons was served.

§ 11.305 Search warrants.

(a) Each magistrate of a Court of Indian Offenses shall have the authority to issue a warrant for the search of premises and for the seizure of physical evidence of a criminal violation under the regulations of this part located within the Indian country over which the court has jurisdiction.

(b) No warrant for search or seizure may be issued unless it is based on a written and signed statement establishing, to the satisfaction of the magistrate, that probable cause exists to believe that the search will lead to discovery of evidence of a criminal violation under the regulations of this part.

(c) No warrant for search or seizure shall be valid unless it contains the name or description of the person, vehicle, or premises to be searched, describes the evidence to be seized, and bears the signature of the magistrate who issued it.

(d) Warrants may be executed only by a BIA or tribal police officer or other official commissioned to enforce the regulations under this part. The executing officer shall return the warrant to the Court of Indian Offenses within the time limit shown on the face of the warrant, which in no case shall be longer than ten (10) days from the date of issuance. Warrants not returned within such time limits shall be void.

§ 11.306 Search without a warrant.

No law enforcement officer shall conduct any search without a valid warrant except:

(a) Incident to making a lawful arrest; or

(b) With the voluntary consent of the person being searched; or

(c) When the search is of a moving vehicle and the officer has probable cause to believe that it contains contraband, stolen property, or property otherwise unlawfully possessed.

§ 11.307 Disposition of seized property.

(a) The officer serving and executing a warrant shall make an inventory of all seized property, and a copy of such inventory shall be left with every person from whom property is seized.

(b) A hearing shall be held by the Court of Indian Offenses to determine the disposition of all seized property. Upon satisfactory proof of ownership, the property shall be delivered immediately to the owner, unless such property is contraband or is to be used as evidence in a pending case. Property seized as evidence shall be returned to the owner after final judgment. Property confiscated as contraband shall be destroyed or otherwise lawfully disposed of as ordered by the Court of Indian Offenses.

§ 11.308 Commitments.

No person may be detained, jailed or imprisoned under the regulations of this part for longer than 48 hours unless the Court of Indian Offenses issues a commitment bearing the signature of a magistrate. A temporary commitment shall be issued for each person held before trial. A final commitment shall be issued for each person sentenced to jail after trial.

§ 11.309 Arraignments.

(a) Arraignment is the bringing of an accused before the court, informing him or her of his or her rights and of the charge(s) against him or her, receiving the plea, and setting conditions of pretrial release as appropriate in accordance with this part.

(b) Arraignment shall be held in open court without unnecessary delay after the accused is taken into custody and in no instance shall arraignment be later than the next regular session of court.

(c) Before an accused is required to plead to any criminal charges the magistrate shall:

(1) Read the complaint to the accused and determine that he or she understands it and the section(s) of this part that he or she is charged with violating, including the maximum authorized penalty; and

(2) Advise the accused that he or she has the right to remain silent, to be tried by a jury if the offense charged is punishable by imprisonment, to be represented by counsel (which shall be paid for by the government if the accused is indigent) and that the arraignment will be postponed should he or she desire to consult with counsel.

(d) The magistrate shall call upon the defendant to plead to the charge:

(1) If the accused pleads "not guilty" to the charge, the magistrate shall then inform the accused of the trial date and set conditions for release prior to trial.

(2) If the accused pleads "guilty" to the charge, the magistrate shall accept the plea only if he or she is satisfied that the plea is made voluntarily and that the accused understands the consequences of the plea, including the rights waived by the plea. The magistrate may then impose sentence or defer sentencing for a reasonable time in order to obtain any information he or she deems necessary for the imposition of a just sentence. The accused shall be afforded an opportunity to be heard by the court prior to sentencing.

(3) If the accused refuses to plead, the judge shall enter a plea of "not guilty" on his or her behalf.

(e) The court may, in its discretion, allow a defendant to withdraw a plea of guilty if it appears that the interest of justice would be served by doing so.

§11.310 Bail.

(a) Each person charged with a criminal offense under this part shall be entitled to release from custody pending trial under whichever one or more of the following conditions is deemed necessary to reasonably assure the appearance of the person at any time lawfully required:

(1) Release on personal recognizance upon execution by the accused of a written promise to appear at trial and all other lawfully required times;

(2) Release to the custody of a designated person or organization agreeing to assure the accused's appearance;

(3) Release with reasonable restrictions on the travel, association, or place of residence of the accused during the period of release;

(4) Release after deposit of a bond or other sufficient collateral in an amount specified by the magistrate or a bail schedule;

(5) Release after execution of a bail agreement by two responsible members of the community; or

(6) Release upon any other condition deemed reasonably necessary to assure the appearance of the accused as required.

(b) Any law enforcement officer authorized to do so by the court may admit an arrested person to bail pending trial pursuant to a bail schedule and conditions prepared by the court.

(c) A convicted person may be released from custody pending appeal on such conditions as the magistrate determines will reasonably assure the appearance of the accused unless the magistrate determines that release of the accused is likely to pose a danger to the community, the accused, or any other person.

(d) The Court of Indian Offenses may revoke its release of the defendant and order him or her committed at any time where it determines that the conditions of release will not reasonably assure the appearance of the defendant, or if any conditions of release have been violated.

§11.311 Subpoenas.

(a) Upon request of any party, the court shall issue subpoenas to compel the testimony of witnesses, or the production of books, records, documents or any other physical evidence relevant to the determination of the case and not an undue burden on the person possessing the evidence. The clerk of the court may act on behalf of the court and issue subpoenas which have been signed either by the clerk of the court or by a magistrate of the Court of Indian Offenses and which are to be served within Indian country over which the Court of Indian Offenses has jurisdiction.

(b) A subpoena shall bear the signature of the chief magistrate of the Court of Indian Offenses, and it shall state the name of the court, the name of the person or description of the physical evidence to be subpoenaed, the title of the proceeding, and the time and place where the witness is to appear or the evidence is to be produced.

(c) A subpoena may be served at any place but any subpoena to be served outside of the Indian country over which the Court of Indian Offenses has jurisdiction shall be issued personally by a magistrate of the Court of Indian Offenses.

(d) A subpoena may be served by any law enforcement officer or other person appointed by the court for such purpose. Service of a subpoena shall be made by delivering a copy of it to the person named or by leaving a copy at his or her place of residence or business with any person 18 years of age or older who also resides or works there.

(e) Proof of service of the subpoena shall be filed with the clerk of the court by noting on the back of the subpoena the date, time and place that it was served and noting the name of the person to whom it was delivered. Proof of service shall be signed by the person who actually served the subpoena.

(f) In the absence of a justification satisfactory to the court, a person who fails to obey a subpoena may be deemed to be in contempt of court and a bench warrant may be issued for his or her arrest.

§ 11.312 Witness fees.

(a) Each fact witness answering a subpoena is entitled to a fee of not less than the hourly minimum wage scale established by 29 U.S.C. 206(a)(1) and any of its subsequent revisions, plus actual cost of travel. Each fact witness testifying at a hearing shall receive pay for a full day (eight hours) plus travel allowance.

(b) The Court of Indian Offenses may order any party calling a witness to testify without a subpoena to compensate the witness for actual traveling and living expenses incurred in testifying.

(c) If the Court of Indian Offenses finds that a complaint was not filed in good faith but with a frivolous or malicious intent, it may order the complainant to reimburse the court for expenditures incurred under this section, and such order may constitute a judgment upon which execution may levy.

§ 11.313 Trial procedure.

(a) The time and place of court sessions, and all other details of judicial procedure shall be set out in rules of court approved by the chief magistrate of the Court of Indian Offenses.

(b) Courts of Indian Offenses shall be bound by the Federal Rules of Evidence, except insofar as such rules are superseded by order of the court or by the existence of inconsistent tribal rules of evidence.

§ 11.314 Jury trials.

(a) A defendant has a right, upon demand, to a jury trial in any criminal case:

(1) That is punishable by a maximum sentence of one year incarceration; or

(2) In which the prosecutor informs the court before the case comes to trial that a jail sentence will be sought.

(b) If the prosecutor informs the court that no sentence of incarceration will be sought, the court may not impose a sentence of incarceration for the offense.

(c) A jury must consist of not less than six residents of the vicinity in which trial is held, selected from a list of eligible jurors prepared each year by the court.

(1) An eligible juror must:

(i) Be at least 18 years of age;

(ii) Not have been convicted of a felony; and

(iii) Be otherwise qualified according to standards established by the Court of Indian Offenses under its general rulemaking authority.

(2) Any party may challenge without cause a maximum of three members of the jury panel chosen under this section.

(d) The magistrate shall instruct the jury with regard to the applicable law and the jury shall decide all questions of fact on the basis of the law.

(e) The jury shall deliberate in secret and return a verdict of guilty or not guilty. Six out of the eight jurors must concur to render a verdict.

(f) Each juror who serves on a jury is entitled to a fee not less than the hourly minimum wage scale established by 29 U.S.C. 206(a)(1), and any of its subsequent revisions, plus mileage not to exceed the maximum rate per mile established by the Federal Government of jurors and witnesses. Each juror shall receive pay for a full day (eight hours) for any portion of a day served, plus travel allowance.

[58 FR 54411, Oct. 21, 1993, as amended at 73 FR 39861, July 11, 2008]

§ 11.315 Sentencing.

(a) Any person who has been convicted in a Court of Indian Offenses of a criminal offense under the regulations of this part may be sentenced to one or a combination of the following penalties:

(1) Imprisonment for a period up to the maximum permitted by the section defining the offense, but in no case for longer than one year; and

(2) A fine in an amount up to the maximum permitted by the section defining the offense, but in no case greater than $5,000.

(b) In addition to or in lieu of the penalties provided in paragraph (a) of this section, the court may require a convicted offender who has inflicted injury upon the person or property of another to make restitution or compensate the injured person by means of the surrender of property, payment of money damages, or the performance of any other act for the benefit of the injured party.

(c) If, solely because of indigence, a convicted offender is unable to pay forthwith a money fine assessed under any applicable section, the court shall allow him or her a reasonable period of time to pay the entire sum or allow him or her to make reasonable installment payments to the clerk of the court at specified intervals until the entire sum is paid. If the offender defaults on such payments the court may find him or her in contempt of court and imprison him or her accordingly.

[58 FR 54411, Oct. 21, 1993, as amended at 73 FR 39861, July 11, 2008]

§ 11.316 Probation.

(a) Where a sentence of imprisonment has been imposed on a convicted offender, the Court of Indian Offenses may, in its discretion, suspend the serving of such sentence and release the person on probation under any reasonable conditions deemed appropriate by the court, provided that the period of probation shall not exceed one year.

(b) Any person who violates the terms of his or her probation may be required by the court to serve the sentence originally imposed or such part of it as the court may determine to be suitable giving consideration to all the circumstances, provided that such revocation of probation shall not be ordered without a hearing before the court at which the offender shall have the opportunity to explain his or her actions.

§ 11.317 Parole.

(a) Any person sentenced by the court of detention or labor shall be eligible for parole at such time and under such reasonable conditions as set by the Court of Indian Offenses.

(b) Any person who violates the conditions of his or her parole may be required by the court to serve the whole original sentence, provided that such revocation or parole shall not be ordered without a hearing before the court at which the offender shall have the opportunity to explain his or her actions.

§ 11.318 Extradition.

Any Court of Indian Offenses may order delivery to the proper state, tribal or BIA law enforcement authorities of any person found within the jurisdiction of the court, who is charged with an offense in another jurisdiction. Prior to delivery to the proper officials, the accused shall be accorded a right to contest the propriety of the court's order in a hearing before the court.

Subpart D—Criminal Offenses

§ 11.400 Assault.

(a) A person is guilty of assault if he or she:

(1) Attempts to cause or purposely, knowingly or recklessly causes bodily injury to another; or

(2) Negligently causes bodily injury to another with a deadly weapon; or

(3) Attempts by physical menace to put another in fear of imminent serious bodily injury.

(b) Assault is a misdemeanor unless committed in a fight or scuffle entered into by mutual consent, in which case it is a petty misdemeanor.

§ 11.401 Recklessly endangering another person.

A person commits a misdemeanor if he or she recklessly engages in conduct which places or may place another person in danger of death or serious bodily injury. Recklessness and danger shall be presumed where a person knowingly points a firearm at or in the direction of another person, whether or not the actor believed the firearm to be loaded.

[58 FR 54411, Oct. 21, 1993; 58 FR 58729, Nov. 3, 1993]

§ 11.402 Terroristic threats.

A person is guilty of a misdemeanor if he or she threatens to commit any crime of violence with purpose to terrorize another or to cause evacuation of a building, place of assembly or facility of public transportation, or otherwise to cause serious public inconvenience or in reckless disregard of the risk of causing such terror or inconvenience.

§ 11.403 Unlawful restraint.

A person commits a misdemeanor if he or she knowingly:

(a) Restrains another unlawfully in circumstances exposing him or her to risk of serious bodily injury; or

(b) Holds another in a condition of involuntary servitude.

§ 11.404 False imprisonment.

A person commits a misdemeanor if he or she knowingly restrains another unlawfully so as to interfere substantially with his or her liberty.

§ 11.405 Interference with custody.

(a) *Custody of children.* A person commits a misdemeanor if he or she knowingly or recklessly takes or entices any child under the age of 18 from the custody of his or her parent, guardian or other lawful custodian, when he or she has no privilege to do so.

(b) *Custody of committed person.* A person is guilty of a misdemeanor if he or she knowingly or recklessly takes or entices any committed person away from lawful custody when he or she does not have the privilege to do so. *Committed person* means, in addition to anyone committed under judicial warrant, any orphan, neglected or delinquent child, mentally defective or insane person, or other dependent or incompetent person entrusted to another's custody by or through a recognized social agency or otherwise by authority of law.

§ 11.406 Criminal coercion.

(a) A person is guilty of criminal coercion if, with purpose to unlawfully restrict another's freedom of action to his or her detriment, he or she threatens to:

(1) Commit any criminal offense; or

(2) Accuse anyone of a criminal offense; or

(3) Take or withhold action as an official, or cause an official to take or withhold action.

(b) Criminal coercion is classified as a misdemeanor.

§ 11.407 Sexual assault.

(a) A person who has sexual contact with another person not his or her spouse, or causes such other person to have sexual contact with him or her, is guilty of sexual assault as a misdemeanor, if:

(1) He or she knows that the conduct is offensive to the other person; or

(2) He or she knows that the other person suffers from a mental disease or

defect which renders him or her incapable of appraising the nature or his or her conduct; or

(3) He or she knows that the other person is unaware that a sexual act is being committed; or

(4) The other person is less than 10 years old; or

(5) He or she has substantially impaired the other person's power to appraise or control his or her conduct, by administering or employing without the other's knowledge drugs, intoxicants or other means for the purpose of preventing resistance; or

(6) The other person is less than 16 years old and the actor is at least four years older than the other person; or

(7) The other person is less than 21 years old and the actor is his or her guardian or otherwise responsible for general supervision of his or her welfare; or

(8) The other person is in custody of law or detained in a hospital or other institution and the actor has supervisory or disciplinary authority over him or her.

(b) Sexual contact is any touching of the sexual or other intimate parts of the person for the purpose of arousing or gratifying sexual desire, or for the purpose of abusing, humiliating, harassing, or degrading the victim.

§11.408 Indecent exposure.

A person commits a misdemeanor if he or she exposes his or her genitals under circumstances in which he or she knows his or her conduct is likely to cause affront or alarm.

§11.409 Reckless burning or exploding.

A person commits a misdemeanor if he or she purposely starts a fire or causes an explosion, whether on his or her property or another's, and thereby recklessly:

(a) Places another person in danger of death or bodily injury; or

(b) Places a building or occupied structure of another in danger of damage or destruction.

§11.410 Criminal mischief.

(a) A person is guilty of criminal mischief if he or she:

(1) Damages tangible property of another purposely, recklessly, or by negligence in the employment of fire, explosives, or other dangerous means; or

(2) Purposely or recklessly tampers with tangible property of another so as to endanger person or property; or

(3) Purposely or recklessly causes another to suffer pecuniary loss by deception or threat.

(b) Criminal mischief is a misdemeanor if the actor purposely causes pecuniary loss in excess of $100, or a petty misdemeanor if he or she purposely or recklessly causes pecuniary loss in excess of $25. Otherwise, criminal mischief is a violation.

§11.411 Criminal trespass.

(a) A person commits an offense if, knowing that he or she is not licensed or privileged to do so, he or she enters or surreptitiously remains in any building or occupied structure. An offense under this subsection is a misdemeanor if it is committed in a dwelling at night. Otherwise it is a petty misdemeanor.

(b) A person commits an offense if, knowing that he or she is not licensed or privileged to do so, he or she enters or remains in any place as to which notice against trespass is given by:

(1) Actual communication to the actor; or

(2) Posting in a manner prescribed by law or reasonably likely to come to the attention of intruders; or

(3) Fencing or other enclosure manifestly designed to exclude intruders.

(c) An offense under this section constitutes a petty misdemeanor if the offender defies an order to leave personally communicated to him or her by the owner of the premises or other authorized person. Otherwise it is a violation.

§11.412 Theft.

A person who, without permission of the owner, shall take, shoplift, possess or exercise unlawful control over movable property not his or her own or under his or her control with the purpose to deprive the owner thereof or who unlawfully transfers immovable property of another or any interest therein with the purpose to benefit himself or herself or another not entitled thereto shall be guilty of theft, a misdemeanor.

§ 11.413 Receiving stolen property.

A person is guilty of receiving stolen property, a misdemeanor, if he or she purposely receives, retains, or disposes of movable property of another knowing that it has been stolen, or believing that it has probably been stolen, unless the property is received, retained, or disposed with purpose to restore it to the owner. *Receiving* means acquiring possession, control or title, or lending on the security of the property.

§ 11.414 Embezzlement.

A person who shall, having lawful custody of property not his or her own, appropriate the same to his or her own use, with intent to deprive the owner thereof, shall be guilty of embezzlement, a misdemeanor.

§ 11.415 Fraud.

A person who shall by willful misrepresentation or deceit, or by false interpreting, or by the use of false weights or measures obtain any money or other property, shall be guilty of fraud, a misdemeanor.

§ 11.416 Forgery.

(a) A person is guilty of forgery, a misdemeanor, if, with purpose to defraud or injure anyone, or with knowledge that he or she is facilitating fraud or injury to be perpetrated by anyone, he or she:

(1) Alters, makes, completes, authenticates, issues or transfers any writing of another without his or her authority; or

(2) Utters any writing which he or she knows to be forged in a manner above specified.

(b) "Writing" includes printing or any other method of recording information, money, coins, tokens, stamps, seals, credit cards, badges, trademarks, and other symbols of value, right, privilege, or identification.

§ 11.417 Extortion.

A person who shall willfully, by making false charges against another person or by any other means whatsoever, extort or attempt to extort any moneys, goods, property, or anything else of any value, shall be guilty of extortion, a misdemeanor.

§ 11.418 Misbranding.

A person who shall knowingly and willfully misbrand or alter any brand or mark on any livestock of another person, shall be guilty of a misdemeanor.

§ 11.419 Unauthorized use of automobiles and other vehicles.

A person commits a misdemeanor if he or she operates another person's automobile, airplane, motorcycle, motorboat, or other motor-propelled vehicle without consent of the owner. It is an affirmative defense to prosecution under this section that the actor reasonably believed that the owner would have consented to the operation had he or she known of it.

§ 11.420 Tampering with records.

A person commits a misdemeanor if, knowing that he or she has no privilege to do so, he or she falsifies, destroys, removes or conceals any writing or record, with purpose to deceive or injure anyone or to conceal any wrongdoing.

§ 11.421 Bad checks.

(a) A person who issues or passes a check or similar sight order for the payment of money, knowing that it will not be honored by the drawee, commits a misdemeanor.

(b) For the purposes of this section, an issuer is presumed to know that the check or order would not be paid, if:

(1) The issuer had no account with the drawee at the time the check or order was issued; or

(2) Payment was refused by the drawee for lack of funds, upon presentation within 30 days after issue, and the issuer failed to make good within 10 days after receiving notice of that refusal.

§ 11.422 Unauthorized use of credit cards.

(a) A person commits a misdemeanor if he or she uses a credit card for the purpose of obtaining property or services with knowledge that:

(1) The card is stolen or forged; or

(2) The card has been revoked or cancelled; or

(3) For any other reason his or her use of the card is unauthorized by the issuer.

(b) *Credit card* means a writing or other evidence of an undertaking to pay for property or services delivered or rendered to or upon the order of a designated person or bearer.

§11.423 Defrauding secured creditors.

A person commits a misdemeanor if he or she destroys, conceals, encumbers, transfers or otherwise deals with property subject to a security interest with purpose to hinder that interest.

§11.424 Neglect of children.

(a) A parent, guardian, or other person supervising the welfare of a child under 18 commits a misdemeanor if he or she knowingly endangers the child's welfare by violating a duty of care, protection or support.

(b) A parent, guardian, or other person supervising the welfare of a child under 18 commits a violation if he or she neglects or refuses to send the child to school.

§11.425 Persistent non-support.

A person commits a misdemeanor if he or she persistently fails to provide support which he or she can provide and which he or she knows he or she is legally obliged to provide to a spouse, child or other dependent.

§11.426 Bribery.

(a) A person is guilty of bribery, a misdemeanor, if he or she offers, confers or agrees to confer upon another, or solicits, accepts or agrees to accept from another:

(1) Any pecuniary benefit as consideration for the recipient's decision, opinion, recommendation, vote or other exercise of discretion as a public servant, party official or voter; or

(2) Any benefit as consideration for the recipient's decision, vote, recommendation or other exercise of official discretion in a judicial or administrative proceeding; or

(3) Any benefit as consideration for a violation of a known legal duty as a public servant or party official.

(b) It is no defense to prosecution under this section that a person whom the actor sought to influence was not qualified to act in the desired way, whether because he or she had not yet assumed office, or lacked jurisdiction, or for any other reason.

§11.427 Threats and other improper influence in official and political matters.

(a) A person commits a misdemeanor if he or she:

(1) Threatens unlawful harm to any person with purpose to influence his or her decision, vote or other exercise of discretion as a public servant, party official or voter; or

(2) Threatens harm to any public servant with purpose to influence his decision, opinion, recommendation, vote or other exercise of discretion in a judicial or administrative proceeding; or

(3) Threatens harm to any public servant with purpose to influence his decision, opinion, recommendation, vote or other exercise of discretion in a judicial or administrative proceeding; or

(b) It is no defense to prosecution under this section that a person whom the actor sought to influence was not qualified to act in the desired way, whether because he or she had not yet assumed office, or lacked jurisdiction, or for any other reason.

§11.428 Retaliation for past official action.

A person commits a misdemeanor if he or she harms another by any unlawful act in retaliation for anything lawfully done by the latter in the capacity of public servant.

§11.429 Perjury.

A person is guilty of perjury, a misdemeanor, if in any official proceeding he or she makes a false statement under oath or equivalent affirmation, or swears or affirms the truth of a statement previously made, when the statement is material and he or she does not believe it to be true.

(a) No person shall be guilty of an offense under this section if he or she retracted the falsification in the course of the proceeding in which it was made before it became manifest that the falsification was or would be exposed and before the falsification substantially affected the proceeding.

(b) No person shall be convicted of an offense under this section where proof of falsity rests solely upon contradiction by testimony of a single person other than the defendant.

§ 11.430 False alarms.

A person who knowingly causes a false alarm of fire or other emergency to be transmitted to, or within any organization, official or volunteer, for dealing with emergencies involving danger to life or property commits a misdemeanor.

§ 11.431 False reports.

(a) A person who knowingly gives false information to any law enforcement officer with the purpose to implicate another commits a misdemeanor.

(b) A person commits a petty misdemeanor if he or she:

(1) Reports to law enforcement authorities an offense or other incident within their concern knowing that it did not occur; or

(2) Pretends to furnish such authorities with information relating to an offense or incident when he or she knows he or she has no information relating to such offense or incident.

§ 11.432 Impersonating a public servant.

A person commits a misdemeanor if he or she falsely pretends to hold a position in the public service with purpose to induce another to submit to such pretended official authority or otherwise to act in reliance upon that pretense to his or her prejudice.

§ 11.433 Disobedience to lawful order of court.

A person who willfully disobeys any order, subpoena, summons, warrant or command duly issued, made or given by any Court of Indian Offenses or any officer thereof is guilty of a misdemeanor.

§ 11.434 Resisting arrest.

A person commits a misdemeanor if, for the purpose of preventing a public servant from effecting a lawful arrest or discharging any other duty, he or she creates a substantial risk of bodily injury to the public servant or anyone else, or employs means justifying or requiring substantial force to overcome the resistance.

§ 11.435 Obstructing justice.

A person commits a misdemeanor if, with purpose to hinder the apprehension, prosecution, conviction or punishment of another for a crime, he or she harbors or conceals the other, provides a weapon, transportation, disguise or other means of escape, warns the other of impending discovery, or volunteers false information to a law enforcement officer.

§ 11.436 Escape.

A person is guilty of the offense of escape, a misdemeanor, if he or she unlawfully removes himself or herself from official detention or fails to return to official detention following temporary leave granted for a specific purpose or limited period.

§ 11.437 Bail jumping.

A person set at liberty by court order, with or without bail, upon condition that he or she will subsequently appear at a specified time or place, commits a misdemeanor if, without lawful excuse, he or she fails to appear at that time and place.

§ 11.438 Flight to avoid prosecution or judicial process.

A person who shall absent himself or herself from the Indian country over which the Court of Indian Offenses exercises jurisdiction for the purpose of avoiding arrest, prosecution or other judicial process shall be guilty of a misdemeanor.

§ 11.439 Witness tampering.

(a) A person commits a misdemeanor if, believing that an official proceeding or investigation is pending or about to be instituted, he or she attempts to induce or otherwise cause a witness or informant to:

(1) Testify or inform falsely; or

(2) Withhold any testimony, information, document or thing; or

(3) Elude legal process summoning him or her to supply evidence; or

(4) Absent himself or herself from any proceeding or investigation to which he or she has been legally summoned.

(b) A person commits a misdemeanor if he or she harms another by any unlawful act in retaliation for anything lawfully done in the capacity of witness or informant.

§ 11.440 Tampering with or fabricating physical evidence.

A person commits a misdemeanor if, believing that an official proceeding or investigation is pending or about to be instituted, he or she:

(a) Alters, destroys, conceals, or removes any record, document or thing with purpose to impair its verity or availability in such proceeding or investigation; or

(b) Makes, presents or uses any record, document or thing knowing it to be false and with the purpose to mislead a public servant who is or may be engaged in such proceeding or investigation.

§ 11.441 Disorderly conduct.

(a) A person is guilty of disorderly conduct if, with purpose to cause public inconvenience, annoyance or alarm or recklessly creating a risk thereof, he or she:

(1) Engages in fighting or threatening, or in violent or tumultuous behavior;

(2) Makes unreasonable noise or offensively coarse utterance, gesture or display, or addresses abusive language to any person present; or

(3) Creates a hazardous or physically offensive condition by any act which serves no legitimate purpose of the actor.

(b) *Public* means affecting or likely to affect persons in a place to which the public has access; among the places included are highways, schools, prisons, apartments, places of business or amusement, or any neighborhood.

(c) An offense under this section is a petty misdemeanor if the actor's purpose is to cause substantial harm or serious inconvenience, or if he or she persists in disorderly conduct after reasonable warning or request to desist. Otherwise, disorderly conduct is a violation.

§ 11.442 Riot; failure to disperse.

(a) A person is guilty of riot, a misdemeanor, if he or she participates with two or more others in a course of disorderly conduct:

(1) With purpose to commit or facilitate the commission of a felony or misdemeanor; or

(2) With purpose to prevent or coerce official action; or

(3) When the actor or any other participant to the knowledge of the actor uses or plans to use a firearm or other deadly weapon.

(b) Where three or more persons are participating in a course of disorderly conduct likely to cause substantial harm or serious inconvenience, a law enforcement officer may order the participants and others in the immediate vicinity to disperse. A person who refuses or knowingly fails to obey such an order commits a misdemeanor.

§ 11.443 Harassment.

A person commits a petty misdemeanor if, with purpose to harass another, he or she:

(a) Makes a telephone call without purpose or legitimate communication; or

(b) Insults, taunts or challenges another in a manner likely to provoke violent or disorderly response; or

(c) Makes repeated communications anonymously or at extremely inconvenient hours, or in offensively coarse language; or

(d) Subjects another to an offensive touching; or

(e) Engages in any other course of alarming conduct serving no legitimate purpose.

§ 11.444 Carrying concealed weapons.

A person who goes about in public places armed with a dangerous weapon concealed upon his or her person is guilty of a misdemeanor unless he or she has a permit to do so signed by a magistrate of the Court of Indian Offenses.

§ 11.445 Driving violations.

(a) A person who shall operate any vehicle in a manner dangerous to the public safety is guilty of reckless driving, a petty misdemeanor, unless it is committed while under the influence of alcohol, in which case it is a misdemeanor.

(b) A person who shall drive, operate or be in physical control of any motor vehicle when his or her alcohol concentration is 0.10 or more shall be guilty of driving while intoxicated, a misdemeanor.

(c) Any person who drives, operates, or is in physical control of a motor vehicle within the Indian country under the jurisdiction of a Court of Indian Offenses consents to a chemical test of his or her blood, breath, or urine for the purpose of determining the presence of alcohol, to be administered at the direction of a law enforcement officer. The test may be required when the officer has reasonable cause to believe that a person is driving while intoxicated, and the person has either been lawfully placed under arrest for a violation of this section, or has been involved in a motor vehicle accident or collision resulting in property damage, personal injury, or death.

(d) In the absence of an applicable tribal traffic code, the provisions of state traffic laws applicable in the state where a Court of Indian Offenses is located shall apply to the operation of motor vehicles within the Indian country under the jurisdiction of the Court of Indian Offenses with the exception that any person found guilty of violating such laws shall, in lieu of the penalties provided under state law, be sentenced according to the standards found in § 11.450 depending on the nature of the traffic code violation, and may be deprived of the right to operate any motor vehicle for a period not to exceed 6 months.

§ 11.446 Cruelty to animals.

A person commits a misdemeanor if he or she purposely or recklessly:

(a) Subjects any animal in his or her custody to cruel neglect; or

(b) Subjects any animal to cruel mistreatment; or

(c) Kills or injures any animal belonging to another without legal privilege or consent of the owner.

(d) Causes one animal to fight with another.

§ 11.447 Maintaining a public nuisance.

A person who permits his or her property to fall into such condition as to injure or endanger the safety, health, comfort, or property of his or her neighbors, is guilty of a violation.

§ 11.448 Abuse of office.

A person acting or purporting to act in an official capacity or taking advantage of such actual or purported capacity commits a misdemeanor if, knowing that his or her conduct is illegal, he or she:

(a) Subjects another to arrest, detention, search, seizure, mistreatment, dispossession, assessment, lien or other infringement of personal or property rights; or

(b) Denies or impedes another in the exercise or enjoyment of any right, privilege, power or immunity.

§ 11.449 Violation of an approved tribal ordinance.

A person who violates the terms of any tribal ordinance duly enacted by the governing body of the tribe occupying the Indian country under the jurisdiction of the Court of Indian Offenses and approved by the Assistant Secretary—Indian Affairs or his or her designee, is guilty of an offense and upon conviction thereof shall be sentenced as provided in the ordinance.

§ 11.450 Maximum fines and sentences of imprisonment.

A person convicted of an offense under the regulations in this part may be sentenced as follows:

Type of offense	Maximum allowable sentence
(a) Misdemeanor	Up to 1 year in prison, or a fine of up to $5,000, or both.
(b) Petty misdemeanor.	Up to 6 months in prison, or a fine of up to $2,500, or both.
(c) Violation	Up to 3 months in prison, or a fine of up to $1,000, or both.

[73 FR 39861, July 11, 2008]

§ 11.451 Abuse of psychotoxic chemical solvents.

(a) It is unlawful to:

(1) Intentionally smell or inhale the fumes of any psychotoxic chemical solvent or possess, purchase, or attempt to possess or purchase any psychotoxic

chemical solvent, for the purpose of causing intoxication, inebriation, excitement, stupefaction, or the dulling of the brain or nervous system; or

(2) Sell, give away, dispense, or distribute, or offer to sell, give away, dispense, or distribute, any psychotoxic chemical solvent knowing or believing that the purchaser or another person intends to use the solvent in violation of this section.

(b) This section does not apply to inhalation of anesthesia for medical or dental purposes.

(c) As used in this section, "psychotoxic chemical solvent" means any glue, gasoline, paint, hair spray, Lysol, or other substance containing one or more of the following chemical compounds:

(1) Acetone and acetate;

(2) Benzene;

(3) Butyl-alcohol;

(4) Methyl ethyl;

(6) Peptone;

(7) Pentachlorophenol;

(8) Petroleum ether; or

(9) Any other chemical substance the inhalation of whose fumes or vapors can cause intoxication, inebriation, excitement, stupefaction, or the dulling of the brain or nervous system.

(d) The statement listing the contents of a substance packaged in a container by the manufacturer or producer thereof is rebuttable proof of the contents of the substance without further expert testimony if it reasonably appears that the substance in the container is the same substance placed therein by the manufacturer or producer.

(e) Abuse of psychotoxic chemical solvents, as defined in this section, is punishable as a petty misdemeanor, and the court may order any person using psychotoxic chemical solvents as described in paragraph (a) of this section to be committed to a facility for treatment for up to 6 months.

(f) Psychotoxic chemical solvents kept or used in violation of this section are declared contraband. Upon proof of a violation, these solvents must be forfeited to the Federal government by order of the court, following public notice and an opportunity for any person claiming an interest in the solvents to be heard.

[73 FR 39861, July 11, 2008]

§11.452 Possession of a controlled substance.

(a) It is unlawful for a person to knowingly or intentionally possess any controlled substance listed in 21 CFR Part 1308, as amended, unless:

(1) The Controlled Substances Act or Drug Enforcement Agency regulations specifically authorizes possession of the substance;

(2) The substance or preparation is excluded or exempted by 21 CFR 1308.21 through 1308.35, as amended; or

(3) The provisions of 42 U.S.C. 1996a (regarding traditional Indian religious use of peyote) apply.

(b) Violations of paragraph (a) of this section are punishable as a misdemeanor.

(c) Any controlled substance involved in violation of this section is declared to be contraband. Upon proof of a violation of this section, the controlled substance must be forfeited to the Federal Government by order of the court, after public notice and an opportunity for any person claiming an interest in the substance to be heard.

(d) Any personal property used to transport, conceal, manufacture, cultivate, or distribute a controlled substance in violation of this section is subject to forfeiture to the Federal Government by order of the court upon proof of this use, following public notice and opportunity for any person claiming an interest in the property to be heard.

[73 FR 39861, July 11, 2008]

§11.453 Prostitution or solicitation.

A person who commits prostitution or solicitation or who knowingly keeps, maintains, rents, or leases, any house, room, tent, or other place for the purpose of prostitution is guilty of a misdemeanor.

[73 FR 39861, July 11, 2008]

§11.454 Domestic violence.

(a) A person who commits domestic violence by inflicting physical harm, bodily injury, or sexual assault, or inflicting the fear of imminent physical harm, bodily injury, or sexual assault on a family member, is guilty of a misdemeanor.

(b) For purposes of this section, a family member is any of the following:

(1) A spouse;

(2) A former spouse;

(3) A person related by blood;

(4) A person related by existing or prior marriage;

(5) A person who resides or resided with the defendant;

(6) A person with whom the defendant has a child in common; or

(7) A person with whom the defendant is or was in a dating or intimate relationship.

[73 FR 39861, July 11, 2008]

Subpart E—Civil Actions

§ 11.500 Law applicable to civil actions.

(a) In all civil cases, the Magistrate of a Court of Indian Offenses shall have discretion to apply:

(1) Any laws of the United States that may be applicable;

(2) Any authorized regulations contained in the Code of Federal Regulations; and

(3) Any laws or customs of the tribe occupying the area of Indian country over which the court has jurisdiction that are not prohibited by Federal laws.

(b) The delineation in paragraph (a) of this section does not establish a hierarchy relative to the applicability of specific law in specific cases.

(c) Where any doubt arises as to the customs of the tribe, the court may request the advice of counselors familiar with those customs.

(d) Any matters that are not covered by the laws or customs of the tribe, or by applicable Federal laws and regulations, may be decided by the Court of Indian Offenses according to the laws of the State in which the matter in dispute lies.

[73 FR 39862, July 11, 2008]

§ 11.501 Judgments in civil actions.

(a) In all civil cases, judgment shall consist of an order of the court awarding damages to be paid to the injured party, or directing the surrender of certain property to the injured party, or the performance of some other act for the benefit of the injured party, including injunctive relief and declaratory judgments.

(b) Where the injury inflicted was the result of carelessness of the defendant, the judgment shall fairly compensate the injured party for the loss he or she has suffered.

(c) Where the injury was deliberately inflicted, the judgment shall impose an additional penalty upon the defendant, which additional penalty may run either in favor of the injured party or in favor of the tribe.

(d) Where the injury was inflicted as a result of accident, or where both the complainant and the defendant were at fault, the judgment shall compensate the injured party for a reasonable part of the loss he or she has suffered.

(e) No judgment shall be given on any suit unless the defendant has actually received notice of such suit and ample opportunity to appear in court in his or her defense.

§ 11.502 Costs in civil actions.

(a) The court may assess the accruing costs of the case against the party or parties against whom judgment is given. Such costs shall consist of the expenses of voluntary witnesses for which either party may be responsible and the fees of jurors in those cases where a jury trial is had, and any further incidental expenses connected with the procedure before the court as the court may direct.

(b) In all civil suits the complainant may be required to deposit with the clerk of the court a fee or other security in a reasonable amount to cover costs and disbursements in the case.

§ 11.503 Applicable civil procedure.

The procedure to be followed in civil cases shall be the Federal Rules of Civil Procedure applicable to United States district courts, except insofar as such procedures are superseded by order of the Court of Indian Offenses or by the existence of inconsistent tribal rules of procedure.

§ 11.504 Applicable rules of evidence.

Courts of Indian Offenses shall be bound by the Federal Rules of Evidence, except insofar as such rules are superseded by order of the Court of Indian Offenses, or by the existence of inconsistent tribal rules of evidence.

Subpart F—Domestic Relations

§ 11.600 Marriages.

(a) A magistrate of the Court of Indian Offenses shall have the authority to perform marriages.

(b) A valid marriage shall be constituted by:

(1) The issuance of a marriage license by the Court of Indian Offenses and by execution of a consent to marriage by both parties to the marriage and recorded with the clerk of the court; or

(2) The recording of a tribal custom marriage with the Court of Indian Offenses within 30 days of the tribal custom marriage ceremony by the signing by both parties of a marriage register maintained by the clerk of the court.

(c) A marriage license application shall include the following information:

(1) Name, sex, occupation, address, social security number, and date and place of birth of each party to the proposed marriage;

(2) If either party was previously married, his or her name, and the date, place, and court in which the marriage was dissolved or declared invalid or the date and place of death of the former spouse;

(3) Name and address of the parents or guardian of each party;

(4) Whether the parties are related to each other and, if so, their relationship; and

(5) The name and date of birth of any child of which both parties are parents, born before the making of the application, unless their parental rights and the parent and child relationship with respect to the child have been terminated.

(6) A certificate of the results of any medical examination required by either applicable tribal ordinances, or the laws of the State in which the Indian country under the jurisdiction of the Court of Indian Offenses is located.

§ 11.601 Marriage licenses.

A marriage license shall be issued by the clerk of the court in the absence of any showing that the proposed marriage would be invalid under any provision of this part or tribal custom, and upon written application of an unmarried male and unmarried female, both of whom must be eighteen (18) years or older. If either party to the marriage is under the age of eighteen (18), that party must have the written consent of parent or his or her legal guardian.

§ 11.602 Solemnization.

(a) In the event a judge, clergyman, tribal official or anyone authorized to do so solemnizes a marriage, he or she shall file with the clerk of the court certification thereof within thirty (30) days of the solemnization.

(b) Upon receipt of the marriage certificate, the clerk of the court shall register the marriage.

§ 11.603 Invalid or prohibited marriages.

(a) The following marriages are prohibited:

(1) A marriage entered into prior to the dissolution of an earlier marriage of one of the parties;

(2) A marriage between an ancestor and a descendant, or between a brother and a sister, whether the relationship is by the half or the whole blood;

(3) A marriage between an aunt and a nephew or between an uncle and a niece, whether the relationship is by the half or the whole blood, except as to marriages permitted by established tribal custom;

(4) A marriage prohibited by custom and usage of the tribe.

(b) Children born of a prohibited marriage are legitimate.

§ 11.604 Declaration of invalidity.

(a) The Court of Indian Offenses shall enter a decree declaring the invalidity of a marriage entered into under the following circumstances:

(1) A party lacked capacity to consent to the marriage, either because of mental incapacity or infirmity or by the influence of alcohol, drugs, or other incapacitating substances; or

(2) A party was induced to enter into a marriage by fraud or duress; or

(3) A party lacks the physical capacity to consummate the marriage by sexual intercourse and at the time the marriage was entered into, the other party did not know of the incapacity; or

(4) The marriage is prohibited under § 11.603.

(b) A declaration of invalidity may be sought by either party to the marriage or by the legal representative of the party who lacked capacity to consent.

§ 11.605 Dissolution.

(a) The Court of Indian Offenses shall enter a decree of dissolution of marriage if:

(1) The court finds that the marriage is irretrievably broken, if the finding is supported by evidence that (i) the parties have lived separate and apart for a period of more than 180 days next preceding the commencement of the proceeding, or (ii) there is serious marital discord adversely affecting the attitude of one or both of the parties towards the marriage;

(2) The court finds that either party, at the time the action was commenced, was domiciled within the Indian country under the jurisdiction of the court, and that the domicile has been maintained for 90 days next preceding the making of the findings; and

(3) To the extent it has jurisdiction to do so, the court has considered, approved, or provided for child custody, the support of any child entitled to support, the maintenance of either spouse, and the disposition of property; or has provided for a separate later hearing to complete these matters.

(b) If a party requests a decree of legal separation rather than a decree of dissolution of marriage, the Court of Indian Offenses shall grant the decree in that form unless the other party objects.

§ 11.606 Dissolution proceedings.

(a) Either or both parties to the marriage may initiate dissolution proceedings.

(b) If a proceeding is commenced by one of the parties, the other party shall be served in the manner provided by the applicable rule of civil procedure and within thirty days after the date of service may file a verified response.

(c) The verified petition in a proceeding for dissolution of marriage or legal separation shall allege that the marriage is irretrievably broken and shall set forth:

(1) The age, occupation, and length of residence within the Indian country under the jurisdiction of the court of each party;

(2) The date of the marriage and the place at which it was registered;

(3) That jurisdictional requirements are met and that the marriage is irretrievably broken in that either (i) the parties have lived separate and apart for a period of more than 180 days next preceding the commencement of the proceeding or (ii) there is a serious marital discord adversely affecting the attitude of one or both of the parties toward the marriage, and there is no reasonable prospect of reconciliation;

(4) The names, age, and addresses of all living children of the marriage and whether the wife is pregnant;

(5) Any arrangement as to support, custody, and visitation of the children and maintenance of a spouse; and

(6) The relief sought.

§ 11.607 Temporary orders and temporary injunctions.

(a) In a proceeding for dissolution of marriage or for legal separation, either party may move for temporary maintenance or temporary support of a child of the marriage entitled to support. The motion shall be accompanied by an affidavit setting forth the factual basis for the motion and the amounts requested.

(b) As a part of a motion for temporary maintenance or support or by an independent motion accompanied by an affidavit, either party may request the Court of Indian Offenses to issue a temporary injunction for any of the following relief:

(1) Restraining any person from transferring, encumbering, concealing, or otherwise disposing of any property except in the usual course of business or for the necessities of life, and, if so restrained, requiring him or her to notify the moving party of any proposed extraordinary expenditures made after the order is issued;

(2) Enjoining a party from molesting or disturbing the peace of the other party or of any child;

(3) Excluding a party from the family home or from the home of the other party upon a showing that physical or emotional harm would otherwise result;

(4) Enjoining a party from removing a child from the jurisdiction of the court; and

(5) Providing other injunctive relief proper in the circumstances.

(c) The court may issue a temporary restraining order without requiring notice to the other party only if it finds on the basis of the moving affidavit or other evidence that irreparable injury will result to the moving party if no order is issued until the time for responding has elapsed.

(d) A response may be filed within 20 days after service of notice of a motion or at the time specified in the temporary restraining order.

(e) On the basis of the showing made, the Court of Indian Offenses may issue a temporary injunction and an order for temporary maintenance or support in amounts and on terms just and proper under the circumstances.

(f) A temporary order or temporary injunction:

(1) Does not prejudice the rights of the parties or the child which are to be adjudicated at subsequent hearings in a proceeding;

(2) May be revoked or modified before the final decree as deemed necessary by the court;

(3) Terminates when the final decree is entered or when the petition for dissolution or legal separation is voluntarily dismissed.

§ 11.608 Final decree; disposition of property; maintenance; child support; custody.

(a) A decree of dissolution of marriage or of legal separation is final when entered, subject to the right of appeal.

(b) The Court of Indian Offenses shall have the power to impose judgment as follows in dissolution or separation proceedings:

(1) Apportion or assign between the parties the non-trust property and non-trust assets belonging to either or both and whenever acquired, and whether the title thereto is in the name of the husband or wife or both;

(2) Grant a maintenance order for either spouse in amounts and for periods of time the court deems just;

(3) Order either or both parents owing a duty of support to a child to pay an amount reasonable or necessary for his or her support, without regard to marital misconduct, after considering all relevant factors. In addition:

(i) When a support order is issued by a Court of Indian Offenses, the order may provide that a portion of an absent parent's wages be withheld to comply with the order on the earliest of the following dates: When an amount equal to one month's support becomes overdue; when the absent parent requests withholding; or at such time as the Court of Indian Offenses selects. The amount to be withheld may include an amount to be applied toward liquidation of any overdue support.

(ii) If the Court of Indian Offenses finds that an absent parent who has been ordered to pay child support is now residing within the jurisdiction of another Court of Indian Offenses, an Indian tribal court, or a state court, it shall petition such court for reciprocal enforcement and provide it with a copy of the support order.

(iii) If the Court of Indian Offenses receives a petition from another Court of Indian Offenses, an Indian tribal court or a state court, it shall take necessary steps to determine paternity, establish an order for child support, register a foreign child support order or enforce orders as requested in the petition.

(iv) The Court of Indian Offenses shall assist a state in the enforcement and collection of past-due support from Federal tax refunds of absent parents living within the Indian country over which the court has jurisdiction.

(v) Any person or agency who has provided support or assistance to a child under 18 years of age shall be a proper person to bring an action under this section and to recover judgment in an amount equal to such past-paid support or assistance, including costs of bringing the action.

(4) Make child custody determinations in accordance with the best interest of the child.

(5) Restore the maiden name of the wife.

§ 11.609 Determination of paternity and support.

The Court of Indian Offenses shall have jurisdiction of all suits brought to determine the paternity of a child and to obtain a judgment for the support of the child. A judgment of the court establishing the identity of the father of the child shall be conclusive of that fact in all subsequent determinations of inheritance by the Court of Indian Offenses or by the Department of the Interior.

§ 11.610 Appointment of guardians.

The court shall have the jurisdiction to appoint or remove legal guardians for minors and for persons who are incapable of managing their own affairs under terms and conditions to be prescribed by the court.

§ 11.611 Change of name.

The Court of Indian Offenses shall have the authority to change the name of any person upon petition of such person or upon the petition of the parents of any minor, if at least one parent is Indian. Any order issued by the court for a change of name shall be kept as a permanent record and copies shall be filed with the agency superintendent, the governing body of the tribe occupying the Indian country under the jurisdiction of the court, and any appropriate agency of the State in which the court is located.

Subpart G—Probate Proceedings

§ 11.700 Probate jurisdiction.

The Court of Indian Offenses shall have jurisdiction to administer in probate the estate of a deceased Indian who, at the time of his or her death, was domiciled or owned real or personal property situated within the Indian country under the jurisdiction of the court to the extent that such estate consists of property which does not come within the jurisdiction of the Secretary of the Interior.

§ 11.701 Duty to present will for probate.

Any custodian of a will shall deliver the same to the Court of Indian Offenses within 30 days after receipt of information that the maker thereof is deceased. Any custodian who fails to do so shall be liable for damages sustained by any person injured thereby.

§ 11.702 Proving and admitting will.

(a) Upon initiating the probate of an estate, the will of the decedent shall be filed with the court. Such will may be proven and admitted to probate by filing an affidavit of an attesting witness which identifies such will as being the will which the decedent executed and declared to be his or her last will. If the evidence of none of the attesting witnesses is available, the court may allow proof of the will by testimony that the signature of the testator is genuine.

(b) At any time within 90 days after a will has been admitted to probate, any person having an interest in the decedent's estate may contest the validity of such will. In the event of such contest, a hearing shall be held to determine the validity of such will.

(c) Upon considering all relevant information concerning the will, the Court of Indian Offenses shall enter an order affirming the admission of such will to probate, or rejecting such will and ordering that the probate of the decedent's estate proceed as if the decedent had died intestate.

§ 11.703 Petition and order to probate estate.

(a) Any person having an interest in the administration of an estate which is subject to the jurisdiction of the court may file a written petition with the court requesting that such estate be administered in probate.

(b) The Court of Indian Offenses shall enter an order directing that the estate be probated upon finding that the decedent was an Indian who, at the time of his or her death, was domiciled or owned real or personal property situated within the Indian country under the jurisdiction of the court other than trust or other restricted property, that the decedent left an estate subject to the jurisdiction of the court, and that it is necessary to probate such estate.

§ 11.704 Appointment and duties of executor or administrator.

(a) Upon ordering the estate to be probated, the court shall appoint an administrator to administer the estate of the decedent. The person nominated by the decedent's will, if any, to be the executor of the estate shall be so appointed, provided such person is willing to serve in such capacity.

(b) The executor or administrator appointed by the court shall have the following duties and powers during the administration of the estate and until discharged by the court:

(1) To send by certified mail true copies of the order to probate the estate and the will of the decedent admitted to probate by such order, if any, to each heir, devisee and legatee of the decedent, at their last known address, to the governing body of the tribe or tribes occupying the Indian country over which the court has jurisdiction, and to the agency superintendent;

(2) To preserve and protect the decedent's property within the estate and the heirs, so far as is possible;

(3) To investigate promptly all claims against the decedent's estate and determine their validity;

(4) To cause a written inventory of all the decedent's property within the estate to be prepared promptly with each article or item being separately set forth and cause such property to be exhibited to and appraised by an appraiser, and the inventory and appraisal thereof to be filed with the court;

(5) To give promptly all persons entitled thereto such notice as is required under these proceedings;

(6) To account for all property within the estate which may come into his or her possession or control, and to maintain accurate records of all income received and disbursements made during the course of the administration.

§ 11.705 Removal of executor or administrator.

The Court of Indian Offenses may order the executor or administrator to show cause why he or she should not be discharged, and may discharge the executor or administrator for failure, neglect or improper performance of his or her duties.

§ 11.706 Appointment and duties of appraiser.

(a) Upon ordering an estate to be probated, the court shall appoint a disinterested and competent person as an appraiser to appraise all of the decedent's real and personal property within the estate.

(b) It shall be the duty of the appraiser to appraise separately the true cash value of each article or item of property within the estate, including debts due the decedent, and to indicate the appraised value of each such article or item of property set forth in the inventory of the estate and to certify such appraisal by subscribing his or her name to the inventory and appraisal.

§ 11.707 Claims against estate.

(a) Creditors of the estate or those having a claim against the decedent shall file their claim with the clerk of the court or with the executor or administrator within 60 days from official notice of the appointment of the executor or administrator published locally in the press or posting of signs at the tribal and agency offices, giving appropriate notice for the filing of claims.

(b) The executor or administrator shall examine all claims within 90 days of his or her appointment and notify the claimant whether his or her claim is accepted or rejected. If the claimant is notified of rejection, he or she may request a hearing before the court by filing a petition requesting such hearing within 30 days following the notice of rejection.

§ 11.708 Sale of property.

After filing the inventory and appraisal, the executor or administrator may petition the court for authority to sell personal property of the estate for purposes of paying the expenses of last illness and burial expenses, expenses of administration, claims, if any, against the estate, and for the purpose of distribution. If, in the court's judgment, such sale is in the best interest of the estate, the court shall order such sale and prescribe the terms upon which the property shall be sold.

§ 11.709 Final account.

(a) When the affairs of an estate have been fully administered, the executor or administrator shall file a final account with the court, verified by his or her oath. Such final account shall affirmatively set forth:

(1) That all claims against the estate have been paid, except as shown, and that the estate has adequate unexpended and unappropriated funds to fully pay such remaining claims;

(2) The amount of money received and expended by him or her, from whom received and to whom paid, referring to the vouchers for each of such payments;

(3) That there is nothing further to be done in the administration of the estate except as shown in the final account;

(4) The remaining assets of the estate, including unexpended and unappropriated money, at the time of filing the final account;

(5) The proposed determination of heirs and indicate the names, ages, addresses and relationship to the decedent of each distributee and the proposed distributive share and value thereof each heir, devisee or legatee is to receive; and

(6) A petition that the court set a date for conducting a hearing to approve the final account, to determine the heirs, devisees and legatees of the decedent and the distributive share each distributee is to receive.

§ 11.710 Determination of the court.

At the time set for hearing upon the final account, the Court of Indian Offenses shall proceed to examine all evidence relating to the distribution of the decedent's estate, and consider objections to the final account which may have been filed by any heir, devisee, legatee, or other person having an interest in the distribution of the estate. Upon conclusion of the hearing, the court shall enter an order:

(a) Providing for payment of approved claims;

(b) Determining the decedent's heirs, devisees and legatees, indicating the names, ages and addresses of each, and the distributive share of the remaining estate which each distributee is to receive; and

(c) Directing the administrator or executor to distribute such distributive share to those entitled thereto.

§ 11.711 Descent and distribution.

(a) The court shall distribute the estate according to the terms of the will of the decedent which has been admitted to probate.

(b) If the decedent died intestate or having left a will which has been rejected by the court, the estate shall be distributed as follows:

(1) According to the laws and customs of the tribe if such laws and customs are proved; or

(2) According to state law absent the existence of tribal laws or customs.

(c) If no person takes under the above subsections, the estate shall escheat to the tribe.

§ 11.712 Closing estate.

(a) Upon finding that the estate has been fully administered and is in a condition to be closed, the court shall enter an order closing the estate and discharging the executor or administrator.

(b) If an order closing the estate has not been entered by the end of nine months following appointment of executor or administrator, the executor or administrator shall file a written report with the court stating the reasons why the estate has not been closed.

§ 11.713 Small estates.

An estate having an appraised value which does not exceed $2,000.00 and which is to be inherited by a surviving spouse and/or minor children of the deceased may, upon petition of the executor or administrator, and a hearing before the court, be distributed without administration to those entitled thereto, upon which the estate shall be closed.

Subpart H—Appellate Proceedings

§ 11.800 Jurisdiction of appellate division.

The jurisdiction of the appellate division shall extend to all appeals from final orders and judgments of the trial division, by any party except the prosecution in a criminal case where there has been a jury verdict. The appellate division shall review all issues of law presented to it which arose in the case, but shall not reverse the trial division decision unless the legal error committed affected a substantial right of a party or the outcome of the case.

§ 11.801 Procedure on appeal.

(a) An appeal must be taken within 15 days from the judgment appealed from by filing a written notice of appeal with the clerk of the court.

(b) The notice of appeal shall specify the party or parties taking the appeal, shall designate the judgment, or part thereof appealed from, and shall contain a short statement of reasons for the appeal. The clerk of the court shall mail a copy of the notice of appeal to all parties other than parties taking the appeal.

(c) In civil cases, other parties shall have 15 days to respond to the notice of appeal.

(d) In civil cases, the appellant may request the trial division to stay the judgment pending action on the notice of appeal, and, if the appeal is allowed, either party may request the trial division to grant or stay an injunction pending appeal. The trial division may condition a stay or injunction pending appeal on the depositing of cash or bond sufficient to cover damages awarded by the court together with interest.

§ 11.802 Judgment against surety.

Any surety to a bond submits himself or herself to the jurisdiction of the Court of Indian Offenses, and irrevocably appoints the clerk of the court as his or her agent upon whom any papers affecting his or her liability on the bond may be served.

§ 11.803 Record on appeal.

Within 20 days after a notice of appeal is filed, the clerk of court shall certify and file with the appellate division the record of the case.

§ 11.804 Briefs and memoranda.

(a) Within 30 days after the notice of appeal is filed, the appellant may file a written brief in support of his or her appeal. An original and one copy for each appellee shall be filed with the clerk of court who shall mail one copy by registered or certified mail to each appellee.

(b) The appellee shall have 30 days after receipt of the appellant's brief within which to file an answer brief. An original and one copy for each appellant shall be filed with the clerk of the court who shall mail one copy, by registered or certified mail, to each appellant.

§ 11.805 Oral argument.

The appellate division shall assign all criminal cases for oral argument. The court may in its discretion assign civil cases for oral argument or may dispose of civil cases on the briefs without argument.

§ 11.806 Rules of court.

The chief magistrate of the appellate division shall prescribe all necessary rules concerning the operation of the appellate division and the time and place of meeting of the court.

Subpart I—Children's Court

§ 11.900 Definitions.

For purposes of sections pertaining to the children's court:

(a) *Abandon* means the leaving of a minor without communication or failing to support a minor for a period of one year or more with no indication of the parents' willingness to assume a parental role.

(b) *Adult* means a person eighteen (18) years or older.

(c) *Counsel* means an attorney admitted to the bar of a state or the District of Columbia or a lay advocate admitted to practice before the Court of Indian Offenses.

(d) *Custodian* means one who has physical custody of a minor and who is providing food, shelter and supervision to the minor.

(e) *Custody* means the power to control the day-to-day activities of the minor.

(f) *Delinquent act* means an act which, if committed by an adult, would be designated a crime under this part or under an ordinance of the tribe.

(g) *Detention* means the placement of a minor in a physically restrictive facility.

(h) *Guardian* means a person other than the minor's parent who is by law responsible for the care of the minor.

(i) *Guardian ad Litem* means a person appointed by the court to represent the minor's interests before the court.

(j) *Juvenile offender* means a person who commits a delinquent act prior to his or her eighteenth birthday.

(k) *Minor* means:

(1) A person under 18 years of age,

(2) A person 18 years of age or older concerning whom proceedings are commenced in the children's court prior to his or her eighteenth birthday, or

(3) A person 18 years of age or older who is under the continuing jurisdiction of the children's court.

(l) *Minor-in-need-of-care* means a minor who:

(1) Has no parent or guardian available and willing to take care of him or her;

(2) Is unwilling to allow his or her parent or guardian to take care of him or her;

(3) Has suffered or is likely to suffer a physical or emotional injury, inflicted by other than accidental means, which causes or creates a substantial risk of death, disfigurement, impairment of bodily functions or emotional health;

(4) Has not been provided with adequate food, clothing, shelter, medical care, education or supervision by his or her parent, guardian or custodian;

(5) Has been sexually abused;

(6) Has been committing delinquent acts as a result of parental pressure, guidance or approval; or,

(7) Has been committing status offenses.

(m) *Status offense* means an offense which, if committed by an adult, would not be designated a crime under this part or under an ordinance of the tribe.

§ 11.901 The children's court established.

When conducting proceedings under §§ 11.900–11.1114 of this part, the Court of Indian Offenses shall be known as the "Children's Court".

§ 11.902 Non-criminal proceedings.

No adjudication upon the status of any minor in the jurisdiction of the children's court shall be deemed criminal or be deemed a conviction of a crime, unless the children's court refers the matter to the Court of Indian Offenses. Neither the disposition nor evidence given before the children's court shall be admissible as evidence against the child in any proceeding in another court.

§ 11.903 Presenting officer.

(a) The agency superintendent and the chief magistrate of the children's court shall jointly appoint a presenting officer to carry out the duties and responsibilities set forth under §§ 11.900–11.1114 of this part. The presenting officer's qualifications shall be the same as the qualifications for the official who acts as prosecutor for the Court of Indian Offenses. The presenting officer may be the same person who acts as prosecutor in the Court of Indian Offenses.

(b) The presenting officer shall represent the tribe in all proceedings under §§ 11.900–11.1114 of this part.

§ 11.904 Guardian ad litem.

The children's court, under any proceeding authorized by this part, shall appoint, for the purposes of the proceeding, a guardian ad litem for a minor, where the court finds that the minor does not have a natural or adoptive parent, guardian or custodian willing and able to exercise effective guardianship, or where the parent, guardian, or custodian has been accused of abusing or neglecting the minor.

§ 11.905 Jurisdiction.

The children's court has exclusive, original jurisdiction of the following proceedings:

(a) Proceedings in which a minor who resides in a community for which the court is established is alleged to be a juvenile offender, unless the children's court transfers jurisdiction to the Court of Indian Offenses pursuant to § 11.907 of this part.

(b) Proceedings in which a minor who resides in a community for which the court is established is alleged to be a minor-in-need-of-care.

§ 11.906 Rights of parties.

(a) In all hearings and proceedings under §§ 11.900–11.1114 of this part the following rights will be observed unless modified by the particular section describing a hearing or proceeding:

(1) Notice of the hearing or proceeding shall be given the minor, his or her parents, guardian or custodian and their counsel. The notice shall be delivered by certified mail. The notice shall contain:

(i) The name of the court;

(ii) The title of the proceeding; and

(iii) The date, time and place of the proceeding.

(b) The children's court magistrate shall inform the minor and his or her parents, guardian or custodian of their right to retain counsel, and, in juvenile delinquency proceedings, shall tell them: "You have a right to have a lawyer or other person represent you at this proceeding. If you cannot afford to hire counsel, the court will appoint counsel for you."

(c) If the children's court magistrate believes there is a potential conflict of interest between the minor and his or her parents, guardian, or custodian with respect to legal representation, the court shall appoint another person to act as counsel for the minor.

(d) The minor need not be a witness against, nor otherwise incriminate, himself or herself.

(e) The children's court shall give the minor, and the minor's parent, guardian or custodian the opportunity to introduce evidence, to be heard on their own behalf and to examine witnesses.

§ 11.907 Transfer to Court of Indian Offenses.

(a) The presenting officer or the minor may file a petition requesting the children's court to transfer the minor to the Court of Indian Offenses if the minor is 14 years of age or older and is alleged to have committed an act that would have been considered a crime if committed by an adult.

(b) The children's court shall conduct a hearing to determine whether jurisdiction of the minor should be transferred to the Court of Indian Offenses.

(1) The transfer hearing shall be held no more than 30 days after the petition is filed.

(2) Written notice of the transfer hearing shall be given to the minor and the minor's parents, guardian or custodian at least 72 hours prior to the hearing.

(c) All the rights listed in § 11.906 shall be afforded the parties at the transfer hearing.

(d) The following factors shall be considered when determining whether to transfer jurisdiction of the minor to the Court of Indian Offenses:

(1) The nature and seriousness of the offense with which the minor is charged.

(2) The nature and condition of the minor, as evidenced by his or her age; mental and physical condition; past record of offenses; and responses to past children's court efforts at rehabilitation.

(e) The children's court may transfer jurisdiction of the minor to the Court of Indian Offenses if the children's court finds clear and convincing evidence that both of the following circumstances exist:

(1) There are no reasonable prospects for rehabilitating the minor through resources available to the children's court; and

(2) The offense allegedly committed by the minor evidences a pattern of conduct which constitutes a substantial danger to the public.

(f) When a minor is transferred to the Court of Indian Offenses, the children's court shall issue a written transfer order containing reasons for its order. The transfer order constitutes a final order for purposes of appeal.

§ 11.908 Court records.

(a) A record of all hearings under §§ 11.900–11.1114 of this part shall be made and preserved.

(b) All children's court records shall be confidential and shall not be open to inspection to anyone but the minor, the minor's parents or guardian, the presenting officer, or others by order of the children's court.

§ 11.909 Law enforcement records.

(a) Law enforcement records and files concerning a minor shall be kept separate from the records and files of adults.

(b) All law enforcement records and files shall be confidential and shall not be open to inspection to anyone but the minor, the minor's parents or guardian, the presenting officer, or others by order of the children's court.

§ 11.910 Expungement.

When a minor who has been the subject of any proceeding before the children's court attains his or her twenty-first birthday, the children's court magistrate shall order the court records and the law enforcement records pertaining to the minor to be destroyed, except for adoption records which shall not be destroyed under any circumstances.

§ 11.911 Appeal.

(a) For purposes of appeal, a record of the proceedings shall be made available to the minor and parents, guardian or custodian. Costs of obtaining the record shall be paid by the party seeking the appeal.

(b) Any party to a children's court hearing may appeal a final order or disposition of the case by filing a written notice of appeal with the children's court within 30 days of the final order of disposition.

(c) No decree or disposition of a hearing shall be stayed by such appeal.

(d) All appeals shall be conducted in accordance with this part.

§ 11.912 Contempt of court.

Any willful disobedience or interference with any order of the children's court constitutes contempt of court which may be punished in accordance with this part.

Subpart J—Juvenile Offender Procedure

§ 11.1000 Complaint.

A complaint must be filed by a law enforcement officer or by the presenting officer and sworn to by a person who has knowledge of the facts alleged. The complaint shall be signed by the complaining witness, and shall contain:

(a) A citation to the specific section(s) of this part which gives the children's court jurisdiction of the proceedings;

(b) A citation to the section(s) of this part which the minor is alleged to have violated;

(c) The name, age, and address of the minor who is the subject of the complaint, if known; and

(d) A plain and concise statement of the facts upon which the allegations are based, including the date, time, and location at which the alleged facts occurred.

§ 11.1001 Warrant.

The children's court may issue a warrant directing that a minor be taken into custody if the court finds there is probable cause to believe the minor committed the delinquent act alleged in the complaint.

§ 11.1002 Custody.

A minor may be taken into custody by a law enforcement officer if:

(a) The officer observes the minor committing a delinquent act; or

(b) The officer has reasonable grounds to believe a delinquent act has been committed that would be a crime if committed by an adult, and that the minor has committed the delinquent act; or

(c) A warrant pursuant to § 11.1001 has been issued for the minor.

§ 11.1003 Law enforcement officer's duties.

A law enforcement officer who takes a minor into custody pursuant to § 11.1002 of this part shall:

(a) Give the following warnings to any minor taken into custody prior to any questioning:

(1) The minor has a right to remain silent;

(2) Anything the minor says can be used against the minor in court;

(3) The minor has the right to the presence of counsel during questioning; and

(4) If he or she cannot afford counsel, the court will appoint one.

(b) Release the minor to the minor's parent, guardian, or custodian and issue a verbal advice or warning as may be appropriate, unless shelter care or detention is necessary.

(c) If the minor is not released, make immediate and recurring efforts to notify the minor's parents, guardian, or custodian to inform them that the minor has been taken into custody and inform them of their right to be present with the minor until an investigation to determine the need for shelter care or detention is made by the court.

§ 11.1004 Detention and shelter care.

(a) A minor alleged to be a juvenile offender may be detained, pending a court hearing, in the following places:

(1) A foster care facility approved by the tribe;

(2) A detention home approved by the tribe; or

(3) A private family home approved by the tribe.

(b) A minor who is 16 years of age or older may be detained in a jail facility used for the detention of adults only if:

(1) A facility in paragraph (a) of this section is not available or would not assure adequate supervision of the minor;

(2) The minor is housed in a separate room from the detained adults; and

(3) Routine inspection of the room where the minor is housed is conducted every 30 minutes to assure his or her safety and welfare.

§ 11.1005 Preliminary inquiry.

(a) If a minor is placed in detention or shelter care, the children's court shall conduct a preliminary inquiry within 24 hours for the purpose of determining:

(1) Whether probable cause exist to believe the minor committed the alleged delinquent act; and

(2) Whether continued detention or shelter care is necessary pending further proceedings.

(b) If a minor has been released to the parents, guardian or custodian, the children's court shall conduct a preliminary inquiry within three days after receipt of the complaint for the sole purpose of determining whether probable cause exists to believe the minor committed the alleged delinquent act.

(c) If the minor's parents, guardian or custodian is not present at the preliminary inquiry, the children's court shall determine what efforts have been made to notify and to obtain the presence of the parents, guardian, or custodian. If it appears that further efforts are likely to produce the parents, guardian or custodian, the children's court shall recess for no more than 24 hours and direct that continued efforts be made to obtain the presence of parents, guardian or custodian.

(d) All the rights listed in § 11.906 shall be afforded the parties in a preliminary inquiry.

(e) The children's court shall hear testimony concerning:

(1) The circumstances that gave rise to the complaint or the taking of the minor into custody; and

(2) The need for detention or shelter care.

(f) If the children's court finds that probable cause exists to believe the minor performed the delinquent act, the minor shall be released to the parents, guardian or custodian, and ordered to appear at the adjudicatory hearing unless:

(1) The act is serious enough to warrant continued detention or shelter care;

(2) There is reasonable cause to believe the minor will run away and be unavailable for further proceedings; or

(3) There is reasonable cause to believe that the minor will commit a serious act causing damage to person or property.

(g) The children's court may release a minor pursuant to paragraph (f) of this section to a relative or other responsible adult tribal member if the parent, guardian, or custodian of the minor consents to the release. If the minor is ten years of age or older, the minor and the parents, guardian or custodian must both consent to the release.

(h) Upon a finding that probable cause exists to believe that the minor has committed the alleged delinquent act and that there is need for detention or shelter care, the minor's detention or shelter care shall be continued. Otherwise, the complaint shall be dismissed and the minor released.

§ 11.1006 Investigation by the presenting officer.

(a) The presenting officer shall make an investigation following the preliminary inquiry or the release of the minor to his or her parents, guardian or custodian to determine whether the interests of the minor and the public require that further action be taken. Upon the basis of this investigation, the presenting officer may:

(1) Determine that no further action be taken;

(2) Begin transfer proceedings to the Court of Indian Offenses pursuant to § 11.907 of this part; or

(3) File a petition pursuant to § 11.1007 of this part to initiate further proceedings. The petition shall be filed within 48 hours of the preliminary inquiry if the minor is in detention or shelter care. If the minor has been previously released to his or her parents, guardian or custodian, relative or responsible adult, the petition shall be filed within ten days of the preliminary inquiry.

§ 11.1007 Petition.

(a) Proceedings under §§ 11.1000–11.1014 of this part shall be instituted by a petition filed by the presenting officer on behalf of the tribe and in the interests of the minor. The petition shall state:

(1) The name, birth date, and residence of the minor;

(2) The names and residences of the minor's parents, guardian or custodian;

(3) A citation to the specific section(s) of this part which gives the children's court jurisdiction of the proceedings;

(4) A citation to the section(s) of this part which the minor is alleged to have violated; and

(5) If the minor is in detention or shelter care, the time the minor was taken into custody.

§ 11.1008 Date of hearing.

Upon receipt of the petition, the children's court shall set a date for the hearing which shall not be more than 15 days after the children's court receives the petition from the presenting officer. If the adjudicatory hearing is not held within 15 days after filing of the petition, the petition shall be dismissed and cannot be filed again, unless;

(a) The hearing is continued upon motion of the minor; or

(b) The hearing is continued upon motion of the presenting officer by reason of the unavailability of material evidence or witnesses and the children's court finds the presenting officer has exercised due diligence to obtain the material evidence or witnesses and reasonable grounds exist to believe that the material evidence or witnesses will become available.

§ 11.1009 Summons.

(a) At least five working days prior to the adjudicatory hearing, the children's court shall issue summons to:

(1) The minor;

(2) The minor's parents, guardian or custodian; and

(3) Any person the children's court or the minor believes necessary for the adjudication of the hearing.

(b) The summons shall contain the name of the court, the title of the proceedings, and the date, time and place of the hearing.

(c) A copy of the petition shall be attached to the summons.

(d) The summons shall be delivered personally by a law enforcement officer or appointee of the children's court. If the summons cannot be delivered personally, the court may deliver it by certified mail.

§ 11.1010 Adjudicatory hearing.

(a) The children's court shall conduct the adjudicatory hearing for the sole purpose of determining the guilt or innocence of the minor. The hearing shall be private and closed.

(b) All the rights listed in § 11.906 shall be afforded the parties at the adjudicatory hearing. The notice requirements of § 11.906(a) are met by a summons issued pursuant to § 11.1009.

(c) If the minor admits the allegations of the petition, the children's court shall proceed to the dispositional stage only if the children's court finds that:

(1) The minor fully understands his or her rights as set forth in § 11.906 of this part and fully understands the potential consequences of admitting the allegations;

(2) The minor voluntarily, intelligently and knowingly admits to all facts necessary to constitute a basis for children's court action; and

(3) The minor has not, in the purported admission to the allegations, set forth facts which, if found to be true, constitute a defense to the allegations.

(d) The children's court shall hear testimony concerning the circumstances which gave rise to the complaint.

(e) If the allegations of the petition are sustained by proof beyond a reasonable doubt, the children's court shall find the minor to be a juvenile offender and proceed to the dispositional hearing.

(f) A finding that a minor is a juvenile offender constitutes a final order for purposes of appeal.

§11.1011 Dispositional hearing.

(a) A dispositional hearing shall take place not more than 15 days after the adjudicatory hearing.

(b) At the dispositional hearing, the children's court shall hear evidence on the question of proper disposition.

(c) All the rights listed in §11.906 shall be afforded the parties in the dispositional hearing.

(d) At the dispositional hearing, the children's court shall consider any predisposition report, physician's report or social study it may have ordered and afford the parents an opportunity to controvert the factual contents and conclusions of the reports. The children's court shall also consider the alternative predisposition report prepared by the minor and his or her attorney, if any.

(e) The dispositional order constitutes a final order for purposes of appeal.

§11.1012 Dispositional alternatives.

(a) If a minor has been adjudged a juvenile offender, the children's court may make the following disposition:

(1) Place the minor on probation subject to conditions set by the children's court;

(2) Place the minor in an agency or institution designated by the children's court; or

(3) Order restitution to the aggrieved party.

(b) The dispositional orders are to be in effect for the time limit set by the children's court, but no order may continue after the minor reaches 18 years of age, unless the dispositional order was made within six months of the minor's eighteenth birthday or after the minor had reached 18 years of age, in which case the disposition may not continue for more than six months.

(c) The dispositional order is to be reviewed at the children's court discretion, but at least once every six months.

§11.1013 Modification of dispositional order.

(a) A dispositional order of the children's court may be modified upon a showing of a change of circumstances.

(b) The children's court may modify a dispositional order at any time upon the motion of the minor or the minor's parents, guardian or custodian.

(c) If the modification involves a change of custody, the children's court shall conduct a hearing pursuant to paragraph (d) of this section.

(d) A hearing to review a dispositional order shall be conducted as follows:

(1) All the rights listed in §11.906 shall be afforded the parties in the hearing to review the dispositional order. The notice required by paragraph (a) of §11.906 shall be given at least 48 hours before the hearing.

(2) The children's court shall review the performance of the minor, the minor's parents, guardian or custodian, and other persons providing assistance to the minor and the minor's family.

(3) In determining modification of disposition, the procedures prescribed in §11.1011 of this part shall apply.

(4) If the request for review of disposition is based upon an alleged violation of a court order, the children's court shall not modify its dispositional order unless it finds clear and convincing evidence of the violation.

§11.1014 Medical examination.

The children's court may order a medical examination for a minor who is alleged to be a juvenile offender.

Subpart K—Minor-in-Need-of-Care Procedure

§ 11.1100 Complaint.

A complaint must be filed by a law enforcement officer or by the presenting officer and sworn to by a person who has knowledge of the facts alleged. The complaint shall be signed by the complaining witness and shall contain:

(a) A citation to the specific section of this part which gives the children's court jurisdiction of the proceedings;

(b) The name, age and address of the minor who is the subject of the complaint, if known; and

(c) A plain and concise statement of the facts upon which the allegations are based, including the date, time and location at which the alleged facts occurred.

§ 11.1101 Warrant.

The children's court may issue a warrant, directing that a minor be taken into custody if the children's court finds there is probable cause to believe the minor is a minor-in-need-of-care.

§ 11.1102 Custody.

A minor may be taken into custody by a law enforcement officer if:

(a) The officer has reasonable grounds to believe that the minor is a minor-in-need-of-care and that the minor is in immediate danger from his or her surroundings and that removal is necessary; or

(b) A warrant pursuant to § 11.1101 of this part has been issued for the minor.

§ 11.1103 Law enforcement officer's duties.

Upon taking a minor into custody the officer shall:

(a) Release the minor to the minor's parents, guardian or custodian and issue a verbal advice or warning as may be appropriate, unless shelter care is necessary.

(b) If the minor is not released, make immediate and recurring efforts to notify the minor's parents, guardian or custodian to inform them that the minor has been taken into custody and inform them of their right to be present with the minor until an investigation to determine the need for shelter care is made by the children's court.

§ 11.1104 Shelter care.

(a) A minor alleged to be a minor-in-need-of-care may be detained, pending a court hearing, in the following places:

(1) A foster care facility authorized under tribal or state law to provide foster care, group care or protective residence;

(2) A private family home approved by the tribe; or

(3) A shelter care facility operated by a licensed child welfare services agency and approved by the tribe.

(b) A minor alleged to be a minor-in-need-of care may not be detained in a jail or other facility used for the detention of adults. If such minor is detained in a facility used for the detention of juvenile offenders, he or she must be detained in a room separate from juvenile offenders, and routine inspection of the room where the minor is detained must be conducted every 30 minutes to assure his or her safety and welfare.

§ 11.1105 Preliminary inquiry.

(a) If a minor is placed in shelter care, the children's court shall conduct a preliminary inquiry with 24 hours for the purpose of determining:

(1) Whether probable cause exists to believe the minor is a minor-in-need-of care; and

(2) Whether continued shelter care is necessary pending further proceedings.

(b) If a minor has been released to the parents, guardian or custodian, the children's court shall conduct a preliminary inquiry within three days after receipt of the complaint for the sole purpose of determining whether probable cause exists to believe the minor is a minor-in-need-of-care.

(c) If the minor's parents, guardian or custodian is not present at the preliminary inquiry, the children's court shall determine what efforts have been made to notify and obtain the presence of the parent, guardian or custodian. If it appears that further efforts are likely to produce the parent, guardian or custodian, the children's court shall recess for no more than 24 hours and direct that continued efforts be made to obtain the presence of the parents, guardian or custodian.

(d) All the rights listed in § 11.906 of this part shall be afforded the parties in the minor-in-need-of care preliminary inquiry except that the court is not required to appoint counsel if the parties cannot afford one. Notice of the inquiry shall be given to the minor, and his or her parents, guardian or custodian and their counsel as soon as the time for the inquiry has been established.

(e) The children's court shall hear testimony concerning:

(1) The circumstances that gave rise to the complaint or the taking of the minor into custody; and

(2) The need for shelter care.

(f) If the children's court finds that probable cause exists to believe the minor is a minor-in-need-of-care, the minor shall be released to the parents, guardian or custodian, and ordered to appear at the adjudicatory hearing, unless:

(1) There is reasonable cause to believe that the minor will run away and be unavailable for further proceedings;

(2) There is reasonable cause to believe that the minor is in immediate danger from parents, guardian or custodian and that removal from them is necessary; or

(3) There is a reasonable cause to believe that the minor will commit a serious act causing damage to person or property.

(g) The children's court may release the minor pursuant to paragraph (f) of this section to a relative or other responsible adult tribal member if the parents, guardian or custodian of the minor consent to the release. If the minor is ten years to age or older, the minor and the parents, guardian or custodian must both consent to the release.

(h) Upon finding that probable cause exists to believe that the minor is a minor-in-need-of-care and that there is a need for shelter care, the minor's shelter care shall be continued. Otherwise, the complaint shall be dismissed and the minor released.

§ 11.1106 Investigation by the presenting officer.

The presenting officer shall make an investigation following the preliminary inquiry or the release of the minor to the parents, guardian or custodian to determine whether the interests of the minor and the public require that further action be taken. Upon the basis of this investigation, the presenting officer may:

(a) Determine that no further action be taken; or

(b) File a petition pursuant to § 11.1107 of this part in the children's court to initiate further proceedings. The petition shall be filed within 48 hours of the preliminary inquiry if the minor is in shelter care. If the minor has been previously released to the parents, guardian or custodian, relative or responsible adult, the petition shall be filed within ten days of the preliminary inquiry.

§ 11.1107 Petition.

Proceedings under §§ 11.1100–11.1114 of this part shall be instituted by a petition filed by the presenting officer on behalf of the tribe and the interests of the minor. The petition shall state:

(a) The name, birth date, and residence of the minor;

(b) The names and residences of the minor's parents, guardian or custodian;

(c) A citation to the specific section of this part which gives the children's court jurisdiction of the proceedings; and

(d) If the minor is in shelter care, the place of shelter care and the time he or she was taken into custody.

§ 11.1108 Date of hearing.

Upon receipt of the minor-in-need-of-care petition, the children's court shall set a date for the hearing which shall not be more than 15 days after the children's court receives the petition from the presenting officer. If the adjudicatory hearing is not held within 15 days after the filing of the petition, it shall be dismissed unless;

(a) The hearing is continued upon motion of the minor; or

(b) The hearing is continued upon motion of the presenting officer by reason of the unavailability of material evidence or witnesses and the children's court finds the presenting officer has exercised due diligence to obtain the material evidence or witnesses and reasonable grounds exist to believe that the material evidence or witnesses will become available.

§ 11.1109 Summons.

(a) At least five working days prior to the adjudicatory hearing for a minor-in-need-of-care, the children's court shall issue summons to:

(1) The minor;

(2) The minor's parents, guardian or custodian; and

(3) Any person the children's court or the minor believes necessary for the proper adjudication of the hearing.

(b) The summons shall contain the name of the court; the title of the proceedings, and the date, time and place of the hearing.

(c) A copy of the petition shall be attached to the summons.

(d) The summons shall be delivered personally by a tribal law enforcement officer or appointee of the children's court. If the summons cannot be delivered personally, the court may deliver it by certified mail.

§ 11.1110 Minor-in-need-of-care adjudicatory hearing.

(a) The children's court shall conduct the adjudicatory hearing for the sole purpose of determining whether the minor is a minor-in-need-of-care. The hearing shall be private and closed.

(b) All the rights listed in § 11.906 of this part shall be afforded the parties in the adjudicatory hearing, except that the court may not appoint counsel if the parties cannot afford one. The notice requirements of § 11.906(a) are met by a summons issued pursuant to § 11.1109.

(c) The children's court shall hear testimony concerning the circumstances which gave rise to the complaint.

(d) If the circumstances of the petition are sustained by clear and convincing evidence, the children's court shall find the minor to be a minor-in-need-of-care and proceed to the dispositional hearing.

(e) A finding that a minor is a minor-in-need-of-care constitutes a final order for purposes of appeal.

§ 11.1111 Minor-in-need-of-care dispositional hearing.

(a) No later than 15 days after the adjudicatory hearing, a dispositional hearing shall take place to hear evidence on the question of proper disposition.

(b) All the rights listed in § 11.906 of this part shall be afforded the parties in the dispositional hearing except the right to free court-appointed counsel. Notice of the hearing shall be given to the parties at least 48 hours before the hearing.

(c) At the dispositional hearing the children's court shall consider any predisposition report or other study it may have ordered and afford the parties an opportunity to controvert the factual contents and conclusions of the reports. The children's court shall also consider the alternative predisposition report prepared by the minor and his or her attorney, if any.

(d) The dispositional order constitutes a final order for purposes of appeal.

§ 11.1112 Dispositional alternatives.

(a) If a minor has been adjudged a minor-in-need-of-care, the children's court may:

(1) Permit the minor to remain with his or her parents, guardian or custodian subject to such limitations and conditions as the court may prescribe; or, if reasonable efforts to have the minor return or remain in his or her own home are unsuccessful, the children's court may make whichever of the following dispositions is in the best interest of the minor;

(2) Place the minor with a relative within the boundaries of the reservation subject to such limitations and conditions as the court may prescribe;

(3) Place the minor in a foster home within the boundaries of the reservation which has been approved by the tribe subject to such limitations and conditions as the court may prescribe;

(4) Place the minor in shelter care facilities designated by the court;

(5) Place the minor in a foster home or a relative's home outside the boundaries of the reservation subject to such limitations and conditions as the court may prescribe; or

(6) Recommend that termination proceedings begin.

(b) Whenever a minor is placed in a home or facility located outside the boundaries of the reservation, the court may require the party receiving custody of the minor to sign an agreement that the minor will be returned to the court upon order of the court.

(c) The dispositional orders are to be in effect for the time limit set by the children's court, but no order may continue after the minor reaches 18 years of age, unless the dispositional order was made within six months of the minor's eighteenth birthday, in which case the disposition may not continue for more than six months.

(d) The dispositional orders are to be reviewed at the children's court discretion, but at least once every six months to determine the continuing need for and appropriateness of placement, to determine the extent of progress made, and to assess the probability of the minor's return to his or her home.

(e) A permanency planning hearing must be held within 18 months after the original placement and every six months thereafter to determine the future status of the minor except when the minor is returned to his or her home and court supervision ceases.

§11.1113 Modification of dispositional order.

(a) A dispositional order of the children's court may be modified upon a showing of a change of circumstances.

(b) The children's court may modify a dispositional order at any time upon motion of the minor or the minor's parents, guardian or custodian.

(c) If the modification involves a change of custody, the children's court shall conduct a hearing pursuant to paragraph (d) of this section to review the dispositional order.

(d) A hearing to review a dispositional order shall be conducted as follows:

(1) All the rights listed in §11.906 of this part shall be afforded the parties in the review of the disposition hearing except the right to free court-appointed counsel. Notice of the hearing shall be given the parties at least 48 hours before the hearing.

(2) The children's court shall review the performance of the minor, the minor's parents, guardian or custodian, and other persons providing assistance to the minor and the minor's family.

(3) In determining modification of disposition, the procedures prescribed in §11.1111 of this part shall apply.

(4) If the request for review of disposition is based upon an alleged violation of a court order, the children's court shall not modify its dispositional order unless it finds clear and convincing evidence of the violation.

§11.1114 Termination.

(a) Parental rights to a child may be terminated by the children's court according to the procedures in this section.

(b) Proceedings to terminate parental rights shall be instituted by a petition filed by the presenting officer on behalf of the tribe or by the parents or guardian of the child. The petition shall state:

(1) The name, birth date, and residence of the minor;

(2) The names and residences of the minor's parents, guardian or custodian;

(3) If the child is in detention or shelter care, the place of detention or shelter care and the time he was taken into custody; and

(4) The reasons for the petition.

(c) Upon receipt of the petition, the children's court shall set a date for the termination hearing which shall not be more than 15 days after the children's court receives the petition from the presenting officer. The hearing may be continued:

(1) On motion of the minor's parents, guardian or custodian; or

(2) Upon motion of the presenting officer by reason of the unavailability of material evidence or witnesses and the children's court finds the presenting officer has exercised due diligence to obtain the material evidence or witnesses and reasonable grounds exist to believe that the material evidence or witnesses will become available.

(d) Summons:

(1) At least five working days prior to the termination hearing, the children's court shall issue summons to the minor, the minor's parents, guardian or custodian, and any other person the court or the minor's parents, guardian or custodian believes necessary for the proper adjudication of the hearing.

(2) The summons shall contain the name of the court, the title of the proceedings, and the date, time and place of the hearing.

(3) A copy of the petition shall be attached to the summons.

(4) The summons shall be delivered personally by a law enforcement officer or appointee of the children's court. If the summons cannot be delivered personally, the court may deliver it by certified mail.

(e) The children's court shall conduct the termination hearing for the sole purpose of determining whether parental rights shall be terminated. The hearing shall be private and closed.

(1) All the rights listed in § 11.906 shall be afforded the parties in the termination hearing except the right to a free court-appointed counsel. The minor's parents may not be compelled to be witnesses against, nor otherwise incriminate themselves.

(2) The children's court shall hear testimony concerning the circumstances that gave rise to the petition, and the need for termination of parental rights.

(3) The children's court may terminate parental rights if, following efforts to prevent or eliminate the need to remove the minor, it finds such efforts to have been unsuccessful, and it finds beyond a reasonable doubt that:

(i) The child has been abandoned;

(ii) The minor has suffered physical injuries, willfully and repeatedly inflicted by his or her parent(s) which cause or create a substantial risk of death, disfigurement, or impairment of bodily functions;

(iii) The parent(s) has subjected the minor to willful and repeated acts of sexual abuse;

(iv) The minor has suffered serious emotional or mental harm due to the act of the parent(s); or

(v) The voluntary written consent of both parents has been acknowledged before the court.

(f) Dispositional alternatives:

(1) If parental rights to a child are terminated, the children's court shall place the minor in a foster care or shelter care facility which has been approved by the tribe, and follow the adoption procedures of the tribe, or, in their absence, the adoption procedures of the state within which it is located.

(2) If parental rights to a child are not terminated, the children's court shall make a disposition according to § 11.1112 of this part.

(g) The termination order constitutes a final order for purposes of appeal.

(h) No adjudication of termination of parental rights shall affect the minor's enrollment status as a member of any tribe or the minor's degree of blood quantum of any tribe.

§ 11.1115 Information collection.

(a) The information collection requirements contained in § 11.600 and § 11.606 have been approved by the Office of Management and Budget under 44 U.S.C. 3501 *et seq.*, and assigned approval number 1076–0094. The information is being collected to obtain a marriage license (§ 11.600) and a divorce decree (§ 11.606) from the Courts of Indian Offenses, and will be used by the courts to issue a marriage license or divorce decree. Response to this request is required to obtain a benefit.

(b) Public reporting for this information collection is estimated to average .25 hours per response, including the time for reviewing instructions, gathering and maintaining data, and completing and reviewing the information collection. Direct comments regarding the burden estimate or any other aspect of this information collection to the Bureau of Indian Affairs, Information Collection Clearance Officer, Room 336–SIB, 1849 C Street, NW., Washington, DC 20240; and the Office of Information and Regulatory Affairs [Project 1076–0094], Office of Management and Budget, Washington, DC 20502.

Subpart L—Child Protection and Domestic Violence Procedures

SOURCE: 73 FR 39862, July 11, 2008, unless otherwise noted.

§ 11.1200 Definitions.

For purposes of this subpart:

Domestic violence means to inflict physical harm, bodily injury, or sexual assault, or the fear of imminent physical harm, bodily injury, or sexual assault on a family member.

Family member means any of the following:

(1) A spouse;

(2) A former spouse;

(3) A person related by blood;

(4) A person related by existing or prior marriage;

(5) A person who resides or resided with the defendant;

(6) A person with whom the defendant has a child in common; or

(7) A person with whom the defendant is or was in a dating or intimate relationship.

Parent means persons who have a child in common, regardless of whether they have been married or have lived together at any time.

§ 11.1202 How to petition for an order of protection.

A victim of domestic violence, or the parent, guardian of a victim, or a concerned adult may petition the court under this subpart for an order of protection.

(a) The petition must be made under oath or accompanied by a sworn affidavit setting out specific facts describing the act of domestic violence.

(b) The petitioner is not required to file for annulment, separation, or divorce in order to obtain an order of protection. However, the petition should state whether any legal action is pending between the petitioner and the respondent.

(c) The Court may develop simplified petition forms with instructions for completion and make them available to petitioners not represented by counsel. Law enforcement agencies may keep the forms on hand and make them available upon request to victims of domestic violence.

§ 11.1204 Obtaining an emergency order of protection.

(a) When a victim files a petition for an order of protection under § 11.202(a), the court may immediately grant an ex parte emergency order of protection if the petition clearly shows that an act of domestic violence has occurred. The order must meet the content requirements of § 11.206 (a) and (b).

(b) If the court does not immediately grant an emergency order of protection under paragraph (a) of this section, the court must either:

(1) Within 72 hours after the victim files a petition, serve notice to appear upon both parties and hold a hearing on the petition for order of protection; or

(2) If a notice of hearing cannot be served within 72 hours, issue an emergency order of protection.

(c) If the court issues an ex parte emergency order of protection under paragraph (a) of this section, it must within 10 days hold a hearing on the question of continuing the order. If notice of hearing cannot be served within 10 days:

(1) The emergency order of protection is automatically extended for 10 days; and

(2) If after the 10-day extension, notice to appear cannot be served, the emergency order of protection expires.

(d) If the court issues an ex parte emergency order of protection under paragraph (b)(2) of this section, it must cause the order to be served on the person alleged to have committed a family violence act and seek to hold a hearing as soon as possible. If a hearing cannot be held within 10 days, the petitioner may ask the court to renew the emergency protection order.

§ 11.1206 Obtaining a regular (non-emergency) order of protection.

Following a hearing and finding that an act of domestic violence occurred, the court may issue an order of protection. The order must meet the requirements of paragraph (a) of this section and may meet the requirements of paragraph (b) of this section. Either party may request a review hearing to amend or vacate the order of protection.

(a) The order of protection must do all of the following:

(1) Specifically describe in clear language the behavior the court has ordered he or she do or refrain from doing;

(2) Give notice that violation of any provision of the order of protection constitutes contempt of court and may result in a fine or imprisonment, or both; and

(3) Indicate whether the order of protection supersedes or alters prior orders pertaining to matters between the parties.

(b) The order of protection may do any of the following:

(1) Order the person who committed the act of domestic violence to refrain from acts or threats of violence against the petitioner or any other family member;

(2) Order that the person who committed the act of domestic violence be removed from the home of the petitioner;

(3) Grant sole possession of the residence or household to the petitioner during the period the order of protection is effective, or order the person who has committed an act of domestic violence to provide temporary suitable alternative housing for the petitioner and other family members to whom the respondent owes a legal obligation of support;

(4) Award temporary custody of any children involved when appropriate and provide for visitation rights, child support, and temporary support for the petitioner on a basis which gives primary consideration to the safety of the petitioner and other household members;

(5) Order the person who is found to have committed an act of domestic violence not to initiate contact with the petitioner;

(6) Restrain the parties from transferring, concealing, encumbering, or otherwise disposing of one another's property or the joint property of the parties except in the usual course of business or for the necessities of life, and order the parties to account to the court for all such transferring, encumbrances, and expenditures made after the order is served or communicated; and

(7) Order other injunctive relief as the court deems necessary for the protection of the petitioner, including orders to law enforcement agencies as provided by this subpart.

§ 11.1208 Service of the protection order.

When an order of protection is granted under this subpart:

(a) The petitioner must file it with the clerk of the court;

(b) The clerk of the court must send a copy to a law enforcement agency with jurisdiction over the area in which the court is located;

(c) The order must be personally served upon the respondent, unless the respondent or his or her attorney was present at the time the order was issued; and

(d) If the court finds the petitioner unable to pay court costs, the order will be served without cost to the petitioner.

§ 11.1210 Duration and renewal of a regular protection order.

An order of protection granted by the court:

(a) Is effective for a fixed period of time, which is up to a maximum of 6 months; and

(b) May be extended for good cause upon motion of the petitioner for an additional period of up to 6 months each time a petition is presented. A petitioner may request as many extensions as necessary provided that the court determines that good cause exists.

§ 11.1212 Consequences of disobedience or interference.

Any willful disobedience or interference with any court order constitutes contempt of court which may result in a fine or imprisonment, or both, in accordance with this part.

§ 11.1214 Relationship of this subpart to other remedies.

The remedies provided in this subpart are in addition to the other civil or criminal remedies available to the petitioner.

PART 12—INDIAN COUNTRY LAW ENFORCEMENT

Subpart A—Responsibilities

AUTHORITY: 5 U.S.C. 301; 25 U.S.C. 2, 9, 13, 2417, 2453, and 2802.

SOURCE: 62 FR 15611, Apr. 2, 1997, unless otherwise noted.

Subpart A—Responsibilities

§ 12.1 Who is responsible for the Bureau of Indian Affairs law enforcement function?

The Commissioner of Indian Affairs, or in the absence of a Commissioner, the Deputy Commissioner, is responsible for Bureau of Indian Affairs-operated and contracted law enforcement programs, and for overall policy development and implementation of the Indian Law Enforcement Reform Act, Public Law 101–379 (25 U.S.C. 2801 *et seq.*).

§ 12.2 What is the role of the Bureau of Indian Affairs Director of Law Enforcement Services?

The Director of the Office of Law Enforcement Services for the Bureau of Indian Affairs (Director) has been delegated the responsibility for the development of law enforcement and detention policies, standards, and management of all Bureau of Indian Affairs (BIA) criminal investigations, drug enforcement, training, internal affairs, inspection and evaluation, emergency response forces, and other national level Indian country law enforcement initiatives. The Director publishes these policies and standards in law enforcement manuals and handbooks. The Director is also directly responsible for developing crime prevention and outreach programs within Indian country law enforcement.

§ 12.3 Who supervises Bureau of Indian Affairs criminal investigators?

All BIA criminal investigators are supervised by other criminal investigators within the Office of Law Enforcement Services.

§ 12.4 Who supervises the Bureau of Indian Affairs uniformed police, detention, and conservation enforcement functions?

The agency superintendent is directly responsible for the operation and management of BIA uniformed police operations, detention facilities, and conservation enforcement operations at any agency having these programs. The agency superintendent must also ensure technical support is provided to any agency contracting the law enforcement and/or detention program.

Subpart B—Policies and Standards

§ 12.11 Do I have to follow these regulations?

You must follow the minimum standards outlined in the regulations in this part if you are part of a BIA or tribal law enforcement program receiving Federal funding or operating under a BIA law enforcement commission.

§ 12.12 What about self-determination?

The regulations in this part are not intended to discourage contracting of Indian country law enforcement programs under the Indian Self-determination and Education Assistance Act (Pub. L. 93–638, as amended, 25 U.S.C. 450). The Deputy Commissioner of Indian Affairs will ensure minimum standards are maintained in high risk activities where the Federal government retains liability and the responsibility for settling tort claims arising from contracted law enforcement programs. It is not fair to law abiding citizens of Indian country to have anything less than a professional law enforcement program in their community. Indian country law enforcement programs that receive Federal funding and/or commissioning will be subject to a periodic inspection or evaluation to provide technical assistance, to ensure compliance with minimum Federal standards, and to identify necessary changes or improvements to BIA policies.

§ 12.13 What happens if I do not follow the rules in this part?

Your BIA law enforcement commission may be revoked, your law enforcement contract may be canceled, and you may no longer be eligible for tribal shares allocated from the law enforcement budget.

§ 12.14 Where can I find specific policies and standards for law enforcement functions in Indian country?

BIA will ensure that all Indian country law enforcement programs are provided a copy of the most current policy manuals and handbooks. Every Indian country law enforcement program covered by the regulations in this part must maintain an effective and efficient law enforcement program meeting minimal qualitative standards and procedures specified in chapter 68 Bureau of Indian Affairs Manual (BIAM) and the Law Enforcement Handbook.

Subpart C—Authority and Jurisdiction

§ 12.21 What authority is given to Indian country law enforcement officers to perform their duties?

BIA law enforcement officers are commissioned under the authority established in 25 U.S.C. 2803. BIA may issue law enforcement commissions to other Federal, State, local and tribal full-time certified law enforcement officers to obtain active assistance in enforcing applicable Federal criminal statutes, including Federal hunting and fishing regulations, in Indian country.

(a) BIA will issue commissions to other Federal, State, local and tribal full-time certified law enforcement officers only after the head of the local government or Federal agency completes an agreement with the Commissioner of Indian Affairs asking that BIA issue delegated commissions. The agreement must include language that allows the BIA to evaluate the effectiveness of these special law enforcement commissions and to investigate any allegations of misuse of authority.

(b) Tribal law enforcement officers operating under a BIA contract or compact are not automatically commissioned as Federal officers; however, they may be commissioned on a case-by-case basis.

§ 12.22 Can Bureau of Indian Affairs law enforcement officers enforce tribal laws?

BIA officers will enforce tribal laws only with the permission of the tribe. Local programs are encouraged to make arrangements and agreements with local jurisdictions to facilitate law enforcement objectives.

§ 12.23 What are the jurisdictional limits in Indian country?

The Department of the Interior and the Department of Justice must maintain and periodically review and update a memorandum of understanding describing the relationship between the Federal Bureau of Investigation and the Bureau of Indian Affairs in the investigation and prosecution of major crimes in Indian country. Any law enforcement programs performing duties under the authority of 25 U.S.C. 2803 must follow the guidelines in the memorandum of understanding and any local United States Attorney's guidelines for the investigation and prosecution of Federal crimes.

Subpart D—Qualifications and Training Requirements

§ 12.31 Are there any minimum employment standards for Indian country law enforcement personnel?

The Director must develop, maintain, and periodically review the qualification standards, including medical qualification standards, for all BIA law enforcement, detention, and conservation enforcement occupational series. The standards will be no less stringent than the minimum standards established by the U.S. Office of Personnel Management (OPM) for these occupational series, and may exceed the OPM standards. BIA standards are available for review at any BIA personnel office. All tribal programs are encouraged to develop standards at least as stringent as those established for BIA officers.

§ 12.32 Do minimum employment standards include a background investigation?

Law enforcement authority is only entrusted to personnel possessing adequate education and/or experience, training, aptitude, and high moral character. All Indian country law enforcement programs receiving Federal funding and/or authority must ensure that all law enforcement officers successfully complete a thorough background investigation no less stringent than required of a Federal officer performing the same duties. The background investigations of applicants and employees must be adjudicated by trained and qualified security professionals. All background investigations must be documented and available for inspection by the Bureau of Indian Affairs.

§ 12.33 Are Indian country law enforcement officers paid less than other law enforcement officers?

An officer's pay is determined by his/her grade and classification. The Commissioner of Indian Affairs must ensure that all BIA law enforcement officer positions are established at no lower grade level on the Federal scale than similar Federal law enforcement officer positions in other agencies. No BIA position performing commissioned law enforcement duties will be classified in other than the GS 0083, police officer series, for uniformed officers and the GS 1811, criminal investigating series, for criminal investigators.

§ 12.34 Do minimum salaries and position classifications apply to a tribe that has contracted or compacted law enforcement under self-determination?

Any contract or compact with the BIA to provide law enforcement services for an Indian tribe must require a law enforcement officer to be paid at least the same salary as a BIA officer performing the same duties.

§ 12.35 Do Indian country law enforcement officers complete any special training?

Law enforcement personnel of any program funded by the Bureau of Indian Affairs must not perform law enforcement duties until they have successfully completed a basic law enforcement training course prescribed by the Director. The Director will also prescribe mandatory supplemental and in-service training courses.

§ 12.36 Does other law enforcement training count?

All requests for evaluation of equivalent training must be submitted to the Indian Police Academy for review, with final determination made by the Director. Requests for a waiver of training requirements to use personnel before completing the required courses of instruction must be submitted to the Director and approved or disapproved by the Commissioner of Indian Affairs. In no case will such a waiver allow personnel to be used in any position for more than one year without achieving training standards. Failure to complete basic training requirements will result in removal from a law enforcement position.

Subpart E—Records and Information

§ 12.41 Who keeps statistics for Indian country law enforcement activities?

The Director maintains a criminal justice information system for Indian country. The Director will prescribe the types of data to be collected and the reporting format to be used to collect information and assemble reports on crime reported in Indian country. These reports may be provided to the Department of Justice. Any law enforcement program receiving funding from the BIA must use the same reporting format and submit the same statistical reports to the Office of Law Enforcement Services as prescribed by the Director and as are required of all BIA law enforcement programs.

§ 12.42 Do Indian country law enforcement programs share information with their own communities or other agencies?

At intervals established by the Director, each BIA criminal investigations program, and any investigations program receiving BIA funds will consult with local tribal leaders and managers of local patrol and detention programs. They will discuss the quality of the local investigations program and offer feedback and technical assistance. There will be no requirement to disclose confidential investigative information or to compromise ongoing investigations during this process.

Subpart F—Conduct

§ 12.51 Must Indian country law enforcement officers follow a code of conduct?

All law enforcement programs receiving Bureau of Indian Affairs funding or commissioning must establish a law enforcement code of conduct which establishes specific guidelines for conduct on and off duty, impartiality, and professional conduct in the performance of duty, and acceptance of gifts or favors. Each officer must acknowledge in writing receiving and understanding of this code of conduct. The acknowledgment will remain on file with the law enforcement program manager as long as the officer is employed there. Training will be conducted on this code of conduct and other ethics issues at least once each year.

§ 12.52 How do I report misconduct?

The Director will develop and maintain a reporting system that allows any resident of or visitor to Indian country to report officer misconduct. Each law enforcement program in Indian country will maintain instructions on how to register a complaint. An overview of these steps must be posted for public viewing at each law enforcement facility in Indian country.

§ 12.53 Who investigates officer misconduct?

The Director, Office of Law Enforcement Services maintains an internal affairs program that investigates all allegations of misconduct by BIA officers, and any officer receiving funding and/or authority from the BIA. All allegations of misconduct must be thoroughly investigated and appropriate action taken when warranted. Any person having knowledge of officer misconduct must report that information to the officer's supervisor. The supervisor must immediately report allegations to the internal affairs unit. Depending upon the severity of the allegation, the matter may be dealt with locally or it will be investigated by the internal affairs unit. Failure of any BIA employee to report known allegations may be considered misconduct in itself. Citizens may report officer misconduct directly to the internal affairs unit if that is more practical.

§12.54 What can I do if I believe my civil rights have been violated?

All allegations of civil rights violations must be reported immediately to the internal affairs unit. That office will ensure that allegations are immediately reported to the Civil Rights Division of the U. S. Department of Justice through established procedures. BIA's internal affairs unit may also investigate the matter and make recommendations for additional action as necessary.

§12.55 Are there any limits on how much force an officer can use when performing law enforcement duties?

The Director will develop and maintain the use of force policy for all BIA law enforcement personnel, and for programs receiving BIA funding or authority. Training in the use of force, to include non-lethal measures, will be provided annually. All officers will successfully complete a course of instruction in firearms, to include judgement pistol shooting, approved by the Indian Police Academy before carrying a firearm on or off duty.

Subpart G—Support Functions

§12.61 Can I be paid for information that helps solve a crime?

The Director can spend money to purchase evidence or information, or to offer a reward, in the investigation of a crime. This is subject to the availability of funds. This authority may be delegated in writing to supervisory criminal investigators within the Office of Law Enforcement Services in the BIA. The Director must develop policies and procedures for the expenditure, control, and audit of these funds before their use.

§12.62 Who decides what uniform an Indian country law enforcement officer can wear and who pays for it?

Each local law enforcement program must establish its own uniform requirements for patrol and detention personnel. Uniformed BIA police officers may be paid an annual uniform allowance not to exceed $400. Local programs may provide uniforms and related equipment to officers in lieu of this payment. All law enforcement officers must also have their official identification on their person at all times when performing law enforcement duties. Uniforms, when worn, will be plainly distinguishable from the uniforms of any non-law enforcement personnel working on the reservation.

§12.63 Do Indian country law enforcement officers perform other duties as well?

Law enforcement commissions will only be issued by the Bureau of Indian Affairs to persons occupying positions as full-time officers. Bureau of Indian Affairs funded or commissioned criminal investigators will not be responsible for supervising or managing any patrol, detention, or other uniformed police programs.

PART 13—TRIBAL REASSUMPTION OF JURISDICTION OVER CHILD CUSTODY PROCEEDINGS

Subpart A—Purpose

Subpart B—Reassumption

AUTHORITY: 25 U.S.C. 1952.

SOURCE: 44 FR 45095, July 31, 1979, unless otherwise noted.

Subpart A—Purpose

§13.1 Purpose.

(a) The regulations of this part establish the procedures by which an Indian tribe that occupies a reservation as defined in 25 U.S.C. 1903(10) over which a state asserts any jurisdiction pursuant to the provisions of the Act of August 15, 1953 (67 Stat. 588) Pub. L. 83–280, or pursuant to any other federal law (including any special federal law applicable only to a tribe or tribes in Oklahoma), may reassume jurisdiction over Indian child custody proceedings as authorized by the Indian Child Welfare Act, Pub. L. 95–608, 92 Stat. 3069, 25 U.S.C. 1918.

(b) On some reservations there are disputes concerning whether certain federal statutes have subjected Indian child custody proceedings to state jurisdiction or whether any such jurisdiction conferred on a state is exclusive of tribal jurisdiction. Tribes located on those reservations may wish to exercise exclusive jurisdiction or other jurisdiction currently exercised by the state without the necessity of engaging in protracted litigation. The procedures in this part also permit such tribes to secure unquestioned exclusive, concurrent or partial jurisdiction over Indian child custody matters without relinquishing their claim that no Federal statute had ever deprived them of that jurisdiction.

(c) Some tribes may wish to join together in a consortium to establish a single entity that will exercise jurisdiction over all their members located on the reservations of tribes participating in the consortium. These regulations also provide a procedure by which tribes may reassume jurisdiction through such a consortium.

(d) These regulations also provide for limited reassumptions including jurisdiction restricted to cases transferred from state courts under 25 U.S.C. 1911(b) and jurisdiction over limited geographical areas.

(e) Unless the petition for reassumption specifically states otherwise, where a tribe reassumes jurisdiction over the reservation it occupies, any land or community occupied by that tribe which subsequently acquires the status of reservation as defined in 25 U.S.C. 1903(10) also becomes subject to tribal jurisdiction over Indian child custody matters.

§ 13.2 Information collection.

The information collection requirement contained in § 13.11 has been approved by the Office of Management and Budget under 44 U.S.C. 3501 *et seq.* and assigned clearance number 1076–0112. The information is being collected when federally recognized tribes request reassumption of jurisdiction over child custody proceedings. The information will be used to determine if reassumption of jurisdiction over Indian child custody proceedings is feasible. Response is required to obtain a benefit.

[53 FR 21994, June 13, 1988]

Subpart B—Reassumption

§ 13.11 Contents of reassumption petitions.

(a) Each petition to reassume jurisdiction over Indian child custody proceedings and the accompanying plan shall contain, where available, the following information in sufficient detail to permit the Secretary to determine whether reassumption is feasible:

(1) Full name, address and telephone number of the petitioning tribe or tribes.

(2) A resolution by the tribal governing body supporting the petition and plan. If the territory involved is occupied by more than one tribe and jurisdiction is to be reassumed over all Indians residing in the territory, the governing body of each tribe involved must adopt such a resolution. A tribe that shares territory with another tribe or tribes may reassume jurisdiction only over its own members without obtaining the consent of the other tribe or tribes. Where a group of tribes form a consortium to reassume jurisdiction, the governing body of each participating tribe must submit a resolution.

(3) The proposed date on which jurisdiction would be reassumed.

(4) Estimated total number of members in the petitioning tribe or tribes, together with an explanation of how the number was estimated.

(5) Current criteria for membership in the tribe or tribes.

(6) Explanation of procedure by which a participant in an Indian child custody proceeding may determine whether a particular individual is a member of a petitioning tribe.

(7) Citation to provision in tribal constitution or similar governing document, if any, that authorizes the tribal

governing body to exercise jurisdiction over Indian child custody matters.

(8) Description of the tribal court as defined in 25 U.S.C. 1903(12) that has been or will be established to exercise jurisdiction over Indian child custody matters. The description shall include an organization chart and budget for the court. The source and amount of non-tribal funds that will be used to fund the court shall be identified. Funds that will become available only when the tribe reassumes jurisdiction may be included.

(9) Copy of any tribal ordinances or tribal court rules establishing procedures or rules for the exercise of jurisdiction over child custody matters.

(10) Description of child and family support services that will be available to the tribe or tribes when jurisdiction reassumed. Such services include any resource to maintain family stability or provide support for an Indian child in the absence of a family—regardless of whether or not they are the type of services traditionally employed by social services agencies. The description shall include not only those resources of the tribe itself, but also any state or federal resources that will continue to be available after reassumption of jurisdiction.

(11) Estimate of the number of child custody cases expected during a year together with an explanation of how the number was estimated.

(12) Copy of any tribal agreements with states, other tribes or non-Indian local governments relating to child custody matters.

(b) If the petition is for jurisdiction other than transferral jurisdiction under 25 U.S.C. 1911(b), the following information shall also be included in the petition and plan:

(1) Citation of the statute or statutes upon which the state has based its assertion of jurisdiction over Indian child custody matters.

(2) Clear and definite description of the territory over which jurisdiction will be reassumed together with a statement of the size of the territory in square miles.

(3) If a statute upon which the state bases its assertion of jurisdiction is a surplus land statute, a clear and definite description of the reservation boundaries that will be reestablished for purposes of the Indian Child Welfare Act.

(4) Estimated total number of Indian children residing in the affected territory together with an explanation of how the number was estimated.

§ 13.12 Criteria for approval of reassumption petitions.

(a) The Assistant Secretary—Indian Affairs shall approve a tribal petition to reassume jurisdiction over Indian child custody matters if:

(1) Any reservation, as defined in 25 U.S.C. 1903(10), presently affected by the petition is presently occupied by the petitioning tribe or tribes;

(2) The constitution or other governing document, if any, of the petitioning tribe or tribes authorizes the tribal governing body or bodies to exercise jurisdiction over Indian child custody matters;

(3) The information and documents required by § 13.11 of this part have been provided;

(4) A tribal court, as defined in 25 U.S.C. 1903(12), has been established or will be established before reassumption and that tribal court will be able to exercise jurisdiction over Indian child custody matters in a manner that meets the requirements of the Indian Civil Rights Act, 25 U.S.C. 1302;

(5) Child care services sufficient to meet the needs of most children the tribal court finds must be removed from parental custody are available or will be available at the time of reassumption of jurisdiction; and

(6) The tribe or tribes have established a procedure for clearly identifying persons who will be subject to the jurisdiction of the tribe or tribes upon reassumption of jurisdiction.

(b) If the technical assistance provided by the Bureau to the tribe to correct any deficiency which the Assistant Secretary—Indian Affairs has identified as a basis for disapproving a petition for reassumption of exclusive jurisdiction has proved unsuccessful in eliminating entirely such problem, the Bureau, at the request of the tribe, shall assist the tribe to assert whatever partial jurisdiction as provided in 25 U.S.C. 1918(b) that is feasible and desired by the tribe. In the alternative, the Bureau, if requested by the concerned tribe, shall assist the tribe to enter into agreements with a state or states regarding the care and custody of Indian children and jurisdiction over Indian child custody proceedings, including agreements which may provide for the orderly transfer of jurisdiction to the tribe on a case-by-case basis or agreements which provide for concurrent jurisdiction between the state and the Indian tribe.

§ 13.13 Technical assistance prior to petitioning.

(a) Upon the request of a tribe desiring to reassume jurisdiction over Indian child custody matters, Bureau agency and Area Offices shall provide technical assistance and make available any pertinent documents, records, maps or reports in the Bureau's possession to enable the tribe to meet the requirements for Secretarial approval of the petition.

(b) Upon the request of such a tribe, to the extent funds are available, the Bureau may provide funding under the procedures established under 25 CFR 23.22 to assist the tribe in developing the tribal court and child care services that will be needed when jurisdiction is reassumed.

§ 13.14 Secretarial review procedure.

(a) Upon receipt of the petition, the Assistant Secretary—Indian Affairs shall cause to be published in the FEDERAL REGISTER a notice stating that the petition has been received and is under review and that it may be inspected and copied at the Bureau agency office that serves the petitioning tribe or tribes.

(1) No final action shall be taken until 45 days after the petition has been received.

(2) Notice that a petition has been disapproved shall be published in the FEDERAL REGISTER no later than 75 days after the petition has been received.

(3) Notice that a petition has been approved shall be published on a date requested by the petitioning tribe or within 75 days after the petition has been received—whichever is later.

(b) Notice of approval shall include a clear and definite description of the territory presently subject to the reassumption of jurisdiction and shall state the date on which the reassumption becomes effective. A copy of the notice shall immediately be sent to the petitioning tribe and to the attorney general, governor and highest court of the affected State or States.

(c) Reasons for disapproval of a petition shall be sent immediately to the petitioning tribe or tribes.

(d) When a petition has been disapproved a tribe or tribes may repetition after taking action to overcome the deficiencies of the first petition.

§ 13.15 Administrative appeals.

The decision of the Assistant Secretary—Indian Affairs may be appealed under procedures established in 43 CFR 4.350–4.369.[1]

§ 13.16 Technical assistance after disapproval.

If a petition is disapproved, the Bureau shall immediately offer technical assistance to the tribal governing body for the purpose of overcoming the defect in the petition or plan that resulted in the disapproval.

---

[1] Sections 4.350–4.369 of 43 CFR part 4, were removed at 46 FR 7335, Jan. 23, 1981.

SUBCHAPTER C—PROBATE

PART 15—PROBATE OF INDIAN ESTATES, EXCEPT FOR MEMBERS OF THE OSAGE NATION AND THE FIVE CIVILIZED TRIBES

AUTHORITY: 5 U.S.C. 301; 25 U.S.C. 2, 9, 372–74, 410, 2201 *et seq.*; 44 U.S.C. 3101 *et seq.*

CROSS REFERENCE: For special rules applying to proceedings in Indian Probate (Determination of Heirs and Approval of Wills, Except for Members of the Five Civilized Tribes and Osage Indians), including hearings and appeals within the jurisdiction of the Office of Hearings and Appeals, see title 43, Code of Federal Regulations, part 4, subpart D, and part 30; Funds of deceased Indians other than the Five Civilized Tribes, see title 25 Code of Federal Regulations, part 115.

SOURCE: 73 FR 67278, Nov. 13, 2008, unless otherwise noted.

Subpart A—Introduction

§ 15.1 What is the purpose of this part?

(a) This part contains the procedures that we follow to initiate the probate of the estate of a deceased person for whom the United States holds an interest in trust or restricted land or trust personalty. This part tells you how to file the necessary documents to probate the estate. This part also describes how probates will be processed by the Bureau of Indian Affairs (BIA), and when probates will be forwarded to the Office of Hearings and Appeals (OHA) for disposition.

(b) The following provisions do not apply to Alaska property interests:

(1) Section 15.202(c), (d), (e)(2), (n), and (o); and

(2) Section 15.401(b).

[73 FR 67278, Nov. 13, 2008, as amended at 76 FR 7505, Feb. 10, 2011]

§ 15.2 What definitions do I need to know?

Act means the Indian Land Consolidation Act and its amendments, including the American Indian Probate Reform Act of 2004 (AIPRA), Pub. L. 108–374, as codified at 25 U.S.C. 2201 *et seq.*

Administrative law judge (ALJ) means an administrative law judge with the Office of Hearings and Appeals appointed under the Administrative Procedure Act, 5 U.S.C. 3105.

Affidavit means a written declaration of facts by a person that is signed by that person, swearing or affirming under penalty of perjury that the facts declared are true and correct to the best of that person's knowledge and belief.

Agency means:

(1) The Bureau of Indian Affairs (BIA) agency office, or any other designated office in BIA, having jurisdiction over trust or restricted land and trust personalty; and

(2) Any office of a tribe that has entered into a contract or compact to fulfill the probate function under 25 U.S.C. 450f or 458cc.

Attorney Decision Maker (ADM) means an attorney with OHA who conducts a summary probate proceeding and renders a decision that is subject to de novo review by an administrative law judge or Indian probate judge.

BIA means the Bureau of Indian Affairs within the Department of the Interior.

Child means a natural or adopted child.

Codicil means a supplement or addition to a will, executed with the same formalities as a will. It may explain, modify, add to, or revoke provisions in an existing will.

Consolidation agreement means a written agreement under the provisions of 25 U.S.C. 2206(e) or 2206(j)(9), entered during the probate process, approved by the judge, and implemented by the probate order, by which a decedent's heirs and devisees consolidate interests in trust or restricted land.

Creditor means any individual or entity that has a claim for payment from a decedent's estate.

Day means a calendar day.

Decedent means a person who is deceased.

Decision or order (or *decision and order*) means:

(1) A written document issued by a judge making determinations as to heirs, wills, devisees, and the claims of creditors, and ordering distribution of trust or restricted land or trust personalty;

(2) The decision issued by an attorney decision maker in a summary probate proceeding; or

(3) A decision issued by a judge finding that the evidence is insufficient to determine that a person is dead by reason of unexplained absence.

Department means the Department of the Interior.

Devise means a gift of property by will. Also, to give property by will.

Devisee means a person or entity that receives property under a will.

Eligible heir means, for the purposes of the Act, any of a decedent's children, grandchildren, great grandchildren, full siblings, half siblings by blood, and parents who are any of the following:

(1) Indian;

(2) Lineal descendents within two degrees of consanguinity of an Indian; or

(3) Owners of a trust or restricted interest in a parcel of land for purposes of inheriting—by descent, renunciation, or consolidation agreement—another trust or restricted interest in such parcel from the decedent.

Estate means the trust or restricted land and trust personalty owned by the decedent at the time of death.

Formal probate proceeding means a proceeding, conducted by a judge, in which evidence is obtained through the testimony of witnesses and the receipt of relevant documents.

Heir means any individual or entity eligible to receive property from a decedent in an intestate proceeding.

Individual Indian Money (IIM) account means an interest bearing account for trust funds held by the Secretary that belong to a person who has an interest in trust assets. These accounts are under the control and management of the Secretary.

Indian means, for the purposes of the Act, any of the following:

(1) Any person who is a member of a federally recognized Indian tribe is eligible to become a member of any federally recognized Indian tribe, or is an owner (as of October 27, 2004) of a trust or restricted interest in land;

(2) Any person meeting the definition of Indian under 25 U.S.C. 479; or

(3) With respect to the inheritance and ownership of trust or restricted land in the State of California under 25 U.S.C. 2206, any person described in paragraph (1) or (2) of this definition or any person who owns a trust or restricted interest in a parcel of such land in that State.

Indian probate judge (IPJ) means an attorney with OHA, other than an ALJ, to whom the Secretary has delegated the authority to hear and decide Indian probate cases.

Interested party means:

(1) Any potential or actual heir;

(2) Any devisee under a will;

(3) Any person or entity asserting a claim against a decedent's estate;

(4) Any tribe having a statutory option to purchase the trust or restricted property interest of a decedent; or

(5) A co-owner exercising a purchase option.

Intestate means that the decedent died without a valid will as determined in the probate proceeding.

Judge means an ALJ or IPJ.

Lockbox means a centralized system within OST for receiving and depositing trust fund remittances collected by BIA.

LTRO means the Land Titles and Records Office within BIA.

OHA means the Office of Hearings and Appeals within the Department of the Interior.

OST means the Office of the Special Trustee for American Indians within the Department of the Interior.

Probate means the legal process by which applicable tribal, Federal, or State law that affects the distribution of a decedent's estate is applied in order to:

(1) Determine the heirs;

(2) Determine the validity of wills and determine devisees;

(3) Determine whether claims against the estate will be paid from trust personalty; and

(4) Order the transfer of any trust or restricted land or trust personalty to the heirs, devisees, or other persons or entities entitled by law to receive them.

Purchase option at probate means the process by which eligible purchasers can purchase a decedent's interest during the probate proceeding.

Restricted property means real property, the title to which is held by an Indian but which cannot be alienated or encumbered without the Secretary's consent. For the purpose of probate proceedings, restricted property is treated as if it were trust property. Except as the law may provide otherwise, the term "restricted property" as used in this part does not include the restricted lands of the Five Civilized Tribes of Oklahoma or the Osage Nation.

Secretary means the Secretary of the Interior or an authorized representative.

Summary probate proceeding means the consideration of a probate file without a hearing. A summary probate proceeding may be conducted if the estate involves only an IIM account that did not exceed $5,000 in value on the date of the decedent's death.

Superintendent means a BIA Superintendent or other BIA official, including a field representative or one holding equivalent authority.

Testate means that the decedent executed a valid will as determined in the probate proceeding.

Testator means a person who has executed a valid will as determined in the probate proceeding.

Trust personalty means all tangible personal property, funds, and securities of any kind that are held in trust in an

IIM account or otherwise supervised by the Secretary.

Trust property means real or personal property, or an interest therein, the title to which is held in trust by the United States for the benefit of an individual Indian or tribe.

We or *us* means the Secretary, an authorized representative of the Secretary, or the authorized employee or representative of a tribe performing probate functions under a contract or compact approved by the Secretary.

Will means a written testamentary document that was executed by the decedent and attested to by two disinterested adult witnesses, and that states who will receive the decedent's trust or restricted property.

You or I means an interested party, as defined herein, with an interest in the decedent's estate unless the context requires otherwise.

[73 FR 67278, Nov. 13, 2008, as amended at 76 FR 7505, Feb. 10, 2011]

§ 15.3 Who can make a will disposing of trust or restricted land or trust personalty?

Any person 18 years of age or over and of testamentary capacity, who has any right, title, or interest in trust or restricted land or trust personalty, may dispose of trust or restricted land or trust personalty by will.

§ 15.4 What are the requirements for a valid will?

You must meet the requirements of § 15.3, date and execute your will, in writing and have it attested by two disinterested adult witnesses.

§ 15.5 May I revoke my will?

Yes. You may revoke your will at any time. You may revoke your will by any means authorized by tribal or Federal law, including executing a subsequent will or other writing with the same formalities as are required for execution of a will.

§ 15.6 May my will be deemed revoked by operation of the law of any State?

No. A will that is subject to the regulations of this subpart will not be deemed to be revoked by operation of the law of any State.

§ 15.7 What is a self-proved will?

A self-proved will is a will with attached affidavits, signed by the testator and the witnesses before an officer authorized to administer oaths, certifying that they complied with the requirements of execution of the will.

§ 15.8 May I make my will, codicil, or revocation self-proved?

Yes. A will, codicil, or revocation may be made self-proved as provided in this section.

(a) A will, codicil, or revocation may be made self-proved by the testator and attesting witnesses at the time of its execution.

(b) The testator and the attesting witnesses must sign the required affidavits before an officer authorized to administer oaths, and the affidavits must be attached to the will, codicil, or revocation.

§ 15.9 What information must be included in an affidavit for a self-proved will, codicil, or revocation?

(a) A testator's affidavit must contain substantially the following content:

Tribe of ______ or
State of ______
County of ______.

I, ______, swear or affirm under penalty of perjury that, on the ___ day of ______, 20___, I requested ______ and ______ to act as witnesses to my will; that I declared to them that the document was my last will; that I signed the will in the presence of both witnesses; that they signed the will as witnesses in my presence and in the presence of each other; that the will was read and explained to me (or read by me), after being prepared and before I signed it, and it clearly and accurately expresses my wishes; and that I willingly made and executed the will as my free and voluntary act for the purposes expressed in the will.

____
Testator

(b) Each attesting witness's affidavit must contain substantially the following content:

We, ______ and ______, swear or affirm under penalty of perjury that on the ___ day of ______, 20___, ______ of the State of ______, published and declared the attached document to be his/her last will, signed the will in the presence of both of us, and requested both of us to sign the will as witnesses; that we, in compliance with his/her request, signed the will as witnesses in his/her presence and in the presence of each other; and that the testator was not acting under duress, menace, fraud, or undue influence of any person, so far as we could determine, and in our opinion was mentally capable of disposing of all his/her estate by will.

____
Witness

____
Witness

Subscribed and sworn to or affirmed before me this ____ day of ______, 20___, by ______ testator, and by ______ and ______, attesting witnesses.

____

____
(Title)

§ 15.10 What assets will the Secretary probate?

(a) We will probate only the trust or restricted land, or trust personalty owned by the decedent at the time of death.

(b) We will not probate the following property:

(1) Real or personal property other than trust or restricted land or trust personalty owned by the decedent at the time of death;

(2) Restricted land derived from allotments made to members of the Five Civilized Tribes (Cherokee, Choctaw, Chickasaw, Creek, and Seminole) in Oklahoma; and

(3) Restricted interests derived from allotments made to Osage Indians in Oklahoma (Osage Nation) and Osage headright interests owned by Osage decedents.

(c) We will probate that part of the lands and assets owned by a deceased member of the Five Civilized Tribes or Osage Nation who owned a trust interest in land or a restricted interest in land derived from an individual Indian who was a member of a Tribe other than the Five Civilized Tribes or Osage Nation.

[76 FR 7505, Feb. 10, 2011]

§ 15.11 What are the basic steps of the probate process?

The basic steps of the probate process are:

(a) We learn about a person's death (see subpart B for details);

(b) We prepare a probate file that includes documents sent to the agency (see subpart C for details);

(c) We refer the completed probate file to OHA for assignment to a judge or ADM (see subpart D for details); and

(d) The judge or ADM decides how to distribute any trust or restricted land and/or trust personalty, and we make the distribution (see subpart D for details).

§ 15.12 What happens if assets in a trust estate may be diminished or destroyed while the probate is pending?

(a) This section applies if an interested party or BIA:

(1) Learns of the death of a person owning trust or restricted property; and

(2) Believes that an emergency exists and the assets in the estate may be significantly diminished or destroyed before the final decision and order of a judge in a probate case.

(b) An interested party, the Superintendent, or other authorized representative of BIA has standing to request relief.

(c) The interested party or BIA representative may request:

(1) That OHA immediately assign a judge or ADM to the probate case;

(2) That BIA transfer a probate file to OHA containing sufficient information on potential interested parties and documentation concerning the alleged emergency for a judge to consider emergency relief in order to preserve estate assets; and

(3) That OHA hold an expedited hearing or consider ex parte relief to prevent impending or further loss or destruction of trust assets.

[73 FR 67278, Nov. 13, 2008, as amended at 76 FR 7505, Feb. 10, 2011]

Subpart B—Starting the Probate Process

§ 15.101 When should I notify the agency of the death of a person owning trust or restricted property?

There is no deadline for notifying us of a death.

(a) Notify us as provided in § 15.103 to assure timely distribution of the estate.

(b) If we find out about the death of a person owning trust or restricted property we may initiate the process to collect the necessary documentation.

§ 15.102 Who may notify the agency of a death?

Anyone may notify us of a death.

§ 15.103 How do I begin the probate process?

As soon as possible, contact any of the following offices to inform us of the decedent's death:

(a) The agency or BIA regional office nearest to where the decedent was enrolled;

(b) Any agency or BIA regional office; or

(c) The Trust Beneficiary Call Center in OST.

§ 15.104 Does the agency need a death certificate to prepare a probate file?

(a) Yes. You must provide us with a certified copy of the death certificate if a death certificate exists. If necessary, we will make a copy from your certified copy for our use and return your copy.

(b) If a death certificate does not exist, you must provide an affidavit containing as much information as you have concerning the deceased, such as:

(1) The State, city, reservation, location, date, and cause of death;

(2) The last known address of the deceased;

(3) Names and addresses of others who may have information about the deceased; and

(4) Any other information available concerning the deceased, such as newspaper articles, an obituary, death notices, or a church or court record.

§ 15.105 What other documents does the agency need to prepare a probate file?

In addition to the certified copy of a death certificate or other reliable evidence of death listed in § 15.104, we need the following information and documents:

(a) Originals or copies of all wills, codicils, and revocations, or other evidence that a will may exist;

(b) The Social Security number of the decedent;

(c) The place of enrollment and the tribal enrollment or census number of the decedent and potential heirs or devisees;

(d) Current names and addresses of the decedent's potential heirs and devisees;

(e) Any sworn statements regarding the decedent's family, including any statements of paternity or maternity;

(f) Any statements renouncing an interest in the estate including identification of the person or entity in whose favor the interest is renounced, if any;

(g) A list of claims by known creditors of the decedent and their addresses, including copies of any court judgments; and

(h) Documents from the appropriate authorities, certified if possible, concerning the public record of the decedent, including but not limited to, any:

(1) Marriage licenses and certificates of the decedent;

(2) Divorce decrees of the decedent;

(3) Adoption and guardianship records concerning the decedent or the decedent's potential heirs or devisees;

(4) Use of other names by the decedent, including copies of name changes by court order; and

(5) Orders requiring payment of child support or spousal support.

§ 15.106 May a probate case be initiated when an owner of an interest has been absent?

(a) A probate case may be initiated when either:

(1) Information is provided to us that an owner of an interest in trust or restricted land or trust personalty has been absent without explanation for a period of at least 6 years; or

(2) We become aware of other facts or circumstances from which an inference may be drawn that the person has died.

(b) When we receive information as described in § 15.106(a), we may begin an investigation into the circumstances, and may attempt to locate the person. We may:

(1) Search available electronic databases;

(2) Inquire into other published information sources such as telephone directories and other available directories;

(3) Examine BIA land title and lease records;

(4) Examine the IIM account ledger for disbursements from the account; and

(5) Engage the services of an independent firm to conduct a search for the owner.

(c) When we have completed our investigation, if we are unable to locate the person, we may initiate a probate case and prepare a file that may include all the documentation developed in the search.

(d) We may file a claim in the probate case to recover the reasonable costs expended to contract with an independent firm to conduct the search.

§ 15.107 Who prepares a probate file?

The agency that serves the tribe where the decedent was an enrolled member will prepare the probate file in consultation with the potential heirs or devisees who can be located, and with other people who have information about the decedent or the estate.

§ 15.108 If the decedent was not an enrolled member of a tribe or was a member of more than one tribe, who prepares the probate file?

Unless otherwise provided by Federal law, the agency that has jurisdiction over the tribe with the strongest association with the decedent will serve as the home agency and will prepare the probate file if the decedent owned interests in trust or restricted land or trust personalty and either:

(a) Was not an enrolled member of a tribe; or

(b) Was a member of more than one tribe.

Subpart C—Preparing the Probate File

§ 15.201 What will the agency do with the documents that I provide?

After we receive notice of the death of a person owning trust or restricted land or trust personalty, we will examine the documents provided under §§ 15.104 and 15.105, and other documents and information provided to us to prepare a complete probate file. We may consult with you and other individuals or entities to obtain additional information to complete the probate file. Then we will transfer the probate file to OHA.

§ 15.202 What items must the agency include in the probate file?

We will include the items listed in this section in the probate file.

(a) The evidence of death of the decedent as provided under § 15.104.

(b) A completed "Data for Heirship Findings and Family History Form" or successor form, certified by BIA, with the enrollment or other identifying number shown for each potential heir or devisee.

(c) Information provided by potential heirs, devisees, or the tribes on:

(1) Whether the heirs and devisees meet the definition of "Indian" for probate purposes, including enrollment or eligibility for enrollment in a tribe; or

(2) Whether the potential heirs or devisees are within two degrees of consanguinity of an "Indian."

(d) If an individual qualifies as an Indian only because of ownership of a trust or restricted interest in land, the date on which the individual became the owner of the trust or restricted interest.

(e) A certified inventory of trust or restricted land, including:

(1) Accurate and adequate descriptions of all land; and

(2) Identification of any interests that represent less than 5 percent of the undivided interests in a parcel.

(f) A statement showing the balance and the source of funds in the decedent's IIM account on the date of death.

(g) A statement showing all receipts and sources of income to and disbursements, if any, from the decedent's IIM account after the date of death.

(h) Originals or copies of all wills, codicils, and revocations that have been provided to us.

(i) A copy of any statement or document concerning any wills, codicils, or revocations the BIA returned to the testator.

(j) Any statement renouncing an interest in the estate that has been submitted to us, and the information necessary to identify any person receiving a renounced interest.

(k) Claims of creditors that have been submitted to us under § 15.302

through 15.305, including documentation required by § 15.305.

(l) Documentation of any payments made on requests filed under the provisions of § 15.301.

(m) All the documents acquired under § 15.105.

(n) The record of each tribal or individual request to purchase a trust or restricted land interest at probate.

(o) The record of any individual request for a consolidation agreement, including a description, such as an Individual/Tribal Interest Report, of any lands not part of the decedent's estate that are proposed for inclusion in the consolidation agreement.

[73 FR 67278, Nov. 13, 2008, as amended at 76 FR 7505, Feb. 10, 2011]

§ 15.203 What information must Tribes provide BIA to complete the probate file?

Tribes must provide any information that we require or request to complete the probate file. This information may include enrollment and family history data or property title documents that pertain to any pending probate matter, and a copy of Tribal probate orders where they exist.

[76 FR 7505, Feb. 10, 2011]

§ 15.204 When is a probate file complete?

A probate file is complete for transfer to OHA when a BIA approving official includes a certification that:

(a) States that the probate file includes all information listed in § 15.202 that is available; and

(b) Lists all sources of information BIA queried in an attempt to locate information listed in § 15.202 that is not available.

Subpart D—Obtaining Emergency Assistance and Filing Claims

§ 15.301 May I receive funds from the decedent's IIM account for funeral services?

(a) You may request an amount of no more than $1,000 from the decedent's IIM account if:

(1) You are responsible for making the funeral arrangements on behalf of the family of a decedent who had an IIM account;

(2) You have an immediate need to pay for funeral arrangements before burial; and

(3) The decedent's IIM account contains more than $2,500 on the date of death.

(b) You must apply for funds under paragraph (a) of this section and submit to us an original itemized estimate of the cost of the service to be rendered and the identification of the service provider.

(c) We may approve reasonable costs of no more than $1,000 that are necessary for the burial services, taking into consideration:

(1) The total amount in the IIM account;

(2) The availability of non-trust funds; and

(3) Any other relevant factors.

(d) We will make payments directly to the providers of the services.

§ 15.302 May I file a claim against an estate?

If a decedent owed you money, you may make a claim against the estate of the decedent.

§ 15.303 Where may I file my claim against an estate?

(a) You may submit your claim to us before we transfer the probate file to OHA or you may file your claim with OHA after the probate file has been transferred if you comply with 43 CFR 30.140 through 30.148.

(b) If we receive your claim after the probate file has been transmitted to OHA but before the order is issued, we will promptly transmit your claim to OHA.

§ 15.304 When must I file my claim?

You must file your claim before the conclusion of the first hearing by OHA or, for cases designated as summary probate proceedings, as allowed under 43 CFR 30.140. Claims not timely filed will be barred.

§ 15.305 What must I include with my claim?

(a) You must include an itemized statement of the claim, including copies of any supporting documents such as signed notes, account records, billing records, and journal entries. The itemized statement must also include:

(1) The date and amount of the original debt;

(2) The dates, amounts, and identity of the payor for any payments made;

(3) The dates, amounts, product or service, and identity of any person making charges on the account;

(4) The balance remaining on the debt on the date of the decedent's death; and

(5) Any evidence that the decedent disputed the amount of the claim.

(b) You must submit an affidavit that verifies the balance due and states whether:

(1) Parties other than the decedent are responsible for any portion of the debt alleged;

(2) Any known or claimed offsets to the alleged debt exist;

(3) The creditor or anyone on behalf of the creditor has filed a claim or sought reimbursement against the decedent's non-trust or non-restricted property in any other judicial or quasi-judicial proceeding, and the status of such action; and

(4) The creditor or anyone on behalf of the creditor has filed a claim or sought reimbursement against the decedent's trust or restricted property in any other judicial or quasi-judicial proceeding, and the status of such action.

(c) A secured creditor must first exhaust the security before a claim against trust personalty for any deficiency will be allowed. You must submit a verified or certified copy of any judgment or other documents that establish the amount of the deficiency after exhaustion of the security.

Subpart E—Probate Processing and Distributions

§ 15.401 What happens after BIA prepares the probate file?

Within 30 days after we assemble all the documents required by §§ 15.202 and 15.204, we will:

(a) Refer the case and send the probate file to OHA for adjudication in accordance with 43 CFR part 30; and

(b) Forward a list of fractional interests that represent less than 5 percent of the entire undivided ownership of each parcel of land in the decedent's estate to the tribes with jurisdiction over those interests.

§ 15.402 What happens after the probate file is referred to OHA?

When OHA receives the probate file from BIA, it will assign the case to a judge or ADM. The judge or ADM will conduct the probate proceeding and issue a written decision or order, in accordance with 43 CFR part 30.

§ 15.403 What happens after the probate order is issued?

(a) If the probate decision or order is issued by an ADM, you have 30 days from the decision mailing date to file a written request for a de novo review.

(b) If the probate decision or order is issued by a judge, you have 30 days from the decision mailing date to file a written request for rehearing. After a judge's decision on rehearing, you have 30 days from the mailing date of the decision to file an appeal, in accordance with 43 CFR parts 4 and 30.

(c) When any interested party files a timely request for de novo review, a request for rehearing, or an appeal, we will not pay claims, transfer title to land, or distribute trust personalty until the request or appeal is resolved.

(d) If no interested party files a request or appeal within the 30-day deadlines in paragraphs (a) and (b) of this section, we will wait at least 15 additional days before paying claims, transferring title to land, and distributing trust personalty. At that time:

(1) The LTRO will change the land title records for the trust and restricted land in accordance with the final decision or order; and

(2) We will pay claims and distribute funds from the IIM account in accordance with the final decision or order.

Subpart F—Information and Records

§ 15.501 How may I find out the status of a probate?

You may get information about the status of an Indian probate by contacting any BIA agency or regional office, an OST fiduciary trust officer, OHA, or the Trust Beneficiary Call Center in OST.

§ 15.502 Who owns the records associated with this part?

(a) The United States owns the records associated with this part if:

(1) They are evidence of the organization, functions, policies, decisions, procedures, operations, or other activities undertaken in the performance of a federal trust function under this part; and

(2) They are either:

(i) Made by or on behalf of the United States; or

(ii) Made or received by a tribe or tribal organization in the conduct of a Federal trust function under this part, including the operation of a trust program under Pub. L. 93–638, as amended, and as codified at 25 U.S.C. 450 *et seq.*

(b) The tribe owns the records associated with this part if they:

(1) Are not covered by paragraph (a) of this section; and

(2) Are made or received by a tribe or tribal organization in the conduct of business with the Department of the Interior under this part.

§ 15.503 How must records associated with this part be preserved?

(a) Any organization that has records identified in § 15.502(a), including tribes and tribal organizations, must preserve the records in accordance with approved Departmental records retention procedures under the Federal Records Act, 44 U.S.C. chapters 29, 31, and 33; and

(b) A tribe or tribal organization must preserve the records identified in § 15.502(b) for the period authorized by the Archivist of the United States for similar Department of the Interior records under 44 U.S.C. chapter 33. If a tribe or tribal organization does not do so, it may be unable to adequately document essential transactions or furnish information necessary to protect its legal and financial rights or those of persons affected by its activities.

§ 15.504 Who may inspect records and records management practices?

(a) You may inspect the probate file at the relevant agency before the file is transferred to OHA. Access to records in the probate file is governed by 25 U.S.C. 2216(e), the Privacy Act, and the Freedom of Information Act.

(b) The Secretary and the Archivist of the United States may inspect records and records management practices and safeguards required under the Federal Records Act.

§ 15.505 How does the Paperwork Reduction Act affect this part?

The collections of information contained in this part have been approved by the Office of Management and Budget under 44 U.S.C. 3501 *et seq.* and assigned OMB Control Number 1076–0169. Response is required to obtain a benefit. A Federal agency may not conduct or sponsor, and you are not required to respond to a collection of information unless the form or regulation requesting the information has a currently valid OMB Control Number.

PART 16—ESTATES OF INDIANS OF THE FIVE CIVILIZED TRIBES

Sec.

AUTHORITY: 5 U.S.C. 301 (Interprets or applies Act of Apr. 26, 1906, ch. 1876, 34 Stat. 137, see 25 U.S.C. 355nt (1970); Act of May 27, 1908, ch. 199, 35 Stat. 312, see 25 U.S.C. 355nt (1970); Act of June 14, 1918, ch. 101, 40 Stat. 606, 25 U.S.C. 355, 375 (1970); Act of Apr. 12, 1926, ch. 115, 44 Stat. 239, see 25 U.S.C. 355nt (1970); Act of June 26, 1936, ch. 831, 49 Stat. 1967, 25 U.S.C. 501-509 (1970); Act of Aug. 4, 1947, ch. 458, 61 Stat. 731, 25 U.S.C. 502 (1970) and see 25 U.S.C. 355nt (1970); Act of Aug. 12, 1953, ch. 409, 67 Stat. 558, 25 U.S.C. 375c (1970) and see 25 U.S.C. 355nt (1970); Act of Aug. 11, 1955, ch. 786, 69 Stat. 666, see 25 U.S.C. 355nt (1970); Act of Aug. 29, 1967, Pub. L. 90-76, 81 Stat. 177, 25 U.S.C. 786-788 (1970); and Act of May 7, 1970, Pub. L. 91-240, 84 Stat. 203, 25 U.S.C. 375d (1970)).

SOURCE: 37 FR 7082, Apr. 8, 1972, unless otherwise noted.

§ 16.1 Definitions.

(a) The term *Secretary* means the Secretary of the Interior and his authorized representatives.

(b) The term *Bureau* means the Bureau of Indian Affairs, acting through the Commissioner of Indian Affairs and his authorized representatives, including field officials who are responsible for matters affecting properties in which a restricted interest is owned by an Indian of the Five Civilized Tribes.

(c) The term *Field Solicitor* means the Regional Solicitor, Southwest Region, Page Belcher Federal Building, P.O. Box 3156, Tulsa, Oklahoma 74101.

(d) The term *Indian of the Five Civilized Tribes* means an individual who is either an enrolled member of the Cherokee, Chickasaw, Choctaw, Creek, or Seminole Tribes of Oklahoma, or a descendant of an enrolled member thereof.

(e) The term *restricted interest* means an interest owned in real or personal property subject to restraints upon alienation imposed either by Federal statute or by administrative action authorized by Federal statute. Although this term includes property subject to restraints which may be removed by administrative action, its use in this part refers primarily to property subject to restraints which State courts have jurisdiction to remove in proceedings such as those specified in § 16.2.

[37 FR 7082, Apr. 8, 1972, as amended at 50 FR 12529, Mar. 29, 1985]

§ 16.2 Scope of regulations.

The regulations in this part set forth procedures for discharging the responsibilities of the Secretary in connection with the performance by State courts, as authorized by Federal statutes, of certain functions which affect properties in which a restricted interest is owned by an Indian of the Five Civilized Tribes. These State court functions pertain to such proceedings as guardianship, heirship determination, will probate, estate administration, conveyance approval, partition of real property, confirmation of title to real property, and appeal from action removing or failing to remove restrictions against alienation. In addition, the regulations in this part set forth procedures for discharging certain other responsibilities of the Secretary not necessarily involving State court functions, such as escheat of estates of deceased Indians of the Five Civilized Tribes.

§ 16.3 Legal representation in State courts.

The statutory duties of the Secretary to furnish legal advice to any Indian of the Five Civilized Tribes, and to represent such Indian in State courts, in matters affecting a restricted interest owned by such Indian, shall be performed by attorneys on the staff of the Solicitor, under the supervision of the Field Solicitor. Such advice and representation shall be undertaken to the extent that the Field Solicitor in his discretion shall consider necessary to discharge said duties, with due regard to the complexity of the legal action contemplated, the availability of staff attorneys for such purposes, the value and extent of the restricted interests involved, possible conflicts between Indians claiming to be owners of such interests, the preference of such owners concerning legal representation, the financial resources available to such owners, the extent to which such owners require similar legal services in connection with their unrestricted properties, and any other factor appropriate for consideration.

§ 16.4 Exchange of information within the Department.

To the extent that information may be useful in discharging the duties covered by the regulations in this part, the Bureau shall furnish to the Field Solicitor, either on a current basis or at periodic intervals, processes and notices received concerning court cases and information, as current and complete as may reasonably be obtainable, concerning the estate and status of an Indian of the Five Civilized Tribes for whom legal assistance should be rendered pursuant to the regulations in this part. Similarly, to the extent that such information may be useful for Bureau action or records, the Field Solicitor shall advise the Bureau of court proceedings, information received, and action taken in furnishing legal services pursuant to the regulations in this part.

§ 16.5 Acceptance and acknowledgement of service of process.

Service by the Field Solicitor or any other person of any process or notice, pursuant to any Federal statute which by its express terms is applicable to Indians of the Five Civilized Tribes, may be accepted and acknowledged by the Field Solicitor, or by any attorney authorized to perform the duties specified in § 16.3, on behalf of the Secretary and the Bureau, notwithstanding any specific designation in such statute of the official to be served (such as the Secretary, superintendent for the Five Civilized Tribes, Probate Attorney, etc.).

§ 16.6 Authority of attorneys in State court litigation.

Attorneys authorized to perform the duties specified in § 16.3 appearing in State court litigation in their official capacities are authorized to take such action as the Secretary could take if he were personally appearing in his official capacity as counsel therein, including but not limited to the filing or decision against filing of initial, responsive, or supplemental pleadings and appeals from adverse judgments, the exercise or decision against exercise of a preferential right to purchase property subject to sale, the removal or decision against removal of actions to Federal courts, and the waiver or decision against waiver of the failure to make timely service of process or notice.

§ 16.7 Performance of Federal functions by successor State courts.

All authority to perform functions relating to Indians of the Five Civilized Tribes which by express provisions of Federal statute had been conferred upon probate or county courts of Oklahoma before such county courts were abolished on January 12, 1969, has since that date been vested in the successor district courts of that State, and all rights of litigants continue undiminished in the successor forum, including the right to appeal from adverse decisions rendered therein to the successor appellate court.

(Interprets or applies Okla. Op. Atty. Gen. No. 68-381 (Dec. 20, 1968))

§ 16.8 Summary distribution of small liquid estates.

Where information, furnished by the Bureau pursuant to § 16.4 or otherwise obtained, reveals that the estate of a deceased Indian of the Five Civilized Tribes contains no restricted land but consists of a restricted interest in funds not exceeding $500 on deposit to the credit of the decedent, the Field Solicitor shall, in the absence of any final decree determining the heirs or legatees of the decedent, prepare and furnish to the Bureau a finding and order of distribution, based on affidavit or other proof of death and heirship or bequest, setting forth the facts of death and heirship or bequest and the amount payable from the estate to each person determined to be an heir or legatee of the decedent. The Field Solicitor shall mail to each person considered a possible claimant to any portion of the estate, as an heir or legatee or otherwise, a copy of the order with a notice that the order shall become final 30 days after the date of mailing thereof unless within that period the officer by whom the order was signed shall have received a written request for reconsideration of the order. After final action on any order has been taken by the Field Solicitor, the Bureau shall distribute the funds in the estate of the decedent in accordance with such final action, unless a timely appeal therefrom has been filed in accordance with part 2 of this title.

§ 16.9 Escheat of estates of decedents.

Where information, furnished by the Bureau pursuant to § 16.4 or otherwise obtained, reveals that the estate of a deceased Indian of the Five Civilized Tribes, who has been dead 5 or more years after having died intestate without heirs, consists of restricted interests in lands or rents or profits therefrom, the Field Solicitor shall, in the absence of any final decree determining that the decedent died without heirs or devisees, prepare and furnish to the Bureau a finding and order of escheat, based on affidavit or other proof of intestate death without heirs, setting forth the restricted interests in lands or rents or profits therefrom which have by escheat vested in the tribe which allotted the lands. The Field Solicitor shall mail to each person considered a possible claimant to any portion of the estate, as an heir or devisee or otherwise, a copy of the order with a notice that the order shall become final 30 days after the date of mailing thereof unless within that period the officer by whom the order was signed shall have received a written request for reconsideration of the order. After final action on any order has been taken by the Field Solicitor, the Bureau shall cause a certified copy thereof to be filed in the land records of each county within which are located any escheated lands described therein and shall cause the tribe to be credited with any funds in said estate which arose from rents or profits from such lands, unless a timely appeal therefrom has been filed in accordance with part 2 of this title.

PART 17—ACTION ON WILLS OF OSAGE INDIANS

Sec.

AUTHORITY: 5 U.S.C. 301.

SOURCE: 22 FR 10530, Dec. 24, 1957, unless otherwise noted.

§17.1 Definitions.

When used in the regulations in this part the following words or terms shall have the meaning shown below:

(a) *Secretary* means the Secretary of the Interior.

(b) *Commissioner* means the Commissioner of Indian Affairs.

(c) *Superintendent* means the superintendent of the Osage Indian Agency.

(d) *Special attorney* means the special attorney for Osage Indians, or other legal officer designated by the Commissioner.

§17.2 Attorneys.

Interested parties may appear in person or by attorneys at law. Attorneys must file written authority to appear for their clients in the proceedings.

§17.3 Pleadings, notice and hearings.

(a) The petition for approval of the will of a deceased Osage Indian may be set down for hearing at a date not less than 30 days from the date the petition is filed. Hearings shall be conducted only after notice of the time and place of such hearings shall have been given by mail. The notice shall be mailed not less than 10 days preceding the date of the hearing and shall state that the special attorney will, at the time and place specified therein, take testimony to determine whether the will of the deceased Osage Indian shall be approved or disapproved. The notice shall list the presumptive heirs of the decedent and the beneficiaries under such will, and shall notify the attesting witnesses to be present and testify. It shall state that all persons interested in the estate of the decedent may be present at the hearing. The notice shall further state that the special attorney may, in his discretion, continue the hearing to another time or place to be announced at the original hearing.

(b) Any interested party desiring to contest approval of the will may, not less than 5 days before the date set for hearing, file written objections in triplicate, showing that a copy thereof was served upon attorneys for the proponent and other attorneys of record in the case. Such contestant shall clearly state the interest he takes under the will and, if a presumptive heir, the interest he would take under the Oklahoma law. The contestant shall further state specifically the ground on which his contest is based.

§17.4 Service on interested parties.

A copy of the notice of hearing shall be served by mail, at his last known place of residence, on each presumptive heir; each beneficiary under the will offered for consideration; and each attesting witness thereto. Such notice must be mailed not less than 10 days preceding the date set for the hearing.

§ 17.5 Minors represented at hearings.

Minor heirs at law, who by the terms of the will are devised a lesser interest in the estate than they would take by descent, of whose interests are challenged, shall, with the approval of the special attorney, be represented at the hearing by guardians ad litem. Such minors 14 years of age or over may indicate in writing their choice of guardians ad litem. If no such choice has been indicated on the date of the hearing, the special attorney shall make the selection and appointment.

§ 17.6 Examination of witness.

All testimony taken at the hearing shall be reduced to writing. Any interested party may cross-examine any witness. Attorneys and others will be required to adhere to the rules of evidence of the State of Oklahoma. If, in addition to oral testimony, affidavits or dispositions are introduced, they must be read, and any opposing claimant may require the presence of the affiant, if practicable, either at that or a subsequent hearing, and opportunity shall be given for cross-examination or for having counter interrogatories answered.

§ 17.7 Limiting number of witnesses.

When the evidence seems clear and conclusive, the special attorney may, in his discretion, limit the number of witnesses to be examined formally upon any matter.

§ 17.8 Supplemental hearing.

When it appears that a supplemental hearing is necessary to secure material evidence, such a hearing may be conducted after notice has been given to those persons on whom notice of the original hearing was served and to such other persons as the testimony taken at the original hearing indicates may have a possible interest in the estate.

§ 17.9 Briefs.

When there are two or more parties with conflicting interests, the party upon whom the burden of proof may fall may be allowed a reasonable time, not to exceed 30 days following the conclusion of the hearing, in which to file a brief or other statement of his contentions, showing service on opposing counsel or litigant. The latter shall then be allowed not to exceed 20 days in which to file an answer brief or statement, and his opponent shall have 10 days thereafter to file a reply brief or statement. Upon proper showing the special attorney may grant extensions of time. Each brief or statement shall be filed in duplicate.

§ 17.10 Record.

After the hearing or hearings on the will have been terminated the special attorney shall make up the record and transmit it with his recommendation to the superintendent. The record shall contain:

(a) Copy of notices mailed to the attesting witnesses and the interested parties.

(b) Proof of mailing of notices.

(c) The evidence received at the hearing or hearings.

(d) The original of the will or wills considered at the hearings.

(e) A copy of all the pleadings.

The record, except the original will, shall be a part of the permanent files of the Osage Agency.

§ 17.11 Inspection of wills and approval as to form during testator's lifetime.

When a will has been executed and filed with the superintendent during the lifetime of the testator, the will shall be considered by the special attorney who may endorse on such will "approved as to form." A will shall be held in absolute confidence and its contents shall not be divulged prior to the death of the testator.

§ 17.12 Approval.

After hearings have been concluded in conformity with this part the superintendent shall approve or disapprove the wills of deceased Osage Indians.

§ 17.13 Government employees as beneficiaries.

In considering the will of a deceased Osage Indian the superintendent may disapprove any will which names as a beneficiary thereunder a government employee who is not related to the testator by blood, or otherwise the natural object of the testator's bounty.

§ 17.14 Appeals.

(a) Notwithstanding the provisions in part 2 of this chapter concerning appeals generally from administrative actions, any appeal from the action of the superintendent of approving or disapproving a will shall be taken to the Secretary. Upon the superintendent's final action of approval or disapproval of a will, he shall immediately notify by mail all attorneys appearing in the case, together with interested parties who are not represented by attorneys, of his decision and of their right to file an appeal.

(b) Any party desiring to appeal from the action of the superintendent shall, within 15 days after the date of the mailing of notice of the decision file with the superintendent a notice in writing of his intention to appeal to the Secretary, and shall, within 30 days after the mailing date of such notice by the superintendent, perfect his appeal to the Secretary by service of the appeal upon the superintendent who will transmit the entire record to the Secretary. If no notice of intention to appeal is given within 15 days, the superintendent's decision will be final.

(c) Upon the filing of notice with the superintendent of intention to appeal or the perfecting of an appeal by service upon the superintendent, at the same time similar notice and service shall be effected by the party taking an appeal upon opposing counsel or litigants, and a statement included in the appeal that this has been done. A party taking an appeal may, within the same 30-day period allowed for perfecting an appeal, file a brief or other written statement of his contentions, showing also service of that brief upon opposing counsel or litigants. Opposing counsel or litigants shall have 30 days from the date of the service of appellant's brief upon them in which to file an answer brief, copies of which also shall be served upon the appellant or opposing counsel and litigants. Except by special permission, no other briefs will be allowed on appeal.

[26 FR 10930, Nov. 22, 1961]

PART 18—TRIBAL PROBATE CODES

Subpart A—General Provisions

Subpart B—Approval of Tribal Probate Codes

Subpart C—Approval of Tribal Probate Code Amendments

Subpart D—Approval of Single Heir Rule

Subpart E—Information and Records

AUTHORITY: 5 U.S.C. 301; 25 U.S.C. 2, 9, 372–74, 410, 2201 *et seq.*; 44 U.S.C. 3101 *et seq.*; 25 CFR part 15; 43 CFR part 4.

SOURCE: 73 FR 67283, Nov. 13, 2008, unless otherwise noted.

Subpart A—General Provisions

§ 18.1 What is the purpose of this part?

This part establishes the Department's policies and procedures for reviewing and approving or disapproving tribal probate codes, amendments, and single heir rules that contain provisions regarding the descent and distribution of trust and restricted lands.

§ 18.2 What definitions do I need to know?

Act means the Indian Land Consolidation Act and its amendments, including the American Indian Probate Reform Act of 2004 (AIPRA), Public Law 108–374, as codified at 25 U.S.C. 2201 *et seq.*

Day means a calendar day.

Decedent means a person who is deceased.

Department means the Department of the Interior.

Devise means a gift of property by will. Also, to give property by will.

Devisee means a person or entity that receives property under a will.

Indian means, for the purposes of the Act:

(1) Any person who is a member of a federally recognized Indian tribe, is eligible to become a member of any federally recognized Indian tribe, or is an owner (as of October 27, 2004) of a trust or restricted interest in land;

(2) Any person meeting the definition of Indian under 25 U.S.C. 479; or

(3) With respect to the inheritance and ownership of trust or restricted land in the State of California under 25 U.S.C. 2206, any person described in paragraph (1) or (2) of this definition or any person who owns a trust or restricted interest in a parcel of such land in that State.

Intestate means that the decedent died without a will.

OHA means the Office of Hearings and Appeals within the Department of the Interior.

Restricted lands means real property, the title to which is held by an Indian but which cannot be alienated or encumbered without the Secretary's consent. For the purpose of probate proceedings, restricted lands are treated as if they were trust lands. Except as the law may provide otherwise, the term "restricted lands" as used in this part does not include the restricted lands of the Five Civilized Tribes of Oklahoma or the Osage Nation.

Testator means a person who has executed a will.

Trust lands means real property, or an interest therein, the title to which is held in trust by the United States for the benefit of an individual Indian or tribe.

Trust personalty means all tangible personal property, funds, and securities of any kind that are held in trust in an IIM account or otherwise supervised by the Secretary.

We or *us* means the Secretary or an authorized representative of the Secretary.

Subpart B—Approval of Tribal Probate Codes

§ 18.101 May a tribe create and adopt its own tribal probate code?

Yes. A tribe may create and adopt a tribal probate code.

§ 18.102 When must a tribe submit its tribal probate code to the Department for approval?

The tribe must submit its probate code to the Department for approval if the tribal probate code contains provisions regarding the descent and distribution of trust and restricted lands.

§18.103 Which provisions within a tribal probate code require the Department's approval?

Only those tribal probate code provisions regarding the descent and distribution of trust and restricted lands require the Department's approval.

§18.104 May a tribe include provisions in its tribal probate code regarding the distribution and descent of trust personalty?

No. All trust personalty will be distributed in accordance with the American Indian Probate Reform Act of 2004, as amended.

§18.105 How does a tribe request approval for a tribal probate code?

The tribe must submit the tribal probate code and a duly executed tribal resolution adopting the code to the Assistant Secretary—Indian Affairs, Attn: Tribal Probate Code, 1849 C Street, NW., Washington, DC 20240, for review and approval or disapproval.

§18.106 What will the Department consider in the approval process?

A tribal probate code must meet the requirements of this section in order to receive our approval under this part.

(a) The code must be consistent with Federal law.

(b) The code must promote the policies of the Indian Land Consolidation Act (ILCA) Amendments of 2000, which are to:

(1) Prevent further fractionation;

(2) Consolidate fractional interests into useable parcels;

(3) Consolidate fractional interests to enhance tribal sovereignty;

(4) Promote tribal self-sufficiency and self-determination; and

(5) Reverse the effects of the allotment policy on Indian tribes.

(c) Unless the conditions in paragraph (d) of this section are met, the code must not prohibit the devise of an interest to:

(1) An Indian lineal descendant of the original allottee; or

(2) An Indian who is not a member of the Indian tribe with jurisdiction over the interest in the land.

(d) If the tribal probate code prohibits the devise of an interest to the devisees in paragraph (c)(1) or (c)(2) of this section, then the code must:

(1) Allow those devisees to renounce their interests in favor of eligible devisees as defined by the tribal probate code;

(2) Allow a devisee who is the spouse or lineal descendant of the testator to reserve a life estate without regard to waste; and

(3) Require the payment of fair market value as determined by the Department on the date of the decedent's death.

§18.107 When will the Department approve or disapprove a tribal probate code?

(a) We have 180 days from receipt by the Assistant Secretary—Indian Affairs of a submitted tribal probate code and duly executed tribal resolution adopting the tribal probate code to approve or disapprove a tribal probate code.

(b) If we do not meet the deadline in paragraph (a) of this section, the tribal probate code will be deemed approved, but only to the extent that it:

(1) Is consistent with Federal law; and

(2) Promotes the policies of the ILCA Amendments of 2000 as listed in §18.106(b).

§18.108 What happens if the Department approves the tribal probate code?

Our approval applies only to those sections of the tribal probate code that govern the descent and distribution of trust or restricted land. We will notify the tribe of the approval and forward a copy of the tribal probate code to OHA.

§18.109 How will a tribe be notified of the disapproval of a tribal probate code?

If we disapprove a tribal probate code, we must provide the tribe with a written notification of the disapproval that includes an explanation of the reasons for the disapproval.

§18.110 When will a tribal probate code become effective?

(a) A tribal probate code may not become effective sooner than 180 days after the date of approval by the Department.

(b) If a tribal probate code is deemed approved through inaction by the Department, then the code will become effective 180 days after it is deemed approved.

(c) The tribal probate code will apply only to the estate of a decedent who dies on or after the effective date of the tribal probate code.

§ 18.111 What will happen if a tribe repeals its probate code?

If a tribe repeals its tribal probate code:

(a) The repeal will not become effective sooner than 180 days from the date we receive notification from the tribe of its decision to repeal the code; and

(b) We will forward a copy of the repeal to OHA.

§ 18.112 May a tribe appeal the approval or disapproval of a probate code?

No. There is no right of appeal within the Department from a decision to approve or disapprove a tribal probate code.

Subpart C—Approval of Tribal Probate Code Amendments

§ 18.201 May a tribe amend a tribal probate code?

Yes. A tribe may amend a tribal probate code.

§ 18.202 How does a tribe request approval for a tribal probate code amendment?

To amend a tribal probate code, the tribe must follow the same procedures as for submitting a tribal probate code to the Department for approval.

§ 18.203 Which probate code amendments require approval?

Only those tribal probate code amendments regarding the descent and distribution of trust and restricted lands require the Department's approval.

§ 18.204 When will the Department approve an amendment?

(a) We have 60 days from receipt by the Assistant Secretary of a submitted amendment to approve or disapprove the amendment.

(b) If we do not meet the deadline in paragraphs (a) of this section, the amendment will be deemed approved, but only to the extent that it:

(1) Is consistent with Federal law; and

(2) Promotes the policies of the ILCA Amendments of 2000 as listed in § 18.106(b).

§ 18.205 What happens if the Department approves the amendment?

Our approval applies only to those sections of the amendment that contain provisions regarding the descent and distribution of trust or restricted land. We will notify the tribe of the approval and forward a copy of the amendment to OHA.

§ 18.206 How will a tribe be notified of the disapproval of an amendment?

If we disapprove an amendment, we must provide the tribe with a written notification of the disapproval that includes an explanation of the reasons for the disapproval.

§ 18.207 When do amendments to a tribal probate code become effective?

(a) An amendment may not become effective sooner than 180 days after the date of approval by the Department.

(b) If an amendment is deemed approved through inaction by the Department, then the amendment will become effective 180 days after it is deemed approved.

(c) The amendment will apply only to the estate of a decedent who dies on or after the effective date of the amendment.

§ 18.208 May a tribe appeal an approval or disapproval of a probate code amendment?

No. There is no right of appeal within the Department from a decision to approve or disapprove a tribal probate code amendment.

Subpart D—Approval of Single Heir Rule

§ 18.301 May a tribe create and adopt a single heir rule without adopting a tribal probate code?

Yes. A tribe may create and adopt a single heir rule for intestate succession. The single heir rule may specify a single recipient other than the one specified in 25 U.S.C. 2206(a)(2)(D).

§ 18.302 How does the tribe request approval for the single heir rule?

The tribe must follow the same procedures as for submitting a tribal probate code to the Department for approval.

§ 18.303 When will the Department approve or disapprove a single heir rule?

We have 90 days from receipt by the Assistant Secretary of a single heir rule submitted separate from a tribal probate code to approve or disapprove a single heir rule.

§ 18.304 What happens if the Department approves the single heir rule?

If we approve the single heir rule, we will notify the tribe of the approval and forward a copy of the single heir rule to OHA.

§ 18.305 How will a tribe be notified of the disapproval of a single heir rule?

If we disapprove a single heir rule, we must provide the tribe with a written notification of the disapproval that includes an explanation of the reasons for the disapproval.

§ 18.306 When does the single heir rule become effective?

(a) A single heir rule may not become effective sooner than 180 days after the date of approval by the Department.

(b) If a single heir rule is deemed approved through inaction by the Department, then the single heir rule will become effective 180 days after it is deemed approved.

(c) The single heir rule will apply only to the estate of a decedent who dies on or after the effective date of the single heir rule.

§ 18.307 May a tribe appeal approval or disapproval of a single heir rule?

No. There is no right of appeal within the Department from a decision to approve or disapprove a single heir rule.

Subpart E—Information and Records

§ 18.401 How does the Paperwork Reduction Act affect this part?

The collection of information contained in this part has been approved by the Office of Management and Budget under the Paperwork Reduction Act, 44 U.S.C. 3501 *et seq.*, and assigned OMB Control Number 1076–0168. Response is required to obtain a benefit. A Federal agency may not conduct or sponsor, and members of the public are not required to respond to, a collection of information unless the form or regulation requesting the information displays a currently valid OMB Control Number.

SUBCHAPTER D—HUMAN SERVICES

PART 20—FINANCIAL ASSISTANCE AND SOCIAL SERVICES PROGRAMS

Subpart A—Definitions, Purpose and Policy

Sec.
20.100 What definitions clarify the meaning of the provisions of this part?
20.101 What is the purpose of this part?
20.102 What is the Bureau's policy in providing financial assistance and social services under this part?
20.103 Have the information collection requirements in this part been approved by the Office of Management and Budget?

Subpart B—Welfare Reform

20.200 What contact will the Bureau maintain with State, tribal, county, local, and other Federal agency programs?
20.201 How does the Bureau designate a service area and what information is required?
20.202 What is a tribal redesign plan?
20.203 Can a tribe incorporate assistance from other sources into a tribal redesign plan?
20.204 Must all tribes submit a tribal redesign plan?
20.205 Can tribes change eligibility criteria or levels of payments for General Assistance?
20.206 Must a tribe get approval for a tribal redesign plan?
20.207 Can a tribe use savings from a tribal redesign plan to meet other priorities of the tribe?
20.208 What if the tribal redesign plan leads to increased costs?
20.209 Can a tribe operating under a tribal redesign plan go back to operating under this part?
20.210 Can eligibility criteria or payments for Burial Assistance, Child Assistance, and Disaster Assistance and Emergency Assistance change?

Subpart C—Direct Assistance

ELIGIBILITY FOR DIRECT ASSISTANCE

20.300 Who qualifies for Direct Assistance under this subpart?
20.301 What is the goal of General Assistance?
20.302 Are Indian applicants required to seek assistance through Temporary Assistance for Needy Families?
20.303 When is an applicant eligible for General Assistance?
20.304 When will the Bureau review eligibility for General Assistance?
20.305 What is redetermination?
20.306 What is the payment standard for General Assistance?

DETERMINING NEED AND INCOME

20.307 What resources does the Bureau consider when determining need?
20.308 What does earned income include?
20.309 What does unearned income include?
20.310 What recurring income must be prorated?
20.311 What amounts will the Bureau deduct from earned income?
20.312 What amounts will the Bureau deduct from income or other resources?
20.313 How will the Bureau compute financial assistance payments?

EMPLOYMENT REQUIREMENTS

20.314 What is the policy on employment?
20.315 Who is not covered by the employment policy?
20.316 What must a person covered by the employment policy do?
20.317 How will the ineligibility period be implemented?
20.318 What case management responsibilities does the social services worker have?
20.319 What responsibilities does the general assistance recipient have?

TRIBAL WORK EXPERIENCE PROGRAM (TWEP)

20.320 What is TWEP?
20.321 Does TWEP allow an incentive payment?
20.322 Who can receive a TWEP incentive payment?
20.323 Will the local TWEP be required to have written program procedures?

BURIAL ASSISTANCE

20.324 When can the Bureau provide Burial Assistance?
20.325 Who can apply for Burial Assistance?
20.326 Does Burial Assistance cover transportation costs?

DISASTER ASSISTANCE

20.327 When can the Bureau provide Disaster Assistance?
20.328 How can a tribe apply for Disaster Assistance?

EMERGENCY ASSISTANCE

20.329 When can the Bureau provide Emergency Assistance payments?
20.330 What is the payment standard for Emergency Assistance?

AUTHORITY: 25 U.S.C. 13; Pub. L. 93–638; Pub. L. 98–473; Pub. L. 102–477; Pub. L. 104–193; Pub. L. 105–83.

SOURCE: 65 FR 63159, Oct. 20, 2000, unless otherwise noted.

Subpart A—Definitions, Purpose and Policy

§ 20.100 What definitions clarify the meaning of the provisions of this part?

Adult means an Indian person age 18 or older.

Adult care assistance means financial assistance provided on behalf of an Indian adult who is not eligible for any other state, federal, or tribal assistance as documented in the case file and who requires non-medical personal care and supervision due to advanced age, infirmity, physical condition or mental impairment.

Appeal means a written request for correction of an action or decision of a specific program decision by a Bureau official (§ 20.700) or a tribal official (§ 20.705).

Applicant means an Indian individual by or on whose behalf an application for financial assistance and/or social services has been made under this part.

Application means the written or oral process through which a request is made for financial assistance or social services.

Assistant Secretary means the Assistant Secretary—Indian Affairs.

Authorized representative means a parent or other caretaker relative, conservator, legal guardian, foster parent, attorney, paralegal acting under the supervision of an attorney, friend or other spokesperson duly authorized and acting on behalf or representing the applicant or recipient.

Bureau means the Bureau of Indian Affairs of the United States Department of the Interior.

Bureau Standard of Assistance means payment standards established by the Assistant Secretary for burial, disaster, emergency, TWEP and adoption and guardian subsidy. In accordance with Public Law 104–193, the Bureau standard of assistance for general assistance is the state rate for TANF in the state where the applicant resides. Where the Bureau provides general assistance on a reservation that extends into another state, the Bureau will provide general assistance to eligible Indians based on the standard of assistance where the applicant resides if the applicant is not eligible for state general assistance or TANF. The Bureau standard of assistance for adult care assistance is the state rate for adult care assistance in the state where the applicant resides. The Bureau standard of assistance for foster care is the state rate for foster care in the state where the applicant resides as provided by Title IV of the Social Security Act (49 Stat. 620).

Burial assistance means a financial assistance payment made on behalf of an indigent Indian who meets the eligibility criteria to provide minimum burial expenses according to Bureau payment standards established by the Assistant Secretary.

Case means a single type of assistance and/or service provided to an individual or household in response to an identified need which requires intervention by social services.

Case management means the activity of a social services worker in assessing client and family problem(s), case planning, coordinating and linking services for clients, monitoring service provisions and client progress, advocacy, tracking and evaluating services provided, such as evaluation of child's treatment being concurrent with parent's treatment, and provision of aftercare service. Activities may also include resource development and providing other direct services such as accountability of funds, data collection, reporting requirements, and documenting activities in the case file.

Case plan means a written plan with time limited goals which is developed and signed by the service recipient and social services worker. The case plan will include documentation of referral and disapproval of eligibility for other services. The plan must incorporate the steps needed to assist individuals and families to resolve social, economic, psychological, interpersonal, and/or other problems, to achieve self-sufficiency and independence. All plans for children in foster care or residential care must include a permanency plan which contains a time specific goal of the return of the child to the natural parents or initiation of a guardianship/adoption.

Child means an Indian person under the age of 18 except that no person who has been emancipated by marriage will be deemed a child.

Child assistance means financial assistance provided on behalf of an Indian child, who has special needs as specified in § 20.100. In addition, assistance includes services to a child who requires placement in a foster home or a residential care facility in accordance with standards of payment levels established by the state or county in which the child resides. Further, assistance includes services to a child in need of adoption or guardianship in accordance with payment levels established by the Assistant Secretary.

Designated representative means an official of the Bureau who is designated by a Superintendent to hold a hearing as prescribed in §§ 20.700 through 20.705 and who has had no prior involvement in the proposed decision under § 20.603 and whose hearing decision under §§ 20.700 through 20.705 will have the same force and effect as if rendered by the Superintendent.

Disaster means a situation where a tribal community is adversely affected by a natural disaster or other forces which pose a threat to life, safety, or health as specified in §§ 20.327 and 20.328.

Emergency means a situation where an individual or family's home and personal possessions are either destroyed or damaged through forces beyond their control as specified in § 20.329.

Employable means an eligible Indian person who is physically and mentally able to obtain employment, and who is not exempt from seeking employment in accordance with the criteria specified in § 20.315.

Essential needs means shelter, food, clothing and utilities, as included in the standard of assistance in the state where the eligible applicant lives.

Extended family means persons related by blood, marriage or as defined by tribal law or custom.

Family assessment means a social services assessment of a family's history and present abilities and resources to provide the necessary care, guidance and supervision for individuals within the family's current living situation who may need social service assistance and/or services.

Financial Assistance means any of the following forms of assistance not provided by other federal, state, local or tribal sources:

(1) Adult Care Assistance for adults who require non-medical personal care and supervision;

(2) Burial Assistance for indigent burials;

(3) Child Assistance for any child with special needs, in need of placement in a foster home or residential care facility, or in need of adoption or guardianship;

(4) Disaster Assistance;

(5) Emergency Assistance for essential needs to prevent hardship caused by burnout, flooding of homes, or other life threatening situations that may cause loss or damage of personal possessions;

(6) General Assistance for basic essential needs; or

(7) Tribal Work Experience Program for participants in work experience and training.

Foster care services means those social services provided to an eligible Indian child that is removed from his or her home due to neglect, abandonment, abuse or other maltreatment and placed in a foster home. Services must also be extended to the affected family members and foster parent(s) with a goal of reuniting and preserving the family.

General Assistance means financial assistance payments to an eligible Indian for essential needs provided under §§ 20.300 through 20.319.

Guardianship means long-term, social services and court approved placement of a child.

Head of household means a person in the household that has primary responsibility and/or obligation for the financial support of others in the household. In the case of a two parent household, one will be considered the head of household for the purpose of making an application for benefits.

Homemaker services means non-medical services provided by social services, in the absence of other resources, to assist an eligible Indian in maintaining self-sufficiency, and preventing placement into foster care or residential care. Examples of services included in homemaker services are: cleaning an individual's home, preparing meals for an individual, and maintaining or performing basic household functions.

Household means persons living together who may or may not be related to the "head of household."

Indian means:

(1) Any person who is a member of an Indian tribe; or

(2) In the Alaska service area only, any person who meets the definition of "Native" as defined under 43 U.S.C. 1602(b): "A citizen of the United States and one-fourth degree or more Alaska Indian (including Tsimshian Indians not enrolled in the Metlakatla Indian Community) Eskimo, or Aleut blood, or combination thereof. The term includes any Native as so defined either or both of whose adoptive parents are

not Natives. It also includes, in the absence of proof of a minimum blood quantum, any citizen of the United States who is regarded as an Alaska Native by the Native village or Native group of which he claims to be a member and whose father or mother is (or, if deceased, was) regarded as Native by any village or group. Any decision of the Secretary regarding eligibility for enrollment shall be final."

Indian court means Indian tribal court or Court of Indian Offenses.

Indian tribe means an Indian or Alaska Native tribe, band, nation, pueblo, village, or community which is recognized as eligible for the special programs and services provided by the United States because of their status as Indians.

Individual Self-sufficiency Plan (ISP) means a plan designed to meet the goal of employment through specific action steps and is incorporated within the case plan for the general assistance recipient. The plan is jointly developed and signed by the recipient and social services worker.

Near Reservation means those areas or communities designated by the Assistant Secretary that are adjacent or contiguous to reservations where financial assistance and social service programs are provided.

Need means the deficit after consideration of income and other resources necessary to meet the cost of essential need items and special need items as defined by the Bureau standard of assistance for the state in which the applicant or recipient resides.

Permanency plan means the documentation in a case plan which provides for permanent living alternatives for the child in foster care, a residential care facility, or in need of adoption or guardianship. Permanency plans are developed and implemented in accordance with tribal, cultural, and tribal/state legal standards when the parent or guardian is unable to resolve the issues that require out-of-home placement of the child.

Protective services means those services necessary to protect an Indian who is the victim of an alleged and/or substantiated incident of abuse, neglect or exploitation or who is under the supervision of the Bureau in regard to the use and disbursement of funds in his or her Individual Indian Money (IIM) account.

Public assistance means those programs of financial assistance provided by state, tribal, county, local and federal organizations including programs under Title IV of the Social Security Act (49 Stat. 620), as amended, and Public Law 104–193.

Recipient is an eligible Indian receiving financial assistance or social services under this part.

Recurring income means any cash or in-kind payment, earned or unearned, received on a monthly, quarterly, semiannual, or annual basis.

Regional Director means the Bureau official in charge of a Regional Office.

Reservation means any federally recognized Indian tribe's reservation, pueblo, or colony, including Alaska Native regions established pursuant to the Alaska Native Claims Settlement Act (85 Stat. 688).

Residential care services means those rehabilitation services provided to an eligible Indian child that is removed from his or her home due to lack of resources in the home to care for him or her and placed in a residential care facility.

Resources means income, both earned and unearned, and other liquid assets available to an Indian person or household to meet current living costs, unless otherwise specifically excluded by federal statute. Liquid assets are those properties in the form of cash or other financial instruments which can be converted to cash, such as savings or checking accounts, promissory notes, mortgages and similar properties, and retirements and annuities.

Secretary means the Secretary of the Interior.

Service area means a geographic area designated by the Assistant Secretary where financial assistance and social services programs are provided. Such a geographic area designation can include a reservation, near reservation, or other geographic location. "The Assistant Secretary has designated the entire State of Alaska as a service area."

Services to children, elderly and families means social services, including protective services provided through the social work skills of casework, group work or community development to assist in solving social problems involving children, elderly and families. These services do not include money payments.

Special needs means a financial assistance payment made to or on behalf of children under social services supervision for circumstances that warrant financial assistance that is not included in the foster care rates; for example, respite care, homemaker service, day care service, and may include basic needs (special diets) which are not considered as a medical need where other resources are not available.

Superintendent means the Bureau official in charge of an agency office.

Supplemental Security Income (SSI) means cash assistance provided under Title XVI of the Social Security Act (49 Stat. 620), as amended.

Temporary Assistance for Needy Families (TANF) means one of the programs of financial assistance provided under the Personal Responsibility and Work Opportunity Reconciliation Act of 1996 (PRWORA).

Tribal governing body means the federally recognized governing body of an Indian tribe.

Tribal redesign plan means a tribally designed method for changing general assistance eligibility and/or payment levels in accordance with 25 U.S.C.A. § 13d-3.

Tribal Work Experience Program (TWEP) means a program operated by tribal contract/grant or self-governance annual funding agreement, which provides eligible participants with work experience and training that promotes and preserves work habits and develops work skills aimed toward self-sufficiency. The Bureau payment standard is established by the Assistant Secretary.

Unemployable means a person who meets the criteria specified in § 20.315.

[65 FR 63159, Oct. 20, 2000; 65 FR 76563, Dec. 7, 2000, as amended at 66 FR 15030, Mar. 15, 2001]

§ 20.101 What is the purpose of this part?

The regulations in this part govern the provision to eligible Indians of the following kinds of financial assistance and social services:

(a) Adult Care Assistance;

(b) Burial Assistance;

(c) Child Assistance;

(d) Disaster Assistance;

(e) Emergency Assistance;

(f) General Assistance;

(g) Services to Children, Elderly and Families; and

(h) Tribal Work Experience Program.

§ 20.102 What is the Bureau's policy in providing financial assistance and social services under this part?

(a) Bureau social services programs are a secondary, or residual resource, and must not be used to supplement or supplant other programs.

(b) The Bureau can provide assistance under this part to eligible Indians when comparable financial assistance or social services are either not available or not provided by state, tribal, county, local or other federal agencies.

(c) Bureau financial assistance and social services are subject to annual Congressional appropriations.

§ 20.103 Have the information collection requirements in this part been approved by the Office of Management and Budget?

The information collection requirements contained in §§ 20.300, 20.400, and 20.500 were submitted for clearance to the Office of Management and Budget under 44 U.S.C. 35d *et seq.* This information collection was approved by OMB with OMB Control #1076–0017. The expiration date is on the form. The information is collected to determine applicant eligibility for services. The information will be used to determine applicant eligibility and to insure uniformity of services. Response is required to obtain a benefit. The public reporting burdens for this form are estimated to average 15 minutes per response including time for reviewing the instructions, gathering and maintaining data, and completing and reviewing the form.

Subpart B—Welfare Reform

§ 20.200 What contact will the Bureau maintain with State, tribal, county, local, and other Federal agency programs?

We will coordinate all financial assistance and social services programs with state, tribal, county, local and other federal agency programs to ensure that the financial assistance and social services program avoids duplication of assistance.

§ 20.201 How does the Bureau designate a service area and what information is required?

The Assistant Secretary can designate or modify service areas for a tribe. If you are a tribe requesting a service area designation, you must submit each of the following:

(a) A tribal resolution that certifies that:

(1) All eligible Indians residing within the service area will be served; and

(2) The proposed service area will not include counties or parts thereof that have reasonably available comparable services.

(b) Additional documentation showing that:

(1) The area is administratively feasible (that is, an adequate level of services can be provided to the eligible Indians residing in the area.);

(2) No duplication of services exists; and

(3) A plan describing how services will be provided to all eligible Indians can be implemented.

(c) Documentation should be sent to the Regional Director or Office of Self-Governance.

The Director or office will evaluate the information and make recommendations to the Assistant Secretary. The Assistant Secretary can make a determination to approve or disapprove and publish notice of the designation of service area and the Indians to be served in the FEDERAL REGISTER. Tribes currently providing services are not required to request designation for service areas unless they make a decision to modify their existing service areas.

§ 20.202 What is a tribal redesign plan?

If you are a tribe administering a general assistance program, you can develop and submit to us a tribal redesign plan to change the way that you administer the program.

(a) A tribal redesign plan allows a tribe to:

(1) Change eligibility for general assistance in the service area; or

(2) Change the amount of general assistance payments for individuals within the service area.

(b) If you develop a tribal redesign plan it must:

(1) Treat all persons in the same situation equally; and

(2) Will not result in additional expenses for the Bureau solely because of any increased level of payments.

§ 20.203 Can a tribe incorporate assistance from other sources into a tribal redesign plan?

Yes, when a tribe redesigns its general assistance program, it may include assistance from other sources (such as Public Law 102–477 federal funding sources) in the plan.

§ 20.204 Must all tribes submit a tribal redesign plan?

No, you must submit a tribal redesign plan under § 20.206 only if you want to change the way that the General Assistance program operates in your service area.

§ 20.205 Can tribes change eligibility criteria or levels of payments for General Assistance?

Yes, if you have a redesign plan, you can change eligibility criteria or levels of payment for general assistance.

(a) The funding level for your redesigned general assistance program will be the same funding received in the most recent fiscal or calendar year, whichever applies.

(b) If you do not have a prior year level of funding, the Bureau or Office of Self-Governance will establish a tentative funding level based upon best estimates for caseload and expenditures.

(c) A Bureau servicing office can administer a tribal redesign plan as requested by a tribal resolution.

§ 20.206 Must a tribe get approval for a tribal redesign plan?

If you have a Public Law 93–638 contract or receive direct services from us, you must obtain our approval before implementing a redesign plan. You can apply for approval to the Regional Director through the Bureau servicing office.

(a) You must submit your redesign plan for approval at least 3 months before the effective date.

(b) If you operate with a self-governance annual funding agreement, you must obtain the approval of the redesign from the Office of Self-Governance.

(c) If you operate with a Public Law 102–477 grant, you must obtain approval from the Bureau Central Office.

[65 FR 63159, Oct. 20, 2000; 65 FR 76563, Dec. 7, 2000]

§ 20.207 Can a tribe use savings from a tribal redesign plan to meet other priorities of the tribe?

Yes, you may use savings from a redesign of the general assistance program to meet other priorities.

§ 20.208 What if the tribal redesign plan leads to increased costs?

The tribe must meet any increase in cost to the General Assistance program that results solely from tribally increased payment levels due to a redesign plan.

§ 20.209 Can a tribe operating under a tribal redesign plan go back to operating under this part?

Yes, a tribe operating under a tribal redesign plan can choose to return to operation of the program as provided in §§ 20.300 through 20.323.

§ 20.210 Can eligibility criteria or payments for Burial Assistance, Child Assistance, and Disaster Assistance and Emergency Assistance change?

No, unless otherwise provided by law, the Bureau nor a tribe may change eligibility criteria or levels of payment for Burial Assistance, Child Assistance, Disaster Assistance, and Emergency Assistance awarded in Public Law 93–638 contracts, Public Law 102–477 grants, or Public Law 103–413 self-governance annual funding agreements.

Subpart C—Direct Assistance

ELIGIBILITY FOR DIRECT ASSISTANCE

§ 20.300 Who qualifies for Direct Assistance under this subpart?

To be eligible for assistance or services under this part, an applicant must meet all of the following criteria:

(a) Meet the definition of Indian as defined in this part;

(b) Not have sufficient resources to meet the essential need items defined by the Bureau standard of assistance for those Bureau programs providing financial payment;

(c) Reside in the service area as defined in § 20.100; and

(d) Meet the additional eligibility criteria for each of the specific programs of financial assistance or social services in §§ 20.301 through 20.516.

[65 FR 63159, Oct. 20, 2000, as amended at 66 FR 15030, Mar. 15, 2001]

§ 20.301 What is the goal of General Assistance?

The goal of the General Assistance program is to increase self-sufficiency. Each General Assistance recipient must work with the social services worker to develop and sign an Individual Self-Sufficiency Plan (ISP). The plan must outline the specific steps the individual will take to increase independence by meeting the goal of employment.

§ 20.302 Are Indian applicants required to seek assistance through Temporary Assistance for Needy Families?

Yes, all Indian applicants with dependent children are required to apply for Temporary Assistance for Needy Families (TANF) and follow TANF regulations.

§ 20.303 When is an applicant eligible for General Assistance?

To be eligible for General Assistance an applicant must:

(a) Meet the criteria contained in § 20.300;

(b) Apply concurrently for financial assistance from other state, tribal, county, local, or other federal agency programs for which he/she is eligible;

(c) Not receive any comparable public assistance; and

(d) Develop and sign an employment strategy in the ISP with the assistance of the social services worker to meet the goal of employment through specific action steps including job readiness and job search activities.

§ 20.304 When will the Bureau review eligibility for General Assistance?

The Bureau will review eligibility for General Assistance:

(a) Every 3 months for individuals who are not exempt from seeking or accepting employment in accordance with § 20.315 or the ISP;

(b) Every 6 months for all recipients; and

(c) Whenever there is a change in status that can affect a recipient's eligibility or amount of assistance. Recipients must immediately inform the social services office of any such changes.

§ 20.305 What is redetermination?

Redetermination is an evaluation by a social services worker to assess the need for continued financial assistance as outlined in § 20.304. It includes:

(a) A home visit;

(b) An estimate of income, living circumstances, household composition for the month(s) for which financial assistance is to be provided; and

(c) Appropriate revisions to the case plan and the ISP.

§ 20.306 What is the payment standard for General Assistance?

(a) Under Public Law 104–193, the Bureau must use the same TANF payment standard (and any associated rateable reduction) that exists in the state or service area where the applicant or recipient resides. This payment standard is the amount from which the Bureau subtracts net income and resources to determine General Assistance eligibility and payment levels;

(b) If the state does not have a standard for an adult, we will use either the difference between the standard for a child and the standard for a household of two, or one-half of the standard for a household of two, whichever is greater; and

(c) If the state does not have a TANF program, we will use the AFDC payment standard which was in effect on September 30, 1995, in the State where the applicant or recipient resides.

Determining Need and Income

§ 20.307 What resources does the Bureau consider when determining need?

When the Bureau determines General Assistance eligibility and payment levels, we consider income and other resources as specified in §§ 20.308 and 20.309.

(a) All income, earned or unearned, must be calculated in the month it is received and as a resource thereafter, except that certain income obtained from the sale of real or personal property may be exempt as provided in § 20.309.

(b) Resources are considered to be available when they are converted to cash.

§ 20.308 What does earned income include?

Earned income is cash or any in-kind payment earned in the form of wages, salary, commissions, or profit, from activities by an employee or self-employed individual. Earned income includes:

(a) Any one-time payment to an individual for activities which were sustained over a period of time (for example, the sale of farm crops, livestock, or professional artists producing art work); and

(b) With regard to self-employment, total profit from a business enterprise (i.e., gross receipts less expenses incurred in producing the goods or services). Business expenses do not include depreciation, personal business and entertainment expenses, personal transportation, capital equipment purchases, or principal payments on loans for capital assets or durable goods.

§ 20.309 What does unearned income include?

Unearned income includes, but is not limited to:

(a) Income from interest; oil and gas and other mineral royalties; gaming income per capita distributions; rental property; cash contributions, such as child support and alimony, gaming winnings; retirement benefits;

(b) Annuities, veteran's disability, unemployment benefits, and federal and state tax refunds;

(c) Per capita payments not excluded by federal statute;

(d) Income from sale of trust land and real or personal property that is set aside for reinvestment in trust land or a primary residence, but has not been reinvested in trust land or a primary residence at the end of one year from the date the income was received;

(e) In-kind contributions providing shelter at no cost to the individual or household, this must equal the amount for shelter included in the state standard, or 25 percent of the state standard, whichever is less; and

(f) Financial assistance provided by a state, tribal, county, local, or other federal agency.

§ 20.310 What recurring income must be prorated?

The social services worker will prorate the following recurring income:

(a) Recurring income received by individuals over a 12-month period for less than a full year's employment (for example, income earned by teachers who are not employed for a full year);

(b) Income received by individuals employed on a contractual basis over the term of a contract; and

(c) Intermittent income received quarterly, semiannually, or yearly over the period covered by the income.

§ 20.311 What amounts will the Bureau deduct from earned income?

(a) The social services worker will deduct the following amounts from earned income:

(1) Other federal, state, and local taxes;

(2) Social Security (FICA);

(3) Health insurance;

(4) Work related expenses, including reasonable transportation costs;

(5) Child care costs for children under the age of 6 except where the other parent in the home is unemployed and physically able to care for the children; and

(6) The cost of special clothing, tools, and equipment directly related to the individual's employment.

(b) For self-employed individuals, the social services worker will deduct the costs of conducting business and all of the amounts in paragraph (a) of this section.

§ 20.312 What amounts will the Bureau deduct from income or other resources?

The social services worker will deduct the following amounts from income, or other resources:

(a) The first $2,000 of liquid resources annually available to the household;

(b) Any home produce from a garden, livestock, and poultry used by the applicant or recipient and his/her household for their consumption; and

(c) Resources specifically excluded by federal statute.

§ 20.313 How will the Bureau compute financial assistance payments?

(a) The social services worker will compute financial assistance payments by beginning with the Bureau standard of assistance and doing the following:

(1) Subtracting from all resources calculated under §§ 20.307 through 20.310;

(2) Subtracting the rateable reduction or maximum payment level used by the state where the applicant lives;

(3) Subtracting an amount for shelter (see paragraph (b) of this section for details on how to calculate a shelter amount); and

(4) Rounding the result down to the next lowest dollar.

(b) The social services worker must calculate a shelter amount for purposes of paragraph (a)(3) of this section. To calculate the shelter amount:

(1) The shelter amount must not exceed the amount for shelter in the state TANF standard;

(2) If the state TANF does not specify an amount for shelter, the social services worker must calculate the amount as 25 percent of the total state TANF payment; and

(3) If there is more than one household in a dwelling, the social services worker must prorate the actual shelter cost among the households receiving General Assistance; this amount cannot exceed the amount in the standard for individuals in similar circumstances. The head of each household is responsible for his/her portion of the documented shelter cost.

(c) The social services worker must not provide General Assistance payments for any period before the date of the application for assistance.

EMPLOYMENT REQUIREMENTS

§ 20.314 What is the policy on employment?

(a) An applicant or recipient must:

(1) Actively seek employment, including the use of available state, tribal, county, local or Bureau-funded employment services;

(2) Make satisfactory progress in an ISP; and

(3) Accept local and seasonable employment when it is available.

(b) A head of household who does not comply with this section will not be eligible for General Assistance for a period of at least 60 days but not more than 90 days. This action must be documented in the case file.

(c) The policy in this section does not apply to any person meeting the criteria in § 20.315.

§ 20.315 Who is not covered by the employment policy?

The employment policy in § 20.314 does not apply to the persons shown in the following table.

The employment policy in § 20.314 does not apply to . . .	if . . .	and . . .
(a) Anyone younger than 16.		
(b) A full-student under the age of 19	He/she is attending an elementary or secondary school or a vocational or technical school equivalent to a secondary school.	He/she is making satisfactory progress.
(c) A person enrolled at least half-time in a program of study under Section 5404 of Pub. L. 100–297.	He/she is making satisfactory progress ..	He/she was an active General Assistance recipient for a minimum of 3 months before determination/redetermination of eligibility.
(d) A person suffering from a temporary medical injury or illness.	It is documented in the case plan that the illness or injury is serious enough to temporarily prevent employment.	He/she must be referred to SSI if the disability status exceeds 3 months.
(e) An incapacitated person who has not yet received Supplemental Security Income (SSI) assistance.	A physician, psychologist, or social services worker certifies that a physical or mental impairment (either by itself, or in conjunction with age) prevents the individual from being employed.	The assessment is documented in the case plan.
(f) A caretaker who is responsible for a person in the home who has a physical or mental impairment.	A physician or certified psychologist verifies the condition.	The case plan documents that: the condition requires the caretaker to be home on a virtually continuous basis; and there is no other appropriate household member available to provide this care.
(g) A parent or other individual who does not have access to child care.	He/she personally provides full-time care to a child under the age of 6.	
(h) A person for whom employment is not accessible.	There is a minimum commuting time of one hour each way.	

§ 20.316 What must a person covered by the employment policy do?

(a) If you are covered by the employment policy in § 20.314, you must seek employment and provide evidence of your monthly efforts to obtain employment in accordance with your ISP.

(b) If you do not seek and accept available local and seasonal employment, or you quit a job without good cause, you cannot receive General Assistance for a period of at least 60 days but not more than 90 days after you refuse or quit a job.

§ 20.317 How will the ineligibility period be implemented?

(a) If you refuse or quit a job, your ineligibility period will continue as provided in § 20.316(b) until you seek and accept appropriate available local and seasonal employment and fulfill your obligations already agreed to in the ISP;

(b) The Bureau will reduce your suspension period by 30 days when you show that you have sought local and seasonal employment in accordance with the ISP; and

(c) Your eligibility suspension will affect only you. The Bureau will not apply it to other eligible members of the household.

§ 20.318 What case management responsibilities does the social services worker have?

In working with each recipient, you, the social services worker must:

(a) Assess the general employability of the recipient;

(b) Assist the recipient in the development of the ISP;

(c) Sign the ISP;

(d) Help the recipient identify the service(s) needed to meet the goals identified in their ISP;

(e) Monitor recipient participation in work related training and other employment assistance programs; and

(f) Document activities in the case file.

§ 20.319 What responsibilities does the general assistance recipient have?

In working with the social services worker, you, the recipient, must:

(a) Participate with the social services worker in developing an ISP and sign the ISP;

(b) Perform successfully in the work related activities, community service, training and/or other employment assistance programs developed in the ISP;

(c) Participate successfully in treatment and counseling services identified in the ISP;

(d) Participate in evaluations of job readiness and/or any other testing required for employment purposes; and

(e) Demonstrate that you are actively seeking employment by providing the social services worker with evidence of job search activities as required in the ISP.

TRIBAL WORK EXPERIENCE PROGRAM (TWEP)

§ 20.320 What is TWEP?

TWEP is a program that provides work experience and job skills to enhance potential job placement for the general assistance recipient. TWEP programs can be incorporated within Public Law 93–638 self-determination contracts, Public Law 102–477 grants, and Public Law 103–413 self-governance annual funding agreements at the request of the tribe.

§ 20.321 Does TWEP allow an incentive payment?

Yes, incentive payments to participants are allowed under TWEP.

(a) Incentive payments are separate. The Bureau will not consider incentive payments as wages or work related expenses, but as grant assistance payments under §§ 20.320 through 20.323.

(b) The approved payment will not exceed the Bureau maximum TWEP payment standard established by the Assistant Secretary.

§ 20.322 Who can receive a TWEP incentive payment?

(a) The head of the family unit normally receives the TWEP assistance payment.

(b) The social services worker can designate a spouse or other adult in the assistance group to receive the TWEP assistance payment. The social services worker will do this only if:

(1) The recognized head of the family unit is certified as unemployable; and

(2) The designation is consistent with the ISP.

(c) Where there are multiple family units in one household, one member of each family unit will be eligible to receive the TWEP incentive payment.

§ 20.323 Will the local TWEP be required to have written program procedures?

Yes, the local TWEP must have specific written program procedures that cover hours of work, acceptable reasons for granting leave from work, evaluation criteria and monitoring plans and ISP's for participants. Work readiness progress must be documented in each ISP.

BURIAL ASSISTANCE

§ 20.324 When can the Bureau provide Burial Assistance?

In the absence of other resources, the Bureau can provide Burial Assistance for eligible indigent Indians meeting the requirements prescribed in § 20.300.

§ 20.325 Who can apply for Burial Assistance?

If you are a relative of a deceased Indian, you can apply for burial assistance for the deceased Indian under this section.

(a) To apply for burial assistance under this section, you must submit the application to the social services worker. You must submit this application within 180 days following death.

(b) The Bureau will determine eligibility based on the income and resources available to the deceased in accordance with § 20.100. This includes but is not limited to SSI, veterans' death benefits, social security, and Individual Indian Money (IIM) accounts. Determination of need will be accomplished on a case-by-case basis using the Bureau payment standard.

(c) The Bureau will not approve an application unless it meets the criteria specified at § 20.300.

(d) The approved payment will not exceed the Bureau maximum burial payment standard established by the Assistant Secretary.

[65 FR 63159, Oct. 20, 2000, as amended at 81 FR 10477, Mar. 1, 2016]

§ 20.326 Does Burial Assistance cover transportation costs?

Transportation costs directly associated with burials are normally a part of the established burial rate. If a provider adds an additional transportation charge to the burial rate because of extenuating circumstances, the social services worker can pay the added charge. To do this, the social services worker must ensure and document in the case plan that:

(a) The charges are reasonable and equitable;

(b) The deceased was an eligible indigent Indian who was socially, culturally, and economically affiliated with his or her tribe; and

(c) The deceased resided in the service area for at least the last 6 consecutive months of his/her life.

DISASTER ASSISTANCE

§ 20.327 When can the Bureau provide Disaster Assistance?

Disaster assistance is immediate and/or short-term relief from a disaster and can be provided to a tribal community in accordance with § 20.328.

§ 20.328 How can a tribe apply for Disaster Assistance?

(a) The tribe affected by the disaster is considered the applicant and must submit the following to the Regional Director through the local Superintendent:

(1) A tribal resolution requesting disaster assistance;

(2) A copy of county, state, or Presidential declaration of disaster; and

(3) The projected extent of need in the service area not covered by other federal funding sources.

(b) The Regional Director must forward the above tribal documents and his/her recommendation to the Assistant Secretary for final decision on whether disaster assistance will be provided and to what extent.

EMERGENCY ASSISTANCE

§ 20.329 When can the Bureau provide Emergency Assistance payments?

Emergency Assistance payments can be provided to individuals or families who suffer from a burnout, flood, or other destruction of their home and loss or damage to personal possessions. The Bureau will make payments only for essential needs and other non-medical necessities.

§ 20.330 What is the payment standard for Emergency Assistance?

The approved payment will not exceed the Bureau's maximum Emergency Assistance payment standard established by the Assistant Secretary.

ADULT CARE ASSISTANCE

§ 20.331 What is Adult Care Assistance?

Adult care assistance provides non-medical care for eligible adult Indians who:

(a) Have needs that require personal care and supervision due to advanced age, infirmity, physical condition, or mental impairments; and

(b) Cannot be cared for in their own home by family members.

§ 20.332 Who can receive Adult Care Assistance?

An adult Indian is eligible to receive adult care assistance under this part if he/she:

(a) Is unable to meet his/her basic needs, including non-medical care and/or protection, with his/her own resources; and

(b) Does not require intermediate or skilled nursing care.

§ 20.333 How do I apply for Adult Care Assistance?

To apply for adult care assistance, you or someone acting on your behalf must submit an application form to the social services worker.

§ 20.334 What happens after I apply?

(a) The Bureau will determine eligibility based upon the income and available resources of the person named in the application.

(b) Upon approval by the Bureau Line Officer, payments will be approved under purchase of service agreements for adult care provided in state or tribally licensed or certified group settings, or by individual service providers licensed or certified for homemaker service.

[65 FR 63159, Oct. 20, 2000; 65 FR 76563, Dec. 7, 2000]

§ 20.335 What is the payment standard for Adult Care Assistance?

The approved payment for adult care assistance will not exceed the applicable state payment rate for similar care.

[65 FR 63159, Oct. 20, 2000; 65 FR 76563, Dec. 7, 2000]

Subpart D—Services to Children, Elderly, and Families

§ 20.400 Who should receive Services to Children, Elderly, and Families?

Services to Children, Elderly, and Families will be provided for Indians meeting the requirements prescribed in § 20.300 who request these services or on whose behalf these services are requested.

§ 20.401 What is included under Services to Children, Elderly, and Families?

Services to Children, Elderly, and Families include, but are not limited to, the following:

(a) Assistance in solving problems related to family functioning and interpersonal relationships;

(b) Referral to the appropriate resource for problems related to illness, physical or mental handicaps, drug abuse, alcoholism, and violation of the law; and

(c) Protective services.

In addition, economic opportunity and money management may also be provided.

§ 20.402 When are protective services provided?

Protective services are provided when children or adults:

(a) Are deprived temporarily or permanently of needed supervision by responsible adults;

(b) Are neglected, abused or exploited;

(c) Need services when they are mentally or physically handicapped or otherwise disabled; or

(d) Are under the supervision of the Bureau in regard to the use and disbursement of funds in the child's or adult's Individual Indian Money (IIM) account. Those IIM accounts that are established for children will be supervised by the Bureau until the child becomes an adult as defined in 25 CFR 115.

§ 20.403 What do protective services include?

Protective services provided to a child, family or elderly person will be documented in the case files and:

(a) Can include, but are not limited to, any of the following:

(1) Providing responses to requests from members of the community on behalf of children or adults alleged to need protective services;

(2) Providing services to children, elderly, and families, including referrals for homemaker and day care services for the elderly and children;

(3) Coordinating with Indian courts to provide services, which may include, but are not limited to, the following:

(i) Investigating and reporting on allegations of child abuse and neglect, abandonment, and conditions that may require referrals (such as mental or physical handicaps);

(ii) Providing social information related to the disposition of a case, including recommendation of alternative resources for treatment; and

(iii) Providing placement services by the court order before and after adjudication.

(4) Coordinating with other community services, including groups, agencies, and facilities in the community. Coordination can include, but are not limited to:

(i) Evaluating social conditions that affect community well-being;

(ii) Treating conditions identified under paragraph (b)(1) of this section that are within the competence of social services workers; and

(iii) Working with other community agencies to identify and help clients to use services available for assistance in solving the social problems of individuals, families, and children.

(5) Coordinating with law enforcement and tribal courts, to place the victim of an alleged and/or substantiated incident of abuse, neglect or exploitation out of the home to assure safety while the allegations are being investigated. Social services workers may remove individuals in life threatening situations. After a social services assessment, the individual must be either returned to the parent(s) or to the home from which they were removed or the social services worker must initiate other actions as provided by the tribal code; and

(6) Providing social services in the home, coordinating and making referrals to other programs/services, including Child Protection, and/or establishing Multi-Disciplinary Teams.

(b) Must include, where the service population includes IIM account holders:

(1) Conducting, upon the request of an account holder or other interested party, a social services assessment to evaluate an adult account holder's circumstances and abilities and the extent to which the account holder needs assistance in managing his or her financial affairs; and

(2) Managing supervised IIM accounts of children and adults (in conjunction with legal guardians), which includes, but is not limited to, the following:

(i) Evaluating the needs of the account holder;

(ii) Developing, as necessary and as permitted under 25 CFR 115, a one-time or an annual distribution plan for funds held in an IIM account along with any amendments to the plan for approval by the Bureau;

(iii) Monitoring the implementation of the approved distribution plan to ensure that the funds are expended in accordance with the distribution plan;

(iv) Reviewing the supervised account every 6 months or more often as necessary if conditions have changed to warrant a recommendation to change the status of the account holder, or to modify the distribution plan;

(v) Reviewing receipts for an account holder's expenses and verifying that expenditures of funds from a supervised IIM account were made in accordance with the distribution plan approved by the Bureau, including any amendments made to the plan; and

(vi) Petitioning a court of competent jurisdiction for the appointment of, or change in, a legal guardian for a client, where appropriate.

[65 FR 63159, Oct. 20, 2000; 65 FR 76563, Dec. 7, 2000]

§ 20.404 What information is contained in a social services assessment?

A social services assessment must contain, but is not limited to, the following:

(a) Identifying information about the client (for example, name, address, age, gender, social security number, telephone number, certificate of Indian blood, education level), family history and medical history of the account holder;

(b) Description of the household composition: information on each member of the household (e.g., name, age, and gender) and that person's relationship to the client;

(c) The client's current resources and future income (e.g., VA benefits, retirement pensions, trust assets, employment income, judgment funds, general assistance benefits, unemployment benefits, social security income, supplemental security income and other governmental agency benefits);

(d) A discussion of the circumstances which justify special services, including ability of the client to handle his or her financial affairs and to conduct day-to-day living activities. Factors to be considered should include, but are not limited to:

(1) Age;

(2) Developmental disability;

(3) Chronic alcoholism or substance abuse;

(4) Lack of family assistance or social support systems, or abandonment;

(5) Self-neglect;

(6) Financial exploitation or abuse;

(7) Physical exploitation, neglect or abuse;

(8) Senility; and

(9) Dementia.

(e) Documentation supporting the need for assistance (e.g., medical reports, police reports, court orders, letters from interested parties, prior assessments or evaluations, diagnosis by psychologist/psychiatrist); and

(f) Summary of findings and proposed services to meet the identified needs of the client.

Subpart E—Child Assistance

§20.500 Who is eligible for Child Assistance?

A child is eligible for Child Assistance under this subpart if all of the following criteria are met:

(a) The child must meet the requirements in §20.300.

(b) The child's legally responsible parent, custodian/guardian, or Indian court having jurisdiction must:

(1) Request assistance under this part in writing;

(2) State that they are unable to provide necessary care and guidance for the child, or to provide for the child's special needs in his/her own home; and

(3) Provide a documented social services assessment from the social services worker of whether parent(s), custodian, guardian(s) are able to care for their child.

(c) All income accruing to the child, except income exempted by federal statute, must be used to meet the cost of special needs, foster home or residential care facility as authorized and arranged by social services.

HOW CHILD ASSISTANCE FUNDS CAN BE USED

§20.501 What services can be paid for with Child Assistance funds?

The social services program can use Child Assistance funds to pay for services as shown in the following table.

Service that can be paid	Conditions that must be met	Maximum payment level
(a) Room and board at residential care facilities licensed by the tribe or state.	There must be no other resources available to pay these costs. See §20.502 for other conditions that must be met.	The state or county residential care rate in the state in which the child resides.
(b) Adoption or guardianship subsidies.	There must be no other resources available to pay for this service. See §20.503 for other conditions that must be met.	The Bureau's maximum adoption and guardianship payment standard.
(c) Short-term homemaker services.	There must be no other resources (such as Medicaid) available to pay for this service. Services can be purchased for a maximum of 3 months. See §20.504 for other conditions that must be met.	As approved by the Bureau line officer.
(d) Temporary foster care	See §20.509 for conditions that must be met	The state or county foster care rate in the state in which the child resides.

§ 20.502 Can Child Assistance funds be used to place Indian children in residential care facilities?

You, the social service program, can use Child Assistance funds to purchase or contract for room and board in licensed residential care facilities.

(a) You can use Child Assistance funds to pay only for room and board. You must pay for other services that may be needed, including mental health, education, and physical therapy from other sources.

(b) Before placement the various funding sources must sign an agreement that specifies the services each source will pay. The Bureau Line Officer must approve this agreement.

§ 20.503 When can Child Assistance funds be used for Indian adoption or guardianship subsidies?

You, the social services program, can use Child Assistance funds to provide either adoption or guardianship subsidies if all of the following are true:

(a) The child is 17 or younger;

(b) The child has been in foster care prior to approval of the subsidy;

(c) The social services worker has considered all other available resources, attempted permanency planning, and documented in the case file that placement was in the best interest of the child; and

(d) The Bureau Line Officer approves the subsidy before it is authorized and redetermines eligibility on a yearly basis.

§ 20.504 What short-term homemaker services can Child Assistance pay for?

You, the social services program, can use Child Assistance funds to pay for homemaker services as specified in § 20.501 and this section. While housekeeping services are covered, homemaker services must focus on training household members in such skills as child care and home management. Homemaker services are provided for:

(a) A child who would otherwise need foster care placement or who would benefit from supportive (protective) supervision;

(b) A severely handicapped or special needs child whose care places undue stress on the family; or

(c) A child whose care would benefit from specialized training and supportive services provided to family members.

§ 20.505 What services are provided jointly with the Child Assistance Program?

The services listed in this section are provided by Services to Children, Elderly, and Families under this subpart jointly with the Child Assistance Program.

(a) Social services provided for children in their own home aimed at strengthening the family's ability to provide for and nurture their child. These supportive services can include:

(1) Social work case management;

(2) Counseling for parents and children;

(3) Group work, day care; and

(4) Homemaker services, when necessary.

(b) Protection of Indian children from abuse, neglect or exploitation in coordination with law enforcement and courts.

(c) A written case plan must be established within 30 days of placement and reviewed within 60 days of placement or as outlined in tribally established standards, when temporary placement outside the home is necessary. The case plan must contain a written agreement signed among the various funding sources to identify the services that will be paid by each source in those instances where the child requires services outside the authority of the Child Assistance program.

FOSTER CARE

§ 20.506 What information is required in the foster care case file?

At a minimum the following information is required:

(a) Tribal enrollment verification in accordance with § 20.100;

(b) A written case plan (established within 30 days of placement), which would include a permanency plan detailing the need for and expected length of placement;

(c) Information on each child's health status and school records, including medications and immunization records;

(d) Parental consent(s) for emergency medical care, school, and transportation;

(e) A signed plan for payment, including financial responsibility of parents and use of other appropriate resources;

(f) A copy of the certification/license of the foster home;

(g) A current photo of each child;

(h) A copy of the social security card, birth certificate, Medicaid card and current court order;

(i) For a placement beyond 30 days, copy of the action taken or authorized by a court of competent jurisdiction that documents the need for protection of the child;

(j) For an involuntary placement, a social services assessment completed by a social services worker within 30 days of placement;

(k) Documentation of a minimum of one visit to the placement setting per month by the social services worker with each child; and

(l) A list of all prior placements, including the names of the foster parents and dates of placements.

§20.507 What requirements must foster care providers meet?

If a child needs foster care, the social services worker must select care that meets the physical, behavioral, and emotional needs of the child. Foster care is intended to be short-term. The case plan must show that all of the requirements in paragraphs (a) through (c) of this section are met:

(a) All foster homes must be certified or licensed by the tribe or other appropriate authority. Foster care placements beyond 30 days must be made through a court of competent jurisdiction to ensure that:

(1) Federal background checks are completed prior to placement as required by Public Law 101–630; and

(2) Training (optional for placements with relatives) is provided to the foster family.

(b) If the child is placed with relatives in an adoption and guardian placement, the case file must contain an approved current home study.

(c) An off-reservation foster home, or residential care facility under contract must meet the licensing standards of the state in which it is located or tribally established certifying/licensing standards.

§20.508 What must the social services agency do when a child is placed in foster care, residential care or guardianship home?

The social services agency must make efforts to secure child support for the child in foster care or residential care through a court of competent jurisdiction.

§20.509 What must the social services worker do when a child is placed in foster care or residential care facility?

When a child is placed in foster care or a residential care facility the social services worker must do all of the following:

(a) Discuss with foster parents or caretakers, the child's special needs, including disabilities;

(b) Provide counseling or referral to available resources;

(c) Refer any child requiring medical, substance abuse, or behavioral (mental) health services to an appropriate health services to be assessed and to receive services;

(d) Ensure that the case plan provides for all necessary costs of care (including clothing, incidentals, and personal allowance) in accordance with established state standards of payments;

(e) Develop a foster family agreement signed and dated by the parties involved that specifies the roles and responsibilities of the biological parents, foster parents, and placing agency; the terms of payment of care; and the need for adherence to the established case plan;

(f) Immediately report any occurrences of suspected child abuse or neglect in a foster home or residential care facility to law enforcement and protective services in accordance with tribal standards and reporting requirements under Public Law 101–630; and

(g) Complete a yearly assessment of each tribal or state licensed foster home or residential care facility evaluating how the home has fulfilled its function relative to the needs of the child placed in the home.

§ 20.510 How is the court involved in child placements?

The court retains custody of a child in placement and the care and supervision must be given to the appropriate social services agency. While the court can issue any court order consistent with tribal law, the courts do not have the authority to require expenditure of federal funds to pay for specifically prescribed or restrictive services or out-of-home placements of children. Case plans must be reviewed with the appropriate court at least every 6 months and a permanency hearing held within 12 months after a child enters foster care or residential care, or according to established tribal standards. These standards can be established in the tribal code and can be in accordance with available funding source requirements.

§ 20.511 Should permanency plans be developed?

Permanency planning must be developed for all child placements within 6 months after initial placement of the child. Every reasonable effort will be made to preserve the family and/or reunify the children with the family and relatives when developing permanency plans. However, the child's health and safety are the paramount concern.

§ 20.512 Can the Bureau/tribal contractors make Indian adoptive placements?

The Bureau is not an authorized adoption agency and staff must not arrange adoptive placements. However, long-term permanency planning can involve the Bureau social services workers cooperating with tribal courts to provide an adoption subsidy. Tribal contractors will provide adoption services as authorized by the tribal courts in accordance with tribal codes/law.

§ 20.513 Should Interstate Compacts be used for the placement of children?

Interstate compact agreements should be used when appropriate for foster care, adoption and guardianship to protect the best interests of the child and to assure the availability of the funding resources and services from the originating placement source.

§ 20.514 What assistance can the courts request from social services on behalf of children?

The courts can request the following:

(a) Investigations of law enforcement reports of child abuse and neglect;

(b) Assessment of the need for out-of-home placement of the child; and

(c) Provision of court-related services following adjudication, such as monitoring, foster care, or residential care, or pre/post placement services.

§ 20.515 What is required for case management?

Social services workers must document regular contact with children and families in accordance with specific program requirements. The social services agency is responsible for implementation of quality case management; this requires the supervisor's review of case plans every 90 days.

§ 20.516 How are child abuse, neglect or exploitation cases to be handled?

Reported child abuse, neglect or exploitation cases and the requirement for background clearances will be handled in accordance with the Indian Child Protection and Family Violence Prevention Act of 1990, Public Law 101–630, 25 CFR part 63, federal and/or state laws where applicable, and tribal codes which protect Indian children and victims of domestic violence. This includes developing and maintaining Child Protection Teams in accordance to Public Law 101–630 and collection of child abuse, neglect and exploitation data according to Public Law 99–570. Those cases referred by the state will be handled according to the Indian Child Welfare Act, Public Law 95–608, and 25 CFR part 23.

Subpart F—Administrative Procedures

§ 20.600 Who can apply for financial assistance or social services?

(a) You can apply for financial assistance or social services under this part if you:

(1) Believe that you are eligible to receive benefits; or

(2) Are applying on behalf of someone who you believe is eligible to receive benefits.

(b) Under paragraph (a) of this section, any of the following may apply for benefits on behalf of another person: relatives, interested individuals, social services agencies, law enforcement agencies, courts, or other persons or agencies.

§ 20.601 How can applications be submitted?

You can apply for financial assistance or social services under this part by:

(a) Completing an application that you can get from your social services worker or tribe; or

(b) Through an interview with a social services worker who will complete an application for you based on the oral interview.

§ 20.602 How does the Bureau verify eligibility for social services?

(a) You, the applicant, are the primary source of information used to determine eligibility and need. If it is necessary to secure information such as medical records from other sources, you must authorize the release of information.

(b) You must immediately report to your social services worker any changes in circumstances that may affect your eligibility or the amount of financial assistance that you receive.

§ 20.603 How is an application approved or denied?

(a) Each application must be approved if the applicant meets the eligibility criteria in this part for the type of assistance requested and all recipients will be redetermined for eligibility every 6 months. Financial assistance will be made retroactive to the application date.

(b) An application must be denied if the applicant does not meet the eligibility criteria in §§ 20.300 through 20.516.

(c) The social services worker must approve or deny an application within 30 days of the application date. The local social services worker must issue written notice of the approval or denial of each application within 45 days of the application date.

(d) If for a good reason the social services worker cannot meet the deadline in paragraph (c) of this section, he or she must notify the applicant in writing of:

(1) The reasons why the decision cannot be made; and

(2) The deadline by which the social services worker will send the applicant a decision.

[65 FR 63159, Oct. 20, 2000; 65 FR 76563, Dec. 7, 2000]

§ 20.604 How is an applicant or recipient notified that benefits or services are denied or changed?

If the Bureau increases, decreases, suspends, or terminates financial assistance, the social services worker must mail or hand deliver to the applicant or recipient a written notice of the action. The notice must:

(a) State the action taken, the effective date, and the reason(s) for the decision;

(b) Inform the applicant or recipient of the right to request a hearing if dissatisfied with the decision;

(c) Advise the applicant or recipient of the right to be represented by an authorized representative at no expense to the Bureau;

(d) Include the address of the local Superintendent or his/her designated representative to whom the request for a hearing must be submitted;

(e) Advise the applicant or recipient that failure to request a hearing within 20 days of the date of the notice will cause the decision to become final and not subject to appeal under 25 CFR part 2; and

(f) Be delivered to the applicant 20 days in advance of the effective date of the action.

§ 20.605 What happens when an applicant or recipient appeals a decision under this subpart?

If you are an applicant or recipient and appeal a decision made under § 20.604, you can continue to receive your assistance while your appeal is pending. For this to happen, you must submit your appeal by the deadline in § 20.604(e).

§ 20.606 How is an incorrect payment adjusted or recovered?

(a) When an incorrect payment of financial assistance has been made to an individual or family, a proper adjustment or recovery is required.

(b) The proper adjustment or recovery is based upon individual need as appropriate to the circumstances that resulted in an incorrect payment.

(c) Before adjustment or recovery, the recipient will be notified of the proposal to correct the payment and given an informal opportunity to resolve the matter.

(d) If an informal resolution cannot be attained, the recipient must be given a written notice of decision and the procedures of § 20.604 will apply.

(e) If a hearing is requested, the hearing will be conducted in accordance with the procedures under §§ 20.700 through 20.705.

§ 20.607 What happens when applicants or recipients knowingly and willfully provide false or fraudulent information?

Applicants or recipients who knowingly and willfully provide false or fraudulent information are subject to prosecution under 18 U.S.C. § 1001, which carries a fine of not more than $10,000 or imprisonment for not more than 5 years, or both. The social services worker will prepare a written report detailing the information considered to be false and submit the report to the Superintendent or his/her designated representative for appropriate investigative action.

Subpart G—Hearings and Appeals

§ 20.700 Can an applicant or recipient appeal the decision of a Bureau official?

Yes, if you are an applicant or recipient, and are dissatisfied with a Bureau decision made under this part, you can request a hearing before the Superintendent or his/her designated representative. You must submit your request by the deadline in § 20.604. The Superintendent or his/her designated representative can extend the deadline if you show good cause.

§ 20.701 Does a recipient receive financial assistance while an appeal is pending?

Yes, if you appeal under this subpart, financial assistance will be continued or reinstated to insure there is no break in financial assistance until the Superintendent or his/her designated representative makes a decision. The Superintendent or his/her designated representative can adjust payments or recover overpayments to conform with his/her decision.

[65 FR 63159, Oct. 20, 2000; 65 FR 76563, Dec. 7, 2000]

§ 20.702 When is an appeal hearing scheduled?

The Superintendent or his/her designated representative must set a date for the hearing within 10 days of the date of request for a hearing and give written notice to the applicant or recipient.

§ 20.703 What must the written notice of hearing include?

The written notice of hearing must include:

(a) The date, time and location of the hearing;

(b) A statement of the facts and issues giving rise to the appeal;

(c) The applicant's or recipient's right to be heard in person, or to be represented by an authorized representative at no expense to the Bureau;

(d) The applicant or recipient's right to present both oral and written evidence during the hearing;

(e) The applicant's or recipient's right to confront and cross-examine witnesses at the hearing;

(f) The applicant's or recipient's right of one continuance of not more than 10 days with respect to the date of hearing; and

(g) The applicant's or recipient's right to examine and copy, at a reasonable time before the hearing, his/her case record as it relates to the proposed action being contested.

§ 20.704 Who conducts the hearing or appeal of a Bureau decision or action and what is the process?

(a) The Superintendent or his/her designated representative conducts the hearing in an informal but orderly manner, records the hearing, and provides the applicant or recipient with a transcript of the hearing upon request.

(b) The Superintendent or his/her designated representative must render a written decision within 10 days of the completion of the hearing. The written decision must include:

(1) A written statement covering the evidence relied upon and reasons for the decision; and

(2) The applicant's or recipient's right to appeal the Superintendent or his/her designated representative's decision pursuant to 25 CFR part 2 and request Bureau assistance in preparation of the appeal.

§ 20.705 Can an applicant or recipient appeal a tribal decision?

Yes, the applicant or recipient must pursue the appeal process applicable to the Public Law 93–638 contract, Public Law 102–477 grant, or Public Law 103–413 self-governance annual funding agreement. If no appeal process exists, then the applicant or recipient must pursue the appeal through the appropriate tribal forum.

PART 23—INDIAN CHILD WELFARE ACT

Subpart A—Purpose, Definitions, and Policy

Subpart B—Notice of Involuntary Child Custody Proceedings and Payment for Appointed Counsel in State Courts

Subpart C—Grants to Indian Tribes for Title II Indian Child and Family Service Programs

Subpart D—Grants to Off-Reservation Indian Organizations for Title II Indian Child and Family Service Programs

Subpart E—General and Uniform Grant Administration Provisions and Requirements

Subpart F—Appeals

Subpart G—Administrative Provisions

Subpart H—Assistance to State Courts

Subpart I—Indian Child Welfare Act Proceedings

GENERAL PROVISIONS

AUTHORITY: 5 U.S.C. 301; 25 U.S.C. 2, 9, 1901–1952.

SOURCE: 59 FR 2256, Jan. 13, 1994, unless otherwise noted.

EDITORIAL NOTE: Nomenclature changes to part 23 appear at 79 FR 27190, May 13, 2014.

Subpart A—Purpose, Definitions, and Policy

§ 23.1 Purpose.

The purpose of the regulations in this part is to govern the provision of funding for, and the administration of Indian child and family service programs as authorized by the Indian Child Welfare Act of 1978 (Pub. L. 95–608, 92 Stat. 3069, 25 U.S.C. 2, 9, 1901–1952).

§23.2 Definitions.

Act means the Indian Child Welfare Act (ICWA), Pub. L. 95–608, 92 Stat. 3069, 25 U.S.C. 1901 *et seq.*

Active efforts means affirmative, active, thorough, and timely efforts intended primarily to maintain or reunite an Indian child with his or her family. Where an agency is involved in the child-custody proceeding, active efforts must involve assisting the parent or parents or Indian custodian through the steps of a case plan and with accessing or developing the resources necessary to satisfy the case plan. To the maximum extent possible, active efforts should be provided in a manner consistent with the prevailing social and cultural conditions and way of life of the Indian child's Tribe and should be conducted in partnership with the Indian child and the Indian child's parents, extended family members, Indian custodians, and Tribe. Active efforts are to be tailored to the facts and circumstances of the case and may include, for example:

(1) Conducting a comprehensive assessment of the circumstances of the Indian child's family, with a focus on safe reunification as the most desirable goal;

(2) Identifying appropriate services and helping the parents to overcome barriers, including actively assisting the parents in obtaining such services;

(3) Identifying, notifying, and inviting representatives of the Indian child's Tribe to participate in providing support and services to the Indian child's family and in family team meetings, permanency planning, and resolution of placement issues;

(4) Conducting or causing to be conducted a diligent search for the Indian child's extended family members, and contacting and consulting with extended family members to provide family structure and support for the Indian child and the Indian child's parents;

(5) Offering and employing all available and culturally appropriate family preservation strategies and facilitating the use of remedial and rehabilitative services provided by the child's Tribe;

(6) Taking steps to keep siblings together whenever possible;

(7) Supporting regular visits with parents or Indian custodians in the most natural setting possible as well as trial home visits of the Indian child during any period of removal, consistent with the need to ensure the health, safety, and welfare of the child;

(8) Identifying community resources including housing, financial, transportation, mental health, substance abuse, and peer support services and actively assisting the Indian child's parents or, when appropriate, the child's family, in utilizing and accessing those resources;

(9) Monitoring progress and participation in services;

(10) Considering alternative ways to address the needs of the Indian child's parents and, where appropriate, the family, if the optimum services do not exist or are not available;

(11) Providing post-reunification services and monitoring.

Assistant Secretary means the Assistant Secretary—Indian Affairs, the Department of the Interior.

Bureau of Indian Affairs (BIA) means the Bureau of Indian Affairs, the Department of the Interior.

Child-custody proceeding. (1) "Child-custody proceeding" means and includes any action, other than an emergency proceeding, that may culminate in one of the following outcomes:

(i) *Foster-care placement*, which is any action removing an Indian child from his or her parent or Indian custodian for temporary placement in a foster home or institution or the home of a guardian or conservator where the parent or Indian custodian cannot have the child returned upon demand, but where parental rights have not been terminated;

(ii) *Termination of parental rights*, which is any action resulting in the termination of the parent-child relationship;

(iii) *Preadoptive placement*, which is the temporary placement of an Indian child in a foster home or institution after the termination of parental rights, but prior to or in lieu of adoptive placement; or

(iv) *Adoptive placement*, which is the permanent placement of an Indian child for adoption, including any action resulting in a final decree of adoption.

(2) An action that may culminate in one of these four outcomes is considered a separate child-custody proceeding from an action that may culminate in a different one of these four outcomes. There may be several child-custody proceedings involving any given Indian child. Within each child-custody proceeding, there may be several hearings. If a child is placed in foster care or another out-of-home placement as a result of a status offense, that status offense proceeding is a child-custody proceeding.

Consortium means an association or partnership of two or more eligible applicants who enter into an agreement to administer a grant program and to provide services under the grant to Indian residents in a specific geographical area when it is administratively feasible to provide an adequate level of services within the area.

Continued custody means physical custody or legal custody or both, under any applicable Tribal law or Tribal custom or State law, that a parent or Indian custodian already has or had at any point in the past. The biological mother of a child has had custody of a child.

Custody means physical custody or legal custody or both, under any applicable Tribal law or Tribal custom or State law. A party may demonstrate the existence of custody by looking to Tribal law or Tribal custom or State law.

Domicile means:

(1) For a parent or Indian custodian, the place at which a person has been physically present and that the person regards as home; a person's true, fixed, principal, and permanent home, to which that person intends to return and remain indefinitely even though the person may be currently residing elsewhere.

(2) For an Indian child, the domicile of the Indian child's parents or Indian custodian or guardian. In the case of an Indian child whose parents are not married to each other, the domicile of the Indian child's custodial parent.

Emergency proceeding means and includes any court action that involves an emergency removal or emergency placement of an Indian child.

Extended family member is defined by the law or custom of the Indian child's Tribe or, in the absence of such law or custom, is a person who has reached age 18 and who is the Indian child's grandparent, aunt or uncle, brother or sister, brother-in-law or sister-in-law, niece or nephew, first or second cousin, or stepparent.

Grant means a written agreement between the BIA and the governing body of an Indian tribe or Indian organization wherein the BIA provides funds to the grantee to plan, conduct or administer specific programs, services, or activities and where the administrative and programmatic provisions are specifically delineated.

Grantee means the tribal governing body of an Indian tribe or Board of Directors of an Indian organization responsible for grant administration.

Grants officer means an officially designated officer who administers ICWA grants awarded by the Bureau of Indian Affairs, the Department of the Interior.

Hearing means a judicial session held for the purpose of deciding issues of fact, of law, or both.

Indian means any person who is a member of an Indian tribe, or who is an Alaska Native and a member of a Regional Corporation as defined in section 7 of the Alaska Native Claims Settlement Act, 43 U.S.C. 1606.

Indian child means any unmarried person who is under age 18 and either:

(1) Is a member or citizen of an Indian Tribe; or

(2) Is eligible for membership or citizenship in an Indian Tribe and is the biological child of a member/citizen of an Indian Tribe.

Indian child's Tribe means:

(1) The Indian Tribe in which an Indian child is a member or eligible for membership; or

(2) In the case of an Indian child who is a member of or eligible for membership in more than one Tribe, the Indian Tribe described in §23.109.

Indian custodian means any Indian who has legal custody of an Indian child under applicable Tribal law or custom or under applicable State law, or to whom temporary physical care, custody, and control has been transferred by the parent of such child. An Indian may demonstrate that he or she is an Indian custodian by looking to Tribal law or Tribal custom or State law.

Indian foster home means a foster home where one or more of the licensed or approved foster parents is an "Indian" as defined in 25 U.S.C. 1903(3).

Indian organization, solely for purposes of eligibility for grants under subpart D of this part, means any legally established group, association, partnership, corporation, or other legal entity which is owned or controlled by Indians, or a majority (51 percent or more) of whose members are Indians.

Indian preference means preference and opportunities for employment and training provided to Indians in the administration of grants in accordance with section 7 (b) of the Indian Self-Determination and Education Assistance Act (25 U.S.C. 450).

Indian tribe means any Indian tribe, band, nation, or other organized group or community of Indians federally recognized as eligible for the services provided to Indians by the Secretary because of their status as Indians, including any Alaska Native village as defined in section 3 (c) of the Alaska Native Claims Settlement Act, 43 U.S.C. 1602 (c).

Involuntary proceeding means a child-custody proceeding in which the parent does not consent of his or her free will to the foster-care, preadoptive, or adoptive placement or termination of parental rights or in which the parent consents to the foster-care, preadoptive, or adoptive placement under threat of removal of the child by a State court or agency.

Off-reservation ICWA program means an ICWA program administered in accordance with 25 U.S.C. 1932 by an off-reservation Indian organization.

Parent or *parents* means any biological parent or parents of an Indian child, or any Indian who has lawfully adopted an Indian child, including adoptions under Tribal law or custom. It does not include an unwed biological father where paternity has not been acknowledged or established.

Reservation means Indian country as defined in 18 U.S.C 1151 and any lands, not covered under that section, title to which is held by the United States in trust for the benefit of any Indian Tribe or individual or held by any Indian Tribe or individual subject to a restriction by the United States against alienation.

Secretary means the Secretary of the Interior or the Secretary's authorized representative acting under delegated authority.

Service areas solely for newly recognized or restored Indian tribes without established reservations means those service areas congressionally established by Federal law to be the equivalent of a reservation for the purpose of determining the eligibility of a newly recognized or restored Indian tribe and its members for all Federal services and benefits.

State court means any agent or agency of a state, including the District of Columbia or any territory or possession of the United States, or any political subdivision empowered by law to terminate parental rights or to make foster care placements, preadoptive placements, or adoptive placements.

Status offenses mean offenses that would not be considered criminal if committed by an adult; they are acts prohibited only because of a person's status as a minor (*e.g.*, truancy, incorrigibility).

Subgrant means a secondary grant that undertakes part of the obligations of the primary grant, and assumes the legal and financial responsibility for the funds awarded and for the performance of the grant-supported activity.

Technical assistance means the provision of oral, written, or other relevant information and assistance to prospective grant applicants in the development of their grant proposals. Technical assistance may include a preliminary review of an application to assist the applicant in identifying the strengths and weaknesses of the proposal, ongoing program planning, design and evaluation, and such other program-specific assistance as is necessary for ongoing grant administration and management.

Title II means title II of Public Law 95–608, the Indian Child Welfare Act of 1978, which authorizes the Secretary to make grants to Indian tribes and off-reservation Indian organizations for the establishment and operation of Indian child and family service programs.

Tribal court means a court with jurisdiction over child-custody proceedings and which is either a Court of Indian Offenses, a court established and operated under the code or custom of an Indian Tribe, or any other administrative body of a Tribe vested with authority over child-custody proceedings.

Tribal government means the federally recognized governing body of an Indian tribe.

Upon demand means that the parent or Indian custodian can regain custody simply upon verbal request, without any formalities or contingencies.

Value means face, par, or market value, or cost price, either wholesale or retail, whichever is greater.

Voluntary proceeding means a child-custody proceeding that is not an involuntary proceeding, such as a proceeding for foster-care, preadoptive, or adoptive placement that either parent, both parents, or the Indian custodian has, of his or her or their free will, without a threat of removal by a State agency, consented to for the Indian child, or a proceeding for voluntary termination of parental rights.

[59 FR 2256, Jan. 13, 1994, as amended at 81 FR 38864, June 14, 2016]

§ 23.3 Policy.

In enacting the Indian Child Welfare Act of 1978, Pub. L. 95–608, the Congress has declared that it is the policy of this Nation to protect the best interests of Indian children and to promote the stability and security of Indian tribes and Indian families by the establishment of minimum Federal standards to prevent the arbitrary removal of Indian children from their families and tribes and to ensure that measures which prevent the breakup of Indian families are followed in child custody proceedings (25 U.S.C. 1902). Indian child and family service programs receiving title II funds and operated by federally recognized Indian tribes and off-reservation Indian organizations shall reflect the unique values of Indian culture and promote the stability and security of Indian children, Indian families and Indian communities. It is the policy of the Bureau of Indian Affairs to emphasize and facilitate the comprehensive design, development and implementation of Indian child and family service programs in coordination with other Federal, state, local, and tribal programs which strengthen and preserve Indian families and Indian tribes.

§ 23.4 Information collection.

(a) The information collection requirements contained in § 23.13 of this part have been approved by the Office of Management and Budget (OMB) under 44 U.S.C. 3501 *et seq.*, and assigned clearance number 1076–0111.

(1) This information will be used to determine eligibility for payment of legal fees for indigent Indian parents and Indian custodians, involved in involuntary Indian child custody proceedings in state courts, who are not eligible for legal services through other mechanisms. Response to this request is required to obtain a benefit.

(2) Public reporting for this information collection is estimated to average 10 hours per response, including the time for reviewing instructions, gathering and maintaining data, and completing and reviewing the information collection. Direct comments regarding the burden estimate or any aspect of this information collection should be mailed or hand-delivered to the Bureau of Indian Affairs, Information Collection Clearance Officer, Room 336–SIB, 1849 C Street, NW., Washington, DC 20240; and the Office of Information and Regulatory Affairs Paperwork Reduction Project—1076–0111, Office of Management and Budget, Washington, DC 20503.

(b) The information collection requirements contained in §§ 23.21; 23.31; 23.46; 23.47, and 23.71 have been approved by the Office of Management and Budget under 44 U.S.C. 3501 *et seq.* and assigned clearance number 1076–0131. The information collection requirements under §§ 23.21 and 23.31 are collected in the form of ICWA grant applications from Indian tribes and off-reservation Indian organizations. A response to this request is required to obtain grant funds. The information collection requirements under § 23.46 are collected in compliance with applicable OMB circulars on financial management, internal and external controls and other fiscal assurances in accordance with existing Federal grant administration and reporting requirements. The grantee information collection requirements under § 23.47 are collected in the form of quarterly and annual program performance narrative reports and statistical data as required by the grant award document. Pursuant to 25 U.S.C. 1951, the information collection requirement under § 23.71 is collected from state courts entering final adoption decrees for any Indian child and is provided to and maintained by the Secretary.

(1) Public reporting for the information collection at §§ 23.21 and 23.31 is estimated to average 32 hours per response, including the time for reviewing the grant application instructions, gathering the necessary information and data, and completing the grant application. Public reporting for the information collection at §§ 23.46 and 23.47 is estimated to average a combined total of 16 annual hours per grantee, including the time for gathering the necessary information and data, and completing the required forms and reports. Public reporting for the information collection at § 23.71 is estimated to average 4 hours per response, including the time for obtaining and preparing the final adoption decree for transmittal to the Secretary.

(2) Direct comments regarding any of these burden estimates or any aspect of these information collection requirements should be mailed or hand-delivered to the Bureau of Indian Affairs, Information Collection Clearance Officer, room 336–SIB, 1849 C Street, NW., Washington, DC, 20240; and the Office of Information and Regulatory Affairs Paperwork Reduction Project—1076–0131, Office of Management and Budget, Washington, DC 20503.

Subpart B—Notice of Involuntary Child Custody Proceedings and Payment for Appointed Counsel in State Courts

§ 23.11 Notice.

(a) In any involuntary proceeding in a State court where the court knows or has reason to know that an Indian child is involved, and where the identity and location of the child's parent or Indian custodian or Tribe is known, the party seeking the foster-care placement of, or termination of parental rights to, an Indian child must directly notify the parents, the Indian custodians, and the child's Tribe by registered or certified mail with return receipt requested, of the pending child-custody proceedings and their right of intervention. Notice must include the requisite information identified in § 23.111, consistent with the confidentiality requirement in § 23.111(d)(6)(ix). Copies of these notices must be sent to the appropriate Regional Director listed in paragraphs (b)(1) through (12) of this section by registered or certified mail with return receipt requested or by personal delivery and must include the information required by § 23.111.

(b)(1) For child-custody proceedings in Alabama, Connecticut, Delaware, District of Columbia, Florida, Georgia, Kentucky, Louisiana, Maine, Maryland, Massachusetts, Mississippi, New Hampshire, New Jersey, New York, North Carolina, Pennsylvania, Rhode Island, South Carolina, Tennessee, Vermont, Virginia, West Virginia, or any territory or possession of the United States, notices must be sent to the following address: Eastern Regional Director, Bureau of Indian Affairs, 545 Marriott Drive, Suite 700, Nashville, Tennessee 37214.

(2) For child-custody proceedings in Illinois, Indiana, Iowa, Michigan, Minnesota, Ohio, or Wisconsin, notices must be sent to the following address: Minneapolis Regional Director, Bureau of Indian Affairs, 5600 American Blvd. W, Ste. 500, Bloomington, MN 55437.

(3) For child-custody proceedings in Nebraska, North Dakota, or South Dakota, notices must be sent to the following address: Aberdeen Regional Director, Bureau of Indian Affairs, 115 Fourth Avenue SE., Aberdeen, South Dakota 57401.

(4) For child-custody proceedings in Kansas, Texas (except for notices to the Ysleta del Sur Pueblo of El Paso County, Texas), or the western Oklahoma counties of Alfalfa, Beaver, Beckman, Blaine, Caddo, Canadian, Cimarron, Cleveland, Comanche, Cotton, Custer, Dewey, Ellis, Garfield, Grant, Greer, Harmon, Harper, Jackson, Kay, Kingfisher, Kiowa, Lincoln,

Logan, Major, Noble, Oklahoma, Pawnee, Payne, Pottawatomie, Roger Mills, Texas, Tillman, Washita, Woods or Woodward, notices must be sent to the following address: Anadarko Regional Director, Bureau of Indian Affairs, P.O. Box 368, Anadarko, Oklahoma 73005. Notices to the Ysleta del Sur Pueblo must be sent to the Albuquerque Regional Director at the address listed in paragraph (b)(6) of this section.

(5) For child-custody proceedings in Wyoming or Montana (except for notices to the Confederated Salish and Kootenai Tribes of the Flathead Reservation, Montana), notices must be sent to the following address: Billings Regional Director, Bureau of Indian Affairs, 316 N. 26th Street, Billings, Montana 59101. Notices to the Confederated Salish and Kootenai Tribes of the Flathead Reservation, Montana, must be sent to the Portland Regional Director at the address listed in paragraph (b)(11) of this section.

(6) For child-custody proceedings in the Texas counties of El Paso and Hudspeth or in Colorado or New Mexico (exclusive of notices to the Navajo Nation from the New Mexico counties listed in paragraph (b)(9) of this section), notices must be sent to the following address: Albuquerque Regional Director, Bureau of Indian Affairs, 615 First Street, P.O. Box 26567, Albuquerque, New Mexico 87125. Notices to the Navajo Nation must be sent to the Navajo Regional Director at the address listed in paragraph (b)(9) of this section.

(7) For child-custody proceedings in Alaska (except for notices to the Metlakatla Indian Community, Annette Island Reserve, Alaska), notices must be sent to the following address: Alaska Regional Director—Attn: Human Services, Bureau of Indian Affairs, 3601 C Street, Suite 1258, Anchorage, Alaska 99503. Notices to the Metlakatla Indian Community, Annette Island Reserve, Alaska, must be sent to the Portland Regional Director at the address listed in paragraph (b)(11) of this section.

(8) For child-custody proceedings in Arkansas, Missouri, or the eastern Oklahoma counties of Adair, Atoka, Bryan, Carter, Cherokee, Craig, Creek, Choctaw, Coal, Delaware, Garvin, Grady, Haskell, Hughes, Jefferson, Johnson, Latimer, LeFlore, Love, Mayes, McCurtain, McClain, McIntosh, Murray, Muskogee, Nowata, Okfuskee, Okmulgee, Osage, Ottawa, Pittsburg, Pontotoc, Pushmataha, Marshall, Rogers, Seminole, Sequoyah, Stephens, Tulsa, Wagoner, or Washington, notices must be sent to the following address: Muskogee Regional Director, Bureau of Indian Affairs, 101 North Fifth Street, Muskogee, Oklahoma 74401.

(9) For child-custody proceedings in the Arizona counties of Apache, Coconino (except for notices to the Hopi Tribe of Arizona and the San Juan Southern Paiute Tribe of Arizona) or Navajo (except for notices to the Hopi Tribe of Arizona); the New Mexico counties of McKinley (except for notices to the Zuni Tribe of the Zuni Reservation), San Juan, or Socorro; or the Utah county of San Juan, notices must be sent to the following address: Navajo Regional Director, Bureau of Indian Affairs, P.O. Box 1060, Gallup, New Mexico 87301. Notices to the Hopi and San Juan Southern Paiute Tribes of Arizona must be sent to the Phoenix Regional Director at the address listed in paragraph (b)(10) of this section. Notices to the Zuni Tribe of the Zuni Reservation must be sent to the Albuquerque Regional Director at the address listed in paragraph (b)(6 of this section).

(10) For child-custody proceedings in Arizona (exclusive of notices to the Navajo Nation from those counties listed in paragraph (b)(9) of this section), Nevada, or Utah (exclusive of San Juan County), notices must be sent to the following address: Phoenix Regional Director, Bureau of Indian Affairs, 1 North First Street, P.O. Box 10, Phoenix, Arizona 85001.

(11) For child-custody proceedings in Idaho, Oregon, or Washington, notices must be sent to the following address: Portland Regional Director, Bureau of Indian Affairs, 911 NE 11th Avenue, Portland, Oregon 97232. All notices to the Confederated Salish and Kootenai Tribes of the Flathead Reservation, located in the Montana counties of Flathead, Lake, Missoula, and Sanders, must also be sent to the Portland Regional Director.

(12) For child-custody proceedings in California or Hawaii, notices must be sent to the following address: Sacramento Regional Director, Bureau of Indian Affairs, Federal Office Building, 2800 Cottage Way, Sacramento, California 95825.

(c) Upon receipt of the notice, the Secretary will make reasonable documented efforts to locate and notify the child's Tribe and the child's parent or Indian custodian. The Secretary will have 15 days, after receipt of the notice, to notify the child's Tribe and parents or Indian custodians and to send a copy of the notice to the court. If within the 15-day period the Secretary is unable to verify that the child meets the criteria of an Indian child as defined in §23.2, or is unable to locate the parents or Indian custodians, the Secretary will so inform the court and state how much more time, if any, will be needed to complete the verification or the search. The Secretary will complete all research efforts, even if those efforts cannot be completed before the child-custody proceeding begins.

(d) Upon request from a party to an Indian child-custody proceeding, the Secretary will make a reasonable attempt to identify and locate the child's Tribe, parents, or Indian custodians to assist the party seeking the information.

[81 FR 38866, June 14, 2016, as amended at 83 FR 55268, Nov. 5, 2018]

§23.12 Designated tribal agent for service of notice.

Any Indian tribe entitled to notice pursuant to 25 U.S.C. 1912 may designate by resolution, or by such other form as the tribe's constitution or current practice requires, an agent for service of notice other than the tribal chairman and send a copy of the designation to the Secretary or his/her designee. The Secretary or his/her designee shall update and publish as necessary the names and addresses of the designated agents in the FEDERAL REGISTER. A current listing of such agents shall be available through the area offices.

§23.13 Payment for appointed counsel in involuntary Indian child custody proceedings in state courts.

(a) When a state court appoints counsel for an indigent Indian party in an involuntary Indian child custody proceeding for which the appointment of counsel is not authorized under state law, the court shall send written notice of the appointment to the BIA Regional Director designated for that state in §23.11. The notice shall include the following:

(1) Name, address, and telephone number of attorney who has been appointed.

(2) Name and address of client for whom counsel is appointed.

(3) Relationship of client to child.

(4) Name of Indian child's tribe.

(5) Copy of the petition or complaint.

(6) Certification by the court that state law makes no provision for appointment of counsel in such proceedings.

(7) Certification by the court that the Indian client is indigent.

(b) The Regional Director shall certify that the client is eligible to have his or her appointed counsel compensated by the BIA unless:

(1) The litigation does not involve a child custody proceeding as defined in 25 U.S.C. 1903 (1);

(2) The child who is the subject of the litigation is not an Indian child as defined in 25 U.S.C. 1903 (4);

(3) The client is neither the Indian child who is the subject of the litigation, the Indian child's parent as defined in 25 U.S.C. 1903 (9), nor the child's Indian custodian as defined in 25 U.S.C. 1903 (6);

(4) State law provides for appointment of counsel in such proceedings;

(5) The notice to the Regional Director of appointment of counsel is incomplete; or

(6) Funds are not available for the particular fiscal year.

(c) No later than 10 days after receipt of the notice of appointment of counsel, the Regional Director shall notify the court, the client, and the attorney in writing whether the client has been certified as eligible to have his or her attorney fees and expenses paid by the BIA. If certification is denied, the notice shall include written reasons for that decision, together with a statement that complies with 25 CFR 2.7 and that informs the applicant that the decision may be appealed to the Assistant Secretary. The Assistant Secretary shall consider appeals under this subsection in accordance with 25 CFR 2.20 (c) through (e). Appeal procedures shall be as set out in part 2 of this chapter.

(d) When determining attorney fees and expenses, the court shall:

(1) Determine the amount of payment due appointed counsel by the same procedures and criteria it uses in determining the fees and expenses to be paid appointed counsel in state juvenile delinquency proceedings; and

(2) Submit approved vouchers to the Regional Director who certified eligibility for BIA payment, together with the court's certification that the amount requested is reasonable under the state standards considering the work actually performed in light of criteria that apply in determining fees and expenses for appointed counsel in state juvenile delinquency proceedings.

(e) The Regional Director shall authorize the payment of attorney fees and expenses in the amount requested in the voucher approved by the court unless:

(1) The amount of payment due the state-appointed counsel is inconsistent with the fees and expenses specified in § 23.13 (d)(1); or

(2) The client has not been certified previously as eligible under paragraph (c) of this section; or

(3) The voucher is submitted later than 90 days after completion of the legal action involving a client certified as eligible for payment of legal fees under paragraph (b) of this section.

(f) No later than 15 days after receipt of a payment voucher, the Regional Director shall send written notice to the court, the client, and the attorney stating the amount of payment, if any, that has been authorized. If the payment has been denied, or the amount authorized is less than the amount requested in the voucher approved by the court, the notice shall include a written statement of the reasons for the decision together with a statement that complies with 25 CFR 2.7 and that informs the client that the decision may be appealed to the Interior Board of Indian Appeals in accordance with 25 CFR 2.4 (e); 43 CFR 4.310 through 4.318 and 43 CFR 4.330 through 4.340.

(g) Failure of the Regional Director to meet the deadline specified in paragraphs (c) and (f) of this section may be treated as a denial for purposes of appeal under paragraph (f) of this section.

(h) Payment for appointed counsel does not extend to Indian tribes involved in state court child custody proceedings or to Indian families involved in Indian child custody proceedings in tribal courts.

Subpart C—Grants to Indian Tribes for Title II Indian Child and Family Service Programs

§ 23.21 Noncompetitive tribal government grants.

(a) *Grant application information and technical assistance.* Information on grant application procedures and related information may be obtained from the appropriate Agency Superintendent or Regional Director. Preaward and ongoing technical assistance to tribal governments shall be provided in accordance with § 23.42 of this part.

(b) *Eligibility requirements for tribal governments.* The tribal government(s) of any Indian tribe or consortium of tribes may submit a properly documented application for a grant to the appropriate Agency Superintendent or Regional Director. A tribe may neither submit more than one application for a grant nor be the beneficiary of more than one grant under this subpart.

(1) Through the publication of a FEDERAL REGISTER announcement at the outset of the implementation of the noncompetitive grant award process during which tribal applications will be solicited, the Assistant Secretary will notify eligible tribal applicants under this subpart of the amount of core funds available for their ICWA program. The funding levels will be based on the service area population to be served. Upon the receipt of this notice from the Agency Superintendent or appropriate Regional Director, tribal applicants shall submit a completed ICWA application no later than 60 days after the receipt of this notice.

(2) A grant to be awarded under this subpart shall be limited to the tribal

governing body(ies) of the tribe(s) to be served by the grant.

(3) For purposes of eligibility for newly recognized or restored Indian tribes without established reservations, such tribes shall be deemed eligible to apply for grants under this subpart to provide ICWA services within those service areas legislatively identified for such tribes.

(4) A grantee under this subpart may make a subgrant to another Indian tribe or an Indian organization subject to the provisions of § 23.45.

(c) *Revision or amendment of grants.* A grantee under this subpart may submit a written request and justification for a post-award grant modification covering material changes to the terms and conditions of the grant, subject to the approval of the grants officer. The request shall include a narrative description of any significant additions, deletions, or changes to the approved program activities or budget in the form of a grant amendment proposal.

(d) Continued annual funding of an ICWA grant under this subpart shall be contingent upon the fulfillment of the requirements delineated at § 23.23(c).

(e) Monitoring and program reporting requirements for grantees under this subpart are delineated at §§ 23.44 and 23.47.

§ 23.22 Purpose of tribal government grants.

(a) Grants awarded under this subpart are for the establishment and operation of tribally designed Indian child and family service programs. The objective of every Indian child and family service program shall be to prevent the breakup of Indian families and to ensure that the permanent removal of an Indian child from the custody of his or her Indian parent or Indian custodian shall be a last resort. Such child and family service programs may include, but need not be limited to:

(1) A system for licensing or otherwise regulating Indian foster and adoptive homes, such as establishing tribal standards for approval of on-reservation foster or adoptive homes;

(2) The operation and maintenance of facilities for counseling and treatment of Indian families and for the temporary custody of Indian children with the goal of strengthening Indian families and preventing parent-child separations;

(3) Family assistance, including homemaker and home counselors, protective day care and afterschool care, recreational activities, respite care, and employment support services with the goal of strengthening Indian families and contributing to family stability;

(4) Home improvement programs with the primary emphasis on preventing the removal of children due to unsafe home environments by making homes safer, but not to make extensive structural home improvements;

(5) The employment of professional and other trained personnel to assist the tribal court in the disposition of domestic relations and child welfare matters, but not to establish tribal court systems;

(6) Education and training of Indians, including tribal court judges and staff, in skills relating to child and family assistance and service programs;

(7) A subsidy program under which Indian adoptive children not eligible for state or BIA subsidy programs may be provided support comparable to that for which they could be eligible as foster children, taking into account the appropriate state standards of support for maintenance and medical needs;

(8) Guidance, legal representation and advice to Indian families involved in tribal, state, or Federal child custody proceedings; and

(9) Other programs designed to meet the intent and purposes of the Act.

(b) Grants may be provided to tribes in the preparation and implementation of child welfare codes within their jurisdiction or pursuant to a tribal-state agreement.

(c) Grantees under this subpart may enhance their capabilities by utilizing ICWA funds as non-Federal matching shares in connection with funds provided under titles IV-B, IV-E and XX of the Social Security Act or other Federal programs which contribute to and promote the intent and purposes of the Act through the provision of comprehensive child and family services in coordination with other tribal, Federal, state, and local resources available for the same purpose.

(d) Program income resulting from the operation of programs under this subpart, such as day care operations, may be retained and used for purposes similar to those for which the grant was awarded.

§ 23.23 Tribal government application contents.

(a) The appropriate Regional Director shall, subject to the tribe's fulfillment of the mandatory application requirements and the availability of appropriated funds, make a grant to the tribal governing body of a tribe or consortium of tribes eligible to apply for a grant under this subpart.

(b) The following mandatory tribal application requirements must be submitted to the appropriate Agency Superintendent or Regional Director in accordance with the timeframe established in § 23.21 (b) of this subpart:

(1) A current tribal resolution requesting a grant by the Indian tribe(s) to be served by the grant. If an applicant is applying for a grant benefiting more than one tribe (consortium), an authorizing resolution from each tribal government to be served must be included. The request must be in the form of a current tribal resolution by the tribal governing body and shall include the following information:

(i) The official name of tribe(s) applying for the grant and who will directly benefit from or receive services from the grant;

(ii) The proposed beginning and ending dates of the grant;

(iii) A provision stating that the resolution will remain in effect for the duration of the program or until the resolution expires or is rescinded; and

(iv) The signature of the authorized representative of the tribal government and the date thereof.

(2) A completed Application for Federal Assistance form, SF–424.

(3) A narrative needs assessment of the social problems or issues affecting the resident Indian population to be served; the geographic area(s) to be served; and estimated number of resident Indian families and/or persons to receive benefits or services from the program.

(4) A comprehensive developmental multi-year plan in narrative form describing what specific services and/or activities will be provided each program year and addressing the above-identified social problems or issues. At a minimum, the plan must include:

(i) The program goals and objectives, stated in measurable terms, to be achieved through the grant;

(ii) A narrative description of how Indian families and communities will benefit from the program; and

(iii) The methodology, including culturally defined approaches, and procedures by which the tribe(s) will accomplish the identified goals and objectives.

(5) An internal monitoring system to measure progress and accomplishments, and to assure that the quality and quantity of actual performance conforms to the requirements of the grant.

(6) A staffing plan that is consistent with the implementation of the above-described program plan of operation and the procedures necessary for the successful delivery of services.

(i) The plan must include proposed key personnel; their qualifications, training or experience relevant to the services to be provided; responsibilities; Indian preference criteria for employment; and position descriptions.

(ii) In accordance with 25 U.S.C. 3201 *et seq.* (Pub. L. 101–630), title IV, the Indian Child Protection and Family Violence Prevention Act, grantees shall conduct character and background investigations of those personnel identified in that statute. Grantees must initiate character and background investigations of said personnel prior to their actual employment, and complete the investigations in a timely manner.

(7) A program budget and budget narrative justification submitted on an annual basis for the amount of the award and supported by the proposed plan, appropriate program services and activities for the applicable grant year.

(8) Identification of any consultants and/or subgrantees the applicant proposes to employ; a description of the consultant and/or subgrantee services to be rendered; the qualifications and experience in performing the identified services; and the basis for the cost and amount to be paid for such services.

(9) A certification by a licensed accountant that the bookkeeping and accounting procedures which the tribe(s) uses or intends to use meet existing Federal standards for grant management and administration specified at §23.46.

(10) A system for managing property and recordkeeping which complies with subpart D of 43 CFR part 2 implementing the Privacy Act (5 U.S.C. 552a) and with existing Federal requirements for grants at 25 CFR 276.5 and 276.11, including the maintenance and safeguarding of direct service case records on families and/or individuals served by the grant.

(11) A listing of equipment, facilities, and buildings necessary to carry out the grant program. Liability insurance coverage for buildings and their contents is recommended for grantees under this subpart.

(12) Pursuant to the Drug-Free Workplace Act of 1988, tribal programs shall comply with the mandatory Drug-Free Workplace Certification, a regulatory requirement for Federal grant recipients.

(c) Continued annual funding of an ICWA program under this subpart shall be contingent upon the existing grant program receiving a satisfactory program evaluation from the area social services office for the previous year of operation. A copy of this evaluation must be submitted together with an annual budget and budget narrative justification in accordance with paragraph (b)(7) of this section. Minimum standards for receiving a satisfactory evaluation shall include:

(1) The timely submission of all fiscal and programmatic reports;

(2) A narrative program report indicating work accomplished in accordance with the applicant's approved multi-year plan and, if applicable, a description of any modification in programs or activities to be funded in the next fiscal year; and

(3) The implementation of mutually determined corrective action measures, if applicable.

Subpart D—Grants to Off-Reservation Indian Organizations for Title II Indian Child and Family Service Programs

§23.31 Competitive off-reservation grant process.

(a) Grant application procedures and related information may be obtained from the Regional Director designated at §23.11 for processing ICWA notices for the state in which the applicant is located. Pre-award and ongoing technical assistance of off-reservation Indian organization grantees shall be provided in accordance with §23.42.

(b) Prior to the beginning of or during the applicable year(s) in which grants for off-reservation programs will be awarded competitively, the Assistant Secretary—Indian Affairs shall publish in the FEDERAL REGISTER an announcement of the grant application process for the year(s), including program priorities or special considerations (if any), applicant eligibility criteria, the required application contents, the amount of available funding and evaluation criteria for off-reservation programs.

(c) Based on the announcement described in paragraph (b) of this section, an off-reservation applicant shall prepare a multi-year developmental application in accordance with §23.33 of this subpart. To be considered in the area competitive review and scoring process, a complete application must be received by the deadline announced in the FEDERAL REGISTER by the Regional Director designated at §23.11 for processing ICWA notices for the state in which the applicant is located.

(d) Eligibility requirements for off-reservation Indian organizations. The Secretary or his/her designee shall, contingent upon the availability of funds, make a multi-year grant under this subpart for an off-reservation program when officially requested by a resolution of the board of directors of the Indian organization applicant, upon the applicant's fulfillment of the mandatory application requirements and upon the applicant's successful competition pursuant to §23.33 of this subpart.

(e) A grant under this subpart for an off-reservation Indian organization shall be limited to the board of directors of the Indian organization which will administer the grant.

(f) Continued annual funding of a multi-year grant award to an off-reservation ICWA program under this subpart shall be contingent upon the grantee's fulfillment of the requirements delineated at § 23.33 (e).

(g) Monitoring and program reporting requirements for grants awarded to off-reservation Indian organizations under this subpart are delineated at §§ 23.44 and 23.47.

§ 23.32 Purpose of off-reservation grants.

The Secretary or his/her designee is authorized to make grants to off-reservation Indian organizations to establish and operate off-reservation Indian child and family service programs for the purpose of stabilizing Indian families and tribes, preventing the breakup of Indian families and, in particular, to ensure that the permanent removal of an Indian child from the custody of his/her Indian parent or Indian custodian shall be a last resort. Child and family service programs may include, but are not limited to:

(a) A system for regulating, maintaining, and supporting Indian foster and adoptive homes, including a subsidy program under which Indian adoptive children may be provided support comparable to that for which they would be eligible as Indian foster children, taking into account the appropriate state standards of support for maintenance and medical needs;

(b) The operation and maintenance of facilities and services for counseling and treatment of Indian families and Indian foster and adoptive children with the goal of strengthening and stabilizing Indian families;

(c) Family assistance (including homemaker and home counselors), protective day care and afterschool care, employment support services, recreational activities, and respite care with the goal of strengthening Indian families and contributing toward family stability; and

(d) Guidance, legal representation and advice to Indian families involved in state child custody proceedings.

§ 23.33 Competitive off-reservation application contents and application selection criteria.

(a) An application for a competitive multi-year grant under this subpart shall be submitted to the appropriate Regional Director prior to or on the announced deadline date published in the FEDERAL REGISTER. The Regional Director shall certify the application contents pursuant to § 23.34 and forward the application within five working days to the area review committee, composed of members designated by the Regional Director, for competitive review and action. Modifications and/or information received after the close of the application period, as announced in the FEDERAL REGISTER, shall not be reviewed or considered by the area review committee in the competitive process.

(b) Mandatory application requirements for Indian organization applicants shall include:

(1) An official request for an ICWA grant program from the organization's board of directors covering the duration of the proposed program;

(2) A completed Application for Federal Assistance form, SF 424;

(3) Written assurances that the organization meets the definition of Indian organization at § 23.2;

(4) A copy of the organization's current Articles of Incorporation for the applicable grant years;

(5) Proof of the organization's non-profit status;

(6) A copy of the organization's IRS tax exemption certificate and IRS employer identification number;

(7) Proof of liability insurance for the applicable grant years; and

(8) Current written assurances that the requirements of Circular A–128 for fiscal management, accounting, and recordkeeping are met.

(9) Pursuant to the Drug-Free Workplace Act of 1988, all grantees under this subpart shall comply with the mandatory Drug-Free Workplace Certification, a regulatory requirement for Federal grant recipients.

(c) *Competitive application selection criteria.* The Regional Director or his/her designated representative shall select those proposals which will in his/her judgment best promote the proposes of the Act. Selection shall be made through the area review committee process in which each application will be scored individually and ranked according to score, taking into consideration the mandatory requirements as specified above and the following selection criteria:

(1) The degree to which the application reflects an understanding of the social problems or issues affecting the resident Indian client population which the applicant proposes to serve;

(2) Whether the applicant presents a narrative needs assessment, quantitative data and demographics of the client Indian population to be served;

(3) Estimates of the number of Indian people to receive benefits or services from the program based on available data;

(4) Program goals and objectives to be achieved through the grant;

(5) A comprehensive developmental multi-year narrative plan describing what specific services and/or activities will be provided each program year and addressing the above-identified social problems or issues. At a minimum, the plan must include a narrative description of the program; the program goals and objectives, stated in measurable terms, to be achieved through the grant; and the methodology, including culturally defined approaches, and procedures by which the grantee will accomplish the identified goals and objectives;

(6) An internal monitoring system the grantee will use to measure progress and accomplishments, and to ensure that the quality and quantity of actual performance conforms to the requirements of the grant;

(7) Documentation of the relative accessibility which the Indian population to be served under a specific proposal already has to existing child and family service programs emphasizing the prevention of Indian family breakups, such as mandatory state services. Factors to be considered in determining accessibility include:

(i) Cultural barriers;

(ii) Discrimination against Indians;

(iii) Inability of potential Indian clientele to pay for services;

(iv) Technical barriers created by existing public or private programs;

(v) Availability of transportation to existing programs;

(vi) Distance between the Indian community to be served under the proposal and the nearest existing programs;

(vii) Quality of services provided to Indian clientele; and

(viii) Relevance of services provided to specific needs of the Indian clientele.

(8) If the proposed program duplicates existing Federal, state, or local child and family service programs emphasizing the prevention of Indian family breakups, proper and current documented evidence that repeated attempts to obtain services have been unsuccessful;

(9) Evidence of substantial support from the Indian community or communities to be served, including but not limited to:

(i) Tribal support evidenced by a tribal resolution or cooperative service agreements between the administrative bodies of the affected tribe(s) and the applicant for the duration of the grant period, or

(ii) Letters of support from social services organizations familiar with the applicant's past work experience;

(10) A staffing plan that is consistent with the implementation of the above-described program plan of operation and the procedures necessary for the successful delivery of services. The plan must include proposed key personnel, their qualifications, training or experience relevant to the services to be provided, responsibilities, Indian preference criteria for employment and position descriptions. In accordance with 25 U.S.C. 3201 *et seq.* (Pub. L. 101-630), title IV, the Indian Child Protection and Family Violence Prevention Act, grantees shall conduct character and background investigations of those personnel identified in that statute prior to their actual employment;

(11) The reasonableness and relevance of the estimated overall costs of the proposed program or services and their overall relation to the organization's funding base, activities, and mission;

(12) The degree to which the detailed annual budget and justification for the requested funds are consistent with, and clearly supported by, the proposed

plan and by appropriate program services and activities for the applicable grant year;

(13) The applicant's identification of any consultants and/or subgrantees it proposes to employ; description of the services to be rendered; the qualifications and experience of said personnel, reflecting the requirements for performing the identified services; and the basis for the cost and the amount to be paid for such services;

(14) Certification by a licensed accountant that the bookkeeping and accounting procedures that the applicant uses or intends to use meet existing Federal standards for grant administration and management specified at § 23.46;

(15) The compliance of property management and recordkeeping systems with subpart D of 43 CFR part 2 (the Privacy Act, 5 U.S.C. 552a), and with existing Federal requirements for grants at 25 CFR 276.5 and 276.11, including the maintenance and safeguarding of direct service case records on families and/or individuals served by the grant;

(16) A description of the proposed facilities, equipment, and buildings necessary to carry out the grant activities; and

(17) Proof of liability insurance coverage for the applicable grant year(s).

(d) Two or more applications receiving the same competitive score will be prioritized in accordance with announcements made in the FEDERAL REGISTER pursuant to § 23.31 (b) for the applicable year(s).

(e) Continued annual funding of a multi-year grant award to an off-reservation ICWA program under this subpart shall be contingent upon the availability of appropriated funds and upon the existing grant program receiving a satisfactory program evaluation from the area social services office for the previous year of operation. A copy of this evaluation shall be submitted together with an annual budget and budget narrative justification in accordance with paragraph (c)(10) of this section. Minimum standards for receiving a satisfactory evaluation shall include the timely submission of all fiscal and programmatic reports; a narrative program report indicating work accomplished in accordance with the initial approved multi-year plan; and the implementation of mutually determined corrective action measures, if applicable.

§ 23.34 Review and decision on off-reservation applications by Regional Director.

(a) *Area office certification.* Upon receipt of an application for a grant by an off-reservation Indian organization at the area office, the Regional Director shall:

(1) Complete and sign the area office certification form. In completing the area certification form, the Regional Director shall assess and certify whether applications contain and meet all the application requirements specified at § 23.33. Regional Directors shall be responsible for the completion of the area office certification forms for all applications submitted by off-reservation Indian organizations.

(2) Acknowledge receipt of the application to the applicant and advise the applicant of the disposition of the application within 10 days of receipt; and

(3) Transmit all applications within five working days of receipt to the area review committee for competitive review and subsequent approval or disapproval of the applications.

(b) *Area office competitive review and decision for off-reservation applications.* Upon receipt of an application for an off-reservation grant under this part requiring the approval of the Regional Director, the Regional Director shall:

(1) Establish and convene an area review committee, chaired by a person qualified by knowledge, training and experience in the delivery of Indian child and family services.

(2) Review the area office certification form required in paragraph (a) of this section.

(3) Review the application in accordance with the competitive review procedures prescribed in § 23.33. An application shall not receive approval for funding under the area competitive review and scoring process unless a review of the application determines that it:

(i) Contains all the information required in § 23.33 which must be received by the close of the application period.

Modifications of the grant application received after the close of the application period shall not be considered in the competitive review process.

(ii) Receives at least the established minimum score in an area competitive review, using the application selection criteria and scoring process set out in §23.33. The minimum score shall be established by the Central Office prior to each application period and announced in the FEDERAL REGISTER for the applicable grants year(s).

(4) Approve or disapprove the application and promptly notify the applicant in writing of the approval or disapproval of the application. If the application is disapproved, the Regional Director shall include in the written notice the specific reasons therefore.

(c) The actual funding amounts for the initial grant year shall be subject to appropriations available nationwide and the continued funding of an approved off-reservation grant application under subpart D of this part shall be subject to available funds received by the respective area office for the applicable grant year. Initial funding decisions and subsequent decisions with respect to funding level amounts for all approved grant applications under this part shall be made by the Regional Director.

§23.35 Deadline for Central Office action.

Within 30 days of the receipt of grant reporting forms from the Regional Directors identifying approved and disapproved applications pursuant to subpart D of this part and recommended funding levels for approved applications, the Secretary or his/her designee shall process the Regional Directors' funding requests.

Subpart E—General and Uniform Grant Administration Provisions and Requirements

§23.41 Uniform grant administration provisions, requirements and applicability.

The general and uniform grant administration provisions and requirements specified at 25 CFR part 276 and under this subpart are applicable to all grants awarded to tribal governments and off-reservation Indian organizations under this part, except to the extent inconsistent with an applicable Federal statute, regulation or OMB circular.

§23.42 Technical assistance.

(a) Pre-award and ongoing technical assistance may be requested by an Indian tribe or off-reservation Indian organization from the appropriate agency or area office to which the tribe or organization will be submitting an application for funds under subparts C and D of this part. A request for pre-award technical assistance by an off-reservation Indian organization must be received by the Regional Director designated at §23.11 for the state in which the applicant is located no later than 10 days prior to the application deadline to assure sufficient time for area response.

(b) Pre-award and ongoing technical assistance may be provided by the appropriate BIA agency or area office for purposes of program planning and design, assistance in establishing internal program monitoring and evaluation criteria for ongoing grant administration and management, and for other appropriate assistance requested.

(c) The area social services staff shall provide technical assistance to grantees upon receipt of an authorized request from the grantee or when review of the grantee's quarterly performance reports shows that:

(1) An ICWA program is yielding results that are or will be detrimental to the welfare of the intended Indian beneficiaries of the program;

(2) A program has substantially failed to implement its goals and objectives;

(3) There are serious irregularities in the fiscal management of the grant; or

(4) The grantee is otherwise deficient in its program performance.

(5) Upon receiving an authorized request from the grantee, the area social services staff and/or grants officer shall provide the necessary technical assistance to arrive at mutually determined corrective action measures and their actual implementation, if necessary, and the timeframes within which said corrective actions will be implemented.

§ 23.43 Authority for grant approval and execution.

(a) *Tribal government programs.* The appropriate Agency Superintendent or Regional Director may approve a grant application and its subsequent execution under subpart C when the intent, purpose and scope of the application pertains solely to reservations located within the service area jurisdiction of the agency or area office.

(b) *Off-reservation programs.* The appropriate Regional Director may approve a grant application and its subsequent execution under subpart D when the intent, purpose and scope of the grant proposal pertains to off-reservation Indian service populations or programs.

§ 23.44 Grant administration and monitoring.

All grantees under this part shall be responsible for managing day-to-day program operations to ensure that program performance goals are being achieved and to ensure compliance with the provisions of the grant award document and other applicable Federal requirements. Unless delegated to the Agency Superintendent, appropriate area office personnel designated by the Regional Director shall be responsible for all grant program and fiscal monitoring responsibilities.

§ 23.45 Subgrants.

A tribal government grantee may make a subgrant under subpart C of this part, provided that such subgrants are for the purpose for which the grant was made and that the grantee retains administrative and financial responsibility over the activity and the funds.

§ 23.46 Financial management, internal and external controls and other assurances.

Grantee financial management systems shall comply with the following standards for accurate, current and complete disclosure of financial activities.

(a) OMB Circular A–87 (Cost principles for state and local governments and federally recognized Indian tribal governments).

(b) OMB Circular A–102 (Common rule 43 CFR part 12).

(c) OMB Circular A–128 (Single Audit Act).

(d) OMB Circular A–110 or 122 (Cost principles for non-profit organizations and tribal organizations, where applicable).

(e) *Internal control.* Effective control and accountability must be maintained for all grants. Grantees must adequately safeguard any property and must ensure that it is used solely for authorized purposes.

(f) *Budget control.* Actual expenditures must be compared with budgeted amounts for the grant. Financial information must be related to program performance requirements.

(g) *Source documentation.* Accounting records must be supported by such source documentation as cancelled checks, paid bills, payrolls, time and attendance records, grant documents, or other information required by the grantee's financial management system. The Secretary or his/her designee may review the adequacy of the financial management system of an Indian tribe(s) or off-reservation Indian organization applying for a grant under this part.

(h) Pursuant to 18 U.S.C. 641, whoever embezzles, steals, purloins, or knowingly converts to his or her use or the use of another, or without authority, sells, conveys or disposes of any record, voucher, money, or thing of value of the United States or of any department or agency thereof, or any property made or being made under contract for the United States or any department or agency thereof; or whoever receives, conceals, or retains the same with intent to convert it to his or her use or gain, knowing it to have been embezzled, stolen, purloined, or converted shall be fined not more than $10,000 or imprisoned not more than 10 years, or both; but if the value of such property does not exceed the sum of $100, he or she shall be fined not more than $1,000 or imprisoned not more than one year, or both.

§ 23.47 Reports and availability of information to Indians.

(a) Any tribal government or off-reservation Indian organization receiving a grant under this part shall make general programmatic information and reports concerning that grant available to the Indian people it serves or represents. Access to this information may be requested in writing and shall be made available within 10 days of receipt of the request. Except as required by title IV of Pub. L. 101–630, the Indian Child Protection and Family Violence Prevention Act, grantees shall hold confidential all information obtained from persons receiving services from the program, and shall not release such information without the individual's written consent. Information may be disclosed in a manner which does not identify or lead to the identification of particular individuals.

(b) Grantees shall submit Standard Form 269 or 269A on a quarterly and an annual basis to report their status of funds by the dates specified in the grant award document.

(c) Grantees shall furnish and submit the following written quarterly and annual program reports by the dates specified in the award document:

(1) Quarterly and annual statistical and narrative program performance reports which shall include, but need not be limited to, the following;

(i) A summary of actual accomplishments and significant activities as related to program objectives established for the grant period;

(ii) The grantee's evaluation of program performance using the internal monitoring system submitted in their application;

(iii) Reports on all significant ICWA direct service grant activities including but not limited to the following information:

(A) Significant title II activities;

(B) Data reflecting numbers of individuals referred for out-of-home placements, number of individuals benefiting from title II services and types of services provided, and

(C) Information and referral activities.

(iv) Child abuse and neglect statistical reports and related information as required by 25 U.S.C. 2434, Pub. L. 99–570, the Indian Alcohol and Substance Abuse Prevention and Treatment Act of 1986;

(v) A summary of problems encountered or reasons for not meeting established objectives;

(vi) Any deliverable or product required in the grant; and

(vii) Additional pertinent information when appropriate.

(2) The BIA may negotiate for the provision of other grant-related reports not previously identified.

(d) Events may occur between scheduled performance reporting dates which have significant impact on the grant-supported activity. In such cases, the grantee must inform the awarding agency as soon as problems, delays, adverse conditions, or serious incidents giving rise to liability become known and which will materially impair its ability to meet the objectives of the grant.

§ 23.48 Matching shares and agreements.

(a) Grant funds provided to Indian tribes under subpart C of this part may be used as non-Federal matching shares in connection with funds provided under titles IV-B, IV-E and XX of the Social Security Act or such other Federal programs which contribute to and promote the purposes of the Act as specified in §§ 23.3 and 23.22 (25 U.S.C. 1931).

(b) Pursuant to 25 U.S.C. 1933, in furtherance of the establishment, operation, and funding of programs funded under subparts C and D of this part, the Secretary may enter into agreements with the Secretary of Health and Human Services. The latter Secretary is authorized by the Act to use funds appropriated for the Department of Health and Human Services for programs similar to those funded under subparts C and D of this part (25 U.S.C. 1931 and 1932), provided that authority to make payment pursuant to such agreements shall be effective only to the extent and in such amounts as may be provided in advance by appropriation Acts.

§ 23.49 Fair and uniform provision of services.

(a) Grants awarded under this part shall include provisions assuring compliance with the Indian Civil Rights

Act; prohibiting discriminatory distinctions among eligible Indian beneficiaries; and assuring the fair and uniform provision by the grantees of the services and assistance they provide to eligible Indian beneficiaries under such grants. Such procedures must include criteria by which eligible Indian beneficiaries will receive services, recordkeeping mechanisms adequate to verify the fairness and uniformity of services in cases of formal complaints, and an explanation of what rights will be afforded an individual pending the resolution of a complaint.

(b) Indian beneficiaries of the services to be rendered under a grant shall be afforded access to administrative or judicial bodies empowered to adjudicate complaints, claims, or grievances brought by such Indian beneficiaries against the grantee arising out of the performance of the grant.

§ 23.50 Service eligibility.

(a) Tribal government Indian child and family service programs. Any person meeting the definition of Indian, Indian child, Indian custodian, or Indian parent of any unmarried person under the age of 18 as defined in § 23.2 is eligible for services provided under 25 U.S.C. 1931 of the Act. Tribal membership status shall be determined by tribal law, ordinance, or custom. The tribe may, under subpart C, extend services to nontribal family members related by marriage to tribal members, provided such services promote the intent and purposes of the Act. A tribe may also, within available resources, extend services under this part to individuals who are members of, or are eligible for membership in other Indian tribes, and who reside within the tribe's designated service area.

(b) Off-reservation Indian child and family service programs and agreements with the Secretary of Health and Human Services pursuant to 25 U.S.C. 1933. For purposes of eligibility for services provided under 25 U.S.C. 1932 and 1933 of the Act, any person meeting the definition of Indian, Indian child, Indian custodian, or Indian parent of any unmarried person under the age of 18 as defined in § 23.2, or the definition of Indian as defined in 25 U.S.C. 1603(c), shall be eligible for services. Tribal membership status shall be determined by tribal law, ordinance, or custom.

§ 23.51 Grant carry-over authority.

Unless restricted by appropriation, and contingent upon satisfactory program evaluations from the appropriate area or agency office for an existing program, grantees are authorized to carry over unliquidated grant funds which remain at the end of a budget period. Such funds may be carried over for a maximum period of two years beyond the initial grant funding period and must be utilized only for the intent, purpose and scope of the original grant. These carry-over grant funds shall not be reprogrammed into other appropriation activities or subactivities. Funds carried over into another fiscal year will be added to the grantee's new fiscal year funding amount.

§ 23.52 Grant suspension.

(a) When a grantee has materially failed to comply and remains out of compliance with the terms and conditions of the grant, the grants officer may, after reasonable notice to the grantee and the provision of requested technical assistance, suspend the grant. The notice preceding the suspension shall include the effective date of the suspension, the corrective measures necessary for reinstatement of the grant and, if there is no immediate threat to safety, a reasonable timeframe for corrective action prior to actual suspension.

(b) No obligation incurred by the grantee during the period of suspension shall be allowable under the suspended grant, except that the grants officer may at his/her discretion allow necessary and proper costs which the grantee could not reasonably avoid during the period of suspension if such costs would otherwise be allowable under the applicable cost principles.

(c) Appropriate adjustments to the payments under the suspended grant will be made either by withholding the payments or by not allowing the grantee credit for disbursements which the grantee may make in liquidation of unauthorized obligations the grantee incurs during the period of suspension.

(d) Suspension shall remain in effect until the grantee has taken corrective action to the satisfaction of the grants officer, or given assurances satisfactory to the grants officer that corrective action will be taken, or until the grants officer cancels the grant.

§23.53 Cancellation.

(a) The grants officer may cancel any grant, in whole or in part, at any time before the date of completion whenever it is determined that the grantee has:

(1) Materially failed to comply with the terms and conditions of the grant;

(2) Violated the rights as specified in §23.49 or endangered the health, safety, or welfare of any person; or

(3) Been grossly negligent in, or has mismanaged the handling or use of funds provided under the grant.

(b) When it appears that cancellation of the grant will become necessary, the grants officer shall promptly notify the grantee in writing of this possibility. This written notice shall advise the grantee of the reason for the possible cancellation and the corrective action necessary to avoid cancellation. The grants officer shall also offer, and shall provide, if requested by the grantee, any technical assistance which may be required to effect the corrective action. The grantee shall have 60 days in which to effect this corrective action before the grants officer provides notice of intent to cancel the grant as provided for in paragraph (c) of this section.

(c) Upon deciding to cancel for cause, the grants officer shall promptly notify the grantee in writing of that decision, the reason for the cancellation, and the effective date. The Regional Director or his/her designated official shall also provide a hearing for the grantee before cancellation. However, the grants officer may immediately cancel the grant, upon notice to the grantee, if the grants officer determines that continuance of the grant poses an immediate threat to safety. In this event, the Regional Director or his/her designated official shall provide a hearing for the grantee within 10 days of the cancellation.

(d) The hearing referred to in paragraph (c) of this section shall be conducted as follows:

(1) The grantee affected shall be notified, in writing, at least 10 days before the hearing. The notice should give the date, time, place, and purpose of the hearing.

(2) A written record of the hearing shall be made. The record shall include written statements submitted at the hearing or within five days following the hearing.

Subpart F—Appeals

§23.61 Appeals from decision or action by Agency Superintendent, Regional Director or Grants Officer.

A grantee or prospective applicant may appeal any decision made or action taken by the Agency Superintendent, Regional Director, or grants officer under subpart C or E of this part. Such an appeal shall be made to the Assistant Secretary who shall consider the appeal in accordance with 25 CFR 2.20 (c) through (e). Appeal procedures shall be as set out in part 2 of this chapter.

§23.62 Appeals from decision or action by Regional Director under subpart D.

A grantee or applicant may appeal any decision made or action taken by the Regional Director under subpart D that is alleged to be in violation of the U.S. Constitution, Federal statutes, or the regulations of this part. These appeals shall be filed with the Interior Board of Indian Appeals in accordance with 25 CFR 2.4 (e); 43 CFR 4.310 through 4.318 and 43 CFR 4.330 through 4.340. However, an applicant may not appeal a score assigned to its application or the amount of grant funds awarded.

§23.63 Appeals from inaction of official.

A person or persons whose interests are adversely affected, or whose ability to protect such interests is impeded by the failure of an official to act on a request to the official, may make the official's inaction the subject of an appeal under part 2 of this chapter.

Subpart G—Administrative Provisions

§ 23.71 Recordkeeping and information availability.

(a) The Division of Human Services, Bureau of Indian Affairs (BIA), is authorized to receive all information and to maintain a central file on all State Indian adoptions. This file is confidential and only designated persons may have access to it.

(b) Upon the request of an adopted Indian who has reached age 18, the adoptive or foster parents of an Indian child, or an Indian Tribe, BIA will disclose such information as may be necessary for purposes of Tribal enrollment or determining any rights or benefits associated with Tribal membership. Where the documents relating to such child contain an affidavit from the biological parent or parents requesting anonymity, BIA must certify to the Indian child's Tribe, where the information warrants, that the child's parentage and other circumstances entitle the child to enrollment under the criteria established by such Tribe.

(c) BIA will ensure that the confidentiality of this information is maintained and that the information is not subject to the Freedom of Information Act, 5 U.S.C. 552, as amended.

[81 FR 38867, June 14, 2016]

Subpart H—Assistance to State Courts

§ 23.81 Assistance in identifying witnesses.

Upon the request of a party in an involuntary Indian child custody proceeding or of a court, the Secretary or his/her designee shall assist in identifying qualified expert witnesses. Such requests for assistance shall be sent to the Regional Director designated in § 23.11(c). The BIA is not obligated to pay for the services of such expert witnesses.

§ 23.82 Assistance in identifying language interpreters.

Upon the request of a party in an Indian child custody proceeding or of a court, the Secretary or his/her designee shall assist in identifying language interpreters. Such requests for assistance should be sent to the Regional Director designated in § 23.11(c). The BIA is not obligated to pay for the services of such language interpreters.

§ 23.83 Assistance in locating biological parents of Indian child after termination of adoption.

Upon the request of a child placement agency, the court or an Indian tribe, the Secretary or his/her designee shall assist in locating the biological parents or prior Indian custodians of an adopted Indian child whose adoption has been terminated pursuant to 25 U.S.C. 1914. Such requests for assistance should be sent to the Regional Director designated in § 23.11(c).

Subpart I—Indian Child Welfare Act Proceedings

SOURCE: 81 FR 38867, June 14, 2016, unless otherwise noted.

GENERAL PROVISIONS

§ 23.101 What is the purpose of this subpart?

The regulations in this subpart clarify the minimum Federal standards governing implementation of the Indian Child Welfare Act (ICWA) to ensure that ICWA is applied in all States consistent with the Act's express language, Congress's intent in enacting the statute, and to promote the stability and security of Indian tribes and families.

§ 23.102 What terms do I need to know?

The following terms and their definitions apply to this subpart. All other terms have the meanings assigned in § 23.2.

Agency means a nonprofit, for-profit, or governmental organization and its employees, agents, or officials that performs, or provides services to biological parents, foster parents, or adoptive parents to assist in the administrative and social work necessary for foster, preadoptive, or adoptive placements.

Indian organization means any group, association, partnership, corporation, or other legal entity owned or controlled by Indians or a Tribe, or a majority of whose members are Indians.

§ 23.103 When does ICWA apply?

(a) ICWA includes requirements that apply whenever an Indian child is the subject of:

(1) A child-custody proceeding, including:

(i) An involuntary proceeding;

(ii) A voluntary proceeding that could prohibit the parent or Indian custodian from regaining custody of the child upon demand; and

(iii) A proceeding involving status offenses if any part of the proceeding results in the need for out-of-home placement of the child, including a foster-care, preadoptive, or adoptive placement, or termination of parental rights.

(2) An emergency proceeding.

(b) ICWA does not apply to:

(1) A Tribal court proceeding;

(2) A proceeding regarding a criminal act that is not a status offense;

(3) An award of custody of the Indian child to one of the parents including, but not limited to, an award in a divorce proceeding; or

(4) A voluntary placement that either parent, both parents, or the Indian custodian has, of his or her or their free will, without a threat of removal by a State agency, chosen for the Indian child and that does not operate to prohibit the child's parent or Indian custodian from regaining custody of the child upon demand.

(c) If a proceeding listed in paragraph (a) of this section concerns a child who meets the statutory definition of "Indian child," then ICWA will apply to that proceeding. In determining whether ICWA applies to a proceeding, the State court may not consider factors such as the participation of the parents or the Indian child in Tribal cultural, social, religious, or political activities, the relationship between the Indian child and his or her parents, whether the parent ever had custody of the child, or the Indian child's blood quantum.

(d) If ICWA applies at the commencement of a proceeding, it will not cease to apply simply because the child reaches age 18 during the pendency of the proceeding.

§ 23.104 What provisions of this subpart apply to each type of child-custody proceeding?

The following table lists what sections of this subpart apply to each type of child-custody proceeding identified in § 23.103(a):

Section	Type of proceeding
23.101–23.106 (General Provisions)	Emergency, Involuntary, Voluntary.
Pretrial Requirements:	
23.107 (How should a State court determine if there is reason to know the child is an Indian child?).	Emergency, Involuntary, Voluntary.
23.108 (Who makes the determination as to whether a child is a member whether a child is eligible for membership, or whether a biological parent is a member of a Tribe?).	Emergency, Involuntary, Voluntary.
23.109 (How should a State court determine an Indian child's Tribe when the child may be a member or eligible for membership in more than one Tribe?).	Emergency, Involuntary, Voluntary.
23.110 (When must a State court dismiss an action?)	Involuntary, Voluntary.
23.111 (What are the notice requirements for a child-custody proceeding involving an Indian child?).	Involuntary (foster-care placement and termination of parental rights).
23.112 (What time limits and extensions apply?)	Involuntary (foster-care placement and termination of parental rights).
23.113 (What are the standards for emergency proceedings involving an Indian child?).	Emergency.
23.114 (What are the requirements for determining improper removal?)	Involuntary.
Petitions to Transfer to Tribal Court:	
23.115 (How are petitions for transfer of a proceeding made?)	Involuntary, Voluntary (foster-care placement and termination of parental rights).
23.116 (What happens after a petition for transfer is made?)	Involuntary, Voluntary (foster-care placement and termination of parental rights).
23.117 (What are the criteria for ruling on transfer petitions?)	Involuntary, Voluntary (foster-care placement and termination of parental rights).

Section	Type of proceeding
23.118 (How is a determination of "good cause" to deny transfer made?)	Involuntary, Voluntary (foster-care placement and termination of parental rights).
23.119 (What happens after a petition for transfer is granted?)	Involuntary, Voluntary (foster-care placement and termination of parental rights).
Adjudication of Involuntary Proceedings:	
23.120 (How does the State court ensure that active efforts have been made?)	Involuntary (foster-care placement and termination of parental rights).
23.121 (What are the applicable standards of evidence?)	Involuntary (foster-care placement and termination of parental rights).
23.122 (Who may serve as a qualified expert witness?)	Involuntary (foster-care placement and termination of parental rights).
23.123 Reserved	N/A.
Voluntary Proceedings:	
23.124 (What actions must a State court undertake in voluntary proceedings?)	Voluntary.
23.125 (How is consent obtained?)	Voluntary.
23.126 (What information must a consent document contain?)	Voluntary.
23.127 (How is withdrawal of consent to a foster-care placement achieved?)	Voluntary.
23.128 (How is withdrawal of consent to a termination of parental rights or adoption achieved?).	Voluntary.
Dispositions:	
23.129 (When do the placement preferences apply?)	Involuntary, Voluntary.
23.130 (What placement preferences apply in adoptive placements?)	Involuntary, Voluntary.
23.131 (What placement preferences apply in foster-care or preadoptive placements?).	Involuntary, Voluntary.
23.132 (How is a determination of "good cause" to depart from the placement preferences made?).	Involuntary, Voluntary.
Access:	
23.133 (Should courts allow participation by alternative methods?)	Emergency, Involuntary.
23.134 (Who has access to reports and records during a proceeding?)	Emergency, Involuntary.
23.135 Reserved.	N/A.
Post-Trial Rights & Responsibilities:	
23.136 (What are the requirements for vacating an adoption based on consent having been obtained through fraud or duress?).	Involuntary (if consent given under threat of removal), voluntary.
23.137 (Who can petition to invalidate an action for certain ICWA violations?)	Emergency (to extent it involved a specified violation), involuntary, voluntary.
23.138 (What are the rights to information about adoptees' Tribal affiliations?)	Emergency, Involuntary, Voluntary.
23.139 (Must notice be given of a change in an adopted Indian child's status?)	Involuntary, Voluntary.
Recordkeeping:	
23.140 (What information must States furnish to the Bureau of Indian Affairs?)	Involuntary, Voluntary.
23.141 (What records must the State maintain?)	Involuntary, Voluntary.
23.142 (How does the Paperwork Reduction Act affect this subpart?)	Emergency, Involuntary, Voluntary.
Effective Date:	
23.143 (How does this subpart apply to pending proceedings?)	Emergency, Involuntary, Voluntary.
Severability:	
23.144 (What happens if some portion of part is held to be invalid by a court of competent jurisdiction?).	Emergency, Involuntary, Voluntary.

Note: For purposes of this table, status-offense child-custody proceedings are included as a type of involuntary proceeding.

§ 23.105 How do I contact a Tribe under the regulations in this subpart?

To contact a Tribe to provide notice or obtain information or verification under the regulations in this subpart, you should direct the notice or inquiry as follows:

(a) Many Tribes designate an agent for receipt of ICWA notices. The BIA publishes a list of Tribes' designated Tribal agents for service of ICWA notice in the FEDERAL REGISTER each year and makes the list available on its Web site at *www.bia.gov*.

(b) For a Tribe without a designated Tribal agent for service of ICWA notice, contact the Tribe to be directed to the appropriate office or individual.

(c) If you do not have accurate contact information for a Tribe, or the Tribe contacted fails to respond to written inquiries, you should seek assistance in contacting the Indian Tribe from the BIA local or regional office or the BIA's Central Office in Washington, DC (see *www.bia.gov*).

§23.106 How does this subpart interact with State and Federal laws?

(a) The regulations in this subpart provide minimum Federal standards to ensure compliance with ICWA.

(b) Under section 1921 of ICWA, where applicable State or other Federal law provides a higher standard of protection to the rights of the parent or Indian custodian than the protection accorded under the Act, ICWA requires the State or Federal court to apply the higher State or Federal standard.

PRETRIAL REQUIREMENTS

§23.107 How should a State court determine if there is reason to know the child is an Indian child?

(a) State courts must ask each participant in an emergency or voluntary or involuntary child-custody proceeding whether the participant knows or has reason to know that the child is an Indian child. The inquiry is made at the commencement of the proceeding and all responses should be on the record. State courts must instruct the parties to inform the court if they subsequently receive information that provides reason to know the child is an Indian child.

(b) If there is reason to know the child is an Indian child, but the court does not have sufficient evidence to determine that the child is or is not an "Indian child," the court must:

(1) Confirm, by way of a report, declaration, or testimony included in the record that the agency or other party used due diligence to identify and work with all of the Tribes of which there is reason to know the child may be a member (or eligible for membership), to verify whether the child is in fact a member (or a biological parent is a member and the child is eligible for membership); and

(2) Treat the child as an Indian child, unless and until it is determined on the record that the child does not meet the definition of an "Indian child" in this part.

(c) A court, upon conducting the inquiry required in paragraph (a) of this section, has reason to know that a child involved in an emergency or child-custody proceeding is an Indian child if:

(1) Any participant in the proceeding, officer of the court involved in the proceeding, Indian Tribe, Indian organization, or agency informs the court that the child is an Indian child;

(2) Any participant in the proceeding, officer of the court involved in the proceeding, Indian Tribe, Indian organization, or agency informs the court that it has discovered information indicating that the child is an Indian child;

(3) The child who is the subject of the proceeding gives the court reason to know he or she is an Indian child;

(4) The court is informed that the domicile or residence of the child, the child's parent, or the child's Indian custodian is on a reservation or in an Alaska Native village;

(5) The court is informed that the child is or has been a ward of a Tribal court; or

(6) The court is informed that either parent or the child possesses an identification card indicating membership in an Indian Tribe.

(d) In seeking verification of the child's status in a voluntary proceeding where a consenting parent evidences, by written request or statement in the record, a desire for anonymity, the court must keep relevant documents pertaining to the inquiry required under this section confidential and under seal. A request for anonymity does not relieve the court, agency, or other party from any duty of compliance with ICWA, including the obligation to verify whether the child is an "Indian child." A Tribe receiving information related to this inquiry must keep documents and information confidential.

§23.108 Who makes the determination as to whether a child is a member, whether a child is eligible for membership, or whether a biological parent is a member of a Tribe?

(a) The Indian Tribe of which it is believed the child is a member (or eligible for membership and of which the biological parent is a member) determines whether the child is a member of the Tribe, or whether the child is eligible for membership in the Tribe and a biological parent of the child is a member of the Tribe, except as otherwise provided by Federal or Tribal law.

(b) The determination by a Tribe of whether a child is a member, whether a child is eligible for membership, or whether a biological parent is a member, is solely within the jurisdiction and authority of the Tribe, except as otherwise provided by Federal or Tribal law. The State court may not substitute its own determination regarding a child's membership in a Tribe, a child's eligibility for membership in a Tribe, or a parent's membership in a Tribe.

(c) The State court may rely on facts or documentation indicating a Tribal determination of membership or eligibility for membership in making a judicial determination as to whether the child is an "Indian child." An example of documentation indicating membership is a document issued by the Tribe, such as Tribal enrollment documentation.

§ 23.109 How should a State court determine an Indian child's Tribe when the child may be a member or eligible for membership in more than one Tribe?

(a) If the Indian child is a member or eligible for membership in only one Tribe, that Tribe must be designated as the Indian child's Tribe.

(b) If the Indian child meets the definition of "Indian child" through more than one Tribe, deference should be given to the Tribe in which the Indian child is already a member, unless otherwise agreed to by the Tribes.

(c) If an Indian child meets the definition of "Indian child" through more than one Tribe because the child is a member in more than one Tribe or the child is not a member of but is eligible for membership in more than one Tribe, the court must provide the opportunity in any involuntary child-custody proceeding for the Tribes to determine which should be designated as the Indian child's Tribe.

(1) If the Tribes are able to reach an agreement, the agreed-upon Tribe should be designated as the Indian child's Tribe.

(2) If the Tribes are unable to reach an agreement, the State court designates, for the purposes of ICWA, the Indian Tribe with which the Indian child has the more significant contacts as the Indian child's Tribe, taking into consideration:

(i) Preference of the parents for membership of the child;

(ii) Length of past domicile or residence on or near the reservation of each Tribe;

(iii) Tribal membership of the child's custodial parent or Indian custodian; and

(iv) Interest asserted by each Tribe in the child-custody proceeding;

(v) Whether there has been a previous adjudication with respect to the child by a court of one of the Tribes; and

(vi) Self-identification by the child, if the child is of sufficient age and capacity to meaningfully self-identify.

(3) A determination of the Indian child's Tribe for purposes of ICWA and the regulations in this subpart do not constitute a determination for any other purpose.

§ 23.110 When must a State court dismiss an action?

Subject to 25 U.S.C. 1919 (Agreements between States and Indian Tribes) and § 23.113 (emergency proceedings), the following limitations on a State court's jurisdiction apply:

(a) The court in any voluntary or involuntary child-custody proceeding involving an Indian child must determine the residence and domicile of the Indian child. If either the residence or domicile is on a reservation where the Tribe exercises exclusive jurisdiction over child-custody proceedings, the State court must expeditiously notify the Tribal court of the pending dismissal based on the Tribe's exclusive jurisdiction, dismiss the State-court child-custody proceeding, and ensure that the Tribal court is sent all information regarding the Indian child-custody proceeding, including, but not limited to, the pleadings and any court record.

(b) If the child is a ward of a Tribal court, the State court must expeditiously notify the Tribal court of the pending dismissal, dismiss the State-court child-custody proceeding, and ensure that the Tribal court is sent all information regarding the Indian child-custody proceeding, including, but not limited to, the pleadings and any court record.

§23.111 What are the notice requirements for a child-custody proceeding involving an Indian child?

(a) When a court knows or has reason to know that the subject of an involuntary foster-care-placement or termination-of-parental-rights proceeding is an Indian child, the court must ensure that:

(1) The party seeking placement promptly sends notice of each such child-custody proceeding (including, but not limited to, any foster-care placement or any termination of parental or custodial rights) in accordance with this section; and

(2) An original or a copy of each notice sent under this section is filed with the court together with any return receipts or other proof of service.

(b) Notice must be sent to:

(1) Each Tribe where the child may be a member (or eligible for membership if a biological parent is a member) (*see* §23.105 for information on how to contact a Tribe);

(2) The child's parents; and

(3) If applicable, the child's Indian custodian.

(c) Notice must be sent by registered or certified mail with return receipt requested. Notice may also be sent via personal service or electronically, but such alternative methods do not replace the requirement for notice to be sent by registered or certified mail with return receipt requested.

(d) Notice must be in clear and understandable language and include the following:

(1) The child's name, birthdate, and birthplace;

(2) All names known (including maiden, married, and former names or aliases) of the parents, the parents' birthdates and birthplaces, and Tribal enrollment numbers if known;

(3) If known, the names, birthdates, birthplaces, and Tribal enrollment information of other direct lineal ancestors of the child, such as grandparents;

(4) The name of each Indian Tribe in which the child is a member (or may be eligible for membership if a biological parent is a member);

(5) A copy of the petition, complaint, or other document by which the child-custody proceeding was initiated and, if a hearing has been scheduled, information on the date, time, and location of the hearing;

(6) Statements setting out:

(i) The name of the petitioner and the name and address of petitioner's attorney;

(ii) The right of any parent or Indian custodian of the child, if not already a party to the child-custody proceeding, to intervene in the proceedings.

(iii) The Indian Tribe's right to intervene at any time in a State-court proceeding for the foster-care placement of or termination of parental rights to an Indian child.

(iv) That, if the child's parent or Indian custodian is unable to afford counsel based on a determination of indigency by the court, the parent or Indian custodian has the right to court-appointed counsel.

(v) The right to be granted, upon request, up to 20 additional days to prepare for the child-custody proceedings.

(vi) The right of the parent or Indian custodian and the Indian child's Tribe to petition the court for transfer of the foster-care-placement or termination-of-parental-rights proceeding to Tribal court as provided by 25 U.S.C. 1911 and §23.115.

(vii) The mailing addresses and telephone numbers of the court and information related to all parties to the child-custody proceeding and individuals notified under this section.

(viii) The potential legal consequences of the child-custody proceedings on the future parental and custodial rights of the parent or Indian custodian.

(ix) That all parties notified must keep confidential the information contained in the notice and the notice should not be handled by anyone not needing the information to exercise rights under ICWA.

(e) If the identity or location of the child's parents, the child's Indian custodian, or the Tribes in which the Indian child is a member or eligible for membership cannot be ascertained, but there is reason to know the child is an Indian child, notice of the child-custody proceeding must be sent to the appropriate Bureau of Indian Affairs Regional Director (see *www.bia.gov*). To establish Tribal identity, as much information as is known regarding the child's direct lineal ancestors should be provided. The Bureau of Indian Affairs will not make a determination of Tribal membership but may, in some instances, be able to identify Tribes to contact.

(f) If there is a reason to know that a parent or Indian custodian possesses limited English proficiency and is therefore not likely to understand the contents of the notice, the court must provide language access services as required by Title VI of the Civil Rights Act and other Federal laws. To secure such translation or interpretation support, a court may contact or direct a party to contact the Indian child's Tribe or the local BIA office for assistance in locating and obtaining the name of a qualified translator or interpreter.

(g) If a parent or Indian custodian of an Indian child appears in court without an attorney, the court must inform him or her of his or her rights, including any applicable right to appointed counsel, right to request that the child-custody proceeding be transferred to Tribal court, right to object to such transfer, right to request additional time to prepare for the child-custody proceeding as provided in § 23.112, and right (if the parent or Indian custodian is not already a party) to intervene in the child-custody proceedings.

§ 23.112 What time limits and extensions apply?

(a) No foster-care-placement or termination-of-parental-rights proceeding may be held until at least 10 days after receipt of the notice by the parent (or Indian custodian) and by the Tribe (or the Secretary). The parent, Indian custodian, and Tribe each have a right, upon request, to be granted up to 20 additional days from the date upon which notice was received to prepare for participation in the proceeding.

(b) Except as provided in 25 U.S.C. 1922 and § 23.113, no child-custody proceeding for foster-care placement or termination of parental rights may be held until the waiting periods to which the parents or Indian custodians and to which the Indian child's Tribe are entitled have expired, as follows:

(1) 10 days after each parent or Indian custodian (or Secretary where the parent or Indian custodian is unknown to the petitioner) has received notice of that particular child-custody proceeding in accordance with 25 U.S.C. 1912(a) and § 23.111;

(2) 10 days after the Indian child's Tribe (or the Secretary if the Indian child's Tribe is unknown to the party seeking placement) has received notice of that particular child-custody proceeding in accordance with 25 U.S.C. 1912(a) and § 23.111;

(3) Up to 30 days after the parent or Indian custodian has received notice of that particular child-custody proceeding in accordance with 25 U.S.C. 1912(a) and § 23.111, if the parent or Indian custodian has requested up to 20 additional days to prepare for the child-custody proceeding as provided in 25 U.S.C. 1912(a) and § 23.111; and

(4) Up to 30 days after the Indian child's Tribe has received notice of that particular child-custody proceeding in accordance with 25 U.S.C. 1912(a) and § 23.111, if the Indian child's Tribe has requested up to 20 additional days to prepare for the child-custody proceeding.

(c) Additional time beyond the minimum required by 25 U.S.C. 1912 and § 23.111 may also be available under State law or pursuant to extensions granted by the court.

§ 23.113 What are the standards for emergency proceedings involving an Indian child?

(a) Any emergency removal or placement of an Indian child under State law must terminate immediately when the removal or placement is no longer necessary to prevent imminent physical damage or harm to the child.

(b) The State court must:

(1) Make a finding on the record that the emergency removal or placement is necessary to prevent imminent physical damage or harm to the child;

(2) Promptly hold a hearing on whether the emergency removal or placement continues to be necessary whenever new information indicates that the emergency situation has ended; and

(3) At any court hearing during the emergency proceeding, determine whether the emergency removal or placement is no longer necessary to

prevent imminent physical damage or harm to the child.

(4) Immediately terminate (or ensure that the agency immediately terminates) the emergency proceeding once the court or agency possesses sufficient evidence to determine that the emergency removal or placement is no longer necessary to prevent imminent physical damage or harm to the child.

(c) An emergency proceeding can be terminated by one or more of the following actions:

(1) Initiation of a child-custody proceeding subject to the provisions of ICWA;

(2) Transfer of the child to the jurisdiction of the appropriate Indian Tribe; or

(3) Restoring the child to the parent or Indian custodian.

(d) A petition for a court order authorizing the emergency removal or continued emergency placement, or its accompanying documents, should contain a statement of the risk of imminent physical damage or harm to the Indian child and any evidence that the emergency removal or placement continues to be necessary to prevent such imminent physical damage or harm to the child. The petition or its accompanying documents should also contain the following information:

(1) The name, age, and last known address of the Indian child;

(2) The name and address of the child's parents and Indian custodians, if any;

(3) The steps taken to provide notice to the child's parents, custodians, and Tribe about the emergency proceeding;

(4) If the child's parents and Indian custodians are unknown, a detailed explanation of what efforts have been made to locate and contact them, including contact with the appropriate BIA Regional Director (see *www.bia.gov*);

(5) The residence and the domicile of the Indian child;

(6) If either the residence or the domicile of the Indian child is believed to be on a reservation or in an Alaska Native village, the name of the Tribe affiliated with that reservation or village;

(7) The Tribal affiliation of the child and of the parents or Indian custodians;

(8) A specific and detailed account of the circumstances that led the agency responsible for the emergency removal of the child to take that action;

(9) If the child is believed to reside or be domiciled on a reservation where the Tribe exercises exclusive jurisdiction over child-custody matters, a statement of efforts that have been made and are being made to contact the Tribe and transfer the child to the Tribe's jurisdiction; and

(10) A statement of the efforts that have been taken to assist the parents or Indian custodians so the Indian child may safely be returned to their custody.

(e) An emergency proceeding regarding an Indian child should not be continued for more than 30 days unless the court makes the following determinations:

(1) Restoring the child to the parent or Indian custodian would subject the child to imminent physical damage or harm;

(2) The court has been unable to transfer the proceeding to the jurisdiction of the appropriate Indian Tribe; and

(3) It has not been possible to initiate a "child-custody proceeding" as defined in § 23.2.

§ 23.114 What are the requirements for determining improper removal?

(a) If, in the course of any child-custody proceeding, any party asserts or the court has reason to believe that the Indian child may have been improperly removed from the custody of his or her parent or Indian custodian, or that the Indian child has been improperly retained (such as after a visit or other temporary relinquishment of custody), the court must expeditiously determine whether there was improper removal or retention.

(b) If the court finds that the Indian child was improperly removed or retained, the court must terminate the proceeding and the child must be returned immediately to his or her parent or Indian custodian, unless returning the child to his parent or Indian custodian would subject the child to substantial and immediate danger or threat of such danger.

PETITIONS TO TRANSFER TO TRIBAL COURT

§ 23.115 How are petitions for transfer of a proceeding made?

(a) Either parent, the Indian custodian, or the Indian child's Tribe may request, at any time, orally on the record or in writing, that the State court transfer a foster-care or termination-of-parental-rights proceeding to the jurisdiction of the child's Tribe.

(b) The right to request a transfer is available at any stage in each foster-care or termination-of-parental-rights proceeding.

§ 23.116 What happens after a petition for transfer is made?

Upon receipt of a transfer petition, the State court must ensure that the Tribal court is promptly notified in writing of the transfer petition. This notification may request a timely response regarding whether the Tribal court wishes to decline the transfer.

§ 23.117 What are the criteria for ruling on transfer petitions?

Upon receipt of a transfer petition from an Indian child's parent, Indian custodian, or Tribe, the State court must transfer the child-custody proceeding unless the court determines that transfer is not appropriate because one or more of the following criteria are met:

(a) Either parent objects to such transfer;

(b) The Tribal court declines the transfer; or

(c) Good cause exists for denying the transfer.

§ 23.118 How is a determination of "good cause" to deny transfer made?

(a) If the State court believes, or any party asserts, that good cause to deny transfer exists, the reasons for that belief or assertion must be stated orally on the record or provided in writing on the record and to the parties to the child-custody proceeding.

(b) Any party to the child-custody proceeding must have the opportunity to provide the court with views regarding whether good cause to deny transfer exists.

(c) In determining whether good cause exists, the court must not consider:

(1) Whether the foster-care or termination-of-parental-rights proceeding is at an advanced stage if the Indian child's parent, Indian custodian, or Tribe did not receive notice of the child-custody proceeding until an advanced stage;

(2) Whether there have been prior proceedings involving the child for which no petition to transfer was filed;

(3) Whether transfer could affect the placement of the child;

(4) The Indian child's cultural connections with the Tribe or its reservation; or

(5) Socioeconomic conditions or any negative perception of Tribal or BIA social services or judicial systems.

(d) The basis for any State-court decision to deny transfer should be stated orally on the record or in a written order.

§ 23.119 What happens after a petition for transfer is granted?

(a) If the Tribal court accepts the transfer, the State court should expeditiously provide the Tribal court with all records related to the proceeding, including, but not limited to, the pleadings and any court record.

(b) The State court should work with the Tribal court to ensure that the transfer of the custody of the Indian child and of the proceeding is accomplished smoothly and in a way that minimizes the disruption of services to the family.

ADJUDICATION OF INVOLUNTARY PROCEEDINGS

§ 23.120 How does the State court ensure that active efforts have been made?

(a) Prior to ordering an involuntary foster-care placement or termination of parental rights, the court must conclude that active efforts have been made to prevent the breakup of the Indian family and that those efforts have been unsuccessful.

(b) Active efforts must be documented in detail in the record.

§23.121 What are the applicable standards of evidence?

(a) The court must not order a foster-care placement of an Indian child unless clear and convincing evidence is presented, including the testimony of one or more qualified expert witnesses, demonstrating that the child's continued custody by the child's parent or Indian custodian is likely to result in serious emotional or physical damage to the child.

(b) The court must not order a termination of parental rights for an Indian child unless evidence beyond a reasonable doubt is presented, including the testimony of one or more qualified expert witnesses, demonstrating that the child's continued custody by the child's parent or Indian custodian is likely to result in serious emotional or physical damage to the child.

(c) For a foster-care placement or termination of parental rights, the evidence must show a causal relationship between the particular conditions in the home and the likelihood that continued custody of the child will result in serious emotional or physical damage to the particular child who is the subject of the child-custody proceeding.

(d) Without a causal relationship identified in paragraph (c) of this section, evidence that shows only the existence of community or family poverty, isolation, single parenthood, custodian age, crowded or inadequate housing, substance abuse, or nonconforming social behavior does not by itself constitute clear and convincing evidence or evidence beyond a reasonable doubt that continued custody is likely to result in serious emotional or physical damage to the child.

§23.122 Who may serve as a qualified expert witness?

(a) A qualified expert witness must be qualified to testify regarding whether the child's continued custody by the parent or Indian custodian is likely to result in serious emotional or physical damage to the child and should be qualified to testify as to the prevailing social and cultural standards of the Indian child's Tribe. A person may be designated by the Indian child's Tribe as being qualified to testify to the prevailing social and cultural standards of the Indian child's Tribe.

(b) The court or any party may request the assistance of the Indian child's Tribe or the BIA office serving the Indian child's Tribe in locating persons qualified to serve as expert witnesses.

(c) The social worker regularly assigned to the Indian child may not serve as a qualified expert witness in child-custody proceedings concerning the child.

§23.123 [Reserved]

VOLUNTARY PROCEEDINGS

§23.124 What actions must a State court undertake in voluntary proceedings?

(a) The State court must require the participants in a voluntary proceeding to state on the record whether the child is an Indian child, or whether there is reason to believe the child is an Indian child, as provided in §23.107.

(b) If there is reason to believe the child is an Indian child, the State court must ensure that the party seeking placement has taken all reasonable steps to verify the child's status. This may include contacting the Tribe of which it is believed the child is a member (or eligible for membership and of which the biological parent is a member) to verify the child's status. As described in §23.107, where a consenting parent requests anonymity, a Tribe receiving such information must keep relevant documents and information confidential.

(c) State courts must ensure that the placement for the Indian child complies with §§23.129–23.132.

§23.125 How is consent obtained?

(a) A parent's or Indian custodian's consent to a voluntary termination of parental rights or to a foster-care, preadoptive, or adoptive placement must be executed in writing and recorded before a court of competent jurisdiction.

(b) Prior to accepting the consent, the court must explain to the parent or Indian custodian:

(1) The terms and consequences of the consent in detail; and

(2) The following limitations, applicable to the type of child-custody proceeding for which consent is given, on withdrawal of consent:

(i) For consent to foster-care placement, the parent or Indian custodian may withdraw consent for any reason, at any time, and have the child returned; or

(ii) For consent to termination of parental rights, the parent or Indian custodian may withdraw consent for any reason, at any time prior to the entry of the final decree of termination and have the child returned; or

(iii) For consent to an adoptive placement, the parent or Indian custodian may withdraw consent for any reason, at any time prior to the entry of the final decree of adoption, and have the child returned.

(c) The court must certify that the terms and consequences of the consent were explained on the record in detail in English (or the language of the parent or Indian custodian, if English is not the primary language) and were fully understood by the parent or Indian custodian.

(d) Where confidentiality is requested or indicated, execution of consent need not be made in a session of court open to the public but still must be made before a court of competent jurisdiction in compliance with this section.

(e) A consent given prior to, or within 10 days after, the birth of an Indian child is not valid.

§ 23.126 What information must a consent document contain?

(a) If there are any conditions to the consent, the written consent must clearly set out the conditions.

(b) A written consent to foster-care placement should contain, in addition to the information specified in paragraph (a) of this section, the name and birthdate of the Indian child; the name of the Indian child's Tribe; the Tribal enrollment number for the parent and for the Indian child, where known, or some other indication of the child's membership in the Tribe; the name, address, and other identifying information of the consenting parent or Indian custodian; the name and address of the person or entity, if any, who arranged the placement; and the name and address of the prospective foster parents, if known at the time.

§ 23.127 How is withdrawal of consent to a foster-care placement achieved?

(a) The parent or Indian custodian may withdraw consent to voluntary foster-care placement at any time.

(b) To withdraw consent, the parent or Indian custodian must file a written document with the court or otherwise testify before the court. Additional methods of withdrawing consent may be available under State law.

(c) When a parent or Indian custodian withdraws consent to a voluntary foster-care placement, the court must ensure that the Indian child is returned to that parent or Indian custodian as soon as practicable.

§ 23.128 How is withdrawal of consent to a termination of parental rights or adoption achieved?

(a) A parent may withdraw consent to voluntary termination of parental rights at any time prior to the entry of a final decree of termination.

(b) A parent or Indian custodian may withdraw consent to voluntary adoption at any time prior to the entry of a final decree of adoption.

(c) To withdraw consent prior to the entry of a final decree of adoption, the parent or Indian custodian must file a written document with the court or otherwise testify before the court. Additional methods of withdrawing consent may be available under State law.

(d) The court in which the withdrawal of consent is filed must promptly notify the person or entity who arranged any voluntary preadoptive or adoptive placement of such filing, and the Indian child must be returned to the parent or Indian custodian as soon as practicable.

DISPOSITIONS

§ 23.129 When do the placement preferences apply?

(a) In any preadoptive, adoptive, or foster-care placement of an Indian child, the placement preferences specified in § 23.130 and § 23.131 apply.

(b) Where a consenting parent requests anonymity in a voluntary proceeding, the court must give weight to the request in applying the preferences.

(c) The placement preferences must be applied in any foster-care, preadoptive, or adoptive placement unless there is a determination on the record that good cause under § 23.132 exists to not apply those placement preferences.

§ 23.130 What placement preferences apply in adoptive placements?

(a) In any adoptive placement of an Indian child under State law, where the Indian child's Tribe has not established a different order of preference under paragraph (b) of this section, preference must be given in descending order, as listed below, to placement of the child with:

(1) A member of the Indian child's extended family;

(2) Other members of the Indian child's Tribe; or

(3) Other Indian families.

(b) If the Indian child's Tribe has established by resolution a different order of preference than that specified in ICWA, the Tribe's placement preferences apply.

(c) The court must, where appropriate, also consider the placement preference of the Indian child or Indian child's parent.

§ 23.131 What placement preferences apply in foster-care or preadoptive placements?

(a) In any foster-care or preadoptive placement of an Indian child under State law, including changes in foster-care or preadoptive placements, the child must be placed in the least-restrictive setting that:

(1) Most approximates a family, taking into consideration sibling attachment;

(2) Allows the Indian child's special needs (if any) to be met; and

(3) Is in reasonable proximity to the Indian child's home, extended family, or siblings.

(b) In any foster-care or preadoptive placement of an Indian child under State law, where the Indian child's Tribe has not established a different order of preference under paragraph (c) of this section, preference must be given, in descending order as listed below, to placement of the child with:

(1) A member of the Indian child's extended family;

(2) A foster home that is licensed, approved, or specified by the Indian child's Tribe;

(3) An Indian foster home licensed or approved by an authorized non-Indian licensing authority; or

(4) An institution for children approved by an Indian Tribe or operated by an Indian organization which has a program suitable to meet the child's needs.

(c) If the Indian child's Tribe has established by resolution a different order of preference than that specified in ICWA, the Tribe's placement preferences apply, so long as the placement is the least-restrictive setting appropriate to the particular needs of the Indian child, as provided in paragraph (a) of this section.

(d) The court must, where appropriate, also consider the preference of the Indian child or the Indian child's parent.

§ 23.132 How is a determination of "good cause" to depart from the placement preferences made?

(a) If any party asserts that good cause not to follow the placement preferences exists, the reasons for that belief or assertion must be stated orally on the record or provided in writing to the parties to the child-custody proceeding and the court.

(b) The party seeking departure from the placement preferences should bear the burden of proving by clear and convincing evidence that there is "good cause" to depart from the placement preferences.

(c) A court's determination of good cause to depart from the placement preferences must be made on the record or in writing and should be based on one or more of the following considerations:

(1) The request of one or both of the Indian child's parents, if they attest that they have reviewed the placement options, if any, that comply with the order of preference;

(2) The request of the child, if the child is of sufficient age and capacity

to understand the decision that is being made;

(3) The presence of a sibling attachment that can be maintained only through a particular placement;

(4) The extraordinary physical, mental, or emotional needs of the Indian child, such as specialized treatment services that may be unavailable in the community where families who meet the placement preferences live;

(5) The unavailability of a suitable placement after a determination by the court that a diligent search was conducted to find suitable placements meeting the preference criteria, but none has been located. For purposes of this analysis, the standards for determining whether a placement is unavailable must conform to the prevailing social and cultural standards of the Indian community in which the Indian child's parent or extended family resides or with which the Indian child's parent or extended family members maintain social and cultural ties.

(d) A placement may not depart from the preferences based on the socioeconomic status of any placement relative to another placement.

(e) A placement may not depart from the preferences based solely on ordinary bonding or attachment that flowed from time spent in a non-preferred placement that was made in violation of ICWA.

ACCESS

§ 23.133 Should courts allow participation by alternative methods?

If it possesses the capability, the court should allow alternative methods of participation in State-court child-custody proceedings involving an Indian child, such as participation by telephone, videoconferencing, or other methods.

§ 23.134 Who has access to reports and records during a proceeding?

Each party to an emergency proceeding or a foster-care-placement or termination-of-parental-rights proceeding under State law involving an Indian child has a right to timely examine all reports and other documents filed or lodged with the court upon which any decision with respect to such action may be based.

§ 23.135 [Reserved]

POST-TRIAL RIGHTS & RESPONSIBILITIES

§ 23.136 What are the requirements for vacating an adoption based on consent having been obtained through fraud or duress?

(a) Within two years after a final decree of adoption of any Indian child by a State court, or within any longer period of time permitted by the law of the State, the State court may invalidate the voluntary adoption upon finding that the parent's consent was obtained by fraud or duress.

(b) Upon the parent's filing of a petition to vacate the final decree of adoption of the parent's Indian child, the court must give notice to all parties to the adoption proceedings and the Indian child's Tribe and must hold a hearing on the petition.

(c) Where the court finds that the parent's consent was obtained through fraud or duress, the court must vacate the final decree of adoption, order the consent revoked, and order that the child be returned to the parent.

§ 23.137 Who can petition to invalidate an action for certain ICWA violations?

(a) Any of the following may petition any court of competent jurisdiction to invalidate an action for foster-care placement or termination of parental rights under state law where it is alleged that 25 U.S.C. 1911, 1912, or 1913 has been violated:

(1) An Indian child who is or was the subject of any action for foster-care placement or termination of parental rights;

(2) A parent or Indian custodian from whose custody such child was removed; and

(3) The Indian child's Tribe.

(b) Upon a showing that an action for foster-care placement or termination of parental rights violated any provision of 25 U.S.C. 1911, 1912, or 1913, the court must determine whether it is appropriate to invalidate the action.

(c) To petition for invalidation, there is no requirement that the petitioner's rights under ICWA were violated; rather, a petitioner may challenge the action based on any violations of 25 U.S.C. 1911, 1912, or 1913 during the course of the child-custody proceeding.

§ 23.138 What are the rights to information about adoptees' Tribal affiliations?

Upon application by an Indian who has reached age 18 who was the subject of an adoptive placement, the court that entered the final decree of adoption must inform such individual of the Tribal affiliations, if any, of the individual's biological parents and provide such other information necessary to protect any rights, which may include Tribal membership, resulting from the individual's Tribal relationship.

§ 23.139 Must notice be given of a change in an adopted Indian child's status?

(a) If an Indian child has been adopted, the court must notify, by registered or certified mail with return receipt requested, the child's biological parent or prior Indian custodian and the Indian child's Tribe whenever:

(1) A final decree of adoption of the Indian child has been vacated or set aside; or

(2) The adoptive parent has voluntarily consented to the termination of his or her parental rights to the child.

(b) The notice must state the current name, and any former name, of the Indian child, inform the recipient of the right to petition for return of custody of the child, and provide sufficient information to allow the recipient to participate in any scheduled hearings.

(c) A parent or Indian custodian may waive his or her right to such notice by executing a written waiver of notice and filing the waiver with the court.

(1) Prior to accepting the waiver, the court must explain the consequences of the waiver and explain how the waiver may be revoked.

(2) The court must certify that the terms and consequences of the waiver and how the waiver may be revoked were explained in detail in English (or the language of the parent or Indian custodian, if English is not the primary language), and were fully understood by the parent or Indian custodian.

(3) Where confidentiality is requested or indicated, execution of the waiver need not be made in a session of court open to the public but still must be made before a court of competent jurisdiction in compliance with this section.

(4) The biological parent or Indian custodian may revoke the waiver at any time by filing with the court a written notice of revocation.

(5) A revocation of the right to receive notice does not affect any child-custody proceeding that was completed before the filing of the notice of revocation.

RECORDKEEPING

§ 23.140 What information must States furnish to the Bureau of Indian Affairs?

(a) Any State court entering a final adoption decree or order in any voluntary or involuntary Indian-child adoptive placement must furnish a copy of the decree or order within 30 days to the Bureau of Indian Affairs, Chief, Division of Human Services, 1849 C Street NW, Mail Stop 3645 MIB, Washington, DC 20240, along with the following information, in an envelope marked "Confidential":

(1) Birth name and birthdate of the Indian child, and Tribal affiliation and name of the Indian child after adoption;

(2) Names and addresses of the biological parents;

(3) Names and addresses of the adoptive parents;

(4) Name and contact information for any agency having files or information relating to the adoption;

(5) Any affidavit signed by the biological parent or parents asking that their identity remain confidential; and

(6) Any information relating to Tribal membership or eligibility for Tribal membership of the adopted child.

(b) If a State agency has been designated as the repository for all State-court adoption information and is fulfilling the duties described in paragraph (a) of this section, the State courts in that State need not fulfill those same duties.

[59 FR 2256, Jan. 13, 1994, as amended at 83 FR 55269, Nov. 5, 2018]

§ 23.141 What records must the State maintain?

(a) The State must maintain a record of every voluntary or involuntary foster-care, preadoptive, and adoptive placement of an Indian child and make the record available within 14 days of a request by an Indian child's Tribe or the Secretary.

(b) The record must contain, at a minimum, the petition or complaint, all substantive orders entered in the child-custody proceeding, the complete record of the placement determination (including, but not limited to, the findings in the court record and the social worker's statement), and, if the placement departs from the placement preferences, detailed documentation of the efforts to comply with the placement preferences.

(c) A State agency or agencies may be designated to be the repository for this information. The State court or agency should notify the BIA whether these records are maintained within the court system or by a State agency.

§ 23.142 How does the Paperwork Reduction Act affect this subpart?

The collections of information contained in this part have been approved by the Office of Management and Budget under 44 U.S.C. 3501 *et seq.* and assigned OMB Control Number 1076–0186. Response is required to obtain a benefit. A Federal agency may not conduct or sponsor, and you are not required to respond to, a collection of information unless the form or regulation requesting the information displays a currently valid OMB Control Number. Send comments regarding this collection of information, including suggestions for reducing the burden, to the Information Collection Clearance Officer—Indian Affairs, 1849 C Street NW., Washington, DC 20240.

EFFECTIVE DATE

§ 23.143 How does this subpart apply to pending proceedings?

None of the provisions of this subpart affects a proceeding under State law for foster-care placement, termination of parental rights, preadoptive placement, or adoptive placement that was initiated prior to December 12, 2016, but the provisions of this subpart apply to any subsequent proceeding in the same matter or subsequent proceedings affecting the custody or placement of the same child.

SEVERABILITY

§ 23.144 What happens if some portion of this part is held to be invalid by a court of competent jurisdiction?

If any portion of this part is determined to be invalid by a court of competent jurisdiction, the other portions of the part remain in effect. For example, the Department has considered separately whether the provisions of this part apply to involuntary and voluntary proceedings; thus, if a particular provision is held to be invalid as to one type of proceeding, it is the Department's intent that it remains valid as to the other type of proceeding.

PART 26—JOB PLACEMENT AND TRAINING PROGRAM

Subpart A—General Applicability

Sec.

AUTHORITY: 25 U.S.C. 13; Sec. 1, Public Law 84–959, 70 Stat. 966 as amended by Public Law 88–230, 77 Stat. 471 (25 U.S.C. 309)

SOURCE: 74 FR 41331, Aug. 17, 2009, unless otherwise noted.

Subpart A—General Applicability

§ 26.1 What terms do I need to know?

As used in this part:

Bureau means the Bureau of Indian Affairs (BIA).

Department means the Department of the Interior.

Gainful Employment means work resulting in self-sufficiency.

Indian means any person who is a member of a federally recognized tribe, including Alaska Natives.

Individual Self-Sufficiency Plan (ISP) means a written plan designed to meet the goal of employment through specific actions that meet the needs of the individual. The plan is jointly developed and is signed by both the applicant and the servicing office. The ISP addresses the client's barriers to employment and a plan of action to address barriers.

Must means a mandatory act or requirement.

On or Near Reservation means those areas or communities adjacent or contiguous to reservations, or service areas where Job Training and Placement programs are provided upon approval of the Assistant Secretary-Indian Affairs or his designated representative. For purposes of this program and services, Alaska is included in this definition.

On-the-Job-Training (OJT) means a written agreement for an employer to provide training to a participant who engages in productive work that provides knowledge or skills essential to the full and adequate performance of the job. The employer receives reimbursement from the Job Training Program for the wage rate of the participant. OJT may be used to meet the goal(s) in the participant's ISP, as long as it does not exceed 24 months.

Permanent Employment means a year-round job or one that re-occurs seasonally, lasting at least 90 days per work season.

Service Area means a location agreed to by the tribe with the Bureau to provide Job Training and Placement Services.

Servicing Office means the Bureau office or the office of the tribal service provider that administers the Job Training and Placement Program.

Tribal Governing Body means the recognized entity empowered to exercise governmental authority over a federally recognized tribe.

Tribal Service Provider means a tribe or tribal organization that administers the Job Training and Placement Program pursuant to Public Law 93–638 or Public Law 102–477.

Tribe means any tribal entity listed in the FEDERAL REGISTER notice that the Secretary of the Interior publishes under Public Law 103–454, 108 Stat. 4791.

Underemployed means an individual who is working but whose income is insufficient to meet essential needs.

Unemployed means an individual who is not currently working or employed.

Unmet need means the difference between available resources and the cost associated with finding gainful employment.

Vocational Training means technical training that leads to permanent and gainful employment.

We, us, or *our* means the Secretary of the Interior, or an official in the Office of the Assistant Secretary—Indian Affairs, or an official in the Bureau of Indian Affairs to whom the Secretary has delegated authority.

§ 26.2 Who authorizes this collection of information?

The information collection requirements contained in this part have been approved by the Office of Management and Budget under the Paperwork Reduction Act of 1995, 44 U.S.C. 3507(d), and assigned OMB clearance number 1076–0062. Response is required to obtain a benefit. A Federal agency may not conduct or sponsor, and you are not required to respond to a collection of information unless the form or regulation requesting the information has a currently valid OMB Control Number.

§ 26.3 What is the purpose of the Job Placement and Training Program?

The purpose of the Job Placement and Training Program is to assist eligible applicants to obtain job skills and to find and retain a job leading to self-sufficiency.

§ 26.4 Who administers the Job Placement and Training Program?

The Job Placement and Training Program is administered by the Bureau of Indian Affairs or a tribal service provider. Tribes are encouraged to provide services directly to Indians by either entering into a Public Law 93–638 contract with the Bureau or a compact with the Office of Self—Governance. Tribes may also consolidate Job Placement and Training Program funds in accordance with the provisions of the Indian Employment, Training, and Related Services Demonstration Act of 1992, Public Law 102–477.

§ 26.5 Who may be eligible for Job Placement and Training?

You may apply for assistance for employment or training if all of the following criteria are met:

(a) You meet the definition of Indian in § 26.1; and

(b) You are residing on or near an Indian reservation or in a service area, or in the agreed contract service area; and

(c) You are unemployed or underemployed or need and can benefit from employment assistance as determined by your servicing office; and

(d) You complete an ISP.

§ 26.6 Who is eligible to receive financial assistance?

Financial assistance is only available to persons:

(a) Approved for training that will lead to permanent, gainful and meaningful employment; or

(b) Who have obtained a job and need financial assistance to retain the job, as determined by the servicing office.

§ 26.7 How is financial need established?

You must show that current income and other available resources are not sufficient to meet employment or training goals.

§ 26.8 Where do I go to apply for Job Placement and Training assistance?

You may apply for Job Placement and Training assistance at the servicing office nearest to your current residence.

§ 26.9 How do I apply for assistance?

(a) You should contact the BIA office or the tribal service provider which is nearest to your current residence to get an application form;

(b) You must complete the application process as established by your servicing office; and

(c) You must complete and sign a comprehensive ISP (or an individual development plan (IDP) or employment development plan (EDP), which are synonymous with an ISP).

§ 26.10 When will I find out if I have been selected for Job Placement and Training assistance?

(a) Your servicing office will notify you in writing within 30 calendar days once it receives a completed job training application request; or

(b) Your servicing office will notify you within 5 business days once it has received a completed Job Placement application and written job offer.

§ 26.11 What type of Job Placement and Training assistance may be approved?

Services provided may include funding for employment, training or supplemental assistance that supports job placement or training activities (see subpart B of this part for Job Placement or subpart C of this part for Training Services).

§ 26.12 Who provides the Job Placement and Training?

The Bureau or a tribal service provider may enter into contracts or agreements to provide facilities and services required for vocational training programs with:

(a) Indian tribal governing bodies or, when approved by the tribal service provider, other provider of meaningful training programs not currently operated by the tribe;

(b) Appropriate Federal, State, or local government agencies;

(c) Public or private schools with a recognized reputation in vocational education and successfully obtaining employment for graduates;

(d) Education firms that operate residential training centers; and

(e) Corporations and associations or small business establishments with apprenticeship or on-the-job training (OJT) programs leading to skilled employment.

§ 26.13 How long may I be in training and how long can I receive other assistance?

(a) Your training at any approved institution, apprenticeship, and/or OJT must not exceed 24 months of full-time actual training hours.

(b) Registered nurse training must not exceed 36 months of full actual training hours.

(c) You may receive other financial assistance under this program determined by your ISP that you have developed with your tribal service provider.

§ 26.14 What or who is a service provider?

A service provider is an administrative unit of a BIA Regional Office, a BIA Agency Office, a BIA Field Office, a Tribal contracted office, or Alaska Native federally recognized tribe, or a tribal organization, that provides grants to help offset the cost of vocational or technical training (at approved places), or immediate job placement services. To the extent resources will allow, other kinds of support service may also be available.

§ 26.15 What makes an applicant eligible for Job Placement and Training services?

You are eligible for services if:

(a) You meet the definition of an American Indian or Alaska Native; and

(b) Either:

(1) You can demonstrate an unmet need and show a need for job training or placement services in order to become gainfully and meaningfully employed; or

(2) You are skilled, but need financial assistance to get to a job, and you show an aptitude and potential to benefit from services.

§ 26.16 If I am awarded financial assistance, how much will I receive?

(a) The amount of financial assistance you receive depends on your unmet needs. If applicable, you should apply for:

(1) A Pell Grant if your training institution offers this grant; and

(2) Other education grants or loans for which you may qualify.

(b) The Bureau or tribal service provider will award financial assistance up to the level of your unmet need to the extent resources are available. It is possible that the combination of available financial assistance will not equal your financial need.

§ 26.17 Can more than one family member be financially assisted at the same time?

Yes, more than one family member can be assisted, providing that each applicant is eligible.

§ 26.18 What kinds of supportive services are available?

The BIA or tribal service provider may provide, but is not limited to, the following supportive services:

(a) Assistance in completing an application and the provision of supporting documents;

(b) A description of the Job Placement and Training Program and related services;

(c) An assessment of eligibility;

(d) An assessment of need for employment services (or a combination of training and employment services);

(e) The creation of an ISP (which may include training and other support services);

(f) Counseling services that address cultural differences and strengthen probability of client success;

(g) Referral to other appropriate services;

(h) Youth work experience;

(i) Tools for employment;

(j) Initial union dues;

(k) Transportation of household effects;

(l) Security and safety deposits;

(m) Items to improve personal appearance such as professional work clothing;

(n) If required, kitchen and other household effects including bedding and appliances; and

(o) Childcare.

§ 26.19 Will I be required to contribute financially to my employment and training goals?

Yes, the Job Placement and Training Program clients are required to seek other funding, including the use of personal resources as a condition of their ISP.

§ 26.20 Can I be required to return portions of my grant?

Yes, grants are awarded for a specific purpose as described in the applicant's ISP. If the funds cannot be spent according to the ISP, the unused portion must be returned to the service provider's job placement and training budget.

§ 26.21 Can this program be combined with other similar programs for maximum benefit?

Yes, combining this program with other programs is encouraged, to the extent that laws governing program services permit partnering with similar programs and resources.

§ 26.22 May a tribe integrate Job Placement and Training funds into its Public Law 102–477 Plan?

Yes, Indian tribes may integrate Job Placement and Training Program funds into their Public Law 102–477 Plan.

§ 26.23 What is an Individual Self-Sufficiency Plan (ISP)?

(a) An ISP is a document that:

(1) Spells out the details necessary for a person to assume a meaningful job (usually within a reasonable period of time);

(2) Supplements the application process and includes needed finances, special clothing, transportation, and support services necessary for employment;

(3) Identifies all financial resources and defines the employment or training objective and activities planned to reach the objective; and

(4) Outlines how the applicant will participate in job placement, where resources will allow.

(b) The employer's job information and offer should be attached to the ISP, which becomes a part of the application (and supporting documents).

(c) The ISP must indicate that the services received will meet the individual's and tribal goals.

(d) Only one comprehensive ISP can be in effect for each applicant at one time. The comprehensive ISP should be coordinated and integrated with other programs offered by the servicing agency.

Subpart B—Job Placement Services

§26.24 What is the scope of the Job Placement Program?

The Job Placement Program assists Indian people who have job skills to obtain and retain gainful employment leading to self-sufficiency.

§26.25 What constitutes a complete Job Placement Program application?

To be complete, a Job Placement Program application must contain all of the items required by this section.

(a) An application signed by the applicant and servicing office representative.

(b) An ISP, including a list of goods and services needed to get the applicant to the job, signed by the applicant and servicing representative.

(c) An accepted official document that shows the formal relationship between the applicant and a federally recognized tribe or a document that shows an applicant's eligibility for services.

(d) A statement by the service provider that the applicant has been declared eligible for services.

(e) A financial statement that reflects the applicant's unmet need.

(f) An employer certification that the applicant has been hired. The certification must include, at a minimum:

(1) Job title;

(2) Beginning date;

(3) Beginning wage;

(4) Date first full paycheck will be issued; and

(5) Expected duration of the job.

§26.26 What Job Placement services may I receive?

As determined by the service provider, you may receive transportation to work for a limited period, funds to finalize your job resume, and job placement assistance.

§26.27 What kind of Job Placement support services can I expect?

Service office representatives will make the determination of what support services are necessary and to be funded. Examples of job placement support services include, but are not limited to resume preparation, interview techniques, job retention, and related living skills.

§26.28 What follow-up services are available after I become employed?

As determined by the service provider, the following type of services may be available: Temporary housing, transportation to work for a limited period of time, work clothing, and childcare.

Subpart C—Training Services

§26.29 What is the scope of the Job Training Program?

A service provider may offer career counseling, assessment, recommend training institutions that properly prepare applicants for entry into their career field, and help prepare applicants for gainful employment to the extent program funding will allow and based on applicants' established need.

§26.30 Does the Job Training Program provide part-time training or short-term training?

Yes, part-time and short-term training are allowable provided the training assists individuals to develop skills necessary to acquire gainful employment, in accordance with the ISP, and depending upon availability of resources. Part-time means no less than six credit units per semester (based on a nine-month school year).

§26.31 May I repeat my training?

Eligibility for repeat training and other financial assistance will be determined by your tribal service provider.

§26.32 What constitutes a complete Job Training Program application?

A request for training includes:

(a) Intake and application data;

(b) Feasible, comprehensive ISP;

(c) Tribal affiliation document;

(d) Selective Service registration;

(e) Selected place of training;

(f) Statement of financial need;

(g) Statement of eligibility; and

(h) Applicant assessment or other documents as required by the servicing agency.

§ 26.33 How do I show I need job training?

The need for Job Placement and Training is shown by completing an application for training that demonstrates financial need.

§ 26.34 What type of job training assistance may be approved?

The following types of training that lead to gainful employment may be approved:

(a) Nationally accredited vocational training;

(b) Training and non-accredited vocational courses provided by a tribe;

(c) Training programs not operated by the tribe but approved by the service provider;

(d) Apprenticeship training supervised by a State apprenticeship agency or council or by the Federal Apprenticeship Training Service that is provided by a corporation or association that has been training bona fide apprentices for at least one year or any other apprenticeship program approved by the service provider; or

(e) OJT offered by a public or private business.

§ 26.35 What kind of support services are available to me?

As determined by the service provider, training support services include, but are not limited to, stipends, transportation, and childcare.

§ 26.36 What follow-up service is available after I complete training?

Job Placement assistance may follow training.

§ 26.37 Are there training standards that I must follow?

Yes, students must maintain the minimum academic requirements and be in good standing as set forth by the training institute. If an applicant is separated from training for good cause, the applicant may be responsible for repaying any portion of misused funds.

Subpart D—Appeal by an Applicant

§ 26.38 May I appeal a decision about my application?

If the servicing agency denies your application you may appeal under part 2 of this chapter by sending your appeal to your service provider. If your servicing agency is a tribal contractor, you should file your appeal with the tribal contractor under their established procedure. The letter informing you of the decision on your application will include information on how to appeal.

SUBCHAPTER E—EDUCATION

PART 30—ADEQUATE YEARLY PROGRESS

AUTHORITY: Public Law 107–110, 115 Stat. 1425.

SOURCE: 70 FR 22200, Apr. 28, 2005, unless otherwise noted.

§ 30.100 What is the purpose of this part?

This part establishes for schools receiving Bureau funding a definition of "Adequate Yearly Progress (AYP)." Nothing in this part:

(a) Diminishes the Secretary's trust responsibility for Indian education or any statutory rights in law;

(b) Affects in any way the sovereign rights of tribes; or

(c) Terminates or changes the trust responsibility of the United States to Indian tribes or individual Indians.

§ 30.101 What definitions apply to terms in this part?

Act means the No Child Left Behind Act, Public Law 107–110, enacted January 8, 2002. The No Child Left Behind Act reauthorizes and amends the Elementary and Secondary Education Act (ESEA) and amends the Education Amendments of 1978.

Bureau means the Bureau of Indian Affairs in the Department of the Interior.

Department means the Department of the Interior.

OIEP means the Office of Indian Education Programs in the Bureau of Indian Affairs.

School means a school funded by the Bureau of Indian Affairs.

Secretary means the Secretary of the Interior or a designated representative.

Secretaries means the Secretary of the Interior and the Secretary of Education.

Subpart A—Defining Adequate Yearly Progress

§ 30.102 Does the Act require the Secretary of the Interior to develop a definition of AYP for Bureau-funded schools?

Yes, the Act requires the Secretary to develop a definition of AYP through negotiated rulemaking. In developing the Secretary's definition of AYP, the No Child Left Behind Negotiated Rulemaking Committee (Committee) considered a variety of options. In choosing the definition in § 30.104, the Committee in no way intended to diminish the Secretary's trust responsibility for Indian education or any statutory rights in law. Nothing in this part:

(a) Affects in any way the sovereign rights of tribes; or

(b) Terminates or changes the trust responsibility of the United States to Indian tribes or individual Indians.

§ 30.103 Did the Committee consider a separate Bureau definition of AYP?

Yes, the Committee considered having the Bureau of Indian Affairs develop a separate Bureau definition of AYP. For a variety of reasons, the Committee reached consensus on the definition in § 30.104. This definition is in no way intended to diminish the United States' trust responsibility for Indian education nor is it intended to give States authority over Bureau-funded schools.

§ 30.104 What is the Secretary's definition of AYP?

The Secretary defines AYP as follows. The definition meets the requirements in 20 U.S.C. 6311(b).

(a) Effective in the 2005–2006 school year, the academic content and student achievement standards, assessments, and the definition of AYP are those of the State where the school is located, unless an alternative definition of AYP is proposed by the tribal governing body or school board and approved by the Secretary.

(1) If the geographic boundaries of the school include more than one State, the tribal governing body or school board may choose the State definition it desires. Such decision shall be communicated to the Secretary in writing.

(2) This section does not mean that the school is under the jurisdiction of the State for any purpose, rather a reference to the State is solely for the purpose of using the State's assessment, academic content and student achievement standards, and definition of AYP.

(3) The use of the State's definition of AYP does not diminish or alter the Federal Government's trust responsibility for Indian education.

(b) School boards or tribal governing bodies may seek a waiver that may include developing their own definition of AYP, or adopting or modifying an existing definition of AYP that has been accepted by the Department of Education. The Secretary is committed to providing technical assistance to a school, or a group of schools, to develop an alternative definition of AYP.

ALTERNATIVE DEFINITION OF AYP

§ 30.105 May a tribal governing body or school board use another definition of AYP?

Yes. A tribal governing body or school board may waive all or part of the Secretary's definition of academic content and achievement standards, assessments, and AYP. However, unless an alternative definition is approved under § 30.113, the school must use the Secretary's definition of academic content and achievement standards, assessments, and AYP.

§ 30.106 How does a tribal governing body or school board propose an alternative definition of AYP?

If a tribal governing body or school board decides that the definition of AYP in § 30.104 is inappropriate, it may decide to waive all or part of the definition. Within 60 days of the decision to waive, the tribal governing body or school board must submit to the Secretary a proposal for an alternative definition of AYP. The proposal must meet the requirements of 20 U.S.C. 6311(b) and 34 CFR 200.13–200.20, taking into account the unique circumstances and needs of the school or schools and the students served.

§ 30.107 What must a tribal governing body or school board include in its alternative definition of AYP?

(a) An alternative definition of AYP must meet the requirements of 20 U.S.C. 6311(b)(2) of the Act and 34 CFR 200.13–200.20, taking into account the unique circumstances and needs of the school or schools and the students served.

(b) In accordance with 20 U.S.C. 6311(b) of the Act and 34 CFR 200.13–200.20, an alternative definition of AYP must:

(1) Apply the same high standards of academic achievement to all students;

(2) Be statistically valid and reliable;

(3) Result in continuous and substantial academic improvement for all students;

(4) Measure the progress of all students based on a high-quality assessment system that includes, at a minimum, academic assessments in mathematics and reading or language arts;

(5) Measure progress separately for reading or language arts and for mathematics;

(6) Unless disaggregation of data cannot yield statistically reliable information or reveals personally identifiable information, apply the same annual measurable objectives to each of the following:

(i) The achievement of all students; and

(ii) The achievement of economically disadvantaged students, students from major racial or ethnic groups, students with disabilities, and students with limited English proficiency;

(7) Establish a starting point;

(8) Create a timeline to ensure that all students are proficient by the 2013–2014 school year;

(9) Establish annual measurable objectives;

(10) Establish intermediate goals;

(11) Include at least one other academic indicator which, for any school with a 12th grade, must be graduation rate; and

(12) Ensure that at least 95 percent of the students enrolled in each group under § 30.107(b)(6) are assessed.

(c) If a Bureau-funded school's alternative definition of AYP does not use a State's academic content and student achievement standards and academic assessments, the school must include with its alternative definition the academic standards and assessment it proposes to use. These standards and assessments must meet the requirements in 20 U.S.C. 6311(b) and 34 CFR 200.1–200.9.

§ 30.108 May an alternative definition of AYP use parts of the Secretary's definition?

Yes, a tribal governing body or school board may take part of the Secretary's definition and propose to waive the remainder. The proposed alternative definition of AYP must, however, include both the parts of the Secretary's AYP definition the tribal governing body or school board is adopting and those parts the tribal governing body or school board is proposing to change.

Technical Assistance

§ 30.109 Will the Secretary provide assistance in developing an alternative AYP definition?

Yes, the Secretary through the Bureau, shall provide technical assistance either directly or through contract to the tribal governing body or the school board in developing an alternative AYP definition. A tribal governing body or school board needing assistance must submit a request to the Director of

OIEP under § 30.110. In providing assistance, the Secretary may consult with the Secretary of Education and may use funds supplied by the Secretary of Education in accordance with 20 U.S.C. 7301.

§ 30.110 What is the process for requesting technical assistance to develop an alternative definition of AYP?

(a) The tribal governing body or school board requesting technical assistance to develop an alternative definition of AYP must submit a written request to the Director of OIEP, specifying the form of assistance it requires.

(b) The Director of OIEP must acknowledge receipt of the request for technical assistance within 10 days of receiving the request.

(c) No later than 30 days after receiving the original request, the Director of OIEP will identify a point of contact. This contact will immediately begin working with the tribal governing body or school board to jointly develop the specifics of the technical assistance, including identifying the form, substance, and timeline for the assistance.

§ 30.111 When should the tribal governing body or school board request technical assistance?

In order to maximize the time the tribal governing body or school board has to develop an alternative definition of AYP and to provide full opportunity for technical assistance, the tribal governing body or school board should request technical assistance before formally notifying the Secretary of its intention to waive the Secretary's definition of AYP.

APPROVAL OF ALTERNATIVE DEFINITION

§ 30.113 How does the Secretary review and approve an alternative definition of AYP?

(a) The tribal governing body or school board submits a proposed alternative definition of AYP to the Director, OIEP within 60 days of its decision to waive the Secretary's definition.

(b) Within 60 days of receiving a proposed alternative definition of AYP, OIEP will notify the tribal governing body or the school board of:

(1) Whether the proposed alternative definition is complete; and

(2) If the definition is complete, an estimated timetable for the final decision.

(c) If the proposed alternative definition is incomplete, OIEP will provide the tribal governing body or school board with technical assistance to complete the proposed alternative definition of AYP, including identifying what additional items are necessary.

(d) The Secretaries will review the proposed alternative definition of AYP to determine whether it is consistent with the requirements of 20 U.S.C. 6311(b). This review must take into account the unique circumstances and needs of the schools and students.

(e) The Secretaries shall approve the alternative definition of AYP if it is consistent with the requirements of 20 U.S.C. 6311(b), taking into consideration the unique circumstances and needs of the school or schools and the students served.

(f) If the Secretaries approve the alternative definition of AYP:

(1) The Secretary shall promptly notify the tribal governing body or school board; and

(2) The alternate definition of AYP will become effective at the start of the following school year.

(g) The Secretaries will disapprove the alternative definition of AYP if it is not consistent with the requirements of 20 U.S.C. 6311(b). If the alternative definition is disapproved, the tribal governing body or school board will be notified of the following:

(1) That the definition is disapproved; and

(2) The reasons why the proposed alternative definition does not meet the requirements of 20 U.S.C. 6311(b).

(h) If the Secretaries deny a proposed definition under paragraph (g) of this section, they shall provide technical assistance to overcome the basis for the denial.

Subpart B—Assessing Adequate Yearly Progress

§ 30.114 Which students must be assessed?

All students in grades three through eight and at least once in grades ten through twelve who are enrolled in a Bureau-funded school must be assessed.

§30.115 Which students' performance data must be included for purposes of AYP?

The performance data of all students assessed pursuant to §30.114 must be included for purposes of AYP if the student is enrolled in a Bureau-funded school for a full academic year as defined by the Secretary or by an approved alternative definition of AYP.

§30.116 If a school fails to achieve its annual measurable objectives, what other methods may it use to determine whether it made AYP?

A school makes AYP if each group of students identified in §30.107(b)(6) meets or exceeds the annual measurable objectives and participation rate identified in §§30.107(b)(9) and 30.107(b)(12) respectively, and the school meets the other academic indicators identified in §30.107(b)(11). If a school fails to achieve its annual measurable objectives for any group identified in §30.107(b)(6), there are two other methods it may use to determine whether it made AYP:

(a) *Method A—"Safe Harbor."* Under "safe harbor," the following requirements must be met for each group referenced under §30.107(b)(6) that does not achieve the school's annual measurable objectives:

(1) In each group that does not achieve the school's annual measurable objectives, the percentage of students who were below the "proficient" level of academic achievement decreased by at least 10 percent from the preceding school year; and

(2) The students in that group made progress on one or more of the other academic indicators; and

(3) Not less than 95 percent of the students in that group participated in the assessment.

(b) *Method B—Uniform Averaging Procedure.* A school may use uniform averaging. Under this procedure, the school may average data from the school year with data from one or two school years immediately preceding that school year and determine if the resulting average makes AYP.

Subpart C—Failure To Make Adequate Yearly Progress

§30.117 What happens if a Bureau-funded school fails to make AYP?

Number of yrs of failing to make AYP in same academic subject	Status	Action required by entity operating school for the following school year
1st year of failing AYP	No status change	Analyze AYP data and consider consultation with outside experts.
2nd year of failing AYP	School improvement, year one.	Develop a plan or revise an existing plan for school improvement in consultation with parents, school staff and outside experts.
3rd year of failing AYP	School Improvement, year two.	Continue revising or modifying the plan for school improvement in consultation with parents, school staff and outside experts.
4th year of failing AYP	Corrective Action	Implement at least one of the six corrective actions steps found in 20 U.S.C. 6316(b)(7)(C)(iv).
5th year of failing AYP	Planning to Restructure	Prepare a restructuring plan and make arrangements to implement the plan.
6th year of failing AYP	Restructuring	Implement the restructuring plan no later than the beginning of the school year following the year in which it developed the plan.
7th year (and beyond) of failing AYP.	Restructuring	Continue implementation of the restructuring plan until AYP is met for two consecutive years.

§30.118 May a Bureau-funded school present evidence of errors in identification before it is identified for school improvement, corrective action, or restructuring?

Yes. The Bureau must give such a school the opportunity to review the data on which the bureau would identify a school for improvement, and present evidence as set out in 20 U.S.C. 6316(b)(2).

§ 30.119 Who is responsible for implementing required remedial actions at a Bureau-funded school identified for school improvement, corrective action or restructuring?

(a) For a Bureau-operated school, implementation of remedial actions is the responsibility of the Bureau.

(b) For a tribally operated contract school or grant school, implementation of remedial actions is the responsibility of the school board of the school.

§ 30.120 Are Bureau-funded schools exempt from offering school choice and supplemental educational services when identified for school improvement, corrective action, and restructuring?

Yes, Bureau-funded schools are exempt from offering public school choice and supplemental educational services when identified for school improvement, corrective action, and restructuring.

§ 30.121 What funds are available to assist schools identified for school improvement, corrective action, or restructuring?

From fiscal year 2004 to fiscal year 2007, the Bureau will reserve 4 percent of its title I allocation to assist Bureau-funded schools identified for school improvement, corrective action, and restructuring.

(a) The Bureau will allocate at least 95 percent of funds under this section to Bureau-funded schools identified for school improvement, corrective action, and restructuring to carry out those schools' responsibilities under 20 U.S.C. 6316(b). With the approval of the school board the Bureau may directly provide for the remedial activities or arrange for their provision through other entities such as school support teams or educational service agencies.

(b) In allocating funds under this section, the Bureau will give priority to schools that:

(1) Are the lowest-achieving schools;

(2) Demonstrate the greatest need for funds; and

(3) Demonstrate the strongest commitment to ensuring that the funds enable the lowest-achieving schools to meet progress goals in the school improvement plans.

(c) Funds reserved under this section must not decrease total funding under title I, part A of the Act, for any school below the level for the preceding year. To the extent that reserving funds under this section would reduce the title I, part A dollar amount of any school below the amount of title I, part A dollars the school received the previous year, the Secretary is authorized to reduce the title I, part A allocations of those schools receiving an increase in the title I, part A funds over the previous year to create the 4 percent reserve. This section does not authorize a school to receive title I, part A dollars it is not otherwise eligible to receive.

(d) The Bureau will publish in the FEDERAL REGISTER a list of schools receiving funds under this section.

§ 30.122 Must the Bureau assist a school it identified for school improvement, corrective action, or restructuring?

Yes, if a Bureau-funded school is identified for school improvement, corrective action, or restructuring, the Bureau must provide technical or other assistance described in 20 U.S.C. 6316(b)(4) and 20 U.S.C. 6316(g)(3) .

§ 30.123 What is the Bureau's role in assisting Bureau-funded schools to make AYP?

The Bureau must provide support to all Bureau-funded schools to assist them in achieving AYP. This includes technical assistance and other forms of support.

§ 30.124 Will the Bureau apply for funds that are available to help schools that fail to meet AYP?

Yes, to the extent that Congress appropriates other funds to assist schools not meeting AYP, the Bureau will apply to the Department of Education for these funds.

§ 30.125 What happens if a State refuses to allow a school access to the State assessment?

(a) The Department will work directly with State officials to assist schools in obtaining access to the State's assessment. This can include direct communication with the Governor of the State. A Bureau-funded school may, if necessary, pay a State for access to its assessment tools and scoring services.

(b) If a State does not provide access to the State's assessment, the Bureau-funded school must submit a waiver for an alternative definition of AYP.

Subpart D—Responsibilities and Accountability

§30.126 What is required for the Bureau to meet its reporting responsibilities?

The Bureau has the following reporting responsibilities to the Department of Education, appropriate Committees of Congress, and the public.

(a) In order to provide information about annual progress, the Bureau must obtain from all Bureau-funded schools the results of assessments administered for all tested students, special education students, students with limited English proficiency, and disseminate such results in an annual report.

(b) The Bureau must identify each school that did not meet AYP in accordance with the school's AYP definition.

(c) Within its annual report to Congress, the Secretary shall include all of the reporting requirements of 20 U.S.C. 6316(g)(5).

§30.150 Information collection.

Notwithstanding any other provision of law, no person is required to respond to, nor shall any person be subject to a penalty for failure to comply with, a collection of information subject to the requirements of the Paperwork Reduction Act of 1995 (44 U.S.C. 3501 *et seq.*)(PRA), unless that collection of information displays a currently valid Office of Management and Budget (OMB) Control Number. This part involves collections of information subject to the PRA in §§30.104(a)(1), 30.104(b), 30.106, 30.107, 30.110, and 30.118. These collections have been approved by OMB under control number 1076–0163.

PART 31—FEDERAL SCHOOLS FOR INDIANS

Sec.

AUTHORITY: Sec. 1, 41 Stat. 410; 25 U.S.C. 282, unless otherwise noted.

SOURCE: 22 FR 10533, Dec. 24, 1957, unless otherwise noted.

§31.0 Definitions.

As used in this part:

(a) *School district* means the local unit of school administration as defined by the laws of the State in which it is located.

(b) *Cooperative school* means a school operated under a cooperative agreement between a school district and the Bureau of Indian Affairs in conformance with State and Federal school laws and regulations.

(35 Stat. 72, 25 U.S.C. 295)

[33 FR 6472, Apr. 27, 1968]

§31.2 Use of Federal school facilities.

Federal Indian school facilities may be used for community activities and for adult education activities upon approval by the superintendent or officer in charge.

§31.3 Non-Indian pupils in Indian schools.

Indian and non-Indian children who are not eligible for enrollment in Bureau-operated schools under §31.1 may be enrolled in such schools under the following conditions:

(a) In boarding schools upon payment of tuition fees, which shall not exceed the per capita cost of maintenance in the school attended, when their presence will not exclude Indian pupils eligible under §31.1.

(b) In day schools in areas where there are no other adequate free school facilities available, tuition fees may be charged for such enrollment at the discretion of the superintendent or other officer in charge provided such fees shall not exceed the tuition fees allowed or charged by the State or county in which such school is located for the children admitted in the public schools of such State or county.

(34 Stat. 1018, 35 Stat. 783, 40 Stat. 564; 25 U.S.C. 288, 289, 297)

[29 FR 5828, May 2, 1964]

§ 31.4 Compulsory attendance.

Compulsory school attendance of Indian children is provided for by law.

(60 Stat. 962; 25 U.S.C. 231)

CROSS REFERENCE: For penalties for the failure of Indians to send children to school and for contributing to the delinquency of minors, see § 11.424 of this chapter.

§ 31.6 Coercion prohibited.

There shall be no coercion of children in the matter of transfers from one school to another, but voluntary enrollment should be effected through maintenance of Federal Indian schools or programs which suit the needs and interests of the areas in which they are located.

(Sec. 1, 29 Stat. 348; 25 U.S.C. 287)

§ 31.7 Handling of student funds in Federal school facilities.

The Secretary or his authorized representative may authorize officials and employees of the Bureau of Indian Affairs to accept and to disburse deposits of funds of students and student activity associations in schools operated by the Bureau in accordance with the purposes of such deposits. The following steps shall be taken to safeguard these funds:

(a) A written plan of operation shall be developed by the membership of each student activity group. The plan of operation subject to the approval of authorized officials shall outline procedures and provide for a system of accounting for the student funds commensurate with the age and grade level of the students yet adequate for financial control purposes and shall stipulate the maximum operating capital of activity.

(b) Appropriate safekeeping facilities shall be provided for all student personal and group funds and for the accounting or bookkeeping records.

(c) Employees handling student funds in cumulative amounts in excess of $100 shall be covered by a comprehensive fidelity bond the penal sum of which shall be appropriately related to fund amounts handled.

(d) Student funds accumulated in excess of the amount authorized for operating purposes by the plan of operation shall be deposited in federally insured depositories.

(e) Periodic administrative inspections and financial audit of student fund operations shall be conducted by authorized Bureau personnel.

[26 FR 10637, Nov. 14, 1961]

PART 32—INDIAN EDUCATION POLICIES

AUTHORITY: Secs. 1130 and 1133 of Title XI of the Education Amendments of 1978 (92 Stat. 2143, 2321 and 2325, Pub. L. 95–561; 25 U.S.C. 2010 and 2013).

SOURCE: 44 FR 58098, Oct. 9, 1979, unless otherwise noted. Redesignated at 47 FR 13327, Mar. 30, 1982.

§ 32.1 Purpose and scope.

The purpose of this part is to state the policies to be followed by all schools and education programs under the jurisdiction of the Bureau of Indian Affairs. Contract schools operated by Indian Tribes or Alaska Native entities may develop their independent policies, consistent with contractual obligations, or adhere to these. The adherence to the appropriate policies shall reflect the best interests of the student, the Federal government, the Tribes and Alaska Native entities, and shall be based on educationally sound judgment.

§ 32.2 Definitions.

As used in this part, the term:

(a) *Agency School Board* means a body, the members of which are appointed by the school boards of the schools located within such agency, and the number of such members shall be determined by the Director in consultation with the affected Tribes or Alaska Native entities except that, in agencies serving a single school, the school board of such school shall fulfill these duties.

(b) *Alaska Native* means an Indian, Eskimo, or Aleut who is a member of an Alaska Native entity.

(c) *Alaska Native Entity* means any Alaska Native village or regional or village corporation as defined in or established pursuant to the Alaska Native Claims Settlement Act (85 Stat. 688; 43 U.S.C. 1601 *et seq.*).

(d) *Alaska Native Village* means any Native village as defined in section 3(c) of the Alaska Native Claims Settlement Act (85 Stat. 689; 43 U.S.C. 1602 (c)).

(e) *Boarding school,* hereinafter referred to as *residential school,* means a Bureau school offering residential care and support services as well as an academic program.

(f) *Bureau* means the Bureau of Indian Affairs of the Department of the Interior.

(g) *Consultation* means a conferring process with Tribes, Alaska Native entities, and Tribal organizations on a periodic and systematic basis in which the Bureau and Department officials listen to and give effect, to the extent they can, to the views of these entities.

(h) *Contract school* means a school (other than a public school) which is Tribally operated and aided by a financial assistance contract with the Bureau.

(i) *Day school* means a Bureau school offering an academic program and certain support services such as counseling, food, transportation, etc., but excluding residential care.

(j) *Director* means the Director, Office of Indian Education Programs, Bureau of Indian Affairs.

(k) *Early childhood education* means comprehensive education activities with continuity of educational approach for children ages 0–8 years and their families, appropriate for their age, development, language and culture which supplement and support usual family responsibilities for child growth and development. They are coordinated with, but do not supplant, existing educational, health, nutritional, social and other necessary services.

(l) *Exceptional Education Programs* mean the provision of services to those children who are identified as handicapped and have been found to meet the criteria of handicapped as defined in Pub. L. 94–142, and programs for gifted and talented students.

(m) *Indian* means a member of an Indian Tribe.

(n) *Indian Organization* means any group, association, partnership, corporation, or other legal entity owned or controlled by a federally recognized Indian Tribe or Tribes, or a majority of whose members are members of federally recognized Indian Tribes.

(o) *Indian Tribe* or *Tribe* means any Indian tribe, band, nation, rancheria, pueblo, colony, or community which is recognized as eligible for the special programs and services provided by the United States to Indians because of their status as Indians.

(p) *Local school board,* when used with respect to a Bureau school, means a body chosen in accordance with the laws of the Tribe or Alaska Native entity to be served or, in the absence of such laws, elected by the parents of the Indian children attending the school, except that in schools serving a substantial number of students from different Tribes or Alaska Native entities the members shall be appointed by the governing bodies of the Tribes and entities affected; and, the number of such members shall be determined by the Director in consultation with the affected Tribes and entities.

(q) *Post-secondary* education means any education program beyond the age of compulsory education, including higher education, career, vocational, and technical.

(r) *Tribal Organization* means an organization composed of or duly representing Tribal governments which may be national or regional in scope and function.

§ 32.3 Mission statement.

Recognizing the special rights of Indian Tribes and Alaska Native entities and the unique government-to-government relationship of Indian Tribes and Alaska Native villages with the Federal Government as affirmed by the

United States Constitution, U.S. Supreme Court decisions, treaties, Federal statutes, and Executive Orders, and as set out in the Congressional declaration in sections 2 and 3 of the Indian Self-Determination and Education Assistance Act (Pub. L. 93–638; 88 Stat. 2203; 25 U.S.C. 450 and 450a), it is the responsibility and goal of the Federal government to provide comprehensive education programs and services for Indians and Alaska Natives. As acknowledged in section 5 of the Indian Child Welfare Act of 1978 (Pub. L. 95–608; 92 Stat. 3069; 25 U.S.C. 1901), in the Federal Government's protection and preservation of Indian Tribes and Alaska Native villages and their resources, there is no resource more vital to such Tribes and villages than their young people and the Federal Government has a direct interest, as trustee, in protecting Indian and Alaska Native children, including their education. The mission of the Bureau of Indian Affairs, Office of Indian Education Programs, is to provide quality education opportunities from early childhood through life in accordance with the Tribes' needs for cultural and economic well-being in keeping with the wide diversity of Indian Tribes and Alaska Native villages as distinct cultural and governmental entities. The Bureau shall manifest consideration of the whole person, taking into account the spiritual, mental, physical and cultural aspects of the person within family and Tribal or Alaska Native village contexts.

§ 32.4 Policies.

In carrying out its Education mission, the Assistant Secretary for Indian Affairs through the Director shall:

(a) *Policy making.* (1) Assure that no new policy shall be established nor any existing policy changed or modified without consultation with affected Tribes and Alaska Native Government entities.

(2) Be guided in policy formulation and funding priorities, including the proposing and awarding of contracts and grants, by periodic and systematic consultation with governing bodies of Tribes and Alaska Native entities.

(3) Ensure that Indian Tribes and Alaska Native entities fully exercise self-determination and control in planning, priority-setting, development, management, operation, staffing and evaluation in all aspects of the education process.

(4) Ensure that each agency or local school board shall be authorized and empowered to function as the policy making body for the school, consistent with the authority granted by the tribes or Alaska Native entity(ies) served by the school(s).

(b) *Student rights.* Ensure the constitutional, statutory, civil and human rights of all Indian and Alaska Native students, and respect the role of Tribal judicial systems where appropriate including, for example, ensuring that students have the right to be free from cruel and unusual punishment and that all disciplinary procedures shall be consistent with appropriate customs and practices of the appropriate Indian Tribe or Alaska Native village.

(c) *Equity funding.* Assure that resources for all education programs are equitably distributed for the benefit of all Indian and Alaska Native students, taking into account special educational needs where they exist, as further described in part 39 of this subchapter.

(d) *Direction of programs.* Ensure that the education function be structured in such a manner that all matters relating to the operation of education programs be administered by or be under the direction of education personnel.

(e) *Respect for family.* Promote, respect and defend the cohesiveness and integrity of the family, and Tribal and Alaska Native community, as they relate to the educational and social prerogatives of the Tribes and Alaska Native entities.

(f) *Religious freedom.* Promote and respect the right to cultural practices and religious freedom for all students, consistent with Tribal and Alaska Native entities' wishes and with the provisions of the American Indian Religious Freedom Act (92 Stat. 469; Pub. L. 95–341; 42 U.S.C. 1996).

(g) *Tribal rights regarding governing bodies and planning.* (1) Develop in consultation with Tribes and Alaska Native entities a plan to include their direct involvement in short and long-range planning of Bureau operated post-secondary schools through the formation of policy making governing boards.

(2) Encourage and defend the right of the Tribes and Alaska Native entities to govern their own internal affairs in all matters relating to education, and their right to determine the equitable and appropriate composition of governing boards at Bureau off-reservation and post-secondary schools.

(h) *Multilingual education.* Provide for a comprehensive multicultural and multilingual educational program including the production and use of instructional materials, culturally appropriate methodologies and teaching and learning strategies that will reinforce, preserve and maintain Indian and Alaska Native languages, cultures, and histories which school boards, Tribes and Alaska Native entities may utilize at their discretion.

(i) *Choice of school.* Afford Indian and Alaska Native students the opportunity to attend local day schools and other schools of choice and the option to attend boarding schools when the student and parent or guardian determine it is in the student's best interest and consistent with the provisions of the Indian Child Welfare Act of 1978 (Pub. L. 95–608) except that, residential schools shall not be used as substitutes for providing adequate local family social services. Each school shall establish its attendance area in cooperation with neighboring schools.

(j) *Tribal education plans.* Assist Tribes and Alaska Native entities at their request in the development of Departments of Education, education codes, and comprehensive education plans.

(k) *Advocacy and coordination.* (1) Serve as an advocate for Indian Tribes and Alaska Native entities in education matters before the Federal, State and local governments.

(2) Assume an assertive role in coordinating comprehensive support for Indian and Alaska Native students internally and from other agencies in education, mental and physical health, juvenile justice, job training, including apprenticeship programs and other related Federal, State and local programs and services.

(3) Serve as an advocate and carry out responsibilities for Indian and Alaska Native students in public and other non-Bureau operated schools consistent with the wishes of the appropriate Indian Tribes and Alaska Native entities, particularly in regard to Impact Aid (Pub. L. 81–874), Johnson-O'Malley, and all Elementary and Secondary Education Act programs.

(l) *Student assessment.* Establish and maintain a program of research and development to provide accurate and culturally specific assessment instruments to measure student performance in cooperation with Tribes and Alaska Native entities.

(m) *Recruitment of Indians.* Adopt procedures to insure that qualified Indian and Alaska Native educators are recruited for positions appropriate to their cultural background and qualifications.

(n) *Priorities in contracts and grants.* Provide financial support through contracts, grants or other funding mechanisms with first priority given to the Tribes and Alaska Native entities, Tribal organizations, Tribally controlled community colleges, and Indian or Alaska Native professional or technical assistance organizations which have the sanction of the benefitting Tribes and Alaska Native entities.

(o) *Community school concept.* Promote the community school concept by encouraging year around multi-use of educational facilities, equipment and services for Tribal, Alaska Native village, and community development.

(p) *Education close to home.* Provide day and residential educational services as close to an Indian or Alaska Native student's home as possible, except when a student elects to attend a school elsewhere for specialized curricular offerings or services.

(q) *Tribal notification and involvement and program flexibility.* (1) Notify Indian Tribes and Alaska Native entities of proposed, pending or final Federal legislation, appropriations, Solicitor's and Attorney General's opinions and court decisions affecting Indian and Alaska Native education for the purposes of information and consultation, providing them ready access at the local level to all evaluations, data records, reports and other relevant information, consistent with the provisions of the Privacy and Freedom of Information Acts.

(2) Implement rules, regulations, procedures, practices, and standards to insure flexibility in the exercise of local Tribal or Alaska Native village options, and provide for input in periodic reviews, evaluations, and revisions to meet changing needs and circumstances.

(r) *Career and higher education.* (1) Ensure to the extent possible that all students who choose to pursue career and post-secondary education, including but not limited to, undergraduate and graduate programs, or preparation for skilled trades, receive adequate academic or other preparation, at the schools of their choice, assuring that students are provided adequate support services to enable them to meet their educational goals.

(2) Extend to Tribes and Alaska Native entities the prerogative of determining those critical professions and fields of study in post-secondary education which are of the highest priority to meet their economic and cultural goals.

(s) *Planning, maintenance and use of facilities.* (1) Ensure that the needs of the students and Tribal or Alaska Native community will receive first priority in the planning, design, construction, operation and maintenance of Bureau schools and residential facilities, rather than other considerations, such as ease of maintenance, and that these facilities assure a supportive environment for learning, living and recreation.

(2) Maintain all school and residential facilities to meet appropriate Tribal, State or Federal safety, health and child care standards. If a conflict exists in these standards, the Federal standard shall be followed; in the absence of a Federal standard, the Tribal standard shall be followed. In case of conflict, any such Tribal health or safety standards shall be no greater than any otherwise applicable State standard.

(t) *Alternative, innovative and exemplary programs.* Vigorously encourage and support alternative, innovative and exemplary programs reflecting Tribal or Alaska Native village specific learning styles, including but not limited to, parent-based early childhood education programs, adult and vocational technical education, library and media services, special education including programs for handicapped, gifted and talented students, summer programs, and career development.

(u) *Training.* Provide support and technical assistance at all levels for the training of duly sanctioned Tribal and Alaska Native education representatives involved in educational decision-making, including pre-service and in-service training for educators.

(v) *Tribally controlled community colleges.* Assist Tribes and Alaska Natives in their planning, designing, construction, operation and maintenance of Tribally controlled community colleges, consistent with all appropriate legislation. (See part 41 of this subchapter.)

(w) *Equal opportunity.* Establish and enforce policies and practices to guarantee equal opportunity and open access to all Indian and Alaska Native students in all matters relating to their education programs consistent with the provisions of the Privacy and Freedom of Information Acts.

(x) *Accountability, evaluation of MIS.* (1) Enforce a strict standard of fiscal, programmatic and contract accountability to the Tribes and Alaska Native entities and assist them in the development of their own standards of accountability and carry out annual evaluations of all Bureau-operated or funded education programs.

(2) Provide and make available a computerized management information system which will provide statistical information such as, but not limited to, student enrollment, curriculum, staff, facilities, student assessments and related educational information.

(y) *Accreditation.* (1) Encourage and assist all Bureau and contract schools to attain appropriate State, regional, Tribal or national accreditation.

(2) Assist and promote the establishment of Indian regional and/or national accrediting associations for all levels of Indian Education.

(z) *Eligibility for services.* Serve Indian and Alaska Native students who are recognized by the Secretary of the Interior as eligible for Federal services, because of their status as Indians or

Alaska Natives, whose Indian blood quantum is ¼ degree or more. In the absence of other available facilities, children of non-Indian Bureau personnel or other non-eligibles may be served subject to the provisions of 25 U.S.C. 288 and 289.

(aa) *Appropriations.* Aggressively seek sufficient appropriations to carry out all policies herein established subject to the president's budget and the Department's budgetary process.

§ 32.5 Evaluation of implementation of Pub. L. 95–561.

The Director, Office Indian Education Programs will develop guidelines for evaluating all functional and programmatic responsibilities associated with title XI of the Education Amendments of 1978 (Pub. L. 95–561), and in the January 1, 1981 annual report, as provided in section 1136, of Pub. L. 95–561 include a statement of the specific program toward implementing these policies.

PART 33—TRANSFER OF INDIAN EDUCATION FUNCTIONS

Sec.

AUTHORITY: Sec. 1126, Pub. L. 95–561, Education Amendments of 1978 (92 Stat. 2143, 2391; 25 U.S.C. 2006).

SOURCE: 44 FR 58103, Oct. 9, 1979, unless otherwise noted. Redesignated at 47 FR 13327, Mar. 30, 1982.

§ 33.1 Definitions.

(a) *Agency* means that organizational unit of the Bureau which provides direct services to the governing body or bodies and members of one or more specified Indian Tribes.

(b) *Early childhood* means education activities serving the 0 to 8 year old child, including pre-natal, child care, kindergarten, homebase, homebound, and special education programs.

(c) *Elementary and secondary education* means those programs serving the child from grade one through grade twelve.

(d) *Operating level* means the organizational level at which direct educational services are performed.

(e) *Personnel directly and substantially involved* means those persons who provide services which affect the operation of Indian education programs, including (but not limited to) school or institution custodial or maintenance personnel, and whose services for Indian education programs require the expenditure of at least 51 percent of the employee's working time.

(f) *Post-secondary* means education programs that are provided for persons past the age for compulsory education to include continuing education, higher education, undergraduate and graduate, career and adult education. As used in this Act, the term Post-Secondary shall include those Bureau of Indian Affairs programs operated at Southwestern Indian Polytechnic Institute, the Institute of American Indian Arts, and Haskell Indian Junior College, and those operated at Tribally controlled community colleges under Pub. L. 95–471.

§ 33.2 Policy.

It is the policy of the Department of the Interior that:

(a) Indian control of Indian affairs in all matters relating to education shall be facilitated.

(b) Authority to perform education functions shall be delegated directly from the Assistant Secretary-Indian Affairs to the Director, Office of Indian Education Programs.

(c) Administrative authority shall be compatible with program authorities; and, both shall be delegated to the operating level to assure efficient and effective delivery of education services to Indian children, youth, and adults.

(d) The Director, Office of Indian Education Programs shall supervise the operation of Indian education program personnel at the Arena, Agency, and the three Bureau of Indian Affairs post-secondary institutions.

(e) Indian Education program functions to be performed at the Area office level shall include those dealing with higher education, Johnson-O'Malley aid to non-Bureau schools, off-reservation boarding schools, those education program operations serving tribes from more than one Agency except those at the three post-secondary institutions, on-reservation education functions located at an Agency where no educational personnel are assigned, education contract operations, and adult education.

§ 33.3 Delegation of authority.

The administrative and programmatic authorities of the Assistant Secretary—Indian Affairs pertaining to Indian education functions shall not be delegated to other than the Director, Office of Indian Education Programs. The Assistant Secretary shall publish delegations of authorities to the Director in the Bureau of Indian Affairs Manual after the effective date of these regulations.

§ 33.4 Redelegation of authority.

The authorities of the Assistant Secretary—Indian Affairs as delegated to the Director, Office of Indian Education Programs may be redelegated by the Director to a Bureau of Indian Affairs Agency Superintendent for Education, to a Bureau Area Education Programs Director, or to a President of a Bureau of Indian Affairs post-secondary education institution.

§ 33.5 Area education functions.

A Bureau Area Education Programs Director shall perform those Bureau of Indian Affairs education functions related to Johnson-O'Malley aid to non-Bureau schools, higher education, Bureau peripheral dormitories, adult education, off-reservation residential schools, on-reservation functions located at an Agency where no education personnel are assigned, education contract operations, and those education program operations serving Tribes from more than one Agency, except those of the Bureau's post-secondary institutions.

§ 33.6 Agency education functions.

A Bureau Agency Superintendent for Education shall perform those education functions related to elementary and secondary education, early childhood education, peripheral dormitories which have been supervised prior to Pub. L. 95–561, and exceptional education programs as defined in 25 CFR part 32. This section shall not be construed to remove higher education, adult education and/or Johnson-O'Malley programs currently administered at the Agency level. Further, the Director under the authority of § 33.4 will periodically review Area programs such as higher education, adult education, and Johnson-O'Malley for consideration to assign to Agency level administration.

§ 33.7 Implementing procedures.

(a) The Assistant Secretary—Indian Affairs shall:

(1) Implement the transfer for Indian education functions from the jurisdiction of Agency Superintendents and Area Office Directors to the Director, Office of Indian Education Programs.

(2) Modify existing descriptions of positions for Area Office Directors, Agency Superintendents, and all other personnel directly and substantially involved with the provisions of education services by the Bureau of Indian Affairs.

(b) The Director, Office of Indian Education Programs shall:

(1) For Area, Agency, and Bureau of Indian Affairs postsecondary institutional personnel:

(i) Properly list the duties of each employee required to perform functions redelegated by the Director;

(ii) Define the responsibilities for monitoring and evaluating education programs; and

(iii) Exercise supervision of these employees.

(2) Define responsibilities for employees providing technical and coordinating assistance for support services to the Director, Office of Indian Education Programs and his/her subordinates, including procurement, contracting, personnel, and other administrative support areas.

[44 FR 58103, Oct. 9, 1979. Redesignated at 47 FR 13327, Mar. 30, 1982, as amended at 49 FR 12702, Mar. 30, 1984]

§ 33.8 Realignment of area and agency offices.

The Assistant Secretary—Indian Affairs shall implement Bureau of Indian Affairs Area Office and Agency Office reorganizations required to structure these offices consistent with education program activities to be undertaken at those levels.

§ 33.9 Development of procedures.

The Director, Office of Indian Education Programs shall prepare and promulgate procedures to govern the provision of support services by the Bureau of Indian Affairs for the education function. These procedures shall be consistent with existing laws, regulations, Executive Orders, and Departmental policies governing administrative support services. These provisions shall be prepared in consultation with those personnel within the Bureau of Indian Affairs who are responsible to the Commissioner of Indian Affairs for providing support services.

§ 33.10 Issuance of procedures.

The Assistant Secretary—Indian Affairs, directly or through the Commissioner of Indian Affairs, shall issue procedures in the Bureau of Indian Affairs Manual governing the provision of support services to the Bureau's Education Office function.

PART 36—MINIMUM ACADEMIC STANDARDS FOR THE BASIC EDUCATION OF INDIAN CHILDREN AND NATIONAL CRITERIA FOR DORMITORY SITUATIONS

Subpart A—General Provisions

Subpart B—Educational Management

Subpart C—Minimum Program of Instruction

Subpart D—Student Instructional Evaluation

Subpart E—Instructional Support

Subpart F—Evaluation of Educational Standards

Subpart G—Homeliving Programs

AUTHORITY: Section 502, 25 U.S.C. 2001; section 5101, 25 U.S.C. 2001; Section 1101, 25 U.S.C. 2002; 5 U.S.C. 301; 25 U.S.C. 2 and 9; 25 U.S.C. 2901, Title I of P.L. 101–477.

SOURCE: 50 FR 36816, Sept. 9, 1985, unless otherwise noted.

Subpart A—General Provisions

§ 36.1 Purpose, scope, and information collection requirements.

(a) The purpose of this rule is to establish minimum academic standards for the basic education of Indian children for Bureau-operated schools and for those Indian-controlled contract schools which adopt these standards and to establish national criteria for dormitory situations for schools operated by the Bureau of Indian Affairs and for Indian-controlled contract schools operating dormitories.

(b) The information collection requirement contained in § 36.61(a) has been approved by the Office of Management and Budget under 44 U.S.C. 3507 and assigned clearance number 1076–0092. The information is being collected to evaluate waiver request(s) from tribal government(s) and school board(s). The information will be used to ascertain the approval of academic waiver request. The obligation to respond is mandatory under 25 U.S.C. 2001. The information collection requirements contained in §§ 36.71(g), 36.74(f), and 36.76(b) of this rule are not required to be approved by the Office of Management and Budget since less than ten persons or tribes are affected by the information collection requirement of this rule. However, when ten or more persons or tribes become affected by this requirement, the Bureau will submit an approval request.

[50 FR 36816, Sept. 9, 1985, as amended at 70 FR 21951, Apr. 28, 2005]

§ 36.2 Applicability.

The national criteria for dormitory situations established under subpart G serve as a minimum requirement and are mandatory for all Bureau-operated and Indian-controlled contract schools.

[77 FR 30891, May 24, 2012]

§ 36.3 Definitions.

For purposes of this part, the following definitions apply:

Accreditation means a school has received an official decision by the State(s) department(s) of education, or another recognized agency having official authority, that, in its judgment, the school has met the established standards of quality.

Agency means the current organizational unit of the Bureau which provides direct services to the governing body or bodies and members of one or more specified Indian tribes.

Agency school board as defined in sec. 1139(1), Pub. L. 95–561, means a body, the members of which are appointed by the school boards of the schools located within such Agency. The number of such members shall be determined by the Director in consultation with the affected tribes. In Agencies serving a single school, the school board of that school shall function as the Agency school board.

Agency Superintendent for Education means the Bureau official in charge of education functions at an Agency and to whom the school supervisor(s) and other educators under the Agency's jurisdiction report.

Area Education Programs Administrator means the Bureau official in charge of Bureau education programs and functions in a Bureau Area Office and is responsible for off-reservation residential schools, and, in some cases, peripheral dormitories and on-reservation day schools not receiving services from the Agency Superintendent for Education.

Assistant Secretary means the Assistant Secretary for Indian Affairs of the Department of the Interior.

Authentic assessment means the testing of higher order thinking skills by monitoring performance of tasks requiring analysis, creativity, and application skills in real life situations.

Average daily membership (ADM) means the aggregate days membership of a given school during a given reporting period divided by the number of days school is in session during this period. Only days on which the students are under the guidance and direction of teachers shall be considered as days in session. The reporting period is generally a given regular school term.

Basic academic skills means the abilities acquired by observation, study, or experience in mental and/or physical performance (e.g., proficiency in planning and investigating, operational techniques, comprehension, organization, execution, remembrance and application of knowledge to acquire a desired result) basic to the mastery of school work or other activity.

Basic education means those components of education emphasizing literacy in language arts, mathematics, natural and physical sciences, history, and related social sciences.

Bureau means the Bureau of Indian Affairs of the Department of the Interior.

Certification means the general process by which the State or Agency authorized by the State adjudges and stipulates that an individual meets the established standards which are prerequisite to employment for a teacher or administrator in education.

Competency means having the requisite abilities, skills, or a specified level of mastery.

Computer literacy used here means the general range of skills and understanding needed to function effectively in a society increasingly dependent on computer and information technology.

Content area means the usual school subjects of instruction, such as: Language arts, mathematics, science, social studies, fine arts, practical arts, health, and physical education.

Counselor means a staff member, including those in both academic and dormitory situations, who helps the students to understand educational, personal, and occupational strengths and limitations; to relate abilities, emotions, and aptitudes to educational and career opportunities; to utilize abilities in formulating realistic plans; and to achieve satisfying personal and social development.

Course of study means a written guide prepared by administrators, supervisors, consultants, and teachers of a school system or school, as an aid to teaching a given course or an aspect of subject-matter content to a given category of pupil.

Criterion-referenced test means an achievement test designed to measure specific skills within a subject area. Test results indicate which skills a student has or has not learned.

Days means calendar days.

Director means the Director of the Office of Indian Education Programs in the Bureau.

Dormitory means a facility which provides students boarding and lodging on a temporary residential basis for the purpose of attending a Bureau-operated or Indian-controlled contract or public school.

Dormitory manager means a staff member who manages the day-to-day, 24-hour operation of one or more dormitories.

Elementary school is defined as any combination of grades K–8 except when any of these grades are included in the junior high or middle school level.

Exceptional child program means a program for students who are eligible to receive education and related services as defined by 25 CFR 39.11(i).

Feeder school means a school whose exiting students are absorbed by a school offering instruction on the next higher grade level.

Formative evaluation is an evaluation of progress during the implementation of a program. Its purpose is to provide immediate feedback on results to enable modifying the processes used in order to enhance success and prevent failure.

Goals means a statement of what the school system is attempting to do to meet the comprehensive educational needs and interests of its pupils, in accordance with its statement of philosophy.

Grade means the portion of a school program which represents the work of one regular school year; identified by a designation such as kindergarten, grade 1 or grade 10.

Grade level is a designation applied to that portion of the curriculum which represents the work of one regular school year.

High school is defined as grades nine through twelve, except when grade nine is included in the junior high or middle school organizational unit.

Higher order thinking skills (or advanced skills) means skills such as reading comprehension, written composition, and mathematical reasoning. They differ from basic or discrete skills such as phonetic decoding and arithmetic operations.

Indian-controlled contract school means a school that is operated by a tribal organization and funded under a contract with the Bureau.

Indian student means a student who is a member of an Indian tribe and is one-quarter (1/4) or more degree of Indian blood quantum.

Indian tribe or *tribe* means any Indian tribe, band, nation, rancheria, pueblo, colony or community, including any Alaska Native village or regional or village corporation as defined in or established pursuant to the Alaska Native Claims Settlement Act (85 Stat. 688), which is recognized as eligible for the special programs and services provided by the United States to Indians because of their status as Indians.

Intense residential guidance means the program for residential students who need special residential services due to one or more of the problems as stated in 25 CFR 39.11(h).

Junior high or *middle school* is defined as grades seven and eight, but may include grade six when it is not included in the elementary school level and/or grade nine when it is not included in the high school level.

Kindergarten means a group of students or a class that is organized to provide educational experiences for children for the year immediately preceding the first grade.

Librarian means a certificated school employee whose principal responsibilities include selection, acquisition, preparation, cataloging, and circulation of books and other printed materials; planning the use of the library by teachers and students; and instructing students in the use of library books and materials, whether the library is maintained separately or as a part of an instructional materials center.

Local school board when used with respect to a Bureau-operated school means a body chosen in accordance with the laws of the tribe to be served or, in the absence of such laws, the body elected by the parents of the Indian children attending a Bureau-operated school. In schools serving a substantial number of students from different tribes, the members shall be appointed by the governing bodies of the tribes affected and the number of such members shall be determined by the Director in consultation with the affected tribes.

Objectives means a statement of the general, long-range aims and the specific, short-range aims which indicate what the school is attempting to do to meet the needs of the students in accordance with the philosophy, goals, and policies of the school system.

Paraprofessional means a staff member who works with and is under the supervision of a professional staff member but who does not have full professional status, e.g., teacher aide. The term denotes a level of knowledge and skills possessed by an individual or required of an individual to perform an assignment. The level of skills is usually at a predetermined minimum level.

Parent means a natural parent or guardian or a person legally acting as parent.

Peripheral dormitory is a facility which provides students boarding and lodging during the school year for the purpose of attending a public school.

Regular program student means all students including those determined to be eligible for services as defined under the Exceptional Child Program, 25 CFR 39.11(i).

Residential school means an educational institution in which students are boarded and lodged as well as taught.

Residential Services under Exceptional Child Program means a program providing specialized residential care as determined by 25 CFR 39.11(i).

School means an educational institution, including elementary, junior high or middle, high school, peripheral, cooperative, and contract schools serving students in grades Kindergarten through 12 and as further defined under 25 CFR 39.2(q).

School board means an Agency or local school board.

School day, instructional day, or *teaching day* is a day on which the school is open and students are under the guidance and direction of teachers in instructional activities where the minimum number of instructional hours are met.

School Supervisor means the official in charge of a school and/or peripheral dormitory who reports to an Agency School Superintendent or an Area Education Programs Administrator, as appropriate.

Secretary means the Secretary of the Interior.

Self-contained class means a class having the same teacher or team of teachers for all or most of the daily session.

Standard means the established criterion and/or specified requirement which must be met and maintained.

Summative evaluation means a systematic analysis of the results or products of a program after it is completed. Its purpose is to determine the extent to which the objectives of the program have or have not been achieved. One form of summative evaluation compares results with those of another "control" program using different procedures. Other forms compare results with past results or predetermined target outcomes.

Teacher means a certified staff member performing assigned professional activities in guiding and directing the learning experiences of pupils in an instructional situation.

Unit/Unit of instruction means a major subdivision of instruction generally composed of several topics including content and learning experiences developed around a central focus such as a limited scope of subject matter, a central program, one or more related concepts, one or more related skills, or a combination of these. One unit equals one full year of instruction in a subdivision thereof. *Unit* and *credit* shall be used interchangeably.

[50 FR 36816, Sept. 9, 1985, as amended at 59 FR 61765, Dec. 1, 1994]

Subpart B—Educational Management

§ 36.10 Standard I—Philosophy and goals.

(a) Each school shall develop a written mission statement and philosophy of education that addresses the accumulation of knowledge and development of skills, interests, appreciations, ideals, and attitudes within the school's total educational program. A statement of expected outcomes shall outline what the school is attempting to do to meet the needs and interests of its students and community in accordance with the school's mission statement and philosophy.

(b) The statement of philosophy and goals shall be developed with the involvement of students, parents, lay citizens, school staff, and tribe(s) and shall be formally adopted by the local school board.

(c) The philosophy and goals shall be reviewed annually and revised as necessary by each school.

(d) A copy of the philosophy and goals shall be submitted to the Agency Superintendent for Education or Area Education Programs Administrator, as appropriate.

(e) Informational provisions shall be developed in the form of a manual, handbook, brochure, or other written document(s) of the minimum academic standards of the school's programs and the basic rules and procedures of the school. The staff, students, and parents shall receive the written document or documents and have same explained to all who request explanation. The topics covered in the document(s) shall include but not be limited to the following:

(1) Statement of philosophy and goals;

(2) Description of how policies are developed and administered;

(3) A brief explanation of curricular offerings;

(4) A copy of student rights handbook;

(5) Basic practices related to:

(i) Grading system;

(ii) Graduation requirements, if applicable;

(iii) Attendance policies;

(iv) Special programs at the school; and

(v) Student activities available for students.

[50 FR 36816, Sept. 9, 1985, as amended at 59 FR 61765, Dec. 1, 1994]

§ 36.11 Standard II—Administrative requirements.

(a) *Staffing*. Each school shall, at a minimum, meet the following requirements:

(1) The overall school ratio of regular program students to regular program teachers in self-contained classrooms shall not exceed the following except under the conditions set forth in paragraphs (a)(4) (i) and (ii) of this section. Average daily membership (ADM) shall be used in meeting the following ratios.

Level	Ratio
Kindergarten	20:1
1st grade—3rd grade	22:1
4th grade—high school	25:1

(2) Multi-grade classrooms that cross grade-level boundaries (e.g., K–1, 3–4, etc.) shall use the maximum of the lower grade. In grades K–8, grades shall be consolidated to meet the teacher ratios listed above.

(3) The daily teaching load per teacher in departmentalized classes shall not exceed 150 students (ADM) except in activity type classes such as music and physical education.

(4) Schools exceeding these specific staffing ratios for over 30 consecutive days during one school year shall submit a justification for a request for a waiver to the Director, through the Agency Superintendent for Education or Area Education Programs Administrator, as appropriate, which may be approved for a period not to exceed one school year and for the following reasons:

(i) Additional classroom space is not available for establishing another class; or

(ii) The school, Agency, Area and Office of Indian Education Programs Applicant Supply File has been exhausted and the required teacher position cannot be filled. However, efforts to fill the vacancy shall be continued.

(5) Each school shall provide, in the absence of a regular teacher, a certified substitute teacher who meets the State substitute teacher qualifications. In the event that such a substitute is not available, coverage will be provided by a school employee designated by the school supervisor. A class cannot have as a teacher an employee without teaching credentials for more than 20 school days during any one school year.

(b) *Written school enrollment and attendance policies*. Each school shall have written school enrollment and attendance policies in compliance with and/or consistent with 25 CFR 31, Federal Schools for Indians, the statutes of the State, and tribal education ordinances.

(c) *Immunization*. School children shall be immunized in accordance with the regulations and requirements of the state in which they attend school or standards of the Indian Health Service.

[50 FR 36816, Sept. 9, 1985, as amended at 59 FR 61765, Dec. 1, 1994; 70 FR 21951, Apr. 28, 2005]

§ 36.12 Standard III—Program needs assessment.

The policy and procedures of each school and its curricula shall be developed and revised based on an assessment of educational needs. This needs assessment shall be conducted at least every seven (7) years at the same frequency as required in § 36.50, School Program Evaluation. This assessment shall include at least the following:

(a) A clear statement of student educational goals and objectives. A student educational goal is defined as a statement of the knowledge, skills, attitudes, or concepts students are expected to exhibit upon completion of a grade level. Student educational objectives are defined as statements of more specific knowledge, skills, attitudes, or concepts students must exhibit in order to achieve the goal.

(b) The collection of appropriate data from which valid determinations, judgments, and decisions can be made with respect to the status of the educational program, e.g.,

(1) Perceptions of the parents, tribes, educators, and the students with regard to the relevance and importance of the goals.

(2) The extent to which educational goals and objectives have been achieved.

(3) The data developed as a result of the evaluation outlined in § 36.50 School Program Evaluation.

(c) A statement of educational needs which identifies the difference between the current status of students and the desired goals for the students.

(d) A plan of action to remediate assessed needs.

§ 36.13 Standard IV—Curriculum development.

(a) Each school shall implement an organized program of curriculum development involving certified and noncertified staff and shall provide the opportunity for involvement by members of the local community.

(b) Curriculum development program activities shall be based on an analysis of school programs and shall be related to needs assessment and evaluation.

(c) Each school shall involve staff and provide the opportunity for involvement by the tribal community in planning programs, objectives, and activities which meet student/teacher needs.

Subpart C—Minimum Program of Instruction

§ 36.20 Standard V—Minimum academic programs/school calendar.

(a) If an emergency arises from an uncontrollable circumstance during the school day which results in the dismissal of students by the school administration, the day may be counted as a school day provided that three-fourths of the instructional hours are met.

(b) The educational program shall include multi-culture and multi-ethnic dimensions designed to enable students to function effectively in a pluralistic society.

(1) The school's language arts program shall assess the English and native language abilities of its students and provide instruction that teaches and/or maintains both the English and the primary native language of the school population. Programs shall meet local tribal approval.

(2) The school program shall include aspects of the native culture in all curriculum areas. Content shall meet local tribal approval.

(3) The school program shall assess the learning styles of its students and provide instruction based upon that assessment. The method for assessing learning styles shall be determined at the local level.

(4) The school program shall provide for at least one field trip per child per year to broaden social and academic experiences.

(c) All intraschool programs (e.g., library, instructional labs, physical education, music, etc.) which are directly related to or affect student instruction shall provide services from the beginning of the school term through the final class period at the close of the school term.

[50 FR 36816, Sept. 9, 1985, as amended at 59 FR 61765, Dec. 1, 1994; 70 FR 21951, Apr. 28, 2005]

§ 36.21 Standard VI—Kindergarten instructional program.

(a) The curriculum for kindergarten shall provide children with experiences which emphasize language development, native language where necessary as determined by 25 CFR 39.11(g), and performance of the requirements in paragraph (b) of this section. Such programs shall assist children in developing positive feelings toward themselves and others.

(b) A kindergarten instructional program shall include but not be limited to:

(1) Language (observing, listening, speaking).

(2) Exploration of the environment (number, space and time relationships, natural science).

(3) Psychomotor and socialization development.

(4) Development of imaginative and creative tendencies.

(5) Health education inclusive of the requirements contained in the Act of May 20, 1886, 24 Stat. 69.

§ 36.22 Standard VII—Elementary instructional program.

(a) The elementary instruction programs, grades one through six, shall include but need not be limited to:

(1) Language arts.

(2) Mathematics.

(3) Social studies.

(4) Sciences.

(5) Fine arts.

(6) Physical education.

(b) Each school shall integrate the following content areas into its curriculum:

(1) Career awareness,

(2) Environmental and safety education,

(3) Health education (includes requirements contained in 24 Stat. 69),

(4) Metric education, and

(5) Computer literacy.

§ 36.23 Standard VIII—Junior high/ middle school instructional program.

(a) The instructional program shall reflect the school's philosophy and the needs of the students and the community. It shall be part of a progressive development that begins in the elementary program which precedes it and continues to the secondary program which follows.

(b) The curriculum shall include the following required instructional content areas at each grade level but need not be limited to:

(1) *Language arts.* One unit shall be required of each student every year.

(2) *Social studies.* One unit shall be required of each student every year.

(3) *Mathematics.* One unit shall be required of each student every year.

(4) *Science.* One unit shall be required of each student every year.

(5) *Fine arts and practical arts.* One unit each shall be required of each student in the junior high/middle school instructional program.

(6) *Computer literacy.* One unit shall be required of each student in the junior high/middle school instructional program.

(7) *Physical education.* One unit shall be required of each student in the junior high/middle school instructional program.

(c) The following content areas shall be integrated into the curriculum.

(1) Career exploration and orientation.

(2) Environmental and safety education.

(3) Metric education.

(4) Consumer economics (including personal finances).

(5) Health education (includes meeting the requirements contained in 24 Stat. 69).

(d) Languages other than English are encouraged to be offered as a content area beginning at junior high/middle school level.

(e) Student enrollment in any laboratory or vocational exploration class shall be consistent with applicable health and safety standards.

§36.24 Standard IX—Secondary instructional program.

(a) The secondary instructional program shall reflect the philosophy of the student, tribe, community, and school, and an awareness of the changing world.

(b) The secondary instructional curriculum shall include the following content areas:

(1) Language arts (communication skills).

(2) Sciences.

(3) Mathematics.

(4) Social studies.

(5) Fine arts and practical arts.

(6) Physical education.

(7) Languages other than English.

(8) Driver education. (See guidelines available from the applicable State Department of Education.)

(9) *Vocational education.* Curriculum shall be designed and directly related to actual occupational trends (national, regional, and local) and to introduce and familiarize students with various occupations in technology, industry and business, as well as required special skills and the training requisites. Programs shall be directed toward assisting students in making career choices and developing consumer skills and may include the following:

(i) Vocational exploration,

(ii) Vocational skill development, and

(iii) School/on-the-job cooperative education programs.

(c) The following shall be integrated into the curriculum:

(1) Consumer economics (including personal finances),

(2) Metric education,

(3) Safety education, and

(4) Health education. (In addition, the program shall meet the requirements contained in 24 Stat. 69.)

(d) The high school program shall provide program coordination with feeder schools, career direction, and preparation for the student entering independent living through employment, post-secondary education, and/or marriage.

(e) Yearly class schedules shall take into account the graduation requirements of each student.

(f) Student enrollment in any laboratory or vocational class shall be consistent with applicable health and safety standards.

(g) Schools are encouraged to provide alternative programs that lead to high school completion for secondary students who do not function successfully in the regular academic setting.

[50 FR 36816, Sept. 9, 1985, as amended at 59 FR 61765, Dec. 1, 1994]

Subpart D—Student Instructional Evaluation

§36.30 Standard X—Grading requirements.

(a) Each school shall implement a uniform grading system which assesses a student's mastery of the prescribed objectives of the courses of study undertaken. The mastery of prescribed course objectives shall be the primary measure of academic attainment for reporting student grades on report cards.

(b) The information derived from student instructional evaluations shall be shared with the student and with the parents and shall be used to give teachers and students direction for subsequent learning activities.

(c) Parent/teacher and parent/teacher/student conferences focused on the student's instructional progress and development shall be held, where feasible and practical, to provide an additional means of communication between home and school. Residential schools may meet this standard by documenting the communication of student grades on report cards to parents.

(d) Each school shall issue a report card to parents of students who are under the age of eighteen (18) and to students eighteen (18) years of age and older on a regular basis, but not less than four (4) times yearly. The report card shall include, but not be limited to, the following sections:

(1) Recommendations and probable promotion status;

(2) Appropriate signatures and request for return of report cards; and

(3) Student attendance record.

(e) A summary of each year's final card shall become part of the student's permanent school record.

§36.31 Standard XI—Student promotion requirements.

Each school shall establish and implement a promotion policy which shall be submitted to and approved by the local school board and Agency Superintendent for Education or Area Education Programs Administrator, as appropriate. The requirements shall include, but not be limited to, the following:

(a) Each grade level or equivalent shall have a minimum criteria for student promotion based primarily on measurable mastery of the instructional objectives.

(b) Criterion-referenced tests that evaluate student skills shall be utilized for measuring the mastery of instructional objectives. The evaluation results shall form the basis for the promotion of each student.

(c) A student who has not participated, either directly or through approved alternative instructional methods or programs, in a minimum of 160 instructional days per academic term or 80 instructional days per semester without a written excused absence shall not be promoted. A school board or a school committee may review a promotion decision and, if warranted due to compelling and/or extenuating circumstances, rescind in writing such action on a case-by-case basis. Alternative instructional methods shall be submitted in writing for approval by the Agency Superintendent for Education or Area Education Programs Administrator, as appropriate.

§36.32 Standard XII—Graduation requirements for a high school diploma.

Graduation requirements contained under this section shall be applied beginning with the graduating class of the 1987–88 school year.

(a) Satisfactory completion of a minimum number of units shall be the measure for the issuance of a high school diploma.

(b) To graduate, a student shall earn 20 units in a four year high school program unless the state in which the school is located exceeds these requirements, in which case the state's requirements shall apply; fifteen (15) units shall be required as follows:

(1) Language arts—four (4) units.

(2) Mathematics—three (3) units.

(3) Social studies—three (3) units.

(i) One (1) unit in United States history;

(ii) One-half (½) unit in civics/government;

(iii) One-half (½) unit in tribal history/government;

(iv) One-half (½) unit in Indian studies; and

(v) One-half (½) unit in any other social studies;

(4) Science—two (2) units.

(i) One (1) unit in the general science area.

(ii) One (1) unit in laboratory science areas, i.e., chemistry, physics, biology, zoology, laboratory anatomy.

(5) Physical education—one (1) unit.

(6) Practical arts—one (1) unit. Credit in any vocational course may also be used to satisfy this required unit.

(7) Fine arts—one (1) unit. Music, art, dance, drama, theatre, and other fine arts courses may be used to satisfy this required unit. These are minimum requirements; local schools may establish academic or vocational requirements beyond those prescribed by these standards.

(c) A school with an average enrollment of fewer than 75 students may offer subjects in alternate years. If schools use this pattern, alternating pairs of subjects shall be listed and approved by the Agency Superintendent for Education or Area Education Programs Administrator, as appropriate.

(d) Credits earned through approved correspondence or extension study may be accepted if such credits are from schools approved or accredited by the state in which they are located or by a college or university which is regionally accredited for such purposes.

(e) Students who successfully complete the requirements of the High School Proficiency Examination in the State in which the school is located shall receive an endorsement so stating on their diplomas.

Subpart E—Instructional Support

§36.40 Standard XIII—Library/media program.

(a) Each school shall provide a library/media program which shall, as a minimum, meet the applicable state and/or regional standards, but shall not be limited to these, and shall include the following:

(1) A written set of instructional and service objectives shall be established that is integrated and consistent with the school's educational goals and philosophy. The librarian or educational media specialist, with students and staff, shall set objectives based on assessed academic and residential needs. The program and services will be evaluated yearly by the principal and the librarian or educational media specialist to determine the degree to which all objectives have been met.

(2) A written policy for the selection of materials and equipment shall be developed by a library committee in collaboration with the librarian and be approved by the school board. The collection of materials shall include as a minimum the following:

(i) A collection of books suitable for the range of student abilities and interests being served in the following ADM ratios.

(A) Elementary K–6, 15 books per student

(B) Middle 7–8, 12 books per student

(C) Secondary 9–12, 10 books per student

It is required that materials pertaining to Indian Tribes and/or Alaskan Natives be integrated within this basic collection.

(ii) Eight (8) to 12 percent of the basic collection must be composed of reference books, currently relevant and in a state of good physical condition, for practical use. Single copies of the principal textbooks used to complement instruction shall be in the collection, but textbooks cannot be counted toward this standard.

(iii) A periodical collection, suitable for the range of student abilities and interests being served, consisting of one (1) periodical for every ten (10) students, shall be maintained. Schools of over 200 will have a base collection of 20 periodicals.

(iv) A professional collection for the school staff shall be developed and maintained by the librarian in cooperation with a faculty committee.

(v) A variety of audio-visual materials, suitable for the range of instruction being provided, of at least 750 items or five (5) items for each student, whichever is larger, and inclusive of materials located in the classrooms shall be maintained. This category includes some of each of the following: Tactile objects, globes, models, maps, films, film-strips, microforms, slides, audio and video tapes, recordings, transparencies and graphics, and the equipment to use all of these. Multiple items within a specific set of materials will be counted as separate items.

(3) There shall be a library media center serviced by a librarian. Schools with fewer than 200 students are encouraged, wherever feasible, to cooperate in sharing librarian resources. Schools within an Agency and/or Area may cooperatively share the costs and services of a librarian who shall facilitate sharing of the combined available resources among the cooperating schools in accordance with the following ratios:

School Enrollment (ADM)

Up to 100—1/5 time librarian

101–200—1/5 time librarian and 1/2 time library aide or 20 hours of library activity

201–400—1 full-time librarian or 2/5 time librarian provided the school has a full-time library aide

401 + —1 full-time librarian and a full-time library aide

(4) All libraries must conduct an annual inventory of available books, materials, and equipment in accordance with the acquisitions and selection policies.

§ 36.41 Standard XIV—Textbooks.

(a) Each school shall establish a textbook review committee composed of teachers, parents, and students, and school board members. Appointment to the textbook review committee shall be subject to school board approval.

(b) The textbook review committee shall establish a procedure and criteria for the annual review of textbooks and other materials used to complement instruction. The criteria shall include, but not be limited to, the following:

(1) The textbook content shall meet the course objectives which are within the adopted school curriculum.

(2) The textbooks shall, as much as possible, reflect cultures accurately.

(3) The textbooks shall be current, in good physical condition, and varied in reading levels.

(c) Each school shall equitably distribute instructional materials to all classrooms. Each school shall inventory all property and equipment annually prior to requisitioning additional materials. Copies of the inventory shall be kept on file by the school staff.

§ 36.42 Standard XV—Counseling services.

Each school shall offer student counseling services concerned with physical, social, emotional, intellectual, and vocational growth for each individual. Counseling services shall be included in a school-wide assessment program.

(a) Each Agency and Area, as appropriate, shall institute and supervise an assessment program for its schools in order to provide for the objective assessment of student academic performance. Required formal tests shall be administered annually to all regular program students in grades 4, 8, and 12. (The testing of special education and gifted/talented students shall be in accordance with respective regulations.) If required by state certification standards, schools may use the state mandated academic achievement tests and accompanying requirements. These formal tests and their subtest contents, as well as the test-related procedures, shall include, but not be limited to, the following:

(1) Each Spring, schools shall conduct testing for grades 4, 8, and 12 using a current version of a standardized academic achievement test based upon the national assessment standards designed to assess higher order thinking skills. All schools shall keep a current record, with the Office of Indian Education Programs, of the test the school administers each Spring and the testing dates.

(2) Schools shall use some form of performance-based or authentic assessment in addition to standardized achievement testing.

(3) Each school shall report the summative results of its assessment program to its respective Agency or Area, as appropriate, and its school board.

(4) Parents/guardians shall be informed of their children's assessment results and provided with an explanation and interpretation to ensure adequate understanding of the results.

(5) Each school's instructional program shall establish an ongoing student academic assessment program to ensure that defined assessment procedures are in place. The program shall include regular training in basic assessment procedures and routines for all teachers and other staff involved in student assessment.

(6) Each Agency and Area, as appropriate, shall report the results of each school's formal Spring tests to the Office of Indian Education Programs by August 1 of each year. Summative information from performance-based and authentic assessments shall be reported at the same time.

(b) Each counseling program shall provide the following:

(1) Each school having a minimum school ADM of 200 students shall make provisions for the full-time professional services of a counselor, and each school enrolling fewer than 200 students shall make provisions for a part-time professional counselor.

(2) The counselors shall be familiar with the unique tribal, social, and economic characteristics of students.

(3) The counseling program shall contain the following:

(i) A written referral procedure;

(ii) Counseling techniques and documentation procedures to provide for the career, academic, social, and personal needs of the students which are based on the cultural beliefs and values of the students being served;

(iii) Preventative and crisis counseling on both individual and group bases;

(iv) Confidentiality and security of counseling records for each student; and

(v) Design and implementation of orientation programs to facilitate the pupil's transition from elementary to junior high/middle school and from junior high/middle school to high school.

(vi) Each junior or middle school and high school student shall receive academic counseling a minimum of twice yearly during which time the counselor shall assist the student in developing a written academic and career plan based on ability, aptitude, and interests. Additionally, counselors will assist high school students in selecting courses which satisfy the school's and the state's graduation requirements and the student's academic and career plan. Further, seniors will be given aid in completing registration and/or financial assistance applications for either vocational or academic post-secondary institutions.

(vii) Each high school counseling program shall be required to have on file for each student a planned academic program of studies which is available from the regular course offerings of the school to meet the student's career objectives and which will show that the student has received counseling.

[50 FR 36816, Sept. 9, 1985, as amended at 59 FR 61766, Dec. 1, 1994]

§ 36.43 Standard XVI—Student activities.

All schools shall provide and maintain a well-balanced student activities program based on assessment of both student and program needs. Each activity program shall help develop leadership abilities and provide opportunities for student participation but not be limited to activities that include special interest clubs, physical activities, student government, and cultural affairs. The activity program shall be an integral part of the overall educational program.

(a) All student activities shall be required to have qualified sponsors and be approved by the school supervisor, and the school board shall approve the overall activity plan. A qualified sponsor is a professional staff member of the school that is given responsibility to provide guidance or supervision for student activities.

(b) A plan of student activity operations shall be submitted, by each activity at the beginning of each school year, to the school supervisor. The plan will include the purpose, structure, coordination, and planned types of fund-raising activities.

(c) School may participate in interscholastic sports and activities on an informal or formal basis. On an informal basis, the Bureau-operated schools will coordinate with other schools in setting up a schedule of sports and games. Schools that participate in state-recognized leagues will abide by those state rules regulating inter-school competition.

(d) Until comparable competitive opportunities are provided to all students, regardless of sex, no student shall be barred from participation in interscholastic competition in noncontact sports except on the basis of individual merit.

(e) Residential schools shall plan and provide an intramural program for all students. The program shall include a variety of scholastic and sport activities.

(f) Students shall be involved only in activities which are sanctioned by the school.

(g) All student activities involved only in fund raising are required to establish a school/student activity bank account following school/student banking procedures outlined under 25 CFR 31.7. All student activity accounts shall be audited annually.

(h) The school shall provide for the safety and welfare of students participating in school-sponsored activities.

(i) Each sponsor of a student activity will be given orientation and training covering the responsibilities of a sponsor by the school supervisor.

Subpart F—Evaluation of Educational Standards

§ 36.50 Standard XVII—School program evaluation and needs assessment.

Each school shall complete a formal, formative evaluation at least once every seven (7) years beginning no later than the second complete school year following the effective date of this part. Schools shall follow state and/or regional accreditation, or accreditation requirements equal to the state in which a school is located. Each school shall follow the prescribed evaluation cycle. The primary purpose of this evaluation will be to determine the effects and quality of school programs and to improve the operations and services of the school programs.

(a) Each school's evaluation design or model will provide objective and quantitative analysis of each area to be evaluated. The analysis shall include product and process evaluation methods. The areas to be reviewed will include, but not be limited to, the following:

(1) School philosophy and objectives.

(2) Administrative and organizational requirements.

(3) Program planning and implementation.

(4) Curriculum development and instruction.

(5) Primary education.

(6) Program of studies for elementary, junior high/middle, and high schools.

(7) Grading requirements.

(8) Promotion requirements.

(9) High school graduation requirements.

(10) Library/media.

(11) Textbooks and other instructional materials.

(12) Counseling services.

(13) Medical and health services.

(14) Student activities.

(15) Transportation services.

(16) Staff certification and performance.

(17) Facilities (school plant).

(18) Parent and community concerns.

(19) School procedures and policies.

(20) School board operations.

(b) The Director, within six (6) months from the effective date of this part, shall distribute to each school, Agency or Area, as appropriate, a standardized needs assessment and evaluation instrument with guidelines for developing and applying a locally appropriate evaluation model for carrying out the requirements of this standard.

§36.51 Standard XVIII—Office of Indian Education Programs and Agency monitoring and evaluation responsibilities.

(a) The Office of Indian Education Programs shall monitor and evaluate the conformance of each Agency or Area, as appropriate, and its schools with the requirements of this part. In addition, it shall annually conduct onsite monitoring at one-third of the Agencies and Areas, thereby monitoring onsite each Agency and/or Area at least once every three (3) years. Within 45 days of the onsite visit, the Director shall issue to each Agency Superintendent for Education or Area Education Programs Administrator, as appropriate, a written report summarizing the monitoring findings and ordering, as necessary, required actions to correct noted deficiencies.

(b) Each Agency or Area, as appropriate, in conjunction with its school board shall monitor and evaluate the conformance of its school with the requirements of this part through an annual onsite evaluation involving one-third of the schools annually, thereby monitoring onsite each school at least once every three (3) years. Within 30 days of the onsite visit, the Agency Superintendent for Education or Area Education Programs Administrator, as appropriate, shall issue to the local school supervisor and local school board a written report summarizing the findings and ordering, as necessary, required actions to correct noted deficiencies.

(c) Schools, Agencies, and Areas shall keep such records and submit to the responsible official or designee accurate reports at such times, in such form, and containing such information as determined by that official to be necessary to ascertain conformance with the requirements of this part.

(d) Schools, Agencies, and Areas shall permit access for examination purposes by the responsible official, or any duly authorized designee, to any school records and other sources of information which are related or pertinent to the requirements of this part.

(e) The Office of Indian Education Programs, Agency Superintendent for Education, or Area Education Programs Administrator, as appropriate, shall annually conduct a summative evaluation to assess the degree to which each Bureau educational policy and administrative procedure assists or hinders schools in complying with the requirements of this part. This will include, but not be limited to, the following actions:

(1) Evaluate current policies and practices not related to this part and the effects thereof on the amount of

time and resources required which otherwise would be available for these standards;

(2) Modify any policies and practices which interfere with or compromise a school's capability to achieve and maintain these standards;

(3) Invite non-Federal agencies to evaluate the effects current policies and procedures have had on complying with the requirements of this part; and

(4) Submit annually to the Director a copy of the summative evaluation.

Subpart G—Homeliving Programs

AUTHORITY: 25 U.S.C. 13; 25 U.S.C. 2008; Pub. L. 107–110 (115 Stat. 1425).

SOURCE: 72 FR 68498, Dec. 5, 2007, unless otherwise noted.

§36.70 What terms do I need to know?

The following definitions apply to this subpart:

Behavioral health professional means a State licensed or State certified Social Worker, School Counselor, Drug and Alcohol Counselor, School Psychologist, or School Psychometrist responsible for coordinating a broad range of needs including:

(1) Support groups;

(2) Individual counseling;

(3) Crisis intervention;

(4) Preventive activities; and

(5) Coordination of referrals and outside services with appropriate providers.

Behavioral Health Program means a homeliving based service designed to decrease barriers to learning or increase positive, personal well-being by:

(1) Providing early intervention services, coordinating crisis intervention and prevention services;

(2) Promoting a positive social and emotional environment;

(3) Reducing the incidence of problems; and

(4) Referring students with behavioral needs that require professional medical care to an appropriate residential care facility.

Behavioral health services means the services provided by a school behavioral health program as defined in this section.

Homeliving Manager means the employee responsible for direct supervision of the homeliving program staff and students.

Homeliving Program means a program that provides room and board in a boarding school or dormitory to residents who are either:

(1) Enrolled in and are current members of a public school in the community in which they reside; or

(2) Members of the instructional program in the same boarding school in which they are counted as residents and:

(i) Are officially enrolled in the residential program of a Bureau-operated or funded school; and

(ii) Are actually receiving a homeliving program provided to all students who are provided room and board in a boarding school or dormitory.

Homeliving Program Staff means the employee(s) responsible for direct supervision of students in the homeliving area.

Homeliving Supervisor means the employee with overall administrative responsibility for supervising students, programs, and personnel in the homeliving area.

§36.71 What is the purpose of this part?

The purpose of this part is to establish standards for homeliving programs.

STAFFING

§36.75 What qualifications must homeliving staff possess?

(a) Homeliving staff must possess the qualifications shown in the following table:

Position	Required training
(1) Homeliving Supervisor.	Must be qualified based on size and complexity of the school, but at minimum possess a bachelor's degree.
(2) Homeliving Manager.	Must be qualified based on the size and complexity of the student body but must at a minimum have an associate's degree no later than 2008.
(3) Homeliving Program Staff.	Must have at least 32 post-secondary semester hours (or 48 quarter hours) in an applicable academic discipline, including fields related to working with children, such as, child development, education, behavioral sciences and cultural studies.

(b) A person employed as a homeliving program staff:

(1) Should meet the requirements of paragraph (a) of this section by the 2009–2010 school year; and

(2) May, upon showing good cause, petition the school supervisor (or the homeliving supervisor for peripheral dorms) for a waiver from the new qualifications.

§36.76 Who is in charge of all homeliving operations?

One staff member who has the authority to ensure the successful functioning of all phases of the homeliving program should be designated as in charge of all homeliving operations. All staff should be advised of the lines of authority through an organizational chart approved by the local board responsible for operations of the homeliving program.

§36.77 What are the homeliving staffing requirements?

Homeliving programs must meet the staffing requirements of this section.

(a) Effective with the 2009–2010 school year, each homeliving program must maintain the following student minimum supervisory requirements on weekdays:

Grade level	Time of day	Ratio
Elementary (Grade 1–6)	Morning	1:20.
	During school	As school needs.
	Evening	1:20.
	Night	1:40.
High School (Gr. 7–12)	Morning	1:20.
	During school	As school needs.
	Evening	1:30.
	Night	1:50.

(b) The following staffing ratios apply on weekends:

Grade level	Time of day	Ratio
Elementary (Grade 1–6)	Morning/day	1:20.
	Evening	1:20.
	Night	1:40.
High School (Gr. 7–12)	Morning/day	1:40.
	Evening	1:40.
	Night	1:50.

§36.78 What are the staffing requirements for homeliving programs offering less than 5 nights service?

For homeliving programs providing less than 5 nights service, the staffing levels from 36.77 apply. To fill this requirement, the program must use only employees who work a minimum of 20 hours per week.

§36.79 What are the homeliving behavioral professional staff/student ratio requirements?

Behavioral health professional(s) is necessary in homeliving programs to address issues, such as abuse, neglect, trauma, cultural conflict, and lack of school success. Each homeliving program must provide a minimum of one half-time behavioral health professional for every 50 students.

(a) The program may fill the staffing requirements of this section by using contract services, other agencies (including the Indian Health Service) or private/nonprofit volunteer service organizations.

(b) Off-reservation homeliving programs should consider providing one full-time behavioral health professional for every 50 students.

(c) For purposes of this section, a one half-time behavioral health professional is one that works for the homeliving program a minimum of 20 hours per week.

(d) For purposes of this section, in instances where the behavioral health services are obtained through other programs, the behavioral health professional must be available at the request of the homeliving program.

§36.80 If a school or dormitory has separated boys' and girls' homeliving programs, may the same behavioral professional be used for each program?

Yes, a program may use the same behavioral professional for both boys' and girls' programs. However, behavioral health staffing requirements are based on the combined enrollment during the homeliving count period.

§36.81 May a homeliving program use support staff or teachers to meet behavioral health staffing requirements?

No, a homeliving program must not use support staff or teachers to meet behavioral health staffing requirements. The only exception is if the individual support staff employee or teacher has the appropriate behavioral health license or certification.

§36.82 May behavioral health professional(s) provide services during the academic school day?

Behavioral health professional(s) must average at least 75 percent of their work hours with students in their dormitories. These work hours must occur outside of the academic school day, except in emergency situations as deemed by the administrative head of the homeliving program or designee. The purpose of this requirement is to maximize contact time with students in their homeliving setting.

§36.83 How many hours can a student be taken out of the academic setting to receive behavioral health services?

A student may spend no more than 5 hours per week out of the academic setting to receive behavioral health services from the homeliving behavioral health professional(s), except for emergency situations.

§36.84 Can a program hire or contract or acquire by other means behavioral health professionals to meet staffing requirements?

A program may hire or contract behavioral health professionals to meet staffing requirements or acquire such services by other means such as through a Memorandum of Understanding with other programs.

(a) At least one individual must be a licensed or certified school counselor or a social worker who is licensed/certified to practice at the location where the services are provided.

(b) For additional staffing, other individuals with appropriate certifications or licenses are acceptable to meet staffing requirements.

§36.85 Is a nurse required to be available in the evenings?

No, a program is not required to make a nurse (LPN or RN) available in the evenings. However, this is encouraged for homeliving programs with an enrollment greater than 300 or for programs that are more than 50 miles from available services.

§36.86 Are there staff training requirements?

(a) All homeliving program staff as well as all employees that supervise students participating in homeliving services and activities must have the appropriate certification or licensing requirements up to date and on file. Programs must provide annual and continuous professional training and development appropriate to the certification and licensing requirements.

(b) All homeliving program staff as well as all employees who supervise students participating in homeliving services and activities must receive annual training in the topics set out in this section before the first day of student occupancy for the year.

(1) First Aid/Safety/Emergency & Crisis Preparedness;

(2) CPR—Automated External Defibrillator;

(3) Student Checkout Policy;

(4) Confidentiality (Health Information Privacy Act and the Family Education Right to Privacy Act.);

(5) Medication Administration;

(6) Student Rights;

(7) Child Abuse Reporting Requirements and Protection Procedures; and

(8) Suicide Prevention.

(c) Homeliving staff as well as all employees that supervise students participating in homeliving services and activities must be given the following training annually:

(1) De-escalation/Conflict Resolution;

(2) Substance Abuse Issues;

(3) Ethics;

(4) Parenting skills/Child Care;

(5) Special Education and Working with Students with Disabilities;

(6) Student Supervision Skills;

(7) Child Development (recognizes various stages of development in the student population);

(8) Basic Counseling Skills; and

(9) Continuity of Operations Plan (COOP).

PROGRAM REQUIREMENTS

§36.90 What recreation, academic tutoring, student safety, and health care services must homeliving programs provide?

All homeliving programs must provide for appropriate student safety, academic tutoring, recreation, and health care services for their students, as deemed necessary by the local school board or homeliving board.

§ 36.91 What are the program requirements for behavioral health services?

(a) The homeliving behavioral health program must make available the following services:

(1) Behavioral Health Screening/Assessment;

(2) Diagnosis;

(3) Treatment Plan;

(4) Treatment and Placement;

(5) Evaluation; and

(6) Record of Services (if applicable, in coordination with the student's Individual Education Plan).

(b) Each homeliving behavioral health program must have written procedures for dealing with emergency behavioral health care issues.

(c) Parents or guardians may opt out of any non-emergency behavioral health services by submitting a written request.

(d) Parents or guardians must be consulted before a child is prescribed behavioral health.

(e) Medication in a non-emergency situation.

§ 36.92 Are there any activities that must be offered by a homeliving program?

Yes, a homeliving program must make available the following activities:

(a) One hour per day of scheduled, structured physical activity Monday through Thursday, and two hours of scheduled physical activities on the weekends for any students who are in residence on the weekends;

(b) One hour per day of scheduled, structured study at least four days per week for all students, and additional study time for students who are failing any classes;

(c) Tutoring during study time;

(d) Native language or cultural activities; and

(e) Wellness program that may include character, health, wellness, and sex education.

§ 36.93 Is a homeliving handbook required?

Yes, each program must publish a homeliving handbook, which may be incorporated into a general student handbook. During the first week the students and staff are in the dormitory, the homeliving program must:

(a) Provide each student with a copy of the handbook that contains all the provisions in 36.94;

(b) Provide all staff, students, and parents or guardians with a current and updated copy of student rights and responsibilities;

(c) Conduct an orientation for all students on the handbook and student rights and responsibilities; and

(d) Ensure that all students, school staff, and to the extent possible, parents and guardians confirm in writing that they have received a copy of and understand the homeliving handbook.

§ 36.94 What must a homeliving handbook contain?

A homeliving handbook must contain all of the following, and may include additional information:

(a) Mission/Vision Statement;

(b) Discipline Policy;

(c) Parent/Student Rights and Responsibilities;

(d) Confidentiality;

(e) Sexual Harassment Policy;

(f) Violence/Bullying Policy;

(g) Homeliving Policies and Procedures;

(h) Services Available;

(i) Personnel and Position Listing;

(j) Emergency Procedures and Contact Numbers;

(k) Bank Procedures;

(l) Transportation Policy;

(m) Check-Out Procedures;

(n) Dress Code;

(o) Drug/Alcohol Policy;

(p) Computer Usage Policy;

(q) Medication Administration Policy and Procedure; and

(r) Isolation/Separation Policy.

§ 36.95 What sanitary standards must homeliving programs meet?

Each homeliving program must meet all of the following standards:

(a) Restrooms, showers, and common areas must be cleaned daily;

(b) Rooms must be cleaned daily;

(c) Linens must be changed and cleaned weekly;

(d) Linens are to be provided;

(e) Basic Toiletries must be provided; and

(f) Functional washing machines and dryers must be provided.

§ 36.96 May students be required to assist with daily or weekly cleaning?

Yes, students can be required to assist with daily or weekly cleaning. However, the ultimate responsibility of cleanliness rests with the homeliving supervisor and local law or rules regarding chemical use must be followed.

§ 36.97 What basic requirements must a program's health services meet?

(a) A homeliving program must make available basic medical, dental, vision, and other necessary health services for all students residing in the homeliving program, subject to agreements between the BIE and the Indian Health Service or between a tribally-operated homeliving program and the Indian Health Service or tribal health program.

(b) A homeliving program must have written procedures for dealing with emergency health care issues.

(c) Parents or guardians may opt out of any non-emergency services by submitting a written request.

(d) The homeliving supervisor or designee must act *in loco parentis* when the parent or guardian cannot be found.

§ 36.98 Must the homeliving program have an isolation room for ill children?

Yes, the homeliving program must have an isolation room(s) available for ill students. The isolation room (or rooms, if needed) must be made available for use by students with contagious conditions. Contagious boys and girls should have separate rooms. The isolation room(s) should have a separate access to shower and restroom facilities. Students isolated for contagious illness must be supervised as frequently and as closely as the circumstances and protocols require, but at least every 30 minutes.

§ 36.99 Are immunizations required for residential program students?

Each student must have all immunizations required by State, local, or tribal governments before being admitted to a homeliving program. Annual flu shots are not required, but are encouraged.

§ 36.100 Are there minimum requirements for student attendance checks?

Yes, there are minimum requirements for student attendance checks as follows:

(a) All students must be physically accounted for four times daily;

(b) Each count must be at least two hours apart;

(c) If students are on an off-campus activity, physical accounts of students must be made at least once every two hours or at other reasonable times depending on the activity;

(d) At night all student rooms should be physically checked at least once every hour;

(e) If a student is unaccounted for, the homeliving program must follow its established search procedures; and

(f) When homeliving staff is aware of a student who is going to be absent from school, the homeliving program is required to notify the school.

§ 36.101 How often must students who have been separated for emergency health or behavioral reasons be supervised?

Students who have been separated for emergency behavioral or health reasons must be supervised as frequently and as closely as the circumstances and protocols require. No student will be left unsupervised for any period until such factors as the student's health based on a medical assessment, the safety of the student, and any other applicable guidance for dealing with behavior or health emergencies are considered.

§ 36.102 What student resources must be provided by a homeliving program?

The following minimum resources must be available at all homeliving programs:

(a) Library resources such as access to books and resource materials, including school libraries and public libraries which are conveniently available;

(b) A copy of each textbook used by the academic program or the equivalent for peripheral dorms; and

(c) Reasonable access to a computer with Internet access to facilitate homework and study.

§36.103 What are the requirements for multipurpose spaces in homeliving programs?

Homeliving programs must provide adequate areas for sleeping, study, recreation, and related activities.

§36.104 What are the requirements for heating, ventilation, cooling and lighting at dormitories?

(a) All dormitories must be designed to meet or exceed the standards for heating, ventilation, cooling, and lighting set out in the building codes in the Bureau of Indian Affairs "School Facilities Design Handbook," dated March 30, 2007, written and published by the Bureau of Indian Affairs Office of Facilities Management and Construction. The Director of the Federal Register has approved this incorporation by reference in accordance with 5 U.S.C. 552(a). To enforce any edition other than that specified in this section, the Bureau of Indian Affairs must publish notice of change in the FEDERAL REGISTER and the material must be available to the public

(1) You may obtain a copy of the Handbook at *http://www.bia.gov/cs/groups/xraca/documents/text/idc008030.pdf.* You can get answers to your questions from the Bureau of Indian Affairs Office of Facilities Management and Construction at: 1011 Indian School Road NW., Suite 335, Albuquerque, NM 87103; email: *OFECT@bia.gov;* Web site: *http://www.bia.gov/WhoWeAre/AS-IA/OFECR/index.htm.*

(2) You may inspect the Handbook at the Department of the Interior Library, Main Interior Building, 1849 C Street NW., Room 1151, Washington, DC 20240; telephone: (202) 208–3796. It is also available for inspection at the National Archives and Records Administration (NARA). For information on the availability of this material at NARA, call (202) 741–6030 or go to *http://www.archives.gov/federal_register/code_of_federal_regulations/ibr_locations.html.*

(b) If an existing dormitory does not comply with the standards in paragraph (a) of this section, we will classify the discrepancy as "deferred capital maintenance" for purposes of prioritizing correction of the discrepancy.

(c) The Bureau must publish in the FEDERAL REGISTER any proposal to change which building codes are included in the Bureau of Indian Affairs "School Facilities Design Handbook" or any successor document, and allow 120 days for public comment and consultation.

[77 FR 30891, May 24, 2012]

PRIVACY

§36.110 Must programs provide space for storing personal effects?

Yes, students are entitled to private personal spaces for storing their own personal effects, including at least one lockable closet, dresser drawer, or storage space. However, all drawers, dressers, storage space, or lockable space are the property of the homeliving program and are subject to random search.

WAIVERS AND ACCOUNTABILITY

§36.111 Can a tribe, tribal governing body, or local school board waive the homeliving standards?

A tribal governing body or local school board may waive some or all of the standards established by this part if the body or board determines that the standards are inappropriate for the needs of the tribe's students.

(a) If a tribal governing body or school board waives standards under this section, it must, within 60 days, submit proposed alternative standards to the Director, BIE.

(b) Within 90 days of receiving a waiver and proposal under paragraph (a) of this section, the Director must either:

(1) Approve the submission; or

(2) Deliver to the governing body or school board a written explanation of

the good cause for rejecting the submission.

(c) If the Director rejects a submission under paragraph (c) of this section, the governing body or school board may submit another waiver and proposal for approval. The standards in this part remain in effect until the Director approves alternative standards.

§ 36.112 Can a homeliving program be closed, transferred, consolidated, or substantially curtailed for failure to meet these standards?

No, a homeliving program cannot be closed, transferred to any other authority, consolidated, or its programs substantially curtailed for failure to meet these standards.

§ 36.120 What type of reporting is required to ensure accountability?

The homeliving program must provide to the appropriate local school board or alternative board such as a homeliving board, the tribal governing body, BIE, and the Secretary of the Interior, an annual accountability report within 45 days following the end of the school year consisting of:

(a) Enrollment figures identified by the homeliving count period;

(b) A brief description of programs offered;

(c) A statement of compliance with the requirements of this part and, if the program is not in compliance, recommendations for achieving compliance; and

(d) Recommendations to improve the homeliving program including identification of issues and needs.

PART 37—GEOGRAPHIC BOUNDARIES

Sec.

AUTHORITY: Public Law 107–110, 115 Stat. 1425.

SOURCE: 70 FR 22204, Apr. 28, 2005, unless otherwise noted.

§ 37.100 What is the purpose of this part?

(a) This part:

(1) Establishes procedures for confirming, establishing, or revising attendance areas for each Bureau-funded school;

(2) Encourages consultation with and coordination between and among all agencies (school boards, tribes, and others) involved with a student's education; and

(3) Defines how tribes may develop policies regarding setting or revising geographic attendance boundaries, attendance, and transportation funding for their area of jurisdiction.

(b) The goals of the procedures in this part are to:

(1) Provide stability for schools;

(2) Assist schools to project and to track current and future student enrollment figures for planning their budget, transportation, and facilities construction needs;

(3) Adjust for geographic changes in enrollment, changes in school capacities, and improvement of day school opportunities; and

(4) Avoid overcrowding or stress on limited resources.

§ 37.101 What definitions apply to the terms in this part?

Act means the No Child Left Behind Act, Public Law 107–110, enacted January 8, 2002. The No Child Left Behind Act reauthorizes and amends the Elementary and Secondary Education Act (ESEA) and the amended Education Amendments of 1978.

Bureau means the Bureau of Indian Affairs in the Department of the Interior.

Geographic attendance area means a physical land area that is served by a Bureau-funded school.

Geographic attendance boundary means a line of demarcation that clearly delineates and describes the limits of the physical land area that is served by a Bureau-funded school.

Secretary means the Secretary of the Interior or a designated representative.

§ 37.102 How is this part organized?

This part is divided into three subparts. Subpart A applies to all Bureau-funded schools. Subpart B applies only to day schools, on-reservation boarding schools, and peripheral dorms—in other words, to all Bureau-funded schools except off-reservation boarding schools. Subpart C applies only to off-reservation boarding schools (ORBS).

§ 37.103 Information collection.

Notwithstanding any other provision of law, no person is required to respond to, nor shall any person be subject to a penalty for failure to comply with, a collection of information subject to the requirements of the Paperwork Reduction Act of 1995 (44 U.S.C. 3501 *et seq.*) (PRA), unless that collection of information displays a currently valid Office of Management and Budget (OMB) Control Number. This part involves collections of information subject to the PRA in §§ 37.122(b), and 37.123(c). These collections have been approved by OMB under control number 1076–0163.

Subpart A—All Schools

§ 37.110 Who determines geographic attendance areas?

The Tribal governing body or the Secretary determines geographic attendance areas.

§ 37.111 What role does a tribe have in issues relating to school boundaries?

A tribal governing body may:

(a) Establish and revise geographical attendance boundaries for all but ORB schools;

(b) Authorize ISEP-eligible students, residing within the tribe's jurisdiction, to receive transportation funding to attend schools outside the geographic attendance area in which the student lives; and

(c) Authorize tribal member students who are ISEP-eligible and are not residing within the tribe's jurisdiction to receive transportation funding to attend schools outside the student's geographic attendance area.

§ 37.112 Must each school have a geographic attendance boundary?

Yes. The Secretary must ensure that each school has a geographic attendance area boundary.

Subpart B—Day Schools, On-Reservation Boarding Schools, and Peripheral Dorms

§ 37.120 How does this part affect current geographic attendance boundaries?

The currently established geographic attendance boundaries of day schools, on-reservation boarding schools, and peripheral dorms remain in place unless the tribal governing body revises them.

§ 37.121 Who establishes geographic attendance boundaries under this part?

(a) If there is only one day school, on-reservation boarding school, or peripheral dorm within a reservation's boundaries, the Secretary will establish the reservation boundary as the geographic attendance boundary;

(b) When there is more than one day school, on-reservation boarding school, or peripheral dorm within a reservation boundary, the Tribe may choose to establish boundaries for each;

(c) If a Tribe does not establish boundaries under paragraph (b) of this section, the Secretary will do so.

§ 37.122 Once geographic attendance boundaries are established, how can they be changed?

(a) The Secretary can change the geographic attendance boundaries of a day school, on-reservation boarding school, or peripheral dorm only after:

(1) Notifying the Tribe at least 6 months in advance; and

(2) Giving the Tribe an opportunity to suggest different geographical attendance boundaries.

(b) A tribe may ask the Secretary to change geographical attendance boundaries by writing a letter to the Director of the Office of Indian Education Programs, explaining the tribe's suggested changes. The Secretary must consult with the affected tribes before deciding whether to accept or reject a suggested geographic attendance boundary change.

(1) If the Secretary accepts the Tribe's suggested change, the Secretary must publish the change in the FEDERAL REGISTER.

(2) If the Secretary rejects the Tribe's suggestion, the Secretary will explain in writing to the Tribe why the suggestion either:

(i) Does not meet the needs of Indian students to be served; or

(ii) Does not provide adequate stability to all affected programs.

§ 37.123 How does a Tribe develop proposed geographic attendance boundaries or boundary changes?

(a) The Tribal governing body establishes a process for developing proposed boundaries or boundary changes. This process may include consultation and coordination with all entities involved in student education.

(b) The Tribal governing body may delegate the development of proposed boundaries to the relevant school boards. The boundaries set by the school boards must be approved by the Tribal governing body.

(c) The Tribal governing body must send the proposed boundaries and a copy of its approval to the Secretary.

§ 37.124 How are boundaries established for a new school or dorm?

Geographic attendance boundaries for a new day school, on-reservation boarding school, or peripheral dorm must be established by either:

(a) The tribe; or

(b) If the tribe chooses not to establish boundaries, the Secretary.

§ 37.125 Can an eligible student living off a reservation attend a school or dorm?

Yes. An eligible student living off a reservation can attend a day school, on-reservation boarding school, or peripheral dorm.

Subpart C—Off-Reservation Boarding Schools

§ 37.130 Who establishes boundaries for Off-Reservation Boarding Schools?

The Secretary or the Secretary's designee, in consultation with the affected Tribes, establishes the boundaries for off-reservation boarding schools (ORBS).

§ 37.131 Who may attend an ORBS?

Any student is eligible to attend an ORBS.

PART 38—EDUCATION PERSONNEL

Sec.

AUTHORITY: 25 U.S.C. 2011 and 2015, Secs. 1131 and 1135 of the Act of November 1, 1978, 92 Stat. 2322 and 2327; Secs. 511 and 512, Pub. L. 98–511; Secs. 8 and 9, Pub. L. 99–89; Title V of Pub. L. 100–297; Pub. L. 105–337.

SOURCE: 53 FR 37678, Sept. 27, 1988, unless otherwise noted.

§ 38.1 Scope.

(a) *Primary scope.* This part applies to all individuals appointed or converted to contract education positions as defined in § 38.3 in the Bureau of Indian Affairs after November 1, 1979. This part applies to elementary and secondary school positions and agency education positions.

(b) *Secondary scope.* Section 38.13 applies to employees with continuing tenure in both the competitive and excepted service who encumber education positions.

(c) *Other.* Where 25 CFR part 38 and a negotiated labor relations agreement conflict, the negotiated agreement will govern.

§ 38.2 Information collection.

(a) The information collection requirements contained in § 38.5 use Standard Form 171 for collection, and have been approved by OMB under 25 U.S.C. 2011 and 2015 and assigned approval number 3206–0012. The sponsoring agency for the Standard Form 171, is the Office of Personnel Management. The information is being collected to determine eligibility for employment. The information will be used to rate the qualifications of applicants for employment. Response is mandatory for employment.

(b) The information collection requirement for § 38.14, Voluntary Services has been approved by the Office of Management and Budget under 44 U.S.C. 3501 *et seq.* and assigned clearance number 1076–0116. The information is being collected to determine an applicants eligibility and selection for appropriate volunteer assignments. Response is voluntary.

§ 38.3 Definitions.

As used in this part, the term:

Agency means the current organizational unit of the Bureau, which provides direct services to the governing body or bodies and members of one or more specified Indian Tribes.

Agency school board as defined in section 1139(1), of Pub. L. 95–561, means a body, the members of which are appointed by the school boards of the schools located within such Agency. The number of such members shall be determined by the Director in consultation with the affected tribes. In Agencies serving a single school, the school board of that school shall function as the Agency School Board.

Agency Superintendent for Education (ASE) means the Bureau official in charge of education functions at an Agency Office and to whom the school supervisor(s) and other educators under the Agency's jurisdiction, report.

Area Education Programs Administrator (AEPA) means the Bureau official in charge of an Area Education Office that provides services to off-reservation residential schools, peripheral dormitories or on-reservation BIA funded schools that are not served by an Agency Superintendent for Education. The AEPA may also provide education program services to tribes not having an Agency Superintendent for Education at their agency. The AEPA has no line authority over agency education programs that are under the jurisdiction of an Agency Superintendent for Education.

Assistant Secretary means the Assistant Secretary for Indian Affairs of the Department of the Interior.

Bureau means the Bureau of Indian Affairs of the Department of the Interior.

Consult, as used in this part and provided in section 1131(d)(1) (B) and (C) of Pub. L. 95–561, means providing pertinent information to and being available for discussion with the school board, giving the school board the opportunity to reply and giving due consideration to the school board's response, subject to appeal rights provided in § 38.7 (a), (b) and (c), and § 38.9(e)(3).

Director means the Deputy to the Assistant Secretary/Director—Indian Affairs (Indian Education Programs) in the Bureau.

Discharge means the separation of an employee during the term of the contract.

Education function means the administration and implementation of the Bureau's education programs and activities (including school operations).

Education position, means a position in the Bureau the duties and responsibilities of which:

(a) Are performed on a school term basis principally in a Bureau elementary and secondary school which involve:

(1) Classroom or other instruction or the supervision or direction of classroom or other instruction;

(2) Any activity (other than teaching) that requires academic credits in educational theory and practice equal to the academic credits in educational theory and practice required for a bachelor's degree in education from an accredited institution of higher education; or

(3) Any activity in or related to the field of education notwithstanding that academic credits in educational theory and practice are not a formal requirement for the conduct of such activity; or

(4) Support services at or associated with the site of the school; or

(b) Are performed at the Agency level of the Bureau and involve the implementation of education-related Bureau programs. The position of Agency Superintendent for Education is excluded.

Educator, as defined in section 1131(n)(2) of Pub. L. 95–561 means an individual whose services are required, or who is employed, in an education position as defined in § 38.3.

Employment contract means a signed agreement executed by and between the Bureau and the individual employee hired or converted under this part, that specifies the position title, period of employment, and compensation attached thereto.

Involuntary change in position means the release of an employee from his/her position instigated by a change in program or other occurrence beyond the control of the employee.

Local school board, as used in this part and defined in section 1139(7) of Pub. L. 95–561, means a body chosen in accordance with the laws of the tribe to be served or, in the absence of such laws, the body elected by the parents of the Indian children attending a Bureau-operated school. In schools serving a substantial number of students from different tribes, the members shall be appointed by the governing bodies of the tribes affected and the number of such members shall be determined by the Director in consultation with the affected tribes.

Probationary period means the extension of the appointed process during which a person's character and ability to satisfactorily meet the requirements of the position are reviewed.

School board means an Agency school board or a local school board.

School supervisor means the Bureau official in charge of a Bureau school who reports to an Agency Superintendent for Education. In the case of an off-reservation residential school(s), and, in some cases, peripheral dormitories and on-reservation day schools, the school supervisor shall report to the Area Education Programs Administrator.

School term is that term which begins usually in the last summer or fall and ends in the Spring. It may be interrupted by one or more vacations.

§ 38.4 Education positions.

(a) The Director shall establish the kinds of positions required to carry out the Bureau's education function. No position will be established or continued for which:

(1) Funds are not available; or

(2) There is not a clearly demonstrable need and intent for it to carry out an education function.

(b) Positions established for regular school operations will be restricted to school term or program duration. Particular care shall be taken to insure that year-long positions are not established unless they are clearly required and involve essential 12-month assignments.

§ 38.5 Qualifications for educators.

(a) *Qualifications related to positions.* Job qualification requirements shall be at least equivalent to those established by the appropriate licensing and certification authorities of the State in which the position is located.

(b) *Qualifications related to individuals.* An applicant for an education position must establish that he/she meets the requirements of the position by submitting an application and a college transcript, as appropriate, to the local school supervisor, Agency Superintendent for Education (ASE), Area Education Programs Administrator (AEPA), or Director and appearing for an interview if requested by the official involved. The applicant's education and experience will be subject to verification by the ASE or the AEPA. Employees who falsify experience and employment history may be subject to disciplinary action or discharge from the position to which he/she is appointed.

(1) School boards may waive formal education and State certification requirements for tribal members who are hired to teach tribal culture and language.

(2) Tribal members appointed under this waiver may not have their basic pay rate set higher than the rate paid to qualified educators in teaching positions at that school.

(c) *Identification of qualified individuals.* The Director shall require each ASE, AEPA, and other appropriate local official in the education program organization to maintain lists of qualified and interviewed applicants for each of the kinds of established positions. Applications on file shall be purged annually. Applicants whose qualifications are established and who indicate an interest in working in specified locations will be included on those local applicant lists. The Director shall maintain a national list of qualified applicants for each of the kinds of positions established. Applicants whose qualifications are established and who either do not indicate an interest in a specific location or indicate an interest in working in any location will be entered on the national list. The national list is a secondary source of applicants.

(d) *Special recruitment and training for Indian educators.* The Director shall review annually the Bureau's "Recruitment of Indian Educators Program" and update as necessary. The Director will define individual training plans for trainees and subsequent promotional opportunities for advancement based upon satisfactory job performance in this program.

§ 38.6 Basic compensation for educators and education positions.

(a) *Schedule of basic compensation rates.* The Director shall establish a schedule for each pay level specified in part 62 of the Bureau of Indian Affairs Manual (BIAM). The schedule will be revised at the same time as and be consistent with rates in effect under the General Schedule or Federal Wage System for individuals with comparable qualifications, and holding comparable positions.

(b) *Range of pay rates for positions within pay levels.* The range of basic compensation rates for positions assigned to each pay level will be consistent with the General Schedule or Federal Wage System rates that would otherwise be applicable if the position were classified under chapter 51 or subchapter IV of chapter 53 of title 5 of the United States Code (U.S.C.). The maximum pay shall not exceed step 10 of the comparable General Schedule position by more than ten percent.

(c) *Schedule of compensation rates for teachers and counselors.* The basic compensation for teachers and counselors, including dormitory counselors and homeliving counselors, shall be determined in accordance with rates set by the Defense Department Overseas Teachers Pay and Personnel Practices Act. The schedule used shall be the current published schedule for the school year beginning on or after July 1 of each year.

(d) *Adjusting employee basic compensation rates.* (1) Except for employees occupying positions of teachers and counselors, including dormitory counselors and homeliving counselors, adjustments in an employee's basic compensation made in connection with each contract renewal will be based on the following:

(i) Contract renewal incentive—one pay increment for each renewal, not to exceed four increments, unless the educator is covered by a negotiated labor union agreement.

(ii) Performance—employees whose performance is rated "above satisfactory"; one pay increment; employees whose performance is rated "outstanding"; two pay increments.

(2) Pay increments based on education may be awarded as outlined in 62 BIAM.

(e) *Special additions to basic compensation.* The Director is authorized to established the following special additions to rates of basic compensation:

(1) The Director may authorize payment of a staffing differential not exceeding 25 per centum of the rate of basic compensation based on a formally-documented request by an ASE or AEPA. Such a staffing differential shall only be authorized in writing when the Director determines that:

(i) It is warranted by the geographic isolation of the work site or other unusually difficult environmental working or living conditions and/or,

(ii) It is necessary as a recruitment or retention incentive. This staffing differential is to be computed on the basic schedule rate before any other additions are computed.

(2) Special rates may be established for recruitment and retention applicable only to a specific position or to specific types of positions in specific locations based on a formally documented request by an ASE or AEPA and submitted to the Director for approval.

(f) *Payment of compensation to educators.* This section applies to those individuals employed under the provisions of section 1131(m) of Pub. L. 95–561 or title 5 U.S.C.

(1) *Pay periods.* Educators shall be paid on the basis of a biweekly pay period during the term of the contract. Chapter 55 of title 5 U.S.C. applies to the administration of pay for educators, except that section 1131(m) of Pub. L. 95–561 provides that 5 U.S.C. 5533 does not apply with respect to the receipt of pay by educators during summer recess under certain circumstances.

(2) *Pay for contract educators.* When an educator is appointed, payment under the contract is to begin as of the effective date of the contract. If an educator resigns or is discharged before the expiration of the term of the contract, pay ceases as of the date of resignation or discharge.

(3) *Prorating of pay.* Within 30 days prior to the beginning of the academic school term, each educator must elect whether to have the annual contractual rate or basic pay prorated over the contractual academic school term, or to have the basic pay prorated over a 12-month period.

(i) Each educator may change such election once during the academic school term, provided notice is given two weeks prior to the end of the fifth month after the beginning of the academic school term.

(ii) An educator who elects a 12-month basis of prorated pay may further elect to be paid in one lump sum at the end of the academic school term for the then remaining amount of rate of basic pay otherwise due, provided notice is given four weeks prior to the end of the academic school term.

(iii) No educator shall suffer a loss of pay or benefits because of elections made under this section.

(4) *Stipends for extracurricular activities.* An employee, if assigned to sponsor an approved extracurricular activity, may elect annually at the beginning of the contract to be paid a stipend in lieu of overtime premium pay or compensatory time when the employee performs additional activities to provide services to students or otherwise support the school's academic and social programs.

(i) The Director is authorized to establish a schedule of stipends for each Bureau Area, taking into consideration types of activities to be compensated and payments provided by public school districts in or near the Area.

(ii) The stipend shall be a supplement to the employee's base pay and is not a part of salary for retirement computation purposes.

(iii) The employee shall be paid the stipend in equal payments over the period of the extracurricular activity.

[53 FR 37678, Sept. 27, 1988, as amended at 54 FR 46374, Nov. 3, 1989]

§ 38.7 Appointment of educators.

(a) *Local school employees.* Local Bureau school employees shall be appointed only by the school supervisor. Before the local school employee is employed, the school board shall be consulted. An individual's appointment may be finalized only upon receipt of a formal written determination certified by the local school board under such uniform procedures as it may adopt.

Written determination by the school board should be received within a reasonable period, but not to exceed 30 days. Failure of the school board to act within this period shall have the effect of approving the proposed appointment. The local school board shall use the same written procedure to disapprove an appointment. The school supervisor may appeal to the ASE, or, where appropriate, to the AEPA, any determination by the local school board concerning an individual's appointment. A written statement of appeal describing the action and the reasons the supervisor believes such action should be overturned must be filed within 10 days of receipt of the action from the local school board. A copy of such statement shall be submitted to the school board and the board shall be afforded an opportunity to respond, not to exceed 10 calendar days, in writing, to the appeal. After reviewing such written appeal and response, the ASE or AEPA may, for cause, overturn the action of the local school board. The ASE or AEPA must transmit the determination of the appeal (in the form of a written opinion) to the board and to the supervisor identifying the reasons for overturning the action within 10 calender days. Failure to act within the 10 calendar day period shall have the effect of approving the local school board's determination.

(b) *School supervisors.* School supervisors may be appointed only by the ASE, except the AEPA shall appoint school supervisors for off-reservation boarding schools and those few other schools supervised by the AEPA. The school board shall be consulted before the school supervisor is employed. The appointment may be finalized upon receipt of a formal written determination certified by the school board under any uniform procedures as it may adopt. Written determination by the school board shall be received within a reasonable period, but not to exceed 30 days. Failure of the school board to act within this period shall have the effect of approving the proposed appointment. The school board shall use the same procedure to disapprove an appointment. Within 20 calendar days of receipt of any determination by the school board concerning an individual's appointment, the ASE or AEPA, as appropriate, may appeal to the Director by filing a written statement describing the determination and the reasons the supervisor believes the determination should be overturned. A copy of the statement shall be submitted to the local school board and the board shall be afforded an opportunity to respond, within 10 calendar days, in writing, to such an appeal. The Director may reverse the determination for cause set out in writing to the school board. Within 20 calendar days of the school board's response, the Director shall transmit the determination of the appeal (in the form of a written opinion) to the board and to the ASE or AEPA identifying the reasons for overturning the determination. Failure by the Director to act within the 20 calendar day period shall have the effect of approving the school board's determination.

(c) *Agency office education program employees.* Appointments to Agency office education positions may be made only by the ASE. The Agency school board shall be consulted before the agency education employee is employed, and the appointment may be finalized upon receipt of a formal, written determination certified by the Agency school board under any uniform procedures as it may adopt. Written determination by the school board shall be received within a reasonable period, but not to exceed 30 days. Failure of the school board to act within this period shall have the effect of approving the proposed appointment. The Agency school board shall use the same written procedure to disapprove an appointment. Within 20 calendar days of receipt of any determination by the school board concerning an individual's appointment, the ASE may appeal to the Director by filing a written statement describing the determination and the reasons the supervisor believes the determination should be overturned. A copy of the statement shall be submitted to the Agency school board and the board shall be afforded an opportunity to respond, within 10 calendar days, in writing, to such appeal. After reviewing the written appeal and response, the Director may, for cause, overturn the determination of the Agency school board.

Within 20 days of the board's response, the Director shall transmit the determination of the appeal (in the form of a written opinion) to the board and to the ASE identifying the reasons for overturning the determination. Failure of the Director to act within the 20 calendar day period shall have the effect of approving the school's board's determination.

(d) *Employment contracts.* The Bureau shall issue employment contracts each year for individuals employed in contract education positions at the Agency or school levels.

(e) *Absence of local school boards.* Where a local school board has not been established in accordance with section 1139(7) Pub. L. 95–561 with respect to a Bureau school, or where a school board is not operational, and the local school board is required to be given a notice or required to be consulted by statute or these regulations, the official involved shall notify or consult with the Agency school board serving the tribe(s) to which the parents of the Indian children atending that school belong, or, in that absence, the tribal organization(s) of the tribe(s) involved.

(f) *Provisional contracts.* Provisional certification or other limited certificates from the State are not considered full certification and only a provisional contract may be issued. There may be circumstances when no individual who has met the full certification or experience requirements is available for a professional position or when a status quo employee who does not meet full certification or experience requirements desires to convert to contract. When this situation exists, a provisional contract may be issued in accordance with the following:

(1) The contract will be made only:

(i) After it is determined that an individual already meeting certification or experience requirements is not available; or

(ii) For conversion of a status quo employee who does not yet meet all established position requirements.

(2) Consultation with the appropriate school board is required prior to the contract.

(3) The contract may be of 12-month or school-term duration.

(4) The employee will be required to make satisfactory progress toward meeting full qualification requirements.

(5) If the employee fails to meet the requirements established under §38.7(f)(4), the contract will be terminated. Such termination cannot be grieved or appealed.

(g) *Conditional appointment.* As provided in section 1131(d)(4), Pub. L. 95–561, if an individual who has applied at both the national and local levels is appointed from a local list of applicants, the appointment shall be conditional for 90 days. During that period, the individual's application and background shall be examined to determine if there is a more qualified individual for the position. Removal during this period is not subject to discharge, hearing or grievance procedures.

(h) *Short-term contracts.* (1) There may be circumstances where immediate action is necessary and it is impossible to consult with the local school board. When this situation exists short-term contracts may be made by the school supervisor in accordance with the following:

(i) The length of the contract will not exceed 60 days, or the next regularly scheduled school board meeting, whichever comes first.

(ii) If the board meets and does not take action on the individual in question, the short-term contract may be extended for the duration of the school year.

(iii) It shall be the responsibility of the school supervisor to fully inform the local school board of all such short-term contracts. Failure to do so may be cited as reason to discharge the school supervisor if so requested by the board.

(2) The local school board may authorize the school supervisor to make an emergency short-term contract to classroom, dormitory and other positions directly related to the health and safety of students. When this situation exists, short-term contracts may be made in accordance with the following:

(i) If local and agency lists of qualified applicants are exhausted, short-term contracts may be made without regard to qualifications for the position;

(ii) The pay level will be based on the qualifications of the individual employed rather than the requirements of the position, if the qualifications of the individual are lower than required;

(iii) The short-term contract may not exceed the school term and may not be renewed or extended;

(iv) Every 60 days the school supervisor will determine if qualified individuals have been placed on the local or agency lists. If a qualified individual on the list accepts employment, the school supervisor must terminate the emergency appointment at the time the qualified individual is appointed.

(i) *Temporary contracts.* There may be circumstances where a specific position is needed for a period of one year or less. Under these conditions a position may be advertised as a temporary position and be filled under a temporary contract. Such contract requires the same school board approval as a school year contract. If required for the completion of the activities specified in the original announcement, the position, may with school board approval be extended for up to one additional year. Temporary contracts may be terminated at any time and this action is not subject to approval or grievance procedures.

(j) *Waiver of Indian preference.* Notwithstanding any provision of the Indian preference laws, such laws shall not apply in the case of any personnel action within the purview of this section respecting an application or employee not entitled to Indian preference if each tribal organization concerned grants, in writing, a waiver of the application of such laws with respect to such personnel action, where such a waiver is in writing deemed to be a necessity by the tribal organization, except that this shall in no way relieve the Bureau of its responsibility to issue timely and adequate announcements and advertisements concerning any such personnel action if it is intended to fill a vacancy (no matter how such vacancy is created). When a waiver is granted, it shall apply only to that particular position and as long as the employee remains in that position.

(k) *Prohibited reappointment.* An educator who voluntarily terminates employment before the end of the school term may not be appointed to another Bureau education position before the beginning of the following school term. An educator will not be deemed to have voluntarily terminated employment if transferred elsewhere with the consent of the local school or Agency boards.

(l) *Contract renewals.* The appropriate school board shall be notified in writing by the school supervisor and/or ASE or AEPA not less than 90 days before the end of the school term whether or not an individual's contract is recommended for renewal.

(1) If the school board disagrees with the school supervisor's or ASE's or AEPA's recommendations, the board will submit a formal, written certification of its determinations to the school supervisor or ASE or AEPA within 25 days. If the board's determinations are not received within the 25 days, the school supervisor or ASE or AEPA shall issue the 60 day notification of renewal or nonrenawal to the individual as required under § 38.8.

(2) When the school board submits its determination within the 25 days and determines that a contract will be renewed, or nonrenewed, the appropriate official shall issue the required renewal notice, or nonrenawal, or appeal the determination of the school board to the appropriate official who will make a determination in accordance with the appeal procedure is § 38.7(a) of this part. After the probationary period, if the determination is that the contract will not be renewed, the procedures specified in § 38.8 shall apply.

§ 38.8 Nonrenewal of contract.

Where the determination is made that an employee's contract shall not be renewed for the following year, the following procedure will apply to those employees who have completed three full continuous school terms of service under consecutive contract appointments and satisfactory performance in the same or comparable education positions.

(a) The employee will be given a written notice of the action and the reasons thereof not less than 60 days before the end of the school term.

(b) The employee will be given 10 calendar days to request an informal hearing before the appropriate official or body. Upon request, the employee may be given official time, not to exceed eight hours, to prepare a written response to the reason(s).

(c) If so requested, an informal hearing shall be held within 30 calendar days of receipt of the request.

(d) The appropriate official or body will render a written determination within seven calendar days after the informal hearing.

(e) The employee has a right to request an administrative review by the ASE or AEPA of the determination within 10 calendar days of that determination. The ASE or AEPA then has 20 calendar days to render a final decision. Where the employee is the supervisor of the school or an agency education employee, any appeal of the ASE or AEPA would be addressed to the Director for a decision. If the Director or ASE's or AEPA's decision overturns the appropriate official or bodies determination, the appropriate official or body will be notified of the reasons in writing. Failure by the Director or ASE or AEPA to act within the 20 days will sustain the determination. This completes the administrative appeal process.

(f) Failure of any of the parties to meet the requirements of the above procedures will serve to negate the particular action sought by the negligent party.

(g) Those employees with less than three full continuous school terms of consecutive contract appointments are serving a probationary period. Nonrenewal of his/her contract will be considered a continuation of the examining process. This action cannot be appealed or grieved.

(h) Independent of the procedures outlined in this section, the school supervisor or ASE or AEPA, for applicable positions, shall be required to submit to the ASE or AEPA or appropriate higher authority all nonrenewal actions. Within 60 days, the ASE or AEPA shall review the nonrenewal actions and may overturn the determination of nonrenewal. In the event that the ASE or AEPA makes a decision to overturn the school board determination, the ASE or AEPA shall notify the school board in writing of his/her reasons for doing so.

(i) No more than the substantial standard of evidence shall be required to sustain the nonrenewal.

(j) A procedural error shall not be grounds for overturning a determination of nonrenewal unless the employee shows harmful error in the application of the Agency's procedures in arriving at such a decision. For purposes of this section, "harmful error" means error by the Agency in the application of its procedures which, in the absence or cure of the error, might have caused the Agency to reach a conclusion different than the one reached. The burden is upon the appellant to show that based upon the record as a whole, the error was harmful. i.e., caused substantial harm or prejudice to his/her rights.

(k) Nonrenewal of a contract is not discharge and will not follow the discharge procedures.

§ 38.9 Discharge of educators.

(a) *Discharge for cause.* Educators covered under the provision of this section are excluded from coverage under 5 U.S.C. 7511 and 4303. In order to provide due process for educators, the Director shall publish in 62 BIAM representative conditions that could result in the discharge of educators for cause and procedures to be followed in discharge cases.

(b) *Discharge for inadequate performance.* Action to remove educators for inadequate performance will be taken for failure to meet performance standards established under 5 U.S.C. 4302. Performance standards for all educators will include, among others, lack of student achievement. Willful failure to exercise properly assigned supervisory responsibilities by supervisors shall also be cause for discharge.

(c) *Other discharge.* The Director shall publish in 62 BIAM a description of the budgetary and programmatic conditions that may result in the discharge of educators for other than cause during the school term. The individual's personnel record will clearly reflect that the action taken is based upon budgetary or programmatic restraints and is not a reflection on the employee's performance.

(d) *Procedures for discharge for cause.* The Director shall publish in 62 BIAM the procedural steps to be followed by school supervisors, ASE's, and AEPA's in discharge for cause cases. These procedures shall provide (among other things) for the following:

(1) The educator to be discharged shall receive a written notice of the proposal, specifying the causes or complaints upon which the proposal is based, not less than 30 calendar days before the discharge. However, this shall not prohibit the exclusion of the individual from the education facility in cases where exclusion is required for the safety of the students or the orderly operation of the facility.

(2) A reasonable time, but not less than 10 calendar days, will be allotted for the individual to make written and/or oral responses to the charge.

(3) An opportunity will be afforded the individual to review the material relied upon to support the charge.

(4) Official time, not to exceed eight hours, will be provided to the individual to prepare a response to the charge.

(5) The educator may elect to have a representative and shall furnish the identity of any representative to the ASE or AEPA. The ASE or AEPA may disallow, as an employee representative, any individual whose activities as a representative would cause a conflict of interest or position, or an employee whose release from his or her official position would give rise to unreasonable costs to the Government, or when priority work assignment precludes his or her release from official duties. The terms of any applicable collective bargaining agreement and 5 U.S.C. 7114(a)(5) shall govern representation of employees in an exclusive bargaining unit.

(6) The individual has a right to a final decision made by the appropriate level of supervision.

(7) The individual has a right to appeal the final decision and have the merits of the case reviewed by a Departmental official not previously involved in the case. This right includes entitlement to a hearing upon request under procedures in accordance with the requirements of due process under section 1131(e)(1)(B) of Pub. L. 95–561.

(e) *School board action.* (1) The appropriate school board shall be notified as soon as possible, but in no case later than 10 calendar days from the date of issue of the notice of intent to discharge.

(2) The appropriate school board, under any uniform procedure as it may adopt, may issue a formal written certification to the school supervisor, ASE, or AEPA either approving or disapproving the discharge before the expiration of the notice period and before actual discharge. Failure to respond before the expiration of the notice period will have the effect of approving the discharge.

(3) The school supervisor initiating a discharge action may appeal the board's determination to the ASE or AEPA within 10 calendar days of receipt of the board's notice. The ASE or AEPA initiating a discharge may appeal the board's determination to the Director within 10 calendar days of receipt of the board's notice. Within 20 calendar days following the receipt of an appeal, the reviewing official may, for good cause, reverse the school board's determination by a notice in writing to the board. Failure to act within 20 calendar days shall have the effect of approving the board's determination.

(f) *School board recommendations for discharge.* School boards may recommend in writing to school supervisors, ASE's, or AEPA's, and the Director that individuals in the education program be discharged. These written recommendations may follow any procedures formally established internally by the school board or tribal government. However, the written recommendations must contain specific causes or complaints that may be verified or established by investigation of factual situations. The official receiving a board recommendation for discharge of an individual shall acknowledge the recommendation in writing within 10 calendar days of receipt and proceed with a fact finding investigation. The official who finally disposes of the recommendation shall notify the school board of the disposition in writing within 60 calendar days of initiation of the fact finding investigation.

§38.10 Conditions of employment of educators.

(a) *Supervision not delegated to school boards.* School boards may not direct, control, or interrupt the day-to-day activities of BIA employees carrying out Bureau-operated education programs.

(b) *Employee handbook.* Employee handbook and recruiting guides shall be developed by each local school or agency to provide specific information regarding:

(1) The working and hiring conditions for various tribal jurisdictions and Bureau locations;

(2) The need for all education personnel to adapt to local situations; and

(3) The requirement of all education personnel to comply with and support duly adopted school board policies, including those relating to tribal culture or language.

(c) *Contract renewal notification.* Employees will be notified 60 calendar days before the end of the school term of the intent to renew or not renew their contract. If an individual's contract is to be renewed, the individual must agree in writing to serve for the next school term. This agreement must be received within 14 calendar days of the date of the notice in order to complete the contract renewal. If this agreement is not received by the fourteenth day, the employee has voluntarily forfeited his or her right to continuing employment. If an individual agrees to serve for the next school term and fails to report for duty at the beginning of the next school term, the contract will be terminated and the individual's future appointment will be subject to the restriction in §38.7(k) of this part.

(d) *Dual compensation.* An employee accepting a renewal of a school term contract may be appointed to another Federal position during the school recess period without regard to the dual compensation regulations in 5 U.S.C. 5533.

(e) *Discrimination complaints.* Equal Employment Opportunity (EEO) procedures established under 29 CFR part 1613 are applicable to contract employees under this part. It is the policy of the BIA that all employees and applicants for employment shall be treated equally when considered for employment or benefits of employment, regardless of race, color, sex, religion, national origin, age, or mental or physical health (handicap), within the parameters of Indian preference.

(f) *Grievance procedures.* The Director shall publish in 62 BIAM procedures for the rapid and equitable resolution of grievances. In locations and for positions covered by an exclusive bargaining agreement, the negotiated grievance procedure is the exclusive avenue of redress for all matters within the scope of the negotiated grievance procedure.

(g) *Performance evaluation.* The minimum number of times a supervisor shall meet with an employee to discuss performance and suggest improvements shall be once every three months for the educator's first year at a school or Agency, and twice annually thereafter during the school term.

§38.11 Length of the regular school term.

The length of the regular school term shall be at least 180 student instructional days, unless a waiver has been granted under the provisions of 25 CFR 36.61.

§38.12 Leave system for education personnel.

(a) *Full-time school-term employees.* Employees on a full-time school-term contract are authorized the following types of leave:

(1) *Personal leave.* A school-term employee will receive 28 hours of personal leave to be used for personal reasons and 12 hours of emergency leave. This leave only accrues provided the length of the contract exceeds 24 weeks.

(i) The school-term employee will request the use of this leave in advance when it is for personal use or personal business (e.g., going to the bank, etc.). When this leave is requested for emergency purposes (e.g., death in immediate family), it will be requested immediately after the emergency is known, if possible, by the employee and before leave is taken or as soon as the supervisor reports to work on the official work day.

(ii) Final approval rests with the supervisor. This leave shall be taken only during the school term. No compensation for or carryover of unused leave is authorized.

(2) *Sick leave.* Sick leave is an absence approved by the supervisor for incapacity from duty due to injury or illness, not related to or incurred on-the-job and not covered by the Federal Employee's Compensation Act Regulations. Medical and dental appointments may be included under this part. However, whenever possible, medical and dental appointments should be scheduled after instructional time.

(i) Sick leave shall accrue at the rate of four hours each biweekly pay period in pay status during the term of the contract; and no precredit or advance of sick leave is authorized.

(ii) Accumulated sick leave at the time of separation will be recredited to an educator who is reemployed within three years of separation.

(3) *School vacation.* School term employees may receive up to 136 hours of school vacation time for use when school is not in session. School vacations are scheduled on the annual school calendar during the instructional year and may not be scheduled before the first day of student instruction or after the last day of student instruction. School vacations are not a right of the employee and cannot be paid for or carried over if the employee is required to work during the school vacation time or if the program will not permit school term employees to take such vacation time.

(b) *Leave for full-time, year-long employees.* Employees who are on a full-time, year-long contract are authorized the following types of leave:

(1) *Vacation leave.* Absence approved in advance by the supervisor for rest and relaxation or other personal reasons is authorized on a per year basis of Federal Government service as follows: years 1 and 2 of employment—120 hours; years 3–5 of employment—160 hours; 6 or more years—200 hours. The supervisor will determine when vacation leave may be used. Vacation leave is to be scheduled and used to the greatest extent possible during periods when school is not in session and the students are not in the dormitories. Vacation leave is credited to an employee on the day following his or her date of employment, provided the length of the contract exceeds 24 weeks. An employee may carry into succeeding years up to 200 hours of vacation leave. Leave unused at the time of separation is forfeited.

(2) *Sick leave.* Sick leave accumulation and use is authorized on the same basis as for school term employees under § 38.12(a)(2) of this part.

(c) *Leave for part-time year-long employees.* Employees who are on part-time year-long contracts exceeding 20 hours per week are authorized the following types of leave:

(1) *Vacation leave.* Absence approved in advance by the supervisor for rest and relaxation or other personal reasons is authorized on a per year basis of Federal Government service as follows: years 1 and 2 of employment—64 hours; years 3–5 of employment—80 hours; 6 or more years—104 hours. The supervisor shall determine when vacation leave may be used. Vacation leave is to be scheduled and used to the greatest extent possible during periods when school is not in session and the students are not in the dormitories. Vacation leave is credited to an employee on the day following his or her date of employment provided the length of the contract exceeds 24 weeks and may not be accumulated in excess of 104 hours from year to year. An employee may carry over up to 104 hours from one contract year to the next. Leave unused at the time of separation is forfeited.

(2) *Sick leave.* Sick leave is accumulated on the basis of three hours each biweekly pay period in pay status; no precredit or advance of sick leave is authorized. Accumulated sick leave at the time of separation will be recredited to an educator who is reemployed within three years of separation.

(d) *Leave for school term employees on a part-time work schedule in excess of 20 hours per week.* (1) Employees on a part-time work schedule in excess of 20 hours per week may receive a maximum of 102 hours of school vacation time; 20 hours of personal/emergency leave; and 63 hours of sick leave accrued at three hours per pay period for the first 21 pay periods of their contracts. Personal/emergency leave only accrues provided the length of the contract exceeds 24 weeks.

(2) The part-time employee will request the use of this leave in writing in advance when it is for personal use or personal business (e.g., going to the bank, etc.). When this leave is requested for emergency purposes (e.g., death in immediate family), it will be requested immediately after the emergency is known, if possible, by the employee and before leave is taken or as soon as the supervisor reports to work on the official work day.

(3) Final approval rests with the supervisor. This leave shall be taken only during the school year. No compensation for or carryover of unused leave is authorized.

(4) *Sick leave.* Sick leave is an absence approved by the supervisor for incapacity from duty due to injury or illness, not related to or incurred on-the-job and not covered by the Federal Employee's Compensation Act Regulations. Medical and dental appointments may be included under this part. However, whenever possible, medical and dental appointments should be scheduled after instructional time.

(i) Sick leave shall accrue at the rate of three hours each biweekly pay period in pay status for the first 21 pay periods of their contract; no precredit or advance for sick leave is authorized.

(ii) Accumulated sick leave at the time of separation will be recredited to an educator who is reemployed within three years of separation.

(5) *School vacation time.* Part-time employees may receive up to 102 hours of school vacation time for use when school is not in session. Approval for the use of this time will be administratively determined by the school supervisor, ASE or AEPA, and this time may not be scheduled before the start of school or after the end of school.

(i) All school vacation time for part-time employees will be approved at the convenience of the program and not as a right of the employee.

(ii) Vacation time cannot be paid for or carried over for a part-time employee if the employee is required to work during the school vacation time or if the program will not permit part-time employees to take such vacation time.

(e) *Accountable absences for all contract employees.* The following are considered accountable absences:

(1) *Approved absence.* If prescheduled and approved by the school supervisor, ASE or AEPA, as appropriate, an employee may be on leave without pay.

(2) *Absence without leave.* Any absence is not prescheduled or approved in advance or excused by the supervisor is considered absence without leave.

(3) *Court and military leave.* Employees are entitled to paid absence for jury or witness service and military duty as a member of the National Guard or Reserve under the same terms or conditions as outlined in sections 6322 and 6323 of title 5 U.S.C., and corresponding provisions of the Federal Personnel Manual, when the absence occurs during the regular contract period. Employees may be requested to schedule their military leave at times other than when school is in session.

(4) *Administrative leave.* Administrative leave is an excused absence from duty administratively authorized without loss of pay or without charge to leave. This leave is not a substitute for other paid or unpaid leave categories. Administrative leave usually is authorized on an individual basis except when a school is closed or a group of employees are excused from work for a particular purpose. The school supervisor, ASE or AEPA will grant administrative leave. A school closing must be approved by the ASE or AEPA.

(f) Educators serving with contracts with work weeks of 20 hours a week or less are not eligible for any type of paid leave.

(g) For school term educators, no paid leave is earned nor may accumulated leave be used during any period of employment with the Bureau between school terms.

(h) Employees issued contracts for intermittent work are not eligible for any type of paid leave.

(i) *Leave transferred in.* Annual leave credited to an employee's accrued leave balance immediately before conversion to a contract education position or appointment under this part will be carried over and made available to the employee. Sick leave credited to an employee's accrued sick leave balance immediately before conversion to a contract education position or appointment under this part shall be credited to the employee's sick leave account under the system in § 38.12(a)(2) and (b)(2).

§ 38.13 Status quo employees in education positions.

(a) *Status quo employees.* Individuals who were Bureau employees on October 31, 1979, with an appointment in either the competitive or excepted service without time limitation, and who are serving in an education position, shall be continued in their positions under the terms and conditions of that appointment with no change in their status or positions. Such employees are entitled to receive any changes in compensation attached to the position. Although such employees occupy "education positions" as defined in this part, the terms and conditions of their appointment, status, and entitlements are determined by competitive service regulations and procedures. Under applicable procedures, these employees are eligible for consideration for movement to other positions that are defined as "contract education" positions. Such movement shall change the terms and conditions of their appointment to the terms and conditions of employment established under this part.

(b) If the tribe or school board waives the Indian preference law, the employee loses the early-out retirement eligibility under Pub. L. 96–135, "early-out for non-Indians," if they are entitled to the early-out retirement. A memorandum for the record on BIA letterhead shall be signed by the employee and placed on the permanent side of his/her Official Personnel Folder, along with the tribal resolution, if the tribe/school board has waived the Indian preference law to employ the non-Indian."

(c) *Conversion of status quo employees to contract positions.* Status quo employees may request in writing to the school supervisor, ASE or AEPA, as applicable, that their position be converted to contract. The appropriate school board will be consulted and a determination made by such school board whether such individual should be converted to a contract employee.

(1) Written determination by the school board should be received within a reasonable period, but not to exceed 30 days from receipt of the request. Failure of the school board to act within this period shall have the effect of disapproving the proposed conversion.

(2) With school board approval, an involuntary change in position shall not affect the current status of status quo education employees.

§ 38.14 Voluntary services.

(a) *Scope.* An ASE or AEPA may, subject to the approval of the local school board concerned, accept voluntary services on behalf of Bureau schools from the private sector, including individuals, groups, or students. Voluntary service shall be for all non-hazardous activities where public services, special projects, or school operations are improved and enhanced. Volunteer service is limited to personal services received without compensation (salary or wages) by the Bureau from individuals, groups, and students. Nothing in this section shall be construed to require Federal employees to work without compensation or to allow the use of volunteer services to displace or replace Federal employees.

(b) *Volunteer service agreement.* An agreement is a written document, jointly completed by the volunteer, the Bureau school supervisor, and the school board, that outlines the responsibilities of each. In the case of students receiving credit for their work (i.e., student teaching) from an education institution, the agreement will be jointly completed by the student, a representative of the institution, and the Bureau school supervisor. In the case of volunteer groups, the agreement shall be signed by an official of the volunteering organization, the Bureau school supervisor, and the school board and a list of signatures and emergency telephone numbers of all participants shall be attached.

(c) *Eligibility.* Although no minimum age requirement exists for volunteers, schools shall comply with appropriate Federal and State laws and standards on using the services of minors. All volunteers under the age of 18 must obtain written permission from their parents or guardians to perform volunteer activities.

(d) *Status.* Volunteers participating under this part are not considered Federal employees for any purpose other than:

(1) Title 5 U.S.C. chapter 81, dealing with compensation for injuries sustained during the performance of work assignments.

(2) Federal tort claims provisions published in 28 U.S.C. chapter 171.

(3) Department of the Interior Regulations Governing Responsibilities and Conduct.

(e) *Travel and other expenses.* The decision to reimburse travel and other incidental expenses, as well as the amount of reimbursement, shall be made by the school supervisor, ASE, AEPA, and the respective school board. Payment is made in the same manner as for regular employees. Payment of travel and per diem expenses to a volunteer on a particular assignment must be supported by a specific travel authorization and cannot exceed the cost of employing a temporary employee of comparable qualification at the school for which a travel authorization is considered.

(f) *Annual report.* School supervisors shall submit reports on volunteers to the ASE or AEPA by October 31 of each year for the preceding year.

§ 38.15 Southwestern Indian Polytechnic Institute.

(a) The Southwestern Indian Polytechnic Institute has an independent personnel system established under Public Law 105–337, the Administrative Systems Act of 1998, 112 Stat. 3171. The details of this system are in the Indian Affairs Manual (IAM) at Part 20. This manual system may be found in Bureau of Indian Affairs Regional and Agency Offices, Education Line Offices, and the Central Office in Washington, DC.

(b) The personnel system is in the excepted service and addresses the areas of classification, staffing, pay, performance, discipline, and separation. Other areas of personnel such as leave, retirement, life insurance, health benefits, thrift savings, etc., remain under the jurisdiction of the Office of Personnel Management.

[65 FR 58183, Sept. 27, 2000]

PART 39—THE INDIAN SCHOOL EQUALIZATION PROGRAM

Subpart A—General

Subpart B—Indian School Equalization Formula

Subpart F—School Board Training Expenses

Subpart G—Student Transportation

ELIGIBILITY FOR FUNDS

CALCULATING TRANSPORTATION MILES

REPORTING REQUIREMENTS

MISCELLANEOUS PROVISIONS

Subpart H—Determining the Amount Necessary To Sustain an Academic or Residential Program

Subpart I—Interim Maintenance and Minor Repair Fund

Subpart J—Administrative Cost Formula

Subpart K—Pre-kindergarten Programs

Subpart L—Contract School Operation and Maintenance Fund

AUTHORITY: 25 U.S.C. 13, 2008; Public Law 107–110, 115 Stat. 1425.

SOURCE: 44 FR 61864, Oct. 26, 1979, unless otherwise noted. Redesignated at 47 FR 13327, Mar. 30, 1982.

Subpart A—General

SOURCE: 70 FR 22205, Apr. 28, 2005, unless otherwise noted.

§ 39.1 What is the purpose of this part?

This part provides for the uniform direct funding of Bureau-operated and tribally operated day schools, boarding schools, and dormitories. This part applies to all schools, dormitories, and administrative units that are funded through the Indian School Equalization Program of the Bureau of Indian Affairs.

§ 39.2 What definitions apply to terms in this part?

Act means the No Child Left Behind Act, Public Law 107–110, enacted January 8, 2002. The No Child Left Behind Act reauthorizes and amends the Elementary and Secondary Education Act (ESEA) and the amended Education Amendments of 1978.

Agency means an organizational unit of the Bureau which provides direct services to the governing body or bodies and members of one or more specified Indian Tribes. The term includes Bureau Area Offices only with respect to off-reservation boarding schools administered directly by such Offices.

Agency school board means a body, the members of which are appointed by the school boards of the schools located within such agency, and the number of such members shall be determined by the Director in consultation with the affected tribes, except that, in agencies serving a single school, the school board of such school shall fulfill these duties.

Assistant Secretary means the Assistant Secretary of Indian Affairs, Department of the Interior, or his or her designee.

At no cost means provided without charge, but does not preclude incidental fees normally charged to non-disabled students or their parents as a part of the regular education program.

Average Daily Membership (ADM) means the aggregated ISEP-eligible membership of a school for a school year, divided by the number of school days in the school's submitted calendar.

Basic program means the instructional program provided to all students at any age level exclusive of any supplemental programs that are not provided to all students in day or boarding schools.

Basic transportation miles means the daily average of all bus miles logged for round trip home-to-school transportation of day students.

Bureau means the Bureau of Indian Affairs in the Department of the Interior.

Bureau-funded school means

(1) Bureau school;

(2) A contract or grant school; or

(3) A school for which assistance is provided under the Tribally Controlled Schools Act of 1988.

Bureau school means a Bureau-operated elementary or secondary day or boarding school or a Bureau-operated dormitory for students attending a school other than a Bureau school.

Count Week means the last full week in September during which schools count their student enrollment for ISEP purposes.

Director means the Director of the Office of Indian Education Programs in the Bureau of Indian Affairs or a designee.

Education Line Officer means the Bureau official in charge of Bureau education programs and functions in an Agency who reports to the Director.

Eligible Indian student means a student who:

(1) Is a member of, or is at least one-fourth degree Indian blood descendant of a member of, a tribe that is eligible for the special programs and services provided by the United States through the Bureau of Indian Affairs to Indians because of their status as Indians;

(2) Resides on or near a reservation or meets the criteria for attendance at a Bureau off-reservation home-living school; and

(3) Is enrolled in a Bureau-funded school.

Home schooled means a student who is not enrolled in a school and is receiving educational services at home at the parent's or guardian's initiative.

Homebound means a student who is educated outside the classroom.

Individual supplemental services means non-base academic services provided to eligible students. Individual supplemental services that are funded by additional WSUs are gifted and talented or language development services.

ISEP means the Indian School Equalization Program.

Limited English Proficient (LEP) means a child from a language background other than English who needs language assistance in his/her own language or in English in the schools. This child has sufficient difficulty speaking, writing, or understanding English to deny him/her the opportunity to learn successfully in English-only classrooms and meets one or more of the following conditions:

(1) The child was born outside of the United States or the child's Native language is not English;

(2) The child comes from an environment where a language other than English is dominant; or

(3) The child is an American Indian or Alaska Native and comes from an environment where a language other than English has had a significant impact on the child's level of English language proficiency.

Local School Board means a body chosen in accordance with the laws of the tribe to be served or, in the absence of such laws, elected by the parents of the Indian children attending the school. For a school serving a substantial number of students from different tribes:

(1) The members of the local school board shall be appointed by the tribal governing bodies affected; and

(2) The Secretary shall determine number of members in consultation with the affected tribes.

OIEP means the Office of Indian Education Programs in the Bureau of Indian Affairs.

Physical education means the development of physical and motor fitness, fundamental motor skills and patterns, and skills in aquatics, dance, and individual and group games and sports (including intramural and lifetime sports). The term includes special physical education, adapted physical education, movement education, and motor development.

Resident means a student who is residing at a boarding school or dormitory during the weeks when student membership counts are conducted and is either:

(1) A member of the instructional program in the same boarding school in which the student is counted as a resident; or

(2) Enrolled in and a current member of a public school or another Bureau-funded school.

Residential program means a program that provides room and board in a boarding school or dormitory to residents who are either:

(1) Enrolled in and are current members of a public school or Bureau-funded school; or

(2) Members of the instructional program in the same boarding school in which they are counted as residents and:

(i) Are officially enrolled in the residential program of a Bureau-operated or -funded school; and

(ii) Are actually receiving supplemental services provided to all students who are provided room and board in a boarding school or a dormitory.

Secretary means the Secretary of the Interior or a designated representative.

School means a school funded by the Bureau of Indian Affairs. The term "school" does not include public, charter, or private schools.

School bus means a passenger vehicle that is:

(1) Used to transport day students to and/or from home and the school; and

(2) Operated by an operator in the employ of, or under contract to, a Bureau-funded school, who is qualified to operate such a vehicle under Tribal, State or Federal regulations governing the transportation of students.

School day means a day as defined by the submitted school calendar, as long as annual instructional hours are as they are reflected in §39.213, excluding passing time, lunch, recess, and breaks.

Special education means:

(1) Specially designed instruction, at no cost to the parents, to meet the

unique needs of a child with a disability, including:

(i) Instruction conducted in the classroom, in the home, in hospitals and institutions, and in other settings; and

(ii) Instruction in physical education.

(2) The term includes each of the following, if it meets the requirements of paragraph (1) of this definition:

(i) Speech-language pathology services, or any other related service, if the service is considered special education rather than a related service under State standards;

(1) Travel training; and

(2) Vocational education.

Specially designed instruction means adapting, as appropriate, to the needs of an eligible child under this part, the content, methodology, or delivery or instruction:

(1) To address the unique needs of the child that result from the child's disability; and

(2) To ensure access of the child to the general curriculum, so that he or she can meet the educational standards within the jurisdiction of the public agency that apply to all children

Three-year average means:

(1) For academic programs, the average daily membership of the 3 years before the current year of operation; and

(2) For the residential programs, the count period membership of the 3 years before the current year of operation.

Travel training means providing instruction, as appropriate, to children with significant cognitive disabilities, and any other children with disabilities who require this instruction, to enable them to:

(1) Develop an awareness of the environment in which they live; and

(2) Learn the skills necessary to move efficiently and safely from place to place within that environment (*e.g.*, in school, in the home, at work, and in the community).

Tribally operated school means an elementary school, secondary school, or dormitory that receives financial assistance for its operation under a contract, grant, or agreement with the Bureau under section 102, 103(a), or 208 of 25 U.S.C. 450 *et seq.*, or under the Tribally Controlled Schools Act of 1988.

Vocational education means organized educational programs that are directly related to the preparation of individuals for paid or unpaid employment, or for additional preparation for a career requiring other than a baccalaureate or advanced degree.

Unimproved roads means unengineered earth roads that do not have adequate gravel or other aggregate surface materials applied and do not have drainage ditches or shoulders.

Weighted Student Unit means:

(1) The measure of student membership adjusted by the weights or ratios used as factors in the Indian School Equalization Formula; and

(2) The factor used to adjust the weighted student count at any school as the result of other adjustments made under this part.

§ 39.3 Information collection.

Notwithstanding any other provision of law, no person is required to respond to, nor shall any person be subject to a penalty for failure to comply with a collection of information, subject to the requirements of the Paperwork Reduction Act of 1995 (44 U.S.C. 3501 *et seq.*) (PRA), unless that collection of information displays a currently valid Office of Management and Budget (OMB) Control Number. This part contains in §§ 39.410 and 39.502 collections of information subject to the PRA. These collections have been approved by OMB under control number 1076–0163.

Subpart B—Indian School Equalization Formula

SOURCE: 70 FR 22205, Apr. 28, 2005, unless otherwise noted.

§ 39.100 What is the Indian School Equalization Formula?

The Indian School Equalization Formula (ISEF) was established to allocate Indian School Equalization Program (ISEP) funds. OIEP applies ISEF to determine funding allocation for Bureau-funded schools as described in §§ 39.204 through 39.206.

§39.101 Does ISEF assess the actual cost of school operations?

No. ISEF does not attempt to assess the actual cost of school operations either at the local level or in the aggregate at the national level. ISEF provides a method of distribution of funds appropriated by Congress for all schools.

BASE AND SUPPLEMENTAL FUNDING

§39.102 What is academic base funding?

Academic base funding is the ADM times the weighted student unit.

§39.103 What are the factors used to determine base funding?

To determine base funding, schools must use the factors shown in the following table. The school must apply the appropriate factor to each student for funding purposes.

Grade level	Base academic funding factor	Base residential funding factor
Kindergarten	1.15	NA
Grades 1–3	1.38	1.75
Grades 4–6	1.15	1.6
Grades 7–8	1.38	1.6
Grades 9–12	1.5	1.6

§39.104 How must a school's base funding provide for students with disabilities?

(a) Each school must provide for students with disabilities by:

(1) Reserving 15 percent of academic base funding to support special education programs; and

(2) Providing resources through residential base funding to meet the needs of students with disabilities under the National Criteria for Home-Living Situations.

(b) A school may spend all or part of the 15 percent academic base funding reserved under paragraph (a)(1) of this section on school-wide programs to benefit all students (including those without disabilities) only if the school can document that it has met all needs of students with disabilities with such funds, and after having done so, there are unspent funds remaining from such funds.

§39.105 Are additional funds available for special education?

(a) Schools may supplement the 15 percent base academic funding reserved under §39.104 for special education with funds available under part B of the Individuals with Disabilities Education Act (IDEA). To obtain part B funds, the school must submit an application to OIEP. IDEA funds are available only if the school demonstrates that funds reserved under §39.104(a) are inadequate to pay for services needed by all eligible ISEP students with disabilities.

(b) The Bureau will facilitate the delivery of IDEA part B funding by:

(1) Providing technical assistance to schools in completing the application for the funds; and

(2) Providing training to Bureau staff to improve the delivery of part B funds.

§39.106 Who is eligible for special education funding?

To receive ISEP special education funding, a student must be under 22 years old and must not have received a high school diploma or its equivalent on the first day of eligible attendance. The following minimum age requirements also apply:

(a) To be counted as a kindergarten student, a child must be at least 5 years old by December 31; and

(b) To be counted as a first grade student; a child must be at least 6 years old by December 31.

§39.107 Are schools allotted supplemental funds for special student and/or school costs?

Yes, schools are allotted supplemental funds for special student and/or school costs. ISEF provides additional funds to schools through add-on weights (called special cost factors). ISEF adds special cost factors as shown in the following table.

Cost Factor	For more information see
Gifted and talented students	§§39.110 through 39.121
Students with language development needs.	§§39.130 through 39.137
Small school size	§§39.140 through 39.156
Geographic isolation of the school.	§39.160

GIFTED AND TALENTED PROGRAMS

§ 39.110 Can ISEF funds be distributed for the use of gifted and talented students?

Yes, ISEF funds can be distributed for the provision of services for gifted and talented students.

§ 39.111 What does the term gifted and talented mean?

The term gifted and talented means students, children, or youth who:

(a) Give evidence of high achievement capability in areas such as intellectual, creative, artistic, or leadership capacity, or in specific academic fields; and

(b) Need services or activities not ordinarily provided by the school in order to fully develop those capabilities.

§ 39.112 What is the limit on the number of students who are gifted and talented?

There is no limit on the number of students that a school can classify as gifted and talented.

§ 39.113 What are the special accountability requirements for the gifted and talented program?

If a school identifies more than 13 percent of its student population as gifted and talented the Bureau will immediately audit the school's gifted and talented program to ensure that all identified students:

(a) Meet the gifted and talented requirement in the regulations; and

(b) Are receiving gifted and talented services.

§ 39.114 What characteristics may qualify a student as gifted and talented for purposes of supplemental funding?

To be funded as gifted and talented under this part, a student must be identified as gifted and talented in at least one of the following areas.

(a) *Intellectual Ability* means scoring in the top 5 percent on a statistically valid and reliable measurement tool of intellectual ability.

(b) *Creativity/Divergent Thinking* means scoring in the top 5 percent of performance on a statistically valid and reliable measurement tool of creativity/divergent thinking.

(c) *Academic Aptitude/Achievement* means scoring in the top 15 percent of academic performance in a total subject area score on a statistically valid and reliable measurement tool of academic achievement/aptitude, or a standardized assessment, such as an NRT or CRT.

(d) *Leadership* means the student is recognized as possessing the ability to lead, guide, or influence the actions of others as measured by objective standards that a reasonable person of the community would believe demonstrates that the student possess leadership skills. These standards include evidence from surveys, supportive documentation portfolios, elected or appointed positions in school, community, clubs and organization, awards documenting leadership capabilities. No school can identify more than 15 percent of its student population as gifted and talented through the leadership category.

(e) *Visual and Performing Arts* means outstanding ability to excel in any imaginative art form; including, but not limited to, drawing, printing, sculpture, jewelry making, music, dance, speech, debate, or drama as documented from surveys, supportive documentation portfolios, awards from judged or juried competitions. No school can identify more than 15 percent of its student population as gifted and talented through the visual and performing arts category.

§ 39.115 How are eligible gifted and talented students identified and nominated?

(a) Screening can be completed annually to identify potentially eligible students. A student may be nominated for gifted and talented designation using the criteria in § 39.114 by any of the following:

(1) A teacher or other school staff;

(2) Another student;

(3) A community member;

(4) A parent or legal guardian; or

(5) The student himself or herself.

(b) Students can be nominated based on information regarding the student's abilities from any of the following sources:

(1) Collections of work;

(2) Audio/visual tapes;

(3) School grades;

(4) Judgment of work by qualified individuals knowledgeable about the student's performances (*e.g.*, artists, musicians, poets, historians, etc.);

(5) Interviews or observations; or

(6) Information from other sources.

(c) The school must have written parental consent to collect documentation of gifts and talents under paragraph (b) of this section.

§39.116 How does a school determine who receives gifted and talented services?

(a) To determine who receives gifted and talented funding, the school must use qualified professionals to perform a multi-disciplinary assessment. The assessment may include the examination of work samples or performance appropriate to the area under consideration. The school must have the parent or guardian's written permission to conduct individual assessments or evaluations. Assessments under this section must meet the following standards:

(1) The assessment must use assessment instruments specified in §39.114 for each of the five criteria for which the student is nominated;

(2) If the assessment uses a multi-criteria evaluation, that evaluation must be an unbiased evaluation based on student needs and abilities;

(3) Indicators for visual and performing arts and leadership may be determined based on national, regional, or local criteria; and

(4) The assessment may use student portfolios.

(b) A multi-disciplinary team will review the assessment results to determine eligibility for gifted and talented services. The purpose of the team is to determine eligibility and placement to receive gifted and talented services.

(1) Team members may include nominator, classroom teacher, qualified professional who conducted the assessment, local experts as needed, and other appropriate personnel such as the principal and/or a counselor.

(2) A minimum of three team members is required to determine eligibility.

(3) The team will design a specific education plan to provide gifted and talented services related in the areas identified.

§39.117 How does a school provide gifted and talented services for a student?

Gifted and talented services are provided through or under the supervision of highly qualified professional teachers. To provide gifted and talented services for a student, a school must take the steps in this section.

(a) The multi-disciplinary team formed under §39.116(b) will sign a statement of agreement for placement of services based on documentation reviewed.

(b) The student's parent or guardian must give written permission for the student to participate.

(c) The school must develop a specific education plan that contains:

(1) The date of placement;

(2) The date services will begin;

(3) The criterion from §39.114 for which the student is receiving services and the student's performance level;

(4) Measurable goals and objectives; and

(5) A list of staff responsible for each service that the school is providing.

§39.118 How does a student receive gifted and talented services in subsequent years?

For each student receiving gifted and talented services, the school must conduct a yearly evaluation of progress, file timely progress reports, and update the specific education plan.

(a) If a school identifies a student as gifted and talented based on §39.114 (a), (b), or (c), then the student does not need to reapply for the gifted and talented program. However, the student must be reevaluated at least every 3 years through the 10th grade to verify eligibility for funding.

(b) If a school identifies a student as gifted and talented based on §39.114 (d) or (e), the student must be reevaluated annually for the gifted and talented program.

§39.119 When must a student leave a gifted and talented program?

A student must leave the gifted and talented program when either:

(a) The student has received all of the available services that can meet the student's needs;

(b) The student no longer meets the criteria that have qualified him or her for the program; or

(c) The parent or guardian removes the student from the program.

§ 39.120 How are gifted and talented services provided?

In providing services under this section, the school must:

(a) Provide a variety of programming services to meet the needs of the students;

(b) Provide the type and duration of services identified in the Individual Education Plan established for each student; and

(c) Maintain individual student files to provide documentation of process and services; and

(d) Maintain confidentiality of student records under the Family Educational Rights and Privacy Act (FERPA).

§ 39.121 What is the WSU for gifted and talented students?

The WSU for a gifted and talented student is the base academic weight (see § 39.103) subtracted from 2.0. The following table shows the gifted and talented weights obtained using this procedure.

Grade level	Gifted and talented WSU
Kindergarten	0.85
Grades 1 to 3	0.62
Grades 4 to 6	0.85
Grades 7 to 8	0.62
Grades 9 to 12	0.50

LANGUAGE DEVELOPMENT PROGRAMS

§ 39.130 Can ISEF funds be used for Language Development Programs?

Yes, schools can use ISEF funds to implement Language Development programs that demonstrate the positive effects of Native language programs on students' academic success and English proficiency. Funds can be distributed to a total aggregate instructional weight of 0.13 for each eligible student.

§ 39.131 What is a Language Development Program?

A Language Development program is one that serves students who either:

(a) Are not proficient in spoken or written English;

(b) Are not proficient in any language;

(c) Are learning their Native language for the purpose of maintenance or language restoration and enhancement;

(d) Are being instructed in their Native language; or

(e) Are learning non-language subjects in their Native language.

§ 39.132 Can a school integrate Language Development programs into its regular instructional program?

A school may offer Language Development programs to students as part of its regular academic program. Language Development does not have to be offered as a stand-alone program.

§ 39.133 Who decides how Language Development funds can be used?

Tribal governing bodies or local school boards decide how their funds for Language Development programs will be used in the instructional program to meet the needs of their students.

§ 39.134 How does a school identify a Limited English Proficient student?

A student is identified as limited English proficient (LEP) by using a nationally recognized scientifically research-based test.

§ 39.135 What services must be provided to an LEP student?

A school must provide services that assist each LEP student to:

(a) Become proficient in English and, to the extent possible, proficient in their Native language; and

(b) Meet the same challenging academic content and student academic achievement standards that all students are expected to meet under 20 U.S.C. 6311(b)(1).

§ 39.136 What is the WSU for Language Development programs?

Language Development programs are funded at 0.13 WSUs per student.

§39.137 May schools operate a language development program without a specific appropriation from Congress?

Yes, a school may operate a language development program without a specific appropriation from Congress, but any funds used for such a program must come from existing ISEP funds. When Congress specifically appropriates funds for Indian or Native languages, the factor to support the language development program will be no more than 0.25 WSU.

SMALL SCHOOL ADJUSTMENT

§39.140 How does a school qualify for a Small School Adjustment?

A school will receive a small school adjustment if either:

(a) Its average daily membership (ADM) is less than 100 students; or

(b) It serves lower grades and has a diploma-awarding high school component with an average instructional daily membership of less than 100 students.

§39.141 What is the amount of the Small School Adjustment?

(a) A school with a 3-year ADM of 50 or fewer students will receive an adjustment equivalent to an additional 12.5 base WSU; or

(b) A school with a 3-year ADM of 51 to 99 students will use the following formula to determine the number of WSU for its adjustment. With X being the ADM, the formula is as follows:

WSU adjustment = ((100 − X)/200)*X

§39.143 What is a small high school?

For purposes of this part, a small high school:

(a) Is accredited under 25 U.S.C. 2001(b);

(b) Is staffed with highly qualified teachers;

(c) Operates any combination of grades 9 through 12;

(d) Offers high school diplomas; and

(e) Has an ADM of fewer than 100 students.

§39.144 What is the small high school adjustment?

(a) The small high school adjustment is a WSU adjustment given to a small high school that meets both of the following criteria:

(1) It has a 3-year average daily membership (ADM) of less than 100 students; and

(2) It operates as part of a school that during the 2003–04 school year also included lower grades.

(b) The following table shows the WSU adjustment given to small high schools. In the table, "X" stands for the ADM.

ADM of high school component	Amount of small high school adjustment	School receives a component small school adjustment under §39.141
50 or fewer students	6.25 base WSU	Yes.
51 to 99 students	determined using the following formula: WSU = ((100–X)/200)*X/2	Yes.
50 or fewer students	12.5 base WSU	No.
51 to 99 students	determined using the following formula: WSU = ((100–X)/200)*X	No.

§39.145 Can a school receive both a small school adjustment and a small high school adjustment?

A school that meets the criteria in §39.140 can receive both a small school adjustment and a small high school adjustment. The following table shows the total amount of adjustments for eligible schools by average daily membership (ADM) category.

ADM—entire school	ADM—high school component	Small school adjustment	Small high school adjustment	Total adjustment
1–50	NA	12.5	NA	12.5
1–50	1–50	12.5	6.25	18.75
51–99	1–50	[2]12.5–0.5	6.25	18.75–6.75
51–99	51–99	[1]12.5–0.5	[2]6.25–0.25	18.75–0.7

ADM—entire school	ADM—high school component	Small school adjustment	Small high school adjustment	Total adjustment
99	1–50	0.5	12.5	12.5
99	51–99	0.5	[2] 12.5–0.5	12.5–0.5

[1] The amount of the adjustment is within this range. The exact figure depends upon the results obtained using the formula in § 39.141.

[2] The amount of the adjustment is within this range. The exact figure depends upon the results obtained using the formula in § 39.144.

§ 39.146 Is there an adjustment for small residential programs?

In order to compensate for the additional costs of operating a small residential program, OIEP will add to the total WSUs of each qualifying school as shown in the following table:

Type of residential program	Number of WSUs added
Residential student count of 50 or fewer ISEP-eligible students.	12.5.
Residential student count of between 51 and 99 ISEP-eligible students.	Determined by the formula ((100-X)/200))X, where X equals the residential student count.

GEOGRAPHIC ISOLATION ADJUSTMENT

§ 39.160 Does ISEF provide supplemental funding for extraordinary costs related to a school's geographic isolation?

Yes. Havasupai Elementary School, for as long as it remains in its present location, will be awarded an additional cost factor of 12.5 WSU.

Subpart C—Administrative Procedures, Student Counts, and Verifications

SOURCE: 70 FR 22205, Apr. 28, 2005, unless otherwise noted.

§ 39.200 What is the purpose of the Indian School Equalization Formula?

OIEP uses the Indian School Equalization Formula (ISEF) to distribute Indian School Equalization Program (ISEP) appropriations equitably to Bureau-funded schools.

§ 39.201 Does ISEF reflect the actual cost of school operations?

ISEF does not attempt to assess the actual cost of school operations either at the local school level or in the aggregate nationally. ISEF is a relative distribution of available funds at the local school level by comparison with all other Bureau-funded schools.

§ 39.202 What are the definitions of terms used in this subpart?

Homebound means a student who is educated outside the classroom.

Home schooled means a student who is not enrolled in a school and is receiving educational services at home at the parent's or guardian's initiative.

School day means a day as defined by the submitted school calendar, as long as annual instructional hours are as they are reflected in § 39.213, excluding passing time, lunch, recess, and breaks.

Three-year average means:

(1) For academic programs, the average daily membership of the 3 years before the current year of operation; and

(2) For the residential programs, the count period membership of the 3 years before the current year of operation.

§ 39.203 When does OIEP calculate a school's allotment?

OIEP calculates a school's allotment no later than July 1. Schools must submit final ADM enrollment figures no later than June 15.

§ 39.204 How does OIEP calculate ADM?

OIEP calculates ADM by:

(a) Adding the total enrollment figures from periodic reports received from each Bureau-funded school; and

(b) Dividing the total enrollment for each school by the number of days in the school's reporting period.

§ 39.205 How does OIEP calculate a school's total WSUs for the school year?

(a) OIEP will add the weights obtained from the calculations in paragraphs (a)(1), (a)(2), and (a)(3) of this section to obtain the total weighted student units (WSUs) for each school.

(1) Each year's ADM is multiplied by the applicable weighted student unit for each grade level;

(2) Calculate any supplemental WSUs generated by the students; and

(3) Calculate any supplemental WSUs generated by the schools.

(b) The total WSU for the school year is the sum of paragraphs (a)(1), (a)(2), and (a)(3) of this section.

§39.206 How does OIEP calculate the value of one WSU?

(a) To calculate the appropriated dollar value of one WSU, OIEP divides the systemwide average number of WSUs for the previous 3 years into the current year's appropriation.

(b) To calculate the average WSU for a 3-year period:

(1) *Step 1.* Add together each year's total WSU (calculated under paragraph (b) of this section); and

(2) *Step 2.* Divide the sum obtained in step 1 by 3.

§39.207 How does OIEP determine a school's funding for the school year?

To determine a school's funding for the school year, OIEP uses the following seven-step process:

(a) *Step 1.* Multiply the appropriate base academic and/or residential weight from §39.103 by the number of students in each grade level category.

(b) *Step 2.* Multiply the number of students eligible for supplemental program funding under §39.107 by the weights for the program.

(c) *Step 3.* Calculate the school-based supplemental weights under §639.107.

(d) *Step 4.* Add together the sums obtained in steps 1 through 3 to obtain each school's total WSU.

(e) *Step 5.* Add together the total WSUs for all Bureau-funded schools.

(f) *Step 6.* Calculate the value of a WSU by dividing the current school year's funds by the average total WSUs as calculated under step 5 for the previous 3 years.

(g) *Step 7.* Multiply each school's WSU total by the base value of one WSU to determine funding for that school.

§39.208 How are ISEP funds distributed?

(a) On July 1, schools will receive 80 percent of their funds as determined in §39.207.

(b) On December 1, the balance will be distributed to all schools after verification of the school count and any adjustments made through the appeals process for the third year.

§39.209 When may a school count a student for membership purposes?

If a student is enrolled, is in attendance during any of the first 10 days of school, and receives at least 5 days' instruction, the student is deemed to be enrolled all 10 days and shall be counted for ADM purposes. The first 10 days of school, for purposes of this section, are determined by the calendar that the school submits to OIEP.

(a) For ISEP purposes, a school can add a student to the membership when he or she has been enrolled and has received a full day of instruction from the school.

(b) Except as provided in §39.210, to be counted for ADM, a student dropped under §39.209 must:

(1) Be re-enrolled; and

(2) Receive a full day of instruction from the school.

§39.210 When must a school drop a student from its membership?

If a student is absent for 10 consecutive school days, the school must drop that student from the membership for ISEP purposes of that school on the 11th day.

§39.211 What other categories of students can a school count for membership purposes?

A school can count other categories of students for membership purposes as shown in the following table.

Type of student	Circumstances under which student can be included in the school's membership
(a) Homebound	(1) The student is temporarily confined to the home for some or all of the school day for medical, family emergency, or other reasons required by law or regulation; (2) The student is being provided by the school with at least 5 documented contact hours each week of academic services by certified educational personnel; and (3) Appropriate documentations is on file at the school.
(b) Located in an institutional setting outside of the school.	The school is either: (1) Paying for the student to receive educational services from the facility; or (2) Providing educational services by certified school staff for at least 5 documented contact hours each week.
(c) Taking college courses during the school day.	The student is both: (1) Concurrently enrolled in, and receiving credits for both the school's courses and college courses; and (2) In physical attendance at the school at least 3 documented contact hours per day.
(d) Taking distance learning courses.	The student is both: (1) Receiving high school credit for grades; and (2) In physical attendance at the school at least 3 documented contact hours per day.
(e) Taking internet courses.	The student is both: (1) Receiving high school credit for grades; and (2) Taking the courses at the school site under a teacher's supervision.

§ 39.212 Can a student be counted as enrolled in more than one school?

Yes, if a student attends more than one school during an academic year, each school may count the student as enrolled once the student meets the criteria in 39.209.

§ 39.213 Will the Bureau fund children being home schooled?

No, the Bureau will not fund any child that is being home schooled.

§ 39.214 What is the minimum number of instructional hours required in order to be considered a full-time educational program?

A full time program provides the following number of instructional/student hours to the corresponding grade level:

Grade	Hours
K	720
1–3	810
4–8	900
9–12	970

§ 39.215 Can a school receive funding for any part-time students?

(a) A school can receive funding for the following part-time students:

(1) Kindergarten students enrolled in a 2-hour program; and

(2) Grade 7–12 students enrolled in at least half but less than a full instructional day.

(b) The school must count students classified as part-time at 50 percent of their basic instructional WSU value.

RESIDENTIAL PROGRAMS

§ 39.216 How does ISEF fund residential programs?

Residential programs are funded on a WSU basis using a formula that takes into account the number of nights of service per week. Funding for residential programs is based on the average of the 3 previous years' residential WSUs.

§ 39.217 How are students counted for the purpose of funding residential services?

For a student to be considered in residence for purposes of this subpart, the school must be able to document that the student was:

(a) In residence at least one night during the first full week of October;

(b) In residence at least one night during the week preceding the first full week in October;

(c) In residence at least one night during the week following the first full week in October; and

(d) Present for both the after school count and the midnight count at least one night during each week specified in this section.

§ 39.218 Are there different formulas for different levels of residential services?

(a) Residential services are funded as shown in the following table:

If a residential program operates . . .	Each student is funded at the level of . . .
(1) 4 nights per week or less	Total WSU × 4/7.
(2) 5, 6 or 7 nights per week	Total WSU × 7/7.

(b) In order to qualify for residential services funding under paragraph (a)(2) of this section, a school must document that at least 10 percent of residents are present on 3 of the 4 weekends during the count period.

(c) At least 50 percent of the residency levels established during the count period must be maintained every month for the remainder of the school year.

(d) A school may obtain waivers from the requirements of this section if there are health or safety justifications.

§39.219 What happens if a residential program does not maintain residency levels required by this subpart?

Each school must maintain its declared nights of service per week as certified in its submitted school calendar. For each month that a school does not maintain 25 percent of the residency shown in its submitted calendar, the school will lose one-tenth of its current year allocation.

§39.220 What reports must residential programs submit to comply with this subpart?

Residential programs must report their monthly counts to the Director on the last school day of the month. To be counted, a student must have been in residence at least 10 nights during each full school month.

§39.221 What is a full school month?

A full school month is each 30-day period following the first day that residential services are provided to students based on the school residential calendar.

PHASE-IN PERIOD

§39.230 How will the provisions of this subpart be phased in?

The calculation of the three-year rolling average of ADM for each school and for the entire Bureau-funded school system will be phased-in as shown in the following table.

Time period	How OIEP must calculate ADM
(a) First school year after May 31, 2005.	Use the prior 3 years' count period to create membership for funding purposes
(b) Second school year after May 31, 2005.	(1) The academic program will use the previous year's ADM school year and the 2 prior years' count periods; and (2) The residential program will use the previous year's count period and the 2 prior years' count weeks
(c) Each succeeding school year after May 31, 2005.	Add one year of ADM or count period and drop one year of prior count weeks until both systems are operating on a 3-year rolling average using the previous 3 years' count after period or ADM, respectively.

Subpart D—Accountability

SOURCE: 70 FR 22205, Apr. 28, 2005, unless otherwise noted.

§39.401 What is the purpose of this subpart?

The purpose of this subpart is to ensure accountability of administrative officials by creating procedures that are systematic and can be verified by a random independent outside auditing procedures. These procedures will ensure the equitable distribution of funds among schools.

§39.402 What definitions apply to terms used in this subpart?

Administrative officials means any persons responsible for managing and operating a school, including the school supervisor, the chief school administrator, tribal officials, Education Line Officers, and the Director, OIEP.

Director means the Director of the Office of Indian Education Programs of the Bureau of Indian Affairs.

Education Line Officer means the Bureau official in charge of Bureau education programs and functions in an Agency who reports to the Director.

§39.403 What certification is required?

(a) Each school must maintain an individual file on each student receiving basic educational and supplemental services. The file must contain written documentation of the following:

(1) Each student's eligibility and attendance records;

(2) A complete listing of all supplemental services provided, including all necessary documentation required by statute and regulations (*e.g.*, a current and complete Individual Education

Plan for each student receiving supplemental services); and

(3) Documentation of expenditures and program delivery for student transportation to and from school provided by commercial carriers.

(b) The School must maintain the following files in a central location:

(1) The school's ADM and supplemental program counts and residential count;

(2) Transportation related documentation, such as school bus mileage, bus routes;

(3) A list of students transported to and from school;

(4) An electronic student count program or database;

(5) Class record books;

(6) Supplemental program class record books;

(7) For residential programs, residential student attendance documentation;

(8) Evidence of teacher certification; and

(9) The school's accreditation certificate.

(c) The Director must maintain a record of required certifications for ELOs, specialists, and school superintendents in a central location.

§ 39.404 What is the certification and verification process?

(a) Each school must:

(1) Certify that the files required by § 39.403 are complete and accurate; and

(2) Compile a student roster that includes a complete list of all students by grade, days of attendance, and supplemental services.

(b) The chief school administrator and the president of the school board are responsible for certifying the school's ADM and residential count is true and accurate to the best of their knowledge or belief and is supported by appropriate documentation.

(c) OIEP's education line officer (ELO) will annually review the following to verify that the information is true and accurate and is supported by program documentation:

(1) The eligibility of every student;

(2) The school's ADM and supplemental program counts and residential count;

(3) Evidence of accreditation;

(4) Documentation for all provided basic and supplemental services, including all necessary documentation required by statute and regulations (*e.g.*, a current and complete Individual Education Plan for each student receiving supplemental services); and

(5) Documentation required by subpart G of this part for student transportation to and from school provided by commercial carriers.

§ 39.405 How will verifications be conducted?

The eligibility of every student shall be verified. The ELO will take a random sampling of five days with a minimum of one day per grading period to verify the information in § 39.404(c). The ELO will verify the count for the count period and verify residency during the remainder of the year.

§ 39.406 What documentation must the school maintain for additional services it provides?

Every school must maintain a file on each student receiving additional services. (Additional services include homebound services, institutional services, distance courses, Internet courses or college services.) The school must certify, and its records must show, that:

(a) Each homebound or institutionalized student is receiving 5 contact hours each week by certified educational personnel;

(b) Each student taking college, distance or internet courses is in physical attendance at the school for at least 3 certified contact hours per day.

§ 39.407 How long must a school maintain records?

The responsible administrative official for each school must maintain records relating to ISEP, supplemental services, and transportation-related expenditures. The official must maintain these records in appropriate retrievable storage for at least the four years prior to the current school year, unless Federal records retention schedules require a longer period.

§ 39.408 What are the responsibilities of administrative officials?

Administrative officials have the following responsibilities:

(a) Applying the appropriate standards in this part for classifying and counting ISEP eligible Indian students at the school for formula funding purposes;

(b) Accounting for and reporting student transportation expenditures;

(c) Providing training and supervision to ensure that appropriate standards are adhered to in counting students and accounting for student transportation expenditures;

(d) Submitting all reports and data on a timely basis; and

(e) Taking appropriate disciplinary action for failure to comply with requirements of this part.

§ 39.409 How does the OIEP Director ensure accountability?

(a) The Director of OIEP must ensure accountability in student counts and student transportation by doing all of the following:

(1) Conducting annual independent and random field audits of the processes and reports of at least one school per OIEP line office to ascertain the accuracy of Bureau line officers' reviews;

(2) Hearing and making decisions on appeals from school officials;

(3) Reviewing reports to ensure that standards and policies are applied consistently, education line officers treat schools fairly and equitably, and the Bureau takes appropriate administrative action for failure to follow this part; and

(4) Reporting the results of the findings and determinations under this section to the appropriate tribal governing body.

(b) The purpose of the audit required by paragraph (a)(1) of this section is to ensure that the procedures outlined in these regulations are implemented. To conduct the audit required by paragraph (a)(1) of this section, OIEP will select an independent audit firm that will:

(1) Select a statistically valid audit sample of recent student counts and student transportation reports; and

(2) Analyze these reports to determine adherence to the requirements of this part and accuracy in reporting.

§ 39.410 What qualifications must an audit firm meet to be considered for auditing ISEP administration?

To be considered for auditing ISEP administration under this subpart, an independent audit firm must:

(a) Be a licensed Certified Public Accountant Firm that meets all requirements for conducting audits under the Federal Single Audit Act;

(b) Not be under investigation or sanction for violation of professional audit standards or ethics;

(c) Certify that it has conducted a conflict of interests check and that no conflict exists; and

(d) Be selected through a competitive bidding process.

§ 39.411 How will the auditor report its findings?

(a) The auditor selected under § 39.410 must:

(1) Provide an initial draft report of its findings to the governing board or responsible Federal official for the school(s) involved; and

(2) Solicit, consider, and incorporate a response to the findings, where submitted, in the final audit report.

(b) The auditor must submit a final report to the Assistant Secretary—Indian Affairs and all tribes served by each school involved. The report must include all documented exceptions to the requirements of this part, including those exceptions that:

(1) The auditor regards as negligible;

(2) The auditor regards as significant, or as evidence of incompetence on the part of responsible officials, and that must be resolved in a manner similar to significant audit exceptions in a fiscal audit; or

(3) Involve fraud and abuse.

(c) The auditor must immediately report exceptions involving fraud and abuse directly to the Department of the Interior Inspector General's office.

§ 39.412 What sanctions apply for failure to comply with this subpart?

(a) The employer of a responsible administrative official must take appropriate personnel action if the official:

(1) Submits false or fraudulent ISEP-related counts;

(2) Submits willfully inaccurate counts of student participation in weighted program areas; or

(3) Certifies or verifies submissions described in paragraphs (a)(1) or (a)(2) of this section.

(b) Unless prohibited by law, the employer must report:

(1) Notice of final Federal personnel action to the tribal governing body and tribal school board; and

(2) Notice of final tribal or school board personnel action to the Director of OIEP.

§ 39.413 Can a school appeal the verification of the count?

Yes, a school may appeal to the Director any administrative action disallowing any academic, transportation, supplemental program or residential count. In this appeal, the school may provide evidence to indicate the student's eligibility, membership or residency or adequacy of a program for all or a portion of school year. The school must follow the applicable appeals process in 25 CFR part 2 or 25 CFR part 900, subpart L.

Subpart E—Contingency Fund

SOURCE: 70 FR 22205, Apr. 28, 2005, unless otherwise noted.

§ 39.500 What emergency and contingency funds are available?

The Secretary:

(a) Must reserve 1 percent of funds from the allotment formula to meet emergencies and unforeseen contingencies affecting educational programs;

(b) Can carry over to the next fiscal year a maximum of 1 percent the current year funds; and

(c) May distribute all funds in excess of 1 percent equally to all schools or distribute excess as a part of ISEP.

§ 39.501 What is an emergency or unforeseen contingency?

An emergency or unforeseen contingency is an event that meets all of the following criteria:

(a) It could not be planned for;

(b) It is not the result of mismanagement, malfeasance, or willful neglect;

(c) It is not covered by an insurance policy in force at the time of the event;

(d) The Assistant Secretary determines that Bureau cannot reimburse the emergency from the facilities emergency repair fund; and

(e) It could not have been prevented by prudent action by officials responsible for the educational program.

§ 39.502 How does a school apply for contingency funds?

To apply for contingency funds, a school must send a request to the ELO. The ELO must send the request to the Director for consideration within 48 hours of receipt. The Director will consider the severity of the event and will attempt to respond to the request as soon as possible, but in any event within 30 days.

§ 39.503 How can a school use contingency funds?

Contingency funds can be used only for education services and programs, including repair of educational facilities.

§ 39.504 May schools carry over contingency funds to a subsequent fiscal year?

Bureau-operated schools may carry over funds to the next fiscal year.

§ 39.505 What are the reporting requirements for the use of the contingency fund?

(a) At the end of each fiscal year, Bureau/OIEP shall send an annual report to Congress detailing how the Contingency Funds were used during the previous fiscal year.

(b) By October 1 of each year, the Bureau must send a letter to each school and each tribe operating a school listing the allotments from the Contingency Fund.

Subpart F—School Board Training Expenses

SOURCE: 70 FR 22205, Apr. 28, 2005, unless otherwise noted.

§ 39.600 Are Bureau-operated school board expenses funded by ISEP limited?

Yes. Bureau-operated schools are limited to $8,000 or one percent (1%) of ISEP allotted funds (not to exceed $15,000).

§ 39.601 Is school board training for Bureau-operated schools considered a school board expense subject to the limitation?

No, school board training for Bureau-operated schools is not considered a school board expense subject to the limitation in § 39.600.

§ 39.603 Is school board training required for all Bureau-funded schools?

Yes. Any new member of a local school board or an agency school board must complete 40 hours of training within one year of appointment, provided that such training is recommended, but is not required, for a tribal governing body that serves in the capacity of a school board.

§ 39.604 Is there a separate weight for school board training at Bureau-operated schools?

Yes. There is an ISEP weight not to exceed 1.2 WSUs to cover school board training and expenses at Bureau-operated schools.

Subpart G—Student Transportation

SOURCE: 70 FR 22205, Apr. 28, 2005, unless otherwise noted.

§ 39.700 What is the purpose of this subpart?

(a) This subpart covers how transportation mileage and funds for schools are calculated under the ISEP transportation program. The program funds transportation of students from home to school and return.

(b) To use this part effectively, a school should:

(1) Determine its eligibility for funds using the provisions of §§ 39.702 through 39.708;

(2) Calculate its transportation miles using the provisions of §§ 39.710 and 39.711; and

(3) Submit the required reports as required by §§ 39.721 and 39.722.

§ 39.701 What definitions apply to terms used in this subpart?

ISEP means the Indian School Equalization Program.

Transportation mileage count week means the last full week in September.

Unimproved roads means unengineered earth roads that do not have adequate gravel or other aggregate surface materials applied and do not have drainage ditches or shoulders.

ELIGIBILITY FOR FUNDS

§ 39.702 Can a school receive funds to transport residential students using commercial transportation?

A school transporting students by commercial bus, train, airplane, or other commercial modes of transportation will be funded at the cost of the commercial ticket for:

(a) The trip from home to school in the Fall;

(b) The round-trip return home at Christmas; and

(c) The return trip home at the end of the school year.

§ 39.703 What ground transportation costs are covered for students traveling by commercial transportation?

This section applies only if a school transports residential students by commercial bus, train or airplane from home to school. The school may receive funds for the ground miles that the school has to drive to deliver the students or their luggage from the bus, train, or plane terminal to the school.

§ 39.704 Are schools eligible to receive chaperone expenses to transport residential students?

Yes. Schools may receive funds for actual chaperone expenses, excluding salaries, during the transportation of students to and from home at the beginning and end of the school year and at Christmas.

§ 39.705 Are schools eligible for transportation funds to transport special education students?

Yes. A school that transports a special education student from home to a treatment center and back to home on a daily basis as required by the student's Individual Education Plan may count those miles for day student funding.

§ 39.706 Are peripheral dormitories eligible for day transportation funds?

Yes. If the peripheral dormitory is required to transport dormitory students to the public school, the dormitory may count those miles driven transporting students to the public school for day transportation funding.

§ 39.707 Which student transportation expenses are currently not eligible for Student Transportation Funding?

(a) The following transportation expenses are currently not eligible for transportation funding, however the data will be collected under the provisions in this subpart:

(1) Fuel and maintenance runs;

(2) Transportation home for medical or other emergencies;

(3) Transportation from school to treatment or special services programs;

(4) Transportation to after-school programs; and

(5) Transportation for day and boarding school students to attend instructional programs less than full-time at locations other than the school reporting the mileage.

(b) Examples of after-school programs covered by paragraph (a)(4) of this section include:

(1) Athletics;

(2) Band;

(3) Detention;

(4) Tutoring, study hall and special classes; and

(5) Extra-curricular activities such as arts and crafts.

§ 39.708 Are miles generated by non-ISEP eligible students eligible for transportation funding?

No. Only miles generated by ISEP-eligible students enrolled in and attending a school are eligible for student transportation funding.

CALCULATING TRANSPORTATION MILES

§ 39.710 How does a school calculate annual bus transportation miles for day students?

To calculate the total annual bus transportation miles for day students, a school must use the appropriate formula from this section. In the formulas, Tu = Miles driven on Tuesday of the transportation mileage count week, W = Miles driven on Wednesday of the transportation mileage count week, and Th = Miles driven on Thursday of the transportation mileage count week.

(a) For ISEP-eligible day students whose route is entirely over improved roads, calculate miles using the following formula:

$$\frac{Tu + W + Th}{3} * 180$$

(b) For ISEP-eligible day students whose route is partly over unimproved roads, calculate miles using the following three steps.

(1) *Step 1.* Apply the following formula to miles driven over improved roads only:

$$\frac{Tu + W + Th}{3} * 180$$

(2) *Step 2.* Apply the following formula to miles driven over unimproved roads only:

$$\frac{Tu + W + Th}{3} * 1.2 * 180$$

(3) *Step 3.* Add together the sums from steps 1 and 2 to obtain the total annual transportation miles.

§ 39.711 How does a school calculate annual bus transportation miles for residential students?

To calculate the total annual transportation miles for residential students, a school must use the procedures in paragraph (b) of this section.

(a) The school can receive funds for the following trips:

(1) Transportation to the school at the start of the school year;

(2) Round trip home at Christmas; and

(3) Return trip to home at the end of the school year.

(b) To calculate the actual miles driven to transport students from home to school at the start of the school year, add together the miles driven for all buses used to transport students from their homes to the school. If a school transports students over unimproved roads, the school must separate the number of miles driven for each bus into improved miles and unimproved miles. The number of miles driven is the sum of:

(1) The number of miles driven on improved roads; and

(2) The number of miles driven on unimproved roads multiplied by 1.2.

(c) The annual miles driven for each school is the sum of the mileage from paragraphs (b)(1) and (b)(2) of this section multiplied by 4.

REPORTING REQUIREMENTS

§ 39.720 Why are there different reporting requirements for transportation data?

In order to construct an actual cost data base, residential and day schools must report data required by §§ 39.721 and 39.722.

§ 39.721 What transportation information must off-reservation boarding schools report?

(a) Each off-reservation boarding school that provides transportation must report annually the information required by this section. The report must:

(1) Be submitted to OIEP by August 1 and cover the preceding school year;

(2) Include a Charter/Commercial and Air Transportation Form signed and certified as complete and accurate by the School Principal and the appropriate ELO; and

(3) Include the information required by paragraph (b) of this section.

(b) Each annual transportation report must include the following information:

(1) Fixed vehicle costs, including: the number and type of buses, passenger size, and local GSA rental rate and duration of GSA contract;

(2) Variable vehicle costs;

(3) Mileage traveled to transport students to and from school on school days, to sites of special services, and to extra-curricular activities;

(4) Medical trips;

(5) Maintenance and Service costs; and

(6) Driver costs;

(7) All expenses referred to in § 39.707.

§ 39.722 What transportation information must day schools, on-reservation boarding schools and peripheral dormitory schools report?

(a) By August 1 of each year, all schools and peripheral dorms that provide transportation must submit a report that covers the preceding year. This report must include:

(1) Fixed vehicle costs and other costs, including: the number and type of buses, passenger size, and local GSA rental rate and duration of GSA contract;

(2) Variable vehicle costs;

(3) Mileage traveled to transport students to and from school on school days, to sites of special services, and to extra-curricular activities;

(4) Mileage driven for student medical trips;

(5) Costs of vehicle maintenance and service cost, including cost of miles driven to obtain maintenance and service;

(6) Driver costs; and

(7) All expenses referred to in § 39.707.

(b) In addition, all day schools and on-reservation boarding schools must include in their report a Day Student Transportation Form signed and certified as complete and accurate by the School Principal and the appropriate ELO.

MISCELLANEOUS PROVISIONS

§ 39.730 Which standards must student transportation vehicles meet?

All vehicles used by schools to transport students must meet or exceed all appropriate Federal motor vehicle safety standards and State or Tribal motor vehicle safety standards. The Bureau will not fund transportation mileage and costs incurred transporting students in vehicles that do not meet these standards.

§ 39.731 Can transportation time be used as instruction time for day school students?

No. Transportation time cannot be used as instruction time for day school students in meeting the minimum required hours for academic funding.

§ 39.732 How does OIEP allocate transportation funds to schools?

OIEP allocates transportation funds based on the types of transportation programs that the school provides. To allocate transportation funds OIEP:

(a) Multiplies the one-way commercial costs for all schools by four to identify the total commercial costs for all schools;

(b) Subtracts the commercial cost total from the appropriated transportation funds and allocates the balance of the transportation funds to each school with a per-mile rate;

(c) Divides the balance of funds by the sum of the annual day miles and the annual residential miles to identify a per-mile rate;

(d) For day transportation, multiplies the per-mile rate times the annual day miles for each school; and

(e) For residential transportation, multiplies the per mile rate times the annual transportation miles for each school.

Subpart H—Determining the Amount Necessary To Sustain an Academic or Residential Program

SOURCE: 70 FR 22205, Apr. 28, 2005, unless otherwise noted.

§ 39.801 What is the formula to determine the amount necessary to sustain a school's academic or residential program?

(a) The Secretary's formula to determine the minimum annual amount necessary to sustain a Bureau-funded school's academic or residential program is as follows:

Student Unit Value × Weighted Student Unit = Annual Minimum Amount per student.

(b) Sections 39.802 through 39.807 explain the derivation of the formula in paragraph (a) of this section.

(c) If the annual minimum amount calculated under this section and §§ 39.802 through 39.807 is not fully funded, OIEP will pro rate funds distributed to schools using the Indian School Equalization Formula.

§ 39.802 What is the student unit value in the formula?

The student unit value is the dollar value applied to each student in an academic or residential program. There are two types of student unit values: the student unit instructional value (SUIV) and the student unit residential value (SURV).

(a) The student unit instructional value (SUIV) applies to a student enrolled in an instructional program. It is an annually established ratio of 1.0 that represents a student in grades 4 through 6 of a typical non-residential program.

(b) The student unit residential value (SURV) applies to a residential student. It is an annually established ratio of 1.0 that represents a student in grades 4 through 6 of a typical residential program.

§ 39.803 What is a weighted student unit in the formula?

A weighted student unit is an adjusted ratio using factors in the Indian School Equalization Formula to establish educational priorities and to provide for the unique needs of specific students, such as:

(a) Students in grades kindergarten through 3 or grades 7 through 12;

(b) Special education students;

(c) Gifted and talented students;

(d) Distance education students;

(e) Vocational and industrial education students;

(f) Native Language Instruction students;

(g) Small schools;

(h) Personnel costs;

(i) Alternative schooling; and

(j) Early Childhood Education programs.

§ 39.804 How is the SUIV calculated?

The SUIV is calculated by the following 5-step process:

(a) *Step 1.* Use the adjusted national average current expenditures (ANACE) of public and private schools determined by data from the U.S. Department of Education-National Center of Education Statistics (NCES) for the last school year for which data is available.

(b) *Step 2.* Subtract the average specific Federal share per student (title I part A and IDEA part B) of the total revenue for Bureau-funded elementary and secondary schools for the last school year for which data is available as reported by NCES (15%).

(c) *Step 3.* Subtract the administrative cost grant/agency area technical services revenue per student as a percentage of the total revenue (current expenditures) of Bureau-funded schools from the last year data is available.

(d) *Step 4.* Subtract the day transportation revenue per student as a percentage of the total revenue (current revenue) Bureau-funded schools for the last school year for which data is available.

(e) *Step 5.* Add Johnson O'Malley funding. (See the table, in § 39.805)

§ 39.805 What was the student unit for instruction value (SUIV) for the school year 1999–2000?

The process described in § 39.804 is illustrated in the table below, using figures for the 1999–2000 school year:

Step 1	$8,030	ANACE.
Step 2	−1205	Average specific Federal share of total revenue for Bureau-funded schools.
Step 3	−993	Cost grant/technical services revenue as a percentage total revenue.
Step 4	−658	Transportation revenue as a percentage of the total revenue.
Step 5	85	Johnson O'Malley funding.
Total	$5,259	SUIV.

§ 39.806 How is the SURV calculated?

(a) The SURV is the adjusted national average current expenditures for residential schools (ANACER) of public and private residential schools. This average is determined using data from the Association of Boarding Schools.

(b) Applying the procedure in paragraph (a) of this section, the SURV for school year 1999–2000 was $11,000.

§ 39.807 How will the Student Unit Value be adjusted annually?

(a) The student unit instructional value (SUIV) and the student unit residential value (SURV) will be adjusted annually to derive the current year Student Unit Value (SUV) by dividing the calculated SUIV and the SURV into two parts and adjusting each one as shown in this section.

(1) The first part consists of 85 percent of the calculated SUIV and the SURV. OIEP will adjust this portion using the personnel cost of living increase of the Department of Defense schools for each year.

(2) The second part consists of 15 percent the calculated SUIV and the SURV. OIEP will adjust this portion using the Consumer Price Index-Urban of the Department of Labor.

(b) If the student unit value amount is not fully funded, the schools will receive their pro rata share using the Indian School Equalization Formula.

§ 39.808 What definitions apply to this subpart?

Adjusted National Average Current Expenditure [ANACE] means the actual current expenditures for pupils in fall enrollment in public elementary and secondary schools for the last school year for which data is available. These expenditures are adjusted annually to reflect current year expenditures of federally financed schools' cost of day and residential programs.

Current expenditures means expenses related to classroom instruction, classroom supplies, administration, support services-students and other support services and operations. Current expenditures do not include facility operations and maintenance, buildings and improvements, furniture, equipment, vehicles, student activities and debt retirement.

§ 39.809 Information collection.

Notwithstanding any other provision of law, no person is required to respond to, nor shall any person be subject to a penalty for failure to comply with, a collection of information subject to the requirements of the Paperwork Reduction Act of 1995 (44 U.S.C. 3501 *et seq.*) (PRA), unless that collection of information displays a currently valid Office of Management and Budget (OMB) Control Number. This part involves collections of information subject to the PRA in §§ 39.410 and 39.502. These collections have been approved by OMB under control numbers 1076–0122, 1076–0134, and 1076–0163.

Subpart I—Interim Maintenance and Minor Repair Fund

SOURCE: 44 FR 61864, Oct. 26, 1979, unless otherwise noted. Redesignated at 47 FR 13327, Mar. 30, 1982. Redesignated at 70 FR 33702, June 9, 2005.

§ 39.900 Establishment and funding of an Interim Maintenance and Minor Repair Fund.

There is established in the Division of Facilities Management a separate temporary fund entitled the Interim Maintenance and Minor Repair Fund. The Assistant Secretary shall cause the distribution of an amount of $1 million, under the FY 1980 Appropriation for the Bureau, from budget activity 3500, "General Management and Facilities Operation", to the direct use of schools, and shall create an appropriate account or subaccount for the Interim Maintenance and Minor Repair Fund and credit these funds thereto.

§ 39.901 Conditions for distribution.

Funds from the Interim Maintenance and Minor Repair Fund shall be distributed to Bureau operated and funded schools and shall be separately earmarked in local school financial plans solely for expenditure at the discretion of the school supervisor for cost of school facility maintenance and minor repair. These funds shall be used to meet immediate minor repair and maintenance needs.

§ 39.902 Allocation.

(a) Interim Maintenance and Minor Repair funds shall be allocated to all Bureau operated and contract schools based on the number of square feet of floor space used for that school's educational program, for student residence and for support facilities. Staff quarters shall be specifically excluded from the computation.

(b) Square footage figures used in determining school allocations shall be taken from the facilities inventory maintained by the Division of Facilities Engineering.

(c) In those cases, such as contract schools, where square footage figures are not now available, it shall be the responsibility of the Bureau's Division of Facilities Engineering to correct the information.

(d) Schools in Alaska shall receive a 25% cost adjustment increase in the computation of their allocation.

§ 39.903 Use of funds.

Funds allocated under this provision for maintenance and minor repair shall be used for no other purpose.

§ 39.904 Limitations.

Nothing in this provision shall be interpreted as relieving the Bureau branch of Facilities Management or its field offices of any responsibility for continuing to provide maintenance and repair service to schools through existing procedures.

Subpart J—Administrative Cost Formula

SOURCE: 56 FR 35795, July 26, 1991, unless otherwise noted. Redesignated at 70 FR 33702, June 9, 2005.

§ 39.1000 Purpose and scope.

The purpose of this subpart is to provide funds at the agency and area education offices for FY 1991 and future years for administration of all Bureau of Indian Affairs education functions, including but not limited to school operations, continuing education, early childhood education, post-secondary education and Johnson-O'Malley Programs.

§ 39.1001 Definitions.

(a) *Agency Education Office* means a field office of the Office of Indian Education Programs providing administrative direction and supervision to one or more Bureau-operated schools as well as being responsible for all other education functions serving tribes within that agency's jurisdiction.

(b) *Area Education Office* means a field office of the Office of Indian Education Programs responsible for all education functions serving tribes not serviced by an agency education office an in some cases providing administrative direction to one or more off-reservation boarding schools not under an agency education office.

§ 39.1002 Allotment of education administrative funds.

The total annual budget for agencies/areas shall be allotted to the Director and through him/her to agency and area education offices. This total budget shall be distributed to the various agency and area education offices as follows:

(a) Each agency or area education office as defined above shall receive a base amount of $50,000 for basic administrative costs; and

(b) Each agency or area education office as defined above shall receive an amount under these funds equal to two percent of the total higher education, Johnson-O'Malley and adult education funds administered by each office, except that the Navajo Agencies are restricted to a maximum of $50,000 for administering the Johnson-O'Malley and higher education programs; and

(c) Eighty percent of the remaining funds shall be distributed proportionately based on the number of schools operated under the jurisdiction of each agency or area education office, with Bureau-operated schools counting as 1 and contract/grant schools counting as 0.6; and

(d) The remaining twenty percent shall be distributed proportionately based on the total weighted student units generated by all schools under the jurisdiction of each agency or area education office.

§ 39.1003 Allotment exception for FY 1991.

For FY 1991 only, the Director may reserve an amount equal to no more than one half of the funds received in FY 1990 by those offices to be closed in FY 1991 to cover severance pay costs, lump sum leave payments and relocation costs for those individuals affected by the closures. Any balance uncommitted by March 31, 1991, shall be distributed in accordance with the formula in § 39.122.

Subpart K—Pre-kindergarten Programs

SOURCE: 44 FR 61864, Oct. 26, 1979, unless otherwise noted. Redesignated at 47 FR 13327, Mar. 30, 1982. Redesignated at 70 FR 33702, June 9, 2005.

§ 39.1100 Interim fiscal year 1980 and fiscal year 1981 funding for pre-kindergarten programs previously funded by the Bureau.

Those schools having pre-kindergarten programs funded fully or in part from Bureau education funds in fiscal year 1979 shall be funded from Bureau education funds by the Director in fiscal year 1980 and fiscal year 1981 at their fiscal year 1979 Bureau education funding levels. The fiscal year 1979 pre-kindergarten Bureau funding amount for each Bureau funded school shall be deducted from the school's fiscal year 1979 Bureau Education Budget amount prior to application of the phase-in provision.

[44 FR 61864, Oct. 26, 1979. Redesignated at 47 FR 13327, Mar. 30, 1982. Redesignated and amended at 70 FR 33702, June 9, 2005]

§ 39.1101 Addition of pre-kindergarten as a weight factor to the Indian School Equalization Formula in fiscal year 1982.

The Director, in consultation with the tribes and school boards, shall determine appropriate weight factors needed to include pre-kindergarten programs in the Indian School Equalization Formula in fiscal year 1982. Based on a needs assessment, to be completed by January 1, 1980, pre-kindergarten programs shall be included in the Bureau's education request for fiscal year 1982.

Subpart L—Contract School Operation and Maintenance Fund

SOURCE: 44 FR 61864, Oct. 26, 1979, unless otherwise noted. Redesignated at 70 FR 33702, June 9, 2005.

§ 39.1200 Definitions.

Contract school operation and maintenance costs for fiscal year 1979 means the sum of costs for custodial salaries and fringe benefits, related supplies and equipment and equipment repair, insurance, and school operation utilities costs, where such costs are not paid by the Division of Facilities Management or other noneducation Bureau sources.

§ 39.1201 Establishment of an interim fiscal year 1980 operation and maintenance fund for contract schools.

There is established in the Division of Facilities Management a separate fund entitled the Contract School Operation and Maintenance Fund. The Secretary shall cause the distribution of an amount of $2.5 million, under the fiscal year 1980 appropriation for the Bureau, from budget activity 3500. "General Management and Facilities Operations", to the schools through this fund and shall create an appropriate account or subaccount for the Contract School Operation and Maintenance Fund.

§ 39.1202 Distribution of funds.

(a) Each contract school shall receive in fiscal year 1980 a portion of the Contract School Operation and Maintenance Fund determined by the percentage share which that school's fiscal year 1979 operation and maintenance cost represents in the total fiscal year 1979 operation and maintenance cost for all such schools.

(b) To be eligible for these funds, a contract school shall submit a detailed report of actual operation and maintenance costs for fiscal year 1979 to the Director by November 23, 1979. These cost figures will be subject to verification by the Director to assure their accuracy prior to the allotment of any funds under this subpart.

(c) Any funds generated under this subpart shall be included in the computation of the phase-in amount if supplemental operation and maintenance funds were included in a school's fiscal year 1979 3100 contract funds.

[44 FR 61864, Oct. 26, 1979. Redesignated at 47 FR 13327, Mar. 30, 1982. Redesignated and amended at 70 FR 33702, June 9, 2005]

§ 39.1203 Future consideration of contract school operation and maintenance funding.

The Assistant Secretary shall arrange for full funding for operation and maintenance of contract schools by fiscal year 1981.

PART 40—ADMINISTRATION OF EDUCATIONAL LOANS, GRANTS AND OTHER ASSISTANCE FOR HIGHER EDUCATION

Sec.

AUTHORITY: Sec. 11, 48 Stat. 986; 25 U.S.C. 471.

SOURCE: 22 FR 10533, Dec. 24, 1957, unless otherwise noted. Redesignated at 47 FR 13327, Mar. 30, 1982.

§ 40.1 Appropriations for loans or grants.

Funds appropriated by Congress for the education of Indians may be used for making educational loans and grants to aid students of one-fourth or more degree of Indian blood attending accredited institutions of higher education or other accredited schools offering vocational and technical training who reside within the exterior boundaries of Indian reservations under the jurisdiction of the Bureau of Indian Affairs or on trust or restricted lands under the jurisdiction of the Bureau of Indian Affairs. Such educational loans and grants may be made also to students of one-fourth or more degree of Indian blood who reside near the reservation when a denial of such loans or grants would have a direct effect upon Bureau programs within the reservation. After students meeting these eligibility requirements are taken care of, Indian students who do not meet the residency requirements but are otherwise eligible may be considered.

[33 FR 9708, July 4, 1968. Redesignated at 47 FR 13327, Mar. 30, 1982]

§40.2 Working scholarships.

Working scholarships may be granted to Indians who wish to earn their board and room by part-time work at Federal boarding schools that are located near a college, trade, or vocational school.

§40.3 Applications.

Applications for educational loans, grants, and working scholarships shall be submitted through the superintendent or officer in charge of the agency at which the applicant is enrolled in the manner prescribed by the Commissioner.

§40.4 Security.

If a borrower or cosigner has security to offer for an educational loan it must be given in an amount adequate to protect the loan.

§40.5 Repayments.

Repayment schedules for educational loans may provide not to exceed two years for repayment for each year in school.

PART 41—GRANTS TO TRIBAL COLLEGES AND UNIVERSITIES AND DINÉ COLLEGE

Subpart A—Applicability and Definitions

Sec.

Subpart B—Tribal Colleges and Universities

Subpart C—Diné College

AUTHORITY: Public Law 95–471, Oct. 17, 1978, 92 Stat. 1325; amended Public Law 98–192, Dec. 1, 1983, 97 Stat. 1335; Public Law 99–428, Sept. 30, 1986, 100 Stat. 982; Public Law 105–244, Oct. 7, 1998, 112 Stat. 1619; Public Law 110–315, Aug. 14, 2008, 122 Stat. 3460; 25 U.S.C. 1801 *et seq.*; Public Law 98–192, Dec. 15, 1971, 85 Stat. 646; and Public Law 110–315, Aug. 14, 2008, 122 Stat. 3468; 25 U.S.C. 640a *et seq.*

SOURCE: 81 FR 38587, June 14, 2016, unless otherwise noted.

Subpart A—Applicability and Definitions

§41.1 When does this subpart apply?

The provisions in this subpart A apply to subparts B and C.

§ 41.3 What definitions are needed?

As used in this part:

Academic facilities mean structures suitable for use as:

(1) Classrooms, laboratories, libraries, and related facilities necessary or appropriate for instruction of students;

(2) Research facilities;

(3) Facilities for administration of educational or research programs;

(4) Dormitories or student services buildings; or

(5) Maintenance, storage, support, or utility facilities essential to the operation of the foregoing facilities.

Academic term means a semester, trimester, or other such period (not less than six weeks in duration) into which a Tribal college or university normally subdivides its academic year, but does not include a summer term.

Academic year means a twelve month period established by a Tribal college or university as the annual period for the operation of the Tribal college's or university's education programs.

Assistant Secretary means the Assistant Secretary—Indian Affairs of the Department of the Interior.

BIE means the Bureau of Indian Education.

College or university means an institution of higher education that is formally controlled, formally sanctioned, or chartered by the governing body of an Indian Tribe or Tribes. To qualify under this definition, the college or university must:

(1) Be the only institution recognized by the Department for the Tribe, excluding Diné College; and

(2) If under the control, sanction, or charter of more than one Tribe, be the only institution recognized by the Department for at least one Tribe that currently has no other formally controlled, formally sanctioned, or chartered college or university.

Department means the Department of the Interior.

Director means the Director of the Bureau of Indian Education.

Eligible continuing education units (CEUs) means non-degree credits that meet the criteria established by the International Association of Continuing Education and Training.

Full-time means registered for 12 or more credit hours for an academic term.

Indian Student Count (ISC) or Indian Full-Time Equivalent (FTE) means a number equal to the total number of Indian students enrolled at a Tribal college or university, determined according to the formula in § 41.5.

Indian student means a student who is a member of an Indian Tribe, or a biological child of a living or deceased member of an Indian Tribe. Documentation is required to verify eligibility as a biological child of a living or deceased member of an Indian Tribe, and may include birth certificate and marriage license; Tribal records of student's parent; Indian Health Service eligibility cards; other documentation necessary to authenticate a student as eligible to be counted as an *Indian student* under this definition.

Indian Tribe means an Indian Tribe, band, nation, pueblo, rancheria, or other organized group or community, including any Alaska Native Village or regional or village corporation as defined in or established pursuant to the Alaska Native Claims Settlement Act, to be listed in the FEDERAL REGISTER pursuant to 25 CFR 83.5(a) as recognized by and eligible to receive services from the Bureau of Indian Affairs.

Institution of higher education means an institution as defined by section 1001(a) of Title 20 of the United States Code, except that clause (2) of such section is not applicable and the reference to Secretary in clause (5)(A) of such section will be deemed to refer to the Secretary of the Interior.

National Indian organization means an organization which the Secretary finds to be nationally based, represents a substantial Indian constituency and has expertise in the fields of Tribal colleges and universities, and Indian higher education.

NCCA means the Navajo Community College Act of 1978, as amended (25 U.S.C. 640a *et seq.*).

Operating expenses of education programs means the obligations and expenditures of a Tribal college or university for postsecondary education, except for obligations and expenditures for acquisition or construction of academic facilities. Permissible expenditures may include:

(1) Administration;

(2) Instruction;

(3) Maintenance and repair of facilities; and

(4) Acquisition and upgrade of equipment, technological equipment, and other physical resources.

Part-time means registered for less than 12 credit hours for an academic term.

Satisfactory progress means satisfactory progress toward a degree or certificate as defined by the Tribal college or university.

Secretary, unless otherwise designated, means the Secretary of the Interior, or his/her duly authorized representative.

TCCUA means the Tribally Controlled Colleges and Universities Assistance Act of 1978, as amended (25 U.S.C. 1801 *et seq.*).

You or *your* means the Tribal college or university.

§41.5 How is ISC/FTE calculated?

(a) ISC is calculated on the basis of eligible registrations of Indian students as of the conclusion of the third week of each academic term.

(b) To calculate ISC for an academic term, begin by adding all credit hours of full-time Indian students and all credit hours of part-time Indian students, including full-time and part-time distance education Indian students, who are registered at the conclusion of the third week of the academic term.

(c) Credit hours earned by Indian students who have not obtained a high school degree or its equivalent may be added if you have established criteria for the admission of such students on the basis of their ability to benefit from the education or training offered. You will be presumed to have established such criteria if your admission procedures include counseling or testing that measures students' aptitude to successfully complete the courses in which they enroll.

(d) No credit hours earned by an Indian student attending high school and applied towards the student's high school degree or its equivalent may be counted toward computation of ISC; and no credit hours earned by an Indian student not making satisfactory progress toward a degree or certificate may count toward the ISC.

(e) If ISC is being calculated for a fall term, add to the calculation in paragraph (b) of this section any credits earned in classes offered during the preceding summer term.

(f) Add to the calculation in paragraph (b) of this section those credits being earned in an eligible continuing education program at the conclusion of the third week of the academic term. Determine the number of those credits as follows:

(1) For institutions on a semester system: One credit for every 15 contact hours and

(2) For institutions on a quarter system: One credit for every 10 contact hours of participation in an organized continuing education experience under responsible sponsorship, capable direction, and qualified instruction, as described in the criteria established by the International Association for Continuing Education and Training. Limit the number of calculated eligible continuing education credits to 10 percent of your ISC.

(g) Divide by 12 the final calculation in paragraph (f) of this section. The formula for the full calculation is expressed mathematically as:

$$ISC = (FTCR + PTCR + SCR + CECR)/12$$

(h) In the formula in paragraph (g) of this section, the abbreviations used have the following meanings:

(1) FTCR = the number of credit hours carried by full-time Indian students (students carrying 12 or more credit hours at the end of the third week of each academic term); and

(2) PTCR = the number of credit hours carried by part-time Indian students (students carrying fewer than 12 credit hours at the end of the third week of each academic term).

(3) SCR = in a fall term, the number of credit hours earned during the preceding summer term.

(4) CECR = the number of credit hours being earned in an eligible continuing education program at the conclusion of the third week of the academic term, in accordance with paragraph (f)(2) of this section.

§ 41.7 What happens if false information is submitted?

Persons submitting or causing to be submitted any false information in connection with any application, report, or other document under this part may be subject to criminal prosecution under provisions such as sections 371 or 1001 of Title 18, U.S. Code.

Subpart B—Tribal Colleges and Universities

§ 41.9 What is the purpose of this subpart?

This subpart prescribes procedures for providing financial and technical assistance under the TCCUA for the operation and improvement of Tribal colleges and universities and advancement of educational opportunities for Indian students. This subpart does not apply to Diné College.

§ 41.11 Who is eligible for financial assistance under this subpart?

(a) A Tribal college or university is eligible for financial assistance under this subpart only if it:

(1) Is governed by a board of directors or board of trustees, a majority of whom are Indians;

(2) Demonstrates adherence to stated goals, a philosophy, or a plan of operation directed to meet the needs of Indians;

(3) Has a student body that is more than 50 percent Indian (unless it has been in operation for less than one year);

(4) Is either:

(i) Accredited by a nationally recognized accrediting agency or association determined by the Secretary of Education to be a reliable authority with regard to the quality of training offered; or

(ii) Is making reasonable progress toward accreditation according to such agency or association;

(5) Has received a positive determination after completion of an eligibility study; and

(6) Complies with the requirements of § 41.19.

(b) Priority in grants is given to institutions that were in operation on October 17, 1978, and that have a history of service to Indian people.

§ 41.13 For what activities can financial assistance to Tribal colleges and universities be used?

Tribal colleges and universities may use financial assistance under this subpart to defray expenditures for academic, educational, and administrative purposes and for the operation and maintenance of the college or university.

§ 41.15 What activities are prohibited?

Tribal colleges and universities must not use financial assistance awarded under this subpart in connection with religious worship or sectarian instruction. However, nothing in this subpart will be construed as barring instruction or practice in comparative religions or cultures or in languages of Indian Tribes.

§ 41.17 What is the role of the Secretary of Education?

(a) The Secretary may enter into an agreement with the Secretary of Education to obtain assistance to:

(1) Develop plans, procedures, and criteria for eligibility studies required under this subpart; and

(2) Conduct such studies.

(b) BIE must consult with the Secretary of Education to determine the reasonable number of students required to support a Tribal college or university.

§ 41.19 How can a Tribal college or university establish eligibility to receive a grant?

(a) Before a Tribal college or university can apply for an initial grant under this part, the governing body of one or more Indian Tribes must request a determination of eligibility on the college's or university's behalf.

(b) Within 30 days of receiving a resolution or other duly authorized request from the governing body of one or more

Indian Tribes, BIE will initiate an eligibility study to determine whether there is justification to encourage and maintain a Tribal college or university.

(c) The eligibility study will analyze the following factors:

(1) Financial feasibility based upon reasonable potential enrollment; considering:

(i) Tribal, linguistics, or cultural differences;

(ii) Isolation;

(iii) Presence of alternate educational sources;

(iv) Proposed curriculum;

(2) Levels of Tribal matriculation in and graduation from postsecondary educational institutions; and

(3) The benefits of continued and expanded educational opportunities for Indian students.

(d) Based upon results of the study, the Director will send the Tribe a written determination of eligibility.

(e) The Secretary and the BIE, to the extent practicable, will consult with national Indian organizations and with Tribal governments chartering the colleges or universities being considered.

§41.21 How can a Tribe appeal the results of an eligibility study?

If a Tribe receives a negative determination under §41.19(d), it may submit an appeal to the Assistant Secretary within 45 days.

(a) Following the timely filing of a Tribe's notice of appeal, the Tribal college or university and the Tribe have a right to a formal review of the eligibility study, including a hearing upon reasonable notice within 60 days. At the hearing, the Tribal college or university and the appealing Tribe may present additional evidence or arguments to justify eligibility.

(b) Within 45 days of the hearing, the Assistant Secretary will issue a written ruling confirming, modifying, or reversing the original determination. The ruling will be final and BIE will mail or deliver it within one week of its issuance.

(c) If the Assistant Secretary does not reverse the original negative determination, the ruling will specify the grounds for the decision and state the manner in which the determination relates to each of the factors in §41.11.

§41.23 Can a Tribal college or university request a second eligibility study?

If a Tribe is not successful in its appeal under §41.21, it can request another eligibility study 12 months or more after the date of the negative determination.

§41.25 How does a Tribal college or university apply for a grant?

(a) If the Tribal college or university receives a positive determination of the eligibility study under §41.19(d), it is entitled to apply for financial assistance under this subpart.

(b) To be considered for assistance, a Tribal college or university must submit an application by or before June 1st of the year preceding the academic year for which the Tribal college or university is requesting assistance. The application must contain the following:

Required information	Required details
(1) Identifying information	(i) Name and address of the Tribal college or university. (ii) Names of the governing board members, and the number of its members who are Indian. (iii) Name and address of the Tribe or Tribes that control or have sanctioned or chartered the Tribal college or university.
(2) Eligibility verification	The date on which an eligibility determination was received.
(3) Curriculum materials	(i) A statement of goals, philosophy, or plan of operation demonstrating how the education program is designed to meet the needs of Indians. (ii) A curriculum, which may be in the form of a college catalog or similar publication, or information located on the Tribal college or university Web site.
(4) Financial information	(i) A proposed budget showing total expected education program operating expenses and expected revenues from all sources for the academic year to which the information applies. (ii) A description of record-keeping procedures used to track fund expenditures and to audit and monitor funded programs.

Required information	Required details
(5) Enrollment information	(i) If the Tribal college or university has been in operation for more than one year, a statement of the total number of ISC (FTE Indian students) and the total number of all FTE students. Grantees may exclude high school students for the purpose of calculating the total number of FTE students. (ii) If the Tribal college or university has not yet begun operations, or has been in operation for less than one year, a statement of expected enrollment, including the total number of FTE students and the ISC (FTE Indian students) and may also require verification of the number of registered students after operations have started.
(6) Assurances and requests	(i) Assurance that the Tribal college or university will not deny admission to any Indian student because that student is, or is not, a member of a specific Tribe. (ii) Assurance that the Tribal college or university will comply with the requirements in §41.39 of this subpart. (iii) A request and justification for a specific waiver of any requirement of 25 CFR part 276 which a Tribal college or university believe to be inappropriate.
(7) Certification	Certification by the chief executive that the information on the application is complete and correct.

(c) Material submitted in a Tribal college's or university's initial successful grant application will be retained by the BIE. A Tribal college or university submitting a subsequent application for a grant, must either confirm the information previously submitted remains accurate or submit updated information, as necessary.

§41.27 When can the Tribal college or university expect a decision on its application?

Within 45 days of receiving an application, the Director will notify the Tribal college or university in writing whether or not the application has been approved.

(a) If the Director approves the application, written notice will explain when the BIE will send the Tribal college or university a grant agreement under §41.19.

(b) If the Director disapproves the application, written notice will include:

(1) The reasons for disapproval; and

(2) A statement advising the Tribal college or university of the right to amend or supplement the Tribal college's or university's application within 45 days.

(c) The Tribal college or university may appeal a disapproval or a failure to act within 45 days of receipt following the procedures in §41.21.

§41.29 How will a grant be awarded?

If the Director approves the Tribal college's or university's application, the BIE will send the Tribal college or university a grant agreement that incorporates the Tribal college's or university's application and the provisions required by §41.25. The Tribal college or university grant will be for the fiscal year starting after the approval date of the application.

(a) The BIE will generally calculate the amount of the Tribal college or university grant using the following procedure:

(1) Begin with a base amount of $8,000 (adjusted annually for inflation);

(2) Multiply the base amount by the number of FTE Indian students in attendance during each academic term; and

(3) Divide the resulting sum by the number of academic terms in the academic year.

(b) All grants under this section are subject to availability of appropriations.

(c) If there are insufficient funds to pay the amount calculated under paragraph (a) of this section, BIE will reduce the grant amount awarded to each eligible Tribal college or university on a pro rata basis.

§41.31 When will the Tribal college or university receive funding?

(a) BIE will authorize payments equal to 95 percent of funds available for allotment by either July 1 or within 14 days after appropriations become available, with the remainder of the payment made no later than September 30.

(b) BIE will not commingle funds appropriated for grants under this subpart with other funds expended by the BIE.

§41.33 What if there isn't enough money to pay the full grant amount?

This section applies if BIE has to reduce payments under §41.29(c).

(a) If additional funds have not been appropriated to pay the full amount of grants under this part on or before June 1st of the year, the BIE will notify all grant recipients in writing. The Tribal college or university must submit a written report to the BIE on or before July 1st explaining how much of the grant money remains unspent.

(b) After receiving the Tribal college's or university's report under paragraph (a) of this section, BIE will:

(1) Reallocate the unspent funds using the formula in §41.29 in proportion to the amount of assistance to which each grant recipient is entitled but has not received;

(2) Ensure that no Tribal college or university will receive more than the total annual cost of its education programs;

(3) Collect unspent funds as necessary for redistribution to other grantees under this section; and

(4) Make reallocation payments on or before August 1st of the academic year.

§41.35 What will happen if the Tribal college or university doesn't receive its appropriate share?

(a) If the BIE determines the Tribal college or university has received financial assistance to which the Tribal college or university was not entitled, BIE will:

(1) Promptly notify the Tribal college or university; and

(2) Reduce the amount of the Tribal college's or university's payments under this subpart to compensate for any overpayments or otherwise attempt to recover the overpayments.

(b) If a Tribal college or university has received less financial assistance than the amount to which the Tribal college or university was entitled, the Tribal college or university should promptly notify the BIE. If the BIE confirms the miscalculation, BIE will adjust the amount of the Tribal college's or university's payments for the same or subsequent academic years to compensate for the underpayments. This adjustment will come from the Department's general funds and not from future appropriated funds.

§41.37 Is the Tribal college or university eligible for other grants?

Yes. Eligibility for grants under this subpart does not bar a Tribal college or university from receiving financial assistance under any other Federal program.

§41.39 What reports does the Tribal college or university need to provide?

(a) The Tribal college or university must provide the BIE, on or before December 1 of each year, a report that includes:

(1) An accounting of the amounts and purposes for which the Tribal college or university spent assistance received under this part during the preceding academic year;

(2) An accounting of the annual cost of the Tribal college's or university's education programs from all sources for the academic year; and

(3) A final performance report based upon the criteria the Tribal college's or university's goals, philosophy, or plan of operation.

(b) The Tribal college or university must report to the BIE their FTE Indian student enrollment for each academic term of the academic year within three (3) weeks of the date the Tribal college or university makes the FTE calculation.

§41.41 Can the Tribal college or university receive technical assistance?

(a) If a Tribal college or university sends the BIE a written request for technical assistance, BIE will respond within 30 days.

(b) The BIE will provide technical assistance either directly or through annual contract to a national Indian organization that the Tribal college or university designates.

(c) Technical assistance may include consulting services for developing programs, plans, and eligibility studies and accounting, and other services or technical advice.

§ 41.43 How must the Tribal college or university administer its grant?

In administering any grant provided under this subpart, a Tribal college or university must:

(a) Provide services or assistance under this subpart in a fair and uniform manner;

(b) Not deny admission to any Indian student because they either are, or are not, a member of a specific Indian Tribe; and

(c) Comply with part 276 of this chapter, unless the BIE expressly waives specific inappropriate provisions of part 276 in response to a Tribal college or university request and justification for a waiver.

§ 41.45 How does the Tribal college or university apply for programming grants?

(a) Tribes and Tribal entities may submit a written request to the BIE for a grant to conduct planning activities for the purpose of developing proposals for the establishment of Tribally controlled colleges and universities, or to determine the need and potential for the establishment of such colleges and universities. BIE will provide written notice to the Tribal college or university of its determination on the grant request within 30 days.

(b) Subject to the availability of appropriations, BIE may provide such grants to up to five Tribes and Tribal entities in the amount of $15,000 each.

§ 41.47 Are Tribal colleges or universities eligible for endowments?

Yes. Tribal colleges and universities are eligible for endowments under a signed agreement between the Tribal college and university and the Secretary as described in 25 U.S.C. 1832. Endowments must be invested in a trust fund and the Tribal college or university may only use the interest deposited for the purpose of defraying expenses associated with the operation of the Tribal college or university (25 U.S.C. 1833).

Subpart C—Diné College

§ 41.49 What is the purpose of this subpart?

The purpose of this subpart is to assist the Navajo Nation in providing education to the members of the Tribe and other qualified applicants through a community college, established by that Tribe, known as Diné College. To that end, the regulations in this subpart prescribe procedures for providing financial and technical assistance for Diné College under the NCCA.

§ 41.51 What is the scope of this subpart?

The regulations in this subpart are applicable to the provision of financial assistance to Diné College pursuant to NCCA, title II of the TCCUA.

§ 41.53 How does Diné College request financial assistance?

To request financial assistance, Diné College must submit an application. The application must be certified by the Diné College chief executive officer and include:

(a) A statement of Indian student enrollment and total FTE enrollment for the preceding academic year;

(b) A curriculum description, which may be in the form of a college catalog or like publication or information located on the Diné College Web site; and

(c) A proposed budget showing total expected operating expenses of educational programs and expected revenue from all sources for the grant year.

§ 41.55 How are grant funds processed?

(a) BIE will identify the budget request for Diné College separately in its annual budget justification.

(b) BIE will not commingle funds appropriated for grants under this subpart with appropriations that are historically expended by the Bureau of Indian Affairs for programs and projects normally provided on the Navajo Reservation for Navajo beneficiaries.

§41.57 When will the application be reviewed?

Within 45 days of receiving the application the BIE will send a grant agreement for signature by the Diné College president or his or her designee in an amount determined under §41.29(a). The grant agreement will incorporate the grant application and include the provisions required by §41.25.

§41.59 When will grant funds be paid?

(a) Initial grant funds will be paid in an advance installment of not less than 40 percent of the funds available for allotment by October 1st.

(b) The remainder of the grant funds will be paid by July 1st after the BIE adjusts the amount to reflect any overpayments or underpayments made in the first disbursement.

§41.61 Is Diné College eligible to receive other grants?

Yes. Eligibility for grants under this subpart does not bar Diné College from receiving financial assistance under any other Federal program.

§41.63 How can financial assistance be used?

(a) The Diné College must use financial assistance under this subpart only for operation and maintenance, including educations programs, annual capital expenditures, major capital improvements, mandatory payments, supplemental student services, and improvement and expansion, as described in 25 U.S.C. 640c–1(b)(1);

(b) The Diné College must not use financial assistance under this subpart for religious worship or sectarian instruction. However, this subpart does not prohibit instruction about religions, cultures or Indian Tribal languages.

§41.65 What reports must be provided?

(a) Diné College must submit on or before December 1st of each year a report that includes:

(1) An accounting of the amounts and purposes for which Diné College spent the financial assistance during the preceding academic year;

(2) The annual cost of Diné College education programs from all sources for the academic year; and

(3) A final report of Diné College's performance based upon the criteria in its stated goals, philosophy, or plan of operation.

(b) Diné College must report its FTE Indian student enrollment for each academic term within six weeks of the date it makes the FTE calculation.

§41.67 Can Diné College receive technical assistance?

Technical assistance will be provided to Diné College as noted in §41.41.

§41.69 How must Diné College administer its grant?

In administering any grant provided under this subpart, Diné College must:

(a) Provide all services or assistance under this subpart in a fair and uniform manner;

(b) Not deny admission to any Indian student because the student is, or is not, a member of a specific Indian Tribe; and

(c) Comply with part 276 of this chapter, unless the BIE expressly waives specific inappropriate provisions of part 276 in response to Diné College's request and its justification for a waiver.

§41.71 Can Diné College appeal an adverse decision under a grant agreement by the Director?

Diné College has the right to appeal to the Assistant Secretary by filing a written notice of appeal within 45 days of the adverse decision. Within 45 days after receiving notice of appeal, the Assistant Secretary will conduct a formal hearing at which time the Diné College may present evidence and argument to support its appeal. Within 45 days of the hearing, the Assistant Secretary will issue a written ruling on the appeal confirming, modifying or reversing the decision of the Director. If the ruling does not reverse the adverse decision, the Assistant Secretary will state in detail the basis of his/her ruling. The ruling of the Assistant Secretary on an appeal will be final for the Department.

PART 42—STUDENT RIGHTS

AUTHORITY: 5 U.S.C. 301, Pub. L. 107–110, 115 Stat. 1425.

SOURCE: 70 FR 22218, Apr. 28, 2005, unless otherwise noted.

§ 42.1 What general principles apply to this part?

(a) This part applies to every Bureau-funded school. The regulations in this part govern student rights and due process procedures in disciplinary proceedings in all Bureau-funded schools. To comply with this part, each school must:

(1) Respect the constitutional, statutory, civil and human rights of individual students; and

(2) Respect the role of Tribal judicial systems where appropriate.

(b) All student rights, due process procedures, and educational practices should, where appropriate or possible, afford students consideration of and rights equal to the student's traditional Native customs and practices.

§ 42.2 What rights do individual students have?

Individual students at Bureau-funded schools have, and must be accorded, at least the following rights:

(a) The right to an education that may take into consideration Native American or Alaska Native values;

(b) The right to an education that incorporates applicable Federal and Tribal constitutional and statutory protections for individuals; and

(c) The right to due process in instances of disciplinary actions.

§ 42.3 How should a school address alleged violations of school policies?

(a) In addressing alleged violations of school policies, each school must consider, to the extent appropriate, the reintegration of the student into the school community.

(b) The school may address a student violation using alternative dispute resolution (ADR) processes or the formal disciplinary process.

(1) When appropriate, the school should first attempt to use the ADR processes described in § 42.4 that may allow resolution of the alleged violation without recourse to punitive action.

(2) Where ADR processes do not resolve matters or cannot be used, the school must address the alleged violation through a formal disciplinary proceeding under § 42.7 consistent with the due process rights described in § 42.7.

§ 42.4 What are alternative dispute resolution processes?

Alternative dispute resolution (ADR) processes are formal or informal processes that may allow resolution of the violation without recourse to punitive action.

(a) ADR processes may:

(1) Include peer adjudication, mediation, and conciliation; and

(2) Involve appropriate customs and practices of the Indian Tribes or Alaska Native Villages to the extent that these practices are readily identifiable.

(b) For further information on ADR processes and how to use them, contact the Office of Collaborative Action and Dispute Resolution by:

(1) Sending an e-mail to: *cadr@ios.doi.gov*; or

(2) Writing to: Office of Collaborative Action and Dispute Resolution, Department of the Interior, 1849 C Street NW., MS 5258, Washington, DC 20240.

§ 42.5 When can a school use ADR processes to address an alleged violation?

(a) The school may address an alleged violation through the ADR processes described in §42.4, unless one of the conditions in paragraph (b) of this section applies.

(b) The school must not use ADR processes in any of the following circumstances:

(1) Where the Act requires immediate expulsion ("zero tolerance" laws);

(2) For a special education disciplinary proceeding where use of ADR would not be compatible with the Individuals with Disabilities Education Act (Pub. L. 105–17); or

(3) When all parties do not agree to using alternative dispute resolution processes.

(c) If ADR processes do not resolve matters or cannot be used, the school must address alleged violations through the formal disciplinary proceeding described in §42.8.

§42.6 When does due process require a formal disciplinary hearing?

Unless local school policies and procedures provide for less, a formal disciplinary hearing is required before a suspension in excess of 10 days or expulsion.

§42.7 What does due process in a formal disciplinary proceeding include?

Due process must include written notice of the charges and a fair and impartial hearing as required by this section.

(a) The school must give the student written notice of charges within a reasonable time before the hearing required by paragraph (b) of this section. Notice of the charges includes:

(1) A copy of the school policy allegedly violated;

(2) The facts related to the alleged violation;

(3) Information about any statements that the school has received relating to the charge and instructions on how to obtain copies of those statements; and

(4) Information regarding those parts of the student's record that the school will consider in rendering a disciplinary decision.

(b) The school must hold a fair and impartial hearing before imposing disciplinary action, except under the following circumstances:

(1) If the Act requires immediate removal (such as, if the student brought a firearm to school) or if there is some other statutory basis for removal;

(2) In an emergency situation that seriously and immediately endangers the health or safety of the student or others; or

(3) If the student (or the student's parent or guardian if the student is less than 18 years old) chooses to waive entitlement to a hearing.

(c) In an emergency situation under paragraph (b)(2) of this section, the school:

(1) May temporarily remove the student;

(2) Must immediately document for the record the facts giving rise to the emergency; and

(3) Must afford the student a hearing that follows due process, as set forth in this part, within ten days.

§42.8 What are a student's due process rights in a formal disciplinary proceeding?

A student has the following due process rights in a formal disciplinary proceeding:

(a) The right to have present at the hearing the student's parents or guardians (or their designee);

(b) The right to be represented by counsel (legal counsel will not be paid for by the Bureau-funded school or the Secretary);

(c) The right to produce, and have produced, witnesses on the student's behalf and to confront and examine all witnesses;

(d) The right to the record of the disciplinary action, including written findings of fact and conclusions;

(e) The right to administrative review and appeal under school policy;

(f) The right not to be compelled to testify against himself or herself; and

(g) The right to have an allegation of misconduct and related information expunged from the student's school record if the student is found not guilty of the charges.

§42.9 What are victims' rights in formal disciplinary proceedings?

In formal disciplinary proceedings, each school must consider victims' rights when appropriate.

(a) The victim's rights may include a right to:

(1) Participate in disciplinary proceedings either in writing or in person;

(2) Provide a statement concerning the impact of the incident on the victim; and

(3) Have the outcome explained to the victim and to his or her parents or guardian by a school official, consistent with confidentiality.

(b) For the purposes of this part, the victim is the actual victim, not his or her parents or guardians.

§ 42.10 How must the school communicate individual student rights to students, parents or guardians, and staff?

Each school must:

(a) Develop a student handbook that includes local school policies, definitions of suspension, expulsion, zero tolerance, and other appropriate terms, and a copy of the regulations in this part;

(b) Provide all school staff a current and updated copy of student rights and responsibilities before the first day of each school year;

(c) Provide all students and their parents or guardians a current and updated copy of student rights and responsibilities every school year upon enrollment; and

(d) Require students, school staff, and to the extent possible, parents and guardians, to confirm in writing that they have received a copy and understand the student rights and responsibilities.

§ 42.11 Information collection.

Notwithstanding any other provision of law, no person is required to respond to, nor shall any person be subject to a penalty for failure to comply with a collection of information, subject to the requirements of the Paperwork Reduction Act of 1995 (44 U.S.C. 3501 *et seq.*) (PRA), unless that collection of information displays a currently valid Office of Management and Budget (OMB) Control Number. This part in §§ 42.6, 42.7, and 42.9 contains collections of information subject to the PRA. These collections have been approved by OMB under control number 1076–0163.

PART 43—MAINTENANCE AND CONTROL OF STUDENT RECORDS IN BUREAU SCHOOLS

Sec.

AUTHORITY: 35 Stat. 72 (25 U.S.C. 295); Pub. L. 93–579, 88 Stat. 1896; Sec. 438, Pub. L. 93–380, as amended; Pub. L. 94–142.

SOURCE: 43 FR 52024, Nov. 8, 1978, unless otherwise noted. Redesignated at 47 FR 13327, Mar. 30, 1982.

§ 43.1 Purpose and scope.

This part contains the regulations of the Bureau of Indian Affairs, U.S. Department of the Interior, governing the maintenance, control, and accessibility of student records. This part will apply to all educational institutions under the jurisdiction of the Bureau of Indian Affairs, whether operated under contract or otherwise.

§ 43.2 Definitions.

As used in this part:

(a) *Assistant Secretary* means the Assistant Secretary—Indian Affairs, Department of the Interior.

(b) *Educational institution* means any institution operated under the jurisdiction of the Bureau of Indian Affairs either directly or by contract, including, but not limited to, schools or dormitories from which Indian students attend public schools.

(c) *Eligible student* means a student who has become 18 years of age or is attending an institution of post-secondary education. When a student becomes an *eligible student*, the permission required of and the rights given to the parents of the student shall thereafter only be required of and given to the student.

(d) *Parent* means a natural parent, an adoptive parent, the legal guardian, or a legal custodian of a student. (Where the natural parents are unavailable, a required written parental consent may be obtained from the person who has assumed custody of the student.) For purposes of the Education of All Handicapped Children Act, the term *parent* also includes a *surrogate* as referred to in 20 U.S.C. 1415(b)(1)(B).

(e) *Student records* means those records, files, documents, and other materials which contain information directly related to a student and which are maintained by an educational institution, or by a person acting for that institution. The term does not include:

(1) Records of any educational personnel which are in the sole possession of the maker and which are not accessible or revealed to any other person except a substitute.

(2) Records made and maintained in the normal course of business which relate exclusively to persons who are employed in an educational institution but do not attend that institution.

(3) Directory information as given in §43.20.

(4) Records on a student who is 18 years of age or older, or is attending an institution of post-secondary education, which are made or maintained by a physician, psychiatrist, psychologist, or other recognized professional or paraprofessional acting in his professional or paraprofessional capacity, or assisting in that capacity, and which are made, maintained, or used only in connection with the provision of treatment to the student, and are not available to anyone other than persons providing such treatment, except that such records can be personally reviewed by a physician or other appropriate professional of the student's choice.

§43.3 Student rights.

The regulations in this part do not prevent educational institutions from giving noneligible students rights similar to those given to parents and eligible students. Educational institutions may do so at their discretion.

§43.4 Annual notification of rights.

(a) Each educational institution to which this part applies and which maintains records on students shall inform parents or eligible students of the rights given them by this part.

(b) In meeting the requirement in paragraph (a) of this section the educational institution shall give notice to parents and eligible students at least annually of the following:

(1) The types of education records and information contained in them which are directly related to students and maintained by the institution.

(2) The name and position of the official responsible for maintaining each type of record, the persons who have access to those records, and the purpose for which they have access.

(3) The policies of the institution for reviewing and expunging those records.

(4) The procedures established by the institution under §43.5.

(5) The procedures for challenging the content of education records including those in §43.10.

(6) The cost, if any, which will be charged to the parent or eligible student for reproducing copies of records under §43.5.

(7) The categories of information which the institution has designated as "directory information" under §43.20.

(c) The notice given to a parent or eligible student under this section shall be in a language considered by the institution to be understandable by the parent or eligible student.

§43.5 Access to records.

Educational institutions shall give parents of students or eligible students, who are or have been in attendance at the institutions, access to student records, except as stated in §43.6.

§43.6 Limitations on access.

Educational institutions are not required to make available to students the following materials:

(a) Financial records of the parents of the student or any information contained in those records.

(b) Confidential letters and statements of recommendations, which were placed in any student's record prior to January 1, 1975, and which are not used for purposes other than those for which they were specifically intended.

(c) Those records listed in § 43.2(e) which are exempt from the definition of *student records*.

§ 43.7 Access rights.

The right of access specified in § 43.5 shall include:

(a) The right to obtain a list of the types of student records which are maintained by the institution.

(b) The right to inspect and review the content of those records.

(c) The right to obtain copies of those records, the cost, if any, not to exceed the actual cost to the educational institution of reproducing the copies.

(d) The right to a response from the institution to reasonable requests for explanations and interpretations of those records.

(e) The right to an opportunity for a hearing to challenge the content of records.

(f) If any material or document in the record of a student includes information on more than one student, the right to inspect and review only that portion of such material or document as relates to that particular student or to be informed of the specific information contained in such part of such materials.

§ 43.8 Destruction of records.

This part does not prevent educational institutions from destroying any records, if not otherwise prevented by law. However, access shall be granted under § 43.5 before destroying student records where the parent or eligible student has requested access. Only records which are no longer relevant or necessary may be destroyed, subject to § 43.23(c).

§ 43.9 Procedures for granting access.

Each educational institution shall establish appropriate procedures for granting a request by parents for access to the records of their children, or by eligible students for access to their own records within a reasonable period of time. In no case shall access be withheld more than forty-five (45) days after the request has been made.

§ 43.10 Right to challenge.

Each educational institution shall give parents of students and eligible students, who are or have been in attendance at the institution, an opportunity to challenge the content of the student's records to:

(a) Insure that the records are not inaccurate, misleading, or otherwise violating the privacy or other rights of students.

(b) Provide an opportunity for correcting or deleting any inaccurate, misleading, or otherwise inappropriate data in the record.

(c) Insert into such records a written comment by the parents or eligible students pertaining to the content of such records.

§ 43.11 Informal proceedings.

Educational institutions may attempt to resolve differences with the parent of a student or the eligible student regarding the content of the student's records through informal meetings and discussions with the parent or eligible student.

§ 43.12 Right to a hearing.

Upon the request of the educational institution, the parent, or eligible student, a hearing shall be conducted under the procedures adopted and published by the institution. Such procedures shall include at least the following elements:

(a) The hearing shall be conducted and decided within a reasonable period of time following the request for the hearing.

(b) The hearing shall be informal and a verbatim record of proceedings will not be required. Interpreters will be utilized when necessary.

(c) The hearing shall be conducted by an institutional official or other party who does not have a direct interest in the outcome of the hearing.

(d) The parents or eligible student shall be given a full and fair opportunity to present evidence relevant to the issues raised under § 43.10.

(e) Within a reasonable period of time after the hearing ends, the hearing official shall make his recommendation in writing to the head of the educational institution. Within 20 days after receipt of the recommendation, the head of the institution shall issue his decision in writing to the parent or eligible student.

§43.13 Right of appeal.

If any parent or eligible student is adversely affected by the decision of the head of the institution, that party shall have appeal rights as given in 25 CFR part 2. However, each official decision shall be issued within 30 days from receipt of the appeal.

§43.14 Consent.

Educational institutions shall not permit access to or the release of student records or personally identifiable information contained in them, other than directory information of students, without the written consent of the parents or of an eligible student, to any party other than the following:

(a) Local school officials, including teachers within the educational institution, who have been determined by the institution to have legitimate educational interests in the records.

(b) Officials of other schools or school systems at which a student is interested in enrolling. The student or parent must be notified of such release except in cases involving Bureau of Indian Affairs schools. All Bureau of Indian Affairs schools are considered to be components of one school system whether operated under contract or otherwise.

(c) Persons having official involvement with a student's application for or grant of financial aid.

(d) Parents of a dependent student as defined in section 152 of the Internal Revenue Code of 1954, as amended.

(e) Accreditation agencies in order to carry out their accrediting functions.

(f) U.S. Office of Education officials and other governmental education officials when deemed necessary by the institution to carry out their official functions.

(g) An education testing center or similar institution as a part of its validation research which has been authorized by the school.

(h) In an emergency, any person to whom the information is necessary in the discretion of the school's administration in order to protect the student's health and safety, subject to §43.17.

(i) Indian groups, contractors, grantees, professional social service organizations and personnel performing professional services, when necessary to carry out an official function authorized by the Bureau of Indian Affairs.

(j) Pursuant to the order of a court of competent jurisdiction; however, the parent or eligible student must be notified of such order in advance of compliance therewith by the educational institution.

§43.15 Content of consent.

The consent of a parent or eligible student requested under this part for the release of student records shall be in writing, signed and dated by the person giving the consent. The consent shall include:

(a) A specification of the records to be released.

(b) The reasons for release.

(c) The names of the parties to whom the records will be released.

§43.16 Copy to be provided to parents or eligible students.

Where the consent of a parent or eligible student is required under this part for the release of student records, a copy of the records to be released shall be provided on request to:

(a) The student's parents or the eligible student.

(b) The student who is not an eligible student, if desired by the parents.

§43.17 Release of information for health or safety emergencies.

(a) Educational institutions may release information from student records to appropriate persons in an emergency if the information is necessary to protect the health or safety of a student or other person. The factors to be used in determining whether records may be released under this section include the following:

(1) The seriousness of the threat to the health or safety of the student or other persons.

(2) The need for those records to meet the emergency.

(3) Whether the persons to whom the records are released are in a position to deal with the emergency.

(4) The extent to which time is of the essence in dealing with the emergency.

§ 43.18 Record of access.

(a) Each educational institution shall maintain a record kept with the student records of each student, which will indicate all parties other than those specified in § 43.14 which have requested or obtained access to those records and which will indicate specifically the legitimate interest that each party had in obtaining this information.

(b) A record of access shall be available only to:

(1) Parents or eligible students.

(2) The school official and his or her assistants who are responsible for the custody of such records.

(3) Persons or organizations authorized in and under the conditions of § 43.14.

§ 43.19 Transfer of information by third parties.

(a) Educational institutions shall not release personal information on a student except on the condition that the party to which the information is being transferred will not permit any other party to have access to the information without the written consent of the parents or of the eligible students.

(b) With any information released to a party under paragraph (a) of this section, educational institutions shall include a written statement which informs the party of the requirement in paragraph (a) of this section.

§ 43.20 Directory information.

(a) Any educational institution making public directory information shall make a reasonable effort to individually notify the parent or eligible student of the categories of information which it has designated as directory information. The institution shall allow a reasonable period of time after notice has been given for a parent or eligible student to inform the institution that any or all of the information designated should not be released without the prior consent of the parent or eligible student.

(b) Directory information may include the following: A student's name, address, telephone listing, date and place of birth, major field of study, participation in officially recognized activities and sports, weight and height of members of athletic teams, dates of attendance, degrees and awards received, and the most recent previous educational agency or institution attended by the student, tribe, agency, area, name of parent, sex, and classification (grade). No other information may be included. Educational institutions have the right to limit the content of directory information.

§ 43.21 Standards for collection and maintenance of student records.

(a) Records shall contain only information about an individual which is relevant and necessary to accomplish a purpose of the Bureau required to be accomplished by statute or Executive order of the President.

(b) Student records which are used in making any determination about any student shall be maintained with such accuracy, relevance, timeliness, and completeness as is reasonably necessary to assure fairness to the student in making the determination.

(c) Information which may be used in determining a student's rights, benefits, and privileges under Federal programs shall be collected directly from the student or his parents, to the greatest extent practicable. In deciding whether collection of information from a parent or eligible student, as opposed to a third-party source is practicable, the following factors among others may be considered:

(1) Whether the nature of the information sought is such that it can only be obtained from a third party.

(2) Whether the cost of collecting the information from the parent or student is unreasonable, when compared with the cost of collecting it from a third party.

(3) Whether there is a risk that information collected from third parties, if inaccurate, could result in an adverse

determination to the student concerned.

(4) Whether the information, if supplied by the parent or student, would have to be verified by a third party.

(5) Whether provisions can be made for verification by the parent of student of information collected from third parties.

(d) Each individual parent or eligible student who is asked to supply information about himself which will be added to a system of student records shall be notified of the basis for requesting the information, how it may be used, and what the consequences, if any, are of not supplying the information. At a minimum, the notice to the parent or eligible student must state:

(1) The authority (whether granted by statute or Executive Order of the President) which authorizes requesting the information and whether disclosure of such information is mandatory or voluntary.

(2) The principle purpose or purposes for which the information is intended to be used.

(3) The routine uses which may be made of the information.

(4) The effects, if any, of not providing all or any part of the requested information.

(e) When information is collected on a standard form, the notice to the parent or eligible student shall be on the form or on a tear-off sheet attached to the form or on a separate sheet, whichever, is most practical.

(f) When information is collected by an interviewer, the interviewer shall provide the parent or eligible student with a written notice which the individual may retain. If the interview is conducted by telephone, however, the interviewer may summarize the notice for the individual and need not provide a copy to the individual unless the individual requests that a copy be mailed to him.

(g) A parent or eligible student may be asked to acknowledge, in writing, that he has been given the notice required by this section.

(h) No student records may be maintained describing how any individual exercises rights guaranteed by the first amendment to the Constitution unless:

(1) Expressly authorized by statute or by the individual about whom the student record is maintained; or

(2) Pertinent to and within the scope of an authorized law enforcement activity.

§43.22 Assuring integrity of records.

(a) Student records shall be maintained with appropriate administrative, technical and physical safeguards to insure the security and confidentiality of records and to protect against any anticipated threats or hazards to their security or integrity which could result in substantial harm, embarrassment, inconvenience, or unfairness to any individual on whom information is maintained.

(b) When maintained in manual form, student records shall be maintained, at a minimum, subject to the following safeguards, or safeguards giving comparable protection:

(1) Areas in which the student records are maintained or regularly used shall be posted with an appropriate warning, stating that access to the records is limited to authorized persons. The warning shall also summarize the requirements of §43.23 and state that employees may be subject to a criminal penalty for the unauthorized disclosure of student records.

(2) During working hours, the area in which the student records are maintained or regularly used shall be occupied by authorized personnel, or access to the student records shall be restricted by their storage in locked metal file cabinets or a locked room.

(3) During nonworking hours, access to the student records shall be restricted by their storage in locked metal file cabinets or a locked room.

(4) Where a locked room is the method of security provided for a system, the educational institution responsible for the system shall, no later than December 31, 1978, supplement that security by:

(i) Providing lockable file cabinets or containers for the student records, or

(ii) Changing the lock or locks for the room so that they may not be opened with a master key. For the purpose of this paragraph, a master is a key which may be used to open rooms other than the room containing student records, unless those rooms are used by officials or employees authorized to have access to the student records.

(c) When maintained in computerized form, student records shall be maintained, at a minimum, subject to safeguards based on those recommended in the National Bureau of Standards' booklet, "Computer Security Guidelines for Implementing the Privacy Act of 1974" (May 30, 1975), and any supplements to it, which are adequate and appropriate to assure the integrity of records in the system.

(d) The education institution responsible for a system of student records shall be responsible for assuring that specific procedures are developed to assure that the student records in the system for which it is responsible are maintained with security meeting the regulations in this section. These procedures shall be in writing and shall be posted or otherwise periodically brought to the attention of employees working with the student records contained in the system.

§ 43.23 Conduct of employees.

(a) Employees whose duties require handling of student records shall, at all times, take care to protect the integrity, security, and confidentiality of these records.

(b) No employee of the educational institution may disclose student records unless disclosure is permitted under § 43.14 or made to the parent of the student or eligible student to whom the record pertains.

(c) No employee of the educational institution may alter or destroy a student record, unless:

(1) Alteration or destruction is properly undertaken in the course of the employee's regular duties, or

(2) Alteration or destruction is required by an authorized administrative decision or the decision of a court of competent jurisdiction.

(d) The educational institution responsible for a system of student records shall be responsible for assuring that employees with access to the system are made aware of the requirements of this section.

PART 44—GRANTS UNDER THE TRIBALLY CONTROLLED SCHOOLS ACT

Sec.

AUTHORITY: Public Law 107–110, Title 10, Part D, the Native American Education Improvement Act, 115 Stat. 2007; Part B, Section 1138, Regional Meetings and Negotiated Rulemaking, 115 Stat. 2057.

SOURCE: 70 FR 22219, Apr. 28, 2005, unless otherwise noted.

§ 44.101 What directives apply to a grantee under this part?

In making a grant under this part the Secretary will use only:

(a) The Tribally Controlled Schools Act;

(b) The regulations in this part; and

(c) Guidelines, manuals, and policy directives agreed to by the grantee.

§ 44.102 Does this part affect existing tribal rights?

This part does not:

(a) Affect in any way the sovereign immunity from suit enjoyed by Indian tribes;

(b) Terminate or change the trust responsibility of the United States to any Indian tribe or individual Indian;

(c) Require an Indian tribe to apply for a grant; or

(d) Impede awards by any other Federal agency to any Indian tribe or tribal organization to administer any Indian program under any other law.

§44.103 Who is eligible for a grant?

The Secretary can make grants to Indian tribes and tribal organizations that operate:

(a) A school under the provisions of 25 U.S.C. 450 *et seq.;*

(b) A tribally controlled school (including a charter school, community-generated school or other type of school) approved by tribal governing body; or

(c) A Bureau-funded school approved by tribal governing body.

§44.104 How can a grant be terminated?

A grant can be terminated only by one of the following methods:

(a) Retrocession;

(b) Revocation of eligibility by the Secretary; or

(c) Reassumption by the Secretary.

§44.105 How does a tribal governing body retrocede a program to the Secretary?

(a) To retrocede a program, the tribal governing body must:

(1) Notify the Bureau in writing, by formal action of the tribal governing body; and

(2) Consult with the Bureau to establish a mutually agreeable effective date. If no date is agreed upon, the retrocession is effective 120 days after the tribal governing body notifies the Bureau.

(b) The Bureau must accept any request for retrocession that meets the criteria in paragraph (a) of this section.

(c) After the tribal governing body retrocedes a program:

(1) The tribal governing body decides whether the school becomes Bureau-operated or contracted under 25 U.S.C. 450 *et seq.;* and

(2) If the tribal governing body decides that the school is to be Bureau-operated, the Bureau must provide education-related services in at least the same quantity and quality as those that were previously provided.

§44.106 How can the Secretary revoke an eligibility determination?

(a) In order to revoke eligibility, the Secretary must:

(1) Provide the tribe or tribal organization with a written notice;

(2) Furnish the tribe or tribal organization with technical assistance to take remedial action; and

(3) Provide an appeal process.

(b) The Secretary cannot revoke an eligibility determination if the tribe or tribal organization is in compliance with 25 U.S.C. 2505(c).

(c) The Secretary can take corrective action if the school fails to be accredited by January 8, 2005.

(d) In order to revoke eligibility for a grant, the Secretary must send the tribe or tribal organization a written notice that:

(1) States the specific deficiencies that are the basis of the revocation or reassumption; and

(2) Explains what actions the tribe or tribal organization must take to remedy the deficiencies.

(e) The tribe or tribal organization may appeal a notice of revocation or reassumption by requesting a hearing under 25 CFR part 900, subpart L or P.

(f) After revoking eligibility, the Secretary will either contract the program under 25 U.S.C. 450 *et seq.* or operate the program directly.

§44.107 Under what circumstances may the Secretary reassume a program?

The Secretary may only reassume a program in compliance with 25 U.S.C. 450m and 25 CFR part 900, subpart P. The tribe or school board shall have a right to appeal the reassumption pursuant to 25 CFR part 900, subpart L.

§44.108 How must the Secretary make grant payments?

(a) The Secretary makes two annual grant payments.

(1) The first payment, consisting of 80 per cent of the amount that the grantee was entitled to receive during the previous academic year, must be made no later than July 1 of each year; and

(2) The second payment, consisting of the remainder to which the grantee is entitled for the academic year, must be made no later than December 1 of each year.

(b) For funds that become available for obligation on October 1, the Secretary must make payments no later than December 1.

(c) If the Secretary does not make grant payments by the deadlines stated in this section, the Secretary must pay interest under the Prompt Payment Act. If the Secretary does not pay this interest, the grantee may pursue the remedies provided under the Prompt Payment Act.

§ 44.109 What happens if the grant recipient is overpaid?

(a) If the Secretary has mistakenly overpaid the grant recipient, then the Secretary will notify the grant recipient of the overpayment. The grant recipient must return the overpayment within 30 days after the final determination that overpayment occurred.

(b) When the grant recipient returns the money to the Secretary, the Secretary will distribute the money equally to all schools in the system.

§ 44.110 What Indian Self-Determination Act provisions apply to grants under the Tribally Controlled Schools Act?

(a) The following provisions of 25 CFR part 900 apply to grants under the Tribally Controlled Schools Act.

(1) Subpart F; Standards for Tribal or Tribal Organization Management Systems, § 900.45.

(2) Subpart H; Lease of Tribally-owned Buildings by the Secretary.

(3) Subpart I; Property Donation Procedures.

(4) Subpart N; Post-award Contract Disputes.

(5) Subpart P; Retrocession and Reassumption Procedures.

(b) To resolve any disputes arising from the Secretary's administration of the requirements of this part, the procedures in subpart N of part 900 apply if the dispute involves any of the following:

(1) Any exception or problem cited in an audit;

(2) Any dispute regarding the grant authorized;

(3) Any dispute involving an administrative cost grant;

(4) Any dispute regarding new construction or facility improvement or repair; or

(5) Any dispute regarding the Secretary's denial or failure to act on a request for facilities funds.

§ 44.111 Does the Federal Tort Claims Act apply to grantees?

Yes, the Federal Tort Claims Act applies to grantees.

§ 44.112 Information collection.

Notwithstanding any other provision of law, no person is required to respond to, nor shall any person be subject to a penalty for failure to comply with a collection of information, subject to the requirements of the Paperwork Reduction Act of 1995 (44 U.S.C. 3501 *et seq.*) (PRA), unless that collection of information displays a currently valid Office of Management and Budget (OMB) Control Number. This part in § 44.105 contains collections of information subject to the PRA. These collections have been approved by OMB under control number 1076–0163.

PART 46—ADULT EDUCATION PROGRAM

Subpart A—General Provisions

Sec.

Subpart B [Reserved]

AUTHORITY: 43 U.S.C. 1457; 25 U.S.C. 2, 9, 13.

SOURCE: 62 FR 44081, Aug. 19, 1997, unless otherwise noted.

Subpart A—General Provisions

§ 46.1 Purpose and scope.

The purpose of the Adult Education Program is to:

(a) Improve educational opportunities for Indian adults who lack the level of literacy skills necessary for effective citizenship and productive employment;

(b) Expand and improve existing programs for delivering adult education services, including delivery of these services to educationally disadvantaged Indian adults; and

(c) Encourage the establishment of adult education programs that will:

(1) Enable Indian adults to acquire adult basic educational skills necessary for literate functioning;

(2) Provide Indian adults with sufficient basic education to enable them to benefit from job training and retraining programs and to obtain and retain productive employment so that they might more fully enjoy the benefits and responsibilities of citizenship; and

(3) Enable Indian adults, who so desire, to continue their education to at least the level of completion of adult secondary education.

§46.2 Definitions.

As used in this part:

Adult means an individual who has attained the age of sixteen or is beyond the age of compulsory school attendance under State or tribal law and not currently enrolled in a formal secondary or post-secondary educational program.

Adult Basic Education (ABE) means instruction designed for an adult who:

(1) Has minimal competence in reading, writing, and computation;

(2) Cannot speak, read, or write the English language sufficiently to allow employment commensurate with the adult's real ability;

(3) Is not sufficiently competent to meet the educational requirements of an adult consumer; or

(4) In grade level measurements that would be designated as grades 0 through 8.

Adult Education means services or instruction below the college level for adults who:

(1) Lack sufficient mastery of basic educational skills to enable them to function effectively in society, or

(2) Do not have a certificate of graduation from a school providing secondary education and have not achieved a GED.

Adult Education Office means the BIA or tribal office administering funds appropriated to the BIA, under the TPA, for Adult Education programs.

Adult Secondary Education means instruction designed for an adult who:

(1) Is literate and can function in everyday life, but is not proficient as a competitive consumer or employee; or

(2) Does not have a certificate of graduation (or its equivalent) from a school providing secondary education and in grade level measurements that would be designated as grades 9 through 12.

Assistant Secretary means the Assistant Secretary—Indian Affairs, Department of the Interior, or his/her designee.

Bureau means the Bureau of Indian Affairs.

Department of Education (ED) means the U.S. Department of Education.

Director means the Director, Office of Indian Education Programs, Bureau of Indian Affairs.

Indian means a person who is a member of, or is at least a one-fourth degree Indian blood descendent of a member of, an Indian tribe, and is eligible for the special programs and services provided by the United States through the Bureau of Indian Affairs to Indians because of their status as Indians;

Indian tribe means any Indian tribe, band, nation, rancheria, pueblo, colony or community, including any Alaska native village or regional or village corporation as defined in, or established pursuant to, the Alaska Native Claims Settlement Act (85 Stat. 668) that is Federally recognized by the United States Government through the Secretary of the Interior for the special programs and services provided by the Secretary to Indians because of their status as Indians.

Tribal Priority Allocation (TPA) means the BIA's budget formulation process that allows direct tribal government involvement in the setting of relative priorities for local operating programs.

Secretary means the Secretary of the Department of the Interior.

Service area means the geographic area served by the local Adult Education Program.

§46.3 Information collection.

Information collection requirements contained in this part have been approved by the Office of Management and Budget under 44 U.S.C. 3501 *et seq.* and assigned control number 1076–0120. This information is being collected to assess the need for adult education programs. The information collection is used to manage program resources and for fiscal accountability and appropriate direct services documentation. Response to this request is necessary to obtain or retain a benefit. Public reporting burden for this form is estimated to average 4 hours per response including time for reviewing instructions, gathering, maintaining data, completing and reviewing the form. Direct comments regarding the burden estimate or any other aspect of this form to the BIA Information Collection Clearance Officer, 1849 C Street NW., Washington, DC 20240.

[67 FR 13570, Mar. 25, 2002]

§ 46.10 Eligible activities.

(a) Subject to availability of funds, funds appropriated for the BIA's Adult Education Program may be used to support local projects or programs designed to:

(1) Enable Indian adults to acquire basic educational skills, including literacy;

(2) Enable Indian adults to continue their education through the secondary school level;

(3) Establish career education projects intended to improve employment opportunities;

(4) Provide educational services or instruction for elderly, disabled, or incarcerated Indian adults;

(5) Prepare individuals to benefit from occupational training; and

(6) Teach employment-related skills.

(b) Funds should not be used to support programs designed solely to prepare Indian adults to enter a specific occupation or cluster of closely related occupations.

(c) The Adult Education Program must be implemented in accordance with a plan established by the tribe(s) affected by the program. The tribe(s) may determine to set standards in addition to those established in this part.

§ 46.20 Program requirements.

(a) The Adult Education Office will implement the program or project that is designed to address the needs of the Indian adults in the service area. To determine the needs of Indian adults in the area, the Adult Education Office must consider:

(1) Elementary/secondary school dropout or absentee rates;

(2) Average grade level completed;

(3) Unemployment rates; and

(4) Other appropriate measures.

(b) The Adult Education Office, to ensure efforts that no duplication of services exists, will identify other services in the area, including those offered by Federal, State and Tribal entities, that are designed to meet the same needs as those to be addressed by the project, and the number of Indian adults who receive those services.

(c) The Adult Education Office must establish and maintain an evaluation plan.

(1) The plan must be designed to measure the project's effectiveness in meeting each objective and the impact of the project on the adults involved; and

(2) The plan must provide procedures for periodic assessment of the progress of the project and, if necessary, modification of the project as a result of that assessment.

(d) Subject to the availability of funds, the project is to be supported under the funding level established for Adult Education in the formulation of the budget under the TPA process.

§ 46.30 Records and reporting requirements.

(a) The Adult Education Office will annually submit a report on the previous project year's activities to the Director, Office of Indian Education Programs. The report must include the following information:

(1) The type of eligible activity, under § 46.10, conducted under the project(s);

(2) The number of participants acquiring the GED, high school diploma, and other certificates of performance; and

(3) A narrative summary of the activities conducted under the project.

(b) Each Adult Education Office must:

(1) Submit any records and information that the Director requires in connection with the administration of the program; and

(2) Comply with any requirements that the Director may impose to ensure the accuracy of the reports required by this part.

Subpart B [Reserved]

PART 47—UNIFORM DIRECT FUNDING AND SUPPORT FOR BUREAU-OPERATED SCHOOLS

AUTHORITY: Pub. L. 107–110, 115 Stat. 1425.

SOURCE: 70 FR 22221, Apr. 28, 2005, unless otherwise noted.

§47.1 What is the purpose of this part?

This part contains the requirements for developing local educational financial plans that Bureau-operated schools need in order to receive direct funding from the Bureau of Indian Affairs under section 1127 of the Act.

§47.2 What definitions apply to terms in this part?

Act means the No Child Left Behind Act, Public Law 107–110, enacted January 8, 2002. The No Child Left Behind Act reauthorizes and amends the Elementary and Secondary Education Act (ESEA) and the amended Education Amendments of 1978.

Budget means that element in the local educational financial plan which shows all costs of the plan by discrete programs and sub-cost categories.

Bureau means the Bureau of Indian Affairs in the Department of the Interior.

Consultation means soliciting and recording the opinions of Bureau-operated school boards regarding each element of the local educational financial plan and incorporating these opinions to the greatest degree feasible in the development of the local educational financial plan at each stage.

Director means the Director, Office of Indian Education Programs.

Local educational financial plan means the plan that:

(1) Programs dollars for educational services for a particular Bureau-operated school; and

(2) Has been ratified in an action of record by the local school board or determined by the superintendent under the appeals process in 25 CFR part 2.

OIEP means the Office of Indian Education Programs in the Bureau of Indian Affairs of the Department of the Interior.

Secretary means the Secretary of the Interior or a designated representative.

§47.3 How does a Bureau-operated school find out how much funding it will receive?

The Office of Indian Education Programs (OIEP) will notify each Bureau-operated school in writing of the annual funding amount it will receive as follows:

(a) No later than July 1 OIEP will let the Bureau-operated school know the amount that is 80 percent of its funding; and

(b) No later than September 30 OIEP will let the Bureau-operated school know the amount of the remaining 20 percent.

§47.4 When does OIEP provide funding?

By July 1 of each year OIEP will make available for obligation 80 percent of the funds for the fiscal year that begins on the following October 1.

§47.5 What is the school supervisor responsible for?

Each Bureau-operated school's school supervisor has the responsibilities in this section. The school supervisor must do all of the following:

(a) Ensure that the Bureau-operated school spends funds in accordance with the local educational financial plan, as ratified or amended by the school board;

(b) Sign all documents required to obligate or pay funds or to record receipt of goods and services;

(c) Report at least quarterly to the local school board on the amounts spent, obligated, and currently remaining in funds budgeted for each program in the local educational financial plan;

(d) Recommend changes in budget amounts to carry out the local educational financial plan, and incorporate these changes in the budget as ratified by the local school board, subject to provisions for appeal and overturn; and

(e) Maintain expenditure records in accordance with financial planning system procedures.

§ 47.6 Who has access to local education financial records?

The Comptroller General, the Assistant Secretary, the Director, or any of their duly authorized representatives have access for audit and explanation purposes to any of the local school's accounts, documents, papers, and records which are related to the Bureau-operated schools' operation.

§ 47.7 What are the expenditure limitations for Bureau-operated schools?

Each Bureau-operated school must spend all allotted funds in accordance with applicable Federal regulations and local education financial plans. If a Bureau-operated school and OIEP region or Agency support services staff disagree over expenditures, the Bureau-operated school must appeal to the Director for a decision.

§ 47.8 Who develops the local educational financial plans?

The local Bureau-operated school supervisor develops the local educational financial plan in active consultation with the local school board, based on the tentative allotment received.

§ 47.9 What are the minimum requirements for the local educational financial plan?

(a) The local educational financial plan must include:

(1) Separate funds for each group receiving a discrete program of services is to be provided, including each program funded through the Indian School Equalization Program;

(2) A budget showing the costs projected for each program; and

(3) A certification provision meeting the requirements of paragraph (b) of this section.

(b) The certification required by paragraph (a)(3) of this section must provide for:

(1) Certification by the chairman of the school board that the plan has been ratified in an action of record by the board; and

(2) Certification by the Education Line Officer that he or she has approved the plan as shown in an action overturning the school board's rejection or amendment of the plan.

§ 47.10 How is the local educational financial plan developed?

(a) The following deadlines apply to development of the local educational financial plan:

(1) Within 15 days after receiving the tentative allotment, the school supervisor must consult with the local school board on the local educational financial plan.

(2) Within 30 days of receiving the tentative allotment, the school board must review the local educational financial plan and, by a quorum vote, ratify, reject, or amend, the plan.

(3) Within one week of the school board action under paragraph (a)(2) of this section, the supervisor must either:

(i) Send the plan to the education line officer (ELO), along with the official documentation of the school board action; or

(ii) Appeal the school board's decision to the ELO.

(4) The ELO will review the local educational financial plan for compliance with laws and regulations and may refer the plan to the Solicitor's Office for legal review. If the ELO notes any problem with the plan, he or she must:

(i) Notify the local board and local supervisor of the problem within two weeks of receiving the plan;

(ii) Make arrangements to assist the local school supervisor and board to correct the problem; and

(iii) Refer the problem to the Director of the Office of Indian Education if it cannot be solved locally.

(b) When consulting with the school board under paragraph (a)(1) of this section, the school supervisor must:

(1) Discuss the present program of the Bureau-operated school and any proposed changes he or she wishes to recommend;

(2) Give the school board members every opportunity to express their own ideas and views on the supervisor recommendations; and

(3) After the discussions required by paragraphs (b)(1) and (b)(2) of this section, present a draft plan to the school board with recommendations concerning each of the elements.

(c) If the school board does not act within the deadline in paragraph (a)(2) of this section, the supervisor must send the plan to the ELO for ratification. The school board may later amend the plan by a quorum vote; the supervisor must transmit this amendment in accordance with paragraph (a)(3) of this section.

§47.11 Can these funds be used as matching funds for other Federal programs?

A Bureau-operated school may use funds that it receives under this part as matching funds for other Federal programs.

§47.12 Information collection.

Notwithstanding any other provision of law, no person is required to respond to, nor shall any person be subject to a penalty for failure to comply with, a collection of information subject to the requirements of the Paperwork Reduction Act of 1995 (44 U.S.C. 3501 *et seq.*) (PRA), unless that collection of information displays a currently valid Office of Management and Budget (OMB) Control Number. This part contains collections of information subject to the PRA in §§47.5, 47.7, 47.9, and 47.10. These collections have been approved by OMB under control number 1076–1063.

SUBCHAPTER F—TRIBAL GOVERNMENT

PART 61—PREPARATION OF ROLLS OF INDIANS

AUTHORITY: 5 U.S.C. 301; 25 U.S.C. 2 and 9, 1300d–3(b), 1401 *et seq.*, and Pub. L. 108–270.

SOURCE: 50 FR 46430, Nov. 8, 1985, unless otherwise noted.

§ 61.1 Definitions.

As used in these regulations:

Act means any act of Congress authorizing or directing the Secretary to prepare a roll of a specific tribe, band, or group of Indians.

Adopted person means a person whose natural parents' parental rights have been given to others to exercise by court order.

Approved roll means a roll of Indians approved by the Secretary.

Assistant Secretary means the Assistant Secretary of the Interior for Indian Affairs or an authorized representative acting under delegated authority.

Basic roll means the specified allotment, annuity, census or other roll designated in the Act or Plan as the basis upon which a new roll is to be compiled.

Commissioner means the Commissioner of Indian Affairs or an authorized representative acting under delegated authority.

Descendant(s) means those persons who are the issue of the ancestor through whom enrollment rights are claimed; namely, the children, grandchildren, etc. It does not include collateral relatives such as brothers, sisters, nieces, nephews, cousins, etc. or adopted children, grandchildren, etc.

Director means the Area Director of the Bureau of Indian Affairs area office which has administrative jurisdiction over the local field office responsible for administering the affairs of the tribe, band, or group for which a roll is being prepared or an authorized representative acting under delegated authority.

Enrollee(s) means persons who have met specific requirements for enrollment and whose names appear on a particular roll of Indians.

Lineal ancestor means an ancestor, living or deceased, who is related to a person by direct ascent; namely, the parent, grandparent, etc. It does not include collateral relatives such as brothers, sisters, aunts, uncles, etc., or adopted parents, grandparents, etc.

Living means born on or before and alive on the date specified.

Plan means any effective plan prepared under the provisions of the Act of October 19, 1973, Pub. L. 93–134, 87 Stat. 466, as amended, which authorizes and directs the Secretary to prepare a roll of a specific tribe, band, or group of Indians.

Secretary means the Secretary of Interior or an authorized representative acting under delegated authority.

Sponsor means any person who files an application for enrollment or appeal on behalf of another person.

Staff Officer means the Enrollment Officer or other person authorized to prepare the roll.

Superintendent means the official or other designated representative of the Bureau of Indian Affairs in charge of the field office which has immediate administrative responsibility for the affairs of the tribe, band, or group for which a roll is being prepared.

Tribal Committee means the body of a federally recognized tribal entity vested with final authority to act on enrollment matters.

Tribal Governing Document means the written organizational statement governing the tribe, band, or group of Indians and/or any valid document, enrollment ordinance, or resolution enacted thereunder.

§61.2 Purpose.

The regulations in this part 61 are to govern the compilation of rolls of Indians by the Secretary of the Interior pursuant to statutory authority. The regulations are not to apply in the compilation of tribal membership rolls where the responsibility for the preparation and maintenance of such rolls rests with the tribes.

§61.3 Information collection.

The Office of Management and Budget has reviewed and approved the information collection for §61.4(k). The OMB Control Number assigned is 1076–0165. A federal agency may not conduct or sponsor, and you are not required to respond to, a collection of information unless it displays a currently valid OMB Control Number.

[72 FR 9840, Mar. 5, 2007]

§61.4 Qualifications for enrollment and the deadline for filing application forms.

(a) The qualifications which must be met to establish eligibility for enrollment and the deadline for filing application forms will be included in this part 61 by appropriate amendments to this section; *except that*, when an Act or Plan states the qualifications for enrollment and the deadline for filing application forms and specifies that the regulations contained in this part 61 will apply, amendment to this section will not be required for the procedures contained in this part 61 to govern the preparation of the roll; *provided further*, the provisions contained in this part 61 that were in effect when the regulations were amended to include paragraphs (r), (s), (w), (x), (y), and (z) shall control the preparation of the rolls under paragraphs (r), (s), (w), (x), (y), and (z) of this section.

(b) *Pembina Band of Chippewa Indians.* (1) Pursuant to section 7(a) of the Act of December 31, 1982, Pub. L. 97–403, 96 Stat. 2022, a roll is to be prepared and used as the basis for the distribution of an apportioned share of judgment funds awarded the Pembina Chippewa Indians in dockets numbered 113, 191, 221 and 246 of the Court of Claims of all persons who:

(i) Are of at least ¼ degree Pembina Chippewa blood;

(ii) Are citizens of the United States;

(iii) Were living on December 31, 1982;

(iv) Are not members of the Red Lake Band of Chippewa Indians, the Turtle Mountain Band of Chippewa Indians, the Chippewa Cree Tribe of the Rocky Boy's Reservation, or Minnesota Chippewa Tribe, or the Little Shell Band of Chippewa Indians of Montana; *and*

(v) Are enrolled or are lineal descendants of persons enrolled:

(A) As Pembina descendants under the provisions of the Act of July 29, 1971 (85 Stat. 158), for the disposition of the 1863 Pembina Award, or

(B) On the McCumber roll of the Turtle Mountain Indians of 1892, or

(C) On the Davis roll of the Turtle Mountain Indians of 1904; or

(D) As Chippewa on the tentative roll of the Rocky Boy Indians of May 30, 1917, or the McLaughlin census report of the Rocky Boy Indians of July 7, 1917, or the Roe Cloud Roll of Landless Indians of Montana; *or*

(vi) Are able to establish Pembina ancestry on the basis of any other rolls or records acceptable to the Secretary.

(2) Application forms for eligibility must be filed with the Superintendent, Turtle Mountain Agency, Bureau of Indian Affairs, Belcourt, North Dakota 58316, by March 10, 1986. Application forms filed after that date will be rejected for failure to file on time regardless of whether the applicant otherwise meets the qualifications for eligibility.

(3) Each application for enrollment as a member of any of the tribes specified in paragraph (b)(1)(iv) of this section, except the Red Lake Band of Chippewa Indians, which may be rejected by the tribes shall be reviewed by the Superintendent to determine whether the applicant meets the qualifications for eligibility as a descendant of the Pembina Band of Chippewas under paragraph (b)(1) of this section. Each rejection notice shall contain a statement to the effect that the application is being given such review.

(c) *Cherokee Band of Shawnee Indians.* (1) Pursuant to section 5 of the Act of December 20, 1982, Pub. L. 97–372, 96 Stat. 1815, a roll is to be prepared and used as the basis for the distribution of an apportioned share of judgment funds awarded the Shawnee Tribe in dockets 64, 335, and 338 by the Indian Claims Commission and in docket 64–A by the U.S. Court of Claims of all persons of Cherokee Shawnee ancestry:

(i) Who were living on December 20, 1982;

(ii) Who are lineal descendants of the Shawnee Nation as it existed in 1854, based on the roll of the Cherokee Shawnee compiled pursuant to the Act of March 2, 1889 (25 Stat. 994), or any other records acceptable to the Secretary including eligibility to share in the distribution of judgment funds awarded the Absentee Shawnee Tribe of Oklahoma on behalf of the Shawnee Nation in Indian Claims Commission docket 334–B as a Cherokee Shawnee descendant; *and*

(iii) Who are not members of the Absentee Shawnee Tribe of Oklahoma or the Eastern Shawnee Tribe of Oklahoma.

(2) Application forms for enrollment must be filed with the Director, Muskogee Area Office, Bureau of Indian Affairs, Federal Building, Muskogee, Oklahoma 74401, by May 9, 1986. Application forms filed after that date will be rejected for inclusion on the roll being prepared for failure to file on time regardless of whether the applicant otherwise meets the qualifications for enrollment.

(d) *Miami Indians of Indiana.* (1) Pursuant to section 3 of the Act of December 21, 1982, Pub. L. 97–376, 96 Stat. 1828, a roll is to be prepared and used as the basis for the distribution of an apportioned share of judgment funds awarded the Miami Tribe of Oklahoma and the Miami Indians of Indiana in dockets 124–B and 254 by the U.S. Court of Claims of all persons of Miami Indian ancestry:

(i) Who were living on December 21, 1982;

(ii) Whose name or the name of a lineal ancestor appears on:

(A) The roll of Miami Indians of Oklahoma and Indiana prepared pursuant to the Act of June 2, 1972 (86 Stat. 199), or

(B) The roll of Miami Indians of Indiana of June 12, 1895, or

(C) The roll of "Miami Indians of Indiana, now living in Kansas, Quapaw Agency, I.T., and Oklahoma Territory," prepared and completed pursuant to the Act of March 2, 1895 (28 Stat. 903), or

(D) The roll of the Eel River Miami Tribe of Indians of May 27, 1889, prepared and completed pursuant to the Act of June 29, 1888 (25 Stat. 223), or

(E) The roll of the Western Miami Tribe of Indians of June 12, 1891 (26 Stat. 1001); *and*

(iii) Who are not members of the Miami Tribe of Oklahoma.

(2) Application forms for enrollment must be filed with the Director, Muskogee Area Office, Bureau of Indian Affairs, Federal Building, Muskogee, Oklahoma 74401, by May 9, 1986. Application forms filed after that date will be rejected for inclusion on the roll being prepared for failure to file on time regardless of whether the applicant otherwise meets the qualifications for enrollment.

(e) *Cow Creek Band of Umpqua Tribe of Indians.* (1) Pursuant to section 5 of the Cow Creek Band of Umpqua Tribe of Indians Distribution of Judgment Funds Act of October 26, 1987, Pub. L. 100–139, a tribal membership roll is to be prepared comprised of all persons who are able to establish that they are of Cow Creek or other Indian ancestry indigenous to the United States based on any rolls or records acceptable to the Secretary and were not members of any other Federally recognized Indian tribe on July 30, 1987; and:

(i) Who are named on the tribal roll dated September 13, 1980, the so-called Interrogatory No. 14 roll;

(ii) Who are descendants of individuals named on the tribal roll dated September 13, 1980, the so-called Interrogatory No. 14 roll, and were born on or prior to October 26, 1987; or

(iii) Who are descendants of individuals who were considered to be members of the Cow Creek Band of Umpqua Tribe of Indians for the purposes of the treaty entered between such Band and the United States on September 19, 1853.

(2) Application forms for enrollment must be filed with the Superintendent, Siletz Agency, Bureau of Indian Affairs, P.O. Box 539, Siletz, Oregon 97380 by June 1, 1990. Application forms filed after that date will be rejected for inclusion on the tribal membership roll for failure to file on time regardless of whether the applicant otherwise meets the qualifications for enrollment.

(f) *Cow Creek Band of Umpqua Tribe of Indians descendants.* (1) Pursuant to section 6(a)(1) of the Cow Creek Band of Umpqua Tribe of Indians Distribution of Judgment Funds Act of October 26, 1987, Pub. L. 100–139, a roll of nontribal members eligible to participate in the Higher Education and Vocational Training Program and the Housing Assistance Program of the Cow Creek Band of Umpqua Tribe of Indians is to be prepared of individuals:

(i) Who are descended from persons considered members of the Cow Creek Band of Umpqua Tribe of Indians for purposes of the treaty entered into between such band and the United States on September 19, 1853 (10 Stat. 1027), as ratified by the Senate on April 12, 1854; and

(ii) Who did not share or are not descendants of persons who shared in the distribution of funds under the Act entitled "An Act to provide for the termination of Federal supervision over the property of the Klamath Tribe of Indians located in the State of Oregon and the individuals members thereof, and for other purposes," approved August 13, 1954 (25 U.S.C. 564 *et seq.*), or under the Act entitled "An Act to provide for the termination of Federal supervision over the property of certain tribes and bands of Indians located in western Oregon and the individual members thereof, and for other purposes," approved August 13, 1954 (25 U.S.C. 691 *et seq.*).

(2) Application forms for enrollment must be filed with the Superintendent, Siletz Agency, Bureau of Indian Affairs, P. O. Box 539, Siletz, Oregon 97380. Upon receipt of an application form, the Superintendent shall furnish a copy to the Cow Creek Band of Umpqua Tribe of Indians.

(g) *Cow Creek Band of Umpqua Tribe of Indians descendants.* (1) Pursuant to section 6(a)(2) of the Cow Creek Band of Umpqua Tribe of Indians Distribution of Judgment Funds Act of October 26, 1987, Pub. L. 100–139, a roll of nontribal members eligible to participate in the Elderly Assistance Program of the Cow Creek Band of Umpqua Tribe of Indians is to be prepared of individuals:

(i) Who are descended from persons considered members of the Cow Creek Band of Umpqua Tribe of Indians for purposes of the treaty entered into between such Band and the United States on September 19, 1853 (10 Stat. 1027), as ratified by the Senate on April 12, 1854;

(ii) Who did not share or are not descendants of persons who shared in the distribution of funds under the Act entitled "An act to provide for the termination of Federal supervision over the property of the Klamath Tribe of Indians located in the State of Oregon and the individual members thereof, and for other purposes," approved August 13, 1954 (25 U.S.C. 564 *et seq.*), or under the Act entitled "An Act to provide for the termination of Federal supervision over the property of certain tribes and bands of Indians located in western Oregon and the individual members thereof, and for other purposes," approved August 13, 1954 (25 U.S.C. 691 *et seq.*); and

(iii) Who were 50 years or older as of December 31, 1985.

(2) Application forms for enrollment must be filed with the Superintendent, Siletz Agency, Bureau of Indian Affairs, P. O. Box 539, Siletz, Oregon 97380 by April 25, 1988, and with the Cow Creek Band of Umpqua Tribe of Indians. Application forms filed after that date will be rejected for failure to file on time regardless of whether the applicant otherwise meets the qualifications for eligibility for inclusion on the roll of persons eligible to participate in the Elderly Assistance Program, but will be considered for inclusion on the roll of persons eligible to participate in the Higher Education and Vocation Training Program and the Housing Assistance Program. Upon receipt of an application form, the Superintendent shall furnish a copy to the Cow Creek Band of Umpqua Tribe of Indians.

(h) *Indians of the Hoopa Valley Indian Reservation.* Pursuant to section 5 of the Hoopa-Yurok Settlement Act of October 31, 1988, Pub. L. 100–580, a roll of Indians of the Reservation eligible to participate in certain settlement provisions is to be prepared of all persons:

(1) Who were born on or prior to and living on October 31, 1988; and

(2) Who are citizens of the United States; and

(3) Who were not, on August 8, 1988, enrolled members of the Hoopa Valley Tribe; and

(4) Who meet the criteria to qualify as an "Indian of the Reservation" under one of the following standards established by the U.S. Court of Claims in its March 31, 1982, decision, and the United States Claims Court in its May 14, 1987, and March 1, 1988, decisions in the cases of *Short* v. *United States,* (Cl. Ct. No. 102–63):

(i) Standards A–E which are:

(A) Allottees of land on any part of the Reservation, living on October 1, 1949, and lineal descendants of allottees living on October 1, 1949;

(B) Persons living on October 1, 1949, and resident on the reservation at that time, who have received Reservation benefits or services, and hold an assignment, or can make other proof that though eligible to receive an allotment, they have not been allotted, and the lineal descendants of such persons, living on October 1, 1949;

(C) Persons living on June 2, 1953, who have at least ¼ degree Reservation blood, as defined in paragraph (h)(6)(i) of this section, have forebears born on the Reservation and were resident on the Reservation for 15 years prior to June 2, 1953;

(D) Persons of at least ¼ degree Indian blood, born after October 1, 1949, and before August 9, 1963, to a parent who is or would have been, when alive a qualified Indian of the Reservation under the standards in paragraphs (h)(4)(i) (A), (B) and (C) of this section, or has previously been held entitled to recover in the *Short* cases;

(E) Persons born on or after August 9, 1963, who are of at least ¼ degree Indian blood, derived exclusively from the qualified parent or parents who is or would have been, when alive, a qualified Indian of the Reservation under the standards in paragraphs (h)(4)(i) (A), (B) and (C) of this section, or has previously been held entitled to recover in the *Short* cases; or

(ii) Manifest Injustice Standard which is: Persons who do not qualify under the standards in paragraph (h)(4)(i) of this section, but who it would be manifestly unjust to exclude from enrollment. To qualify under the manifest injustice standard, persons must adequately demonstrate all of the following:

(A) A significant degree of Indian blood (at least ¼ degree Indian blood, and

(B) Personal connections to the Reservation shown through a substantial period of residence on the Reservation (nearly ten years of residence), and

(C) Personal ties to the land of the Reservation and/or ties to the land through a lineal ancestor; and

(5) Who file or have filed on their behalf application forms for enrollment with the Superintendent, Northern California Agency, Bureau of Indian Affairs, P.O. Box 494879, Redding, California 96049, by April 10, 1989. Applications filed after that date will not be considered for inclusion on the roll regardless of whether the applicant otherwise meets the qualifications for enrollment, except for plaintiffs determined to be an "Indian of the Reservation" in the *Short* cases, who will, if they otherwise meet the requirements of the Act, be included on the roll.

(6) As used in paragraph (h) of this section:

(i) *Reservation blood* means the blood of the following tribes or bands: Yurok; Hoopa/Hupa; Grouse Creek; Hunstand/ Hoonsotton/Hoonsolton; Miskut/ Miscotts/Miscolts; Redwood/Chilula; Saiaz/Nongatl/Siahs; Sermaltion; South Fork; Tish-tang-atan; Karok; Tolowa; Sinkyone/Sinkiene; Wailake/ Wylacki; Wiyot/Humboldt; and Wintun.

(ii) *Short* cases means the cases entitled *Jessie Short et al.* v. *United States,* (Cl. Ct. No. 102–63); *Charlene Ackley* v. *United States,* (Cl. Ct. No. 460–78); *Bret Aastadt* v. *United States,* (Cl. Ct. No. 146–85L); and *Norman Giffen* v. *United States,* (Cl. Ct. No. 746–85L).

(i) [Reserved]

(j) *Coquille Tribe of Indians.* (1) Pursuant to section 7 of the Coquille Restoration Act of June 28, 1989, Pub. L. 101–42, a tribal membership roll is to be prepared comprised of persons of Coquille Indian ancestry:

(i) Who were born on or before and living on June 28, 1989;

(ii) Who possess at least one-eighth (1/8) degree or more Indian blood;

(iii) Who are not enrolled members of another federally recognized tribe; and

(iv) Whose names were listed on the Coquille roll prepared pursuant to the Act of August 30, 1954 (68 Stat. 979; 25 U.S.C. 771), and approved by the Bureau of Indian Affairs on August 29, 1960;

(v) Whose names were not listed on but who met the requirements to be listed on the Coquille roll prepared pursuant to the Act of August 30, 1954, and approved by the Bureau of Indian Affairs on August 29, 1960; or

(vi) Who are lineal descendants of persons, living or dead, identified in paragraphs (j)(1)(iv) and (j)(1)(v) of this section.

(2) To establish eligibility for inclusion on the tribal membership roll, all persons must file an application form with the Superintendent, Siletz Agency, Bureau of Indian Affairs, P.O. Box 539, Siletz, Oregon 97380 by January 10, 1991. Application forms filed after that date will be rejected for inclusion on the roll being prepared for failure to file on time regardless of whether the applicant otherwise meets the qualifications for enrollment.

(3) For the purposes of establishing eligibility under paragraph (j) of this section, any available evidence establishing Coquille ancestry and the required degree of Indian blood shall be accepted. However, information shown on the Coquille roll prepared pursuant to the Act of August 30, 1954, shall be accepted as conclusive evidence of Coquille ancestry and blood degree information shown on the January 1, 1940, census roll of nonreservation Indians of the Grand Ronde-Siletz Agency shall be accepted as conclusive evidence in determining degree of Indian blood for applicants.

(4) For the purposes of establishing eligibility under paragraph (j) of this section, persons who may be enrolled members of another federally recognized tribe or tribes may submit a conditional relinquishment of membership document in the other tribe or tribes with their application forms. A conditional relinquishment of membership document in the other tribe or tribes with their application forms. A conditional relinquishment will be accepted by the Superintendent only if it is executed by the person himself or herself unless the person is legally incompetent, in which case the legal guardian and only the legal guardian may execute the conditional relinquishment document. In the case of minors, only the parent or legal guardian may execute a conditional relinquishment document.

(k) *Western Shoshone Identifiable Group of Indians.* (1) Under section 3(b)(1) of the Act of July 7, 2004, Pub. L. 108–270, 118 Stat. 805, the Secretary will prepare a roll of all individuals who meet the eligibility criteria established under the Act and who file timely applications prior to a date that will be established by a notice published in the FEDERAL REGISTER. The roll will be used as the basis for distributing the judgment funds awarded by the Indian Claims Commission to the Western Shoshone Identifiable Group of Indians in Docket No. 326–K. To be eligible a person must:

(i) Have at least 1/4 degree of Western Shoshone blood;

(ii) Be living on July 7, 2004;

(iii) Be a citizen of the United States; and

(iv) Not be certified by the Secretary to be eligible to receive a per capita payment from any other judgment fund based on an aboriginal land claim awarded by the Indian Claims Commission, the United States Claims Court, or the United States Court of Federal Claims, that was appropriated on or before July 7, 2004.

(2) Indian census rolls prepared by the Agents or Superintendents at Carson or Western Shoshone Agencies between the years of 1885 and 1940, and other documents acceptable to the Secretary will be used in establishing proof of eligibility of an individual to:

(i) Be listed on the judgment roll; and

(ii) Receive a per capita payment under the Western Shoshone Claims Distribution Act.

(3) Application forms for enrollment must be mailed to Tribal Government Services, BIA-Western Shoshone, Post

Office Box 3838, Phoenix, Arizona 85030–3838.

(4) The application period will remain open until further notice.

(l)–(q) [Reserved]

(r) *Mdewakanton and Wahpakoota Tribe of Sioux Indians.* (1) All lineal descendants of the Mdewakanton and Wahpakoota Tribe of Sioux Indians who were born on or prior to and were living on October 25, 1972, whose names or the name of a lineal ancestor appears on any available records and rolls acceptable to the Secretary of the Interior and who are not members of the Flandreau Santee Sioux Tribe of South Dakota, the Santee Sioux Tribe of Nebraska, the Lower Sioux Indian Community at Morton, Minn., the Prairie Island Indian Community at Welch, Minn., or the Shakopee Mdewakanton Sioux Community of Minnesota shall be entitled to be enrolled under title I, section 101(b) of the act of October 25, 1972 (86 Stat. 1168), to share in the distribution of funds derived from a judgment awarded the Mississippi Sioux Indians.

(2) Applications for enrollment must have been filed with the Director, Aberdeen Area Office, Bureau of Indian Affairs, 820 South Main Street, Aberdeen, S. Dak. 57401, and must have been received no later than November 1, 1973. Applications received after that date will be denied for failure to file in time regardless of whether the applicant otherwise meets the requirements for enrollment.

(3) Each application for enrollment with any of the tribes named in paragraph (r)(1) of this section which may be rejected by the tribes shall be reviewed by the Director to determine whether the applicant meets the requirements for enrollment as a descendant of the Mdewakanton and Wahpakoota Tribe of Sioux Indians under paragraph (r)(1) of this section. Each rejection notice issued by the tribes shall contain a statement to the effect that the application is being given such review.

(s) *Sisseton and Wahpeton Mississippi Sioux Tribe.* (1) Persons meeting the criteria in this paragraph are entitled to enroll under 25 U.S.C. 1300d–3(b) to share in the distribution of certain funds derived from a judgment awarded to the Mississippi Sioux Indians. To be eligible a person must:

(i) Be a lineal descendent of the Sisseton and Wahpeton Mississippi Sioux Tribe;

(A) Those individuals who applied for enrollment before January 1, 1998, and whose applications were approved by the Aberdeen Area Director before that same date, are deemed to appear in records and rolls acceptable to the Secretary or have a lineal ancestor whose name appears in these records;

(B) Those individuals who apply for enrollment after January 1, 1998, or whose application was not approved by the Aberdeen Area Director before that same date, must be able to trace ancestry to a specific Sisseton or Wahpeton Mississippi Sioux Tribe lineal ancestor who was listed on:

(*1*) The 1909 Sisseton and Wahpeton annuity roll;

(*2*) The list of Sisseton and Wahpeton Sioux prisoners convicted for participating in the outbreak referred to as the "1862 Minnesota Outbreak";

(*3*) The list of Sioux scouts, soldiers, and heirs identified as Sisseton and Wahpeton Sioux on the roll prepared under the Act of March 3, 1891 (26 Stat. 989 *et seq.*, Chapter 543); or

(*4*) Any other Sisseton or Wahpeton payment or census roll that preceded a roll referred to in paragraphs (s)(1)(i)(B)(*1*), (*2*), or (*3*) of this section.

(ii) Be living on October 25, 1972;

(iii) Be a citizen of the United States;

(iv) Not be listed on the membership rolls for the following tribes:

(A) The Flandreau Santee Sioux Tribe of South Dakota;

(B) The Santee Sioux Tribe of Nebraska;

(C) The Lower Sioux Indian Community at Morton, Minnesota;

(D) The Prairie Island Indian Community at Welch, Minnesota;

(E) The Shakopee Mdewakanton Sioux Community of Minnesota;

(F) The Spirit Lake Tribe (formerly known as the Devils Lake Sioux of North Dakota);

(G) The Sisseton-Wahpeton Sioux Tribe of South Dakota; or

(H) The Assiniboine and Sioux Tribes of the Fort Peck Reservation.

(v) Not be listed on the roll of Mdewakantan and Wahpakoota lineal descendants prepared under 25 U.S.C. 1300d–1(b).

(2) The initial enrollment application period that closed on November 1, 1973, is reopened as of May 24, 1999. The application period will remain open until further notice.

(t)–(v) [Reserved]

(w) *Lower Skagit Tribe of Indians.* (1) All persons of Lower Skagit ancestry born on or prior to and living on February 18, 1975, who are lineal descendants of a member of the tribe as it existed in 1859 based on the 1919 Roblin Roll and other records acceptable to the Assistant Secretary, shall be entitled to have their names placed on the roll, to be prepared and used as the basis to distribute the judgment funds awarded the Lower Skagit Tribe in Indian Claims Commission docket 294. Proof of Upper Skagit ancestry will not be acceptable as proof of Lower Skagit ancestry.

(2) Applications for enrollment must have been filed with the Superintendent, Puget Sound Agency, Bureau of Indian Affairs, 3006 Colby Avenue, Everett, Washington 88201, and must have been received by close of business on May 31, 1977. Applications received after that date will be denied for failure to file in time regardless of whether the applicant otherwise meets the requirements for enrollment.

(3) Payment of shares will be made in accordance with parts 87 and 115 of this chapter.

(x) *Kikiallus Tribe of Indians.* (1) All persons of Kikiallus ancestry born on or prior to and living on February 18, 1975, who are lineal descendants of a member of the tribe as it existed in 1859 based on the 1919 Roblin Roll and other records acceptable to the Assistant Secretary, shall be entitled to have their names placed on the roll, to be prepared and used as the basis to distribute the judgment funds awarded the Kikiallus Tribe in Indian Claims Commission docket 263.

(2) Applications for enrollment must have been filed with the Superintendent, Puget Sound Agency, Bureau of Indian Affairs, 3006 Colby Avenue, Everett, Washington 98021, and must have been received by close of business on May 31, 1977. Applications received after that date will be denied for failure to file in time regardless of whether the applicant otherwise meets the requirements for enrollment.

(3) Payment of shares will be made in accordance with parts 87 and 115 of this chapter.

(y) *Swinomish Tribe of Indians.* (1) All persons of Swinomish ancestry born on or prior to and living on December 10, 1975, who are lineal descendants of a member of the tribe as it existed in 1859 based on the 1919 Roblin Roll and other records acceptable to the Assistant Secretary, shall be entitled to have their names placed on the roll, to be prepared and used as the basis to distribute the judgment funds awarded the Swinomish Tribe in Indian Claims Commission docket 233.

(2) Application for enrollment must have been filed with the Superintendent, Puget Sound Agency, Bureau of Indian Affairs, 3006 Colby Avenue, Everett, Washington 98201, and must have been received by close of business on May 31, 1977. Applications received after that date will be denied for failure to file in time regardless of whether the applicant otherwise meets the requirements for enrollment.

(3) Payment of shares will be made in accordance with parts 87 and 115 of this chapter.

(z) *Samish Tribe of Indians.* (1) All persons of Samish ancestry born on or prior to and living on December 10, 1975, who are lineal descendants of a member of the tribe as it existed in 1859 based on any records acceptable to the Secretary, shall be entitled to have their names placed on the roll to be prepared and used as the basis to distribute the judgment funds awarded the Samish Tribe in Indian Claims Commission docket 261.

(2) Applications for enrollment must have been filed with the Superintendent, Puget Sound Agency, Bureau of Indian Affairs, 3006 Colby Avenue, Everett, Washington 98201, and must have been received by close of business on May 31, 1977. Applicants received after that date will be denied for failure to file in time regardless of whether the applicant otherwise meets the requirements for enrollment.

(3) Payment of shares will be made in accordance with parts 87 and 115 of this chapter.

[50 FR 46430, Nov. 8, 1985, as amended at 53 FR 11272, Apr. 6, 1988; 54 FR 14193, Apr. 7, 1989; 55 FR 7494, Mar. 2, 1990; 55 FR 41519, Oct. 12, 1990; 56 FR 10806, Mar. 14, 1991; 64 FR 19898, Apr. 23, 1999; 72 FR 9840, Mar. 5, 2007]

§61.5 Notices.

(a) The Director or Superintendent shall give notice to all Directors of the Bureau of Indian Affairs and all Superintendents within the jurisdiction of the Director, of the preparation of the roll for public display in Bureau field offices. Reasonable efforts shall be made to place notices for public display in community buildings, tribal buildings, and Indian centers.

(b) The Director or Superintendent shall, on the basis of available residence data, publish, and republish when advisable, notices of the preparation of the roll in appropriate locales utilizing media suitable to the circumstances.

(c) The Director or Superintendent shall, when applicable, mail notices of the preparation of the roll to previous enrollees or tribal members at the last address of record or in the case of tribal members, the last address available.

(d) Notices shall advise of the preparation of the roll and the relevant procedures to be followed including the qualifications for enrollment and the deadline for filing application forms to be eligible for enrollment. The notices shall also state how and where application forms may be obtained as well as the name, address, and telephone number of a person who may be contacted for further information.

§61.6 Application forms.

(a) Application forms to be filed by or for applicants for enrollment will be furnished by the Director, Superintendent, or other designated persons, upon written or oral request. Each person furnishing application forms shall keep a record of the names of individuals to whom forms are given, as well as the control numbers of the forms and the date furnished. Instructions for completing and filing applications shall be furnished with each form. The form shall indicate prominently the deadline for filing application forms.

(b) Among other information, each application form shall contain:

(1) Certification as to whether application form is for a natural child or an adopted child of the parent through whom eligibility is claimed.

(2) If the application form is filed by a sponsor, the name and address of sponsor and relationship to applicant.

(3) A control number for the purpose of keeping a record of forms furnished interested individuals.

(4) Certification that the information given on the application form is true to the best of the knowledge and belief of the person filing the application. Criminal penalties are provided by statute for knowingly filing false information in such applications (18 U.S.C. 1001).

(c) Application forms may be filed by sponsors on behalf of other persons.

(d) Every applicant or sponsor shall furnish the applicant's mailing address on the application form. Thereafter, the applicant or sponsor shall promptly notify the Director or Superintendent of any change in address, giving appropriate identification of the application, otherwise the mailing address as stated on the form shall be acceptable as the address of record for all purposes under the regulations in this part 61.

§61.7 Filing of application forms.

(a) Application forms filed by mail must be postmarked no later than midnight on the deadline specified. Where there is no postmark date showing on the envelope or the postmark date is illegible, application forms mailed from within the United States, including Alaska and Hawaii, received more than 15 days and application forms mailed from outside of the United States received more than 30 days after the deadline specified in the office of the designated Director or Superintendent, will be denied for failure to file in time.

(b) Application forms filed by personal delivery must be received in the office of the designated Director or Superintendent no later than close of business on the deadline specified.

(c) If the deadline for filing application forms falls on a Saturday, Sunday, legal holiday, or other nonbusiness day, the deadline will be the next working day thereafter.

(d) The provisions of this section shall not apply in the preparation of the rolls under paragraphs (r), (s), (w), (x), (y) and (z) of §61.4.

§61.8 Verification forms.

If the Director or Superintendent is preparing a roll of Indians by adding names of eligible persons to and deleting names of ineligible persons from a previously approved roll, *and* individuals whose names appear on the previously approved roll are not required to file applications for enrollment, a verification form, to be completed and returned, shall be mailed to each previous enrollee using the last address of record. The verification form will be used to ascertain the previous enrollee's current name and address and that the enrollee is living, or if deceased, the enrollee's date of death. Name and/or address changes will only be made if the verification form is signed by an adult enrollee, if living, or the parent or guardian having legal custody of a minor enrollee, or an authorized sponsor. The verification form may also be used by any sponsor to notify the Director or Superintendent of the date of death of a previous enrollee.

§61.9 Burden of proof.

The burden of proof rests upon the applicant or tribal member to establish eligibility for enrollment. Documentary evidence such as birth certificates, death certificates, baptismal records, copies of probate findings, or affidavits, may be used to support claim of eligibility for enrollment. Records of the Bureau of Indian Affairs may be used to establish eligibility.

§61.10 Review of applications by tribal authorities.

(a) If tribal review is applicable, the Director or Superintendent shall submit all applications to the Tribal Committee for review and recommendations or determinations; except that, in the cases of adopted persons where the Bureau of Indian Affairs has assured confidentiality to obtain the information necessary to determine the eligibility for enrollment of the individual or has the statutory obligation to maintain the confidentiality of the information, the confidential information may not be released to the Tribal Committee, but the Director or Superintendent shall certify as to the eligibility for enrollment of the individual to the Tribal Committee.

(b) The Tribal Committee shall review all applications and make its recommendations or determinations in writing stating the reasons for acceptance or rejection for enrollment.

(c) The Tribal Committee shall return the applications to the Director or Superintendent with its recommendations or determinations and any additional evidence used in determining eligibility for enrollment within 30 days of receipt of the applications by the Tribal Committee. The Director or Superintendent may grant the Tribal Committee additional time, upon request, for its review.

(d) Acceptance of an individual for enrollment by the Tribal Committee does not insure the individual's eligibility to share in the distribution of the judgment funds.

§61.11 Action by the Director or Superintendent.

(a) The Director or Superintendent shall consider each application, all documentation, and when applicable, tribal recommendations or determinations.

(b) The Director or Superintendent, when tribal recommendations or determinations are applicable, shall accept the recommendations or determinations of the Tribal Committee unless clearly erroneous.

(1) If the Director or Superintendent does not accept the tribal recommendation or determination, the Tribal Committee shall be notified in writing, by certified mail, return receipt requested, or by personal delivery, of the action and the reasons therefor.

(2) The Tribal Committee may appeal the decision of the Director or Superintendent not to accept the tribal recommendation or determination. Such appeal must be in writing and must be filed pursuant to part 62 of this chapter.

(3) Unless otherwise specified by law or in a tribal governing document, the

determination of the Director or Superintendent shall only affect the individual's eligibility to share in the distribution of judgment funds.

(c) The Director or Superintendent, upon determining an individual's eligibility, shall notify the individual, parent or guardian having legal custody of a minor, or sponsor, as applicable, in writing of the decision. If an individual files applications on behalf of more than one person, one notice of eligibility or adverse action may be addressed to the person who filed the applications. However, the notice must list the name of each person involved. Where an individual is represented by a sponsor, notification of the sponsor of eligibility or adverse action shall be considered to be notification of the individual.

(1) If the Director or Superintendent determines that the individual is eligible, the name of the individual shall be placed on the roll.

(2) If the Director or Superintendent determines that the individual is not eligible, he/she shall notify the individual's parent or guardian having legal custody of a minor, or sponsor, as applicable, in writing by certified mail, to be received by the addressee only, return receipt requested, and shall explain fully the reasons for the adverse action and the right to appeal to the Secretary. If correspondence is sent out of the United States, registered mail will be used. If a certified or registered notice is returned as "Unclaimed" the Director or Superintendent shall remail the notice by regular mail together with an acknowledgment of receipt form to be completed by the addressee and returned to the Director or Superintendent. If the acknowledgment of receipt is not returned, computation of the appeal period shall begin on the date the notice was remailed. Certified or registered notices returned for any reason other than "Unclaimed" need not be remailed.

(d) Except as provided in paragraph (c)(2) of this section, a notice of adverse action is considered to have been made and computation of the appeal period shall begin on the earliest of the following dates:

(1) Of delivery indicated on the return receipt;

(2) Of acknowledgment of receipt;

(3) Of personal delivery; or

(4) Of the return by the post office of an undelivered certified or registered letter.

(e) In all cases where an applicant is represented by an attorney, the attorney shall be recognized as fully controlling the application on behalf of the applicant and service on the attorney of any document relating to the application shall be considered to be service on the applicant. Where an applicant is represented by more than one attorney, service upon one of the attorneys shall be sufficient.

(f) To avoid hardship or gross injustice, the Director or Superintendent may waive technical deficiencies in applications or other submissions. Failure to file by the deadline does not constitute a technical deficiency.

§61.12 Appeals.

Appeals from or on behalf of tribal members or applicants who have been denied enrollment must be in writing and must be filed pursuant to part 62 of this chapter. When the appeal is on behalf of more than one person, the name of each person must be listed in the appeal. A copy of part 62 of this chapter shall be furnished with each notice of adverse action.

§61.13 Decision of the Assistant Secretary on appeals.

The decision of the Assistant Secretary on an appeal shall be final and conclusive and written notice of the decision shall be given the individual, parent or guardian having legal custody of a minor, or sponsor, as applicable. The name of any person whose appeal has been sustained will be added to the roll. Unless otherwise specified by law or in a tribal governing document, the determination of the Assistant Secretary shall only affect the individual's eligibility to share in the distribution of the judgment funds.

§61.14 Preparation, certification and approval of the roll.

(a) The staff officer shall prepare a minimum of five copies of the roll of those persons determined to be eligible for enrollment. The roll shall contain for each person a roll number, name, address, sex, date of birth, date of death, when applicable, and when required by law, degree of Indian blood, and, in the remarks column, when applicable, the basic roll number, date of the basic roll, name and relationship of ancestor on the basic roll through whom eligibility was established.

(b) A certificate shall be attached to the roll by the staff officer or Superintendent certifying that to the best of his/her knowledge and belief the roll contains only the names of those persons who were determined to meet the qualifications for enrollment.

(c) The Director shall approve the roll.

§61.15 Special instructions.

To facilitate the work of the Director or Superintendent, the Assistant Secretary may issue special instructions not inconsistent with the regulations in this part 61.

PART 62—ENROLLMENT APPEALS

Sec.

AUTHORITY: 5 U.S.C. 301, 25 U.S.C. 2 and 9.

SOURCE: 52 FR 30160, Aug. 13, 1987, unless otherwise noted.

§62.1 Definitions.

As used in these regulations:

Assistant Secretary means the Assistant Secretary of the Interior for Indian Affairs or an authorized representative acting under delegated authority.

Bureau means the Bureau of Indian Affairs of the Department of the Interior.

Commissioner means the Commissioner of Indian Affairs or an authorized representative acting under delegated authority.

Department means the Department of the Interior.

Director means the Area Director of the Bureau of Indian Affairs area office which has administrative jurisdiction over the local field office responsible for administering the affairs of a tribe, band, or group of Indians or an authorized representative acting under delegated authority.

Secretary means the Secretary of the Interior or an authorized representative acting under delegate authority.

Sponsor means any authorized person, including an attorney, who files an appeal on behalf of another person.

Superintendent means the official or other designated representative of the Bureau of Indian Affairs in charge of the field office which has immediate administrative responsibility with respect to the affairs of a tribe, band, or group of Indians or an authorized representative acting under delegated authority.

Tribal committee means the body of a federally recognized tribal entity vested with final authority to act on enrollment matters.

Tribal governing document means the written organizational statement governing a tribe, band or group of Indians and/or any valid document, enrollment ordinance or resolution enacted thereunder.

Tribal member means a person who meets the requirements for enrollment in a tribal entity and has been duly enrolled.

§62.2 Purpose.

(a) The regulations in this part are to provide procedures for the filing and processing of appeals from adverse enrollment actions by Bureau officials.

(b) The regulations in this part are not applicable and do not provide procedures for the filing of appeals from adverse enrollment actions by tribal committees, unless:

(1) The adverse enrollment action is incident to the preparation of a tribal roll subject to Secretarial approval; or

(2) An appeal to the Secretary is provided for in the tribal governing document.

§ 62.3 Information collection.

In accordance with the Office of Management and Budget regulations contained in 5 CFR 1320.3, approval of the information collection requirements contained in this part is not required.

§ 62.4 Who may appeal.

(a) A person who is the subject of an adverse enrollment action may file or have filed on his/her behalf an appeal. An adverse enrollment action is:

(1) The rejection of an application for enrollment by a Bureau official incident to the preparation of a roll for Secretarial approval;

(2) The removal of a name from a tribal roll by a Bureau official incident to review of the roll for Secretarial approval;

(3) The rejection of an application for enrollment or the disenrollment of a tribal member by a tribal committee when the tribal governing document provides for an appeal of the action to the Secretary;

(4) The change in degree of Indian blood by a tribal committee which affects a tribal member when the tribal governing document provides for an appeal of the action to the Secretary;

(5) The change in degree of Indian blood by a Bureau official which affects an individual; and

(6) The certification of degree of Indian blood by a Bureau official which affects an individual.

(b) A tribal committee may file an appeal as provided for in § 61.11 of this chapter.

(c) A sponsor may file an appeal on behalf of another person who is subject to an adverse enrollment action.

§ 62.5 An appeal.

(a) An appeal must be in writing and must be filed with the Bureau official designated in the notification of an adverse enrollment action, or in the absence of a designated official, with the Bureau official who issued the notification of an adverse enrollment action; or when the notification of an adverse action is made by a tribal committee with the Superintendent.

(b) An appeal may be on behalf of more than one person. However, the name of each appellant must be listed in the appeal.

(c) An appeal filed by mail or filed by personal delivery must be received in the office of the designated Bureau official or of the Bureau official who issued the notification of an adverse enrollment action by close of business within 30 days of the notification of an adverse enrollment action, except when the appeal is mailed from outside the United States, in which case the appeal must be received by the close of business within 60 days of the notification of an adverse enrollment action.

(d) The appellant or sponsor shall furnish the appellant's mailing address in the appeal. Thereafter, the appellant or sponsor shall promptly notify the Bureau official with whom the appeal was filed of any change of address, otherwise the address furnished in the appeal shall be the address of record.

(e) An appellant or sponsor may request additional time to submit supporting evidence. A period considered reasonable for such submissions may be granted by the Bureau official with whom the appeal is filed. However, no additional time will be granted for the filing of the appeal.

(f) In all cases where an appellant is represented by a sponsor, the sponsor shall be recognized as fully controlling the appeal on behalf of the appellant. Service of any document relating to the appeal shall be on the sponsor and shall be considered to be service on the appellant. Where an appellant is represented by more than one sponsor, service upon one of the sponsors shall be sufficient.

§ 62.6 Filing of an appeal.

(a) Except as provided in paragraph (b) of this section, a notification of an adverse enrollment action will be mailed to the address of record or the last available address and will be considered to have been made and computation of the appeal period shall begin on:

(1) The date of delivery indicated on the return receipt when notice of the adverse enrollment action has been sent by certified mail, return receipt requested; or

(2) Ten (10) days after the date of the decision letter to the individual when notice of the adverse enrollment action

has not been sent by certified mail return receipt requested and the letter has not been returned by the post office; or

(3) The date the letter is returned by the post office as undelivered whether the notice of the adverse enrollment action has been sent by certified mail return receipt requested or by regular mail.

(b) When notification of an adverse enrollment action is under the regulations contained in part 61 of this chapter, computation of the appeal period shall be in accordance with § 61.11.

(c) In computing the 30 or 60 day appeal period, the count begins with the day following the notification of an adverse enrollment action and continues for 30 or 60 calendar days. If the 30th or 60th day falls on a Saturday, Sunday, legal holiday, or other nonbusiness day, the appeal period will end on the first working day thereafter.

§ 62.7 Burden of proof.

(a) The burden of proof is on the appellant or sponsor. The appeal should include any supporting evidence not previously furnished and may include a copy or reference to any Bureau or tribal records having a direct bearing on the action.

(b) Criminal penalties are provided by statute for knowingly filing false or fraudulent information to an agency of the U.S. government (18 U.S.C. 1001).

§ 62.8 Advising the tribal committee.

Whenever applicable, the Superintendent or Director shall notify the tribal committee of the receipt of the appeal and shall give the tribal committee the opportunity to examine the appeal and to present such evidence as it may consider pertinent to the action being appealed. The tribal committee shall have not to exceed 30 days from receipt of notification of the appeal in which to present in writing such statements as if may deem pertinent, supported by any tribal records which have a bearing on the case. The Director or Superintendent may grant the tribal committee additional time, upon request, for its review.

§ 62.9 Action by the Superintendent.

When an appeal is from an adverse enrollment action taken by a Superintendent or tribal committee, the Superintendent shall acknowledge in writing receipt of the appeal and shall forward the appeal to the Director together with any relevant information or records; the recommendations of the tribal committee, when applicable; and his/her recommendations on the appeal.

§ 62.10 Action by the Director.

(a) Except as provided in paragraph (c) of this section, when an appeal is from an adverse enrollment action taken by a Superintendent or tribal committee, the Director will consider the record as presented together with such additional information as may be considered pertinent. Any additional information relied upon shall be specifically identified in the decision. The Director shall make a decision on the appeal which shall be final for the Department and which shall so state in the decision. The appellant or sponsor will be notified in writing of the decision. Provided that, the Director may waive his/her authority to make a final decision and forward the appeal to the Assistant Secretary for final action.

(b) When an appeal is from an adverse enrollment action taken by a Director, the Director shall acknowledge in writing receipt of the appeal and shall forward the appeal to the Assistant Secretary for final action together with any relevant information or records; the recommendations of the tribal committee, when applicable; and his/her recommendations.

(c) The Director shall forward the appeal to the Assistant Secretary for final action together with any relevant information or records; the recommendations of the tribal committee, when applicable; and his/her recommendations when the adverse enrollment action which is being appealed is either:

(1) The change in degree of Indian blood by a tribal committee which affects a tribal member and the tribal governing document provides for an appeal of the action to the Secretary; or

(2) The change in degree of Indian blood by a Bureau official which affects an individual.

§ 62.11 Action by the Assistant Secretary.

The Assistant Secretary will consider the record as presented, together with such additional information as may be considered pertinent. Any additional information relied upon shall be specifically identified in the decision. The Assistant Secretary shall make a decision on the appeal which shall be final for the Department and which shall so state in the decision. The appellant or sponsor will be notified in writing of the decision.

§ 62.12 Special instructions.

To facilitate the work of the Director, the Assistant Secretary may issue special instructions not inconsistent with the regulations in this part 62.

PART 63—INDIAN CHILD PROTECTION AND FAMILY VIOLENCE PREVENTION

Subpart A—Purpose, Policy, and Definitions

Sec.

Subpart B—Minimum Standards of Character and Suitability for Employment

Subpart C—Indian Child Protection and Family Violence Prevention Program

AUTHORITY: 5 U.S.C. 301; 25 U.S.C. 2, 9, 13, 200, 3201 *et seq.*; 42 U.S.C. 13041.

SOURCE: 61 FR 32274, June 21, 1996, unless otherwise noted.

Subpart A—Purpose, Policy, and Definitions

§ 63.1 Purpose.

The purpose of these regulations is to prescribe minimum standards of character and suitability for employment for individuals whose duties and responsibilities allow them regular contact with or control over Indian children, and to establish the method for distribution of funds to support tribally operated programs to protect Indian children and reduce the incidents of family violence in Indian country as authorized by the Indian Child Protection and Family Violence Prevention Act of 1990, Pub. L. 101–630, 104 Stat. 4544, 25 U.S.C. 3201 3211.

§ 63.2 Policy.

In enacting the Indian Child Protection and Family Violence Prevention Act, the Congress recognized there is no resource more vital to the continued existence and integrity of Indian tribes than their children and that the United States has a direct interest, as trustee, in protecting Indian children who are members of, or are eligible for membership in, an Indian tribe. The minimum standards of character and suitability of employment for individuals ensure that Indian children are protected, and the Indian child protection and family violence prevention programs will emphasize the unique values of Indian culture and community involvement in the prevention and treatment of child abuse, child neglect and family violence.

§ 63.3 Definitions.

Bureau means the Bureau of Indian Affairs of the Department of the Interior;

Child means an individual who is not married, and has not attained 18 years of age.

Child abuse includes but is not limited to any case in which a child is dead, or exhibits evidence of skin bruising, bleeding, malnutrition, failure to thrive, burns, fracture of any bone, subdural hematoma, or soft tissue swelling, and this condition is not justifiably explained or may not be the product of an accidental occurrence; and any case in which a child is subjected to sexual assault, sexual molestation, sexual exploitation, sexual contact, or prostitution.

Child neglect includes but is not limited to, negligent treatment or maltreatment of a child by a person, including a person responsible for the child's welfare, under circumstances which indicate that the child's health or welfare is harmed or threatened.

Crimes against persons are defined by local law. Adjudicating officers must contact local law enforcement agencies to determine if the crime for which an applicant or employee was found guilty (or entered a plea of nolo contendere or guilty) is defined as a crime against persons.

Family violence means any act, or threatened act, of violence, including any forceful detention of an individual, which results, or threatens to result, in physical or mental injury, and is committed by an individual against another individual to whom such person is, or was, related by blood or marriage or otherwise legally related, or with whom such person is, or was, residing, or with whom such person has, or had, intimate or continuous social contact and household access.

Indian means any individual who is a member of an Indian tribe.

Indian child means any unmarried person who is under age eighteen and is either a member of an Indian tribe or eligible for membership in an Indian tribe and is the biological child of a member of an Indian tribe.

Indian country means:

(1) All land within the limits of any Indian reservation under the jurisdiction of the United States Government, notwithstanding the issuance of any patent, and, including rights-of-way running through the reservation;

(2) All dependent Indian communities within the borders of the United States whether within the original or subsequently acquired territory thereof; and,

(3) All Indian allotments, the Indian titles to which have not been extinguished, including rights-of-way running through the same. Unless otherwise indicated, the term "Indian country" is used instead of "Indian reservation" for consistency.

Indian reservation means any Indian reservation, public domain Indian allotment, former Indian reservation in Oklahoma, or lands held by incorporated Native groups, regional corporations, or village corporations under the provisions of the Alaska Native Claims Settlement Act (43 U.S.C. 1601 *et seq.*).

Indian tribe means any Indian tribe, band, nation, or other organized group or community, including any Alaska Native village or regional or village corporation as defined in or established pursuant to the Alaska Native Claims Settlement Act (43 U.S.C. 1601 *et seq.*) which is recognized as eligible for the special programs and services provided by the United States to Indians because of their status as Indians.

Inter-tribal consortium means a partnership between an Indian tribe or tribal organization of an Indian tribe, and one or more Indian tribes or tribal organizations of one or more Indian tribes.

Local child protective services agency is an agency of the Federal Government, state, or Indian tribe that has the primary responsibility for child protection on any Indian reservation, or within any community in Indian country.

Local law enforcement agency is that Federal, tribal, or state law enforcement agency that has primary responsibility for the investigation of an instance of alleged child abuse within the involved Indian jurisdiction.

Must is used in place of shall and indicates a mandatory or imperative act or requirement.

Person responsible for a child's welfare is any person who has legal or other recognized duty for the care and safety of a child, and may include any employee or volunteer of a children's residential facility, and any person providing out-of-home care, education, or services to children.

Related assistance means the counseling and self-help services for abusers, victims, and dependents in family violence situations; referrals for appropriate health-care services (including alcohol and drug abuse treatment); and may include food, clothing, child care, transportation, and emergency services for victims of family violence and their dependents.

Secretary means the Secretary of the Interior.

Service means the Indian Health Service of the Department of Health and Human Services.

Shelter means the temporary refuge and related assistance in compliance with applicable Federal and tribal laws and regulations governing the provision, on a regular basis, of shelter, safe homes, meals, and related assistance to victims of family violence or their dependents.

Tribal organization means the recognized governing body of any Indian tribe; any legally established organization of Indians which is controlled, sanctioned, or chartered by such governing body or which is democratically elected by the adult members of the Indian community to be served by such organization and which includes the maximum participation of Indians in all phases of its activities: *Provided*, That in any case where a contract is let, a grant is awarded, or funding agreement is made to an organization to perform services benefitting more than one Indian tribe, the approval of each such Indian tribe must be a prerequisite to the letting or making of such contract, grant, or funding agreement.

§ 63.4 Information collection.

The information collection requirement contained in § 63.15, § 63.33 and § 63.34 will be approved by the Office of Management and Budget under the Paperwork Reduction Act of 1995, 44 U.S.C. 3507(d), and assigned clearance number ________.

§§ 63.5–63.9 [Reserved]

Subpart B—Minimum Standards of Character and Suitability for Employment

§ 63.10 Purpose.

The purpose of this part is to establish:

(a) Procedures for determining suitability for employment and efficiency of service as mandated by the Indian Child Protection and Family Violence Prevention Act; and

(b) *Minimum standards of character* to ensure that individuals having regular contact with or control over Indian children have not been convicted of certain types of crimes or acted in a manner that placed others at risk or raised questions about their trustworthiness.

§63.11 What is a determination of suitability for employment and efficiency of service?

(a) *Determinations of suitability measure the fitness or eligibility* of an applicant, volunteer, or employee for a particular position. Suitability for employment does not evaluate an applicant's education, skills, knowledge, experience, etc. Rather, it requires that the employer investigate the background of each applicant, volunteer, and employee to:

(1) Determine the degree of risk the applicant, volunteer, or employee brings to the position; and

(2) Certify that the applicant's, volunteer's, or employee's past conduct would not interfere with his/her performance of duties, nor would it create an immediate or long-term risk for any Indian child.

(b) *Efficiency of service* is the employer's verification that the applicant or employee is able to perform the duties and responsibilities of the position, and his/her presence on the job will not inhibit other employees or the agency from performing their functions.

§63.12 What are minimum standards of character?

Minimum standards of character are established by an employer and refer to identifiable character traits and past conduct. An employer may use character traits and past conduct to determine whether an applicant, volunteer, or employee can effectively perform the duties of a particular position without risk of harm to others. Minimum standards of character ensure that no applicant, volunteer, or employee will be placed in a position with regular contact with or control over Indian children if he/she has been found guilty of or entered a plea of nolo contendere or guilty to any offense under Federal, state, or tribal law involving crimes of violence, sexual assault, sexual molestation, sexual exploitation, sexual contact or prostitution, or crimes against persons.

§63.13 What does the Indian Child Protection and Family Violence Prevention Act require of the Bureau of Indian Affairs and Indian tribes or tribal organizations receiving funds under the Indian Self-Determination and Education Assistance Act or the Tribally Controlled Schools Act?

(a) The *Bureau of Indian Affairs* must compile a list of all authorized positions which involve regular contact with or control over Indian children; investigate the character of each individual who is employed, or is being considered for employment; and, prescribe minimum standards of character which each individual must meet to be appointed to such positions.

(b) All *Indian tribes or tribal organizations* receiving funds under the authority of the Indian Self-Determination and Education Assistance Act or the Tribally Controlled Schools Act of 1988 must conduct a background investigation for individuals whose duties and responsibilities would allow them regular contact with or control over Indian children, and employ only individuals who meet standards of character that are no less stringent than those prescribed for the Bureau of Indian Affairs.

§63.14 What positions require a background investigation and determination of suitability for employment or retention?

All positions that allow an applicant, employee, or volunteer regular contact with or control over Indian children are subject to a background investigation and determination of suitability for employment.

§63.15 What questions should an employer ask?

Employment applications must:

(a) Ask whether the applicant, volunteer, or employee has been arrested or convicted of a crime involving a child, violence, sexual assault, sexual molestation, sexual exploitation, sexual contact or prostitution, or crimes against persons;

(b) Ask the disposition of the arrest or charge;

(c) Require that an applicant, volunteer or employee sign, under penalty of perjury, a statement verifying the truth of all information provided in the employment application; and

(d) Inform the applicant, volunteer or employee that a criminal history record check is a condition of employment and require the applicant, volunteer or employee to consent, in writing, to a record check.

§ 63.16 Who conducts the background investigation and prepares the determination of suitability for employment?

(a) The *Bureau of Indian Affairs* must use the United States Office of Personnel Management (OPM) to conduct background investigations for Federal employees. The BIA must designate qualified security personnel to adjudicate the results of background investigations.

(b) *Indian tribes and tribal organizations* may conduct their own background investigations, contract with private firms, or request the OPM to conduct an investigation. The investigation should cover the past five years of the individual's employment, education, etc.

§ 63.17 How does an employer determine suitability for employment and efficiency of service?

(a) *Adjudication* is the process employers use to determine suitability for employment and efficiency of service. The adjudication process protects the interests of the employer and the rights of applicants and employees. Adjudication requires uniform evaluation to ensure fair and consistent judgment.

(b) Each case is judged on its own merits. All available information, both favorable and unfavorable, must be considered and assessed in terms of accuracy, completeness, relevance, seriousness, overall significance, and how similar cases have been handled in the past.

(c) An *adjudicating official* conducts the adjudication. Each Federal agency, Indian tribe, or tribal organization must appoint an adjudicating official, who must first have been the subject of a favorable background investigation.

(1) Indian tribes and tribal organizations must ensure that persons charged with the responsibility for adjudicating employee background investigations are well-qualified and trained.

(2) Indian tribes and tribal organizations should also ensure that individuals who are not trained to adjudicate these types of investigations are supervised by someone who is experienced and receive the training necessary to perform the task.

(d) Each adjudicating official must be thoroughly familiar with all laws, regulations, and criteria involved in making a determination for suitability.

(e) The adjudicating official must review the background investigation to determine the character, reputation, and trustworthiness of the individual. At a minimum, the adjudicating official must:

(1) Review each security investigation form and employment application and compare the information provided;

(2) Review the results of written record searches requested from local law enforcement agencies, former employers, former supervisors, employment references, and schools; and

(3) Review the results of the fingerprint charts maintained by the Federal Bureau of Investigation or other law enforcement information maintained by other agencies.

(f) Relevancy is a key objective in evaluating investigative data. The adjudicating official must consider prior conduct in light of:

(1) The nature and seriousness of the conduct in question;

(2) The recency and circumstances surrounding the conduct in question;

(3) The age of the individual at the time of the incident;

(4) Societal conditions that may have contributed to the nature of the conduct;

(5) The probability that the individual will continue the type of behavior in question; and,

(6) The individual's commitment to rehabilitation and a change in the behavior in question.

§63.18 Are the requirements for Bureau of Indian Affairs adjudication different from the requirements for Indian tribes and tribal organizations?

Yes.

(a) In addition to the minimum requirements for background investigations found in §63.12, *Bureau of Indian Affairs'* adjudicating officials must review the OPM National Agency Check and Inquiries which includes a search of the OPM Security/Suitability Investigations Index (SII) and the Defense Clearance and Investigations Index (DCII), and any additional standards which may be established by the BIA.

(b) *All* Bureau of Indian Affairs employees who have regular contact with or control over Indian children must be reinvestigated every five years during their employment in that or any other position which allows regular contact with or control over Indian children.

(c) *Indian tribes and tribal organizations* may adopt these additional requirements but are not mandated to do so by law.

§63.19 When should an employer deny employment or dismiss an employee?

(a) An employer must deny employment or dismiss an employee when an individual has been found guilty of or entered a plea of guilty or nolo contendere to any Federal, state or tribal offense involving a crime of violence, sexual assault, sexual molestation, child exploitation, sexual contact, prostitution, or crimes against persons.

(b) An employer may deny employment or dismiss an employee when an individual has been convicted of an offense involving a child victim, a sex crime, or a drug felony.

[61 FR 32274, June 21, 1996, as amended at 64 FR 66771, Nov. 30, 1999]

§63.20 What should an employer do if an individual has been charged with an offense but the charge is pending or no disposition has been made by a court?

(a) The employer may deny the applicant employment until the charge has been resolved.

(b) The employer may deny the employee any on-the-job contact with children until the charge is resolved.

(c) The employer may detail or reassign the employee to other duties that do not involve contact with children.

(d) The employer may place the employee on administrative leave until the court has disposed of the charge.

§63.21 Are there other factors that may disqualify an applicant, volunteer or employee from placement in a position which involves regular contact with or control over Indian children?

Yes.

(a) An applicant, volunteer, or employee may be disqualified from consideration or continuing employment if it is found that:

(1) The individual's misconduct or negligence interfered with or affected a current or prior employer's performance of duties and responsibilities.

(2) The individual's criminal or dishonest conduct affected the individual's performance or the performance of others.

(3) The individual made an intentional false statement, deception or fraud on an examination or in obtaining employment.

(4) The individual has refused to furnish testimony or cooperate with an investigation.

(5) The individual's alcohol or substance abuse is of a nature and duration that suggests the individual could not perform the duties of the position or would directly threaten the property or safety of others.

(6) The individual has illegally used narcotics, drugs, or other controlled substances without evidence of substantial rehabilitation.

(7) The individual knowingly and willfully engaged in an act or activities designed to disrupt government programs.

(b) An individual must be disqualified for Federal employment if any statutory or regulatory provision would prevent his/her lawful employment.

§ 63.22 Can an employer certify an individual with a prior conviction or substantiated misconduct as suitable for employment?

(a) The *Bureau of Indian Affairs* must use Federal adjudicative standards which allow the BIA to certify that an individual is suitable for employment in a position that does not involve regular contact with or control over Indian children. The adjudicating officer must determine that the individual's prior conduct will not interfere with the performance of duties and will not create a potential for risk to the safety and well-being of Indian children.

(b) *Indian tribes and tribal organizations* must identify those positions which permit contact with or control over Indian children and establish standards to determine suitability for employment. Those standards should then be used to determine whether an individual is suitable for employment in a position that permits contact with or control over Indian children. If not, the individual may only be placed in a position that does not permit contact with or control over Indian children.

§ 63.23 What rights does an applicant, volunteer or employee have during this process?

(a) The applicant, volunteer, or employee must be provided an opportunity to explain, deny, or refute unfavorable and incorrect information gathered in an investigation, before the adjudication is final. The applicant, volunteer, or employee should receive a written summary of all derogatory information and be informed of the process for explaining, denying, or refuting unfavorable information.

(b) Employers and adjudicating officials must not release the actual background investigative report to an applicant, volunteer, or employee. However, they may issue a written summary of the derogatory information.

(c) The applicant, volunteer, or employee who is the subject of a background investigation may obtain a copy of the reports from the originating (Federal, state, or other tribal) agency and challenge the accuracy and completeness of any information maintained by that agency.

(d) The results of an investigation cannot be used for any purpose other than to determine suitability for employment in a position that involves regular contact with or control over Indian children.

(e) Investigative reports contain information of a highly personal nature and should be maintained confidentially and secured in locked files. Investigative reports should be seen only by those officials who in performing their official duties need to know the information contained in the report.

§ 63.24 What protections must employers provide to applicants, volunteers and employees?

(a) Indian tribes and tribal organizations must comply with the privacy requirements of any Federal, state, or other tribal agency providing background investigations. Indian tribes and tribal organizations must establish and comply with personnel policies that safeguard information derived from background investigations.

(b) The Bureau of Indian Affairs must comply with all policies, procedures, criteria, and guidance contained in the Bureau of Indian Affairs Manual or other appropriate guidelines.

(c) Federal agencies exercising authority under this part by delegation from OPM must comply with OPM policies, procedures, criteria, and guidance.

§§ 63.25–63.29 [Reserved]

Subpart C—Indian Child Protection and Family Violence Prevention Program

§ 63.30 What is the purpose of the Indian child protection and family violence prevention program?

The purpose of this program is to develop tribally-operated programs to protect Indian children and reduce the incidence of family violence on Indian reservations.

§ 63.31 Can both the Bureau of Indian Affairs and tribes operate Indian child protection and family violence prevention programs?

Yes. However, tribes are encouraged to develop and operate programs to protect Indian children and reduce the incidence of family violence in Indian country.

§63.32 Under what authority are Indian child protection and family violence prevention program funds awarded?

The Secretary is authorized to enter into contracts with Indian tribes, tribal organizations, or tribal consortia pursuant to the Indian Self-Determination and Education Assistance Act, as amended, 25 U.S.C. 450 *et seq.*, for the development and establishment of Indian child protection and family violence prevention programs. This includes compacting with tribes under the Self-Governance program procedures.

§63.33 What must an application for Indian child protection and family violence prevention program funds include?

In addition to the Indian Self-Determination and Education Assistance Act, as amended, 25 U.S.C. 450 *et seq.*, contracting requirements, each application must provide the following information:

(a) The name and address of the agency or official to be responsible for the investigation of reported cases of child abuse and child neglect, the treatment and prevention of incidents of family violence, and the provision of immediate shelter and related assistance for victims of family violence and their dependents;

(b) Projected service population of the program;

(c) Projected service area of the program; and

(d) Projected number of cases per month.

§63.34 How are Indian child protection and family violence prevention program funds distributed?

(a) Funds will be distributed, subject to the availability of appropriations, and:

(1) In any fiscal year that the appropriation exceeds 50 percent of the level of funding authorized for this purpose by the Act, 49 percent must be distributed equally to all tribes and tribal organizations and 49 percent must be distributed on a per capita basis according to the population of children residing in the service area. Two percent of the annual appropriation will be set aside for distribution to tribes demonstrating special circumstances.

(2) In any fiscal year that the appropriation does not exceed 50 percent of the level of funding authorized for this purpose by the Act, funding must be distributed in equal amounts to all tribes. Two percent of the annual appropriation will be set aside for distribution to tribes demonstrating special circumstances.

(3) Special circumstances include but are not limited to a high incidence of child sexual abuse, a high incidence of violent crimes, a high incidence of violent crimes against women, or the existence of a significant victim population within the community.

(i) This 2 percent will be subject to discretionary distribution by the Assistant Secretary—Indian Affairs, or his or her designee. Tribes may request these funds through their respective area offices. All requests must demonstrate a high incidence of child sexual abuse, a high incidence of violent crimes, a high incidence of violent crimes against women, or the existence of a significant victim population within the community.

(ii) Special circumstances funds will remain available through the third quarter of each fiscal year. In the fourth quarter, unallocated special circumstances funds will be redistributed as set forth in paragraphs (a)(1) and (a)(2) of this section, except that there will be no additional set aside for special circumstances.

(b) Any tribe not wishing to receive Indian child protection and family violence prevention funds must inform its respective area office in writing within 90 days after receiving notice of the allocation from the area office. Each area office may reallocate unused Indian child protection and family violence prevention program funds as provided in this section.

(c) Funds may be used as matching shares for other federally funded programs which contribute to and promote prevention of child abuse, child neglect, and family violence on Indian reservations, but may not be used to supplant funds available for the same general purposes.

(d) Any income resulting from the operation of Indian child protection and family violence prevention programs may be retained and used to promote prevention of child abuse, child neglect, and family violence on Indian reservations.

§ 63.35 How may Indian child protection and family violence prevention program funds be used?

Indian child protection and family violence prevention program funds may be used to:

(a) Establish child protective services programs.

(b) Establish family violence prevention and treatment programs.

(c) Develop and implement multidisciplinary child abuse investigation and prosecution programs.

(d) Provide immediate shelter and related assistance to victims of family violence and their dependents, including construction or renovation of facilities to establish family violence shelters.

(e) Purchase equipment to assist in the investigation of cases of child abuse and child neglect.

(f) Develop protocols and intergovernmental or interagency agreements among tribal, Federal, state law enforcement, courts of competent jurisdiction, and related agencies to ensure investigations of child abuse cases to minimize the trauma to the child victim, to define and specify each party's responsibilities, and to provide for the coordination of services to victims and their families.

(g) Develop child protection codes and regulations that provide for the care and protection of children and families on Indian reservations.

(h) Establish community education programs for tribal members and school children on issues of family violence, child abuse, and child neglect.

(i) Establish training programs for child protective services, law enforcement, judicial, medical, education, and related services personnel in the investigation, prevention, protection, and treatment of child abuse, child neglect, and family violence.

(j) Establish other innovative and culturally relevant programs and projects that show promise of successfully preventing and treating family violence, child abuse, and child neglect.

§ 63.36 What are the special requirements for Indian child protection and family violence prevention programs?

(a) Each tribe must develop appropriate standards of service, including caseload standards and staffing requirements. The following caseload standards and staffing requirements are comparable to those recommended by the Child Welfare League of America, and are included to assist tribes in developing standards for Indian child protection and family violence prevention programs:

(1) Caseworkers providing services to abused and neglected children and their families have a caseload of 20 active ongoing cases and five active investigations per caseworker.

(2) Caseworkers providing services to strengthen and preserve families with children have a caseload of 20 families. If intensive family-centered crisis services are provided, a caseload of 10 families per caseworker is recommended.

(3) It is recommended that there be one supervisor for every six caseworkers.

(b) The negotiation and award of contracts, grants, or funding agreements under these regulations must include the following requirements:

(1) Performance of background investigations to ensure that only those individuals who meet the standards of character contained in § 63.12 are employed in positions which involve regular contact with or control over Indian children.

(2) Submission of an annual report to the contracting officer's representative which details program activities, number of children and families served, and the number of child abuse, child neglect, and family violence reports received.

(3) Assurance that the identity of any person making a report of child abuse or child neglect will not be disclosed without the consent of the individual and that all reports and records collected under these regulations are confidential and to be disclosed only as provided by Federal or tribal law.

(4) Assurance that persons who, in good faith, report child abuse or child neglect will not suffer retaliation from their employers.

§§63.37–63.50 [Reserved]

PART 67—PREPARATION OF A ROLL OF INDEPENDENT SEMINOLE INDIANS OF FLORIDA

AUTHORITY: 5 U.S.C. 301; 25 U.S.C. 2 and 9; and Pub.L. 101–277, 104 Stat. 143.

SOURCE: 59 FR 3291, Jan. 20, 1994, unless otherwise noted.

§67.1 Definitions.

As used in this part:

Act means the Act of Congress approved April 30, 1990, Public Law 101–277, 104 Stat. 143, which authorizes the use and distribution of funds awarded the Seminole Indians in Dockets 73, 151, and 73–A of the Indian Claims Commission.

Adopted person means a person whose natural parents' parental rights have been terminated by court order and persons other than the natural parents have exercised or do exercise parental rights with regard to the adopted person.

Applicant means a person who is making application for inclusion on the roll prepared by the Secretary pursuant to the Act of April 30, 1990, by either personally filing an application or by having a sponsor complete and file an application on his or her behalf.

Assistant Secretary means the Assistant Secretary for Indian Affairs or authorized representative.

BIA means the Bureau of Indian Affairs, Department of the Interior.

Commissioner means the Commissioner of Indian Affairs or authorized representative.

Director means the Area Director, Eastern Area Office, Bureau of Indian Affairs or authorized representative.

Lineal descendant(s) means those persons who are the issue of the ancestor through whom enrollment rights are claimed; namely, the children, grandchildren, etc. It does not include collateral relatives such as brothers, sisters, nieces, nephews, cousins, etc., or adopted children, adopted grandchildren, etc.

Living means born on or before and alive on the date specified.

Secretary means the Secretary of the Interior or authorized representative.

Sponsor means any person who files an application for enrollment or an appeal on behalf of another person.

Superintendent means the Superintendent, Seminole Agency, Bureau of Indian Affairs or authorized representative.

§67.2 Purpose.

The regulations in this part govern the compilation of a roll of persons who meet the requirements specified in section 7 of the Act who will be eligible to share in the distribution of a portion of the judgment funds awarded the Seminole Indians in Dockets 73, 151, and 73–A of the Indian Claims Commission.

§67.3 Information collection.

The information collection requirement contained in this part does not require approval by the Office of Management and Budget under 44 U.S.C. 3501 *et seq.*

§67.4 Qualifications for enrollment and the deadline for filing application forms.

(a) The roll shall contain the names of persons of Seminole Indian descent who:

(1) Were born on or before, and living on April 30, 1990;

(2) Are listed on or who are lineal descendants of persons listed on the annotated Seminole Agency Census of 1957 as Independent Seminoles; and

(3) Are not members of an Indian tribe recognized by the Secretary on the most recent list of such Indian tribes published in the FEDERAL REGISTER.

(b) To qualify for enrollment, all persons must file application forms with the Superintendent, Seminole Agency, Bureau of Indian Affairs, 6075 Stirling Road, Hollywood, Florida 33024 by June 19, 1994. An application filed after June 19, 1994 will be rejected for failure to file on time regardless of whether the applicant otherwise meets the qualifications for enrollment.

§ 67.5 Notices.

(a) The Director shall give notice to all Area Directors of the BIA and all Superintendents within the jurisdiction of the Director of the preparation of the roll for public display in BIA field offices. Notices shall be placed for public display in community buildings, tribal buildings and Indian centers.

(b) The Superintendent shall, on the basis of available residence data, publish, and republish when advisable, notices of the preparation of the roll in appropriate localities utilizing media suitable to the circumstances.

(c) Notices shall advise of the preparation of the roll and the relevant procedures to be followed, including the qualifications for enrollment and the deadline for filing application forms to be eligible for enrollment. The notices shall also state how and where application forms may be obtained, as well as the name, address, and telephone number of a person who may be contacted for further information.

§ 67.6 Application forms.

(a) Application forms to be filed by or for applicants for enrollment shall be furnished by the Area Director, Superintendent, or other designated persons upon written or oral request. Each person furnishing application forms shall keep a record of the names of individuals to whom forms are given, as well as the control numbers of the forms and the date furnished. Instructions for completing and filing application forms shall be furnished with each form. The form shall indicate prominently the deadline date for filing application forms.

(b) Among other information, each application form shall contain:

(1) Certification as to whether the application form is for a natural child or an adopted child of the parent through whom eligibility is claimed.

(2) If the application form is filed by a sponsor, the name and address of the sponsor and the sponsor's relationship to the applicant.

(3) A control number for the purpose of keeping a record of forms furnished to interested individuals.

(4) Certification that the information given on the application form is true to the best of the knowledge and belief of the person filing the application. Criminal penalties are provided by statute for knowingly filing false information in such applications (18 U.S.C. 1001).

(5) An election by the applicant as to whether the applicant, if determined to meet the qualifications for enrollment, wishes to share in the per capita payment.

(c) Sponsors may file application forms on behalf of other persons, but may not file elections to share in the per capita payment.

(1) The election to share in the per capita payment shall be made as follows:

(i) If the applicant is a competent adult, the election shall be made by the applicant.

(ii) If the applicant is not a competent adult, the election shall be made by the applicant's legal guardian.

(iii) If the applicant is a minor, the election shall be made by the applicant's parent or legal guardian.

(2) When an application is filed by a sponsor, the Superintendent shall:

(i) Furnish the sponsor a copy of the application for forwarding to the applicant or his/her guardian for completion of the election to share in the per capita payment; and

(ii) Make a reasonable effort to furnish a copy of the application directly to the applicant or his/her guardian for completion of the election to share in the per capita payment.

(d) Every applicant or sponsor shall furnish the applicant's mailing address on the application form. Thereafter, the applicant or sponsor shall promptly notify the Superintendent of any change in address, giving appropriate identification of the applicant. Otherwise, the mailing address as stated on the application form shall be accepted as the address of record for all purposes under the regulations in this part.

§67.7 Filing of application forms.

(a) Application forms filed by mail must be postmarked no later than midnight on the deadline date specified in §67.4(b). Where there is no postmark date showing on the envelope or the postmark date is illegible, application forms mailed from within the United States, including Alaska and Hawaii, received more than 15 days after the specified deadline, and application forms mailed from outside of the United States received more than 30 days after the specified deadline in the office of the Superintendent, will be rejected for failure to file in time.

(b) Application forms filed by personal delivery must be received in the office of the Superintendent no later than close of business on the deadline date specified in §67.4(b).

(c) If the deadline date for filing application forms falls on a Saturday, Sunday, legal holiday, or other nonbusiness day, the deadline will be the next working day thereafter.

§67.8 Burden of proof.

The burden of proof rests upon the applicant to establish eligibility for enrollment. Documentary evidence such as birth certificates, death certificates, baptismal records, copies of probate findings, or affidavits may be used to support claims of eligibility for enrollment. Records of the BIA may be used to establish eligibility.

§67.9 Action by Superintendent.

(a) The Superintendent shall notify each individual applicant or sponsor, as applicable, upon receipt of an application. The Superintendent shall consider each application and all documentation. Upon determining an individual's eligibility, the Superintendent shall notify the individual; the parent or guardian having legal custody of a minor or incompetent adult; or the sponsor, as applicable.

(1) Written notification of the Superintendent's decision shall be sent to the applicant by certified mail, for receipt by the addressee only, return receipt requested.

(2) If a decision by the Superintendent is sent out of the United States, registered mail will be used. If a certified or registered notice is returned as "Unclaimed," the Superintendent shall remail the notice by regular mail together with an acknowledgment of receipt form to be completed by the addressee and returned to the Superintendent. If the acknowledgment of receipt is not returned, computation of the period specified for changes in election and for appeals shall begin on the date the notice was remailed. A certified or registered notice returned for any reason other than "Unclaimed" need not be remailed.

(3) If an individual files an application on behalf of more than one person, one notice of eligibility or adverse action may be addressed to the person who filed the applications. However, the notice must list the name of each person to whom the notice is applicable. Where an individual is represented by a sponsor, notification to the sponsor of eligibility or adverse action shall be considered notification to the individual.

(b) On the basis of an applicant's election with regard to whether he or she wishes to share in the per capita payment, the Superintendent's decision shall also state whether the applicant's name will be included on the per capita payment roll. If no election has been made by the applicant, parent, or legal guardian on the application form, the individual applicant's name will not be included on the per capita payment roll.

(1) The eligible individual will have 30 days from notification of his or her eligibility in which to request a change in the election of whether to share in the per capita payment. Computation of the 30-day period will be in accordance with §67.9(a)(2) and §67.9(d). Upon written request received within the 30-day period, to avoid hardship or gross injustice, the Superintendent may

grant an applicant additional time, not to exceed 30 days, in which to submit a request for a change in election.

(2) A change in the election of whether to share in the per capita payment can only be made by competent adult applicants; by the legal guardian of an incompetent adult; or, in the case of a minor, by the minor's parent or legal guardian.

(c) If the Superintendent determines that an applicant is not eligible for enrollment as an Independent Seminole Indian of Florida, the Superintendent shall notify the applicant of the decision and shall fully explain the reasons for the adverse action and explain the rejected applicant's right to appeal to the Area Director. The decision of the Area Director shall be final and conclusive.

(d) Except as provided in paragraph (a)(2) of this section, a notice of adverse action concerning an individual's enrollment eligibility or the inclusion or exclusion of an individual's name on the per capita payment roll is considered to have been made, and computation of the period for appeal shall begin on the earliest of the following dates:

(1) Delivery date indicated on the return receipt;

(2) Date of acknowledgment of receipt;

(3) Date of personal delivery; or

(4) Date of return by the post office of an undelivered certified or registered letter.

(e) To avoid hardship or gross injustice, the Area Director or the Superintendent may waive technical deficiencies in application forms or other submittals. Failure to file by the deadline date does not constitute a technical deficiency.

§ 67.10 Appeals.

(a) Appeals from or on behalf of applicants who have been rejected for enrollment must be in writing and must be filed pursuant to part 62 of this chapter. When the appeal is on behalf of more than one person, the name of each person must be listed in the appeal.

(b) A copy of part 62 of this chapter shall be furnished with each notice of adverse action. All sections of part 62 shall be applicable to appeals filed under this part except §§ 62.10, 62.11 and 62.12.

§ 67.11 Decision of the Area Director on appeals.

(a) The Area Director will consider the record as presented, together with such additional information as may be considered pertinent. Any additional information relied upon shall be specifically identified in the decision.

(b) The decision of the Area Director on an appeal shall be final and conclusive, and written notice, which shall state that the decision is final and conclusive, shall be given to the individual applicant, parent, legal guardian, or sponsor, as applicable.

(c) If an individual files an appeal on behalf of more than one applicant, one notice of the Area Director's decision may be addressed to the person who filed the appeal. The Area Director's decision must list the name of each person to whom the decision is applicable. Where an individual applicant is represented by a sponsor, notification to the sponsor of the Area Director's decision is sufficient.

(d) Written notice of the Area Director's decision on the appeal shall be sent to the applicant by certified mail, to be received by the addressee only, return receipt requested.

(1) On the basis of the individual's election with regard to whether he or she wishes to share in the per capita payment, the Area Director's decision shall also state whether the individual's name will be included on the per capita payment roll. If no election is made by the individual applicant, parent, or legal guardian, the individual's name will not be included on the per capita payment roll.

(2) The eligible individual will have 30 days from notification of his or her eligibility in which to request a change in the election of whether to share in the per capita payment. Computation of the 30-day period will be in accordance with § 67.9(a)(2) and § 67.9(d). Upon written request received within the 30-day period, to avoid hardship or gross injustice, the Area Director may grant additional time, not to exceed 30 days, in which to submit a request for a change in election.

(3) The change in the election of whether to share in the per capita payment can only be made by adult applicants, or by the legal guardian of an incompetent adult, or in the case of minors, by the parents or legal guardian of such minors.

§67.12 Exhaustion of administrative remedies.

The decision of the Area Director on appeal, which shall be final for the Department, is subject to judicial review under 5 U.S.C. 704.

§67.13 Preparation, certification and approval of the roll.

(a) The Superintendent shall prepare a minimum of three (3) copies of the roll of those persons determined to be qualified for enrollment as an Independent Seminole Indian of Florida. The roll shall contain for each person a roll number or identification number, name, address, sex, date of birth, date of death (when applicable), and the name and relationship of the ancestor on the annotated Seminole Agency Census of 1957 through whom eligibility for enrollment was established.

(b) A certificate shall be attached to the roll by the Superintendent certifying that to the best of his or her knowledge and belief, the roll contains only the names of those persons who were determined to meet the qualifications for enrollment.

(c) The Area Director shall approve the roll.

§67.14 Preparation of a per capita payment roll.

(a) The Superintendent shall, based on the roll approved under §67.12(c), prepare a per capita payment roll. The payment roll shall be comprised of those persons whose names appear on the approved roll and who have elected to share in the per capita payment.

(b) The per capita payment roll shall contain for each person a roll number or identification number, name, and address.

(c) The Area Director shall authorize the distribution of the judgment funds to those persons named on the per capita payment roll.

§67.15 Special instructions.

To facilitate the work of the Superintendent and Area Director, the Assistant Secretary may issue special instructions not inconsistent with the regulations in this part.

PART 75—REVISION OF THE MEMBERSHIP ROLL OF THE EASTERN BAND OF CHEROKEE INDIANS, NORTH CAROLINA

Sec.

AUTHORITY: Sec. 2, 71 Stat. 374.

SOURCE: 24 FR 201, Jan. 8, 1959, unless otherwise noted. Redesignated at 47 FR 13327, Mar. 30, 1982.

§75.1 Definitions.

As used in this part:

(a) *Band* means the Eastern Band of Cherokee Indians in North Carolina.

(b) *Reservation* means the lands of the Eastern Band of Cherokee Indians in the counties of Jackson, Swain, Graham, Cherokee and Haywood in North Carolina.

(c) *Tribal Council* means the Tribal Council of the Eastern Band of Cherokee Indians in North Carolina.

(d) *Announcement* means the announcement of the revision of the membership roll issued as required in §75.3.

(e) *Tribal Enrollment Office* means the Tribal Enrollment Clerk working in concert with the Enrollment Committee.

(f) *Tribal Enrollment Clerk* means the individual working in the Tribal Enrollment Office.

(g) *Enrollment Committee* means the three individuals appointed by the Tribal Council in accordance with § 75.12.

[24 FR 201, Jan. 8, 1959, as amended at 25 FR 2516, Mar. 25, 1960; 38 FR 9998, Apr. 23, 1973. Redesignated at 47 FR 13327, Mar. 30, 1982]

§ 75.2 Purpose.

The regulations in this part are to govern the revision, as authorized by the Act approved August 21, 1957 (71 Stat. 374), of the membership roll of the Eastern Band of Cherokee Indians, North Carolina, prepared and approved in accordance with the Act of June 4, 1924 (43 Stat. 376), and the Act of March 4, 1931 (46 Stat. 1518).

§ 75.3 Announcement of revision of roll.

When the Tribal Council has authorized the expenditure of tribal funds to supply sufficient staff to perform the work necessary to revise the membership roll of the Band and such staff has been employed and when the application forms and other necessary documents have been devised and printed, the Principal Chief, or in his absence the Vice Chief or the Chairman of the Tribal Council shall announce that a revision of the membership roll of the Band shall commence on a specified date. The date specified shall be not less than 15 days nor more than 30 days from the date of issuance of the announcement. A press release should be prepared announcing the date the revision of the roll shall begin, together with other pertinent information such as the membership requirements and where application forms may be obtained. The press release should be distributed to all newspapers and radio stations within the region of the Reservation with a request that it be given wide publicity. Copies of the press release should also be posted in the Agency Office and at various other public places throughout the Reservation as well as in Post Offices of the towns adjacent to the Reservation.

§ 75.4 Basic membership roll.

All persons whose names appear on the roll of the Eastern Band of Cherokee Indians of North Carolina, prepared and approved pursuant to the act of June 4, 1924 (43 Stat. 376), and the act of March 4, 1931 (46 Stat. 1518), shall be members of the Band.

§ 75.5 Removal of deceased persons from the roll.

The name of any person who was not alive as of midnight August 21, 1957, shall be stricken from the basic membership roll by the Tribal Enrollment Office upon receipt of a death certificate or other evidence of death acceptable to the Tribal Enrollment Office.

[38 FR 9998, Apr. 23, 1973. Redesignated at 47 FR 13327, Mar. 30, 1982]

§ 75.6 Additions to the roll.

There shall be added to the roll of the Band the names of persons living on August 21, 1957, who meet the following qualifications:

(a) Persons born during the period, beginning on or after June 4, 1924, and ending midnight August 21, 1957, who are direct descendants of persons whose names appear on the roll prepared and approved pursuant to the act of June 4, 1924 (43 Stat. 376), and the act of March 4, 1931 (46 Stat. 1518); provided, such persons:

(1) Who applied for membership before August 14, 1963 possess at least 1/32 degree of Eastern Cherokee Indian blood, and those persons who apply for membership on or after August 14, 1963, possess at least 1/16 degree Eastern Cherokee Indian blood, except that persons who also possess Indian blood of another tribe shall not be enrolled if they are enrolled as members of the other tribe.

(2) Have themselves or have parents who have maintained and dwelt in a home at sometime during the period from June 4, 1924, through August 21, 1957, on the lands of the Eastern Band of Cherokee Indians in the counties of Swain, Jackson, Graham, Cherokee and Haywood in North Carolina, except that this specific part of this section shall not apply to those persons and members of their families who were

temporarily away from the Reservation due to one or both parents being in the U.S. Armed Services or who were employed by the U.S. Government and neither shall it apply to those individuals who were in mental or penal institutions during this period of time.

(3) Have filed an application for enrollment with the Band in accordance with the procedures set forth in this part.

(b) A child born out of wedlock to a mother who is either an enrolled member of the Band, or who meets the qualifications for enrollment as a member, may be enrolled if such child otherwise meets the requirements for enrollment as set forth in this section.

(c) A child born out of wedlock to a mother who is not a member of the Band may be enrolled if the mother files with the Enrollment Committee proof established in accordance with the laws of North Carolina as to the paternity of the child and the person adjudged to be the father is either an enrolled member of the Band, or meets the requirements for enrollment as a member, and if the child otherwise meet the requirements for enrollment as set forth in this section.

[24 FR 201, Jan. 8, 1959, as amended at 25 FR 2516, Mar. 25, 1960; 28 FR 8314, Aug. 14, 1963. Redesignated at 47 FR 13327, Mar. 30, 1982]

§75.7 Applications for enrollment.

Each adult person who believes he meets the requirements for enrollment established herein may submit to the Tribal Enrollment Office an application for enrollment as a member of the Eastern Band of Cherokee Indians.

[38 FR 9998, Apr. 23, 1973. Redesignated at 47 FR 13327, Mar. 30, 1982]

§75.8 Applications for minors and incompetents.

Applications for enrollment of minors may be filed by the parent, next of kin, recognized guardian, or other person responsible for their care. Applications for enrollment of persons known to be in mental or penal institutions may be filed by the Principal Chief of the Eastern Band of Cherokee.

[38 FR 9998, Apr. 23, 1973. Redesignated at 47 FR 13327, Mar. 30, 1982]

§75.9 Application form.

The form of application for enrollment will be prepared by the Tribal Enrollment Office and, in addition to whatever information the Enrollment Committee may deem necessary, shall contain the following:

(a) The name and address of the applicant. If the application is filed on behalf of a minor, the name and address of the person filing the application and his relationship to the minor.

(b) The name, relationship, tribe and roll number of the ancestor or ancestors through whom enrollment rights are claimed, and whether applicant is enrolled with another tribe.

(c) The date of death of such ancestor, if deceased.

[38 FR 9998, Apr. 23, 1973. Redesignated at 47 FR 13327, Mar. 30, 1982]

§75.10 Where application forms may be obtained.

Application forms will be supplied by the Tribal Enrollment Office of the Eastern Band of Cherokee Indians, Council House, Cherokee, N.C. 28719, upon request, either in person or by mail.

[38 FR 9998, Apr. 23, 1973. Redesignated at 47 FR 13327, Mar. 30, 1982]

§75.11 Proof of relationship.

If the applicant's parents or other Eastern Cherokee ancestors through whom the applicant claims enrollment rights are unknown to the Tribal Enrollment Office, the Tribal Enrollment Office may request the applicant to furnish such additional information and evidence as it may deem necessary to determine the applicant's eligibility for enrollment. Failure of the applicant to furnish the information requested may be deemed sufficient cause for rejection.

[38 FR 9998, Apr. 23, 1973. Redesignated at 47 FR 13327, Mar. 30, 1982]

§75.12 Enrollment Committee.

The Tribal Council shall appoint either from within or without the membership of the Council, but not from without the membership of the Band, a committee of three (3) persons to serve as the Enrollment Committee. The Enrollment Committee shall review all applications for enrollment filed in accordance with the existing regulations, and shall determine the qualifications of the applicant for enrollment with the Band. The Enrollment Committee may perform such other functions relating to the enrollment and membership in the Band as the Tribal Council may from time to time direct.

[38 FR 9999, Apr. 23, 1973. Redesignated at 47 FR 13327, Mar. 30, 1982]

§ 75.13 Tenure of Enrollment Committee.

The members of the Enrollment Committee shall be appointed to serve a term of office of 2 years by each newly elected Tribal Council.

[38 FR 9999, Apr. 23, 1973. Redesignated at 47 FR 13327, Mar. 30, 1982]

§ 75.14 Appeals.

Any person whose application for enrollment has been rejected by the Enrollment Committee shall have the right to appeal to the Tribal Council from the determination made by the Enrollment Committee: *Provided*, That such appeal shall be made in writing and shall be filed in the office of the Principal Chief for presentation to the Tribal Council within sixty (60) days from the date on which the Enrollment Committee issues notice to the applicant of his rejection. The applicant may submit with his appeal any additional data to support his claim to enrollment not previously furnished. The decision of the Tribal Council as to whether the applicant meets the requirements for enrollment set forth in this part shall be final. The Tribal Council shall review no applications for enrollment except in those cases where the rejected applicant appeals to the Council in writing from the determination made by the Enrollment Committee.

[38 FR 9999, Apr. 23, 1973. Redesignated at 47 FR 13327, Mar. 30, 1982]

§ 75.15 Current membership roll.

The membership roll of the Eastern Band of Cherokee Indians shall be kept current by striking therefrom the names of persons who have relinquished their membership in the Band as provided in § 75.17 and of deceased persons upon receipt of a death certificate or other evidence of death acceptable to the Tribal Enrollment Office, and by adding thereto the names of individuals who meet the qualifications and are accepted for membership in the Band as set forth in this part.

[38 FR 9999, Apr. 23, 1973. Redesignated at 47 FR 13327, Mar. 30, 1982]

§ 75.16 Eligibility for enrollment of persons born after August 21, 1957.

(a) Persons possessing one-sixteenth or more degree Eastern Cherokee Indian blood and born after August 21, 1957, may be enrolled in either of the following manners:

(1) An application to have the person enrolled must be filed by or on behalf of the person by the parent or recognized guardian or person responsible for his care, which application shall be accompanied by the applicant's birth certificate or by other evidence of eligibility of the applicant for enrollment that the Tribal Enrollment Office may require.

(2) In the absence of such application within 6 months after a person's birth, the Tribal Enrollment Office shall be authorized and encouraged to obtain evidence relating to the eligibility of the person for enrollment in the Eastern Band, and present an application in his behalf to the Enrollment Committee which may proceed to enroll the person if the evidence submitted meets the criteria.

(b) A person adopted in accordance with applicable laws by either tribal members or nonmembers, shall be considered for enrollment as a tribal member if the person otherwise meets the requirements for enrollment.

(c) A person born to an enrolled member of the Band and an enrolled member of another Tribe, and said person is enrolled in the other Tribe, may be transferred from the rolls of the other and added to the rolls of the Eastern Band if he meets the general requirements for enrollment and, in addition:

(1) A death certificate or other acceptable evidence of the death of the parent enrolled in the other Tribe is received and the surviving parent who is a member of the Eastern Band makes

application for enrollment by way of transfer.

(2) Upon receipt of divorce documents in the Tribal Enrollment Office, there is evidence of custody of the minors being awarded to the parent who is a member of the Band and the parent awarded custody makes application for enrollment of the minors with the Eastern Band by way of transfer.

(d) In order for a child to be enrolled under paragraph (b) or (c) of this section, either:

(1) An application to have the child enrolled must be filed on behalf of the child by the parent or recognized guardian or person responsible for his care, which application shall be accompanied by the child's birth certificate or by other evidence as to the eligibility of the child for enrollment as the Enrollment Committee may require, which application must be filed within one year from the date of birth of such child, or

(2) In the absence of such application, the Tribal Enrollment Committee may on its own motion, proceed to enroll any eligible child upon receipt by it of such evidence as shall satisfy the Committee as to the eligibility of the child to be enrolled, within one year from date of birth of such child.

[28 FR 8315, Aug. 14, 1963, as amended at 29 FR 9326, July 8, 1964; 38 FR 9999, Apr. 23, 1973. Redesignated at 47 FR 13327, Mar. 30, 1982]

§ 75.17 Relinquishment of membership.

Any member of the Eastern Band of Cherokee Indians may relinquish his membership in the Band by filing notice in writing that he no longer desires to be enrolled as a member of the Band. On receipt of such notice the name of the members shall be stricken from the roll and he shall no longer be considered as a member of the Band and shall not be entitled to share in any use or in any distribution of tribal assets which may be made in the future to the enrolled members of the Band.

§ 75.18 Adoption.

The Tribal Council of the Eastern Band of Cherokee Indians shall be empowered to enact ordinances governing the adoption of new members.

[39 FR 43391, Dec. 13, 1974. Redesignated at 47 FR 13327, Mar. 30, 1982]

§ 75.19 Distribution of judgment funds.

The membership roll of the Eastern Band of Cherokee Indians of North Carolina will be brought up to date as of October 10, 1974, to serve as the basis for distributing certain judgment funds awarded to the Band in Indian Claims Commission dockets 282–A through L.

(a) Filing of and action on applications shall be in accordance with regulations in this part 75, except as otherwise provided in paragraphs (b) through (g) of this section.

(b) In lieu of notice provisions contained in § 75.3, the Commissioner of Indian Affairs or his authorized representative shall provide notice of the bringing up to date of the membership roll through publication of these amended regulations in the FEDERAL REGISTER and through appropriate press releases and other public notices.

(c) Application forms may be obtained from the Tribal Enrollment Office of the Eastern Band of Cherokee Indians, Council House, Cherokee, North Carolina 28719. Completed applications must be received by the Tribal Enrollment Office no later than midnight January 8, 1975.

(d) Requests for applications for enrollment in the Band received after midnight of the deadline date will not be furnished until after the funds have been distributed.

(e) In lieu of the procedures given in § 75.14, appeals from rejected applicants must be in writing and filed pursuant to part 62 of this subchapter, a copy of which shall be furnished with each notice of rejection.

(f) The Tribal Council and the Superintendent shall attach separate statements to the roll certifying that to the best of their knowledge and belief, the roll contains only the names of those persons who were determined to meet the requirements for enrollment. The roll shall then be submitted through the Area Director to the Commissioner for approval.

(g) To facilitate the work of the Tribal Enrollment Committee the Commissioner may issue special instructions not inconsistent with the regulations in this part 75.

[39 FR 43391, Dec. 13, 1974. Redesignated at 47 FR 13327, Mar. 30, 1982]

PART 81—SECRETARIAL ELECTION PROCEDURES

Subpart A—Purpose and Scope

Subpart B—Definitions

Subpart C—Provisions Applicable to All Secretarial Elections

Subpart D—The Secretarial Election Process under the Indian Reorganization Act (IRA)

Subpart E—The Secretarial Election Process under the Oklahoma Indian Welfare Act (OIWA)

Subpart F—Formulating Petitions to Request a Secretarial Election

AUTHORITY: : 25 U.S.C. 473a, 476, 477, as amended, and 503.

SOURCE: 80 FR 63106, Oct. 19, 2015, unless otherwise noted.

Subpart A—Purpose and Scope

§81.1 What is the purpose of this part?

This part prescribes the Department's procedures for authorizing and conducting elections when Federal statute or the terms of a tribal governing document require the Secretary to conduct and approve an election to:

(a) Adopt, amend, or revoke tribal governing documents; or

(b) Adopt or amend charters.

§81.2 When does this part apply?

(a) This part applies only to federally recognized tribes, in the circumstances shown in the following table.

If a tribe wants to . . .	And . . .
(1) Adopt a new governing document to reorganize under Federal statute.	The Federal statute requires an election before or after Secretarial approval.
(2) Adopt a new governing document to reorganize outside Federal statute.	The governing document requires approval under the Secretary's general authority to approve.
(3) Amend or revoke a governing document adopted under Federal statute.	The Federal statute requires an election and approval for amendment or revocation.
(4) Amend or revoke a governing document adopted outside Federal statute.	The governing document requires Secretarial approval of an amendment or revocation.
(5) Ratify a federal charter of incorporation.	The charter requires Secretarial approval or is being ratified under the Oklahoma Indian Welfare Act (OIWA).
(6) Amend a federal charter of incorporation.	The charter requires a Secretarial election to amend.
(7) Take other action	A Federal statute or tribal law requires a Secretarial election in order to take that action.
(8) Remove the requirement for a Secretarial approval from a governing document.	A Federal statute or tribal law requires a Secretarial election in order to take that action.

(b) Secretarial elections will be conducted in accordance with the procedures in this part unless the amendment article of the tribe's governing document provides otherwise and is not contrary to Federal voting qualifications or substantive provisions, in which case the provisions of those documents shall rule, where applicable.

(c) If the amendment provisions of a tribal governing document have become outdated and the amendment cannot be effected under them, and the recognized tribal governing body requests a Secretarial election, the Bureau may authorize a Secretarial election under this part to amend the documents.

§81.3 Information collection.

The information collection requirements contained in this part are approved by the Office of Management and Budget under the Paperwork Reduction Act of 1995, 44 U.S.C. 3507(d), and has been assigned OMB control number 1076–0183. This information is collected when, under Federal statute or the tribe's governing documents, the Secretarial election is authorized to adopt, amend, or revoke governing documents; or adopt or amend charters. This information is required to obtain or retain benefits. A Federal agency may not collect or sponsor an information collection without a valid OMB control number.

Subpart B—Definitions

§81.4 What terms do I need to know?

For purposes of this part:

Absentee ballot means a ballot the Secretarial Election Board provides to a registered voter, upon request, to allow him or her to vote by mail even though polling sites are used.

Amendment means any modification or change to one or more provisions of an existing governing document or charter.

Applicable law means any treaty, statute, Executive Order, regulation, or final decision of a Federal court, which is applicable to the tribe.

Authorizing Official means the Bureau official with delegated Federal authority to authorize a Secretarial election.

Bureau means the Bureau of Indian Affairs, Department of the Interior.

Business day means a weekday (Monday through Friday), excluding Federal holidays.

Cast means the action of a registered voter, when the ballot is received through the mail by the Secretarial Election Board, or placed in the ballot box at the polling site.

Charter means a charter of incorporation issued under a Federal statute and ratified by the governing body in accordance with tribal law or, if adopted before May 24, 1990, by a majority vote in an election conducted by the Secretary.

Day means a calendar day. A Secretarial election may be held on a Saturday, Sunday or Federal holiday.

Department means the Department of the Interior.

Director means the Director of the Bureau of Indian Affairs or his or her authorized representative.

Electioneering means campaigning for or against the adoption, ratification, revocation or amendment of a proposed governing document or a charter.

Eligible voter means a tribal member who will be 18 years of age or older on the date of the Secretarial election (and, if the tribe's governing document imposes additional requirements for voting in a Secretarial election, also meets those requirements).

Eligible Voters List means a list of eligible voters, including their birthdates and their last known mailing addresses. The Eligible Voters List is compiled and certified by the tribe's governing body or the Bureau if the Bureau maintains the current membership roll for the tribe.

Federal statute means the Indian Reorganization Act (IRA), 25 U.S.C. 476, 477, as amended, the Oklahoma Indian Welfare Act (OIWA), 25 U.S.C. 503, and any tribe-specific Federal statute that requires a Secretarial election for the adoption of a governing document.

Final agency action means the Authorizing Official's approval or disapproval of a Secretarial election or acknowledgment of the tribe's or petitioners' withdrawal of a request for Secretarial election, and is final for the Department.

Governing document means any written document that prescribes the extent, limitations, and manner in which the tribe exercises its sovereign powers.

Local Bureau office means the local administrative office of the Bureau that is the primary point of contact between the Bureau and the tribe.

Local Bureau Official means the Superintendent, Field Representative, or other official having delegated Federal administrative responsibility under this part.

Mailout ballot means a ballot the Secretarial Election Board provides to a registered voter to allow him or her to vote by mail in an election conducted entirely by mail.

Member of a tribe or *tribal member* means any person who meets the criteria for membership in a tribe and, if required by the tribe, is formally enrolled.

Petition means the official document submitted by the petitioners to the Secretary to call a Secretarial election for the purpose of adopting or ratifying a new governing document, amending the tribe's existing governing document, or revoking the tribe's existing governing document.

Petitioner means a tribal member who is 18 years of age or older (and, if the tribe's governing document imposes additional requirements for petitioning, also meets those requirements), and signs a petition.

Polling site ballot means the ballot the Secretarial Election Board provides to a registered voter, allowing him or her to vote when polling sites are required by the amendment and adoption article of the tribe's governing document.

Recognized governing body means the tribe's governing body recognized by the Bureau for the purposes of government-to-government relations.

Registered Voter means an eligible voter who has registered to vote in the Secretarial election.

Registered Voters List means the list of all Registered Voters showing only names and, where applicable, voting districts.

Registration means the process by which an eligible voter signs up to vote in the Secretarial election.

Revocation means that act whereby the registered voters of a tribe vote to revoke their current governing document.

Secretarial election means a Federal election conducted by the Secretary under a Federal statute or tribal governing document under this part.

Secretarial Election Board means the body of officials appointed by the Bureau and the tribe (and the spokesperson for petitioners, as applicable) to conduct the Secretarial election.

Secretary means the Secretary of the Interior or his or her authorized representative.

Spoiled ballot means the ballot is mismarked, mutilated, rendered impossible to determine the voter's intent, or marked so as to violate the secrecy of the ballot.

Spokesperson for the petitioners or *spokesperson* means a tribal member who provides a document signed by other tribal members that provides him or her authority to speak or submit a petition on their behalf.

Tribal request means a request that includes all of the components set out in 81.6.

Tribe means any Indian or Alaska Native tribe, band, nation, pueblo, village or community that is listed in the FEDERAL REGISTER under 25 U.S.C. 479a—1(a), as recognized and receiving services from the Bureau of Indian Affairs.

Voting district means a geographic area established to facilitate the voting process, if required, by the amendment and adoption articles of the tribe's governing document.

Subpart C—Provisions Applicable to All Secretarial Elections

§81.5 What informal review is available to a tribe or petitioner when anticipating adopting or amending a governing document?

A tribe that plans to adopt or amend a governing document or a spokesperson for a petitioner may, but is not required to, submit the proposed document with a request for informal review to the Local Bureau Official.

(a) During the informal review:

(1) Bureau personnel will help the tribal government or petitioner spokesperson in drafting governing documents, bylaws, charters, amendments and revocations, explain the Secretarial election process, and provide guidance on methods for voter education, such as informational meetings.

(2) The Local Bureau Official will review the proposed document and will offer technical assistance and comments to the tribe or petitioner spokesperson, including but not limited to guidance on whether any of the provisions of the proposed document or amendment may be contrary to applicable laws.

(b) The Bureau will provide technical assistance for a petition only upon request of the spokesperson. Bureau personnel will provide a courtesy copy to the tribe's governing body of all correspondence regarding technical assistance to the petitioners. The spokesperson will be responsible for obtaining the approval of the tribal members it represents on changes to the content of the petition.

§81.6 How is a Secretarial election requested?

To request a Secretarial election:

(a) The tribe or petitioner must submit:

(1) A duly adopted tribal resolution, tribal ordinance, other appropriate tribal document requesting the Secretary to call a Secretarial election, or, in the absence of an existing governing document or if authorized or required by the existing governing documents, a petition that has been verified by the Bureau as having the minimum

number of required signatures of tribal members; and

(2) The exact document or amended language to be voted on; and

(b) The tribe must submit a list in an electronically sortable format with names, last known addresses, dates of birth, and voting district, if any, of all tribal members who:

(1) Will be 18 years of age or older within 120 days of the date of the request; and

(2) Meet any other voting restrictions imposed by the tribe's governing document for voting in the Secretarial election.

§ 81.7 What technical assistance will the Bureau provide after receiving a request for election?

After receiving a tribal request for election under § 81.6, the Bureau will provide the following technical assistance.

(a) The Local Bureau Official will review and make a recommendation on the proposed document or amendment, prepare background information on the tribe, and submit to the Authorizing Official.

(b) The Authorizing Official must do all of the following:

(1) Review the proposed document or amendment and offer technical assistance to the tribe (and spokesperson, for petitions);

(2) Consult with the Office of the Solicitor to determine whether any of the provisions of the proposed document or amendment may be contrary to applicable law; and

(3) Notify the tribe (and spokesperson, for petitions) in writing of the results of the review.

(i) If the review finds that a provision is or may be contrary to applicable law, the notification must explain how the provision may be contrary to applicable law and list changes to the document that would be required to allow the Authorizing Official to approve the document as not contrary to applicable law.

(ii) The notification must be sent to the tribe (and spokesperson, for petitions) promptly but in no case less than 30 days before calling the election.

(iii) For IRA elections, the tribe may choose to proceed with the election without incorporating required changes, but the Authorizing Official may not approve election results ratifying provisions that are contrary to applicable law.

(iv) For OIWA elections, the Authorizing Official may not authorize a Secretarial election on any proposed document that contains provisions that may be contrary to applicable law.

§ 81.8 What happens if a governing Federal statute and this part disagree?

If a conflict appears to exist between this part and a specific requirement of the Federal statute, this part must be interpreted to conform to the statute.

§ 81.9 Will the Secretary give deference to the Tribe's interpretation of its own documents?

The Secretary will give deference to the tribe's reasonable interpretation of the amendment and adoption articles of the tribe's governing documents. The Secretary retains authority, however, to interpret tribal law when necessary to carry out the government-to-government relationship with the tribe or when a provision, result, or interpretation may be contrary to Federal law.

§ 81.10 Who may cast a vote in a Secretarial election?

If the tribe:	Then the following individuals may cast a vote:
(a) Is reorganizing under Federal statute for the first time,.	Any member of the tribe who: (1) Will be 18 years of age or older on the date of the Secretarial election; and (2) Has duly registered, regardless of residence or other qualifications contained in the tribe's governing documents or charter
(b) Is already reorganized under Federal statute,.	Any member of the tribe who: (1) Will be 18 years of age or older on the date of the Secretarial election; and (2) Otherwise meets the qualifications required by the tribe's governing documents or charter for that particular type of Secretarial election; and (3) Has duly registered.

If the tribe:	Then the following individuals may cast a vote:
(c) Is not reorganized under a Federal statute but tribal law requires a Secretarial election.	Any member of the tribe who: (1) Will be 18 years of age or older on the date of the Secretarial election; and (2) Otherwise meets the qualifications, if any, required by the tribe's governing documents or charter for that particular type of Secretarial election, if any; and (3) Has duly registered.

§81.11 May a tribe establish a voting age different from 18 years of age for Secretarial elections?

No. A Secretarial election is a Federal election. According to the 26th Amendment of the U.S. Constitution, adopted July 1, 1971, all individuals 18 years of age and older must be allowed to vote in Federal elections.

§81.12 What type of electioneering is allowed before and during Secretarial election?

There shall be no electioneering within 50 feet of the entrance of a polling site.

§81.13 What types of voting assistance are provided for a Secretarial election?

If polling sites are required by the amendment or adoption article of the tribe's governing document, the Chair of the Secretarial Election Board will:

(a) Appoint interpreters;

(b) Ensure that audio or visual aids for the hearing or visually impaired are provided;

(c) Ensure that reasonable accommodations are made for others with impairments that would impede their ability to vote; and

(d) Allow the interpreter or Secretarial Election Board member to explain the election process and voting instructions. At the request of the voter, the interpreter or Board member may accompany the voter into the voting booth, but must not influence the voter in casting the ballot.

§81.14 May Secretarial elections be scheduled at the same time as tribal elections?

The Secretarial Election Board will, generally, avoid scheduling Secretarial elections at the same time as tribal elections to avoid confusion. If the Secretarial Election Board decides to schedule a Secretarial election at the same time as a tribal election, the Secretarial Election Board must clearly inform eligible voters of any differences between the tribal election and the Secretarial election and separate ballots must be used for each type of election.

§81.15 How are conflicting proposals to amend a single document handled?

When conflicting proposals to amend a single provision of a tribal governing document or charter provision are submitted, the proposal first received by the Local Bureau Official, if properly submitted as a complete tribal request, must be voted on before any consideration is given other proposals. Other proposals must be considered in order of their receipt if they are resubmitted following final agency action on the first submission. This procedure applies regardless of whether the proposal is a new or revised tribal governing document.

§81.16 Who pays for holding the Secretarial election?

(a) A Secretarial election is a Federal election; therefore, Federal funding will be used to cover costs. The Bureau will pay for the costs, unless the tribe has received funding for this function through contracts or self-governance compacts entered into under the Indian Self-Determination and Education Assistance Act, as amended, 25 U.S.C. 450f, *et seq.*

(b) Once a tribe removes the requirement for Secretarial approval, all subsequent elections it holds to amend the governing document are tribal elections and the tribe is responsible for the costs of those elections.

§81.17 May a tribe use its funds to pay non-Federal election officials?

A recognized tribal governing body may use tribal funds to compensate non-Federal personnel to respond to the needs of the tribal government in the conduct of the Secretarial election.

§ 81.18 Who can withdraw a request for a Secretarial election?

The tribe may withdraw the request for Secretarial election in the same manner in which the Secretarial election was requested. The petitioners may withdraw the request for Secretarial election by submitting a new petition, with signatures of at least a majority of the signers of the original petition, seeking withdrawal of the original petition. However, the request for a Secretarial election cannot be withdrawn after the established deadline for voter registration.

Subpart D—The Secretarial Election Process under the Indian Reorganization Act (IRA)

§ 81.19 How does the Bureau proceed after receiving a request for a Secretarial election?

(a) Upon receiving a request for a Secretarial election, the Local Bureau Official will forward the request to the Authorizing Official with any appropriate background information.

(b) The Authorizing Official will issue a memorandum to the Local Bureau official. The memorandum will do all of the following:

(1) Direct the Local Bureau Official to call and conduct a Secretarial election by one of the following deadlines:

(i) If the tribal request is to amend an existing governing document, within 90 days from the date of receipt of the request;

(ii) If the tribal request is to adopt a new governing document (including an amendment to a governing document in the nature of an entire substitute) or to revoke an existing governing document, within 180 days after receiving the request.

(2) Include as an attachment the document or proposed language to be voted upon;

(3) Include as an attachment the Certificate of Results of Election with instructions to return it after the Secretarial election. The Certificate shall read as follows:

CERTIFICATE OF RESULTS OF ELECTION

Under a Secretarial election authorized by (name and title of authorizing official) on (date), the attached [insert: Governing document and Bylaws, charter of incorporation, amendment or revocation] of the (official name of tribe) was submitted to the registered voters of the tribe and on (date) duly (insert: adopted, ratified, rejected or revoked) by a vote of (number) for and (number) against and (number) cast ballots found spoiled in an election in which at least 30 percent (or such "percentages" as may be required to amend according the governing document) of the (number) registered voters cast their ballot in accordance with (appropriate Federal statute).

Signed: ____________________
(by the Chair of the Secretarial Election Board and Board Members)
Date: ________; and

(4) Advise that no changes or modifications can be made to any attached document, without the Authorizing Official's prior approval.

(c) The Local Bureau Official will appoint a Bureau employee to serve as the Chair of the Secretarial Election Board and notify the tribe of the need to appoint at least two tribal members, who are at least 18 years of age, to the Secretarial Election Board. If the election is to be held as the result of a petition, then the Local Bureau Official will appoint a Bureau employee to serve as the Chair of the Secretarial Election Board and notify the tribe and the spokesperson for the petitioners of the need to appoint one tribal member each, who is at least 18 years of age, to the Secretarial Election Board. If the tribe or spokesperson for the petitioners declines or fails for any reason to make the appointment(s) by close of business on the 10th day after the date the notice letter is issued, the Chair of the Secretarial Election Board must appoint the representative(s), who are tribal members, if available, on the 11th day after the notice letter is issued.

§ 81.20 What is the first action to be taken by the Chair of the Election Board?

Within 5 days after the Secretarial Election Board representatives are appointed, the Chair must hold the first meeting of the Secretarial Election Board to set the election date.

§81.21 What are the responsibilities of the Secretarial Election Board in conducting a Secretarial election?

The Secretarial Election Board conducts the Secretarial election. Except as provided in §81.43, decisions of the Secretarial Election Board are not subject to administrative appeal.

§81.22 How is the Secretarial election conducted?

The Secretarial Election Board:

(a) Uses the list provided in the tribal request as the basis for the Eligible Voters List;

(b) Assembles and mails the Secretarial Election Notice Packet at least 30 days, but no more than 60 days, before the date of the Secretarial election to all persons on the Eligible Voters List;

(c) Confirms that registration forms were received on or before the deadline date;

(d) Retains the completed registration form as part of the record;

(e) Develops the Registered Voters List for posting;

(f) Where the election is conducted entirely by mailout ballot, notes on a copy of the Registered Voters List, by the individual's name, the date the ballot was mailed, and the date the ballot was returned; and

(g) Where polling sites are required and an individual requests an absentee ballot, notes on a copy of the Registered Voters List, by the individual's name, the date his or her absentee ballot request was received, the date the absentee ballot was mailed, and the date the absentee ballot was returned.

§81.23 What documents are included in the Secretarial Election Notice Packet?

The Secretarial Election Notice Packet includes the following:

(a) Mailout Balloting:

(1) The Secretarial election notice;

(2) A registration form with instructions for returning the completed form by mail;

(3) An addressed envelope with which to return the completed registration form;

(4) If the entire document is to be amended or adopted, a copy of the proposed document including proposed language; and if applicable, a copy of the current document proposed for change; and

(5) A side-by-side comparison showing the current language to be changed, if applicable, in the left column and the proposed language in the right column.

(b) Polling Sites (if required by the amendment or adoption articles of the tribe's governing document):

(1) The Secretarial election notice;

(2) A registration form with instructions for returning the completed form by mail;

(3) An absentee ballot request form with instructions for returning the completed form by mail;

(4) An addressed envelope with which to return the completed registration form and absentee ballot request form;

(5) If the entire document is to be amended or adopted, a copy of the proposed document including proposed language; and if applicable, a copy of the current document proposed for change; and

(6) A side-by-side comparison showing the current language to be changed, if applicable, in the left column and the proposed language in the right column.

§81.24 What information must be included on the Secretarial election notice?

The Secretarial election notice must contain all of the following items.

(a) The date of the Secretarial election;

(b) The date which registration forms must be received by the Secretarial Election Board;

(c) A description of the purpose of the Secretarial election;

(d) A description of the statutory and tribal authority under which the Secretarial election is held;

(e) The deadline for filing challenges to the Registered Voters List;

(f) If polling sites are to be used, the date an absentee ballot request must be received by the Secretarial Election Board;

(g) A statement as to whether the Secretarial election is being held entirely by mailout ballot or with polling sites, in accordance with the tribe's governing document's amendment or adoption articles; and

(h) The locations and hours of established polling sites, if any.

§ 81.25 Where will the Secretarial election notice be posted?

The Secretarial election notice will be posted at the local Bureau office, if any, the tribal headquarters, and other public places determined by the Secretarial Election Board.

§ 81.26 How does BIA use the information I provide on the registration form?

We use the information you provide on the registration form to determine whether you will be registered for and vote in the Secretarial election. The registration form must include the following statements:

(a) Completing and returning this registration is necessary if you desire to vote in the forthcoming Secretarial election;

(b) This form, upon completion and return to the Secretarial Election Board, will be the basis for determining whether your name will be placed upon the list of registered voters, and therefore may receive a ballot, and

(c) Completion and return of this form is voluntary, but failure to do so will prevent you from participating in the Secretarial election.

§ 81.27 Must I re-register if I have already registered for a tribal or Secretarial election?

Yes. A Secretarial election is a Federal election and you must register for each Secretarial election.

§ 81.28 How do I submit my registration form?

You must submit your registration form to the Secretarial Election Board by U.S. mail.

§ 81.29 Why does the Secretarial Election Board compile a Registered Voters List?

The Registered Voters List is a list of eligible voters who have registered and are, therefore, entitled to vote in the Secretarial election. We use this list, after all challenges have been resolved, to determine whether voter participation in the Secretarial election satisfies the minimum requirements of the tribe's governing documents and Federal law.

§ 81.30 What information is contained in the Registered Voters List?

The Registered Voters List must contain the names, in alphabetical order, of all registered voters and their voting districts, if voting districts are required by the tribe's governing document's amendment or adoption articles.

§ 81.31 Where is the Registered Voters List posted?

A copy of the Registered Voters List, showing only names and, where applicable, voting districts, must be posted at the local Bureau office, the tribal headquarters, and other public places the Secretarial Election Board designates.

§ 81.32 May the Registered Voters List be challenged?

(a) It is possible to challenge in writing the inclusion or exclusion or omission of a name on the Registered Voters List. The written challenge must be received by the Secretarial Election Board by the established deadline and include the following:

(1) The name of the affected individual or individuals;

(2) The reason why the individual's name should be added to or removed from the Registered Voters List; and

(3) Supporting documentation.

(b) If an individual failed to submit his or her registration form on time, that individual is precluded from challenging the omission of his/her name from the list.

§ 81.33 How does the Secretarial Election Board respond to challenges?

All challenges must be resolved by close of business on the third day after the date of the challenge deadline established by the Secretarial Election Board and all determinations of the Secretarial Election Board are final for the purpose of determining who can vote in the Secretarial election.

(a) If the challenge was received after the deadline, the Secretarial Election Board must deny the challenge.

(b) If the challenge was received on or before the deadline, the Secretarial Election Board will decide the challenge by reviewing the documentation submitted. Thereafter, the Secretarial Election Board will include the name of any individual whose name should appear or remove the name of any individual who should not appear on the Registered Voters List.

§81.34 How are the official ballots prepared?

(a) The Secretarial Election Board must prepare the official ballot so that it is easy for the voters to indicate a choice between no more than two alternatives (*i.e.*, adopting or rejecting the proposed language). Separate ballots should be prepared for each proposed amendment or a single ballot for adoption of a proposed document (with a reference to the document provided in the Secretarial election notice).

(b) The following information must appear on the face of the mailout or absentee ballot:

OFFICIAL BALLOT

(Facsimile Signature)

CHAIR, SECRETARIAL ELECTION BOARD

(c) When polling places are required by the tribe's governing document, the official ballot may be a paper ballot, voting machine ballot, or other type of ballot supporting the secret ballot process.

§81.35 When must the Secretarial Election Board send ballots to voters?

(a) Unless the amendment or adoption articles of the tribe's governing document require the use of polling sites in the election, the election must be conducted entirely by mailout ballots, and the Secretarial Election Board must send mailout ballots to registered voters promptly upon completion of the Registered Voters List.

(b) When the amendment or adoption articles of the tribe's governing document require the use of polling sites in the election, the Secretarial Election Board must send an absentee ballot to every registered voter who requests an absentee ballot, as long as the request is received before the Secretarial election date.

(c) All mailout or absentee ballot deliveries must be via U.S. Mail or by hand-delivery to the location identified in the Secretarial election notice before the date of the Secretarial election.

§81.36 What will the mailout or absentee ballot packet include?

The mailout or absentee ballot packet contains:

(a) A cover letter summarizing what the ballot packet contains and, if there is more than one ballot included in the packet, enumerating the ballots and advising voters to give consideration to each enumerated ballot;

(b) A mailout or absentee ballot (or, if several amendments are to be voted on, multiple ballots, each printed on a different colored sheet if possible);

(c) Instructions for voting by mailout or absentee ballot including the date the ballot must be received by the Secretarial Election Board;

(d) An inner envelope with the words "Mailout Ballot" or "Absentee Ballot" printed on the outside, as applicable;

(e) A copy of the proposed governing document or amendment, if the full text is not printed on the mailout ballot and if the entire document is to be amended or adopted; and

(f) A pre-addressed outer envelope with the following certification printed on the back:

I, (print name of voter), hereby certify I am a registered voter of the (name of Tribe); I will be 18 years of age or older on the day of the Secretarial election; I am entitled to vote in the Secretarial election to be held on (date of Secretarial election). I further certify that I marked the enclosed mailout ballot in secret.

Signed:
(voter's signature) ____________________

§81.37 How do I cast my vote at a polling site?

If polling sites are required by the tribe's governing document's amendment or adoption articles, the Secretarial Election Board will establish procedures for how polling site ballots will be presented and collected, including, but not limited to, paper ballots, voting machines, or other methods supporting a secret ballot.

§81.38 When are ballots counted?

The ballots will be counted under the supervision of the Secretarial Election Board, after the deadline established for receiving all ballots or closing of the polls, if polling sites are required by the tribe's governing document's amendment or adoption articles.

§81.39 How does the Board determine whether the required percentage of registered voters have cast ballots?

The Secretarial Election Board must count the number of valid ballots and cast spoiled ballots to determine total voter participation. The Board must take the total voter participation and divide it by the total number of Registered Voters. This total is used to determine whether the percentage of Registered Voters who cast votes meets the requirements of the tribe's governing documents or Federal statute that requires at least 30 percent voter participation. For example:

(a) If there were 200 registered voters of which 75 cast valid ballots and 5 cast spoiled ballots for a total of 80 cast ballots (75 + 5 = 80). The percentage of voter participation would be determined as follows:

Total number of votes cast (80) divided by the total number registered voters (200) or 80 ÷ 200 = 0.40 or 40 percent voter participation.

(b) This example meets the Federal statutory requirement of at least 30 percent voter participation.

§81.40 What happens if a ballot is spoiled before it is cast?

If a ballot is spoiled before it is cast, this section applies.

(a) The registered voter may return the spoiled ballot to the Secretarial Election Board by mail or in person at the local Bureau office with a request for a new ballot before the election date. The new ballot will be promptly provided to the registered voter. The Secretarial Election Board must retain all "spoiled uncast ballots" for recordkeeping purposes.

(b) If polling sites are required, the voter may return the spoiled ballot to the polling site worker and request a new ballot. Upon receiving the new ballot, the voter must then complete the voting process. The polling site worker will mark the spoiled ballot "spoiled uncast" and record that the ballot has been spoiled. The polling site worker must retain all "spoiled uncast ballots" for recordkeeping purposes.

§81.41 Who certifies the results of the Election?

The Chair and all members of the Secretarial Election Board must be present during the counting of the ballots and must sign the Certificate of Results of Election.

§81.42 Where are the results of the Election posted?

The Secretarial Election Board must post a copy of the Certificate of Results of Election at the local Bureau office, the tribal headquarters, and at other public places listed in the election notice. The Board also has the discretion to publicize the results using additional methods, such as by posting on the tribe's Web site.

§81.43 How are the results of the Election challenged?

Any person who was listed on the Eligible Voters List and who submitted a voter registration form may challenge the results of the Secretarial election. The written challenge, with substantiating evidence, must be received by the Chairman of the Secretarial Election Board within 5 days after the Certificate of Results of Election is posted, not including the day the Certificate of Results of Election is posted. Challenges received after the deadline for filing challenges will not be considered. If the third day falls on a weekend or Federal holiday, the challenge must be received by close of business on the next business day.

§81.44 What documents are sent to the Authorizing Official?

The Chair of the Secretarial Election Board must transmit all documents pertaining to the Secretarial election to the Authorizing Official, including:

(a) The original text of the material voted on;

(b) The Eligible Voters List;

(c) The Registered Voters List;

(d) The Secretarial Election Notice Packet;

(e) Any challenges to the Secretarial election results; and

(f) The Certificate of Results of Election.

§81.45 When are the results of the Secretarial election final?

The Authorizing Official will review election results and challenges, if any, as follows:

(a) If a challenge alleges errors that would invalidate the election, and the Authorizing Official sustains any such challenges, the Authorizing Official must authorize a recount or call for a new Secretarial election. The Authorizing Official will take the appropriate steps necessary to provide for a recount or a new Secretarial election.

(b) If all challenges are denied or dismissed, the Authorizing Official will review and make a decision based on the following:

(1) The percentage of total votes cast was at least 30 percent, or other percentages required according to the tribe's governing document's amendment or adoption articles.

(2) The voters rejected or accepted the proposed document or each proposed amendment; and

(3) The proposed documents or amendments are not contrary to Federal law.

(c) The Authorizing Official must notify, in writing, the recognized governing body of the tribe, and the Director of the Bureau, of the following:

(1) The decisions on challenges;

(2) The outcome of the voting;

(3) Whether the proposed governing document, proposed amendment(s) or charter or charter amendments are approved or ratified, or if the proposed documents contain language that is contrary to Federal law and, therefore, disapproved; and

(4) That the decision is a final agency action.

(d) The Authorizing Official must:

(1) Forward the original text of the document, Original Certificate of Approval or Disapproval, and the Certificate of Results of Election to the tribe and a copy of all documents to the Bureau Director; and

(2) Retain, as required by the Records Disposition Schedule, a copy of all document(s) relevant to the Secretarial election.

(e) If the certified election results show that the tribal members ratified the documents, but the Authorizing Official does not approve or disapprove the governing document or amendment by close of business on the 45th day after the date of the Secretarial election, the Secretary's approval of the documents must be considered as given.

(f) The Authorizing Official's decision to approve or disapprove the governing document or amendment is a final agency action.

Subpart E—The Secretarial Election Process Under the Oklahoma Indian Welfare Act (OIWA)

§81.46 How does the Bureau proceed upon receiving a request for an OIWA Election if no provisions are contrary to applicable law?

If the proposed document does not contain any provision that may be contrary to applicable law, the Bureau will take the following steps.

(a) The Authorizing Official will issue a memorandum to the Local Bureau Official:

(1) Approving the proposed document or proposed amendments;

(2) Authorizing the Local Bureau Official to call and conduct a Secretarial election, within 90 days from the date of receiving the tribal request;

(3) Attaching the document or proposed language to be voted upon;

(4) Attaching the Certificate of Results of Election, with instructions to return it at the conclusion of the Secretarial election. The Certificate shall read as follows:

CERTIFICATE OF RESULTS OF ELECTION

Under a Secretarial election authorized by (name and title of authorizing official) on (date), the attached [insert: Governing document and Bylaws, charter of incorporation, amendment or revocation] of the (official name of tribe) was submitted to the registered voters of the tribe and on (date) duly (insert: adopted, ratified, rejected or revoked) by a vote of (number) for and (number) against and (number) cast ballots found spoiled in an election in which at least 30 percent (or such "percentages" as may be required to amend according the governing document) of the (number) registered voters cast their ballot in accordance with (appropriate Federal statute).

Signed: ____________________________

(by the Chair of the Secretarial Election Board and Board Members)

Date: ____________________________.; and

(5) Advising that no changes or modifications can be made to any of the attached documents, without prior approval from the Authorizing Official.

(b) The Local Bureau Official will appoint the Chair of the Secretarial Election Board and notify the tribe of the need to appoint at least two tribal members to the Secretarial Election Board. If the election is to be held as the result of a petition, then the Local Bureau Official will appoint a Bureau employee to serve as the Chair of the Secretarial Election Board and notify the tribe and the spokesperson for the petitioners of the need to appoint one tribal member each, who is at least 18 years of age, to the Secretarial Election Board. If the tribe or spokesperson declines or fails for any reason to make the appointment(s) by close of business on the 10th day after the date the notice letter is issued, the Chair of the Secretarial Election Board must appoint the representative(s), who are tribal members, if available, on the 11th day after the notice letter is issued.

§ 81.47 How is the OIWA Secretarial election conducted?

After the Chair of the Election Board receives the authorization of the Election, the Chair of the Secretarial Election Board will conduct the election following the procedures set out in §§ 81.19 through § 81.45 of subpart D.

§ 81.48 When are the results of the OIWA Election final?

(a) If a challenge is sustained and has an effect on the outcome of the election, the Authorizing Official must authorize a recount or call for a new Secretarial election. The Authorizing Official will take the appropriate steps necessary to provide for a recount or a new Secretarial election.

(b) If the challenges are denied or dismissed, the Authorizing Official will review and determine whether:

(1) The percentage of total votes cast was at least 30 percent, or such percentages as may be required according to the tribe's governing document's amendment or adoption articles; and

(2) The voters ratified or rejected the proposed document, proposed amendment or revocation.

(c) The Authorizing Official must notify, in writing, the recognized governing body of the tribe, and the Director of the Bureau, of the following:

(1) The decisions on challenges;

(2) The outcome of the voting; and

(3) That the proposed document, proposed amendments or revocation becomes effective as of the date of the Secretarial election; and

(4) That the decision is a final agency action.

(d) The Authorizing Official must:

(1) Forward the original text of the document, Original Certificate of Approval, and the Certificate of Results of Election to the tribe and a copy of all documents to the Director of the Bureau; and

(2) Retain, as required by the Records Disposition Schedule, a copy of all document(s) relevant to the Secretarial election.

Subpart F—Formulating Petitions To Request a Secretarial Election

§ 81.49 What is the purpose of this subpart?

This subpart establishes requirements for formulating and submitting petitions to request the Secretary to call a Secretarial election as required by the governing documents or charters of incorporation of tribes issued under the Indian Reorganization Act (IRA), 25 U.S.C. 476 and 477, as amended, and the Oklahoma Indian Welfare Act (OIWA), 25 U.S.C. 503. This Subpart may also be used by a federally recognized tribe that is adopting a governing document, under Federal statute, for the first time.

§ 81.50 Who must follow these requirements?

Any tribe meeting the criteria in paragraphs (a) or (b) of this section must follow the requirements of this subpart.

(a) A tribe whose governing document or charter of incorporation provides for petitioning the Secretary to call a Secretarial election for any of the following purposes:

(1) Amending or revoking the governing document;

(2) Amending a charter of incorporation ratified under 25 U.S.C. 477 of the IRA before May 24, 1990 where the amendments section or article specifically requires it;

(3) Amending or ratifying a charter of incorporation under 25 U.S.C. 503 of the OIWA; or

(4) Taking any other action authorized by the governing document or charter of incorporation.

(b) A federally recognized tribe, without an existing governing document, adopting a governing document under Federal statute, for the first time.

§ 81.51 How do tribal members circulate a petition to adopt or amend the tribe's governing document?

Tribal members wishing to circulate a petition to adopt or amend the tribe's governing document may submit the proposed document to the Local Bureau Official for review and comment. The Local Bureau Official may help the petitioners in drafting governing documents, bylaws, charters, amendments and revocations. The Bureau may also explain the Secretarial election process.

§ 81.52 Who may initiate a petition?

A member of the tribe who is 18 years of age or older whose tribe's governing document or charter of incorporation permits tribal members to petition the Secretary to authorize a Secretarial election.

§ 81.53 Who may sign a petition?

A member of the tribe who is 18 years of age or older may sign a petition. Where the tribe's governing document imposes additional requirements (other than age requirements) on who may petition, those requirements also apply.

§ 81.54 Who is authorized to submit a petition to the Secretary?

The petitioners must designate a spokesperson to submit the petition and act on their behalf for the petitioning process.

§ 81.55 How is the petition formatted and signed?

(a) Each page of the petition must contain:

(1) A summary of the purpose of the petition, or proposed document, or proposed amendment language;

(2) Numbered lines for each individual to print their legal name, current mailing address, date, and signature, and;

(3) The following declaration at the bottom of each page to confirm the collector was present when each signature was collected:

"I, *(Collector's Printed Name)* , hereby declare that each individual whose name appears above signed and dated the petition. To the best of my knowledge, the individual signing the petition is a member of the tribe and is 18 years or older.

(Signature of Collector)

(Notary Certification)",

(b) Each individual must print their legal name, current mailing address, date, and sign on a numbered line.

(c) Each collector must complete and sign the declaration on each page in front of a notary, who will sign and certify.

§ 81.56 Do petitions have a minimum or maximum number of pages?

A petition can have as many pages as necessary to obtain the required signatures. However, each page must have the information shown in § 81.58 of this subpart.

§ 81.57 How do I determine how many signatures are needed for a petition to be valid?

(a) For a tribe whose governing document or charter of incorporation provides for petitioning the Secretary to call a Secretarial election:

(1) The spokesperson for the petitioners may ask the tribe or the Local Bureau Official how many signatures are required.

(2) The Local Bureau Official will:

(i) Contact the tribal governing body to obtain the current number of tribal members, 18 years of age or older, to determine the number of tribal members who must sign a petition as required by the tribe's governing document; and

(ii) Notify the petitioners' spokesperson how many signatures are required and that the number is valid for 180 days from the date of this notification.

(b) For a federally recognized tribe adopting a governing document under Federal statute for the first time, the petition must have signatures of 50 percent of the tribal members who are 18 years of age or older.

§ 81.58 How long do tribal members have to gather the signatures?

Tribal members have one year from the date of the first signature to gather the required signatures.

§ 81.59 How does the spokesperson file a petition?

The spokesperson must submit the original petition to the Local Bureau Official.

§ 81.60 How does the Local Bureau Official process the petition?

(a) The Local Bureau Official must, on the date of receipt, date stamp the petition to record the Official Filing Date, and make four copies of the petition for use as follows:

(1) Posting at the local Bureau office for 30 days from the Official Filing Date, including a statement of the proposal contained in the petition and instructions for filing a challenge;

(2) Use in determining sufficiency of petition; and

(3) For viewing at the Local Bureau Office by a member of the tribe, 18 years of age or older.

(b) The Local Bureau Official must, within one week of the Official Filing Date:

(1) Provide the spokesperson written acknowledgment of receiving the petition, which contains the Official Filing Date, the exact number of signatures submitted on the petition, and the statement "The petitioners may not add or withdraw any signatures from the petition after the Official Filing Date"; and

(2) Provide a copy of the written acknowledgment of receipt and petition to the recognized tribal governing body.

(c) The Local Bureau Official must:

(1) Consult with the Office of the Solicitor to determine if any of the provisions that are the subject of the petition are or may be contrary to applicable law; and

(2) If it appears that a provision is or may be contrary to applicable law, notify the petitioner's spokesperson in writing (with a copy to the recognized tribal governing body) how the provision may be contrary to applicable law.

(d) The Local Bureau Official must promptly notify the petitioners (with a copy to the recognized tribal governing body) of any problems identified under paragraph (c) of this section at least 30 days before calling the election.

§ 81.61 How can signatures to the petition be challenged?

Any member of the tribe, 18 years of age or older, may challenge in writing the signatures appearing on the petition. The challenge must be submitted to the Local Bureau Official, within 30 days of the Official Filing Date of the petition and must:

(a) Identify the page and line on which a signature appears; and

(b) Provide documentation supporting a challenge that at least one of the following is true:

(1) A signature was forged;

(2) An individual was ineligible to sign the petition;

(3) A petition page is inconsistent or improperly formatted; or

(4) A petition page contains an incomplete or un-notarized declaration statement.

§ 81.62 How is the petition validated?

(a) The Local Bureau Official must:

(1) Confirm the petition has the required number of signatures;

(2) Indicate any signatures appearing more than once and include only one in the count;

(3) Make recommendations regarding any challenge to the validity of signatures based upon the documentation provided by the challenger; and

(4) Verify the petitioning procedures complied with this Subpart.

(5) Transmit within 45 calendar days of the Official Filing Date the original

petition, challenges, and recommendations to the Authorizing Official.

(b) The Authorizing Official must within 60 calendar days of the Official Filing Date:

(1) Determine whether the petition complies with the requirements of this Subpart;

(2) Inform the spokesperson for the petitioners and the recognized tribal governing body, in writing, whether the petition is valid, the basis for that determination, and a statement that the decision of the Authorizing Official is a final agency action.

(i) If the petition is determined valid for the purposes of calling a Secretarial election, it will be deemed a "tribal request" for the purposes of this part, and the Authorizing Official will instruct the Local Bureau Official to call and conduct the Secretarial election in accordance with §§81.19 through 81.45 of subpart D.

(ii) If the petition is determined invalid, the Authorizing Official will notify the spokesperson for the petitioners, with a courtesy copy to the tribe's governing body, that the petition was not valid and a Secretarial election will not be called.

§81.63 May the same petition be used for more than one Secretarial election?

No. A petition may not be used for more than one Secretarial election. Each request for a Secretarial election requires a new petition.

PART 82 [RESERVED]

PART 83—PROCEDURES FOR FEDERAL ACKNOWLEDGMENT OF INDIAN TRIBES

Subpart A—General Provisions

Sec.

Subpart B—Criteria for Federal Acknowledgment

Subpart C—Process for Federal Acknowledgment

DOCUMENTED PETITION SUBMISSION

REVIEW OF DOCUMENTED PETITION

PROPOSED FINDING

COMMENT AND RESPONSE PERIODS, HEARING

AUTHORITY: 5 U.S.C. 301; 25 U.S.C. 2, 9, 479a–1; Pub. L. 103–454 Sec. 103 (Nov. 2, 1994); and 43 U.S.C. 1457.

SOURCE: 80 FR 37887, July 1, 2015, unless otherwise noted.

Subpart A—General Provisions

§ 83.1 What terms are used in this part?

As used in this part:

ALJ means an administrative law judge in the Departmental Cases Hearings Division, Office of Hearings and Appeals (OHA), Department of the Interior, appointed under 5 U.S.C. 3105.

Assistant Secretary or *AS–IA* means the Assistant Secretary—Indian Affairs within the Department of the Interior, or that officer's authorized representative, but does not include representatives of the Office of Federal Acknowledgment.

Autonomous means independent of the control of any other Indian governing entity.

Bureau means the Bureau of Indian Affairs within the Department of the Interior.

Continental United States means the contiguous 48 states and Alaska.

Department means the Department of the Interior, including the Assistant Secretary and OFA.

Documented petition means the detailed arguments and supporting documentary evidence submitted by a petitioner claiming that it meets the Indian Entity Identification (§ 83.11(a)), Governing Document (§ 83.11(d)), Descent (§ 83.11(e)), Unique Membership (§ 83.11(f)), and Congressional Termination (§ 83.11(g)) Criteria and claiming that it:

(1) Demonstrates previous Federal acknowledgment under § 83.12(a) and meets the criteria in § 83.12(b); or

(2) Meets the Community (§ 83.11(b)) and Political Authority (§ 83.11(c)) Criteria.

Federally recognized Indian tribe means an entity listed on the Department of the Interior's list under the Federally Recognized Indian Tribe List Act of 1994, which the Secretary currently acknowledges as an Indian tribe and with which the United States maintains a government-to-government relationship.

Historical means before 1900.

Indigenous means native to the continental United States in that at least part of the petitioner's territory at the time of first sustained contact extended into what is now the continental United States.

Member of a petitioner means an individual who is recognized by the petitioner as meeting its membership criteria and who consents to being listed as a member of the petitioner.

Office of Federal Acknowledgment or *OFA* means the Office of Federal Acknowledgment within the Office of the Assistant Secretary—Indian Affairs, Department of the Interior.

Petitioner means any entity that has submitted a documented petition to OFA requesting Federal acknowledgment as a federally recognized Indian tribe.

Previous Federal acknowledgment means action by the Federal government clearly premised on identification of a tribal political entity and indicating clearly the recognition of a relationship between that entity and the United States.

Roll means a list exclusively of those individuals who have been determined by the tribe to meet the tribe's membership requirements as set forth in its governing document. In the absence of such a document, a roll means a list of those recognized as members by the tribe's governing body. In either case, those individuals on a roll must have affirmatively demonstrated consent to being listed as members.

Secretary means the Secretary of the Interior within the Department of the Interior or that officer's authorized representative.

Tribe means any Indian tribe, band, nation, pueblo, village or community.

§ 83.2 What is the purpose of the regulations in this part?

The regulations in this part implement Federal statutes for the benefit of Indian tribes by establishing procedures and criteria for the Department to use to determine whether a petitioner is an Indian tribe eligible for the special programs and services provided by the United States to Indians because of their status as Indians. A positive determination will result in Federal recognition status and the petitioner's addition to the Department's list of federally recognized Indian tribes. Federal recognition:

(a) Is a prerequisite to the protection, services, and benefits of the Federal Government available to those that qualify as Indian tribes and possess a government-to-government relationship with the United States;

(b) Means the tribe is entitled to the immunities and privileges available to other federally recognized Indian tribes;

(c) Means the tribe has the responsibilities, powers, limitations, and obligations of other federally recognized Indian tribes; and

(d) Subjects the Indian tribe to the same authority of Congress and the United States as other federally recognized Indian tribes.

§ 83.3 Who does this part apply to?

This part applies only to indigenous entities that are not federally recognized Indian tribes.

§ 83.4 Who cannot be acknowledged under this part?

The Department will not acknowledge:

(a) An association, organization, corporation, or entity of any character formed in recent times unless the entity has only changed form by recently incorporating or otherwise formalizing its existing politically autonomous community;

(b) A splinter group, political faction, community, or entity of any character that separates from the main body of a currently federally recognized Indian tribe, petitioner, or previous petitioner unless the entity can clearly demonstrate it has functioned from 1900 until the present as a politically autonomous community and meets § 83.11(f), even though some have regarded them as part of or associated in some manner with a federally recognized Indian tribe;

(c) An entity that is, or an entity whose members are, subject to congressional legislation terminating or forbidding the government-to-government relationship; or

(d) An entity that previously petitioned and was denied Federal acknowledgment under these regulations or under previous regulations in part 83 of this title (including reconstituted, splinter, spin-off, or component groups who were once part of previously denied petitioners).

§ 83.5 How does a petitioner obtain Federal acknowledgment under this part?

To be acknowledged as a federally recognized Indian tribe under this part, a petitioner must meet the Indian Entity Identification (§ 83.11(a)), Governing Document (§ 83.11(d)), Descent (§ 83.11(e)), Unique Membership (§ 83.11(f)), and Congressional Termination (§ 83.11(g)) Criteria and must:

(a) Demonstrate previous Federal acknowledgment under § 83.12(a) and meet the criteria in § 83.12(b); or

(b) Meet the Community (§ 83.11(b)) and Political Authority (§ 83.11(c)) Criteria.

§ 83.6 What are the Department's duties?

(a) The Department will publish in the FEDERAL REGISTER, by January 30 each year, a list of all Indian tribes which the Secretary recognizes to be eligible for the special programs and services provided by the United States to Indians because of their status as Indians, in accordance with the Federally Recognized Indian Tribe List Act of 1994. The list may be published more frequently, if the Assistant Secretary deems it necessary.

(b) OFA will maintain guidelines limited to general suggestions on how and where to conduct research. The guidelines may be supplemented or updated as necessary. OFA will also make available examples of portions of documented petitions in the preferred format, though OFA will accept other formats.

(c) OFA will, upon request, give prospective petitioners suggestions and advice on how to prepare the documented petition. OFA will not be responsible for the actual research on behalf of the petitioner.

§ 83.7 How does this part apply to documented petitions submitted before August 17, 2015?

(a) Any petitioner who has not submitted a complete documented petition as of July 31, 2015 must proceed under these revised regulations. We will notify these petitioners and provide them with a copy of the revised regulations by July 31, 2015.

(b) By August 31, 2015, OFA will notify each petitioner that has submitted complete documented petitions but has not yet received a final agency decision that it must proceed under these revised regulations unless it chooses by September 29, 2015 to complete the petitioning process under the previous version of the acknowledgment regulations as published in 25 CFR part 83, revised as of April 1, 1994.

(c) Any petitioner who has submitted a documented petition under the previous version of the acknowledgment regulations and chooses to proceed under these revised regulations does not need to submit a new documented petition, but may supplement its petition.

§ 83.8 May the deadlines in this part be extended?

(a) The AS–IA may extend any of the deadlines in this part upon a finding of good cause.

(b) For deadlines applicable to the Department, AS–IA may extend the deadlines upon the consent of the petitioner.

(c) If AS–IA grants a time extension, it will notify the petitioner and those listed in § 83.22(d).

§ 83.9 How does the Paperwork Reduction Act affect the information collections in this part?

The collections of information contained in this part have been approved by the Office of Management and Budget under 44 U.S.C. 3501 *et seq.* and assigned OMB Control Number 1076–0104. Response is required to obtain a benefit. A Federal agency may not conduct or sponsor, and you are not required to respond to, a collection of information unless the form or regulation requesting the information displays a currently valid OMB Control Number. Send comments regarding this collection of information, including suggestions for reducing the burden, to the Information Collection Clearance Officer—Indian Affairs, 1849 C Street, NW., Washington, DC 20240.

Subpart B—Criteria for Federal Acknowledgment

§ 83.10 How will the Department evaluate each of the criteria?

(a) The Department will consider a criterion in § 83.11 to be met if the available evidence establishes a reasonable likelihood of the validity of the facts relating to that criterion.

(1) The Department will not require conclusive proof of the facts relating to a criterion in order to consider the criterion met.

(2) The Department will require existence of community and political influence or authority be demonstrated on a substantially continuous basis, but this demonstration does not require meeting these criteria at every point in time. Fluctuations in tribal activity during various years will not in themselves be a cause for denial of acknowledgment under these criteria.

(3) The petitioner may use the same evidence to establish more than one criterion.

(4) Evidence or methodology that the Department found sufficient to satisfy any particular criterion in a previous decision will be sufficient to satisfy the criterion for a present petitioner.

(b) When evaluating a petition, the Department will:

(1) Allow criteria to be met by any suitable evidence, rather than requiring the specific forms of evidence stated in the criteria;

(2) Take into account historical situations and time periods for which evidence is demonstrably limited or not available;

(3) Take into account the limitations inherent in demonstrating historical existence of community and political influence or authority;

(4) Require a demonstration that the criteria are met on a substantially continuous basis, meaning without substantial interruption; and

(5) Apply these criteria in context with the history, regional differences, culture, and social organization of the petitioner.

§83.11 What are the criteria for acknowledgment as a federally recognized Indian tribe?

The criteria for acknowledgment as a federally recognized Indian tribe are delineated in paragraphs (a) through (g) of this section.

(a) *Indian entity identification.* The petitioner has been identified as an American Indian entity on a substantially continuous basis since 1900. Evidence that the group's character as an Indian entity has from time to time been denied will not be considered to be conclusive evidence that this criterion has not been met. Evidence to be relied upon in determining a group's Indian identity may include one or a combination of the following, as well as other evidence of identification.

(1) Identification as an Indian entity by Federal authorities.

(2) Relationships with State governments based on identification of the group as Indian.

(3) Dealings with a county, parish, or other local government in a relationship based on the group's Indian identity.

(4) Identification as an Indian entity by anthropologists, historians, and/or other scholars.

(5) Identification as an Indian entity in newspapers and books.

(6) Identification as an Indian entity in relationships with Indian tribes or with national, regional, or state Indian organizations.

(7) Identification as an Indian entity by the petitioner itself.

(b) *Community.* The petitioner comprises a distinct community and demonstrates that it existed as a community from 1900 until the present. Distinct community means an entity with consistent interactions and significant social relationships within its membership and whose members are differentiated from and distinct from nonmembers. Distinct community must be understood flexibly in the context of the history, geography, culture, and social organization of the entity. The petitioner may demonstrate that it meets this criterion by providing evidence for known adult members or by providing evidence of relationships of a reliable, statistically significant sample of known adult members.

(1) The petitioner may demonstrate that it meets this criterion at a given point in time by some combination of two or more of the following forms of evidence or by other evidence to show that a significant and meaningful portion of the petitioner's members constituted a distinct community at a given point in time:

(i) Rates or patterns of known marriages within the entity, or, as may be culturally required, known patterned out-marriages;

(ii) Social relationships connecting individual members;

(iii) Rates or patterns of informal social interaction that exist broadly among the members of the entity;

(iv) Shared or cooperative labor or other economic activity among members;

(v) Strong patterns of discrimination or other social distinctions by nonmembers;

(vi) Shared sacred or secular ritual activity;

(vii) Cultural patterns shared among a portion of the entity that are different from those of the non-Indian populations with whom it interacts. These patterns must function as more than a symbolic identification of the group as Indian. They may include, but are not limited to, language, kinship organization or system, religious beliefs or practices, and ceremonies;

(viii) The persistence of a collective identity continuously over a period of more than 50 years, notwithstanding any absence of or changes in name;

(ix) Land set aside by a State for the petitioner, or collective ancestors of the petitioner, that was actively used by the community for that time period;

(x) Children of members from a geographic area were placed in Indian boarding schools or other Indian educational institutions, to the extent that supporting evidence documents the community claimed; or

(xi) A demonstration of political influence under the criterion in § 83.11(c)(1) will be evidence for demonstrating distinct community for that same time period.

(2) The petitioner will be considered to have provided more than sufficient evidence to demonstrate distinct community and political authority under § 83.11(c) at a given point in time if the evidence demonstrates any one of the following:

(i) More than 50 percent of the members reside in a geographical area exclusively or almost exclusively composed of members of the entity, and the balance of the entity maintains consistent interaction with some members residing in that area;

(ii) At least 50 percent of the members of the entity were married to other members of the entity;

(iii) At least 50 percent of the entity members maintain distinct cultural patterns such as, but not limited to, language, kinship system, religious beliefs and practices, or ceremonies;

(iv) There are distinct community social institutions encompassing at least 50 percent of the members, such as kinship organizations, formal or informal economic cooperation, or religious organizations; or

(v) The petitioner has met the criterion in § 83.11(c) using evidence described in § 83.11(c)(2).

(c) *Political influence or authority*. The petitioner has maintained political influence or authority over its members as an autonomous entity from 1900 until the present. Political influence or authority means the entity uses a council, leadership, internal process, or other mechanism as a means of influencing or controlling the behavior of its members in significant respects, making decisions for the entity which substantially affect its members, and/or representing the entity in dealing with outsiders in matters of consequence. This process is to be understood flexibly in the context of the history, culture, and social organization of the entity.

(1) The petitioner may demonstrate that it meets this criterion by some combination of two or more of the following forms of evidence or by other evidence that the petitioner had political influence or authority over its members as an autonomous entity:

(i) The entity is able to mobilize significant numbers of members and significant resources from its members for entity purposes.

(ii) Many of the membership consider issues acted upon or actions taken by entity leaders or governing bodies to be of importance.

(iii) There is widespread knowledge, communication, or involvement in political processes by many of the entity's members.

(iv) The entity meets the criterion in § 83.11(b) at greater than or equal to the percentages set forth under § 83.11(b)(2).

(v) There are internal conflicts that show controversy over valued entity goals, properties, policies, processes, or decisions.

(vi) The government of a federally recognized Indian tribe has a significant relationship with the leaders or the governing body of the petitioner.

(vii) Land set aside by a State for petitioner, or collective ancestors of the petitioner, that is actively used for that time period.

(viii) There is a continuous line of entity leaders and a means of selection or acquiescence by a significant number of the entity's members.

(2) The petitioner will be considered to have provided sufficient evidence of political influence or authority at a given point in time if the evidence demonstrates any one of the following:

(i) Entity leaders or other internal mechanisms exist or existed that:

(A) Allocate entity resources such as land, residence rights, and the like on a consistent basis;

(B) Settle disputes between members or subgroups by mediation or other means on a regular basis;

(C) Exert strong influence on the behavior of individual members, such as the establishment or maintenance of norms or the enforcement of sanctions to direct or control behavior; or

(D) Organize or influence economic subsistence activities among the members, including shared or cooperative labor.

(ii) The petitioner has met the requirements in §83.11(b)(2) at a given time.

(d) *Governing document.* The petitioner must provide:

(1) A copy of the entity's present governing document, including its membership criteria; or

(2) In the absence of a governing document, a written statement describing in full its membership criteria and current governing procedures.

(e) *Descent.* The petitioner's membership consists of individuals who descend from a historical Indian tribe (or from historical Indian tribes that combined and functioned as a single autonomous political entity).

(1) The petitioner satisfies this criterion by demonstrating that the petitioner's members descend from a tribal roll directed by Congress or prepared by the Secretary on a descendancy basis for purposes of distributing claims money, providing allotments, providing a tribal census, or other purposes, unless significant countervailing evidence establishes that the tribal roll is substantively inaccurate; or

(2) If no tribal roll was directed by Congress or prepared by the Secretary, the petitioner satisfies this criterion by demonstrating descent from a historical Indian tribe (or from historical Indian tribes that combined and functioned as a single autonomous political entity) with sufficient evidence including, but not limited to, one or a combination of the following identifying present members or ancestors of present members as being descendants of a historical Indian tribe (or of historical Indian tribes that combined and functioned as a single autonomous political entity):

(i) Federal, State, or other official records or evidence;

(ii) Church, school, or other similar enrollment records;

(iii) Records created by historians and anthropologists in historical times;

(iv) Affidavits of recognition by tribal elders, leaders, or the tribal governing body with personal knowledge; and

(v) Other records or evidence.

(f) *Unique membership.* The petitioner's membership is composed principally of persons who are not members of any federally recognized Indian tribe. However, a petitioner may be acknowledged even if its membership is composed principally of persons whose names have appeared on rolls of, or who have been otherwise associated with, a federally recognized Indian tribe, if the petitioner demonstrates that:

(1) It has functioned as a separate politically autonomous community by satisfying criteria in paragraphs (b) and (c) of this section; and

(2) Its members have provided written confirmation of their membership in the petitioner.

(g) *Congressional termination.* Neither the petitioner nor its members are the subject of congressional legislation that has expressly terminated or forbidden the Federal relationship. The Department must determine whether the petitioner meets this criterion, and the petitioner is not required to submit evidence to meet it.

§83.12 What are the criteria for a previously federally acknowledged petitioner?

(a) The petitioner may prove it was previously acknowledged as a federally recognized Indian tribe, or is a portion that evolved out of a previously federally recognized Indian tribe, by providing substantial evidence of unambiguous Federal acknowledgment, meaning that the United States Government recognized the petitioner as an Indian tribe eligible for the special programs and services provided by the United States to Indians because of their status as Indians with which the United States carried on a relationship at some prior date including, but not limited to, evidence that the petitioner had:

(1) Treaty relations with the United States;

(2) Been denominated a tribe by act of Congress or Executive Order;

(3) Been treated by the Federal Government as having collective rights in tribal lands or funds; or

(4) Land held for it or its collective ancestors by the United States.

(b) Once the petitioner establishes that it was previously acknowledged, it must demonstrate that it meets:

(1) At present, the Community Criterion; and

(2) Since the time of previous Federal acknowledgment or 1900, whichever is later, the Indian Entity Identification Criterion and Political Authority Criterion.

Subpart C—Process for Federal Acknowledgment

DOCUMENTED PETITION SUBMISSION AND REVIEW

§ 83.20 How does an entity request Federal acknowledgment?

Any entity that believes it can satisfy the criteria in this part may submit a documented petition under this part to: Department of the Interior, Office of the Assistant Secretary—Indian Affairs, Attention: Office of Federal Acknowledgment, Mail Stop 4071 MIB, 1849 C Street NW, Washington, DC 20240.

[83 FR 33826, July 18, 2018]

§ 83.21 What must a documented petition include?

(a) The documented petition may be in any readable form and must include the following:

(1) A certification, signed and dated by the petitioner's governing body, stating that it is the petitioner's official documented petition;

(2) A concise written narrative, with citations to supporting documentation, thoroughly explaining how the petitioner meets each of the criteria in § 83.11, except the Congressional Termination Criterion (§ 83.11 (g))—

(i) If the petitioner chooses to provide explanations of and supporting documentation for the Congressional Termination Criterion (§ 83.11 (g)), the Department will accept it; but

(ii) The Department will conduct the research necessary to determine whether the petitioner meets the Congressional Termination Criterion (§ 83.11 (g)).

(3) Supporting documentation cited in the written narrative and containing specific, detailed evidence that the petitioner meets each of the criteria in § 83.11;

(4) Membership lists and explanations, including:

(i) An official current membership list, separately certified by the petitioner's governing body, of all known current members of the petitioner, including each member's full name (including maiden name, if any), date of birth, and current residential address;

(ii) A statement describing the circumstances surrounding the preparation of the current membership list;

(iii) A copy of each available former list of members based on the petitioner's own defined criteria; and

(iv) A statement describing the circumstances surrounding the preparation of the former membership lists, insofar as possible.

(b) If the documented petition contains any information that is protectable under Federal law such as the Privacy Act and Freedom of Information Act, the petitioner must provide a redacted version, an unredacted version of the relevant pages, and an explanation of the legal basis for withholding such information from public release. The Department will not publicly release information that is protectable under Federal law, but may release redacted information if not protectable under Federal law.

§ 83.22 What notice will OFA provide upon receipt of a documented petition?

When OFA receives a documented petition, it will do all of the following:

(a) Within 30 days of receipt, acknowledge receipt in writing to the petitioner.

(b) Within 60 days of receipt:

(1) Publish notice of receipt of the documented petition in the FEDERAL REGISTER and publish the following on the OFA Web site:

(i) The narrative portion of the documented petition, as submitted by the petitioner (with any redactions appropriate under § 83.21(b));

(ii) The name, location, and mailing address of the petitioner and other information to identify the entity;

(iii) The date of receipt;

(iv) The opportunity for individuals and entities to submit comments and evidence supporting or opposing the petitioner's request for acknowledgment within 120 days of the date of the Web site posting; and

(v) The opportunity for individuals and entities to request to be kept informed of general actions regarding a specific petitioner.

(2) Notify, in writing, the following:

(i) The governor of the State in which the petitioner is located;

(ii) The attorney general of the State in which the petitioner is located;

(iii) The government of the county-level (or equivalent) jurisdiction in which the petitioner is located; and

(iv) Notify any recognized tribe and any petitioner that appears to have a historical or present relationship with the petitioner or that may otherwise be considered to have a potential interest in the acknowledgment determination.

(c) Publish the following additional information to the OFA Web site:

(1) Other portions of the documented petition, to the extent feasible and allowable under Federal law, except documentation and information protectable from disclosure under Federal law, as identified by Petitioner under § 83.21(b) or otherwise;

(2) Any comments or materials submitted by third parties to OFA relating to the documented petition;

(3) Any substantive letter, proposed finding, recommended decision, and final determination issued by the Department;

(4) OFA's contact list for each petitioner, including the point of contact for the petitioner; attorneys, and representatives; and

(5) Contact information for any other individuals and entities that request to be kept informed of general actions regarding the petitioner.

(d) All subsequent notices that the Department provides under this part will be provided via the most efficient means for OFA to:

(1) The governor of the State in which the petitioner is located;

(2) The attorney general of the State in which the petitioner is located;

(3) The government of the county-level (or equivalent) jurisdiction in which the petitioner is located;

(4) Any recognized tribe and any petitioner that appears to have a historical or present relationship with the petitioner or that may otherwise be considered to have a potential interest in the acknowledgment determination; and

(5) Any individuals and entities that request to be kept informed of general actions regarding a specific petitioner.

REVIEW OF DOCUMENTED PETITION

§ 83.23 How will OFA determine which documented petition to consider first?

(a) OFA will begin reviews of documented petitions in the order of their receipt.

(1) At each successive review stage, there may be points at which OFA is waiting on additional information or clarification from the petitioner. Upon receipt of the additional information or clarification, OFA will return to its review of the documented petition as soon as possible.

(2) To the extent possible, OFA will give highest priority to completing reviews of documented petitions it has already begun to review.

(b) OFA will maintain a numbered register of documented petitions that have been received.

(c) OFA will maintain a numbered register of any letters of intent, which were allowable prior to July 31, 2015, or incomplete (*i.e.*, not fully documented) petitions and the original dates of their filing with the Department. If two or more documented petitions are ready for review on the same date, this register will determine the order of consideration.

§ 83.24 What opportunity will the petitioner have to respond to comments before OFA reviews the petition?

Before beginning review of a documented petition, OFA will provide the petitioner with any comments on the petition received from individuals or entities under § 83.22(b) and provide the petitioner with 90 days to respond to such comments. OFA will not begin review until it receives the petitioner's response to the comments or the petitioner requests that OFA proceed without its response.

§ 83.25 Who will OFA notify when it begins review of a documented petition?

OFA will notify the petitioner and those listed in § 83.22(d) when it begins review of a documented petition and will provide the petitioner and those listed in § 83.22(d) with:

(a) The name, office address, and telephone number of the staff member with primary administrative responsibility for the petition;

(b) The names of the researchers conducting the evaluation of the petition; and

(c) The name of their supervisor.

§ 83.26 How will OFA review a documented petition?

(a) *Phase I.* When reviewing a documented petition, OFA will first determine if the petitioner meets the Governing Document Criterion (§ 83.11(d)), Descent Criterion (§ 83.11(e)), Unique Membership Criterion (§ 83.11(f)), and Termination Criterion (§ 83.11(g)), in accordance with the following steps.

(1)(i) OFA will conduct a Phase I technical assistance review and notify the petitioner by letter of any deficiencies that would prevent the petitioner from meeting the Governing Document, Descent, Unique Membership, or Termination Criteria. Upon receipt of the letter, the petitioner must submit a written response that:

(A) Withdraws the documented petition to further prepare the petition;

(B) Submits additional information and/or clarification; or

(C) Asks OFA to proceed with the review.

(ii) If the documented petition claims previous Federal acknowledgment and/or includes evidence of previous Federal acknowledgment, the Phase I technical assistance review will include a review to determine whether that evidence meets the requirements of previous Federal acknowledgment (§ 83.12).

(2) Following the receipt of the petitioner's written response to the Phase I technical assistance review, OFA will provide the petitioner with:

(i) Any comments and evidence OFA may consider that the petitioner does not already have, to the extent allowable by Federal law; and

(ii) The opportunity to respond in writing to the comments and evidence provided.

(3) OFA will publish a negative proposed finding if it issues a deficiency letter under paragraph (a)(1)(i) of this section, and the petitioner:

(i) Does not withdraw the documented petition or does not respond with information or clarification sufficient to address the deficiencies; or

(ii) Asks OFA in writing to proceed with the review.

(4) OFA will publish a positive proposed finding and proceed to Phase II if it determines that the petitioner meets the Governing Document, Descent, Unique Membership, and Termination criteria.

(b) *Phase II.* If the petitioner meets the Governing Document, Descent, Unique Membership, and Termination criteria, OFA will next review whether the petitioner meets the Indian Entity Identification Criterion (§ 83.11(a)), the Community Criterion (§ 83.11(b)), and the Political Influence/Authority Criterion (§ 83.11(c)). If the petitioner claims previous Federal acknowledgment, the Department will also review whether petitioner proves previous Federal acknowledgment and, if so, will review whether the petitioner meets the criteria under § 83.12(b).

(1) OFA will conduct a Phase II technical assistance review and notify the petitioner by letter of any deficiencies that would prevent the petitioner from meeting these criteria. Upon receipt of the letter, the petitioner must submit a written response that:

(i) Withdraws the documented petition to further prepare the petition;

(ii) Provides additional information and/or clarification; or

(iii) Asks OFA to proceed with the review.

(2) Following receipt of the petitioner's written response to the Phase II technical assistance review, OFA will provide the petitioner with:

(i) Any comments and evidence OFA may consider in preparing the proposed finding that the petitioner does not already have, to the extent allowable by Federal law; and

(ii) The opportunity to respond in writing to the comments and evidence provided.

(3) OFA will then review the record to determine:

(i) For petitioners with previous Federal acknowledgment, whether the criteria at § 83.12(b) are met; or

(ii) For petitioners without previous Federal acknowledgment, whether the Indian Entity Identification (§ 83.11(a)), Community (§ 83.11(b)) and Political Authority (§ 83.11(c)) Criteria are met.

(4) OFA will publish a negative proposed finding if it issues a deficiency letter under paragraph (a)(1) of this section, and the petitioner:

(i) Does not withdraw the documented petition or does not respond with information or clarification sufficient to address the deficiencies; or

(ii) Asks OFA in writing to proceed with the review.

(5) OFA will publish a positive proposed finding if it determines that the petitioner meets the Indian Entity Identification (§ 83.11(a)), Community (§ 83.11(b)) and Political Authority (§ 83.11(c)) Criteria or, for petitioners with previous Federal acknowledgment, that the petitioner meets the criteria at § 83.12(b).

§ 83.27 What are technical assistance reviews?

Technical assistance reviews are preliminary reviews for OFA to tell the petitioner where there appear to be evidentiary gaps for the criteria that will be under review in that phase and to provide the petitioner with an opportunity to supplement or revise the documented petition.

§ 83.28 When does OFA review for previous Federal acknowledgment?

(a) OFA reviews the documented petition for previous Federal acknowledgment during the Phase II technical assistance review of the documented petition.

(b) If OFA cannot verify previous Federal acknowledgment during this technical assistance review, the petitioner must provide additional evidence. If a petitioner claiming previous Federal acknowledgment does not respond or does not demonstrate the claim of previous Federal acknowledgment, OFA will consider its documented petition on the same basis as documented petitions submitted by petitioners not claiming previous Federal acknowledgment.

§ 83.29 What will OFA consider in its reviews?

(a) In any review, OFA will consider the documented petition and evidence submitted by the petitioner, any comments and evidence on the petition received during the comment period, and petitioners' responses to comments and evidence received during the response period.

(b) OFA may also:

(1) Initiate and consider other research for any purpose relative to analyzing the documented petition and obtaining additional information about the petitioner's status; and

(2) Request and consider timely submitted additional explanations and information from commenting parties to support or supplement their comments on the proposed finding and from the petitioner to support or supplement their responses to comments.

(c) OFA must provide the petitioner with the additional material obtained in paragraph (b) of this section, and provide the petitioner with the opportunity to respond to the additional material. The additional material and any response by the petitioner will become part of the record.

§ 83.30 Can a petitioner withdraw its documented petition?

A petitioner can withdraw its documented petition at any point in the process but the petition will be placed at the end of the numbered register of documented petitions upon re-submission and may not regain its initial priority number.

§ 83.31 Can OFA suspend review of a documented petition?

(a) OFA can suspend review of a documented petition, either conditionally or for a stated period, upon:

(1) A showing to the petitioner that there are technical or administrative

problems that temporarily preclude continuing review; and

(2) Approval by the Assistant Secretary.

(b) Upon resolution of the technical or administrative problems that led to the suspension, the documented petition will have the same priority on the numbered register of documented petitions to the extent possible.

(1) OFA will notify the petitioner and those listed in § 83.22(d) when it suspends and when it resumes review of the documented petition.

(2) Upon the resumption of review, OFA will have the full six months to issue a proposed finding.

PROPOSED FINDING

§ 83.32 When will OFA issue a proposed finding?

(a) OFA will issue a proposed finding as shown in the following table:

OFA must	within . . .
(1) Complete its review under Phase I and either issue a negative proposed finding and publish a notice of availability in the FEDERAL REGISTER, or proceed to review under Phase II.	six months after notifying the petitioner under § 83.25 that OFA has begun review of the petition.
(2) Complete its review under Phase II and issue a proposed finding and publish a notice of availability in the FEDERAL REGISTER.	six months after the deadline in paragraph (a)(1) of this section.

(b) The times set out in paragraph (a) of this section will be suspended any time the Department is waiting for a response or additional information from the petitioner.

(c) OFA will strive to limit the proposed finding and any reports to no more than 100 pages, cumulatively, excluding source documents.

§ 83.33 What will the proposed finding include?

The proposed finding will summarize the evidence, reasoning, and analyses that are the basis for OFA's proposed finding regarding whether the petitioner meets the applicable criteria.

(a) A Phase I negative proposed finding will address that the petitioner fails to meet any one or more of the following criteria: Governing Document (§ 83.11(d)), Descent (§ 83.11(e)), Unique Membership (§ 83.11(f)), or Congressional Termination (§ 83.11(g)).

(b) A Phase II proposed finding will address whether the petitioner meets the following criteria: Indian Entity Existence (§ 83.11(a)), Community (§ 83.11(b)), and Political Influence/Authority (§ 83.11(c)).

§ 83.34 What notice of the proposed finding will OFA provide?

In addition to publishing notice of the proposed finding in the FEDERAL REGISTER, OFA will:

(a) Provide copies of the proposed finding and any supporting reports to the petitioner and those listed in § 83.22(d); and

(b) Publish the proposed finding and reports on the OFA Web site.

PROPOSED FINDING—COMMENT AND RESPONSE PERIODS, HEARING

§ 83.35 What opportunity to comment will there be after OFA issues the proposed finding?

(a) Publication of notice of the proposed finding will be followed by a 120-day comment period. During this comment period, the petitioner or any individual or entity may submit the following to OFA to rebut or support the proposed finding:

(1) Comments, with citations to and explanations of supporting evidence; and

(2) Evidence cited and explained in the comments.

(b) Any individual or entity that submits comments and evidence must provide the petitioner with a copy of their submission.

§ 83.36 What procedure follows the end of the comment period on a favorable proposed finding?

(a) At the end of the comment period for a favorable proposed finding, AS–IA will automatically issue a final determination acknowledging the petitioner as a federally recognized Indian tribe if OFA does not receive a timely objection with evidence challenging the proposed finding that the petitioner meets the acknowledgment criteria.

(b) If OFA has received a timely objection and evidence challenging the favorable proposed finding, then the petitioner will have 60 days to submit a written response, with citations to and explanations of supporting evidence, and the supporting evidence cited and explained in the response. The Department will not consider additional comments or evidence on the proposed finding submitted by individuals or entities during this response period.

§83.37 What procedure follows the end of the comment period on a negative proposed finding?

If OFA has received comments on the negative proposed finding, then the petitioner will have 60 days to submit a written response, with citations to and explanations of supporting evidence, and the supporting evidence cited and explained in the response. The Department will not consider additional comments or evidence on the proposed finding submitted by individuals or entities during this response period.

§83.38 What options does the petitioner have at the end of the response period on a negative proposed finding?

(a) At the end of the response period for a negative proposed finding, the petitioner will have 60 days to elect to challenge the proposed finding before an ALJ by sending to the Departmental Cases Hearings Division, Office of Hearings and Appeals, with a copy to OFA a written election of hearing that lists:

(1) Grounds for challenging the proposed finding, including issues of law and issues of material fact; and

(2) The witnesses and exhibits the petitioner intends to present at the hearing, other than solely for impeachment purposes, including:

(i) For each witness listed, his or her name, address, telephone number, and qualifications and a brief narrative summary of his or her expected testimony; and

(ii) For each exhibit listed, a statement confirming that the exhibit is in the administrative record reviewed by OFA or is a previous final determination of a petitioner issued by the Department.

(b) The Department will not consider additional comments or evidence on the proposed finding submitted by individuals or entities during this period.

§83.39 What is the procedure if the petitioner elects to have a hearing before an ALJ?

(a) If the petitioner elects a hearing to challenge the proposed finding before an ALJ, OFA will provide to the Departmental Cases Hearings Division, Office of Hearings and Appeals, copies of the negative proposed finding, critical documents from the administrative record that are central to the portions of the negative proposed finding at issue, and any comments and evidence and responses sent in response to the proposed finding.

(1) Within 5 business days after receipt of the petitioner's hearing election, OFA will send notice of the election to each of those listed in §83.22(d) and the Departmental Cases Hearings Division by express mail or courier service for delivery on the next business day.

(2) OFA will retain custody of the entire, original administrative record.

(b) *Hearing process.* The assigned ALJ will conduct the hearing process in accordance with 43 CFR part 4, subpart K.

(c) *Hearing record.* The hearing will be on the record before an ALJ. The hearing record will become part of the record considered by AS–IA in reaching a final determination.

(d) *Recommended decision.* The ALJ will issue a recommended decision and forward it along with the hearing record to the AS–IA in accordance with the timeline and procedures in 43 CFR part 4, subpart K.

AS–IA EVALUATION AND PREPARATION OF FINAL DETERMINATION

§83.40 When will the Assistant Secretary begin review?

(a) AS–IA will begin his/her review in accordance with the following table:

If the PF was:	And:	AS–IA will begin review upon:
(1) Negative	The petitioner did not elect a hearing	Expiration of the period for the petitioner to elect a hearing.
(2) Negative	The petitioner elected a hearing	Receipt of the ALJ's recommended decision.
(3) Positive	No objections with evidence were received	Expiration of the comment period for the positive PF.
(4) Positive	Objections with evidence were received	Expiration of the period for the petitioner to respond to comments on the positive PF.

(b) AS–IA will notify the petitioner and those listed in § 83.22(d) of the date he/she begins consideration.

§ 83.41 What will the Assistant Secretary consider in his/her review?

(a) AS–IA will consider all the evidence in the administrative record, including any comments and responses on the proposed finding and any the hearing transcript and recommended decision.

(b) AS–IA will not consider comments submitted after the close of the comment period in § 83.35, the response period in § 83.36 or § 83.37, or the hearing election period in § 83.38.

§ 83.42 When will the Assistant Secretary issue a final determination?

(a) AS–IA will issue a final determination and publish a notice of availability in the FEDERAL REGISTER within 90 days from the date on which he/she begins its review. AS–IA will also

(1) Provide copies of the final determination to the petitioner and those listed in § 83.22(d); and

(2) Make copies of the final determination available to others upon written request.

(b) AS–IA will strive to limit the final determination and any reports to no more than 100 pages, cumulatively, excluding source documents.

§ 83.43 How will the Assistant Secretary make the determination decision?

(a) AS–IA will issue a final determination granting acknowledgment as a federally recognized Indian tribe when AS–IA finds that the petitioner meets the Governing Document (§ 83.11(d)), Descent (§ 83.11(e)), Unique Membership (§ 83.11(f)), and Congressional Termination (§ 83.11(g)) Criteria and:

(1) Demonstrates previous Federal acknowledgment under § 83.12(a) and meets the criteria in § 83.12(b); or

(2) Meets the Indian Entity Identification (§ 83.11(a)), Community (§ 83.11(b)) and Political Authority (§ 83.11(c)) Criteria.

(b) AS–IA will issue a final determination declining acknowledgement as a federally recognized Indian tribe when he/she finds that the petitioner:

(1) In Phase I, does not meet the Governing Document (§ 83.11(d)), Descent (§ 83.11(e)), Unique Membership (§ 83.11(f)), or Congressional Termination (§ 83.11(g)) Criteria: or

(2) In Phase II, does not:

(i) Demonstrate previous Federal acknowledgment under § 83.12(a) and meet the criteria in § 83.12(b); or

(ii) Meet the Indian Entity Identification (§ 83.11(a)), Community (§ 83.11(b)) and Political Authority (§ 83.11(c)) Criteria.

§ 83.44 Is the Assistant Secretary's final determination final for the Department?

Yes. The AS–IA's final determination is final for the Department and is a final agency action under the Administrative Procedure Act (5 U.S.C. 704).

§ 83.45 When will the final determination be effective?

The final determination will become immediately effective. Within 10 business days of the decision, the Assistant Secretary will submit to the FEDERAL REGISTER a notice of the final determination to be published in the FEDERAL REGISTER.

§ 83.46 How is a petitioner with a positive final determination integrated into Federal programs as a federally recognized Indian tribe?

(a) Upon acknowledgment, the petitioner will be a federally recognized Indian tribe entitled to the privileges and immunities available to federally recognized Indian tribes. It will be included on the list of federally recognized Indian tribes in the next scheduled publication.

(b) Within six months after acknowledgment, the appropriate Bureau of Indian Affairs Regional Office will consult with the newly federally recognized Indian tribe and develop, in cooperation with the federally recognized Indian tribe, a determination of needs and a recommended budget. These will be forwarded to the Assistant Secretary. The recommended budget will then be considered with other recommendations by the Assistant Secretary in the usual budget request process.

(c) While the newly federally acknowledged Indian tribe is eligible for benefits and services available to federally recognized Indian tribes, acknowledgment as a federally recognized Indian tribe does not create immediate access to existing programs. The newly federally acknowledged Indian tribe may participate in existing programs after it meets the specific program requirements, if any, and upon appropriation of funds by Congress. Requests for appropriations will follow a determination of the needs of the newly federally acknowledged Indian tribe.

PART 84—ENCUMBRANCES OF TRIBAL LAND—CONTRACT APPROVALS

Sec.

AUTHORITY: 25 U.S.C. 81, Pub. L. 106–179.

SOURCE: 66 FR 38923, July 26, 2001, unless otherwise noted.

§ 84.001 What is the purpose of this part?

The purpose of this part is to implement the provisions of the Indian Tribal Economic Development and Contract Encouragement Act of 2000, Public Law 106–179, which amends section 2103 of the Revised Statutes, found at 25 U.S.C. 81.

§ 84.002 What terms must I know?

The *Act* means the Indian Tribal Economic Development and Contract Encouragement Act of 2000, Public Law 106–179, which amends section 2103 of the Revised Statutes, found at 25 U.S.C. 81.

Encumber means to attach a claim, lien, charge, right of entry or liability to real property (referred to generally as encumbrances). Encumbrances covered by this part may include leasehold mortgages, easements, and other contracts or agreements that by their terms could give to a third party exclusive or nearly exclusive proprietary control over tribal land.

Indian tribe, as defined by the Act, means any Indian tribe, nation, or other organized group or community, including any Alaska Native Village or regional or village corporation as defined in or established under the Alaska Native Claims Settlement Act, which is recognized as eligible for special programs and services provided by the Secretary to Indians because of their status as Indians.

Secretary means the Secretary of the Interior or his or her designated representative.

Tribal lands means those lands held by the United States in trust for an Indian tribe or those lands owned by an Indian tribe subject to federal restrictions against alienation, as referred to Public Law 106–179 as "Indian lands."

§ 84.003 What types of contracts and agreements require Secretarial approval under this part?

Unless otherwise provided in this part, contracts and agreements entered into by an Indian tribe that encumber trial lands for a period of seven or more years require Secretarial approval under this part.

§ 84.004 Are there types of contracts and agreements that do not require Secretarial approval under this part?

Yes, the following types of contracts or agreements do not require Secretarial approval under this part:

(a) Contracts or agreements otherwise reviewed and approved by the Secretary under this title or other federal law or regulation. See, for example, 25 CFR parts 152 (patents in fee, certificates or competency); 162 (non-mineral leases, leasehold mortgages); 163 (timber contracts); 166 (grazing permits); 169 (rights-of-way); 200 (coal leases); 211 (mineral leases); 216 (surface mining permits and leases); and 225 (mineral development agreements);

(b) Leases of tribal land that are exempt from approval by the Secretary under 25 U.S.C. 415 or 25 U.S.C. 477;

(c) Sublease and assignments of leases of tribal land that do not require approval by the Secretary under part 162 of this title;

(d) Contracts or agreements that convey to tribal members any rights for temporary use of tribal lands, assigned by Indian tribes in accordance with tribal laws or custom;

(e) Contracts or agreements that do not convey exclusive or nearly exclusive proprietary control over tribal lands for a period of seven years or more;

(f) Contracts or agreements that are exempt from Secretarial approval under the terms of a corporate charter authorized by 25 U.S.C. 477;

(g) Tribal attorney contracts, including those for the Five Civilized Tribes that are subject to our approval under 25 U.S.C. 82a;

(h) Contracts or agreements entered into in connection with a contract under the Indian Self-Determination Act, 25 U.S.C. 450f, or a compact under the Tribal Self-Governance Act, 25 U.S.C. 458aa.

(i) Contracts or agreements that are subject to approval by the National Indian Gaming Commission under the Indian Gaming Regulatory Act, 25 U.S.C. 2701 *et seq.*, and the Commission's regulations; or

(j) Contracts or agreements relating to the use of tribal lands for hydropower projects where the tribal lands meet the definition of a "reservation" under the Federal Power Act (FPA), provided that:

(1) Federal Energy Regulatory Commission (FERC) has issued a license or an exemption;

(2) FERC has made the finding under section 4(e) of the FPA (16 U.S.C. 797(e)) that the license or exemption will not interfere or be inconsistent with the purpose for which such reservation was created or acquired; and

(3) FERC license or exemption includes the Secretary's conditions for protection and utilization of the reservation under section 4(e) and payment of annual use charges to the tribe under section 10(e) of the FPA (16 U.S.C. 803(e)).

§ 84.005 Will the Secretary approve contracts or agreements even where such approval is not required under this part?

No, the Secretary will not approve contracts or agreements that do not encumber tribal lands for a period of seven or more years. Within thirty days after receipt of final, executed documents, the Secretary will return such contracts and agreements with a statement explaining why Secretarial approval is not required. The provisions of the Act will not apply to those contracts or agreements the Secretary determines are not covered by the Act.

§ 84.006 Under what circumstances will the Secretary disapprove a contract or agreement that requires Secretarial approval under this part?

(a) The Secretary will disapprove a contract or agreement that requires Secretarial approval under this part if the Secretary determines that such contract or agreement:

(1) Violates federal law; or

(2) Does not contain at least one of the following provisions that:

(i) Provides for remedies in the event the contract or agreement is breached;

(ii) References a tribal code, ordinance or ruling of a court of competent jurisdiction that discloses the right of the tribe to assert sovereign immunity as a defense in an action brought against the tribe; or

(iii) Includes an express waiver of the right of the tribe to assert sovereign immunity as a defense in any action brought against the tribe, including a waiver that limits the nature of relief that may be provided or the jurisdiction of a court with respect to such an action.

(b) The Secretary will consult with the Indian tribe as soon as practicable before disapproving a contract or agreement regarding the elements of the contract or agreement that may lead to disapproval.

§84.007 What is the status of a contract or agreement that requires Secretarial approval under this part but has not yet been approved?

A contract or agreement that requires Secretarial approval under this part is not valid until the Secretary approves it.

§84.008 What is the effect of the Secretary's disapproval of a contract or agreement that requires Secretarial approval under this part?

If the Secretary disapproves a contract or agreement that requires Secretarial approval under this part, the contract or agreement is invalid as a matter of law.

PART 87—USE OR DISTRIBUTION OF INDIAN JUDGMENT FUNDS

AUTHORITY: 5 U.S.C. 301; 87 Stat. 466, 467, 468.

SOURCE: 39 FR 1835, Jan. 15, 1974, unless otherwise noted. Redesignated at 47 FR 13327, Mar. 30, 1982.

§87.1 Definitions.

As used in this part 87, terms shall have the meanings set forth in this section.

(a) *Act* means the Act of October 19, 1973 (Pub. L. 93–134; 87 Stat. 466, 467, 468).

(b) *Secretary* means the Secretary of the Interior or his authorized representative.

(c) *Commissioner* means the Commissioner of Indian Affairs or his authorized representative.

(d) *Area Director* means the Area Director or his equivalent of any one of the Area Offices of the Bureau of Indian Affairs or his authorized representative.

(e) *Superintendent* means the Superintendent or Officer in Charge of any one of the Agency Offices or other local offices of the Bureau of Indian Affairs or his authorized representative.

(f) *Congressional Committees* means the Committees on Interior and Insular Affairs of the Senate and House of Representatives of the United States.

(g) *Indian tribe or group* means any Indian tribe, nation, band, pueblo, community or identifiable group of Indians, or Alaska Native entity.

(h) *Tribal governing body* means, as recognized by the Secretary, the governing body of a formally organized or recognized tribe or group; the governing body of any informally organized tribe or group, the governing body of a formally organized Alaska Native entity or recognized tribe in Oklahoma, and for the purposes of the Act the recognized spokesmen or representatives of any descendant group.

(i) *Plan* means the document submitted by the Secretary, together with all pertinent records, for the use or distribution of judgment funds, to the Congressional Committees.

(j) *Enrollment* means that aspect of a plan which pertains to making or bringing current a roll of members of an organized, reservation-based tribe with membership criteria approved or accepted by the Secretary, a roll of members of an organized or recognized entity in Oklahoma, or Alaska or elsewhere, or a roll prepared for the purpose of making per capita payments for judgments awarded by the Indian Claims Commission or United States Court of Claims; or which pertains to using an historical roll or records of names, including tribal rolls closed and made final, for research or other purposes.

(k) *Program* means that aspect of a plan which pertains to using part or all of the judgment funds for tribal social and economic development projects.

(l) *Per capita payment* means that aspect of a plan which pertains to the individualization of the judgment funds in the form of shares to tribal members or to individual descendants.

(m) *Use or distribution* means any utilization or disposition of the judgment funds, including programming, per capita payments, or a combination thereof.

(n) *Individual beneficiary* means a tribal member or any individual descendant, found by the Secretary to be eligible to participate in a plan, who was born on or prior to, and is living on, the approval date of the plan.

(o) *Approval date* means the date that a plan is approved by the Congress. Except for a plan disapproved by either House, the approval date of a plan shall be the sixtieth (60) day after formal submittal of a plan by the Secretary to the Congressional Committees, excluding days on which either the House of Representatives or the Senate is not in session because of an adjournment of more than three (3) calendar days to a day certain. In the event a proposed plan is disapproved by either House, or in the event the Secretary is unable to submit a plan and therefore proposes legislation, the approval date shall be the date of the enabling legislation for the disposition of the judgment funds.

(p) *Minor* is an individual beneficiary who is eligible to participate in a per capita payment and who has not reached the age of eighteen (18) years.

(q) *Legal incompetent* is an individual beneficiary eligible to participate in a per capita payment and who has been declared to be under a legal disability, other than being a minor, by a court of competent jurisdiction, including tribal courts.

(r) *Attorney fees and litigation expenses* means all fees and expenses incurred in litigating and processing tribal claims before the Indian Claims Commission or the United States Court of Claims.

§ 87.2 Purpose.

The regulations in this part govern the preparation of proposed plans for the use or distribution, pursuant to the Act, of all judgment funds awarded from the date of the Act to Indian tribes and groups by the Indian Claims Commission or the United States Court of Claims, excepting any tribe or group whose trust relationship with the Federal Government has been terminated and for which there exists legislation authorizing the disposition of its judgment funds; and of all funds deriving from judgments entered prior to the date of the Act for which there has been no enabling legislation.

§ 87.3 Time limits.

(a) The Secretary shall cause to begin as early as possible the necessary research to determine the identity of the ultimate or present day beneficiaries of judgments. Such research shall be done under the direction of the Commissioner of Indian Affairs. The affected tribes or groups shall be encouraged to submit pertinent data. All pertinent data, including cultural, political and historical material, and records, including membership, census and other rolls shall be considered. If more than one entity is determined to be eligible to participate in the use or distribution of the funds, the results of the research shall include a proposed formula for the division or apportionment of the judgment funds among or between the involved entities.

(b) The results of all research shall be provided to the governing bodies of all affected tribes and groups. The Area Director shall assist the affected tribe or group in arranging for preliminary sessions or meetings of the tribal governing body, or public meetings. The Area Director shall make a presentation of the results of the research and shall arrange for expertise of the Bureau of Indian Affairs to be available at these meetings to assist the tribe or group in developing a use or distribution proposal, bearing in mind that under the Act not less than twenty (20) per centum of the judgment funds, including investment income thereon, is to be used for tribal programs unless the Secretary determines that the particular circumstances of the affected Indian tribe clearly warrant otherwise.

§ 87.4 Conduct of hearings of record.

(a) As soon as appropriate after the tribal meetings have been held and the Commissioner has reviewed the tribal proposal(s), the Area Director, or such other official of the Department of the Interior as he shall designate to act for him, shall hold a hearing of record to receive testimony on the tribal proposal(s).

(b) The hearing shall be held after appropriate public notice beginning at least twenty (20) days prior to the date of such hearing, and after consultation with the governing body of the tribe or group regarding the date and location of the hearing, to obtain the testimony of members of the governing body and other representatives, spokesmen or members of the tribe or group on the proposal(s).

(c) All testimony at the hearing shall be transcribed and a transcript thereof shall be furnished to the Commissioner and the tribal governing body immediately subsequent to the hearing. Particular care shall be taken to insure that minority views are given full opportunity for expression either during the hearing or in the form of written communications by the date of the hearing.

(d) Whenever two or more tribes or groups are involved in the use or distribution of the judgment funds, including situations in which two or more Area Offices are concerned, every effort shall be made by the Area Director or Directors to arrange for a single hearing to be conducted at a time and location as convenient to the involved tribes and groups as possible. Should the tribes and groups fail to reach agreement on such time or place, or on the number of entities to be represented at the hearing, the Commissioner, after considering the views of the affected tribes and groups, shall within twenty (20) days of receipt of such advice by the Area Director, designate a location and date for such hearing and invite the participation of all entities he considers to be involved and the Commissioner's decision shall be final.

§87.5 Submittal of proposed plan by Secretary.

Subsequent to the hearing of record, the Commissioner shall prepare all pertinent materials for the review of the Secretary. Pertinent materials shall include:

(a) The tribal use or distribution proposal or any alternate proposals;

(b) A copy of the transcript of the hearing of record;

(c) A statement on the hearing of record and other evidence reflecting the extent to which such proposal(s) meets the desires of the affected tribe or group, including minorities views;

(d) Copies of all pertinent resolutions and other communications or documents received from the affected tribe or group, including minorities;

(e) A copy of the tribal constitution and bylaws, or other organizational document, if any; a copy of the tribal enrollment ordinance, if any; and a statement as to the availability or status of the membership roll of the affected tribe or group;

(f) A statement reflecting the nature and results of the investment of the judgment funds as of thirty (30) days of the submittal of the proposed plan, including a statement concerning attorney fees and litigation expenses;

(g) A statement justifying any compromise proposal developed by the Commissioner in the event of the absence of agreement among any and all entities on the division or apportionment of the funds, should two or more entities be involved;

(h) And a statement regarding the feasibility of the proposed plan, including a timetable prepared in cooperation with the tribal governing body, for the implementation of programming and roll preparation.

Within one hundred and eighty (180) days of the appropriation of the judgment funds the Secretary shall submit a proposed plan, together with the pertinent materials described above, simultaneously to each of the Chairmen of the Congressional Committees, at the same time sending copies of the proposed plan and materials to the governing body of the affected tribe or group. The one hundred and eighty (180) day period shall begin on the date of the Act with respect to all judgments for which funds have been appropriated and for which enabling legislation has not been enacted.

§87.6 Extension of period for submitting plans.

An extension of the one hundred and eighty (180) day period, not to exceed ninety (90) days, may be requested by the Secretary or by the governing body of any affected tribe or group submitting such request to both Congressional Committees through the Secretary, and any such request shall be subject to the approval of both Congressional Committees.

§ 87.7 Submittal of proposed legislation by Secretary.

(a) Within thirty (30) calendar days after the date of a resolution by either House disapproving a plan, the Secretary shall simultaneously submit proposed legislation authorizing the use or distribution of the funds, together with a report thereon, to the Chairmen of both Congressional Committees, at the same time sending copies of the proposed legislation to the governing body of the affected tribe or group. Such proposed legislation shall be developed on the basis of further consultation with the affected tribe or group.

(b) In any instance in which the Secretary determines that circumstances are not conducive to the preparation and submission of a plan, he shall, after appropriate consultation with the affected tribe or group, submit proposed legislation within the 180-day period to both Congressional Committee simultaneously.

§ 87.8 Enrollment aspects of plans.

An approved plan that includes provisions for enrollment requiring formal adoption of enrollment rules and regulations shall be implemented through the publication of such rules and regulations in the FEDERAL REGISTER. Persons not members of organized or recognized tribes and who are not citizens of the United States shall not, unless otherwise provided by Congress, be eligible to participate in the use or distribution of judgment funds, excepting heirs or legatees of deceased individual beneficiaries.

§ 87.9 Programming aspects of plans.

In assessing any tribal programming proposal the Secretary shall consider all pertinent factors, including the following: the percentage of tribal members residing on or near the subject reservation, including former reservation areas in Oklahoma, or Alaska Native villages; the formal educational level and the general level of social and economic adjustment of such reservation residents; the nature of recent programming affecting the subject tribe or group and particularly the reservation residents; the needs and aspirations of any local Indian communities or districts within the reservation and the nature of organization of such local entities; the feasibility of the participation of tribal members not in residence on the reservation; the availability of funds for programming purposes derived from sources other than the subject judgment; and all other pertinent social and economic data developed to support any proposed program.

§ 87.10 Per capita payment aspects of plans and protection of funds accruing to minors, legal incompetents and deceased beneficiaries.

(a) The per capita shares of living competent adults shall be paid directly to them. The shares of minors, legal incompetents and deceased individual beneficiaries, enhanced by investment earnings, shall be held in individual Indian money (IIM) accounts unless otherwise provided as set out in this section. While held in IIM accounts, said shares shall be invested pursuant to 25 U.S.C. 162a and shall be the property of the minors and legal incompetents or the estates of the deceased individual beneficiaries to whom the per capita payments were made.

(b)(1) Unless otherwise provided in paragraph (b)(2) of this section, minors' per capita shares, until the minors attain the age of 18 years, shall be retained in individually segregated IIM accounts and handled as provided in § 115.4 of this chapter. Should it be determined that the funds are to be invested pursuant to a trust, minors who will have reached the age of 18 years within six months after the establishment of the trust shall have their funds retained at interest in IIM accounts and paid to them upon attaining their majority.

(2) A private trust for the minors' per capita shares may be established subject to the approval of the tribal governing body and the Secretary on the following conditions:

(i) The tribal governing body specifically requests the establishment of such trust, and the trust provides for segregated amounts to each individual minor, based on his per capita share, and

(ii) The trust agreement specifically provides that the investment policy to be followed is that of preserving the trust corpus and of obtaining the highest interest rates current money markets can safely provide. The trust agreement must further provide that maturity dates of investments cannot exceed the period of the trust and that only the following types of investment shall be made: United States Treasury obligations; Federal agency obligations; repurchase/resell agreements; United States Treasury bills; Bankers' acceptance, provided the assets of the issuing bank exceed $1 billion or the issuing bank pledges full collateral; Certificates of deposit, provided the assets of the issuing bank exceed $1 billion or the issuing bank pledges full collateral; Commercial paper, provided it is rated prime-2 by Moody or A–2 by Standard and Poor or is obligation of a company with outstanding unsecured debt rated Aa by Standard and Poor.

(c) The per capita shares of legal incompetents shall be held in IIM accounts and administered pursuant to the provisions of §115.5 of this chapter.

(d) The shares of deceased individual beneficiaries, plus all interest and investment income accruing thereto, shall be paid to their heirs and legatees upon their determination as provided in 43 CFR part 4, subpart D.

(e) All per capita shares, including all interest and investment income accruing thereto, while they are held in trust under the provisions of this section, shall be exempt from Federal and State income taxes and shall not be considered as income or resources when determining the extent of eligibility for assistance under the Social Security Act, as amended.

(f) All per capita shares or portions thereof, including all interest and investment income accruing thereto, which are not paid out but which remain unclaimed with the Federal Government shall be maintained separately and be enhanced by investment, and shall, unless otherwise provided in an effective plan or in enabling legislation, be subject to the provisions of the Act of September 22, 1961, 75 Stat. 584. No per capita share or portion thereof shall be transferred to the U.S. Treasury as "Monies Belonging to Individuals Whose Whereabouts are Unknown."

[41 FR 48735, Nov. 5, 1976. Redesignated at 47 FR 13327, Mar. 30, 1982]

§87.11 Investment of judgment funds.

As soon as possible after the appropriation of judgment funds and pending approval of a plan or the enactment of legislation authorizing the use or distribution of the funds, the Commissioner shall invest such funds pursuant to 25 U.S.C. 162a. Investments of judgment funds and of investment income therefrom will continue to be made by the Commissioner after the approval of a plan or enactment of use or distribution legislation to the extent funds remain available for investment under such plan or legislation, and provided that thereafter investments of judgment funds made available for tribal use are not undertaken by the tribe pursuant to authorizing law. Invested judgment funds, including investment income therefrom, shall be withdrawn from investment only as currently needed under approved plans or legislation authorizing the use or distribution of such funds.

§87.12 Insuring the proper performance of approved plans.

A timetable prepared in cooperation with the tribal governing body shall be included in the plan submitted by the Secretary for the implementation of all programming and enrollment aspects of a plan. At any time within one calendar year after the approval date of a plan, the Area Director shall report to the Commissioner on the status of the implementation of the plan, including all enrollment and programming aspects, and thenceforth shall report to the Commissioner on an annual basis regarding any remaining or unfulfilled aspects of a plan. The Area Director shall include in his first and all subsequent annual reports a statement regarding the maintenance of the timetable, a full accounting of any per capita distribution, and the expenditure of all programming funds. The Commissioner shall report the deficient performance of any aspect of a plan to the Secretary, together with the corrective measures he has taken or intends to take.

PART 88—RECOGNITION OF ATTORNEYS AND AGENTS TO REPRESENT CLAIMANTS

AUTHORITY: 5 U.S.C. 301.

CROSS REFERENCES: For law and order regulations on Indian reservations, see part 11 of this chapter. For probate procedure, see part 15 of this chapter. For regulations governing the admission of attorneys to practice before the Department of the Interior and the offices and bureaus thereof, see 43 CFR part 1. For regulations governing the execution of attorney contracts with Indians, see part 89 of this subchapter.

§ 88.1 Employment of attorneys.

(a) Indian tribes organized pursuant to the Indian Reorganization Act of June 18, 1934 (48 Stat. 984; 25 U.S.C. 461–479), as amended, may employ legal counsel. The choice of counsel and the fixing of fees are subject under 25 U.S.C. 476 to the approval of the Secretary of the Interior or his authorized representative.

(b) Attorneys may be employed by Indian tribes not organized under the Act of June 18, 1934, under contracts subject to approval under 25 U.S.C. 81 and the Reorganization Plan No. 3 of 1950, 5 U.S.C. 481, note, by the Secretary of the Interior or his authorized representative.

(c) Any action of the authorized representative of the Secretary of the Interior which approves, disapproves or conditionally approves a contract pursuant to paragraph (a) or (b) of this section shall be final.

(d) Practice of such attorneys before the Bureau of Indian Affairs and the Department of the Interior is subject to the requirements of 43 CFR 1.1 through 1.7.

[27 FR 11548, Nov. 24, 1962. Redesignated at 47 FR 13327, Mar. 30, 1982]

§ 88.2 Employment by tribes or individual claimants.

All such attorneys or agents seeking approval of their employment by Indian tribes or desiring to represent individual claimants before the Indian Bureau shall be required to comply fully with the regulations of the Department promulgated September 27, 1917, governing admission to practice, and to take the oath of allegiance and to support the Constitution of the United States, as required by section 3478 of the United States Revised Statutes (31 U.S.C. 204).

[22 FR 10538, Dec. 24, 1957. Redesignated at 47 FR 13327, Mar. 30, 1982]

PART 89—ATTORNEY CONTRACTS WITH INDIAN TRIBES

AUTHORITY: 5 U.S.C. 301; secs. 89.30 to 89.35 also issued under 25 U.S.C. 2, 9, and 82a; secs. 89.40 to 89.43 also issued under 25 U.S.C. 13, 450 *et seq.*

CROSS REFERENCE: For recognition of attorneys and agents to represent claimants, see part 88 of this subchapter.

TRIBES ORGANIZED UNDER THE INDIAN REORGANIZATION ACT

§§ 89.1–89.26 [Reserved]

FIVE CIVILIZED TRIBES

§ 89.30 Contents and approval of contracts.

All contracts for the services of legal counsel or technical specialists negotiated and executed with the Choctaw,

Chickasaw, Cherokee, Creek, or Seminole Tribes or Nations, also known as the Five Civilized Tribes, shall be in strict compliance with the requirements of section 2103 of the Revised Statutes of the United States (25 U.S.C. 81).

[37 FR 10440, May 23, 1972. Redesignated at 47 FR 13327, Mar. 30, 1982]

§ 89.31 Negotiation of contract.

That person or governing entity recognized as having authority to act for and in behalf of any one of the Five Civilized Tribes in matters of importance may, when it is found there is a substantial need and demand therefor, negotiate and contract for services of a tribal counsel or counsels and technical specialist or specialists, subject to the approval of the Secretary of the Interior or his authorized representative.

[37 FR 10440, May 23, 1972. Redesignated at 47 FR 13327, Mar. 30, 1982]

§ 89.32 Notice from the principal officer.

Notice of intention to negotiate with attorneys or with technical specialists shall be sent by the principal tribal officer to the Superintendent. Such notice shall be accompanied by a full statement concerning the need for retaining counsel or specialists, as the case may be, the purpose for which such assistance is needed and the scope of the intended employment. The notice and statement shall be transmitted to the Area Director by the Superintendent together with the latter's report and recommendations with respect to the approval of such contract.

[37 FR 10440, May 23, 1972. Redesignated at 47 FR 13327, Mar. 30, 1982]

§ 89.33 Notice from attorney.

Attorneys desiring to execute contracts with any one of the Five Civilized Tribes shall be required to give written notice to the Area Director through the Superintendent having jurisdiction over said tribe.

[37 FR 10440, May 23, 1972. Redesignated at 47 FR 13327, Mar. 30, 1982]

§ 89.34 Tentative form of contract.

The principal officer of any one of the Choctaw, Cherokee, Creek, Seminole, and Chickasaw Tribes may, if he desires, obtain a tentative form of contract by written application to the office of the appropriate Agency Superintendent. Requests for forms for an attorney contract should include a statement reciting whether the attorney is desired as a general legal counsel in connection with the business of the tribe or as counsel in respect to specific problems on which legal counsel is desired, or specific matters requiring representation in court or before committees of Congress and the Departments of Government. Requests for forms for technical service contracts should include a statement of the particular type of service required and the purpose for which it is needed. The anticipated term of each proposed contract should be stated.

[37 FR 10440, May 23, 1972. Redesignated at 47 FR 13327, Mar. 30, 1982]

§ 89.35 Execution in quintuplet.

The contract should be executed in quintuplet, and all copies of it shall be transmitted by the Superintendent to the Area Director.

[37 FR 10440, May 23, 1972. Redesignated at 47 FR 13327, Mar. 30, 1982]

PAYMENT OF TRIBAL ATTORNEY FEES WITH APPROPRIATED FUNDS

SOURCE: 48 FR 3969, Jan. 28, 1983, unless otherwise noted.

§ 89.40 General policy.

In ordinary circumstances, legal services with respect to trust resources are provided for Indian tribe(s):

(a) By private counsel employed by tribes when such tribe is financially able and elects to do so, or

(b) By the United States as trustee through the Office of the Solicitor and/or the Department of Justice.

It is the policy of the Department of the Interior not to use federally appropriated funds to pay for private counsel to represent Indian tribes. Exceptions to that policy are listed in § 89.41 of this part.

§ 89.41 Exceptions to policy.

The Assistant Secretary—Indian Affairs upon concurrence of the Solicitor and receipt of a recommendation as provided by § 89.43 may, in his/her discretion, authorize the direct or indirect expenditure of appropriated funds to pay reasonable attorney's fees in order to permit an Indian tribe to secure private legal representation in the following circumstances:

(a) When a tribe determines it necessary to bring a court action or to defend itself to protect its trust resources, rights claimed under a treaty, agreement, executive order, or statute, or its governmental powers and the Attorney General refuses assistance or advises that assistance is not otherwise available (Comptroller General's Opinion B–114868, December 6, 1976).

(b) When a tribe determines it necessary to institute or to defend itself in an administrative proceeding to protect its trust resources, rights claimed under a treaty, agreement, executive order, or statute, or to protect its governmental powers and the Solicitor is unable to provide representation due to a conflict of interest or other reasons.

(c) When a tribe determines legal assistance necessary, other than for litigation, pursuant to a contract executed under Pub. L. 93–638 and the Solicitor has determined that the services of his office are not available.

(d) When a tribe determines it critical, and the Assistant Secretary—Indian Affairs finds the concerns of the tribe to have merit after consultation with and the advice of the Solicitor, to intervene, in a lawsuit being handled by the Justice Department or in an administrative proceeding being handled by the Solicitor because the responsible Government Attorney refuses either to exclude or to include some facet of the suit or proceedings which the tribe claims renders such legal representation completely inadequate to protect or in contravention of the rights and interests of the tribe. Prior to consulting with and advising the Assistant Secretary—Indian Affairs, in a lawsuit being handled by the Justice Department, the Solicitor shall seek the comments and advice of the Attorney General.

(e) When a tribe determines, and the Assistant Secretary—Indian Affairs, after consultation with the Solicitor concurs, that a substantial possibility of a negotiated settlement or agreement exists.

(f) Payment of fees will not be allowed if such payment was not authorized before services were performed.

(g) This rule applies to expenditure of appropriated Federal funds and not a tribe's own funds on deposit in the U.S. Treasury.

§ 89.42 Factors to be considered.

The following factors are to be considered in determining whether funds should be paid to provide private legal representation for a tribe.

(a) The merits of the legal position which the tribe asserts. Greater weight will be given to those cases where the tribe's legal argument is deemed particularly meritorious than to those cases where the tribe's position, although not entirely without merit, may be relatively weak;

(b) The ability of the tribe to pay all or a part of its legal expenses out of its own funds. A review of the tribe's financial resources under this subsection will include an examination of the tribe's total expenditures to determine whether its expenditures for other purposes comport with the asserted importance of the case for which it seeks funds;

(c) Whether the question the tribe seeks to litigate is being litigated in another case by another tribe;

(d) Whether, as a matter of strategy, the issues the tribe seeks to litigate could be more satisfactorily resolved in another forum, in a different factual context, or a different time; and

(e) Whether the issue should be litigated at all in preference to a legislative or other solution.

§ 89.43 Procedures.

The information collection requirements contained in this section do not require approval by the Office of Management and Budget under 44 U.S.C. 3051 *et seq.*, because it is anticipated there will be fewer than 10 respondents annually.

(a) A tribe or other organization seeking funds under § 89.41 shall submit a written request through the Agency Superintendent and the Area Director, including

(1) A detailed statement describing the nature and scope of the problems for which legal services are sought;

(2) A statement of the terms, including total anticipated costs, of the requested legal services contract;

(3) A current financial statement and a statement that the tribe does not possess sufficient tribal funds or assets to pay for all or a part of the legal services sought; and

(4) A statement of why the matter must be handled by a private attorney as opposed to Department of Justice or Department of Interior attorneys.

All requests shall be considered by a committee consisting of the Deputy Assistant Secretary—Indian Affairs (Policy), or his delegate, the Director of the Office of Trust Responsibilities in BIA or his delegate, and the Associate Solicitor—Indian Affairs or his delegate.

(b) If two of the three committee members recommend approval of a tribe's request, the request, along with the committee's recommendation, shall be submitted to the Assistant Secretary for final determination after consultation with and the advice of the Solicitor. The committee's recommendation shall indicate the amount of funds recommended to assist the tribe, the hourly rate allowed, the maximum amount permitted to be expended in the recommended action and the tribal contributions, if any. The Assistant Secretary shall approve the request only with the concurrence of the Solicitor.

(c) The requirements imposed by this policy are supplementary to those contained in all existing regulations dealing with attorney contracts with Indian tribes and, in particular, those contained in parts 88 and 89 of this title.

PART 90—ELECTION OF OFFICERS OF THE OSAGE TRIBE

GENERAL

AUTHORITY: Sec. 9, 34 Stat. 539; sec. 7, 45 Stat. 1478; 71 Stat. 471, unless otherwise noted.

SOURCE: 23 FR 1948, Mar. 25, 1958; 23 FR 2026, Mar. 27, 1958, unless otherwise noted. Redesignated at 47 FR 13327, Mar. 30, 1982.

GENERAL

§90.1 Definitions.

As used in this part:

(a) The term *supervisor* means the tribal election official chosen and appointed by the Principal Chief or Assistant Principal Chief to act as chairman of the election board and shall in the absence of the supervisor denote the Assistant Supervisor.

§90.2 Statutory provisions.

Section 7 of the Act of March 2, 1929 (45 Stat. 1481) provides in part as follows:

That there shall be a quadrennial election of officers of the Osage Tribe as follows: A principal chief, an assistant principal chief, and eight members of the Osage tribal council, to succeed the officers elected in the year 1928, said officers to be elected at a general election to be held in the town of Pawhuska, Oklahoma, on the first Monday in June 1930 and on the first Monday in June each four years thereafter, in the manner to be prescribed by the Commissioner of Indian Affairs, and said officers shall be elected for a period of four years commencing on the 1st day of July following said elections. * * *

ELIGIBILITY

§ 90.21 General.

Only members of the Osage Tribe who will be eighteen years of age or over on election day and whose names appear on the quarterly annuity roll at the Osage Agency as of the last quarterly payment immediately preceding the date of election will be entitled to hold office or vote for any tribal officers. Each such voter shall be entitled to cast one ballot and each ballot shall have exactly the same value as the voter's headright interest shown on the last quarterly annuity roll. Any fraction of a headright, however, shall be valued as to the first two decimals only unless such interest is less than one-hundredth of a share, then it shall have its full value.

(45 Stat. 1481)

[43 FR 8798, Mar. 3, 1978. Redesignated at 47 FR 13327, Mar. 30, 1982]

ELECTIONS

§ 90.30 Nominating conventions and petitions.

Conventions shall be held on or before the first Monday in April of the year in which a quadrennial election is held, and there shall be written reports of such conventions, duly certified by the secretary or presiding officer showing total number of qualified voters in attendance, together with the names of candidates nominated for the various offices: *Provided*, That at least 25 qualified voters shall have been in attendance at any such convention; also, names of any independent candidates nominated by petition of not less than 25 qualified voters, each signature to be witnessed by two persons, shall be filed with the supervisor not later than 5 p.m. on the first Monday in April of the year in which a quadrennial election is held in order that such names may be placed on the official ballot. No person shall be considered a candidate for tribal office unless and until the requirements of this section have been met.

[32 FR 10253, July 12, 1967. Redesignated at 47 FR 13327, Mar. 30, 1982]

§ 90.31 Applicability.

The manner of carrying out elections to be held under the act of June 28, 1906 (34 Stat. 539), as amended by the act of March 2, 1929 (45 Stat. 1478), as amended by the act of August 28, 1957 (71 Stat. 471), is covered in the regulations set forth in this part. The next election will be held on the first Monday in June 1958 and subsequent elections will be held on the first Monday in June each four years thereafter.

§ 90.32 Election Board.

The Principal Chief, or in his absence, the Assistant Principal Chief shall, not more than seventy-five days nor less than sixty-five days preceding the day appointed by law for the holding of an election of officers of the Osage Tribe, issue in the form and manner prescribed in § 90.37, an election notice and appoint an election board consisting of a Supervisor who shall be chairman, Assistant Supervisor, five judges, one of whom in addition to his regular duties shall act as interpreter, and five clerks, whose duties shall be to conduct the election as provided in the regulations in this part:

Provided further, That the Superintendent on the recommendation of the election board may designate extra clerical assistants. Prior to the date of the election, the election board shall assemble and make necessary arrangements for the election in a building to be designated by the Superintendent of the Osage Agency as the polling site and make the necessary preparation for receiving prospective voters, for receiving absentee ballots, and see to it that voting booths are arranged to afford privacy. Members of the election board and any extra clerical assistants designated by the Superintendent under authority contained in this section, other than employees of the Osage Agency when duly appointed or designated as provided for in this part may be compensated for conducting each quadrennial election at rates to be fixed by the Osage Tribal Council. If a member of the election board desires to be relieved from duty for any cause, he shall notify the Principal Chief or in his absence the Assistant Principal Chief, in writing to that effect and the Principal Chief, or in his absence the

Assistant Principal Chief shall designate someone else to serve as a member of the election board. The Supervisor, or in his absence the Assistant Supervisor, shall see that the rules prescribed for conducting the election are faithfully carried out. The ballots shall be handed out by a judge to the voters as they present themselves to vote, after being identified by a clerk who shall be supplied with a copy of the list of voters prepared pursuant to §90.35. The judge before handing out a ballot shall remove the detachable portion. A judge shall receive the ballot after the voter has indicated his choice thereon by placing an "X" mark opposite the name of each candidate for whom he desires his vote counted and shall deposit same in the ballot box. The duties of the remaining judges in conjunction with the Supervisor will be to read the names on the ballot when requested so as to identify the candidates or furnish such other information as may be desired in that connection and also to assist prospective voters unable because of language difficulties or physical incapacity to cast votes for candidates of their choice, and to undertake such other duties as may be assigned by the Supervisor.

[27 FR 2458, Mar. 15, 1962. Redesignated at 47 FR 13327, Mar. 30, 1982]

§90.33 Watchers and challengers.

Any candidate or political party may name a person to act as watcher and challenger at any election provided for by the regulations in this part. Each watcher and challenger shall be appointed in writing by the candidate or political party he or she represents. The watchers and challengers shall have the right to be present in the polling place but outside the voting booths and to watch the election officials, the balloting, the call, the tally, and the recording of the result of the vote. It shall be the duty of the watcher to watch, listen, and observe the count for all candidates voted for to insist upon an honest and fair count but shall have no further authority than to have the election judges and clerks note or record any objections to the count and to challenge the result thereof. The challenger shall have the right to question any voter and his right to vote. Watchers shall not divulge or give out any intimation or information as to the count prior to announcement by the election board and shall be subject to the same rules governing the election board with regard to leaving and returning to the polling place. A watcher or challenger shall receive no compensation for his services.

[27 FR 2458, Mar. 15, 1962. Redesignated at 47 FR 13327, Mar. 30, 1982]

§90.35 List of voters.

The Superintendent of the Osage Agency shall compile a list of the voters of the Tribe who are qualified under §90.21. Such list shall set forth only the name and last known address of each voter. The Superintendent shall furnish copies of the list to the Supervisor of the election board and shall post copies at the headquarters of the Osage Agency at Pawhuska, Okla., and such other places as the election board may determine to be appropriate. The compilation, posting and distribution of copies to the Supervisor of the election board shall be done as soon as possible after preparation of the last quarterly annuity roll preceding the election. Copies of the list shall also be made available to all qualified candidates for office and for the purpose of checking off the name of each voter as his ballot is cast and for determining, in the event of question, the right of any individual to vote.

[27 FR 2458, Mar. 15, 1962. Redesignated at 47 FR 13327, Mar. 30, 1982]

§90.36 Disputes on eligibility of voters.

(a) The election board shall fix a date not less than five days before the election at which time all complaints will be heard. The election board shall, at least three days before the date of election, determine any claim or challenge as to the right of any person to be listed on the roll of eligible voters.

(b) Any voter of the tribe shall have the right to challenge any person presenting himself to vote and it shall be the duty of the supervisor and a judge of the board to make such investigation then and there as they deem essential, and decide the question of whether or not a person is a listed voter.

§ 90.37 Election notices.

The election notice shall set forth the place, date and time for holding the election, qualification of voters, method of nominating candidates, and closing date for same, method of locating each name on the ballot and the names of each member of the election board. As soon as possible a copy of the notice of the election, after approval by the Superintendent of the Osage Agency, shall be mailed to each qualified voter at his last known address.

§ 90.38 Opening and closing of poll.

The poll shall remain open without intermission from 8 a.m. to 8 p.m. on the date of the election. When all else is in readiness for the opening of the poll the supervisor shall open the ballot box in view of the other election officers, shall turn same top down to show that no ballots are contained therein, and shall then lock the box and retain the key in his possession.

[32 FR 10253, July 12, 1967. Redesignated at 47 FR 13327, Mar. 30, 1982]

§ 90.39 Voters to announce name and residence.

Each voter shall upon presenting himself to vote announce to the clerk his name, and address.

§ 90.40 Ballots.

The Superintendent of the Osage Agency shall have ballots printed showing the name and the office for which each candidate has been nominated and also space for showing the value of the respective ballots. The Superintendent shall have recorded on a detachable portion of each ballot the name of the voter. The value of each voter's ballot shall be recorded on the principal portion of the respective ballots. Any faction or group has the right to nominate any candidate it chooses, in accordance with the regulations prescribed in this part. The names of such candidates shall be printed on the ballot in the manner set forth as follows:

(a) Under the heading, Principal Chief, with notation to vote for one, shall appear names of all candidates for that office. Under the heading, Assistant Chief, with notation to vote for one, shall appear the names of all candidates for that office. Under the heading, Members of Council, with notation to vote for eight, shall appear names of all candidates for council. Names of candidates for office shall appear only once on ballot, regardless of the fact that they may have been nominated on more than one ticket. The order in which names of qualified candidates for office will be placed on the ballot shall be by lot method of drawing in a manner to be determined by the tribal council, and to be free from or regardless of party or factional affiliations. A candidate may use one nickname. Titles and professional designations will not be shown on the ballot. A record shall be kept of any ballots that may be mutilated, canceled, or used as samples.

(b) A space will be provided on each ballot in which the clerk prior to issuing the ballot shall note the value of the ballot which shall be exactly the same value as the voter's headright interest as shown on the last quarterly annuity roll, except any fraction of a headright shall be valued as to the first two decimals only unless such interest is less than one one-hundredth then it shall have its full value. As verification the clerk shall initial the ballot so numbered in the margin. In addition each ballot shall be stamped "Official Ballot" (facsimile signature Supervisor Osage Election Board). Should any voter spoil or mutilate his ballot in his effort to vote he may surrender the ballot to the supervisor who shall give the voter in lieu thereof another ballot which shall show its appropriate value. The spoiled or mutilated ballot or any portion of a spoiled or mutilated ballot shall be retained with other records pertaining to the election.

[32 FR 10253, July 12, 1967. Redesignated at 47 FR 13327, Mar. 30, 1982]

§ 90.41 Absentee voting.

(a) An eligible voter who will be unable to appear at the poll in Pawhuska on election day shall be entitled to vote by absentee ballot. Absentee ballots shall be identical to the ballots described in § 90.40 with the exception that each such ballot shall be stamped "Absentee Ballot," and reflect the date of issuance. All applications for absentee ballots shall be made in writing by the voter. Each ballot shall indicate the value of the vote to which the voter is entitled. The supervisor shall maintain a file of all applications, together with a record of the names and addresses of all persons to whom absentee ballots are mailed or delivered, including the date of mailing or delivery. All absentee ballots must be postmarked and be in the Pawhuska Post Office prior to 8 a.m. on election day.

(b) It shall be the duty of the supervisor, upon receipt of an application, to mail or deliver to the applicant an envelope containing a ballot (after removing the detachable portion), and an inner and outer envelope as described herein. This shall be done not more than 30 days before the election, except that the envelopes and ballots may be mailed to absentee voters residing outside the continental limits of the United States at any time after mailing of the election notice.

(c) If the absentee ballot and accompanying envelopes are to be mailed to the prospective voter, the written request must be submitted to the supervisor on or before 5 p.m. of the Wednesday preceding the election. The absentee ballot and accompanying envelopes may be delivered personally to the prospective voter any time prior to the opening of the poll.

(d) The absentee voter shall mark the ballot and seal it only in the inner envelope. The following shall be printed on the inner envelope:

ABSENTEE BALLOT

ELECTION OF OFFICERS OF THE OSAGE TRIBE

JUNE __, 19___

(e) The absentee voter shall enclose the inner envelope in the outer envelope and after sealing same shall execute the certificate imprinted thereon which certificate shall be in the following form:

I will be unable to appear at the poll in Pawhuska, Oklahoma, on the _________ day of June 19____ and have enclosed my ballot for the election of officers of the Osage Tribe.[1]

(Voter's signature)_________________.

The outer envelope shall be preaddressed as follows: Supervisor, Osage Election Board, Post Office Box ____, Pawhuska, Okla. 74056.

(45 Stat. 1481)

[23 FR 1948, Mar. 25, 1958; 23 FR 2026, Mar. 27, 1958, as amended at 43 FR 8799, Mar. 3, 1978. Redesignated at 47 FR 13327, Mar. 30, 1982]

§ 90.42 Absentee ballots.

The absentee ballots shall remain in the locked box in the post office, Pawhuska, Okla., until 8 a.m. on the day of election at which time the supervisor or assistant supervisor of the election board, accompanied by the Superintendent of the Osage Agency or his designated representatives, shall receive the locked box from the post office and shall personally transport the locked box to the polling site where it shall be delivered immediately to the supervisor or assistant supervisor of the election board. The supervisor or the assistant supervisor in the presence of at least two judges shall unlock the locked box containing the absentee ballots and shall then determine whether the person whose name is signed to the statement is a qualified voter of the Osage Tribe and check said voter off the poll list before opening the outer envelope. After it has been determined which of the absentee ballots have been cast by duly qualified electors, the supervisor in the presence of the election board shall cause the valid ballots in the sealed inner envelopes to be placed in the ballot box.

[32 FR 10254, July 12, 1967. Redesignated at 47 FR 13327, Mar. 30, 1982]

§ 90.43 Canvass of election returns.

(a) Immediately after the polls are closed at 8 p.m., the counting of the ballots shall commence. The supervisor and not less than two judges shall remain continuously in the room until the ballots are finally counted. One or more judges shall act as official counters and two or more clerks shall record the value of each vote and shall comprise a vote tallying team. The

[1] Criminal penalties are provided by statute for knowingly filing false information in such statements (18 U.S.C. 1001).

vote shall be recorded on two tally sheets by each team of judges and clerks under the name of each candidate for whom the voter designated his choice. The count shall continue until all votes have been recorded. The duties of the remaining officials of the election board will be to assist in conducting the election. After the vote of each ballot is recorded, the ballot shall be pierced by needle and string and after the ballots have been so counted, the ends of the string shall be tied together. After all other ballots have been counted, the sealed inner envelopes containing the absentee ballots shall be opened and all ballots found to be valid shall be counted and treated in the same manner as other valid ballots. All ballots and mutilated ballots; registration lists of voters, both absentee and those appearing at the poll; all tally sheets; and all other election materials shall be placed in the ballot box which shall be locked. The supervisor shall then deliver the locked ballot box and keys to same to the Superintendent, Osage Agency, and the box shall be retained in a safe place until opened by order of the supervisor or election board in the event a contest is filed. If no contest is filed, the ballots shall be destroyed 180 days after the election. No information concerning voting shall be posted or made public information until after 8 p.m.

(b) Should any ballot be marked for more than one principal chief or assistant chief or for more than eight councilmen, only that section of the ballot wherein the error was made shall be declared void and the remaining section or sections shall be counted in the same manner as other ballots. Absentee ballots shall be declared void when items other than the ballot are enclosed in the inner envelope, the voter fails to sign the statement appearing on the outer envelope, and for failure to seal the inner envelope or enclose the inner envelope in the outer envelope. Votes cast for individuals whose names are not printed on the official ballot shall not be counted.

[32 FR 10254, July 12, 1967, as amended at 43 FR 8799, Mar. 3, 1978. Redesignated at 47 FR 13327, Mar. 30, 1982]

§ 90.44 Statement of supervisor.

Following the election a statement is to be prepared by the supervisor pertaining to the conduct of the election and certifying to the correct tabulation of the votes for each candidate. The statement shall also set forth the names of the elected candidates and the office to which each was elected. The statement shall be duly acknowledged before an officer qualified to administer oaths and delivered to the Superintendent of the Osage Agency.

[32 FR 10254, July 12, 1967. Redesignated at 47 FR 13327, Mar. 30, 1982]

§ 90.45 Electioneering.

No person shall be allowed to electioneer within the building where and when the election is in progress and it will be the duty of the supervisor to request the detail of a police officer to assist him in maintaining order about the building during the progress of the election.

§ 90.46 Notification of election of tribal officers.

The Superintendent of the Osage Indian Agency shall in due time give written notice to candidates of their election to the various tribal offices and as soon thereafter as practicable such tribal officers shall appear and subscribe to oath of office before an officer qualified to administer oaths and such oaths shall be delivered to the Superintendent and by him transmitted to the Commissioner of Indian Affairs.

§ 90.47 Contesting elections.

Any unsuccessful candidate may before noon on Monday next following the tribal election file with the supervisor a challenge to the correctness of the vote cast for the office for which he was a candidate, which challenge must be accompanied by a deposit of $500. The election board or the supervisor shall order a recount and proceed with same as provided in this part. If the recount results in the contestant being elected, the deposit shall be refunded; otherwise, the deposit shall be used to defray all expenses of said recount and any balance not so used shall be returned to the contestant.

[32 FR 10254, July 12, 1967. Redesignated at 47 FR 13327, Mar. 30, 1982]

§90.48 Notice of contest.

It shall be the duty of the supervisor, to serve upon the contestee, or contestees, directly affected by such challenge or contest, a true copy of said written application, the original of which is required to be filed with the supervisor. Said service shall be made in person, where possible, within twenty-four hours after the filing of said original challenge or contest, and where personal service is impossible within such time, on account of the absence of contestee, or contestees, from Osage County, or for any other reason, it is hereby made the duty of the supervisor to serve a true copy upon the Superintendent of the Osage Indian Agency: *Provided*, That for the purpose of such constructive service, the Superintendent is hereby made and constituted the service agent of each and every candidate in all tribal elections, and by filing petition as a candidate, such candidate shall thereby be presumed conclusively to have accepted the terms and provisions hereof and specifically the constructive service as aforesaid.

§90.49 Expenses of elections.

All expenses of elections including compensation to the members of the election board and any clerical assistants designated by the Superintendent under §90.32, stationery supplies, meals, printing and postage shall be borne by the Osage Tribe as set forth in an appropriate Osage Tribal Council resolution establishing current pay scale.

[27 FR 2459, Mar. 15, 1962. Redesignated at 47 FR 13327, Mar. 30, 1982]

PART 91—GOVERNMENT OF INDIAN VILLAGES, OSAGE RESERVATION, OKLAHOMA

Sec.

AUTHORITY: Subdivision 9 of sec. 2, sec. 12, Act of June 28, 1906 (34 Stat. 539), sec. 3, Act of June 24, 1938 (52 Stat. 1034). Interpret or apply Act of April 18, 1912 (37 Stat. 86).

SOURCE: 28 FR 10203, Sept. 18, 1963, unless otherwise noted. Redesignated at 47 FR 13327, Mar. 30, 1982.

§91.1 Purpose.

The purpose of the regulations in this part is to establish policies and procedures for the government of Indian villages, Osage Reservation, Oklahoma.

§91.2 Definitions.

As used in this part:

(a) *Secretary* means the Secretary of the Interior or his authorized representative.

(b) *Superintendent* means the Superintendent or other officer in charge of Osage Agency.

(c) *Council* means the Osage Tribal Council, that elected governing body of the Osage Tribe of Indians.

(d) *Tribal Member* means any person of Osage Indian blood of whatever degree, allotted or unallotted.

(e) *Minor* means any person under 21 years of age.

(f) *Resident* means an adult tribal member who has resided in the village for thirty (30) days, in the 12-month period preceding the election.

§91.3 Description of village reserves.

The act of June 28, 1906 (34 Stat. 539), as amended by the act of June 24, 1938 (52 Stat. 1034), set aside certain tribal lands exclusively as dwelling sites for the use and benefit of the Osage Indians until January 1, 1984, unless otherwise provided by Act of Congress. These lands are described as follows:

(a) *Grayhorse Indian Village.* The southeast quarter (SE ½) of the southeast quarter (SE ¼), and the west half (W ½) of the southwest quarter (SW ¼) of the southeast quarter (SE ¼), and the south half (S ½) of the northeast quarter (NE ¼) of the southeast quarter (SE ¼) of the southwest quarter (SW ¼), and the south half (S ½) of the north half (N ½) of the northeast quarter (NE ¼) of the southeast quarter (SE ¼) of the southwest quarter (SW ¼), and the southeast quarter (SE ½) of the southeast quarter (SE ¼) of the southwest quarter (SW ¼) of sec. fifteen (15); and the north half (N ½) of the northeast quarter (NE ¼), and the northeast quarter (NE ¼) of the northwest quarter (NW ¼) of sec. twenty-two (22), all in township twenty-four (24) north, range six (6) east of the Indian meridian, and containing 197.5 acres, more or less.

(b) *Hominy Indian Village.* Lots Six (6) and Seven (7), and the East Half (E ½) of the Southwest Quarter (SW ¼) of Section Six (6) in Township Twenty-two (22) North, Range Nine (9) East of the Indian Meridian, and containing 160 acres, more or less.

(c) *Pawhuska Indian Village.* Lots One (1) and Two (2), and the South Half (S ½) of the Northeast Quarter (NE ¼) of Section Three (3) in Township Twenty-five (25) North, Range Nine (9) East of the Indian Meridian, and containing 160 acres, more or less.

[28 FR 10203, Sept. 18, 1963, as amended at 33 FR 8270, June 4, 1968. Redesignated at 47 FR 13327, Mar. 30, 1982]

§ 91.4 Plats of village reserves.

Plats of the Grayhorse Indian Village, the Pawhuska Indian Village, and the Hominy Indian Village, certified by Ralph M. Tolson, Registered Engineer, on July 5, 1966, are the official plats of dedication of said villages and shall be filed of record with the county clerk of Osage County, State of Oklahoma.

[33 FR 8270, June 4, 1968. Redesignated at 47 FR 13327, Mar. 30, 1982]

§ 91.5 Tracts reserved from selection by individuals.

The following described tracts, as shown on the plats of the three villages, are reserved from selection by individuals and are set aside for sepultural use or for public use by tribal members:

(a) Grayhorse Indian Village:

(1) Public Squares.

(2) Parks, and

(3) Cemetery.

(b) Hominy Indian Village:

(1) Public squares.

(2) Cemetery, and

(3) Lot 1 in block 1 set aside for religious and educational purposes to the Society of Friends, its Associate Executive Committee of Friends on Indian Affairs and its or their representative at Hominy, Okla., by Resolution of the Osage Tribal Council dated June 6, 1956, and approved by the Assistant Secretary of the Interior, September 7, 1956.

(c) Pawhuska Indian Village:

(1) Wakon Iron Square.

(d) Those individuals who have summer homes or dance arbors located on the Public Square of the Hominy Indian Village shall be permitted to retain said summer homes or dance arbors during their lifetimes if they are maintained in a condition satisfactory to the Hominy Indian Village Committee. Following the owner's death, the improvements shall be removed within ninety (90) days or become the property of the Hominy Indian Village.

[33 FR 8270, June 4, 1968. Redesignated at 47 FR 13327, Mar. 30, 1982]

§ 91.6 Custody of public buildings and tracts reserved from selection by individuals; village committees.

Each of the three (3) villages described herein shall organize a village committee to provide for the health, safety and welfare of its inhabitants, for the maintenance of tribal property, and to serve as custodian and manager of tribal property and improvements located within said village except that tract described in § 91.5(b)(3). Each village committee shall be composed of five (5) members, domiciled in the village, one of whom shall be designated by the committee as chairman. The committees shall be elected biennially by the residents of the villages, except in the Grayhorse Indian Village where the committee shall be appointed by the Council from among those tribal members residing in or historically associated with the village. The procedure for initial committee elections shall be established by the Council. Each village committee shall prepare a constitution and by-laws to be approved by the Council and the Superintendent before said committee will have any authority to govern, and any changes or amendments thereto must likewise be approved by the Council and the Superintendent. All actions of the committee are subject to appeal to the Council whose decision shall be final: *Provided*, That such committee shall have no control or authority to grant permission for the use of tribal property described in §91.5 for the holding of dances. Such authority shall remain in the Council and any group or individual using the property for dance purposes without the written permission of the Council shall be in violation of these regulations: *Provided, further*, That the village committee shall not permit the use of any of the tracts described in §91.5 in any manner that would conflict with Council authorization for dance purposes.

§91.7 Permits to occupy land for dwelling purposes.

The issuance of permits for the use of land for dwelling purposes within any village reserve described in §91.3 except tracts reserved for specific purposes by §91.5 will be under the jurisdiction of the Superintendent. Permits may be issued only to tribal members upon application to the Superintendent: *Provided*, That only one permit shall be issued to any one individual and that erection of a dwelling house shall be started on such land within six (6) months from date of approval of the permit or such permit shall be automatically terminated except that upon written application the Superintendent may extend such permit for an addition six (6) months: *Provided, further*, That only one dwelling shall be constructed under any one permit. Permits shall be issued for the use of one to three contiguous lots, depending upon the quality and permanency of the improvements to be placed thereon. Permits issued under this section shall be made in duplicate in a manner to be prescribed by the Superintendent. The original copy shall be filed in the Branch of Realty, Osage Agency, and the duplicate copy shall be mailed to the permittee.

[33 FR 8270, June 4, 1968. Redesignated at 47 FR 13327, Mar. 30, 1982]

§91.8 Sale or mortgage of improvements.

No improvements located within the village reserves described in §91.3 shall be sold, mortgaged, transferred or assigned without the approval of the Superintendent.

(a) Improvements may be mortgaged for home improvements or the erection of new improvements. Such mortgages shall be made with acceptable lending agencies and shall be approved by the Superintendent. The lending agency shall have the right:

(1) To foreclose the mortgage and to sell the improvements within six (6) months of the date of foreclosure judgment to any eligible tribal member with the understanding that the use of the land on which the improvements are situated shall be transferable to the new owner; or

(2) To foreclose the mortgage and to sell the improvements to a non-tribal member, who shall remove the improvements from the village reserve within six (6) months of the date of sale. In the event of removal of the mortgaged property, it shall be the responsibility of the lending agency to level the land on which such improvements were located and to remove all debris, sidewalks, etc., leaving the premises in an orderly condition. Failure to make such disposition within the time stated in this paragraph shall result in forfeiture of the improvements to the village committee.

(b) Improvements may be sold by the owner thereof with the approval of the Superintendent. Sale of such improvements shall be accomplished by bill of sale executed by the owner in triplicate who shall file all copies with the Superintendent. If the purchaser of such improvements is a member of the Osage

Tribe, the bill of sale shall be accompanied by a relinquishment of the permit in favor of the vendee for the occupancy of the land on which such improvements are located. If the purchaser is not a member of the Osage Tribe, such purchaser shall be required to endorse an agreement on the reverse of all copies of the bill of sale that he will:

(1) Remove the improvements from the village reserve within six (6) months of date of approval of the bill of sale;

(2) Transfer the title thereof as provided in this section to a tribal member who is eligible; or

(3) Failing to make such disposition within the time stated forfeit title to the village committee.

(c) Upon approval of the bill of sale by the Superintendent, the original or certified copy shall be filed in the Branch of Realty, Osage Agency, the duplicate copy mailed to the purchaser, and the triplicate copy mailed to the seller.

§ 91.9 Inheritance of improvements.

(a) Upon the death of the owner of improvements in a village reserve, such improvements shall, in probate matters, be subject to the jurisdiction of the county courts, State of Oklahoma, and shall be subject to inheritance or bequest in accordance with applicable State and Federal laws. The land within a village reserve is held in trust for the benefit of tribal members and is not subject to inheritance or purchase.

(b) When such improvements or interests therein are inherited by or bequeathed to a non-tribal member, he or she shall dispose of such improvements in the manner provided for disposition of improvements by purchaser under § 91.8: *Provided*, That when such non-tribal member is a legally adopted minor child such child may continue to occupy the land during its minority: *Provided, further*, That when such non-tribal member is the surviving spouse such individual, so long as he or she remains single may continue to occupy the land during his or her lifetime or may sell the improvements as provided herein and may receive a proceeds therefrom. In the event such surviving spouse remarries, the right to continuous occupancy of the land pursuant to this § 91.9 shall terminate and such surviving spouse shall make disposition of such improvements as provided for purchasers in § 91.8. If upon the death of the surviving spouse title to the improvements vests in a non-tribal member, they shall be sold as provided in § 91.8 and the proceeds distributed to the persons entitled thereto.

(c) Improvements inherited by tribal members may be occupied or rented in accordance with § 91.10: *Provided*, No tribal member shall be issued more than two permits or own more than two sets of improvements, one of which must be inherited property and one occupied by the tribal member: *Provided, further*, No tribal member shall be permitted to retain more than one set of improvements for rental. If this provision is violated, the tribal member will have three years, from the date of written notice from the Superintendent that such provision has been violated, within which to dispose of the surplus property in accordance with § 91.8.

§ 91.10 Renting of improvements.

The Superintendent may issue a certificate of permission to rent for a period of one (1) year improvements located on land held under valid permit, subject to renewal in the discretion of the Superintendent, upon written application by the owner of such improvements and the prospective tenant: *Provided*, That such prospective tenant is a tribal member and the property to be rented is that heretofore occupied or inherited by the owner. Certificates of permission issued under this section may be withdrawn upon 30-day notice to the tenant by the Superintendent and such tenant expelled from the village reserve. The application and certificate of permission on a form to be prescribed by the Superintendent shall be made in triplicate and all copies forwarded to the Superintendent for action. Upon approval by the Superintendent, the original copy of the application and certificate shall be filed in the Branch of Realty, Osage Agency, the duplicate copy of each forwarded to the owner, and the triplicate copy of each forwarded to the tenant.

§91.11 Domestic animals in village reserves.

(a) No livestock shall be permitted to trespass in any village reserve except that unassigned lots or unplatted areas enclosed by adequate fences may be leased by the village committee with the approval of the Superintendent and the proceeds therefrom credited to the account of the village committee. Trespassing livestock may be impounded by the village committee. The village committee shall give notice of impoundment to the owner of the animal, if known, by certified mail or by posting in the village square. The notice shall advise the owner that a $10 charge shall be assessed per day for each animal impounded and a reasonable charge for forage consumed and that the animal or animals shall be sold at the expiration of twenty (20) days from the date of mailing or posting the notice. In the event an animal is sold, the balance after deducting $10 per day for impoundment and a reasonable forage charge, shall be deposited at the Osage Agency and the owner may claim said funds if satisfactory proof of ownership is presented to the Superintendent of the Osage Agency within six (6) months of the date of sale. After six (6) months, any funds remaining on deposit will become the property of the village in which the animal was trespassing.

(b) No horses, mules, bovine, hogs, sheep, or goats shall be penned on assigned lots.

[33 FR 8270, June 4, 1968. Redesignated at 47 FR 13327, Mar. 30, 1982]

§91.12 Business enterprises and public buildings.

No permanent business enterprises shall be carried on within the boundaries of a village reserve and no public buildings shall be erected on lands within the boundaries of a village reserve except on tracts described in §91.5 maintained for the use and benefit of tribal members. The construction or acquisition of dwellings for rental purposes is prohibited. The village committee may grant permission and charge fees for temporary concessions within the village reserve during Indian celebrations, dances, community gatherings, etc., such temporary permits to last only for the term of activities for which granted.

§91.13 Health, sanitation, and sewerage disposal.

Health, sanitation, and sewerage disposal problems within the village reserves shall be subject to and controlled by applicable County and State laws.

§91.14 Confirmation of permits.

The Superintendent shall prepare a certified list of all current permittees with a description of lots held, which descriptions shall conform to the plats certified July 5, 1966. Said list shall be served by certified mail on the individual permittees and the village committee chairman and shall be posted at the Osage Agency and each of the three village squares. Unless a protest is filed with the Superintendent within ninety (90) days of the mailing and posting, said certified list of assigned lots and the individual permittees shall be final and conclusive. Protests may be filed by tribal members claiming an interest in an assigned lot and such protest shall be determined by the Superintendent after notice and hearing.

[33 FR 8271, June 4, 1968. Redesignated at 47 FR 13327, Mar. 30, 1982]

§91.15 Suspension or amendment of regulations.

The regulations in this part may be suspended or amended at any time by the Secretary of the Interior: *Provided*, That such amendments or suspension shall not serve to change the terms or conditions of any mortgage approved in accordance with §91.8(a).

SUBCHAPTER G—FINANCIAL ACTIVITIES

PART 101—LOANS TO INDIANS FROM THE REVOLVING LOAN FUND

AUTHORITY: 25 U.S.C. 1469.

SOURCE: 40 FR 3587, Jan. 23, 1975, unless otherwise noted. Redesignated at 47 FR 13327, Mar. 30, 1982.

§ 101.1 Definitions.

As used in this part 101:

Applicant means an applicant for a United States Direct Loan from the revolving loan fund or a loan from a relending organization.

Commissioner means the Commissioner of Indian Affairs or an authorized representative.

Cooperative association means an association of individuals organized pursuant to state, Federal, or tribal law, for the purpose of owning and operating an economic enterprise for profit with profits distributed or allocated to patrons who are members of the organization.

Corporation means an entity organized as a corporation pursuant to state, Federal, or tribal law, with or without stock, for the purpose of owning and operating an economic enterprise.

Default means failure of a borrower to:

(1) Make scheduled payments on a loan when due,

(2) Obtain the lender's approval for disposal of assets mortgaged as security for a loan, or

(3) Comply with the covenants, obligations, or other provisions of a loan agreement.

Economic enterprise means any Indian-owned commercial, industrial, agricultural, or business activity established or organized for the purpose of profit, provided that eligible Indian ownership constitutes not less than 51 percent of the enterprise.

Equity means the borrower's residual ownership, after deducting all business debt, of tangible business assets used in the business being financed, on which a lender can perfect a first lien position.

Financing statement means the document filed or recorded in county or state offices pursuant to the provisions of the Uniform Commercial Code notifying third parties that a lender has a lien on the chattels and/or crops of a borrower.

Indian means a person who is a member of an Indian tribe as defined in this part.

Organization means the governing body of any Indian tribe, or entity established or recognized by such governing body for the purpose of the Indian Financing Act.

Other organization means any non-Indian individual, firm, corporation, partnership, or association.

Partnership means a form of business organization in which two or more legal persons are associated as co-owners for the purposes of business or professional activities for private pecuniary gain, organized pursuant to tribal, state, or Federal law.

Reservation means Indian reservation, California rancheria, public domain Indian allotment, former Indian reservation in Oklahoma, and land held by Alaska Native groups incorporated under the provisions of the Alaska Native Claims Settlement Act (85 Stat. 688), as amended.

Revolving loan fund means all funds that are now or hereafter a part of the revolving fund authorized by the Act of June 18, 1934 (48 Stat. 986), the Act of June 26, 1936 (49 Stat. 1968) and the Act of April 14, 1950 (64 Stat. 44), as amended and supplemented including sums received in settlement of debts for livestock pursuant to the Act of May 24, 1950, (64 Stat. 190) and sums collected in repayment of loans made, including interest or other charges on loans, and any funds appropriated pursuant to section 108 of the Indian Financing Act of 1974 (88 Stat. 77).

Secretary means the Secretary of the Interior.

Tribe means any Indian tribe, bank, nation, rancheria, pueblo, colony or community, including any Alaska Native village or any regional, village, urban or group corporation as defined in or established pursuant to the Alaska Native Claims Settlement Act (85 Stat. 688), as amended, which is recognized by the Federal Government as eligible for services from the Bureau of Indian Affairs.

[57 FR 46471, Oct. 8, 1992]

§101.2 Kinds of loans.

Loans from the Indian Revolving Loan Fund shall be made for purposes which will improve and promote the economic development on Indian reservations.

(a) Loans may be made by the United States to eligible relending organizations for relending to members for economic enterprises and to eligible tribes for relending to members, eligible corporations, cooperative associations, partnerships and subordinate bands and for financing tribal economic enterprises, which will promote the economic development of a reservation and/or the group or members thereon. Loans made by tribes or relending organizations may be for the following purposes:

(1) To individual Indians or Natives, cooperative associations, corporations and partnerships, to finance economic enterprises operated for profit, the operation of which will contribute to the improvement of the economy of a reservation and/or the members thereon.

(2) To individual Indians or Natives for purposes of purchasing, constructing or improving housing on a reservation and to be occupied by the borrower.

(3) To individual Indians and Natives for purposes of obtaining a college or graduate education and degree in a field which will provide employment opportunities, provided that adequate funds are not available from sources such as grants, scholarships or other loan sources.

(4) To individual Indians and Natives for purposes of attending vocational schools which provide training in desired skills in a field in which there are employment opportunities, provided that adequate funds and/or training are not available from grant or scholarship sources, or federal or state training programs.

Loans may also be made by the United States to tribes for loaning to or investing in other organizations subject to the provisions in paragraph (d) of this section.

(b) Direct loans may be made by the United States to eligible tribes, tribal organizations or corporations and tribal cooperative associations without fund restrictions. Direct loans to individual Indians, partnerships, and other non-tribal organizations shall not exceed $350,000. Direct loans from the United States shall be made for the following purposes:

(1) To eligible tribes, individual Indians, Natives, or associations thereof, corporations and partnerships, to finance economic enterprises operated for profit, the operation of which will contribute to the improvement of the economy of a reservation and/or the members thereon.

(2) To individual Indians and Natives for purposes of purchasing, constructing or improving housing on a reservation and to be occupied by the borrower.

(3) To individual Indians and Natives for purposes of obtaining a college or

graduate education and degree in a field which will provide employment opportunities, provided that adequate funds are not available from sources such as grants, scholarships or other loan sources.

(4) To individual Indians and Natives for purposes of attending vocational schools which provide training in desired skills in a field in which there are employment opportunities, provided that adequate funds and/or training are not available from grants or scholarship sources or federal or state training programs.

(c) Before a United States direct loan is approved, the Commissioner may require the applicants to prepare a market and capacity report on existing or proposed economic enterprises for which financing is requested if the operation involves manufacturing, selling or providing services.

(d) Loans may be made to eligible tribes and Indian organizations for use in attracting industries and economic enterprises, the operation of which will contribute to the economy of a reservation. Tribes and Indian organizations may receive loans from the revolving loan fund for investment in or lending to other organizations regardless of whether they are organizations of Indians. However, not more than 50 percent of the loan made to an Indian organization may be used for the purpose of making a loan to or investing in other organizations. Applications for loans to provide funds for lending to or investing in other organizations already in operation will be accompanied by:

(1) Audited balance sheets and operating statements of the other organization for the immediate three preceding years;

(2) Pro forma operating statement and balance sheets for the succeeding three years reflecting the results of operations after injection of the additional funds;

(3) Names of owners or if a corporation and stock has been issued, names of major stockholders and shares of stock owned by each;

(4) A copy of the articles of incorporation and bylaws, if incorporated, or other organization papers if not incorporated;

(5) Names of members of the board of directors and officers with a resume of education and experience, and the number of shares of stock owned by each in the corporation;

(6) Purposes for which loan or investment will be used; and

(7) If for manufacturing, selling or providing services, a market and capacity report will be prepared. If a proposed operation is to be established, the information in paragraphs (d)(2) through (7) of this section will be furnished. The Commissioner may require additional information on the other organization, if needed, to adequately evaluate the benefits which the Indian organization will receive and the economic benefits which will accrue to a reservation. If the loan is for relending to another organization, the application must show what security is being offered. If the loan is for investment in another organization, the equity to be obtained must be shown. Copies of all agreements, contracts or other documents to be executed by the Indian organization and the other organization in connection with a loan or investment shall be submitted with the application for a loan and will require Commissioner approval prior to disbursement of loan funds to the Indian organization.

[40 FR 3587, Jan. 23, 1975. Redesignated at 47 FR 13327, Mar. 30, 1982, as amended at 54 FR 34974, Aug. 23, 1989]

§ 101.3 Eligible borrowers under United States direct loan program.

(a) Loans may be made from the revolving loan fund to Indians, eligible tribes and relending organizations, and corporations, cooperative associations and partnerships having a form of organization satisfactory to the Commissioner. Loans may be made to applicants only when, in the judgment of the Commissioner, there is a reasonable prospect of repayment. Loans may be made only to an applicant who, in the opinion of the Commissioner, is unable to obtain financing on reasonable terms and conditions from other sources such as tribal relending programs, banks, Farmers Home Administration, Small Business Administration, Production Credit Associations, or Federal Land Banks, and is also unable to obtain a guaranteed or insured loan pursuant to title II of the Indian Financing Act of 1974 (88 Stat. 77). In addition, the applicant will be required to have equity equal to 20 percent of the total cost of a new enterprise, or 20 percent of the total cost of expansion of an existing enterprise.

(b) The establishment of a United States direct revolving loan program on a reservation(s) for making direct loans will require the approval of the Commissioner. All requests for establishing a United States direct revolving loan program on a reservation will be accompanied by reasons for need, estimate of financing needs, and other sources of financing available to meet the needs. The Commissioner, in approving a United States direct loan program, may require the preparation and approval of a plan of operation for conducting the program.

(c) If local lending conditions and/or the information in an application for a loan indicate a probability that an applicant may be able to obtain the loan from other sources, the Commissioner, before approving a United States direct loan, will require the applicant to furnish letters from two customary lenders in the area who are making loans for similar purposes, stating whether or not they are willing to make a loan to the applicant for the same purposes and amount. If a customary lender will make the loan on reasonable terms and conditions, the Commissioner will not approve a United States direct loan.

[40 FR 3587, Jan. 23, 1975. Redesignated at 47 FR 13327, Mar. 30, 1982, as amended at 54 FR 34974, Aug. 23, 1989; 57 FR 46471, Oct. 8, 1992]

§ 101.4 Applications.

An applicant for a United States direct loan or a loan from a relending organization conducting a relending program under this part will submit an application on a form approved by the Commissioner. Applications shall include the name, current address and telephone number of the applicant(s); current and prior Taxpayer Identification Number—Employer Identification Number if a business entity, Social Security Number if an individual; and current employer's name, address, and telephone number; amount of the loan requested; purpose for which loan funds will be used; and security to be offered; period of the loan, assets, liabilities and repayment capacity of the applicant; budgets reflecting income and expenditures of the applicant; and any other information necessary to adequately evaluate the application. The borrower must sign a statement declaring no delinquency on Federal taxes or other Federal debt and borrower's good standing on dealings in procurement or non-procurement with the Federal Government. The Bureau will obtain a current credit bureau report and prescribe procedures to be used in handling loan proceeds. In addition, applications for loans to finance economic enterprises already in operation will be accompanied by:

(a) A copy of operating statements, balance sheets and budgets for the prior two operating years or applicable period thereof preceding submittal of the application;

(b) Current budget, balance sheet and operating statements; and

(c) Pro forma budgets operating statements and balance sheets showing the estimated results for operating the enterprise for two years after injection of the loan funds into the operation.

A resume of the applicant's management experience will be submitted with the application. Applications for loans and requests for advance of tribal trust funds for relending under the provisions of this part shall be accompanied by a declaration of policy and plan of operation or other acceptable plan for conducting the program. Applications for loans or modifications thereof, to establish, acquire, operate, or expand an economic enterprise shall be accompanied by a plan of operation. Declarations of policy or other plans for conducting a relending program and plans of operation for economic enterprises require the approval of the Commissioner before becoming effective. An application from a corporation, partnership or cooperative association, for a United States direct loan or a loan under a relending program for financing an economic enterprise must, in addition to financial statements and budgets, include a copy of documents establishing the entity, or the proposed documents to be used in establishing it.

[40 FR 3587, Jan. 23, 1975. Redesignated at 47 FR 13327, Mar. 30, 1982, as amended at 57 FR 46471, Oct. 8, 1992]

§ 101.5 Approval of loans.

(a) Loan agreements, including those used by relending organizations in operating a relending program, must be executed on a form approved by the Commissioner. On direct United States loans, the Commissioner will approve the loan by issuing a commitment order covering the terms and conditions for making the loan.

(b) Applications for loans from relending organizations must be approved, if a tribe, by the governing body or designated committee, or other approving committee or body authorized to act on credit matters for a relending organization, before the Commissioner takes action on the application. This designated governing body of the tribe or committee must be authorized to act on behalf of the relending organization as evidenced in the organization's declaration of policy and plan of operation.

(c) Corporations, partnerships and cooperative associations organized for the purpose of establishing, acquiring, expanding, and operating an economic enterprise shall be organized pursuant to federal, state or tribal law. The form of organization shall be acceptable to the Commissioner. Economic enterprises which are or will be operated on a reservation(s) must comply with the requirements of applicable rules, resolutions and ordinances enacted by the governing body of the tribe.

§ 101.6 Modification of loans.

(a) *United States direct loans.* Any modification of the terms and provisions of a United States direct loan agreement must be requested in writing by the borrower and approved by the Commissioner. The borrower will submit the request for modification and will indicate the section(s) of the loan agreement to be modified together with a justification for the modification. Requests for modifications of loan agreements will include an agreement to abide by the provisions of the regulations in this part and future amendments and modifications thereof. In addition, a current credit bureau report, obtained by the Bureau of Indian Affairs, will be made a part of the modification request.

(b) *Relending program.* Any modification of the terms and provisions of a loan agreement of a borrower from an organization conducting a relending program must be in writing, agreed to by the borrower, and must be approved by the body authorized to act on loans and modifications thereof as provided in an approved declaration of policy and plan of operation or other plan. If a request for modification of a loan has been disapproved by the body authorized to act on the request, the rejected borrower may request the Commissioner to make a direct loan from the revolving loan fund if the Commissioner determines that the rejection is unwarranted.

[40 FR 3587, Jan. 23, 1975. Redesignated at 47 FR 13327, Mar. 30, 1982, as amended at 57 FR 46472, Oct. 8, 1992]

§ 101.7 Management and technical assistance.

Prior to and concurrent with the approval of a United States direct loan to finance an economic enterprise, the Commissioner will assure under title V of the Indian Financing Act of 1974 that competent management and technical assistance is available to the loan applicant for preparation of the application and/or administration of funds loaned consistent with the nature of the enterprise proposed to be or in fact funded by the loan. Assistance may be provided by available Bureau of Indian Affairs staff, the tribe or other sources which the Commissioner considers competent to provide needed assistance. Contracting for management and technical assistance may be used only when adequate assistance is not available without additional cost. Contracts for providing borrowers with competent management and technical assistance shall be in accordance with applicable Federal Procurement Regulations and the Buy Indian Act of April 30, 1908, chapter 153 (35 Stat. 71), as amended June 25, 1910, chapter 431, section 25 (36 Stat. 861).

[40 FR 3587, Jan. 23, 1975. Redesignated at 47 FR 13327, Mar. 30, 1982, as amended at 54 FR 34975, Aug. 23, 1989]

§ 101.8 Environmental and Flood Disaster Acts.

Loans will not be approved until there is assurance of compliance with any applicable provisions of the Flood Disaster Protection Act of 1973 (Pub. L. 93–234, 87 Stat. 975), the National Environmental Policy Act of 1969 (Pub. L. 91–190), (42 U.S.C. 4321) and Executive Order 11514.

§ 101.9 Preservation of historical and archeological data.

(a) On United States direct loans from the revolving loan fund and modifications thereof to provide additional loan funds which will involve excavations, road or street construction, land development or disturbance of land on known or reported historical or archeological sites, the Commissioner will take or require appropriate action to assure compliance with the applicable provisions of the Act of June 27, 1960 (74 Stat. 220; (16 U.S.C. 469)), as amended by the Act of May 24, 1974 (Pub. L. 93–291, 88 Stat. 174).

(b) On loans made by relending organizations conducting a relending program using revolving loan funds, the body authorized to act on loan applications and modifications thereof will, at the time of taking action on a loan or request for modification, inform the applicant of the applicability of this Act to the loan and advise the Commissioner of compliance or the need to obtain compliance.

§ 101.10 Federal Reserve Regulation Z and Fair Credit Reporting Act.

(a) United States direct loans and loans made by a relending organization are subject to the provisions of Federal Reserve Regulation Z (Truth In Lending, 12 CFR part 226; Pub. L. 91–508, 84 Stat. 1127). Economic enterprises which extend credit and require payment of finance charges on unpaid balances will determine the applicability of Regulation Z and comply with the requirements thereof. The Commissioner will issue any necessary instructions to assure compliance with Regulation Z on United States direct loans.

(b) Relending organizations, through their committee or other body authorized to act on loan matters on its behalf, will assure compliance with the applicable provisions of this Act.

(c) The Commissioner will require adherence to the provisions and requirements of title VI of the Fair Credit Reporting Act in making United States direct loans. Relending organizations, through the body authorized to act on credit matters, will require compliance with the requirements of the Fair Credit Reporting Act.

§ 101.11 Interest.

(a) The interest to be charged on loans by the United States shall be at a rate determined by the Secretary of the Treasury in accordance with section 104, title I, of the Indian Financing Act of 1974 (Pub. L. 93-262, 88 Stat. 77). The interest rate shall be determined monthly and shall be effective on advances made on loans during the current calendar month. The interest rate shall be stated in the promissory note(s) executed by the borrower(s) evidencing the advance(s).

(b) Additional charges to cover loan administration costs, including credit reports, may be charged to borrowers.

(c) Education loans may provide for deferral of interest while the borrower is in school full time or in the military service.

(d) The interest rate on loans made by relending organizations which are conducting relending programs shall not be less than the rate the organization pays on its loan(s) from the United States. Relending organizations which adopt and follow the same procedure in calculating interest on educational loans as is followed on educational loans made by the United States, will not be charged interest on loans from the United States on the amount outstanding on educational loans during the period the organization is not charging its borrowers interest.

(e) Interest rates on loan advances made by the United States as shown on promissory notes dated before April 12, 1974, will remain in effect until the loan is paid in full, refinanced, or modified to extend the repayment terms. Unless otherwise specifically provided in a loan contract, the interest rate on advances made after April 12, 1974, will be at a rate determined pursuant to section 104 of title I of the Indian Financing Act of 1974. The interest rate on loans for expert assistance will be at a rate established in § 101.25 herein.

[40 FR 3587, Jan. 23, 1975. Redesignated at 47 FR 13327, Mar. 30, 1982, as amended at 57 FR 46472, Oct. 8, 1992]

§ 101.12 Records and reports.

Loan agreements between the United States and tribes, corporations, partnerships, cooperative associations and individual Indians for financing economic enterprises, and to relending organizations, will require that borrowers establish and maintain accounting and operating records that are satisfactory to the Commissioner and submit written reports as required by the Commissioner. The records, accounts, and loan files shall be available for examination and audit by the Commissioner at any reasonable time. Unless an exception is approved by the Commissioner, borrowers will be required to have an annual audit made of the records of relending programs and economic enterprises financed with revolving loan funds, by a certified public accountant or a firm of certified public accountants or other qualified public accountants satisfactory to the Commissioner.

§ 101.13 Security.

(a) United States direct loans shall be secured by such security as the Commissioner may require. A lack of security will not preclude the making of a loan if the proposed use of the funds is sound and the information in the application and supporting papers correctly show that expected income will be adequate to pay all expenses and the loan principal and interest payments, indicating reasonable assurance that the loan will be repaid. Loans made by relending organizations conducting a relending program using revolving loan funds will require borrowers to give security for loans, if available, but the absence of security will not preclude the making of a loan if the proposed use of the funds is sound and the information in the application and supporting papers correctly show that expected income will be adequate to pay all expenses and the loan principal and interest payments, indicating reasonable assurance that the loan will be repaid. The declaration of policy and plan of operation of relending organizations conducting relending programs will include provisions covering the type and amount of security to be taken to secure loans made.

(b) Land purchased by an individual Indian with the proceeds of a loan and land already held in trust or restricted status by the individual Indian may be mortgaged as security for a loan in accordance with 25 CFR 152.34 and the Act of March 29, 1956 (70 Stat. 62; (25 U.S.C. 483a)). Mortgages of individually held trust or restricted land will include only an acreage of the borrower's land which the Commissioner determines is necessary to protect the loan in case of default. On proposed foreclosures which involve the sale of individually held trust or restricted land given as security for a loan, the tribe of the reservation on which the land is located will be notified in writing at least thirty calendar days in advance of the anticipated date of sale. Land purchased by a tribe with the proceeds of a loan from the revolving loan fund with title taken in a trust or restricted status, and land already held in a trust or restricted status by a tribe may not be mortgaged as security for a loan.

(1) Title to any land purchased by a tribe or by an individual Indian with revolving loan funds may be taken in trust or restricted status unless the land is located outside the boundaries of a reservation or a tribal consolidation area approved by the Secretary. Title to any land purchased by a tribe or an individual Indian which is outside the boundaries of a reservation or approved consolidation area may be taken in trust if the purchaser was the owner of trust or restricted interests in the land before the purchase. Otherwise, title shall be taken in the name of the purchaser without any restrictions on alienation, control, or use.

(c) Mortgages of leasehold interests in land held in trust or restricted status by an individual Indian, may be taken for the purpose of borrowing capital for the development and improvement of the leased premises when permitted in the lease or lease modification agreement. Such mortgages must be approved by the lessor and Commissioner. (70 Stat. 62, (25 U.S.C. 483a)).

(d) Individuals may give assignments of income from trust property as security for loans. Tribes may give assignments of trust income as security for loans provided that the assignment shall be specific as to the source(s) of income being assigned. All assignments of trust income require approval by the Commissioner before becoming effective.

(e) Chattels may be given as security for a loan. A mortgage on chattels, the title to which is known to be in trust, requires Commissioner approval. Non-trust chattels may be mortgaged without approval of any federal official.

(f) Crops grown on lands held in trust or restricted status for the benefit of an individual Indian may be given as security for a loan when approved by the Commissioner. Crops grown on leased, trust or restricted land may be given as security for a loan when permitted by the provisions of a lease or when the owner gives written consent. Approval of the lien document by the Commissioner is required. Crops grown on trust or restricted land held by a tribe which has been assigned to an individual for use may be given as security for a loan, provided the terms of the assignment permit the assignee to give the crops as security for a loan or the tribe's governing body specifically gives consent. The lien document requires Commissioner approval. Crops grown on non-trust or non-restricted land may be mortgaged without the approval of any federal official.

(g) Title to any personal property purchased with a loan shall be taken in the name of the purchaser and mortgaged to secure the loan unless the loan is otherwise adequately secured. Tribes must adhere to the provisions of their constitutions and bylaws, corporate charters, or other organizational documents when mortgaging tribal property and assigning trust income as security for loans.

(h) Relending organizations receiving a loan from the United States for relending shall be required to assign to the United States as security for the loan all securities acquired in connection with loans made to its members, sub-organizations, or associations from such funds, unless the Commissioner determines that repayment of the loan to the United States is otherwise reasonably assured. Funds advanced to finance a tribal economic enterprise shall be secured by an assignment of net income and net assets of the economic enterprise, unless the Commissioner determines that it is not feasible to require an assignment or that repayment of the loan to the United States is otherwise reasonably assured.

(i) Securing documents or financing statements shall be filed or recorded in accordance with applicable state or federal laws except for those customarily filed in Bureau of Indian Affairs offices. Mortgages on documented vessels will be filed at the customs house designated as the home port of the vessel as shown on the marine document.

§101.14 Maturity.

The maturity of any United States direct loan shall not exceed thirty years. Loans made will be scheduled for repayment at the earliest possible date consistent with the purpose of the loan and the repayment capacity of the borrower.

§101.15 Penalties on default.

Unless otherwise provided in the loan agreement between the United States and a borrower, failure on the part of a borrower to conform to the terms of the loan agreement will be deemed grounds for the taking of any one or all of the following steps by the Commissioner:

(a) Discontinue any further advance of funds contemplated by the loan agreement.

(b) Take possession of any or all collateral given as security and in the case of individuals, corporation, partnerships or cooperative associations, the property purchased with the borrowed funds.

(c) Prosecute legal action against the borrower or against officers of corporations, tribes, bands, credit associations, cooperative associations, and other organizations.

(d) Declare the entire amount advanced immediately due and payable.

(e) Prevent further disbursement of credit funds under the control of the borrower.

(f) Withdraw any unobligated funds from the borrower.

(g) Require relending organizations conducting a relending program to apply all collections on loans to liquidate the debt to the United States.

(h) Take possession of the assets of a relending organization conducting a relending program and exercise or arrange to exercise its powers until the Commissioner has received acceptable assurance of its repayment of the revolving loan and compliance with the provisions of the terms of the loan agreement.

(i) Liquidate, operate or arrange for the operation of economic enterprises financed with revolving loans made to individuals, tribes, corporations, partnerships and cooperative associations until the indebtedness is paid or until the Commissioner has received acceptable assurance of its repayment and compliance with the terms of the loan agreement.

(j) Report the name and account information of a delinquent borrower to a credit bureau.

(k) Assess additional interest and penalty charges for the period of time that payment is not made.

(l) Assess charges to cover additional administrative costs incurred by the Government to service the account.

(m) Offset amounts owed the borrower under other Federal programs including other programs administered by the Bureau of Indian Affairs.

(n) Refer the account to a private collection agency to collect the amount due.

(o) Refer the account to the U.S. Department of Justice for collection by litigation.

(p) If the borrower is a current or retired Federal employee, take action to offset the borrower's salary or civil service retirement benefits.

(q) Refer the debt to the Internal Revenue Service for offset against any amount owed the borrower as an income tax refund.

(r) Report any written-off debt to the Internal Revenue Service as taxable income to the borrower.

(s) Recommend suspension or debarment from conducting further business with the Federal Government.

[40 FR 3587, Jan. 23, 1975. Redesignated at 47 FR 13327, Mar. 30, 1982, as amended at 57 FR 46472, Oct. 8, 1992]

§ 101.16 Default on loans made by relending organizations.

Relending organizations conducting relending programs using revolving loan funds will follow prudent lending practices in making and servicing loans and take appropriate actions to protect their interests in the security given to secure repayment of loans. Declarations of policy and plans of operation shall include procedures which will be followed in acting to correct a default, such as modification of loan agreement or foreclosure and liquidation of security. Relending organizations employing a general counsel will refer legal questions on foreclosure procedures and sale of security to their counsel.

§ 101.17 Uncollectable loans made by the United States.

If the Secretary determines that a United States direct loan is uncollectable in whole or in part or is collectable only at an unreasonable cost, or when such action would be in the best interest of the United States, the Secretary may cancel, adjust, compromise, or reduce the amount of any loan made from the revolving loan fund. The Commissioner may adjust, compromise, subordinate, or modify the terms of any mortgage, lease, assignment, contract, agreement, or other document taken as security for loans. The cancellation of all or part of a loan shall become effective when signed by the Secretary.

[54 FR 34975, Aug. 23, 1989]

§ 101.18 Uncollectible loans made by relending organizations.

(a) Relending organizations conducting relending programs using revolving loan funds may, when approved by the Commissioner, chargeoff as uncollectible all or part of the balance of principal and interest owing on loans which are considered to be uncollectible. Usually a chargeoff includes both principal and interest and provides for cessation of interest accruals on the principal balance owing as of the date of the chargeoff.

(b) Action to chargeoff a loan will be in the form of a resolution enacted by the committee or body authorized and responsible for actions on loan matters for the relending organization. Before action is taken to chargeoff a loan as uncollectible, the lender will make an effort, to the extent feasible, to liquidate the security given for a loan and apply the net proceeds as a repayment on the balance of principal and interest owed. The chargeoff of a loan by a relending organization as uncollectible will not reduce the principal balance owed to the United States. A chargeoff will not release the borrower of the obligation or the responsibility to make payments when his or her financial situation will permit. Chargeoff action will not release the lender of responsibility to continue its efforts to collect the loan.

§101.19 Assignment of loans.

A borrower of a direct loan from the United States may not assign the loan agreement or any interest in it to a third party without the consent of the Commissioner. Relending organizations which are conducting relending programs may not assign the loan agreements of borrowers, or any interest therein, to third parties without the approval of the Commissioner and the borrower.

§101.20 Relending by borrower.

(a) A relending organization may reloan funds loaned to it by the United States with the approval of the Commissioner. The Commissioner may authorize such lenders to approve applications for particular types of loans up to a specified amount.

(b) Loans shall be secured by such securities as the lender and the Commissioner may require. With the Commissioner's approval, mortgages of individually held trust or restricted land, leasehold interests, chattels, crops grown on trust or restricted land, and assignments of trust income may all be taken as security for loans.

(c) Title to personal property purchased with loans received from relending organizations using revolving loan funds in its relending program shall be taken in the name of the borrower.

(d) The term of a loan made by a relending organization conducting a relending program shall not extend beyond the maturity date of its loan from the United States, unless an exception is approved by the Commissioner and the organization has funds available from which to make scheduled repayment on its loan from the United States. Loans made will be scheduled for repayment at the earliest possible date consistent with the purpose for which a loan is made and the indicated repayment capacity of the borrower.

(e) Securing documents or financing statements shall be filed or recorded in accordance with federal or state law except those customarily filed in Bureau of Indian Affairs offices. Mortgages on documented vessels will be filed at the custom house designated as the home port of the vessel as shown on the marine document.

[40 FR 3587, Jan. 23, 1975. Redesignated at 47 FR 13327, Mar. 30, 1982. Further redesignated and amended at 57 FR 46472, Oct. 8, 1992]

§101.21 Repayments on United States direct loans.

Repayments on United States direct loans shall be made to the authorized collection officer of the Bureau of Indian Affairs who shall issue an official receipt for the repayment and deposit the collection into the revolving loan fund. Collections will first be applied to pay interest to date of payment and the balance applied on the principal installment due. Collections on loans made by relending organizations which have been declared in default in which the Commissioner has taken control of the assets of the program (including loans made with balances owing) will be made to an authorized collection officer of the Bureau of Indian Affairs who shall issue a receipt to the payor and deposit the collection in the United States revolving loan fund. The relending organization's loan from the United States will be credited with the amounts collected from its borrowers, with the collections applied first on interest accrued and the balance applied to the principal. Payments on United States direct loans may be made in advance of due dates without penalty.

[40 FR 3587, Jan. 23, 1975. Redesignated at 47 FR 13327, Mar. 30, 1982. Further redesignated at 57 FR 46472, Oct. 8, 1992]

§ 101.22 Repayments on loans made by relending organizations.

Repayments on loans made by a relending organization conducting a relending program will be made to the officers of the lending organization or individuals designated and authorized in a declaration of policy and plan of operation. Collections on loans and other income to a relending program will be deposited in the lender's revolving loan account as designated in a declaration of policy and plan of operation. Collections on loans will be first applied to pay interest to date of payment with the balance applied to the principal.

[40 FR 3587, Jan. 23, 1975. Redesignated at 47 FR 13327, Mar. 30, 1982. Further redesignated at 57 FR 46472, Oct. 8, 1992]

§ 101.23 Approval of articles of association and bylaws.

Articles of association and bylaws of relending organizations and cooperative associations require approval of the Commissioner if they make application for a revolving credit loan.

[40 FR 3587, Jan. 23, 1975. Redesignated at 47 FR 13327, Mar. 30, 1982. Further redesignated at 57 FR 46472, Oct. 8, 1992]

§ 101.24 Loans for expert assistance for preparation and trial of Indian claims.

(a) Loans may be made to Indian tribes, bands and other identifiable groups of Indians from funds authorized and appropriated under the provisions of section 1 of the Act of November 4, 1963 (Pub. L. 88–168, 77 Stat. 301; 25 U.S.C. 70n–1), as amended by the Act of September 19, 1966 (Pub. L. 89–592, 80 Stat. 814) and section 2 of the Act of May 24, 1973 (Pub. L. 93–37, 87 Stat. 73). Loan proceeds may only be used for the employment of expert assistance, other than the assistance of counsel, for the preparation and trial of claims pending before the Indian Claims Commission. Applications for loans will be submitted on forms approved by the Commissioner and shall include a justification of the need for a loan. The justification shall include a statement from the applicant's claims attorney regarding the need for a loan. The application will be accompanied by a statement signed by an authorized officer of the applicant certifying that the applicant does not have adequate funds available to obtain and pay for the expert assistance needed. The Superintendent and the Area Director will attest to the accuracy of the statement or point out any inaccuracies. Loans will be approved by issuance of a commitment order by the Commissioner.

(b) No loan shall be approved if the applicant has funds available on deposit in the United States Treasury or elsewhere in an amount adequate to obtain the expert assistance needed or if, in the opinion of the Commissioner, the fees to be paid the experts are unreasonable on the basis of the services to be performed by them.

(c) Contracts for the employment of experts are subject to the provisions of 25 U.S.C. 81 and require approval by the Commissioner.

(d) Vouchers or claims submitted by experts for payment for services rendered and reimbursement for expenses will be in accordance with the provisions of the expert assistance contract and shall be sufficiently detailed and itemized to permit an audit to determine that the amounts are in accordance with the contract. Vouchers or claims shall be reviewed by the borrower's claims attorney who will certify on the last page of the voucher or by attachment thereto, that the services have been rendered and payment is due the expert and that expenses and charges for work performed are in accordance with the provisions of the contract.

(e) Requests for advances under the loan agreement shall be accompanied by a certificate signed by an authorized officer of the borrower certifying that the borrower does not have adequate funds available from its own financial resources with which to pay the expert. The Superintendent and Area Director will attest to the accuracy of the statement or point out inaccuracies. A copy of the voucher or claim from the expert will accompany the request for advance.

(f) Loan funds will be advanced only as needed to pay obligations incurred under approved contracts for expert assistance. The funds will be deposited in a separate account, shall not be commingled with other funds of the borrower, and shall not be disbursed for any other purpose.

(g) Loans shall bear interest at the rate of 5½ percent per annum from the date funds are advanced until the loan is repaid.

(h) The principal amount of the loan advanced plus interest shall be repayable from the proceeds of any judgment received by the borrower at the time funds from the award become available to make the payment.

(77 Stat. 301 (25 U.S.C. 70n-1 to 70n-7))

[40 FR 3587, Jan. 23, 1975. Redesignated at 47 FR 13327, Mar. 30, 1982. Further redesignated at 57 FR 46472, Oct. 8, 1992]

§ 101.25 Information collection.

(a) The collections of information contained in §§ 101.3, 101.4, 101.12, and 101.25 have been approved by the Office of Management and Budget under 44 U.S.C. 3501 *et seq.* and assigned clearance number 1076–0020. The information will be used to rate applicants in accordance with the terms and conditions set forth in section 103 of the Indian Financing Act, as amended. Response is required to obtain a benefit in accordance with 25 U.S.C. 1451.

(b) Public reporting burden for this information is estimated to vary from 15 minutes to 3 hours per response, with an average of one hour per response, including the time for reviewing instructions, searching existing data sources, gathering and maintaining the data needed, and completing and reviewing the collection of information. Send comments regarding this burden estimate or any other aspects of this collection of information, including suggestions for reducing the burden, to the Information Collection Clearance Officer, Bureau of Indian Affairs, Mailstop 337–SIB, 18th and C Streets NW., Washington, DC 20240; and the Paperwork Reduction Project (1076–0020), Office of Management and Budget, Washington, DC 20503.

[54 FR 34975, Aug. 23, 1989. Redesignated at 57 FR 46472, Oct. 8, 1992]

PART 103—LOAN GUARANTY, INSURANCE, AND INTEREST SUBSIDY

Subpart A—General Provisions

Subpart B—How a Lender Obtains a Loan Guaranty or Insurance Coverage

Subpart C—Interest Subsidy

AUTHORITY: 25 U.S.C. 1498, 1511.

SOURCE: 66 FR 3867, Jan. 17, 2001, unless otherwise noted.

Subpart A—General Provisions

§ 103.1 What does this part do?

This part explains how to obtain and use a BIA loan guaranty or loan insurance agreement under the Program, and who may do so. It also describes how to obtain and use interest subsidy payments under the Program, and who may do so.

§ 103.2 Who does the Program help?

The purpose of the Program is to encourage eligible borrowers to develop viable Indian businesses through conventional lender financing. The direct function of the Program is to help lenders reduce excessive risks on loans they make. That function in turn helps borrowers secure conventional financing that might otherwise be unavailable.

§ 103.3 Who administers the Program?

Authority for administering the Program ultimately rests with the Secretary, who may exercise that authority directly at any time. Absent a direct exercise of authority, however, the Secretary delegates Program authority to BIA officials through the U.S. Department of Interior Departmental Manual. A lender should submit all applications and correspondence to the BIA office serving the borrower's location.

§ 103.4 What kinds of loans will BIA guarantee or insure?

In general, BIA may guarantee or insure any loan made by an eligible lender to an eligible borrower to conduct a lawful business organized for profit. There are several important exceptions:

(a) The business must contribute to the economy of an Indian reservation or tribal service area recognized by BIA;

(b) The borrower may not use the loan for relending purposes;

(c) If any portion of the loan is used to refinance an existing loan, the borrower must be current on the existing loan; and

(d) BIA may not guarantee or insure a loan if it believes the lender would be willing to extend the requested financing without a BIA guaranty or insurance coverage.

§ 103.5 What size loan will BIA guarantee or insure?

BIA can guarantee or insure a loan or combination of loans of up to $500,000 for an individual Indian, or more for an acceptable Indian business entity, Tribe, or tribal enterprise involving two or more persons. No individual Indian may have an outstanding principal balance of more than $500,000 in guaranteed or insured loans at any time. BIA can limit the size of loans it will guarantee or insure, depending on the resources BIA has available.

§ 103.6 To what extent will BIA guarantee or insure a loan?

(a) BIA can guarantee up to 90 percent of the unpaid principal and accrued interest due on a loan.

(b) BIA can insure up to the lesser of:

(1) 90 percent of the unpaid principal and accrued interest due on a loan; or

(2) 15 percent of the aggregate outstanding principal amount of all loans the lender has insured under the Program as of the date the lender makes a claim under its insurance coverage.

(c) BIA's guaranty certificate or loan insurance agreement should reflect the lowest guaranty or insurance percentage rate that satisfies the lender's risk management requirements.

(d) Absent exceptional circumstances, BIA will allow no more than:

(1) Two simultaneous guarantees under the Program covering outstanding loans from the same lender to the same borrower; or

(2) One loan guaranty under the Program when the lender simultaneously has one or more outstanding loans insured under the Program to the same borrower.

§ 103.7 Must the borrower have equity in the business being financed?

The borrower must be projected to have at least 20 percent equity in the business being financed, immediately after the loan is funded. If a substantial portion of the loan is for construction or renovation, the borrower's equity may be calculated based upon the reasonable estimated value of the borrower's assets after completion of the construction or renovation.

§ 103.8 Is there any cost for a BIA guaranty or insurance coverage?

BIA charges the lender a premium for a guaranty or insurance coverage.

(a) The premium is:

(1) Two percent of the portion of the original loan principal amount that BIA guarantees; or

(2) One percent of the portion of the original loan principal amount that BIA insures, without considering the 15 percent aggregate outstanding principal limitation on the lender's insured loans.

(b) Lenders may pass the cost of the premium on to the borrower, either by charging a one-time fee or by adding the cost to the principal amount of the borrower's loan. Adding the premium to the principal amount of the loan will not make any further premium due. BIA will guarantee or insure the additional principal to the same extent as the original approved principal amount.

Subpart B—How a Lender Obtains a Loan Guaranty or Insurance Coverage

§ 103.9 Who applies to BIA under the Program?

The lender is responsible for determining whether it will require a BIA guaranty or insurance coverage, based upon the loan application it receives from an eligible borrower. If the lender requires a BIA guaranty or insurance coverage, the lender is responsible for completing and submitting a guaranty application or complying with a loan insurance agreement under the Program.

§ 103.10 What lenders are eligible under the Program?

(a) Except as specified in paragraph (b) of this section, a lender is eligible under the Program, and may be considered for BIA approval, if the lender is:

(1) Regularly engaged in the business of making loans;

(2) Capable of evaluating and servicing loans in accordance with reasonable and prudent industry standards; and

(3) Otherwise reasonably acceptable to BIA.

(b) The following lenders are not qualified to issue loans under the Program:

(1) An agency or instrumentality of the Federal Government;

(2) A lender that borrows money from any Federal Government source, other than the Federal Reserve Bank System, for purposes of relending;

(3) A lender that does not include the interest on loans it makes in gross income, for purposes of chapter 1, title 26 of the United States Code; and

(4) A lender that does not keep any ownership interest in loans it originates.

§ 103.11 How does BIA approve lenders for the Program?

(a) BIA approves each lender by entering into a loan guaranty agreement and/or a loan insurance agreement with it. BIA may provide up to three different levels of approval for a lender making guaranteed loans, depending on factors such as:

(1) The number of loans the lender makes under the Program;

(2) The total principal balance of the lender's Program loans;

(3) The number of years the lender has been involved with the Program;

(4) The relative benefits and opportunities the lender has given to Indian business efforts through the Program; and

(5) The lender's historical compliance with Program requirements.

(b) BIA will consider a lender's loan guaranty agreement and/or loan insurance agreement suspended as of:

(1) The effective date of a change in the lender's corporate structure;

(2) The effective date of a merger between the lender and any other entity, when the lender is not the surviving entity; or

(3) The start of any legal proceeding in which substantially all of the lender's assets may be subject to disposition through laws governing bankruptcy, insolvency, or receivership.

(c) A change in a lender's name, without any other change specified under paragraph (b) of this section, will not cause a suspension of the lender's loan guaranty agreement and/or loan insurance agreement. The lender should notify BIA of its name change as soon as possible.

(d) If a lender's loan guaranty agreement and/or loan insurance agreement is suspended under paragraph (b) of this section, the lender, or its successor in interest, must enter into a new loan guaranty agreement and/or loan insurance agreement with BIA in order to secure any new BIA loan guarantees or insurance coverage.

(e) The suspension of a loan guaranty agreement and/or loan insurance agreement does not affect the validity of any guaranty certificate or insurance coverage in effect before the date of the suspension. Any such certificate or insurance coverage will remain governed by applicable terms of the suspended loan guaranty agreement and/or loan insurance agreement.

§ 103.12 How does a lender apply for a loan guaranty?

To apply for a loan guaranty, a BIA-approved lender must submit to BIA a loan guaranty application request form, together with each of the following:

(a) A written explanation from the lender indicating why it needs a BIA guaranty for the loan, and the minimum loan guarantee percentage it will accept;

(b) A copy of the borrower's complete loan application;

(c) A description of the borrower's equity in the business being financed;

(d) A copy of the lender's independent credit analysis of the borrower's business, repayment ability, and loan collateral (including insurance);

(e) An original report from a nationally-recognized credit bureau, dated within 90 days of the date of the lender's loan guaranty application package, outlining the credit history of the borrower, and to the extent permitted by law, each co-maker or guarantor of the loan (if any);

(f) A copy of the lender's loan commitment letter to the borrower, showing at a minimum the proposed loan amount, purpose, interest rate, schedule of payments, and security (including insurance requirements), and the lender's terms and conditions for funding;

(g) The lender's good faith estimate of any loan-related fees and costs it will charge the borrower, as authorized under this part;

(h) If any significant portion of the loan will be used to finance construction, renovation, or demolition work, the lender's:

(1) Insurance and bonding requirements for the work;

(2) Proposed draw requirements; and

(3) Proposed work inspection procedures;

(i) If any significant portion of the loan will be used to refinance or otherwise retire existing indebtedness:

(1) A clear description of all loans being paid off, including the names of all makers, cosigners and guarantors, maturity dates, payment schedules, uncured delinquencies, collateral, and payoff amounts as of a specific date; and

(2) A comparison of the terms of the loan or loans being paid off and the terms of the new loan, identifying the advantages of the new loan over the loan being paid off.

§ 103.13 How does a lender apply for loan insurance coverage?

BIA-approved lenders can make loans insured under the Program in two ways, depending on the size of the loan:

(a) For loans in an original principal amount of up to $100,000 per borrower, the lender can make each loan in accordance with the lender's loan insurance agreement, without specific prior approval from BIA.

(b) For loans in an original principal amount of over $100,000, the lender must seek BIA's specific prior approval in each case. The lender must submit a loan insurance coverage application request form, together with the same information required for a loan guaranty under § 103.12, except for the information required by § 103.12(a).

(c) The lender must submit a loan insurance application package even for a loan of less than $100,000 if:

(1) The total outstanding balance of all insured loans the lender is extending to the borrower under the Program exceeds $100,000; or

(2) the lender makes a request for interest subsidy, pursuant to § 103.21.

§ 103.14 Can BIA request additional information?

BIA may require the lender to provide additional information, whenever BIA believes it needs the information to properly evaluate a new lender, guaranty application, or insurance application. After BIA issues a loan guaranty or insurance coverage, the lender must let BIA inspect the lender's records at any reasonable time for information concerning the Program.

§ 103.15 Are there any prohibited loan terms?

A loan agreement guaranteed or insured under the Program may not contain:

(a) Charges by the lender styled as "points," loan origination fees, or any similar fees (however named), except that if authorized in the loan agreement, the lender may charge the borrower a reasonable annual loan servicing fee that:

(1) Is not included as part of the loan principal; and

(2) Does not bear interest;

(b) Charges of any kind by the lender or by any third party except for the reasonable and customary cost of legal and architectural services, broker commissions, surveys, compliance inspections, title inspection and/or insurance, lien searches, appraisals, recording costs, premiums for required hazard, liability, key man life, and other kinds of insurance, and such other charges as BIA may approve in writing;

(c) A loan repayment term of over 30 years;

(d) Payments scheduled less frequently than annually;

(e) A prepayment penalty, unless the terms of the penalty are clearly specified in BIA's loan guaranty or loan insurance conditions;

(f) An interest rate greater than what BIA considers reasonable, taking into account the range of rates prevailing in the private market for similar loans;

(g) A variable interest rate, unless the rate is tied to a specific prime rate published from time to time by a nationally recognized financial institution or news source;

(h) An increased rate of interest based on default;

(i) A fee imposed for the late repayment of any installment due, except for a late fee that:

(1) Is imposed only after the borrower is at least 30 days late with payment;

(2) Does not bear interest; and

(3) Equals no more than 5 percent of the late installment;

(j) An "insecurity" clause, or any similar provision permitting the lender to declare a loan default solely on the basis of its subjective view of the borrower's changed repayment prospects;

(k) A requirement that the borrower take title to any real or personal property purchased with loan proceeds by a title instrument containing restrictions on alienation, control or use of the property, unless otherwise required by applicable law; or

(l) A requirement that a borrower which is a tribe provide as security a general assignment of the tribe's trust income. If otherwise lawful, a tribe may provide as loan security an assignment of trust income from a specific source.

§ 103.16 How does BIA approve or reject a loan guaranty or insurance application?

(a) BIA reviews each guaranty or insurance application, and may evaluate each loan application independently from the lender. BIA bases its loan guaranty or insurance decisions on many factors, including compliance with this part, and whether there is a reasonable prospect of loan repayment from business cash flow, or if necessary, from liquidating loan collateral. Lenders are expected to obtain a first lien security interest in enough collateral to reasonably secure repayment of each loan guaranteed or insured under the Program, to the extent that collateral is available.

(b) BIA approves applications by issuing an approval letter, followed by the procedures in § 103.18. If the guaranty or insurance application is incomplete, BIA may return the application to the lender, or hold the application while the lender submits the missing information. If BIA denies the application, it will provide the lender with a written explanation, with a copy to the borrower.

§ 103.17 Must the lender follow any special procedures to close the loan?

(a) BIA officials or their representatives may attend the closing of any loan or loan modification that BIA agrees to guarantee or insure. For guaranteed loans, and insured loans that BIA must individually review under this part, the lender must give BIA notice of the date of closing at least 5 business days before closing occurs.

(b) At or prior to closing, the lender must obtain appropriate, satisfactory title and/or lien searches for each asset to be used as loan collateral.

(c) At or prior to closing, the lender must obtain recent appraisals for all real property and improvements to be used as collateral for the loan, to the extent required by law.

(d) At or prior to closing, the lender must document that the lender and borrower have complied with all applicable Federal, State, local, and tribal laws implicated by financing the borrower's business, for example by securing:

(1) Copies of all permits and licenses required to operate the borrower's business;

(2) Environmental studies required for construction and/or business operations under NEPA and other environmental laws;

(3) Archeological or historical studies required by law; and

(4) Certification by a registered surveyor or appropriate BIA official indicating that the proposed business will not be located in a special flood hazard area, as defined by applicable law.

(e) The lender must supply BIA with copies of all final, signed loan closing documents within 30 days following closing. To the extent applicable, loan closing documents must include the following:

(1) Promissory notes;

(2) Security agreements, including pledge and similar agreements, and related financing statements (together

with BIA's written approval of any assignment of specific tribal trust assets under § 103.15(l), or of any security interest in an individual Indian money account);

(3) Mortgage instruments or deeds of trust (together with BIA's written approval, if required by 25 U.S.C. 483a, or if the mortgage is of a leasehold interest in tribal trust property);

(4) Guarantees (other than from BIA);

(5) Construction contracts, and plans and specifications;

(6) Leases related to the business (together with BIA's written approval, if required under 25 CFR part 162);

(7) Attorney opinion letters;

(8) Resolutions made by a Tribe or business entity;

(9) Waivers or partial waivers of sovereign immunity; and

(10) Similar instruments designed to document the loan, establish the basis for a security interest in loan collateral, and comply with applicable law.

(f) Unless BIA indicates otherwise in writing, the lender must close a guaranteed or insured loan within 90 days of any approval provided under § 103.16.

§ 103.18 How does BIA issue a loan guaranty or confirm loan insurance?

(a) A loan is guaranteed under the Program when all of the following occur:

(1) BIA issues a signed loan guaranty certificate bearing a series number, an authorized signature, a guaranty percentage rate, the lender's name, the borrower's name, the original principal amount of the loan, and such other terms and conditions as BIA may require;

(2) The loan closes and funds;

(3) The lender pays BIA the applicable loan guaranty premium; and

(4) The lender meets all of the conditions listed in the loan guaranty certificate.

(b) A loan is insured under the Program when all of the following occur:

(1) The loan's purpose and terms meet the requirements of the Program and the lender's loan insurance agreement with BIA;

(2) The loan closes and funds;

(3) The lender notifies BIA of the borrower's identity and organizational structure, the amount of the loan, the interest rate, the payment schedule, and the date on which the loan closing and funding occurred;

(4) The lender pays BIA the applicable loan insurance premium;

(5) If over $100,000 or if the loan requires interest subsidy, BIA approves the loan in writing; and

(6) If over $100,000 or if the loan requires interest subsidy, the lender meets all of the conditions listed in BIA's written loan approval.

§ 103.19 When must the lender pay BIA the loan guaranty or insurance premium?

The premium is due within 30 calendar days of the loan closing. If not paid on time, BIA will send the lender written notice by certified mail (return receipt requested), or by a nationally-recognized overnight delivery service (signature of recipient required), stating that the premium is due immediately. If the lender fails to make the premium payment within 30 calendar days of the date of BIA's notice, BIA's guaranty certificate or insurance coverage with respect to that particular loan is void, without further action.

Subpart C—Interest Subsidy

§ 103.20 What is interest subsidy?

Interest subsidy is a payment BIA makes for the benefit of the borrower, to reimburse part of the interest payments the borrower has made on a loan guaranteed or insured under the Program. It is available to borrowers whose projected or historical earnings before interest and taxes, after adjustment for extraordinary items, is less than the industry norm.

§ 103.21 Who applies for interest subsidy payments, and what is the application procedure?

(a) An eligible lender must request interest subsidy payments on behalf of an eligible borrower, after determining that the borrower qualifies. Typically, the lender should include a request for interest subsidy at the time it applies for a guaranty or insurance coverage under the Program. A request for interest subsidy must be supported by the information required in §§ 103.12 and

103.13 (relating to loan guaranty and insurance coverage applications). BIA approves, returns, or rejects interest subsidy requests in the same manner indicated in § 103.16, based on the factors in § 103.20 and BIA's available resources.

(b) BIA's approval of interest subsidy for an insured loan may provide for specific limitations on the manner in which the lender and borrower can modify the loan.

§ 103.22 How does BIA determine the amount of interest subsidy?

Interest subsidy payments should equal the difference between the lender's rate of interest and the rate determined in accordance with 25 U.S.C. 1464. BIA will fix the amount of interest subsidy as of the date it approves the interest subsidy request.

[66 FR 3867, Jan. 17, 2001, as amended at 67 FR 63543, Oct. 15, 2002]

§ 103.23 How does BIA make interest subsidy payments?

The lender must send BIA reports at least quarterly on the borrower's loan payment history, together with a calculation of the interest subsidy then due. The lender's reports and calculation do not have to be in any specific format, but in addition to the calculation the reports must contain at least the information required by § 103.33(a). Based on the lender's reports and calculation, BIA will send interest subsidy payments to the borrower in care of the lender. The payments belong to the borrower, but the borrower and lender may agree in advance on how the borrower will use interest subsidy payments. BIA may verify and correct interest subsidy calculations and payments at any time.

§ 103.24 How long will BIA make interest subsidy payments?

(a) BIA will issue interest subsidy payments for the term of the loan, up to 3 years. If interest subsidy payments still are justified, the lender may apply for up to two 1-year extensions of this initial term. BIA will make interest subsidy payments on a single loan for no more than 5 years.

(b) BIA will choose the date from which it calculates interest subsidy years, usually the date the lender first extends the loan funds. Interest subsidy payments will apply to all loan payments made in the calendar years following that date.

(c) Interest subsidy payments will not be due for any loan payment made after the corresponding loan guaranty or insurance coverage stops under the Program, regardless of the circumstances.

Subpart D—Provisions Relating to Borrowers

§ 103.25 What kind of borrower is eligible under the Program?

(a) A borrower is eligible for a BIA-guaranteed or insured loan if the borrower is:

(1) An Indian individual;

(2) An Indian-owned business entity organized under Federal, State, or tribal law, with an organizational structure reasonably acceptable to BIA;

(3) A tribe; or

(4) A business enterprise established and recognized by a tribe.

(b) To be eligible for a BIA-guaranteed or insured loan, a business entity or tribal enterprise must be at least 51 percent owned by Indians. If at any time a business entity or tribal enterprise becomes less than 51 percent Indian owned, the lender either may declare a default as of the date the borrower stopped being at least 51 percent Indian owned and exercise its remedies under this part, or else continue to extend the loan to the borrower and allow BIA's guaranty or insurance coverage to become invalid.

[66 FR 3867, Jan. 17, 2001; 66 FR 46307, Sept. 4, 2001]

§ 103.26 What must the borrower supply the lender in its loan application?

The lender may use any form of loan application it chooses. However, the borrower must supply the lender the information listed in this section in order for BIA to process a guaranty or insurance coverage application:

(a) The borrower's precise legal name, address, and tax identification number or social security number;

(b) Proof of the borrower's eligibility under the Program;

(c) A statement signed by the borrower, indicating that it is not delinquent on any Federal tax or other debt obligation;

(d) The borrower's business plan, including resumes of all principals and a detailed discussion of the product or service to be offered, market factors, the borrower's marketing strategy, and any technical assistance the borrower may require;

(e) A detailed description of the borrower's equity in the business being financed, including the method(s) of valuation;

(f) The borrower's balance sheets and operating statements for the preceding 3 years, or so much of that period that the borrower has been in business;

(g) The borrower's current financial statement, and the financial statements of all co-makers and guarantors of the loan (other than BIA);

(h) At least 3 years of financial projections for the borrower's business, consisting of pro-forma balance sheets, operating statements, and cash flow statements;

(i) A detailed list of all proposed collateral for the loan, including asset values and the method(s) of valuation;

(j) A detailed list of all proposed hazard, liability, key man life, and other kinds of insurance the borrower will maintain on its business assets and operations;

(k) If any significant portion of the loan will be used to finance construction, renovation, or demolition work:

(1) Written quotes for the work from established and reputable contractors; and

(2) To the extent available, copies of all construction and architectural contracts for the work, plans and specifications, and applicable building permits;

(l) If the borrower is a tribe or a tribal enterprise, resolutions by the tribe and proof of authority under tribal law permitting the borrower to borrow the loan amount and offer the proposed loan collateral; and

(m) If the borrower is a business entity, resolutions by the appropriate governing officials and proof of authority under its organizing documents permitting the borrower to borrow the loan amount and offer the proposed loan collateral.

§ 103.27 Can the borrower get help preparing its loan application or putting its loan funds to use?

A borrower may seek BIA's assistance when preparing a loan application or when planning business operations, including assistance identifying and complying with applicable laws as indicated by § 103.17(d). The borrower should contact the BIA field or agency office serving the area in which the borrower's business is to be located, or if there is no separate field or agency office serving the area, then the borrower should contact the BIA regional office serving the area.

Subpart E—Loan Transfers

§ 103.28 What if the lender transfers part of the loan to another person?

(a) A lender may transfer one or more interests in a guaranteed loan to another person or persons, as long as the parties have in place an agreement that designates one person to perform all of the duties required of the lender under the Program and the loan guaranty certificate. Starting on the date of the transfer, only the person designated to perform the duties of the lender will be entitled to exercise the rights conferred by BIA's loan guaranty certificate, and will from that point forward be considered the lender for purposes of the Program. A lender under the Program must both service the guaranteed loan and own at least a 10 percent interest in the guaranteed loan. BIA will not consider more than one person at any given time to be the lender with respect to any loan guaranty certificate. If the person designated to perform the duties of the lender in an agreement among loan participants is not the original lender, then the provisions of § 103.29(a) will apply (relating to sale or assignment of guaranteed loans), and the person designated to perform the duties of the lender must give BIA notice of its interest in the loan. Failure to provide notice in accordance with § 103.29(a) will void BIA's loan guaranty certificate, without further action.

(b) Transferring any interest in an insured loan to another person will void the insurance coverage for that loan, except where the transfer is effected by a merger.

§ 103.29 What if the lender transfers the entire loan?

(a) A lender may transfer all of its rights in a guaranteed loan to any other person. The acquiring person must send BIA written notice of the transfer, describing the borrower, the loan, BIA's loan guaranty certificate number, and the acquiring person's name and address. Starting on the date of the transfer, only the acquiring person will be entitled to exercise the rights conferred by BIA's loan guaranty certificate, and will from that point forward be considered the lender for purposes of the Program. The acquiring person must service the guaranteed loan and otherwise perform all of the duties required of the lender under the Program and the loan guaranty certificate. Except when a transfer is effected by a merger, any failure by the acquiring person to send BIA proper notice of the transfer within 30 calendar days of the transfer date will void BIA's loan guaranty certificate, without further action.

(b) Transferring an insured loan to another person will void the insurance coverage for that loan, except where the transfer is effected by a merger.

(c) If a lender is not the surviving entity after a merger, the lender's successor must notify BIA in writing of the change within 30 calendar days of the merger. The lender also must reapply to become an approved lender under the Program, as indicated in § 103.11.

Subpart F—Loan Servicing Requirements

§ 103.30 What standard of care must a lender meet?

Lenders must service all loans guaranteed or insured under the Program in a commercially reasonable manner, in accordance with standards and procedures adopted by prudent lenders in the BIA region in which the borrower's business is located, and in accordance with this part. If the lender fails to follow any of these standards, BIA may reduce or eliminate entirely the amount payable under its guaranty or insurance coverage to the extent BIA can reasonably attribute the loss to the lender's failure. BIA also may deny payment completely if the lender gets a loan guaranty or insurance coverage through fraud, or negligently allows a borrower's fraudulent loan application or use of loan funds to go undetected. In particular, and without limitation, lenders must:

(a) Check and verify information contained in the borrower's loan application, such as the borrower's eligibility, the authority of persons acting on behalf of the borrower, and the title status of any proposed collateral;

(b) Take reasonable precautions to assure that loan proceeds are used as specified in BIA's guaranty certificate or written insurance approval, or if not so specified, then in descending order of importance:

(1) BIA's written loan guaranty approval;

(2) The loan documents;

(3) The terms of the lender's final loan commitment to the borrower; or

(4) The borrower's loan application;

(c) When feasible, require the borrower to use automatic bank account debiting to make loan payments;

(d) Require the borrower to take title to real and personal property purchased with loan proceeds in the borrower's own name, except for real property to be held in trust by the United States for the benefit of a borrower that is a tribe;

(e) Promptly record all security interests and subsequently keep them in effect. Lenders must record all mortgages and other security interests in accordance with State and local law, including the laws of any tribe that may have jurisdiction. Lenders also must record any leasehold mortgages or assignments of income involving individual Indian or tribal trust land with the BIA office having responsibility for maintaining records on that trust land;

(f) Assure, to the extent reasonably practicable, that the borrower and any guarantor of the loan (other than BIA) keep current on all taxes levied on real and personal property used in the borrower's business or as collateral for the loan, and on all applicable payroll taxes;

(g) Assure, to the extent reasonably practicable, that all required insurance policies remain in effect, including hazard, liability, key man life, and other kinds of insurance, in amounts reasonably necessary to protect the interests of the borrower, the borrower's business, and the lender;

(h) Assure, to the extent reasonably practicable, that the borrower remains in compliance with all applicable Federal, State, local and tribal laws, including environmental laws and laws concerning the preservation of historical and archeological sites and data;

(i) Assure, to the extent reasonably practicable, that the borrower causes any construction, renovation, or demolition work funded by the loan to proceed in accordance with approved construction contracts and plans and specifications, which must be sufficient in scope and detail to adequately govern the work;

(j) Reserve for itself and BIA the right to inspect the borrower's business records and all loan collateral at any reasonable time;

(k) Promptly notify the borrower in writing of any material breach by the borrower of the terms of its loan, with specific instructions on how to cure the breach and a deadline for doing so;

(l) Participate in any probate, receivership, bankruptcy, or similar proceeding involving the borrower and any guarantor or co-maker of the borrower's debt, to the extent necessary to maintain the greatest possible rights to repayment; and

(m) Otherwise seek to avoid and mitigate any potential loss arising from the loan, using at least that level of care the lender would use if it did not have a BIA loan guaranty or insurance coverage.

§ 103.31 What loan servicing requirements apply to BIA?

Once a lender extends a loan that is guaranteed or insured under the Program, BIA has no responsibility for decisions concerning it, except for:

(a) Any approvals required under this part;

(b) Any decisions reserved to BIA under conditions of BIA's guaranty certificate or insurance coverage; and

(c) Decisions concerning a loan that the lender has assigned to BIA or to which BIA is subrogated by virtue of paying a claim based on a guaranty certificate or insurance coverage.

§ 103.32 What sort of loan documentation does BIA expect the lender to maintain?

For every loan guaranteed or insured under the Program, the lender must maintain:

(a) BIA's original loan guaranty certificate or insurance coverage approval letter, if applicable;

(b) Original signed and/or certified counterparts of all final loan documents, including those listed in § 103.17 (concerning documents required for loan closing), all renewals, modifications, and additions to those documents, and signed settlement statements;

(c) Originals or copies, as appropriate, of all documents gathered by the lender under §§ 103.12, 103.13 and 103.26 (concerning information submitted by the borrower in its loan application, and information supplied to BIA in the lender's loan guaranty or insurance coverage application);

(d) Originals or copies, as appropriate, of all applicable insurance binders or certificates, including without limitation hazard, liability, key man life, and title insurance;

(e) A complete and current history of all loan transactions, including dated disbursements, payments, adjustments, and notes describing all contacts with the borrower;

(f) Originals or copies, as appropriate, of all correspondence with the borrower, including default notices and evidence of receipt;

(g) Originals or copies, as appropriate, of all correspondence, notices, news items or other information concerning the borrower, whether gathered by the lender or furnished to it, containing material information about the borrower and its business operations;

(h) Originals or copies, as appropriate, of all advertisements, notices, title instruments, accountings, and other documentation of efforts to liquidate loan collateral; and

(i) Originals or copies, as appropriate, of all notices, pleadings, motions, orders, and other documents associated with any legal proceeding involving the lender and the borrower or its assets, including without limitation judicial or non-judicial foreclosure proceedings, suits to collect payment, bankruptcy proceedings, probate proceedings, and any settlement associated with threatened or actual litigation.

§ 103.33 Are there reporting requirements?

(a) The lender must periodically report the borrower's loan payment history so that BIA can recalculate the government's contingent liability. Loan payment history reports must be quarterly unless BIA provides otherwise for a particular loan. These reports can be in any format the lender desires, as long as they contain:

(1) The lender's name;

(2) The borrower's name;

(3) A reference to BIA's Loan Guaranty Certificate or Loan Insurance Agreement number;

(4) The lender's internal loan number; and

(5) The date and amount of all loan balance activity for the reporting period.

(b) If applicable, the lender must supply a calculation of any interest subsidy payments that are due, as indicated in § 103.23.

(c) If there is a transfer of any or all of the lender's ownership interest in the loan, the party receiving the ownership interest may be required to notify BIA, as indicated in §§ 103.28 and 103.29.

(d) If there is a default on the loan, the lender must notify BIA, as indicated in §§ 103.35 and 103.36.

(e) If the borrower ceases to qualify for a BIA-guaranteed or insured loan under § 103.25(b), the lender must promptly notify BIA even if the lender does not pursue default remedies under §§ 103.35 and 103.36. This notice allows BIA to eliminate the guaranty or insurance coverage from its active recordkeeping system.

(f) If the loan is prepaid in full, the lender must promptly notify BIA in writing so that BIA can eliminate the guaranty or insurance coverage from its active recordkeeping system.

(g) If a lender changes its name, it should notify BIA in accordance with § 103.11(c).

§ 103.34 What if the lender and borrower decide to change the terms of the loan?

(a) The lender must obtain written BIA approval before modifying a loan guaranteed or insured under the Program, if the change will:

(1) Increase the borrower's outstanding principal amount (if a term loan), or maximum available credit (if a revolving loan).

(i) BIA will approve or disapprove a loan increase based upon the lender's explanation of the borrower's need for additional funding, and updated information of the sort required under §§ 103.12, 103.13, and 103.26, as applicable.

(ii) Upon approval by BIA and payment of an additional guaranty or insurance premium in accordance with §§ 103.8 and 103.19 and this section, the entire outstanding loan amount, as modified, will be guaranteed or insured (as the case may be) to the extent BIA specifies. The lender must pay the additional premium only on the increase in the outstanding principal amount of the loan (if a term loan) or the increase in the credit limit available to the borrower (if a revolving loan).

(iii) Lenders may not increase the outstanding principal amount of a loan guaranteed or insured under the Program if a significant purpose of doing so would be to allow the borrower to pay accrued loan interest it otherwise would have difficulty paying.

(2) Permanently adjust the loan repayment schedule.

(3) Increase a fixed interest rate, convert a fixed interest rate to an adjustable interest rate, or convert an adjustable interest rate to a fixed interest rate.

(4) Allow any changes in the identity or organizational structure of the borrower.

(5) Allow any material change in the use of loan proceeds or the nature of the borrower's business.

(6) Release any collateral taken as security for the loan, except items sold

in the ordinary course of business and promptly replaced by similar items of collateral, such as inventory.

(7) Allow the borrower to move any significant portion of its business operations to a location that is not on or near an Indian reservation or tribal service area recognized by BIA.

(8) Be likely to materially increase the risk of a claim on BIA's guaranty or insurance coverage, or materially reduce the aggregate value of the collateral securing the loan.

(9) Cure a default for which BIA is to receive notice under § 103.35(b).

(b) In the case of an insured loan, the amount of which will not exceed $100,000 when combined with all other insured loans from the lender to the borrower, the lender need not obtain BIA's prior approval to make any of the loan modifications indicated in § 103.34(a), except as provided in § 103.21(b). However, all loan modifications must remain consistent with the lender's loan insurance agreement with BIA, and in the event of an increase in the borrower's outstanding principal amount (if a term loan), or maximum available credit (if a revolving loan), the lender must send BIA an additional premium payment in accordance with §§ 103.8, 103.19 and this section. The lender must pay the additional premium only on the increase in the outstanding principal amount of the loan (if a term loan) or the increase in the credit limit available to the borrower (if a revolving loan). To the extent a loan modification changes any of the information supplied to BIA under § 103.18(b)(3), the lender also must promptly notify BIA of the new information.

(c) Subject to any applicable BIA loan guaranty or insurance coverage conditions, a lender may extend additional loans to a borrower without BIA approval, if the additional loans are not to be guaranteed or insured under the Program.

Subpart G—Default and Payment by BIA

§ 103.35 What must the lender do if the borrower defaults on the loan?

(a) The lender must send written notice of the default to the borrower, and otherwise meet the standard of care established for the lender in this part. The lender's notice to the borrower should be sent as soon as possible after the default, but in any event before the lender's notice to BIA under paragraph (b) of this section. For purposes of the Program, "default" will mean a default as defined in this part.

(b) The lender also must send written notice of the default to BIA by certified mail (return receipt requested), or by a nationally-recognized overnight delivery service (signature of recipient required) within 60 calendar days of the default, unless the default is fully cured before that deadline. This notice is required even if the lender grants the borrower a forbearance under § 103.36(a). One purpose of the notice is to give BIA the opportunity to intervene and seek assistance for the borrower, even though BIA has no duty, either to the lender or the borrower, to do so. Another purpose of the notice is to permit BIA to plan for a possible loss claim from the lender, under § 103.36(d). The lender's notice must clearly indicate:

(1) The identity of the borrower;

(2) The applicable Program guaranty certificate or insurance agreement number;

(3) The date and nature of all bases for default;

(4) If a monetary default, the amount of past due principal and interest, the date through which interest has been calculated, and the amount of any late fees, precautionary advances, or other amounts the lender claims;

(5) The nature and outcome of any correspondence or other contacts with the borrower concerning the default; and

(6) The precise nature of any action the borrower could take to cure the default.

§ 103.36 What options and remedies does the lender have if the borrower defaults on the loan?

(a) The lender may grant the borrower a temporary forbearance, even beyond any default cure periods specified in the loan documents, if doing so is likely to result in the borrower curing the default. However, BIA must approve in writing any forbearance or other agreement that:

(1) Permanently modifies the terms of the loan in any manner indicated by § 103.34(a);

(2) Would allow the borrower's default to extend beyond the deadline established in § 103.36(d) for the lender to elect a remedy; or

(3) Is not likely to result in the borrower curing the default.

(b) The lender may make precautionary advances on the borrower's behalf during the default, if doing so is reasonably necessary to ensure that loan recovery prospects do not significantly deteriorate. Items for which the lender may make precautionary advances include, for example:

(1) Hazard, liability, or key man life insurance premiums;

(2) Security measures to safeguard abandoned business assets;

(3) Real or personal property taxes;

(4) Corrective actions required by court or administrative orders; or

(5) Essential maintenance.

(c) BIA will guaranty or insure the amount of precautionary advances from the date of each advance to the same extent as other amounts due under the loan, if:

(1) The borrower has demonstrated its inability or unwillingness to make the payment or perform the duty that jeopardizes loan recovery, including by undue delay in making the payment or performing the duty;

(2) The total expense of all precautionary advances by the lender does not at the time of the advance exceed 10 percent of the outstanding principal balance of the loan;

(3) Where loan document provisions do not require the borrower to repay precautionary advances (however termed) when made by the lender, or where the total expense of all precautionary advances by the lender will exceed 10 percent of the outstanding principal balance of the loan when made, the lender secures BIA's prior written approval; and

(4) The lender properly claims and documents all precautionary advances, if and when it submits a claim for loss under § 103.37.

(d) If the default remains uncured, the lender must send BIA a written notice by certified mail (return receipt requested), or by a nationally-recognized overnight delivery service (signature of recipient required) within 90 calendar days of the default to select one of the following remedies:

(1) In the case of a guaranteed loan, the lender may submit a claim to BIA for its loss;

(2) In the case of either a guaranteed or insured loan, the lender may liquidate all collateral securing the loan, and upon completion, if it has a residual loss on the loan, it may submit a claim to BIA for that loss; or

(3) The lender may negotiate a loan modification agreement with the borrower to permanently change the terms of the loan in a manner that will cure the default. If the lender chooses this remedy, it may take no longer than 45 calendar days from the date BIA receives the notice of remedy selection to finalize a loan modification agreement and secure BIA's written approval of it, unless BIA specifically extends this deadline in writing. However, the lender may at any time before the expiration of the 45-day period (or any extension thereof) change its choice of remedy by sending BIA a notice otherwise complying with § 103.36(d)(1) or (2). If the lender fails to send BIA a notice changing its choice of remedy and does not finalize an approved loan modification agreement within the 45-day period (or any extension thereof), the lender's only permissible remedy under the Program will be to pursue the procedure specified in § 103.36(d)(2).

(e) Failure by the lender to provide BIA with notice of the lender's election of remedy within 90 calendar days of the default, as indicated in § 103.36(d), will invalidate BIA's loan guaranty certificate or insurance coverage for that particular loan, absent an express waiver of this provision by BIA. BIA may preserve the validity of a loan guaranty certificate or insurance coverage through waiver of this provision only when BIA determines, in its discretion, that:

(1) The lender consistently has acted in good faith, and

(2) The lender's failure to provide timely notice either:

(i) Has not caused any actual or potential prejudice to BIA; or

(ii) Was the result of the lender relying upon specific written advice from a BIA official.

§ 103.37 What must the lender do to collect payment under its loan guaranty certificate or loan insurance coverage?

(a) For guaranteed loans, the lender must submit a claim for its loss on a form approved by BIA.

(1) If the lender makes an immediate claim under § 103.36(d)(1), it must send BIA the claim for loss within 90 calendar days of the default by certified mail (return receipt requested), or by a nationally-recognized overnight delivery service (signature of recipient required). The lender's claim for loss may include interest that has accrued on the outstanding principal amount of the loan only through the date it submits the claim.

(2) If the lender elects first to liquidate the collateral securing the loan under § 103.36(d)(2), and has a residual loss after doing so, it must send BIA the claim for loss within 30 calendar days of completing all liquidation efforts. The lender must perform collateral liquidation as expeditiously and thoroughly as is reasonably possible, within the standards established by this part. The lender's claim for loss may include interest that has accrued on the outstanding principal amount of the loan only through the earlier of:

(i) The date it submits the claim;

(ii) The date the lender gets a judgment of foreclosure or sale (or the non-judicial equivalent) on the principal collateral securing the loan; or

(iii) One hundred eighty calendar days after the date of the default.

(b) For insured loans, after liquidating all loan collateral, the lender must submit a claim for its loss (if any) on a form approved by BIA. The lender must send BIA the claim for loss by certified mail (return receipt requested), or by a nationally-recognized overnight delivery service (signature of recipient required) within 30 calendar days of completing all liquidation efforts. The lender must perform collateral liquidation as expeditiously and thoroughly as is reasonably possible, within the standards established by this part. The lender's claim for loss may include interest that has accrued on the outstanding principal amount of the loan through the earlier of:

(1) The date it submits the claim;

(2) The date the lender gets a judgment of foreclosure or sale (or the non-judicial equivalent) on the principal collateral securing the loan; or

(3) One hundred eighty calendar days after the date of the default.

(c) Whenever the lender liquidates loan collateral under § 103.36(d)(2), it must vigorously pursue all reasonable methods of collection concerning the loan collateral before submitting a claim for its residual loss (if any) to BIA. Without limiting the generality of the preceding sentence, the lender must:

(1) Foreclose, either judicially or non-judicially, all rights of redemption the borrower or any co-maker or guarantor of the loan (other than BIA) may have in collateral under any mortgage securing the loan;

(2) Gather and dispose of all personal property pledged as collateral under the loan, in accordance with applicable law;

(3) Exercise all set-off rights the lender may have under contract or applicable law;

(4) Make demand for payment on the borrower, all co-makers, and all guarantors of the loan (other than BIA); and

(5) Participate fully in all bankruptcy proceedings that may arise involving the borrower and any co-maker or guarantor of the loan. Full participation might include, for example, filing a proof of claim in the case, attending creditors' meetings, and seeking a court order releasing the automatic stay of collection efforts so that the lender can liquidate affected loan collateral.

(d) BIA may require further information, including without limitation copies of any documents the lender is to maintain under § 103.32 and all documentation of liquidation efforts, to help BIA evaluate the lender's claim for loss.

(e) BIA will pay the lender the guaranteed or insured portion of the lender's claim for loss, to the extent the claim is based upon reasonably sufficient evidence of the loss and compliance with the requirements of this part. BIA will render a decision on a claim for loss within 90 days of receiving all information it requires to properly evaluate the loss.

§ 103.38 Is there anything else for BIA or the lender to do after BIA makes payment?

When BIA pays the lender on its claim for loss, the lender must sign and deliver to BIA an assignment of rights to its loan agreement with the borrower, in a document acceptable to BIA. Immediately upon payment, BIA is subrogated to all rights of the lender under the loan agreement with the borrower, and must pursue collection efforts against the borrower and any co-maker and guarantor, as required by law.

§ 103.39 When will BIA refuse to pay all or part of a lender's claim?

BIA may deny all or part of a lender's claim for loss when:

(a) The loan is not guaranteed or insured as indicated in § 103.18;

(b) The guarantee or insurance coverage has become invalid under §§ 103.28, 103.29, or 103.36(e);

(c) The lender has not met the standard of care indicated in § 103.30;

(d) The lender presents a claim for a residual loss after attempting to liquidate loan collateral, and:

(1) The lender has not made a reasonable effort to liquidate all security for the loan;

(2) The lender has taken an unreasonable amount of time to complete its liquidation efforts, the probable consequence of which has been to reduce overall prospects of loss recovery; or

(3) The lender's loss claim is inflated by unreasonable liquidation expenses or unjustifiable deductions from collateral liquidation proceeds applied to the loan balance; or

(e) The lender has otherwise failed in any material respect to follow the requirements of this part, and BIA can reasonably attribute some or all of the lender's loss to that failure.

§ 103.40 Will BIA make exceptions to its criteria for denying payment?

(a) BIA will not reduce or deny payment solely on the basis of §§ 103.39(c) or (e) when the lender making the claim for loss:

(1) Is a person to whom a previous lender transferred the loan under §§ 103.28 or 103.29 before maturity for value;

(2) Notified BIA of its acquisition of the loan interest as required by §§ 103.28 or 103.29;

(3) Had no involvement in or knowledge of the actions or circumstances that would have allowed BIA to reduce or deny payment to a previous lender; and

(4) Has not itself violated the standards set forth in §§ 103.39(c) or (e).

(b) If BIA makes payment to a lender under this section, it may seek reimbursement from the previous lender or lenders who contributed to the loss by violating §§ 103.39(c) or (e).

§ 103.41 What happens if a lender violates provisions of this part?

In addition to reducing or eliminating payment on a specific claim for loss, BIA may either temporarily suspend, or permanently bar, a lender from making or acquiring loans under the Program if the lender repeatedly fails to abide by the requirements of this part, or if the lender significantly violates the requirements of this part on any single occasion.

§ 103.42 How long must a lender comply with Program requirements?

(a) A lender must comply in general with Program requirements during:

(1) The effective period of its loan guaranty agreement or loan insurance agreement; and

(2) Whatever additional period is necessary to resolve any outstanding loan guaranty or insurance claims or coverage the lender may have.

(b) Except as otherwise required by law, a lender must maintain records with respect to a particular loan for 6 years after either:

(1) The loan is repaid in full; or

(2) The lender accepts payment from BIA for a loss on the loan, pursuant to a guaranty certificate or an insurance agreement.

(c) At any time 2 years or more following one of the events specified in paragraphs (b)(1) or (2) of this section, a lender may convert its records for corresponding loans to any electronic format that is readily retrievable and that provides an accurate, detailed image of the original records. Upon converting its records in this manner, the lender may dispose of its original loan records.

(d) This section does not restrict any claims BIA may have against the lender or any other party arising from the lender's participation in the Program.

§ 103.43 What must the lender do after repayment in full?

The lender must completely and promptly release of record all remaining collateral for a guaranteed or insured loan after the loan has been paid in full. The release must be at the lender's sole cost. In addition, if the loan is prepaid the lender must notify BIA in accordance with § 103.33(f).

Subpart H—Definitions and Miscellaneous Provisions

§ 103.44 What certain terms mean in this part.

BIA means the Bureau of Indian Affairs within the United States Department of the Interior.

Default means:

(1) The borrower's failure to make a scheduled loan payment when it is due;

(2) The borrower's failure to meet a material condition of the loan agreement;

(3) The borrower's failure to comply with any other condition, covenant or obligation under the terms of the loan agreement within applicable grace or cure periods;

(4) The borrower's failure to remain at least 51 percent Indian owned, as provided in § 103.25(b);

(5) The filing of a voluntary or involuntary petition in bankruptcy listing the borrower as debtor;

(6) The imposition of a Federal, State, local, or tribal government lien on any assets of the borrower or assets otherwise used as collateral for the loan, except real property tax liens imposed by law to secure payments that are not yet due;

(7) Any default defined in the loan agreement, to the extent the definition is not inconsistent with this part.

Equity means the value, after deducting all debt, of the borrower's tangible assets in the business being financed, on which a lender can perfect a first lien security interest. It can include cash, securities, or other cash equivalent instruments, but cannot include the value of contractual options, the right to pay below market rental rates, or similar rights if those rights:

(1) Are unassignable; or

(2) Can expire before maturity of the loan.

Indian means a person who is a member of a tribe as defined in this part.

Loan agreement means the collective terms and conditions under which the lender extends a loan to a borrower, as reflected by the documents that evidence the loan.

Mortgage means a consensual lien on real or personal property in favor of the lender, given by the borrower or a co-maker or guarantor of the loan (other than BIA), to secure loan repayment. The term "mortgage" includes "deed of trust."

NEPA means the National Environmental Policy Act of 1969, 42 U.S.C. 4321 *et seq.*

Person means any individual or distinct legal entity.

Program means the BIA's Loan Guaranty, Insurance, and Interest Subsidy Program, established under 25 U.S.C. 1481 *et seq.*, 25 U.S.C. 1511 *et seq.*, and this part 103.

Reservation means any land that is an Indian reservation, California rancheria, public domain Indian allotment, pueblo, Indian colony, former Indian reservation in Oklahoma, or land held by an Alaska Native corporation under the provisions of the Alaska Native Claims Settlement Act (85 Stat. 688), as amended.

Secretary means the Secretary of the United States Department of the Interior, or his authorized representative.

Tribe means any Indian or Alaska Native tribe, band, nation, pueblo, rancheria, village, community or corporation that the Secretary acknowledges to exist as an Indian tribe, and that is eligible for services from BIA.

§ 103.45 Information collection.

(a) The information collection requirements of §§ 103.11, 103.12, 103.13, 103.14, 103.17, 103.21, 103.23, 103.26, 103.32, 103.33, 103.34, 103.35, 103.36, 103.37, and 103.38 have been approved by the Office of Management and Budget under 44 U.S.C. 3501 *et seq.*, and assigned approval number 1076–0020. The information will be used to approve and make payments on Federal loan guarantees, insurance agreements, and interest subsidy awards. Response is required to obtain a benefit.

(b) The burden on the public to report this information is estimated to average from 15 minutes to 2 hours per response, including the time for reviewing instructions, gathering and maintaining data, and completing and reviewing the information collection. Direct comments regarding the burden estimate or any other aspect of this information collection to the Information Collection Control Officer, Bureau of Indian Affairs, MS 4613, 1849 C Street, NW., Washington, DC 20240.

PART 111—ANNUITY AND OTHER PER CAPITA PAYMENTS

Sec.

AUTHORITY: 5 U.S.C. 301.

SOURCE: 22 FR 10549, Dec. 24, 1957, unless otherwise noted. Redesignated at 47 FR 13327, Mar. 30, 1982.

§ 111.1 Persons to share payments.

In making all annuity and other per capita payments, the funds shall be equally divided among the Indians entitled thereto share and share alike. The roll for such payments should be prepared on Form 5–322,[1] in strict alphabetical order by families of husband, wife, and unmarried dependent minor children. Unless otherwise instructed,

(a) Indians of both sexes may be considered adults at the age of 18 years;

(b) Deceased enrollees may be carried on the rolls for one payment after death;

(c) Where final rolls have been prepared constituting the legal membership of the tribe, only Indians whose names appear thereon are entitled to share in future payments, after-born children being excluded and the shares of deceased enrollees paid to the heirs if determined or if not determined credited to the estate pending determination; and

(d) The shares of competent Indians will be paid to them directly and the shares of incompetents and minors deposited for expenditure under the individual Indian money regulations.

CROSS REFERENCES: For regulations pertaining to the determination of heirs and approval of wills, see part 15 and subpart G of part 11 of this chapter. For individual Indian money regulations, see part 115 of this chapter.

§ 111.2 Enrolling non-full-blood children.

Where an Indian woman was married to a white man prior to June 7, 1897, and was at the time of her marriage a recognized member of the tribe even though she left it after marriage and lived away from the reservation, the children of such a marriage should be enrolled—and, also in the case of an Indian woman married to a white man subsequent to the above date but who still maintains her affiliation with the tribe and she and her children are recognized members thereof; however, where an Indian woman by marriage with a white man after June 7, 1897, has, in effect, withdrawn from the tribe and is no longer identified with it, her children should not be enrolled. In case of doubt all the facts should be submitted to the Bureau of Indian Affairs, Washington, D.C., for a decision.

§ 111.3 Payments by check.

All payments should be made by check. In making payments to competent Indians, each check should be drawn to the order of the enrollee and given or sent directly to him. Powers of attorney and orders given by an Indian to another person for his share in

[1] Forms may be obtained from the Commissioner of Indian Affairs, Washington, D.C.

a payment will not be recognized. Superintendents will note in the "Remarks" column on the roll the date of birth of each new enrollee and the date of death of deceased annuitants.

§ 111.4 Election of shareholders.

An Indian holding equal rights in two or more tribes can share in payments to only one of them and will be required to elect with which tribe he wishes to be enrolled and to relinquish in writing his claims to payments to the other. In the case of a minor the election will be made by the parent or guardian.

§ 111.5 Future payments.

Indians who have received or applied for their pro rata shares of an interest-bearing tribal fund under the act of March 2, 1907 (34 Stat. 1221; 25 U.S.C. 119, 121), as amended by the act of May 18, 1916 (39 Stat. 128), will not be permitted to participate in future payments made from the accumulated interest.

PART 114—SPECIAL DEPOSITS [RESERVED]

PART 115—TRUST FUNDS FOR TRIBES AND INDIVIDUAL INDIANS

Subpart A—Purpose, Definitions, and Public Information

Subpart B—IIM Accounts

Subpart C—IIM Accounts: Minors

Subpart D—IIM Accounts: Estate Accounts

Subpart E—IIM Accounts: Hearing Process for Restricting an IIM Account

Subpart F—Trust Fund Accounts: General Information

AUTHORITY: R.S. 441, as amended, R.S. 463, R.S. 465; 5 U.S.C. 301; 25 U.S.C. 2; 25 U.S.C. 9; 43 U.S.C. 1457; 25 U.S.C. 4001; 25 U.S.C. 161(a); 25 U.S.C. 162a; 25 U.S.C. 164; Pub. L. 87–283; Pub. L. 97–100; Pub. L. 97–257; Pub. L. 103–412; Pub. L. 97–458; 44 U.S.C. 3101 *et seq.*

SOURCE: 66 FR 7094, Jan. 22, 2001, unless otherwise noted.

Subpart A—Purpose, Definitions, and Public Information

§ 115.001 What is the purpose of this part?

This part sets forth guidelines for the Secretary of the Interior, including any tribe or tribal organization if that entity is administering specific programs, functions, services or activities, previously administered by the Secretary of the Interior, but now authorized under a Self-Determination Act contract (pursuant to 25 U.S.C. § 450f) or a Self-Governance compact (pursuant to 25 U.S.C. § 558cc), to carry out the trust duties owed to tribes and individual Indians to manage and administer trust assets for the exclusive benefit of tribal and individual Indian beneficiaries pursuant to federal law, including the American Indian Trust Fund Management Reform Act of 1994, Public Law 103–412, 108 Stat. 4239, 25 U.S.C. § 4001 (Trust Reform Act).

§ 115.002 What definitions do I need to know?

As used in this part:

Account holder means a tribe or a person who owns the funds in a tribal or Individual Indian Money (IIM) account that is maintained by the Secretary.

Account means a record of trust funds that is maintained by the Secretary for the benefit of a tribe or a person.

Administratively restricted account means an IIM account that is placed on temporary hold by OTFM where an account holder's current address of record is unknown or where more documentation is needed to make a distribution from an account.

Adult means an individual who has reached 18 years of age, except when the individual's tribe has determined the age for adulthood to be older than 18 for access to tribal trust fund per capita proceeds.

Adult in need of assistance means an individual who has been determined to be "incapable of managing or administering his or her property, including his or her financial affairs" either (a) through a BIA administrative process that is based on a finding by a licensed medical professional or licensed mental health professional, or (b) by an order or judgment of a court of competent jurisdiction.

BIA means the Bureau of Indian Affairs, Department of the Interior, or its authorized representative.

Bond means security for the performance of certain obligations or a guaranty of such performance as furnished by a third-party surety. As used in this part, bonds may include cash bonds, performance bonds, and surety bonds.

Court of competent jurisdiction means a federal or tribal court with jurisdiction; however, if there is no tribal court with jurisdiction, then a state court with jurisdiction.

Day means a calendar day unless otherwise specified.

Department means the Department of the Interior or its authorized representative.

Deposits mean receiving funds, ordinarily through a Federal Reserve Bank, for credit to a trust fund account.

Emancipated minor means a person under 18 years of age who is married or who is determined by a court of competent jurisdiction to be legally able to care for himself or herself.

Encumber or encumbrance means to attach trust assets held by the Secretary with a claim, lien, or charge that has been approved by the Secretary.

Encumbered account means a trust fund account where some portion of the proceeds are obligated to another party.

Estate account means an account for a deceased IIM account holder.

FOIA means the Freedom of Information Act, 5 U.S.C. § 552.

Guardian means a person who is legally responsible for the care and management of an individual and his or her estate. This definition includes, but is not limited to, conservator or guardian of the property. However, this definition does not apply to property subject to § 115.106 of this part.

Individual Indian Money (IIM) accounts means an interest bearing account for trust funds held by the Secretary that belong to a person who has an interest in trust assets. These accounts are under the control and management of the Secretary. There are three types of IIM accounts: unrestricted, restricted, and estate accounts.

Legal disability means the lack of legal capability to perform an act which includes the ability to manage or administer his or her financial affairs as determined by a court of competent jurisdiction or another federal agency where the federal agency has determined that the adult requires a representative payee and there is no legal guardian to receive federal benefits on his or her behalf.

MSW means a Master of Social Work degree from an accredited college or university.

Minor means an individual who is not an adult as defined in this part.

Non-compos mentis means a person who has been determined by a court of competent jurisdiction to be of unsound mind or incapable of managing his or her own affairs.

OST means the Office of the Special Trustee for American Indians, Department of the Interior, or its authorized representative.

OTFM means the Office of Trust Funds Management, within the Office of the Special Trustee for American Indians, Department of the Interior, or its authorized representative.

Privacy Act means the Federal Privacy Act, 5 U.S.C. § 552a.

Restricted fee land(s) means land the title to which is held by an individual Indian or a tribe and which can only be alienated or encumbered by the owner with the approval of the Secretary because of limitations contained in the conveyance instrument pursuant to federal law.

Secretary means the Secretary of the Interior or an authorized representative; it also means a tribe or tribal organization if that entity is administering specific programs, functions, services or activities, previously administered by the Secretary of the Interior, but now authorized under a Self-Determination Act contract (pursuant to 25 U.S.C. § 450f) or a Self-Governance compact (pursuant to 25 U.S.C. § 558cc).

Special deposit account means a temporary account for the deposit of trust funds that cannot immediately be credited to the rightful account holders.

Supervised account means a restricted IIM account, from which all disbursements must be approved by the BIA, that is maintained for minors, emancipated minors, adults who are in need of assistance, adults who under legal disability, or adults who are non-compos mentis.

Tribal account or tribal trust account generally means a trust fund account for a federally recognized tribe that is maintained and held in trust by the Secretary.

Tribe means any Indian tribe, nation, band, pueblo, rancheria, colony, or community, including any Alaska Native Village or regional or village corporation as defined or established under the Alaska Native Claims Settlement Act which is federally recognized by the United States government for special programs and services provided by the Secretary to Indians because of their status as Indians. Tribe also means two or more tribes joined for any purpose, the joint assets of which include funds held in trust by the Secretary.

Trust account means a tribal account, an IIM account, or a special deposit account for trust funds maintained by the Secretary.

Trust assets mean trust lands, natural resources, trust funds, or other assets held by the federal government in trust for Indian tribes and individual Indians.

Trust funds means money derived from the sale or use of trust lands, restricted fee lands, or trust resources and any other money that the Secretary must accept into trust.

Trust land(s) means any tract or interest therein, that the United States holds in trust status for the benefit of a tribe or an individual Indian.

Trust Reform Act means the American Indian Trust Fund Management Reform Act of 1994, Pub. L. 103–412, 108 Stat. 4239, 25 U.S.C. § 4001.

Trust resources means any element or matter directly derived from Indian trust property.

Unrestricted account means an IIM account in which an Indian account holder may determine the timing and amount of disbursements from the account.

Voluntary hold means a request by an individual Indian with an unrestricted IIM account to keep his or her trust funds in a trust account instead of having the trust funds automatically disbursed.

We or *Us* or *Our* means the Secretary as defined in this part.

You or *Your* means an IIM account holder.

Subpart B—IIM Accounts

§ 115.100 Osage Agency.

The provisions of this part do not apply to funds the deposit or expenditure of which is subject to the provisions of part 117 of this subchapter.

§ 115.101 Individual accounts.

Except as otherwise provided in this part, adults shall have the right to withdraw funds from their accounts. Upon their application, or an application made in their behalf by the Secretary or his authorized representative, their funds shall be disbursed to them. All such disbursements will be made at such convenient times and places as the Secretary or his authorized representatives may designate.

§ 115.102 Adults under legal disability.

The funds of an adult who is non compos mentis or under other legal disability may be disbursed for his benefit for such purposes deemed to be for his best interest and welfare, or the funds may be disbursed to a legal guardian or curator under such conditions as the Secretary or his authorized representative may prescribe.

§ 115.103 Payments by other Federal agencies.

Moneys received from the Veterans Administration or other Government agency pursuant to the Act of February 25, 1933 (47 Stat. 907; 25 U.S.C. 14), may be accepted and administered for the benefit of adult Indians under legal disability or minors for whom no legal guardian or fiduciary has been appointed.

§ 115.104 Restrictions.

Funds of individuals may be applied by the Secretary or his authorized representative against delinquent claims of indebtedness to the United States or any of its agencies or to the tribe of which the individual is a member, unless such payments are prohibited by acts of Congress, and against money judgments rendered by courts of Indian offenses or under any tribal law and order code. Funds derived from the sale of capital assets which by agreement approved prior to such sale by the Secretary or his authorized representative are to be expended for specific purposes, and funds obligated under contractual arrangements approved in advance by the Secretary or his authorized representative or subject to deductions specifically authorized or directed by acts of Congress, shall be disbursed only in accordance with the agreements (including any subsequently approved modifications thereof) or acts of Congress. The funds of an adult whom the Secretary or his authorized representative finds to be in need of assistance in managing his affairs, even though such adult is not non compos mentis or under other legal disability, may be disbursed to the adult, within his best interest, under approved plans. Such finding and the basis for such finding shall be recorded and filed with the records of the account. For rules governing the payment of judgments from individual Indian money accounts, see § 11.208 of this chapter.

§ 115.105 Funds of deceased Indians of the Five Civilized Tribes.

Funds of a deceased Indian of the Five Civilized Tribes may be disbursed to pay ad valorem and personal property taxes, Federal and State estate and income taxes, obligations approved by the Secretary or his authorized representative prior to death of decedent, expenses of last sickness and burial and claims found to be just and reasonable which are not barred by the statute of limitations, costs of determining heirs to restricted property by the State courts, and claims allowed pursuant to part 16 of this chapter.

§ 115.106 Assets of members of the Agua Caliente Band of Mission Indians.

(a) The provisions of this section apply to money or other property, except real property, held by the United States in trust for such Indians, which may be used, advanced, expended, exchanged, deposited, disposed of, invested, and reinvested by the Director, Palm Springs Office, in accordance with the Act of October 17, 1968 (Pub. L. 90–597). The management or disposition of real property is covered in other parts of this chapter.

(b) Investments made by the Director, Palm Springs Office, under the Act of October 17, 1968, supra, shall be of such a nature as will afford reasonable protection of the assets of the individual Indian involved. The Director is authorized to enter into contracts for the management of the assets (except real property) of individual Indians. The consent of the individual Indian concerned must be obtained prior to the taking of actions affecting his assets, unless the Director determines, under the provisions of section (e) of the Act, that consent is not required.

(c) The Director may, consistent with normal business practices, establish appropriate fees for reports he requires from guardians, conservators, or other fiduciaries appointed under State law for members of the Band.

§ 115.107 Appeals.

Appeals from an action taken by an official of the Bureau of Indian Affairs may be taken pursuant to 25 CFR part 2, subject to the terms of subpart E.

Subpart C—IIM Accounts: Minors

§ 115.400 Will a minor's IIM account always be supervised?

Yes, all IIM accounts established by BIA for minors will be a supervised by the BIA.

§ 115.401 What is a minor's supervised account?

A minor's supervised account is a restricted IIM account from which all disbursements must be made pursuant to a distribution plan approved by the BIA that is established for:

(a) A minor, or

(b) An emancipated minor.

§ 115.402 Will a minor have access to information about his or her account?

A minor will not have access to information about his or her IIM account without approval of the custodial parent(s) or legal guardian. However, an emancipated minor will have access to information about his or her IIM account.

§ 115.403 Who will receive information regarding a minor's supervised account?

(a) The parent(s) with legal custody of the minor or the minor's legal guardian will receive a minor's statement of performance at the address of record for the minor's supervised account.

(b) An emancipated minor will receive his or her statement of performance at the address of record for the minor's supervised account.

§ 115.404 What information will be provided in a minor's statement of performance?

A minor's statement of performance will identify the source, type, and status of the funds deposited and held in the account; the beginning balance; the gains and losses; receipts and disbursements, if any; and the ending balance of the quarterly statement period for the minor's supervised account.

§ 115.405 How frequently will a minor's statement of performance be mailed?

We will mail a minor's statement of performance to the address of record quarterly, within and no later than 20 business days after the close of the quarterly statement period.

§ 115.406 Who provides an address of record for a minor's supervised account?

(a) The custodial parent or the legal guardian must provide an address to the BIA and this address will be the address of record for the minor's supervised account. Where applicable, a parent or legal guardian must provide a copy of the custodial order or guardianship order from a court of competent jurisdiction when providing the address of record for the minor's supervised IIM account.

(b) The emancipated minor must provide his or her address of record to the BIA.

(c) Upon receipt of the change of address of record from the parent or legal guardian, the BIA must provide the change of the address of record to the OTFM.

§ 115.407 How is an address of record for a minor's supervised account changed?

(a) To change an address of record for a minor's supervised IIM account, a custodial parent(s), legal guardian, or emancipated minor must provide BIA with the following information:

(1) The minor's or emancipated minor's name;

(2) The name of the custodial parent(s) or legal guardian, if applicable;

(3) A custody order from a court of competent jurisdiction or a copy of a guardianship, if applicable;

(4) The new address of the custodial parent(s), legal guardian, or emancipated minor; and

(5) The signature, mark or thumb print of a custodial parent, legal guardian, or emancipated minor that has been notarized by a notary public and/or witnessed by a DOI employee who has been shown verifiable photo identification. See § 115.410

(b) When requesting a change of an address of record, the following information will further assist us to identify the minor's account:

(1) The minor's or emancipated minor's IIM account number;

(2) The minor's or emancipated minor's date of birth;

(3) The minor's or emancipated minor's tribal enrollment number; and

(4) The minor's or emancipated minor's social security number.

§ 115.408 May a minor's supervised account have more than one address on file with the BIA?

Yes, a minor's supervised account may have more than one address on file with the BIA. We request that the parent, legal guardian, or the person who has been recognized by the BIA as having control and custody of the minor, notify us of the following addresses for the minor:

(a) The minor's residence;

(b) The address of record where the statement of performance will be mailed;

(c) The address where disbursement checks will be mailed or financial institution information for direct deposits of trust funds as authorized under an approved distribution plan.

§ 115.409 How is an address for a minor's residence changed?

(a) To change an address for a minor's residence, the custodial parent, legal guardian, or the person who has been recognized by the BIA as having control and custody of the minor must provide BIA with the following information:

(1) The minor's name;

(2) The name of the custodial parent(s) or legal guardian;

(3) A copy of a custodial order from a court of competent jurisdiction or a guardianship order, where applicable;

(4) The new address of the minor's residence; and

(5) The signature, mark or thumb print of the individual who is providing the updated address for the minor's residence that has been notarized by a notary public and/or witnessed by a DOI employee who has been shown verifiable photo identification. See § 115.410

(b) When requesting a change of an address for a minor's residence, the following information will further assist us to identify the minor's account:

(1) The minor's IIM account number;

(2) The minor's date of birth;

(3) The minor's tribal enrollment number (if known); and

(4) The minor's social security number (where known).

§ 115.410 What types of identification will the BIA or OTFM accept as "verifiable photo identification"?

BIA or OTFM will accept the following forms of identification as "verifiable photo identification":

(a) A valid driver's license;

(b) A government-issued photo identification card, such as a passport, security badge, etc.; or

(c) A tribal photo identification card.

§ 115.411 What if the individual making a request regarding a minor's supervised account does not have any verifiable photo identification?

If the individual making a request regarding a minor's supervised account does not have any verifiable photo identification, the individual may make a request in person at the BIA and we will talk with the individual and review information in the minor's file to see if we can attest to the individual's identity. If we cannot establish the identity of the individual, we will not accept the request.

§ 115.412 Will child support payments be accepted for deposit into a minor's supervised account?

The Secretary will not accept child support payments for deposit into a minor's supervised account.

§ 115.413 Who may receive funds from a minor's supervised account?

A custodial parent, a legal guardian, a person who has been recognized by the BIA as having control and custody of the minor, or an emancipated minor may be eligible to withdraw funds from a minor's supervised account if there is an authorized disbursement request that is based upon the terms of a BIA-approved distribution plan.

§ 115.414 What is an authorized disbursement request?

An authorized disbursement request is the form or letter that must be approved by the BIA that specifies the funds to be disbursed from an IIM account. The authorized disbursement request may not be issued to disburse funds from a minor's supervised account unless an approved distribution plan exists, the amount to be disbursed is in conformity with the distribution plan and the disbursement will be made to an individual or third party specified in the plan.

§ 115.415 How will an authorized disbursement from a minor's supervised account be sent?

OTFM will make an authorized disbursement based on the approved distribution plan from a minor's supervised account by:

(a) Making a direct deposit to a specified account at a financial institution (a direct deposit into the specified account will eliminate lost, stolen or damaged checks and will also eliminate delays associated with mailing the check);

(b) Mailing a check to the address of record or to a specified disbursement address; or

(c) Mailing a check to a specified third party's address.

§ 115.416 Will the United States post office forward mail regarding a minor's supervised account to a forwarding address left with the United States post office?

(a) Federal law does not allow the United States post office to forward checks that are issued by the federal government. Therefore, a check from a minor's supervised account will not be forwarded to an address left with the United States post office. The new address of record must be provided directly to BIA.

(b) Where a forwarding address has been provided to the United States post office, the United States post office will forward a statement of performance and general correspondence regarding a minor's supervised account that is mailed to the minor's address of record for a limited time period. However, it is the responsibility of a custodial parent, legal guardian, or emancipated minor to give BIA the new address of record for the minor's supervised account.

§ 115.417 What portion of funds in a minor's supervised account may be withdrawn under a distribution plan?

Trust money in a minor's supervised account will not be distributed without a review of other resources that may be available to meet the needs of the minor. Any trust funds of a minor that are distributed must be used for the direct benefit of the minor and in accordance with any additional limitations (*e.g.*, statutory, court order, tribal resolution, etc.) placed on the use of specific trust funds. Allowable uses may include health, education, or welfare when based upon a justified unmet need. The BIA will require receipts for expenditures of funds disbursed from a minor's account to a custodial parent, legal guardian, person who has been recognized by the BIA as having control and custody of the minor, or an emancipated minor.

§ 115.418 What types of trust funds may a minor have?

A minor may have one or more of the following types of trust funds:

(a) Judgment per capita funds: Withdrawals may only be made upon BIA approval of an application made under Public Law 97–458. See 25 CFR 1.2.

(b) Tribal per capita funds: Withdrawals may only be made under a BIA approved distribution plan and in accordance with the terms of the tribe's per capita resolution/document.

(c) Other trust funds: Withdrawals may only be made under a minor's BIA-approved distribution plan that is based on a justified unmet need for the minor's health, education, or welfare.

(d) Funds from other federal agencies (e.g., SSA, SSI, VA) received for the benefit of the minor: Withdrawals must be made only under a BIA-approved distribution plan that must be consistent with the disbursing agency's (e.g., SSA, SSI, VA) allowable uses for the funds.

§ 115.419 Who develops a minor's distribution plan?

A social service provider will develop a minor's distribution plan for approval by the BIA after evaluating the needs of the minor in consultation with a custodial parent, a legal guardian, the person who has been recognized by the BIA as having control and custody of the minor, or emancipated minor. A minor's distribution plan may only provide for those expenditures outlined in part § 115.417.

§ 115.420 When developing a minor's distribution plan, what information must be considered and included in the evaluation?

When developing a minor's distribution plan, the following information must be considered and included in the evaluation:

(a) Documentation which establishes who has physical custody of the minor (e.g., home visits, school records, medical records, etc.);

(b) A copy of any custodial orders or guardianship orders from a court of competent jurisdiction;

(c) The name(s) of the person and his or her relationship to the minor, if any, who make a request for a disbursement from the minor's account;

(d) An evaluation of other resources, including parental income, that may be available to meet the unmet needs of the minor;

(e) A list of the amounts, purposes, and dates for which disbursements will be made;

(f) The name(s) of the person to whom disbursements may be made, including, as applicable:

(1) A custodial parent;

(2) A legal guardian;

(3) The person who has been recognized by the BIA as having control and custody of the minor;

(4) An emancipated minor; and/or

(5) Any third parties to whom the BIA will make direct payment for goods or services provided to the minor and supported by an invoice or bill of sale;

(g) The date(s) (at least every six months) when the custodial parent, the legal guardian, the person who has been recognized by the BIA as having control and custody of the minor, or the emancipated minor must provide receipts to the BIA to show that expenditures were made in accordance with the approved distribution plan;

(h) Additional requirements and justification for those requirements, as necessary to ensure that any distribution(s) will benefit the minor;

(i) The dates the disbursement plan was developed, approved, and reviewed, and the date for the next scheduled review;

(j) The date(s) the distribution plan was amended and an explanation for any amendment(s) to the distribution plan, when an amendment is necessary;

(k) The signature of the BIA official approving the plan with the certification that the plan is in the best interest of the account holder; and

(l) The signature(s) of the custodial parent, legal guardian, with date(s) signed, certifying that he or she has been consulted and has agreed to the terms of the evaluation and the distribution plan.

§ 115.421 What information will be included in the copy of the minor's distribution plan that will be provided to OTFM?

A minor's distribution plan must contain the following:

(a) A copy of any custodial order or guardianship order from a court of competent jurisdiction;

(b) A list of the amounts, purposes, and dates for which disbursements will be made;

(c) The name(s) of the person(s) to whom disbursements may be made, including, as applicable:

(1) A custodial parent;

(2) A legal guardian;

(3) The person who has been recognized by the BIA as having control and custody of the minor and the address of that person;

(4) An emancipated minor; and/or

(5) Any third parties and the address(es) of the third parties to whom the direct payment will be made for goods or services provided to the minor and supported by an invoice or bill of sale, where applicable;

(d) The date that the disbursement plan was approved and the expiration date of the distribution plan; and

(e) The date and signature of the BIA official approving the plan with a certification that the plan is in the best interest of the account holder.

§ 115.422 As a custodial parent, the legal guardian, the person who BIA has recognized as having control and custody of the minor, or an emancipated minor, what are your responsibilities if you receive trust funds from a minor's supervised account?

If you are a custodial parent, the legal guardian, the person who BIA has recognized as having control and custody of the minor, or an emancipated minor who receives funds from a minor's supervised account, you must:

(a) Consult with the social service provider on the development of an evaluation;

(b) Sign an acknowledgment that you have reviewed the evaluation;

(c) Follow the terms of a distribution plan approved by the BIA;

(d) Follow any applicable court order;

(e) Provide receipts to the social services provider in accordance with terms of the evaluation for all expenses paid out of the minor's IIM funds;

(f) Review the statements of performance for the supervised account for discrepancies, if applicable;

(g) File tax returns on behalf of the account holder, if applicable; and

(h) Notify the social service provider of any change in circumstances that impairs your performance of your obligations under this part or inform the social service provider of any information regarding misuse of a minor's trust funds.

§ 115.423 If you are a custodial parent, a legal guardian, or an emancipated minor, may BIA authorize the disbursement of funds from a minor's supervised account without your knowledge?

At the Secretary's discretion, the BIA may authorize the disbursement of funds from a minor's supervised account for the benefit of the minor.

§ 115.424 Who receives a copy of the BIA-approved distribution plan and any amendments to the plan?

The BIA-approved distribution plan will be provided to:

(a) The custodial parent; or

(b) A legal guardian; or

(c) At the Secretary's discretion, in unusual circumstances, to a family member who has been recognized as having control and custody of the minor; or

(d) An emancipated minor; and

(e) OTFM.

§ 115.425 What will we do if we find that a distribution plan has not been followed or an individual has acted improperly in regard to his or her duties involving a minor's trust funds?

If we find that a distribution plan has not been followed or that a custodial parent, a legal guardian, or the person who has been recognized by the BIA as having control and custody of the minor has failed to satisfactorily account for expenses or has not used the minor's funds for the primary benefit of the minor, we will:

(a) Notify the individual; and

(b) Take action to protect the interests of the minor, which may include:

(1) Referring the matter for civil or criminal legal action;

(2) Demanding repayment from the individual who has improperly expended trust funds or failed to account for the use of trust funds;

(3) Liquidating a bond posted by the legal guardian, where applicable, to recover improperly expended trust funds up to the amount of the bond; or

(4) Immediately modifying the distribution plan for up to sixty days, including suspending the authority of the individual to receive further disbursements.

§ 115.426 What is the BIA's responsibility regarding the management of a minor's supervised account?

The BIA's responsibility in regard to the management of a minor's supervised account is to:

(a) Review and approve the evaluation and the distribution plan;

(b) Authorize OTFM to disburse IIM funds in accordance with an approved distribution plan; and

(c) Conduct annual reviews of case records for minors' supervised accounts to ensure that the social service providers have managed the accounts in accordance with the approved evaluation and distribution plan.

§ 115.427 What is the BIA's annual review process for a minor's supervised account?

A BIA social worker with an MSW will conduct an annual review of minors' supervised accounts by:

(a) Verifying that all receipts for disbursements made under a distribution plan were collected in accordance with the terms specified in the evaluation;

(b) Reviewing the receipts for disbursements made from a minor's supervised account to ensure that all expenditures were made in accordance with the distribution plan;

(c) Reviewing all case worker reports and notes;

(d) Reviewing account records to insure that withdrawals and payments were made in accordance with the distribution plan;

(e) Verifying current addresses, including the address of record, the address of the minor's residence, and the disbursement address; and

(f) Deciding whether the distribution plan needs to be modified.

§ 115.428 Will you automatically receive all of your trust funds when you reach the age of 18?

No, we will not automatically send your trust funds to you when you reach the age of 18.

§ 115.429 What do you need to do when you reach 18 years of age to access your trust funds?

You must contact OTFM to request withdrawal of any or all of your trust funds that may be available to you. OTFM may require certain information from you to verify your identity, etc. prior to the release of your trust funds. All signatures must be notarized by a notary public or witnessed by a DOI employee. In addition, if you choose to have a check mailed to you, you must provide us with your address of record. If you choose to have your trust funds electronically transferred to you, you must provide your financial institution account information to OTFM.

§ 115.430 Will your account lose its supervised status when you reach the age of 18?

Your account will no longer be supervised when you reach the age of 18 unless statutory language or a tribal resolution specifies an age other than 18 years of age for access to specific trust funds. However, if a court of competent jurisdiction has found you to be non-compos mentis, under legal disability, or the BIA has determined you to be an adult in need of assistance, your account will remain supervised and you will be notified in accordance with subpart E.

§ 115.431 If you are an emancipated minor may you withdraw trust funds from your account?

If you are an emancipated minor, you may have access to some or all of your trust funds as follows:

(a) For judgment per capita funds: you may not make withdrawals from your account until you have reached the age specified in the judgment. Exceptions are only granted upon the approval of an application made under Public Law 97–458. See 25 CFR 1.2.

(b) Tribal per capita funds: access to these funds will be determined by tribal resolution.

(c) Other trust funds: You may be able to have supervised access to some or all of your funds, but the BIA must approve all requests for withdrawals from your account. You must work with the BIA to develop a distribution plan to access the funds in your account. In no instance will the BIA allow an emancipated minor to make unsupervised withdrawals.

(d) For funds from other federal agencies (*e.g.*, SSA, SSI, VA), you may be able to receive funds directly, but you must contact and make arrangements with the other federal agency. Direct receipt of funds from another federal agency will not change the supervised status of an emancipated minor's trust account.

Subpart D—IIM Accounts: Estate Accounts

§ 115.500 When is an estate account established?

An estate account is established when we receive notice of an account holder's death.

§ 115.501 How long will an estate account remain open?

An estate account will remain open until the funds have been distributed in accordance with the distribution and/or probate order.

§ 115.502 Who inherits the money in an IIM account when an account holder dies?

At the end of all probate procedures, funds remaining in a decedent's estate account will be distributed from the decedent's estate account and paid directly to or deposited into an IIM account of the decedent's heirs, beneficiaries, or other persons or entities entitled by law to receive the funds, where applicable. See 25 CFR part 15.

§ 115.503 May money in an IIM account be withdrawn after the death of an account holder but prior to the end of the probate proceedings?

(a) If you are responsible for making the funeral arrangements of a decedent who had an IIM account and you have an immediate need for emergency assistance to pay for funeral arrangements prior to burial, you may make a request to the BIA for up to $1,000 from the decedent's IIM account if the decedent's IIM account has more than $2,500 in the account at the date of death.

(b) You must apply for this assistance and submit to the BIA an original itemized estimate of the cost of the service to be rendered and the identification of the service provider.

(c) We may approve reasonable costs up to $1,000 that are necessary for the burial services.

(d) We will make payments directly to the providers of the service(s).

§ 115.504 If you have a life estate interest in income-producing trust assets, how will you receive the income?

If you have a life estate interest in income-producing trust assets, which is earning income, OTFM will open an IIM-life estate account for you and funds will be distributed after BIA has certified ownership of the trust funds.

Subpart E—IIM Accounts: Hearing Process for Restricting an IIM Account

§ 115.600 If BIA decides to restrict your IIM account under § 115.102 or § 115.104, what procedures must the BIA follow?

If under § 115.102 or § 115.104, the BIA has decided to limit your access to your IIM account (*i.e.*, decided to supervise the IIM account), or if the BIA has decided to pay creditors with funds from your IIM account, including creditors with judgments from Courts of Indian Offenses for which preliminary procedures are prescribed in 25 CFR 11.208, the BIA must notify you or your guardian, as applicable, to provide you or your guardian, as applicable, with an opportunity to challenge the BIA's decision to restrict your IIM account as specified in subpart E.

§ 115.601 Under what circumstances may the BIA restrict your IIM account through supervision or an encumbrance?

(a) The BIA may restrict your IIM account through supervision if the BIA:

(1) Receives an order from a court of competent jurisdiction that you are non-compos mentis; or

(2) Receives an order or judgment from a court of competent jurisdiction that you are an adult in need of assistance because you are "incapable of

managing or administering property, including your financial affairs;" or

(3) Determines through an administrative process that you are an adult in need of assistance based on a finding by a licensed medical or mental health professional that you are "incapable of managing or administering property, including your financial affairs;" or

(4) Receives information from another federal agency that you are under a legal disability and that the agency has appointed a representative payee to receive federal benefits on your behalf.

(b) The BIA may restrict your IIM account through an encumbrance if the BIA:

(1) Receives an order from a court of competent jurisdiction awarding child support from your IIM account; or

(2) Receives from a third party:

(i) A copy of the original contract between you and the third party in which you used your IIM funds as security/collateral for the transaction;

(ii) A copy of the document showing that the BIA approved in advance the use of your IIM funds as security/collateral for the contract;

(iii) Proof of your default on the contract according to the terms of the contract; and

(iv) A copy of the original assignment of IIM income as security/collateral for the contract that is signed and dated by you and is notarized;

(3) Receives a money judgment from a Court of Indian Offenses pursuant to 25 CFR 11.208 or under any tribal law and order code;

(4) Is provided documentation showing that BIA or OTFM caused an administrative error which resulted in a deposit into your IIM account, or a disbursement to you, or to a third party on your behalf; or

(5) Is provided with proof of debts owed to the United States pursuant to § 115.104 of this part.

§ 115.602 How will the BIA notify you or your guardian, as applicable, of its decision to restrict your IIM account?

The BIA will notify you or your guardian, as applicable, of its decision to restrict your IIM account by:

(a) United States certified mail to your address of record;

(b) Personal delivery to you or your guardian, as applicable, or to your address of record;

(c) Publication for four consecutive weeks in your tribal newspaper if your whereabouts are unknown and in the local newspaper serving your last known address of record; or

(d) United States certified mail to you in care of the warden, if you are incarcerated. The BIA may send a copy of the notification to your attorney, if known.

§ 115.603 What happens if BIA's notice of its decision to place a restriction on your IIM account that is sent by United States certified mail is returned to the BIA as undeliverable for any reason?

If BIA's notice of its decision to place a restriction on your IIM account that is sent by United States certified mail is returned to the BIA as undeliverable for any reason, the BIA will remove the restriction on your account, which was placed five days after the notice was mailed, and will publish a notice in accordance with § 115.602(c) and § 115.605(b).

§ 115.604 When will BIA authorize OTFM to place a restriction on your IIM account?

BIA will authorize OTFM to place a restriction on your IIM account after providing OTFM with supporting documentation (i.e., receipts, notice of publication, etc.) of the following:

(a) Five (5) days after the date BIA mails you or your guardian, as applicable, notice of its decision to restrict your account by United States certified mail to your address of record;

(b) One (1) day after BIA has made personal delivery to you or your guardian, as applicable, or to your address of record of its notice of the BIA's decision to restrict your account; or

(c) Five (5) days after the fourth publication of the public notice of BIA's decision to restrict your account.

§ 115.605 What information will the BIA include in its notice of the decision to restrict your IIM account?

(a) When the BIA provides notice of its decision to restrict your IIM account by certified mail or personal delivery to you or your guardian, as applicable, the notice must contain:

(1) The name on the IIM account;

(2) The reason for the restriction;

(3) The amount to be encumbered, if applicable;

(4) A statement that your IIM account will be restricted 5 days after the date the notice was sent United States certified mail to your address of record;

(5) An explanation that you have 40 days from the date the notice was sent United States certified mail to request a hearing to challenge BIA's decision to restrict your IIM account;

(6) An explanation of how to request a hearing;

(7) A statement that the BIA will conduct the hearing and that you are assured a fair hearing;

(8) A copy of the fair hearing guidelines;

(9) A statement that you may contact the BIA to authorize immediate payment from your IIM account to pay the claim, if applicable;

(10) The address and phone number of the BIA office that made the decision to restrict your IIM account and provided the notice; and

(11) Other information as may be determined appropriate by the BIA.

(b) When the BIA provides public notice of its decision to restrict your account, the only information the public notice will include is:

(1) The name on the account;

(2) The date of first publication of the public notice;

(3) A statement that the BIA has decided to place a restriction on your IIM account;

(4) A statement that the public notice will be published once a week for four consecutive weeks;

(5) A statement that the BIA will place a restriction on your account five (5) days after the date of the fourth publication of the public notice;

(6) A statement that your opportunity to request a hearing to challenge BIA's decision to restrict your account will expire 30 days after the date of the fourth publication of the public notice; and

(7) An address and telephone number of the BIA office publishing the notice to request further information and instructions on how to request a hearing.

§ 115.606 What happens if you do not request a hearing to challenge BIA's decision to restrict your IIM account during the allotted time period?

If you or your guardian, as applicable, do not request a hearing to challenge BIA's decision to restrict your IIM account during the allotted time period, BIA's decision to restrict your IIM account will become final. BIA will follow the procedures outlined in § 115.616 through § 115.618, and § 115.620, as applicable.

§ 115.607 How do you request a hearing to challenge the BIA's decision to restrict your IIM account?

You or your guardian, as applicable, must request a hearing to challenge the BIA's decision to restrict your IIM account from the BIA office that made the decision and notified you of the restriction. Your request must:

(a) Be in writing;

(b) Specifically request a hearing to challenge the restriction; and

(c) Be hand delivered to the BIA office or postmarked within:

(i) 40 days of the date that BIA's notice was sent United States certified mail or personally delivered to the address of record, or

(ii) 30 days of the date of the final publication of the public notice.

§ 115.608 If you request a hearing to challenge BIA's decision to restrict your IIM account, when will BIA conduct the hearing?

BIA will conduct a hearing within ten (10) working days from its receipt of a written request from you or your guardian, as applicable, for a hearing to challenge the decision to restrict your IIM account.

§ 115.609 Will you be allowed to present testimony and/or evidence at the hearing?

Yes, you or your guardian, as applicable, will be provided the opportunity to present testimony and/or evidence as to the reasons the BIA should not restrict your IIM account, including information showing how an encumbrance may create an undue financial hardship, if applicable. You may not challenge a court order or judgment in this proceeding. However, if you have appealed an order or judgment from a court of competent jurisdiction, you or your guardian, as applicable, may present evidence of your appeal and the BIA hearing will be postponed until there is a final order from the court. The restriction on your IIM account will remain in place until after the hearing is concluded.

§ 115.610 Will you be allowed to present witnesses during a hearing?

Yes, you or your guardian, as applicable, may present witnesses during a hearing. You are responsible for any and all expenses which may be associated with presenting witnesses.

§ 115.611 Will you be allowed to question opposing witnesses during a hearing?

Yes, you or your guardian, as applicable, may question all opposing witnesses testifying during your hearing. You may also present witnesses to challenge opposing witness testimony.

§ 115.612 May you be represented by an attorney during your hearing?

Yes, you may have an attorney or other person represent you during your hearing. However, you are responsible for any and all expenses associated with having an attorney or other person represent you.

§ 115.613 Will the BIA record the hearing?

Yes, the BIA will record the hearing.

§ 115.614 Why is the BIA hearing recorded?

The BIA hearing will be recorded so that it will be available for review if the hearing process is appealed under § 115.107. The BIA hearing record must be preserved as a trust record.

§ 115.615 How long after the hearing will BIA make its final decision?

BIA will make its final decision within 10 business days of the end of the hearing.

§ 115.616 What information will be included in BIA's final decision?

BIA's final written decision to the parties involved in the proceeding will include:

(a) BIA's decision to remove or retain the restriction on the IIM account;

(b) A detailed justification for the supervision or encumbrance of the IIM account, where applicable;

(c) The amount(s) to be paid, the name and address of a third party to whom payment will be made, and the time period for repayment established under 617(a) of this part, where applicable;

(d) Any provision to allow for distributions to the account holder because of an undue financial hardship created by the encumbrance, if applicable; and

(e) Any other information the hearing officer deems necessary.

§ 115.617 What happens when the BIA decides to supervise or encumber your IIM account after your hearing?

BIA will provide OTFM with a copy of the distribution plan, after the BIA decides to:

(a) Supervise your IIM account. BIA social services staff will consult with you and/or your guardian to develop a distribution plan. Upon BIA approval, the distribution plan will be valid for one year.

(b) Encumber your IIM account. BIA will review your account balance and your future IIM income to develop a distribution plan that establishes the amount(s) to be paid and the dates payment(s) will be made to the specified party. Payments may need to be made over the course of one or more years if the amount owed to the specified party is greater than your current IIM account balance.

§115.618 What happens if at the conclusion of the notice and hearing process we decide to encumber your IIM account because of an administrative error which resulted in funds that you do not own being deposited in your account or distributed to you or to a third party on your behalf?

If we decide at the conclusion of the notice and hearing process to encumber your account because of an administrative error which resulted in funds that you do not own being deposited into your IIM account or distributed to you or to a third party on your behalf, we will consult with you or your guardian, as applicable, to determine how the funds will be re-paid.

§115.619 If the BIA decides that the restriction on your IIM account will be continued after your hearing, do you have the right to appeal that decision?

Yes, if the BIA decides after your hearing to continue the restriction on your IIM account, you or your guardian, as applicable, have the right to appeal the decision under the procedures proscribed in §115.107.

§115.620 If you decide to appeal the BIA's final decision pursuant to §115.107, will the BIA restrict your IIM account during the appeal?

Yes, if under §115.107 you or your guardian, as applicable, decide to appeal the BIA's final decision to:

(a) Supervise your IIM account, your IIM account will remain restricted during the appeal period.

(b) Encumber your IIM account, your IIM account will remain restricted up to the amount at issue during the appeal period. If your account balance is greater than the amount encumbered, those funds will be available to you upon request to and by approval of the Secretary.

Subpart F—Trust Fund Accounts: General Information

§115.700 Why is money held in trust for tribes and individual Indians?

Congress has passed a number of laws that require the Secretary to establish and administer trust fund accounts for Indian tribes and certain individual Indians who have an interest(s) in trust lands, trust resources, or trust assets.

§ 115.701 What types of accounts are maintained for Indian trust funds?

Indian trust funds are deposited in tribal accounts, Individual Indian Money (IIM) accounts, and special deposit accounts. The illustration below provides information on each of these trust accounts.

<table>
<tr><th colspan="3">Types of Trust Fund Accounts</th><th>Descriptions</th></tr>
<tr><td rowspan="5">Individual Indian Money (IIM) Accounts</td><td colspan="2">Unrestricted IIM accounts</td><td>There are no restrictions on these accounts. Funds may be left on deposit, or paid to the account holder based upon instructions by the account holder.</td></tr>
<tr><td rowspan="3">Restricted IIM accounts:</td><td>Administratively Restricted</td><td>A temporary hold is placed on an account by OTFM where an address of record for an account holder is unknown or where more documentation is needed to make a distribution from an account.</td></tr>
<tr><td>Supervised</td><td>A restriction is placed on the account by the BIA and funds from these accounts may only be withdrawn under a BIA approved distribution plan. The following account holders will have supervised accounts:
• minors,
• emancipated minors,
• adults who are non-compos mentis,
• adults in need of assistance; and/or
• adults under legal disability as defined in this part.</td></tr>
<tr><td>Encumbered</td><td>A restriction is placed on the account by the BIA until money owed from an the account is paid to a specified party. The account holder may withdraw any money available in the account that is above the amount owed to specified parties.</td></tr>
<tr><td colspan="2">IIM Estate accounts</td><td>An account for a deceased IIM account holder.</td></tr>
<tr><td colspan="3">Tribal Accounts</td><td>Generally, an account for a federally recognized tribe.</td></tr>
<tr><td colspan="3">Special Deposit Accounts</td><td>An account for the temporary deposit of trust funds that cannot be distributed immediately to its rightful owners.</td></tr>
</table>

[66 FR 7094, Jan. 22, 2001, as amended at 66 FR 8768, Feb. 2, 2001]

§115.702 What specific sources of money will be accepted for deposit into a trust account?

We must accept proceed on behalf of tribes or individuals from the following sources:

SOURCES	TRUST ACCOUNTS				
	Tribal	Individual Indian Money (IIM)			
		Unrestricted IIM Accounts	Restricted IIM Accounts		
			Administratively restricted	Supervised	Encumbered
Payments from the United States as a Result of —					
Federal laws requiring funds to be deposited in trust accounts.	✓	✓	✓	✓	✓
Settlement of a claim related to trust assets that requires the funds to be deposited in trust accounts	✓	✓	✓	✓	✓
A final order from a United States court for a cause of action directly related to trust assets requiring funds to be deposited in trust accounts	✓	✓	✓	✓	✓
Unobligated or unspent forestry funds specifically appropriated for the benefit of such Indian tribe	✓				
Designation of the BIA as the representative payee (by another federal agency) to receive certain Federal assistance payments, such as VA benefits, Social Security, or Supplemental Security Income, on behalf of an individual Indian because there is no legal guardian for that individual			✓	✓	
Payments resulting from —					
Money directly derived from the title conveyance (e.g. sale, probate, condemnation) or use of trust lands or restricted fee lands or trust resources, including any late payment penalties, when paid directly to the Secretary on behalf of the account holder	✓	✓	✓	✓	✓
Penalties for trespass on trust lands or restricted fee lands	✓	✓	✓	✓	✓

Default or breach of the terms of a contract for the sale or use of trust lands, restricted fee lands, or trust resources arising from cash performance or surety bonds, or other source(s)	✓	✓	✓	✓	✓
A final order from a court of competent jurisdiction for a cause of action directly related to trust assets requiring funds to be deposited in trust accounts	✓	✓	✓	✓	✓
Deposits from an Indian Tribe —					
Redeposit of tribal trust funds previously withdrawn under an investment plan submitted and approved pursuant to the American Indian Trust Fund Management Reform Act of 1994, Pub. L. 103-412, 108 Stat. 4239, 25 U.S.C. § 4001 (Trust Reform Act)	✓				
Where a tribe under 25 U.S.C. 450f et seq. has contracted or compacted with the federal government to operate a federal program and the tribe, operating the federal program on behalf of the Secretary, receives trust funds for the sale or use of trust assets pursuant to a contract that specifies that payments are to be made to the Secretary on behalf of a tribe or an individual	✓	✓	✓	✓	✓
Legislative settlement funds or judgment funds withdrawn, but not spent, for a specific project. Documentation showing source of funds is required.	✓				
Deposits from other sources –					
Interest earned on trust fund deposits	✓	✓	✓	✓	✓
Disbursements of tribal trust funds held by OTFM to tribal members as per capita payments	✓			✓	
As permitted by law (25 U.S.C. § 3109) to be deposited into an Indian forest land assistance account	✓				
Funds derived directly from trust lands, restricted fee lands, or trust resources that are presented to the Secretary, on behalf of the tribe or individual Indian owner(s) of the trust asset, by the payor after being mailed to the owner(s) as required by contract (i.e., direct pay) and returned by mail to the payor as undeliverable	✓	✓	✓		✓

Funds derived directly from trust lands, restricted fee lands, or trust resources that are presented to the Secretary, on behalf of the tribe or individual Indian owner(s) of the trust asset, by the payor after being mailed to the owner(s) as required by contract (i.e., direct pay) and returned by mail to the payor as undeliverable	✓	✓	✓		✓

[66 FR 7094, Jan. 22, 2001. Redesignated at 66 FR 8768, Feb. 2, 2001]

§115.703 May we accept for deposit into a trust account money not specified in §115.702?

No, we will not accept funds from sources that are not identified in the table in §115.702 for deposit into a trust account.

§115.704 May we accept for deposit into a trust account retirement checks/payments or pension fund checks/payments even though those funds are not specified in §115.702?

No, we will not accept retirement checks/payments or pension fund checks/payments or any funds from sources that are not identified in the table in §115.702 for deposit into a trust account.

§115.705 May we accept for deposit into a trust account money awarded or assessed by a court of competent jurisdiction?

We will accept money awarded or assessed by a court of competent jurisdiction for a cause of action directly related to trust assets to be deposited into a trust account. Other funds awarded by a court of competent jurisdiction may not be deposited into a trust account.

§115.706 When funds are awarded or assessed by a court of competent jurisdiction in a cause of action involving trust assets, what documentation is required to deposit the trust funds into a trust account?

When funds are awarded or assessed by a court of competent jurisdiction in a cause of action involving trust assets, we must receive the funds awarded as stipulated in the court order and a copy of the court's order.

§115.707 Will the Secretary accept administrative fees for deposit into a trust account?

No. The Secretary will not accept administrative fees for deposit into a trust account because administrative fees are not trust funds. However, administrative fees may be deposited into a non-interest bearing, non-trust account with the BIA.

§115.708 How quickly will trust funds received by the Secretary on behalf of tribes or individual Indians be deposited into a trust account?

Trust funds received by the Secretary on behalf of a tribe or individual Indians will be deposited into a trust account within twenty-four hours, or no later than the close of business on the next business day following the receipt of funds at a location with a designated federal depository.

§115.709 Will an annual audit be conducted on trust funds?

Yes, in accordance with the Trust Reform Act an annual audit will be conducted on trust funds. Each tribe and IIM account holder will be notified when the Secretary has conducted an annual audit on a fiscal year basis of all the trust funds held by the United States for the benefit of tribes and individual Indians. This notice will be provided in the first quarterly statement of performance following the publication of the audit.

INVESTMENTS AND INTERESTS

§ 115.710 Does money in a trust account earn interest?

Yes, all money deposited in a trust account is invested and earns interest or yield returns, or both.

§ 115.711 How is money in a trust account invested?

OTFM manages trust fund investments and its investment decisions are governed by federal statute. See 25 U.S.C. §§ 161(a) and 162a.

§ 115.712 What is the interest rate earned on money in a trust account?

The rate of interest on a trust account changes based on how the money is invested and how those investments perform.

§ 115.713 When does money in a trust account start earning interest?

Funds must remain on deposit at least one business day before interest is earned. Interest earnings of less than one cent are not credited to any account.

Subpart G—Tribal Accounts

§ 115.800 When does OTFM open a tribal account?

A tribal account is opened when OTFM receives income from the sources described in § 115.702.

§ 115.801 How often will a tribe receive information about its trust account(s)?

The OTFM is required to provide each tribe with a statement of performance quarterly, within or no later than 20 business days after the close of every quarterly statement period.

§ 115.802 May a tribe make a request to OTFM to receive information about its trust account more frequently?

Yes, a tribe may contact OTFM at any time to:

(a) Request information about account transactions and balances;

(b) Make arrangements to access account information electronically; or

(c) Receive a monthly statement.

§ 115.803 What information will be provided in a statement of performance?

The statement of performance will identify the source, type, and status of the trust funds deposited and held in a trust account; the beginning balance; the gains and losses; receipts and disbursements; and the ending account balance of the quarterly statement period.

§ 115.804 Will we account to a tribe for those trust funds the tribe receives through direct pay?

No, under the Trust Reform Act we are only responsible for accounting for those trust funds received into, and maintained by, the Department's trust funds management system.

§ 115.805 If a tribe is paid directly under a contract for the sale or use of trust assets, will we accept those trust funds for deposit into a tribal trust account?

If a contract for the sale or use of trust assets specifies that payments are to be made directly to a tribe, we will not accept these trust funds into a tribal trust account. Where a tribe under 25 U.S.C. 450f *et seq.* has contracted or compacted with the federal government to operate a federal program and the tribe, operating the federal program on behalf of the Secretary, receives trust funds for the sale or use of trust assets pursuant to a contract that specifies that payments are to be made to the Secretary on behalf of a tribe or an individual [the owner of the trust assets], the tribe must follow § 115.708 for the deposit of the trust funds into the trust account.

§ 115.806 How will the BIA assist in the administration of tribal judgment fund accounts?

(a) If the tribe requests assistance or if Congress directs the Secretary to provide assistance, BIA will provide technical assistance on developing a judgment use and distribution plan to a tribe.

(b) BIA will review all tribal requests for distribution of tribal judgment funds to ensure that each request complies with any requirements associated with the use of that money found in statutory language, congressional directives, court orders, court-approved settlements, settlement agreements, use and distribution plans, or bond or loan payments.

INVESTING AND MANAGING TRIBAL TRUST FUNDS

§115.807 Will OTFM consult with tribes about investments of tribal trust funds?

Upon the request of a tribe, OTFM will consult with the tribe annually to develop investment strategies to accommodate the cash flow needs of the tribe.

§115.808 Could trust fund investments made by OTFM lose money?

The value of trust fund investments made by OTFM will vary depending on the type of investment and, including but not limited to, the following:

(a) Current interest rates;

(b) Whether the security/investment is held to its maturity; and

(c) Original purchase price.

However, as long as the purchase price of the security/investment is made at or below face value and the security/investment is held until maturity or payoff, the security/investment will not lose principal invested funds.

§115.809 May a tribe recommend to OTFM how to invest the tribe's trust funds?

Tribes may recommend certain investments to OTFM, but the recommendations must be in accordance with the statutory requirements set forth in 25 U.S.C. §§161a and 162a. The OTFM will make the final investment decision based on prudent investment practices.

§115.810 May a tribe directly invest and manage its trust funds?

A tribe may apply to withdraw its trust funds from OTFM for investment and management by the tribe. The tribe's request to withdraw funds must be in accordance with the requirements of the Trust Reform Act and 25 CFR part 1200, subpart B, unless otherwise specified by statutory language or the controlling document which governs the use of the trust funds.

§115.811 Under what conditions may a tribe redeposit funds with OTFM that were previously withdrawn under the Trust Reform Act?

Tribal trust funds withdrawn under the Trust Reform Act may be returned to OTFM under the following conditions:

(a) A tribe must make a written request to OTFM to redeposit all or part of the withdrawn trust funds;

(b) No tribal trust funds may be redeposited to a tribal trust account during the first six months after being withdrawn, except with the approval of the Secretary;

(c) Tribal trust funds may only be returned to OTFM a maximum of twice a year, except with the approval of the Secretary; and

(d) A tribe must return withdrawn trust funds in accordance with the requirements of the Trust Reform Act in 25 CFR, part 1200, subpart C.

§115.812 Is a tribe responsible for its expenditures of trust funds that are not made in compliance with statutory language or other federal law?

If a tribe's use of trust funds is limited by statutory language or other federal law(s) and a tribe uses those trust funds in direct violation of those laws, absent an approved modification which allows for the expenditures, we will require the tribe to reimburse its trust fund account.

§115.813 Is there a limit to the amount of trust funds OTFM will disburse from a tribal trust account?

OTFM will only disburse the available balance of the trust funds in a tribal trust account in accordance with a use and distribution plan, if applicable, and will not overdraw a tribal trust account. If a tribe's trust funds are invested in securities that have not matured, OTFM will only sell the asset to make cash available to the tribe if:

(a) There are no restrictions against the sale, and

(b) A tribe provides OTFM with a tribal resolution stating that:

(1) The security must be sold;

(2) The tribe acknowledges that they may incur a penalty when the security is sold; and

(3) The tribe acknowledges that the security may lose value if it is sold prior to maturity.

§ 115.814 If a tribe withdraws money from its trust account for a particular purpose or project, may the tribe redeposit any money that was not used for its intended purpose?

A tribe may redeposit funds not used for a particular purpose or project if:

(a) The funds were withdrawn in accordance with:

(1) The terms of Trust Reform Act;

(2) The terms of the legislative settlement; or

(3) The terms of a judgment use and distribution plan; and

(b) The tribe can provide documentation showing the source of the funds to be redeposited.

WITHDRAWING TRIBAL TRUST FUNDS

§ 115.815 How does a tribe request trust funds from a tribal trust account?

To request trust funds from a tribal trust account, a tribe may:

(a) Make a written request to the BIA or the OTFM that is signed by the proper authorizing official(s), list the amount of trust funds to be withdrawn, provide any additional documentation or information required by law to withdraw certain trust funds, and must include a tribal resolution approving the withdrawal of the specified amount of trust funds; or

(b) Contact the OTFM to withdraw funds in accordance with the Trust Reform Act and 25 CFR part 1200.

§ 115.816 May a tribe's request for a withdrawal of trust funds from its trust account be delayed or denied?

(a) Action on a tribe's request for a withdrawal of trust funds may be delayed or denied if:

(1) The tribe did not submit all the necessary documentation;

(2) The tribe's request is not signed by the proper authorizing official(s);

(3) OTFM does not have documentation from the tribe certifying its recognized, authorizing officials;

(4) The tribe's request is in conflict with statutory language or the controlling document governing the use of the trust funds; or

(5) The BIA or OTFM requires clarification regarding the tribe's request.

(b) If action on a tribe's request to withdraw trust funds will be delayed or denied, the BIA or the OTFM will:

(1) Notify the tribe within ten (10) working days of the date of a request made under § 115.815(a);

(2) Notify the tribe under the time frames established in 25 CFR part 1200 for requests made under the Trust Reform Act; and

(3) Provide technical assistance to the tribe to address any problems.

§ 115.817 How does OTFM disburse money to a tribe?

Upon receipt of all necessary documentation, OTFM will process the request for disbursement and send the tribe the requested amount of trust funds within one business day. Whenever possible, trust funds will be disbursed electronically to an account in a financial institution designated by the tribe. If there are circumstances that preclude electronic payments, OTFM will mail a check.

UNCLAIMED PER CAPITA FUNDS

§ 115.818 What happens if an Indian adult does not cash his or her per capita check?

(a) If an Indian adult does not cash his or her per capita check within twelve (12) months of the date the check was issued, the check will be canceled and the trust funds will be deposited into a "returned per capita account" where the funds will be maintained until we receive a request for disbursement by the Indian adult or for disposition by a tribe pursuant to § 115.820.

(b) If an Indian adult's per capita check is returned to us as undeliverable, the trust funds will be immediately deposited into a "returned per capita account" where the funds will be maintained until we receive a request for disbursement by the individual or for disposition by a tribe pursuant to § 115.820.

§ 115.819 What steps will be taken to locate an individual whose per capita check is returned as undeliverable or not cashed within twelve (12) months of issuance?

The OTFM will notify a tribe of the names of the individuals whose per capita checks were returned as undeliverable or not cashed within twelve (12) months of issuance and will take reasonable action, including utilizing electronic search tools, to locate the individual entitled to receive the per capita funds.

§ 115.820 May OTFM transfer money in a returned per capita account to a tribal account?

Funds in a returned per capita account will not automatically be returned to a tribe. However, a tribe may apply under 25 U.S.C. 164 and Public Law 87–283, 75 Stat. 584 (1961), to have the unclaimed per capita funds transferred to its account for the tribe's use after six years have passed from the date of distribution.

Subpart H—Special Deposit Accounts

§ 115.900 Who receives the interest earned on trust funds in a special deposit account?

Generally, any interest earned on trust funds in a special deposit account will follow the principal (i.e., the tribe or individual who owns the trust funds in the special deposit account will receive the interest earned).

§ 115.901 When will the trust funds in a special deposit account be credited or paid out to the owner of the funds?

OTFM will disburse the trust funds from a special deposit account and deposit the trust funds in the owner's trust account following the BIA certification of the ownership of the funds and OTFM's receipt of such certification.

§ 115.902 May administrative or land conveyance fees paid as federal reimbursements be deposited in a special deposit account?

No, administrative or land conveyance fees paid as federal reimbursements may not be deposited with OTFM, which includes special deposit accounts. These fees must be deposited in the Federal Financial System.

§ 115.903 May cash bonds (e.g., performance bonds, appeal bonds, etc.) be deposited into a special deposit account?

No, cash bonds may not be deposited with OTFM, which includes the special deposit accounts at OTFM. Cash bonds held by the Secretary are to be deposited in non-interest bearing accounts until the term of the bonds expire.

§ 115.904 Where earnest money is paid prior to Secretarial approval of a conveyance or contract instrument involving trust assets, may the BIA deposit that earnest money into a special deposit account?

No, any money received prior to Secretarial approval of conveyance or contract instrument involving trust assets must be deposited into a non-interest bearing, non-trust account. After the Secretary approves the conveyance or contract instrument involving trust assets, the money designated by the conveyance or contract instrument will be deposited into a trust fund account.

Subpart I—Records

§ 115.1000 Who owns the records associated with this part?

(a) Records are the property of the United States if they:

(1) Are made or received by a tribe or tribal organization in the conduct of a federal trust function under this part, including the operation of a trust program pursuant to 25 U.S.C. 450f *et seq.*; and

(2) Evidence the organization, functions, policies, decisions, procedures, operations, or other activities undertaken in the performance of a federal trust function under this part.

(b) Records not covered by paragraph (a) of this section that are made or received by a tribe or tribal organization in the conduct of business with the Department of the Interior under this part are the property of the tribe.

§ 115.1001 How must records associated with this part be preserved?

(a) Any organization, including tribes and tribal organizations, that have records identified in § 115.1000(a) must preserve the records in accordance with approved Departmental records retention procedures under the Federal Records Act, 44 U.S.C. Chapters 29, 31 and 33. These records and related records management practices and safeguards required under the Federal Records Act are subject to inspection by the Secretary and the Archivist of the United States.

(b) A tribe or tribal organization should preserve the records identified in § 115.1000(b) for the period of time authorized by the Archivist of the United States for similar Department of the Interior records in accordance with 44 U.S.C. Chapter 33. If a tribe or tribal organization does not preserve records associated with its conduct of business with the Department of the Interior under this part, the tribe or tribal organization may be prevented from being able to adequately document essential transactions or furnish information necessary to protect its legal and financial rights or those of persons directly affected by its activities.

PART 117—DEPOSIT AND EXPENDITURE OF INDIVIDUAL FUNDS OF MEMBERS OF THE OSAGE TRIBE OF INDIANS WHO DO NOT HAVE CERTIFICATES OF COMPETENCY

Sec.

AUTHORITY: 5 U.S.C. 301.

SOURCE: 22 FR 10554, Dec. 24, 1957, unless otherwise noted. Redesignated at 47 FR 13327, Mar. 30, 1982.

§ 117.1 Definitions.

When used in the regulations in this part the following words or terms shall have the meaning shown below:

(a) *Secretary* means the Secretary of the Interior or his authorized representative.

(b) *Commissioner* means the Commissioner of Indian Affairs or his authorized representative.

(c) *Superintendent* means the superintendent of the Osage Agency.

(d) *Quarterly payment* means the payment of not to exceed $1,000 which is made each fiscal quarter to or on behalf of an adult Indian, from the following sources:

(1) The pro rata distribution of tribal mineral income and other tribal revenues.

(2) The interest on segregated trust funds.

(3) Surplus funds in addition to the income from the foregoing sources in the amount necessary to aggregate $1,000 when the income from those sources is less than $1,000 and the Indian has a balance of accumulated surplus funds in excess of $10,000.

(e) *Surplus funds* means all those moneys and securities readily convertible into cash, except allowance funds and segregated trust funds, which are held to the credit of an Indian at the

Osage Agency and which may be disbursed, expended or invested only upon authorization by the Secretary. The term includes:

(1) That portion of the quarterly distribution of tribal income and interest on segregated trust funds, in excess of $1,000, belonging to an adult Indian.

(2) The proceeds, including appreciation, of the sale or conversion of restricted real or personal property (other than partition sales).

(3) Payments made by insurance companies or others for loss or damage to restricted real or personal property.

(4) All moneys and securities, other than segregated trust funds, to the credit of an Indian who is less than 21 years of age (except the income from restricted lands payable as provided by § 117.3).

(5) Funds and securities placed to the credit of an Indian upon the distribution of an Osage estate.

(f) *Allowance funds* means that income payable to or on behalf of a living adult Indian, the expenditure and disbursement of which is not subject to supervision unless authorized pursuant to the procedure contained in § 117.5. The term includes:

(1) The quarterly payment in an amount not to exceed $1,000.

(2) The rentals and income from restricted lands owned by the Indian.

(3) The rentals and income from restricted lands owned by the minor children of the Indian, as provided in § 117.3.

(4) Income from investments.

(5) Interest on deposits to the credit of the Indian.

(g) *Segregated trust funds* means those moneys held in the United States Treasury at interest to the credit of an Indian which represent pro rata shares of the segregation of tribal trust funds and the proceeds of the partition of restricted lands.

§ 117.2 Payment of taxes of adult Indians.

The superintendent may cause to be paid out of any money heretofore accrued or hereafter accruing to the credit of any adult Indian all taxes of every kind and character for which such Indian is or may be liable before paying to or for such person any funds as required by law. All checks in payment of taxes shall be made payable to the proper collector. For the purpose of establishing a fund with which to meet the payment of such taxes when due, the Superintendent may cause the funds of an adult Indian to be hypothecated in the following manner:

(a) For the payment of ad valorem taxes, one-fourth of the estimated amount ad valorem taxes from each quarterly payment unless this procedure would cause the obligation of more than 25 percent of such quarterly payments, in which event the necessary additional funds shall be retained from other allowance funds payable to such person under the law. If there be no other allowance funds available, or if the funds from these sources are insufficient, one-fourth of the estimated amount of such ad valorem taxes may be obligated from each quarterly payment. If an Indian who is liable for ad valorem taxes has no allowance funds, or such funds are insufficient for the payment thereof, surplus funds may be used for such payment.

(b)(1) For the payment of income taxes, one-half of the estimated amount of income taxes from each semi-annual payment of interest on deposits, but if such interest payments are insufficient to meet this obligation, additional funds shall be retained from interest on investments, rentals, or other allowance funds.

(2) Whenever funds are withheld for the purpose of establishing a fund to meet the payment of taxes, the Indian shall be notified of the action taken.

§ 117.3 Payment of taxes of Indians under 21 years of age.

All taxes assessed against the restricted lands of Indians less than 21 years of age shall be paid by the superintendent direct to the collector from the rents and income derived from such lands, and the balance, if any, of such rents and income shall be paid to the living parents or parent. If the parents are separated, the balance shall be paid to the parent having custody of the Indian under 21 years of age. All other taxes for which an Indian under 21 years of age may be liable shall be paid from his surplus funds.

§ 117.4 Disbursement of allowance funds.

Except as provided in § 117.5, all allowance funds shall be disbursed to the Indian owner unless the Indian owner directs otherwise in writing. At the request of the Indian owner, such funds may be retained by the superintendent as voluntary deposits subject to withdrawal or other disposition upon demand or direction of the Indian owner. The superintendent may recognize a power of attorney executed by the Indian and may disburse the allowance funds of the Indian in conformity therewith so long as the power of attorney remains in force and effect.

§ 117.5 Procedure for hearings to assume supervision of expenditure of allowance funds.

(a) Whenever the superintendent has reason to believe that an adult Indian is wasting or squandering his allowance funds the superintendent may cause an investigation and written report of the facts to be made. If the report indicates that the Indian is wasting or squandering his allowance funds the following notice shall be served upon the Indian, in person or by registered mail, and a copy thereof shall likewise be served upon his guardian if the Indian is under guardianship:

Section 1 of the act of February 27, 1925 (43 Stat. 1008) provides in part as follows:

"All payments to adults not having certificates of competency, including amounts paid for each minor, shall, in case the Secretary of the Interior finds that such adults are wasting or squandering said income, be subject to the supervision of the Superintendent of the Osage Agency: . . ."

Enclosed is a copy of a report which has been made to me concerning your handling and management of the income paid to you through the Osage Agency. This report indicates that you have been wasting and squandering your payments.

You are hereby notified that a hearing will be held in the Osage Indian Agency, Pawhuska, Oklahoma, at ____ m., on the ________ day of ___________, 19___, before the Superintendent, for the purpose of taking testimony and evidence to be submitted to the Commissioner of Indian Affairs for his consideration in determining whether your payments shall be subject to the supervision of the Superintendent.

You are requested to be present at the hearing at the time and place designated above. You may introduce at the hearing such testimony and evidence as you deem appropriate to show that you are not wasting or squandering your payments and that your payments should continue to be made to you without supervision for your unrestricted use.

You are entitled to employ an attorney to assist you in this matter. Upon your request the employees of the Osage Agency will furnish you with any information you desire concerning your accounts at the Osage Agency or any of your transactions handled through the Osage Agency.

Date.

Superintendent.

(b) A hearing shall be held pursuant to the notice, the date of which shall be not less than 30 days after the date of the notice. For good cause shown to exist the superintendent may continue the hearing to a later date.

(c) A record of the proceedings, consisting of the superintendent's preliminary report, the notice and proof of service, all testimony and evidence introduced at the hearing, and all briefs and letters filed by the Indian or his attorney shall be submitted to the Commissioner, together with a recommendation from the superintendent.

(d) Upon a finding by the Commissioner that the Indian is wasting or squandering his income, his allowance funds shall thereafter be subject to the supervision of the superintendent. Notice of the decision of the Commissioner shall be furnished all interested parties.

§ 117.6 Allowance for minors.

The superintendent may disburse from the surplus funds of an Indian under 21 years of age not to exceed $300 quarterly for the support and maintenance of the minor. Disbursement may be made to the parent, guardian, or other person, school or institution having actual custody of the minor, or, when the minor is 18 years of age or over, disbursement may be made direct to the minor.

§ 117.7 Disbursement or expenditure of surplus funds.

Except as provided in the regulations in this part, no disbursement or expenditure of surplus funds of Indians shall be made without the consent of the Indian owner and until authorization has been obtained from the Commissioner. Application by an Indian or his legal guardian, or if he is a minor, by his parent or legal guardian, for the expenditure of surplus funds shall be presented to the Commissioner, fully justified with the appropriate attachments such as court orders, decrees or other papers. Such application shall contain full information regarding the individual including his cash balance, the sum invested, the number of shares in the Osage mineral estate, total income from all sources including that paid on behalf of minors, the family status and the occupation or industry of the applicant. When request is made for payment to the individual without supervision, the record of said individual and his ability to handle such funds shall be shown.

§ 117.8 Purchase of land.

Upon written application of an adult Indian, the superintendent may disburse not to exceed $10,000 from the surplus funds of such Indian for the purchase of land, the title to which has been examined and accepted by the special attorney for the Osage Indians or other legal officer designated by the Commissioner. In all cases title must be taken by deed containing a clause restricting alienation or encumbrance without the consent of the Secretary of the Interior or his authorized representative.

§ 117.9 Construction and repairs.

Upon written application by an adult Indian, the superintendent may disburse not to exceed $1,000 during any one fiscal year from the surplus funds of such Indian to make repairs and improvements to restricted real property and in addition not to exceed $300 for new construction. When such expenditures are being made on property producing an income, reimbursement shall be required from such income unless otherwise directed by the Commissioner. When an Indian refuses to make application for funds to defray the cost of repairs necessary to preserve restricted property, the superintendent may, when authorized by the Commissioner, expend the surplus funds of the Indian for such repairs.

§ 117.10 Purchase of automotive equipment.

The superintendent may disburse from the surplus funds of an adult Indian not to exceed $2,000 for the purchase of automotive equipment when the Indian agrees in writing to carry property and liability insurance on the automotive equipment and to reimburse his surplus funds account from allowance funds within 24 months. No disbursement of surplus funds for the purchase of automotive equipment shall be made if the fulfillment of the reimbursable agreement will endanger the payment of taxes, insurance or other obligations, or result in the inability of the Indian to meet his current living expenses from allowance funds.

§ 117.11 Insurance.

The superintendent may obtain policies of insurance covering the restricted property, real or personal, of minor Indians and pay the premiums thereon from the funds of the minors. Upon application by an adult Indian the superintendent may procure insurance on any restricted property, real or personal, owned by the applicant and pay the necessary premiums from his surplus or allowance funds. When authorized by the Commissioner, the superintendent may also procure insurance on restricted property, real or personal, of any adult Indian who neglects or refuses to take out such insurance.

§ 117.12 Costs of recording and conveyancing.

The superintendent may expend the surplus funds of an Indian to make direct payment of recording fees and costs, of conveyancing, including abstracting costs, which are properly payable by the Indian.

§ 117.13 Telephone and telegraph messages.

The superintendent may expend the surplus funds of an Indian to make direct payment for telephone and telegraph messages sent by the agency or received at the agency at the instance of the Indian or his guardian or attorney.

§ 117.14 Miscellaneous expenditure of surplus funds.

Upon application by an adult Indian the superintendent may disburse the surplus funds of such Indian for the following purposes:

(a) Medical, dental, and hospital expenses for the applicant or a member of his family, not to exceed one thousand dollars ($1,000) during any one fiscal year.

(b) Funeral expenses, including the funeral feast, of a deceased member of his family, in an amount not to exceed one thousand dollars ($1,000).

(c) A tombstone or monument to mark the grave of a deceased member of his family in amount not to exceed five hundred dollars ($500).

(d) Court costs in any judicial proceeding to which the applicant is a party.

(e) Bond premiums, except bail and supersedeas bonds.

(f) For miscellaneous purposes, not to exceed five hundred dollars ($500) during any one fiscal year.

§ 117.15 Collections from insurance companies.

Moneys collected from insurance companies for loss or damage to restricted real or personal property shall be deposited to the credit of the Indian owner as surplus funds. Moneys so deposited to the credit of an adult Indian may, upon the written application of the Indian, be disbursed by the superintendent for the purpose of repairing or replacing the property. Moneys collected from insurance companies for loss or damage to unrestricted real or personal property shall be paid to the Indian for his unrestricted use.

§ 117.16 Reimbursement to surplus funds.

When expenditures have been made from surplus funds upon the condition, and with the written agreement of the Indian, that reimbursement or repayment shall be made from future allowance funds, the superintendent is authorized to withhold from succeeding quarterly payments or other allowance funds such amounts as may be necessary to effect reimbursement within a period not exceeding 24 months from date of the first expenditure under the given authority.

§ 117.17 Inactive surplus funds accounts.

When the balance of surplus funds to the credit of an adult Indian is less than $300 and when there is no likelihood of its increase within 90 days, the superintendent may disburse the entire balance to the Indian owner for his unrestricted use.

§ 117.18 Withdrawal and payment of segregated trust funds.

The withdrawal and payment of segregated trust funds will be made only upon application and satisfactory evidence that the withdrawal and payment of such funds would be to the best interest of the Indian in view of all the circumstances shown to exist. The segregated trust funds of an Indian under guardianship or an Indian under 21 years of age shall not be released and paid except to a guardian appointed by a proper court and after the filing of a bond approved by the court conditioned upon the faithful handling of the funds. Applications for the withdrawal and payment of segregated trust funds must be made upon the forms prescribed by the Secretary for that purpose.

§ 117.19 Debts of Indians.

No indebtedness of Indians will be paid from their funds under the control or supervision of the Secretary unless authorized in writing and obligated against their accounts by the superintendent or some other designated employee except in cases of emergency involving the protection or preservation of life or property, which emergency must be clearly shown. With this exception, no authorization or obligation against the account of any Indian for indebtedness incurred by him shall be made by the superintendent unless specifically authorized by the regulations in this part.

§ 117.20 Purchase orders.

Purchase orders may be issued by the superintendent for expenditures authorized by the regulations in this part or for expenditures specifically authorized by the Commissioner. When necessary to prevent hardship or suffering, purchase orders may be issued by the superintendent against the future income of an Indian in an amount not to exceed 80 percent of the anticipated quarterly payment. The payment of purchase orders issued against future income shall be contingent upon the availability of funds.

§117.21 Fees and expenses of attorneys.

When payment of an attorney fee for services to an Indian is to be made from his surplus funds, the employment of the attorney by the Indian must be approved in advance. All fees will be determined on a quantum merit basis and paid upon completion of the services. The superintendent may approve the employment of an attorney, determine the fee, and disburse the surplus funds of the Indian in payment thereof when the fee does not exceed $500. Upon application by the Indian and upon the presentation of properly authenticated vouchers, the superintendent may disburse the surplus funds of the Indian in an amount not to exceed $200 in payment of necessary expenses incurred by the attorney.

§117.22 Disbursements to legal guardians.

Any disbursement authorized to be made to an Indian by the regulations of this part may, when the Indian is under guardianship, be made by the superintendent to the guardian. All expenditures by a guardian of the funds of his ward must be approved in writing by the court and the superintendent.

§117.23 Transactions between guardian and ward.

Business dealings between the guardian and his ward involving the sale or purchase of any property, real or personal, by the guardian to or from the ward, or to or from any store, company or organization in which the guardian has a direct interest or concern or contrary to the policy of the Department and shall not be approved by the superintendent without specific authority from the Commissioner.

§117.24 Compensation for guardians and their attorneys.

(a) The superintendent may approve compensation for services rendered by the guardian of an Indian on an annual basis, the amount of the compensation to be determined by application of the following schedule to the moneys collected by the guardian:

First $1,000 or portion thereof, not to exceed 10 percent.
Second $1,000 or portion thereof, not to exceed 9 percent.
Third $1,000 or portion thereof, not to exceed 8 percent.
Fourth $1,000 or portion thereof, not to exceed 7 percent.
Fifth $1,000 or portion thereof, not to exceed 6 percent.
Sixth $1,000 or portion thereof, not to exceed 5 percent.
Seventh $1,000 or portion thereof, not to exceed 4 percent.
Eighth $1,000 or portion thereof, not to exceed 3 percent.
Ninth $1,000 or portion thereof, not to exceed 2 percent.
All above $9,000 not to exceed 1 percent.

(b) Balance carried forward from previous reports and moneys received by a guardian or his attorney as compensation shall be excluded in determining the compensation of the guardian or his attorney.

(c) The attorney for a guardian shall be allowed compensation in an amount equal to one-half of the amount allowed the guardian under the foregoing schedule except when such attorney is himself the guardian and acting as his own attorney, in which event he shall be allowed a fee of not to exceed one-fourth of the amount allowed the guardian under the foregoing schedule in addition to the fee as guardian.

(d) The superintendent may in his discretion permit the guardian to collect rentals from restricted city or town properties belonging to his ward.

§117.25 Charges for services to Indians.

The superintendent shall make the following charges for services to Indians: Five per cent of all interest and non-liquidating dividends received from all types of securities, including stocks, bonds, and mortgages held in trust for individual Indians and interest on group investments. Such fees shall be deposited in the Treasury of the United States to the credit of the fund "Proceeds of Oil and Gas Leases, Royalties, etc., Osage Reservation, Oklahoma".

§ 117.26 Expenses incurred pending qualification of an executor or administrator.

Pending the qualification of the executor or administrator of the estate of a deceased Indian of one-half or more Indian blood who did not have a certificate of competency at the time of his death, the superintendent may authorize the extension of credit for the following purposes, subject to allowance of claims by the executor or administrator and approval thereof by the court:

(a) Funeral expenses, including the cost of a funeral feast, in an amount not to exceed $1,000.

(b) Necessary expenses in hearings before the Osage Agency involving the approval or disapproval of last wills and testaments.

(c) Expenses necessary to preserve restricted property.

§ 117.27 Custody of funds pending administration of estates.

(a) *Estates of Indians of less than one-half Indian blood and estates of Indians who had certificates of competency.* Upon the death of an Indian of less than one-half Indian blood or an Indian who had a certificate of competency, the superintendent shall pay to the executor or administrator of the estate all moneys and securities, other than segregated trust funds to the credit of the Indian and all funds which accrue pending administration of the estate.

(b) *Estates of Indians of one-half or more Indian blood who did not have certificates of competency.* Upon the death of an Indian of one-half or more Indian blood who did not have a certificate of competency at the time of his death, the following classes of funds, less any amount hypothecated for the payment of taxes as provided in § 117.2 shall be paid by the superintendent to the executor or administrator of the estate:

(1) Allowance funds to the credit of the Indian.

(2) Any quarterly payment authorized prior to the death of the Indian.

(3) Interest on segregated trust funds and deposits computed to the date of death.

(4) Rentals and income from restricted lands collected after the death of the Indian which were due and payable to the Indian prior to his death.

Except as provided in § 117.28, the superintendent shall not pay to the executor or administrator any surplus funds to the credit of the Indian or any funds, other than those listed in paragraphs (b) (1), (2), (3) and (4) of this section which accrue pending administration of the estate.

§ 117.28 Payment of claims against estates.

The superintendent may disburse to the executor or administrator of the estate of a deceased Indian of one-half or more Indian blood who did not have a certificate of competency at the time of his death sufficient funds out of the estate to pay the following classes of claims approved by the court:

(a) Debts authorized by the superintendent during the lifetime of the Indian.

(b) Expenses incurred pending the qualifications of an executor or administrator under authority contained in § 117.26.

(c) Expenses of administration, including court costs, premium on bond of executor or administrator, transcript fees and appraiser fees.

(d) Living expenses incurred within 90 days immediately preceding the date of death of the Indian.

(e) Allowance for reasonable living expenses each month for 12 months to a surviving spouse who is entitled to participate in the distribution of the estate and who is in need of such support.

(f) Allowance for reasonable living expenses each month for 12 months for each child of the decedent under 21 years of age who is entitled to participate in the distribution of the estate and who is in need of such support.

(g) Insurance premiums and license fees on restricted property.

(h) Not to exceed $1,000 for the preservation and upkeep of restricted property including the services of a caretaker when necessary.

(i) Debts incurred during the lifetime of the Indian but not authorized by the superintendent, if found by the Commissioner to be just and payable. The superintendent shall disburse no funds to an executor or administrator for the payment of the foregoing classes of claims unless the executor or administrator has no other funds in his hands available for the payment of such claims.

[22 FR 10554, Dec. 24, 1957, as amended at 35 FR 10005, June 18, 1970. Redesignated at 47 FR 13327, Mar. 30, 1982]

§117.29 Sale of improvements.

The superintendent may approve the sale of improvements on restricted Indian lands when such improvements are appraised at not more than $500 and when the owner has submitted a written request that the sale be made and a statement that the improvements can no longer be used by him. The proceeds of all such sales shall be deposited to the credit of the Indian as surplus funds. Improvements consisting of buildings, etc., located on property within the Osage villages of Pawhuska, Hominy, and Grayhorse may, upon approval of the superintendent, be disposed of to other Osage Indians. The superintendent may disburse the surplus funds of the purchaser to consummate the transaction. Sale of such improvements to non-Indian or non-Osage Indians must be approved by the Commissioner.

§117.30 Sale of personal property.

The superintendent may approve the sale of restricted personal property other than livestock. The superintendent may also approve the sale of livestock when authorized so to do by special or general instructions from the Commissioner. The proceeds from the sale of personal property other than livestock shall be deposited to the credit of the Indian as surplus funds unless the surplus funds from which said property was purchased have been reimbursed from allowance funds, in which case the proceeds from such sale shall be disbursed as allowance funds. If partial reimbursement only has been made, such portion of the proceeds of sale as may be necessary to complete the reimbursable agreement shall be deposited to the credit of the Indian as surplus funds and the balance, if any, shall be disbursed as allowance funds. The proceeds from the sale of livestock shall be deposited in conformity with general or specific instructions from the Commissioner.

§117.31 Removal of restrictions from personal property.

The superintendent may relinquish title to personal property (other than livestock) held by the United States in trust for the Indian when to do so will enable the Indian to use the property as part payment in the purchase of other personal property and when the remainder of the purchase price is to be made from other than surplus funds of the Indian.

§117.32 Funds of Indians of other tribes.

The funds of restricted non-Osage Indians, both adults and minors, residing within the jurisdiction of the Osage Agency, derived from sources within the Osage Nation and collected through the Osage Agency, may be disbursed by the superintendent, subject to the condition that all payments to third persons, including taxes and insurance premiums, shall be made upon the written authorization of the individual whose funds are involved, if an adult, and upon the written authorization of the parent or guardian, if a minor. The funds of restricted non-Osage Indians who do not reside within the jurisdiction of the Osage Agency shall be transferred to the superintendent of the jurisdiction within which the Indian resides, to be disbursed under regulations of the receiving agency.

§117.33 Signature of illiterates.

An Indian who cannot write shall be required to endorse checks payable to his order and sign receipts or other documents by making an imprint of the ball of the right thumb (or the left, if he has lost his right) after his name. This imprint shall be clear and distinct, showing the central whorl and striations and witnessed by two reputable persons whose addresses shall be given opposite or following their names. An Indian may sign by marking "X" before two witnesses where he is unable to attach his thumb mark for physical reasons.

§ 117.34 Financial status of Indians confidential.

The financial status of Indians shall be regarded as confidential and shall not be disclosed except to the owner of the account or his authorized agent, unless authorized in advance by the Commissioner.

§ 117.35 Appeals.

Any decision by the superintendent may be appealed to the area director, any decision by the area director may be appealed to the Commissioner, and any decision by the Commissioner may be appealed to the Secretary.

PART 122—MANAGEMENT OF OSAGE JUDGMENT FUNDS FOR EDUCATION

Sec.

AUTHORITY: 86 Stat. 1295, 98 Stat. 3103 (25 U.S.C. 331 note).

SOURCE: 54 FR 34155, Aug. 18, 1989, unless otherwise noted.

§ 122.1 Purpose and scope.

(a) The purpose of this part is to set forth procedures and guidelines to govern the use of authorized funds in education programs for the benefit of Osage Tribal members, along with application requirements and procedures used by those eligible persons.

(b) The Osage Tribe by act of Congress, October 27, 1972 (25 U.S.C. 883, 86 Stat. 12950, as amended by Pub. L. 98–605) on October 30, 1984, provides that $1 million, together with other funds which revert to the Osage Tribe, may be advanced, expended, invested, or reinvested for the purpose of financing an education program of benefit to the Osage Tribe of Indians of Oklahoma, with said program to be administered as authorized by the Secretary of the Interior.

§ 122.2 Definitions.

Act means Osage Tribe by Act of Congress, October 27, 1972 (25 U.S.C. 883, 86 Stat. 1295), as amended by Pub. L. 98–605.

Allottee means a person whose name appears on the roll of Osage Tribe of Indians approved by the Secretary of the Interior on April 11, 1908, pursuant to the Act of June 28, 1906 (34 Stat. 539).

Assistant Secretary means the Assistant Secretary—Indian Affairs.

Osage Tribal Education Committee means the committee selected to administer the provisions of this part as specified by § 122.6.

Reverted funds means the unpaid portions of the per capita distribution fund, as provided by the Act, which were not distributed because the funds were:

(1) Unclaimed within the period specified by the Act; or

(2) For an amount totaling less than $20 due an individual from one or more shares of one or more Osage allottees.

Secretary means the Secretary of the Department of the Interior or his/her authorized representative.

§ 122.3 Information collection.

(a) The information collection requirements contained in §§ 122.6 and 122.9 have been approved by the Office of Management and Budget under U.S.C. 3501 *et seq.* and assigned clearance numbers 1076–0098 and 1076–0106, respectively. The information collected in § 122.6 is used to determine the eligibility of Osage Indian student applicants for educational assistance grants. The information collected in § 122.9 provides summary review for program evaluation and program planning. Response to the information collections is required to obtain a benefit in accordance with 25 U.S.C. 883.

(b) Public reporting burden for this information collection is estimated to average 30 minutes per response, including the time for reviewing instructions, searching existing data sources, gathering and maintaining the data needed, and completing and reviewing the collection of information. Send comments regarding this burden estimate or any other aspect of this collection of information, including suggestions for reducing the burden, to the Bureau of Indian Affairs, Information Collection Clearance Officer, Room 337 SIB, 18th & C Streets, NW., Washington, DC 20240; and the Office of Management and Budget, Paperwork Reduction Project (1076–0106), Washington DC 20503.

§ 122.4 Establishment of the Osage Tribal Education Committee.

(a) The Osage Tribe, to maintain its right of Tribal autonomy, shall, at the direction of the Bureau of Indian Affairs, establish the Osage Tribal Education Committee (OTEC) to fulfill the responsibilities and provisions of this part as set out in § 122.6.

(b) This committee shall be composed of seven (7) members. Five (5) of the members shall be of Osage blood or descendents of Osage, and two (2) from the education staff of the Bureau of Indian Affairs.

(1) Of the five Osage members, at least three shall be legal residents and/or live within a 20-mile radius of one of the three Osage Indian villages. Of these, at least one member shall reside within the specified radius of the Pawhuska Indian village; at least one member shall reside within the specified radius of the Hominy Indian village; and at least one member shall reside within the specified radius of the Greyhorse Indian village.

(2) The two remaining Osage committee members will be members at large.

§ 122.5 Selection/nomination process for committee members.

(a) Selection of the five (5) OTEC members shall be made by the Assistant Secretary in accordance with the following:

(1) Any adult person of Osage Indian blood who is an allottee or a descendant of an allottee is eligible to serve on the Osage Tribal Education Committee.

(2) Nominees for committee membership shall include a brief statement of interest and qualifications for serving on the committee.

(b) Nominations may be made by any Osage organization, including the Osage village communities of Greyhorse, Hominy and Pawhuska, by requesting its candidates to follow procedures outlined in paragraph (a)(2) of this section.

(c) Nominations shall be delivered by registered mail to the following address: Osage Tribal Education Committee, c/o Area Education Programs Administrator, Bureau of Indian Affairs, Muskogee Area Office—Room 152, 5th & W, Okmulgee, Muskogee, Oklahoma 74401.

(d) A Nominee Selection Committee composed of OTEC members so designated by the Assistant Secretary will review all nominations. Upon completion of this process, the Nominee Selection Committee will forward its recommendations for final consideration to the Assistant Secretary.

(e) Each member shall be sworn in for a four year term. At the discretion of the Assistant Secretary, members may succeed themselves with a recommendation for reappointment from the Nominee Selection Committee.

(f) The Assistant Secretary may, until a vacancy is filled, appoint an individual to serve for a temporary period not to exceed 120 days.

§ 122.6 Duties of the Osage Tribal Education Committee.

(a) For the purpose of providing financial assistance to eligible Osage applicants for educational assistance, the Osage Tribal Education Committee shall maintain an office and retain all official records at the Bureau of Indian Affairs offices located at the Federal Building, Muskogee, Oklahoma.

(b) The Osage Tribal Education Committee shall be responsible for implementing an overall plan of operation consistent with the policy of Indian self-determination which incorporates a systematic sequential process whereby all student applications for financial aid are rated and ranked simultaneously to enable a fair distribution of available funds.

(1) All applicants shall be rated by a point system appropriate to applications for education assistance. After all

applications are rated, the Osage Tribal Education Committee will rank the applications in a descending order for award purposes. No awards shall be made until all applications are rated against the point system.

(2) Monetary awards shall be for fixed amounts as determined by the Osage Tribal Education Committee. The fixed amounts shall be itemized in the committee's annual budgetary request, and the monetary award amounts shall be consistent with the fixed amounts itemized in the approved budget.

(3) Payment of the monetary awards shall be made directly to the student, with half of the amount payable on or before September 15 and the second half payable on or before February 15, provided the student is successfully enrolled in an accredited institution of higher education and meeting the institution's requirement for passing work.

(4) No student will be funded beyond 10 semesters or five academic years, not to include summer sessions, nor shall any student with a baccalaureate degree be funded for an additional undergraduate degree.

§ 122.7 Budget.

(a) By August 1 of each year, the Osage Tribal Education Committee will submit a proposed budget to the Assistant Secretary or to his/her designated representative for formal approval. Unless the Assistant Secretary or his/her designated representative informs the committee in writing of budget restrictions by September 1, the proposed budget is considered to be accepted.

(b) The investment principal, composed of the one million dollars appropriated by the Act and reverted funds, must be invested in a federally insured banking or savings institution or invested in obligations of the Federal Government. There are no provisions in this part which shall limit the right of the Osage Tribal Education Committee to withdraw interest earned from the investment principal; however, expenditures shall be made against only the interest generated from investment principal and reverted funds.

(c) All funds deposited will accumulate interest at a rate not less than that generally available for similar funds deposited at the same banking or savings institution or invested in the same obligations of the United States Government for the same period of time.

§ 122.8 Administrative costs for management of the fund.

Funds available for expenditures may be used by the Osage Tribal Education Committee in the performance of its duties and responsibilities. Recordkeeping is required and proposed expenditures are to be attached with the August 1 proposed annual budget to the Assistant Secretary or his/her designated representative.

§ 122.9 Annual report.

The Osage Tribal Education Committee shall submit an annual report on OMB approved Form 1076–0106, Higher Education Annual Report, to the Assistant Secretary or his/her designated representative on or before November 1, for the preceding 12 month period.

§ 122.10 Appeal.

The procedure for appealing any decision regarding the awarding of funds under this part shall be made in accordance with 25 CFR part 2, Appeals from Administrative Action.

§ 122.11 Applicability.

These regulations shall cease upon determination of the legal and appropriate body to administer the fund and upon the establishment of succeeding regulations.

PART 124—DEPOSITS OF PROCEEDS FROM LANDS WITHDRAWN FOR NATIVE SELECTION

Sec.

AUTHORITY: 43 U.S.C. 1601 *et seq.*; Pub. L. 92–203, 85 Stat. 688; 25 U.S.C. 4001 *et seq.*; Pub L. 103–402, 108 Stat. 4239.

SOURCE: 70 FR 40661, July 14, 2005, unless otherwise noted.

§ 124.1 What is the purpose of this part?

This part provides contact information on depositing proceeds from contracts, leases, permits, rights-of-way, or easements pertaining to lands withdrawn for Native selection under the Alaska Native Claims Settlement Act. All Federal agencies and the State of Alaska must use this part when making deposits of this type.

§ 124.2 Who should an agency or the State of Alaska contact for information?

When a Federal agency or the State of Alaska receives proceeds covered by this part, it must deposit the proceeds to the credit of the United States Department of the Interior, Office of the Special Trustee for American Indians. For further information including depositing instructions, contact: Office of the Special Trustee for American Indians, Attention: Division of Trust Funds Accounting, 4400 Masthead Street NE., Albuquerque, New Mexico 87109.

PART 134—PARTIAL PAYMENT CONSTRUCTION CHARGES ON INDIAN IRRIGATION PROJECTS

Sec.

AUTHORITY: Secs. 1, 3, 36 Stat. 270, 272, as amended; 25 U.S.C. 385. Interpret or apply sec. 1, 41 Stat. 409; 25 U.S.C. 386.

SOURCE: 22 FR 10643, Dec. 24, 1957, unless otherwise noted. Redesignated at 47 FR 13327, Mar. 30, 1982.

§ 134.1 Partial reimbursement of irrigation charges; 5 percent per annum of cost of system, June 30, 1920.

In pursuance of the act of February 14, 1920 (41 Stat. 409; 25 U.S.C. 386), regulations governing partial payment of construction charges on Indian irrigation projects, with the exception of certain ones mentioned therein, where approved by the Department June 21, 1920, and require that each owner of irrigable land under any irrigation system constructed for the benefit of Indians under provisions of law requiring reimbursement of the cost of such system and to which land, water for irrigation purposes can be delivered from such system, shall pay, on or before November 15, 1920, a sum equal to 5 percent of the per acre cost, as of June 30, 1920, of the construction of the system under which such land is situated. The per acre cost of a given system as of June 30, 1920, shall be determined by dividing the total amount expended for construction purposes on such system up to that day by the total area of land to which water for irrigation purposes can be delivered on that date; and on November 15 of each year following the year 1920, until further notice, the land owners, as therein prescribed, shall pay 5 percent of the per acre construction cost as of June 30, of the current year, such per acre cost to be determined by dividing the cost of the system to June 30 of that year by the total area of land to which water for irrigation purposes can be delivered from the system on that date. Provision is contained that no payments shall be required under the regulations in behalf of lands still in process of allotment or prior to the issuance of the first or trust patent therefor, nor for lands reserved for school, agency, or other administrative purposes where the legal title still remains in the United States.

§ 134.2 Landowners financially unable to pay.

Considerable difficulty has been encountered in collecting charges under the regulations in this part owing to the fact that Indians have been financially unable to pay the charges, the result being that the construction charges have accrued against the lands and in cases where the land is sold for the benefit of the allottee or his heirs under the regulations, the purchaser is to pay the accrued and future irrigation charges which make it difficult in some instances, to sell the land at as favorable terms as might otherwise be secured.

§ 134.3 Period for payments extended.

Furthermore, in recent legislation dealing with specific projects in the Bureau and also all reclamation projects the policy has been to extend the payment of such charges over a longer period of years.

§ 134.4 Annual payment reduced.

In view of these conditions the regulations governing this matter are hereby modified so as to distribute the unaccrued installments over a period of time so that 2½ percent of the total amount yet due shall be due and payable on November 15 of each year until further notice. You shall accordingly ascertain the per acre cost after deducting the amount of the accrued charges and take 2½ percent of that amount and a like sum each year so that the amount of the annual installments will be the same each year. Superintendents are obligated to submit all proposed lists of sales involving allotments containing irrigable allotments to the project or supervising engineer for checking, as to the irrigable acreage and amounts of unpaid construction, operation, and maintenance charges against such allotments. Each sale forwarded to the Bureau for action shall be accompanied by contract executed on Form 5–462b where irrigable acreage is involved and after approval thereof a copy of contract on said form shall be sent to the project engineer for his records and the charges paid by the purchaser shall be turned over to the disbursing agent for credit and deposit as instructed in the next paragraph. The regulations in this part shall not apply to lands in the Wapato project, on the Yakima Indian Reservation, nor to the irrigation projects on the Blackfeet, Fort Peck, Flathead, and Crow Reservations, Montana, for which special regulations have been issued nor to the Fort Hall Reservation, Idaho, or the San Carlos project, Arizona.[1]

CROSS REFERENCES: For special regulations applying to San Carlos project, see part 137 of this chapter. For further information concerning Form 5–462b, see part 159 of this chapter.

§ 134.4a Assessment and collection of additional construction costs.

(a) Upon the completion of the construction of an Indian irrigation project, or unit thereof, subsequent to the determination of the partial per acre construction assessment rate which was fixed prior to July 1, 1957, pursuant to § 134.4 the Secretary of the Interior or his authorized representative shall determine such additional construction cost and distribute that cost on a per acre basis against all of the irrigable lands of the project, or unit thereof, and 1/40th of such per acre additional construction cost thus determined shall be assessed and collected annually from the non-Indian landowner of the project, or unit, thereof. The first installment shall be due and payable on November 15 of the year following the completion of such additional construction work or, if such additional construction work on the project, or unit thereof, has been completed prior to July 1, 1957, and the per acre annual rate determined, the first installment of the additional construction cost to be repaid by such non-Indian landowners shall be due and payable on November 15, 1958. This annual per acre rate shall be in addition to, and run concurrently with, the per acre construction rate assessed annually under § 134.4.

(b) Project lands in Indian ownership are not subject to assessment for their proportionate share of the per acre construction cost of the project, or unit thereof, until after the Indian title to the land has been extinguished. At that time the total annual per acre assessment rate against non-Indian lands of the project, or unit thereof, shall be assessed against the former Indian lands for each and every acre of irrigable land to which water can be delivered through the project works, beginning on November 15 of the year following the extinguishment of the Indian title to the land and on November 15 of each year thereafter over a forty year period. In cases where the Indian title to project land was extinguished prior to July 1, 1957, the assessment

[1] The special regulations for Wapato, Fort Peck, and Flathead, were not codified. Operations of the Blackfeet project were discontinued by the Bureau, July 20, 1938, effective September 30, 1933.

rate shall be due and payable on November 15, 1958.

§134.5 Payments to disbursing officer.

Payments under this part shall be made to the disbursing officer for the supervising engineer of the Indian Irrigation Service having jurisdiction over the irrigation system under which the land for which payment is made may lie. The sum so collected will then, after proper credit has been made to the land for which collected, be deposited in the Treasury of the United States to the credit of the respective funds used in constructing irrigation systems toward which reimbursement shall have been made.

§134.6 "Owner" defined.

The word "owner" as used in this part shall be construed to include any person, Indian or white, or any firm, partnership, corporation, association, or other organization to whom title to the land capable of irrigation, as provided in the act of February 14, 1920 (41 Stat. 409; 25 U.S.C. 386), has passed, either by fee or trust patent, or otherwise.

§134.7 Modifications.

The act of July 1, 1932 (47 Stat. 564; 25 U.S.C. 386a), cancelled all irrigation assessments for construction costs against lands in Indian ownership which were unpaid at that date and deferred all future assessments for construction costs until the Indian title to the land shall have been extinguished.

PART 135—CONSTRUCTION ASSESSMENTS, CROW INDIAN IRRIGATION PROJECT

Subpart A—Charges Assessed Against Irrigation District Lands

Sec.

Subpart B—Charges Assessed Against Non-Indian Lands Not Included in an Irrigation District

AUTHORITY: Sec. 15, 60 Stat. 338.

SOURCE: 22 FR 10644, Dec. 24, 1957, unless otherwise noted. Redesignated at 47 FR 13327, Mar. 30, 1982.

Subpart A—Charges Assessed Against Irrigation District Lands

§135.1 Contracts.

Under provisions of the act of Congress approved June 28, 1946 (60 Stat. 333-338), contracts were executed June 28, 1951, by the United States with the Lower Little Horn and Lodge Grass Irrigation District and the Upper Little Horn Irrigation District providing for the payment, over a period of 40 years, by each of the Districts of its respective share of the sum of $210,726 expended for the construction of the Willow Creek storage works on account of non-Indian lands within the Districts entitled to share in the storage water, directly or by substitution.

§135.2 Annual rate of assessments.

Within the Lower Little Horn and Lodge Grass Irrigation District there are 3,196.8 acres for which the District is obligated by contract to pay its proper share of the total construction costs. Within the Upper Little Horn Irrigation District there are 1,554.7 acres for which the District is obligated by contract to pay its proper share of the total construction costs. There are 3,237.6 acres, more or less, covered by contracts with private landowners, obligating such owners to pay their proper share of such construction costs. The total per acre charge against all such lands is $26.38. This amounts to an annual per acre rate of $0.6595. For the purpose of this notice the annual per acre rate is hereby fixed at $0.66. This annual per acre rate of assessment will continue for a 40-year period within which the total amount of construction costs of $210,726 is to be repaid without interest. The amount of each annual installment chargeable against each of the Districts for the acreage covered by their respective contracts shall be determined by multiplying the total acreage, under each contract entitled to Willow Creek storage rights, either directly or by subsituation, by the per acre annual rate.

§ 135.3 Annual assessments.

Notice is hereby given of an annual assessment of $2,108.05 to be repaid by the Lower Little Horn and Lodge Grass Irrigation District for the 3,196.8 acres of irrigable land of the District, and an annual assessment of $1,025.06 to be repaid by the Upper Little Horn Irrigation District for the 1,554.7 acres of irrigable land of the District. Against the amounts due annually by the Districts under this notice, there shall be allowed any credits due under section 6 of the act of June 28, 1946. Credits due on behalf of any land shall be reflected by the respective Districts when placing against such land the annual assessment on the tax rolls.

§ 135.4 Time of payment.

Annual assessments shall be paid by the Districts to the United States, one-half thereof on or before February 1 and one-half thereof on or before July 1 following, of each year commencing with the calendar year 1952.

§ 135.5 Penalty.

To all assessments not paid on the due date, there shall be added a penalty of one-half of one percent per month or fraction thereof, from the due date so long as the delinquency continues.

§ 135.6 Refusal of water delivery.

The right is reserved to the United States to refuse the delivery of water to each of the said Irrigation Districts in the event of default in the payment of assessments, including penalties on account of delinquencies.

Subpart B—Charges Assessed Against Non-Indian Lands Not Included in an Irrigation District

§ 135.20 Private contract lands; assessments.

In addition to 4,751.5 acres of non-Indian land included within the two irrigation Districts dealt with in subpart A, there are 3,237.6 acres of land, more or less, in non-Indian ownership under private ditches, covered by repayment contracts executed pursuant to the act of June 28, 1946 (60 Stat. 333–338), obligating such owners to pay their proper share of such construction costs. The total per acre charge against all such lands is $26.38. This amounts to an annual per acre rate of $0.6595. For the purposes of this notice the annual per acre rate is hereby fixed at $0.66. This annual rate of assessment will continue for a 40-year period within which the total amount of construction cost of $210,726 is to be repaid without interest. The amount of each annual installment chargeable against the lands covered by each of the several contracts with individual landowners whose lands are served under private ditches, shall be determined by multiplying the total acreage, under each contract entitled to Willow Creek storage rights, either directly or by substitution, by the per acre annual rate. Against the amounts due annually by the individual landowners whose lands are served by private ditches, under this notice there shall be allowed any credits due under section 6 of the act of June 28, 1946. Credits due on behalf of any land shall be reflected in any statement submitted to the landowners.

§ 135.21 Time of payment.

The amount of each annual installment, payable under the private landowner contracts, determined as provided in this part shall be paid by the landowners to the United States, on or before November 15 of each year commencing with the calendar year 1951.

§ 135.22 Penalty.

To all assessments not paid on the due date there shall be added a penalty of one-half of one percent per month or fraction thereof, from the due date so long as the delinquency continues.

§ 135.23 Refusal of water delivery.

The right is reserved to refuse the delivery of water to any landowner in the event of default in the payment of assessments, including penalties on account of delinquencies.

PART 136—FORT HALL INDIAN IRRIGATION PROJECT, IDAHO

AUTHORITY: Sec. 9, 46 Stat. 1063.

SOURCE: 22 FR 10645, Dec. 24, 1957, unless otherwise noted. Redesignated at 47 FR 13327, Mar. 30, 1982.

§ 136.1 Repayment contracts.

A rehabilitation program was established on the Fort Hall Unit of the Fort Hall Project in 1936. Based upon the estimated construction costs, contracts were signed by all non-Indian landowners within the project, including such landowners within the Little Indian Unit, now a part of the Fort Hall Unit. Under the terms of their contracts, the landowners agreed to repay to the Government their pro rata share, on an acreage basis, of all expenditures for construction and other necessary improvements for carrying out the approved program, payments not to exceed $7.50 per acre, based upon an estimated expenditure of $450,000.00 for a project then considered as covering approximately 60,000 acres.

§ 136.2 Construction costs.

The program of rehabilitation has now been completed at a cost of $419,186.52. This amount, chargeable on an equal per acre basis against 60,000 acres, amounts to a rate of $6.986 per acre, which rate is hereby determined to be the per acre cost to be repaid to the United States under the 1936 contracts.

§ 136.3 Repayment of construction costs.

Under the terms of the contracts, the landowners agreed to repay the construction cost in forty (40) equal annual installments. Therefore, the annual per acre installment is hereby fixed at seventeen and one-half cents (17½ cents) per acre, due and payable on December 1st of each year, the first payment being due on December 1, 1955. Under section 4 of the repayment contracts of the landowners and the act of March 10, 1928 (45 Stat. 210), the charges remain a lien against the lands until paid.

PART 137—REIMBURSEMENT OF CONSTRUCTION COSTS, SAN CARLOS INDIAN IRRIGATION PROJECT, ARIZONA

AUTHORITY: Sec. 5, 43 Stat. 476.

SOURCE: 22 FR 10645, Dec. 24, 1957, unless otherwise noted. Redesignated at 47 FR 13327, Mar. 30, 1982.

§ 137.1 Water supply.

The engineering report dealt with in section 1 of the act of June 7, 1924 (43 Stat. 475) and other available records show that the storage capacity of the San Carlos reservoir created by the Coolidge Dam and the water supply therefor over a period of years will provide for the irrigation of only 80,000 acres of lands in Indian and public or private ownership within the San Carlos irrigation project, the balance of the water supply needed for the additional 20,000 acres of the project to be provided for by recaptured and return flow water and by means of pumping the underground supply. The cost of providing the proposed supply and of operating the works for this latter acreage to be equally distributed over the entire 100,000 acres of the project regardless of where the works are placed and operated.

§ 137.2 Availability of water.

Pursuant to section 3 of the act of June 7, 1924 (43 Stat. 475), requiring the Secretary of the Interior by public notice to announce when water is actually available for lands in private ownership under the project and the amount of the construction charges per irrigable acre against the same which charges shall be payable in annual installments as provided for therein, this public notice, of which § 137.1 is made a part hereof, is hereby given:

The date when a reasonable water supply is actually available for lands in private ownership under the San Carlos irrigation project is hereby declared to be the 1st day of December 1932.

§ 137.3 Construction charges.

Each acre of land in private ownership of said project is hereby charged with $95.25 of construction cost assessable thereto at the date hereof (Dec. 1, 1932), which sum is based upon 50,000 acres of such privately owned lands, making a total charge or assessment due from the owners thereof of $4,762,250 on this date (Dec. 1, 1932), excluding the cost of operation and maintenance for the calendar year of 1933 which may be carried into construction cost as provided for by section 3 of the act of June 7, 1924 (43 Stat. 476), and also excluding interest at the rate of 4 percent which is charged against such lands by said act. Of the 50,000 acres constituting the lands in private ownership within the said project only 46,107.49 acres have at this date (Dec. 1, 1932) actually been designated as coming within the project. Should this present designated area be not increased within a reasonable time herefrom and prior to the due date of the first installment of the charge fixed in this section, namely, on December 1, 1935, so as to bring the total designated area up to the 50,000 acres, the per acre charge fixed in this section shall be proportionately increased against the then designated area so as to assure reimbursement of the total indebtedness due the Government by the owners of the lands in private ownership from the lesser designated acreage.

§ 137.4 Future charges.

The payment of said construction cost and costs of future operation and maintenance of said project as provided for in said section 3 of the act of June 7, 1924 (43 Stat. 476), as supplemented or amended and such contingent project liabilities which may be incurred in accordance with the provisions of said repayment contract shall be made in accordance with the provisions of said act of June 7, 1924, as supplemented or amended and the repayment contract by and between the San Carlos irrigation and drainage district and the Secretary of the Interior bearing date of June 8, 1931; the said construction cost incurred subsequent to this public notice assessable against the lands in private ownership and costs of operation and maintenance assessed against such privately owned lands within the project for the first year after this public notice to be included in the construction cost and such contingent project liabilities which may be incurred in accordance with provisions of the repayment contract shall also be repaid to the Government pursuant to the terms of said act of June 7, 1924, as supplemented or amended, and the repayment contract and this public notice.

§ 137.5 Construction costs limited.

The repayment contract[1] with the San Carlos irrigation and drainage district, page 13 thereof, contains the following:

> In accordance with the foregoing the costs of the San Carlos project as fixed by the public notice to be issued as aforesaid, unless further sums shall be agreed to by the Secretary of the Interior and the district after the execution of this instrument, may amount to but shall not exceed the sum of $9,556,313.77, except that said total may be exceeded by the inclusion of any sums expended to safeguard the project as hereinabove provided for, and any sums expended on account of contingent liabilities as in the next paragraph hereof provided.
>
> The foregoing and subsequent statements of project costs, the district's shares of which are to be repaid hereunder, unless otherwise provided by Congress more favorably to the lands of the project, may be increased

[1] Contract available at the Bureau of Indian Affairs, Washington, D.C.

by the addition of sums not now fixed as project charges but which possibly constitute contingent project liabilities incurred after the date of the San Carlos Act of June 7, 1924 (43 Stat. 476), or incurred on account of the Florence-casa Grande project, and so may become project charges by the judgment of courts of competent jurisdiction or of other proper authority.

The limitations therein fixed has approximately been reached, there remaining but $32,815.02 yet to be expended on project works before reaching that limitation. Upon the expenditure of this additional sum there shall be no further expenditures of funds for construction, operation and maintenance of the San Carlos project so far as the private lands are concerned until the San Carlos irrigation and drainage district shall, through appropriate action, authorize pursuant to the terms of the said repayment contract such additional expenditures. This limitation does not apply to project expenditures for the extension of the distributing and pumping system regardless of where they may arise. This class of expenditures being excepted from the limitation on expenditures contained in the said repayment contract by section 14, page 10, thereof, which section is known as the "Equalization of Expenditures."

§ 137.6 Power development.

The cost of the power development at the Coolidge Dam is hereby fixed at $735,000. The net revenues derived from the operation of this power development shall be disposed of as required by the terms and conditions of the act of March 7, 1928 (45 Stat. 210) as supplemented or amended.

§ 137.7 Private ownership defined.

The term "private ownership" used in this public notice includes all lands of the San Carlos irrigation project that have or may be designated by the Secretary of the Interior that are situated outside of the boundaries of the Gila River Indian Reservation.

§ 137.8 Indian lands excluded.

This public notice, with the exception of that part dealing with payment in advance each year of operation and maintenance charges against lands in Indian ownership operated under lease, does not apply in so far as payments are concerned to Indian lands within the project. The act of July 1, 1932 (47 Stat. 564; 25 U.S.C. 386a) defers the collection of construction costs from Indian owned lands so long as the title to such lands remains in the Indian ownership.

PART 138—REIMBURSEMENT OF CONSTRUCTION COSTS, AHTANUM UNIT, WAPATO INDIAN IRRIGATION PROJECT, WASHINGTON

AUTHORITY: Secs. 1, 3, 36 Stat. 270, 272, as amended; 25 U.S.C. 385.

SOURCE: 22 FR 10646, Dec. 24, 1957, unless otherwise noted. Redesignated at 47 FR 13327, Mar. 30, 1982.

§ 138.1 Construction costs and assessable acreage.

The construction program has been completed on the Ahtanum Unit of the Wapato Indian Irrigation Project and the construction costs have been established as $79,833.64. The area benefited by this development has been established at 4,765.2 acres. Under the requirements of the acts of February 14, 1920 (41 Stat. 409) and March 7, 1928 (45 Stat. 210), these costs are to be repaid to the United States Treasury by the owners of the lands benefited.

§ 138.2 Repayment of construction costs.

The cost per acre under § 138.1 is, therefore, established at $16.7535. Under the provisions of the acts of February 14, 1920 (41 Stat. 409) and March 7, 1928 (45 Stat. 210) is based on forty equal annual payments, the annual per acre assessment is hereby fixed at $0.42 per acre for the year 1957 and each succeeding year until the entire cost for each tract shall have been repaid to the United States Treasury. On those tracts where payments have been made pursuant to part 134 of this chapter, annual assessments beginning with the year 1957 at the rate of $0.42 per acre will be made until the entire cost of $16.7535 per acre shall have been repaid to the United States Treasury. Landowners may pay at any time the total of the then remaining indebtedness. Under the act of March 10, 1928 (45 Stat. 210) the unpaid charges stand as a lien against the lands until paid.

[22 FR 10646, Dec. 24, 1957. Redesignated at 47 FR 13327, Mar. 30, 1982; 48 FR 13414, Mar. 31, 1983]

§ 138.3 Payments.

Payments are due on December 31 of each year and shall be made to the official in charge of collections for the project.

§ 138.4 Deferment of assessments on lands remaining in Indian ownership.

In conformity with the act of July 1, 1932 (47 Stat. 564); 25 U.S.C. 386(a) no assessment shall be made on behalf of construction costs against Indian-owned land within the project until the Indian title thereto has been extinguished.

§ 138.5 Assessments after the Indian title has been extinguished.

Indian-owned lands passing to non-Indian ownership shall be assessed for construction costs and the first assessment shall be due on December 31 of the year that Indian title is extinguished. Assessments against this land will be at the annual rate of $0.42 per acre and shall be due as provided in § 138.3, and payable promptly thereafter until the total construction cost of $16.7535 per acre chargeable against the land has been paid in full.

PART 139—REIMBURSEMENT OF CONSTRUCTION COSTS, WAPATO-SATUS UNIT, WAPATO INDIAN IRRIGATION PROJECT, WASHINGTON

Sec.

AUTHORITY: Sec. 1, 41 Stat. 409, 45 Stat. 210; 25 U.S.C. 386, 387.

SOURCE: 28 FR 6536, June 26, 1963, unless otherwise noted. Redesignated at 47 FR 13327, Mar. 30, 1982.

§ 139.1 Construction costs and assessable acreage.

The construction program has been completed on the Wapato-Satus Unit of the Wapato Indian Irrigation Project, and the construction costs have been established by Designation Report dated August 1962 as $7,903,823.12 for the project and $1,499,073.62 for the "B" lands share of the construction costs in the Bureau of Reclamation reservoirs on the Yakima River. The area benefited by this development has been established at 136,559.59 acres divided into 79,025.68 acres of "A" land and 57,533.91 acres of "B" land. Under the requirements of the acts of February 14, 1920 (41 Stat. 409), and March 7, 1928 (45 Stat. 210), these costs are to be repaid to the U.S. Treasury by the owners of the lands benefited.

§ 139.2 Repayment of construction costs.

The cost per acre of the construction under § 139.1 is, therefore, calculated at $57.8782 for "A" lands and $83.9337 for "B" lands in non-Indian ownership as established by Designation Report dated August 1962. Under the provisions of the acts cited in § 139.1 the annual per acre assessment for forty equal annual payments, is hereby fixed at $1.45 per acre for "A" lands and $2.10 per acre for "B" lands for the year 1962 and each succeeding year, until the entire cost for each tract shall have been repaid to the U.S. Treasury. On those tracts where payments have been made pursuant to uncodified special regulations, annual assessments beginning with the year 1962 at the rate of $1.45 per acre for "A" lands and $2.10 per acre for "B" lands will be made until the entire cost of $57.8782 per acre for "A" lands and $83.9337 per acre for "B" lands shall have been repaid to the U.S. Treasury. Landowners may pay at any time the total of the then remaining indebtedness. Under the act of March 10, 1928 (45 Stat. 210), the unpaid charges stand as a lien against the lands until paid.

§ 139.3 Payments.

Payments are due on December 31 of each year and shall be made to the official in charge of collections for the project.

§ 139.4 Deferment of assessments on lands remaining in Indian ownership.

In conformity with the act of July 1, 1932 (47 Stat. 564; U.S.C. 386(a)), no assessment shall be made on behalf of construction costs against Indian-owned land within the project until the Indian title thereto has been extinguished.

§ 139.5 Assessments after the Indian title has been extinguished.

Indian-owned lands passing to non-Indian ownership shall be assessed for construction costs and the first assessment shall be due on December 31 of the year that the Indian title is extinguished. The construction costs against this land will be established as provided by section 5 of the act of September 26, 1961 (75 Stat. 680). The annual per acre assessment rate will be determined by dividing the established construction cost per acre into forty equal payments. "B" lands will also be assessed for reservoir construction costs in the annual per-acre rate as established in the Designation Report dated August 1962. Assessments against this land will continue until the entire established construction costs shall have been repaid to the U.S. Treasury. Landowners may pay at any time the total of the then remaining indebtedness. Under the act of March 10, 1928 (45 Stat. 210), the unpaid charges stand as a lien against the lands until paid.

PART 140—LICENSED INDIAN TRADERS

Sec.

AUTHORITY: Sec. 5, 19 Stat. 200, sec. 1, 31 Stat. 1066 as amended; 25 U.S.C. 261, 262; 94 Stat. 544, 18 U.S.C. 437; 25 U.S.C. 2 and 9; 5 U.S.C. 301; and Sec. 701, Pub. L. 114–74, 129 Stat. 599, unless otherwise noted.

CROSS REFERENCES: For law and order regulations on Indian Reservations, see part 11 of this chapter. For regulations pertaining to business practices on Navajo, Hopi and Zuni reservations, see part 141 of this chapter. For additional regulation of certain employees trading with Indians, see 43 CFR part 20.735–28 and 29.

SOURCE: 22 FR 10670, Dec. 24, 1957, unless otherwise noted. Redesignated at 47 FR 13327, Mar. 30, 1982.

§ 140.1 Sole power to appoint.

The Commissioner of Indian Affairs shall have the sole power and authority to appoint traders to the Indian tribes. Any person desiring to trade with the Indians on any reservation may, upon establishing the fact, to the satisfaction of the Commissioner of Indian Affairs, that he is a proper person to engage in such trade, be permitted to do so under such rules and regulations as the Commissioner of Indian Affairs may prescribe.

§ 140.2 Presidential prohibition.

The President is authorized, whenever in his opinion the public interest may require, to prohibit the introduction of goods, or of any particular articles, into the country belonging to any Indian tribe, and to direct that all licenses to trade with such tribe be revoked, and all applications therefor rejected. No trader shall, so long as such prohibition exists, trade with any Indians of or for said tribe.

(R.S. 2132; 25 U.S.C. 263)

§ 140.3 Forfeiture of goods.

Any person other than an Indian of the full blood who shall attempt to reside in the Indian country, or on any Indian reservation, as a trader, or to introduce goods, or to trade therein, without a license, shall forfeit all merchandise offered for sale to the Indians or found in his possession, and shall moreover be liable to a penalty of $1,296: *Provided*, That this section shall not apply to any person residing among or trading with the Choctaws, Cherokee, Chickasaws, Creeks, or Seminoles, commonly called the Five Civilized Tribes: *And provided further*, That no white person shall be employed as a clerk by any Indian trader, except as such trade with said Five Civilized Tribes, unless first authorized so to do by the Commissioner of Indian Affairs.

(R.S. 2133, as amended; 25 U.S.C. 264)

[22 FR 10670, Dec. 24, 1957, as amended at 81 FR 42481, June 30, 2016; 82 FR 7652, Jan. 23, 2017; 83 FR 5195, Feb. 6, 2018]

§ 140.5 Bureau of Indian Affairs employees not to contract or trade with Indians except in certain cases.

(a) Definitions of terms as used in this part:

(1) *Indian* means any member of an Indian tribe recognized as eligible for the services provided by the Bureau of Indian Affairs who is residing on a Federal Indian Reservation, on land held in trust by the United States for Indians, or on land subject to a restriction against alienation imposed by the United States. The term shall also include any such tribe and any Indian owned or controlled organization located on such a reservation or land.

(2) *Bureau* or the "Bureau of Indian Affairs" means the Bureau of Indian Affairs and the Office of the Assistant Secretary for Indian Affairs, both in the Department of the Interior.

(3) *Employee* means an officer, employee, or agent of the Bureau of Indian Affairs.

(4) *Secretary* means the Secretary of the Interior.

(5) *Contract* means any agreement made or under negotiation with any Indian for the purchase, transportation or delivery of goods or supplies.

(6) *Trading* means buying, selling, bartering, renting, leasing, permitting and any other transaction involving the acquisition of property or services.

(7) *Commercial trading* means any trading transaction where an employee engages in the business of buying or selling services or items which he/she is trading.

(b) With the exceptions provided in subsection (b) of section 437 of title 18 U.S. Code, section 437 provides that whoever, being an officer, employee, or agent of the Bureau of Indian Affairs, has (other than as a lawful representative of the United States) any interest, in such officer, employee, or agent's name, or in the name of another person where such officer, employee, or agent benefits or appears to benefit from such interest:

(1) In any contract made or under negotiation with any Indian, for the purchase, transportation or delivery of goods or supplies for any Indian, or

(2) In any purchase or sale of any service or real or personal property (or any interest therein) from or to any Indian, or colludes with any person attempting to obtain any such contract, purchase, or sale, shall be fined not more than $5,000 or imprisoned not more than six months or both, and shall be removed from office, notwithstanding any other provision of law concerning termination from Federal employment.

(c) The further subsections of this section authorize certain employees contracting and trading with Indians as authorized by the exceptions in section 437 of title 18 U.S. Code. All such contracting and trading is subject to the express provision of section 437 that none of the sales or purchases so authorized may be made if the purpose of any such sale, trade, or purchase is that of commercially selling, reselling, trading, or bartering such property.

(d)(1) Under authority granted by section 437(b)(1) of title 18 U.S. Code, employees of the Bureau of Indian Affairs may with the approval of an authorized officer of the Bureau, as designated in paragraph (d)(2) of this section, purchase from or sell to an Indian any service or any real or personal property, not held in trust by the

United States or subject to a restriction against alienation imposed by the United States, or any interest in such property. In addition, employees may purchase from Indians without approval from an authorized officer of the Bureau any non-trust or unrestricted personal property for home use or consumption the value of which property does not exceed $1000. Where the purchase or sale price is less than $1,000, employees may also purchase motor vehicles for their personal use from Indians or sell their personal motor vehicles to Indians without obtaining approval of such purchases or sales from an authorized officer of the Bureau. Approval must be obtained if the purchase or sale price is $1,000 or more.

(2) As used in paragraph (d)(1) of this section an authorized officer of the Bureau of Indian Affairs for employees on reservations and in agencies or in field service units shall be the superintendent or other officer in charge of the unit in which the employee is employed. The authorized officer for the superintendent or officer in charge is his or her immediate supervisor. The authorized officer for employees in area offices is the Area Director, and the authorized officer for an Area Director is his or her immediate supervisor. The authorized officer for employees in the Central Office is the Deputy Assistant Secretary—Indian Affairs (Operations).

(e) No employee of the Bureau of Indian Affairs may have any interest in any purchase or sale involving property or funds which are either held in trust by the United States for Indians or which are purchased, sold, utilized, or received in connection with a contract or grant to an Indian from the Bureau if such employee is employed in the office or installation of the Bureau which recommends, approves, executes, or administers such transaction, grant, or contract on behalf of the United States, except that, as authorized by section 437(b)(1) of title 18 U.S. Code an employee of the Bureau may have such an interest if such purchase or sale is approved by an authorized officer of the Bureau, as designated in paragraphs (e) (3) to (5) of this section, and the conditions in (e) (1) and (2) of this section are satisfied to the extent to which they are applicable to the transaction concerned:

(1) The conveyance or granting of any interest in property held in trust or subject to restriction against alienation imposed by the United States is otherwise authorized by law.

(2) Trading by employees with Indians which involves property or funds which are either held in trust by the United States or are subject to restrictions against alienation imposed by the United States must be conducted on the basis of sealed bid or public auction. If the trading involves leases or sales of trust or restricted Indian land it must be conducted on the basis of sealed bids. Such requirements for sealed bid or public auction may only be waived by the Assistant Secretary for Indian Affairs on the basis of a full report showing:

(i) The need for the transaction,

(ii) The benefits accruing to both parties,

(iii) That the consideration for the proposed transaction shall be not less than the fair market value of the trust or restricted property or interest therein, unless the employee is involved in a transaction in accordance with § 152.25(c) or (d) or § 162.5(b)(1), (2), or (3) of this title or the employee is the recipient of a benefit for tribal members for which a uniform charge to all members is made, and

(iv) An affidavit as follows shall accompany each proposed transaction: "I (name) (title), swear (or affirm) that I have not exercised any undue influence nor used any special knowledge received by reason of my employment in the Bureau in obtaining the (grantor's, purchaser's, vendor's) consent to the instant transaction."

(3) The authorized officer of the Bureau for employees employed on reservations, in agencies or service units is one who is not a relative by blood or marriage of the employee, and is not employed at the employee's reservation, agency or service unit. That officer must also be employed at not less than one grade level higher than such employee at the Washington, District of Columbia, Central Office or at an Area Office other than that with authority over the employee's reservation, agency, or service unit.

(4) The authorized officer of the Bureau for employees employed in Area offices is one who is not a relative by blood or marriage of the employee, is not employed at the employee's area office, and must be employed at not less than one grade level higher than the employee at the Washington, District of Columbia, Central Office.

(5) The authorized officer of the Bureau for employees employed at the Washington, District of Columbia, Central Office is the Secretary.

(f) Except as provided in subsection (b)(2) of section 437 of title 18 U.S. Code as implemented by this section, nothing in the cited law shall be construed as preventing any employee of the Bureau who is an Indian, of whatever degree of Indian blood, from obtaining or receiving any benefit or benefits made available to Indians generally or to any member of his or her particular tribe, under any Act of Congress, nor to prevent any such employee who is an Indian from being a member of or receiving benefits by reason of his or her membership in any Indian tribe, corporation, or cooperative association organized by Indians, when authorized under such rules and regulations as the Secretary or his/her designee has prescribed or shall prescribe.

[49 FR 25434, June 21, 1984]

§ 140.9 Application for license.

(a) Application for license must be made in writing on Form 5–052, setting forth the full name and residence of the applicant; if a firm, the firm name and the name of each member thereof; the place where it is proposed to carry on the trade; the capital to be invested; the names of the clerks to be employed; and the business experience of the applicant. The application must be forwarded through the Superintendent to the Commissioner of Indian Affairs, accompanied by two satisfactory testimonials on Form 2–077 as to the character of the applicant and his employees and their fitness to be in the Indian country, and by an affidavit of the Superintendent on Form 5–053 that neither he nor any person for him has any interest, direct or indirect, present or prospective, in the proposed business or the profits arising therefrom, and that no arrangement for any benefit to himself or to any other person on his behalf is contemplated in case the license is granted. Licensed traders will be held responsible for the conduct of their employees.

(b) Itinerant peddlers or purveyors of foodstuffs and other merchandise shall be considered as traders and shall obtain a license or permit from the Superintendent setting forth the class of trade or peddling to be carried on, furnishing such character or credit references, or both, as may be required by the Superintendent. The period of the license for such itinerant peddlers shall be determined by the Superintendent.

(c) When a license or permit to trade is issued under the regulations in this part 140, a fee of $5, payable when the license is issued, shall be levied against the licensee.

[30 FR 8267, June 29, 1965. Redesignated at 47 FR 13327, Mar. 30, 1982]

§ 140.11 License period.

Licenses to trade shall not be issued unless the proposed licensee has a right to the use of the land on which the business is to be conducted. The license period shall correspond to the period of the lease or permit held by the licensee on restricted Indian land, except that where the proposed licensee is the owner or beneficial owner or holds a use right to the land on which the business is to be conducted, the license period shall be fixed by the Commissioner of Indian Affairs or his authorized representative, but in no case shall the license period exceed 25 years.

[30 FR 8268, June 29, 1965. Redesignated at 47 FR 13327, Mar. 30, 1982]

§ 140.12 License renewal.

Application for renewal of license must be made to the Commissioner of Indian Affairs on Form 5-054, through the superintendent, at least 30 days prior to the expiration of the existing license, and the superintendent must report as to the record the applicant has made as a trader and his fitness to continue as such under a new license.

§ 140.13 Power to close unlicensed stores.

If persons carry on trade within a reservation with the Indians without a license, or continue to trade after expiration of the license without applying for renewal, the superintendent will immediately report the facts in the case to the Commissioner of Indian Affairs, who may, if necessary, direct the superintendent to close the stores of such traders.

§ 140.14 Trade limited to specified premises.

No trade with Indians is permitted at any other place than that specified in the license. Licenses to not cover branch stores. A separate license and bond must be furnished for each such store. The business of a licensed trader must be managed by the bonded principal, who must habitually reside upon the reservation, and not by an unbonded subordinate.

§ 140.15 License applicable for trading only by original licensee.

No trader will be allowed to lease, sublet, rent, or sell any of the buildings which he occupies, for any purpose to any other person or concern, without the approval of the Commissioner of Indian Affairs. A license to trade with Indians does not confer upon the trader any right or privileges in respect to the herding or raising of livestock upon the reservation. The use of reservation lands, whether tribal or allotted, for such purposes can be obtained by a trader only upon the terms and under the restrictions which apply to other persons. His license gives him no advantage over others in this respect.

§ 140.16 Trade in annuities or gratuities prohibited.

Traders are forbidden to buy, trade for, or have in their possession any annuity or other goods of any description which have been purchased or furnished by the Government for the use or welfare of the Indians. Livestock or their increase purchased by the Government and in possession or control of the Indians may not be purchased by any trader, not a member of the tribe to which the owners or possessors of the cattle belong, except with the written consent of the agent of said tribe.

§ 140.17 Tobacco sales to minors.

No trader shall sell tobacco, cigars, or cigarettes to any Indian under 18 years of age.

§ 140.18 Intoxicating liquors.

No trader shall use or permit to be used his premises for any unlawful conduct or purpose whatsoever. No trader shall use of permit to be used any part of his premises for the manufacture, sale, gift, transportation, drinking or storage of intoxicating liquors or beverages in violation of existing laws relating thereto. Violation of this section will subject the trader to criminal prosecution, revocation of license and such other action as may be necessary.

§ 140.19 Drugs.

Traders shall not keep for sale, or sell, give away, or use any opium, chloral, cocaine, peyote or mescal bean, hashish or Indian hemp or marihuana, or any compound containing either ingredient, and for violation hereof the trader's license shall be revoked.

§ 140.21 Gambling.

Gambling, by dice, cards, or in any way whatever, is strictly prohibited in any licensed trader's store or on the premises.

§ 140.22 Inspection of traders' prices.

It is the duty of the superintendent to see that the prices charged by licensed traders are fair and reasonable. To this end the traders shall on request submit to the superintendent or inspecting officials the original invoice, showing cost, together with a statement of transportation charges, retail price of articles sold by them, the amount of Indian accounts carried on their books, the total annual sales, the value of buildings, livestock owned on reservation, the number of employees, and any other business information such officials may desire. The quality of all articles kept on sale must be good and merchantable.

§ 140.23 Credit at trader's risk.

Credit given Indians will be at the trader's own risk, as no assistance will be given by Government officials in the collection of debts against Indians.

Traders shall not accept pawns or pledges of personal property by Indians to obtain credit or loans.

§ 140.24 Cash payments only to Indians.

Traders must not pay Indians in tokens, tickets, store orders, or anything else of that character. Payment must be made in money, or in credit if the Indian is indebted to the trader.

§ 140.25 Trade in antiquities prohibited.

Traders shall not deal in objects of antiquity removed from any historic or prehistoric ruin or monument on land owned or controlled by the United States.

CROSS REFERENCE: For regulations pertaining to archaeological resources, see part 262 of this chapter. For regulations of the Bureau of Land Management regarding antiquities, see 43 CFR part 3.

§ 140.26 Infectious plants.

Traders shall not introduce into, sell, or spread within Indian reservations any plant, plant product, seed, or any type of vegetation, which is infested, or infected or which might act as a carrier of any pests of infectious, transmissible, or contagious diseases, as determined by the laws and regulations of the State for plant quarantine and pest control. For the purpose of enforcement of this provision State officers may enter Indian reservations, with the consent of the superintendent, to inspect the premises of such traders and otherwise to execute such State laws and regulations.

PART 141—BUSINESS PRACTICES ON THE NAVAJO, HOPI AND ZUNI RESERVATIONS

Subpart A—Interpretation and Construction Guides

Sec.

Subpart B—Licensing Requirements and Procedures

Subpart C—General Business Practices

Subpart D—Pawnbroker Practices

Subpart E—Consumer Credit Transactions Other Than Pawn

Subpart F—Enforcement Powers, Procedures and Remedies

AUTHORITY: 5 U.S.C. 301; 25 U.S.C. 2 and 9; and Sec. 701, Pub. L. 114-74, 129 Stat. 599, unless otherwise noted.

SOURCE: 40 FR 39835, Aug. 29, 1975, unless otherwise noted. Redesignated at 47 FR 13327, Mar. 30, 1982.

Subpart A—Interpretation and Construction Guides

§ 141.1 Purpose.

The purpose of the regulations of this part is to prescribe rules for the regulation of reservation businesses for the protection of Indian consumers on the Navajo, Hopi and Zuni Reservations as required by 25 U.S.C. 261, 262, 263, and 264.

§ 141.2 Scope.

The regulations of this part apply to all non-members of the Navajo, Hopi and Zuni Tribes, who engage in retail businesses on the above respective reservations. These regulations do not apply to businesses that are wholly owned and operated by either the Navajo, Hopi or Zuni Tribes, or by individual tribal members within their respective reservations.

[45 FR 64906, Oct. 1, 1980. Redesignated at 47 FR 13327, Mar. 30, 1982]

§ 141.3 Definitions.

For the purposes of this part—

(a) *Annual percentage rate* means the annual percentage rate of finance charge determined in accordance with 12 CFR 226.5, which defines annual percentage rates.

(b) *Consumer credit transaction* means a grant of credit or a loan that is made by a person regularly engaged in the business of making loans or granting credit primarily for a personal, family, household, or agricultural purpose.

(c) *Draft* means a writing that is a direction to pay that:

(1) Identifies the person to pay with reasonable certainty;

(2) Is signed by the drawer;

(3) Contains an unconditional order to pay a sum certain in money and no other promise, order, obligation or power given by the drawer;

(4) Is payable on demand or at a definite time; and

(5) Is payable to order.

(d) *Finance charge* means the cost of credit determined in accordance with 12 CFR 226.4, which defines "finance charge".

(e) *Firm* means a corporation or a partnership.

(f) *Gross receipts* include the following:

(1) All cash received from the conduct and operation of the licensee's business at the premises described in the application for license.

(2) Receipts from both wholesale and retail transactions.

(3) Receipts resulting from transactions concluded off the reservation that originate from the conduct and operation of the licensee's business on the reservation.

(4) The market value of all property taken in trade on the date when received and either held by the licensee for purposes other than resale or credited on any account in payment for merchandise.

(5) Proceeds from the sale of any goods bought from Indians regardless of where the sale takes place.

(6) Finance charge received on loans, but not the return of principal.

(g) *Open end credit* means consumer credit transactions made on an account by a plan under which:

(1) The creditor may permit the customer to make purchases or obtain loans, from time to time, directly from the creditor or indirectly by use of a credit card, check, or other device, as the plan may provide;

(2) The customer has the privilege of paying the balance in full or in installments; and

(3) A finance charge may be computed by the creditor from time to time on an outstanding unpaid balance.

(h) *Pawnbroker* means a person whose business includes lending money secured by personal property deposited with the lender.

(i) *Peddler* means a person who offers goods for sale within the exterior boundaries of the Hopi, Navajo or Zuni Reservations, but does not do business from a fixed location or site on any of those reservations.

(j) *Person* includes a natural person, a corporation, trust, estate, partnership, cooperative or association.

(k) *Replacement value* means the present cost to the owner of replacing an item with one having the same quality and usefulness.

(l) *Reservation business* means a person that engages at a fixed location or site within the exterior boundaries of the Navajo, Hopi or Zuni Reservations in the sale or purchase of goods or services or in consumer credit transactions with Indians and is not a bank, saving bank, trust company, savings or building and loan association or credit union operating under the laws of the United States or the laws of New Mexico, Arizona or Utah, a business on the Hopi Reservation that is wholly owned and operated by members of the Hopi Tribe, or a business on the Zuni Reservation that is wholly owned and operated by members of the Zuni Tribe.

§ 141.4 Interpretation and construction.

(a) *Area Director* refers to the Area Director of the Bureau of Indian Affairs or the Administrator of the Joint Use Area of the Bureau of Indian Affairs who has jurisdiction over the land on which a person does business or intends to do business with Indians.

(b) *Commissioner* refers to the Commissioner of Indian Affairs or a person to whom the Commissioner of Indian Affairs has delegated authority under this part or under 25 U.S.C. 261, 262, 263, or 264.

(c) *Superintendent* refers to the Superintendent of the Bureau of Indian Affairs who has jurisdiction over the land on which a person does business or intends to do business with Indians.

(d) *Tribe* refers to the tribe that has jurisdiction over the land on which a person does business or intends to do business with Indians.

Subpart B—Licensing Requirements and Procedures

§ 141.5 Reservation business license required.

(a) No person may own or lease a reservation business without a license issued under the provisions of this subpart.

(b) The applicant shall apply in writing on a form provided by the Commissioner setting forth the following:

(1) The full name and residence of the applicant.

(2) Three (3) responsible references.

(3) The firm name and the name of each member of the board of directors if the applicant is a firm.

(4) Satisfactory evidence as to the character, experience and business ability of the applicant and the employees of the applicant.

(5) Satisfactory evidence of the general fitness of the applicant and employees of the applicant to reside on the Indian reservation.

(c) Upon the request of the Commissioner, the applicant shall furnish the following:

(1) The capital invested or to be invested and, of this, the amount of capital owned and the amount borrowed or to be borrowed.

(2) The name of the lender of any borrowed capital, the date due, the rate of interest to be paid, and the names of any endorsers and security.

(3) A copy of any contract or trade agreement whether oral or written with creditors or financing individuals or institutions, including any stipulations whereby financing fees are to be paid.

(d) Information that if released might adversely affect the competitive position of the applicant shall remain confidential.

[40 FR 39837, Aug. 29, 1975, as amended at 41 FR 3288, Jan. 22, 1976. Redesignated at 47 FR 13327, Mar. 30, 1982]

§ 141.6 Approval or denial of license application.

(a) The Commissioner shall approve or deny each license application and notify the applicant no later than thirty (30) days after receipt of a completed application.

(b) No application is complete until any clearance or tribal council approval required by tribal or Federal regulations has been obtained.

(c) The Commissioner may not deny a license to an applicant for the purpose of limiting competition.

(d) If the application is approved the license shall be issued on a form provided by the Commissioner.

(e) If the Commissioner denies the license application the applicant may appeal under the provisions of part 2 of this title no later than thirty (30) days after the date on which notice of denial of the application was sent.

§ 141.7 Bond requirement for a reservation business.

(a) An applicant for a license or renewal of a license to operate a reservation business shall at the time the application is submitted furnish a bond on a form provided by the Commissioner in the name of the applicant in the amount of ten thousand dollars ($10,000) or such larger sum as the Commissioner may designate, with two (2) on more sureties approved by the Commissioner or with a guaranty company qualified under the Act of August 13, 1894 (28 Stat. 279; 6 U.S.C. 6–13). The bond shall be for the same period covered by the license. No licensee may trade without a bond. Except as provided in paragraph (d) of this section, no surety may be released from liability until the license expires.

(b) The bond shall be in favor of the United States for the benefit of the United States and any customer of the licensee who recovers a judgment for damages resulting from violation of any law or regulation affecting or relating to reservation businesses. Any customer who recovers such a judgment may bring suit on the bond in his or her own name. The bond shall be conditioned on payment by the licensee of all judgments for damages resulting from violations of the regulations of this part.

(c) Any surety for a reservation business on the Hopi or Zuni Reservation shall agree in writing to submit itself voluntarily to the jurisdiction of the tribal court for the purpose of adjudicating any claim arising under the bond.

(d) Any surety on the bond of a licensed reservation business may be relieved from liabilities by complying with the provisions of § 141.57 of this title.

[40 FR 39837, Aug. 29, 1975, as amended at 41 FR 22937, June 8, 1976. Redesignated at 47 FR 13327, Mar. 30, 1982]

§ 141.8 License period for reservation businesses.

A license to operate a reservation business may not be issued unless the applicant has a right to use the land on which the business is to be conducted. The license period shall correspond to the period of the lease held by the licensee. The license period in no event may exceed twenty-five (25) years.

§ 141.9 Application for license renewal.

(a) An applicant for renewal of the license to trade shall file an application on a form provided by the Commissioner with the Area Director not less than three (3) months prior to the expiration of the existing license. The Area Director shall report in writing to the Commissioner on the record the applicant has made as a reservation business owner and the applicant's present fitness to reside on the Indian reservation.

(b) The Commissioner may issue a temporary permit for three (3) months pending consideration of application for license renewal.

(c) Prior to expiration of the existing license or, if issued, the temporary permit, the Commissioner shall approve or deny the application for license renewal and notify the applicant.

(d) No license may be renewed until any clearance or tribal council approval required by tribal or other federal regulations has been obtained.

(e) If the Commissioner denies the application for renewal, the applicant may appeal under the provisions of part 2 of this title.

§ 141.10 License fees for reservation businesses.

(a) Prior to the issuance of an initial license, each licensee who is not a member of the Navajo tribe shall pay the following amount:

(1) If the license is issued before July 1, the licensee shall pay fifty dollars ($50).

(2) If the license is issued on or after July 1, the licensee shall pay twenty-five dollars ($25).

(b) Each licensed business owner who is not a member of the Navajo tribe shall pay on or before January 10 of each year an annual license fee determined as follows based on the licensee's most recent annual report:

(1) If the licensee's gross receipts are less than one hundred thousand dollars ($100,000) for the year or the licensee has not yet been required to file its first annual report, the license fee is fifty dollars ($50).

(2) If the licensee's gross receipts for the year are at least one hundred thousand dollars ($100,000) but not more than four hundred and ninety-nine thousand nine hundred and ninety-nine dollars ($499,999) the fee is one hundred dollars ($100).

(3) If the licensee's gross receipts for the year are at least five hundred thousand dollars ($500,000) but not more than seven hundred and forty-nine thousand nine hundred and ninety-nine dollars ($749,999), the fee is two hundred dollars ($200).

(4) If the licensee's gross receipts for the year are seven hundred fifty thousand dollars ($750,000) or more, the fee is three hundred dollars ($300).

(c) The Navajo Area Director shall determine the annual license fee payable by licensees who are enrolled members of the Navajo Tribe. The license fee for an enrolled member of the Navajo Tribe may not be less than twenty percent (20%) nor greater than one hundred percent (100 percent) of the amount the licensee would be required to pay if the licensee were not a tribal member.

(d) All fees are payable to the Area Director and shall be deposited to the credit of the account "Special Deposits."

[40 FR 39835, Aug. 29, 1975, as amended at 59 FR 54502, Oct. 31, 1994]

§ 141.11 Tribal fees, taxes, and enforcement.

(a) The regulations in this part do not preclude the Hopi, Navajo, or Zuni tribal councils from assessing and collecting such fees or taxes as they may deem appropriate from reservation businesses.

(b) Nothing in the regulations of this part may be construed to preclude tribal enforcement of these regulations or consistent tribal ordinances.

[40 FR 39837, Aug. 29, 1975, as amended at 41 FR 3288, Jan. 22, 1976. Redesignated at 47 FR 13327, Mar. 30, 1982]

§ 141.12 Peddler's permits.

(a) Except as provided in paragraph (b) of this section, no peddler may offer goods for sale within the exterior boundaries of the Hopi, Navajo, or Zuni reservations without a peddler's permit. The permit shall state on its face the class of goods that may be offered for sale. No peddler may offer for sale any class of goods other than those listed on the face of the permit.

(b) No peddler who is an enrolled member of a federally recognized Indian tribe is required to obtain a peddler's permit for offering to sell the following items:

(1) Coal and wood for non-commercial use,

(2) Homegrown fresh products,

(3) Meat products raised locally by the peddler, or

(4) Arts and crafts made by the peddler or the peddler's family.

(c) The applicant shall apply for a permit in writing on a form provided by the Commissioner.

(d) Peddlers shall pay such fee and post such surety bond on a form provided by the Commissioner as the Commissioner requires. The surety bond required may not be less than five hundred dollars ($500) nor more than ten thousand dollars ($10,000).

(e) Any surety on the bond of a peddler may be relieved of liability by complying with the provisions of § 141.57.

(25 U.S.C. 261 *et seq.*)

[43 FR 27826, June 27, 1978. Redesignated at 47 FR 13327, Mar. 30, 1982]

§ 141.13 Amusement company licenses.

(a) No person may operate a portable dance pavilion, mechanical amusement device such as a ferris wheel or carousel, or commercial games of skill within the exterior boundaries of the Navajo, Hopi, or Zuni Reservations without a license from the Commissioner.

(b) The licensee shall pay such fee as the Commissioner requires. The fee shall be not less than five dollars ($5) nor more than twenty-five dollars ($25) per unit.

(c) The licensee shall post a surety bond on a form provided by the Commissioner in an amount not exceeding ten thousand dollars ($10,000) and a personal injury and property damage liability bond of not less than five thousand dollars ($5,000) nor more than fifty thousand dollars ($50,000) as may be required by the Commissioner.

(d) The provisions of this section do not apply to amusement companies where the contract between the tribe and the amusement company provides for the payment of a fee to the tribe and for the protection of the public against personal injury and property damage by bond in the amounts specified in paragraph (c) of this section.

(e) Any surety on a bond under this section may be relieved of liability by complying with the provisions of § 141.57.

§ 141.14 Trade in livestock restricted.

(a) No person other than an enrolled member of the tribe or any association, partnership, corporation or business entity wholly owned by enrolled members of the tribe may purchase livestock from tribal members without a special permit issued by the Commissioner.

(b) The Commissioner shall issue a permit to each applicant who establishes to the Commissioner's satisfaction that the applicant is a fit person to engage in the purchase of livestock and who posts a bond on a form provided by the Commissioner in the amount of ten thousand dollars ($10,000). This paragraph does not require a person who has posted a bond of ten thousand dollars ($10,000) or more under other provisions of this part to post an additional bond to obtain a permit under this section.

(c) Any surety on a bond under this section may be relieved of liability by complying with the provisions of § 141.57.

(d) The provisions of this section do not apply to purchases of livestock made at an organized public auction.

[40 FR 39837, Aug. 29, 1975, as amended at 41 FR 22937, June 8, 1976. Redesignated at 47 FR 13327, Mar. 30, 1982]

§ 141.15 Consent to jurisdiction of Hopi and Zuni tribal courts.

As a condition to doing business on the Hopi or the Zuni Reservation each applicant for license under this part shall, in accordance with the constitutions of those tribes, voluntarily submit the applicant and the applicant's employees or agents to the jurisdiction of the tribal court for the purpose of the adjudication of any dispute, claim or obligation arising under tribal ordinance relating to commerce carried out by the licensee.

Subpart C—General Business Practices

§ 141.16 Price marking.

The price of each article offered for sale shall be marked on the article, its containers or in any other manner that is plain and visible to the customer and that affords the customer a reasonable opportunity to learn the price of the article prior to purchase.

§ 141.17 Health and sanitation requirements.

(a) Each licensee shall keep both the premises and the place of business in a clean and sanitary condition at all times and shall avoid exposure of foodstuffs to contamination. No licensee may offer for sale any goods that are banned for health or sanitation reasons from retail sale by any Federal agency or by the tribe or, where not in conflict with the tribal regulations, by the State or by any State agency. No licensee may knowingly offer for sale any food that is contaminated.

(b) All weights and measure shall conform to standards set by the National Bureau of Standards and to standards, if any, set by the tribe and, if not in conflict with tribal regulations, to the standards set by the State.

(c) If training in foodhandling is available from the Indian Health Service, each person working in a reservation business shall complete the foodhandler training offered by the Indian Health Service before handling any food sold by a reservation business.

(d) Any person whom the Service Unit Director of the Indian Health Service determines is infected with or is a carrier of any communicable disease in a stage likely to be communicable to persons exposed as a result of the infected employee's normal duties as a foodhandler may not be employed by a reservation business.

(e) Each business shall comply with all Federal health regulations and with all tribal health regulations that are consistent with Federal regulations. Each business shall comply with State health regulations that are consistent with tribal and Federal health regulations.

(f) Except as otherwise provided herein, nothing in this section may be construed as a grant of enforcement powers to any agency of a State or its subdivisions.

(g) It is the duty of the health officers of the Indian Health Service to make periodic inspections, recommend improvements, and report thereon to the Commissioner.

§ 141.18 Availability of employee authorized to transact business.

Each licensee shall provide during normal business hours an employee authorized in writing to engage in all business transactions that the licensee normally offers to customers.

§ 141.19 Check cashing.

(a) A reservation business may give a fully negotiable check in addition to U.S. currency when cashing a draft, check or money order. A reservation business may not give scrip, credit or other substitute for U.S. currency when cashing a draft, check or money order.

(b) A reservation business owner or employee may advise a customer cashing checks, money orders or drafts of the amount due on the customer's credit accounts, pawn accounts or any other obligation the customer owes to the business, but in no event may the owner or employee withhold the proceeds of the check, money order or draft from the customer on the basis of existing credit obligations.

[40 FR 39837, Aug. 29, 1975, as amended at 41 FR 3288, Jan. 22, 1976. Redesignated at 47 FR 13327, Mar. 30, 1982]

§ 141.20 Payment for purchase of Indian goods or services.

(a) A reservation business shall pay for the purchase of Indian goods or services with cash or a fully negotiable check. A reservation business may not pay for Indian goods or services with trade slips or future credit. In any transaction involving the purchase of Indian goods on the Navajo Reservation, the reservation business shall furnish a bill of sale indicating the name of the seller, a description of the goods, the amount paid for the goods, the date of sale, and the signature of both parties and shall retain a copy of the bill of sales in its business records.

(b) A reservation business owner or employee may advise a customer selling Indian goods or services of the amount due on the customer's credit accounts, pawn accounts or any other obligation the customer owes to the business, but in no event may the owner or employee withhold the proceeds of the sale from the customer on the basis of existing credit obligations.

§ 141.21 Trade confined to premises.

The licensee shall confine all trade on the reservation to the premises specified in the license, except, where permitted under § 141.14, the buying and selling of livestock and livestock products.

§ 141.22 Subleasing prohibited.

No licensee may lease, sublet, rent, or sell any building that the licensee occupies for any purpose to any person without the approval of the Commissioner and the consent of the tribe.

§ 141.23 Posted statement of ownership.

The licensee of a reservation business shall display in a prominent place a notice that is legible to customers stating the form of the business entity, the names and addresses of all other reservation businesses owned in whole or in part by the business entity, and if the licensee is not a corporation, the names and addresses of the owner or owners of the business. If the licensee is a corporation the notice shall list the names and addresses of the members of the Board of Directors.

§ 141.24 Attendance at semi-annual meetings.

Upon the request of a tribal official designated by the governing body, each licensee shall attend a semi-annual public meeting of a tribal governing body to respond to customer inquiries.

§ 141.25 Withholding of mail prohibited.

No owner or employee of a reservation business may open, withhold, or otherwise delay the delivery of mail.

§ 141.26 Trade in antiquities prohibited.

No licensee may knowingly buy, sell, rent or lease any artifact created before 1930 that was removed from an historic ruin or monument.

§ 141.27 Trade in imitation Indian crafts prohibited.

No person may introduce or possess for disposition or sale within the exterior boundaries of the Hopi, Navajo or Zuni Reservations any object that is represented to be an Indian handicraft unless the object was produced by an Indian or Indians with the help of only such devices as allow the manual skill of the maker to condition the shape and design of each individual's product.

§ 141.28 Gambling prohibited.

No licensee may permit any person to gamble by dice, cards, or in any way whatever, including the use of any mechanical device, on the premises of any licensed business.

§ 141.29 Political contributions restricted.

No reservation business owner who is ineligible to vote in a Navajo tribal election may grant or donate any money or goods to any candidate for election to Navajo tribal office.

§ 141.30 Retaliation prohibited.

No licensee may refuse service to any customer for the purpose of retaliating against that customer for enforcing or attempting to enforce the regulations of this part.

§ 141.31 Trade by Indian Affairs employees restricted.

(a) Except as authorized in this section, no person employed by the U.S. Government in Indian Affairs may have any interest in any trade with an Indian or an Indian organization. Employees of the U.S. Government may trade with an Indian or Indian organization for any purpose other than to engage in a profit-making activity under the following conditions:

(1) Where the amount involved is $500 or less a U.S. Government employee may purchase goods or services from an Indian or Indian organization.

(2) Where the amount involved is greater than $500 a U.S. Government employee may, with the approval of the Secretary of the Interior, purchase goods or services from any Indian or Indian organization.

(b) Lease or sale of home sites or allotments on trust or restricted Indian land to or from Indian employees of the U.S. Government shall be made on sealed bids, unless the Commissioner waives this requirement on the basis of a report showing:

(1) The need for the transaction,

(2) The benefits accruing to both parties, and

(3) That the consideration for the proposed transaction is not less than the appraised value of the land or leasehold interest unless the Indian employee qualifies and is intending a transaction in accordance with § 152.5 (b) and (c) of this chapter or § 162.5(b)(1), (2) and (3) of this chapter.

An affidavit, as follows, shall accompany each proposed land transaction:

I,____________________(Name)

____________________________(Title)
swear (or affirm) that I have not exercised any undue influence nor used any special knowledge received by reason of my office in obtaining the (grantor's, purchaser's, vendor's) consent to the instant transaction.

(c) This section does not prohibit any reservation business from contracting with the Federal Government to provide postal services to Indian communities in which Government postal service is unavailable.

(d) Nothing in this section prohibits an Indian employee from receiving benefits by reason of membership in a tribe or corporation or cooperative association organized by and operated for Indians.

(e) U.S. Government employees who violate this section are liable to a penalty of five thousand dollars ($5,000) and shall be removed from office, see 25 U.S.C. 68.

[40 FR 39837, Aug. 29, 1975, as amended at 41 FR 3288, Jan. 22, 1976. Redesignated at 47 FR 13327, Mar. 30, 1982]

Subpart D—Pawnbroker Practices

§ 141.32 Reservation pawnbroker license required.

(a) No person may accept pawns or pledges of personal property as security for monies or accounts due by an Indian within the exterior boundaries of the Navajo, Hopi or Zuni Reservations unless such person is an agent of a bank, saving bank, trust company, savings or building and loan association, or credit union operating under the laws of the United States or the laws of New Mexico, Arizona, or Utah or unless such person—

(1) Holds a valid license to operate a reservation business,

(2) Holds a valid reservation pawnbroker license, and

(3) Posts a bond on a form provided by the commissioner in the name of the licensee in the amount of twenty-five thousand dollars ($25,000) or such larger sum as may be designated by the Commissioner with two (2) or more sureties approved by the Commissioner or with a guaranty company qualified under the Act of August 13, 1894 (28 Stat. 279; 6 U.S.C. 6–13).

(b) An applicant for a reservation pawnbroker license shall apply in writing on a form provided by the Commissioner.

(c) The bond required by paragraph (a) of this section shall be in favor of the United States for the benefits of the customers of the licensee and shall specifically indemnify all customers who have recovered judgment against the licensee for destroyed, lost, misplaced or misappropriated pawn or other property. Any customer recovering such a judgment may bring suit on the bond in his or her own name. The bond shall be for the same period as the license.

(d) Any surety on a bond under this section may be relieved of liability by complying with the provisions of § 141.57.

(e) No person may accept pawns or pledges of personal property as security for monies or accounts due by an Indian after the effective date of a tribal ordinance banning the acceptance of pawn on the reservation.

[40 FR 39837, Aug. 29, 1975, as amended at 41 FR 3288, Jan. 22, 1976; 41 FR 22937, June 8, 1976. Redesignated at 47 FR 13327, Mar. 30, 1982]

§ 141.33 Fees for pawnbroker license.

(a) Prior to the issuance of an initial pawnbroker license, each licensee who is not a member of the Navajo Tribe shall pay the following amount:

(1) If the license is issued before July 1, the licensee shall pay two hundred dollars ($200).

(2) If the license is issued on or after July 1, the licensee shall pay one hundred dollars ($100).

(b) Each licensed pawnbroker who is not a member of the Navajo Tribe shall pay on or before January 10 of each year an annual license fee of two hundred dollars ($200).

(c) The Area Director shall determine the annual license fee payable by licensees who are enrolled members of the Navajo Tribe. The license fee for a member of the Navajo Tribe may not be less than twenty percent (20 percent) nor greater than one hundred percent (100 percent) of the amount the licensee would be required to pay if the licensee were not tribal member.

(d) All fees are payable to the Area Director and shall be deposited to the credit of the account "Special Deposits."

[40 FR 39837, Aug. 29, 1975, as amended at 41 FR 3288, Jan. 22, 1976. Redesignated at 47 FR 13327, Mar. 30, 1982; 59 FR 54502, Oct. 31, 1994]

§ 141.34 Pawnbroker records.

Each pawnbroker shall keep a written record of the following information:

(a) Transaction number.

(b) Name of pledgor.

(c) Address of pledgor.

(d) Census number or social security number of pledgor.

(e) Date of transaction.

(f) Replacement value of pawn.

(g) Description of pawned item.

(h) Amount loaned in cash.

(i) Amount loaned as credit.

(j) Finance charge.

(k) Amount financed.

(l) Date and amount of payments made by pledgor.

(m) Date notice of default sent to pledgor.

(n) Date pawned item sold.

(o) Name and address of purchaser.

(p) Amount received upon sale.

(q) Amount of any surplus returned to the pledgor.

(r) Such other information as the Commissioner may require.

§ 141.35 Pawnbroker disclosure requirements.

In all transactions in which pawn is taken the lender shall give the borrower a written ticket or receipt disclosing the following information to the extent applicable:

(a) Clear identification of the property pledged.

(b) The date of the transaction.

(c) Amount of the loan.

(d) Name and social security or census number of the pledgor.

(e) Replacement value of the pawn as agreed upon by the pledgor and pledgee.

(f) Date on which loan is due.

(g) The amount, expressed as a dollar amount, of any finance charges.

(h) The finance charges expressed as an annual percentage rate and computed in accordance with the provisions of 12 CFR 226.5(b).

(i) The amount, or method of computing the amount, of any charges to be assessed after the date the loan is due.

(j) A statement of the conditions of default and the pledgor's rights upon default, as defined by this part.

(k) Identification of the method of computing any unearned portion of the finance charges in the event of prepayment of the obligation.

§ 141.36 Maximum finance charges on pawn transactions.

No pawnbroker may impose an annual finance charge greater than twenty-four percent (24 percent) of the unpaid balance for the period of the loan nor assess late charges or delinquency charges on any loan.

§ 141.37 Prepayment.

(a) Subject to the provisions of paragraph (b) of this section, the pledgor may prepay in full or in any part the unpaid balance of a loan at any time without penalty.

(b) When a loan is prepaid the lender may collect the earned portion of the finance charge or may charge an administrative fee not to exceed ten percent (10 percent) of the unearned finance charge or two dollars ($2) whichever is greater.

§ 141.38 Pawn loans, period, notice and sale.

(a) The proceeds of all loans secured by pawn and for which a finance charge is imposed shall be paid only in cash or with a fully negotiable check.

(b) The period of all such loans shall be no less than twelve (12) months, subject to the provisions of paragraph (c).

(c) Thirty (30) days prior to the end of the loan period the pledgee may make a declaration of intention to proceed with sale of the pawned item by sending notice of intent to the pledgor.

(d) The notice required in paragraph (c) of this section shall be sent to the pledgor and proof of delivery obtained and shall contain a description of the item pawned, a statement of the principal and finance charge owed, a statement of the intention to sell, the date of the sale, and the procedure for redemption.

(e) Nothing in this section requires the business owner to proceed with notice and sale if the business owner desires to hold the pawn for a period longer than the loan period stated in the original agreement.

(f) Unless notice is given under paragraph (c) of this section, or the loan is refinanced under the provisions of § 141.41, no finance charge may be imposed for the time the loan remains unpaid after the end of the loan period stated on the pawn ticket.

§ 141.39 Sale and redemption of pawn.

(a) If the retention period has expired and notice as required under § 141.38 of this part has been sent and received, the pledgee may proceed with the sale of the pawn.

(b) The pawn shall be sold no sooner than thirty (30) days but no later than twelve (12) months after notice of intent to sell has been given. The sale shall be a public sale, with notice of the time, place, and manner to be given in a tribal newspaper of general circulation not less than fourteen (14) days prior to the sale, or in the absence of such a newspaper, in a commercially reasonable manner. The sale itself shall also be conducted in a commercially reasonable manner.

(c) A pledgor may redeem pawn which has been put up for sale at any time before the day it is to be sold by tendering to the pledgee the face amount of the loan, plus the finance charge assessed on the original loan. The pledgee may also collect an additional charge covering the period between the date due and the date of redemption, provided that the rate of charge does not exceed the finance charge on the original loan.

(d) The pledgee may buy at the pledgee's own sale if the collateral is of a type customarily sold in a recognized market or which is the subject of widely distributed standard price quotations.

(e) Pawn held for more than twelve (12) months after notice of intent to sell has been given may not be sold, but the pledgor may redeem the pawn at any time by tendering to the pledgee the face amount of the loan, plus the finance charge that accrued before the end of the sale period provided in paragraph (b) of this section.

[40 FR 39837, Aug. 29, 1975, as amended at 41 FR 3288, Jan. 22, 1976. Redesignated at 47 FR 13327, Mar. 30, 1982]

§ 141.40 Proceeds of sale.

(a) The following items shall be deducted from the proceeds of the sale of pawned items in the following order of priority:

(1) The expense of advertising and conducting the sale, not to exceed ten percent (10%) of the amount loaned.

(2) The principal amount of the loan, plus any accrued finance charges.

(3) The finance charge calculated at the annual percentage rate of the original loan on the unpaid balance of the loan for the period from the date of default to the date of sale.

(b) Within ten (10) days after the sale of the pledge under this section, the pledgee shall send a notice to the pledgor informing the pledgor of the date of the sale, the proceeds of the sale, the allowable costs of the sale, any additional finance charges, and the amount of any surplus realized. The pledgee shall obtain proof that the notice was delivered.

(c) Any proceeds of the sale remaining after the deductions authorized in paragraph (a) of this section are deemed to be "surplus" and shall be paid over to the pledgor or the pledgor's estate in U.S. currency.

(d) The sale of pledged goods and the application of the proceeds in accordance with this section extinguishes all rights of action of the pledgee for any unpaid principal or finance charge on the original loan.

§ 141.41 Refinancing transaction.

(a) Any pawn agreement may be refinanced, either with or without an increase in the principal amount of the loan, prior to or following the date of expiration of the original period of the loan upon agreement between the parties.

(b) Such refinancing constitutes a new transaction for purposes of all disclosure and record keeping requirements of this part and requires the issuance of a new ticket or receipt.

(c) The rate of the additional finance charge imposed as part of the refinancing agreement may not exceed the maximum rate imposed by § 141.36.

(d) The total finance charges in a refinancing agreement may not exceed the sum of the following amounts:

(1) The finance charge that the pledgor would have been required to pay upon prepayment on the date of refinancing under § 141.37 of this part, except that, for the purpose of computing this amount, no minimum finance charge or administrative fee may be included, and

(2) Such additional finance charge as is permissible on the balance of the loan over the remaining period of the loan as extended.

(e) The default and sale procedures of this part apply to a refinanced pawn transaction in the same manner as they apply to an original pawn transaction.

§ 141.42 Lost pawn receipts or tickets.

(a) Redemption may not be denied on the sole ground that the pledgor is unable to produce a receipt or pawn ticket, provided the pledgor gives a reasonable description of the pawned item or makes an actual identification of the item. The pledgee may require the pledgor to sign a receipt for the redeemed pawn. No person other than the pledgor may redeem pawn without a ticket.

(b) No additional charges may be imposed for the loss of a pawn receipt or ticket.

§ 141.43 Outstanding obligations owed to pledgee.

If the pledgor tenders payment to be applied toward redemption of a pawned item, it shall be so applied by the pledgee, irrespective of other outstanding obligations owed by the pledgor to the pledgee. The pledgee may not deny the pledgor the right to redeem the pawn.

§ 141.44 Insurance on pawn.

(a) Any licensee under this part who lends money or extends credit with personal property as security and holds such property as a pledge shall maintain invault all risk insurance coverage running in favor of the pledgor for such property in amounts based upon a report issued monthly to the insurer. Such monthly report shall be an amount not less than the total agreed replacement value of all pawned items then held by the licensee.

(b) A copy of the insurance policy shall be available for inspection at the licensee's place of business and a copy shall be filed with the Commissioner.

Subpart E—Consumer Credit Transactions Other Than Pawn

§ 141.45 Consumer credit applications.

Any reservation business offering credit which is not secured by pawn shall provide an application for credit to any customer requesting credit. Within thirty (30) days of the date of application, the lender shall act upon the application and notify the customer in writing of the decision with the reason therefor. A business owner who reduces the amount of credit available to a customer or terminates a credit account shall provide written notice to the customer stating the reason for the reduction or termination of such credit.

§ 141.46 Credit disclosure statements.

Upon approval of a credit application the lender shall give the applicant the following information where applicable in a written disclosure statement:

(a) The maximum credit limit of the account.

(b) The conditions under which a finance charge may be imposed.

(c) The period in which payment may be made without incurring a finance charge.

(d) The method used in determining the balance on which the finance charge is calculated.

(e) The method used to calculate the finance charge.

(f) The periodic rates used and the range of balances to which each rate applies.

(g) The conditions under which additional charges may be made and the method for calculating those charges.

(h) A description of any lien that may be acquired on a customer's property.

(i) The minimum payment that must be made on each billing.

§ 141.47 Monthly billing statement.

On all credit accounts on which a finance charge may be imposed and for all other credit accounts when requested by the customer, a licensee shall issue a monthly billing statement to the customer stating the following information where applicable:

(a) The unpaid balance at the start of the billing period.

(b) The amount and date of each extension of credit and identification of each item costing more than ten dollars ($10).

(c) Payments made by a customer and other credits, including returns, rebates, and adjustments.

(d) The finance charge shown in dollars and cents.

(e) The rates used in calculating the finance charge plus the range of balances to which the finance charge was calculated.

(f) The closing date of the billing cycle.

(g) The unpaid balance at that time.

§ 141.48 Translation of disclosure statements.

Disclosure required by §§ 141.46 and 141.47 shall be made in writing regardless of the customer's ability to speak, read, or write the English language. Disclosure to non-English speaking persons shall be translated orally into the appropriate language.

§ 141.49 Usury prohibited.

No reservation business may take or receive money, goods, or other things of value for a loan or forbearance on a debt that exceeds in value the principal plus twenty-four percent (24 percent) per annum finance charge. Any reservation business contracting for, reserving, or receiving directly or indirectly, any greater amount shall forfeit the finance charge.

Subpart F—Enforcement Powers, Procedures and Remedies

§ 141.50 Penalty and forfeiture of merchandise.

Any person other than an enrolled member of the tribe who either resides as a reservation business owner within the exterior boundaries of the Navajo, Hopi, or Zuni Reservations or introduces or attempts to introduce goods or to trade therein without a license shall forfeit all merchandise offered for sale to the Indians or found in the person's possession and is liable to a penalty of $1,296. This section may be enforced by commencing an action in the appropriate United States District Court under the provisions of 28 U.S.C. 1345.

[40 FR 39835, Aug. 29, 1975, as amended at 81 FR 42481, June 30, 2016; 82 FR 7652, Jan. 23, 2017; 83 FR 5195, Feb. 6, 2018]

§ 141.51 Authority to close unlicensed reservation businesses.

The Commissioner shall close any reservation business subject to the provisions of this part that does not hold a valid license or temporary permit.

§ 141.52 Revocation of license and lease and recovery on bond.

The reservation business owner is subject to revocation of license and lease and recovery on the bond in whole or in part in the event of any violation of the regulations of this part after a show cause proceeding according to the provisions of § 141.56.

[41 FR 22937, June 8, 1976. Redesignated at 47 FR 13327, Mar. 30, 1982]

§ 141.53 Cease and desist orders.

(a) If the Commissioner believes that violation of the regulations in this part is occurring, the Commissioner may order the person believed to be in violation to show cause according to the provisions of § 141.56 why a cease and desist order should not be issued.

(b) If the person accused of the violations fails to show cause at the hearing why such an order should not issue, the Commissioner shall issue the order.

(c) A person subject to a cease and desist order issued under this section who violates the order is liable to revocation of license after a show cause proceeding according to the provisions of § 141.56 of this part.

§ 141.54 Periodic review of performance.

(a) The Commissioner shall review licenses at ten (10) year intervals to determine whether or not the business is operating in accordance with these regulations and all other applicable laws and regulations and whether the business is adequately serving the economic needs of the community.

(b) If, as a result of the review provided in paragraph (a) of this section, the Commissioner finds that the licensee has repeatedly violated these regulations, the Commissioner may order the licensee to show cause according to the provisions of §141.56 why the licensee's license should not be revoked.

(c) If the licensee fails to show cause why the license should not be revoked, the Commissioner shall revoke the license.

§141.55 Price monitoring and control.

(a) A reservation business may not charge its customers unfair or unreasonable prices. To insure compliance with this section, the Commissioner shall perform audits as provided in §141.58. In performing those audits the Commissioner may inspect all original books, records, and other evidences of the cost of doing business. In addition, at least once a year the Commissioner shall cause to be made a survey of the prices of flour, sugar, fresh eggs, lard, coffee, ground beef, bread, cheese, fresh milk, canned fruit, and such other goods as the Commissioner deems appropriate in all stores licensed under these regulations and in a representative number of similar stores located in communities immediately adjoining the reservations. The results of the survey shall be posted publicly, sent to each licensed business, and made available to the appropriate agency of the tribal government. Copies of the survey shall be available at the office of the Area Director.

(b) If the Commissioner finds that a reservation business is charging higher prices, especially for basic consumer commodities, than those charged on the average based on the studies conducted under the provisions of paragraph (a) of this section, the Commissioner may order the business owner to show cause under the provisions of §141.56 why an order should not be issued to reduce prices. If the Commissioner determines that the prices charged by the business are not economically justified, based on all of the information, then the Commissioner may order the business to reduce its price on all items determined to be priced too high to a reasonable price as determined by the Commissioner, but in no event to a lower price than the cost of the item increased by a reasonable mark-up.

§141.56 Show cause procedures.

(a) When the Commissioner believes there has been a violation of this part the Commissioner shall serve the licensee with written notice setting forth in detail the nature of the alleged violation and stating what remedial action the Commissioner proposes to take.

(b) The licensee shall have ten (10) days from the date of receipt of notice in which to show cause why the contemplated remedial action should not be ordered.

(c) If within the ten (10) day period the Commissioner determines that the violation may be corrected and the licensee agrees to take the necessary corrective measure, the licensee shall be given the opportunity to take the necessary corrective measures.

(d) If the licensee fails within a reasonable time to correct the violation or to show cause why the contemplated remedial action should not be ordered, the Commissioner shall order the appropriate remedial action.

(e) If the Commissioner orders remedial action the licensee may appeal under the provisions of part 2 of this title not later than thirty (30) days after the date on which the remedial action is ordered.

§141.57 Procedures to cancel liability on bond.

(a) Any surety who wishes to be relieved from liability arising on a bond issued under this part shall file with the Commissioner a statement in writing setting forth the desire of the surety to be relieved of liability and the reasons therefor.

(b) The surety shall mail a copy of the statement by certified mail, return receipt requested, to the last known address of the licensee named in the bond.

(c) Twenty (20) days after the statement required in paragraph (b) of this section is mailed to the licensee and the statement required in paragraph (a) of this section is filed with the Commissioner, the surety from all liability thereafter arising on the bond.

(d) If the licensee does not have other bond sufficient to meet the requirements of this part or has not executed and filed a new or substitute bond within twenty (20) days after the service of the statement, the Commissioner shall declare the license and lease void.

(e) No surety is released from liability under the bond for claims which arose prior to the issuance of the Commissioner's order releasing the surety.

[40 FR 39837, Aug. 29, 1975, as amended at 41 FR 3288, Jan. 22, 1976; 41 FR 22937, June 8, 1976. Redesignated at 47 FR 13327, Mar. 30, 1982]

§ 141.58 Records, reports, and obligations of reservation business owners.

(a) The Commissioner may, in consultation with interested persons and agencies, promulgate a model bookkeeping system for use in reservation businesses. Until such model bookkeeping system is promulgated, each business owner shall keep records in accordance with generally accepted accounting principles.

(b) Each reservation business owner shall file with the Area Director an annual report on or before April 15 in a form approved by the Commissioner. Reports shall be subject to a yearly audit. The reports shall contain the names and respective interests of all persons participating in the business.

(c) The business owner or an employee shall record all sales and purchases whether for cash or credit. If the business is on the Navajo Reservation the owner or an employee shall supply the customer with a copy of the sale transaction containing a description of the article purchased or sold, the date of the transaction, and the price. A cash register receipt complies with this paragraph for grocery or dry goods purchases for cash.

(d) The licensee shall keep a duplicate copy of any writing required by paragraph (c) of this section for a period of not less than three (3) years and shall provide the customer or the customer's representative one copy of those writings upon request.

[40 FR 39837, Aug. 29, 1975, as amended at 41 FR 3288, Jan. 22, 1976; 41 FR 13937, Apr. 1, 1976. Redesignated at 47 FR 13327, Mar. 30, 1982]

§ 141.59 Customer complaint procedures.

(a) Any customer of a licensee may file a complaint with the Commissioner alleging that the licensee has committed a violation of this part.

(b) Upon receipt of a customer complaint the Commissioner shall initiate show cause proceedings under the provisions of § 141.56 of this part.

(c) If the Commissioner fails to order remedial action within forty (40) days from the date the complaint is filed, the complainant may appeal under the provisions of part 2 of this title not later than seventy (70) days after the date the complaint is filed.

(d) If the Commissioner orders remedial action, the complainant may appeal under the provisions of part 2 of this title not later than thirty (30) days after the date on which the remedial action is ordered.

PART 142—ALASKA RESUPPLY OPERATION

Sec.

AUTHORITY: 5 U.S.C. 301; R.S. 463; 25 U.S.C. 2; R.S. 465; 25 U.S.C. 9; 42 Stat. 208; 25 U.S.C. 13; 38 Stat. 586.

SOURCE: 62 FR 18516, Apr. 16, 1997, unless otherwise noted.

§ 142.1 Definitions.

Area Director means the Area Director, Juneau Area Office, Bureau of Indian Affairs.

Bureau means Bureau of Indian Affairs.

Department means Department of the Interior.

Manager means Manager of the Seattle Support Center.

Must is used in place of shall and indicates a mandatory or imperative act or requirement.

Indian means any individual who is a member of an Indian tribe.

Indian tribe means an Indian or Alaska Native tribe, band, nation, pueblo, village, or community that the Secretary of the Interior acknowledges to exist as an Indian tribe pursuant to Public Law 103–454, 108 Stat. 4791.

Alaska Native means a member of an Alaska Native village or a Native shareholder in a corporation as defined in or established pursuant to the Alaska Native Claims Settlement Act, 43 U.S.C. 1601 *et seq.*

§ 142.2 What is the purpose of the Alaska Resupply Operation?

The Alaska Resupply Operation provides consolidated purchasing, freight handling and distribution, and necessary transportation services from Seattle, Washington to and from other points in Alaska or en route in support of the Bureau's mission and responsibilities.

§ 142.3 Who is responsible for the Alaska Resupply Operation?

The Seattle Support Center, under the direction of the Juneau Area Office, is responsible for the operation of the Alaska Resupply Operation, including the management of all facilities and equipment, personnel, and procurement of goods and services.

(a) The Seattle Support Center is responsible for publishing the rates and conditions that must be published in a tariff.

(b) All accounts receivable and accounts payable are handled by the Seattle Support Center.

(c) The Manager must make itineraries for each voyage in conjunction with contracted carriers. Preference is to be given to the work of the Bureau.

(d) The Area Director is authorized to direct the Seattle Support Center to perform special services that may arise and to act in any emergency.

§ 142.4 For whom is the Alaska Resupply Operation operated?

The Manager is authorized to purchase and resell food, fuel, clothing, supplies and materials, and to order, receive, stage, package, store and transport these goods and materials for:

(a) Alaska Native Tribes, Alaska Natives, Indian or Native owned businesses, profit or nonprofit Alaska Native corporations, Native cooperatives or organizations, or such other groups or individuals as may be sponsored by any Native or Indian organization.

(b) Other Federal agencies and the State of Alaska and its subsidiaries, as long as the ultimate beneficiaries are the Alaska Natives or their communities.

(c) Non-Indians and Non-Natives and commercial establishments that economically or materially benefit Alaska Natives or Indians.

(d) The Manager must make reasonable efforts to restrict competition with private enterprise.

§ 142.5 Who determines the rates and conditions of service of the Alaska Resupply Operation?

The general authority of the Assistant Secretary—Indian Affairs to establish rates and conditions for users of the Alaska Resupply Operation is delegated to the Area Director.

(a) The Manager must develop a tariff that establishes rates and conditions for charging users.

(1) The tariff must be approved by the Area Director.

(2) The tariff must be published on or before March 1 of each year.

(3) The tariff must not be altered, amended, or published more frequently

than once each year, except in an extreme emergency.

(4) The tariff must be published, circulated and posted throughout Alaska, particularly in the communities commonly and historically served by the resupply operation.

(b) The tariff must include standard freight categories and rate structures that are recognized within the industry, as well as any appropriate specialized warehouse, handling and storage charges.

(c) The tariff must specify rates for return cargo and cargo hauled between ports.

(1) The rates and conditions for the Bureau, other Federal agencies, the State of Alaska and its subsidiaries must be the same as that for Native entities.

(2) Different rates and conditions may be established for non-Indian and non-Native commercial establishments, if those establishments do not meet the standard in § 142.4(c) and no other service is available to that location.

§ 142.6 How are the rates and conditions for the Alaska Resupply Operation established?

The Manager must develop tariff rates using the best modeling techniques available to ensure the most economical service to the Alaska Natives, Indian or Native owned businesses, profit or nonprofit Alaska Native corporations, Native cooperatives or organizations, or such other groups or individuals as may be sponsored by any Native or Indian organization, without enhancing the Federal treasury.

(a) The Area Director's approval of the tariff constitutes a final action for the Department for the purpose of establishing billing rates.

(b) The Bureau must issue a supplemental bill to cover excess cost in the event that the actual cost of a specific freight substantially exceeds the tariff price.

(c) If the income from the tariff substantially exceeds actual costs, a prorated payment will be issued to the shipper.

§ 142.7 How are transportation and scheduling determined?

(a) The Manager must arrange the most economical and efficient transportation available, taking into consideration lifestyle, timing and other needs of the user. Where practical, shipping must be by consolidated shipment that takes advantage of economies of scale and consider geographic disparity and distribution of sites.

(b) Itineraries and scheduling for all deliveries must be in keeping with the needs of the users to the maximum extent possible. Planned itineraries with dates set as to the earliest and latest anticipated delivery dates must be provided to users prior to final commitment by them to utilize the transportation services. Each shipping season the final departure and arrival schedules must be distributed prior to the commencement of deliveries.

§ 142.8 Is economy of operation a requirement for the Alaska Resupply Operation?

Yes. The Manager must ensure that purchasing, warehousing and transportation services utilize the most economical delivery. This may be accomplished by memoranda of agreement, formal contracts, or cooperative arrangements. Whenever possible joint arrangements for economy will be entered into with other Federal agencies, the State of Alaska, Alaska Native cooperatives or other entities providing services to rural Alaska communities.

§ 142.9 How are orders accepted?

(a) The Manager must make a formal determination to accept an order, for goods or services, and document the approval by issuing a permit or similar instrument.

(b) The Seattle Support Center must prepare proper manifests of the freight accepted at the facility or other designated location. The manifest must follow industry standards to ensure a proper legal contract of carriage is executed, upon which payment can be exacted upon the successful delivery of the goods and services.

§ 142.10 How is freight to be prepared?

All freight must be prepared in accordance with industry standards, unless otherwise specified, for overseas shipment, including any pickup, delivery, staging, sorting, consolidating, packaging, crating, boxing, containerizing, and marking that may be deemed necessary by the Manager.

§ 142.11 How is payment made?

(a) Unless otherwise provided in this part, all regulations implementing the Financial Integrity Act, Anti-Deficiency Act, Prompt Payments Act, Debt Collection Act of 1982, 4 CFR Ch. II—Federal Claims Collection Standards, and other like acts apply to the Alaska Resupply Operation.

(b) Payment for all goods purchased and freight or other services rendered by the Seattle Support Center are due and payable upon final receipt of the goods or services. If payment is not received within the time specified on the billing document, interest and penalty fees at the current treasury rate will be charged, and handling and administrative fees may be applied.

(c) Where fuel and other goods are purchased on behalf of commercial enterprises, payment for those goods must be made within 30 days of delivery to the Seattle Support Center Warehouse. Payment for freight must be made within 30 days from receipt of the goods by the shipper.

§ 142.12 What is the liability of the United States for loss or damage?

(a) The liability of the United States for any loss or damage to, or non-delivery of freight is limited by 46 U.S.C. 746 and the Carriage of Goods by Sea Act (46 U.S.C. 1300 *et seq.*). The terms of such limitation of liability must be contained in any document of title relating to the carriage of goods by sea. This liability may be further restricted in specialized instances as specified in the tariff.

(b) In addition to the standards of conduct and ethics applicable to all government employees, the employees of the Seattle Support Center shall not conduct any business with, engage in trade with, or accept any gifts or items of value from any shipper or permittee.

(c) The Seattle Support Center will continue to function only as long as the need for assistance to Native village economies exits. To that end, a review of the need for the serve must be conducted every five years.

§ 142.13 Information collection.

In accordance with Office of Management and Budget regulations in 5 CFR 1320.4, approval of information collections contained in this regulation is not required.

PART 143—CHARGES FOR GOODS AND SERVICES PROVIDED TO NON-FEDERAL USERS

Sec.

AUTHORITY: 31 U.S.C. 9701; 25 U.S.C. 2, 13, 413.

SOURCE: 55 FR 19621, May 10, 1990, unless otherwise noted.

§ 143.1 Definitions.

As used in this part:

(a) *Assistant Secretary* means the Assistant Secretary—Indian Affairs, Department of the Interior, or other employee to whom authority has been delegated.

(b) *Reservation* means any bounded geographical area established or created by treaty, statute, executive order, or interpreted by court decision and over which a federally recognized Indian Tribal entity may exercise certain jurisdiction.

(c) *Flat fee* is the amount prorated to each user based on the total costs incurred by the Government for the goods/services being provided.

(d) *Non-Federal users* are persons not employed by the Federal Government who receive goods/services provided by the BIA.

(e) *Goods/Services* for the purpose of these regulations are those provided or performed at the request of an indentifiable recipient and are above and beyond those which accrue to the public at large.

§ 143.2 Purpose.

(a) The purpose of the regulations in this part is to establish procedures for the assessment, billing, and collection of charges for goods/services provided to non-Federal users.

(b) The Assistant Secretary may sell or contract to sell to non-Federal users within, or in the immediate vicinity of an Indian Reservation (or former Reservation), any of the following goods/services if it is determined that the goods/services are not available from another local source or providing that goods/services is in the best interest of the Indian tribes or individual Indians. The goods/services include, but are not limited to:

(1) Electric power;

(2) Water;

(3) Sewage operations;

(4) Landfill operations;

(5) Steam;

(6) Compressed air;

(7) Telecommunications;

(8) Natural, manufactured, or mixed gas;

(9) Fuel oil;

(10) Landscaping; and

(11) Garbage collections.

§ 143.3 Procedures.

(a) All non-Federal users who receive the above listed goods/services must sign a standard agreement adopted by the Assistant Secretary for the goods/services. This agreement shall contain the following statement:

"Application for _________ (specify good(s)/service(s)) is hereby requested at the noted address. In exchange for receiving the requested good(s)/service(s), the applicant agrees to accept and abide by all applicable rules, regulations, and rate schedules, including any future amendments, additions, or changes thereto. If the applicant should fail to comply with any of the rules, regulations, or rate schedules, the cost incurred by the United States Government for enforcement of same shall be charged to the applicant."

(b) Lack of a signed agreement does not invalidate payment requirements. Any user will be responsible for payment of actual goods/services received or delivered.

§ 143.4 Charges.

(a) Charges shall be established by the Assistant Secretary and shall be based upon the total costs (including both direct and indirect) of goods/services to the Government at that locale. A schedule of charges will be made available to the public upon request.

(b) All documentation used in establishing charges must be maintained at the appropriate Bureau of Indian Affairs agency or Area Office and shall be made available for review by the public upon request.

(c) Established charges may be reviewed, amended, and adjusted monthly, but not less than annually.

(d) A flat fee may be charged where it is impractical to measure actual usage by recipients.

(e) Security deposits are authorized under this regulation at the discretion of the Assistant Secretary. The deposit may not exceed the amount of one billing cycle. All deposits will be applied to the final bill.

§ 143.5 Payment.

(a) The Assistant Secretary—Indian Affairs will establish a billing cycle that is appropriate to the goods/services being provided.

(b) Payment is due within 30 days after the billing date.

(c) Upon non-payment by the non-Federal user, the Assistant Secretary may discontinue service. Service may be discontinued after proper notification by letter. Proper notification shall include:

(1) Written notice to user that payment is due. Such notice shall afford the user the opportunity to challenge payment or excuse non-payment within 14 days of the date on the notification letter.

(2) Following the expiration of the 14 day deadline for response, and after consideration of any such response, the Assistant Secretary—Indian Affairs may notify the user by letter that if payment is not received within 10 days of the date on the letter, the service will be discontinued.

(d) The Assistant Secretary has the discretion to continue services for health and safety reasons. However, the non-Federal user is still responsible for payment for goods/services provided.

(e) Once service has been discontinued based on delinquency of payment, the discontinuance may be appealed under part 2 of this title.

SUBCHAPTER H—LAND AND WATER

PART 150—LAND RECORDS AND TITLE DOCUMENTS

Sec.

AUTHORITY: Act of June 30, 1834 (4 Stat. 738; 25 U.S.C. 9). Act of July 26, 1892 (27 Stat. 272; 25 U.S.C. 5). Reorganization Plan No. 3 of 1950 approved June 20, 1949 (64 Stat. 1262). (Act of April 26, 1906 (34 Stat. 137); Act of May 27, 1908 (35 Stat. 312); Act of August 1, 1914 (38 Stat. 582, 598) deal specifically with land records of the Five Civilized Tribes.)

CROSS REFERENCE: For further regulations pertaining to proceedings in Indian probate, see 43 CFR part 4, subpart D.

SOURCE: 46 FR 47537, Sept. 29, 1981, unless otherwise noted. Redesignated at 47 FR 13327, Mar. 30, 1982.

§ 150.1 Purpose and scope.

These regulations set forth authorities, policy and procedures governing the recording, custody, maintenance, use and certification of title documents, and the issuance of title status reports for Indian land.

§ 150.2 Definitions.

As used in this part.

(a) *Secretary* is the Secretary of the Interior or his authorized representative.

(b) *Commissioner* is the Commissioner of Indian Affairs or his authorized representative.

(c) *Agency* is an Indian Agency or other field unit of the Bureau of Indian Affairs having Indian land under its immediate jurisdiction.

(d) *Superintendent* is the designated officer in charge of an Agency.

(e) *Tribe* is a tribe, band, nation, community, rancheria, colony, pueblo, or other Federally-acknowledged group of Indians.

(f) *Bureau* is the Bureau of Indian Affairs.

(g) *Land* is real property, including any interests, benefits, and rights inherent in the ownership of the real property.

(h) *Indian land* is an inclusive term describing all lands held in trust by the United States for individual Indians or tribes, or all lands, titles to which are held by individual Indians or tribes, subject to Federal restrictions against alienation or encumbrance, or all lands which are subject to the rights of use, occupancy and/or benefit of certain tribes. For purposes of this part, the term Indian land also includes land for which the title is held in fee status by Indian tribes, and U.S. Government-owned land under Bureau jurisdiction.

(i) *Administrative Law Judge* is an employee of the Office of Hearing and Appeals, Department of the Interior, upon whom authority has been conferred by the Secretary to probate the trust or restricted estates of deceased Indians in accordance with 43 CFR part 4, subpart D.

(j) *Land Titles and Records Offices* are those offices within the Bureau of Indian Affairs charged with the Federal responsibility to record, provide custody, and maintain records that affect titles to Indian lands, to examine titles, and to provide title status reports for such land.

(k) *Manager* is the designated officer in charge of a Land Titles and Records Office.

(l) *Title document* is any document that affects the title to or encumbers Indian land and is required to be recorded by regulation or Bureau policy.

(m) *Recordation* or *recording* is the acceptance of a title document by the appropriate Land Titles and Records Office. The purpose of recording is to provide evidence of a transaction, event, or happening that affects land titles; to preserve a record of the title document; and to give constructive notice of the ownership and change of ownership and the existence of encumbrances to the land.

(n) *Title examination* means an examination and evaluation by a qualified title examiner of the completeness and accuracy of title documents affecting a particular tract of Indian land with certification of the findings by the Manager of the Land Titles and Records Office.

(o) *Title status report* means a report issued after a title examination which shows the proper legal description of a tract of Indian land; current ownership, including any applicable conditions, exceptions, restrictions or encumbrances on record; and whether the land is in unrestricted, restricted, trust, or other status as indicated by the records in a Land Titles and Records Office.

§ 150.3 Maintenance of land records and title documents.

The Land Titles and Records Offices within the Bureau are hereby designated as the offices of record for land records and title documents and are hereby charged with the Federal responsibility to record, provide custody, and maintain records that affect titles to Indian land, to examine titles, and to provide title status reports.

§ 150.4 Locations and service areas for land titles and records offices.

Shown below are present Land Titles and Records Offices and the jurisdictional area served by each office.

(a) Aberdeen, S. Dakota Office provides title service for Indian land located under the jurisdiction of the Aberdeen and Minneapolis Area Offices, except for Indian land on the White Earth, Isabella, and Oneida Indian Reservations.

(b) Albuquerque, New Mexico Office provides title services for Indian land located under the jurisdiction of the Albuquerque, Navajo, and Phoenix Area Offices.

(c) Anadarko, Oklahoma Office provides title services for Indian land located under the jurisdiction of the Anadarko Area Office and under the Miami Agency of the Muskogee Area Office.

(d) Billings, Montana Office provides title services for Indian land located under the jurisdiction of the Billings Area Office.

(e) Portland, Oregon Office provides title services for Indian land located under the jurisdiction of the Portland and Sacramento Area Offices.

§ 150.5 Other Bureau offices with title service responsibility.

(a) Muskogee Area Office is the office of record and performs limited title functions for all Indian land of the Five Civilized Tribes. The regulations in this part apply to the Muskogee Area Office to the extent that they relate to the title services performed by that office.

(b) The Juneau Area Office has title service responsibility for the Juneau Area. This authority has been largely delegated to the agencies. The regulations in this part apply to the Juneau Area Office to the extent practicable.

(c) The Cherokee Agency has title service responsibility for the Eastern Cherokee Reservation. The regulations in this part apply to the Cherokee Agency to the extent practicable.

(d) The Bureau Central Office, Washington, DC, provides title services for all other Indian land not shown above in § 150.4 or in this section, including the land of the Absentee Wyandottes. The regulations in this part apply to the Central Office.

§ 150.6 Recordation of title documents.

All title documents shall be submitted to the appropriate Land Titles and Records Office for recording immediately after final approval, issuance, or acceptance. Bureau officials delegated authority by the Secretary to approve title documents or accept title are responsible for prompt compliance with the recording requirement. Documents submitted for recording shall be completed in accordance with prescribed Bureau regulations or instructions.

(a) *Title documents other than probate records.* The original, a signed duplicate, or a certified copy of such documents shall be submitted for recording. Following the recording process, the

Land Titles and Records Office will return those title documents that are required to be returned to the originating office with appropriate recording information.

(b) *Probate records.* In accordance with 43 CFR part 4, subpart D, Administrative Law Judges shall forward the original record of Indian probate decisions and copies of petitions for rehearing, reopening, and other appeals to the Land Titles and Records Office which provides service to the originating Agency. If trust land or Indian heirs involved in the probate are located within the jurisdictional area of another Land Titles and Records Office, the Administrative Law Judge shall also send a duplicate copy to that office. Probate records submitted by an Administrative Law Judge for recording will be retained by the Land Titles and Records Office.

§ 150.7 Curative action to correct title defects.

Land Titles and Records Office shall initiate such action as described below to cure defects in the record discovered during the recording of title documents or examination of titles.

(a) If an error is traced to a defective title document other than probate records, the Land Titles and Records Office shall notify the originating office of the defect.

(b) If errors are discovered in probate records, the Land Titles and Records Office may initiate corrective action as follows:

(1) An administrative modification shall be issued to modify probate records to include any Indian land omitted from the inventory if such property is located in the same state and takes the same line of descent as that shown in the original probate decision. Authority is delegated to the Commissioner by 43 CFR 4.272 to make such modifications except on those Indian reservations covered by special Inheritance Acts (43 CFR 4.300). Copies of administrative modifications shall be distributed to the appropriate Administrative Law Judge, Agencies with jurisdiction over the Indian land, and to all persons who share in the estate.

(2) Land Titles and Records Offices shall notify the Superintendent when modifications are required by Administrative Law Judges for other types of probate errors. Corrective action is then initiated in accordance with 43 CFR part 4, subpart D.

(3) Land Titles and Records Offices shall issue administrative corrections to correct probate errors which are clerical in nature and which do not affect vested property rights or involve questions of due process. Copies of administrative corrections are distributed to the appropriate Administrative Law Judge and Agency.

§ 150.8 Title status reports.

Land Titles and Records Offices may conduct a title examination of a tract of Indian land provide a title status report upon request to those persons authorized by law to receive such information. Requests for title status reports shall be submitted by or through the Bureau office that has administrative jurisdiction over the Indian land. All requests must clearly identify the tract of Indian land.

§ 150.9 Land status maps.

The Land Titles and Records Offices shall prepare and maintain maps of all reservations and similar entities within their jurisdictions to assist Bureau personnel in the execution of their title service responsibilities. Base maps shall be prepared from plats of official survey made by the General Land Office and the Bureau of Land Management. These base maps, showing prominent physical features and section, township and range lines, shall be used to prepare land status maps. The land status maps shall reflect the individual tracts, tract numbers, and current status of the tract. Other special maps, such as plats and townsite maps, may also be prepared and maintained to meet the needs of individual Land Titles and Records Offices, Agencies, and Indian tribes.

§ 150.10 Certification of land records and title documents.

Under the provisions of the Act of July 26, 1892 (27 Stat. 273; 25 U.S.C. 6), an official seal was created for the use of the Commissioner of Indian Affairs in authenticating and certifying copies of Bureau records. Managers of Land

Titles and Records Offices are designated as Certifying Officers for this purpose. When a copy or reproduction of a title document is authenticated by the official seal and certified by a Manager, Land Titles and Records Office, the copy or reproduction shall be admitted into evidence the same as the original from which it was made. The fees for furnishing such certified copies are established by a uniform fee schedule applicable to all constituent units of the Department of the Interior and published in 43 CFR part 2, appendix A.

§150.11 Disclosure of land records, title documents, and title reports.

(a) The usefulness of a Land Titles and Records Office depends in large measure on the ability of the public to consult the records contained therein. It is therefore, the policy of the Bureau of Indian Affairs to allow access to land records and title documents unless such access would violate the Privacy Act, 5 U.S.C. 552a or other law restricting access to such records, or there are strong policy grounds for denying access where such access is not required by the Freedom of Information Act, 5 U.S.C. 552. It shall be the policy of the Bureau of Indian Affairs that, unless specifically authorized, monetary considerations will not be disclosed insofar as leases of tribal land are concerned.

(b) Before disclosing information concerning any living individual, the Manager, Land Titles and Records Office, shall consult 5 U.S.C. 552a(b) and the notice of routine users then in effect to determine whether the information may be released without the written consent of the person to whom it pertains.

PART 151—LAND ACQUISITIONS

Sec.

AUTHORITY: R.S. 161: 5 U.S.C. 301. Interpret or apply 46 Stat. 1106, as amended; 46 Stat. 1471, as amended; 48 Stat. 985, as amended; 49 Stat. 1967, as amended, 53 Stat. 1129; 63 Stat. 605; 69 Stat. 392, as amended; 70 Stat. 290, as amended; 70 Stat. 626; 75 Stat. 505; 77 Stat. 349; 78 Stat. 389; 78 Stat. 747; 82 Stat. 174, as amended, 82 Stat. 884; 84 Stat. 120; 84 Stat. 1874; 86 Stat. 216; 86 Stat. 530; 86 Stat. 744; 88 Stat. 78; 88 Stat. 81; 88 Stat. 1716; 88 Stat. 2203; 88 Stat. 2207; 25 U.S.C. 2, 9, 409a, 450h, 451, 464, 465, 487, 488, 489, 501, 502, 573, 574, 576, 608, 608a, 610, 610a, 622, 624, 640d–10, 1466, 1495, and other authorizing acts.

CROSS REFERENCE: For regulations pertaining to: The inheritance of interests in trust or restricted land, see parts 15, 16, and 17 of this title and 43 CFR part 4; the purchase of lands under the BIA Loan Guaranty, Insurance and Interest Subsidy program, see part 103 of this title; the exchange and partition of trust or restricted lands, see part 152 of this title; land acquisitions authorized by the Indian Self-Determination and Education Assistance Act, see parts 900 and 276 of this title; the acquisition of allotments on the public domain or in national forests, see 43 CFR part 2530; the acquisition of Native allotments and Native townsite lots in Alaska, see 43 CFR parts 2561 and 2564; the acquisition of lands by Indians with funds borrowed from the Farmers Home Administration, see 7 CFR part 1823, subpart N; the acquisition of land by purchase or exchange for members of the Osage Tribe not having certificates of competency, see §§117.8 and 158.54 of this title.

SOURCE: 45 FR 62036, Sept. 18, 1980, unless otherwise noted. Redesignated at 47 FR 13327, Mar. 30, 1982.

§151.1 Purpose and scope.

These regulations set forth the authorities, policy, and procedures governing the acquisition of land by the United States in trust status for individual Indians and tribes. Acquisition of land by individual Indians and tribes in fee simple status is not covered by these regulations even though such land may, by operation of law, be held in restricted status following acquisition. Acquisition of land in trust status by inheritance or escheat is not covered by these regulations.

[79 FR 76897, Dec. 23, 2014]

§ 151.2 Definitions.

(a) *Secretary* means the Secretary of the Interior or authorized representative.

(b) *Tribe* means any Indian tribe, band, nation, pueblo, community, rancheria, colony, or other group of Indians, including the Metlakatla Indian Community of the Annette Island Reserve, which is recognized by the Secretary as eligible for the special programs and services from the Bureau of Indian Affairs. For purposes of acquisitions made under the authority of 25 U.S.C. 488 and 489, or other statutory authority which specifically authorizes trust acquisitions for such corporations, "Tribe" also means a corporation chartered under section 17 of the Act of June 18, 1934 (48 Stat. 988; 25 U.S.C. 477) or section 3 of the Act of June 26, 1936 (49 Stat. 1967; 25 U.S.C. 503).

(c) *Individual Indian* means:

(1) Any person who is an enrolled member of a tribe;

(2) Any person who is a descendent of such a member and said descendant was, on June 1, 1934, physically residing on a federally recognized Indian reservation;

(3) Any other person possessing a total of one-half or more degree Indian blood of a tribe;

(4) For purposes of acquisitions outside of the State of Alaska, *Individual Indian* also means a person who meets the qualifications of paragraph (c)(1), (2), or (3) of this section where "Tribe" includes any Alaska Native Village or Alaska Native Group which is recognized by the Secretary as eligible for the special programs and services from the Bureau of Indian Affairs.

(d) *Trust land* or *land in trust status* means land the title to which is held in trust by the United States for an individual Indian or a tribe.

(e) *Restricted land* or *land in restricted status* means land the title to which is held by an individual Indian or a tribe and which can only be alienated or encumbered by the owner with the approval of the Secretary because of limitations contained in the conveyance instrument pursuant to Federal law or because of a Federal law directly imposing such limitations.

(f) Unless another definition is required by the act of Congress authorizing a particular trust acquisition, *Indian reservation* means that area of land over which the tribe is recognized by the United States as having governmental jurisdiction, except that, in the State of Oklahoma or where there has been a final judicial determination that a reservation has been disestablished or diminished, *Indian reservation* means that area of land constituting the former reservation of the tribe as defined by the Secretary.

(g) *Land* means real property or any interest therein.

(h) *Tribal consolidation area* means a specific area of land with respect to which the tribe has prepared, and the Secretary has approved, a plan for the acquisition of land in trust status for the tribe.

[45 FR 62036, Sept. 18, 1980, as amended at 60 FR 32879, June 23, 1995]

§ 151.3 Land acquisition policy.

Land not held in trust or restricted status may only be acquired for an individual Indian or a tribe in trust status when such acquisition is authorized by an act of Congress. No acquisition of land in trust status, including a transfer of land already held in trust or restricted status, shall be valid unless the acquisition is approved by the Secretary.

(a) Subject to the provisions contained in the acts of Congress which authorize land acquisitions, land may be acquired for a tribe in trust status:

(1) When the property is located within the exterior boundaries of the tribe's reservation or adjacent thereto, or within a tribal consolidation area; or

(2) When the tribe already owns an interest in the land; or

(3) When the Secretary determines that the acquisition of the land is necessary to facilitate tribal self-determination, economic development, or Indian housing.

(b) Subject to the provisions contained in the acts of Congress which authorize land acquisitions or holding land in trust or restricted status, land may be acquired for an individual Indian in trust status:

(1) When the land is located within the exterior boundaries of an Indian reservation, or adjacent thereto; or

(2) When the land is already in trust or restricted status.

§151.4 Acquisitions in trust of lands owned in fee by an Indian.

Unrestricted land owned by an individual Indian or a tribe may be conveyed into trust status, including a conveyance to trust for the owner, subject to the provisions of this part.

§151.5 Trust acquisitions in Oklahoma under section 5 of the I.R.A.

In addition to acquisitions for tribes which did not reject the provisions of the Indian Reorganization Act and their members, land may be acquired in trust status for an individual Indian or a tribe in the State of Oklahoma under section 5 of the Act of June 18, 1934 (48 Stat. 985; 25 U.S.C. 465), if such acquisition comes within the terms of this part. This authority is in addition to all other statutory authority for such an acquisition.

§151.6 Exchanges.

An individual Indian or tribe may acquire land in trust status by exchange if the acquisition comes within the terms of this part. The disposal aspects of an exchange are governed by part 152 of this title.

§151.7 Acquisition of fractional interests.

Acquisition of a fractional land interest by an individual Indian or a tribe in trust status can be approved by the Secretary only if:

(a) The buyer already owns a fractional interest in the same parcel of land; or

(b) The interest being acquired by the buyer is in fee status; or

(c) The buyer offers to purchase the remaining undivided trust or restricted interests in the parcel at not less than their fair market value; or

(d) There is a specific law which grants to the particular buyer the right to purchase an undivided interest or interests in trust or restricted land without offering to purchase all of such interests; or

(e) The owner of a majority of the remaining trust or restricted interests in the parcel consent in writing to the acquisition by the buyer.

§151.8 Tribal consent for nonmember acquisitions.

An individual Indian or tribe may acquire land in trust status on a reservation other than its own only when the governing body of the tribe having jurisdiction over such reservation consents in writing to the acquisition; provided, that such consent shall not be required if the individual Indian or the tribe already owns an undivided trust or restricted interest in the parcel of land to be acquired.

§151.9 Requests for approval of acquisitions.

An individual Indian or tribe desiring to acquire land in trust status shall file a written request for approval of such acquisition with the Secretary. The request need not be in any special form but shall set out the identity of the parties, a description of the land to be acquired, and other information which would show that the acquisition comes within the terms of this part.

§151.10 On-reservation acquisitions.

Upon receipt of a written request to have lands taken in trust, the Secretary will notify the state and local governments having regulatory jurisdiction over the land to be acquired, unless the acquisition is mandated by legislation. The notice will inform the state or local government that each will be given 30 days in which to provide written comments as to the acquisition's potential impacts on regulatory jurisdiction, real property taxes and special assessments. If the state or local government responds within a 30-day period, a copy of the comments will be provided to the applicant, who will be given a reasonable time in which to reply and/or request that the Secretary issue a decision. The Secretary will consider the following criteria in evaluating requests for the acquisition of land in trust status when the land is located within or contiguous to an Indian reservation, and the acquisition is not mandated:

(a) The existence of statutory authority for the acquisition and any limitations contained in such authority;

(b) The need of the individual Indian or the tribe for additional land;

(c) The purposes for which the land will be used;

(d) If the land is to be acquired for an individual Indian, the amount of trust or restricted land already owned by or for that individual and the degree to which he needs assistance in handling his affairs;

(e) If the land to be acquired is in unrestricted fee status, the impact on the State and its political subdivisions resulting from the removal of the land from the tax rolls;

(f) Jurisdictional problems and potential conflicts of land use which may arise; and

(g) If the land to be acquired is in fee status, whether the Bureau of Indian Affairs is equipped to discharge the additional responsibilities resulting from the acquisition of the land in trust status.

(h) The extent to which the applicant has provided information that allows the Secretary to comply with 516 DM 6, appendix 4, National Environmental Policy Act Revised Implementing Procedures, and 602 DM 2, Land Acquisitions: Hazardous Substances Determinations. (For copies, write to the Department of the Interior, Bureau of Indian Affairs, Branch of Environmental Services, 1849 C Street NW., Room 4525 MIB, Washington, DC 20240.)

[45 FR 62036, Sept. 18, 1980, as amended at 60 FR 32879, June 23, 1995]

§ 151.11 Off-reservation acquisitions.

The Secretary shall consider the following requirements in evaluating tribal requests for the acquisition of lands in trust status, when the land is located outside of and noncontiguous to the tribe's reservation, and the acquisition is not mandated:

(a) The criteria listed in § 151.10 (a) through (c) and (e) through (h);

(b) The location of the land relative to state boundaries, and its distance from the boundaries of the tribe's reservation, shall be considered as follows: as the distance between the tribe's reservation and the land to be acquired increases, the Secretary shall give greater scrutiny to the tribe's justification of anticipated benefits from the acquisition. The Secretary shall give greater weight to the concerns raised pursuant to paragraph (d) of this section.

(c) Where land is being acquired for business purposes, the tribe shall provide a plan which specifies the anticipated economic benefits associated with the proposed use.

(d) Contact with state and local governments pursuant to § 151.10 (e) and (f) shall be completed as follows: Upon receipt of a tribe's written request to have lands taken in trust, the Secretary shall notify the state and local governments having regulatory jurisdiction over the land to be acquired. The notice shall inform the state and local government that each will be given 30 days in which to provide written comment as to the acquisition's potential impacts on regulatory jurisdiction, real property taxes and special assessments.

[60 FR 32879, June 23, 1995, as amended at 60 FR 48894, Sept. 21, 1995]

§ 151.12 Action on requests.

(a) The Secretary shall review each request and may request any additional information or justification deemed necessary to reach a decision.

(b) The Secretary's decision to approve or deny a request shall be in writing and state the reasons for the decision.

(c) A decision made by the Secretary, or the Assistant Secretary—Indian Affairs pursuant to delegated authority, is a final agency action under 5 U.S.C. 704 upon issuance.

(1) If the Secretary or Assistant Secretary denies the request, the Assistant Secretary shall promptly provide the applicant with the decision.

(2) If the Secretary or Assistant Secretary approves the request, the Assistant Secretary shall:

(i) Promptly provide the applicant with the decision;

(ii) Promptly publish in the FEDERAL REGISTER a notice of the decision to acquire land in trust under this part; and

(iii) Immediately acquire the land in trust under § 151.14 on or after the date such decision is issued and upon fulfillment of the requirements of § 151.13 and any other Departmental requirements.

(d) A decision made by a Bureau of Indian Affairs official pursuant to delegated authority is not a final agency action of the Department under 5 U.S.C. 704 until administrative remedies are exhausted under part 2 of this chapter or until the time for filing a notice of appeal has expired and no administrative appeal has been filed.

(1) If the official denies the request, the official shall promptly provide the applicant with the decision and notification of any right to file an administrative appeal under part 2 of this chapter.

(2) If the official approves the request, the official shall:

(i) Promptly provide the applicant with the decision;

(ii) Promptly provide written notice of the decision and the right, if any, to file an administrative appeal of such decision pursuant to part 2 of this chapter, by mail or personal delivery to:

(A) Interested parties who have made themselves known, in writing, to the official prior to the decision being made; and

(B) The State and local governments having regulatory jurisdiction over the land to be acquired;

(iii) Promptly publish a notice in a newspaper of general circulation serving the affected area of the decision and the right, if any, of interested parties who did not make themselves known, in writing, to the official to file an administrative appeal of the decision under part 2 of this chapter; and

(iv) Immediately acquire the land in trust under § 151.14 upon expiration of the time for filing a notice of appeal or upon exhaustion of administrative remedies under part 2 of this title, and upon the fulfillment of the requirements of § 151.13 and any other Departmental requirements.

(3) The administrative appeal period under part 2 of this chapter begins on:

(i) The date of receipt of written notice by the applicant or interested parties entitled to notice under paragraphs (d)(1) and (d)(2)(ii) of this section;

(ii) The date of first publication of the notice for unknown interested parties under paragraph (d)(2)(iii) of this section.

(4) Any party who wishes to seek judicial review of an official's decision must first exhaust administrative remedies under 25 CFR part 2.

[78 FR 67937, Nov. 13, 2013]

§ 151.13 Title review.

(a) If the Secretary determines that she will approve a request for the acquisition of land from unrestricted fee status to trust status, she shall require the applicant to furnish title evidence as follows:

(1) The deed or other conveyance instrument providing evidence of the applicant's title or, if the applicant does not yet have title, the deed providing evidence of the transferor's title and a written agreement or affidavit from the transferor, that title will be transferred to the United States on behalf of the applicant to complete the acquisition in trust; and

(2) Either:

(i) A current title insurance commitment; or

(ii) The policy of title insurance issued to the applicant or current owner and an abstract of title dating from the time the policy of title insurance was issued to the applicant or current owner to the present.

(3) The applicant may choose to provide title evidence meeting the title standards issued by the U.S. Department of Justice, in lieu of the evidence required by paragraph (a)(2) of this section.

(b) After reviewing submitted title evidence, the Secretary shall notify the applicant of any liens, encumbrances, or infirmities that the Secretary identified and may seek additional information from the applicant needed to address such issues. The Secretary may require the elimination of any such liens, encumbrances, or infirmities prior to taking final approval action on the acquisition, and she shall require elimination prior to such approval if she determines that the liens, encumbrances or infirmities make title to the land unmarketable.

[81 FR 30177, May 16, 2016]

§ 151.14 Formalization of acceptance.

Formal acceptance of land in trust status shall be accomplished by the issuance or approval of an instrument of conveyance by the Secretary as is appropriate in the circumstances.

[45 FR 62036, Sept. 18, 1980. Redesignated at 60 FR 32879, June 23, 1995]

§ 151.15 Information collection.

(a) The information collection requirements contained in §§ 151.9; 151.10; 151.11(c), and 151.13 have been approved by the Office of Management and Budget under 44 U.S.C. 3501 *et seq.* and assigned clearance number 1076–0100. This information is being collected to acquire land into trust on behalf of the Indian tribes and individuals, and will be used to assist the Secretary in making a determination. Response to this request is required to obtain a benefit.

(b) Public reporting for this information collection is estimated to average 4 hours per response, including the time for reviewing instructions, gathering and maintaining data, and completing and reviewing the information collection. Direct comments regarding the burden estimate or any other aspect of this information collection to the Bureau of Indian Affairs, Information Collection Clearance Officer, Room 337–SIB, 18th and C Streets, NW., Washington, DC 20240; and the Office of Information and Regulatory Affairs [Project 1076–0100], Office of Management and Budget, Washington, DC 20502.

[60 FR 32879, June 23, 1995; 64 FR 13895, Mar. 23, 1999]

PART 152—ISSUANCE OF PATENTS IN FEE, CERTIFICATES OF COMPETENCY, REMOVAL OF RESTRICTIONS, AND SALE OF CERTAIN INDIAN LANDS

Sec.

AUTHORITY: R.S. 161; 5 U.S.C. 301. Interpret or apply sec. 7, 32 Stat. 275, 34 Stat. 1018, sec. 1, 35 Stat. 444, sec. 1 and 2, 36 Stat. 855, as amended, 856, as amended, sec. 17, 39 Stat. 127, 40 Stat. 579, 62 Stat. 236, sec. 2, 40 Stat. 606, 68 Stat. 358, 69 Stat. 666: 25 U.S.C. 378, 379, 405, 404, 372, 373, 483, 355, unless otherwise noted.

CROSS REFERENCES: For further regulations pertaining to the sale of irrigable lands, see parts 160, 159 and §134.4 of this chapter. For Indian money regulations, see parts 115, 111, 116, and 112 of this chapter. For regulations pertaining to the determination of heirs and approval of wills, see part 15 and subpart G of part 11 of this chapter.

SOURCE: 38 FR 10080, Apr. 24, 1973, unless otherwise noted. Redesignated at 47 FR 13327, Mar. 30, 1982.

§ 152.1 Definitions.

As used in this part:

(a) *Secretary* means the Secretary of the Interior or his authorized representative acting under delegated authority.

(b) *Agency* means an Indian agency or other field unit of the Bureau of Indian Affairs having trust or restricted Indian land under its immediate jurisdiction.

(c) *Restricted land* means land or any interest therein, the title to which is held by an individual Indian, subject to Federal restrictions against alienation or encumbrance.

(d) *Trust land* means land or any interest therein held in trust by the United States for an individual Indian.

(e) *Competent* means the possession of sufficient ability, knowledge, experience, and judgment to enable an individual to manage his business affairs, including the administration, use, investment, and disposition of any property turned over to him and the income or proceeds therefrom, with such reasonable degree of prudence and wisdom as will be apt to prevent him from losing such property or the benefits thereof. (Act of August 11, 1955 (69 Stat. 666)).

(f) *Tribe* means a tribe, band, nation, community, group, or pueblo of Indians.

§ 152.2 Withholding action on application.

Action on any application, which if approved would remove Indian land from restricted or trust status, may be withheld, if the Secretary determines that such removal would adversely affect the best interest of other Indians, or the tribes, until the other Indians or the tribes so affected have had a reasonable opportunity to acquire the land from the applicant. If action on the application is to be withheld, the applicant shall be advised that he has the right to appeal the withholding action pursuant to the provisions of part 2 of this chapter.

ISSUING PATENTS IN FEE, CERTIFICATES OF COMPETENCY OR ORDERS REMOVING RESTRICTIONS

§ 152.3 Information regarding status of applications for removal of Federal supervision over Indian lands.

The status of applications by Indians for patents in fee, certificates of competency, or orders removing restrictions shall be disclosed to employees of the Department of the Interior whose duties require that such information be disclosed to them; to the applicant or his attorney, upon request; and to Members of Congress who inquire on behalf of the applicant. Such information will be available to all other persons, upon request, 15 days after the fee patent has been issued by the Bureau of Land Management, or 15 days after issuance of certificate of competency or order removing restrictions, or after the application has been rejected and the applicant notified. Where the termination of the trust or restricted status of the land covered by the application would adversely affect the protection and use of Indian land remaining in trust or restricted status, the owners of the land that would be so affected may be informed that the application has been filed.

§ 152.4 Application for patent in fee.

Any Indian 21 years of age or over may apply for a patent in fee for his trust land. A written application shall be made in the form approved by the Secretary and shall be completed and filed with the agency having immediate jurisdiction over the land.

§ 152.5 Issuance of patent in fee.

(a) An application may be approved and fee patent issued if the Secretary, in his discretion, determines that the applicant is competent. When the patent in fee is delivered, an inventory of the estate covered thereby shall be given to the patentee. (Acts of Feb. 8, 1887 (24 Stat. 388), as amended (25 U.S.C. 349); June 25, 1910 (36 Stat. 855), as amended (25 U.S.C. 372); and May 14, 1948 (62 Stat. 236; 25 U.S.C. 483), and other authorizing acts.)

(b) If an application is denied, the applicant shall be notified in writing, given the reasons therefor and advised of his right to appeal pursuant to the provisions of part 2 of this chapter.

(c) White Earth Reservation: The Secretary will, pursuant to the Act of March 1, 1907 (34 Stat. 1015), issue a patent in fee to any adult mixed-blood Indian owning land within the White Earth Reservation in the State of Minnesota upon application from such Indian, and without consideration as to whether the applicant is competent.

(d) Fort Peck Reservation: Pursuant to the Act of June 30, 1954 (68 Stat. 358), oil and gas underlying certain allotments in the Fort Peck Reservation were granted to certain Indians to be held in trust for such Indians and provisions was made for issuance of patents in fee for such oil and gas or patents in fee for land in certain circumstances.

(1) Where an Indian or Indians were the grantees of the entire interest in the oil and gas underlying a parcel of land, and such Indian or Indians had before June 30, 1954, been issued a patent or patents in fee for any land within the Fort Peck Reservation, the title to the oil and gas was conveyed by the act in fee simple status.

(2) Where the entire interest in the oil and gas granted by the act is after June 30, 1954, held in trust for Indians to whom a fee patent has been issued at any time, for any land within the Fort Peck Reservation, or who have been or are determined by the Secretary to be competent, the Secretary will convey, by patent, without application, therefor, unrestricted fee simple title to the oil and gas.

(3) Where the Secretary determines that the entire interest in a tract of land on the Fort Peck Reservation is owned by Indians who were grantees of oil and gas under the act and he determines that such Indians are competent, he will issue fee patents to them covering all interests in the land without application.

§ 152.6 Issuance of patents in fee to non-Indians and Indians with whom a special relationship does not exist.

Whenever the Secretary determines that trust land, or any interest therein, has been acquired through inheritance or devise by a non-Indian, or by a person of Indian descent to whom the United States owes no trust responsibility, the Secretary may issue a patent in fee for the land or interest therein to such person without application.

§ 152.7 Application for certificate of competency.

Any Indian 21 years old or over, except certain adult members of the Osage Tribe as provided in § 152.9, who holds land or an interest therein under a restricted fee patent may apply for a certificate of competency. The written application shall be made in the form approved by the Secretary and filed with the agency having immediate jurisdiction over the land.

§ 152.8 Issuance of certificate of competency.

(a) An application may be approved and a certificate of competency issued if the Secretary, in his discretion, determines that the applicant is competent. The delivery of the certificate shall have the effect of removing the restrictions from the land described therein. (Act of June 25, 1910 (36 Stat. 855), as amended (25 U.S.C. 372).)

(b) If the application is denied, the applicant shall be notified in writing, given the reasons therefor and advised of his right to appeal pursuant to the provisions of part 2 of this chapter.

§ 152.9 Certificates of competency to certain Osage adults.

Applications for certificates of competency by adult members of the Osage Tribe of one-half or more Indian blood shall be in the form approved by the

Secretary. Upon the finding by the Secretary that an applicant is competent, a certificate of competency may be issued removing restrictions against alienation of all restricted property and terminating the trust on all restricted property, except Osage headright interests, of the applicant.

CROSS REFERENCES: For regulations pertaining to the issuance of certificates of competency to adult Osage Indians of less than one-half Indian blood, see part 154 of this chapter.

§ 152.10 Application for orders removing restrictions, except Five Civilized Tribes.

Any Indian not under legal disability under the laws of the State where he resides or where the land is located, or the court-appointed guardian or conservator of any Indian, may apply for an order removing restrictions from his restricted land or the restricted land of his ward. The application shall be in writing setting forth reasons for removal of restrictions and filed with the agency having immediate jurisdiction over the lands.

§ 152.11 Issuance of orders removing restrictions, except Five Civilized Tribes.

(a) An application for an order removing restrictions may be approved and such order issued by the Secretary, in his discretion, if he determines that the applicant is competent or that removal of restrictions is in the best interests of the Indian owner. The effect of the order will be to remove the restrictions from the land described therein.

(b) If the application is denied, the applicant will be notified in writing, given the reasons therefor and advised of his right to appeal pursuant to the provisions of part 2 of this chapter.

§ 152.12 Removal of restrictions, Five Civilized Tribes, after application under authority other than section 2(a) of the Act of August 11, 1955.

When an Indian of the Five Civilized Tribes makes application for removal of restrictions from his restricted lands under authority other than section 2(a) of the Act of August 11, 1955 (69 Stat. 666), such application may be for either unconditional removal of restrictions or conditional removal of restrictions, but shall not include lands or interest in lands acquired by inheritance or devise.

(a) If the application is for unconditional removal of restrictions and the Secretary, in his discretion, determines the applicant should have the unrestricted control of that land described in his application, the Secretary may issue an order removing restrictions therefrom.

(b) When the Secretary, in his discretion, finds that in the best interest of the applicant all or part of the land described in the application should be sold with conditions concerning terms of sale and disposal of the proceeds, the Secretary may issue a conditional order removing restrictions which shall be effective only and simultaneously with the execution of a deed by said applicant upon completion of an advertised sale or negotiated sale acceptable to the Secretary.

§ 152.13 Removal of restrictions, Five Civilized Tribes, after application under section 2(a) of the Act of August 11, 1955.

When an Indian of the Five Civilized Tribes makes application for removal of restrictions under authority of section 2(a) of the Act of August 11, 1955 (69 Stat. 666), the Secretary will determine the competency of the applicant.

(a) If the Secretary determines the applicant to be competent, he shall issue an order removing restrictions having the effect stated in § 152.16.

(b) If the Secretary rejects the application, his action is not subject to administrative appeal, notwithstanding the provisions concerning appeals in part 2 of this chapter.

(c) If the Secretary rejects the application, or neither rejects nor approves the application within 90 days of the application date, the applicant may apply to the State district court in the county in which he resides for an order removing restrictions. If that State district court issues such order, it will have the effect stated in § 152.16.

§ 152.14 Removal of restrictions, Five Civilized Tribes, without application.

Section 2(b) of the Act of August 11, 1955 (69 Stat. 666), authorizes the Secretary to issue an order removing restrictions to an Indian of the Five Civilized Tribes without application therefor. When the Secretary determines an Indian to be competent, he shall notify the Indian in writing of his intent to issue an order removing restrictions 30 days after the date of the notice. This decision may be appealed under the provisions of part 2 of this chapter within such 30 days. All administrative appeals under that part will postpone the issuance of the order. When the decision is not appealed within 30 days after the date of notice, or when any dismissal of an appeal is not appealed within the prescribed time limit, or when the final appeal is dismissed, an order removing restrictions will be issued.

§ 152.15 Judicial review of removal of restrictions, Five Civilized Tribes, without application.

When an order removing restrictions is issued, pursuant to § 152.14, a copy of such order will be delivered to the Indian, to any person acting in his behalf, and to the Board of County Commissioners for the county in which the Indian resides. At the time the order is delivered written notice will be given the parties that under the terms of the Act of August 11, 1955 (69 Stat. 666), the Indian or the Board of County Commissioners has, within 6 months of the date of notification, the right to appeal to the State district court for the district in which the Indian resides for an order setting aside the order removing restrictions. The timely initiation of proceedings in the State district court will stay the effective date of the order removing restrictions until such proceedings are concluded. If the State district court dismisses the appeal, the order removing restrictions will become effective 6 months after notification to the parties of such dismissal. The effect of the issuance of such order will be as prescribed in § 152.16.

§ 152.16 Effect of order removing restrictions, Five Civilized Tribes.

An order removing restrictions issued pursuant to the Act of August 11, 1955 (69 Stat. 666), on its effective date shall serve to remove all jurisdiction and supervision of the Bureau of Indian Affairs over money and property held by the United States in trust for the individual Indian or held subject to restrictions against alienation imposed by the United States. The Secretary shall cause to be turned over to the Indian full ownership and control of such money and property and issue in the case of land such title document as may be appropriate: *Provided*, That the Secretary may make such provisions as he deems necessary to insure payment of money loaned to any such Indian by the Federal Government or by an Indian tribe; *And provided further*, That the interest of any lessee or permittee in any lease, contract, or permit that is outstanding when an order removing restrictions becomes effective shall be preserved as provided in section 2(d) of the Act of August 11, 1955 (69 Stat. 666).

SALES, EXCHANGES AND CONVEYANCES OF TRUST OR RESTRICTED LANDS

§ 152.17 Sales, exchanges, and conveyances by, or with the consent of the individual Indian owner.

Pursuant to the Acts of May 27, 1902 (32 Stat. 275; 25 U.S.C. 379); May 17, 1906 (34 Stat. 197), as amended August 2, 1956 (70 Stat. 954; 48 U.S.C. 357); March 1, 1907 (34 Stat. 1018; 25 U.S.C. 405); May 29, 1908 (35 Stat. 444; 25 U.S.C. 404); June 25, 1910 (36 Stat. 855; 25 U.S.C. 372), as amended May 25, 1926 (44 Stat. 629; 48 U.S.C. 355a-355d); June 18, 1934 (48 Stat. 984; 25 U.S.C. 464); and May 14, 1948 (62 Stat. 236; 25 U.S.C. 483); and pursuant to other authorizing acts, trust or restricted lands acquired by allotment, devise, inheritance, purchase, exchange, or gift may be sold, exchanged, and conveyed by the Indian owner with the approval of the Secretary or by the Secretary with the consent of the Indian owner.

§ 152.18 Sale with the consent of natural guardian or person designated by the Secretary.

Pursuant to the Act of May 29, 1908 (35 Stat. 444; 25 U.S.C. 404), the Secretary may, with the consent of the natural guardian of a minor, sell trust or restricted land belonging to such minor; and the Secretary may, with the consent of a person designated by him, sell trust or restricted land belonging to Indians who are minor orphans without a natural guardian, and Indians who are non compos mentis or otherwise under legal disability. The authority contained in this act is not applicable to lands in Oklahoma, Minnesota, and South Dakota, nor to lands authorized to be sold by the Act of May 14, 1948 (62 Stat. 236; 25 U.S.C. 483).

§ 152.19 Sale by fiduciaries.

Guardians, conservators, or other fiduciaries appointed by State courts, or by tribal courts operating under approved constitutions or law and order codes, may, upon order of the court, convey with the approval of the Secretary or consent to the conveyance by the Secretary of trust or restricted land belonging to their Indian wards who are minors, non compos mentis or otherwise under legal disability. This section is subject to the exceptions contained in 25 U.S.C. 954(b).

§ 152.20 Sale by Secretary of certain land in multiple ownership.

Pursuant to the Act of June 25, 1910 (36 Stat. 855), as amended (25 U.S.C. 372), if the Secretary decides that one or more of the heirs who have inherited trust land are incapable of managing their own affairs, he may sell any or all interests in that land. This authority is not applicable to lands authorized to be sold by the Act of May 14, 1948 (62 Stat. 236; 25 U.S.C. 483).

§ 152.21 Sale or exchange of tribal land.

Certain tribal land may be sold or exchanged pursuant to the Acts of February 14, 1920 (41 Stat. 415; 25 U.S.C. 294); June 18, 1934 (48 Stat. 984; 25 U.S.C. 464); August 10, 1939 (53 Stat. 1351; 25 U.S.C. 463(e)); July 1, 1948 (62 Stat. 1214); June 4, 1953 (67 Stat. 41; 25 U.S.C. 293(a)); July 28, 1955 (69 Stat. 392), as amended August 31, 1964 (78 Stat. 747; 25 U.S.C. 608-608c); June 18, 1956 (70 Stat. 290; 25 U.S.C. 403a-2); July 24, 1956 (70 Stat. 626); May 19, 1958 (72 Stat. 121; 25 U.S.C. 463, Note); September 2, 1958 (72 Stat. 1762); April 4, 1960 (74 Stat. 13); April 29, 1960 (74 Stat. 85); December 11, 1963 (77 Stat. 349); August 11, 1964 (78 Stat. 389), and pursuant to other authorizing acts. Except as otherwise provided by law, and as far as practicable, the regulations in this part 152 shall be applicable to sale or exchanges of such tribal land.

§ 152.22 Secretarial approval necessary to convey individual-owned trust or restricted lands or land owned by a tribe.

(a) *Individual lands.* Trust or restricted lands, except inherited lands of the Five Civilized Tribes, or any interest therein, may not be conveyed without the approval of the Secretary. Moreover, inducing an Indian to execute an instrument purporting to convey any trust land or interest therein, or the offering of any such instrument for record, is prohibited and criminal penalties may be incurred. (See 25 U.S.C. 202 and 348.)

(b) *Tribal lands.* Lands held in trust by the United States for an Indian tribe, lands owned by a tribe with Federal restrictions against alienation and any other land owned by an Indian tribe may only be conveyed where specific statutory authority exists and then only with the approval of the Secretary unless the Act of Congress authorizing sale provides that approval is unnecessary. (See 25 U.S.C. 177.)

§ 152.23 Applications for sale, exchange or gift.

Applications for the sale, exchange or gift of trust or restricted land shall be filed in the form approved by the Secretary with the agency having immediate jurisdiction over the land. Applications may be approved if, after careful examination of the circumstances in each case, the transaction appears to be clearly justified in the light of the long-range best interest of the owner or owners or as under conditions set out in § 152.25(d).

§ 152.24 Appraisal.

Except as otherwise provided by the Secretary, an appraisal shall be made indicating the fair market value prior to making or approving a sale, exchange, or other transfer of title of trust or restricted land.

§ 152.25 Negotiated sales, gifts and exchanges of trust or restricted lands.

Those sales, exchanges, and gifts of trust or restricted lands specifically described in the following paragraphs (a), (b), (c), and (d) of this section may be negotiated; all other sales shall be by advertised sale, except as may be otherwise provided by the Secretary.

(a) *Consideration not less than the appraised fair market value.* Indian owners may, with the approval of the Secretary, negotiate a sale of and sell trust or restricted land for not less than the appraised fair market value:

(1) When the sale is to the United States, States, or political subdivisions thereof, or such other sale as may be for a public purpose;

(2) When the sale is to the tribe or another Indian; or

(3) When the Secretary determines it is impractical to advertise.

(b) *Exchange at appraised fair market value.* With the approval of the Secretary, Indian owners may exchange trust or restricted land, or a combination of such land and other things of value, for other lands or combinations of land and other things of value. The value of the consideration received by the Indian in the exchange must be at least substantially equal to the appraised fair market value of the consideration given by him.

(c) *Sale to coowners.* With the approval of the Secretary, Indian owners may negotiate a sale of and sell trust or restricted land to a coowner of that land. The consideration may be less than the appraised fair market value, if in the opinion of the Secretary there is a special relationship between the coowners or special circumstances exist.

(d) *Gifts and conveyances for less than the appraised fair market value.* With the approval of the Secretary, Indian owners may convey trust or restricted land, for less than the appraised fair market value or for no consideration when the prospective grantee is the owner's spouse, brother, sister, lineal ancestor of Indian blood or lineal descendant, or when some other special relationship exists between the grantor and grantee or special circumstances exist that in the opinion of the Secretary warrant the approval of the conveyance.

§ 152.26 Advertisement.

(a) Upon approval of an application for an advertised sale, notice of the sale will be published not less than 30 days prior to the date fixed for the sale unless for good cause a shorter period is authorized by the Secretary.

(b) The notice of sale will include:

(1) Terms, conditions, place, date, hour, and methods of sale, including explanation of auction procedure as set out in § 152.27(b)(2) if applicable;

(2) Where and how bids shall be submitted;

(3) A statement warning all bidders against violation of 18 U.S.C. 1860 prohibiting unlawful combination or intimidation of bidders or potential bidders; and

(4) Description of tracts, all reservations to which title will be subject and any restrictions and encumbrances of record with the Bureau of Indian Affairs and any other information that may improve sale prospects.

§ 152.27 Procedure of sale.

Advertised sales shall be by sealed bids except as otherwise provided herein.

(a)(1) Bids, conforming to the requirements set out in the advertisement of sale, along with a certified check, cashier's check, money order, or U.S. Treasury check, payable to the Bureau of Indian Affairs, for not less than 10 percent of the amount of the bid, must be enclosed in a sealed envelope marked as prescribed in the notice of sale. A cash deposit may be submitted in lieu of the above-specified negotiable instruments at the bidder's risk. Tribes submitting bids pursuant to this paragraph may guarantee the required 10 percent deposit by an appropriate resolution;

(2) The sealed envelopes containing the bids will be publicly opened at the

time fixed for sale. The bids will be announced and will be appropriately recorded.

(b) The policy of the Secretary recognizes that in many instances a tribe or a member thereof has a valid interest in acquiring trust or restricted lands offered for sale.

(1) With the consent of the owner and when the notice of sale so states, the tribe or members of such tribe shall have the right to meet the high bid.

(2) Provided the tribe is not the high bidder and when one or more acceptable sealed bids are received and when so stated in the notice of sale, an oral auction may be held following the bid opening. Bidding in the auction will be limited to the tribe, and to those who submitted sealed bids at 75 percent or more of the appraised value of the land being auctioned. At the conclusion of the auction the highest bidder must increase his deposit to not less than 10 percent of his auction bid.

§ 152.28 Action at close of bidding.

(a) The officer in charge of the sale shall publicly announce the apparent highest acceptable bid. The deposits submitted by the unsuccessful bidders shall be returned immediately. The deposit submitted by the apparent successful bidder shall be held in a special account.

(b) If the highest bid received at an advertised sale is less than the appraised fair market value of the land, the Secretary with the consent of the owner may accept that bid if the amount bid approximates said appraised fair market value and in the Secretary's judgment is the highest price that may be realized in the circumstances.

(c) The Secretary shall award the bid and notify the apparent successful bidder that the remainder of the purchase price must be submitted within 30 days.

(1) Upon a showing of cause the Secretary may, in his discretion, extend the time of payment of the balance due.

(2) If the remainder of the purchase price is not paid within the time allowed, the bid will be rejected and the apparent successful bidder's 10 percent deposit will be forfeited to the landowner's use.

(d) The issuance of the patent or delivery of a deed to the purchaser will not be authorized until the balance of the purchase price has been paid, except that the fee patent may be ordered in cases where the purchaser is obtaining a loan from an agency of the Federal Government and such agency has given the Secretary a commitment that the balance of the purchase price will be paid when the fee patent is issued.

§ 152.29 Rejection of bids; disapproval of sale.

The Secretary reserves the right to reject any and all bids before the award, after the award, or at any time prior to the issuance of a patent or delivery of a deed, when he shall have determined such rejection to be in the best interests of the Indian owner.

§ 152.30 Bidding by employees.

Except as authorized by the provisions of part 140 of this chapter, no person employed in Indian Affairs shall directly or indirectly bid, make, or prepare any bid, or assist any bidder in preparing his bid. Sales between Indians, either of whom is an employee of the U.S. Government, are governed by the provisions of part 140 of this chapter (see 25 U.S.C. 68 and 441).

§ 152.31 Cost of conveyance; payment.

Pursuant to the Act of February 14, 1920 (41 Stat. 415), as amended by the Act of March 1, 1933 (47 Stat. 1417; 25 U.S.C. 413), the Secretary may in his discretion collect from a purchaser reasonable fees for work performed or expense incurred in the transaction. The amount so collected shall be deposited to the credit of the United States as general fund receipts, except as stated in paragraph (b) of this section.

(a)(1) The amount of the fee shall be $22.50 for each transaction.

(2) The fee may be reduced to a lesser amount or may be waived, if the Secretary determines circumstances justify such action.

(b)(1) If any or all of the costs of the work performed or expenses incurred are paid with tribal funds, an alternate schedule of fees may be established, subject to approval of the Secretary, and that part of such fees deemed appropriate may be credited to the tribe.

(2) When the purchaser is the tribe which bears all or any part of such costs, the collection of the proportionate share from the tribe may be waived.

§ 152.32 Irrigation fee; payment.

Collection of all construction costs against any Indian-owned lands within Indian irrigation projects is deferred as long as Indian title has not been extinguished. (Act of July 1, 1932 (47 Stat. 564; 25 U.S.C. 386a)). This statute is interpreted to apply only where such land is owned by Indians either in trust or restricted status.

(a) When any person whether Indian or non-Indian acquires Indian lands in a fee simple status that are part of an Indian irrigation project he must enter into an agreement,

(1) To pay the pro rata share of the construction of the project chargeable to the land,

(2) To pay all construction costs that accrue in the future, and

(3) To pay all future charges assessable to the land which are based on the annual cost of operation and maintenance of the irrigation system.

(b) Any operation and maintenance charges that are delinquent when Indian land is sold will be deducted from the proceeds of sale unless other acceptable arrangements are made to provide for their payment prior to the approval of the sale.

(c) A lien clause covering all unpaid irrigation construction costs, past and future, will be inserted in the patent or other instrument of conveyance issued to all purchasers of restricted or trust lands that are under an Indian irrigation project.

CROSS REFERENCE: See part 159 and part 160 and cross-references thereunder in this chapter for further regulations regarding sale of irrigable lands.

PARTITIONS IN KIND OF INHERITED ALLOTMENTS

§ 152.33 Partition.

(a) *Partition without application.* If the Secretary of the Interior shall find that any inherited trust allotment or allotments (as distinguished from lands held in a restricted fee status or authorized to be sold under the Act of May 14, 1948 (62 Stat. 236; 25 U.S.C. 483)), are capable of partition in kind to the advantage of the heirs, he may cause such lands to be partitioned among them, regardless of their competency, patents in fee to be issued to the competent heirs for their shares and trust patents to be issued to the incompetent heirs for the lands respectively or jointly set apart to them, the trust period to terminate in accordance with the terms of the original patent or order of extension of the trust period set out in said patent. (Act of May 18, 1916 (39 Stat. 127; 25 U.S.C. 378)). The authority contained in the Act of May 18, 1916, is not applicable to lands authorized to be sold by the Act of May 14, 1948, nor to land held in restricted fee status.

(b) *Application for partition.* Heirs of a deceased allottee may make written application, in the form approved by the Secretary, for partition of their trust or restricted land. If the Secretary finds the trust lands susceptible of partition, he may issue new patents or deeds to the heirs for the portions set aside to them. If the allotment is held under a restricted fee title (as distinguished from a trust title), partition may be accomplished by the heirs executing deeds approved by the Secretary, to the other heirs for their respective portions.

MORTGAGES AND DEEDS OF TRUST TO SECURE LOANS TO INDIANS

§ 152.34 Approval of mortgages and deeds of trust.

Any individual Indian owner of trust or restricted lands, may with the approval of the Secretary execute a mortgage or deed of trust to his land. Prior to approval of such mortgage or deed of trust, the Secretary shall secure appraisal information as he deems advisable. Such lands shall be subject to foreclosure or sale pursuant to the terms of the mortgage or deed of trust in accordance with the laws of the State in which the lands are located. For the purpose of foreclosure or sale proceedings under this section, the Indian owners shall be regarded as vested with unrestricted fee simple title to the lands (Act of March 29, 1956).

(70 Stat. 62; 25 U.S.C. 483a)

§152.35 Deferred payment sales.

When the Indian owner and purchaser desire, a sale may be made or approved on the deferred payment plan. The terms of the sale will be incorporated in a memorandum of sale which shall constitute a contract for delivery of title upon payment in full of the amount of the agreed consideration. The deed executed by the grantor or grantors will be held by the Superintendent and will be delivered only upon full compliance with the terms of sale. If conveyance of title is to be made by fee patent, request therefor will be made only upon full compliance with the terms of the sale. The terms of the sale shall require that the purchaser pay not less than 10 percent of the purchase price in advance as required by the Act of June 25, 1910 (36 Stat. 855), as amended (25 U.S.C. 372); terms for the payment of the remaining installments plus interest shall be those acceptable to the Secretary and the Indian owner. If the purchaser on any deferred payment plan makes default in the first or subsequent payments, all payments, including interest, previously made will be forfeited to the Indian owner.

PART 153—DETERMINATION OF COMPETENCY: CROW INDIANS

Sec.

AUTHORITY: Sec. 12, 41 Stat. 755, 46 Stat. 1495, as amended.

SOURCE: 22 FR 10563, Dec. 24, 1957, unless otherwise noted. Redesignated at 47 FR 13327, Mar. 30, 1982.

§153.1 Purpose of regulations.

The regulations in this part govern the procedures in determining the competency of Crow Indians under Public Law 303, 81st Congress, approved September 8, 1949.

§153.2 Application and examination.

The Commissioner of Indian Affairs or his duly authorized representative, upon the application of any unenrolled adult member of the Crow Tribe, shall classify him by placing his name to the competent or incompetent rolls established pursuant to the act of June 4, 1920 (41 Stat. 751), and upon application shall determine whether those persons whose names now or hereafter appear on the incompetent roll shall be reclassified as competent and their names placed on the competent roll.

§153.3 Application form.

The application form shall include, among other things:

(a) The name of the applicant;

(b) His age, residence, degree of Indian blood, and education;

(c) His experience in farming, cattle raising, business, or other occupation (including home-making);

(d) His present occupation, if any;

(e) A statement concerning the applicant's financial status, including his average earned and unearned income for the last two years from restricted leases and from other sources, and his outstanding indebtedness to the United States, to the tribe, or to others;

(f) A description of his property and its value, including his allotted and inherited lands; and

(g) The name of the applicant's spouse, if any, and the names of his minor children, if any, and their ages, together with a statement regarding the land, allotted and inherited, held by each.

§153.4 Factors determining competency.

Among the matters to be considered by the Commissioner of Indian Affairs in determining competency are the amount of the applicant's indebtedness to the tribe, to the United States Government, and to others; whether he is a public charge or a charge on friends and relatives, or will become such a charge, by reason of being classed as competent; and whether the applicant has demonstrated that he possesses the ability to take care of himself and his property, to protect the interests of himself and his family, to lease his land and collect the rentals therefrom, to lease the land of his minor children, to prescribe in lease agreements those provisions which will protect the land from deterioration through over-grazing and other improper practices, and to assume full responsibility for obtaining compliance with the terms of any lease.

§ 153.5 Children of competent Indians.

Children of competent Indians who have attained or upon attaining their majority shall automatically become competent except any such Indian who is declared incompetent by a court of competent jurisdiction or who is incompetent under the laws of the State within which he resides.

§ 153.6 Appeals.

An appeal to the Secretary of the Interior may be made within 30 days from the date of notice to the applicant of the decision of the Commissioner of Indian Affairs.

PART 158—OSAGE LANDS

AUTHORITY: 5 U.S.C. 301. Interpret or apply 62 Stat. 18; 25 U.S.C. 331 note.

SOURCE: 22 FR 10565, Dec. 24, 1957, unless otherwise noted. Redesignated at 47 FR 13327, Mar. 30, 1982.

§ 158.51 Definitions.

When used in this part:

(a) *Homestead* means the restricted nontaxable lands, not exceeding 160 acres, allotted to an enrolled member of the Osage Tribe pursuant to the act of June 28, 1906 (34 Stat. 539), or the restricted surplus lands designated in lieu thereof pursuant to the act of May 25, 1918 (40 Stat. 578).

(b) *Surplus land* means those restricted lands, other than the homestead, allotted to an enrolled member of the Osage Tribe pursuant to the act of June 28, 1906 (34 Stat. 539).

§ 158.52 Application for change in designation of homestead.

Any Osage allottee or the legal guardian thereof may make application to change his homestead for an equal area of his surplus land. The application shall give in detail the reasons why such change is desired and shall be submitted to the Osage Indian Agency on the form "Application to Change Designation of Homestead."

§ 158.53 Order to change designation of homestead.

The application of an Osage allottee, or his legal guardian, may be approved by the Secretary of the Interior, or his authorized representative, and an order issued to change designation of homestead, if it is found that the applicant owns an equal area of surplus land. The expense of recording the order shall be borne by the applicant. The order to change designation shall be made on the form "Order to Change Designation of Homestead."

§ 158.54 Exchanges of restrictive lands.

Upon written application of the Indians involved, the exchange of restricted lands between adult Indians, and between adult Indians and non-Indians, may be approved by the Secretary of the Interior, or his authorized representative. Title to all lands acquired under this part by an Indian who does not have a certificate of competency shall be taken by deed containing a clause restricting alienation or encumbrance without the consent of the Secretary, or his authorized representative. In case of differences in the appraised value of lands under consideration for exchange, the application of an Indian for funds to equalize such differences may be approved to the extent authorized by § 117.8 of this chapter.

§ 158.55 Institution of partition proceedings.

(a) Prior authorization should be obtained from the Secretary, or his authorized representative, before the institution of proceedings to partition the lands of deceased Osage allottees in which any interest is held by an Osage Indian not having a certificate of competency. Requests for authority to institute such partition proceedings shall contain a description of the lands involved, the names of the several owners and their respective interests and the reasons for such court action. Authorization may be given for the institution of partition proceedings in a court of competent jurisdiction when it appears to the best interest of the Indians involved to do so and the execution of voluntary exchange deeds is impracticable.

(b) When it appears to the best interest of the Indians to do so, the Secretary's, or his authorized representative's, authorization to institute partition proceedings may require that title to the lands be quieted in the partition action in order that the deeds issued pursuant to the proceedings shall convey good and merchantable title to the grantee therein. (See section 6, 37 Stat. 87.)

§ 158.56 Partition records.

Upon completion of an action in partition, a copy of the judgment roll showing schedule of costs and owelty moneys having accrued to or from the several parties, together with deeds, or other instruments vesting title on partition, in triplicate, shall be furnished to the Osage Agency. The original allotment number shall follow the legal description on all instruments vesting title. When a grantee is a member of the Osage Tribe who has not received a certificate of competency, deeds or other instruments vesting title shall contain the following clause against alienation:

> Subject to the condition that while title to the above-described lands shall remain in the grantee or his Osage Indian heirs or devisees who do not have certificates of competency, the same shall not be alienated or encumbered without approval of the Secretary of the Interior or his authorized representative.

§ 158.57 Approval of deeds or other instruments vesting title on partition and payment of costs.

Upon completion of the partition proceedings in accordance with the law and in conformity with the regulations in this part, the Secretary, or his authorized representative, may approve the deeds, or other instruments vesting title on partition, and may disburse from the restricted (accounts) funds of the Indians concerned, such amounts as may be necessary for payment of their share of court costs, attorney fees, and owelty moneys.

§ 158.58 Disposition of proceeds of partition sales.

Owelty moneys due members of the Osage Tribe who do not have certificates of competency shall be paid into the Treasury of the United States and placed to the credit of the Indians upon the same conditions as attach to segregated shares of the Osage national fund.

PART 159—SALE OF IRRIGABLE LANDS, SPECIAL WATER CONTRACT REQUIREMENTS

CROSS REFERENCES: For additional regulations pertaining to the payment of fees and charges in connection with the sale of irrigable lands, see part 160 and §§ 134.4 and 152.21 of this chapter. For general regulations pertaining to the issuance of patents in fee, see part 152 of this chapter.

§ 159.1 Conditions of contract.

(a) The form of contract (Form 5-462b)[1] for sale of irrigable lands specifically provides that the purchaser will obligate and pay on a per acre basis all irrigation charges assessed or to be assessed against the land purchased including accrued assessment, which accrued assessment shall be paid prior to the approval of the sale, and for the payment of the construction and operation and maintenance assessments on the due dates of each year. The agreement is to be acknowledged and recorded in the county records in which county the land is situated. The charges incidental to the recording of

[1] Forms may be obtained from the Commissioner of Indian Affairs, Washington, D.C.

the instrument shall be paid by the purchaser at the time of executing the agreement.

(b) A strict compliance with the terms of paragraph (a) of this section is absolutely necessary and required.

(Secs. 1, 3, 36 Stat. 270, 272, as amended; 25 U.S.C. 385. Interprets or applies sec. 1, 41 Stat. 409; 25 U.S.C. 386)

[22 FR 10566, Dec. 24, 1957. Redesignated at 47 FR 13327, Mar. 30, 1982]

NOTE: On May 12, 1921, Circular No. 1677, re sale of irrigable lands, was addressed to all superintendents. It was pointed out therein that the collection of irrigation construction charges was required by the terms of an act approved February 14, 1920 (41 Stat. 409; 25 U.S.C. 386), and that in addition to the construction charge there was an operation and maintenance charge assessable annually that must be paid by the landowners benefited; furthermore, that the purpose of this circular was to point out to the superintendents the necessity of advising prospective purchasers that irrigation charges must be paid and that a so-called paid-up water right was not conveyed with the land. A form of agreement to be executed by the prospective purchaser accompanied this circular.

It has been brought to the attention of the Bureau that irrigation construction charges and operation and maintenance charges have accrued against irrigable allotments prior to the time of their being advertised for sale and that the superintendents have failed to provide for payment of the accrued irrigation charges, with the result that no means are apparent for their collection.

With a view of preventing any future misunderstanding the form of contract accompanying Circular No. 1677 has been redrafted and Form 5-462b assigned to it. The circular has been designated "No. 1677a."

PART 160—INCLUSION OF LIENS IN ALL PATENTS AND INSTRUMENTS EXECUTED

AUTHORITY: Secs. 1, 3, 36 Stat. 270, 272, as amended; 25 U.S.C. 385.

SOURCE: 22 FR 10566, Dec. 24, 1957, unless otherwise noted. Redesignated at 47 FR 13327, Mar. 30, 1982.

§ 160.1 Liens.

The act of March 7, 1928 (45 Stat. 210; 25 U.S.C. 387) creates a first lien against irrigable lands under all Indian irrigation projects where the construction, operation and maintenance costs of such projects remain unpaid and are reimbursable, and directs that such lien shall be recited in any patent or instrument issued for such lands to cover such unpaid charges. Prior to the enactment of this legislation similar liens had been created by legislative authority against irrigable lands of the projects on the Fort Yuma, Colorado River, and Gila River Reservations, in Arizona; Blackfeet, Fort Peck, Flathead, Fort Belknap, and Crow Reservations, Mont.; Wapato project, Yakima Reservation, Wash.; the irrigable lands on the Colville Reservation within the West Okanogan irrigation district, Washington, and the Fort Hall Reservation, Idaho. This legislation, therefore, extends protection similar to that existing in the legislation applicable to the projects on the reservations above mentioned.

CROSS REFERENCES: For operation and maintenance charges and construction costs, see parts 134 and 137 of this chapter.

§ 160.2 Instructions.

All superintendents and other officers are directed to familiarize themselves with this provision of law, and in all cases involving the issuance of patents or deeds direct to the Indian or purchaser of Indian allotments embracing irrigable lands, they will recite in the papers forwarded to the Department for action the fact that the lands involved are within an irrigation project (giving the name) and accordingly are subject to the provisions of this law. This requirement will be in addition to the existing regulations requiring the superintendents in case of sales of irrigable lands to obtain from the project engineer a written statement relative to the irrigability of the lands to be sold, and whether or not there are any unpaid irrigation charges, together with the estimated per acre construction cost assessable against the land involved in the sale. Each sale will also be accompanied by contract executed in accordance with regulations obligating the purchaser to pay the accrued charges, namely, construction, operation, and maintenance, prior to the approval of the sale and to assume and pay the unassessed irrigation charges in accordance with regulations promulgated by the Secretary of the Interior.

CROSS REFERENCES: For additional regulations pertaining to the payment of fees and charges in connection with the sale of irrigable lands, see part 159 and §§134.4 and 152.21 of this chapter.

§ 160.3 Leases to include description of lands.

It is important, also, for superintendents in leasing irrigable lands to present to the project engineer lists containing descriptions of the lands involved for his approval of the irrigable acreage and for checking as to whether or not such lands are in fact irrigable under existing works. Strict compliance with this section is required for the purpose of avoiding error.

§ 160.4 Prompt payment of irrigation charges by lessees.

Superintendents will also see that irrigation charges are promptly paid by lessees, and where such charges are not so paid take appropriate and prompt action for their collection. Such unpaid charges are a lien against the land, and accordingly any failure on the part of the superintendents to collect same increases the obligation against the land.

PART 161—NAVAJO PARTITIONED LANDS GRAZING PERMITS

Subpart A—Definitions, Authority, Purpose and Scope

Sec.

Subpart B—Tribal Policies and Laws Pertaining to Permits

Subpart C—General Provisions

Subpart D—Permit Requirements

Subpart E—Reissuance of Grazing Permits

Subpart F—Modifying A Permit

Subpart G—Permit Violations

Subpart H—Trespass

NOTIFICATION

ACTIONS

PENALTIES, DAMAGES, AND COSTS

Subpart I—Concurrence/Appeals/ Amendments

AUTHORITY: 25 U.S.C. 2; 5 U.S.C. 301; 25 U.S.C. 640d *et seq.*

SOURCE: 70 FR 58888, Oct. 7, 2005, unless otherwise noted.

Subpart A—Definitions, Authority, Purpose, and Scope

§ 161.1 What definitions do I need to know?

Agricultural Act means the American Indians Agricultural Resource Management Act (AIARMA) of December 3, 1993 (107 Stat. 2011, 25 U.S.C. 3701 *et seq.*), and amended on November 2, 1994 (108 Stat. 4572).

Agricultural resource management plan means a 10-year plan developed through the public review process specifying the tribal management goals and objectives developed for tribal agricultural and grazing resources. Plans developed and approved under AIARMA will govern the management and administration of Indian agricultural resources and Indian agricultural lands by BIA and Indian tribal governments.

Allocation means the number of animal units authorized in each grazing permit.

Animal Unit (AU) means one adult cow and her 6-month-old calf or the equivalent thereof based on comparable forage consumption. Thus as defined in the following:

(1) One adult sheep or goat is equivalent to one-fifth (0.20) of an AU;

(2) One adult horse, mule, or burro is equivalent to one and one quarter (1.25) AU; or

(3) One adult llama is equivalent to three-fifths (0.60) of an AU.

Appeal means a written request for review of an action or the inaction of an official of the Bureau of Indian Affairs that is claimed to adversely affect the interested party making the request.

Appeal Bond means a bond posted upon filing of an appeal that provides a security or guaranty if an appeal creates a delay in implementing our decision that could cause a significant and measurable financial loss to another party.

BIA means the Bureau of Indian Affairs within the Department of the Interior.

Bond means security for the performance of certain permit obligations, as furnished by the permittee, or a guaranty of such performance as furnished by a third-party surety.

Business day means Monday through Friday, excluding federally or tribally recognized holidays.

Carrying capacity means the number of livestock and/or wildlife, which may be sustained on a management unit compatible with management objectives for the unit.

Concurrence means the written agreement of the Navajo Nation with a policy, action, decision or finding submitted for consideration by BIA.

Conservation practice refers to any management measure taken to maintain or improve the condition, productivity, sustainability, or usability of targeted resources.

Customary Use Area refers to an area to which an individual traditionally confined his or her traditional grazing use and occupancy and/or an area traditionally inhabited by his or her ancestors.

Day means a calendar day, unless otherwise specified.

Enumeration means the list of persons living on and identified improvements located within the Former Joint Use Area obtained through interviews conducted by BIA in 1974 and 1975.

Former Joint Use Area means the area that was divided between the Navajo Nation and the Hopi Tribe by the Judgment of Partition issued April 18, 1979, by the United States District Court for the District of Arizona. This area was established by the United States District Court for the District of Arizona in *Healing* v. *Jones*, 210 F. Supp. 125 (1962), aff'd. 373 U.S. 758 (1963) and is located:

(1) Inside the Executive Order area (Executive Order of December 16, 1882); and

(2) Outside Land Management District 6.

Grazing Committee means the District Grazing Committee established by the Navajo Nation Council, that is responsible for enforcing and implementing tribal grazing regulations on the Navajo Partitioned Lands.

Grazing Permit means a revocable privilege granted in writing and limited to entering on and utilizing forage by domestic livestock on a specified range unit. The term as used herein shall include authorizations issued to enable the crossing or trailing of domestic livestock within an assigned range unit.

Historical Land Use see Customary Use Area.

Improvement means any structure or excavation to facilitate management of the range for livestock, such as: Fences, cattle guards, spring developments, windmills, stock ponds, and corrals.

Livestock means horses, cattle, sheep, goats, mules, burros, donkeys, and llamas.

Management Unit is a subdivision of a geographic area where unique resource conditions, goals, concerns, or opportunities require specific and separate management planning.

Navajo Nation means all offices/entities/programs under the direct jurisdiction of the Navajo Nation Government.

Navajo Partitioned Lands (NPL) means that portion of the Former Joint Use Area awarded to the Navajo Nation under the Judgment of Partition issued April 18, 1979, by the United States District Court for the District of Arizona, and now a separate administrative entity within the Navajo Indian Reservation.

Non-Concurrence means the official written denial of approval by the Navajo Nation of a policy, action, decision, or finding submitted for consideration by BIA.

Range management plan is a statement of management objectives for grazing, farming, or other agriculture management including contract stipulations defining required uses, operations, and improvements.

Range Unit means a tract of land designated as a separate management subdivision for the administration of grazing.

Resident means a person who lives on the Navajo Partitioned Lands.

Resources Committee means the oversight committee for the Division of Natural Resources within the Navajo Nation Government. The Resources Committee of the Navajo Nation Council to whom authority is delegated to exercise the powers of the Navajo Nation with regards to the range development and grazing management of the Navajo Partitioned Lands.

Secretary means the Secretary of the Interior or his or her designated representative.

Settlement Act means the Navajo Hopi Settlement Act of December 22, 1974 (88 Stat. 1712, 25 U.S.C. 64d *et seq.*, as amended).

Sheep Unit means an adult ewe with un-weaned lamb. It is also the basic unit in which forage allocations are expressed.

Special land use means all land usage for purposes other than for grazing withdrawn in accordance with Navajo Nation laws, Federal laws, and BIA policies and procedures, such as but not limited to: Housing permits, farm leases, governmental facilities, rights-of-way, schools, parks, business leases, etc.

Stocking rate means the maximum number of sheep units, or animal units authorized to graze on a particular pasture, management unit, or range unit during a specified period of time.

Trespass means any unauthorized occupancy, grazing, use of, or action on the Navajo Partitioned Lands.

§ 161.2 What are the Secretary's authorities under this part?

(a) Under Section 640d–9(e) of the Settlement Act, lands partitioned under the Settlement Act are subject to the jurisdiction of the tribe to whom partitioned. The laws of the tribe apply to the partitioned lands as in paragraphs (a)(1) and (a)(2) of this section.

(1) Effective October 6, 1980:

(i) All conservation practices on the Navajo Partitioned Lands, including control and range restoration activities, must be coordinated and executed with the concurrence of the Navajo Nation; and

(ii) All grazing and range restoration matters on the Navajo Reservation lands must be administered by BIA, under applicable laws and regulations.

(2) Effective April 18, 1981, the Navajo Nation has jurisdiction and authority over any lands partitioned to it and over all persons on these lands. This jurisdiction and authority apply:

(i) To the same extent as is applicable to those other portions of the Navajo reservation; and

(ii) Notwithstanding any provision of law to the contrary, except where there is a conflict with the laws and regulations referred to in paragraph (a) of this section.

(b) Under the Agricultural Act, the Secretary is authorized to:

(1) Carry out the trust responsibility of the United States and promote Indian tribal self-determination by providing for management of Indian agricultural lands and renewable resources consistent with tribal goals and priorities for conservation, multiple use, and sustained yield;

(2) Take part in managing Indian agricultural lands, with the participation of the land's beneficial owners, in a manner consistent with the Secretary's trust responsibility and with the objectives of the beneficial owners;

(3) Provide for the development and management of Indian agricultural lands; and

(4) Improve the expertise and technical abilities of Indian tribes and their members by increasing the educational and training opportunities available to Indian people and communities in the practical, technical, and professional aspects of agricultural and land management.

§ 161.3 What is the purpose of this part?

The purpose of this part is to describe the goals and objectives of grazing management on the Navajo Partitioned Lands:

(a) To respect and recognize the importance that livestock and land have in sustaining Navajo tradition and culture.

(b) Provide resources to rehabilitate range resources in the preservation of forage, soil, and water on the Navajo Partitioned Lands;

(c) Monitor the recovery of those resources where they have deteriorated;

(d) Protect, conserve, utilize, and maintain the highest productive potential on the Navajo Partitioned Lands through the application of sound conservation practices and techniques. These practices and techniques will be applied to planning, development, inventorying, classification, and management of agricultural resources;

(e) Increase production and expand the diversity and availability of agricultural products for subsistence, income, and employment of Indians, through the development of agricultural resources on the Navajo Partitioned Lands;

(f) Manage agricultural resources consistent with integrated resource management plans in order to protect and maintain other values such as wildlife, fisheries, cultural resources, recreation and to regulate water runoff and minimize soil erosion;

(g) Enable the Navajo Nation to maximize the potential benefits available to its members from their lands by providing technical assistance, training, and education in conservation practices, management and economics of agribusiness, sources and use of credit and marketing of agricultural products, and other applicable subject areas;

(h) Develop the Navajo Partitioned Lands to promote self-sustaining communities; and

(i) Assist the Navajo Nation with permitting the Navajo Partitioned Lands, consistent with prudent management and conservation practices, and community goals as expressed in the tribal management plans and appropriate tribal ordinances.

§161.4 To what lands does this part apply?

The grazing regulations in this part apply to the Navajo Partitioned Lands within the boundaries of the Navajo Indian Reservation held in trust by the United States for the Navajo Nation. Contiguous areas outside of the Navajo Partitioned Lands may be included under this part for management purposes by BIA in consultation with the affected permittees and other affected land users, and with the concurrence of the Resources Committee. Other affected land users include those holding approved assignments, permits, leases, and rights of way for activities such as: home sites, farm plots, roads, utilities, businesses, and schools.

§161.5 Can BIA waive the application of this part?

Yes. If a provision of this part conflicts with the objectives of the agricultural resource management plan provided for in §161.200, or with a tribal law, BIA may waive the application of this part unless the waiver would either:

(a) Constitute a violation of a federal statute or judicial decision; or

(b) Conflict with BIA's general trust responsibility under federal law.

§161.6 Are there any other restrictions on information given to BIA?

Information that the BIA collects in connection with permits for NPL in sections 161.102, 161.206, 161.301, 161.302, 161.304, 161.402, 161.500, 161.502, 161.604, 161.606, 161.703, 161.704, 161.708, 161.717, 161.800, 161.801, and 161.802 have been reviewed and approved by the Office of Management and Budget. The OMB Control Number assigned is 1076–0162. Please note that a federal agency may not conduct or sponsor, and you are not required to respond to, a collection of information unless it displays a currently valid OMB control number.

Subpart B—Tribal Policies and Laws Pertaining to Permits

§161.100 Do tribal laws apply to grazing permits?

Navajo Nation laws generally apply to land under the jurisdiction of the Navajo Nation, except to the extent that those Navajo Nation laws are inconsistent with this part or other applicable federal law. This part may be superseded or modified by Navajo Nation laws with Secretarial approval, however, so long as:

(a) The Navajo Nation laws are consistent with the enacting Navajo Nation's governing documents;

(b) The Navajo Nation has notified BIA of the superseding or modifying effect of the Navajo Nation laws;

(c) The superseding or modifying of the regulation would not violate a federal statute or judicial decision, or conflict with the Secretary's general trust responsibility under federal law; and

(d) The superseding or modifying of the regulation applies only to Navajo Partitioned Lands.

§ 161.101 How will tribal laws be enforced on the Navajo Partitioned Lands?

(a) Unless prohibited by federal law, BIA will recognize and comply with tribal laws regulating activities on the Navajo Partitioned Lands, including tribal laws relating to land use, environmental protection, and historic or cultural preservation.

(b) While the Navajo Nation is primarily responsible for enforcing tribal laws pertaining to the Navajo Partitioned Lands, BIA will:

(1) Assist in the enforcement of Navajo Nation laws;

(2) Provide notice of Navajo Nation laws to persons or entities undertaking activities on the Navajo Partitioned Lands; and

(3) Require appropriate federal officials to appear in tribal forums when requested by the tribe, so long as the appearance would not:

(i) Be inconsistent with the restrictions on employee testimony set forth at 43 CFR part 2, subpart E;

(ii) Constitute a waiver of the sovereign immunity of the United States; or

(iii) Authorize or result in a review of (BIA) actions by the tribal court.

(c) Where the provisions in this subpart are inconsistent with a Navajo Nation law, but the provisions cannot be superseded or modified by the Navajo Nation laws under § 161.5, BIA may waive the provisions under part 1 of 25 CFR, so long as the new waiver does not violate a federal statute or judicial decision or conflict with the Secretary's trust responsibility under federal law.

§ 161.102 What notifications are required that tribal laws apply to grazing permits on the Navajo Partitioned Lands?

(a) The Navajo Nation must provide BIA with an official copy of any tribal law or tribal policy that relates to this part. The Navajo Nation must notify BIA of the content and effective dates of tribal laws.

(b) BIA will then notify affected permittees of the effect of the Navajo Nation law on their grazing permits. BIA will:

(1) Provide individual written notice; or

(2) Post public notice. This notice will be posted at the tribal community building, U.S. Post Office, announced on local radio station, and/or published in the local newspaper nearest to the permitted Navajo Partitioned Lands where activities are occurring.

Subpart C—General Provisions

§ 161.200 Is an Indian agricultural resource management plan required?

(a) Yes, Navajo Partitioned Lands must be managed in accordance with the goals and objectives in the agricultural resource management plan developed by the Navajo Nation, or by BIA in close consultation with the Navajo Nation, under the Agricultural Act.

(b) The 10-year agricultural resource management and monitoring plan must be developed through public meetings and completed within 3 years of the initiation of the planning activity. The plan must be based on the public meeting records and existing survey documents, reports, and other research from Federal agencies, tribal community colleges, and land grant universities. When completed, the plan must:

(1) Determine available agricultural resources;

(2) Identify specific tribal agricultural resource goals and objectives;

(3) Establish management objectives for the resources;

(4) Define critical values of the tribe and its members and provide identified resource management objectives; and

(5) Identify actions to be taken to reach established objectives.

(c) Where the provisions in this subpart are inconsistent with the Navajo Nation's agricultural resource management plan, the Secretary may waive the provisions under part 1 of this title, so long as the waiver does not violate a federal statute or judicial decision or conflict with the Secretary's trust responsibility under federal law.

§161.201 Is environmental compliance required?

Actions taken by BIA under this part must comply with the National Environmental Policy Act of 1969, 42 U.S.C. 4321 *et seq.*, applicable provisions of the Council on Environmental Quality, 40 CFR part 1500, and applicable tribal laws and provisions of the Navajo Nation Environmental Policy Act CAP-47-95, where the tribal laws and provisions do not violate a federal or judicial decision or conflict with the Secretary's trust responsibility under federal law.

§161.202 How are range units established?

(a) BIA, with the concurrence of the Navajo Nation, will establish range units on the Navajo Partitioned Lands to provide unified areas for which range management plans can be developed to improve and maintain soil and forage resources. Physical land features, watersheds, drainage patterns, vegetation, soil, resident concentration, problem areas, historical land use patterns, chapter boundaries, special land uses and comprehensive land use planning will be considered in the determination of range unit boundaries.

(b) BIA may modify range unit boundaries with the concurrence of the Navajo Nation. This may include small and/or isolated portions of Navajo Partitioned Lands contiguous to Navajo tribal lands in order to develop more efficient land management.

§161.203 Are range management plans required?

Yes. BIA will:

(a) Consult with the Navajo Nation in planning conservation practices, including grazing control and range restoration activities for the Navajo Partitioned Lands.

(b) Develop range management plans with the concurrence of the Navajo Nation.

(c) Approve the range management plans, after concurrence with the Navajo Nation, and the implementation of the plan may begin immediately. The plan will address, but is not limited to, the following issues:

(1) Goals for improving vegetative productivity and diversity;

(2) Stocking rates;

(3) Grazing schedules;

(4) Wildlife management;

(5) Needs assessment for range and livestock improvements;

(6) Schedule for operation and maintenance of existing range improvements and development for cooperative funded projects;

(7) Cooperation in the implementation of range studies;

(8) Control of livestock diseases and parasites;

(9) Fencing or other structures necessary to implement any of the other provisions in the range management plan;

(10) Special land uses; and

(11) Water development and management.

§161.204 How are carrying capacities and stocking rates established?

(a) BIA, with the concurrence of the Navajo Nation, will prescribe, review and adjust the carrying capacity of each range unit by determining the number of livestock, and/or wildlife, that can be grazed on the Navajo Partitioned Lands without inducing damage to vegetation or related resources on each range unit and the season or seasons of use to achieve the objectives of the agricultural resource management plan and range unit management plan.

(b) BIA, with the concurrence of the Navajo Nation, will establish the stocking rate of each range or management unit. The stocking rate will be based on forage production, range utilization, the application of land management practices, and range improvements in place to achieve uniformity of grazing under sustained yield management principles on each range or management unit.

(c) BIA will review the carrying capacity of the grazing units on a continuing basis and, in consultation with the Grazing Committee and affected permittees, adjust the stocking rate for each range or management unit as conditions warrant.

(d) Any adjustments in stocking rates will be applied equally to each permittee within the management unit requiring adjustment.

§ 161.205 How are range improvements treated?

(a) Improvements placed on the Navajo Partitioned Lands will be considered affixed to the land unless specifically exempted in the permit. No improvement may be constructed or removed from Navajo Partitioned Lands without the written consent of BIA and the Navajo Nation.

(b) Before undertaking an improvement, BIA, Navajo Nation and permittee will negotiate who will complete and maintain improvements. The improvement agreement will be reflected in the permit.

§ 161.206 What must a permittee do to protect livestock from exposure to disease?

In accordance with applicable law, permittees must:

(a) Vaccinate livestock;

(b) Treat all livestock exposed to or infected with contagious or infectious diseases; and

(c) Restrict the movement of exposed or infected livestock.

§ 161.207 What livestock are authorized to graze?

The following livestock are authorized to graze on the Navajo Partitioned Lands: horses, cattle, sheep, goats, mules, burros, donkeys, and llamas.

Subpart D—Permit Requirements

§ 161.300 When is a permit needed to authorize grazing use?

Unless otherwise provided for in this part, any person or legal entity, including an independent legal entity owned and operated by the Navajo Nation, must obtain a permit under this part before using Navajo Partitioned Land for grazing purposes.

§ 161.301 What will a grazing permit contain?

(a) All grazing permits will contain the following provisions:

(1) Name of permit holder;

(2) Range management plan requirements;

(3) Applicable stocking rate;

(4) Range unit number and description of the permitted area;

(5) Animal identification requirements (*i.e.*, brand, microchip, freeze brand, earmark, tattoo, etc.);

(6) Term of permit (including beginning and ending dates of the term allowed, as well as an option to renew, or extend);

(7) A provision stating that the permittee agrees that he or she will not use, cause, or allow to be used any part of the permitted area for any unlawful conduct or purpose;

(8) A provision stating that the permit authorizes no other privilege than grazing use;

(9) A provision stating that no person is allowed to hold a grazing permit in more than one range unit of the Navajo Partitioned Lands, unless the customary use area extends beyond the range unit boundary;

(10) A provision reserving a right of entry by BIA and the Navajo Nation for range survey, inventory and inspection or compliance purposes;

(11) A provision prohibiting the creation of a nuisance, any illegal activity, and negligent use or waste of resources;

(12) A provision stating how trespass proceeds are to be distributed;

(13) A provision stating whether mediation will be used in the event of a permit violation; and

(14) A provision stating that the permit cannot be subdivided once it has been issued.

(b) Grazing permits will contain any other provision that in the discretion of BIA with the concurrence of the Navajo Nation is necessary to protect the land and/or resources.

(c) Grazing permits containing any special land use authorized under §161.503 of this part must be included on the permit.

§ 161.302 What restrictions are placed on grazing permits?

Only a grazing permit issued under this part authorizes the grazing of livestock within the Navajo Partitioned Lands. Grazing permits are subject to the following restrictions:

(a) Grazing permits should not be issued for less than 2 animal units (10 sheep units) or exceed 70 animal units (350 sheep units). However, all grazing permits issued before the adoption of this regulation will be honored and reissued with an adjusted stocking rate if the permittee meets the eligibility and priority criteria found in § 161.400 of this part, and only if the carrying capacity and stocking rate as determined under §§ 161.204 and 161.403 allows.

(b) A grazing permit will be issued in the name of one individual.

(c) Only two horses will be permitted on a grazing permit.

(d) Grazing permits may contain additional conditions authorized by Federal law or Navajo Nation law.

(e) A state/tribal brand only identifies the owner of the livestock, but does not authorize the grazing of any livestock within the Navajo Partitioned Lands.

(f) A permit cannot be subdivided once it has been issued.

§ 161.303 How long is a permit valid?

After its initial issuance, each grazing permit is valid for one year beginning on the following January 1. All permits will be automatically renewed annually if the permittee is in compliance with all applicable laws including tallies and permit requirements.

§ 161.304 Must a permit be recorded?

A permit must be recorded by BIA following approval under this subpart.

§ 161.305 When is a decision by BIA regarding a permit effective?

BIA approval of a permit will be effective immediately upon signature, notwithstanding any appeal, which may be filed under part 2 of this title. Copies of the approved permit will be provided to the permittee and made available to the Navajo Nation upon request.

§ 161.306 When are permits effective?

Unless otherwise provided in the permit, a permit will be effective on the date on which BIA approves the permit.

§ 161.307 When may a permittee commence grazing on Navajo Partitioned Land?

The permittee may graze on Navajo Partitioned Land on the date specified in the permit as the beginning date of the term, but not before BIA approves the permit.

§ 161.308 Must a permittee comply with standards of conduct if granted a permit?

Yes. Permittees are expected to:

(a) Conduct grazing operations in accordance with the principles of sustained yield management, agricultural resource management planning, sound conservation practices, and other community goals as expressed in Navajo Nation laws, agricultural resource management plans, and similar sources.

(b) Comply with all applicable laws, ordinances, rules, provisions, and other legal requirements. Permittee must also pay all applicable penalties that may be assessed for non-compliance.

(c) Fulfill all financial permit obligations owed to the Navajo Nation and the United States.

(d) Conduct only those activities authorized by the permit.

Subpart E—Reissuance of Grazing Permits

§ 161.400 What are the criteria for reissuing grazing permits?

(a) The Navajo Nation may prescribe eligibility requirements for grazing allocations within 180 days following the effective date of this part. BIA will prescribe the eligibility requirements after expiration of the 180-day period if the Navajo Nation does not prescribe eligibility requirements, or if satisfactory action is not taken by the Navajo Nation.

(b) With the written concurrence of the Navajo Nation, BIA will prescribe the following eligibility requirements, where only those applicants who meet the following criteria are eligible to receive permits to graze livestock:

(1) Those who had grazing permits on Navajo Partitioned Lands under 25 CFR part 167 (formerly part 152), and whose permits were canceled on October 14, 1973;

(2) Those who are listed in the 1974 and 1975 Former Joint Use Area enumeration;

(3) Those who are current residents on Navajo Partitioned Lands; and

(4) Those who have a customary use area on Navajo Partitioned Lands.

(c) Permits re-issued to applicants under this section may be granted by BIA based on the following priority criteria:

(1) The first priority will go to individuals currently the age of 65 or older; and

(2) The second priority will go to individuals under the age of 65.

(d) Upon the recommendation of the NPL District Grazing Committee and Resources Committee, BIA or Navajo Nation will have authority to waive one of the eligibility or priority criteria.

§ 161.401 Will new permits be granted after the initial reissuance of permits?

(a) Following the initial reissuance of permits under § 161.400, the Navajo Nation can grant new permits, subject to BIA approval, if:

(1) Additional permits become available; and

(2) The carrying capacity and stocking rates as determined under §§ 161.204 and 161.403 allow.

(b) The Navajo Nation must inform BIA if it grants any permits under paragraph (a) of this section.

§ 161.402 What are the procedures for reissuing permits?

BIA, with the concurrence of the Navajo Nation, will reissue grazing permits only to individuals that meet the eligibility requirements in § 161.400. Responsibilities for reissuance of grazing permits are as follows:

(a) BIA will develop a complete list consisting of all former permittees whose permits were cancelled and the number of animal units previously authorized in prior grazing permits. This list will be provided to the Grazing Committee and Resources Committee for their review. BIA will also provide the Grazing Committee and Resources Committee with the current carrying capacity and stocking rate for each range unit within the Navajo Partitioned Lands, as determined under § 161.204.

(b) Within 90 days of receipt, the Grazing Committee will review the list developed under § 161.402(a), and make recommendations to the Resources Committee for the granting of grazing permits according to the eligibility and priority criteria in § 161.400.

(c) If the Grazing Committee fails to make its recommendation to the Resources Committee within 90 days after receiving the list of potential permittees, BIA will submit its recommendations to the Resources Committee.

(d) The Resources Committee will review and concur with the list of proposed permit grantees, and then forward a final list to BIA for the reissuance of grazing permits. If the Resources Committee does not concur, the procedures outlined in § 161.800 will govern.

(e) The final determination list of eligible permittees will be published. Permits will not be issued sooner than 90 days following publication of the final list.

§ 161.403 How are grazing permits allocated within each range unit?

(a) Initial allocation of the number of animal units authorized in each grazing permit will be determined by considering the number of animal units previously authorized in prior grazing permits and the current authorized stocking rate on a given range unit.

(b) Grazing permit allocations may vary from range unit to range unit depending on the stocking rate of each unit, the range management plan, and the number of eligible grazing permittees in the unit.

Subpart F—Modifying A Permit

§ 161.500 May permits be transferred, assigned or modified?

(a) Grazing permits may be transferred, assigned, or modified only as provided in this section. Permits may only be transferred or assigned as a single permit under Navajo Nation procedures and with the approval of BIA. Permittees must reside within the same range unit as the original permittee.

(b) Permits may be transferred, assigned, or modified with the written consent of the permittee, District Grazing Committee and/or Resources Committee and approved by BIA.

(c) BIA must record each transfer, assignment, or modification that it approves under a permit.

§ 161.501 When will a permit modification be effective?

BIA approval of a transfer, assignment, or modification under a permit will be effective immediately, notwithstanding any appeal, which may be filed under part 2 of this title. Copies of approved documents will be provided to the permittee and made available to the Navajo Nation upon request.

§ 161.502 Will a special land use require permit modification?

Yes. When the Navajo Nation and BIA approve a special land use, the grazing permit will be modified to reflect the change in available forage. If a special land use is inconsistent with grazing activities authorized in the permit, the special land use area will be withdrawn from the permit, and grazing cannot take place on that part of the range unit.

Subpart G—Permit Violations

§ 161.600 What permit violations are addressed by this subpart?

This subpart addresses violations of permit provisions other than trespass. Trespass is addressed under subpart H.

§ 161.601 How will BIA monitor permit compliance?

Unless the permit provides otherwise, BIA and/or Navajo Nation may enter the range unit at any reasonable time, without prior notice, to protect the interests of the Navajo Nation and ensure that the permittee is in compliance with the operating requirements of the permit.

§ 161.602 Will my permit be canceled for non-use?

(a) If a grazing permit is not used by the permittee for a 2-year period, BIA may cancel the permit upon the recommendation of the Grazing Committee and with the concurrence of the Resources Committee under § 161.606(c). Non-use consists of, but is not limited to, absence of livestock on the range unit, and/or abandonment of a permittee's grazing permit.

(b) Unused grazing permits or portions of grazing permits that are set aside for range recovery will not be cancelled for non-use.

§ 161.603 Can mediation be used in the event of a permit violation or dispute?

A permit may provide for permit disputes or violations to be resolved with the District Grazing Committee through mediation.

(a) The District Grazing Committee will conduct the mediation before the Navajo Nation's appropriate hearing body, before BIA invokes any cancellation remedies.

(b) Conducting the mediation may substitute for permit cancellation. However, BIA retains the authority to cancel the permit under § 161.606.

(c) The Navajo Nation's appropriate hearing body decision will be final, unless it is appealed to the Navajo Nation Supreme Court on a question of law. BIA will defer to any ongoing proceedings, as appropriate, in deciding whether to exercise any of the remedies available to BIA under § 161.606.

§ 161.604 What happens if a permit violation occurs?

(a) If the Resources Committee notifies BIA that a specific permit violation has occurred, BIA will initiate an appropriate investigation within 5 business days of that notification.

(b) Unless otherwise provided under tribal law, when BIA has reason to believe that a permit violation has occurred, BIA or the authorized tribal representative will provide written notice to the permittee within 5 business days.

§ 161.605 What will a written notice of a permit violation contain?

The written notice of a permit violation will provide the permittee with 10 days from the receipt of the written notice to:

(a) Cure the permit violation and notify BIA that the violation is cured;

(b) Explain why BIA should not cancel the permit;

(c) Request in writing additional time to complete corrective actions. If additional time is granted, BIA may require that certain actions be taken immediately; or

(d) Request mediation under § 161.603.

§ 161.606 What will BIA do if the permittee doesn't cure a violation on time?

(a) If the permittee does not cure a violation within the required time period, or if the violation is not referred to District Grazing Committee for mediation, BIA will consult with the Navajo Nation, as appropriate, and determine whether:

(1) The permit may be canceled by BIA under paragraph (c) of this section and §§ 161.607 through 161.608;

(2) BIA may invoke any other remedies available to BIA under the permit;

(3) The Navajo Nation may invoke any remedies available to them under the permit; or

(4) The permittee may be granted additional time in which to cure the violation.

(b) If BIA grants a permittee a time extension to cure a violation, the permittee must proceed diligently to complete the necessary corrective actions within a reasonable or specified time from the date on which the extension is granted.

(c) If BIA cancels the permit, BIA will send the permittee and the District Grazing Committee a written notice of cancellation within 5 business days of the decision. BIA will also provide actual or constructive notice of the cancellation to the Navajo Nation, as appropriate. The written notice of cancellation will:

(1) Explain the grounds for cancellation;

(2) Notify the permittee of the amount of any unpaid fees and other financial obligations due under the permit;

(3) Notify the permittee of his or her right to appeal under 25 CFR part 2 of this title, as modified by § 161.607, including the amount of any appeal bond that must be posted with an appeal of the cancellation decision; and

(4) Order the permittee to cease grazing livestock on the next anniversary date of the grazing permit or 180 days following the receipt of the written notice of cancellation, whichever is sooner.

§ 161.607 What appeal bond provisions apply to permit cancellation decisions?

(a) The appeal bond provisions in § 2.5 of part 2 of this title will not apply to appeals from permit cancellation decision. Instead, when BIA decides to cancel a permit, BIA may require the permittee to post an appeal bond with an appeal of the cancellation decision. The requirement to post an appeal bond will apply in addition to all of the other requirements in part 2 of this title.

(b) An appeal bond should be set in an amount necessary to protect the Navajo Nation against financial losses that will likely result from the delay caused by an appeal. Appeal bond requirements will not be separately appealable, but may be contested during the appeal of the permit cancellation decision.

§ 161.608 When will a permit cancellation be effective?

A cancellation decision involving a permit will not be effective for 30 days after the permittee receives a written notice of cancellation from BIA. The cancellation decision will remain ineffective if the permittee files an appeal under § 161.607 and part 2 of this title, unless the decision is made immediately effective under part 2. While a cancellation decision is ineffective, the permittee must continue to comply with the other terms of the permit. If an appeal is not filed in accordance with § 161.607 and part 2 of this title, the cancellation decision will be effective on the 31st day after the permittee receives the written notice of cancellation from BIA.

§ 161.609 Can BIA take emergency action if the rangeland is threatened?

Yes, if a permittee or any other party causes or threatens to cause immediate, significant and irreparable harm to the Navajo Nation land during the term of a permit, BIA will take appropriate emergency action. Emergency action may include trespass proceedings under subpart H, or judicial action seeking immediate cessation of the activity resulting in or threatening harm. Reasonable efforts will be made to notify the Navajo Nation, either before or after the emergency action is taken.

§ 161.610 What will BIA do if livestock is not removed when a permit expires or is cancelled?

If the livestock is not removed after the expiration or cancellation of a permit, BIA will treat the unauthorized use as a trespass. BIA may remove the livestock on behalf of the Navajo Nation, and pursue any additional remedies available under applicable law, including the assessment of civil penalties and costs under subpart H.

Subpart H—Trespass

§ 161.700 What is trespass?

Under this part, trespass is any unauthorized use of, or action on, Navajo partitioned grazing lands.

§ 161.701 What is BIA's trespass policy?

BIA will:

(a) Investigate accidental, willful, and/or incidental trespass on Navajo Partitioned Lands;

(b) Respond to alleged trespass in a prompt, efficient manner;

(c) Assess trespass penalties for the value of products used or removed, cost of damage to the Navajo Partitioned Lands, and enforcement costs incurred as a consequence of the trespass; and

(d) Ensure, to the extent possible, that damage to Navajo Partitioned Lands resulting from trespass is rehabilitated and stabilized at the expense of the trespasser.

§ 161.702 Who will enforce this subpart?

(a) BIA enforces the provisions of this subpart. If the Navajo Nation adopts the provisions of this subpart, the Navajo Nation will have concurrent jurisdiction to enforce this subpart. Additionally, if the Navajo Nation so requests, BIA will defer to tribal prosecution of trespass on Navajo Partitioned Lands.

(b) Nothing in this subpart will be construed to diminish the sovereign authority of the Navajo Nation with respect to trespass.

NOTIFICATION

§ 161.703 How are trespassers notified of a trespass determination?

(a) Unless otherwise provided under tribal law, when BIA has reason to believe that a trespass on Navajo Partitioned Lands has occurred, BIA or the authorized tribal representative will provide written notice within 5 business days to:

(1) The alleged trespasser;

(2) The possessor of trespass property; and

(3) Any known lien holder.

(b) The written notice under paragraph (a) of this section will include the following:

(1) The basis for the trespass determination;

(2) A legal description of where the trespass occurred;

(3) A verification of ownership of unauthorized property (*e.g.*, brands in the State Brand Book for cases of livestock trespass, if applicable);

(4) Corrective actions that must be taken;

(5) Time frames for taking the corrective actions;

(6) Potential consequences and penalties for failure to take corrective action; and

(7) A statement that unauthorized livestock or other property may not be removed or disposed of unless authorized by BIA under paragraph (b)(4) of this section.

(c) If BIA determines that the alleged trespasser or possessor of trespass property is unknown or refuses delivery of the written notice, a public trespass notice will be posted at the tribal community building, U.S. Post Office, and published in the local newspaper nearest to the Indian agricultural lands where the trespass is occurring.

(d) Trespass notices under this subpart are not subject to appeal under part 2 of this title.

§ 161.704 What can a permittee do if they receive a trespass notice?

The trespasser will within the time frame specified in the notice:

(a) Comply with the ordered corrective actions; or

(b) Contact BIA in writing to explain why the trespass notice is in error. The trespasser may contact BIA by telephone but any explanation of trespass must be provided in writing. If BIA determines that a trespass notice was issued in error, the notice will be withdrawn.

§ 161.705 How long will a written trespass notice remain in effect?

A written trespass notice will remain in effect for the same action identified in that written notice for a period of one year from the date of receipt of the written notice by the trespasser.

ACTIONS

§ 161.706 What actions does BIA take against trespassers?

If the trespasser fails to take the corrective action as specified, BIA may take one or more of the following actions, as appropriate:

(a) Seize, impound, sell or dispose of unauthorized livestock or other property involved in the trespass. BIA may keep the property seized for use as evidence.

(b) Assess penalties, damages, and costs under § 161.712.

§ 161.707 When will BIA impound unauthorized livestock or other property?

BIA will impound unauthorized livestock or other property under the following conditions:

(a) Where there is imminent danger of severe injury to growing or harvestable crop or destruction of the range forage.

(b) When the known owner or the owner's representative of the unauthorized livestock or other property refuses to accept delivery of a written notice of trespass and the unauthorized livestock or other property are not removed within the period prescribed in the written notice.

(c) Any time after 5 days of providing notice of impoundment if the trespasser failed to correct the trespass.

§ 161.708 How are trespassers notified of impoundments?

(a) If the trespass is not corrected in the time specified in the initial trespass notice, BIA will send written notice of its intent to impound unauthorized livestock or other property to:

(1) The unauthorized livestock or property owner or representative; and

(2) Any known lien holder of the unauthorized livestock or other property.

(b) If BIA determines that the owner of the unauthorized livestock or other property or the owner's representative is unknown or refuses delivery of the written notice, a public notice of intent to impound will be posted at the tribal community building, U.S. Post Office, and published in the local newspaper nearest to the Indian agricultural lands where the trespass is occurring.

(c) After BIA has given notice as described in § 161.707, unauthorized livestock or other property will be impounded without any further notice.

§ 161.709 What happens after unauthorized livestock or other property are impounded?

Following the impoundment of unauthorized livestock or other property, BIA will provide notice that the impounded property will be sold as follows:

(a) BIA will provide written notice of the sale to the owner, the owner's representative, and any known lien holder. The written notice must include the procedure by which the impounded property may be redeemed before the sale.

(b) BIA will provide public notice of sale of impounded property by posting at the tribal community building, U.S. Post Office, and publishing in the local newspaper nearest to the Indian agricultural lands where the trespass is occurring. The public notice will include a description of the impounded property, and the date, time, and place of the public sale. The sale date must be at least 5 days after the publication and posting of notice.

§ 161.710 How can impounded livestock or other property be redeemed?

Impounded livestock or other property may be redeemed by submitting proof of ownership and paying all penalties, damages, and costs under § 161.712 and completing all corrective actions identified by BIA under § 161.704.

§ 161.711 How will BIA sell impounded livestock or other property?

(a) Unless the owner or known lien holder of the impounded livestock or other property redeems the property before the time set by the sale, by submitting proof of ownership and settling all obligations under §§ 161.704 and 161.712, the property will be sold by public sale to the highest bidder.

(b) If a satisfactory bid is not received, the livestock or property may be re-offered for sale, returned to the owner, condemned and destroyed, or otherwise disposed of.

(c) BIA will give the purchaser a bill of sale or other written receipt evidencing the sale.

PENALTIES, DAMAGES, AND COSTS

§ 161.712 What are the penalties, damages, and costs payable by trespassers?

Trespassers on Navajo Partitioned Lands must pay the following penalties and costs:

(a) Collection of the value of the products illegally used or removed plus a penalty of double their values;

(b) Costs associated with any damage to Navajo Partitioned Lands and/or property;

(c) The costs associated with enforcement of the provisions, including field examination and survey, damage appraisal, investigation assistance and reports, witness expenses, demand letters, court costs, and attorney fees;

(d) Expenses incurred in gathering, impounding, caring for, and disposal of livestock in cases which necessitate impoundment under § 161.707; and

(e) All other penalties authorized by law.

§ 161.713 How will BIA determine the amount of damages to Navajo Partitioned Lands?

(a) BIA will determine the damages by considering the costs of rehabilitation and re-vegetation, loss of future revenue, loss of profits, loss of productivity, loss of market value, damage to other resources, and other factors.

(b) BIA will determine the value of forage or crops consumed or destroyed based upon the average rate received per month for comparable property or grazing privileges, or the estimated commercial value or replacement costs of the products or property.

(c) BIA will determine the value of the products or property illegally used or removed based upon a valuation of similar products or property.

§ 161.714 How will BIA determine the costs associated with enforcement of the trespass?

Costs of enforcement may include detection and all actions taken by us through prosecution and collection of damages. This includes field examination and survey, damage appraisal, investigation assistance and report preparation, witness expenses, demand letters, court costs, attorney fees, and other costs.

§ 161.715 What will BIA do if a trespasser fails to pay penalties, damages and costs?

This section applies if a trespasser fails to pay the assessed penalties, damages, and costs as directed. Unless otherwise provided by applicable Navajo Nation law, BIA will:

(a) Refuse to issue the permittee a permit for any use of Navajo Partitioned Lands; and

(b) Forward the case for appropriate legal action.

§ 161.716 How are the proceeds from trespass distributed?

Unless otherwise provided by Navajo Nation law:

(a) BIA will treat any amounts recovered under § 161.712 as proceeds from the sale of agricultural property from the Navajo Partitioned Lands upon which the trespass occurred.

(b) Proceeds recovered under § 161.712 may be distributed to:

(1) Repair damages of the Navajo Partitioned Lands and property; or

(2) Reimburse the affected parties, including the permittee for loss due to the trespass, as negotiated and provided in the permit.

(c) Reimburse for costs associated with the enforcement.

(d) If any money is left over after the distribution of the proceeds described in paragraph (b) of this section, BIA will return it to the trespasser or, where the owner of the impounded property cannot be identified within

180 days, the net proceeds of the sale will be deposited into the appropriate Navajo Nation account or transferred to the Navajo Nation under applicable tribal law.

§ 161.717 What happens if BIA does not collect enough money to satisfy the penalty?

BIA will send written notice to the trespasser demanding immediate settlement and advising the trespasser that unless settlement is received within 5 business days from the date of receipt, BIA will forward the case for appropriate legal action. BIA may send a copy of the notice to the Navajo Nation, permittee, and any known lien holders.

Subpart I—Concurrence/Appeals/ Amendments

§ 161.800 How does the Navajo Nation provide concurrence to BIA?

(a) Actions taken by BIA under this part require concurrence of the Navajo Nation under section 640d–9(e)(1)(A) of the Settlement Act.

(b) For any action requiring the concurrence of the Resources Committee, the following procedures will apply:

(1) Unless a longer time is specified in a particular section, or unless BIA grants an extension of time, the Resources Committee will have 45 days to review and concur with the proposed action;

(2) If the Resources Committee concurs in writing with all or part of BIA proposed action, the action or a portion of it may be immediately implemented;

(3) If the Resources Committee does not concur with all or part of the proposed action within the time prescribed in paragraph (b)(1) of this section, BIA will submit to the Resources Committee a written declaration of non-concurrence. BIA will then notify the Resources Committee in writing of a formal hearing to be held not sooner than 30 days from the date of the non-concurrence declaration;

(4) The formal hearing on non-concurrence will permit the submission of written evidence and argument concerning the proposal. BIA will take minutes of the hearing. Following the hearing, BIA may amend, alter, or otherwise change the proposed action. If, following a hearing, BIA alters or amends portions of the proposed plan of action, BIA will submit the altered or amended portions of the plan to the Resources Committee for its concurrence; and

(5) If the Resources Committee fails or refuses to give its concurrence to the proposal, BIA may implement the proposal only after issuing a written order, based upon findings of fact, that the proposed action is necessary to protect the land under the Settlement Act and the Agricultural Act.

§ 161.801 May decisions under this part be appealed?

(a) Appeals of BIA decisions issued under this part may be taken in accordance with procedures in part 2 of 25 CFR.

(b) All appeals of decisions by the Grazing Committee and Resources Committee will be forwarded to the Navajo Nation's Office of Hearings and Appeals.

§ 161.802 How will the Navajo Nation recommend amendments to this part?

The Resources Committee will have final authority on behalf of the Navajo Nation to approve amendments to the Navajo Partitioned Lands grazing provisions, upon the recommendation of the Grazing Committee and the Navajo-Hopi Land Commission, and the concurrence of BIA.

PART 162—LEASES AND PERMITS

Subpart A—General Provisions

PURPOSE, DEFINITIONS, AND SCOPE

HOW TO GET A LEASE

LEASE ADMINISTRATION

Subpart B—Agricultural Leases

GENERAL PROVISIONS

HOW TO OBTAIN A LEASE

LEASE REQUIREMENTS

LEASE ADMINISTRATION

LEASE ENFORCEMENT

Subpart C—Residential Leases

RESIDENTIAL LEASING GENERAL PROVISIONS

LEASE REQUIREMENTS

Subpart D—Business Leases

BUSINESS LEASING GENERAL PROVISIONS

LEASE REQUIREMENTS

MONETARY COMPENSATION REQUIREMENTS

BONDING AND INSURANCE

APPROVAL

AMENDMENTS

ASSIGNMENTS

SUBLEASES

LEASEHOLD MORTGAGES

Subpart F—Special Requirements for Certain Reservations

Subpart G—Records

AUTHORITY: 5 U.S.C. 301, R.S. 463 and 465; 25 U.S.C. 2 and 9. Interpret or apply sec. 3, 26 Stat. 795, sec. 1, 28 Stat. 305, secs. 1, 2, 31 Stat. 229, 246, secs. 7, 12, 34 Stat. 545, 34 Stat. 1015, 1034, 35 Stat. 70, 95, 97, sec. 4, 36 Stat. 856, sec. 1, 39 Stat. 128, 41 Stat. 415, as amended, 751, 1232, sec. 17, 43 Stat. 636, 641, 44 Stat. 658, as amended, 894, 1365, as amended, 47 Stat. 1417, sec. 17, 48 Stat. 984, 988, 49 Stat. 115, 1135, sec. 55, 49 Stat. 781, sec. 3, 49 Stat. 1967, 54 Stat. 745, 1057, 60 Stat. 308, secs. 1, 2, 60 Stat. 962, sec. 5, 64 Stat. 46, secs. 1, 2, 4, 5, 6, 64 Stat. 470, 69 Stat. 539, 540, 72 Stat. 968, 107 Stat. 2011, 108 Stat. 4572, March 20, 1996, 110 Stat. 4016; 25 U.S.C. 380, 393, 393a, 394, 395, 397, 402, 402a, 403, 403a, 403b, 403c, 409a, 413, 415, 415a, 415b, 415c, 415d, 416, 477, 635, 2201 *et seq.*, 3701, 3702, 3703, 3712, 3713, 3714, 3715, 3731, 3733, 4211; 44 U.S.C. 3101 *et seq.*

SOURCE: 66 FR 7109, Jan. 22, 2001, unless otherwise noted.

Subpart A—General Provisions

SOURCE: 77 FR 72467, Dec. 5, 2012, unless otherwise noted.

PURPOSE, DEFINITIONS, AND SCOPE

§ 162.001 What is the purpose of this part?

(a) The purpose of this part is to promote leasing on Indian land for housing, economic development, and other purposes.

(b) This part specifies:

(1) Conditions and authorities under which we will approve leases of Indian land and may issue permits on Government land;

(2) How to obtain leases;

(3) Terms and conditions required in leases;

(4) How we administer and enforce leases; and

(5) Special requirements for leases made under special acts of Congress that apply only to certain Indian reservations.

(c) If any section, paragraph, or provision of this part is stayed or held invalid, the remaining sections, paragraphs, or provisions of this part remain in full force and effect.

§ 162.002 How is this part subdivided?

(a) This part includes multiple subparts relating to:

(1) General Provisions (Subpart A);

(2) Agricultural Leases (Subpart B);

(3) Residential Leases (Subpart C);

(4) Business Leases (Subpart D);

(5) Wind Energy Evaluation, Wind Resource, and Solar Resource Leases (Subpart E);

(6) Special Requirements for Certain Reservations (Subpart F); and

(7) Records (Subpart G).

(b) Leases covered by subpart B are not subject to the provisions in subpart A. Leases covered by subpart B are subject to the provisions in subpart G, except that if a provision in subpart B conflicts with a provision of subpart G, then the provision in subpart B will govern.

(c) Subpart F applies only to leases made under special acts of Congress covering particular Indian reservations. Leases covered by subpart F are also subject to the provisions in subparts A through G, except to the extent that subparts A through G are inconsistent with the provisions in subpart F or any act of Congress under which the lease is made, in which case the provisions in subpart F or any act of Congress under which the lease is made will govern.

§ 162.003 What key terms do I need to know?

Adult means a person who is 18 years of age or older.

Appeal bond means a bond posted upon filing of an appeal.

Approval means written authorization by the Secretary or a delegated official or, where applicable, the "deemed approved" authorization of an amendment or sublease.

Assignment means an agreement between a lessee and an assignee, whereby the assignee acquires all or some of the lessee's rights, and assumes all or some of the lessee's obligations, under a lease.

BIA means the Secretary of the Interior or the Bureau of Indian Affairs within the Department of the Interior and any tribe acting on behalf of the Secretary or Bureau of Indian Affairs under § 162.018.

Business day means Monday through Friday, excluding federally recognized holidays and other days that the applicable office of the Federal Government is closed to the public.

Cancellation means BIA action to end a lease.

Consent or consenting means written authorization by an Indian landowner to a specified action.

Constructive notice means notice:

(1) Posted at the tribal government office, tribal community building, and/or the United States Post Office; and

(2) Published in the local newspaper(s) nearest to the affected land and/or announced on a local radio station(s).

Court of competent jurisdiction means a Federal, tribal, or State court with jurisdiction.

Day means a calendar day, unless otherwise specified.

Emancipated minor means a person less than 18 years of age who is married or who is determined by a court of competent jurisdiction to be legally able to care for himself or herself.

Equipment installation plan means a plan that describes the type and location of any improvements to be installed by the lessee to evaluate the wind resources and a schedule showing the tentative commencement and completion dates for installation of those improvements.

Fair market rental means the amount of rental income that a leased tract of Indian land would most probably command in an open and competitive market, or as determined by competitive bidding.

Fee interest means an interest in land that is owned in unrestricted fee status, and is thus freely alienable by the fee owner.

Fractionated tract means a tract of Indian land owned in common by Indian landowners and/or fee owners holding undivided interests therein.

Government land means any tract, or interest therein, in which the surface estate is owned and administered by the United States, not including Indian land.

Holdover means circumstances in which a lessee remains in possession of the leased premises after the lease term expires.

Housing for public purposes means multi-family developments, single-family residential developments, and single-family residences:

(1) Administered by a tribe or tribally designated housing entity (TDHE); or

(2) Substantially financed using a tribal, Federal, or State housing assistance program or TDHE.

Immediate family means, in the absence of a definition under applicable tribal law, a spouse, brother, sister, aunt, uncle, niece, nephew, first cousin, lineal ancestor, lineal descendant, or member of the household.

Indian means:

(1) Any person who is a member of any Indian tribe, is eligible to become a member of any Indian tribe, or is an owner as of October 27, 2004, of a trust or restricted interest in land;

(2) Any person meeting the definition of Indian under the Indian Reorganization Act (25 U.S.C. 479) and the regulations promulgated thereunder; and

(3) With respect to the inheritance and ownership of trust or restricted land in the State of California under 25 U.S.C. 2206, any person described in paragraph (1) or (2) of this definition or any person who owns a trust or restricted interest in a parcel of such land in that State.

Indian land means any tract in which any interest in the surface estate is owned by a tribe or individual Indian in trust or restricted status and includes both individually owned Indian land and tribal land.

Indian landowner means a tribe or individual Indian who owns an interest in Indian land.

Individually owned Indian land means any tract, or interest therein, in which the surface estate is owned by an individual Indian in trust or restricted status.

Indian tribe means an Indian tribe under section 102 of the Federally Recognized Indian Tribe List Act of 1994 (25 U.S.C. 479a).

Interest, when used with respect to Indian land, means an ownership right to the surface estate of Indian land.

Lease means a written contract between Indian landowners and a lessee, whereby the lessee is granted a right to possess Indian land, for a specified purpose and duration. The lessee's right to possess will limit the Indian landowners' right to possess the leased premises only to the extent provided in the lease.

Lease document means a lease, amendment, assignment, sublease, or leasehold mortgage.

Leasehold mortgage means a mortgage, deed of trust, or other instrument that pledges a lessee's leasehold interest as security for a debt or other obligation owed by the lessee to a lender or other mortgagee.

Lessee means person or entity who has acquired a legal right to possess Indian land by a lease under this part.

Life estate means an interest in property held only for the duration of a designated person(s)' life. A life estate may be created by a conveyance document or by operation of law.

LTRO means the Land Titles and Records Office of the BIA.

Mail means to send something by U.S. Postal Service or commercial delivery service.

Minor means an individual who is less than 18 years of age.

Mortgagee means the holder of a leasehold mortgage.

NEPA means the National Environmental Policy Act of 1969, 42 U.S.C. 4321 *et seq.*

Nominal rental or nominal compensation means a rental amount that is so insignificant that it bears no relationship to the value of the property that is being leased.

Non compos mentis means that the person to whom the term is applied has been legally determined by a court of competent jurisdiction to be of unsound mind or incapable of managing his or her own affairs.

Notice of violation means a letter notifying the lessee of a violation of the lease and providing the lessee with a specified period of time to show cause why the lease should not be cancelled for the violation. A 10-day show cause letter is one type of notice of violation.

Orphaned minor means a minor whose parents are deceased.

Performance bond means security for the performance of certain lease obligations, as furnished by the lessee, or a guaranty of such performance as furnished by a third-party surety.

Permanent improvements means buildings, other structures, and associated infrastructure attached to the leased premises.

Permit means a written, non-assignable agreement between Indian landowners or BIA and the permittee, whereby the permittee is granted a temporary, revocable privilege to use Indian land or Government land, for a specified purpose.

Permittee means a person or entity who has acquired a privilege to use Indian land or Government land by a permit.

Power of attorney means an authority by which one person enables another to act for him or her as attorney-in-fact.

Remainder interest means an interest in Indian land that is created at the same time as a life estate, for the use and enjoyment of its owner after the life estate terminates.

Restoration and reclamation plan means a plan that defines the reclamation, revegetation, restoration, and soil stabilization requirements for the project area, and requires the expeditious reclamation of construction areas and revegetation of disturbed areas to reduce invasive plant infestation and erosion.

Secretary means the Secretary of the Interior.

Single-family residence means a building with one to four dwelling units on a tract of land under a single residential lease, or as defined by applicable tribal law or other tribal authorization.

Single-family residential development means two or more single-family residences owned, managed, or developed by a single entity.

Sublease means a written agreement by which the lessee grants to an individual or entity a right to possession no greater than that held by the lessee under the lease.

Surety means one who guarantees the performance of another.

TDHE means a tribally designated housing entity under 25 U.S.C. 4103(22), a tribally-sponsored or tribally sanctioned not-for-profit entity, or any limited partnership or other entity organized for the purpose of developing or improving low-income housing utilizing tax credits.

Termination means action by Indian landowners to end a lease.

Trespass means any unauthorized occupancy, use of, or action on any Indian land or Government land.

Tribal authorization means a duly adopted tribal resolution, tribal ordinance, or other appropriate tribal document authorizing the specified action.

Tribal land means any tract, or interest therein, in which the surface estate is owned by one or more tribes in trust or restricted status, and includes such lands reserved for BIA administrative purposes. The term also includes the surface estate of lands held by the United States in trust for an Indian corporation chartered under section 17 of the Act of June 18, 1934 (48 Stat. 988; 25 U.S.C. 477).

Tribal land assignment means a contract or agreement that conveys to tribal members or wholly owned tribal corporations any rights for the use of tribal lands, assigned by an Indian tribe in accordance with tribal laws or customs.

Tribal law means the body of non-Federal law that governs lands and activities under the jurisdiction of a tribe, including ordinances or other enactments by the tribe, and tribal court rulings.

Trust or restricted land means any tract, or interest therein, held in trust or restricted status.

Trust or restricted status means:

(1) That the United States holds title to the tract or interest in trust for the benefit of one or more tribes or individual Indians; or

(2) That one or more tribes or individual Indians holds title to the tract or interest, but can alienate or encumber it only with the approval of the United States because of limitations in the conveyance instrument under Federal law or limitations in Federal law.

Undivided interest means a fractional share in the surface estate of Indian land, where the surface estate is owned in common with other Indian landowners or fee owners.

USPAP means the Uniform Standards of Professional Appraisal Practice promulgated by the Appraisal Standards Board of the Appraisal Foundation to establish requirements and procedures for professional real property appraisal practice.

Us/we/our means the BIA.

Violation means a failure to take an action, including payment of compensation, when required by the lease, or to otherwise not comply with a term of the lease. This definition applies for purposes of our enforcement of a lease under this part no matter how "violation" or "default" is defined in the lease.

§ 162.004 To what land does this part apply?

(a) This part applies to Indian land and Government land, including any tract in which an individual Indian or Indian tribe owns an interest in trust or restricted status.

(1) We will not take any action on a lease of fee interests or collect rent on behalf of fee interest owners. We will not condition our approval of a lease of the trust and restricted interests on your having obtained a lease from the owners of any fee interests. The lessee will be responsible for accounting to the owners of any fee interests that may exist in the property being leased.

(2) We will not include the fee interests in a tract in calculating the applicable percentage of interests required for consent to a lease document.

(b) This paragraph (b) applies if there is a life estate on the land to be leased.

(1) When all of the trust or restricted interests in a tract are subject to a single life estate, the life tenant may lease the land without the consent of

the owners of the remainder interests or our approval, for the duration of the life estate.

(i) The lease will terminate upon the death of the life tenant.

(ii) The life tenant must record the lease in the LTRO.

(iii) The lessee must pay rent directly to the life tenant under the terms of the lease unless the whereabouts of the life tenant are unknown, in which case we may collect rents on behalf of the life tenant.

(iv) We may monitor the use of the land on behalf of the owners of the remainder interests, as appropriate, but will not be responsible for enforcing the lease on behalf of the life tenant.

(v) We will not lease the remainder interests or join in a lease by the life tenant on behalf of the owners of the remainder interests except as needed to preserve the value of the land.

(vi) We will be responsible for enforcing the terms of the lease on behalf of the owners of the remainder interests.

(2) When less than all of the trust or restricted interests in a tract are subject to a single life estate, the life tenant may lease his or her interest without the consent of the owners of the remainder interests, but must obtain the consent of the co-owners and our approval.

(i) We will not lease on the life tenant's behalf.

(ii) The lease must provide that the lessee pays the life tenant directly, unless the life tenant's whereabouts are unknown in which case we may collect rents on behalf of the life tenant.

(iii) The lease must be recorded in the LTRO, even where our approval is not required.

(iv) We will be responsible for enforcing the terms of the lease on behalf of the owners of the remainder interests.

(3) Where the remaindermen and the life tenant have not entered into a lease or other written agreement approved by the Secretary providing for the distribution of rent monies under the lease, the life tenant will receive payment in accordance with the distribution and calculation scheme set forth in Part 179 of this chapter.

(4) The life tenant may not cause or allow permanent injury to the land.

(5) The life tenant must provide a copy of the executed lease to all owners of the remainder interests.

WHEN TO GET A LEASE

§ 162.005 When do I need a lease to authorize possession of Indian land?

(a) You need a lease under this part to possess Indian land if you meet one of the criteria in the following table, unless you are authorized to possess or use the Indian land by a land use agreement not subject to this part under § 162.006(b) or by a permit.

If you are . . .	then you must obtain a lease under this part . . .
(1) A person or legal entity (including an independent legal entity owned and operated by a tribe) who is not an owner of the Indian land.	from the owners of the land before taking possession of the land or any portion thereof.
(2) An Indian landowner of a fractional interest in the land.	from the owners of other trust and restricted interests in the land, unless all of the owners have given you permission to take or continue in possession without a lease.

(b) You do not need a lease to possess Indian land if:

(1) You are an Indian landowner who owns 100 percent of the trust or restricted interests in a tract; or

(2) You meet any of the criteria in the following table.

You do not need a lease if you are . . .	but the following conditions apply . . .
(i) A parent or guardian of a minor child who owns 100 percent of the trust or restricted interests in the land.	We may require you to provide evidence of a direct benefit to the minor child and when the child is no longer a minor, you must obtain a lease to authorize continued possession.
(ii) A 25 U.S.C. 477 corporate entity that manages or has the power to manage the tribal land directly under its Federal charter or under a tribal authorization (not under a lease from the Indian tribe).	You must record documents in accordance with § 162.343, § 162.443, and § 162.568.

§ 162.006 To what types of land use agreements does this part apply?

(a) This part applies to leases of Indian land entered into under 25 U.S.C. 380, 25 U.S.C. 415(a), and 25 U.S.C. 4211, and other tribe-specific statutes authorizing surface leases of Indian land with our approval.

(b) This part does not apply to:

(1) Land use agreements entered into under other statutory authority, such as the following:

This part does not apply to . . .	which are covered by . . .
(i) Contracts or agreements that encumber tribal land under 25 U.S.C. 81.	25 CFR part 84.
(ii) Traders' licenses	25 CFR part 140.
(iii) Timber contracts	25 CFR part 163.
(iv) Grazing permits	25 CFR part 166.
(v) Rights-of-way	25 CFR part 169.
(vi) Mineral leases, prospecting permits, or mineral development agreements.	25 CFR parts 211, 212, 213, 225, 226, 227.
(vii) Tribal land assignments and similar instruments authorizing uses of tribal land.	tribal laws.

(2) Leases of water rights associated with Indian land, except to the extent the use of water rights is incorporated in a lease of the land itself.

(3) The following leases, which do not require our approval, except that you must record these leases in accordance with §§ 162.343, 162.443, and 162.568:

(i) A lease of tribal land by a 25 U.S.C. 477 corporate entity under its charter to a third party for a period not to exceed 25 years; and

(ii) A lease of Indian land under a special act of Congress authorizing leasing without our approval.

§ 162.007 To what permits does this part apply?

(a) Permits for the use of Indian land do not require our approval; however, you must fulfill the following requirements:

(1) Ensure that permitted activities comply with all applicable environmental and cultural resource laws; and

(2) Submit all permits to the appropriate BIA office to allow us to maintain a copy of the permit in our records. If we determine within 10 days of submission that the document does not meet the definition of "permit" and grants a legal interest in Indian land, we will notify you that a lease is required.

(b) The following table provides examples of some common characteristics of permits versus leases.

Permit	Lease
Does not grant a legal interest in Indian land.	Grants a legal interest in Indian land.
Shorter term	Longer term.
Limited use	Broader use with associated infrastructure.
Permittee has non-possessory right of access.	Lessee has right of possession, ability to limit or prohibit access by others.
Indian landowner may terminate at any time.	Indian landowner may terminate under limited circumstances.

(c) We will not administer or enforce permits on Indian land.

(d) We may grant permits for the use of Government land. The leasing regulations in this part will apply to such permits, as appropriate.

§ 162.008 Does this part apply to lease documents I submitted for approval before January 4, 2013?

This part applies to all lease documents, except as provided in § 162.006. If you submitted your lease document to us for approval before January 4, 2013, the qualifications in paragraphs (a) and (b) of this section also apply.

(a) If we approved your lease document before January 4, 2013, this part applies to that lease document; however, if the provisions of the lease document conflict with this part, the provisions of the lease govern.

(b) If you submitted a lease document but we did not approve it before January 4, 2013, then:

(1) We will review the lease document under the regulations in effect at the time of your submission; and

(2) Once we approve the lease document, this part applies to that lease document; however, if the provisions of the lease document conflict with this part, the provisions of the lease document govern.

§ 162.009 Do I need BIA approval of a subleasehold mortgage?

Unless the lease provides otherwise, sublease, or by request of the parties, you do not need our approval of a subleasehold mortgage. If the lease or sublease requires, or parties request, our approval, we will use the procedures governing our review of leasehold mortgages.

How to Get a Lease

§ 162.010 How do I obtain a lease?

(a) This section establishes the basic steps to obtain a lease.

(1) Prospective lessees must:

(i) Directly negotiate with Indian landowners for a lease; and

(ii) For fractionated tracts, notify all Indian landowners and obtain the consent of the Indian landowners of the applicable percentage of interests, under § 162.012; and

(2) Prospective lessees and Indian landowners must:

(i) Prepare the required information and analyses, including information to facilitate our analysis under applicable environmental and cultural resource requirements; and

(ii) Ensure the lease complies with the requirements in subpart C for residential leases, subpart D for business leases, or subpart E for wind energy evaluation, wind resource, or solar resource leases; and

(3) Prospective lessees or Indian landowners must submit the lease, and required information and analyses, to the BIA office with jurisdiction over the lands covered by the lease, for our review and approval.

(b) Generally, residential, business, wind energy evaluation, wind resource, and solar resource leases will not be advertised for competitive bid.

§ 162.011 How does a prospective lessee identify and contact individual Indian landowners to negotiate a lease?

(a) Prospective lessees may submit a written request to us to obtain the following information. The request must specify that it is for the purpose of negotiating a lease:

(1) Names and addresses of the individual Indian landowners or their representatives;

(2) Information on the location of the parcel; and

(3) The percentage of undivided interest owned by each individual Indian landowner.

(b) We may assist prospective lessees in contacting the individual Indian landowners or their representatives for the purpose of negotiating a lease, upon request.

(c) We will assist individual Indian landowners in lease negotiations, upon their request.

§ 162.012 What are the consent requirements for a lease?

(a) For fractionated tracts:

(1) Except in Alaska, the owners of the following percentage of undivided trust or restricted interests in a fractionated tract of Indian land must consent to a lease of that tract:

If the number of owners of the undivided trust or restricted interest in the tract is . . .	Then the required percentage of the undivided trust or restricted interest is . . .
(i) One to five,	90 percent;
(ii) Six to 10,	80 percent;
(iii) 11 to 19,	60 percent;
(iv) 20 or more,	Over 50 percent.

(2) Leases in Alaska require consent of all of the Indian landowners in the tract.

(3) If the prospective lessee is also an Indian landowner, his or her consent will be included in the percentages in paragraphs (a)(1) and (2) of this section.

(4) Where owners of the applicable percentages in paragraph (a)(1) of this section consent to a lease document:

(i) That lease document binds all non-consenting owners to the same extent as if those owners also consented to the lease document; and

(ii) That lease document will not bind a non-consenting Indian tribe, except with respect to the tribally owned fractional interest, and the non-consenting Indian tribe will not be treated as a party to the lease. Nothing in this paragraph affects the sovereignty or sovereign immunity of the Indian tribe.

(5) We will determine the number of owners of, and undivided interests in, a fractionated tract of Indian land, for the purposes of calculating the percentages in paragraph (a)(1) of this section based on our records on the date on which the lease is submitted to us for approval.

(b) Tribal land subject to a tribal land assignment may only be leased with the consent of the tribe.

§ 162.013 Who is authorized to consent to a lease?

(a) Indian tribes, adult Indian landowners, and emancipated minors, may consent to a lease of their land, including undivided interests in fractionated tracts.

(b) The following individuals or entities may consent on behalf of an individual Indian landowner:

(1) An adult with legal custody acting on behalf of his or her minor children;

(2) A guardian, conservator, or other fiduciary appointed by a court of competent jurisdiction to act on behalf of an individual Indian landowner;

(3) Any person who is authorized to practice before the Department of the Interior under 43 CFR 1.3(b) and has been retained by the Indian landowner for this purpose;

(4) BIA, under the circumstances in paragraph (c) of this section; or

(5) An adult or legal entity who has been given a written power of attorney that:

(i) Meets all of the formal requirements of any applicable law under § 162.014;

(ii) Identifies the attorney-in-fact; and

(iii) Describes the scope of the powers granted, to include leasing land, and any limits on those powers.

(c) BIA may give written consent to a lease, and that consent must be counted in the percentage ownership described in § 162.012, on behalf of:

(1) The individual owner if the owner is deceased and the heirs to, or devisees of, the interest of the deceased owner have not been determined;

(2) An individual whose whereabouts are unknown to us, after we make a reasonable attempt to locate the individual;

(3) An individual who is found to be non compos mentis or determined to be an adult in need of assistance who does not have a guardian duly appointed by a court of competent jurisdiction, or an individual under legal disability as defined in part 115 of this chapter;

(4) An orphaned minor who does not have a guardian duly appointed by a court of competent jurisdiction;

(5) An individual who has given us a written power of attorney to lease their land; and

(6) The individual Indian landowners of a fractionated tract where:

(i) We have given the Indian landowners written notice of our intent to consent to a lease on their behalf;

(ii) The Indian landowners are unable to agree upon a lease during a 3 month negotiation period following the notice; and

(iii) The land is not being used by an Indian landowner under § 162.005(b)(1).

LEASE ADMINISTRATION

§ 162.014 What laws will apply to leases approved under this part?

(a) In addition to the regulations in this part, leases approved under this part:

(1) Are subject to applicable Federal laws and any specific Federal statutory requirements that are not incorporated in this part;

(2) Are subject to tribal law, subject to paragraph (b) of this section; and

(3) Are not subject to State law or the law of a political subdivision thereof except that:

(i) State law or the law of a political subdivision thereof may apply in the specific areas and circumstances in Indian country where the Indian tribe with jurisdiction has made it expressly applicable;

(ii) State law may apply in the specific areas and circumstances in Indian country where Congress has made it expressly applicable; and

(iii) State law may apply where a Federal court has expressly applied State law to a specific area or circumstance in Indian country in the absence of Federal or tribal law.

(b) Tribal laws generally apply to land under the jurisdiction of the tribe enacting the laws, except to the extent that those tribal laws are inconsistent with these regulations or other applicable Federal law. However, these regulations may be superseded or modified by tribal laws, as long as:

(1) The tribe has notified us of the superseding or modifying effect of the tribal laws;

(2) The superseding or modifying of the regulation would not violate a Federal statute or judicial decision, or conflict with our general trust responsibility under Federal law; and

(3) The superseding or modifying of the regulation applies only to tribal land.

(c) Unless prohibited by Federal law, the parties to a lease may subject that lease to State or local law in the absence of Federal or tribal law, if:

(1) The lease includes a provision to this effect; and

(2) The Indian landowners expressly agree to the application of State or local law.

(d) An agreement under paragraph (c) of this section does not waive a tribe's sovereign immunity unless the tribe expressly states its intention to waive sovereign immunity in the lease of tribal land.

§ 162.015 May a lease contain a preference consistent with tribal law for employment of tribal members?

A lease of Indian land may include a provision, consistent with tribal law, requiring the lessee to give a preference to qualified tribal members, based on their political affiliation with the tribe.

§ 162.016 Will BIA comply with tribal laws in making lease decisions?

Unless contrary to Federal law, BIA will comply with tribal laws in making decisions regarding leases, including tribal laws regulating activities on leased land under tribal jurisdiction, including, but not limited to, tribal laws relating to land use, environmental protection, and historic or cultural preservation.

§ 162.017 What taxes apply to leases approved under this part?

(a) Subject only to applicable Federal law, permanent improvements on the leased land, without regard to ownership of those improvements, are not subject to any fee, tax, assessment, levy, or other charge imposed by any State or political subdivision of a State. Improvements may be subject to taxation by the Indian tribe with jurisdiction.

(b) Subject only to applicable Federal law, activities under a lease conducted on the leased premises are not subject to any fee, tax, assessment, levy, or other charge (e.g., business use, privilege, public utility, excise, gross revenue taxes) imposed by any State or political subdivision of a State. Activities may be subject to taxation by the Indian tribe with jurisdiction.

(c) Subject only to applicable Federal law, the leasehold or possessory interest is not subject to any fee, tax, assessment, levy, or other charge imposed by any State or political subdivision of a State. Leasehold or possessory interests may be subject to taxation by the Indian tribe with jurisdiction.

§ 162.018 May tribes administer this part on BIA's behalf?

A tribe or tribal organization may contract or compact under the Indian Self-Determination and Education Assistance Act (25 U.S.C. 450f *et seq.*) to administer any portion of this part that is not an approval or disapproval of a lease document, waiver of a requirement for lease approval (including but not limited to waivers of fair market rental and valuation, bonding, and insurance), cancellation of a lease, or an appeal.

§ 162.019 May a lease address access to the leased premises by roads or other infrastructure?

A lease may address access to the leased premises by roads or other infrastructure, as long as the access complies with applicable statutory and regulatory requirements, including 25 CFR part 169. Roads or other infrastructure within the leased premises do not require compliance with 25 CFR part 169 during the term of the lease, unless otherwise stated in the lease.

§ 162.020 May a lease combine tracts with different Indian landowners?

(a) We may approve a lease that combines multiple tracts of Indian land into a unit, if we determine that unitization is:

(1) In the Indian landowners' best interest; and

(2) Consistent with the efficient administration of the land.

(b) For a lease that covers multiple tracts, the minimum consent requirements apply to each tract separately.

(c) Unless the lease provides otherwise, the rent or other compensation will be prorated in proportion to the acreage each tract contributes to the entire lease. Once prorated per tract, the rent will be distributed to the owners of each tract based upon their respective percentage interest in that particular tract.

§ 162.021 What are BIA's responsibilities in approving leases?

(a) We will work to provide assistance to Indian landowners in leasing their land, either through negotiations or advertisement.

(b) We will promote tribal control and self-determination over tribal land and other land under the tribe's jurisdiction, including through contracts and self-governance compacts entered into under the Indian Self-Determination and Education Assistance Act, as amended, 25 U.S.C. 450f *et. seq.*

(c) We will promptly respond to requests for BIA approval of leases, as specified in §§ 162.340, 162.440, 162.530, and 162.565.

(d) We will work to ensure that the use of the land is consistent with the Indian landowners' wishes and applicable tribal law.

§ 162.022 What are BIA's responsibilities in administering and enforcing leases?

(a) Upon written notification from an Indian landowner that the lessee has failed to comply with the terms and conditions of the lease, we will promptly take appropriate action, as specified in §§ 162.364, 162.464, and 162.589. Nothing in this part prevents an Indian landowner from exercising remedies available to the Indian landowners under the lease or applicable law.

(b) We will promptly respond to requests for BIA approval of amendments, assignments, leasehold mortgages, and subleases, as specified in subparts C, D, and E.

(c) We will respond to Indian landowners' concerns regarding the management of their land.

(d) We will take emergency action as needed to preserve the value of the land under § 162.024.

§ 162.023 What if an individual or entity takes possession of or uses Indian land without an approved lease or other proper authorization?

If an individual or entity takes possession of, or uses, Indian land without a lease and a lease is required, the unauthorized possession or use is a trespass. We may take action to recover possession, including eviction, on behalf of the Indian landowners and pursue any additional remedies available under applicable law. The Indian landowners may pursue any available remedies under applicable law.

§ 162.024 May BIA take emergency action if Indian land is threatened?

(a) We may take appropriate emergency action if there is a natural disaster or if an individual or entity causes or threatens to cause immediate and significant harm to Indian land. Emergency action may include judicial action seeking immediate cessation of the activity resulting in or threatening the harm.

(b) We will make reasonable efforts to notify the individual Indian landowners before and after taking emergency action. In all cases, we will notify the Indian landowners after taking emergency action by actual or constructive notice. We will provide written notification of our action to the Indian tribe exercising jurisdiction over the Indian land before and after taking emergency action.

§ 162.025 May decisions under this part be appealed?

Appeals from BIA decisions under this part may be taken under part 2 of this chapter, except for deemed approvals and as otherwise provided in this part. For purposes of appeals from BIA decisions under this part, "interested party" is defined as any person whose own direct economic interest is adversely affected by an action or decision. Our decision to disapprove a lease may be appealed only by an Indian landowner. Our decision to disapprove any other lease document may be appealed only by the Indian landowners or the lessee.

§ 162.026 Who can answer questions about leasing?

An Indian landowner or prospective lessee may contact the local BIA realty office (or of any tribe acting on behalf of BIA under § 162.018) with jurisdiction over the land for answers to questions about the leasing process.

§ 162.027 What documentation may BIA require in approving, administering, and enforcing leases?

(a) We may require that the parties provide any pertinent environmental and technical records, reports, and other information (e.g., records of lease payments), related to approval of lease documents and enforcement of leases.

(b) We will adopt environmental assessments and environmental impact statements prepared by another Federal agency, Indian tribe, entity, or person under 43 CFR 46.320 and 42 CFR 1506.3, including those prepared under 25 U.S.C. 4115 and 25 CFR part 1000, but may require a supplement. We will use any reasonable evidence that another Federal agency has accepted the environmental report, including but not limited to, letters of approval or acceptance.

(c) Upon our request, the parties must make appropriate records, reports, or information available for our inspection and duplication. We will keep confidential any information that is marked confidential or proprietary and will exempt it from public release to the extent allowed by law and in accordance with 43 CFR part 2. We may, at our discretion, treat a lessee's failure to cooperate with such request, provide data, or grant access to information or records as a lease violation.

§ 162.028 How may an Indian tribe obtain information about leases on its land?

Upon request of the Indian tribe with jurisdiction, BIA will promptly provide information on the status of leases on tribal land, without requiring a Freedom of Information Act request.

§ 162.029 How does BIA provide notice to the parties to a lease?

(a) When this part requires us to notify the parties of the status of our review of a lease document (including but not limited to, providing notice to the parties of the date of receipt of a lease document, informing the parties of the need for additional review time, and informing the parties that a lease proposal package is not complete):

(1) For leases of tribal land, we will notify the lessee and the tribe by mail; and

(2) For leases of individually owned Indian land, we will notify the lessee by mail and, where feasible, the individual Indian landowners either by constructive notice or by mail.

(b) When this part requires us to notify the parties of our determination to approve or disapprove a lease document, and to provide any right of appeal:

(1) For leases of tribal land, we will notify the lessee and the tribe by mail; and

(2) For leases of individually owned Indian land, we will notify the lessee by mail and the individual Indian landowners either by constructive notice or by mail.

Subpart B—Agricultural Leases

§ 162.101 What key terms do I need to know for this subpart?

For purposes of this subpart:

Adult means an individual who is 18 years of age or older.

Agricultural land means Indian land or Government land suited or used for the production of crops, livestock or other agricultural products, or Indian land suited or used for a business that supports the surrounding agricultural community.

Agricultural lease means a lease of agricultural land for farming and/or grazing purposes.

AIARMA means the American Indian Agricultural Resources Management Act of December 3, 1993 (107 Stat. 2011, 25 U.S.C. 3701 *et seq.*), as amended on November 2, 1994 (108 Stat. 4572).

Assignment means an agreement between a tenant and an assignee, whereby the assignee acquires all of the tenant's rights, and assumes all of the tenant's obligations, under a lease.

BIA means the Bureau of Indian Affairs within the Department of the Interior and any tribe acting on behalf of BIA under § 162.109 of this part.

Bond means security for the performance of certain lease obligations, as furnished by the tenant, or a guaranty of such performance as furnished by a third-party surety.

Day means a calendar day.

Emancipated minor means a person under 18 years of age who is married or who is determined by a court of competent jurisdiction to be legally able to care for himself or herself.

Fair annual rental means the amount of rental income that a leased tract of Indian land would most probably command in an open and competitive market.

Fee interest means an interest in land that is owned in unrestricted fee status, and is thus freely alienable by the fee owner.

Fractionated tract means a tract of Indian land owned in common by Indian landowners and/or fee owners holding undivided interests therein.

Government land means any tract, or interest therein, in which the surface estate is owned by the United States and administered by BIA, not including tribal land that has been reserved for administrative purposes.

Immediate family means a spouse, brother, sister, lineal ancestor, lineal descendant, or member of the household of an individual Indian landowner.

Indian land means any tract in which any interest in the surface estate is owned by a tribe or individual Indian in trust or restricted status.

Indian landowner means a tribe or individual Indian who owns an interest in Indian land in trust or restricted status.

Individually-owned land means any tract, or interest therein, in which the surface estate is owned by an individual Indian in trust or restricted status.

Interest, when used with respect to Indian land, means an ownership right to the surface estate of Indian land that is unlimited or uncertain in duration, including a life estate.

Lease means a written agreement between Indian landowners and a tenant or lessee, whereby the tenant or lessee is granted a right to possession of Indian land, for a specified purpose and duration. Unless otherwise provided, the use of this term will also include permits, as appropriate.

Lessee means tenant, as defined in this section.

Life estate means an interest in Indian land that is limited, in duration, to the life of the life tenant holding the interest, or the life of some other person.

Majority interest means more than 50% of the trust or restricted interests in a tract of Indian land.

Minor means an individual who is less than 18 years of age.

Mortgage means a mortgage, deed of trust or other instrument that pledges a tenant's leasehold interest as security for a debt or other obligation owed by the tenant to a lender or other mortgagee.

NEPA means the National Environmental Policy Act (42 U.S.C. § 4321, *et seq.*)

Non compos mentis means a person who has been legally determined by a court of competent jurisdiction to be of unsound mind or incapable of managing his or her own affairs.

Permit means a written agreement between Indian landowners and the applicant for the permit, also referred to as a permittee, whereby the permittee is granted a revocable privilege to use Indian land or Government land, for a specified purpose.

Remainder means an interest in Indian land that is created at the same time as a life estate, for the use and enjoyment of its owner after the life estate terminates.

Restricted land or restricted status means land the title to which is held by an individual Indian or a tribe and which can only be alienated or encumbered by the owner with the approval of the Secretary because of limitations contained in the conveyance instrument pursuant to federal law.

Secretary means the Secretary of the Interior or an authorized representative.

Sublease means a written agreement by which the tenant grants to an individual or entity a right to possession no greater than that held by the tenant under the lease.

Surety means one who guarantees the performance of another.

Tenant means a person or entity who has acquired a legal right of possession to Indian land by a lease or permit under this part.

Trespass means an unauthorized possession, occupancy or use of Indian land.

Tribal land means the surface estate of land or any interest therein held by the United States in trust for a tribe, band, community, group or pueblo of Indians, and land that is held by a tribe, band, community, group or pueblo of Indians, subject to federal restrictions against alienation or encumbrance, and includes such land reserved for BIA administrative purposes when it is not immediately needed for such purposes. The term also includes lands held by the United States in trust for an Indian corporation chartered under section 17 of the Act of June 18, 1934 (48 Stat. 984; 25 U.S.C. §476).

Tribal laws means the body of law that governs land and activities under the jurisdiction of a tribe, including ordinances and other enactments by the tribe, tribal court rulings, and tribal common law.

Trust land means any tract, or interest therein, that the United States holds in trust status for the benefit of a tribe or individual Indian.

Undivided interest means a fractional share in the surface estate of Indian land, where the surface estate is owned in common with other Indian landowners or fee owners.

Us/We/Our means the Secretary or BIA and any tribe acting on behalf of the Secretary or BIA under §162.110 of this part.

USPAP means the Uniform Standards of Professional Appraisal Practice, as promulgated by the Appraisal Standards Board of the Appraisal Foundation to establish requirements and procedures for professional real property appraisal practice.

[66 FR 7109, Jan. 22, 2001, as amended at 77 FR 72474, Dec. 5, 2012]

§ 162.105 Can tracts with different Indian landowners be unitized for agricultural leasing purposes?

(a) An agricultural lease negotiated by Indian landowners may cover more than one tract of Indian land, but the minimum consent requirements for leases granted by Indian landowners under subparts B through D of this part will apply to each tract separately. We may combine multiple tracts into a unit for leases negotiated or advertised by us, if we determine that unitization is in the Indian landowners' best interests and consistent with the efficient administration of the land.

(b) Unless otherwise provided in the agricultural lease, the rent or other consideration derived from a unitized agricultural lease will be distributed based on the size of each landowner's interest in proportion to the acreage within the entire unit.

[66 FR 7109, Jan. 22, 2001, as amended at 77 FR 72474, Dec. 5, 2012; 78 FR 19100, Mar. 29, 2013]

§ 162.106 What will BIA do if possession is taken without an approved agricultural lease or other proper authorization?

(a) If an agricultural lease is required, and possession is taken without an agricultural lease by a party other than an Indian landowner of the tract, we will treat the unauthorized use as a trespass. Unless we have reason to believe that the party in possession is engaged in negotiations with the Indian landowners to obtain an agricultural lease, we will take action to recover possession on behalf of the Indian landowners, and pursue any additional remedies available under applicable law.

(b) Where a trespass involves Indian agricultural land, we will also assess civil penalties and costs under part 166, subpart I, of this chapter.

[66 FR 7109, Jan. 22, 2001, as amended at 77 FR 72474, Dec. 5, 2012; 78 FR 19100, Mar. 29, 2013]

§ 162.107 What are BIA's objectives in granting or approving agricultural leases?

We will assist Indian landowners in leasing their land for agricultural purposes. For the purposes of §§162.102 through 162.256:

(a) We will assist Indian landowners in leasing their land, either through negotiations or advertisement. In reviewing a negotiated lease for approval, we will defer to the landowners' determination that the lease is in their best interest, to the maximum extent possible. In granting a lease on the landowners' behalf, we will obtain a fair annual rental and attempt to ensure (through proper notice) that the use of the land is consistent with the landowners' wishes. We will also recognize the rights of Indian landowners to use their own land, so long as their Indian co-owners are in agreement and the value of the land is preserved.

(b) We will recognize the governing authority of the tribe having jurisdiction over the land to be leased, preparing and advertising leases in accordance with applicable tribal laws and policies. We will promote tribal control and self-determination over tribal land and other land under the tribe's jurisdiction, through contracts and self-governance compacts entered into under the Indian Self-Determination and Education Assistance Act, as amended, 25 U.S.C. § 450f *et seq.*

[66 FR 7109, Jan. 22, 2001, as amended at 77 FR 72474, Dec. 5, 2012]

§ 162.108 What are BIA's responsibilities in administering and enforcing agricultural leases?

(a) We will ensure that tenants meet their payment obligations to Indian landowners, through the collection of rent on behalf of the landowners and the prompt initiation of appropriate collection and enforcement actions. We will also assist landowners in the enforcement of payment obligations that run directly to them, and in the exercise of any negotiated remedies that apply in addition to specific remedies made available to us under these or other regulations.

(b) We will ensure that tenants comply with the operating requirements in their agricultural leases, through appropriate inspections and enforcement actions as needed to protect the interests of the Indian landowners and respond to concerns expressed by them. We will take immediate action to recover possession from trespassers operating without an agricultural lease, and take other emergency action as needed to preserve the value of the land.

[66 FR 7109, Jan. 22, 2001, as amended at 77 FR 72474, Dec. 5, 2012]

§ 162.109 What laws, other than these regulations, will apply to agricultural leases granted or approved under this part?

(a) Agricultural leases granted or approved under this part will be subject to federal laws of general applicability and any specific federal statutory requirements that are not incorporated in these regulations.

(b) Tribal laws generally apply to land under the jurisdiction of the tribe enacting such laws, except to the extent that those tribal laws are inconsistent with these regulations or other applicable federal law. These regulations may be superseded or modified by tribal laws, however, so long as:

(1) The tribal laws are consistent with the enacting tribe's governing documents;

(2) The tribe has notified us of the superseding or modifying effect of the tribal laws;

(3) The superseding or modifying of the regulation would not violate a federal statute or judicial decision, or conflict with our general trust responsibility under federal law; and

(4) The superseding or modifying of the regulation applies only to tribal land.

(c) State law may apply to agricultural lease disputes or define the remedies available to the Indian landowners in the event of an agricultural lease violation by the tenant, if the agricultural lease so provides and the Indian landowners have expressly agreed to the application of state law.

[66 FR 7109, Jan. 22, 2001, as amended at 77 FR 72474, Dec. 5, 2012]

§ 162.110 Can these regulations be administered by tribes, on the Secretary's or on BIA's behalf?

Except insofar as these regulations provide for the granting, approval, or enforcement of agricultural leases and permits, the provisions in these regulations that authorize or require us to take certain actions will extend to any tribe or tribal organization that is administering specific programs or providing specific services under a contract or self-governance compact entered into under the Indian Self-Determination and Education Assistance Act (25 U.S.C. § 450f *et seq.*).

[66 FR 7109, Jan. 22, 2001, as amended at 77 FR 72474, Dec. 5, 2012]

§ 162.111 Who owns the records associated with this subpart?

(a) Records associated with this subpart are the property of the United States if they:

(1) Are made or received by a tribe or tribal organization in the conduct of a federal trust function under 25 U.S.C. § 450f *et seq.*, including the operation of a trust program; and

(2) Evidence the organization, functions, policies, decisions, procedures, operations, or other activities undertaken in the performance of a federal trust function under this part.

(b) Records associated with this subpart not covered by paragraph (a) of this section that are made or received by a tribe or tribal organization in the conduct of business with the Department of the Interior under this subpart are the property of the tribe.

[66 FR 7109, Jan. 22, 2001, as amended at 77 FR 72474, Dec. 5, 2012]

§ 162.112 How must records associated with this part be preserved?

(a) Any organization, including tribes and tribal organizations, that have records identified in § 162.111(a) must preserve the records in accordance with approved Departmental records retention procedures under the Federal Records Act, 44 U.S.C. Chapters 29, 31 and 33. These records and related records management practices and safeguards required under the Federal Records Act are subject to inspection by the Secretary and the Archivist of the United States.

(b) A tribe or tribal organization should preserve the records identified in § 162.111(b) for the period of time authorized by the Archivist of the United States for similar Department of the Interior records in accordance with 44 U.S.C. Chapter 33. If a tribe or tribal organization does not preserve records associated with its conduct of business with the Department of the Interior under this part, it may prevent the tribe or tribal organization from being able to adequately document essential transactions or furnish information necessary to protect its legal and financial rights or those of persons directly affected by its activities.

§ 162.113 May decisions under this subpart be appealed?

Yes. Except where otherwise provided in this subpart, appeals from decisions by the BIA under this subpart may be taken pursuant to 25 CFR subpart 2.

[66 FR 7109, Jan. 22, 2001, as amended at 77 FR 72474, Dec. 5, 2012]

General Provisions

§ 162.200 What types of leases are covered by this subpart?

The regulations in this subpart apply to agricultural leases, as defined in this part. The regulations in this subpart may also apply to business leases on agricultural land, where appropriate.

§ 162.201 Must agricultural land be managed in accordance with a tribe's agricultural resource management plan?

(a) Agricultural land under the jurisdiction of a tribe must be managed in accordance with the goals and objectives in any agricultural resource management plan developed by the tribe, or by us in close consultation with the tribe, under AIARMA.

(b) A ten-year agricultural resource management and monitoring plan must be developed through public meetings and completed within three years of the initiation of the planning activity. Such a plan must be developed through public meetings, and be based on the public meeting records and existing survey documents, reports, and other research from federal agencies, tribal community colleges, and land grant universities. When completed, the plan must:

(1) Determine available agricultural resources;

(2) Identify specific tribal agricultural resource goals and objectives;

(3) Establish management objectives for the resources;

(4) Define critical values of the Indian tribe and its members and identify holistic management objectives; and

(5) Identify actions to be taken to reach established objectives.

(c) Where the regulations in this subpart are inconsistent with a tribe's agricultural resource management plan, we may waive the regulations under part 1 of this title, so long as the waiver does not violate a federal statute or judicial decision or conflict with our general trust responsibility under federal law.

§ 162.202 How will tribal laws be enforced on agricultural land?

(a) Unless prohibited by federal law, we will recognize and comply with tribal laws regulating activities on agricultural land, including tribal laws relating to land use, environmental protection, and historic or cultural preservation.

(b) While the tribe is primarily responsible for enforcing tribal laws pertaining to agricultural land, we will:

(1) Assist in the enforcement of tribal laws;

(2) Provide notice of tribal laws to persons or entities undertaking activities on agricultural land, under § 162.204(c) of this subpart; and

(3) Require appropriate federal officials to appear in tribal forums when requested by the tribe, so long as such an appearance would not:

(i) Be inconsistent with the restrictions on employee testimony set forth at 43 CFR Part 2, Subpart E;

(ii) Constitute a waiver of the sovereign immunity of the United States; or

(iii) Authorize or result in a review of our actions by a tribal court.

(c) Where the regulations in this subpart are inconsistent with a tribal law, but such regulations cannot be superseded or modified by the tribal law under § 162.109 of this part, we may waive the regulations under part 1 of this chapter, so long as the waiver does not violate a federal statute or judicial decision or conflict with our general trust responsibility under federal law.

§ 162.203 When can the regulations in this subpart be superseded or modified by tribal laws and leasing policies?

(a) The regulations in this subpart may be superseded or modified by tribal laws, under the circumstances described in § 162.109(b) of this part.

(b) When specifically authorized by an appropriate tribal resolution establishing a general policy for the leasing of tribal and individually-owned agricultural land, we will:

(1) Waive the general prohibition against tenant preferences in leases advertised for bid under § 162.212 of this subpart, by allowing prospective Indian tenants to match the highest responsible bid (unless the tribal leasing policy specifies some other manner in which the preference must be afforded);

(2) Waive the requirement that a tenant post a bond under § 162.234 of this subpart;

(3) Modify the requirement that a tenant post a bond in a form described in § 162.235 of this subpart;

(4) Approve leases of tribal land at rates established by the tribe, as provided in § 162.222(b) of this subpart.

(c) When specifically authorized by an appropriate tribal resolution establishing a general policy for the leasing of "highly fractionated undivided heirship lands" (as defined in the tribal leasing policy), we may waive or modify the three-month notice requirement in § 162.209(b) of this subpart, so long as:

(1) The tribal law or leasing policy adopts an alternative plan for providing notice to Indian landowners, before an agricultural lease is granted by us on their behalf; and

(2) A waiver or modification of the three-month notice requirement is needed to prevent waste, reduce idle land acreage, and ensure lease income to the Indian landowners.

(d) Tribal leasing policies of the type described in paragraphs (b) through (c) of this section will not apply to individually-owned land that has been made exempt from such laws or policies under § 162.205 of this subpart.

§ 162.204 Must notice of applicable tribal laws and leasing policies be provided?

(a) A tribe must provide us with an official copy of any tribal law or leasing policy that supersedes or modifies these regulations under §§ 162.109 or 162.203 of this part. If the tribe has not already done so, we will provide notice of such a tribal law or leasing policy to affected Indian landowners and persons or entities undertaking activities on agricultural land. Such notice will be provided in the manner described in paragraphs (b) through (c) of this section.

(b) We will provide notice to Indian landowners, as to the superseding or modifying effect of any tribal leasing policy and their right to exempt their land from such a policy. Such notice will be provided by:

(1) Written notice included in a notice of our intent to lease the land, issued under § 162.209(b) of this subpart; or

(2) Public notice posted at the tribal community building or the United States Post Office, or published in the local newspaper that serves the area in which the Indian owners' land is located, at the time the tribal leasing policy is adopted.

(c) We will provide notice to persons or entities undertaking activities on agricultural land, as to the general applicability of tribal laws and the superseding or modifying effect of particular tribal laws and leasing policies. Such notice will be provided by:

(1) Written notice included in advertisements for lease, issued under § 162.212 of this subpart; or

(2) Public notice posted at the tribal community building or the United States Post Office, or published in a local newspaper of general circulation, at the time the tribal law is enacted or the leasing policy adopted.

§ 162.205 Can individual Indian landowners exempt their agricultural land from certain tribal leasing policies?

(a) Individual Indian landowners may exempt their agricultural land from the application of a tribal leasing policy of a type described in § 162.203(b) through (c) of this subpart, if the Indian owners of at least 50% of the trust or restricted interests in the land submit a written objection to us before a lease is granted or approved.

(b) Upon our receipt of a written objection from the Indian landowners that satisfies the requirements of paragraph (a) of this section, we will notify the tribe that the owners' land has been exempted from a specific tribal leasing policy. If the exempted land is part of a unitized lease tract, such land will be removed from the unit and leased separately, if appropriate.

(c) The procedures described in paragraphs (a) and (b) of this section will also apply to withdrawing an approved exemption.

How to Obtain a Lease

§ 162.206 Can the terms of an agricultural lease be negotiated with the Indian landowners?

An agricultural lease may be obtained through negotiation. We will assist prospective tenants in contacting the Indian landowners or their representatives for the purpose of negotiating a lease, and we will assist the landowners in those negotiations upon request.

§ 162.207 When can the Indian landowners grant an agricultural lease?

(a) Tribes grant leases of tribally-owned agricultural land, including any tribally-owned undivided interest(s) in a fractionated tract, subject to our approval. Where tribal land is subject to a land assignment made to a tribal member or some other individual under tribal law or custom, the individual and the tribe must both grant the lease, subject to our approval.

(b) Adult Indian owners, or emancipated minors, may grant agricultural leases of their land, including undivided interests in fractionated tracts, subject to our approval.

(c) An agricultural lease of a fractionated tract may be granted by the owners of a majority interest in the tract, subject to our approval. Although prior notice to non-consenting individual Indian landowners is generally not needed prior to our approval of such a lease, a right of first refusal must be offered to any non-consenting Indian landowner who is using the entire lease tract at the time the lease is entered into by the owners of a majority interest. Where the owners of a majority interest grant such a lease on behalf of all of the Indian owners of a fractionated tract, the non-consenting Indian landowners must receive a fair annual rental.

(d) As part of the negotiation of a lease, Indian landowners may advertise their land to identify potential tenants with whom to negotiate.

§ 162.208 Who can represent the Indian landowners in negotiating or granting an agricultural lease?

The following individuals or entities may represent an individual Indian landowner:

(a) An adult with custody acting on behalf of his or her minor children;

(b) A guardian, conservator, or other fiduciary appointed by a court of competent jurisdiction to act on behalf of an individual Indian landowner;

(c) An adult or legal entity who has been given a written power of attorney that:

(1) Meets all of the formal requirements of any applicable tribal or state law;

(2) Identifies the attorney-in-fact and the land to be leased; and

(3) Describes the scope of the power granted and any limits thereon.

§ 162.209 When can BIA grant an agricultural lease on behalf of an Indian landowner?

(a) We may grant an agricultural lease on behalf of:

(1) Individuals who are found to be non compos mentis by a court of competent jurisdiction;

(2) Orphaned minors;

(3) The undetermined heirs and devisees of deceased Indian owners;

(4) Individuals who have given us a written power of attorney to lease their land; and

(5) Individuals whose whereabouts are unknown to us, after reasonable attempts are made to locate such individuals; and

(6) The individual Indian landowners of fractionated Indian land, when necessary to protect the interests of the individual Indian landowners.

(b) We may grant an agricultural lease on behalf of all of the individual Indian owners of a fractionated tract, where:

(1) We have provided the Indian landowners with written notice of our intent to grant a lease on their behalf, but the Indian landowners are unable to agree upon a lease during a three-month negotiation period immediately following such notice, or any other notice period established by a tribe under § 162.203(c) of this subpart; and

(2) The land is not being used by an Indian landowner under § 162.104(b) of this part.

§ 162.210 When can BIA grant a permit covering agricultural land?

(a) We may grant a permit covering agricultural land in the same manner as we would grant an agricultural lease under § 162.209 of this part. We may also grant a permit on behalf of individual Indian landowners, without prior notice, if it is impractical to provide notice to the owners and no substantial injury to the land will occur.

(b) We may grant a permit covering agricultural land, but not an agricultural lease, on government land.

(c) We will not grant a permit on tribal agricultural land, but a tribe may grant a permit, subject to our approval, in the same manner as it would grant a lease under § 162.207(a) of this subpart.

§ 162.211 What type of valuation or evaluation methods will be applied in estimating the fair annual rental of Indian land?

(a) To support the Indian landowners in their negotiations, and to assist in our consideration of whether an agricultural lease is in the Indian landowners' best interest, we must determine the fair annual rental of the land prior to our grant or approval of the lease, unless the land may be leased at less than a fair annual rental under § 162.222(b) through (c) of this subpart.

(b) A fair annual rental may be determined by competitive bidding, appraisal, or any other appropriate valuation method. Where an appraisal or other valuation is needed to determine the fair annual rental, the appraisal or valuation must be prepared in accordance with USPAP.

§ 162.212 When will the BIA advertise Indian land for agricultural leases?

(a) We will generally advertise Indian land for agricultural leasing:

(1) At the request of the Indian landowners; or

(2) Before we grant a lease under § 162.209(b) of this subpart.

(b) Advertisements will provide prospective tenants with notice of any superseding tribal laws and leasing policies that have been made applicable to the land under §§ 162.109 and 162.203 of this part, along with certain standard terms and conditions to be included in the lease. Advertisements will prohibit tenant preferences, and bidders at lease sales will not be afforded any preference, unless a preference in favor of individual Indians is required by a superseding tribal law or leasing policy.

(c) Advertisements will require sealed bids, and they may also provide for further competitive bidding among the prospective tenants at the conclusion of the bid opening. Competitive bidding should be supported, at a minimum, by a market study or rent survey that is consistent with USPAP.

§ 162.213 What supporting documents must be provided prior to BIA's grant or approval of an agricultural lease?

(a) If the tenant is a corporation, partnership or other legal entity, it must provide organizational and financial documents, as needed to show that the lease will be enforceable against the tenant and the tenant will be able to perform all of its lease obligations.

(b) Where a bond is required under § 162.234 of this subpart, the bond must be furnished before we grant or approve the lease.

(c) The tenant must provide environmental and archaeological reports, surveys, and site assessments, as needed to document compliance with NEPA and other applicable federal and tribal land use requirements.

§ 162.214 How and when will BIA decide whether to approve an agricultural lease?

(a) Before we approve a lease, we must determine in writing that the lease is in the best interest of the Indian landowners. In making that determination, we will:

(1) Review the lease and supporting documents;

(2) Identify potential environmental impacts and ensure compliance with all applicable environmental laws, land use laws, and ordinances (including preparation of the appropriate review documents under NEPA);

(3) Assure ourselves that adequate consideration has been given, as appropriate, to:

(i) The relationship between the use of the leased premises and the use of neighboring lands;

(ii) The height, quality, and safety of any structures or other facilities to be constructed on the leased premises;

(iii) The availability of police and fire protection, utilities, and other essential community services;

(iv) The availability of judicial forums for all criminal and civil matters arising on the leased premises; and

(v) The effect on the environment of the proposed land use.

(4) Require any lease modifications or mitigation measures that are needed to satisfy any requirements of this subpart, or any other federal or tribal land use requirements.

(b) Where an agricultural lease is in a form that has previously been accepted or approved by us, and all of the documents needed to support the findings required by paragraph (a) of this section have been received, we will decide whether to approve the lease within 30 days of the date of our receipt of the lease and supporting documents. If we decide to approve or disapprove a lease, we will notify the parties immediately and advise them of their right to appeal the decision under part 2 of this chapter. Copies of agricultural leases that have been approved will be provided to the tenant, and made available to the Indian landowners upon request.

§ 162.215 When will an agricultural lease be effective?

Unless otherwise provided in the lease, an agricultural lease will be effective on the date on which the lease is approved by us. An agricultural lease may be made effective on some past or future date, by agreement, but such a lease may not be approved more than one year prior to the date on which the lease term is to commence.

§ 162.216 When will a BIA decision to approve an agricultural lease be effective?

Our decision to approve an agricultural lease will be effective immediately, notwithstanding any appeal that may be filed under part 2 of this chapter.

§ 162.217 Must an agricultural lease or permit be recorded?

(a) An agricultural lease or permit must be recorded in our Land Titles and Records Office with jurisdiction over the land. We will record the lease or permit immediately following our approval under this subpart.

(b) Agricultural leases of tribal land that do not require our approval, under § 162.102 of this part, must be recorded by the tribe in our Land Titles and Records Office with jurisdiction over the land.

LEASE REQUIREMENTS

§ 162.218 Is there a standard agricultural lease form?

Based on the need for flexibility in advertising, negotiating and drafting of appropriate lease terms and conditions, there is no standard agricultural lease form that must be used. We will assist the Indian landowners in drafting lease provisions that conform to the requirements of this part.

§ 162.219 Are there any provisions that must be included in an agricultural lease?

In addition to the other requirements of this part, all agricultural leases must provide that:

(a) The obligations of the tenant and its sureties to the Indian landowners will also be enforceable by the United States, so long as the land remains in trust or restricted status;

(b) Nothing contained in this lease shall operate to delay or prevent a termination of federal trust responsibilities with respect to the land by the issuance of a fee patent or otherwise during the term of the lease; however, such termination shall not serve to abrogate the lease. The owners of the land and the lessee and his surety or sureties shall be notified of any such change in the status of the land;

(c) There must not be any unlawful conduct, creation of a nuisance, illegal activity, or negligent use or waste of the leased premises; and

(d) The tenant must comply with all applicable laws, ordinances, rules, regulations, and other legal requirements, including tribal laws and leasing policies.

§ 162.220 Are there any formal requirements that must be satisfied in the execution of an agricultural lease?

(a) An agricultural lease must identify the Indian landowners and their respective interests in the leased premises, and the lease must be granted by or on behalf of each of the Indian landowners. One who executes a lease in a representative capacity under § 162.208 of this subpart must identify the owner being represented and the authority under which such action is being taken.

(b) An agricultural lease must be executed by individuals having the necessary capacity and authority to bind the tenant under applicable law.

(c) An agricultural lease must include a citation of the provisions in this subpart that authorize our approval, along with a citation of the formal documents by which such authority has been delegated to the official taking such action.

§ 162.221 How should the land be described in an agricultural lease?

An agricultural lease should describe the leased premises by reference to a public or private survey, if possible. If the land cannot be so described, the lease must include a legal description or other description that is sufficient to identify the leased premises, subject to our approval. Where there are undivided interests owned in fee status, the aggregate portion of trust and restricted interests should be identified in the description of the leased premises.

§ 162.222 How much rent must be paid under an agricultural lease?

(a) An agricultural lease must provide for the payment of a fair annual rental at the beginning of the lease term, unless a lesser amount is permitted under paragraphs (b) through (d) of this section. The tenant's rent payments may be:

(1) In fixed amounts; or

(2) Based on a share of the agricultural products generated by the lease,

or a percentage of the income to be derived from the sale of such agricultural products.

(b) We will approve an agricultural lease of tribal land at a nominal rent, or at less than a fair annual rental, if such a rent is negotiated or established by the tribe.

(c) We will approve an agricultural lease of individually-owned land at a nominal rent or at less than a fair annual rental, if:

(1) The tenant is a member of the Indian landowner's immediate family, or a co-owner in the lease tract; or

(2) The tenant is a cooperative or other legal entity in which the Indian landowners directly participate in the revenues or profits generated by the lease.

(d) We will grant or approve a lease at less than a fair annual rental, as previously determined by an appraisal or some other appropriate valuation method, if the land is subsequently advertised and the tenant is the highest responsible bidder.

§ 162.223 Must the rent be adjusted under an agricultural lease?

(a) Except as provided in paragraph (c) of this section, an agricultural lease must provide for one or more rental adjustments if the lease term runs more than five years, unless the lease provides for the payment of:

(1) Less than a fair annual rental, as permitted under § 162.222(b) through (c) of this part; or

(2) A rental based primarily on a share of the agricultural products generated by the lease, or a percentage of the income derived from the sale of agricultural products.

(b) If rental adjustments are required, the lease must specify:

(1) How adjustments are made;

(2) Who makes the adjustments;

(3) When the adjustments are effective; and

(4) How disputes about the adjustments are resolved.

(c) An agricultural lease of tribal land may run for a term of more than five years, without providing for a rental adjustment, if the tribe establishes such a policy under § 162.203(b)(4) and negotiates such a lease.

§ 162.224 When are rent payments due under an agricultural lease?

An agricultural lease must specify the dates on which all rent payments are due. Unless otherwise provided in the lease, rent payments may not be made or accepted more than one year in advance of the due date. Rent payments are due at the time specified in the lease, regardless of whether the tenant receives an advance billing or other notice that a payment is due.

§ 162.225 Will untimely rent payments made under an agricultural lease be subject to interest charges or late payment penalties?

An agricultural lease must specify the rate at which interest will accrue on any rent payment not made by the due date or any other date specified in the lease. A lease may also identify additional late payment penalties that will apply if a rent payment is not made by a specified date. Unless otherwise provided in the lease, such interest charges and late payment penalties will apply in the absence of any specific notice to the tenant from us or the Indian landowners, and the failure to pay such amounts will be treated as a lease violation under § 162.251 of this subpart.

§ 162.226 To whom can rent payments be made under an agricultural lease?

(a) An agricultural lease must specify whether rent payments will be made directly to the Indian landowners or to us on behalf of the Indian landowners. If the lease provides for payment to be made directly to the Indian landowners, the lease must also require that the tenant retain specific documentation evidencing proof of payment, such as canceled checks, cash receipt vouchers, or copies of money orders or cashier's checks, consistent with the provisions of §§ 162.112 and 162.113 of this part.

(b) Rent payments made directly to the Indian landowners must be made to the parties specified in the lease, unless the tenant receives notice of a change of ownership. Unless otherwise provided in the lease, rent payments may not be made payable directly to anyone other than the Indian landowners.

(c) A lease that provides for rent payments to be made directly to the Indian landowners must also provide for such payments to be suspended and the rent thereafter paid to us, rather than directly to the Indian landowners, if:

(1) An Indian landowner dies;

(2) An Indian landowner requests that payment be made to us;

(3) An Indian landowner is found by us to be in need of assistance in managing his/her financial affairs; or

(4) We determine, in our discretion and after consultation with the Indian landowner(s), that direct payment should be discontinued.

§ 162.227 What form of rent payment can be accepted under an agricultural lease?

(a) When rent payments are made directly to the Indian landowners, the form of payment must be acceptable to the Indian landowners.

(b) Payments made to us may be delivered in person or by mail. We will not accept cash, foreign currency, or third-party checks. We will accept:

(1) Personal or business checks drawn on the account of the tenant;

(2) Money orders;

(3) Cashier's checks;

(4) Certified checks; or

(5) Electronic funds transfer payments.

§ 162.228 What other types of payments are required under an agricultural lease?

(a) The tenant may be required to pay additional fees, taxes, and/or assessments associated with the use of the land, as determined by the tribe having jurisdiction over the land. The tenant must pay these amounts to the appropriate tribal official.

(b) Except as otherwise provided in part 171 of this chapter, if the leased premises are within an Indian irrigation project or drainage district, the tenant must pay all operation and maintenance charges that accrue during the lease term. The tenant must pay these amounts to the appropriate official in charge of the irrigation project or drainage district. Failure to make such payments will constitute a violation of the lease under § 162.251.

§ 162.229 How long can the term of an agricultural lease run?

(a) An agricultural lease must provide for a definite lease term, specifying the commencement date. The commencement date of the lease may not be more than one year after the date on which the lease is approved.

(b) The lease term must be reasonable, given the purpose of the lease and the level of investment required. Unless otherwise provided by statute, the maximum term may not exceed ten years, unless a substantial investment in the improvement of the land is required. If such a substantial investment is required, the maximum term may be up to 25 years.

(c) Where all of the trust or restricted interests in a tract are owned by a deceased Indian whose heirs and devisees have not yet been determined, the maximum term may not exceed two years.

(d) An agricultural lease may not provide the tenant with an option to renew, and such a lease may not be renewed or extended by holdover.

§ 162.230 Can an agricultural lease be amended, assigned, sublet, or mortgaged?

(a) An agricultural lease may authorize amendments, assignments, subleases, or mortgages of the leasehold interest, but only with the written consent of the parties to the lease in the same manner the original lease was approved, and our approval. An attempt by the tenant to mortgage the leasehold interest or authorize possession by another party, without the necessary consent and approval, will be treated as a lease violation under § 162.251 of this subpart.

(b) An agricultural lease may authorize us, one or more of the Indian landowners, or a designated representative of the Indian landowners, to consent to an amendment, assignment, sublease, mortgage, or other type of agreement, on the landowners' behalf. A designated landowner or representative may not negotiate or consent to an amendment, assignment, or sublease that would:

(1) Reduce the rentals payable to the other Indian landowners; or

(2) Terminate or modify the term of the lease.

(c) Where the Indian landowners have not designated a representative for the purpose of consenting to an amendment, assignment, sublease, mortgage, or other type of agreement, such consent may be granted by or on behalf of the landowners in the same manner as a new lease, under §§ 162.207 through 162.209 of this subpart.

§ 162.231 How can the land be used under an agricultural lease?

(a) An agricultural lease must describe the authorized uses of the leased premises. Any use of the leased premises for an unauthorized purpose, or a failure by the tenant to maintain continuous operations throughout the lease term, will be treated as a lease violation under § 162.251 of this subpart.

(b) An agricultural lease must require that farming and grazing operations be conducted in accordance with recognized principles of sustained yield management, integrated resource management planning, sound conservation practices, and other community goals as expressed in applicable tribal laws, leasing policies, or agricultural resource management plans. Appropriate stipulations or conservation plans must be developed and incorporated in all agricultural leases.

§ 162.232 Can improvements be made under an agricultural lease?

An agricultural lease must generally describe the type and location of any improvements to be constructed by the lessee. Unless otherwise provided in the lease, any specific plans for the construction of those improvements will not require the consent of the Indian owners or our approval.

§ 162.233 Who will own the improvements made under an agricultural lease?

(a) An agricultural lease may specify who will own any improvements constructed by the tenant, during the lease term. The lease must indicate whether any improvements constructed by the tenant will remain on the leased premises upon the expiration or termination of the lease, providing for the improvements to either:

(1) Remain on the leased premises, in a condition satisfactory to the Indian landowners and us; or

(2) Be removed within a time period specified in the lease, at the tenant's expense, with the leased premises to be restored as close as possible to their condition prior to construction of such improvements.

(b) If the lease allows the tenant to remove the improvements, it must also provide the Indian landowners with an option to waive the removal requirement and take possession of the improvements if they are not removed within the specified time period. If the Indian landowners choose not to exercise this option, we will take appropriate enforcement action to ensure removal at the tenant's expense.

§ 162.234 Must a tenant provide a bond under an agricultural lease?

Unless otherwise provided by a tribe under § 162.203 of this subpart, or waived by us at the request of the owners of a majority interest in an agricultural lease tract, the tenant must provide a bond to secure:

(a) The payment of one year's rental;

(b) The construction of any required improvements;

(c) The performance of any additional lease obligations, including the payment of operation and maintenance charges under § 162.228(b) of this subpart; and

(d) The restoration and reclamation of the leased premises, to their condition at the commencement of the lease term or some other specified condition.

§ 162.235 What form of bond can be accepted under an agricultural lease?

(a) Except as provided in paragraph (b) of this section, a bond must be deposited with us and made payable only to us, and such a bond may not be modified or withdrawn without our approval. We will only accept a bond in one of the following forms:

(1) Cash;

(2) Negotiable Treasury securities that:

(i) Have a market value at least equal to the bond amount; and

(ii) Are accompanied by a statement granting full authority to us to sell such securities in case of a violation of the terms of the lease.

(3) Certificates of deposit that indicate on their face that our approval is required prior to redemption by any party;

(4) Irrevocable letters of credit issued by federally-insured financial institutions authorized to do business in the United States. A letter of credit must:

(i) Contain a clause that grants us the authority to demand immediate payment if the tenant violates the lease or fails to replace the letter of credit at least 30 days prior to its expiration date;

(ii) Be payable to us;

(iii) Be irrevocable during its term and have an initial expiration date of not less than one year following the date of issuance; and

(iv) Be automatically renewable for a period of not less than one year, unless the issuing financial institution provides us with written notice that it will not be renewed, at least 90 calendar days before the letter of credit's expiration date.

(5) A surety bond issued by a company approved by the U.S. Department of the Treasury; or

(6) Any other form of highly liquid, non-volatile security that is easily convertible to cash and for which our approval is required prior to redemption by any party.

(b) A tribe may accept and hold any form of bond described in paragraph (a) of this section, to secure performance under an agricultural lease of tribal land.

§ 162.236 How will a cash bond be administered?

(a) If a cash bond is submitted, we will retain the funds in an account established in the name of the tenant.

(b) We will not pay interest on a cash performance bond.

(c) If the bond is not forfeited under § 162.252(a) of this subpart, we will refund the bond to the tenant upon the expiration or termination of the lease.

§ 162.237 What insurance is required under an agricultural lease?

When necessary to protect the interests of the Indian landowners, an agricultural lease must require that a tenant provide insurance. Such insurance may include property, crop, liability and/or casualty insurance. If insurance is required, it must identify both the Indian landowners and the United States as insured parties, and be sufficient to protect all insurable improvements on the leased premises.

§ 162.238 What indemnities are required under an agricultural lease?

(a) An agricultural lease must require that the tenant indemnify and hold the United States and the Indian landowners harmless from any loss, liability, or damages resulting from the tenant's use or occupation of the leased premises, unless:

(1) The tenant would be prohibited by law from making such an agreement; or (2) The interests of the Indian landowners are adequately protected by insurance.

(b) Unless the tenant would be prohibited by law from making such an agreement, an agricultural lease must specifically require that the tenant indemnify the United States and the Indian landowners against all liabilities or costs relating to the use, handling, treatment, removal, storage, transportation, or disposal of hazardous materials, or the release or discharge of any hazardous materials from the leased premises that occurs during the lease term, regardless of fault.

§ 162.239 How will payment rights and obligations relating to agricultural land be allocated between the Indian landowners and the tenant?

(a) Unless otherwise provided in an agricultural lease, the Indian landowners will be entitled to receive any settlement funds or other payments arising from certain actions that diminish the value of the land or the improvements thereon. Such payments may include (but are not limited to) :

(1) Insurance proceeds;

(2) Trespass damages; and

(3) Condemnation awards.

(b) An agricultural lease may provide for the tenant to assume certain cost-share or other payment obligations that have attached to the land through past farming and grazing operations, so long as those obligations are specified in the lease and considered in any determination of fair annual rental made under this subpart.

§ 162.240 Can an agricultural lease provide for negotiated remedies in the event of a violation?

(a) A lease of tribal agricultural land may provide the tribe with certain negotiated remedies in the event of a lease violation, including the power to terminate the lease. An agricultural lease of individually-owned land may provide the individual Indian landowners with similar remedies, so long as the lease also specifies the manner in which those remedies may be exercised by or on behalf of the landowners.

(b) The negotiated remedies described in paragraph (a) of this section will apply in addition to the cancellation remedy available to us under § 162.252(c) of this subpart. If the lease specifically authorizes us to exercise any negotiated remedies on behalf of the Indian landowners, the exercise of such remedies may substitute for cancellation.

(c) An agricultural lease may provide for lease disputes to be resolved in tribal court or any other court of competent jurisdiction, or through arbitration or some other alternative dispute resolution method. We may not be bound by decisions made in such forums, but we will defer to ongoing proceedings, as appropriate, in deciding whether to exercise any of the remedies available to us under § 162.252 of this subpart.

LEASE ADMINISTRATION

§ 162.241 Will administrative fees be charged for actions relating to agricultural leases?

(a) We will charge an administrative fee each time we approve an agricultural lease, amendment, assignment, sublease, mortgage, or related document. These fees will be paid by the tenant, assignee, or subtenant, to cover our costs in preparing or processing the documents and administering the lease.

(b) Except as provided in paragraph (c) of this section, we will charge administrative fees based on the rent payable under the lease. The fee will be 3% of the annual rent payable, including any percentage-based rent that can be reasonably estimated.

(c) The minimum administrative fee is $10.00 and the maximum administrative fee is $500.00, and any administrative fees that have been paid will be non-refundable. However, we may waive all or part of these administrative fees, in our discretion.

(d) If all or part of the expenses of the work are paid from tribal funds, the tribe may establish an additional or alternate schedule of fees.

§ 162.242 How will BIA decide whether to approve an amendment to an agricultural lease?

We will approve an agricultural lease amendment if:

(a) The required consents have been obtained from the parties to the lease under § 162.230 and any sureties; and

(b) We find the amendment to be in the best interest of the Indian landowners, under the standards set forth in § 162.213 of this subpart.

§ 162.243 How will BIA decide whether to approve an assignment or sublease under an agricultural lease?

(a) We will approve an assignment or sublease under an agricultural lease if:

(1) The required consents have been obtained from the parties to the lease under § 162.230 and the tenant's sureties;

(2) The tenant is not in violation of the lease;

(3) The assignee agrees to be bound by, or the subtenant agrees to be subordinated to, the terms of the lease; and

(4) We find no compelling reason to withhold our approval in order to protect the best interests of the Indian owners.

(b) In making the finding required by paragraph (a)(4) of this section, we will consider whether:

(1) The Indian landowners should receive any income derived by the tenant from the assignment or sublease, under the terms of the lease;

(2) The proposed use by the assignee or subtenant will require an amendment of the lease;

(3) The value of any part of the leased premises not covered by the assignment or sublease would be adversely affected; and

(4) The assignee or subtenant has bonded its performance and provided supporting documents that demonstrate that the lease or sublease will be enforceable against the assignee or subtenant, and that the assignee or subtenant will be able to perform its obligations under the lease or sublease.

§ 162.244 How will BIA decide whether to approve a leasehold mortgage under an agricultural lease?

(a) We will approve a leasehold mortgage under an agricultural lease if:

(1) The required consents have been obtained from the parties to the lease under § 162.230 and the tenant's sureties;

(2) The mortgage covers only the tenant's interest in the leased premises, and no unrelated collateral;

(3) The loan being secured by the mortgage will be used only in connection with the development or use of the leased premises, and the mortgage does not secure any unrelated debts owed by the tenant to the mortgagee; and

(4) We find no compelling reason to withhold our approval in order to protect the best interests of the Indian landowners.

(b) In making the finding required by paragraph (a)(4) of this section, we will consider whether:

(1) The tenant's ability to comply with the lease would be adversely affected by any new loan obligations;

(2) Any lease provisions would be modified by the mortgage;

(3) The remedies available to us or to the Indian landowners would be limited (beyond any additional notice and cure rights to be afforded to the mortgagee), in the event of a lease violation; and

(4) Any rights of the Indian landowners would be subordinated or adversely affected in the event of a loan default by the tenant.

§ 162.245 When will a BIA decision to approve an amendment, assignment, sublease, or mortgage under an agricultural lease be effective?

Our decision to approve an amendment, assignment, sublease, or mortgage under an agricultural lease will be effective immediately, notwithstanding any appeal that may be filed under part 2 of this chapter. Copies of approved documents will be provided to the party requesting approval, and made available to the Indian landowners upon request.

§ 162.246 Must an amendment, assignment, sublease, or mortgage approved under an agricultural lease be recorded?

An amendment, assignment, sublease, or mortgage approved under an agricultural lease must be recorded in our Land Titles and Records Office that has jurisdiction over the leased premises. We will record the document immediately following our approval under this subpart.

LEASE ENFORCEMENT

§ 162.247 Will BIA notify a tenant when a rent payment is due under an agricultural lease?

We may issue bills or invoices to a tenant in advance of the dates on which rent payments are due under an agricultural lease, but the tenant's obligation to make such payments in a timely manner will not be excused if such bills or invoices are not delivered or received.

§ 162.248 What will BIA do if rent payments are not made in the time and manner required by an agricultural lease?

(a) A tenant's failure to pay rent in the time and manner required by an agricultural lease will be a violation of the lease, and a notice of violation will be issued under § 162.251 of this subpart. If the lease requires that rent payments be made to us, we will send the tenant and its sureties a notice of violation within five business days of the date on which the rent payment was due. If the lease provides for payment directly to the Indian landowners, we will send the tenant and its sureties a notice of violation within five business days of the date on which we receive actual notice of non-payment from the landowners.

(b) If a tenant fails to provide adequate proof of payment or cure the violation within the requisite time period described in § 162.251(b) of this subpart, and the amount due is not in dispute, we may immediately take action to recover the amount of the unpaid rent and any associated interest charges or late payment penalties. We may also cancel the lease under § 162.252 of this subpart, or invoke any other remedies available under the lease or applicable law, including collection on any available bond or referral of the debt to the Department of the Treasury for collection. An action to recover any unpaid amounts will not be conditioned on the prior cancellation of the lease or any further notice to the tenant, nor will such an action be precluded by a prior cancellation.

(c) Partial payments may be accepted by the Indian landowners or us, but acceptance will not operate as a waiver with respect to any amounts remaining unpaid or any other existing lease violations. Unless otherwise provided in the lease, overpayments may be credited as an advance against future rent payments, or refunded.

(d) If a personal or business check is dishonored, and a rent payment is therefore not made by the due date, the failure to make the payment in a timely manner will be a violation of the lease, and a notice of violation will be issued under § 162.251 of this subpart. Any payment made to cure such a violation, and any future payments by the same tenant, must be made by one of the alternative payment methods listed in § 162.227(b) of this subpart.

§ 162.249 Will any special fees be assessed on delinquent rent payments due under an agricultural lease?

The following special fees will be assessed if rent is not paid in the time and manner required, in addition to any interest or late payment penalties that must be paid to the Indian landowners under an agricultural lease. The following special fees will be assessed to cover administrative costs incurred by the United States in the collection of the debt:

The tenant will pay * * *	For * * *
(a) $50.00	Administrative fee for dishonored checks.
(b) $15.00	Administrative fee for BIA processing of each notice or demand letter.
(c) 18% of balance due.	Administrative fee charged by Treasury following referral for collection of delinquent debt.

§ 162.250 How will BIA determine whether the activities of a tenant under an agricultural lease are in compliance with the terms of the lease?

(a) Unless an agricultural lease provides otherwise, we may enter the leased premises at any reasonable time, without prior notice, to protect the interests of the Indian landowners and ensure that the tenant is in compliance with the operating requirements of the lease.

(b) If an Indian landowner notifies us that a specific lease violation has occurred, we will initiate an appropriate investigation within five business days of that notification.

§ 162.251 What will BIA do in the event of a violation under an agricultural lease?

(a) If we determine that an agricultural lease has been violated, we will send the tenant and its sureties a notice of violation within five business days of that determination. The notice of violation must be provided by certified mail, return receipt requested.

(b) Within ten business days of the receipt of a notice of violation, the tenant must:

(1) Cure the violation and notify us in writing that the violation has been cured;

(2) Dispute our determination that a violation has occurred and/or explain why we should not cancel the lease; or

(3) Request additional time to cure the violation.

§ 162.252 What will BIA do if a violation of an agricultural lease is not cured within the requisite time period?

(a) If the tenant does not cure a violation of an agricultural lease within the requisite time period, we will consult with the Indian landowners, as appropriate, and determine whether:

(1) The lease should be canceled by us under paragraph (c) of this section and §§ 162.253 through 162.254 of this subpart;

(2) We should invoke any other remedies available to us under the lease, including collecting on any available bond;

(3) The Indian landowners wish to invoke any remedies available to them under the lease; or

(4) The tenant should be granted additional time in which to cure the violation.

(b) If we decide to grant a tenant additional time in which to cure a violation, the tenant must proceed diligently to complete the necessary corrective actions within a reasonable or specified time period from the date on which the extension is granted.

(c) If we decide to cancel the lease, we will send the tenant and its sureties a cancellation letter within five business days of that decision. The cancellation letter must be sent to the tenant by certified mail, return receipt requested. We will also provide actual or constructive notice of a cancellation decision to the Indian landowners, as appropriate. The cancellation letter will:

(1) Explain the grounds for cancellation;

(2) Notify the tenant of the amount of any unpaid rent, interest charges, or late payment penalties due under the lease;

(3) Notify the tenant of its right to appeal under part 2 of this chapter, as modified by §162.253 of this subpart, including the amount of any appeal bond that must be posted with an appeal of the cancellation decision; and

(4) Order the tenant to vacate the property within 30 days of the date of receipt of the cancellation letter, if an appeal is not filed by that time.

§162.253 Will BIA's regulations concerning appeal bonds apply to cancellation decisions involving agricultural leases?

(a) The appeal bond provisions in §2.5 of part 2 of this chapter will not apply to appeals from lease cancellation decisions made under §162.252 of this subpart. Instead, when we decide to cancel an agricultural lease, we may require that the tenant post an appeal bond with an appeal of the cancellation decision. The requirement to post an appeal bond will apply in addition to all of the other requirements in part 2 of this chapter.

(b) An appeal bond should be set in an amount necessary to protect the Indian landowners against financial losses that will likely result from the delay caused by an appeal. Appeal bond requirements will not be separately appealable, but may be contested during the appeal of the lease cancellation decision.

§162.254 When will a cancellation of an agricultural lease be effective?

A cancellation decision involving an agricultural lease will not be effective until 30 days after the tenant receives a cancellation letter from us. The cancellation decision will remain ineffective if the tenant files an appeal under §162.253 of this subpart and part 2 of this chapter, unless the decision is made immediately effective under part 2. While a cancellation decision is ineffective, the tenant must continue to pay rent and comply with the other terms of the lease. If an appeal is not filed in accordance with §162.253 of this subpart and part 2 of this chapter, the cancellation decision will be effective on the 31st day after the tenant receives the cancellation letter from us.

§162.255 Can BIA take emergency action if the leased premises are threatened with immediate and significant harm?

If a tenant or any other party causes or threatens to cause immediate and significant harm to the leased premises during the term of an agricultural lease, we will take appropriate emergency action. Emergency action may include trespass proceedings under part 166, subpart I, of this chapter, or judicial action seeking immediate cessation of the activity resulting in or threatening the harm. Reasonable efforts will be made to notify the Indian landowners, either before or after the emergency action is taken.

§162.256 What will BIA do if a tenant holds over after the expiration or cancellation of an agricultural lease?

If a tenant remains in possession after the expiration or cancellation of an agricultural lease, we will treat the unauthorized use as a trespass. Unless we have reason to believe that the tenant is engaged in negotiations with the Indian landowners to obtain a new lease, we will take action to recover possession on behalf of the Indian landowners, and pursue any additional remedies available under applicable law, including the assessment of civil penalties and costs under part 166, subpart I, of this chapter.

Subpart C—Residential Leases

SOURCE: 77 FR 72474, Dec. 5, 2012, unless otherwise noted.

RESIDENTIAL LEASING GENERAL PROVISIONS

§ 162.301 What types of leases does this subpart cover?

(a) This subpart covers both ground leases (undeveloped land) and leases of developed land (together with the permanent improvements thereon) on Indian land, for housing purposes. Leases covered by this subpart would authorize the construction or use of:

(1) A single-family residence; and

(2) Housing for public purposes, which may include office space necessary to administer programs for housing for public purposes.

(b) Leases for other residential development (for example, single-family residential developments and multi-family developments that are not housing for public purposes) are covered under subpart D of this part.

§ 162.302 Is there a model residential lease form?

(a) We will make available one or more model lease forms that satisfy the formal requirements of this part, including, as appropriate, the model tribal lease form jointly developed by BIA, the Department of Housing and Urban Development, the Department of Veterans' Affairs, and the Department of Agriculture. Use of a model lease form is not mandatory, provided all requirements of this part are met.

(b) If a model lease form prepared by us is not used by the parties to a residential lease, we will assist the Indian landowners, upon their request, in drafting lease provisions or in using tribal lease forms that conform to the requirements of this part.

§ 162.303 Who needs a lease for housing for public purposes?

A TDHE or tribal housing authority must obtain an approved residential lease under this subpart from the Indian landowners if, under the terms of its charter, it is a legal entity independent from the tribe, regardless of whether it is owned and operated by the tribe. A TDHE or tribal housing authority does not need an approved residential lease under this subpart if the tribe has authorized the TDHE's or tribal housing authority's possession through a tribal land assignment.

LEASE REQUIREMENTS

§ 162.311 How long may the term of a residential lease run?

(a) A residential lease must provide for a definite lease term, state if there is an option to renew, and if so, provide for a definite term for the renewal period.

(1) The maximum term of a lease approved under 25 U.S.C. 4211 may not exceed 50 years or may be month-to-month. The lease may provide for an initial term of less than 50 years with a provision for one or more renewals, so long as the maximum term, including all renewals, does not exceed 50 years.

(2) The maximum term of a lease approved under 25 U.S.C. 415(a) may not exceed 50 years (consisting of an initial term not to exceed 25 years and one renewal not to exceed 25 years), unless a Federal statute provides for a longer maximum term (e.g., 25 U.S.C. 415(a) allows for a maximum term of 99 years for certain tribes), a different initial term, renewal term, or number of renewals.

(b) For tribal land, we will defer to the tribe's determination that the lease term, including any renewal, is reasonable. For individually owned Indian land, we will review the lease term, including any renewal, to ensure it is reasonable, given the:

(1) Purpose of the lease;

(2) Type of financing; and

(3) Level of investment.

(c) Unless the lease provides otherwise, a residential lease may not be extended by holdover.

§ 162.312 What must the lease include if it contains an option to renew?

(a) If the lease provides for an option to renew, the lease must specify:

(1) The time and manner in which the option must be exercised or is automatically effective;

(2) That confirmation of the renewal will be submitted to us, unless the lease provides for automatic renewal;

(3) Whether Indian landowner consent to the renewal is required;

(4) That the lessee must provide notice of the renewal to the Indian landowners and any mortgagees;

(5) The additional consideration, if any, that will be due upon the exercise of the option to renew or the start of the renewal term; and

(6) Any other conditions for renewal (e.g., that the lessee not be in violation of the lease at the time of renewal).

(b) We will record any renewal of a lease in the LTRO.

§ 162.313 Are there mandatory provisions that a residential lease must contain?

(a) All residential leases must identify:

(1) The tract or parcel of land being leased;

(2) The purpose of the lease and authorized uses of the leased premises;

(3) The parties to the lease;

(4) The term of the lease;

(5) The ownership of permanent improvements and the responsibility for constructing, operating, maintaining, and managing permanent improvements under § 162.315; and

(6) Payment requirements and late payment charges, including interest.

(b) Where a representative executes a lease on behalf of an Indian landowner or lessee, the lease must identify the landowner or lessee being represented and the authority under which the action is taken.

(c) All residential leases must include the following provisions:

(1) The obligations of the lessee to the Indian landowners are also enforceable by the United States, so long as the land remains in trust or restricted status;

(2) There must not be any unlawful conduct, creation of a nuisance, illegal activity, or negligent use or waste of the leased premises;

(3) The lessee must comply with all applicable laws, ordinances, rules, regulations, and other legal requirements under § 162.014;

(4) If historic properties, archeological resources, human remains, or other cultural items not previously reported are encountered during the course of any activity associated with this lease, all activity in the immediate vicinity of the properties, resources, remains, or items will cease and the lessee will contact BIA and the tribe with jurisdiction to determine how to proceed and appropriate disposition;

(5) BIA has the right, at any reasonable time during the term of the lease and upon reasonable notice in accordance with § 162.364, to enter the leased premises for inspection and to ensure compliance; and

(6) BIA may, at its discretion, treat as a lease violation any failure by the lessee to cooperate with a BIA request to make appropriate records, reports, or information available for BIA inspection and duplication.

(d) Unless the lessee would be prohibited by law from doing so, the lease must also contain the following provisions:

(1) The lessee holds the United States and the Indian landowners harmless from any loss, liability, or damages resulting from the lessee's use or occupation of the leased premises; and

(2) The lessee indemnifies the United States and the Indian landowners against all liabilities or costs relating to use, handling, treatment, removal, storage, transportation, or disposal of hazardous materials, or release or discharge of any hazardous material from the leased premises that occurs during the lease term, regardless of fault, with the exception that the lessee is not required to indemnify the Indian landowners for liability or cost arising from the Indian landowners' negligence or willful misconduct.

(e) We may treat any provision of a lease document that violates Federal law as a violation of the lease.

§ 162.314 May permanent improvements be made under a residential lease?

(a) The lessee may construct permanent improvements under a residential lease if the residential lease authorizes the construction and generally describes the type and location of the permanent improvements to be constructed during the lease term.

(b) The lessee must provide reasonable notice to the Indian landowners of the construction of any permanent improvements not generally described in the lease.

§ 162.315 How must a residential lease address ownership of permanent improvements?

(a) A residential lease must specify who will own any permanent improvements the lessee constructs during the lease term. In addition, the lease must indicate whether each specific permanent improvement the lessee constructs will:

(1) Remain on the leased premises upon expiration, termination, or cancellation of the lease, in a condition satisfactory to the Indian landowners and become the property of the Indian landowners;

(2) Be removed within a time period specified in the lease, at the lessee's expense, with the leased premises to be restored as closely as possible to their condition before construction of the permanent improvements; or

(3) Be disposed of by other specified means.

(b) A lease that requires the lessee to remove the permanent improvements must also provide the Indian landowners with an option to take possession of and title to the permanent improvements if the improvements are not removed within the specified time period.

§ 162.316 How will BIA enforce removal requirements in a residential lease?

We may take appropriate enforcement action to ensure removal of the permanent improvements and restoration of the premises at the lessee's expense:

(a) In consultation with the tribe for tribal land or, where feasible, with Indian landowners for individually owned Indian land; and

(b) Before or after expiration, termination, or cancellation of the lease.

§ 162.317 How must a residential lease describe the land?

(a) A residential lease must describe the leased premises by reference to a public or private survey, if possible. If the land cannot be so described, the lease must include one or more of the following:

(1) A legal description;

(2) A survey-grade global positioning system description; or

(3) Another description prepared by a registered land surveyor that is sufficient to identify the leased premises.

(b) If the tract is fractionated, we will identify the undivided trust or restricted interests in the leased premises.

RENTAL REQUIREMENTS

§ 162.320 How much rent must be paid under a residential lease of tribal land?

(a) A residential lease of tribal land may allow for any payment amount negotiated by the tribe, and we will defer to the tribe and not require a valuation, if:

(1) The lease is for housing for public purposes; or

(2) The tribe submits a signed certification or tribal authorization stating that it has determined the negotiated amount to be in its best interest.

(b) The tribe may request, in writing, that we determine fair market rental, in which case we will use a valuation in accordance with § 162.322. After providing the tribe with the fair market rental, we will defer to a tribe's decision to allow for any payment amount negotiated by the tribe.

(c) If the conditions in paragraph (a) or (b) of this section are not met, we will require that the lease provide for fair market rental based on a valuation in accordance with § 162.322.

§ 162.321 How much rent must be paid under a residential lease of individually owned Indian land?

(a) A residential lease of individually owned Indian land must require payment of not less than fair market rental except that we may approve a lease of individually owned Indian land that provides for the payment of nominal rent, or less than a fair market rental, if:

(1) One hundred percent of the Indian landowners execute a written waiver of the right to receive fair market rental; or

(2) We waive the requirement under paragraph (c) of this section.

(b) We will require a valuation in accordance with § 162.322, unless:

(1) One hundred percent of the Indian landowners submit to us a written request to waive the valuation requirement; or

(2) We waive the requirement under paragraph (c) of this section.

(c) If the owners of the applicable percentage of interests under § 162.012 consent to a residential lease on behalf of all the Indian landowners of a fractionated tract, the lease must provide that the non-consenting Indian landowners (and those on whose behalf we have consented) receive fair market rental, as determined by a valuation, unless we waive the requirement because:

(1) The lessee is a co-owner who, as of January 4, 2013, has been residing on the tract for at least 7 years, and no other co-owner raises an objection to BIA by July 3, 2013 to the lessee's continued possession of the tract; or

(2) The tribe or lessee will construct infrastructure improvements on, or serving, the leased premises, and we determine it is in the best interest of all the landowners.

§ 162.322 How will BIA determine fair market rental for a residential lease?

(a) We will use a market analysis, appraisal, or other appropriate valuation method to determine the fair market rental for residential leases of individually owned Indian land. We will also do this, at the request of the tribe, for tribal land.

(b) We will either:

(1) Prepare, or have prepared, a market analysis, appraisal, or other appropriate valuation method; or

(2) Use an approved market analysis, appraisal, or other appropriate valuation method from the Indian landowners or lessee.

(c) We will use or approve a market analysis, appraisal, or other appropriate valuation method for use only if it:

(1) Has been prepared in accordance with USPAP or a valuation method developed by the Secretary under 25 U.S.C. 2214; and

(2) Complies with Department policies regarding appraisals, including third-party appraisals.

§ 162.323 When are rental payments due under a residential lease?

(a) A residential lease must specify the dates on which payments are due.

(b) Unless the lease provides otherwise, payments may not be made or accepted more than one year in advance of the due date.

(c) Payments are due at the time specified in the lease, regardless of whether the lessee receives an advance billing or other notice that a payment is due.

§ 162.324 Must a residential lease specify who receives rental payments?

(a) A residential lease must specify whether the lessee will make payments directly to the Indian landowners (direct pay) or to us on their behalf.

(b) The lessee may make payments directly to the Indian landowners if:

(1) The Indian landowners' trust accounts are unencumbered;

(2) There are 10 or fewer beneficial owners; and

(3) One hundred percent of the beneficial owners (including those on whose behalf we have consented) agree to receive payment directly from the lessee at the start of the lease.

(c) If the lease provides that the lessee will directly pay the Indian landowners, then:

(1) The lease must include provisions for proof of payment upon our request.

(2) When we consent on behalf of an Indian landowner, the lessee must

make payment to us on behalf of that landowner.

(3) The lessee must send direct payments to the parties and addresses specified in the lease, unless the lessee receives notice of a change of ownership or address.

(4) Unless the lease provides otherwise, payments may not be made payable directly to anyone other than the Indian landowners.

(5) Direct payments must continue through the duration of the lease, except that:

(i) The lessee must make all Indian landowners' payments to us if 100 percent of the Indian landowners agree to suspend direct pay and provide us with documentation of their agreement; and

(ii) The lessee must make an individual Indian landowner's payment to us if that individual Indian landowner who dies, is declared non compos mentis, owes a debt resulting in a trust account encumbrance, or his or her whereabouts become unknown.

§ 162.325 What form of payment is acceptable under a residential lease?

(a) When payments are made directly to Indian landowners, the form of payment must be acceptable to the Indian landowners.

(b) When payments are made to us, our preferred method of payment is electronic funds transfer payments. We will also accept:

(1) Money orders;

(2) Personal checks;

(3) Certified checks; or

(4) Cashier's checks.

(c) We will not accept cash or foreign currency.

(d) We will accept third-party checks only from financial institutions or Federal agencies.

§ 162.326 May a residential lease provide for non-monetary or varying types of compensation?

(a) A lease may provide for the following, subject to the conditions in paragraphs (b) and (c) of this section:

(1) Alternative forms of rental, including, but not limited to in-kind consideration; or

(2) Varying types of compensation at specific stages during the life of the lease.

(b) For tribal land, we will defer to the tribe's determination that the compensation under paragraph (a) of this section is in its best interest, if either:

(1) The lease is for housing for public purposes; or

(2) The tribe submits a signed certification or tribal authorization stating that it has determined the compensation under paragraph (a) of this section to be in its best interest.

(c) For individually owned Indian land, we may approve a lease that provides for compensation under paragraph (a) of this section if we determine that it is in the best interest of the Indian landowners.

§ 162.327 Will BIA notify a lessee when a payment is due under a residential lease?

Upon request of the Indian landowners, we may issue invoices to a lessee in advance of the dates on which payments are due under a residential lease. The lessee's obligation to make these payments in a timely manner will not be excused if invoices are not issued, delivered, or received.

§ 162.328 Must a residential lease provide for rental reviews or adjustments?

(a) For a residential lease of tribal land, unless the lease provides otherwise, no periodic review of the adequacy of rent or rental adjustment is required if:

(1) The tribe states in a tribal certification or authorization that it has determined that not having rental reviews and/or adjustments is in its best interest; or

(2) The lease is for housing for public purposes.

(b) For a residential lease of individually Indian owned land, unless the lease provides otherwise, no periodic review of the adequacy of rent or rental adjustment is required if:

(1) The lease is for housing for public purposes;

(2) The term of the lease is 5 years or less;

(3) The lease provides for automatic rental adjustments; or

(4) We determine it is in the best interest of the Indian landowners not to

require a review or automatic adjustment based on circumstances including, but not limited to, the following:

(i) The lease provides for payment of less than fair market rental; or

(ii) The lease provides for most or all rent to be paid during the first 5 years of the lease term or before the date the review would be conducted.

(c) If the conditions in paragraph (a) or (b) of this section are not met, a review of the adequacy of rent must occur at least every fifth year, in the manner specified in the lease. The lease must specify:

(1) When adjustments take effect;

(2) Who can make adjustments;

(3) What the adjustments are based on; and

(4) How to resolve disputes arising from the adjustments.

(d) When a review results in the need for adjustment of rent, the Indian landowners must consent to the adjustment in accordance with § 162.012, unless the lease provides otherwise.

§ 162.329 What other types of payments are required under a residential lease?

(a) The lessee may be required to pay additional fees, taxes, and assessments associated with the use of the land, as determined by entities having jurisdiction, except as provided in § 162.017. The lessee must pay these amounts to the appropriate office.

(b) If the leased premises are within an Indian irrigation project or drainage district, except as otherwise provided in part 171 of this chapter, the lessee must pay all operation and maintenance charges that accrue during the lease term. The lessee must pay these amounts to the appropriate office in charge of the irrigation project or drainage district. We will treat failure to make these payments as a violation of the lease.

BONDING AND INSURANCE

§ 162.334 Is a performance bond required for a residential lease document?

We will not require a lessee or assignee to provide a performance bond or alternative form of security for a residential lease document.

§ 162.335 Is insurance required for a residential lease document?

We will not require a lessee or assignee to provide insurance for a residential lease document.

§§ 162.336–162.337 [Reserved]

APPROVAL

§ 162.338 What documents are required for BIA approval of a residential lease?

A lessee or the Indian landowners must submit the following documents to us to obtain BIA approval of a residential lease:

(a) A lease executed by the Indian landowners and the lessee that meets the requirements of this part;

(b) For tribal land, a tribal authorization for the lease and, if applicable, meeting the requirements of §§ 162.320(a), 162.326(b), and 162.328(a), or a separate signed certification meeting the requirements of §§ 162.320(a), 162.326(b), and 162.328(a);

(c) A valuation, if required under § 162.320 or § 162.321;

(d) A statement from the appropriate tribal authority that the proposed use is in conformance with applicable tribal law, if required by the tribe;

(e) Reports, surveys, and site assessments as needed to facilitate compliance with applicable Federal and tribal environmental and land use requirements, including any documentation prepared under § 162.027(b);

(f) A preliminary site plan identifying the proposed location of residential development, roads, and utilities, if applicable, unless the lease is for housing for public purposes;

(g) A legal description of the land under § 162.317;

(h) If the lease is being approved under 25 U.S.C. 415, information to assist us in our evaluation of the factors in 25 U.S.C. 415(a); and

(i) If the lessee is a corporation, limited liability company, partnership, joint venture, or other legal entity, except a tribal entity, information such as organizational documents, certificates, filing records, and resolutions, that demonstrates that:

(1) The representative has authority to execute a lease;

(2) The lease will be enforceable against the lessee; and

(3) The legal entity is in good standing and authorized to conduct business in the jurisdiction where the land is located.

§ 162.339 Will BIA review a proposed residential lease before or during preparation of the NEPA review documentation?

Upon request of the Indian landowners, we will review the proposed residential lease after negotiation by the parties, before or during preparation of the NEPA review documentation and any valuation. Within 10 days of receiving the proposed lease, we will provide an acknowledgement of the terms of the lease and identify any provisions that, based on this acknowledgment review, would justify disapproval of the lease, pending results of the NEPA review and any valuation.

§ 162.340 What is the approval process for a residential lease?

(a) Before we approve a residential lease, we must determine that the lease is in the best interest of the Indian landowners. In making that determination, we will:

(1) Review the lease and supporting documents;

(2) Ensure compliance with applicable laws and ordinances;

(3) If the lease is being approved under 25 U.S.C. 415, assure ourselves that adequate consideration has been given to the factors in 25 U.S.C. 415(a); and

(4) Require any lease modifications or mitigation measures necessary to satisfy any requirements including any other Federal or tribal land use requirements.

(b) Upon receiving a residential lease package, we will promptly notify the parties whether the package is or is not complete. A complete package includes all the information and supporting documents required under this subpart, including but not limited to, NEPA review documentation and valuation documentation, where applicable.

(1) If the residential lease package is not complete, our letter will identify the missing information or documents required for a complete package. If we do not respond to the submission of a residential lease package, the parties may take action under § 162.363.

(2) If the residential lease package is complete, we will notify the parties of the date of receipt. Within 30 days of the receipt date, we will approve or disapprove the lease or return the package for revision.

(c) If we do not meet the deadlines in this section, then the parties may take action under § 162.363.

(d) We will provide any lease approval or disapproval and the basis for the determination, along with notification of any appeal rights under part 2 of this chapter, in writing to the parties to the lease.

(e) Any residential lease issued under the authority of the Native American Housing Assistance and Self-Determination Act, 25 U.S.C 4211(a), whether on tribal land or on individually owned Indian land, must be approved by us and by the affected tribe.

(f) We will provide approved residential leases on tribal land to the lessee and provide a copy to the tribe. We will provide approved residential leases on individually owned Indian land to the lessee, and make copies available to the Indian landowners upon written request.

§ 162.341 How will BIA decide whether to approve a residential lease?

(a) We will approve a residential lease unless:

(1) The required consents have not been obtained from the parties to the lease;

(2) The requirements of this subpart have not been met; or

(3) We find a compelling reason to withhold our approval in order to protect the best interests of the Indian landowners.

(b) We will defer, to the maximum extent possible, to the Indian landowners' determination that the residential lease is in their best interest.

(c) We may not unreasonably withhold approval of a lease.

§ 162.342 When will a residential lease be effective?

(a) A residential lease will be effective on the date that we approve the lease, even if an appeal is filed under part 2 of this chapter.

(b) The lease may specify a date on which the obligations between the parties to a residential lease are triggered. Such date may be before or after the approval date under paragraph (a) of this section.

§ 162.343 Must a residential lease document be recorded?

(a) Any residential lease, amendment, assignment, or leasehold mortgage must be recorded in the LTRO with jurisdiction over the leased land. A residential sublease need not be recorded.

(1) We will record the lease or other document immediately following our approval.

(2) When our approval of an assignment is not required, the parties must record the assignment in the LTRO with jurisdiction over the leased land.

(b) The tribe must record lease documents for the following types of leases in the LTRO with jurisdiction over the leased lands, even though BIA approval is not required:

(1) Leases of tribal land that a corporate entity leases to a third party under 25 U.S.C. 477; and

(2) Leases of tribal land under a special act of Congress authorizing leases without our approval under certain conditions.

§ 162.344 Will BIA require an appeal bond for an appeal of a decision on a residential lease document?

BIA will not require an appeal bond for an appeal of a decision on a residential lease document.

AMENDMENTS

§ 162.345 May the parties amend a residential lease?

The parties may amend a residential lease by obtaining:

(a) The lessee's signature;

(b) The Indian landowners' consent under the requirements in § 162.346; and

(c) BIA approval of the amendment under §§ 162.347 and 162.348.

§ 162.346 What are the consent requirements for an amendment of a residential lease?

(a) Unless the lease provides otherwise, the lessee must notify all Indian landowners of the proposed amendment.

(b) The Indian landowners, or their representatives under § 162.013, must consent to an amendment of a residential lease in the same percentages and manner as a new residential lease under § 162.012, unless the lease:

(1) Provides that individual Indian landowners are deemed to have consented if they do not object in writing to the amendment within a specified period of time following Indian landowners' receipt of the amendment and the lease meets the requirements of paragraph (c) of this section;

(2) Authorizes one or more representatives to consent to an amendment on behalf of all Indian landowners; or

(3) Designates us as the Indian landowners' representative for the purposes of consent to an amendment.

(c) If the lease provides for deemed consent under paragraph (b)(1) of this section, it must require the parties to submit to us:

(1) A copy of the executed amendment or other documentation of any Indian landowners' actual consent;

(2) Proof of mailing of the amendment to any Indian landowners who are deemed to have consented; and

(3) Any other pertinent information for review.

(d) Unless specifically authorized in the lease, a written power of attorney, or a court document, Indian landowners may not be deemed to have consented to, and an Indian landowner's designated representative may not negotiate or consent to, an amendment that would:

(1) Reduce the payment obligations to the Indian landowners;

(2) Increase or decrease the lease area; or

(3) Terminate or change the term of the lease.

§ 162.347 What is the approval process for an amendment of a residential lease?

(a) When we receive an amendment that meets the requirements of this subpart, we will notify the parties of the date we receive it. We have 30 days from receipt of the executed amendment, proof of required consents, and required documentation to approve or disapprove the amendment. Our determination whether to approve the amendment will be in writing and will state the basis for our approval or disapproval.

(b) If we do not send a determination within 30 days from receipt of the required documents, the amendment is deemed approved to the extent consistent with Federal law. Unless the lease provides otherwise, provisions of the amendment that are inconsistent with Federal law will be severed and unenforceable; all other provisions of the amendment will remain in force.

§ 162.348 How will BIA decide whether to approve an amendment of a residential lease?

(a) We may disapprove a residential lease amendment only if at least one of the following is true:

(1) The Indian landowners have not consented and their consent is required;

(2) The lessee's mortgagees have not consented;

(3) The lessee is in violation of the lease;

(4) The requirements of this subpart have not been met; or

(5) We find a compelling reason to withhold our approval in order to protect the best interests of the Indian landowners.

(b) We will defer, to the maximum extent possible, to the Indian landowners' determination that the amendment is in their best interest.

(c) We may not unreasonably withhold approval of an amendment.

Assignments

§ 162.349 May a lessee assign a residential lease?

(a) A lessee may assign a residential lease by meeting the consent requirements in § 162.350 and obtaining our approval of the assignment under §§ 162.351 and 162.352 or by meeting the conditions in paragraph (b) of this section.

(b) The lessee may assign the lease without our approval or meeting consent requirements if:

(1) The lease is for housing for public purposes, or the assignee is a leasehold mortgagee or its designee, acquiring the lease either through foreclosure or by conveyance;

(2) The assignee agrees in writing to assume all of the obligations and conditions of the lease; and

(3) The assignee agrees in writing that any transfer of the lease will be in accordance with applicable law under § 162.014.

§ 162.350 What are the consent requirements for an assignment of a residential lease?

(a) Unless the lease provides otherwise, the lessee must notify all Indian landowners of the proposed assignment.

(b) The Indian landowners, or their representatives under § 162.013, must consent to an assignment of a residential lease in the same percentages and manner as a new residential lease under § 162.012, unless the lease:

(1) Provides for assignments without further consent of the Indian landowners or with consent in specified percentages and manner;

(2) Provides that individual Indian landowners are deemed to have consented where they do not object in writing to the assignment within a specified period of time following the landowners' receipt of the assignment and the lease meets the requirements of paragraph (c) of this section;

(3) Authorizes one or more of the Indian landowners to consent on behalf of all Indian landowners; or

(4) Designates us as the Indian landowners' representative for the purposes of consenting to an assignment.

(c) If the lease provides for deemed consent under paragraph (b)(2) of this section, it must require the parties to submit to us:

(1) A copy of the executed assignment or other documentation of any Indian landowners' actual consent;

(2) Proof of mailing of the assignment to any Indian landowners who are deemed to have consented; and

(3) Any other pertinent information for us to review.

(d) The lessee must obtain the consent of the holders of any mortgages.

§ 162.351 What is the approval process for an assignment of a residential lease?

(a) When we receive an assignment that meets the requirements of this subpart, we will notify the parties of the date we receive it. If our approval is required, we have 30 days from receipt of the executed assignment, proof of required consents, and required documentation to approve or disapprove the assignment. Our determination whether to approve the assignment will be in writing and will state the basis for our approval or disapproval.

(b) If we do not meet the deadline in this section, the lessee or Indian landowners may take appropriate action under § 162.363.

§ 162.352 How will BIA decide whether to approve an assignment of a residential lease?

(a) We may disapprove an assignment of a residential lease only if at least one of the following is true:

(1) The Indian landowners have not consented, and their consent is required;

(2) The lessee's mortgagees have not consented;

(3) The lessee is in violation of the lease;

(4) The assignee does not agree to be bound by the terms of the lease;

(5) The requirements of this subpart have not been met; or

(6) We find a compelling reason to withhold our approval in order to protect the best interests of the Indian landowners.

(b) In making the finding required by paragraph (a)(6) of this section, we may consider whether the value of any part of the leased premises not covered by the assignment would be adversely affected.

(c) We will defer, to the maximum extent possible, to the Indian landowners' determination that the assignment is in their best interest.

(d) We may not unreasonably withhold approval of an assignment.

SUBLEASES

§ 162.353 May a lessee sublease a residential lease?

(a) A lessee may sublease a residential lease by meeting the consent requirements in § 162.354 and obtaining our approval of the sublease under §§ 162.355 and 162.356, or by meeting the conditions in paragraph (b) of this section.

(b) The lessee may sublease without meeting consent requirements or obtaining BIA approval of the sublease, if:

(1) The lease provides for subleasing without meeting consent requirements or obtaining BIA approval; and

(2) The sublease does not relieve the lessee/sublessor of any liability.

§ 162.354 What are the consent requirements for a sublease of a residential lease?

(a) Unless the lease provides otherwise, the lessee must notify all Indian landowners of the proposed sublease.

(b) The Indian landowners must consent to a sublease of a residential lease in the same percentages and manner as a new residential lease under § 162.012, unless the lease:

(1) Provides that individual Indian landowners are deemed to have consented where they do not object in writing to the sublease within a specified period of time following the landowners' receipt of the sublease and the lease meets the requirements of paragraph (c) of this section;

(2) Authorizes one or more of the Indian landowners to consent on behalf of all Indian landowners; or

(3) Designates us as the Indian landowners' representative for the purposes of consenting to a sublease.

(c) If the lease provides for deemed consent under paragraph (b)(1) of this section, it must require the parties to submit to us:

(1) A copy of the executed sublease or other documentation of any landowner's actual consent;

(2) Proof of mailing of the sublease to any Indian landowners who are deemed to have consented; and

(3) Any other pertinent information for us to review.

(d) The lessee must obtain the consent of any mortgagees.

§ 162.355 What is the approval process for a sublease of a residential lease?

(a) When we receive a sublease that meets the requirements of this subpart, we will notify the parties of the date we receive it. If our approval is required, we have 30 days from receipt of the executed sublease, proof of required consents, and required documentation to approve or disapprove the sublease.

(b) If we do not send a determination within 30 days from receipt of required documents, the sublease is deemed approved to the extent consistent with Federal law. Unless the lease provides otherwise, provisions of the sublease that are inconsistent with Federal law will be severed and unenforceable; all other provisions of the sublease will remain in force.

§ 162.356 How will BIA decide whether to approve a sublease of a residential lease?

(a) We may disapprove a sublease of a residential lease only if at least one of the following is true:

(1) The Indian landowners have not consented, and their consent is required;

(2) The lessee's mortgagees have not consented;

(3) The lessee is in violation of the lease;

(4) The lessee will not remain liable under the lease;

(5) The requirements of this subpart have not been met; or

(6) We find a compelling reason to withhold our approval in order to protect the best interests of the Indian landowners.

(b) In making the finding required by paragraph (a)(6) of this section, we may consider whether the value of any part of the leased premises not covered by the sublease would be adversely affected.

(c) We will defer, to the maximum extent possible, to the Indian landowners' determination that the sublease is in their best interest.

(d) We may not unreasonably withhold approval of a sublease.

LEASEHOLD MORTGAGES

§ 162.357 May a lessee mortgage a residential lease?

(a) A lessee may mortgage a residential lease by meeting the consent requirements in § 162.358 and obtaining BIA approval of the leasehold mortgage under in §§ 162.359 and 162.360.

(b) Refer to § 162.349(b) for information on what happens if a sale or foreclosure under an approved mortgage of the leasehold interest occurs.

§ 162.358 What are the consent requirements for a leasehold mortgage of a residential lease?

(a) Unless the lease provides otherwise, the lessee must notify all Indian landowners of the proposed leasehold mortgage.

(b) The Indian landowners, or their representatives under § 162.013, must consent to a leasehold mortgage of a residential lease in the same percentages and manner as a new residential lease under § 162.012, unless the lease:

(1) States that landowner consent is not required for a leasehold mortgage and identifies what law would apply in case of foreclosure;

(2) Provides that individual Indian landowners are deemed to have consented where they do not object in writing to the leasehold mortgage within a specified period of time following the landowners' receipt of the leasehold mortgage and the lease meets the requirements of paragraph (c) of this section;

(3) Authorizes one or more representatives to consent to a leasehold mortgage on behalf of all Indian landowners; or

(4) Designates us as the Indian landowners' representative for the purposes of consenting to a leasehold mortgage.

(c) If the lease provides for deemed consent under paragraph (b)(2) of this section, it must require the parties to submit to us:

(1) A copy of the executed leasehold mortgage or other documentation of any Indian landowners' actual consent;

(2) Proof of mailing of the leasehold mortgage to any Indian landowners who are deemed to have consented; and

(3) Any other pertinent information for us to review.

§ 162.359 What is the approval process for a leasehold mortgage of a residential lease?

(a) When we receive leasehold mortgage that meets the requirements of this subpart, we will notify the parties of the date we receive it. We have 20 days from receipt of the executed leasehold mortgage, proof of required consents, and required documentation to approve or disapprove the leasehold mortgage. Our determination whether to approve the leasehold mortgage will be in writing and will state the basis for our approval or disapproval.

(b) If we do not meet the deadline in this section, the lessee may take appropriate action under § 162.363.

§ 162.360 How will BIA decide whether to approve a leasehold mortgage of a residential lease?

(a) We may disapprove a leasehold mortgage of a residential lease only if at least one of the following is true:

(1) The Indian landowners have not consented, and their consent is required;

(2) The requirements of this subpart have not been met; or

(3) We find a compelling reason to withhold our approval in order to protect the best interests of the Indian landowners.

(b) In making the finding required by paragraph (a)(3) of this section, we may consider whether:

(1) The leasehold mortgage proceeds would be used for purposes unrelated to the leased premises; and

(2) The leasehold mortgage is limited to the leasehold.

(c) We will defer, to the maximum extent possible, to the Indian landowners' determination that the leasehold mortgage is in their best interest.

(d) We may not unreasonably withhold approval of a leasehold mortgage.

EFFECTIVENESS, COMPLIANCE, AND ENFORCEMENT

§ 162.361 When will an amendment, assignment, sublease, or leasehold mortgage of a residential lease be effective?

(a) An amendment, assignment, sublease, or leasehold mortgage of a residential lease will be effective when approved, even if an appeal is filed under part 2 of this chapter, except:

(1) If the amendment or sublease was deemed approved under § 162.347(b) or § 162.355(b), the amendment or sublease becomes effective 45 days from the date the parties mailed or delivered the document to us for our review; and

(2) An assignment that does not require our approval under § 162.349(b) or a sublease that does not require our approval under § 162.353(b) becomes effective on the effective date specified in the assignment or sublease. If the assignment or sublease does not specify the effective date, it becomes effective upon execution by the parties.

(b) We will provide copies of approved documents to the party requesting approval, to the tribe for tribal land, and upon request, to other parties to the lease document.

§ 162.362 What happens if BIA disapproves an amendment, assignment, sublease, or leasehold mortgage?

If we disapprove an amendment, assignment, sublease, or leasehold mortgage of a residential lease, we will notify the parties immediately and advise the landowners of their right to appeal the decision under part 2 of this chapter.

§ 162.363 What happens if BIA does not meet a deadline for issuing a decision on a lease document?

(a) If a Superintendent does not meet a deadline for issuing a decision on a lease, assignment, or leasehold mortgage, the parties may file a written notice to compel action with the appropriate Regional Director.

(b) The Regional Director has 15 days from receiving the notice to:

(1) Issue a decision; or

(2) Order the Superintendent to issue a decision within the time set out in the order.

(c) The parties may file a written notice to compel action with the BIA Director if:

(1) The Regional Director does not meet the deadline in paragraph (b) of this section;

(2) The Superintendent does not issue a decision within the time set by the Regional Director under paragraph (b)(2) of this section; or

(3) The initial decision on the lease, assignment, or leasehold mortgage is with the Regional Director, and he or she does not meet the deadline for such decision.

(d) The BIA Director has 15 days from receiving the notice to:

(1) Issue a decision; or

(2) Order the Regional Director or Superintendent to issue a decision within the time set out in the order.

(e) If the Regional Director or Superintendent does not issue a decision within the time set out in the order under paragraph (d)(2) of this section, then the BIA Director must issue a decision within 15 days from the expiration of the time set out in the order.

(f) The parties may file an appeal from our inaction to the Interior Board of Indian Appeals if the Director does not meet the deadline in paragraph (d) or (e) of this section.

(g) The provisions of 25 CFR 2.8 do not apply to the inaction of BIA officials with respect to a decision on a lease, amendment, assignment, sublease, or leasehold mortgage under this subpart.

§ 162.364 May BIA investigate compliance with a residential lease?

(a) We may enter the leased premises at any reasonable time, upon reasonable notice, and consistent with any notice requirements under applicable tribal law and applicable lease documents, to protect the interests of the Indian landowners and ensure that the lessee is in compliance with the requirements of the lease.

(b) If an Indian landowner notifies us that a specific lease violation has occurred, we will promptly initiate an appropriate investigation.

§ 162.365 May a residential lease provide for negotiated remedies if there is a violation?

(a) A residential lease of tribal land may provide either or both parties with negotiated remedies in the event of a lease violation, including, but not limited to, the power to terminate the lease. If the lease provides one or both parties with the power to terminate the lease:

(1) BIA approval of the termination is not required;

(2) The termination is effective without BIA cancellation; and

(3) The Indian landowners must notify us of the termination so that we may record it in the LTRO.

(b) A residential lease of individually owned Indian land may provide either or both parties with negotiated remedies, so long as the lease also specifies the manner in which those remedies may be exercised by or on behalf of the Indian landowners of the applicable percentage of interests under § 162.012 of this part. If the lease provides one or both parties with the power to terminate the lease:

(1) BIA concurrence with the termination is required to ensure that the Indian landowners of the applicable percentage of interests have consented; and

(2) BIA will record the termination in the LTRO.

(c) The parties must notify any mortgagee of any violation that may result in termination and the termination of a residential lease.

(d) Negotiated remedies may apply in addition to, or instead of, the cancellation remedy available to us, as specified in the lease. The landowners may request our assistance in enforcing negotiated remedies.

(e) A residential lease may provide that lease violations will be addressed by the tribe, and that lease disputes will be resolved by a tribal court, any other court of competent jurisdiction, or by a tribal governing body in the absence of a tribal court, or through an alternative dispute resolution method. We may not be bound by decisions made in such forums, but we will defer to ongoing actions or proceedings, as appropriate, in deciding whether to exercise any of the remedies available to us.

162.366 What will BIA do about a violation of a residential lease?

(a) In the absence of actions or proceedings described in § 162.365(e), or if it is not appropriate for us to defer to the actions or proceedings, we will follow the procedures in paragraphs (b), (c), and (d) of this section and, as applicable, ensure consistency with 25 U.S.C. 4137.

(b) If we determine there has been a violation of the conditions of a residential lease other than a violation of payment provisions covered by paragraph (c) of this section, we will promptly send the lessee and any mortgagee a notice of violation by certified mail, return receipt requested.

(1) We will send a copy of the notice of violation to the tribe for tribal land, or provide constructive notice to Indian landowners for individually owned Indian land.

(2) The notice of violation will advise the lessee that, within 10 business days of the receipt of a notice of violation, the lessee must:

(i) Cure the violation and notify us, and the tribe for tribal land, in writing that the violation has been cured;

(ii) Dispute our determination that a violation has occurred; or

(iii) Request additional time to cure the violation.

(3) The notice of violation may order the lessee to cease operations under the lease.

(c) A lessee's failure to pay rent in the time and manner required by a residential lease is a violation of the lease, and we will issue a notice of violation in accordance with this paragraph.

(1) We will send the lessee and any mortgagee a notice of violation by certified mail, return receipt requested:

(i) Promptly following the date on which the payment was due, if the lease requires that rental payments be made to us; or

(ii) Promptly following the date on which we receive actual notice of non-payment from the Indian landowners, if the lease provides for payment directly to the Indian landowners.

(2) We will send a copy of the notice of violation to the tribe for tribal land, or provide constructive notice to Indian landowners for individually owned Indian land.

(3) The notice of violation will require the lessee to provide adequate proof of payment.

(d) The lessee will continue to be responsible for the obligations in the lease until the lease expires or is terminated or cancelled.

§ 162.367 What will BIA do if the lessee does not cure a violation of a residential lease on time?

(a) If the lessee does not cure a violation of a residential lease within the required time period, or provide adequate proof of payment as required in the notice of violation, we will consult with the tribe for tribal land or, where feasible, with Indian landowners for individually owned Indian land, and determine whether:

(1) We should cancel the lease;

(2) The Indian landowners wish to invoke any remedies available to them under the lease;

(3) We should invoke other remedies available under the lease or applicable law, including collection on any available performance bond or, for failure to pay rent, referral of the debt to the Department of the Treasury for collection; or

(4) The lessee should be granted additional time in which to cure the violation.

(b) Following consultation with the tribe for tribal land or, where feasible, with Indian landowners for individually owned Indian land, we may take action to recover unpaid rent and any associated late payment charges.

(1) We do not have to cancel the lease or give any further notice to the lessee before taking action to recover unpaid rent.

(2) We may still take action to recover any unpaid rent if we cancel the lease.

(c) If we decide to cancel the lease, we will send the lessee and any mortgagee a cancellation letter by certified mail, return receipt requested within 5 business days of our decision. We will send a copy of the cancellation letter to the tribe for tribal land, and will provide Indian landowners for individually owned Indian land with actual or constructive notice of the cancellation. The cancellation letter will:

(1) Explain the grounds for cancellation;

(2) If applicable, notify the lessee of the amount of any unpaid rent or late payment charges due under the lease;

(3) Notify the lessee of the lessee's right to appeal under part 2 of this chapter;

(4) Order the lessee to vacate the property within 31 days of the date of receipt of the cancellation letter, if an appeal is not filed by that time; and

(5) Order the lessee to take any other action BIA deems necessary to protect the Indian landowners.

(d) We may invoke any other remedies available to us under the lease, including collecting on any available performance bond, and the Indian landowners may pursue any available remedies under tribal law.

(e) We will ensure that any action we take is consistent with 25 U.S.C. 4137, as applicable.

§ 162.368 Will late payment charges or special fees apply to delinquent payments due under a residential lease?

(a) Late payment charges will apply as specified in the lease. The failure to pay these amounts will be treated as a lease violation.

(b) We may assess the following special fees to cover administrative costs incurred by the United States in the collection of the debt, if rent is not paid in the time and manner required, in addition to late payment charges that must be paid to the Indian landowners under the lease:

The lessee will pay . . .	For . . .
(1) $50.00	Any dishonored check.
(2) $15.00	Processing of each notice or demand letter.
(3) 18 percent of balance due.	Treasury processing following referral for collection of delinquent debt.

§ 162.369 How will payment rights relating to a residential lease be allocated?

The residential lease may allocate rights to payment for insurance proceeds, trespass damages, condemnation awards, settlement funds, and other payments between the Indian landowners and the lessee. If not specified in the lease, insurance policy, order, award, judgment, or other document, the Indian landowners will be entitled to receive these payments.

§ 162.370 When will a cancellation of a residential lease be effective?

(a) A cancellation involving a residential lease will not be effective until 31 days after the lessee receives a cancellation letter from us, or 41 days from the date we mailed the letter, whichever is earlier.

(b) The cancellation decision will not be effective if an appeal is filed unless the cancellation is made immediately effective under part 2 of this chapter. While a cancellation decision is ineffective, the lessee must continue to pay rent and comply with the other terms of the lease.

§ 162.371 What will BIA do if a lessee remains in possession after a residential lease expires or is terminated or cancelled?

If a lessee remains in possession after the expiration, termination, or cancellation of a residential lease, we may treat the unauthorized possession as a trespass under applicable law in consultation with the Indian landowners. Unless the Indian landowners of the applicable percentage of interests under § 162.012 have notified us in writing that they are engaged in good faith negotiations with the holdover lessee to obtain a new lease, we may take action to recover possession on behalf of the Indian landowners, and pursue any additional remedies available under applicable law, such as a forcible entry and detainer action.

§ 162.372 Will BIA appeal bond regulations apply to cancellation decisions involving residential leases?

(a) Except as provided in paragraph (b) of this section, the appeal bond provisions in part 2 of this chapter will apply to appeals from lease cancellation decisions.

(b) The lessee may not appeal the appeal bond decision. The lessee may, however, request that the official to whom the appeal is made reconsider the appeal bond decision, based on extraordinary circumstances. Any reconsideration decision is final for the Department.

§ 162.373 When will BIA issue a decision on an appeal from a residential leasing decision?

BIA will issue a decision on an appeal from a leasing decision within 30 days of receipt of all pleadings.

§ 162.374 What happens if the lessee abandons the leased premises?

If a lessee abandons the leased premises, we will treat the abandonment as a violation of the lease. The lease may specify a period of non-use after which the lease premises will be considered abandoned.

Subpart D—Business Leases

SOURCE: 77 FR 72474, Dec. 5, 2012, unless otherwise noted.

BUSINESS LEASING GENERAL PROVISIONS

§ 162.401 What types of leases does this subpart cover?

(a) This subpart covers both ground leases (undeveloped land) and leases of developed land (together with the permanent improvements thereon) on Indian land that are not covered in another subpart of this part, including:

(1) Leases for residential purposes that are not covered in subpart C;

(2) Leases for business purposes that are not covered in subpart E;

(3) Leases for religious, educational, recreational, cultural, or other public purposes; and

(4) Commercial or industrial leases for retail, office, manufacturing, storage, biomass, waste-to-energy, or other business purposes.

(b) Leases covered by this subpart may authorize the construction of single-purpose or mixed-use projects designed for use by any number of lessees or occupants.

§ 162.402 Is there a model business lease form?

There is no model business lease form because of the need for flexibility in negotiating and writing business leases; however, we may:

(a) Provide other guidance, such as checklists and sample lease provisions, to assist in the lease negotiation process; and

(b) Assist the Indian landowners, upon their request, in developing appropriate lease provisions or in using tribal lease forms that conform to the requirements of this part.

LEASE REQUIREMENTS

§ 162.411 How long may the term of a business lease run?

(a) A business lease must provide for a definite term, state if there is an option to renew, and if so, provide for a definite term for the renewal period. The maximum term of a lease approved under 25 U.S.C. 415(a) may not exceed 50 years (consisting of an initial term not to exceed 25 years and one renewal not to exceed 25 years), unless a Federal statute provides for a longer maximum term (e.g., 25 U.S.C. 415(a) allows for a maximum term of 99 years for certain tribes), a different initial term, renewal term, or number of renewals.

(b) For tribal land, we will defer to the tribe's determination that the lease term, including any renewal, is reasonable. For individually owned Indian land, we will review the lease term, including any renewal, to ensure it is reasonable, given the:

(1) Purpose of the lease;

(2) Type of financing; and

(3) Level of investment.

(c) The lease may not be extended by holdover.

§ 162.412 What must the lease include if it contains an option to renew?

(a) If the lease provides for an option to renew, the lease must specify:

(1) The time and manner in which the option must be exercised or is automatically effective;

(2) That confirmation of the renewal will be submitted to us, unless the lease provides for automatic renewal;

(3) Whether Indian landowner consent to the renewal is required;

(4) That the lessee must provide notice of the renewal to the Indian landowners and any sureties and mortgagees;

(5) The additional consideration, if any, that will be due upon the exercise of the option to renew or the start of the renewal term; and

(6) Any other conditions for renewal (e.g., that the lessee not be in violation of the lease at the time of renewal).

(b) We will record any renewal of a lease in the LTRO.

§ 162.413 Are there mandatory provisions that a business lease must contain?

(a) All business leases must identify:

(1) The tract or parcel of land being leased;

(2) The purpose of the lease and authorized uses of the leased premises;

(3) The parties to the lease;

(4) The term of the lease;

(5) The ownership of permanent improvements and the responsibility for constructing, operating, maintaining, and managing permanent improvements under § 162.415;

(6) Payment requirements and late payment charges, including interest;

(7) Due diligence requirements under § 162.417 (unless the lease is for religious, educational, recreational, cultural, or other public purposes);

(8) Insurance requirements under § 162.437; and

(9) Bonding requirements under § 162.434. If a performance bond is required, the lease must state that the lessee must obtain the consent of the surety for any legal instrument that directly affects their obligations and liabilities.

(b) Where a representative executes a lease on behalf of an Indian landowner or lessee, the lease must identify the landowner or lessee being represented and the authority under which the action is taken.

(c) All business leases must include the following provisions:

(1) The obligations of the lessee and its sureties to the Indian landowners are also enforceable by the United States, so long as the land remains in trust or restricted status;

(2) There must not be any unlawful conduct, creation of a nuisance, illegal activity, or negligent use or waste of the leased premises;

(3) The lessee must comply with all applicable laws, ordinances, rules, regulations, and other legal requirements under § 162.014;

(4) If historic properties, archeological resources, human remains, or other cultural items not previously reported are encountered during the course of any activity associated with this lease, all activity in the immediate vicinity of the properties, resources, remains, or items will cease and the lessee will contact BIA and the tribe with jurisdiction over the land to determine how to proceed and appropriate disposition;

(5) BIA has the right, at any reasonable time during the term of the lease and upon reasonable notice, in accordance with § 162.464, to enter the leased premises for inspection and to ensure compliance; and

(6) BIA may, at its discretion, treat as a lease violation any failure by the lessee to cooperate with a BIA request to make appropriate records, reports, or information available for BIA inspection and duplication.

(d) Unless the lessee would be prohibited by law from doing so, the lease must also contain the following provisions:

(1) The lessee holds the United States and the Indian landowners harmless from any loss, liability, or damages resulting from the lessee's use or occupation of the leased premises; and

(2) The lessee indemnifies the United States and the Indian landowners against all liabilities or costs relating to the use, handling, treatment, removal, storage, transportation, or disposal of hazardous materials, or the release or discharge of any hazardous material from the leased premises that occurs during the lease term, regardless of fault, with the exception that the lessee is not required to indemnify the Indian landowners for liability or cost arising from the Indian landowners' negligence or willful misconduct.

(e) We may treat any provision of a lease document that violates Federal law as a violation of the lease.

§ 162.414 May permanent improvements be made under a business lease?

The lessee may construct permanent improvements under a business lease if the business lease specifies, or provides for the development of:

(a) A plan that describes the type and location of any permanent improvements to be constructed by the lessee; and

(b) A general schedule for construction of the permanent improvements, including dates for commencement and completion of construction.

§ 162.415 How must a business lease address ownership of permanent improvements?

(a) A business lease must specify who will own any permanent improvements the lessee constructs during the lease term and may specify under what conditions, if any, permanent improvements the lessee constructs may be conveyed to the Indian landowners during the lease term. In addition, the lease must indicate whether each specific permanent improvement the lessee constructs will:

(1) Remain on the leased premises, upon the expiration, cancellation, or termination of the lease, in a condition satisfactory to the Indian landowners, and become the property of the Indian landowners;

(2) Be removed within a time period specified in the lease, at the lessee's expense, with the leased premises to be restored as closely as possible to their condition before construction of the permanent improvements; or

(3) Be disposed of by other specified means.

(b) A lease that requires the lessee to remove the permanent improvements must also provide the Indian landowners with an option to take possession of and title to the permanent improvements if the improvements are not removed within the specified time period.

§ 162.416 How will BIA enforce removal requirements in a business lease?

(a) We may take appropriate enforcement action to ensure removal of the permanent improvements and restoration of the premises at the lessee's expense:

(1) In consultation with the tribe, for tribal land or, where feasible, with Indian landowners for individually owned Indian land; and

(2) Before or after expiration, termination, or cancellation of the lease.

(b) We may collect and hold the performance bond or alternative form of security until removal and restoration are completed.

§ 162.417 What requirements for due diligence must a business lease include?

(a) If permanent improvements are to be constructed, the business lease must include due diligence requirements that require the lessee to complete construction of any permanent improvements within the schedule specified in the lease or general schedule of construction, and a process for changing the schedule by mutual consent of the parties. If construction does not occur, or is not expected to be completed, within the time period specified in the lease, the lessee must provide the Indian landowners and BIA with an explanation of good cause as to the nature of any delay, the anticipated date of construction of facilities, and evidence of progress toward commencement of construction.

(b) Failure of the lessee to comply with the due diligence requirements of the lease is a violation of the lease and may lead to cancellation of the lease under § 162.467.

(c) BIA may waive the requirements in this section if such waiver is in the best interest of the Indian landowners.

(d) The requirements of this section do not apply to leases for religious, educational, recreational, cultural, or other public purposes.

§ 162.418 How must a business lease describe the land?

(a) A business lease must describe the leased premises by reference to an official or certified survey, if possible. If the land cannot be so described, the lease must include one or more of the following:

(1) A legal description;

(2) A survey-grade global positioning system description; or

(3) Another description prepared by a registered land surveyor that is sufficient to identify the leased premises.

(b) If the tract is fractionated we will identify the undivided trust or restricted interests in the leased premises.

§ 162.419 May a business lease allow compatible uses?

A business lease may provide for the Indian landowners to use, or authorize others to use, the leased premises for other uses compatible with the purpose of the business lease and consistent with the terms of the business lease. Any such use or authorization by the Indian landowners will not reduce or offset the monetary compensation for the business lease.

MONETARY COMPENSATION REQUIREMENTS

§ 162.420 How much monetary compensation must be paid under a business lease of tribal land?

(a) A business lease of tribal land may allow for any payment amount negotiated by the tribe, and we will defer to the tribe and not require a valuation if the tribe submits a tribal authorization expressly stating that it:

(1) Has negotiated compensation satisfactory to the tribe;

(2) Waives valuation; and

(3) Has determined that accepting such negotiated compensation and waiving valuation is in its best interest.

(b) The tribe may request, in writing, that we determine fair market rental, in which case we will use a valuation in accordance with § 162.422. After providing the tribe with the fair market rental, we will defer to a tribe's decision to allow for any payment amount negotiated by the tribe.

(c) If the conditions in paragraph (a) or (b) of this section are not met, we will require that the lease provide for fair market rental based on a valuation in accordance with § 162.422.

§ 162.421 How much monetary compensation must be paid under a business lease of individually owned Indian land?

(a) A business lease of individually owned Indian land must require payment of not less than fair market rental before any adjustments, based on a fixed amount, a percentage of the projected income, or some other method, unless paragraphs (b) or (c) of this section permit a lesser amount. The lease must establish how the fixed amount, percentage, or combination will be calculated and the frequency at which the payments will be made.

(b) We may approve a lease of individually owned Indian land that provides for the payment of nominal compensation, or less than a fair market rental, if:

(1) The Indian landowners execute a written waiver of the right to receive fair market rental; and

(2) We determine it is in the Indian landowners' best interest, based on factors including, but not limited to:

(i) The lessee is a member of the immediate family, as defined in § 162.003, of an individual Indian landowner;

(ii) The lessee is a co-owner in the leased tract;

(iii) A special relationship or circumstances exist that we believe warrant approval of the lease;

(iv) The lease is for religious, educational, recreational, cultural, or other public purposes;

(v) We have waived the requirement for a valuation under paragraph (e) of this section.

(c) We may approve a lease that provides for payment of less than a fair market rental during the pre-development or construction periods, if we determine it is in the Indian landowners' best interest. The lease must specify the amount of the compensation and the applicable periods.

(d) We will require a valuation in accordance with § 162.422, unless:

(1) 100 percent of the Indian landowners submit to us a written request to waive the valuation requirement; or

(2) We waive the requirement under paragraph (e) of this section.

(e) If the owners of the applicable percentage of interests under § 162.012 of this part execute a business lease on behalf of all of the Indian landowners of a fractionated tract, the lease must provide that the non-consenting Indian landowners, and those on whose behalf we have consented, receive a fair market rental, as determined by a valuation, unless we waive the requirement because the tribe or lessee will construct infrastructure improvements on, or serving, the leased premises, and we determine it is in the best interest of all the landowners.

§ 162.422 How will BIA determine fair market rental for a business lease?

(a) We will use a market analysis, appraisal, or other appropriate valuation method to determine the fair market rental before we approve a business lease of individually owned Indian land or, at the request of the tribe, for tribal land.

(b) We will either:

(1) Prepare, or have prepared, a market analysis, appraisal, or other appropriate valuation method; or

(2) Use an approved market analysis, appraisal, or other appropriate valuation method from the Indian landowners or lessee.

(c) We will use or approve use of a market analysis, appraisal, or other appropriate valuation method only if it:

(1) Has been prepared in accordance with USPAP or a valuation method developed by the Secretary under 25 U.S.C. 2214; and

(2) Complies with Departmental policies regarding appraisals, including third-party appraisals.

(d) Indian landowners may use competitive bidding as a valuation method.

§ 162.423 When are monetary compensation payments due under a business lease?

(a) A business lease must specify the dates on which all payments are due.

(b) Unless the lease provides otherwise, payments may not be made or accepted more than one year in advance of the due date.

(c) Payments are due at the time specified in the lease, regardless of whether the lessee receives an advance billing or other notice that a payment is due.

§ 162.424 Must a business lease specify who receives monetary compensation payments?

(a) A business lease must specify whether the lessee will make payments directly to the Indian landowners (direct pay) or to us on their behalf.

(b) The lessee may make payments directly to the Indian landowners if:

(1) The Indian landowners' trust accounts are unencumbered;

(2) There are 10 or fewer beneficial owners; and

(3) One hundred percent of the beneficial owners (including those on whose behalf we have consented) agree to receive payment directly from the lessee at the start of the lease.

(c) If the lease provides that the lessee will directly pay the Indian landowners, then:

(1) The lease must include provisions for proof of payment upon our request.

(2) When we consent on behalf of an Indian landowner, the lessee must make payment to us on behalf of that landowner.

(3) The lessee must send direct payments to the parties and addresses specified in the lease, unless the lessee receives notice of a change of ownership or address.

(4) Unless the lease provides otherwise, compensation payments may not be made payable directly to anyone other than the Indian landowners.

(5) Direct payments must continue through the duration of the lease, except that:

(i) The lessee must make all Indian landowners' payments to us if 100 percent of the Indian landowners agree to suspend direct pay and provide us with documentation of their agreement; and

(ii) The lessee must make that individual Indian landowner's payment to us if any individual Indian landowner who dies, is declared non compos mentis, owes a debt resulting in a trust account encumbrance, or his or her whereabouts become unknown.

§ 162.425 What form of monetary compensation payment is acceptable under a business lease?

(a) When payments are made directly to Indian landowners, the form of payment must be acceptable to the Indian landowners.

(b) When payments are made to us, our preferred method of payment is electronic funds transfer payments. We will also accept:

(1) Money orders;

(2) Personal checks;

(3) Certified checks; or

(4) Cashier's checks.

(c) We will not accept cash or foreign currency.

(d) We will accept third-party checks only from financial institutions or Federal agencies.

§ 162.426 May the business lease provide for non-monetary or varying types of compensation?

(a) A lease may provide for the following, subject to the conditions in paragraphs (b) and (c) of this section:

(1) Alternative forms of compensation, including but not limited to, in-kind consideration and payments based on percentage of income; or

(2) Varying types of compensation at specific stages during the life of the lease, including but not limited to fixed annual payments during construction, payments based on income during an operational period, and bonuses.

(b) For tribal land, we will defer to the tribe's determination that the compensation under paragraph (a) of this section is in its best interest, if the tribe submits a signed certification or tribal authorization stating that it has determined the compensation under paragraph (a) of this section to be in its best interest.

(c) For individually owned land, we may approve a lease that provides for compensation under paragraph (a) of this section if we determine that it is in the best interest of the Indian landowners.

§ 162.427 Will BIA notify a lessee when a payment is due under a business lease?

Upon request of the Indian landowners, we may issue invoices to a lessee in advance of the dates on which payments are due under a business lease. The lessee's obligation to make these payments in a timely manner will not be excused if invoices are not issued, delivered, or received.

§ 162.428 Must a business lease provide for compensation reviews or adjustments?

(a) For a business lease of tribal land, unless the lease provides otherwise, no periodic review of the adequacy of compensation or adjustment is required if the tribe states in its tribal certification or authorization that it has determined that not having compensation reviews and/or adjustments is in its best interest.

(b) For a business lease of individually owned Indian land, unless the lease provides otherwise, no periodic review of the adequacy of compensation or adjustment is required if:

(1) If the term of the lease is 5 years or less;

(2) The lease provides for automatic adjustments; or

(3) We determine it is in the best interest of the Indian landowners not to require a review or automatic adjustment based on circumstances including, but not limited to, the following:

(i) The lease provides for payment of less than fair market rental;

(ii) The lease is for religious, educational, recreational, cultural, or other public purposes;

(iii) The lease provides for most or all of the compensation to be paid during the first 5 years of the lease term or before the date the review would be conducted; or

(iv) The lease provides for graduated rent or non-monetary or various types of compensation.

(c) If the conditions in paragraph (a) or (b) of this section are not met, a review of the adequacy of compensation must occur at least every fifth year, in the manner specified in the lease. The lease must specify:

(1) When adjustments take effect;

(2) Who can make adjustments;

(3) What the adjustments are based on; and

(4) How to resolve disputes arising from the adjustments.

(d) When a review results in the need for adjustment of compensation, the Indian landowners must consent to the adjustment in accordance with § 162.012, unless the lease provides otherwise.

§ 162.429 What other types of payments are required under a business lease?

(a) The lessee may be required to pay additional fees, taxes, and assessments associated with the use of the land, as determined by entities having jurisdiction, except as provided in § 162.017. The lessee must pay these amounts to the appropriate office.

(b) If the leased premises are within an Indian irrigation project or drainage district, except as otherwise provided in part 171 of this chapter, the lessee must pay all operation and maintenance charges that accrue during the lease term. The lessee must pay these amounts to the appropriate office in charge of the irrigation project or drainage district. We will treat failure to make these payments as a violation of the lease.

(c) Where the property is subject to at least one other lease for another compatible use, the lessees may agree among themselves how to allocate payment of the Indian irrigation operation and maintenance charges.

BONDING AND INSURANCE

§ 162.434 Must a lessee provide a performance bond for a business lease?

The lessee must provide a performance bond or alternative form of security, except as provided in paragraph (f) of this section.

(a) The performance bond or alternative form of security must be in an amount sufficient to secure the contractual obligations including:

(1) No less than:

(i) The highest annual rental specified in the lease, if compensation is paid annually; or

(ii) If the compensation is not paid annually, another amount established by BIA in consultation with the tribe for tribal land or, where feasible, with Indian landowners for individually owned Indian land;

(2) The construction of any required permanent improvements;

(3) The operation and maintenance charges for any land located within an irrigation project; and

(4) The restoration and reclamation of the leased premises, to their condition at the start of the lease term or some other specified condition.

(b) The performance bond or other security:

(1) Must be deposited with us and made payable only to us, and may not be modified without our approval, except as provided in paragraph (b)(2) of this section; and

(2) For tribal land, if the lease so provides, may be deposited with the tribe and made payable to the tribe, and may not be modified without the approval of the tribe.

(c) The lease must specify the conditions under which we may adjust security or performance bond requirements to reflect changing conditions, including consultation with the tribal landowner for tribal land before the adjustment.

(d) We may require that the surety provide any supporting documents needed to show that the performance bond or alternative forms of security will be enforceable, and that the surety will be able to perform the guaranteed obligations.

(e) The performance bond or other security instrument must require the surety to provide notice to us at least 60 days before canceling a performance bond or other security. This will allow us to notify the lessee of its obligation to provide a substitute performance bond or other security and require collection of the bond or security before the cancellation date. Failure to provide a substitute performance bond or security is a violation of the lease.

(f) We may waive the requirement for a performance bond or alternative form of security if either:

(1) The lease is for religious, educational, recreational, cultural, or other public purposes; or

(2) The Indian landowners request it and we determine a waiver is in the Indian landowners' best interest.

(g) For tribal land, we will defer, to the maximum extent possible, to the tribe's determination that a waiver of a performance bond or alternative form of security is in its best interest.

§ 162.435 What forms of security are acceptable under a business lease?

(a) We will accept a performance bond only in one of the following forms:

(1) Certificates of deposit issued by a federally insured financial institution authorized to do business in the United States;

(2) Irrevocable letters of credit issued by a federally insured financial institution authorized to do business in the United States;

(3) Negotiable Treasury securities; or

(4) Surety bonds issued by a company approved by the U.S. Department of the Treasury.

(b) We may accept an alternative form of security approved by us that provides adequate protection for the Indian landowners and us, including but not limited to an escrow agreement and assigned savings account.

(c) All forms of performance bonds or alternative security must, if applicable:

(1) Indicate on their face that BIA approval is required for redemption;

(2) Be accompanied by a statement granting full authority to BIA to make an immediate claim upon or sell them if the lessee violates the lease;

(3) Be irrevocable during the term of the performance bond or alternative security; and

(4) Be automatically renewable during the term of the lease.

(d) We will not accept cash bonds.

§ 162.436 What is the release process for a performance bond or alternative form of security under a business lease?

(a) Upon expiration, termination, or cancellation of the lease, the lessee may ask BIA in writing to release the performance bond or alternative form of security.

(b) Upon receiving a request under paragraph (a) of this section, BIA will:

(1) Confirm with the tribe, for tribal land or, where feasible, with the Indian landowners for individually owned Indian land, that the lessee has complied with all lease obligations; and

(2) Release the performance bond or alternative form of security to the lessee, unless we determine that the bond or security must be redeemed to fulfill the contractual obligations.

§ 162.437 Must a lessee provide insurance for a business lease?

Except as provided in paragraph (c) of this section, a lessee must provide insurance necessary to protect the interests of the Indian landowners and in the amount sufficient to protect all insurable permanent improvements on the premises.

(a) The insurance may include property, crop, liability, and casualty insurance, depending on the Indian landowners' interests to be protected.

(b) Both the Indian landowners and the United States must be identified as additional insured parties.

(c) We may waive the requirement for insurance upon the request of the Indian landowner, if a waiver is in the best interest of the Indian landowner, including if the lease is for less than fair market rental or nominal compensation. For tribal land, we will defer, to the maximum extent possible, to the tribe's determination that a waiver is in its best interest.

APPROVAL

§ 162.438 What documents are required for BIA approval of a business lease?

A lessee or the Indian landowners must submit the following documents to us to obtain BIA approval of a business lease:

(a) A lease executed by the Indian landowners and the lessee that meets the requirements of this part;

(b) For tribal land, a tribal authorization for the lease and, if applicable, meeting the requirements of §§ 162.420(a), 162.426(b), and 162.428(a), or a separate signed certification meeting the requirements of §§ 162.426(b) and 162.428(a));

(c) A valuation, if required under § 162.420 or § 162.421;

(d) Proof of insurance, if required under § 162.437;

(e) A performance bond or other security, if required under § 162.434;

(f) Statement from the appropriate tribal authority that the proposed use is in conformance with applicable tribal law, if required by the tribe;

(g) Environmental and archeological reports, surveys, and site assessments as needed to facilitate compliance with applicable Federal and tribal environmental and land use requirements, including any documentation prepared under § 162.027(b);

(h) A restoration and reclamation plan (and any subsequent modifications to the plan), if appropriate;

(i) Where the lessee is not an entity owned and operated by the tribe, documents that demonstrate the technical capability of the lessee or lessee's agent to construct, operate, maintain, and terminate the proposed project and the lessee's ability to successfully design, construct, or obtain the funding for a project similar to the proposed project, if appropriate;

(j) A preliminary plan of development that describes the type and location of any permanent improvements the lessee plans to construct and a schedule showing the tentative commencement and completion dates for those improvements, if appropriate;

(k) A legal description of the land under § 162.418;

(l) If the lease is being approved under 25 U.S.C. 415, information to assist us in our evaluation of the factors in 25 U.S.C. 415(a); and

(m) If the lessee is a corporation, limited liability company, partnership, joint venture, or other legal entity, except a tribal entity, information such as organizational documents, certificates, filing records, and resolutions, that demonstrates that:

(1) The representative has authority to execute a lease;

(2) The lease will be enforceable against the lessee; and

(3) The legal entity is in good standing and authorized to conduct business in the jurisdiction where the land is located.

§ 162.439 Will BIA review a proposed business lease before or during preparation of the NEPA review documentation?

Upon request of the Indian landowners, we will review the proposed business lease after negotiation by the parties, before or during preparation of the NEPA review documentation and any valuation. Within 60 days of receiving the proposed lease, we will provide an acknowledgement of the terms of the lease and identify any provisions that, based on this acknowledgment review, would justify disapproval of the lease, pending results of the NEPA review and any valuation.

§ 162.440 What is the approval process for a business lease?

(a) Before we approve a business lease, we must determine that the lease is in the best interest of the Indian landowners. In making that determination, we will:

(1) Review the lease and supporting documents;

(2) Identify potential environmental impacts and ensure compliance with all applicable environmental laws, land use laws, and ordinances;

(3) If the lease is being approved under 25 U.S.C. 415, assure ourselves that adequate consideration has been given to the factors in 25 U.S.C. 415(a); and

(4) Require any lease modifications or mitigation measures necessary to satisfy any requirements including any other Federal or tribal land use requirements.

(b) Upon receiving a business lease package, we will promptly notify the parties whether the package is or is not complete. A complete package includes all the information and supporting documents required under this subpart, including but not limited to, NEPA review documentation and valuation documentation, where applicable.

(1) If the business lease package is not complete, our letter will identify the missing information or documents required for a complete package. If we do not respond to the submission of a business lease package, the parties may take action under § 162.463.

(2) If the business lease package is complete, we will notify the parties of the date of our receipt. Within 60 days of the receipt date, we will approve or disapprove the lease, return the package for revision, or inform the parties in writing that we need additional review time. If we inform the parties in writing that we need additional time, then:

(i) Our letter informing the parties that we need additional review time must identify our initial concerns and invite the parties to respond within 15 days of the date of the letter; and

(ii) We have 30 days from sending the letter informing the parties that we need additional time to approve or disapprove the lease.

(c) If we do not meet the deadlines in this section, then the parties may take appropriate action under § 162.463.

(d) We will provide any lease approval or disapproval and the basis for the determination, along with notification of any appeal rights under part 2 of this chapter, in writing to the parties to the lease.

(e) We will provide approved business leases on tribal land to the lessee and provide a copy to the tribe. We will provide approved business leases on individually owned Indian land to the lessee, and make copies available to the Indian landowners upon written request.

§ 162.441 How will BIA decide whether to approve a business lease?

(a) We will approve a business lease unless:

(1) The required consents have not been obtained from the parties to the lease;

(2) The requirements of this subpart have not been met; or

(3) We find a compelling reason to withhold our approval in order to protect the best interests of the Indian landowners.

(b) We will defer, to the maximum extent possible, to the Indian landowners' determination that the lease is in their best interest.

(c) We may not unreasonably withhold approval of a lease.

§ 162.442 When will a business lease be effective?

(a) A business lease will be effective on the date that we approve the lease, even if an appeal is filed under part 2 of this chapter.

(b) The lease may specify a date on which the obligations between the parties to the business lease are triggered. Such date may be before or after the approval date under paragraph (a) of this section.

§ 162.443 Must a business lease document be recorded?

(a) Any business lease document must be recorded in our LTRO with jurisdiction over the leased land.

(1) We will record the lease document immediately following our approval.

(2) If our approval of an assignment or sublease is not required, the parties must record the assignment or sublease in the LTRO with jurisdiction over the leased land.

(b) The tribe must record lease documents for the following types of leases in the LTRO with jurisdiction over the leased lands, even though BIA approval is not required:

(1) Leases of tribal land a corporate entity leases to a third party under 25 U.S.C. 477; and

(2) Leases of tribal land under a special act of Congress authorizing leases without our approval under certain conditions.

§ 162.444 Will BIA require an appeal bond for an appeal of a decision on a business lease document?

(a) If a party appeals our decision on a lease, assignment, amendment, or sublease, then the official to whom the appeal is made may require the appellant to post an appeal bond in accordance with part 2 of this chapter. We will not require an appeal bond:

(1) For an appeal of a decision on a leasehold mortgage; or

(2) If the tribe is a party to the appeal and requests a waiver of the appeal bond.

(b) The appellant may not appeal the appeal bond decision. The appellant may, however, request that the official to whom the appeal is made reconsider the bond decision, based on extraordinary circumstances. Any reconsideration decision is final for the Department.

AMENDMENTS

§ 162.445 May the parties amend a business lease?

The parties may amend a business lease by obtaining:

(a) The lessee's signature;

(b) The Indian landowners' consent under the requirements in § 162.446; and

(c) BIA approval of the amendment under §§ 162.447 and 162.448.

§ 162.446 What are the consent requirements for an amendment to a business lease?

(a) Unless the lease provides otherwise, the lessee must notify all Indian landowners of the proposed amendment.

(b) The Indian landowners, or their representatives under § 162.013, must consent to an amendment of a business lease in the same percentages and manner as a new business lease under § 162.012, unless the lease:

(1) Provides that individual Indian landowners are deemed to have consented where they do not object in writing to the amendment within a specified period of time following the landowners' receipt of the amendment and the lease meets the requirements of paragraph (c) of this section;

(2) Authorizes one or more representatives to consent to an amendment on behalf of all Indian landowners; or

(3) Designates us as the Indian landowners' representative for the purposes of consenting to an amendment.

(c) If the lease provides for deemed consent under paragraph (b)(1) of this section, it must require the parties to submit to us:

(1) A copy of the executed amendment or other documentation of any Indian landowners' actual consent;

(2) Proof of mailing of the amendment to any Indian landowners who are deemed to have consented; and

(3) Any other pertinent information for us to review.

(d) Unless specifically authorized in the lease, a written power of attorney, or a court document, Indian landowners may not be deemed to have consented to, and an Indian landowner's designated representative may not negotiate or consent to, an amendment that would:

(1) Reduce the payment obligations to the Indian landowners;

(2) Increase or decrease the lease area;

(3) Terminate or change the term of the lease; or

(4) Modify the dispute resolution procedures.

§ 162.447 What is the approval process for an amendment to a business lease?

(a) When we receive an amendment that meets the requirements of this subpart, we will notify the parties of the date we receive it. We have 30 days from receipt of the executed amendment, proof of required consents, and required documentation to approve or disapprove the amendment or inform the parties in writing that we need additional review time. Our determination whether to approve the amendment will be in writing and will state the basis for our approval or disapproval.

(b) Our letter informing the parties that we need additional review time must identify our initial concerns and invite the parties to respond within 15 days of the date of the letter. We have 30 days from sending the letter informing the parties that we need additional time to approve or disapprove the amendment.

(c) If we do not meet the deadline in paragraph (a) or this section, or paragraph (b) of this section if applicable, the amendment is deemed approved to the extent consistent with Federal law. Unless the lease provides otherwise, provisions of the amendment that are inconsistent with Federal law will be severed and unenforceable; all other provisions of the amendment will remain in force.

§ 162.448 How will BIA decide whether to approve an amendment to a business lease?

(a) We may disapprove a business lease amendment only if at least one of the following is true:

(1) The Indian landowners have not consented and their consent is required;

(2) The lessee's mortgagees or sureties have not consented;

(3) The lessee is in violation of the lease;

(4) The requirements of this subpart have not been met; or

(5) We find a compelling reason to withhold our approval in order to protect the best interests of the Indian landowners.

(b) We will defer, to the maximum extent possible to the Indian landowners' determination that the amendment is in their best interest.

(c) We may not unreasonably withhold approval of an amendment.

ASSIGNMENTS

§ 162.449 May a lessee assign a business lease?

(a) A lessee may assign a business lease by meeting the consent requirements in § 162.450 and obtaining our approval of the assignment under §§ 162.451 and 162.452, or by meeting the conditions in paragraphs (b) or (c) of this section.

(b) Where provided in the lease, the lessee may assign the lease to the following without meeting consent requirements or obtaining BIA approval of the assignment, as long as the lessee notifies BIA of the assignment within 30 days after it is executed:

(1) Not more than three distinct legal entities specified in the lease; or

(2) The lessee's wholly owned subsidiaries.

(c) The lessee may assign the lease without our approval or meeting consent requirements if:

(1) The assignee is a leasehold mortgagee or its designee, acquiring the lease either through foreclosure or by conveyance;

(2) The assignee agrees in writing to assume all of the obligations and conditions of the lease; and

(3) The assignee agrees in writing that any transfer of the lease will be in accordance with applicable law under § 162.014.

§ 162.450 What are the consent requirements for an assignment of a business lease?

(a) Unless the lease provides otherwise, the lessee must notify all Indian landowners of the proposed assignment.

(b) The Indian landowners, or their representatives under § 162.013, must consent to an amendment of a business lease in the same percentages and manner as a new business lease under § 162.012, unless the lease:

(1) Provides that individual Indian landowners are deemed to have consented where they do not object in writing to the amendment within a specified period of time following the landowners' receipt of the amendment and the lease meets the requirements of paragraph (c) of this section;

(2) Authorizes one or more representatives to consent to an amendment on behalf of all Indian landowners; or

(3) Designates us as the Indian landowners' representative for the purposes of consenting to an amendment.

(c) If the lease provides for deemed consent under paragraph (b)(1) of this section, it must require the parties to submit to us:

(1) A copy of the executed amendment or other documentation of any Indian landowners' actual consent;

(2) Proof of mailing of the amendment to any Indian landowners who are deemed to have consented; and

(3) Any other pertinent information for us to review.

(d) The lessee must obtain the consent of the holders of any bonds or mortgages.

§ 162.451 What is the approval process for an assignment of a business lease?

(a) When we receive an assignment that meets the requirements of this subpart, we will notify the parties of the date we receive it. If our approval is required, we have 30 days from receipt of the executed assignment, proof of required consents, and required documentation to approve or disapprove the assignment. Our determination whether to approve the assignment will be in writing and will state the basis for our approval or disapproval.

(b) If we do not meet the deadline in this section, the lessee or Indian landowners may take appropriate action under § 162.463.

§ 162.452 How will BIA decide whether to approve an assignment of a business lease?

(a) We may disapprove an assignment of a business lease only if at least one of the following is true:

(1) The Indian landowners have not consented and their consent is required;

(2) The lessee's mortgagees or sureties have not consented;

(3) The lessee is in violation of the lease;

(4) The assignee does not agree to be bound by the terms of the lease;

(5) The requirements of this subpart have not been met; or

(6) We find a compelling reason to withhold our approval in order to protect the best interests of the Indian landowners.

(b) In making the finding required by paragraph (a)(6) of this section, we may consider whether:

(1) The value of any part of the leased premises not covered by the assignment would be adversely affected; and

(2) If a performance bond is required, the assignee has posted the bond or security and provided supporting documents that demonstrate that:

(i) The lease will be enforceable against the assignee; and

(ii) The assignee will be able to perform its obligations under the lease or assignment.

(c) We will defer, to the maximum extent possible, to the Indian landowners' determination that the assignment is in their best interest.

(d) We may not unreasonably withhold approval of an assignment.

SUBLEASES

§ 162.453 May a lessee sublease a business lease?

(a) A lessee may sublease a business lease by meeting the consent requirements in § 162.454 and obtaining our approval of the sublease under §§ 162.455 and 162.456, or by meeting the conditions in paragraph (b) of this section.

(b) Where the sublease is part of a commercial development or residential development, the lessee may sublease without meeting consent requirements or obtaining BIA approval of the sublease, if:

(1) The lease provides for subleasing without meeting consent requirements or obtaining BIA approval;

(2) The sublease does not relieve the lessee/sublessor of any liability; and

(3) The parties provide BIA with a copy of the sublease within 30 days after it is executed.

§ 162.454 What are the consent requirements for a sublease of a business lease?

(a) Unless the lease provides otherwise, the lessee must notify all Indian landowners of the proposed sublease.

(b) The Indian landowners must consent to a sublease of a business lease in the same percentages and manner as a new business lease under § 162.012, unless the lease:

(1) Provides that individual Indian landowners are deemed to have consented where they do not object in writing to the sublease within a specified period of time following the landowners' receipt of the sublease and the lease meets the requirements of paragraph (c) of this section;

(2) Authorizes one or more representatives to consent to a sublease on behalf of all Indian landowners; or

(3) Designates us as the Indian landowners' representative for the purposes of consenting to a sublease.

(c) If the lease provides for deemed consent under paragraph (b)(1) of this section, it must require the parties to submit to us:

(1) A copy of the executed sublease or other documentation of any Indian landowners' actual consent;

(2) Proof of mailing of the sublease to any Indian landowners who are deemed to have consented; and

(3) Any other pertinent information for us to review.

§ 162.455 What is the approval process for a sublease of a business lease?

(a) When we receive a sublease that meets the requirements of this subpart, we will notify the parties of the date we receive it. If our approval is required, we have 30 days from receipt of the executed sublease, proof of required consents, and required documentation to approve or disapprove the sublease or inform the parties in writing that we need additional review time. Our determination whether to approve the sublease will be in writing and will state the basis for our approval or disapproval.

(b) Our letter informing the parties that we need additional review time must identify our initial concerns and invite the parties to respond within 15 days of the date of the letter. We have 30 days from sending the letter informing the parties that we need additional time to approve or disapprove the sublease.

(c) If we do not meet the deadline in paragraph (a) of this section, or paragraph (b) of this section if applicable, the sublease is deemed approved to the extent consistent with Federal law. Unless the lease provides otherwise, provisions of the sublease that are inconsistent with Federal law will be severed and unenforceable; all other provisions of the sublease will remain in force.

§ 162.456 How will BIA decide whether to approve a sublease of a business lease?

(a) We may disapprove a sublease of a business lease only if at least one of the following is true:

(1) The Indian landowners have not consented and their consent is required;

(2) The lessee's mortgagees or sureties have not consented;

(3) The lessee is in violation of the lease;

(4) The lessee will not remain liable under the lease;

(5) The requirements of this subpart have not been met; or

(6) We find a compelling reason to withhold our approval in order to protect the best interests of the Indian landowners.

(b) In making the finding required by paragraph (a)(6) of this section, we may consider whether the value of any part of the leased premises not covered by the sublease would be adversely affected.

(c) We will defer, to the maximum extent possible, to the Indian landowners' determination that the sublease is in their best interest.

(d) We may not unreasonably withhold approval of a sublease.

LEASEHOLD MORTGAGES

§ 162.457 May a lessee mortgage a business lease?

(a) A lessee may mortgage a business lease by meeting the consent requirements in § 162.458 and obtaining our approval of the leasehold mortgage under §§ 162.459 and 162.460.

(b) Refer to § 162.449(c) for information on what happens if a sale or foreclosure under an approved mortgage of the leasehold interest occurs.

§ 162.458 What are the consent requirements for a leasehold mortgage of a business lease?

(a) Unless the lease provides otherwise, the lessee must notify all Indian landowners of the proposed leasehold mortgage.

(b) The Indian landowners, or their representatives under § 162.013, must consent to a leasehold mortgage of a business lease in the same percentages and manner as a new business lease under § 162.012, unless the lease:

(1) States that landowner consent is not required for a leasehold mortgage and identifies what law would apply in case of foreclosure;

(2) Provides that individual Indian landowners are deemed to have consented where they do not object in writing to the leasehold mortgage within a specified period of time following the landowners' receipt of the leasehold mortgage and the lease meets the requirements of paragraph (c) of this section;

(3) Authorizes one or more representatives to consent to a leasehold mortgage on behalf of all Indian landowners; or

(4) Designates us as the Indian landowners' representative for the purposes of consenting to a leasehold mortgage.

(c) If the lease provides for deemed consent under paragraph (b)(2) of this section, it must require the parties to submit to us:

(1) A copy of the executed leasehold mortgage or other documentation of any Indian landowners' actual consent;

(2) Proof of mailing of the leasehold mortgage to any Indian landowners who are deemed to have consented; and

(3) Any other pertinent information for us to review.

§ 162.459 What is the approval process for a leasehold mortgage of a business lease?

(a) When we receive a leasehold mortgage that meets the requirements of this subpart, we will notify the parties of the date we receive it. We have 20 days from receipt of the executed leasehold mortgage, proof of required consents, and required documentation to approve or disapprove the leasehold mortgage. Our determination whether to approve the leasehold mortgage will be in writing and will state the basis for our approval or disapproval.

(b) If we do not meet the deadline in this section, the lessee may take appropriate action under § 162.463.

§ 162.460 How will BIA decide whether to approve a leasehold mortgage of a business lease?

(a) We may disapprove a leasehold mortgage of a business lease only if at least one of the following is true:

(1) The Indian landowners have not consented and their consent is required;

(2) The lessee's mortgagees or sureties have not consented;

(3) The requirements of this subpart have not been met; or

(4) We find a compelling reason to withhold our approval in order to protect the best interests of the Indian landowners.

(b) In making the finding required by paragraph (a)(4) of this section, we may consider whether:

(1) The leasehold mortgage proceeds would be used for purposes unrelated to the leased premises; and

(2) The leasehold mortgage is limited to the leasehold.

(c) We will defer, to the maximum extent possible, to the Indian landowners' determination that the leasehold mortgage is in their best interest.

(d) We may not unreasonably withhold approval of a leasehold mortgage.

EFFECTIVENESS, COMPLIANCE, AND ENFORCEMENT

§ 162.461 When will an amendment, assignment, sublease, or leasehold mortgage of a business lease be effective?

(a) An amendment, assignment, sublease, or leasehold mortgage of a business lease will be effective when approved, even if an appeal is filed under part 2 of this chapter, except:

(1) If the amendment or sublease was deemed approved under § 162.447(c) or § 162.455(c), the amendment or sublease becomes effective 45 days from the date the parties mailed or delivered the document to us for our review or, if we sent a letter informing the parties that we need additional time to approve or disapprove the lease, the amendment or sublease becomes effective 45 days from the date of the letter informing the parties that we need additional time to approve or disapprove the lease; and

(2) An assignment that does not require our approval under § 162.449(b) or § 162.449(c) or a sublease that does not require our approval under § 152.453(b) becomes effective on the effective date specified in the assignment or sublease. If the assignment or sublease does not specify the effective date, it becomes effective upon execution by the parties.

(b) We will provide copies of approved documents to the party requesting approval, to the tribe for tribal land, and upon request, to other parties to the lease document.

§ 162.462 What happens if BIA disapproves an amendment, assignment, sublease, or leasehold mortgage of a business lease?

If we disapprove an amendment, assignment, sublease, or leasehold mortgage of a business lease, we will notify the parties immediately and advise the landowners of their right to appeal the decision under part 2 of this chapter.

§ 162.463 What happens if BIA does not meet a deadline for issuing a decision on a lease document?

(a) If a Superintendent does not meet a deadline for issuing a decision on a lease, assignment, or leasehold mortgage, the parties may file a written notice to compel action with the appropriate Regional Director.

(b) The Regional Director has 15 days from receiving the notice to:

(1) Issue a decision; or

(2) Order the Superintendent to issue a decision within the time set out in the order.

(c) The parties may file a written notice to compel action with the BIA Director if:

(1) The Regional Director does not meet the deadline in paragraph (b) of this section;

(2) The Superintendent does not issue a decision within the time set by the Regional Director under paragraph (b)(2) of this section; or

(3) The initial decision on the lease, assignment, or leasehold mortgage is with the Regional Director, and he or she does not meet the deadline for such decision.

(d) The BIA Director has 15 days from receiving the notice to:

(1) Issue a decision; or

(2) Order the Regional Director or Superintendent to issue a decision within the time set out in the order.

(e) If the Regional Director or Superintendent does not issue a decision within the time set out in the order under paragraph (d)(2), then the BIA Director must issue a decision within 15 days from the expiration of the time set out in the order.

(f) The parties may file an appeal from our inaction to the Interior Board of Indian Appeals if the Director does not meet the deadline in paragraph (d) or (e) of this section.

(g) The provisions of 25 CFR 2.8 do not apply to the inaction of BIA officials with respect to a decision on a lease, amendment, assignment, sublease, or leasehold mortgage under this subpart.

§ 162.464 May BIA investigate compliance with a business lease?

(a) We may enter the leased premises at any reasonable time, upon reasonable notice, and consistent with any notice requirements under applicable tribal law and applicable lease documents, to protect the interests of the Indian landowners and to determine if the lessee is in compliance with the requirements of the lease.

(b) If an Indian landowner notifies us that a specific lease violation has occurred, we will promptly initiate an appropriate investigation.

§ 162.465 May a business lease provide for negotiated remedies if there is a violation?

(a) A business lease of tribal land may provide either or both parties with negotiated remedies in the event of a lease violation, including, but not limited to, the power to terminate the lease. If the lease provides one or both parties with the power to terminate the lease:

(1) BIA approval of the termination is not required;

(2) The termination is effective without BIA cancellation; and

(3) The Indian landowners must notify us of the termination so that we may record it in the LTRO.

(b) A business lease of individually owned Indian land may provide either or both parties with negotiated remedies, so long as the lease also specifies the manner in which those remedies may be exercised by or on behalf of the Indian landowners of the applicable percentage of interests under § 162.012 of this part. If the lease provides one or both parties with the power to terminate the lease:

(1) BIA concurrence with the termination is required to ensure that the Indian landowners of the applicable percentage of interests have consented; and

(2) BIA will record the termination in the LTRO.

(c) The parties must notify any surety or mortgagee of any violation that may result in termination and the termination of a business lease.

(d) Negotiated remedies may apply in addition to, or instead of, the cancellation remedy available to us, as specified in the lease. The landowners may request our assistance in enforcing negotiated remedies.

(e) A business lease may provide that lease violations will be addressed by a tribe, and that lease disputes will be resolved by a tribal court, any other court of competent jurisdiction, or by a tribal governing body in the absence of a tribal court, or through an alternative dispute resolution method. We may not be bound by decisions made in such forums, but we will defer to ongoing actions or proceedings, as appropriate, in deciding whether to exercise any of the remedies available to us.

§ 162.466 What will BIA do about a violation of a business lease?

(a) In the absence of actions or proceedings described in § 162.465(e), or if it is not appropriate for us to defer to the actions or proceedings, we will follow the procedures in paragraphs (b) and (c) of this section.

(b) If we determine there has been a violation of the conditions of a business lease, other than a violation of payment provisions covered by paragraph (c) of this section, we will promptly send the lessee and any surety and mortgagee a notice of violation by certified mail, return receipt requested.

(1) We will send a copy of the notice of violation to the tribe for tribal land, or provide constructive notice to Indian landowners for individually owned Indian land.

(2) The notice of violation will advise the lessee that, within 10 business days of the receipt of a notice of violation, the lessee must:

(i) Cure the violation and notify us, and the tribe for tribal land, in writing that the violation has been cured;

(ii) Dispute our determination that a violation has occurred; or

(iii) Request additional time to cure the violation.

(3) The notice of violation may order the lessee to cease operations under the lease.

(c) A lessee's failure to pay compensation in the time and manner required by a business lease is a violation of the lease, and we will issue a notice of violation in accordance with this paragraph.

(1) We will send the lessees and any surety and mortgagee a notice of violation by certified mail, return receipt requested:

(i) Promptly following the date on which the payment was due, if the lease requires that payments be made to us; or

(ii) Promptly following the date on which we receive actual notice of nonpayment from the Indian landowners, if the lease provides for payment directly to the Indian landowners.

(2) We will send a copy of the notice of violation to the tribe for tribal land, or provide constructive notice to the Indian landowners for individually owned Indian land.

(3) The notice of violation will require the lessee to provide adequate proof of payment.

(d) The lessee and its sureties will continue to be responsible for the obligations in the lease until the lease expires, or is terminated or cancelled.

§ 162.467 What will BIA do if the lessee does not cure a violation of a business lease on time?

(a) If the lessee does not cure a violation of a business lease within the required time period, or provide adequate proof of payment as required in the notice of violation, we will consult with the tribe for tribal land or, where feasible, with Indian landowners for individually owned Indian land, and determine whether:

(1) We should cancel the lease;

(2) The Indian landowners wish to invoke any remedies available to them under the lease;

(3) We should invoke other remedies available under the lease or applicable law, including collection on any available performance bond or, for failure to pay compensation, referral of the debt to the Department of the Treasury for collection; or

(4) The lessee should be granted additional time in which to cure the violation.

(b) Following consultation with the tribe for tribal land or, where feasible, with Indian landowners for individually owned Indian land, we may take action to recover unpaid compensation and any associated late payment charges.

(1) We do not have to cancel the lease or give any further notice to the lessee before taking action to recover unpaid compensation.

(2) We may still take action to recover any unpaid compensation if we cancel the lease.

(c) If we decide to cancel the lease, we will send the lessee and any surety and mortgagee a cancellation letter by certified mail, return receipt requested, within 5 business days of our decision. We will send a copy of the cancellation letter to the tribe for tribal land, and will provide Indian landowners for individually owned Indian land with actual or constructive notice of the cancellation. The cancellation letter will:

(1) Explain the grounds for cancellation;

(2) If applicable, notify the lessee of the amount of any unpaid compensation or late payment charges due under the lease;

(3) Notify the lessee of the lessee's right to appeal under part 2 of this chapter, including the possibility that the official to whom the appeal is made may require the lessee to post an appeal bond;

(4) Order the lessee to vacate the property within 31 days of the date of receipt of the cancellation letter, if an appeal is not filed by that time; and

(5) Order the lessee to take any other action BIA deems necessary to protect the Indian landowners.

(d) We may invoke any other remedies available to us under the lease, including collecting on any available performance bond, and the Indian landowners may pursue any available remedies under tribal law.

§ 162.468 Will late payment charges or special fees apply to delinquent payments due under a business lease?

(a) Late payment charges will apply as specified in the lease. The failure to pay these amounts will be treated as a lease violation.

(b) We may assess the following special fees to cover administrative costs incurred by the United States in the collection of the debt, if compensation is not paid in the time and manner required, in addition to the late payment charges that must be paid to the Indian landowners under the lease:

The lessee will pay . . .	For . . .
(1) $50.00	Any dishonored check.
(2) $15.00	Processing of each notice or demand letter.
(3) 18 percent of balance due.	Treasury processing following referral for collection of delinquent debt.

§ 162.469 How will payment rights relating to a business lease be allocated?

The business lease may allocate rights to payment for insurance proceeds, trespass damages, condemnation awards, settlement funds, and other payments between the Indian landowners and the lessee. If not specified in the lease, insurance policy, order, award, judgment, or other document, the Indian landowners or lessees will be entitled to receive these payments.

§ 162.470 When will a cancellation of a business lease be effective?

(a) A cancellation involving a business lease will not be effective until 31 days after the lessee receives a cancellation letter from us, or 41 days from the date we mailed the letter, whichever is earlier.

(b) The cancellation decision will not be effective if an appeal is filed unless the cancellation is made immediately effective under part 2 of this chapter. While a cancellation decision is ineffective, the lessee must continue to pay compensation and comply with the other terms of the lease.

§ 162.471 What will BIA do if a lessee remains in possession after a business lease expires or is terminated or cancelled?

If a lessee remains in possession after the expiration, termination, or cancellation of a business lease, we may treat the unauthorized possession as a trespass under applicable law in consultation with the Indian landowners. Unless the Indian landowners of the applicable percentage of interests under § 162.012 have notified us in writing that they are engaged in good faith negotiations with the holdover lessee to obtain a new lease, we may take action to recover possession on behalf of the Indian landowners, and pursue any additional remedies available under applicable law, such as a forcible entry and detainer action.

§ 162.472 Will BIA appeal bond regulations apply to cancellation decisions involving business leases?

(a) Except as provided in paragraph (b) of this section, the appeal bond provisions in part 2 of this chapter will apply to appeals from lease cancellation decisions

(b) The lessee may not appeal the appeal bond decision. The lessee may, however, request that the official to whom the appeal is made reconsider the appeal bond decision, based on extraordinary circumstances. Any reconsideration decision is final for the Department.

§ 162.473 When will BIA issue a decision on an appeal from a business leasing decision?

BIA will issue a decision on an appeal from a business leasing decision within 60 days of receipt of all pleadings.

§ 162.474 What happens if the lessee abandons the leased premises?

If a lessee abandons the leased premises, we will treat the abandonment as a violation of the lease. The lease may specify a period of non-use after which the lease premises will be considered abandoned.

Subpart E—Wind and Solar Resource Leases

SOURCE: 77 FR 72494, Dec. 5, 2012, unless otherwise noted.

GENERAL PROVISIONS APPLICABLE TO WEELS AND WSR LEASES

§ 162.501 What types of leases does this subpart cover?

(a) This subpart covers:

(1) Wind energy evaluation leases (WEELs), which are short-term leases that authorize possession of Indian land for the purpose of installing, operating, and maintaining instrumentation, and associated infrastructure, such as meteorological towers, to evaluate wind resources for electricity generation; and

(2) Wind and solar resource (WSR) leases, which are leases that authorize possession of Indian land for the purpose of installing, operating, and maintaining instrumentation, facilities, and associated infrastructure, such as wind turbines and solar panels, to harness wind and/or solar energy to generate and supply electricity:

(i) For resale on a for-profit or nonprofit basis;

(ii) To a utility grid serving the public generally; or

(iii) To users within the local community (e.g., on and adjacent to a reservation).

(b) If the generation of electricity is solely to support a use approved under subpart B, Agricultural Leases; subpart C, Residential Leases; or subpart D Business Leases (including religious, educational, recreational, cultural, or other public purposes), for the same parcel of land, then the installation, operation, and maintenance of instrumentation, facilities, and associated infrastructure are governed by subpart B, C, or D, as appropriate.

§ 162.502 Who must obtain a WEEL or WSR lease?

(a) Anyone seeking to possess Indian land to conduct activities associated with the evaluation of wind resources must obtain a WEEL, except that a WEEL is not required if use or possession of the Indian land to conduct wind energy evaluation activities is authorized:

(1) Under § 162.005(b);

(2) By a permit from the Indian landowners under § 162.007; or

(3) By a tribe on its land under 25 U.S.C. 81.

(b) Except as provided in §§ 162.005(b), 162.501, and paragraph (c) of this section, anyone seeking to possess Indian land to conduct activities associated with the development of wind and/or solar resources must obtain a WSR lease.

(c) A tribe that conducts wind and solar resource activities on its tribal land does not need a WEEL or WSR under this subpart.

§ 162.503 Is there a model WEEL or WSR lease?

There is no model WEEL or WSR lease because of the need for flexibility in negotiating and writing WEELs and WSR leases; however, we may:

(a) Provide other guidance, such as checklists and sample lease provisions, to assist in the lease negotiation process; and

(b) Assist the Indian landowners, upon their request, in developing appropriate lease provisions or in using tribal lease forms that conform to the requirements of this part.

WEELS

§ 162.511 What is the purpose of a WEEL?

A WEEL is a short-term lease that allows the lessee to possess trust or restricted lands for the purpose of evaluating wind resources. The lessee may use information collected under the WEEL to assess the potential for wind energy development, and determine future placement and type of wind energy technology to use in developing the energy resource potential of the leased area.

§ 162.512 How long may the term of a WEEL run?

(a) A WEEL must provide for a definite term, state if there is an option to renew and if so, provide for a definite term for the renewal period. WEELs are for project evaluation purposes, and therefore may have:

(1) An initial term that is no longer than 3 years; and

(2) One renewal period not to exceed 3 years.

(b) The exercise of the option to renew must be in writing and the WEEL must specify:

(1) The time and manner in which the option must be exercised or is automatically effective;

(2) That confirmation of the renewal will be submitted to us, unless the WEEL provides for automatic renewal; and

(3) Additional consideration, if any, that will be due upon the exercise of the option to renew or the start of the renewal term.

§ 162.513 Are there mandatory provisions a WEEL must contain?

(a) All WEELs must identify:

(1) The tract or parcel of land being leased;

(2) The purpose of the WEEL and authorized uses of the leased premises;

(3) The parties to the WEEL;

(4) The term of the WEEL;

(5) The ownership of permanent improvements and the responsibility for constructing, operating, maintaining, and managing permanent improvements, under § 162.515;

(6) Payment requirements and late payment charges, including interest;

(7) Due diligence requirements, under § 162.517; and

(8) Insurance requirements, under § 162.527.

(b) Where a representative executes a lease on behalf of an Indian landowner or lessee, the lease must identify the landowner or lessee being represented and the authority under which the action is taken.

(c) All WEELs must include the following provisions:

(1) The obligations of the lessee and its sureties to the Indian landowners are also enforceable by the United States, so long as the land remains in trust or restricted status;

(2) There must not be any unlawful conduct, creation of a nuisance, illegal activity, or negligent use or waste of leased premises;

(3) The lessee must comply with all applicable laws, ordinances, rules, regulations, and other legal requirements under § 162.014;

(4) If historic properties, archeological resources, human remains, or other cultural items, not previously reported are encountered during the course of any activity associated with this lease, all activity in the immediate vicinity of the properties, resources, remains, or items will cease, and the lessee will contact BIA and the tribe with jurisdiction to determine how to proceed and appropriate disposition;

(5) BIA has the right, at any reasonable time during the term of the lease, and upon reasonable notice, in accordance with § 162.589, to enter the leased premises for inspection; and

(6) BIA may, at its discretion, treat as a lease violation any failure by the lessee to cooperate with a BIA request to make appropriate records, reports, or information available for BIA inspection and duplication.

(d) Unless the lessee would be prohibited by law from doing so, the lease must also contain the following provisions:

(1) The lessee holds the United States and the Indian landowners harmless from any loss, liability, or damages resulting from the lessee's use or occupation of the leased premises;

(2) The lessee indemnifies the United States and the Indian landowners against all liabilities or costs relating to the use, handling, treatment, removal, storage, transportation, or disposal of hazardous materials, or the release or discharge of any hazardous material from the leased premises that occurs during the lease term, regardless of fault, with the exception that the lessee is not required to indemnify the Indian landowners for liability or cost arising from the Indian landowners' negligence or willful misconduct.

(e) We may treat any provision of a lease document that violates Federal law as a violation of the lease.

[77 FR 72494, Dec. 5, 2012, as amended at 78 FR 19100, Mar. 29, 2013]

§ 162.514 May permanent improvements be made under a WEEL?

(a) A WEEL anticipates the installation of facilities and associated infrastructure of a size and magnitude necessary for evaluation of wind resource capacity and potential effects of development. These facilities and associated infrastructure are considered permanent improvements. An equipment installation plan must be submitted with the lease under § 162.528(g).

(b) If any of the following changes are made to the equipment installation plan, the Indian landowners must approve the revised plan and the lessee must provide a copy of the revised plan to BIA:

(1) Location of permanent improvements;

(2) Type of permanent improvements; or

(3) Delay of 90 days or more in any phase of development.

§ 162.515 How must a WEEL address ownership of permanent improvements?

(a) A WEEL must specify who will own any permanent improvements the lessee installs during the lease term. In addition, the WEEL must indicate whether any permanent improvements the lessee installs:

(1) Will remain on the premises upon expiration, termination, or cancellation of the lease whether or not the WEEL is followed by a WSR lease, in a condition satisfactory to the Indian landowners;

(2) May be conveyed to the Indian landowners during the WEEL term and under what conditions the permanent improvements may be conveyed;

(3) Will be removed within a time period specified in the WEEL, at the lessee's expense, with the leased premises to be restored as closely as possible to their condition before installation of the permanent improvements; or

(4) Will be disposed of by other specified means.

(b) A WEEL that requires the lessee to remove the permanent improvements must also provide the Indian landowners with an option to take possession and title to the permanent improvements if the improvements are not removed within the specified time period.

§ 162.516 How will BIA enforce removal requirements in a WEEL?

We may take appropriate enforcement action to ensure removal of the permanent improvements and restoration of the premises at the lessee's expense:

(a) In consultation with the tribe, for tribal land or, where feasible, with Indian landowners for individually owned Indian land; and

(b) After termination, cancellation, or expiration of the WEEL.

§ 162.517 What requirements for due diligence must a WEEL include?

(a) A WEEL must include due diligence requirements that require the lessee to:

(1) Install testing and monitoring facilities within 12 months after the effective date of the WEEL or other period designated in the WEEL and consistent with the plan of development; and

(2) If installation does not occur, or is not expected to be completed, within the time period specified in paragraph (a)(1) of this section, provide the Indian landowners and BIA with an explanation of good cause for any delay, the anticipated date of installation of facilities, and evidence of progress toward installing or completing testing and monitoring facilities.

(b) Failure of the lessee to comply with the due diligence requirements of the WEEL is a violation of the WEEL and may lead to:

(1) Cancellation of the WEEL under § 162.592; and

(2) Application of the requirement that the lessee transfer ownership of energy resource information collected under the WEEL to the Indian landowners under § 162.520.

§ 162.518 How must a WEEL describe the land?

(a) A WEEL must describe the leased premises by reference to a public or private survey, if possible. If the land cannot be so described, the lease must include one or more of the following:

(1) A legal description;

(2) A survey-grade global positioning system description; or

(3) Another description prepared by a registered land surveyor that is sufficient to identify the leased premises.

(b) If the tract is fractionated, we will identify the undivided trust or restricted interests in the leased premises.

§ 162.519 May a WEEL allow for compatible uses by the Indian landowner?

The WEEL may provide for the Indian landowners to use, or authorize others to use, the leased premises for other noncompeting uses compatible with the purpose of the WEEL. This may include the right to lease the premises for other compatible purposes. Any such use by the Indian landowners will not reduce or offset the monetary compensation for the WEEL.

§ 162.520 Who owns the energy resource information obtained under the WEEL?

(a) The WEEL must specify the ownership of any energy resource information the lessee obtains during the WEEL term.

(b) Unless otherwise specified in the WEEL, the energy resource information the lessee obtains through the leased activity becomes the property of Indian landowners at the expiration, termination, or cancellation of the WEEL or upon failure by the lessee to diligently install testing and monitoring facilities on the leased premises in accordance with § 162.517.

(c) BIA will keep confidential any information it is provided that is marked confidential or proprietary and that is exempt from public release, to the extent allowed by law.

§ 162.521 May a lessee incorporate its WEEL analyses into its WSR lease analyses?

Any analyses a lessee uses to bring a WEEL activity into compliance with applicable laws, ordinances, rules, regulations under § 162.014 and any other legal requirements may be incorporated by reference, as appropriate, into the analyses of a proposed WSR lease.

§ 162.522 May a WEEL contain an option for the lessee to enter into a WSR lease?

(a) A WEEL may provide for an option period following the expiration of the WEEL term during which the lessee and the Indian landowners may enter into a WSR lease.

(b) Our approval of a WEEL that contains an option to enter into a WSR lease does not guarantee or imply our approval of any WSR lease.

WEEL MONETARY COMPENSATION REQUIREMENTS

§ 162.523 How much compensation must be paid under a WEEL?

(a) The WEEL must state how much compensation will be paid.

(b) A WEEL must specify the date on which compensation will be due.

(c) Failure to make timely payments is a violation of the WEEL and may lead to cancellation of the WEEL.

(d) The lease compensation requirements of §§ 162.552 through 162.558 also apply to WEELs.

§ 162.524 Will BIA require a valuation for a WEEL?

We will not require a valuation for a WEEL.

WEEL BONDING AND INSURANCE

§ 162.525 Must a lessee provide a performance bond for a WEEL?

We will not require the lessee to provide a performance bond or alternative form of security for a WEEL.

§ 162.526 [Reserved]

§ 162.527 Must a lessee provide insurance for a WEEL?

Except as provided in paragraph (d) of this section, a lessee must provide insurance necessary to protect the interests of Indian landowners and in the amount sufficient to protect all insurable permanent improvements on the leased premises.

(a) The insurance may include property, crop, liability, and casualty insurance, depending on the Indian landowners' interests to be protected.

(b) Both the Indian landowners and the United States must be identified as additional insured parties.

(c) Lease insurance may be increased and extended for use as the required WSR lease insurance.

(d) We may waive the requirement for insurance upon the request of the Indian landowner, if a waiver is in the best interest of the Indian landowner, including if the lease is for less than fair market rental or nominal compensation. For tribal land, we will defer, to the maximum extent possible, to the tribe's determination that a waiver is in its best interest.

WEEL APPROVAL

§ 162.528 What documents are required for BIA approval of a WEEL?

A lessee or the Indian landowners must submit the following documents to us to obtain BIA approval of a WEEL:

(a) A WEEL executed by the Indian landowners and the lessee that meets the requirements of this part;

(b) For tribal land, a tribal authorization for the WEEL;

(c) Proof of insurance, as required by § 162.527;

(d) Statement from the appropriate tribal authority that the proposed use is in conformance with applicable tribal law, if required by the tribe;

(e) Environmental and archeological reports, surveys, and site assessments as needed to facilitate compliance with applicable Federal and tribal environmental and land use requirements, including any documentation prepared under § 162.027(b);

(f) An equipment installation plan;

(g) A restoration and reclamation plan (and any subsequent modifications to the plan);

(h) Where the lessee is not an entity owned and operated by the tribe, documents that demonstrate the technical capability of the lessee or lessee's agent to construct, operate, maintain, and terminate the proposed project and the lessee's ability to successfully design, construct, or obtain the funding for a project similar to the proposed project, if appropriate;

(i) A legal description of the land under § 162.518;

(j) If the lease is being approved under 25 U.S.C. 415, information to assist us in our evaluation of the factors in 25 U.S.C. 415(a); and

(k) If the lessee is a corporation, limited liability company, partnership, joint venture, or other legal entity, except a tribal entity, information such as organizational documents, certificates, filing records, and resolutions, that demonstrates that:

(1) The representative has authority to execute a lease;

(2) The lease will be enforceable against the lessee; and

(3) The legal entity is in good standing and authorized to conduct business in the jurisdiction where the land is located.

§ 162.529 Will BIA review a proposed WEEL before or during preparation of the NEPA review documentation?

Upon request of the Indian landowners, we will review the proposed WEEL after negotiation by the parties, before or during preparation of the NEPA review documentation. Within 10 days of receiving the proposed WEEL, we will provide an acknowledgement of the terms of the lease and identify any provisions that, based on this acknowledgment review, would justify disapproval of the lease, pending results of the NEPA review.

§ 162.530 What is the approval process for a WEEL?

(a) Before we approve a WEEL, we must determine that the WEEL is in the best interest of the Indian landowners. In making that determination, we will:

(1) Review the WEEL and supporting documents;

(2) Identify potential environmental impacts and ensure compliance with all applicable environmental laws, land use laws, and ordinances;

(3) If the lease is being approved under 25 U.S.C. 415, assure ourselves that adequate consideration has been given to the factors in 25 U.S.C. 415(a); and

(4) Require any lease modifications or mitigation measures necessary to satisfy any requirements including any other Federal or tribal land use requirements.

(b) Upon receiving the WEEL package, we will promptly notify the parties whether the package is or is not complete. A complete package includes all the information and supporting documents required for a WEEL, including but not limited to, NEPA review documentation, where applicable.

(1) If the WEEL package is not complete, our letter will identify the missing information or documents required for a complete package. If we do not respond to the submission of a WEEL package, the parties may take action under § 162.588.

(2) If the WEEL package is complete, we will notify the parties of the date we receive the complete package, and, within 20 days of the date of receipt of the package at the appropriate BIA office, approve or disapprove the WEEL or return the package for revision.

(c) If we do not meet the deadline in this section, then the parties may take appropriate action under § 162.588.

(d) We will provide any WEEL approval determination and the basis for the determination, along with notification of appeal rights under part 2 of this chapter, in writing to the parties to the WEEL.

(e) We will provide any WEEL disapproval determination and the basis for the determination, along with notification of rights to an informal conference, in writing to the parties. Within 30 days of receipt of the disapproval determination, the parties may request an informal conference with the official who issued the determination. Within 30 days of receiving this request, the official must hold the informal conference with the parties. Within 10 days of the informal conference, the official must issue a decision and the basis for the decision, along with a notification of appeal rights under part 2 of this chapter, in writing to the parties to the WEEL.

(f) We will provide the approved WEEL on tribal land to the lessee and provide a copy to the tribe. We will provide the approved WEEL on individually owned Indian land to the lessee, and make copies available to the Indian landowners upon written request.

§ 162.531 How will BIA decide whether to approve a WEEL?

(a) We will approve a WEEL unless:

(1) The required consents have not been obtained from the parties to the WEEL;

(2) The requirements applicable to WEELs have not been met; or

(3) We find a compelling reason to withhold our approval in order to protect the best interests of the Indian landowners.

(b) We will defer, to the maximum extent possible, to the Indian landowners' determination that the WEEL is in their best interest.

(c) We may not unreasonably withhold approval of a WEEL.

§ 162.532 When will a WEEL be effective?

(a) A WEEL will be effective on the date on which we approve the WEEL, even if an appeal is filed under part 2 of this chapter.

(b) The WEEL may specify a date on which the obligations between the parties to a WEEL are triggered. Such date may be before or after the approval date under paragraph (a) of this section.

(c) WEEL lease documents not requiring our approval are effective upon execution by the parties, or on the effective date specified in the lease document. If the WEEL lease document does not specify an effective date, it becomes effective upon execution by the parties.

§ 162.533 Must a WEEL lease document be recorded?

(a) Any WEEL lease document must be recorded in our LTRO with jurisdiction over the leased land.

(1) We will record the lease document immediately following our approval.

(2) If our approval of an assignment or sublease is not required, the parties must record the assignment or sublease in the LTRO with jurisdiction over the leased land.

(b) The tribe must record lease documents for the following types of leases in the LTRO with jurisdiction over the tribal lands, even though BIA approval is not required:

(1) Leases of tribal land that a corporate entity leases to a third party under 25 U.S.C. 477; and

(2) Leases of tribal land under a special act of Congress authorizing leases without our approval.

WEEL ADMINISTRATION

§ 162.534 May the parties amend, assign, sublease, or mortgage a WEEL?

The parties may amend, assign, sublease, or mortgage a WEEL by following the procedures and requirements for amending, assigning, subleasing, or mortgaging a WSR lease.

WEEL COMPLIANCE AND ENFORCEMENT

§ 162.535 What effectiveness, compliance, and enforcement provisions apply to WEELs?

(a) The provisions at § 162.586 apply to WEEL lease documents.

(b) The provisions at §§ 162.587 through 162.589 and 162.591 through 162.599 apply to WEELs, except that any references to § 162.590 will apply instead to § 162.536.

§ 162.536 Under what circumstances may a WEEL be terminated?

A WEEL must state whether, and under what conditions, the Indian landowners may terminate the WEEL.

§ 162.537 [Reserved]

WSR LEASES

§ 162.538 What is the purpose of a WSR lease?

A WSR lease authorizes a lessee to possess Indian land to conduct activities related to the installation, operation, and maintenance of wind and/or solar energy resource development projects. Activities include installing instrumentation facilities and infrastructure associated with the generation, transmission, and storage of electricity and other related activities. Leases for biomass or waste-to-energy purposes are governed by subpart D of this part.

§ 162.539 Must I obtain a WEEL before obtaining a WSR lease?

You may enter into a WSR lease without a WEEL. While you may enter into a lease as a direct result of energy resource information gathered from a WEEL activity, obtaining a WEEL is not a precondition to entering into a WSR lease.

§ 162.540 How long may the term of a WSR lease run?

(a) A WSR lease must provide for a definite lease term, state if there is an option to renew, and if so, provide for a definite term for the renewal period. The maximum term of a lease approved under 25 U.S.C. 415(a) may not exceed 50 years (consisting of an initial term not to exceed 25 years and one renewal not to exceed 25 years), unless a Federal statute provides for a longer maximum term (e.g., 25 U.S.C. 415(a) allows for a maximum term of 99 years for certain tribes), a different initial term, renewal term, or number of renewals.

(b) For tribal land, we will defer to the tribe's determination that the lease term, including any renewal, is reasonable. For individually owned Indian land, we will review the lease term, including any renewal, to ensure it is reasonable, given the:

(1) Purpose of the lease;

(2) Type of financing; and

(3) Level of investment.

(c) The lease may not be extended by holdover.

§ 162.541 What must the lease include if it contains an option to renew?

(a) If the lease provides for an option to renew, the lease must specify:

(1) The time and manner in which the option must be exercised or is automatically effective;

(2) That confirmation of the renewal will be submitted to us, unless the lease provides for automatic renewal;

(3) Whether Indian landowner consent to the renewal is required;

(4) That the lessee must provide notice of the renewal to the Indian landowners and any sureties and mortgagees;

(5) The additional consideration, if any, that will be due upon the exercise of the option to renew or the start of the renewal term; and

(6) Any other conditions for renewal (e.g., that the lessee not be in violation of the lease at the time of renewal).

(b) We will record any renewal of a lease in the LTRO.

§ 162.542 Are there mandatory provisions a WSR lease must contain?

(a) All WSR leases must identify:

(1) The tract or parcel of land being leased;

(2) The purpose of the lease and authorized uses of the leased premises;

(3) The parties to the lease;

(4) The term of the lease;

(5) The ownership of permanent improvements and the responsibility for constructing, operating, maintaining, and managing, WSR equipment, roads, transmission lines and related facilities under § 162.543;

(6) Who is responsible for evaluating the leased premises for suitability; purchasing, installing, operating, and maintaining WSR equipment; negotiating power purchase agreements; and transmission;

(7) Payment requirements and late payment charges, including interest;

(8) Due diligence requirements, under § 162.546;

(9) Insurance requirements, under § 162.562; and

(10) Bonding requirements under § 162.559. If a performance bond is required, the lease must state that the lessee must obtain the consent of the surety for any legal instrument that directly affects their obligations and liabilities.

(b) Where a representative executes a lease on behalf of an Indian landowner or lessee, the lease must identify the landowner or lessee being represented and the authority under which such action is taken.

(c) All WSR leases must include the following provisions:

(1) The obligations of the lessee and its sureties to the Indian landowners are also enforceable by the United States, so long as the land remains in trust or restricted status;

(2) There must not be any unlawful conduct, creation of a nuisance, illegal activity, or negligent use or waste of the leased premises;

(3) The lessee must comply with all applicable laws, ordinances, rules, regulations, and other legal requirements under § 162.014;

(4) If historic properties, archeological resources, human remains, or other cultural items not previously reported are encountered during the course of any activity associated with the lease, all activity in the immediate vicinity of the properties, resources, remains, or items will cease and the lessee will contact BIA and the tribe with jurisdiction to determine how to proceed and appropriate disposition;

(5) BIA has the right, at any reasonable time during the term of the lease and upon reasonable notice, in accordance with § 162.589, to enter the leased premises for inspection and to ensure compliance; and

(6) BIA may, at its discretion, treat as a lease violation any failure by the lessee to cooperate with a BIA request to make appropriate records, reports, or information available for BIA inspection and duplication.

(d) Unless the lessee would be prohibited by law from doing so, the lease must also contain the following provisions:

(1) The lessee holds the United States and the Indian landowners harmless from any loss, liability, or damages resulting from the lessee's use or occupation of the leased premises; and

(2) The lessee indemnifies the United States and the Indian landowners against all liabilities or costs relating to the use, handling, treatment, removal, storage, transportation, or disposal of hazardous materials, or the release or discharge of any hazardous material from the leased premises that occurs during the lease term, regardless of fault, with the exception that the lessee is not required to indemnify the Indian landowners for liability or cost arising from the Indian landowners' negligence or willful misconduct.

(e) We may treat any provision of a lease document that violates Federal law as a violation of the lease.

§ 162.543 May permanent improvements be made under a WSR lease?

(a) A WSR lease must provide for the installation of a facility and associated infrastructure of a size and magnitude necessary for the generation and delivery of electricity, in accordance with § 162.019. These facilities and associated infrastructure are considered permanent improvements. A resource development plan must be submitted for approval with the lease under § 162.563(h).

(b) If the parties agree to any of the following changes to the resource development plan after lease approval, they must submit the revised plan to BIA for the file:

(1) Location of permanent improvements;

(2) Type of permanent improvements; or

(3) Delay of 90 days or more in any phase of development.

§ 162.544 How must a WSR lease address ownership of permanent improvements?

(a) A WSR lease must specify who will own any permanent improvements the lessee installs during the lease term and may specify under what conditions, if any, permanent improvements the lessee constructs may be conveyed to the Indian landowners during the lease term. In addition, the lease must indicate whether each specific permanent improvement the lessee installs will:

(1) Remain on the leased premises upon the expiration, termination, or cancellation of the lease, in a condition satisfactory to the Indian landowners and become the property of the Indian landowners;

(2) Be removed within a time period specified in the lease, at the lessee's expense, with the leased premises to be restored as closely as possible to their condition before installation of the permanent improvements; or

(3) Be disposed of by other specified means.

(b) A lease that requires the lessee to remove the permanent improvements must also provide the Indian landowners with an option to take possession of and title to the permanent improvements if the improvements are not removed within the specified time period.

§ 162.545 How will BIA enforce removal requirements in a WSR lease?

(a) We may take appropriate enforcement action to ensure removal of the permanent improvements and restoration of the premises at the lessee's expense:

(1) In consultation with the tribe, for tribal land or, where feasible, with Indian landowners for individually owned Indian land; and

(2) Before or after expiration, termination, or cancellation of the lease.

(b) We may collect and hold the performance bond until removal and restoration are completed.

§ 162.546 What requirements for due diligence must a WSR lease include?

(a) A WSR lease must include due diligence requirements that require the lessee to:

(1) Commence installation of energy facilities within 2 years after the effective date of the lease or consistent with a timeframe in the resource development plan;

(2) If installation does not occur, or is not expected to be completed, within the time period specified in paragraph (a)(1) of this section, provide the Indian landowners and BIA with an explanation of good cause as to the nature of any delay, the anticipated date of installation of facilities, and evidence of progress toward commencement of installation;

(3) Maintain all on-site electrical generation equipment and facilities and related infrastructure in accordance with the design standards in the resource development plan; and

(4) Repair, place into service, or remove from the site within a time period specified in the lease any idle, improperly functioning, or abandoned equipment or facilities that have been inoperative for a continuous period specified in the lease (unless the equipment or facilities were idle as a result of planned suspension of operations, for example, for grid operations or during bird migration season).

(b) Failure of the lessee to comply with the due diligence requirements of the lease is a violation of the lease and may lead to cancellation of the lease under § 162.592.

§ 162.547 How must a WSR lease describe the land?

(a) A WSR lease must describe the leased premises by reference to a private or public survey, if possible. If the land cannot be so described, the lease must include one or more of the following:

(1) A legal description;

(2) A survey-grade global positioning system description; or

(3) Another description prepared by a registered land surveyor that is sufficient to identify the leased premises.

(b) If the tract is fractionated, we will identify the undivided trust or restricted interests in the leased premises.

§ 162.548 May a WSR lease allow compatible uses?

The lease may provide for the Indian landowners to use, or authorize others to use, the leased premises for other uses compatible with the purpose of the WSR lease and consistent with the terms of the WSR lease. This may include the right to lease the premises for other compatible purposes. Any such use or authorization by the Indian landowners will not reduce or offset the monetary compensation for the WSR lease.

WSR Lease Monetary Compensation Requirements

§ 162.549 How much monetary compensation must be paid under a WSR lease of tribal land?

(a) A WSR lease of tribal land may allow for any payment negotiated by the tribe, and we will defer to the tribe and not require a valuation if the tribe submits a tribal authorization expressly stating that it:

(1) Has negotiated compensation satisfactory to the tribe;

(2) Waives valuation; and

(3) Has determined that accepting such negotiated compensation and waiving valuation is in its best interest.

(b) The tribe may request, in writing, that we determine fair market rental, in which case we will use a valuation in accordance with § 162.551. After providing the tribe with the fair market rental, we will defer to a tribe's decision to allow for any payment amount negotiated by the tribe.

(c) If the conditions in paragraph (a) or (b) of this section are not met, we will require that the lease provide for fair market rental based on a valuation in accordance with § 162.551.

§ 162.550 How much monetary compensation must be paid under a WSR lease of individually owned Indian land?

(a) A WSR lease of individually owned Indian land must require payment of not less than fair market rental before any adjustments, based on a fixed amount, a percentage of the projected gross income, megawatt capacity fee, or some other method, unless paragraphs (b) or (c) of this section permit a lesser amount. The lease must establish how the fixed amount, percentage or combination will be calculated and the frequency at which the payments will be made.

(b) We may approve a lease of individually owned Indian land that provides for the payment of nominal compensation, or less than a fair market rental, if:

(1) The Indian landowners execute a written waiver of the right to receive fair market rental; and

(2) We determine it is in the Indian landowners' best interest, based on factors including, but not limited to:

(i) The lessee is a member of the immediate family, as defined in § 162.003, of an Indian landowner;

(ii) The lessee is a co-owner of the leased tract;

(iii) A special relationship or circumstances exist that we believe warrant approval of the lease;

(iv) The lease is for public purposes; or

(v) We have waived the requirement for a valuation under paragraph (e) of this section.

(c) We may approve a lease that provides for the payment of less than a fair market rental during the periods before the generation and transmission of electricity begins, if we determine it is in the Indian landowners' best interest. The lease must specify the amount of the compensation and the applicable periods.

(d) We will require a valuation in accordance with § 162.422, unless:

(1) 100 percent of the landowners submit to us a written request to waive the valuation requirement; or

(2) We waive the requirement under paragraph (e) of this section; or

(3) We determine it is in the best interest of the Indian landowners to accept an economic analysis in lieu of an appraisal and:

(i) The Indian landowners submit an economic analysis that is approved by the Office of Indian Energy & Economic Development (IEED); or

(ii) IEED prepares an economic analysis at the request of the Indian landowners.

(e) If the owners of the applicable percentage of interests under § 162.011 of this part grant a WSR lease on behalf of all of the Indian landowners of a fractionated tract, the lease must provide that the non-consenting Indian landowners, and those on whose behalf we have consented, receive a fair market rental, as determined by a valuation, unless we waive the requirement because the tribe or lessee will construct infrastructure improvements on, or serving, the leased premises, and we determine it is in the best interest of all the landowners.

§ 162.551 How will BIA determine fair market rental for a WSR lease?

(a) We will use a market analysis, appraisal, or other appropriate valuation method to determine the fair market rental before we approve a WSR lease of individually owned Indian land or, at the request of the tribe, for tribal land.

(b) We will either:

(1) Prepare, or have prepared, a market analysis, appraisal, or other appropriate valuation method; or

(2) Use an approved market analysis, appraisal, or other appropriate valuation method from the Indian landowners or lessee.

(c) We will use or approve use of a market analysis, appraisal, or other appropriate valuation method only if it:

(1) Has been prepared in accordance with USPAP or a valuation method developed by the Secretary under 25 U.S.C. 2214; and

(2) Complies with Department policies regarding appraisals, including third-party appraisals.

(d) Indian landowners may use competitive bidding as a valuation method.

§ 162.552 When are monetary compensation payments due under a WSR lease?

(a) A WSR lease must specify the dates on which all payments are due.

(b) Unless the lease provides otherwise, payments may not be made or accepted more than one year in advance of the due date.

(c) Payments are due at the time specified in the lease, regardless of whether the lessee receives an advance billing or other notice that a payment is due.

§ 162.553 Must a WSR lease specify who receives monetary compensation payments?

(a) A WSR lease must specify whether the lessee will make payments directly to the Indian landowners (direct pay) or to us on their behalf.

(b) The lessee may make payments directly to the Indian landowners if:

(1) The Indian landowners' trust accounts are unencumbered;

(2) There are 10 or fewer beneficial owners; and

(3) One hundred percent of the beneficial owners (including those on whose behalf we have consented) agree to receive payment directly from the lessee at the start of the lease.

(c) If the lease provides that the lessee will directly pay the Indian landowners, then:

(1) The lease must include provisions for proof of payment upon our request.

(2) When we consent on behalf of an Indian landowner, the lessee must make payment to us on behalf of that landowner.

(3) The lessee must send direct payments to the parties and addresses specified in the lease, unless the lessee receives notice of a change of ownership or address.

(4) Unless the lease provides otherwise, payments may not be made payable directly to anyone other than the Indian landowners.

(5) Direct payments must continue through the duration of the lease, except that:

(i) The lessee must make all Indian landowners' payments to us if 100 percent of the Indian landowners agree to suspend direct pay and provide us with documentation of their agreement; and

(ii) The lessee must make that individual Indian landowner's payment to us if any individual Indian landowner who dies, is declared non compos mentis, owes a debt resulting in a trust account encumbrance, or his or her whereabouts become unknown.

§ 162.554 What form of monetary compensation payment is acceptable under a WSR lease?

(a) When payments are made directly to Indian landowners, the form of payment must be acceptable to the Indian landowners.

(b) When payments are made to us, our preferred method of payment is electronic funds transfer payments. We will also accept:

(1) Money orders;

(2) Personal checks;

(3) Certified checks; or

(4) Cashier's checks.

(c) We will not accept cash or foreign currency.

(d) We will accept third-party checks only from financial institutions or Federal agencies.

§ 162.555 May a WSR lease provide for non-monetary or varying types of compensation?

(a) A WSR lease may provide for the following, subject to the conditions in paragraphs (b) and (c) of this section:

(1) Alternative forms of compensation, including but not limited to, in-kind consideration and payments based on percentage of income; or

(2) Varying types of consideration at specific stages during the life of the lease, including but not limited to fixed annual payments during installation, payments based on income during an operational period, and bonuses.

(b) For tribal land, we will defer to the tribe's determination that the compensation in paragraph (a) of this section is in its best interest, if the tribe submits a signed certification or tribal authorization stating that it has determined the compensation in paragraph (a) of this section to be in its best interest.

(c) For individually owned land, we may approve a lease that provides for compensation under paragraph (a) of this section if we determine that it is in the best interest of the Indian landowners.

§ 162.556 Will BIA notify a lessee when a payment is due under a WSR lease?

Upon request of the Indian landowners, we may issue invoices to a lessee in advance of the dates on which payments are due under a WSR lease. The lessee's obligation to make these payments in a timely manner will not be excused if invoices are not delivered or received.

§ 162.557 Must a WSR lease provide for compensation reviews or adjustments?

(a) For a WSR lease of tribal land, unless the lease provides otherwise, no periodic review of the adequacy of compensation or adjustment is required if the tribe states in its tribal certification or authorization that it has determined that not having reviews and/or adjustments is in its best interest.

(b) For a WSR lease of individually owned Indian land, unless the lease provides otherwise, no periodic review of the adequacy of compensation or adjustment is required if:

(1) If the term of the lease is 5 years or less;

(2) The lease provides for automatic adjustments; or

(3) We determine it is in the best interest of the Indian landowners not to require a review or automatic adjustment based on circumstances including, but not limited to, the following:

(i) The lease provides for payment of less than fair market rental;

(ii) The lease is for public purposes;

(iii) The lease provides for most or all of the compensation to be paid during the first 5 years of the lease term or before the date the review would be conducted; or

(iv) The lease provides for graduated rent or non-monetary or various types of compensation.

(c) If the conditions in paragraph (a) or (b) of this section are not met, a review of the adequacy of compensation must occur at least every fifth year, in the manner specified in the lease. The lease must specify:

(1) When adjustments take effect;

(2) Who can make adjustments;

(3) What the adjustments are based on; and

(4) How to resolve disputes arising from the adjustments.

(d) When a review results in the need for adjustment of compensation, the Indian landowners must consent to the adjustment in accordance with § 162.012, unless the lease provides otherwise.

§ 162.558 What other types of payments are required under a WSR lease?

(a) The lessee may be required to pay additional fees, taxes, and assessments associated with the use of the land, as determined by entities having jurisdiction, except as provided in § 162.017. The lessee must pay these amounts to the appropriate office.

(b) If the leased premises are within an Indian irrigation project or drainage district, except as otherwise provided in part 171 of this chapter, the lessee must pay all operation and maintenance charges that accrue during the lease term. The lessee must pay these amounts to the appropriate office in charge of the irrigation project or drainage district. We will treat failure to make these payments as a violation of the lease.

(c) Where the property is subject to at least one other lease for another compatible use, such as grazing, the lessees may agree among themselves how to allocate payment of the operation and maintenance charges.

WSR LEASE BONDING AND INSURANCE

§ 162.559 Must a lessee provide a performance bond for a WSR lease?

The lessee must provide a performance bond or alternative form of security, except as provided in paragraph (f) of this section.

(a) The performance bond or alternative form of security must be in an amount sufficient to secure the contractual obligations including:

(1) No less than:

(i) The highest annual rental specified in the lease, if the compensation is paid annually; or

(ii) If the compensation is not paid annually, another amount established by BIA in consultation with the tribe for tribal land or, where feasible, with Indian landowners for individually owned Indian land;

(2) The installation of any required permanent improvements;

(3) The operation and maintenance charges for any land located within an irrigation project; and

(4) The restoration and reclamation of the leased premises, to their condition at the start of the lease term or some other specified condition.

(b) The performance bond or other security:

(1) Must be deposited with us and made payable only to us, and may not be modified without our approval, except as provided in paragraph (b)(2) of this section; and

(2) For tribal land, if the lease so provides, may be deposited with the tribe and made payable to the tribe, and may not be modified without the approval of the tribe.

(c) The lease must specify the conditions under which we may adjust security or performance bond requirements to reflect changing conditions, including consultation with the tribal landowner for tribal land before adjustment.

(d) We may require that the surety provide any supporting documents needed to show that the performance bond or alternative forms of security will be enforceable, and that the surety will be able to perform the guaranteed obligations.

(e) The performance bond or other security instrument must require the surety to provide notice to us at least 60 days before canceling a performance bond or other security. This will allow us to notify the lessee of its obligation to provide a substitute performance bond or other security and require collection of the bond or security before the cancellation date. Failure to provide a substitute performance bond or security is a violation of the lease.

(f) We may waive the requirement for a performance bond or alternative forms of security if:

(1) The lease is for public purposes; or

(2) The Indian landowners request it and we determine a waiver is in the Indian landowners' best interest.

(g) For tribal land, we will defer to the tribe's determination that a waiver of the performance bond or alternative form of security is in its best interest, to the maximum extent possible.

§ 162.560 What forms of security are acceptable under a WSR lease?

(a) We will accept a performance bond only in one of the following forms:

(1) Certificates of deposit issued by a federally insured financial institution authorized to do business in the United States;

(2) Irrevocable letters of credit issued by a federally insured financial institution authorized to do business in the United States;

(3) Negotiable Treasury securities; or

(4) Surety bonds issued by a company approved by the U.S. Department of the Treasury.

(b) We may accept an alternative form of security approved by us that provides adequate protection for the Indian landowners and us, including but not limited to an escrow agreement and assigned savings account.

(c) All forms of performance bonds or alternative security must, if applicable:

(1) Indicate on their face that BIA approval is required for redemption;

(2) Be accompanied by a statement granting full authority to BIA to make an immediate claim upon or sell them if the lessee violates the terms of the lease;

(3) Be irrevocable during the term of the performance bond or alternative security; and

(4) Be automatically renewable during the term of the lease.

(d) We will not accept cash bonds.

§ 162.561 What is the release process for a performance bond or alternative form of security under a WSR lease?

(a) Upon expiration, termination, or cancellation of the lease, the lessee must ask BIA in writing to release the performance bond or alternative form of security.

(b) Upon receiving the request under paragraph (a) of this section, BIA will:

(1) Confirm with the tribe, for tribal land or, where feasible, with the Indian landowners for individually owned Indian land, that the lessee has complied with all lease obligations; and

(2) Release the performance bond or alternative form of security to the lessee unless we determine that the bond or security must be redeemed to fulfill the contractual obligations.

§ 162.562 Must a lessee provide insurance for a WSR lease?

Except as provided in paragraph (c) of this section, a lessee must provide insurance when necessary to protect the interests of Indian landowners and in the amount sufficient to protect all insurable permanent improvements on the leased premises.

(a) The insurance may include property, liability, and casualty insurance, depending on the Indian landowners' interests to be protected.

(b) Both the Indian landowners and the United States must be identified as additional insured parties.

(c) We may waive the requirement for insurance upon the request of the Indian landowner, if a waiver is in the best interest of the Indian landowner, including if the lease is for less than fair market rental or nominal compensation. For tribal land, we will defer, to the maximum extent possible, to the tribe's determination that a waiver is in its best interest.

WSR Lease Approval

§ 162.563 What documents are required for BIA approval of a WSR lease?

A lessee or the Indian landowners must submit the following documents to us to obtain BIA approval of a WSR lease:

(a) A lease executed by the Indian landowners and the lessee that meets the requirements of this part;

(b) For tribal land, a tribal authorization for the lease and, if applicable, meeting the requirements of §§ 162.549(a), 162.555(b), and 162.557(a), or a separate signed certification meeting the requirements of §§ 162.555(b) and 162.557(a));

(c) A valuation, if required under § 162.549 or § 162.550;

(d) Proof of insurance, if required under § 162.562;

(e) A performance bond or other security, if required under § 162.559;

(f) Statement from the appropriate tribal authority that the proposed use is in conformance with applicable tribal law, if required by the tribe;

(g) Environmental and archeological reports, surveys, and site assessments as needed to facilitate compliance with applicable Federal and tribal environmental and land use requirements, including any documentation prepared under § 162.027(b);

(h) A resource development plan that describes the type and location of any permanent improvements the lessee plans to install and a schedule showing the tentative commencement and completion dates for those improvements;

(i) A restoration and reclamation plan (and any subsequent modifications to the plan);

(j) Where the lessee is not an entity owned and operated by the tribe, documents that demonstrate the technical capability of the lessee or lessee's agent to construct, operate, maintain, and terminate the proposed project and the lessee's ability to successfully design, construct, or obtain the funding for a project similar to the proposed project, if appropriate;

(k) A legal description of the land under § 162.547;

(l) If the lease is being approved under 25 U.S.C. 415, information to assist us in our evaluation of the factors in 25 U.S.C. 415(a); and

(m) If the lessee is a corporation, limited liability company, partnership, joint venture, or other legal entity, except a tribal entity, information such as organizational documents, certificates, filing records, and resolutions, that demonstrates that:

(1) The representative has authority to execute a lease;

(2) The lease will be enforceable against the lessee; and

(3) The legal entity is in good standing and authorized to conduct business in the jurisdiction where the land is located.

§ 162.564 Will BIA review a proposed WSR lease before or during preparation of the NEPA review documentation?

Upon request of the Indian landowners, we will review the proposed WSR lease after negotiation by the parties, before or during preparation of the NEPA review documentation and any valuation. Within 60 days of receiving the proposed lease, we will provide an acknowledgement of the terms of the lease and identify any provisions that, based on this acknowledgment review, would justify disapproval of the lease, pending results of the NEPA review and any valuation.

§ 162.565 What is the approval process for a WSR lease?

(a) Before we approve a WSR lease, we must determine that the lease is in the best interest of the Indian landowners. In making that determination, we will:

(1) Review the lease and supporting documents;

(2) Identify potential environmental impacts and ensure compliance with all applicable environmental laws, land use laws, and ordinances;

(3) If the lease is being approved under 25 U.S.C. 415, assure ourselves that adequate consideration has been given to the factors in 25 U.S.C. 415(a); and

(4) Require any lease modifications or mitigation measures necessary to satisfy any requirements including any other Federal or tribal land use requirements.

(b) Upon receiving a WSR lease package, we will promptly notify the parties whether the package is or is not complete. A complete package includes all the information and supporting documents required under this subpart, including but not limited to, NEPA review documentation and valuation documentation, where applicable.

(1) If the WSR lease package is not complete, our letter will identify the missing information or documents required for a complete package. If we do not respond to the submission of a WSR lease package, the parties may take action under § 162.588.

(2) If the WSR lease package is complete, we will notify the parties of the date of receipt. Within 60 days of the receipt date, we will approve or disapprove the lease, return the package for revision, or inform the parties in writing that we need additional review time. If we inform the parties in writing that we need additional time, then:

(i) Our letter informing the parties that we need additional review time must identify our initial concerns and invite the parties to respond within 15 days of the date of the letter; and

(ii) We have 30 days from sending the letter informing the parties that we need additional time to approve or disapprove the lease.

(c) If we do not meet the deadlines in this section, then the parties may take appropriate action under § 162.588.

(d) We will provide any lease approval or disapproval and the basis for the determination, along with notification of any appeal rights under part 2 of this chapter, in writing to the parties to the lease.

(e) We will provide approved WSR leases on tribal land to the lessee and provide a copy to the tribe. We will provide approved WSR leases on individually owned Indian land to the lessee, and make copies available to the Indian landowners upon written request.

§ 162.566 How will BIA decide whether to approve a WSR lease?

(a) We will approve a WSR lease unless:

(1) The required consents have not been obtained from the parties to the lease;

(2) The requirements of this subpart have not been met; or

(3) We find a compelling reason to withhold our approval in order to protect the best interests of the Indian landowners.

(b) We will defer, to the maximum extent possible, to the Indian landowners' determination that the WSR lease is in their best interest.

(c) We may not unreasonably withhold approval of a WSR lease.

§ 162.567 When will a WSR lease be effective?

(a) A WSR lease will be effective on the date that we approve the lease, even if an appeal is filed under part 2 of this chapter.

(b) The lease may specify a date on which the obligations between the parties to the lease are triggered. Such date may be before or after the approval date under paragraph (a) of this section.

§ 162.568 Must a WSR lease document be recorded?

(a) Any WSR lease document must be recorded in the LTRO with jurisdiction over the leased land.

(1) We will record the lease document immediately following our approval.

(2) If our approval of an assignment or sublease is not required, the parties must record the assignment or sublease in the LTRO with jurisdiction over the leased land.

(b) The tribe must record lease documents for the following types of leases in the LTRO with jurisdiction over the tribal lands, even though BIA approval is not required:

(1) Leases of tribal land that a corporate entity leases to a third party under 25 U.S.C. 477; and

(2) Leases of tribal land under a special act of Congress authorizing leases without our approval.

§ 162.569 Will BIA require an appeal bond for an appeal of a decision on a WSR lease document?

(a) If a party appeals our decision on a WSR lease, assignment, amendment, or sublease, then the official to whom the appeal is made may require the appellant to post an appeal bond in accordance with part 2 of this chapter. We will not require an appeal bond:

(1) For an appeal of a decision on a leasehold mortgage; or

(2) If the tribe is a party to the appeal and requests a waiver of the appeal bond.

(b) The appellant may not appeal the appeal bond decision. The appellant may, however, request that the official to whom the appeal is made reconsider the bond decision, based on extraordinary circumstances. Any reconsideration decision is final for the Department.

WSR Lease Amendments

§ 162.570 May the parties amend a WSR lease?

The parties may amend a WSR lease by obtaining:

(a) The lessee's signature;

(b) The Indian landowners' consent under the requirements in § 162.571; and

(c) BIA approval of the amendment under §§ 162.572 and 162.573.

§ 162.571 What are the consent requirements for an amendment to a WSR lease?

(a) Unless the lease provides otherwise, the lessee must notify all Indian landowners of the proposed amendment.

(b) The Indian landowners, or their representatives under § 162.013, must consent to an amendment of a WSR lease in the same percentages and manner as a new WSR lease under § 162.012, unless the lease:

(1) Provides that individual Indian landowners are deemed to have consented if they do not object in writing to the amendment within a specified period of time following the landowners' receipt of the amendment and the lease meets the requirements of paragraph (c) of this section;

(2) Authorizes one or more representatives to consent to an amendment on behalf of all Indian landowners; or

(3) Designates us as the Indian landowners' representative for the purposes of consenting to an amendment.

(c) If the lease provides for deemed consent under paragraph (b)(1) of this section, it must require the parties to submit to us:

(1) A copy of the executed amendment or other documentation of any Indian landowners' actual consent;

(2) Proof of mailing of the amendment to any Indian landowners who are deemed to have consented; and

(3) Any other pertinent information for review.

(d) Unless specifically authorized in the lease, a written power of attorney, or a court document, Indian landowners may not be deemed to have consented to, and an Indian landowner's designated representative may not negotiate or consent to, an amendment that would:

(1) Reduce the payment obligations to the Indian landowners;

(2) Increase or decrease the lease area;

(3) Terminate or change the term of the lease; or

(4) Modify dispute resolution procedures.

§ 162.572 What is the approval process for an amendment to a WSR lease?

(a) When we receive an amendment that meets the requirements of this subpart, we will notify the parties of the date we receive it. We have 30 days from receipt of the executed amendment, proof of required consents, and required documentation to approve or disapprove the amendment or inform the parties in writing that we need additional review time. Our determination whether to approve the amendment will be in writing and will state the basis for our approval or disapproval.

(b) Our letter informing the parties that we need additional review time must identify our initial concerns and invite the parties to respond within 15 days of the date of the letter. We have 30 days from sending the letter informing the parties that we need additional time to approve or disapprove the amendment.

(c) If we do not meet the deadline in paragraph (a) of this section, or paragraph (b) of this section if applicable, the amendment is deemed approved to the extent consistent with Federal law. Unless the lease provides otherwise, provisions of the amendment that are inconsistent with Federal law will be severed and unenforceable; all other provisions of the amendment will remain in force.

§ 162.573 How will BIA decide whether to approve an amendment to a WSR lease?

(a) We may disapprove a WSR lease amendment only if at least one of the following is true:

(1) The Indian landowners have not consented and their consent is required;

(2) The lessee's mortgagees or sureties have not consented;

(3) The lessee is in violation of the lease;

(4) The requirements of this subpart have not been met; or

(5) We find a compelling reason to withhold our approval in order to protect the best interests of the Indian landowners.

(b) We will defer, to the maximum extent possible, to the Indian landowners' determination that the amendment is in their best interest.

(c) We may not unreasonably withhold approval of an amendment.

WSR LEASE ASSIGNMENTS

§ 162.574 May a lessee assign a WSR lease?

(a) A lessee may assign a WSR lease by meeting the consent requirements in § 162.575 and obtaining our approval of the assignment under §§ 162.576 and 162.577 or by meeting the conditions in paragraphs (b) or (c) of this section.

(b) Where provided in the lease, the lessee may assign the lease to the following without meeting consent requirements or obtaining BIA approval of the assignment, as long as the lessee notifies BIA of the assignment within 30 days after it is executed:

(1) Not more than three distinct legal entities specified in the lease; or

(2) The lessee's wholly owned subsidiaries.

(c) The lessee may assign the lease without our approval or meeting consent requirements if:

(1) The assignee is a leasehold mortgagee or its designee, acquiring the lease either through foreclosure or by conveyance;

(2) The assignee agrees in writing to assume all of the obligations and conditions of the lease; and

(3) The assignee agrees in writing that any transfer of the lease will be in accordance with applicable law under § 162.014.

§ 162.575 What are the consent requirements for an assignment of a WSR lease?

(a) Unless the lease provides otherwise, the lessee must notify all Indian landowners of the proposed assignment.

(b) The Indian landowners, or their representatives under § 162.013, must consent to an assignment in the same percentages and manner as a new WSR lease under § 162.012, unless the lease:

(1) Provides that individual Indian landowners are deemed to have consented where they do not object in writing to the assignment within a specified period of time following the landowners' receipt of the assignment and the lease meets the requirements of paragraph (c) of this section;

(2) Authorizes one or more representatives to consent to an assignment on behalf of all Indian landowners; or

(3) Designates us as the Indian landowners' representative for the purposes of consenting to an assignment.

(c) If the lease provides for deemed consent under paragraph (b)(1) of this section, it must require the parties to submit to us:

(1) A copy of the executed assignment or other documentation of any Indian landowners' actual consent;

(2) Proof of mailing of the assignment to any Indian landowners who are deemed to have consented; and

(3) Any other pertinent information for us to review.

(d) The lessee must obtain the consent of the holders of any bonds or mortgages.

§ 162.576 What is the approval process for an assignment of a WSR lease?

(a) When we receive an assignment that meets the requirements of this subpart, we will notify the parties of the date we receive it. If our approval is required, we have 30 days from receipt of the executed assignment, proof of required consents, and required documentation to approve or disapprove the assignment. Our determination whether to approve the assignment will be in writing and will state the basis for our approval or disapproval.

(b) If we do not meet any of the deadlines in this section, the lessee or Indian landowners may take appropriate action under § 162.588.

§ 162.577 How will BIA decide whether to approve an assignment of a WSR lease?

(a) We may disapprove an assignment of a WSR lease only if at least one of the following is true:

(1) The Indian landowners have not consented and their consent is required;

(2) The lessee's mortgagees or sureties have not consented;

(3) The lessee is in violation of the lease;

(4) The assignee does not agree to be bound by the terms of the lease;

(5) The requirements of this subpart have not been met; or

(6) We find a compelling reason to withhold our approval in order to protect the best interests of the Indian landowners.

(b) In making the finding required by paragraph (a)(6) of this section, we may consider whether:

(1) The value of any part of the leased premises not covered by the assignment would be adversely affected; and

(2) If a performance bond is required, the assignee has posted the bond or security and provided supporting documents that demonstrate that:

(i) The lease will be enforceable against the assignee; and

(ii) The assignee will be able to perform its obligations under the lease or assignment.

(c) We will defer, to the maximum extent possible, to the Indian landowners' determination that the assignment is in their best interest.

(d) We may not unreasonably withhold approval of an assignment.

WSR LEASE SUBLEASES

§ 162.578 May a lessee sublease a WSR lease?

(a) A lessee may sublease a WSR lease by meeting the consent requirements in § 162.579 and obtaining our approval of the sublease under §§ 162.580 and 162.581, or by meeting the conditions in paragraph (b) of this section.

(b) The lessee may sublease without meeting consent requirements or obtaining BIA approval of the sublease, if:

(1) The lease provides for subleasing without meeting consent requirements or obtaining BIA approval;

(2) The sublease does not relieve the lessee/sublessor of any liability; and

(3) The parties provide BIA with a copy of the sublease within 30 days after it is executed.

§ 162.579 What are the consent requirements for a sublease of a WSR lease?

(a) Unless the lease provides otherwise, the lessee must notify all Indian landowners of the proposed sublease.

(b) The Indian landowners, or their representatives under § 162.013, must consent to a sublease in the same percentages and manner as a new WSR lease under § 162.012, unless the lease:

(1) Provides that individual Indian landowners are deemed to have consented where they do not object in writing to the sublease within a specified period of time following the landowners' receipt of the sublease and the lease meets the requirements in paragraph (c) of this section;

(2) Authorizes one or more representatives to consent to a sublease on behalf of all Indian landowners; or

(3) Designates us as the Indian landowners' representative for the purposes of consenting to a sublease.

(c) If the lease provides for deemed consent under paragraph (b)(1) of this section, it must require the parties to submit to us:

(1) A copy of the executed sublease or other documentation of any Indian landowners' actual consent;

(2) Proof of mailing of the sublease to any Indian landowners who are deemed to have consented; and

(3) Any other pertinent information for us to review.

§ 162.580 What is the approval process for a sublease of a WSR lease?

(a) When we receive a sublease that meets the requirements of this subpart, we will notify the parties of the date we receive it. If our approval is required, we have 30 days from receipt of the executed sublease, proof of required consents, and required documentation to approve or disapprove the sublease or inform the parties to the sublease and Indian landowners in writing that we need additional review time. Our determination whether to approve the sublease will be in writing and will state the basis for our approval or disapproval.

(b) Our letter informing parties that we need additional review time must identify our initial concerns and invite the parties to respond within 15 days of the date of the letter. We have 30 days from sending the letter informing the parties that we need additional time to approve or disapprove the sublease.

(c) If we do not meet the deadline in paragraph (a) of this section, or paragraph (b) of this section if applicable, the sublease is deemed approved to the extent consistent with Federal law.

Unless the lease provides otherwise, provisions of the sublease that are inconsistent with Federal law will be severed and unenforceable; all other provisions of the sublease will remain in force.

§ 162.581 How will BIA decide whether to approve a sublease of a WSR lease?

(a) We may disapprove a sublease of a WSR lease only if at least one of the following is true:

(1) The Indian landowners have not consented and their consent is required;

(2) The lessee's mortgagees or sureties have not consented;

(3) The lessee is in violation of the lease;

(4) The lessee will not remain liable under the lease; and

(5) We find a compelling reason to withhold our approval in order to protect the best interests of the Indian landowners.

(b) In making the finding required by paragraph (a)(5) of this section, we may consider whether the value of any part of the leased premises not covered by the sublease would be adversely affected.

(c) We will defer, to the maximum extent possible, to the Indian landowners' determination that the sublease is in their best interest.

(d) We may not unreasonably withhold approval of a sublease.

WSR Leasehold Mortgages

§ 162.582 May a lessee mortgage a WSR lease?

(a) A lessee may mortgage a WSR lease by meeting the consent requirements in § 162.583 and obtaining our approval of the leasehold mortgage under §§ 162.584 and 162.585.

(b) Refer to § 162.574(c) for information on what happens if a sale or foreclosure under an approved mortgage of the leasehold interest occurs.

§ 162.583 What are the consent requirements for a leasehold mortgage of a WSR lease?

(a) Unless the lease provides otherwise, the lessee must notify all Indian landowners of the proposed leasehold mortgage.

(b) The Indian landowners, or their representatives under § 162.013, must consent to a leasehold mortgage in the same percentages and manner as a new WSR lease under § 162.012, unless the lease:

(1) States that landowner consent is not required for a leasehold mortgage and identifies what law would apply in case of foreclosure;

(2) Provides that individual Indian landowners are deemed to have consented where they do not object in writing to the leasehold mortgage within a specified period of time following the landowners' receipt of the leasehold mortgage and the lease meets the requirements of paragraph (c) of this section;

(3) Authorizes one or more representatives to consent to a leasehold mortgage on behalf of all Indian landowners; or

(4) Designates us as the Indian landowners' representative for the purposes of consenting to a leasehold mortgage.

(c) If the lease provides for deemed consent under paragraph (b)(2) of this section, it must require the parties to submit to us:

(1) A copy of the executed leasehold mortgage or other documentation of any Indian landowners' actual consent;

(2) Proof of mailing of the leasehold mortgage to any Indian landowners who are deemed to have consented; and

(3) Any other pertinent information for us to review.

§ 162.584 What is the approval process for a leasehold mortgage of a WSR lease?

(a) When we receive a leasehold mortgage that meets the requirements of this subpart, we will notify the parties of the date we receive it. We have 20 days from receipt of the executed leasehold mortgage, proof of required consents, and required documentation to approve or disapprove the leasehold mortgage. Our determination whether to approve the leasehold mortgage will be in writing and will state the basis for our approval or disapproval.

(b) If we do not meet the deadline in this section, the lessee may take appropriate action under § 162.588.

§ 162.585 How will BIA decide whether to approve a leasehold mortgage of a WSR lease?

(a) We may disapprove a leasehold mortgage of a WSR lease only if at least one of the following is true:

(1) The Indian landowners have not consented and their consent is required;

(2) The lessee's mortgagees or sureties have not consented;

(3) The requirements of this subpart have not been met; or

(4) We find a compelling reason to withhold our approval in order to protect the best interests of the Indian landowners.

(b) In making the finding required by paragraph (a)(4) of this section, we may consider whether:

(1) The leasehold mortgage proceeds would be used for purposes unrelated to the leased premises; and

(2) The leasehold mortgage is limited to the leasehold.

(c) We will defer, to the maximum extent possible, to the Indian landowners' determination that the leasehold mortgage is in their best interest.

(d) We may not unreasonably withhold approval of a leasehold mortgage.

WSR LEASE EFFECTIVENESS, COMPLIANCE, AND ENFORCEMENT

§ 162.586 When will an amendment, assignment, sublease, or leasehold mortgage of a WSR lease be effective?

(a) An amendment, assignment, sublease, or leasehold mortgage of a WSR lease will be effective when approved, even if an appeal is filed under part 2 of this chapter, except:

(1) If the amendment or sublease was deemed approved under § 162.572(b) or § 162.580(b), the amendment or sublease becomes effective 45 days from the date the parties mailed or delivered the document to us for our review or, if we sent a letter informing the parties that we need additional time to approve or disapprove the lease, the amendment or sublease becomes effective 45 days from the date of the letter informing the parties that we need additional time to approve or disapprove the lease; and

(2) An assignment that does not require our approval under § 162.574(b) or a sublease that does not require our approval under § 162.578(b) becomes effective on the effective date specified in the assignment or sublease. If the assignment or sublease does not specify the effective date, it becomes effective upon execution by the parties.

(b) We will provide copies of approved documents to the party requesting approval, to the tribe for tribal land, and upon request, to other parties to the lease document.

§ 162.587 What happens if BIA disapproves an amendment, assignment, sublease, or leasehold mortgage of a WSR lease?

If we disapprove an amendment, assignment, sublease, or leasehold mortgage of a WSR lease, we will notify the parties immediately and advise the landowners of their right to appeal the decision under part 2 of this chapter.

§ 162.588 What happens if BIA does not meet a deadline for issuing a decision on a lease document?

(a) If a Superintendent does not meet a deadline for issuing a decision on a lease, assignment, or leasehold mortgage, the parties may file a written notice to compel action with the appropriate Regional Director.

(b) The Regional Director has 15 days from receiving the notice to:

(1) Issue a decision; or

(2) Order the Superintendent to issue a decision within the time set out in the order.

(c) The parties may file a written notice to compel action with the BIA Director if:

(1) The Regional Director does not meet the deadline in paragraph (b) of this section;

(2) The Superintendent does not issue a decision within the time set by the Regional Director under paragraph (b)(2) of this section; or

(3) The initial decision on the lease, assignment, or leasehold mortgage is with the Regional Director, and he or she does not meet the deadline for such decision.

(d) The BIA Director has 15 days from receiving the notice to:

(1) Issue a decision; or

(2) Order the Regional Director or Superintendent to issue a decision within the time set out in the order.

(e) If the Regional Director or Superintendent does not issue a decision within the time set out in the order under paragraph (d)(2), then the BIA Director must issue a decision within 15 days from the expiration of the time set out in the order.

(f) The parties may file an appeal from our inaction to the Interior Board of Indian Appeals if the Director does not meet the deadline in paragraph (d) or (e) of this section.

(g) The provisions of 25 CFR 2.8 do not apply to the inaction of BIA officials with respect to a decision on a lease, amendment, assignment, sublease, or leasehold mortgage under this subpart.

§ 162.589 May BIA investigate compliance with a WSR lease?

(a) We may enter the leased premises at any reasonable time, upon reasonable notice, and consistent with any notice requirements under applicable tribal law and applicable lease documents, to protect the interests of the Indian landowners and to determine if the lessee is in compliance with the requirements of the lease.

(b) If an Indian landowner notifies us that a specific lease violation has occurred, we will promptly initiate an appropriate investigation.

§ 162.590 May a WSR lease provide for negotiated remedies if there is a violation?

(a) A WSR lease of tribal land may provide either or both parties with negotiated remedies in the event of a lease violation, including, but not limited to, the power to terminate the lease. If the lease provides one or both parties with the power to terminate the lease:

(1) BIA approval of the termination is not required;

(2) The termination is effective without BIA cancellation; and

(3) The Indian landowners must notify us of the termination so that we may record it in the LTRO.

(b) A WSR lease of individually owned Indian land may provide either or both parties with negotiated remedies, so long as the lease also specifies the manner in which those remedies may be exercised by or on behalf of the Indian landowners of the applicable percentage of interests under § 162.012 of this part. If the lease provides one or both parties with the power to terminate the lease:

(1) BIA concurrence with the termination is required to ensure that the Indian landowners of the applicable percentage of interests have consented; and

(2) BIA will record the termination in the LTRO.

(c) The parties must notify any surety or mortgagee of any violation that may result in termination and the termination of a WSR lease.

(d) Negotiated remedies may apply in addition to, or instead of, the cancellation remedy available to us, as specified in the lease. The landowners may request our assistance in enforcing negotiated remedies.

(e) A WSR lease may provide that lease violations will be addressed by the tribe, and that lease disputes will be resolved by a tribal court, any other court of competent jurisdiction, or by a tribal governing body in the absence of a tribal court, or through an alternative dispute resolution method. We may not be bound by decisions made in such forums, but we will defer to ongoing actions and proceedings, as appropriate, in deciding whether to exercise any of the remedies available to us.

§ 162.591 What will BIA do about a violation of a WSR lease?

(a) In the absence of actions or proceedings described in § 162.590(e), or if it is not appropriate for us to defer to the actions or proceedings, we will follow the procedures in paragraphs (b) and (c) of this section.

(b) If we determine there has been a violation of the conditions of a WSR lease, other than a violation of payment provisions covered by paragraph (c) of this section, we will promptly send the lessee and any surety and mortgagee a notice of violation by certified mail, return receipt requested.

(1) We will send a copy of the notice of violation to the tribe for tribal land, or provide constructive notice to Indian landowners for individually owned Indian land.

(2) The notice of violation will advise the lessee that, within 10 business days

of the receipt of a notice of violation, the lessee must:

(i) Cure the violation and notify us, and the tribe for tribal land, in writing that the violation has been cured;

(ii) Dispute our determination that a violation has occurred; or

(iii) Request additional time to cure the violation.

(3) The notice of violation may order the lessee to cease operations under the lease.

(c) A lessee's failure to pay compensation in the time and manner required by a WSR lease is a violation of the lease, and we will issue a notice of violation in accordance with this paragraph.

(1) We will send the lessees and any surety and mortgagee a notice of violation by certified mail, return receipt requested:

(i) Promptly following the date on which payment was due, if the lease requires that payments be made to us; or

(ii) Promptly following the date on which we receive actual notice of nonpayment from the Indian landowners, if the lease provides for payment directly to the Indian landowners.

(2) We will send a copy of the notice of violation to the tribe for tribal land, or provide constructive notice to the Indian landowners for individually owned Indian land.

(3) The notice of violation will require the lessee to provide adequate proof of payment.

(d) The lessee and its sureties will continue to be responsible for the obligations in the lease until the lease expires or is terminated or cancelled.

§ 162.592 What will BIA do if a lessee does not cure a violation of a WSR lease on time?

(a) If the lessee does not cure a violation of a WSR lease within the required time period, or provide adequate proof of payment as required in the notice of violation, we will consult with the tribe for tribal land or, where feasible, with Indian landowners for individually owned Indian land, and determine whether:

(1) We should cancel the lease;

(2) The Indian landowners wish to invoke any remedies available to them under the lease;

(3) We should invoke other remedies available under the lease or applicable law, including collection on any available performance bond or, for failure to pay compensation, referral of the debt to the Department of the Treasury for collection; or

(4) The lessee should be granted additional time in which to cure the violation.

(b) Following consultation with the tribe for tribal land or, where feasible, with Indian landowners for individually owned Indian land, we may take action to recover unpaid compensation and any associated late payment charges.

(1) We do not have to cancel the lease or give any further notice to the lessee before taking action to recover unpaid compensation.

(2) We may still take action to recover any unpaid compensation if we cancel the lease.

(c) If we decide to cancel the lease, we will send the lessee and any surety and mortgagee a cancellation letter by certified mail, return receipt requested, within 5 business days of our decision. We will send a copy of the cancellation letter to the tribe for tribal land, and will provide Indian landowners for individually owned Indian land with actual or constructive notice of the cancellation. The cancellation letter will:

(1) Explain the grounds for cancellation;

(2) If applicable, notify the lessee of the amount of any unpaid compensation or late payment charges due under the lease;

(3) Notify the lessee of the lessee's right to appeal under part 2 of this chapter, including the possibility that the official to whom the appeal is made may require the lessee to post an appeal bond;

(4) Order the lessee to vacate the property within 31 days of the date of receipt of the cancellation letter, if an appeal is not filed by that time; and

(5) Order the lessee to take any other action BIA deems necessary to protect the Indian landowners.

(d) We may invoke any other remedies available to us under the lease, including collecting on any available performance bond, and the Indian landowners may pursue any available remedies under tribal law.

§ 162.593 Will late payment charges or special fees apply to delinquent payments due under a WSR lease?

(a) Late payment charges will apply as specified in the lease. The failure to pay these amounts will be treated as a lease violation.

(b) We may assess the following special fees to cover administrative costs incurred by the United States in the collection of the debt, if compensation is not paid in the time and manner required, in addition to late payment charges that must be paid to the Indian landowners under the lease:

The lessee will pay . . .	For . . .
(1) $50.00	Any dishonored check.
(2) $15.00	Processing of each notice or demand letter.
(3) 18 percent of balance due.	Treasury processing following referral for collection of delinquent debt.

§ 162.594 How will payment rights relating to WSR leases be allocated?

The WSR lease may allocate rights to payment for insurance proceeds, trespass damages, compensation awards, settlement funds, and other payments between the Indian landowners and the lessee. If not specified in the lease, insurance policy, order, award, judgment, or other document, the Indian landowners will be entitled to receive these payments.

§ 162.595 When will a cancellation of a WSR lease be effective?

(a) A cancellation involving a WSR lease will not be effective until 31 days after the lessee receives a cancellation letter from us, or 41 days from the date we mailed the letter, whichever is earlier.

(b) The cancellation decision will not be effective if an appeal is filed unless the cancellation is made immediately effective under part 2 of this chapter. While a cancellation decision is ineffective, the lessee must continue to pay compensation and comply with the other terms of the lease.

§ 162.596 What will BIA do if a lessee remains in possession after a WSR lease expires or is terminated or cancelled?

If a lessee remains in possession after the expiration, termination, or cancellation of a WSR lease, we may treat the unauthorized possession as a trespass under applicable law in consultation with the Indian landowners. Unless the Indian landowners of the applicable percentage of interests under § 162.012 have notified us in writing that they are engaged in good faith negotiations with the holdover lessee to obtain a new lease, we may take action to recover possession on behalf of the Indian landowners, and pursue any additional remedies available under applicable law, such as a forcible entry and detainer action.

§ 162.597 Will BIA appeal bond regulations apply to cancellation decisions involving WSR leases?

(a) Except as provided in paragraph (b) of this section, the appeal bond provisions in part 2 of this chapter will apply to appeals from lease cancellation decisions.

(b) The lessee may not appeal the appeal bond decision. The lessee may, however, request that the official to whom the appeal is made reconsider the appeal bond decision, based on extraordinary circumstances. Any reconsideration decision is final for the Department.

§ 162.598 When will BIA issue a decision on an appeal from a WSR leasing decision?

BIA will issue a decision on an appeal from a WSR leasing decision within 60 days of receipt of all pleadings.

§ 162.599 What happens if the lessee abandons the leased premises?

If a lessee abandons the leased premises, we will treat the abandonment as a violation of the lease. The lease may specify a period of non-use after which the lease premises will be considered abandoned.

Subpart F—Special Requirements for Certain Reservations

§ 162.600 Crow Reservation.

(a) Notwithstanding the regulations in other sections of this part 162, Crow Indians classified as competent under the Act of June 4, 1920 (41 Stat. 751), as amended, may lease their trust lands and the trust lands of their minor children for farming or grazing purposes without the approval of the Secretary pursuant to the Act of May 26, 1926 (44 Stat. 658), as amended by the Act of March 15, 1948 (62 Stat. 80). However, at their election Crow Indians classified as competent may authorize the Secretary to lease, or assist in the leasing of such lands, and an appropriate notice of such action shall be made a matter of record. When this prerogative is exercised, the general regulations contained in this part 162 shall be applicable. Approval of the Secretary is required on leases signed by Crow Indians not classified as competent or made on inherited or devised trust lands owned by more than five competent devisees or heirs.

(b) The Act of May 26, 1926 (44 Stat. 658), as amended by the Act of March 15, 1948 (62 Stat. 80), provides that no lease for farming or grazing purposes shall be made for a period longer than five years, except irrigable lands under the Big Horn Canal; which may be leased for periods of ten years. No such lease shall provide the lessee a preference right to future leases which, if exercised, would thereby extend the total period of encumbrance beyond the five or ten years authorized by law.

(c) All leases entered into by Crow Indians classified as competent, under the above-cited special statutes, must be recorded at the Crow Agency. Such recording shall constitute notice to all persons. Under these special statutes, Crow Indians classified as competent are free to lease their property within certain limitations. The five-year (ten-year in the case of lands under the Big Horn Canal) limitation is intended to afford a protection to the Indians. The essence of this protection is the right to deal with the property free, clear, and unencumbered at intervals at least as frequent as those provided by law. If lessees are able to obtain new leases long before the termination of existing leases, they are in a position to set their own terms. In these circumstances lessees could perpetuate their leaseholds and the protection of the statutory limitations as to terms would be destroyed. Therefore, in implementation of the foregoing interpretation, any lease which, on its face, is in violation of statutory limitations or requirements, and any grazing lease executed more than 12 months, and any farming lease executed more than 18 months, prior to the commencement of the term thereof or any lease which purports to cancel an existing lease with the same lessee as of a future date and take effect upon such cancellation will not be recorded. Under a Crow tribal program, approved by the Department of the Interior, competent Crow Indians may, under certain circumstances, enter into agreements which require that, for a specified term, their leases be approved. Information concerning whether a competent Crow Indian has executed such an instrument is available at the office of the Superintendent of the Crow Agency, Bureau of Indian Affairs, Crow Agency, Montana. Any lease entered into with a competent Crow Indian during the time such instrument is in effect and which is not in accordance with such instrument will be returned without recordation.

(d) Where any of the following conditions are found to exist, leases will be recorded but the lessee and lessor will be notified upon discovery of the condition:

(1) The lease in single or counterpart form has not been executed by all owners of the land described in the lease;

(2) There is, of record, a lease on the land for all or a part of the same term;

(3) The lease does not contain stipulations requiring sound land utilization plans and conservation practices; or

(4) There are other deficiencies such as, but not limited to, erroneous land descriptions, and alterations which are not clearly endorsed by the lessor.

(e) Any adult Crow Indian classified as competent shall have the full responsibility for obtaining compliance with the terms of any lease made by him pursuant to this section. This shall not preclude action by the Secretary to assure conservation and protection of these trust lands.

(f) Leases made by competent Crow Indians shall be subject to the right to issue permits and leases to prospect for, develop, and mine oil, gas, and other minerals, and to grant rights-of-way and easements, in accordance with applicable law and regulations. In the issuance or granting of such permits, leases, rights-of-way or easements due consideration will be given to the interests of lessees and to the adjustment of any damages to such interests. In the event of a dispute as to the amount of such damage, the matter will be referred to the Secretary whose determination will be final as to the amount of said damage.

[66 FR 7109, Jan. 22, 2001. Redesignated at 77 FR 72494, Dec. 5, 2012 and correctly redesignated at 78 FR 27860, May 13, 2013]

§ 162.601 Fort Belknap Reservation.

Not to exceed 20,000 acres of allotted and tribal lands (non-irrigable as well as irrigable) on the Fort Belknap Reservation in Montana may be leased for the culture of sugar beets and other crops in rotation for terms not exceeding ten years.

[66 FR 7109, Jan. 22, 2001. Redesignated at 77 FR 72494, Dec. 5, 2012 and correctly redesignated at 78 FR 27860, May 13, 2013]

§ 162.602 Cabazon, Augustine, and Torres-Martinez Reservations, California.

(a) Upon a determination by the Secretary that the owner or owners are not making beneficial use thereof, restricted lands on the Cabazon, Augustine, and Torres-Martinez Indian Reservations which are or may be irrigated from distribution facilities administered by the Coachella Valley County Water District in Riverside County, California, may be leased by the Secretary in accordance with the regulations in this part for the benefit of the owner or owners.

(b) All leases granted or approved on restricted lands of the Cabazon, Augustine, and Torres-Martinez Indian Reservations shall be filed for record in the office of the county recorder of the county in which the land is located, the cost thereof to be paid by the lessee. A copy of each such lease shall be filed by the lessee with the Coachella Valley County Water District or such other irrigation or water district within which the leased lands are located. All such leases shall include a provision that the lessee, in addition to the rentals provided for in the lease, shall pay all irrigation charges properly assessed against the land which became payable during the term of the lease. Act of August 25, 1950 (64 Stat. 470); Act of August 28, 1958 (72 Stat. 968).

[66 FR 7109, Jan. 22, 2001. Redesignated at 77 FR 72494, Dec. 5, 2012 and correctly redesignated at 78 FR 27860, May 13, 2013]

§ 162.603 San Xavier and Salt River Pima-Maricopa Reservations.

(a) *Purpose and scope*. The Act of November 2, 1966 (80 Stat. 1112), provides statutory authority for long-term leasing on the San Xavier and Salt River Pima-Maricopa Reservations, Arizona, in addition to that contained in the Act of August 9, 1955 (69 Stat. 539), as amended (25 U.S.C. 415). When leases are made under the 1955 Act on the San Xavier or Salt River Pima-Maricopa Reservations, the regulations in part 162 apply. The purpose of this section is to provide regulations for implementation of the 1966 Act. The 1966 Act does not apply to leases made for purposes that are subject to the laws governing mining leases on Indian lands.

(b) *Duration of leases*. Leases made under the 1966 Act for public, religious, educational, recreational, residential, or business purposes may be made for terms of not to exceed 99 years. The terms of a grazing lease shall not exceed ten years; the term of a farming lease that does not require the making of a substantial investment in the improvement of the land shall not exceed ten years; and the term of a farming lease that requires the making of a substantial investment in the improvement of the land shall not exceed 40 years. No lease shall contain an option to renew which extends the total term beyond the maximum term permitted by this section.

(c) *Required covenant and enforcement thereof*. Every lease under the 1966 Act shall contain a covenant on the part of the lessee that he will not commit or permit on the leased land any act that causes waste or a nuisance or which creates a hazard to health of persons or to property wherever such persons or property may be.

(d) *Notification regarding leasing proposals.* If the Secretary determines that a proposed lease to be made under the 1966 Act for public, religious, educational, recreational, residential, or business purposes will substantially affect the governmental interests of a municipality contiguous to the San Xavier Reservation or the Salt River Pima-Maricopa Reservation, as the case may be, he shall notify the appropriate authority of such municipality of the pendency of the proposed lease. The Secretary may, in his discretion, furnish such municipality with an outline of the major provisions of the lease which affect its governmental interests and shall consider any comments on the terms of the lease affecting the municipality or on the absence of such terms from the lease that the authorities may offer. The notice to the authorities of the municipality shall set forth a reasonable period, not to exceed 30 days, within which any such comments shall be submitted.

(e) *Applicability of other regulations.* The regulations in part 162 of this title shall apply to leases made under the 1966 Act except where such regulations are inconsistent with this section.

(f) *Mission San Xavier del Bac.* Nothing in the 1966 Act authorizes development that would detract from the scenic, historic, and religious values of the Mission San Xavier del Bac owned by the Franciscan Order of Friars Minor and located on the San Xavier Reservation.

[66 FR 7109, Jan. 22, 2001. Redesignated at 77 FR 72494, Dec. 5, 2012 and correctly redesignated at 78 FR 27860, May 13, 2013]

Subpart G—Records

SOURCE: 77 FR 72494, Dec. 5, 2012, unless otherwise noted.

§ 162.701 Who owns the records associated with this part?

(a) Records are the property of the United States if they:

(1) Are made or received by a tribe or tribal organization in the conduct of a Federal trust function under 25 U.S.C. 450f *et seq.*, including the operation of a trust program; and

(2) Evidence the organization, functions, policies, decisions, procedures, operations, or other activities undertaken in the performance of a Federal trust function under this part.

(b) Records not covered by paragraph (a) of this section that are made or received by a tribe or tribal organization in the conduct of business with the Department of the Interior under this part are the property of the tribe.

§ 162.702 How must records associated with this part be preserved?

(a) Any organization, including a tribe or tribal organization, that has records identified in § 162.701(a) of this part, must preserve the records in accordance with approved Departmental records retention procedures under the Federal Records Act, 44 U.S.C. chapters 29, 31 and 33. These records and related records management practices and safeguards required under the Federal Records Act are subject to inspection by the Secretary and the Archivist of the United States.

(b) A tribe or tribal organization should preserve the records identified in § 162.701(b) of this part, for the period of time authorized by the Archivist of the United States for similar Department of the Interior records under 44 U.S.C. chapter 33. If a tribe or tribal organization does not preserve records associated with its conduct of business with the Department of the Interior under this part, it may prevent the tribe or tribal organization from being able to adequately document essential transactions or furnish information necessary to protect its legal and financial rights or those of persons directly affected by its activities.

§ 162.703 How does the Paperwork Reduction Act affect this part?

The collections of information in this part have been approved by the Office of Management and Budget under 44 U.S.C. 3501 *et seq.* and assigned OMB Control Number 1076–0155. Response is required to obtain a benefit. A Federal agency may not conduct or sponsor, and you are not required to respond to, a collection of information unless it displays a currently valid OMB Control Number.

PART 163—GENERAL FORESTRY REGULATIONS

AUTHORITY: 25 U.S.C. 2, 5, 9, 13, 406, 407, 413, 415, 466; and 3101–3120.

SOURCE: 60 FR 52260, Oct. 5, 1995, unless otherwise noted.

Subpart A—General Provisions

§163.1 Definitions.

Advance deposits means, in Timber Contract for the Sale of Estimated Volumes, contract-required deposits in advance of cutting which the purchaser furnishes to maintain an operating balance against which the value of timber to be cut will be charged.

Advance payments means, in Timber Contract for the Sale of Estimated Volumes, non-refundable partial payments of the estimated value of the timber to be cut. Payments are furnished within 30 days of contract approval and prior to cutting. Advance payments are normally 25 percent of the estimated value of the forest products on each allotment. Advance payments may be required for tribal land.

Alaska Native means native as defined in section 3(b) of the Alaska Native Claims Settlement Act of December 18, 1971 (43 U.S.C. 1604).

ANCSA corporation means both profit and non-profit corporations established pursuant to the Alaska Native Claims Settlement Act (43 U.S.C. 1604).

Approval means authorization by the Secretary, Area Director, Superintendent, tribe or individual Indian in accordance with appropriate delegations of authority.

Approving officer means the officer approving instruments of sale for forest products or his/her authorized representative.

Authorized representative means an individual or entity duly empowered to make decisions under a direct, clear, and specific delegation of authority.

Authorized tribal representative means an individual or entity duly empowered to make decisions under a direct, clear, and specific delegation of authority from an Indian tribe.

Beneficial owner means an individual or entity who holds an ownership interest in Indian land.

Bid deposit means, in Timber Contract for the Sale of Estimated Volumes or in Timber Contract for the Sale of Predetermined Volumes, a deposit with bid furnished by prospective purchasers. At contract execution, the bid deposit of the successful bidder becomes a portion of the contract required advance deposit in estimated volume contracts or an installment payment in predetermined volume contracts.

Commercial forest land means forest land that is producing or capable of producing crops of marketable forest products and is administratively available for intensive management and sustained production.

Expenditure plan means a written agreement between an Indian tribe and the Secretary documenting tribal commitment to undertake specified forest land management activities within general time frames.

Forest or forest land means an ecosystem at least one acre in size, including timberland and woodland, which: Is characterized by a more or less dense and extensive tree cover; contains, or once contained, at least ten percent tree crown cover, and is not developed or planned for exclusive non-forest resource use.

Forest land management activities means all activities performed in the management of Indian forest land including:

(a) All aspects of program administration and executive direction such as:

(1) Development and maintenance of policy and operational procedures, program oversight, and evaluation;

(2) Securing of legal assistance and handling of legal matters;

(3) Budget, finance, and personnel management; and

(4) Development and maintenance of necessary data bases and program reports.

(b) All aspects of the development, preparation and revision of forest inventory and management plans, including aerial photography, mapping, field management inventories and re- inventories, inventory analysis, growth studies, allowable annual cut calculations, environmental assessment, and forest history, consistent with and reflective of tribal integrated resource management plans where such plans exist.

(c) Forest land development, including forestation, thinning, tree improvement activities, and the use of silvicultural treatments to restore or increase growth and yield to the full productive capacity of the forest environment.

(d) Protection against losses from wildfire, including acquisition and maintenance of fire fighting equipment and fire detection systems, construction of fire breaks, hazard reduction, prescribed burning, and the development of cooperative wildfire management agreements.

(e) Protection against insects and disease, including:

(1) All aspects of detection and evaluation;

(2) Preparation of project proposals containing project descriptions, environmental assessments and statements, and cost- benefit analyses necessary to secure funding;

(3) Field suppression operations and reporting.

(f) Assessment of damage caused by forest trespass, infestation or fire, including field examination and survey, damage appraisal, investigation assistance and report, demand letter, and testimony preparation.

(g) All aspects of the preparation, administration, and supervision of timber sale contracts, paid and free use permits, and other Indian forest product harvest sale documents, including;

(1) Cruising, product marketing, silvicultural prescription, appraisal and harvest supervision;

(2) Forest product marketing assistance, including evaluation of marketing and development opportunities related to Indian forest products and consultation and advice to tribes, tribal and Indian enterprises on maximization of return on forest products;

(3) Archeological, historical, environmental and other land management reviews, clearances, and analyses;

(4) Advertising, executing, and supervising contracts;

(5) Marking and scaling of timber; and

(6) Collecting, recording and distributing receipts from sales.

(h) Provision of financial assistance for the education of Indians and Alaska Natives enrolled in accredited programs of postsecondary and postgraduate forestry and forestry-related fields of study, including the provision of scholarships, internships, relocation assistance, and other forms of assistance to cover educational expenses.

(i) Participation in the development and implementation of tribal integrated resource management plans, including activities to coordinate current and future multiple uses of Indian forest lands.

(j) Improvement and maintenance of extended season primary and secondary Indian forest land road systems.

(k) Research activities to improve the basis for determining appropriate management measures to apply to Indian forest land.

Forest management deduction means a percentage of the gross proceeds from the sales of forest products harvested from Indian land which is collected by the Secretary pursuant to 25 U.S.C. 413 to cover in whole or in part the cost of managing and protecting such Indian forest lands.

Forest management plan means the principal document, approved by the Secretary, reflecting and consistent with an integrated resource management plan, which provides for the regulation of the detailed, multiple-use operation of Indian forest land by methods ensuring that such lands remain in a continuously productive state while meeting the objectives of the tribe and which shall include: Standards setting forth the funding and staffing requirements necessary to carry out each management plan, with a report of current forestry funding and staffing levels; and standards providing quantitative criteria to evaluate performance against the objectives set forth in the plan.

Forest products means marketable products extracted from Indian forests, such as: Timber; timber products, including lumber, lath, crating, ties, bolts, logs, pulpwood, fuelwood, posts, poles, and split products; bark; Christmas trees, stays, branches, firewood, berries, mosses, pinyon nuts, roots, acorns, syrups, wild rice, mushrooms, and herbs; other marketable material; and gravel which is extracted from, and utilized on, Indian forest land.

Forestry-related field or *forestry-related curriculum* means a renewable natural resource management field necessary to manage Indian forest land and other professionally recognized fields as approved by the education committee established pursuant to §163.40(a)(1).

Forest resources means all the benefits derived from Indian forest land, including forest products, soil productivity, water, fisheries, wildlife, recreation, and aesthetic or other traditional values of Indian forest land.

Forester intern means an Indian or Alaska Native who: Is employed as a forestry or forestry-related technician with the Bureau of Indian Affairs, an Indian tribe, or tribal forest-related enterprise; is acquiring necessary academic qualifications to become a forester or a professional trained in forestry-related fields; and is appointed to one of the Forester Intern positions established pursuant to §163.40(b).

Indian means a member of an Indian tribe.

Indian enterprise means an enterprise which is designated as such by the Secretary or tribe.

Indian forest land means Indian land, including commercial, non-commercial, productive and non-productive timberland and woodland, that are considered chiefly valuable for the production of forest products or to maintain watershed or other land values enhanced by a forest cover, regardless of whether a formal inspection and land classification action has been taken.

Indian land means land title which is held by: The United States in trust for an Indian, an individual of Indian or Alaska Native ancestry who is not a member of a federally-recognized Indian tribe, or an Indian tribe; or by an Indian, an individual of Indian or Alaska Native ancestry who is not a member of a federally recognized tribe, or an Indian tribe subject to a restriction by the United States against alienation.

Indian tribe or *tribe* means any Indian tribe, band, nation, rancheria, Pueblo or other organized group or community which is recognized as eligible for the special programs and services provided by the United States to Indians because of their status as Indians and shall mean, where appropriate, the recognized tribal government of such tribe's reservation.

Installment payments means, in Timber Contract for the Sale of Predetermined Volumes, scheduled partial payments of the total contract value based on purchaser bid. Payments made are normally not refundable.

Integrated resource management plan means a document, approved by an Indian tribe and the Secretary, which provides coordination for the comprehensive management of the natural resources of such tribe's reservation.

Noncommercial forest land means forest land that is available for extensive management, but is incapable of producing sustainable forest products within the general rotation period. Such land may be economically harvested, but the site quality does not warrant significant investment to enhance future crops.

Productive forest land means forest land producing or capable of producing marketable forest products that is unavailable for harvest because of administrative restrictions or because access is not practical.

Reservation means an Indian reservation established pursuant to treaties, Acts of Congress, or Executive Orders and public domain Indian allotments, Alaska Native allotments, rancherias, and former Indian reservations in Oklahoma.

Secretary means the Secretary of the Interior or his or her authorized representative.

Stumpage rate means the stumpage value per unit of measure for a forest product.

Stumpage value means the value of a forest product prior to extraction from Indian forest land.

Sustained yield means the yield of forest products that a forest can produce continuously at a given intensity of management.

Timberland means forest land stocked, or capable of being stocked, with tree species that are regionally utilized for lumber, pulpwood, poles or veneer products.

Trespass means the removal of forest products from, or damaging forest products on, Indian forest land, except when authorized by law and applicable federal or tribal regulations. Trespass can include any damage to forest resources on Indian forest land resulting from activities under contracts or permits or from fire.

Tribal forest enterprise means an Indian enterprise that is initiated and organized by a reservation's recognized tribal government.

Unproductive forest land means forest land that is not producing or capable of producing marketable forest products and is also unavailable for harvest because of administrative restrictions or because access is not practical.

Woodland means forest land not included within the timberland classification, stocked, or capable of being stocked, with tree species of such form and size to produce forest products that are generally marketable within the region for products other than lumber, pulpwood, or veneer.

§ 163.2 Information collection.

The information collection requirements contained in 25 CFR part 163 do not require the approval of the Office of Management and Budget under 44 U.S.C. 3504(h) *et seq.*

§ 163.3 Scope and objectives.

(a) The regulations in this part are applicable to all Indian forest land except as this part may be superseded by legislation.

(b) Indian forest land management activities undertaken by the Secretary shall be designed to achieve the following objectives:

(1) The development, maintenance and enhancement of Indian forest land in a perpetually productive state in accordance with the principles of sustained yield and with the standards and objectives set forth in forest management plans by providing effective management and protection through the application of sound silvicultural and economic principles to the harvesting of forest products, forestation, timber stand improvement and other forestry practices;

(2) The regulation of Indian forest land through the development and implementation, with the full and active consultation and participation of the appropriate Indian tribe, of forest management plans which are supported by written tribal objectives;

(3) The regulation of Indian forest land in a manner that will ensure the use of good method and order in harvesting so as to make possible, on a sustained yield basis, continuous productivity and a perpetual forest business;

(4) The development of Indian forest land and associated value-added industries by Indians and Indian tribes to promote self-sustaining communities, so that Indians may receive from their Indian forest land not only stumpage value, but also the benefit of all the labor and profit that such Indian forest land is capable of yielding;

(5) The retention of Indian forest land in its natural state when an Indian tribe determines that the recreational, cultural, aesthetic, or traditional values of the Indian forest land represents the highest and best use of the land;

(6) The management and protection of forest resources to retain the beneficial effects to Indian forest land of regulating water run-off and minimizing soil erosion; and

(7) The maintenance and improvement of timber productivity, grazing, wildlife, fisheries, recreation, aesthetic, cultural and other traditional values.

§163.4 Secretarial recognition of tribal laws.

Subject to the Secretary's trust responsibilities, and unless otherwise prohibited by Federal statutory law, the Secretary shall comply with tribal laws pertaining to Indian forest land, including laws regulating the environment or historic or cultural preservation, and shall cooperate with the enforcement of such laws on Indian forest land. Such cooperation does not constitute a waiver of United States sovereign immunity and shall include:

(a) Assistance in the enforcement of such laws;

(b) Provision of notice of such laws to persons or entities undertaking activities on Indian forest land; and

(c) Upon the request of an Indian tribe, the appearance in tribal forums.

Subpart B—Forest Management and Operations

§163.10 Management of Indian forest land.

(a) The Secretary shall undertake forest land management activities on Indian forest land, either directly or through contracts, cooperative agreements, or grants under the Indian Self-Determination and Education Assistance Act (Pub. L. 93–638, as amended).

(b) Indian forest land management activities undertaken by the Secretary shall be designed to achieve objectives enumerated in §163.3 of this part.

§163.11 Forest management planning and sustained yield management.

(a) To further the objectives identified in §163.3 of this part, an appropriate forest management plan shall be prepared and revised as needed for all Indian forest lands. Such documents shall contain a statement describing the manner in which the policies of the tribe and the Secretary will be applied, with a definite plan of silvicultural management, analysis of the short term and long term effects of the plan, and a program of action, including a harvest schedule, for a specified period in the future. Forest management plans shall be based on the principle of sustained yield management and objectives established by the tribe and will require approval of the Secretary.

(b) Forest management planning for Indian forest land shall be carried out through participation in the development and implementation of integrated resource management plans which provide coordination for the comprehensive management of all natural resources on Indian land. If the integrated resource management planning process has not been initiated, or is not ongoing or completed, a stand-alone forest management plan will be prepared.

(c) The harvest of forest products from Indian forest land will be accomplished under the principles of sustained yield management and will not be authorized until practical methods of harvest based on sound economic and silvicultural and other forest management principles have been prescribed. Harvest schedules will be prepared for a specified period of time and updated annually. Such schedules shall support the objectives of the beneficial land owners and the Secretary and shall be directed toward achieving an approximate balance between net growth and harvest at the earliest practical time.

§ 163.12 Harvesting restrictions.

(a) Harvesting timber on commercial forest land will not be permitted unless provisions for natural and/or artificial reforestation of acceptable tree species is included in harvest plans.

(b) Clearing of large contiguous areas will be permitted only on land that, when cleared, will be devoted to a more beneficial use than growing timber crops. This restriction shall not prohibit clearcutting when it is silviculturally appropriate, based on ecological principles, to harvest a particular stand of timber by such method and it otherwise conforms with objectives in § 163.3 of this part.

§ 163.13 Indian tribal forest enterprise operations.

Indian tribal forest enterprises may be initiated and organized with consent of the authorized tribal representatives. Such enterprises may contract for the purchase of non-Indian owned forest products. Subject to approval by the Secretary the following actions may be taken:

(a) Authorized tribal enterprises may enter into formal agreements with tribal representatives for the use of tribal forest products, and with individual beneficial Indian owners for their forest products;

(b) Authorized officials of tribal enterprises, operating under approved agreements for the use of Indian-owned forest products pursuant to this section, may sell the forest products produced according to generally accepted trade practices;

(c) With the consent of the beneficial Indian owners, such enterprises may, without advertisement, contract for the purchase of forest products on Indian land at stumpage rates authorized by the Secretary;

(d) Determination of and payment for stumpage and/or products utilized by such enterprises will be authorized in accordance with § 163.22. However, the Secretary may issue special instructions for payment by methods other than those in § 163.22 of this part; and

(e) Performance bonds may or may not be required in connection with operations on Indian land by such enterprises as determined by the Secretary.

§ 163.14 Sale of forest products.

(a) Consistent with the economic objectives of the tribe and with the consent of the Secretary and authorized by tribal resolution or resolution of recognized tribal government, open market sales of Indian forest products may be authorized. Such sales require consent of the authorized representatives of the tribe for the sale of tribal forest products, and the owners of a majority Indian interest on individually owned lands. Open market sales of forest products from Indian land located off reservations will be permitted with the consent of the Secretary and majority Indian interest of the beneficial Indian owner(s).

(b) On individually owned Indian forest land not formally designated for retention in its natural state, the Secretary may, after consultation, sell the forest products without the consent of the owner(s) when in his or her judgment such action is necessary to prevent loss of value resulting from fire, insects, diseases, windthrow or other catastrophes.

(c) Unless otherwise authorized by the Secretary, each sale of forest products having an estimated stumpage value exceeding $15,000 will not be approved until:

(1) An examination of the forest products to be sold has been made by a forest officer; and

(2) A report setting forth all pertinent information has been submitted to the approving officer as provided in §163.20 of this part.

(d) With the approval of the Secretary, authorized beneficial Indian owners who have been duly apprised as to the value of the forest products to be sold, may sell or transfer forest products for less than the appraised value.

(e) Except as provided in §163.14(d) of this part, in all such sales, the forest products shall be appraised and sold at stumpage rates not less than those established by the Secretary.

§163.15 Advertisement of sales.

Except as provided in §§163.13, 163.14, 163.16, and 163.26 of this part, sales of forest products shall be made only after advertising.

(a) The advertisement shall be approved by the officer who will approve the instrument of sale. Advertised sales shall be made under sealed bids, or at public auction, or under a combination thereof. The advertisement may limit sales of Indian forest products to Indian forest enterprises, members of the tribe, or may grant to Indian forest enterprises and/or members of the tribe who submitted bids the right to meet the higher bid of a nonmember. If the estimated stumpage value of the forest products offered does not exceed $15,000, the advertisement may be made by posters and circular letters. If the estimated stumpage value exceeds $15,000, the advertisement shall also be made in at least one edition of a newspaper of general circulation in the locality where the forest products are situated. If the estimated stumpage value does not exceed $50,000, the advertisement shall be made for not less than 15 days; if the estimated stumpage value exceeds $50,000 but not $250,000, for not less than 30 days; and if the estimated stumpage value exceeds $250,000, for not less than 60 days.

(b) The approving officer may reduce the advertising period because of emergencies such as fire, insect attack, blowdown, limitation of time, or when there would be no practical advantage in advertising for the prescribed period.

(c) If no instrument of sale is executed after such advertisement, the approving officer may, within one year from the last day on which bids were to be received as defined in the advertisement, permit the sale of such forest products. The sale will be made upon the terms and conditions in the advertisement and at not less than the advertised value or the appraised value at the time of sale, whichever is greater.

§163.16 Forest product sales without advertisement.

(a) Sales of forest products may be made without advertisement to Indians or non-Indians with the consent of the authorized tribal representatives for tribal forest products or with the consent of the beneficial owners of a majority Indian interest of individually owned Indian land, and the approval of the Secretary when:

(1) Forest products are to be cut in conjunction with the granting of a right-of-way;

(2) Granting an authorized occupancy;

(3) Tribal forest products are to be purchased by an Indian tribal forest enterprise;

(4) It is impractical to secure competition by formal advertising procedures;

(5) It must be cut to protect the forest from injury; or

(6) Otherwise specifically authorized by law.

(b) The approving officer shall establish a documented record of each negotiated transaction. This will include:

(1) A written determination and finding that the transaction is a type allowing use of negotiation procedures;

(2) The extent of solicitation and competition, or a statement of the facts upon which a finding of impracticability of securing competition is based; and

(3) A statement of the factors on which the award is based, including a determination as to the reasonability of the price accepted.

§ 163.17 Deposit with bid.

(a) A deposit shall be made with each proposal for the purchase of Indian forest products. Such deposits shall be at least:

(1) Ten (10) percent if the appraised stumpage value is less than $100,000 and in any event not less than $1,000 or full value whichever is less;

(2) Five (5) percent if the appraised stumpage value is $100,000 to $250,000 but in any event not less than $10,000; and

(3) Three (3) percent if the appraised stumpage value exceeds $250,000 but in any event not less than $12,500.

(b) Deposits shall be in the form of either a certified check, cashier's check, bank draft, postal money order, or irrevocable letter-of-credit, drawn payable as specified in the advertisement, or in cash.

(c) The deposit of the apparent high bidder, and of others who submit a written request to have their bids considered for acceptance will be retained pending acceptance or rejection of the bids. All other deposits will be returned following the opening and posting of bids.

(d) The deposit of the successful bidder will be forfeited and distributed as damages to the beneficial owners if the bidder does not:

(1) Furnish the performance bond required by § 163.21 of this part within the time stipulated in the advertisement for sale of forest products;

(2) Execute the contract; or

(3) Perform the contract.

(e) Forfeiture of a deposit does not limit or waive any further claims for damages available under applicable law or terms of the contract.

(f) In the event of an administrative appeal under 25 CFR part 2, the Secretary may hold such bid deposits in an escrow account pending resolution of the appeal.

§ 163.18 Acceptance and rejection of bids.

(a) The high bid received in accordance with any advertisement issued under authority of this part shall be accepted, except that the approving officer, having set forth the reason(s) in writing, shall have the right to reject the high bid if:

(1) The high bidder is considered unqualified to fulfill the contractual requirement of the advertisement; or

(2) There are reasonable grounds to consider it in the interest of the Indians to reject the high bid.

(b) If the high bid is rejected, the approving officer may authorize:

(1) Rejection of all bids; or

(2) Acceptance of the offer of another bidder who, at bid opening, makes written request that their bid and bid deposit be held pending a bid acceptance.

(c) The officer authorized to accept the bid shall have the discretion to waive minor technical defects in advertisements and proposals, such as typographical errors and misplaced entries.

§ 163.19 Contracts for the sale of forest products.

(a) In sales of forest products with an appraised stumpage value exceeding $15,000, the contract forms approved by the Secretary must be used unless a special form for a particular sale or class of sales is approved by the Secretary.

(b) Unless otherwise directed, the contracts for forest products from individually-owned Indian land will be paid by remittance drawn to the Bureau of Indian Affairs and transmitted to the Superintendent. Upon the request of the tribe, the contracts for tribal forest products may require that the proceeds be paid promptly and directly into a bank depository account designated by such tribe, or by remittance drawn to the Bureau of Indian Affairs and transmitted to the Superintendent.

(c) By mutual agreement of the parties to a contract, contracts may be extended, modified, or assigned subject to approval by the approving officer, and may be terminated by the approving officer upon completion or by mutual agreement.

§ 163.20 Execution and approval of contracts.

(a) All contracts for the sale of tribal forest products shall be executed by the authorized tribal representative(s). There shall be included with the contract an affidavit executed by the authorized tribal representative(s) setting forth the resolution or other authority of the governing body of the tribe. Contracts must be approved by the Secretary to be valid.

(b) Contracts for the sale of individually owned forest products shall be executed by the beneficial Indian owner(s) or the Secretary acting pursuant to a power of attorney from the beneficial Indian owner(s). Contracts must be approved by the Secretary to be valid.

(1) The Secretary may, after consultation with any legally appointed guardian, execute contracts on behalf of minors and beneficial Indian owners who are non compos mentis.

(2) The Secretary may execute contracts for a decedent's estate where ownership has not been determined or for those persons who cannot be located after a reasonable and diligent search and the giving of notice by publication.

(3) Upon the request of the owner of an undivided but unrestricted interest in land in which there are trust or restricted Indian interests, the Secretary may include such unrestricted interest in a sale of the trust or restricted interests in the timber, pursuant to this part, and perform any functions required of him/her by the contract of sale for both the restricted and the unrestricted interests, including the collection and disbursement of payments for timber and the forest management deductions from such payments.

(4) When consent of only a majority interest has been obtained, the Secretary may execute the sale on behalf of all owners to fulfill responsibilities to the beneficiaries of the trust. In such event, the contract file must contain evidence of the effort to obtain consent of all owners. When an individual cannot be located, the Secretary, after a reasonable and diligent search and the giving of notice by publication, may sign a power of attorney consenting to the sale for particular interests. For Indian forest land containing undivided restricted and unrestricted interests, only the restricted interests are considered in determining if a majority interest has been obtained.

§ 163.21 Bonds required.

(a) Performance bonds will be required in connection with all sales of forest products, except they may or may not be required, as determined by the approving officer, in connection with the use of forest products by Indian tribal forest enterprises pursuant to this part in § 163.13 or in timber cutting permits issued pursuant to § 163.26 of this part.

(1) In sales in which the estimated stumpage value, calculated at the appraised stumpage rates, does not exceed $15,000, the bond shall be at least 20 percent of the estimated stumpage value.

(2) In sales in which the estimated stumpage value exceeds $15,000 but is not over $150,000, the bond shall be at least 15 percent of the estimated stumpage value but not less than $3,000.

(3) In sales in which the estimated stumpage value exceeds $150,000, but is not over $350,000, the bond shall be at least 10 percent of the estimated stumpage value but not less than $22,500.

(4) In sales in which the estimated stumpage value exceeds $350,000, the bond shall be at least 5 percent of the estimated stumpage value but not less than $35,000.

(b) Bonds shall be in a form acceptable to the approving officer and may include:

(1) A corporate surety bond by an acceptable surety company;

(2) A cash bond designating the approving officer to act as trustee under terms of an appropriate trust;

(3) Negotiable U.S. Government securities supported by an appropriate trust instrument; or

(4) An irrevocable letter of credit.

§ 163.22 Payment for forest products.

(a) The basis of volume determination for forest products sold shall be the Scribner Decimal C log rules, cubic volume, lineal measurement, piece count, weight, or such other form of measurement as the Secretary may authorize for use. With the exception of Indian tribal forest enterprises pursuant to § 163.13 of this part, payment for forest products will be required in advance of cutting for timber, or removal for other forest products.

(b) Upon the request of an Indian tribe, the Secretary may provide that the purchaser of the forest products of such tribe, which are harvested under a timber sale contract, permit, or other harvest sale document to make advanced deposits, or direct payments of the gross proceeds of such forest products, less any amounts segregated as forest management deductions pursuant to § 163.25 of this part, into accounts designated by such Indian tribe. Such accounts may be in one or more of the following formats:

(1) Escrow accounts at a tribally designated financial institution for receiving deposits with bids and advance deposits from which direct disbursements for timber harvested shall be made to tribes and forest management deductions accounts; or

(2) Tribal depository accounts for receiving advance payments, installment payments, payments from Indian tribal forest enterprises, and/or disbursements from advance deposit accounts or escrow accounts.

(c) The format must allow the Secretary to maintain trust responsibility through written verification that all required deposits, payments, and disbursements have been made.

(d) Terms and conditions for payment of forest products under lump sum (predetermined volume) sales shall be specified in forest product contract documents.

§ 163.23 Advance payment for timber products.

(a) Unless otherwise authorized by the Secretary, and except in the case of lump sum (predetermined volume) sales, contracts for the sale of timber from allotted, trust or restricted Indian forest land shall provide for an advance payment of up to 25 percent of the stumpage value, calculated at the bid price, within 30 days from the date of approval and before cutting begins. Additional advance payments may be specified in contracts. However, no advance payment will be required that would make the sum of such payment and of advance deposits and advance payments previously applied against timber cut from each ownership in a sale exceed 50 percent of the bid stumpage value. Advance payments shall be credited against the timber of each ownership in the sale as the timber is cut and scaled at stumpage rates governing at the time of scaling. Advance payments are not refundable.

(b) Advance payments may be required on tribal land. When required, advance payments will operate the same as provided for in § 163.23(a) of this part.

§ 163.24 Duration of timber contracts.

After the effective date of a forest product contract, unless otherwise authorized by the Secretary, the maximum period which shall be allowed for harvesting the estimated volume of timber purchased, shall be five years.

§ 163.25 Forest management deductions.

(a) Pursuant to the provisions of 25 U.S.C. 413 and 25 U.S.C. 3105, a forest management deduction shall be withheld from the gross proceeds of sales of forest products harvested from Indian forest land as described in this section.

(b) Gross proceeds shall mean the value in money or money's worth of consideration furnished by the purchaser of forest products purchased under a contract, permit, or other document for the sale of forest products.

(c) Forest management deductions shall not be withheld where the total consideration furnished under a contract, permit or other document for the sale of forest products is less than $5,001.

(d) Except as provided in § 163.25(e) of this part, the amount of the forest management deduction shall not exceed the lesser amount of ten percent (10%) of the gross proceeds or, the actual percentage in effect on November 28, 1990.

(e) The Secretary may increase the forest management deduction percentage for Indian forest land upon receipt of a written request from a tribe supported by a resolution executed by the authorized tribal representatives. At the request of the authorized tribal representatives and at the discretion of the Secretary the forest management deduction percentage may be decreased to not less than one percent (1%) or the requirement for collection may be waived.

(f) Forest management deductions are to be utilized to perform forest land management activities in accordance with an approved expenditure plan. Expenditure plans shall describe the forest land management activities anticipated to be undertaken, establish a time period for their completion, summarize anticipated obligations and expenditures, and specify the method through which funds are to be transferred or credited to tribal accounts from special deposit accounts established to hold amounts withheld as forest management deductions. Any forest management deductions that have not been incorporated into an approved expenditure plan by the end of the fiscal year following the fiscal year in which the deductions are withheld, shall be collected into the general funds of the United States Treasury pursuant to 25 U.S.C. 413.

(1) For Indian forest lands located on an Indian reservation, a written expenditure plan for the use of forest management deductions shall be prepared annually and approved by the authorized tribal representative(s) and the Secretary. The approval of the expenditure plan by the authorized tribal representatives constitutes allocation of tribal funds for Indian forest land management activities. Approval of the expenditure plan by the Secretary shall constitute authority for crediting of forest management deductions to tribal account(s). The full amount of any deduction collected by the Secretary plus any income or interest earned thereon shall be available for expenditure according to the approved expenditure plan for the performance of forest land management activities on the reservation from which the forest management deduction is collected.

(2) Forest management deductions shall be handled in the same manner as described under §163.25(f)(1) of this part if the expenditure plan approved by an Indian tribe and the Secretary provides for the conduct of forest land management activities on Indian forest lands located outside the boundaries of an Indian reservation.

(3) For public domain and Alaska Native allotments held in trust for Indians by the United States, forest management deductions may be utilized to perform forest land management activities on such lands in accordance with an expenditure plan approved by the Secretary.

(g) Forest management deductions withheld pursuant to this section shall not be available to cover the costs that are paid from funds appropriated for fire suppression or pest control or otherwise offset federal appropriations for meeting the Federal trust responsibility for management of Indian forest land.

(h) Within 120 days after the close of the tribal fiscal year, tribes shall submit to the Secretary a written report detailing the actual expenditure of forest management deductions during the past fiscal year. The Secretary shall have the right to inspect accounts, books, or other tribal records supporting the report.

(i) Forest management deductions incorporated into an expenditure plan approved by the Secretary shall remain available until expended.

(j) As provided in §163.25(f) of this part, only forest management deductions that have not been incorporated into an approved expenditure plan may be deposited to a U.S. Treasury miscellaneous receipt account. No amount collected as forest management deductions shall be credited to any Federal appropriation. No other forest management deductions or fees derived from Indian forest land shall be collected to be covered into the general funds of the United States Treasury.

§ 163.26 Forest product harvesting permits.

(a) Except as provided in §§163.13 and 163.27 of this part, removal of forest products that are not under formal contract, pursuant to §163.19, shall be under forest product harvesting permit forms approved by the Secretary. Permits will be issued only with the written consent of the beneficial Indian owner(s) or the Secretary, for harvest of forest products from Indian forest land, as authorized in §163.20 of this part. To be valid, permits must be approved by the Secretary. Minimum stumpage rates at which forest products may be sold will be set at the time consent to issue the permit is obtained. Payment and bonding requirements will be stipulated in the permit document as appropriate.

(b) Free use harvesting permits issued shall specify species and types of forest products to be removed. It may be stipulated that forest products removed under this authority cannot be sold or exchanged for other goods or services. The estimated value which may be harvested in a fiscal year by any individual under this authority shall not exceed $5,000. For the purpose of issuance of free use permits, individual shall mean an individual Indian or any organized group of Indians.

(c) Paid permits subject to forest management deductions, as provided in § 163.25 of this part, may be issued. Unless otherwise authorized by the Secretary, the stumpage value which may be harvested under paid permits in a fiscal year by any individual under this authority shall not exceed $25,000. For the purpose of issuance of paid permits, individual shall mean an individual or any operating entity comprised of more than one individual.

(d) A Special Allotment Timber Harvest Permit may be issued to an Indian having sole beneficial interest in an allotment to harvest and sell designated forest products from his or her allotment. The special permit shall include provision for payment by the Indian of forest management deductions pursuant to § 163.25 of this part. Unless waived by the Secretary, the permit shall also require the Indian to make a bond deposit with the Secretary as required by § 163.21. Such bonds will be returned to the Indian upon satisfactory completion of the permit or will be used by the Secretary in his or her discretion for planting or other work to offset damage to the land or the timber caused by failure to comply with the provisions of the permit. As a condition to granting a special permit under authority of this paragraph, the Indian shall be required to provide evidence acceptable to the Secretary that he or she has arranged a bona fide sale of the forest products, on terms that will protect the Indian's interests.

§ 163.27 Free-use harvesting without permits.

With the consent of the beneficial Indian owners and the Secretary, Indians may harvest designated types of forest products from Indian forest land without a permit or contract, and without charge. Forest products harvested under this authority shall be for the Indian's personal use, and shall not be sold or exchanged for other goods or services.

§ 163.28 Fire management measures.

(a) The Secretary is authorized to maintain facilities and staff, hire temporary labor, rent fire fighting equipment, purchase tools and supplies, and pay for their transportation as needed, to maintain an adequate level of readiness to meet normal wildfire protection needs and extinguish forest or range fires on Indian land. No expenses for fighting a fire outside Indian lands may be incurred unless the fire threatens Indian land or unless the expenses are incurred pursuant to an approved cooperative agreement with another protection agency. The rates of pay for fire fighters and for equipment rental shall be the rates for fire fighting services that are currently in use by public and private wildfire protection agencies adjacent to Indian reservations on which a fire occurs, unless there are in effect at the time different rates that have been approved by the Secretary. The Secretary may also enter into reciprocal agreements with any fire organization maintaining protection facilities in the vicinity of Indian reservations or other Indian land for mutual aid in wildfire protection. This section does not apply to the rendering of emergency aid, or agreements for mutual aid in fire protection pursuant to the Act of May 27, 1955 (69 Stat. 66).

(b) The Secretary is authorized to conduct a wildfire prevention program to reduce the number of person-caused fires and prevent damage to natural resources on Indian land.

(c) The Secretary is authorized to expend funds for emergency rehabilitation measures needed to stabilize soil and watershed on Indian land damaged by wildfire.

(d) Upon consultation with the beneficial Indian owners, the Secretary may use fire as a management tool on Indian land to achieve land and/or resource management objectives.

§ 163.29 Trespass.

(a) Trespassers will be liable for civil penalties and damages to the enforcement agency and the beneficial Indian owners, and will be subject to prosecution for acts of trespass.

(1) *Cases in Tribal Court.* For trespass actions brought in tribal court pursuant to these regulations, the measure of damages, civil penalties, remedies and procedures will be as set forth in this § 163.29 of this part. All other aspects of a tribal trespass prosecution brought under these regulations will be that prescribed by the law of the tribe in whose reservation or within whose jurisdiction the trespass was committed, unless otherwise prescribed under federal law. Absent applicable tribal or federal law, the measure of damages shall be that prescribed by the law of the state in which the trespass was committed.

(2) *Cases in Federal Court.* For trespass actions brought in Federal court pursuant to these regulations, the measure of damages, civil penalties, remedies and procedures will be as set forth in this § 163.29. In the absence of applicable federal law, the measure shall be that prescribed by the law of the tribe in whose reservation or within whose jurisdiction the trespass was committed, or in the absence of tribal law, the law of the state in which it was committed.

(3) Civil penalties for trespass include, but are not limited to:

(i) Treble damages, whenever any person, without lawful authority injures, severs, or carries off from a reservation any forest product as defined in § 163.1 of this part. Proof of Indian ownership of the premises and commission of the acts by the trespasser are prima facie evidence sufficient to support liability for treble damages, with no requirement to show willfulness or intent. Treble damages shall be based upon the highest stumpage value obtainable from the raw materials involved in the trespass.

(ii) Payment of costs associated with damage to Indian forest land includes, but is not limited to, rehabilitation, reforestation, lost future revenue and lost profits, loss of productivity, and damage to other forest resources.

(iii) Payment of all reasonable costs associated with the enforcement of these trespass regulations beginning with detection and including all processes through the prosecution and collection of damages, including but not limited to field examination and survey, damage appraisal, investigation assistance and reports, witness expenses, demand letters, court costs, and attorney fees.

(iv) Interest calculated at the statutory rate prescribed by the law of the tribe in whose reservation or within whose jurisdiction the trespass was committed, or in the absence of tribal law in the amount prescribed by federal law. Where tribal law or federal law does not supply a statutory interest rate, the rate of interest shall be statutory rate upon judgments as prescribed by the law of the state in which the trespass was committed. Interest shall be based on treble the highest stumpage value obtainable from the raw materials involved in the trespass, and calculated from the date of the trespass until payment is rendered.

(b) Any cash or other proceeds realized from forfeiture of equipment or other goods or from forest products damaged or taken in the trespass shall be applied to satisfy civil penalties and other damages identified under § 163.29(a) of this part. After disposition of real and personal property to pay civil penalties and damages resulting from trespass, any residual funds shall be returned to the trespasser. In the event that collection and forfeiture actions taken against the trespasser result in less than full recovery, civil penalties shall be distributed as follows:

(1) Collection of damages up to the highest stumpage value of the trespass products shall be distributed pro rata between the Indian beneficial owners and any costs and expenses needed to restore the trespass land; or

(2) Collections exceeding the highest stumpage value of the trespass product, but less than full recovery, shall be proportionally distributed pro rata between the Indian beneficial owners, the law enforcement agency, and the cost to restore the trespass land. Forest management deductions shall not be withheld where less than the highest

stumpage value of the unprocessed forest products taken in trespass has been recovered.

(c) Indian beneficial owners who trespass, or who are involved in trespass upon their own land, or undivided land in which such owners have a partial interest, shall not receive their beneficial share of any civil penalties and damages collected in consequence of the trespass. Any civil penalties and damages defaulted in consequence of this provision instead shall be distributed first toward restoration of the land subject of the trespass and second toward costs of the enforcement agency in consequence of the trespass, with any remainder to the forest management deduction account of the reservation in which the trespass took place.

(d) Civil penalties and other damages collected under these regulations, except for penalties and damages provided for in §§ 163.29(a)(3) (ii) and (iii) of this part, shall be treated as proceeds from the sale of forest products from the Indian forest land upon which the trespass occurred.

(e) When a federal official or authorized tribal representative pursuant to § 163.29(j) of this part has reason to believe that Indian forest products are involved in trespass, such individual may seize and take possession of the forest products involved in the trespass if the products are located on reservation. When forest products are seized, the person seizing the products must at the time of the seizure issue a Notice of Seizure to the possessor or claimant of the forest products. The Notice of Seizure shall indicate the date of the seizure, a description of the forest products seized, the estimated value of forest products seized, an indication of whether the forest products are perishable, and the name and authority of the person seizing the forest products. Where the official initiates seizure under these regulations only, the Notice of Seizure shall further include the statement that any challenge or objection to the seizure shall be exclusively through administrative appeal pursuant to part 2 of title 25, and shall provide the name and the address of the official with whom the appeal may be filed. Alternately, an official may exercise concurrent tribal seizure authority under these regulations using applicable tribal law. In such case, the Notice of Seizure shall identify the tribal law under which the seizure may be challenged, if any. A copy of a Notice of Seizure shall be given to the possessor or claimant at the time of the seizure. If the claimant or possessor is unknown or unavailable, Notice of Seizure shall be posted on the trespass property, and a copy of the Notice shall be kept with any incident report generated by the official seizing the forest products. If the property seized is perishable and will lose substantial value if not sold or otherwise disposed of, the representative of the Secretary, or authorized tribal representative where deferral has been requested, may cause the forest products to be sold. Such sale action shall not be stayed by the filing of an administrative appeal nor by a challenge of the seizure action through a tribal forum. All proceeds from the sale of the forest products shall be placed into an escrow account and held until adjudication or other resolution of the underlying trespass. If it is found that the forest products seized were involved in a trespass, the proceeds shall be applied to the amount of civil penalties and damages awarded. If it is found that a trespass has not occurred or the proceeds are in excess of the amount of the judgment awarded, the proceeds or excess proceeds shall be returned to the possessor or claimant.

(f) When there is reason to believe that Indian forest products are involved in trespass and that such products have been removed to land not under federal or tribal government supervision, the federal official or authorized tribal representative pursuant to § 163.29(k) of this part responsible for the trespass shall immediately provide the following notice to the owner of the land or the party in possession of the trespass products:

(1) That such products could be Indian trust property involved in a trespass; and

(2) That removal or disposition of the forest products may result in criminal and/or civil action by the United States or tribe.

(g) A representative of the Secretary or authorized tribal representative pursuant to § 163.29(j) of this part will promptly determine if a trespass has occurred. The appropriate representative will issue an official Notice of Trespass to the alleged trespasser and, if necessary, the possessor or potential buyer of any trespass products. The Notice is intended to inform the trespasser, buyer, or the processor:

(1) That a determination has been made that a trespass has occurred;

(2) The basis for the determination;

(3) An assessment of the damages, penalties and costs;

(4) Of the seizure of forest products, if applicable; and

(5) That disposition or removal of Indian forest products taken in the trespass may result in civil and/or criminal action by the United States or the tribe.

(h) The Secretary may accept payment of damages in the settlement of civil trespass cases. In the absence of a court order, the Secretary will determine the procedure and approve acceptance of any settlements negotiated by a tribe exercising its concurrent jurisdiction pursuant to § 163.29(j) of this part.

(i) The Secretary may delegate by written agreement or contract, responsibility for detection and investigation of forest trespass.

(j) Indian tribes that adopt the regulations set forth in this section, conformed as necessary to tribal law, shall have concurrent civil jurisdiction to enforce 25 U.S.C. 3106 and this section against any person.

(1) The Secretary shall acknowledge said concurrent civil jurisdiction over trespass, upon:

(i) Receipt of a formal tribal resolution documenting the tribe's adoption of this section; and

(ii) Notification of the ability of the tribal court system to properly adjudicate forest trespass cases, including a statement that the tribal court will enforce the Indian Civil Rights Act or a tribal civil rights law that contains provisions for due process and equal protection that are similar to or stronger than those contained in the Indian Civil Rights Act.

(2) Where an Indian tribe has acquired concurrent civil jurisdiction over trespass cases as set forth in § 163.29(j)(1) of this part, the Secretary and tribe's authorized representatives will be jointly responsible to coordinate prosecution of trespass actions. The Secretary shall, upon timely request of the tribe, defer prosecution of forest trespasses to the tribe. Where said deferral is not requested, the designated Bureau of Indian Affairs forestry trespass official shall coordinate with the authorized forest trespass official of each tribe the exercise of concurrent tribal and Federal trespass jurisdiction as to each trespass. Such officials shall review each case, determine in which forums to recommend bringing an action, and promptly provide their recommendation to the Federal officials responsible for initiating and prosecuting forest trespass cases. Where an Indian tribe has acquired concurrent civil jurisdiction, but does not request deferral of prosecution, the federal officials responsible for initiating and prosecuting such cases may file and prosecute the action in the tribal court or forum.

(3) The Secretary may rescind an Indian tribe's concurrent civil jurisdiction over trespass cases under this regulation if the Secretary or a court of competent jurisdiction determines that the tribal court has not adhered to the due process or equal protection requirements of the Indian Civil Rights Act. If it is determined that said rescission is justified, the Secretary shall provide written Notice of the rescission, including the findings justifying the rescission and the steps needed to remedy the violations causing the rescission, to the chief judge of the tribal judiciary or other authorized tribal official should there be no chief judge. If said steps are not taken within 60 days, the Secretary's rescission of concurrent civil jurisdiction shall become final. The affected tribe(s) may appeal a Notice of Rescission under part 2 of title 25.

(4) Nothing shall be construed to prohibit or in any way diminish the authority of a tribe to prosecute individuals under its criminal or civil trespass laws where it has jurisdiction over those individuals.

§ 163.30 Revocable road use and construction permits for removal of commercial forest products.

(a) In accordance with 25 U.S.C. 415 as amended, the Secretary may request tribes and/or other beneficial owners to sign revocable permits designating the Secretary as agent for the landowner and empowering him or her to issue revocable road use and construction permits to users for the purpose of removing forest products.

(b) When a majority of trust interest in a tract has consented, the Secretary may issue revocable road use and construction permits for removal of forest products over and across such land. In addition, the Secretary may act for individual owners when:

(1) One or more of the individual owner(s) of the land or of an interest therein is a minor or a person non compos mentis, and the Secretary finds that such grant, in total or for an interest therein, will cause no substantial injury to the land or the owner, which cannot be adequately compensated for by monetary damages;

(2) The whereabouts of the owner(s) of the land or those with an interest therein are unknown so long as the majority of owner(s) of interests whose whereabouts are known, consent to the grant;

(3) The heirs or devisees of a deceased owner of the land or interest have not been determined, and the Secretary finds the grant will cause no substantial injury to the land or any land owner; or

(4) The owners of interests in the land are so numerous that the Secretary finds it would be impractical to obtain the consent of the majority and finds that such grant in total or an interest therein will cause no substantial injury to the land or the owner(s), that cannot be adequately compensated for by monetary damages.

(c) Nothing in this section shall preclude acquisition of rights-of-way over Indian lands, under 25 CFR part 169, or conflict with provisions of that part.

§ 163.31 Insect and disease control.

(a) The Secretary is authorized to protect and preserve Indian forest land from disease or insects (Sept. 20, 1922, Ch. 349, 42 Stat. 857). The Secretary shall consult with the authorized tribal representatives and beneficial owners of Indian forest land concerning control actions.

(b) The Secretary is responsible for controlling and mitigating harmful effects of insects and diseases on Indian forest land and will coordinate control actions with the Secretary of Agriculture in accordance with 92 Stat. 365, 16 U.S.C. 2101.

§ 163.32 Forest development.

Forest development pertains to forest land management activities undertaken to improve the sustainable productivity of commercial Indian forest land. The program shall consist of reforestation, timber stand improvement projects, and related investments to enhance productivity of commercial forest land with emphasis on accomplishing on-the-ground projects. Forest development funds will be used to reestablish, maintain, and/or improve growth of commercial timber species and control stocking levels on commercial forest land. Forest development activities will be planned and executed using benefit-cost analyses as one of the determinants in establishing priorities for project funding.

§ 163.33 Administrative appeals.

Any challenge to action under 25 CFR part 163 taken by an approving officer or subordinate official exercising delegated authority from the Secretary shall be exclusively through administrative appeal or as provided in the Indian Self-Determination and Education Assistance Act (Pub. L. 93–638, as amended). Such appeal(s) shall be filed in accordance with the provisions of 25 CFR part 2, Appeals from administrative actions, except that an appeal of any action under part 163 of this title shall:

(a) Not stay any action unless otherwise directed by the Secretary; and

(b) Define "interested party" for purposes of bringing such an appeal or participating in such an appeal as any person whose own direct economic interest is adversely affected by an action or decision.

§163.34 Environmental compliance.

Actions taken by the Secretary under the regulations in this part must comply with the National Environmental Policy Act of 1969, applicable Council on Environmental Quality Regulations, and tribal laws and regulations.

§163.35 Indian forest land assistance account.

(a) At the request of a tribe's authorized representatives, the Secretary may establish tribal-specific forest land assistance accounts within the trust fund system.

(b) Deposits shall be credited either to forest transportation or to general forest land management accounts.

(c) Deposits into the accounts may include:

(1) Funds from non-federal sources related to activities on or for the Indian forest land of such tribe's reservation;

(2) Donations or contributions;

(3) Unobligated forestry appropriations for the tribe;

(4) User fees; and

(5) Funds transferred under Federal interagency agreements if otherwise authorized by law.

(d) For purposes of §163.35(c)(3) of this part; unobligated forestry appropriations shall consist of balances that remain unobligated at the end of the fiscal year(s) for which funds are appropriated for the benefit of an Indian tribe.

(e) Funds in the Indian forest land assistance account plus any interest or other income earned shall remain available until expended and shall not be available to otherwise offset Federal appropriations for the management of Indian forest land.

(f) Funds in the forest land assistance account shall be used only for forest land management activities on the reservation for which the account is established.

(g) Funds in a tribe's forest land assistance account shall be expended in accordance with a plan approved by the tribe and the Secretary.

(h) The Secretary may, where circumstances warrant, at the request of the tribe, or upon the Secretary's own volition, conduct audits of the forest land assistance accounts and shall provide the audit results of to the tribe(s).

§163.36 Tribal forestry program financial support.

(a) The Secretary shall maintain a program to provide financial support to qualifying tribal forestry programs. A qualifying tribal forestry program is an organization or entity established by a tribe for purposes of carrying out forest land management activities. Such financial support shall be made available through the Indian Self-Determination and Education Assistance Act (Pub. L. 93–638, as amended).

(b) The authorized tribal representatives of any category 1, 2, or 3 reservation (as defined under §163.36(b)(1)–(3)) with an established tribal forestry program or with an intent to establish such a program for the purpose of carrying out forest land management activities may apply and qualify for tribal forestry program financial support. Reservation categories, as determined by the Secretary, are defined as:

(1) Category 1 includes major forested reservations comprised of more than 10,000 acres of trust or restricted commercial timberland or having more than a one million board foot harvest of forest products annually.

(2) Category 2 includes minor forested reservations comprised of less than 10,000 acres of trust or restricted commercial timberland and having less than a one million board foot harvest of forest products annually, or whose forest resource is determined by the Secretary to be of significant commercial timber value.

(3) Category 3 includes significant woodland reservations comprised of an identifiable trust or restricted forest area of any size which is lacking a timberland component, and whose forest resource is determined by the Secretary to be of significant commercial woodland value.

(c) A group of tribes that has either established or intends to establish a cooperative tribal forestry program to provide forest land management services to their reservations may apply and qualify for tribal forestry program financial support. For purposes of financial support under this provision, the cooperative tribal forestry program and the commercial forest acreage and annual allowable cut which it represents may be considered as a single reservation.

(d) Before the beginning of each Federal fiscal year, tribes applying to qualify for forestry program financial support shall submit application packages to the Secretary which:

(1) Document that a tribal forestry program exists or that there is an intent to establish such a program;

(2) Describe forest land management activities and the time line for implementing such activities which would result from receiving tribal forestry program financial support; and

(3) Document commitment to sustained yield management.

(e) Tribal forestry program financial support shall provide professional and technical services to carry out forest land management activities and shall be based on levels of funding assistance as follows:

(1) Level one funding assistance shall be equivalent to a Federal Employee General Pay Schedule GS 9 step 5 position salary plus an additional 40 percent of the annual salary for such a position to pay for fringe benefits and support costs;

(2) Level two funding assistance shall be equivalent to an additional Federal Employee General Pay Schedule GS 9 step 5 position salary plus an additional 40 percent of the annual salary for such a position to pay for fringe benefits and support costs; and

(3) Level three funding assistance shall be based on equal distribution of remaining funds among qualifying applicants.

(f) Determination of qualification for level of funding assistance shall be as follows:

(1) A funding level qualification value shall be determined for each eligible applicant using the formula below. Such formula shall only be used to determine which applicants qualify for level one funding assistance. Acreage and allowable cut data used in the formula shall be as maintained by the Secretary. Eligible applicants with a funding level qualification value of one (1) or greater shall qualify for level one assistance.

Funding Level Qualification Formula

$$\left[\frac{.5\times \text{CA}}{\text{Tot. CA}}+\frac{.5\times \text{AAC}}{\text{Tot. AAC}}\right]\times 1000$$

where:

CA = applicant's total commercial Indian forest land acres;

Tot. CA = national total commercial Indian forest land acres;

AAC = applicant's total allowable annual cut from commercial Indian forest land acres; and

Tot. AAC = national total allowable annual cut from commercial Indian forest land acres.

(2) All category 1 or 2 reservations that are eligible applicants under § 163.36(d) of this part are qualified and eligible for level two assistance.

(3) All category 1, 2 or 3 reservations that are eligible applicants under § 163.36(d) of this part are qualified and eligible for level three assistance.

(g) Tribal forestry program financial support funds shall be distributed based on the following:

(1) All requests from reservations qualifying for level one funding assistance must be satisfied before funds are made available for level two funding assistance;

(2) All requests from reservations qualifying for level two funding assistance must be satisfied before funds are made available for level three funding assistance; and

(3) If available funding is not adequate to satisfy all requests at a particular level of funding, funds will be evenly divided among tribes qualifying at that level.

§ 163.37 Forest management research.

The Secretary, with the consent of the authorized Indian representatives' is authorized to perform forestry research activities to improve the basis for determining appropriate land management activities to apply to Indian forest land.

Subpart C—Forestry Education, Education Assistance, Recruitment and Training

§ 163.40 Indian and Alaska Native forestry education assistance.

(a) *Establishment and evaluation of the forestry education assistance programs.* (1) The Secretary shall establish within the Bureau of Indian Affairs Division of Forestry an education committee to coordinate and implement the forestry education assistance programs and to select participants for all the forestry education assistance programs with the exception of the cooperative education program. This committee will be, at a minimum, comprised of a professional educator, a personnel specialist, an Indian or Alaska Native who is not employed by the Bureau of Indian Affairs, and a professional forester from the Bureau of Indian Affairs.

(2) The Secretary, through the Bureau of Indian Affairs Division of Forestry, shall monitor and evaluate the forestry education assistance programs to ensure that there are adequate Indian and Alaska Native foresters and forestry-related professionals to manage the Bureau of Indian Affairs forestry programs and forestry programs maintained by or for tribes and ANCSA Corporations. Such monitoring and evaluating shall identify the number of participants in the intern, cooperative education, scholarship, and outreach programs; the number of participants who completed the requirements to become a professional forester or forestry-related professional; and the number of participants completing advanced degree requirements.

(b) *Forester intern program.* (1) The purpose of the forester intern program is to ensure the future participation of trained, professional Indians and Alaska Natives in the management of Indian and Alaska Native forest land. In keeping with this purpose, the Bureau of Indian Affairs in concert with tribes and Alaska Natives will work:

(i) To obtain the maximum degree of participation from Indians and Alaska Natives in the forester intern program;

(ii) To encourage forester interns to complete an undergraduate degree program in a forestry or forestry-related field which could include courses on indigenous culture; and

(iii) To create an opportunity for the advancement of forestry and forestry-related technicians to professional resource management positions with the Bureau of Indian Affairs, a tribe, tribal forest enterprise or ANCSA Corporation.

(2) The Secretary, through the Bureau of Indian Affairs Division of Forestry, subject to the availability of personnel resource levels established in agency budgets, shall establish and maintain in the Bureau of Indian Affairs at least 20 positions for the forester intern program. All Indians and Alaska Natives who satisfy the qualification criteria in § 163.40(b)(3) of this part may compete for such positions.

(3) To be considered for selection, applicants for forester intern positions must meet the following criteria:

(i) Be eligible for Indian preference as defined in 25 CFR part 5, subchapter A;

(ii) Possess a high school diploma or its recognized equivalent;

(iii) Be able to successfully complete the intern program within a three year maximum time period; and

(iv) Possess a letter of acceptance to an accredited post-secondary school or demonstrate that such a letter of acceptance will be acquired within 90 days.

(4) The Bureau of Indian Affairs shall advertise vacancies for forester intern positions semiannually, no later than the first day of April and October, to accommodate entry into school.

(5) Selection of forester interns will be based on the following guidelines:

(i) Selection will be on a competitive basis selecting applicants who have the greatest potential for success in the program;

(ii) Selection will take into consideration the amount of time which will be required for individual applicants to complete the intern program;

(iii) Priority in selection will be given to candidates currently employed with and recommended for participation by the Bureau of Indian Affairs, a tribe, a tribal forest enterprise or ANCSA Corporation; and

(iv) Selection of individuals to the program awaiting the letter of acceptance required by § 163.40(b)(3)(iv) of this part may be canceled if such letter of acceptance is not secured and provided to the education committee in a timely manner.

(6) Forester interns shall comply with each of the following program requirements:

(i) Maintain full-time status in a forestry related curriculum at an accredited post-secondary school having an agreement which assures the transferability of a minimum of 55 semester hours from the post-secondary institution which meet the program requirements for a forestry related program at a bachelor degree granting institution accredited by the American Association of Universities;

(ii) Maintain good academic standing;

(iii) Enter into an obligated service agreement to serve as a professional forester or forestry-related professional with the Bureau of Indian Affairs, the recommending tribe, tribal forest enterprise or ANCSA Corporation for two years for each year in the program; and

(iv) Report for service with the Bureau of Indian Affairs, a tribe, tribal forest enterprise or ANCSA Corporation during any break in attendance at school of more than three weeks duration. Time spent in such service shall be counted toward satisfaction of the intern's obligated service.

(7) The education committee established pursuant to §163.40(a)(1) of this part will evaluate annually the performance of forester intern program participants against requirements enumerated in §163.40(b)(6) of this part to ensure that they are satisfactorily progressing toward completing program requirements.

(8) The Secretary shall pay all costs for tuition, books, fees and living expenses incurred by a forester intern while attending an accredited post-secondary school.

(c) *Cooperative education program.* (1) The purpose of the cooperative education program is to recruit and develop promising Indian and Alaska Native students who are enrolled in secondary schools, tribal or Alaska Native community colleges, and other post-secondary schools for employment as professional foresters and other forestry-related professionals by the Bureau of Indian Affairs, a tribe, tribal forest enterprise or ANCSA Corporation.

(2) The program shall be operated by the Bureau of Indian Affairs Division of Forestry in accordance with the provisions of 5 CFR 213.3202(a) and 213.3202(b).

(3) To be considered for selection, applicants for the cooperative education program must meet the following criteria:

(i) Meet eligibility requirements stipulated in 5 CFR 213.3202;

(ii) Be accepted into or enrolled in a course of study at a high school offering college preparatory course work, an accredited institution which grants bachelor degrees in forestry or forestry-related curriculums or a post-secondary education institution which has an agreement with a college or university which grants bachelor degrees in forestry or forestry-related curriculums. The agreement must assure the transferability of a minimum of 55 semester hours from the post-secondary institution which meet the program requirements for a forestry related program at the bachelor degree-granting institution.

(4) Cooperative education steering committees established at the field level shall select program participants based on eligibility requirements stipulated in §163.40(c)(3) of this part without regard to applicants' financial needs.

(5) A recipient of assistance under the cooperative education program shall be required to enter into an obligated service agreement to serve as a professional forester or forestry- related professional with the Bureau of Indian Affairs, a recommending tribe, tribal forest enterprise or ANCSA Corporation for one year in return for each year in the program.

(6) The Secretary shall pay all costs of tuition, books, fees, and transportation to and from the job site to school, for an Indian or Alaska Native student who is selected for participation in the cooperative education program.

(d) *Scholarship program.* (1) The Secretary is authorized, within the Bureau of Indian Affairs Division of Forestry, to establish and grant forestry scholarships to Indians and Alaska Natives enrolled in accredited programs for post-secondary and graduate forestry and forestry-related programs of study as full-time students.

(2) The education committee established pursuant to this part in § 163.40(a)(1) shall select program participants based on eligibility requirements stipulated in §§ 163.40(d)(5), 163.40(d)(6) and 163.40(d)(7) without regard to applicants' financial needs or past scholastic achievements.

(3) Recipients of scholarships must reapply annually to continue funding beyond the initial award period. Students who have been recipients of scholarships in past years, who are in good academic standing and have been recommended for continuation by their academic institution will be given priority over new applicants for selection for scholarship assistance.

(4) The amount of scholarship funds an individual is awarded each year will be contingent upon the availability of funds appropriated each fiscal year and, therefore, may be subject to yearly changes.

(5) Preparatory scholarships are available for a maximum of two and one half academic years of general, undergraduate course work leading to a degree in forestry or forestry-related curriculums and may be awarded to individuals who meet the following criteria:

(i) Must possess a high school diploma or its recognized equivalent; and

(ii) Be enrolled and in good academic standing or accepted for enrollment at an accredited post-secondary school which grants degrees in forestry or forestry-related curriculums or be in a post-secondary institution which has an agreement with a college or university which grants bachelor degrees in forestry or forestry-related curriculums. The agreement must assure the transferability of a minimum of 55 semester hours from the post-secondary institution which meet the program requirements for a forestry-related curriculum at the bachelor degree granting institution.

(6) Pregraduate scholarships are available for a maximum of three academic years and may be awarded to individuals who meet the following criteria:

(i) Have completed a minimum of 55 semester hours towards a bachelor degree in a forestry or forestry-related curriculum; and

(ii) Be accepted into a forestry or forestry-related bachelor degree-granting program at an accredited college or university.

(7) Graduate scholarships are available for a maximum of three academic years for individuals selected into the graduate program of an accredited college or university that grants advanced degrees in forestry or forestry-related fields.

(8) A recipient of assistance under the scholarship program shall be required to enter into an obligated service agreement to serve as a professional forester or forestry-related professional with the Bureau of Indian Affairs, a tribe, tribal forest enterprise or ANCSA Corporation for one year for each year in the program.

(9) The Secretary shall pay all scholarships approved by the education committee established pursuant to this part in § 163.40(a)(1), for which funding is available.

(e) *Forestry education outreach.* (1) The Secretary shall establish and maintain a forestry education outreach program within the Bureau of Indian Affairs Division of Forestry for Indian and Alaska Native youth which will:

(i) Encourage students to acquire academic skills needed to succeed in post-secondary mathematics and science courses;

(ii) Promote forestry career awareness that could include modern technologies as well as native indigenous forestry technologies;

(iii) Involve students in projects and activities oriented to forestry related professions early so students realize the need to complete required precollege courses; and

(iv) Integrate Indian and Alaska Native forestry program activities into the education of Indian and Alaska Native students.

(2) The program shall be developed and carried out in consultation with appropriate community education organizations, tribes, ANCSA Corporations, and Alaska Native organizations.

(3) The program shall be coordinated and implemented nationally by the education committee established pursuant to § 163.40(a)(1) of this part.

(f) *Postgraduate studies.* (1) The purpose of the postgraduate studies program is to enhance the professional and technical knowledge of Indian and Alaska Native foresters and forestry-related professionals working for the Bureau of Indian Affairs, a tribe, tribal forest enterprise or ANCSA Corporations so that the best possible service is provided to Indian and Alaska Native publics.

(2) The Secretary is authorized to pay the cost of tuition, fees, books and salary of Alaska Natives and Indians who are employed by the Bureau of Indian Affairs, a tribe, tribal forest enterprise or ANCSA Corporation who have previously received diplomas or degrees in forestry or forestry-related curriculums and who wish to pursue advanced levels of education in forestry or forestry-related fields.

(3) Requirements of the postgraduate study program are:

(i) The goal of the advanced study program is to encourage participants to obtain additional academic credentials such as a degree or diploma in a forestry or forestry-related field;

(ii) The duration of course work cannot be less than one semester or more than three years; and

(iii) Students in the postgraduate studies program must meet performance standards as required by the graduate school offering the study program during their course of study.

(4) Program applicants will submit application packages to the education committee established by § 163.40(a)(1). At a minimum, such packages shall contain a complete SF 171 and an endorsement, signed by the applicant's supervisor clearly stating the needs and benefits of the desired training.

(5) The education committee established pursuant to § 163.40(a)(1) shall select program participants based on the following criteria:

(i) Need for the expertise sought at both the local and national levels;

(ii) Expected benefits, both to the location and nationally; and

(iii) Years of experience and the service record of the employee.

(6) Program participants will enter into an obligated service agreement in accordance with § 163.42(a), to serve as a professional forester or forestry-related professional with the Bureau of Indian Affairs, a tribe, tribal forest enterprise or ANCSA Corporation for two years for each year in the program. However, the obligated service requirement may be reduced by the Secretary if the employee receives supplemental funding such as research grants, scholarships or graduate stipends and, as a result, reduces the need for financial assistance. If the obligated service agreement is breached, the Secretary is authorized to pursue collection in accordance with § 163.42(b) of this part.

§ 163.41 Postgraduation recruitment, continuing education and training programs.

(a) *Postgraduation recruitment program.* (1) The purpose of the postgraduation recruitment program is to recruit Indian and Alaska Native graduate foresters and trained forestry technicians into the Bureau of Indian Affairs forestry program or forestry programs conducted by a tribe, tribal forest enterprise or ANCSA Corporation.

(2) The Secretary is authorized to assume outstanding student loans from established lending institutions of Indian and Alaska Native foresters and forestry technicians who have successfully completed a post-secondary forestry or forestry- related curriculum at an accredited institution.

(3) Indian and Alaska Natives receiving benefits under this program shall enter into an obligated service agreement in accordance with § 163.42(a) of this part. Obligated service required under this program will be one year for every $5,000 of student loan debt repaid.

(4) If the obligated service agreement is breached, the Secretary is authorized to pursue collection of the student loan(s) in accordance with § 163.42(b) of this part.

(b) *Postgraduate intergovernmental internships.* (1) Forestry personnel working for the Bureau of Indian Affairs, a tribe, tribal forest enterprise or ANCSA Corporation may apply to the Secretary and be granted an internship within forestry-related programs of agencies of the Department of the Interior.

(2) Foresters or forestry-related personnel from other Department of the Interior agencies may apply through proper channels for internships within Bureau of Indian Affairs forestry programs and, with the consent of a tribe or Alaska Native organization, within tribal or Alaska Native forestry programs.

(3) Forestry personnel from agencies not within the Department of the Interior may apply, through proper agency channels and pursuant to an interagency agreement, for an internship within the Bureau of Indian Affairs and, with the consent of a tribe or Alaska Native organization, within a tribe, tribal forest enterprise or ANCSA Corporation.

(4) Forestry personnel from a tribe, tribal forest enterprise or ANCSA Corporation may apply, through proper channels and pursuant to a cooperative agreement, for an internship within another tribe, tribal forest enterprise or ANCSA Corporation forestry program.

(5) The employing agency of participating Federal employees will provide for the continuation of salary and benefits.

(6) The host agency for participating tribal, tribal forest enterprise or ANCSA Corporation forestry employees will provide for salaries and benefits.

(7) A bonus pay incentive, up to 25 percent of the intern's base salary, may be provided to intergovernmental interns at the conclusion of the internship period. Bonus pay incentives will be at the discretion of and funded by the host organization and will be conditioned upon the host agency's documentation of the intern's superior performance, in accordance with the agency's performance standards, during the internship period.

(c) *Continuing education and training.* (1) The purpose of continuing education and training is to establish a program to provide for the ongoing education and training of forestry personnel employed by the Bureau of Indian Affairs, a tribe, tribal forest enterprise or ANCSA Corporation. This program will emphasize continuing education and training in three areas:

(i) Orientation training, including tribal-Federal relations and responsibilities;

(ii) Technical forestry education; and

(iii) Developmental training in forest land-based enterprises and marketing.

(2) The Secretary shall implement within the Bureau of Indian Affairs Division of Forestry, an orientation program designed to increase awareness and understanding of Indian culture and its effect on forest management practices and on Federal laws that affect forest management operations and administration in the Indian forestry program.

(3) The Secretary shall implement within the Bureau of Indian Affairs Division of Forestry, a continuing technical forestry education program to assist foresters and forestry-related professionals to perform forest management on Indian forest land.

(4) The Secretary shall implement, within the Bureau of Indian Affairs Division of Forestry, a forest land-based forest enterprise and marketing training program to assist with the development and use of Indian and Alaska Native forest resources.

§ 163.42 Obligated service and breach of contract.

(a) *Obligated service.* (1) Individuals completing forestry education programs with an obligated service requirement may be offered full time permanent employment with the Bureau of Indian Affairs, a tribe, tribal forest enterprise or ANCSA Corporation to fulfill their obligated service within 90 days of the date all program education requirements have been completed. If such employment is not offered within the 90-day period, the student shall be relieved of obligated service requirements. Not less than 30 days prior to the commencement of employment, the employer shall notify the participant of the work assignment, its location and the date work must begin. If the employer is other than the Bureau of Indian Affairs, the employer shall notify the Secretary of the offer for employment.

(2) Qualifying employment time eligible to be credited to fulfilling the obligated service requirement will begin

the day after all program education requirements have been completed, with the exception of the forester intern program, which includes the special provisions outlined in § 163.40(b)(6)(iv). The minimum service obligation period shall be one year of full-time employment.

(3) The Secretary or other qualifying employer reserves the right to designate the location of employment for fulfilling the service obligation.

(4) A participant in any of the forestry education programs with an obligated service requirement who receives a degree may, within 30 days of the degree completion date, request a deferment of obligated service to pursue postgraduate or postdoctoral studies. In such cases, the Secretary shall issue a decision within 30 days of receipt of the request for deferral. The Secretary may grant such a request, however, deferments granted in no way waive or otherwise affect obligated service requirements.

(5) A participant in any of the forestry education programs with an obligated service requirement may, within 30 days of the date all program education requirements have been completed, request a waiver of obligated service based on personal or family hardship. The Secretary may grant a full or partial waiver or deny the request for waiver. In such cases, the Secretary shall issue a decision within 30 days of receipt of the request for waiver.

(b) *Breach of contract.* Any individual who has participated in and accepted financial support under forestry education programs with an obligated service requirement and who does not accept employment or unreasonably terminates such employment by their own volition will be required to repay financial assistance as follows:

(1) *Forester intern program*—Amount plus interest equal to the sum of all salary, tuition, books, and fees that the forester intern received while occupying the intern position. The amount of salary paid to the individual during breaks in attendance from school, when the individual was employed by the Bureau of Indian Affairs, a tribe, tribal forest enterprise, or ANCSA Corporation, shall not be included in this total.

(2) *Cooperative education program*—Amount plus interest equal to the sum of all tuition, books, and fees that the individual received under the cooperative education program.

(3) *Scholarship program*—Amount plus interest equal to scholarship(s) provided to the individual under the scholarship program.

(4) *Postgraduation recruitment program*—Amount plus interest equal to the sum of all the individual's student loans assumed by the Secretary under the postgraduation recruitment program.

(5) *Postgraduate studies program*—Amount plus interest equal to the sum of all salary, tuition, books, and fees that the individual received while in the postgraduate studies program. The amount of salary paid to that individual during breaks in attendance from school, when the individual was employed by the Bureau of Indian Affairs, a tribe, a tribal enterprise, or ANCSA Corporation, shall not be included in this total.

(c) *Adjustment of repayment for obligated service performed.* Under forestry education programs with an obligated service requirement, the amount required for repayment will be adjusted by crediting time of obligated service performed prior to breach of contract toward the final amount of debt.

Subpart D—Alaska Native Technical Assistance Program

§ 163.60 Purpose and scope.

(a) The Secretary shall provide a technical assistance program to ANCSA corporations to promote sustained yield management of their forest resources and, where practical and consistent with the economic objectives of the ANCSA Corporations, promote local processing and other value-added activities. For the purpose of this subpart, technical assistance means specialized professional and technical help, advice or assistance in planning, and providing guidance, training and review for programs and projects associated with the management of, or impact upon, Indian forest land, ANCSA corporation forest land,

and their related resources. Such technical assistance shall be made available through contracts, grants or agreements entered into in accordance with the Indian Self-Determination and Education Assistance Act (Pub. L. 93–638, as amended).

(b) Nothing in this part shall be construed as: Affecting, modifying or increasing the responsibility of the United States toward ANCSA corporation forest land, or affecting or otherwise modifying the Federal trust responsibility towards Indian forest land; or requiring or otherwise mandating an ANCSA corporation to apply for a contract, grant, or agreement for technical assistance with the Secretary. Such applications are strictly voluntary.

§ 163.61 Evaluation committee.

(a) The Secretary shall establish an evaluation committee to assess and rate technical assistance project proposals. This committee will include, at a minimum, local Bureau of Indian Affairs and Alaska Native representatives with expertise in contracting and forestry.

§ 163.62 Annual funding needs assessment and rating.

(a) Each year, the Secretary will request a technical assistance project needs assessment from ANCSA corporations. The needs assessments will provide information on proposed project goals and estimated costs and benefits and will be rated by the evaluation committee established pursuant to § 163.61 for the purpose of making funding recommendations to the Secretary. To the extent practicable, such recommendations shall achieve an equitable funding distribution between large and small ANCSA corporations and shall give priority for continuation of previously approved multi-year projects.

(b) Based on the recommendations of the evaluation committee, the Secretary shall fund such projects, to the extent available appropriations permit.

§ 163.63 Contract, grant, or agreement application and award process.

(a) At such time that the budget for ANCSA corporation technical assistance projects is known, the Secretary shall advise the ANCSA corporations on which projects were selected for funding and on the deadline for submission of complete and detailed contract, grant or agreement packages.

(b) Upon the request of an ANCSA corporation and to the extent that funds and personnel are available, the Bureau of Indian Affairs shall provide technical assistance to ANCSA corporations to assist them with:

(1) Preparing the technical parts of the contract, grant, or agreement application; and

(2) Obtaining technical assistance from other Federal agencies.

Subpart E—Cooperative Agreements

§ 163.70 Purpose of agreements.

(a) To facilitate administration of the programs and activities of the Department of the Interior, the Secretary is authorized to negotiate and enter into cooperative agreements between Indian tribes and any agency or entity within the Department. Such cooperative agreements include engaging tribes to undertake services and activities on all lands managed by Department of the Interior agencies or entities or to provide services and activities performed by these agencies or entities on Indian forest land to:

(1) Engage in cooperative manpower and job training and development programs;

(2) Develop and publish cooperative environmental education and natural resource planning materials; and

(3) Perform land and facility improvements, including forestry and other natural resources protection, fire protection, reforestation, timber stand improvement, debris removal, and other activities related to land and natural resource management.

(b) The Secretary may enter into such agreements when he or she determines the public interest will be benefited. Nothing in § 163.70(a) shall be construed to limit the authority of the Secretary to enter into cooperative agreements otherwise authorized by law.

§ 163.71 Agreement funding.

In cooperative agreements, the Secretary is authorized to advance or reimburse funds to contractors from any appropriated funds available for similar kinds of work or by furnishing or sharing materials, supplies, facilities, or equipment without regard to the provisions of 31 U.S.C. 3324, relating to the advance of public moneys.

§ 163.72 Supervisory relationship.

In any agreement authorized by the Secretary, Indian tribes and their employees may perform cooperative work under the supervision of the Department of the Interior in emergencies or otherwise, as mutually agreed to, but shall not be deemed to be Federal employees other than for purposes of 28 U.S.C. 2671 through 2680, and 5 U.S.C. 8101 through 8193.

Subpart F—Program Assessment

§ 163.80 Periodic assessment report.

The Secretary shall commission every ten years an independent assessment of Indian forest land and Indian forest land management practices under the guidelines established in § 163.81 of this part.

(a) Assessments shall be conducted in the first year of each decade (e.g., 2000, 2010, etc.) and shall be completed within 24 months of their initiation date. Each assessment shall be initiated no later than November 28 of the designated year.

(b) Except as provided in § 163.83 of this part, each assessment shall be conducted by a non-Federal entity knowledgeable of forest management practices on Federal and private land. Assessments will evaluate and compare investment in and management of Indian forest land with similar Federal and private land.

(c) Completed assessment reports shall be submitted to the Committee on Interior and Insular Affairs of the United States House of Representatives and the Select Committee on Indian Affairs of the United States Senate and shall be made available to Indian tribes.

§ 163.81 Assessment guidelines.

Assessments shall be national in scope and shall include:

(a) An in-depth analysis of management practices on, and the level of funding by management activity for, specific Indian forest land compared with similar Federal and private forest land;

(b) A survey of the condition of Indian forest land, including health and productivity levels;

(c) An evaluation of the staffing patterns, by management activity, of forestry organizations of the Bureau of Indian Affairs and of Indian tribes;

(d) An evaluation of procedures employed in forest product sales administration, including preparation, field supervision, and accountability for proceeds;

(e) An analysis of the potential for streamlining administrative procedures, rules and policies of the Bureau of Indian Affairs without diminishing the Federal trust responsibility;

(f) A comprehensive review of the intensity and utility of forest inventories and the adequacy of Indian forest land management plans, including their compatibility with other resource inventories and applicable integrated resource management plans and their ability to meet tribal needs and priorities;

(g) An evaluation of the feasibility and desirability of establishing or revising minimum standards against which the adequacy of the forestry program of the Bureau of Indian Affairs in fulfilling its trust responsibility to Indian forest land can be measured;

(h) An evaluation of the effectiveness of implementing the Indian Self-Determination and Education Assistance Act (Pub. L. 93–638, as amended) in regard to the Bureau of Indian Affairs forestry program;

(i) A recommendation of any reforms and increased funding and other resources necessary to bring Indian forest land management programs to a state-of-the-art condition; and

(j) Specific examples and comparisons from across the United States where Indian forest land is located.

§ 163.82 Annual status report.

The Secretary shall, within 6 months of the end of each fiscal year, submit to the Committee on Interior and Insular Affairs of the United States House of Representatives, the Select Committee on Indian Affairs of the United States Senate, and to the affected Indian tribes, a report on the status of Indian forest land with respect to attaining the standards, goals and objectives set forth in approved forest management plans. The report shall identify the amount of Indian forest land in need of forestation or other silvicultural treatment, and the quantity of timber available for sale, offered for sale, and sold, for each Indian tribe.

§ 163.83 Assistance from the Secretary of Agriculture.

The Secretary of the Interior may ask the Secretary of Agriculture, through the Forest Service, on a nonreimbursable basis, for technical assistance in the conduct of such research and evaluation activities as may be necessary for the completion of any reports or assessments required by § 163.80 of this part.

PART 166—GRAZING PERMITS

Subpart A—Purpose, Scope, and Definitions

Subpart B—Tribal Policies and Laws Pertaining to Permits

Subpart C—Permit Requirements

GENERAL REQUIREMENTS

OBTAINING A PERMIT

PERMIT (LEASEHOLD) MORTGAGE

Subpart J—Agriculture Education, Education Assistance, Recruitment, and Training

Subpart K—Records

AUTHORITY: 5 U.S.C. 301; R.S. 463, 25 U.S.C. 2; R.S. 465, 25 U.S.C. 9; Sec. 6, 96 Stat. 986, 25 U.S.C. 466. Interpret or apply R.S. 2078, 25 U.S.C. 68; R.S. 2117, 25 U.S.C. 179; Sec. 3, 26 Stat. 795, 25 U.S.C. 397; Sec. 1, 28 Stat. 305, 25 U.S.C. 402; Sec. 4, 36 Stat. 856, 25 U.S.C. 403; Sec. 1, 39 Stat. 128, 25 U.S.C. 394; Sec. 1, 41 Stat. 1232, 25 U.S.C. 393; Sec. 16, 17, 48 Stat. 987, 988, 25 U.S.C. 476, 477; Sec. 1, 2, 4, 5, 6, 69 Stat. 539, 540, 25 U.S.C. 415, 415a, 415b, 415c, 415d, 25 U.S.C. 3701, 3702, 3703, 3711, 3712, 3713, 3714, 3731, 3732, 3733, 3734, 3741, 3742, 3743, 3744, 3745, 107 Stat. 2011; 44 U.S.C. §3101, *et seq.*)

SOURCE: 66 FR 7126, Jan. 22, 2001, unless otherwise noted.

Subpart A—Purpose, Scope, and Definitions

§ 166.1 What is the purpose and scope of this part?

(a) The purpose of this part is to describe the authorities, policies, and procedures the BIA uses to approve, grant, and administer a permit for grazing on tribal land, individually-owned Indian land, or government land.

(b) If the BIA's approval is not required for a permit, these regulations will not apply.

(c) These regulations do not apply to any tribal land which is permitted under a corporate charter issued by us pursuant to 25 U.S.C. §477, or under a special act of Congress authorizing permits without our approval under certain conditions, except to the extent that the authorizing statutes require us to enforce such permits on behalf of the Indian landowners.

(d) To the extent that any provisions of this part conflict with Section 213 of the Indian Land Consolidation Act Amendments of 2000, the provisions of that act will govern.

(e) In approving a permit on behalf of the Indian landowners, the BIA will not permit for fee interest owners nor will we collect rent on behalf of fee interest owners. Our permitting of the trust and restricted interests of the Indian landowners will not be conditioned on a permit having been obtained from any fee interest owners. However, where all of the trust or restricted interests in a tract are subject to a life estate held in fee status, we will approve a permit of the remainder interests of the Indian landowners only if such action is necessary to preserve the value of the land or protect the interests of the Indian landowners. Where a life estate and remainder interest are both owned in trust or restricted status, the life estate and remainder interest must both be permitted under these regulations, unless the permit is for less than one year in duration. Unless otherwise provided by the document creating the life estate or by agreement, rent payable under the permit must be paid to the holder of the life estate under part 179 of this title.

§ 166.2 Can the BIA waive the application of these regulations?

Yes. In any case in which these regulations conflict with the objectives of the agricultural resource management plan provided for in §166.311 of this part, or with a tribal law, the BIA may waive the application of such regulations unless the waiver would constitute a violation of a federal statute or judicial decision or would conflict with the BIA's general trust responsibility under federal law.

§ 166.3 May decisions under this part be appealed?

Yes. Except where otherwise provided in this part, appeals from decisions by the BIA under this part may be taken pursuant to 25 CFR part 2.

§ 166.4 What terms do I need to know?

Adult means an individual Indian who is 18 years of age or older.

Agency means the agency or field office or any other designated office in the Bureau of Indian Affairs (BIA) having jurisdiction over trust or restricted property or money.

Agricultural product means:

(1) Crops grown under cultivated conditions whether used for personal consumption, subsistence, or sold for commercial benefit;

(2) Domestic livestock, including cattle, sheep, goats, horses, buffalo, swine, reindeer, fowl, or other animals specifically raised and used for food or fiber or as a beast of burden;

(3) Forage, hay, fodder, food grains, crop residues and other items grown or harvested for the feeding and care of livestock, sold for commercial profit, or used for other purposes; and

(4) Other marketable or traditionally used materials authorized for removal from Indian agricultural lands.

Agricultural resource management plan means a ten-year plan developed through the public review process specifying the tribal management goals and objectives developed for tribal agricultural and grazing resources. Plans developed and approved under AIARMA will govern the management and administration of Indian agricultural resources and Indian agricultural lands by the BIA and Indian tribal governments.

AIARMA means American Indian Agricultural Resources Management Act of December 3, 1993 (107 Stat. 2011, 25 U.S.C. 3701 *et seq.*), and amended on November 2, 1994 (108 Stat. 4572).

Allocation means the apportionment of grazing privileges without competition to tribal members or tribal entities, including the tribal designation of permittees and the number and kind of livestock to be grazed.

Animal Unit Month (AUM) means the amount of forage required to sustain one cow or one cow with one calf for one month.

Approving/approval means the action taken by the BIA to approve a permit.

Assign/assignment means an agreement between a permittee and an assignee, whereby the assignee acquires all of the permittee's rights, and assumes all of the permittee's obligations under a permit.

Assignee means the person to whom the permit rights for use of Indian land are assigned.

BIA means the Bureau of Indian Affairs within the Department of the Interior and any tribe acting on behalf of the BIA under this part.

Bond means security for the performance of certain permit obligations, as furnished by the permitee, or a guaranty of such performance as furnished by a third-party surety.

Conservation plan means a statement of management objectives for grazing, including contract stipulations defining required uses, operations, and improvements.

Conservation practice means a management action to protect, conserve, utilize, and maintain the sustained yield productivity of Indian agricultural land.

Day means a calendar day.

Encumbrance means mortgage, deed of trust or other instrument which secures a debt owed by a permittee to a lender or other holder of a leasehold mortgage on the permit interest.

Emancipated minor means a person under 18 years of age who is married or who is determined by a court of competent jurisdiction to be legally able to care for himself or herself.

Fair annual rental means the amount of rental income that a permitted parcel of Indian land would most probably command in an open and competitive market.

Farmland means Indian land, excluding Indian forest land, that is used for production of food, feed, fiber, forage, and seed, oil crops, or other agricultural products, and may be either dry land, irrigated land, or irrigated pasture.

Fee interest means an interest in land that is owned in unrestricted fee status, and is thus freely alienable by the fee owner.

Fractionated tract means a tract of Indian land owned in common by Indian landowners and/or fee owners holding undivided interests therein.

Government land means any tract, or interest therein, in which the surface estate is owned by the United States and administered by the BIA, not including tribal land which has been reserved for administrative purposes.

Grant/granting means the process of the BIA or the Indian landowner agreeing or consenting to a permit.

Grazing capacity means the maximum sustainable number of livestock that may be grazed on a defined area and within a defined period, usually expressed in an Animal Unit Month (AUM).

Grazing rental payment means the total of the grazing rental rate multiplied by the number of AUMs or acres in the permit.

Grazing rental rate means the amount you must pay for an AUM or acre based on the fair annual rental.

I/You means the person to whom these regulations directly apply.

Immediate family means the spouse, brothers, sisters, lineal ancestors, lineal descendants, or members of the household of an individual Indian landowner.

Indian agricultural land means Indian land, including farmland and rangeland, excluding Indian forest land, that is used for production of agricultural products, and Indian lands occupied by industries that support the agricultural community, regardless of whether a formal inspection and land classification has been conducted.

Indian land means any tract in which any interest in the surface estate is owned by a tribe or individual Indian in trust or restricted status.

Indian landowner means a tribe or individual Indian who owns an interest in Indian land in trust or restricted status.

Individually-owned Indian land means any tract, or interest therein, in which the surface estate is owned by an individual Indian in trust or restricted status.

Interest means, when used with respect to Indian land, an ownership right to the surface estate of Indian land that is unlimited or uncertain in duration, including a life estate.

Life estate means an interest in Indian land which is limited in duration to the life of the permittor holding the interest, or the life of some other person.

Majority interest means the ownership interest(s) that are greater than 50 percent of the trust or restricted ownership interest(s) in a tract of Indian land.

Minor means an individual who is less than 18 years of age.

Mortgage means a mortgage, deed of trust or other instrument which pledges a permittee's permit (leasehold) interest as security for a debt or other obligation owed by the permittee to a lender or other mortgagee.

Non compos mentis means a person who has been legally determined by a court of competent jurisdiction to be of unsound mind or incapable of transacting or conducting business and managing one's own affairs.

On-and-off grazing permit means a written agreement with a permittee for additional grazing capacity for other rangeland not covered by the permit.

Permit means a written agreement between Indian landowners and a permittee, whereby the permittee is granted a revocable privilege to use Indian land or Government land, for a specified purpose.

Permittee means an a person or entity who has acquired a legal right of possession to Indian land by a permit for grazing purposes under this part.

Range unit means rangelands consolidated to form a unit of land for the management and administration of grazing under a permit. A range unit may consist of a combination of tribal, individually-owned Indian, and/or government land.

Rangeland means Indian land, excluding Indian forest land, on which native vegetation is predominantly grasses, grass-like plants, half-shrubs or shrubs suitable for grazing or browsing use, and includes lands re-vegetated naturally or artificially to provide a forage cover that is managed as native vegetation.

Restricted land or restricted status means land the title to which is held by an individual Indian or a tribe and which can only be alienated or encumbered by the owner with the approval of the Secretary because of limitations contained in the conveyance instrument pursuant to federal law.

Subpermit means a written agreement, whereby the permittee grants to an individual or entity a right to possession (i.e., pasturing authorization), no greater than that held by the permittee under the permit.

Surety means one who guarantees the performance of another.

Sustained yield means the yield of agricultural products that a unit of land can produce continuously at a given level of use.

Trespass means any unauthorized occupancy, use of, or action on Indian lands.

Tribal land means the surface estate of land or any interest therein held by the United States in trust for a tribe, band, community, group or pueblo of Indians, and land that is held by a tribe, band, community, group or pueblo of Indians, subject to federal restrictions against alienation or encumbrance, and includes such land reserved for BIA administrative purposes when it is not immediately needed for such purposes. The term also includes lands held by the United States in trust for an Indian corporation chartered under section 17 of the Act of June 18, 1934 (48 Stat. 984; 25 U.S.C. 476).

Tribal law means the body of non-federal law that governs lands and activities under the jurisdiction of a tribe, including ordinances or other enactments by the tribe, tribal court rulings, and tribal common law.

Trust land means any tract, or interest therein, that the United States holds in trust status for the benefit of a tribe or individual Indian.

Undivided interest means a fractional share in the surface estate of Indian land, where the surface estate is owned in common with other Indian landowners or fee owners.

Us/We/Our means the BIA and any tribe acting on behalf of the BIA under 166.1 of this part.

Uniform Standards of Professional Appraisal Practices (USPAP) means the standards promulgated by the Appraisal Standards Board of the Appraisal Foundation to establish requirements and procedures for professional real property appraisal practice.

Written notice means a written letter mailed by way of United States mail, certified return receipt requested, postage prepaid, or hand-delivered letter.

Subpart B—Tribal Policies and Laws Pertaining to Permits

§ 166.100 What special tribal policies will we apply to permitting on Indian agricultural lands?

(a) When specifically authorized by an appropriate tribal resolution establishing a general policy for permitting of Indian agricultural lands, the BIA will:

(1) Waive the general prohibition against Indian operator preferences in permits advertised for bid under § 166.221 of this part, by allowing prospective Indian operators to match the highest responsible bid (unless the tribal law or leasing policy specifies some other manner in which the preference must be afforded);

(2) Waive or modify the requirement that a permittee post a surety or performance bond;

(3) Provide for posting of other collateral or security in lieu of surety or other bonds; and

(4) Approve permits of tribally-owned agricultural lands at rates determined by the tribal governing body.

(b) When specifically authorized by an appropriate tribal resolution establishing a general policy for permitting of Indian agricultural lands, and subject to paragraph (c) of this section, the BIA may:

(1) Waive or modify any general notice requirement of federal law; and

(2) Grant or approve a permit on "highly fractionated undivided heirship lands" as defined by tribal law.

(c) The BIA may take the action specified in paragraph (b) of this section only if:

(1) The tribe defines by resolution what constitutes "highly fractionated undivided heirship lands";

(2) The tribe adopts an alternative plan for notifying individual Indian landowners; and

(3) The BIA's action is necessary to prevent waste, reduce idle land acreage and ensure income.

§ 166.101 May individual Indian landowners exempt their land from certain tribal policies for permitting on Indian agricultural lands?

(a) The individual Indian landowners of Indian land may exempt their land from our application of a tribal policy referred to under § 166.100 of this part if:

(1) The Indian landowners have at least a 50% interest in such fractionated tract; and

(2) The Indian landowners submit a written objection to the BIA of all or any part of such tribal policies to the permitting of such parcel of land.

(b) Upon verification of the written objection we will notify the tribe of the Indian landowners' exemption from the specific tribal policy.

(c) The procedures described in paragraphs (a) and (b) of this section will also apply to withdrawing an approved exemption.

§ 166.102 Do tribal laws apply to permits?

Tribal laws will apply to permits of Indian land under the jurisdiction of the tribe enacting such laws, unless those tribal laws are inconsistent with applicable federal law.

§ 166.103 How will tribal laws be enforced on Indian agricultural land?

(a) Unless prohibited by federal law, we will recognize and comply with tribal laws regulating activities on Indian agricultural land, including tribal laws relating to land use, environmental protection, and historic or cultural preservation.

(b) While the tribe is primarily responsible for enforcing tribal laws pertaining to Indian agricultural land, we will:

(1) Assist in the enforcement of tribal laws;

(2) Provide notice of tribal laws to persons or entities undertaking activities on Indian agricultural land, under § 166.104(b) of this part; and

(3) Require appropriate federal officials to appear in tribal forums when requested by the tribe, so long as such an appearance would not:

(i) Be inconsistent with the restrictions on employee testimony set forth at 43 CFR Part 2, Subpart E;

(ii) Constitute a waiver of the sovereign immunity of the United States; or

(iii) Authorize or result in a review of our actions by a tribal court.

(c) Where the regulations in this subpart are inconsistent with a tribal law, but such regulations cannot be superseded or modified by the tribal law under § 166.2 of this part, we may waive the regulations under part 1 of this title, so long as the waiver does not violate a federal statute or judicial decision or conflict with our general trust responsibility under federal law.

§ 166.104 What notifications are required that tribal laws apply to permits on Indian agricultural lands?

(a) Tribes must notify us of the content and effective dates of new tribal laws.

(b) We will then notify affected Indian landowners and any persons or entities undertaking activities on Indian agricultural lands of the superseding or modifying effect of the tribal law. We will:

(1) Provide individual written notice; or

(2) Post public notice. This notice will be posted at the tribal community building, U.S. Post Office, and/or published in the local newspaper nearest to the Indian lands where activities are occurring.

Subpart C—Permit Requirements

GENERAL REQUIREMENTS

§ 166.200 When is a permit needed to authorize possession of Indian land for grazing purposes?

(a) Unless otherwise provided for in this part, any person or legal entity, including an independent legal entity owned and operated by a tribe, must obtain a permit under these regulations before taking possession of Indian land for grazing purposes.

(b) An Indian landowner who owns 100% of the trust or restricted interests in a tract may take possession of that Indian land without a permit or any other prior authorization from us.

(c) If an Indian landowner does not own 100 percent (%) of his or her Indian land and wants to use the Indian land for grazing purposes, a permit must be granted by the majority interest of the fractionated tract.

§ 166.201 Must parents or guardians of Indian minors who own Indian land obtain a permit before using land for grazing purposes?

Parents or guardians need not obtain a permit for Indian lands owned by their minor Indian children if:

(a) Those minor children own 100 percent (%) of the land; and

(b) The minor children directly benefit from the use of the land. We may require the user to provide evidence of the direct benefits to the minor children. When one of the minor children becomes an adult, the permit will have to be obtained from the majority interest.

§ 166.202 May an emancipated minor grant a permit?

Yes. An emancipated minor may grant a permit.

§ 166.203 When can the Indian landowners grant a permit?

(a) Tribes grant permits of tribal land, including any tribally-owned undivided interest(s) in a fractionated tract. A permit granted by the tribe must be approved by us, unless the permit is authorized by a charter approved by us under 25 U.S.C. § 477, or unless our approval is not required under other applicable federal law. In order to permit tribal land in which the beneficial interest has been assigned to another party, the assignee and the tribe must both grant the permit, subject to our approval.

(b) Individual Indian landowners may grant a permit of their land, including their undivided interest in a fractionated tract, subject to our approval. Except as otherwise provided in this part, these Indian landowners may include the owner of a life estate holding 100 percent (%) interest in their land.

(c) The owners of a majority interest in the Indian ownership of a fractionated tract may grant a permit, subject to our approval, without giving prior notice to the minority Indian landowners as long as the minority interest owners receive fair annual rental.

§ 166.204 Who may represent an individual Indian landowner in granting a permit?

The following individuals or entities may represent an individual Indian landowner in granting a permit:

(a) An adult with custody acting on behalf of their minor children;

(b) A guardian, conservator, or other fiduciary appointed by a court of competent jurisdiction to act on behalf of an individual Indian landowner;

(c) An adult or legal entity who has been given a written power of attorney that:

(1) Meets all of the formal requirements of any applicable tribal or state law;

(2) Identifies the attorney-in-fact and the land to be permitted; and

(3) Describes the scope of the power granted and any limits thereon.

§ 166.205 When can the BIA grant a permit on behalf of Indian landowners?

(a) We may grant a permit on behalf of:

(1) An individual who is adjudicated to be non compos mentis by a court of competent jurisdiction;

(2) An orphaned minor;

(3) An Indian landowner who has granted us written authority to permit his or her land;

(4) The undetermined heirs and devisees of a deceased Indian landowner;

(5) An Indian landowner whose whereabouts are unknown to us after a reasonable attempt is made to locate the Indian landowner;

(6) Indian landowners, where:

(i) We have provided written notice of our intent to grant a permit on their behalf, but the Indian landowners are unable to agree upon a permit during a three-month negotiation period immediately following such notice, or any other notice period established by a tribe under § 166.100(c)(2) of this part; and

(ii) The land is not being used by an individual Indian landowner under § 166.200 of this part.

(7) The individual Indian owners of fractionated Indian land, when necessary to protect the interests of the individual Indian landowners.

§ 166.206 What requirements apply to a permit on a fractionated tract?

We may grant a permit on behalf of all Indian landowners of a fractionated tract as long as the owners receive fair annual rental. Before granting such a permit, we may offer a preference right to any Indian landowner who:

(a) Is in possession of the entire tract;

(b) Submits a written offer to permit the land, subject to any required or negotiated terms and conditions, prior to our granting a permit to another party; and

(c) Provides any supporting documents needed to demonstrate the ability to perform all of the obligations under the proposed permit.

§ 166.207 What provisions will be contained in a permit?

A permit, at a minimum, must include:

(a) Authorized user(s);

(b) Conservation plan requirements;

(c) Prohibition against creating a nuisance, any illegal activity, and negligent use or waste or resources;

(d) Numbers and types of livestock allowed;

(e) Season(s) of use;

(f) Grazing rental payment, payment schedule, and late payment interest and penalties;

(g) Administrative fees;

(h) Tribal fees, if applicable;

(i) Payment method;

(j) Range unit number or name;

(k) Animal identification requirements;

(l) A description (preferably a legal description) of the permitted area;

(m) Term of permit (including beginning and ending dates of the term allowed, as well as any option to renew, extend or terminate);

(n) Conditions for making improvements, if any;

(o) A right of entry by the BIA for purposes of inspection or enforcement purposes;

(p) A provision concerning the applicability of tribal jurisdiction;

(q) A provision stating how trespass proceeds are to be distributed; and

(r) A provision for the permittee to indemnify the United States and the Indian landowners against all liabilities or costs relating to the use, handling, treatment, removal, storage, transportation, or disposal of hazardous materials or the release or discharge of any hazardous material from the permitted premises that occur during the permit term, regardless of fault.

§ 166.208 How long is a permit term?

(a) The duration must be reasonable given the purpose of the permit and the level of investment required by the permittee to place the property into productive use.

(b) On behalf of the undetermined heirs of an individual Indian decedent owning 100 percent (%) interest in the land, we will grant or approve permits for a maximum term of two years.

(c) Permits granted for agricultural purposes will not usually exceed ten years. A term longer than ten years, but not to exceed 25 years unless authorized by other federal law, may be authorized when a longer term is determined by us to be in the best interest of the Indian landowners and when such permit requires substantial investment in the development of the lands by the permittee.

(d) A tribe may determine the duration of permits composed entirely of its tribal land or in combination with government land, subject to the same limitations provided in paragraph (d) of this section.

(e) A permit will specify the beginning and ending dates of the term allowed, as well as any option to renew, extend, or terminate.

(f) Permits granted by us for protection of the Indian land will be for no more than two years.

§ 166.209 Must a permit be recorded?

A permit must be recorded in our Land Titles and Records Office which has jurisdiction over the land. We will record the permit immediately following our approval under this subpart.

§ 166.210 When is a decision by the BIA regarding a permit effective?

Our decision to approve a permit will be effective immediately, notwithstanding any appeal which may be filed under Part 2 of this title. Copies of the approved permit will be provided to the permitee and made available to the Indian landowners upon request.

§ 166.211 When are permits effective?

Unless otherwise provided in the permit, a permit will be effective on the date on which the permit is approved by us. A permit may be made effective on some past or future date, by agreement, but such a permit may not be granted or approved more than one year prior to the date on which the permit term is to commence.

§ 166.212 When may a permittee take possession of permitted Indian land?

The permittee may take possession of permitted Indian land on the date specified in the permit as the beginning date of the term, but not before we approve the permit.

§ 166.213 Must I comply with any standards of conduct if I am granted a permit?

Yes. Permittees are expected to:

(a) Conduct grazing operations in accordance with the principles of sustained yield management, agricultural resource management planning, sound conservation practices, and other community goals as expressed in tribal laws, agricultural resource management plans, and similar sources.

(b) Comply with all applicable laws, ordinances, rules, regulations, and other legal requirements. You must also pay all applicable penalties that may be assessed for non-compliance.

(c) Fulfill all financial obligations of your permit owed to the Indian landowners and the United States.

(d) Conduct only those activities authorized by the permit.

§ 166.214 Will the BIA notify the permittee of any change in land title status?

Yes. We will notify the permittee if a fee patent is issued or if restrictions are removed. After we notify the permittee our obligation under § 166.228 of this part ceases.

OBTAINING A PERMIT

§ 166.215 How can I find Indian land available for grazing?

You may contact a local BIA office or tribal office to determine what Indian land may be available for grazing permits.

§ 166.216 Who is responsible for permitting Indian land?

The Indian landowner is primarily responsible for granting permits on their Indian land, with the assistance and approval of the BIA, except where otherwise provided by law. You may contact the local BIA or tribal office for assistance in obtaining a permit for grazing purposes on Indian land.

§ 166.217 In what manner may a permit on Indian land be granted?

(a) A tribe may grant a permit on tribal land through tribal allocation, negotiation, or advertisement in accordance with § 166.203 of this part. We must approve all permits of tribal land in order for the permit to be valid, except where otherwise provided by law.

(b) Individual Indian landowners may grant a permit on their Indian land through negotiation or advertisement in accordance with § 166.203 of this part. We must approve all permits of Individual Indian land in order for the permit to be valid.

(c) We will grant permits through negotiation or advertisement for range units containing, in whole or part, individually-owned Indian land and range units that consist of, or in combination with individually-owned Indian land, tribal or government land, under § 166.205 of this part. We will consult with tribes prior to granting permits for range units that include tribal land.

§ 166.218 How do I acquire a permit through tribal allocation?

(a) A tribe may allocate grazing privileges on range units containing trust or restricted land which is entirely tribally-owned or which contains only tribal and government land under the control of the tribe.

(b) A tribe may allocate grazing privileges to its members and to tribally-authorized entities without competitive bidding on tribal and tribally-controlled government land.

(c) We will implement the tribe's allocation procedure by authorizing the grazing privileges on individually-owned Indian land and government land, subject to the rental rate provisions in § 166.400(b) and (c) of this part.

(d) A tribe may prescribe the eligibility requirements for allocations 60 days before granting a new permit or before an existing permit expires.

(e) 120 days before the expiration of existing permits, we will notify the tribe of the 60-day period during which the tribe may prescribe eligibility requirements.

(f) We will prescribe the eligibility requirements after the expiration of the 60-day period in the event satisfactory action is not taken by the tribe.

(g) Grazing rental rates for grazing privileges allocated from an existing permit, in whole or in part, must equal or exceed the rates paid by the preceding permittee(s). Tribal members will pay grazing rental rates established by the tribe on tribal lands.

§ 166.219 How do I acquire a permit through negotiation?

(a) Permits may be negotiated and granted by the Indian landowners with the permittee of their choice. The BIA may negotiate and grant permits on behalf of Indian landowners pursuant to § 166.205 of this part.

(b) Upon the conclusion of negotiations with the Indian landowners or their representatives, and the satisfaction of any applicable conditions, you may submit an executed permit and any required supporting documents to us for appropriate action. Where a permit is in a form that has previously been accepted or approved by us, and all of the documents needed to support the findings required by this part have been received, we will decide whether to approve the permit within 30 days of the date of our receipt of the permit and supporting documents. If we decide to approve or disapprove a permit, we will notify the parties immediately and advise them of their right to appeal the decision under part 2 of this title.

(c) In negotiating a permit, the Indian landowners may choose to include their land in the permit in exchange for their receipt of a share of the revenues or profits generated by the permit. Under such an arrangement, the permit may be granted to a joint venture or other legal entity owned, in part, by the Indian landowners.

(d) Receipt of permit payments based upon income received from the land will not, of itself, make the Indian landowner a partner, joint venturer, or associate of the permittees.

(e) We will assist prospective permittees in contacting the Indian landowners or their representatives, for the purpose of negotiating a permit.

§ 166.220 What are the basic steps for acquiring a permit through negotiation?

The basic steps for acquiring a permit by negotiation are as follows:

(a) The BIA or the Indian landowner will:

(1) Receive a request to permit from an Indian landowner or the potential permittee;

(2) Prepare the permit documents; and

(3) Grant the permit.

(b) A potential permittee will complete the requirements for securing a permit, (e.g., bond, insurance, payment of administrative fee, etc.);

(c) We will:

(1) Review the permit for proper documentation and compliance with all applicable laws and regulations;

(2) Approve the permit after our review;

(3) Send the approved permit to the permittee and, upon request, to the Indian landowner; and

(4) Record and maintain the approved permit.

§ 166.221 How do I acquire an advertised permit through competitive bidding?

(a) As part of the negotiation of a permit, Indian landowners may advertise their Indian land to identify potential permittees with whom to negotiate.

(b) When the BIA grants and approves a permit on behalf of an individual Indian landowner using an advertisement for bids, we will:

(1) Prepare and distribute an advertisement of lands available for permit that identifies the terms and conditions of the permit sale, including, for agricultural permits, any preference rights;

(2) Solicit sealed bids and conduct the public permit sale;

(3) Determine and accept the highest or best responsible bidder(s), which may require further competitive bidding after the bid opening; and

(4) Prepare permits for successful bidders.

(c) After completion of the steps in paragraph (b) of this section, the successful bidder must complete and submit the permit and satisfy all applicable requirements, (e.g., bond, insurance, payment of administrative fee, etc.).

(d) After review of the permit documentation for proper completion and compliance with all applicable laws and regulations, within 30 days we will:

(1) Grant and approve the permit on behalf of Indian landowners where we are authorized to do so by law;

(2) Distribute the approved permit to the permittee(s) and, upon request, to the Indian landowner(s); and

(3) Record and maintain the approved permit.

§ 166.222 Are there standard permit forms?

Yes. Standard permit forms, including bid forms, permit forms, and permit modification forms are available at our agency offices.

Permit (Leasehold) Mortgage

§ 166.223 Can I use a permit as collateral for a loan?

We may approve a permit containing a provision that authorizes the permittee to encumber the permit interest, known as a leasehold mortgage, for the development and improvement of the permitted Indian land. We must approve the leasehold mortgage that encumbers the permit interest before it can be effective. We will record the approved leasehold mortgage instrument.

§ 166.224 What factors does the BIA consider when reviewing a leasehold mortgage?

(a) We will approve the leasehold mortgage if:

(1) All consents required in the permit have been obtained from the Indian landowners and any surety or guarantor;

(2) The mortgage covers only the permit interest, and no unrelated collateral belonging to the permittee;

(3) The financing being obtained will be used only in connection with the development or use of the permitted premises, and the mortgage does not secure any unrelated obligations owed by the permittee to the mortgagee; and

(4) We find no compelling reason to withhold our approval, in order to protect the best interests of the Indian landowner.

(b) In making the finding required by paragraph (a)(4) of this section, we will consider whether:

(1) The ability to perform the permit obligations would be adversely affected by the cumulative mortgage obligations;

(2) Any negotiated permit provisions as to the allocation or control of insurance or condemnation proceeds would be modified;

(3) The remedies available to us or the Indian landowners would be limited (beyond the additional notice and cure rights to be afforded to the mortgagee), if the permittee defaults on the permit;

(4) Any rights of the Indian landowners would be subordinated or adversely affected in the event of a foreclosure, assignment in lieu of foreclosure, or issuance of a "new permit" to the mortgagee.

(c) We will notify the Indian landowners of our approval of the leasehold mortgage.

§ 166.225 May a permittee voluntarily assign a leasehold interest under an approved encumbrance?

With our approval, under an approved encumbrance, a permittee voluntarily may assign the leasehold interest to someone other than the holder of a leasehold mortgage if the assignee agrees in writing to be bound by the terms of the permit. A permit may provide the Indian landowners with a right of first refusal on the conveyance of the leasehold interest.

§ 166.226 May the holder of a leasehold mortgage assign the leasehold interest after a sale or foreclosure of an approved encumbrance?

Yes. The holder of a leasehold mortgage may assign a leasehold interest obtained by a sale or foreclosure of an approved encumbrance without our approval if the assignee agrees in writing to be bound by the terms of the permit. A permit may provide the Indian landowners with a right of first refusal on the conveyance of the permit interest (leasehold).

MODIFYING A PERMIT

§ 166.227 How can Indian land be removed from an existing permit?

(a) We will remove Indian land from the permit if:

(1) The trust status of the Indian land terminates;

(2) The Indian landowners request removal of their interest, with the written approval of the majority interest of the fractionated tract to be removed, and we determine that the removal is beneficial to such interests;

(3) A tribe allocates grazing privileges for Indian land covered by your permit under § 166.218 of this part;

(4) The permittee requests removal of the Indian land, the owners of the majority interest of the Indian land provides written approval of the removal of the Indian land, and we determine that the removal is warranted; or

(5) We determine that removal of the Indian land is appropriate, with the written approval of the owners of the majority interest of the Indian land.

(b) We will revise the grazing capacity to reflect the removal of Indian land and show it on the permit.

§ 166.228 How will the BIA provide notice if Indian land is removed from an existing permit?

If the reason for removal is:

(a) Termination of trust status. We will notify the parties to the permit in writing within 30 days. The removal will be effective on the next anniversary date of the permit.

(b) A request from Indian landowners or the permittee, or our determination. We will notify the parties to the permit in writing within 30 days of such request. The removal will be effective immediately if all sureties, Indian landowners, and permittee agree. Otherwise, the removal will be effective upon the next anniversary date of the permit. If our written notice is within 180 days of the anniversary date of the permit, the removal of Indian land will be effective 180 days after the written notice.

(c) Tribal allocation under § 166.218 of this part. We will notify the parties to the permit in writing within 180 days of such action. The removal of tribal land will be effective on the next anniversary date of the permit. If our written notice is within 180 days of the anniversary date of the permit, the removal of Indian land will be effective 180 days after the written notice.

§ 166.229 Other than to remove land, how can a permit be amended, assigned, subpermitted, or mortgaged?

(a) We must approve an amendment, assignment, subpermit, or mortgage with the written consent of the parties to the permit in the same manner that the permit was approved, and the consent of the sureties.

(b) Indian landowners may designate in writing one or more of their co-owners or representatives to negotiate and/or agree to amendments on their behalf.

(1) The designated landowner or representative may:

(i) Negotiate or agree to amendments; and

(ii) Consent to or approve other items as necessary.

(2) The designated landowner or representative may not:

(i) Negotiate or agree to amendments that reduce the grazing rental payments payable to the other Indian landowners; or

(ii) Terminate the permit or modify the term of the permit.

(c) We may approve a permit for tribal land to individual members of a tribe which contains a provision permitting the assignment of the permit by the permittee or the lender without our approval when a lending institution or an agency of the United States:

(1) Accepts the interest in the permit (leasehold) as security for the loan; and

(2) Obtains the interest in the permit (leasehold) through foreclosure or otherwise.

(d) We will revise the grazing capacity and modify the permit.

§ 166.230 When will a BIA decision to approve an amendment, assignment, subpermit, or mortgage under a permit be effective?

Our decision to approve an amendment, assignment, subpermit, or mortgage under a permit will be effective immediately, notwithstanding any appeal which may be filed under Part 2 of this title. Copies of approved documents will be provided to the party requesting approval, and made available to the Indian landowners upon request.

§ 166.231 Must an amendment, assignment, subpermit, or mortgage approved under a permit be recorded?

An amendment, assignment, subpermit, or mortgage approved under a permit must be recorded in our Land Titles and Records Office which has jurisdiction over the Indian land. We will record the document immediately following our approval.

Subpart D—Land and Operations Management

§ 166.300 How is Indian agricultural land managed?

Tribes, individual Indian landowners, and the BIA will manage Indian agricultural land either directly or through contracts, compacts, cooperative agreements, or grants under the Indian Self-Determination and Education Assistance Act (Public Law 93–638, as amended).

§ 166.301 How is Indian land for grazing purposes described?

Indian land for grazing purposes should be described by legal description (e.g., aliquot parts, metes and bounds) or other acceptable description. Where there are undivided interests owned in fee status, the aggregate portion of trust and restricted interests should be identified in the description of the permitted land.

§ 166.302 How is a range unit created?

We create a range unit after we consult with the Indian landowners of rangeland, by designating units of compatible size, availability, and location.

§ 166.303 Can more than one parcel of Indian land be combined into one permit?

Yes. A permit may include more than one parcel of Indian land. Permits may include tribal land, individually-owned Indian land, or government land, or any combination thereof.

§ 166.304 Can there be more than one permit for each range unit?

Yes. There can be more than one permit for each range unit.

§ 166.305 When is grazing capacity determined?

Before we grant, modify, or approve a permit, in consultation with the Indian landowners, we will establish the total grazing capacity for each range unit based on the summation of each parcel's productivity. We will also establish the season(s) of use on Indian lands.

§ 166.306 Can the BIA adjust the grazing capacity?

Yes. In consultation with the Indian landowners or in the BIA's discretion based on good cause, we may adjust the grazing capacity using the best evaluation method(s) relevant to the ecological region.

§ 166.307 Will the grazing capacity be increased if I graze adjacent trust or non-trust rangelands not covered by the permit?

No. You will not receive an increase in grazing capacity in the permit if you graze trust or non-trust rangeland in common with the permitted land. Grazing capacity will be established only for Indian land covered by your permit.

§ 166.308 Can the number of animals and/or season of use be modified on the permitted land if I graze adjacent trust or non-trust rangelands under an on-and-off grazing permit?

Yes. The number of animals and/or season of use may be modified on permitted Indian land with an on-and-off grazing permit only when a conservation plan includes the use of adjacent trust or non-trust rangelands not covered by the permit and when that land is used in common with permitted land.

§ 166.309 Who determines livestock class and livestock ownership requirements on permitted Indian land?

(a) Tribes determine the class of livestock and livestock ownership requirements for livestock that may be grazed on range units composed entirely of tribal land or which include government land, subject to the grazing capacity prescribed by us under § 166.305 of this part.

(b) For permits on range units containing, in whole or part, individually-owned Indian land, we will adopt the tribal determination in paragraph (a) of this section.

§ 166.310 What must a permittee do to protect livestock from exposure to disease?

In accordance with applicable law, permittees must:

(a) Vaccinate livestock;

(b) Treat all livestock exposed to or infected with contagious or infectious diseases; and

(c) Restrict the movement of exposed or infected livestock.

MANAGEMENT PLANS AND ENVIRONMENTAL COMPLIANCE

§ 166.311 Is an Indian agricultural resource management plan required?

(a) Indian agricultural land under the jurisdiction of a tribe must be managed in accordance with the goals and objectives in any agricultural resource management plan developed by the tribe, or by us in close consultation with the tribe, under the AIARMA.

(b) The ten-year agricultural resource management and monitoring plan must be developed through public meetings and completed within three years of the initiation of the planning activity. Such a plan must be developed through public meetings, and be based on the public meeting records and existing survey documents, reports, and other research from federal agencies, tribal community colleges, and land grant universities. When completed, the plan must:

(1) Determine available agricultural resources;

(2) Identify specific tribal agricultural resource goals and objectives;

(3) Establish management objectives for the resources;

(4) Define critical values of the tribe and its members and provide identified holistic management objectives; and

(5) Identify actions to be taken to reach established objectives.

(c) Where the regulations in this subpart are inconsistent with a tribe's agricultural resource management plan, we may waive the regulations under part 1 of this title, so long as the waiver does not violate a federal statute or judicial decision or conflict with our general trust responsibility under federal law.

§ 166.312 Is a conservation plan required?

A conservation plan must be developed for each permit with the permittee and approved by us prior to the issuance of the permit. The conservation plan must be consistent with the tribe's agricultural resource management plan and must address the permittee's management objectives regarding animal husbandry and resource conservation. The conservation plan must cover the entire permit period and reviewed by us on an annual basis.

§ 166.313 Is environmental compliance required?

Actions taken by the BIA under the regulations in this part must comply with the National Environmental Policy Act of 1969 (42 U.S.C. 4321 *et seq.*), applicable regulations of the Council on Environmental Quality (40 CFR part

1500), and applicable tribal laws and regulations.

CONSERVATION PRACTICES AND IMPROVEMENTS

§ 166.314 Can a permittee apply a conservation practice on permitted Indian land?

Yes. A permittee can apply a conservation practice on permitted Indian land as long as the permittee has approval from the BIA and majority interest and the conservation practice is consistent with the conservation plan.

§ 166.315 Who is responsible for the completion and maintenance of a conservation practice if the permit expires or is canceled before the completion of the conservation practice?

Prior to undertaking a conservation practice, the BIA, landowner, and permittee will negotiate who will complete and maintain a conservation practice if the permit expires or is canceled before the conservation practice is completed. That conservation practice agreement will be reflected in the conservation plan and permit.

§ 166.316 Can a permittee construct improvements on permitted Indian land?

Improvements may be constructed on permitted Indian land if the permit contains a provision allowing improvements.

§ 166.317 What happens to improvements constructed on Indian lands when the permit has been terminated?

(a) If improvements are to be constructed on Indian land, the permit must contain a provision that improvements will either:

(1) Remain on the land upon termination of the permit, in a condition that is in compliance with applicable codes, to become the property of the Indian landowner; or

(2) Be removed and the land restored within a time period specified in the permit. The land must be restored as close as possible to the original condition prior to construction of such improvements. At the request of the permittee we may, at our discretion, grant an extension of time for the removal of improvements and restoration of the land for circumstances beyond the control of the permittee.

(b) If the permittee fails to remove improvements within the time allowed in the permit, the permittee may forfeit the right to remove the improvements and the improvements may become the property of the Indian landowner or at the request of the Indian landowner, we will apply the bond for the removal of the improvement and restoration of the land.

Subpart E—Grazing Rental Rates, Payments, and Late Payment Collections

RENTAL RATE DETERMINATION AND ADJUSTMENT

§ 166.400 Who establishes grazing rental rates?

(a) For tribal lands, a tribe may establish a grazing rental rate that is less or more than the grazing rental rate established by us. We will assist a tribe to establish a grazing rental rate by providing the tribe with available information concerning the value of grazing on tribal lands.

(b) We will establish the grazing rental rate by determining the fair annual rental for:

(1) Individually-owned Indian lands; and

(2) Tribes that have not established a rate under paragraph (a) of this section.

(c) Indian landowners may give us written authority to grant grazing privileges on their individually-owned Indian land at a grazing rental rate that is:

(1) Above the grazing rental rate set by us; or

(2) Below the grazing rental rate set by us, subject to our approval, when the permittee is a member of the Indian landowner's immediate family as defined in this part.

§ 166.401 How does the BIA establish grazing rental rates?

An appraisal can be used to determine the rental value of real property. The development and reporting of the valuation will be completed in accordance with the Uniform Standards of Professional Appraisal Practices (USPAP). If an appraisal is not desired, competitive bids, negotiations, advertisements, or any other method can be used in conjunction with a market study, rent survey, or feasibility analysis developed in accordance with the USPAP.

§ 166.402 Why must the BIA determine the fair annual rental of Indian land?

The BIA must determine the fair annual rental of Indian land to:

(a) Assist the Indian landowner in negotiating a permit with potential permittees; and

(b) Enable us to determine whether a permit is in the best interests of the Indian landowner.

§ 166.403 Will the BIA ever grant or approve a permit at less than fair annual rental?

(a) We will grant a permit for grazing on individually-owned Indian land at less than fair annual rental if, after competitive bidding of the permit, we determine that such action would be in the best interests of the individual Indian landowners.

(b) We may approve a permit for grazing on individually-owned Indian land at less than fair annual rental if:

(1) The permit is for the Indian landowner's immediate family or co-owner; or

(2) We determine it is in the best interest of the Indian landowners.

(c) We may approve a permit for grazing on tribal land at less than fair annual rental if the tribe sets the rate.

§ 166.404 Whose grazing rental rate will be applicable for a permit on tribal land?

The following grazing rental rate schedule will apply for tribal land:

If you are * * *	And if * * *	Then you will pay * * *
(a) Grazing livestock on tribal land	The tribe established the grazing rental rate.	The rate set by the tribe.
(b) Grazing livestock on tribal land	No tribal grazing rental rate has been established.	The rate set by the BIA.
(c) The successful bidder for use of any of these specific parcels of Indian land.		Your rental rate bid, but not less than the minimum bid rate advertised.

§ 166.405 Whose grazing rental rate will be applicable for a permit on individually-owned Indian land?

The following grazing rental rate schedule will apply for individually-owned Indian land:

If you are * * *	Then you will pay * * *
(a) Grazing livestock on Individually-owned Indian land.	The rate set by the BIA or by the individual Indian landowner and approved by us.
(b) The successful bidder for use of any of these specific parcels of Indian land.	Your rental rate bid, but not less than the minimum bid rate advertised, unless the permit is granted at less than fair annual rental under § 166.403.
(c) The recipient of an allocation from a bid unit.	The bid rate or the appraised rate, whichever is higher.

§ 166.406 Whose grazing rental rate will be applicable for a permit on government land?

The following grazing rental rate schedule will apply for government land:

If you are * * *	And if * * *	Then you will pay * * *
(a) Grazing livestock on government land	The tribe has control over the land or the tribe has authority to set the rate.	The rate set by the tribe.
(b) Grazing livestock on government land	Government controls all use of the land	The rate set by the BIA.

§ 166.407 If a range unit consists of tribal and individually-owned Indian lands, what is the grazing rental rate?

The grazing rental rate for tribal land will be the rate set by the tribe. The grazing rental rate for individually-owned Indian land will be the grazing rental rate set by us.

§ 166.408 Is the grazing rental rate established by the BIA adjusted periodically?

Yes. To ensure that Indian landowners are receiving the fair annual return, we may adjust the grazing rental rate established by the BIA, based upon an appropriate valuation method, taking into account the value of improvements made under the permit, unless the permit provides otherwise, following the Uniform Standards of Professional Appraisal Practice.

(a) We will:

(1) Review the grazing rental rate prior to each anniversary date or when specified by the permit.

(2) Provide you with written notice of any adjustment of the grazing rental rate 60 days prior to each anniversary date.

(3) Allow the adjusted grazing rental rate to be less than the fair annual rental if we determine that such a rate is in the best interest of the Indian landowner.

(b) If adjusted, the grazing rental rate will become effective on the next anniversary date of the permit.

(c) These adjustments will be retroactive, if they are not made at the time specified in the permit.

(d) For permits granted by tribes, we will consult with the granting tribe to determine whether an adjustment of the grazing rental payment should be made. The permit must be modified to document the granting tribe's waiver of the adjustment. A tribe may grant a permit without providing for a rental adjustment, if the tribe establishes such a policy under § 166.100(a)(4) of this part and negotiates such a permit.

RENTAL PAYMENTS

§ 166.409 How is my grazing rental payment determined?

The grazing rental payment is the total of the grazing rental rate multiplied by the number of AUMs or acres covered by the permit.

§ 166.410 When are grazing rental payments due?

The initial grazing rental payment is due and payable as specified in the permit or 15 days after the BIA approves the permit, whichever is later. Subsequent payments are due as specified in the permit.

§ 166.411 Will a permittee be notified when a grazing rental payment is due?

Each permit states the schedule of rental payments agreed to by the parties. We will issue an invoice to the permittee 30 to 60 days prior to the rental payment due date.

§ 166.412 What if the permittee does not receive an invoice that a grazing rental payment is due?

If we fail to send an invoice or if we send an invoice and the permittee does not receive it, the permittee is still responsible for making timely payment of all amounts due under the permit.

§ 166.413 To whom are grazing rental payments made?

(a) A permit must specify whether grazing rental payments will be made directly to the Indian landowners or to us on behalf of the Indian landowners. If the permit provides for payment to be made directly to the Indian landowners, the permit must also require that the permittee retain specific documentation evidencing proof of payment, such as canceled checks, cash receipt vouchers, or copies of money orders or cashier's checks, consistent with the provisions of §§ 166.1000 and 166.1001 of this part.

(b) Grazing rental payments made directly to the Indian landowners must be made to the parties specified in the permit, unless the permittee receives a notice of a change of ownership. Unless otherwise provided in the permit, grazing rental payments may not be made payable directly to anyone other than the Indian landowners.

(c) A permit which provides for grazing rental payments to be made directly to the Indian landowners must also provide for such payments to be suspended and rent thereafter paid to us, rather than directly than to the Indian landowners, if:

(1) An Indian landowner dies;

(2) An Indian landowner requests that payment be made to us;

(3) An Indian landowner is found by us to be in need of assistance in managing his/her financial affairs; or

(4) We determine, in our discretion and after consultation with the Indian landowner(s), that direct payment should be discontinued.

§ 166.414 What forms of grazing rental payments are acceptable?

(a) When grazing rental payments are made directly to the Indian landowners, the form of payment must be acceptable to the Indian landowners.

(b) Payments made to us may be delivered in person or by mail. We will not accept cash, foreign currency, or third-party checks. We will accept:

(1) Personal or business checks drawn on the account of the permittee;

(2) Money orders;

(3) Cashier's checks;

(4) Certified checks; or

(5) Electronic funds transfer payments.

§ 166.415 What will the BIA do if the permittee fails to make a direct payment to an Indian landowner?

Within five business days of the Indian landowner's notification to us that a payment has not been received, we will contact the permittee either in writing or by telephone requesting that the permittee provide documentation (e.g., canceled check, cash receipt voucher, copy of a money order or cashier's check) showing that payment has been made to the Indian landowner. If the permitee fails to provide such documentation, we will follow the procedures identified in § 166.419 of this part to collect the money on behalf of the Indian landowner or to cancel the permit.

§ 166.416 May a permittee make a grazing rental payment in advance of the due date?

Rent may be paid no more than 30 days in advance, unless otherwise specified in the permit.

§ 166.417 May an individual Indian landowner modify the terms of the permit on a fractionated tract for advance grazing rental payment?

No. An individual Indian landowner of a fractionated tract may not modify a permit to allow a grazing rental payment in advance of the due date specified in the initial approved permit.

§ 166.418 When is a grazing rental payment late?

A grazing rental payment is late if it is not received on or before the due date.

LATE RENTAL PAYMENT COLLECTIONS

§ 166.419 What will the BIA do if grazing rental payments are not made in the time and manner required by the permit?

(a) A permitee's failure to pay grazing rental payments in the time and manner required by a permit will be a violation of the permit, and a notice of violation will be issued under § 166.703 of this part. If the permit requires that grazing rental payments be made to us, we will send the permittee and its sureties a notice of violation within five business days of the date on which the grazing rental payment was due. If the permit provides for payment directly to the Indian landowner(s), we will send the permittee and its sureties a notice of violation within five business days of the date on which we receive actual notice of non-payment from the Indian landowner(s).

(b) If a permittee fails to provide adequate proof of payment or cure the violation within the requisite time period described in § 166.704 of this part, and the amount due is not in dispute, we may immediately take action to recover the amount of the unpaid rent and any associated interest charges or late payment penalties. We may also cancel the permit under § 166.705 of this part, or invoke any other remedies available under the permit or applicable law, including collection on any available bond or referral of the debt to the Department of the Treasury for collection. An action to recover any unpaid amounts will not be conditioned on the prior cancellation of the permit or any further notice to the permittee, nor will such an action be precluded by a prior cancellation.

(c) Partial payments may be accepted, under special circumstances, by the Indian landowners or us, but acceptance will not operate as a waiver with respect to any amounts remaining unpaid or any other existing permit violations. Unless otherwise provided in the permit, overpayments may be credited as an advance against future grazing rental payments.

(d) If a personal or business check is dishonored, and a grazing rental payment is therefore not made by the due date, the failure to make the payment in a timely manner will be a violation of the permit, and a written notice of violation will be issued under § 166.703 of this part. Any payment made to cure such a default, and any future payments by the same permittee, must be made by one of the alternative payment methods listed in § 166.414(b) of this part.

§ 166.420 Will any special fees be assessed on delinquent grazing rental payments due under a permit?

The following special fees will be assessed if a grazing rental payment is not paid in the time and manner required, in addition to any interest or late payment penalties which must be paid to the Indian landowners under a permit. The following special fees will be assessed to cover administrative costs incurred by the United States in the collection of the debt:

The permittee will pay * * *	For * * *
(a) $50.00	Administrative fee for checks returned by the bank for insufficient funds.
(b) $15.00	Administrative fee for the BIA processing of each demand letter.
(c) 18% of balance due.	Administrative fee charged by the Department of Treasury for collection.

§ 166.421 If a permit is canceled for non-payment, does that extinguish the permittee's debt?

No. The permittee remains liable for any delinquent payment. No future permits will be issued until all outstanding debts related to Indian agricultural lands are paid.

COMPENSATION TO INDIAN LANDOWNERS

§ 166.422 What does the BIA do with grazing rental payments received from permittees?

Unless arrangements for direct payment to the Indian landowners has been provided, the rent will be deposited to the appropriate account maintained by the Office of Trust Funds Management in accordance with part 115 of this title.

§ 166.423 How do Indian landowners receive grazing rental payments that the BIA has received from permittees?

Funds will be paid to the Indian landowners by the Office of Trust Funds Management in accordance with 25 CFR part 115.

§ 166.424 How will the BIA determine the grazing rental payment amount to be distributed to each Indian landowner?

Unless otherwise specified in the permit, the grazing rental payment will be distributed to each Indian landowner according to the forage production that each parcel of Indian land contributes to the permit, annual rental rate of each parcel, and the Indian landowner's interest in each parcel.

Subpart F—Administrative and Tribal Fees

§ 166.500 Are there administrative fees for a permit?

Yes. We will charge an administrative fee before approving any permit, subpermit, assignment, encumbrance, modification, or other related document.

§ 166.501 How are annual administrative fees determined?

(a) Except as provided in subsection (b), we will charge a three percent (%) administrative fee based on the annual grazing rent.

(b) The minimum administrative fee is $10.00 and the maximum administrative fee is $500.00.

(c) If a tribe performs all or part of the administrative duties for this part, the tribe may establish, collect, and use reasonable fees to cover its costs associated with the performance of administrative duties.

§ 166.502 Are administrative fees refundable?

No. We will not refund administrative fees.

§ 166.503 May the BIA waive administrative fees?

Yes. We may waive the administrative fee for a justifiable reason.

§ 166.504 Are there any other administrative or tribal fees, taxes, or assessments that must be paid?

Yes. The permittee may be required to pay additional fees, taxes, and/or assessments associated with the use of the land as determined by us or by the tribe. Failure to make such payments will constitute a permit violation under subpart H of this part.

Subpart G—Bonding and Insurance Requirements

§ 166.600 Must a permittee provide a bond for a permit?

Yes. A permittee, assignee or subpermittee must provide a bond for each permit interest acquired. Upon request by an Indian landowner, we may waive the bond requirement.

§ 166.601 How is the amount of the bond determined?

(a) The amount of the bond for each permit is based on the:

(1) Value of one year's grazing rental payment;

(2) Value of any improvements to be constructed;

(3) Cost of performance of any additional obligations; and

(4) Cost of performance of restoration and reclamation.

(b) Tribal policy made applicable by § 166.100 of this part may establish or waive specific bond requirements for permits.

§ 166.602 What form of bonds will the BIA accept?

(a) We will only accept bonds in the following forms:

(1) Cash;

(2) Negotiable Treasury securities that:

(i) Have a market value equal to the bond amount; and

(ii) Are accompanied by a statement granting full authority to the BIA to sell such securities in case of a violation of the terms of the permit.

(3) Certificates of deposit that indicate on their face that Secretarial approval is required prior to redemption by any party;

(4) Irrevocable letters of credit (LOC) issued by federally-insured financial institutions authorized to do business in the United States. LOC's must:

(i) Contain a clause that grants the BIA authority to demand immediate payment if the permittee defaults or fails to replace the LOC within 30 calendar days prior to its expiration date;

(ii) Be payable to the "Department of the Interior, BIA";

(iii) Be irrevocable during its term and have an initial expiration date of not less than one year following the date we receive it; and

(iv) Be automatically renewable for a period of not less than one year, unless the issuing financial institution provides the BIA with written notice at least 90 calendar days before the letter of credit's expiration date that it will not be renewed;

(5) Surety bond; or

(6) Any other form of highly liquid, non-volatile security subsequently approved by us that is easily convertible to cash by us and for which our approval is required prior to redemption by any party.

(b) Indian landowners may negotiate a permit term that specifies the use of any of the bond forms described in paragraph (a) of this section.

(c) A tribe may accept and hold any form of bond described in paragraph (a) of this section, to secure performance under a permit of tribal land.

§ 166.603 If cash is submitted as a bond, how is it administered?

If cash is submitted as a bond, we will establish an account in the name of the permittee and retain it.

§ 166.604 Is interest paid on a cash performance bond?

No. Interest will not be paid on a cash performance bond.

§ 166.605 Are cash performance bonds refunded?

If the cash performance bond has not been forfeited for cause, the amount deposited will be refunded to the depositor at the end of the permit period.

§ 166.606 What happens to a bond if a violation occurs?

We may apply the bond to remedy the violation, in which case we will require the permittee to submit a replacement bond of an appropriate amount.

§ 166.607 Is insurance required for a permit?

When we determine it to be in the best interest of the Indian landowners, we will require a permittee to provide insurance. If insurance is required, it must:

(a) Be provided in an amount sufficient to:

(1) Protect any improvements on the permit premises;

(2) Cover losses such as personal injury or death; and

(3) Protect the interest of the Indian landowner.

(b) Identify the tribe, individual Indian landowners, and United States as insured parties.

§ 166.608 What types of insurance may be required?

We may require liability or casualty insurance (such as for fire, hazard, or flood), depending upon the activity conducted under the permit.

Subpart H—Permit Violations

§ 166.700 What permit violations are addressed by this subpart?

This subpart addresses violations of permit provisions other than trespass. Trespass is addressed under subpart I of this part.

§ 166.701 How will the BIA determine whether the activities of a permittee under a permit are in compliance with the terms of the permit?

Unless the permit provides otherwise, we may enter the range unit at any reasonable time, without prior notice, to protect the interests of the Indian landowners and ensure that the permittee is in compliance with the operating requirements of the permit.

§ 166.702 Can a permit provide for negotiated remedies in the event of a permit violation?

(a) A permit of tribal land may provide the tribe with certain negotiated remedies in the event of a permit violation, including the power to terminate the permit. A permit of individually-owned Indian land may provide the individual Indian landowners with similar remedies, so long as the permit also specifies the manner in which those remedies may be exercised by or on behalf of the Indian landowners. Any notice of violation must be provided by written notice.

(b) The negotiated remedies described in paragraph (a) of this section will apply in addition to the cancellation remedy available to us under § 166.705(c) of this subpart. If the permit specifically authorizes us to exercise any negotiated remedies on behalf of the Indian landowners, the exercise of such remedies may substitute for cancellation.

(c) A permit may provide for permit disputes to be resolved in tribal court or any other court of competent jurisdiction, or through arbitration or some other alternative dispute resolution method. We may not be bound by decisions made in such forums, but we will defer to any ongoing proceedings, as appropriate, in deciding whether to exercise any of the remedies available to us under § 166.705 of this subpart.

§ 166.703 What happens if a permit violation occurs?

(a) If an Indian landowner notifies us that a specific permit violation has occurred, we will initiate an appropriate investigation within five business days of that notification.

(b) If we determine that a permit violation has occurred based on facts known to us, we will provide written notice to the permittee and the sureties of the violation within five business days.

§ 166.704 What will a written notice of a permit violation contain?

The written notice of a permit violation will provide the permittee with ten days from the receipt of the written notice to:

(a) Cure the permit violation and notify us that the violation is cured.

(b) Explain why we should not cancel the permit; or

(c) Request in writing additional time to complete corrective actions. If additional time is granted, we may require that certain corrective actions be taken immediately.

§ 166.705 What will the BIA do if a permit violation is not cured within the required time period?

(a) If the permittee does not cure a violation within the required time period, we will consult with the Indian landowners, as appropriate, and determine whether:

(1) The permit should be canceled by us under paragraph (c) of this section and §§ 166.706 through 166.707 of this subpart;

(2) We should invoke any other remedies available to us under the permit, including collecting on any available bond;

(3) The Indian landowners wish to invoke any remedies available to them under the permit; or

(4) The permittee should be granted additional time in which to cure the violation.

(b) If we decide to grant a permittee additional time in which to cure a violation, the permittee must proceed diligently to complete the necessary corrective actions within a reasonable or specified time period from the date on which the extension is granted.

(c) If we decide to cancel the permit, we will send the permittee and its sureties a written notice of cancellation within five business days of that decision. We will also provide actual or constructive notice of a cancellation decision to the Indian landowners, as appropriate. The written notice of cancellation will:

(1) Explain the grounds for cancellation;

(2) Notify the permittee of the amount of any unpaid rent, interest charges, or late payment penalties due under the permit;

(3) Notify the permittee of its right to appeal under Part 2 of this chapter, as modified by § 166.706 of this subpart, including the amount of any appeal bond that must be posted with an appeal of the cancellation decision; and

(4) Order the permittee to vacate the property within 30 days of the date of receipt of the written notice of cancellation, if an appeal is not filed by that time.

§ 166.706 Will the BIA's regulations concerning appeal bonds apply to cancellation decisions involving permits?

(a) The appeal bond provisions in § 2.5 of part 2 of this chapter will not apply to appeals from permit cancellation decisions made under § 166.705 of this subpart. Instead, when we decide to cancel a permit, we may require the permittee to post an appeal bond with an appeal of the cancellation decision. The requirement to post an appeal bond will apply in addition to all of the other requirements in part 2 of this chapter.

(b) An appeal bond should be set in an amount necessary to protect the Indian landowners against financial losses that will likely result from the delay caused by an appeal. Appeal bond requirements will not be separately appealable, but may be contested during the appeal of the permit cancellation decision.

§ 166.707 When will a cancellation of a permit be effective?

A cancellation decision involving a permit will not be effective for 30 days after the permittee receives a written notice of cancellation from us. The cancellation decision will remain ineffective if the permittee files an appeal under § 166.706 of this subpart and part 2 of this chapter, unless the decision is made immediately effective under part

2. While a cancellation decision is ineffective, the permittee must continue to pay rent and comply with the other terms of the permit. If an appeal is not filed in accordance with § 166.706 of this subpart and part 2 of this chapter, the cancellation decision will be effective on the 31st day after the permittee receives the written notice of cancellation from us.

§ 166.708 Can the BIA take emergency action if the rangeland is threatened with immediate, significant, and irreparable harm?

Yes. If a permittee or any other party causes or threatens to cause immediate, significant and irreparable harm to the Indian land during the term of a permit, we will take appropriate emergency action. Emergency action may include trespass proceedings under subpart I of this part, or judicial action seeking immediate cessation of the activity resulting in or threatening the harm. Reasonable efforts will be made to notify the Indian landowners, either before or after the emergency action is taken.

§ 166.709 What will the BIA do if a permittee holds over after the expiration or cancellation of a permit?

If a permittee remains in possession of Indian land after the expiration or cancellation of a permit, we will treat the unauthorized use as a trespass. Unless we have reason to believe that the permittee is engaged in negotiations with the Indian landowners to obtain a new permit, we will take action to recover possession of the Indian land on behalf of the Indian landowners, and pursue any additional remedies available under applicable law, including the assessment of civil penalties and costs under subpart I of this part.

Subpart I—Trespass

§ 166.800 What is trespass?

Under this part, trespass is any unauthorized occupancy, use of, or action on Indian agricultural lands. These provisions also apply to Indian agricultural land managed under an agricultural lease or permit under part 162 of this title.

§ 166.801 What is the BIA's trespass policy?

We will:

(a) Investigate accidental, willful, and/or incidental trespass on Indian agricultural land;

(b) Respond to alleged trespass in a prompt, efficient manner;

(c) Assess trespass penalties for the value of products used or removed, cost of damage to the Indian agricultural land, and enforcement costs incurred as a consequence of the trespass.

(d) Ensure that damage to Indian agricultural lands resulting from trespass is rehabilitated and stabilized at the expense of the trespasser.

§ 166.802 Who can enforce this subpart?

(a) The BIA enforces the provisions of this subpart. If the tribe adopts the provisions of this subpart, the tribe will have concurrent jurisdiction to enforce this subpart. Additionally, if the tribe so requests, we will defer to tribal prosecution of trespass on Indian agricultural lands.

(b) Nothing in this subpart shall be construed to diminish the sovereign authority of Indian tribes with respect to trespass.

NOTIFICATION

§ 166.803 How are trespassers notified of a trespass determination?

(a) Unless otherwise provided under tribal law, when we have reason to believe that a trespass on Indian agricultural land has occurred, within five business days, we or the authorized tribal representative will provide written notice to the alleged trespasser, the possessor of trespass property, any known lien holder, and beneficial Indian landowner, as appropriate. The written notice will include the following:

(1) The basis for the trespass determination;

(2) A legal description of where the trespass occurred;

(3) A verification of ownership of unauthorized property (*e.g.*, brands in the State Brand Book for cases of livestock trespass, if applicable);

(4) Corrective actions that must be taken;

(5) Time frames for taking the corrective actions;

(6) Potential consequences and penalties for failure to take corrective action; and

(7) A statement that unauthorized livestock or other property may not be removed or disposed of unless authorized by us.

(b) If we determine that the alleged trespasser or possessor of trespass property is unknown or refuses delivery of the written notice, a public trespass notice will be posted at the tribal community building, U.S. Post Office, and published in the local newspaper nearest to the Indian agricultural lands where the trespass is occurring.

(c) Trespass notices under this subpart are not subject to appeal under 25 CFR part 2.

§ 166.804 What can I do if I receive a trespass notice?

If you receive a trespass notice, you will within the time frame specified in the notice:

(a) Comply with the ordered corrective actions; or

(b) Contact us in writing to explain why the trespass notice is in error. You may contact us by telephone but any explanation of trespass you wish to provide must be in writing. If we determine that we issued the trespass notice in error, we will withdraw the notice.

§ 166.805 How long will a written trespass notice remain in effect?

A written trespass notice will remain in effect for the same conduct identified in that written notice for a period of one year from the date of receipt of the written notice by the trespasser.

Actions

§ 166.806 What actions does the BIA take against trespassers?

If the trespasser fails to take the corrective action specified by us, we may take one or more of the following actions, as appropriate:

(a) Seize, impound, sell or dispose of unauthorized livestock or other property involved in the trespass. We may keep such property we seize for use as evidence.

(b) Assess penalties, damages, and costs, under § 166.812 of this subpart.

§ 166.807 When will we impound unauthorized livestock or other property?

We will impound unauthorized livestock or other property under the following conditions:

(a) Where there is imminent danger of severe injury to growing or harvestable crop or destruction of the range forage.

(b) When the known owner or the owner's representative of the unauthorized livestock or other property refuses to accept delivery of a written notice of trespass and the unauthorized livestock or other property are not removed within the period prescribed in the written notice.

(c) Any time after five days of providing notice of impoundment if you failed to correct the trespass.

§ 166.808 How are trespassers notified if their unauthorized livestock or other property are to be impounded?

(a) If the trespass is not corrected in the time specified in the initial trespass notice, we will send written notice of our intent to impound unauthorized livestock or other property to the unauthorized livestock or property owner or representative, and any known lien holder of the unauthorized livestock or other property.

(b) If we determine that the owner of the unauthorized livestock or other property or the owner's representative is unknown or refuses delivery of the written notice, we will post a public notice of intent to impound at the tribal community building, U.S. Post Office, and published in the local newspaper nearest to the Indian agricultural lands where the trespass is occurring.

(c) After we have given notice as described above, we will impound unauthorized livestock or other property without any further notice.

§ 166.809 What happens after my unauthorized livestock or other property are impounded?

Following the impoundment of unauthorized livestock or other property, we will provide notice that we will sell the impounded property as follows:

(a) We will provide written notice of the sale to the owner, the owner's representative, and any known lien holder. The written notice must include the procedure by which the impounded property may be redeemed prior to the sale.

(b) We will provide public notice of sale of impounded property by posting at the tribal community building, U.S. Post Office, and publishing in the local newspaper nearest to the Indian agricultural lands where the trespass is occurring. The public notice will include a description of the impounded property, and the date, time, and place of the public sale. The sale date must be at least five days after the publication and posting of notice.

§ 166.810 How do I redeem my impounded livestock or other property?

You may redeem impounded livestock or other property by submitting proof of ownership and paying all penalties, damages, and costs under § 166.812 of this subpart and completing all corrective actions identified by us under § 166.804 of this subpart.

§ 166.811 How will the sale of impounded livestock or other property be conducted?

(a) Unless the owner or known lien holder of the impounded livestock or other property redeems the property prior to the time set by the sale, by submitting proof of ownership and settling all obligations under § 166.804 and § 166.812 of this subpart, the property will be sold by public sale to the highest bidder.

(b) If a satisfactory bid is not received, the livestock or property may be re-offered for sale, returned to the owner, condemned and destroyed, or otherwise disposed of.

(c) We will give the purchaser a bill of sale or other written receipt evidencing the sale.

PENALTIES, DAMAGES, AND COSTS

§ 166.812 What are the penalties, damages, and costs payable by trespassers on Indian agricultural land?

Trespassers on Indian agricultural land must pay the following penalties and costs:

(a) Collection of the value of the products illegally used or removed plus a penalty of double their values;

(b) Costs associated with any damage to Indian agricultural land and/or property;

(c) The costs associated with enforcement of the regulations, including field examination and survey, damage appraisal, investigation assistance and reports, witness expenses, demand letters, court costs, and attorney fees;

(d) Expenses incurred in gathering, impounding, caring for, and disposal of livestock in cases which necessitate impoundment under § 166.807 of this subpart; and

(e) All other penalties authorized by law.

§ 166.813 How will the BIA determine the value of forage or crops consumed or destroyed?

We will determine the value of forage or crops consumed or destroyed based upon the average rate received per month for comparable property or grazing privileges, or the estimated commercial value or replacement costs of such products or property.

§ 166.814 How will the BIA determine the value of the products or property illegally used or removed?

We will determine the value of the products or property illegally used or removed based upon a valuation of similar products or property.

§ 166.815 How will the BIA determine the amount of damages to Indian agricultural land?

We will determine the damages by considering the costs of rehabilitation and revegetation, loss of future revenue, loss of profits, loss of productivity, loss of market value, damage to other resources, and other factors.

§ 166.816 How will the BIA determine the costs associated with enforcement of the trespass?

Costs of enforcement may include detection and all actions taken by us through prosecution and collection of damages. This includes field examination and survey, damage appraisal, investigation assistance and report preparation, witness expenses, demand letters, court costs, attorney fees, and other costs.

§ 166.817 What happens if I do not pay the assessed penalties, damages and costs?

Unless otherwise provided by applicable tribal law:

(a) We will refuse to issue you a permit for use, development, or occupancy of Indian agricultural lands; and

(b) We will forward your case for appropriate legal action.

§ 166.818 How are the proceeds from trespass distributed?

Unless otherwise provided by tribal law:

(a) We will treat any amounts recovered under § 166.812 of this subpart as proceeds from the sale of agricultural property from the Indian agricultural land upon which the trespass occurred.

(b) Proceeds recovered under § 166.812 of this subpart may be distributed to:

(1) Repair damages of the Indian agricultural land and property;

(2) Reimburse the affected parties, including the permittee for loss due to the trespass, as negotiated and provided in the permit; and

(3) Reimburse for costs associated with the enforcement of this subpart.

(c) If any money is left over after the distribution of the proceeds described in paragraph (b) of this section, we will return it to the trespasser or, where we cannot identify the owner of the impounded property within 180 days, we will deposit the net proceeds of the sale into the accounts of the landowners where the trespass occurred.

§ 166.819 What happens if the BIA does not collect enough money to satisfy the penalty?

We will send written notice to the trespasser demanding immediate settlement and advising the trespasser that unless settlement is received within five business days from the date of receipt, we will forward the case for appropriate legal action. We may send a copy of the notice to the Indian landowner, permittee, and any known lien holders.

Subpart J—Agriculture Education, Education Assistance, Recruitment, and Training

§ 166.900 How are the Indian agriculture education programs operated?

(a) The purpose of the Indian agriculture education programs is to recruit and develop promising Indian and Alaska Natives who are enrolled in secondary schools, tribal or Alaska Native community colleges, and other post-secondary schools for employment as professional resource managers and other agriculture-related professionals by approved organizations.

(b) We will operate the student educational employment program as part of our Indian agriculture education programs in accordance with the provisions of 5 CFR 213.3202(a) and (b).

(c) We will establish an education committee to coordinate and carry out the agriculture education assistance programs and to select participants for all agriculture education assistance programs. The committee will include at least one Indian professional educator in the field of natural resources or agriculture, a personnel specialist, a representative of the Intertribal Agriculture Council, and a natural resources or agriculture professional from the BIA and a representative from American Indian Higher Education Consortium. The committee's duties will include the writing of a manual for the Indian and Alaska Native Agriculture Education and Assistance Programs.

(d) We will monitor and evaluate the agriculture education assistance programs to ensure that there are adequate Indian and Alaska Native natural resources and agriculture-related professionals to manage Indian natural resources and agriculture programs by or for tribes and Alaska Native Corporations. We will identify the number of participants in the intern, student educational employment program, scholarship, and outreach programs; the number of participants who completed the requirements to become a natural resources or agriculture-related professional; and the number of participants completing advanced degree requirements.

§ 166.901 How will the BIA select an agriculture intern?

(a) The purpose of the agriculture intern program is to ensure the future participation of trained, professional Indians and Alaska Natives in the management of Indian and Alaska Native agricultural land. In keeping with this purpose, we will work with tribes and Alaska Natives:

(1) To obtain the maximum degree of participation from Indians and Alaska Natives in the agriculture intern program;

(2) To encourage agriculture interns to complete an undergraduate degree program in natural resources or agriculture-related field; and

(3) To create an opportunity for the advancement of natural resources and agriculture-related technicians to professional resource management positions with the BIA, other federal agencies providing an agriculture service to their respective tribe, a tribe, or tribal agriculture enterprise.

(b) Subject to restrictions imposed by agency budgets, we will establish and maintain in the BIA at least 20 positions for the agriculture intern program. All Indians and Alaska Natives who satisfy the qualification criteria may compete for positions.

(c) Applicants for intern positions must meet the following criteria:

(1) Be eligible for Indian preference as defined in 25 CFR part 5;

(2) Possess a high school diploma or its recognized equivalent;

(3) Be able to successfully complete the intern program within a three-year period; and

(4) Possess a letter of acceptance to an accredited post-secondary school or demonstrate that one will be sent within 90 days.

(d) We will advertise vacancies for agriculture intern positions semi-annually, no later than the first day of April and October, to accommodate entry into school.

(e) In selecting agriculture interns, we will seek to identify candidates who:

(1) Have the greatest potential for success in the program;

(2) Will take the shortest time period to complete the intern program; and

(3) Provide the letter of acceptance required by paragraph (c)(4) of this section.

(f) Agriculture interns must:

(1) Maintain full-time status in an agriculture-related curriculum at an accredited post-secondary school;

(2) Maintain good academic standing;

(3) Enter into an obligated service agreement to serve as a professional resource manager or agriculture-related professional with an approved organization for one year in exchange for each year in the program; and

(4) Report for service with the approved organization during any break in attendance at school of more than three weeks.

(g) The education committee will evaluate annually the performance of the agriculture intern program participants against requirements to ensure that they are satisfactorily progressing toward completion of program requirements.

(h) We will pay all costs for tuition, books, fees, and living expenses incurred by an agriculture intern while attending an accredited post-secondary school.

§ 166.902 How can I become an agriculture educational employment student?

(a) To be considered for selection, applicants for the student educational employment program must:

(1) Meet the eligibility requirements in 5 CFR part 308; and

(2) Be accepted into or enrolled in a course of study at an accredited post-secondary institution which grants degrees in natural resources or agriculture-related curricula.

(b) Student educational employment steering committees established at the field level will select program participants based on eligibility requirements without regard to applicants' financial needs.

(c) A recipient of assistance under the student educational employment program will be required to enter into an obligated service agreement to serve as a natural resources or agriculture-related professional with an approved organization for one year in exchange for each year in the program.

(d) We will pay all costs of tuition, books, fees, and transportation to and from the job site to school, for an Indian or Alaska Native student who is selected for the cooperative education program.

§ 166.903 How can I get an agriculture scholarship?

(a) We may grant agriculture scholarships to Indians and Alaska Natives enrolled as full-time students in accredited post-secondary and graduate programs of study in natural resources and agriculture-related curricula.

(b) The education committee established in § 166.900(c) of this subpart will select program participants based on eligibility requirements stipulated in paragraphs (e) through (g) of this section without regard to applicants' financial needs or past scholastic achievements.

(c) Recipients of scholarships must reapply annually to continue to receive funding beyond the initial award period. Students who have received scholarships in past years, are in good academic standing, and have been recommended for continuation by their academic institution will be given priority over new applicants for scholarship assistance.

(d) The amount of scholarship funds an individual is awarded each year will be contingent upon the availability of funds appropriated each fiscal year and is subject to yearly change.

(e) Preparatory scholarships may be available for a maximum of three academic years of general, undergraduate course work leading to a degree in natural resources or agriculture-related curricula and may be awarded to individuals who:

(1) Possess a high school diploma or its recognized equivalent; and

(2) Are enrolled and in good academic standing at an acceptable post-secondary school.

(f) Undergraduate scholarships are available for a maximum of three academic years and may be awarded to individuals who:

(1) Have completed a minimum of 55 semester hours toward a bachelor's degree in a natural resources or agriculture-related curriculum; and

(2) Have been accepted into a natural resource or agriculture-related degree-granting program at an accredited college or university.

(g) Graduate scholarships are available for a maximum of five academic years for individuals selected into the graduate program of an accredited college or university that grants advanced degrees in natural resources or agriculture-related fields.

(h) A recipient of assistance under the scholarship program must enter into an obligated service agreement to serve as a natural resources or agriculture-related professional with the BIA, other federal agency providing assistance to their respective tribe, a tribe, tribal agriculture enterprise, or an ANCSA Corporation for one year for each year in the program.

(i) We will pay all scholarships approved by the education committee established in § 166.900 of this subpart for which funding is available.

§ 166.904 What is agriculture education outreach?

(a) We will establish and maintain an agriculture education outreach program for Indian and Alaska Native youth that will:

(1) Encourage students to acquire academic skills needed to succeed in post-secondary mathematics and science courses;

(2) Promote agriculture career awareness;

(3) Involve students in projects and activities oriented to agriculture related professions early so students realize the need to complete required pre-college courses; and

(4) Integrate Indian and Alaska Native agriculture program activities into the education of Indian and Alaska Native students.

(b) We will develop and carry out the program in consultation with appropriate community education organizations, tribes, ANCSA Corporations,

Alaska Native organizations, and other federal agencies providing agriculture services to Indians.

(c) The education committee established under § 166.900(c) of this subpart will coordinate and implement the program nationally.

§ 166.905 Who can get assistance for postgraduate studies?

(a) The purpose of the postgraduate studies program is to enhance the professional and technical knowledge of Indian and Alaska Native natural resource and agriculture-related professionals working for an approved organization so that the best possible service is provided to Indian and Alaska Natives.

(b) We may pay the cost of tuition, fees, books, and salary of Alaska Natives and Indians who are employed by an approved organization and who wish to pursue advanced levels of education in natural resource or agriculture-related fields.

(c) The goal of the advanced study program is to encourage participants to obtain additional academic credentials such as a degree or diploma in a natural resources or agriculture-related field. Requirements of the postgraduate study program are:

(1) The duration of course work cannot be less than one semester or more than three years; and

(2) Students in the postgraduate studies program must meet performance standards as required by the graduate school offering the study program.

(d) Program applicants must submit application packages to the education committee. At a minimum, such packages must contain a resume and an endorsement signed by the applicant's supervisor clearly stating the need for and benefits of the desired training.

(e) The education committee must use the following criteria to select participants:

(1) Need for the expertise sought at both the local and national levels;

(2) Expected benefits, both locally and nationally; and

(3) Years of experience and the service record of the employee.

(f) Program participants will enter into an obligated service agreement to serve as a natural resources or agriculture-related professional with an approved organization for one year for each year in the program. We may reduce the obligated service requirement if the employee receives supplemental funding such as research grants, scholarships, or graduate stipends and, as a result, reduces the need for financial assistance under this part. If the obligated service agreement is breached, we will collect the amount owed us in accordance with § 166.910 of this subpart.

§ 166.906 What can happen if we recruit you after graduation?

(a) The purpose of the post graduation recruitment program is to recruit Indian and Alaska Native natural resource and trained agriculture technicians into the agriculture programs of approved organizations.

(b) We may assume outstanding student loans from established lending institutions of Indian and Alaska Native natural resources and agriculture technicians who have successfully completed a post-secondary natural resources or agriculture-related curriculum at an accredited institution.

(c) Indian and Alaska Natives receiving benefits under this program will enter into an obligated service agreement in accordance with § 166.901 of this subpart. Obligated service required under this program will be one year for every $5,000 of student loan debt repaid.

(d) If the obligated service agreement is breached, we will collect student loan(s) in accordance with § 166.910 of this subpart.

§ 166.907 Who can be an intern?

(a) Natural resources or agriculture personnel working for an approved organization may apply for an internship within agriculture-related programs of agencies of the Department of the Interior or other federal agencies providing an agriculture service to their respective reservations.

(b) Natural resources or agriculture-related personnel from other Department of the Interior agencies may apply through proper channels for "internships" within the BIA's agriculture programs. With the consent of a tribe or Alaska Native organization, the BIA can arrange for an Intergovernmental

Personnel Act assignment in tribal or Alaska Native agriculture programs.

(c) Natural resources and agriculture personnel from agencies not within the Department of the Interior may apply, through proper agency channels and pursuant to an interagency agreement, for an "internship" within the BIA and, with the consent of a tribe or Alaska Native organization, we can facilitate an Intergovernmental Personnel Act assignment in a tribe, tribal agriculture enterprise, or Alaska Native Corporation.

(d) Natural resources or agriculture personnel from a tribe, tribal agriculture enterprise, or Alaska Native Corporation may apply, through proper channels and pursuant to a cooperative agreement, for an internship within another tribe, tribal forest enterprise, or ANCSA Corporation agriculture program.

(e) The employing agency of participating federal employees will provide for the continuation of salary and benefits.

(f) The host agency for participating tribal, tribal agriculture enterprise, or Alaska Native Corporation agriculture employees will provide for salaries and benefits.

(g) A bonus pay incentive, up to 25 percent (%) of the intern's base salary, may be provided to intergovernmental interns at the conclusion of the internship period. Bonus pay incentives will be at the discretion of and funded by the host organization and must be conditioned upon the host agency's documentation of the intern's superior performance, in accordance with the agency's performance standards, during the internship period.

§ 166.908 Who can participate in continuing education and training?

(a) The purpose of continuing education and training is to establish a program to provide for the ongoing education and training of natural resources and agriculture personnel employed by approved organizations. This program will emphasize continuing education and training in three areas:

(1) Orientation training including tribal-federal relations and responsibilities;

(2) Technical agriculture education; and

(3) Developmental training in agriculture-based enterprises and marketing.

(b) We will maintain an orientation program to increase awareness and understanding of Indian culture and its effect on natural resources management and agriculture practices and on federal laws that effect natural resources management and agriculture operations and administration in the Indian agriculture program.

(c) We will maintain a continuing technical natural resources and agriculture education program to assist natural resources managers and agriculture-related professionals to perform natural resources and agriculture management on Indian land.

(d) We will maintain an agriculture land-based enterprise and marketing training program to assist with the development and use of Indian and Alaska Native agriculture resources.

§ 166.909 What are my obligations to the BIA after I participate in an agriculture education program?

(a) Individuals completing agriculture education programs with an obligated service requirement may be offered full time permanent employment with an approved organization to fulfill their obligated service within 90 days of the date all program education requirements have been completed. If employment is not offered within the 90-day period, the student will be relieved of obligated service requirements. Not less than 30 days before the start of employment, the employer must notify the participant of the work assignment, its location and the date work must begin. If the employer is other than the BIA, the employer must also notify us.

(b) Employment time that can be credited toward obligated service requirement will begin the day after all program education requirements have been completed, with the exception of the agriculture intern program which includes the special provisions outlined in § 166.901(f)(4) of this subpart. The minimum service obligation period will be one year of full time employment.

(c) The employer has the right to designate the location of employment for fulfilling the service obligation.

(d) A participant in any of the agriculture education programs with an obligated service requirement may, within 30 days of completing all program education requirements, request a deferment of obligated service to pursue postgraduate or post-doctoral studies. In such cases, we will issue a decision within 30 days of receipt of the request for deferral. We may grant such a request; however, deferments granted in no way waive or otherwise affect obligated service requirements.

(e) A participant in any of the agriculture education programs with an obligated service requirement may, within 30 days of completing all program education requirements, request a waiver of obligated service based on personal or family hardship. We may grant a full or partial waiver or deny the request for wavier. In such cases, we will issue a decision within 30 days of receiving the request for waiver.

§ 166.910 What happens if I do not fulfill my obligation to the BIA?

(a) Any individual who accepts financial support under agriculture education programs with an obligated service requirement, and who does not accept employment or unreasonably terminates employment must repay us in accordance with the following table:

If you are...	Then the costs that you must repay are...	And then the costs that you do not need to repay are...
(1) Agriculture intern	Living allowance, tuition, books, and fees received while occupying position plus interest.	Salary paid during school breaks or when recipient was employed by an approved organization.
(2) Cooperative education	Tuition, books, and fees plus interest.	
(3) Scholarship	Costs of scholarship plus interest.	
(4) Post graduation recruitment.	All student loans assumed by us under the program plus interest.	
(5) Postgraduate studies	Living allowance, tuition, books, and fees received while in the program plus interest.	Salary paid during school breaks or when recipient was employed by an approved organization.

(b) For agriculture education programs with an obligated service requirement, we will adjust the amount required for repayment by crediting toward the final amount of debt any obligated service performed before breach of contract.

Subpart K—Records

§ 166.1000 Who owns the records associated with this part?

(a) Records are the property of the United States if they:

(1) Are made or received by a tribe or tribal organization in the conduct of a federal trust function under 25 U.S.C. § 450f *et seq.*, including the operation of a trust program; and

(2) Evidence the organization, functions, policies, decisions, procedures, operations, or other activities undertaken in the performance of a federal trust function under this part.

(b) Records not covered by paragraph (a) of this section that are made or received by a tribe or tribal organization in the conduct of business with the Department of the Interior under this part are the property of the tribe.

§ 166.1001 How must a records associated with this part be preserved?

(a) Any organization, including tribes and tribal organizations, that have records identified in § 166.1000(a) of this part must preserve the records in accordance with approved Departmental records retention procedures under the Federal Records Act, 44 U.S.C. Chapters 29, 31 and 33. These records and related records management practices and safeguards required under the Federal Records Act are subject to inspection by the Secretary and the Archivist of the United States.

(b) A tribe or tribal organization should preserve the records identified in § 166.1000(b) of this part for the period of time authorized by the Archivist of the United States for similar Department of the Interior records in accordance with 44 U.S.C. Chapter 33. If a tribe or tribal organization does not preserve records associated with its conduct of business with the Department of the Interior under this part, it may prevent the tribe or tribal organization from being able to adequately document essential transactions or furnish information necessary to protect its legal and financial rights or those of persons directly affected by its activities.

PART 167—NAVAJO GRAZING REGULATIONS

AUTHORITY: R.S. 465, 2117, as amended, sec. 3, 26 Stat. 795, sec. 1, 28 Stat. 305, as amended; 25 U.S.C. 9, 179, 397, 345, 402.

SOURCE: 22 FR 10578, Dec. 24, 1957, unless otherwise noted. Redesignated at 47 FR 13327, Mar. 30, 1982.

§ 167.1 Authority.

It is within the authority of the Secretary of the Interior to protect Indian tribal lands against waste. Subject to regulations of this part, the right exists for Indian tribes to authorize the granting of permits upon their tribal lands and to prescribe by appropriate tribal action the conditions under which their lands may be used.

§ 167.2 General regulations.

Part 166 of this subchapter authorizes the Commissioner of Indian Affairs to regulate the grazing of livestock on Indian lands under conditions set forth therein. In accordance with this authority and that of the Navajo Tribal Council, the Central Grazing Committee and the District Grazing Committees, the grazing of livestock on the Navajo Reservation shall be governed by the regulations in this part.

§ 167.3 Objectives.

It is the purpose of the regulations in this part to aid the Navajo Indians in achievement of the following objectives:

(a) The preservation of the forage, the land, and the water resources on the Navajo Reservation, and the building up of those resources where they have deteriorated.

(b) The protection of the interests of the Navajo Indians from the encroachment of unduly aggressive and anti-social individuals who may or may not be members of the Navajo Tribe.

(c) The adjustment of livestock numbers to the carrying capacity of the range in such a manner that the livestock economy of the Navajo Tribe will be preserved.

(d) To secure increasing responsibility and participation of the Navajo people, including tribal participation in all basic policy decisions, in the sound management of one of the Tribe's greatest assets, its grazing lands, and to foster a better relationship and a clearer understanding between the Navajo people and the Federal Government in carrying out the grazing regulations.

(e) The improvement of livestock through proper breeding practices and the maintenance of a sound culling policy. Buck and bull pastures may be established and maintained either on or off the reservation through District Grazing Committee and Central Grazing Committee action.

§ 167.4 Regulations; scope; exceptions.

The grazing regulations in this part apply to all lands within the boundaries of the Navajo Reservation held in trust by the United States for the Navajo Tribe and all the trust lands hereafter added to the Navajo Reservation. The regulations in this part do not apply to any of the area described in the Executive order of December 16, 1882, to individually owned allotted lands within the Navajo Reservation nor to tribal purchases, allotted or privately owned Navajo Indian lands outside the exterior boundaries of the Navajo Reservation.

[34 FR 14599, Sept. 19, 1969. Redesignated at 47 FR 13327, Mar. 30, 1982]

§167.5 Land management districts.

The Commissioner of Indian Affairs has established and will retain the present land management districts within the Navajo Indian Reservation, based on the social and economic requirements of the Navajo Indians and the necessity of rehabilitating the grazing lands. District boundary changes may be made when deemed necessary and advisable by the District Grazing Committees, Central Grazing Committee and Tribal Council, with approval by the Superintendent, Area Director, and the Commissioner of Indian Affairs.

§167.6 Carrying capacities.

(a) The Commissioner of Indian Affairs on June 26, 1943, promulgated the authorized carrying capacity for each land management district of the Navajo Reservation.

(b) Recommended adjustments in carrying capacities shall be referred by the Superintendent to District Grazing Committee, Central Grazing Committee, and the Navajo Tribal Council for review and recommendations prior to presentation to the Area Director and the Commissioner of Indian Affairs for approval.

(c) Upon the request of the District Grazing Committee, Central Grazing Committee and Navajo Tribal Council to the Superintendent; recommendations for future adjustments to the established carrying capacities shall be made by Range Technicians based on the best information available through annual utilization studies and range condition studies analyzed along with numbers of livestock and precipitation data. The recommendations of the Range Technicians shall be submitted to the Superintendent, the Area Director and the Commissioner of Indian Affairs.

(d) Carrying capacities shall be stated in terms of sheep units yearlong, in the ratio of horses, mules, and burros 1 to 5; cattle 1 to 4; goats 1 to 1. The latter figure in each case denotes sheep units. Sheep, goats, cattle, horses, mules, and burros one year of age or older shall be counted against the carrying capacity.

§167.7 Records.

The District Grazing Committee, the Superintendent, and his authorized representatives shall keep accurate records of all grazing permits and ownership of all livestock. Master files shall be maintained by the Superintendent or his authorized representatives.

(a) The District Grazing Committee shall be responsible for and assist in organizing the sheep and goat dipping and horse and cattle branding program and obtaining the annual live- stock count.

(b) In order to obtain true records of ownership the permittee shall personally appear at the dipping vat or tallying point designated by the Grazing Committee with his or her sheep and goats and at branding and tallying points for cattle and horses. Should the permittee be unable to appear personally he or she shall designate a representative to act for and in his or her behalf. The sheep and goats will be dipped and the cattle and horses will be branded and recorded in the name of the permittee.

(c) The Superintendent shall prepare and keep current a register containing the names of all permittees using the range, the number of each class of stock by age classes grazed annually and the periods during which grazing shall be permitted in each part thereof. An annual stock census will be taken to insure that the carrying capacity is not exceeded. All classes of livestock twelve months of age or over will be counted against range use and permitted number, except that yearling colts will not be counted against permitted numbers on all permits with less than six horses. (Cross Reference §167.9.)

§167.8 Grazing rights.

(a) The Superintendent shall determine grazing rights of bona fide livestock owners based on recommendations of District Grazing Committees. Grazing rights shall be recognized for those permittees having ownership records as established in accordance with § 167.7 or who have acquired grazing rights by marriage, inheritance, purchase or division of permits. Whenever the permitted number of sheep units within a district is less than the carrying capacity, new permits to the carrying capacity limit may be granted as provided in § 167.9.

(b) All enrolled members of the Navajo Tribe over 18 years of age are eligible to acquire and hold grazing permits. Minors under 18 years of age can get possession of grazing permits only through inheritance or gift, and in each case Trustees must be appointed by the Tribal Courts to manage the permits and livestock of such minors until they become 18 years of age and can hold grazing permits in their own right.

(c) No person can hold a grazing permit in more than one district on the Navajo Reservation.

(d) Determination of rights to grazing permits involved in cases of divorce, separation, threatened family disruption, and permits of deceased permittees shall be the responsibility of the Navajo Court of Indian Offenses under existing laws, rules, and regulations.

§ 167.9 Grazing permits.

(a) All livestock grazed on the Navajo Reservation must be covered by an authorized grazing permit issued by the Superintendent based upon the recommendations of the District Grazing Committee. All such grazing permits will be automatically renewed annually until terminated. District Grazing Committees shall act on all grazing permit changes resulting from negotiability within their respective Districts. The number of livestock that may be grazed under each permit shall be the number originally permitted plus or minus any changes as indicated by Transfer Agreements and Court Judgment Orders.

(b) Any permittee who has five or more horses on his current permit will be required to apply any acquired sheep units in classes of stock other than horses. If the purchaser wishes more than his present number of horses, he must have his needs evaluated by the District Grazing Committee. Yearling colts will be counted against permitted number on all permits with six or more horses. Yearling colts will not be counted against permitted number on all permits with less than six horses. In hardship cases the District Grazing Committee may reissue horses removed from grazing permits through negotiability to permit holders who are without sufficient horses on their present permits to meet minimum needs.

(c) No permittee shall be authorized to graze more than ten head of horses or to accumulate a total of over 350 sheep units.

(d) Upon recommendation of the District Grazing Committee and with the approval of the Superintendent, grazing permits may be transferred from one permittee to another in accordance with instructions provided by the Advisory Committee of the Navajo Tribal Council, or may be inherited; provided that the permitted holdings of any individual permittee shall not exceed 350 sheep units or the equivalent thereof. Should inheritance or other acquisition of permits increase the holdings of any permittee to more than 350 sheep units, said permittee shall dispose of all livestock in excess of 350 sheep units not later than November 15 following date of inheritance or other acquisition, and that portion of his or her permit in excess of 350 sheep units within one year from date of inheritance.

(e) By request of a permittee to sublet all or a part of his or her regular grazing permit to a member of his family or to any person who would receive such permit by inheritance, such subletting of permits may be authorized by the District Grazing Committee and the Superintendent or his authorized representative.

§ 167.10 Special grazing permits.

The problem of special grazing permits shall be settled by the Bureau of Indian Affairs working in cooperation with the Tribal Council, or any Committee designated by it, with a view to terminating these permits at a suitable date and with the least hardship to the Indians concerned.

§ 167.11 Tenure of grazing permits.

(a) All active regular grazing permits shall be for one year and shall be automatically renewed annually until terminated. Any Navajo eligible to hold a grazing permit as defined in § 167.8 may become a livestock operator by obtaining an active grazing permit through negotiability or inheritance or both.

(b) In many Districts, and portions of all districts, unused grazing permits or portions of grazing permits are beneficial in aiding range recovery. Each District Grazing Committee will handle each matter of unused grazing permit or portions of grazing permits on individual merits. Where ample forage is available operators will be encouraged to fill their permits with livestock or dispose of their unused permits through negotiability. In those areas where forage is in need of rehabilitation permittees will not be encouraged to stock to their permitted numbers until the range has sufficiently recovered to justify the grazing of additional livestock.

§ 167.12 Grazing fees.

Grazing fees shall not be charged at this time.[1]

§ 167.13 Trespass.

The owner of any livestock grazing in trespass in Navajo Tribal ranges shall be subject to action by the Navajo Court of Indian Offenses as provided in part 11 of this chapter, however, upon recommendations of the District Grazing Committee, first offenses may be referred to the Central Grazing Committee and the Superintendent or his authorized representative for proper settlement out of court. The following acts are considered as trespass:

(a) Any person who sells an entire permit must dispose of all his livestock or be in trespass. Any person selling a portion of his permit must not run more stock than covered by his remaining permit, or be subject to immediate trespass.

(b) All persons running livestock in excess of their permitted number must by April 25, 1959, either obtain permits to cover their total livestock numbers or reduce to their permitted number, or be in trespass. Additional time may be granted in unusual individual cases as determined and approved by the District Grazing Committee, General Grazing Committee, and the Superintendent or his authorized representative.

(c) Failure to comply with the provisions in § 167.9, shall be considered as trespass.

(d) Any person who willfully allows his livestock to drift from one district to another shall be subject to trespass action. The grazing of livestock in customary use areas extending over District Boundary lines, when such customary use areas are defined and agreed upon by the District Grazing Committees involved, shall not be considered as willful trespass.

(e) The owner of any livestock who violates the customary or established use units of other permittees shall be subject to trespass action.

[22 FR 10578, Dec. 24, 1957, as amended at 24 FR 1178, Feb. 17, 1959. Redesignated at 47 FR 13327, Mar. 30, 1982]

§ 167.14 Movement of livestock.

Annually, prior to the normal lamb buying season, the Central Grazing Committee after consultation with District Grazing Committees shall issue regulations covering the buying period and the procedures and methods to be used in moving livestock to market. All movements of livestock other than trucking from buying areas to loading or shipping points must be authorized by Trailing Permits issued by the District Grazing Committees on the approved forms. Failure to comply with

[1] Grazing Committees were organized in May 1953. These committees have not had ample time to fully acquaint themselves or the stockmen in their respective districts with all of the various items of range administration and range management. Also the drought of several years has not broken. The Navajo Tribe therefore requests that the matter of establishing regulations regarding the adoption of grazing fees be deferred until such a time as a full understanding of the advantages of fees can be had by the majority of the stockmen in all Districts. The assessment of grazing fees will not aid materially in obtaining proper range use. At this time it is more important that other sections of these grazing regulations be adopted and enforced. Resolution of Navajo Tribal Council No. CJ-22-54 of June 9, 1954.

this section and with annual lamb buying regulations will be considered as trespass.

§ 167.15 Control of livestock disease and introduction of livestock.

(a) The District Grazing Committees with the approval of the Superintendent shall require livestock to be dipped, vaccinated, inspected and be restricted in movement when necessary to prevent the introduction and spread of contagious or infectious disease in the economic interest of the Navajo stock owners. Upon the recommendation of the District Grazing Committee livestock shall be dipped annually when such dipping is necessary to prevent the spread of contagious diseases. These annual dippings shall be completed on or before September 1st each year. Livestock, however, may be dipped at other times when necessary. The Superintendent or his authorized representative and the District Grazing Committee may also require the rounding up of cattle, horses, mules, etc., in each District for the purpose of inspection for disease, vaccinating, branding and other related operations.

(b) No livestock shall be brought onto the Reservation without a permit issued by the Superintendent or his authorized representative following inspection, in order to safeguard Indian livestock from infections and contagious disease and to insure the introduction of good quality sires and breeding stock.

(c) Any unusual disease conditions beyond the control measures provided herein shall be immediately reported by the District Grazing Committee to the Chairman of the Navajo Tribal Council and the Superintendent who shall attempt to obtain specialists and provide emergency funds to control and suppress the disease.

§ 167.16 Fences.

Favorable recommendation from the District Grazing Committee and a written authorization from the Superintendent or his authorized representative must be secured before any fences may be constructed in non-agricultural areas. The District Grazing Committee shall recommend to the Superintendent the removal of unauthorized existing fences, or fences enclosing demonstration areas no longer used as such, if it is determined that such fences interfere with proper range management or an equitable distribution of range privileges. All enclosures fenced for the purpose of protecting agricultural land shall be kept to a size commensurate with the needs for protection of agricultural land and must be enclosed by legal four strand barbed wire fence or the equivalent.

§ 167.17 Construction near permanent livestock water developments.

(a) The District Grazing Committee shall regulate the construction of all dwellings, corrals and other structures within one-half mile of Government or Navajo Tribal developed permanent livestock waters such as springs, wells, and charcos or deep reservoirs.

(b) A written authorization from the District Grazing Committee must be secured before any dwellings, corrals, or other structures may be constructed within one-half mile of Government or Navajo Tribal developed springs, wells and charcos or deep reservoirs.

(c) No sewage disposal system shall be authorized to be built which will drain into springs or stream channels in such a manner that it would cause contamination of waters being used for livestock or human consumption.

PART 168—GRAZING REGULATIONS FOR THE HOPI PARTITIONED LANDS AREA

Sec.

AUTHORITY: 5 U.S.C. 301; 25 U.S.C. 2, 640d–8, and 640d–18.

SOURCE: 47 FR 39817, Sept. 10, 1982, unless otherwise noted.

§ 168.1 Definitions.

As used in this part, terms shall have the meanings set forth in this section.

(a) *Secretary* means the Secretary of Interior or his designee;

(b) *Area Director* means the officer in charge of the Phoenix Bureau of Indian Affairs Area Office (or his successor; and/or his authorized representative) to whom has been delegated the authority of the Assistant Secretary—Indian Affairs to act in all matters pertaining to lands partitioned to the Hopi Tribe under its jurisdiction, within the boundaries of the former Joint Use Area.

(c) *Superintendent* means the Superintendent, Hopi Agency or his designee.

(d) *Tribal Government* means the Hopi Tribal Council, or its duly designated representative.

(e) *Project Officer* means the former Special Project Officer of the Bureau of Indian Affairs, Administrative Office, Flagstaff, Arizona 86001, who had been delegated the authority of the Commissioner of Indian Affairs to act in matters respecting the former Joint Use Area.

(f) *Former Joint Use Area* means the area established by the United States District Court for the District of Arizona in the case entitled *Healing* v. *Jones*, 210 F. Supp. 125 (1962), which is inside the Executive order area (Executive order of December 16, 1882) but outside Land Management District 6 and which was partitioned by the judgment of partition dated April 18, 1979.

(g) *Hopi Partition Area* means that portion of the Former Joint Use Area which has been added to the Hopi Tribe's reservation.

(h) *Range Unit* means a tract of range land designated as a management unit for administration of grazing.

(i) *Range improvements* means fences, stockwater devices, corrals, trails and other similar devices or practices which are applied to the land to enhance range productivity or usability.

(j) *Permit* means a revocable privilege granted in writing limited to entering on and utilizing forage by domestic livestock on a specified tract of land. The term as used herein shall include written authorizations issued to enable the crossing or trailing of domestic livestock across specified tracts or range units.

(k) *Interim permit* means a permit granted to members of the Navajo tribe residing on Hopi Partitioned Lands who meet the qualifications of § 168.6(b) in accordance with Pub. L. 93–531 as amended.

(l) *Animal unit* (AU) means one adult cow with unweaned calf by her side or equivalent thereof based on comparative forage consumption. Accepted conversion factors are: sheep and goats, one ewe, doe, buck or ram equals 0.25 A.U.; one sheep unit year long (SUYL) equals 0.25 Animal Unit year long; horses and mules, one horse, mule, donkey or burro equals 1.25 A.U.

(m) *Tribe* means the Hopi Tribe including all villages and clans.

(n) *Allocate* means to apportion grazing, including the determination of who may graze livestock, the number and kind of livestock, and the place such livestock will be grazed.

(o) *Person awaiting relocation* means a resident of the Hopi Partitioned Area who meets each of the following criteria:

(1) Is listed on the Bureau of Indian Affairs enumeration (as defined in (q) below);

(2) Has a livestock inventory listed with the project Officer (see (r) below);

(3) Is awaiting relocation under the Settlement Act; and

(4) Was grazing livestock on the date of the entry of the Judgment of Partition, April 18, 1979.

(p) *Carrying capacity* means the maximum stocking rate possible without inducing damage to vegetation or related resources.

(q) *BIA enumeration* means the list of persons living on and improvements located within the former Joint Use Area obtained by interviews by the Project Officer's staff.

(r) *Livestock inventory* means the original list as amended (developed by the Project Officer in 1976–77) of livestock owned by persons having customary grazing use in the former Joint Use Area.

(s) *Settlement Act* means the Act of December 22, 1974, 88 Stat. 1712, as amended.

(t) *Life tenant* means a person who has applied for and been granted a life estate lease pursuant to section 30 of the Settlement Act, 25 U.S.C. 640d–28.

§ 168.2 Authority.

It is within the general authority of the Secretary to protect Indian trust lands against waste and to prescribe rules and regulations under which these lands may be leased or permitted for grazing. Also, under the Navajo-Hopi Settlement Act as amended, 25 U.S.C. 640d–8 and 18, the Secretary is authorized and directed to:

(a) Reduce livestock grazing within the former Joint Use Area to carrying capacity,

(b) Restore the grazing range potential of the resource to maximum grazing extent feasible,

(c) Survey, monument and fence the partition boundary,

(d) Protect the rights and property of individuals awaiting relocation or authorized to reside on life estates, and

(e) To administer conservation practices, including grazing control and range restoration activities on the Hopi Partitioned Lands.

§ 168.3 Purpose.

These regulations are issued to implement the Secretary's responsibilities mandated by the Settlement Act and subsequent U.S. District Court Judgement filed May 4, 1982, in the case, *Hopi Tribe* v. *Watt,* Civ. No. 81-272 PCT-EHC. This portion of the regulations apply only to lands partitioned to the Hopi Tribe within the former Joint Use Area.

§ 168.4 Establishment of range units.

The Area Director will use Soil and Range Inventory data to establish range units on the Hopi Partitioned Area to provide for a surface land management program to restore the land to its full grazing potential and maintain that potential to the maximum extent feasible. The establishment of range units on Hopi Partitioned Lands is subject to the concurrence of the Hopi Tribe in accordance with § 168.17 of these regulations.

§ 168.5 Grazing capacity.

(a) The Area Director shall prescribe the maximum number of each kind of livestock which may be grazed on land under his jurisdiction without inducing damage to vegetation or related resources on each range unit and the season or seasons of use to achieve the objectives of the land recovery program required by the Settlement Act.

(b) The Area Director shall review the stocking rate upon which the grazing permits are issued on a continuing basis and adjust that rate as conditions warrant.

§ 168.6 Grazing on range units authorized by permit.

Grazing use on range units is authorized only by permits granted under paragraph (a) or (b) of this section.

(a) *Grazing permits to Hopi tribal members on their partitioned lands.* The Area Director shall assign grazing privileges to the Hopi Tribe for lands within Hopi Partitioned Lands. The tribal government will then allocate use to their tribal members for permit periods not to exceed five years. Grazing use by Hopi tribal enterprises may be authorized. The Area Director will issue permits based on the determination of the Hopi tribal government.

(b) *Interim Grazing Permit for persons awaiting relocation.* Navajo Tribal members who have maintained both a permanent residence on Hopi Partitioned lands; a livestock inventory since enumeration; and meet all the criteria listed in § 168.1(o), shall be eligible for an interim grazing allocation on Hopi Partitioned Lands under the following terms and conditions:

(1) The Area Director shall first verify that an applicant meets the criteria of the definition in § 168.1(o) and will issue all permits.

(2) The permitted number shall not exceed either (i) 10 SUYL (See § 168.1(1)) for each eligible family member, or (ii) the grazing applicant's livestock inventory reduced by voluntary sales as adjusted by reproduction, in accordance with procedures developed by the

Project Officer based upon the study by Stubblefield and Camfield, 1975 page 5. The determination of the person to whom permits will be issued and the number of livestock to be permitted will be based on information provided by the permit applicant and an assessment of the number of dependents residing in the immediate household.

(3) The permit shall authorize grazing for a specific number and kind of animal(s) in a specified range unit. Interim grazing permits will not be issued in excess of one-half the authorized carrying capacity of the Hopi Partition area.

(4) Subject to the provisions of § 168.9(b), permits shall expire when the person awaiting relocation is relocated pursuant to the Settlement Act. No interim permit will be issued for a term greater than one year. Permits may be reissued upon application and redetermination of eligibility. All interim permits will expire at the end of the period provided for completion of relocation, Pub. L. 99–190. When a Navajo permit holder discontinues grazing livestock or reduces the number being grazed whether by reason of his relocating or for any other reason, his grazing permit will be cancelled or reduced and no permit will be issued in lieu thereof. The total number of authorized animal units grazed by the Navajo permit holders awaiting relocation will reduced by the number of animal units authorized under the cancelled or reduced permit.

[47 FR 39817, Sept. 10, 1982, as amended at 51 FR 23052, June 25, 1986]

§ 168.7 Kind of livestock.

Unless determined otherwise by the Area Director for conservation purposes, the Hopi Tribe may determine, subject to the authorized carrying capacity, the kind of livestock that may be grazed by their tribal members on the range units within the Hopi Partitioned Land area.

§ 168.8 Grazing fees.

(a) The rental value of all uses of Hopi Partitioned lands by persons who are not members of the Hopi Tribe, including eligible holders of interim permits, will be determined, and assessed by the Area Director and paid in accordance with 25 U.S.C. 640d–15.

(b) The Hopi Tribe has established an annual grazing fee to be assessed all range users on Hopi Partitioned Lands. The annual Hopi grazing fee shall be paid in full in advance of the annual effective date of the permit, prior to the issuance of a grazing permit. All interim permits will expire at the end of the period provided for completion of relocation, Pub. L. 99–190. Failure of the permittee to make payment in full in advance will be cause to deny issuance of the grazing permit.

[47 FR 39817, Sept. 10, 1982, as amended at 51 FR 23052, June 25, 1986]

§ 168.9 Assignment, modification and cancellation of permits.

(a) Grazing permits to Hopi tribal members shall not be reassigned, subpermitted or transferred without the approval of the permit issuer(s).

(b) The Area Director may revoke or withdraw all or any part of any grazing permit in Hopi Partitioned Lands by cancellation or modification on 30 days written notice of a violation of the permit or special conditions affecting the land or the safety of the livestock thereon, as may result from flood, disaster, drought, contagious diseases, etc. Except in the case of extreme necessity, cancellation or modification shall be effected on the next annual anniversay date of the grazing permit following the date of notice. Revocation or withdrawal of all or any of the grazing permit by cancellation or modification as provided herein is effective on the date the notice of cancellation or modification is received and shall be appealable under 25 CFR

part 2.

§ 168.10 Conservation and land use provisions.

Grazing operations shall be conducted in accordance with recognized principles of good range management. Conservation management plans necessary to accomplish this will be made a part of the grazing permit by stipulation.

§ 168.11 Range improvements; ownership; new construction.

Except as provided by the Relocation Act, range improvements placed on the permitted land shall be considered affixed to the land unless specifically excepted therefrom under the permit terms. Written permission to construct or remove improvements must be obtained from the Hopi Tribe.

§ 168.12 Special permit requirements and provisions.

All grazing permits shall contain the following provisions:

(a) Because the lands covered by the permit are in trust status, all of the permittees' obligations on the permit and the obligations of his sureties are to the United States as well as to the beneficial owners of the lands.

(b) The permittee agrees he will not use, cause, or allow to be used any part of the permitted area for any unlawful conduct or purpose.

(c) The permit authorizes only the grazing of livestock.

§ 168.13 Fences.

Fencing will be erected by the Federal Government around the perimeter of the 1882 Executive Order Area, Land Management District 6, and on the boundary of the former Joint Use Area partitioned to each tribe by the Judgment of Partition of April 18, 1979. Fencing of other areas in the former Joint Use Area will be required for a range recovery program in accordance with the range units established under § 168.4. Such fencing shall be erected at Government expense and ownership shall be clearly identified by appropriate posting on the fencing. Intentional destruction of Federal property will be treated as a violation of 18 U.S.C. 1164.

§ 168.14 Livestock trespass.

The owner of any livestock grazing in trespass on the Hopi Partitioned Lands Area is liable to a civil penalty of $1 per head per day for each animal in trespass, together with the replacement value of the forage consumed and a reasonable value for damages to property injured or destroyed. The Superintendent may take appropriate action to collect all such penalties and damages and seek injunctive relief when appropriate. All payments for such penalties and damages shall be credited to the Tribe. The following acts are prohibited:

(a) The grazing upon or driving across any of the Hopi Partitioned Lands of any livestock without an approved grazing or crossing permit;

(b) Allowing livestock to drift and graze on lands without an approved permit;

(c) The grazing of livestock upon lands within an area closed to grazing of that class of livestock;

(d) The grazing of livestock by permittees upon any land withdrawn from use for grazing purpose to protect it from damage, after the receipt of notice from the Area Director; and

(e) Grazing livestock in excess of those numbers and kinds authorized on a livestock grazing permit approved by the Area Director.

§ 168.15 Control of livestock diseases and parasites.

Whenever livestock within the Hopi Partitioned Lands become infected with contagious or infectious diseases or parasites or have been exposed thereto, such livestock must be treated and the movement thereof restricted in accordance with applicable laws.

§ 168.16 Impoundment and disposal of unauthorized livestock.

Unauthorized livestock within any range unit of the Hopi Partitioned Lands which are not removed therefrom within the periods prescribed by the regulation will be impounded and disposed of by the Superintendent as provided herein.

(a) When the Area Director determines that unauthorized livestock use is occurring and has definite knowledge of the kind of unauthorized livestock, and knows the name and address of the owners, such livestock may be impounded any time five days after written notice of intent to impound unauthorized livestock is mailed by certified mail or personally delivered to such owners or their agent.

(b) When the Area Director determines that unauthorized livestock use is occurring but does not have complete knowledge of the number and class of livestock or if the name and address of the owner thereof are unknown, such livestock will be impounded anytime 15 days after the date of a General Notice of Intent to Impound unauthorized livestock is first published in the local newspaper, posted at the nearest chapter house, and in one or more local trading posts.

(c) Unauthorized livestock on the Hopi Partitioned Lands which are owned by persons given notice under paragraph (a) of this section, and any unauthorized livestock in areas for which a notice has been posted and published under paragraph (b) of this section, will be impounded without further notice anytime within the twelve-month period immediately following the effective date of the notice.

(d) Following the impoundment of unauthorized livestock a notice of sale of impounded livestock will be published in the local newspaper, posted at the nearest chapter house, and in one or more local trading posts. The notice will describe the livestock and specify the date, time and place of sale. The date set shall be at least 5 days after the publication and posting of such notice.

(e) The owners or their agent may redeem the livestock anytime before the time set for the sale by submitting proof of ownership and paying for all expenses incurred in gathering, impounding and feeding or pasturing the livestock and any trespass fees and/or damages caused by the animals.

(f) Livestock erroneously impounded shall be returned to the rightful owner and all expenses accruing thereto shall be waived.

(g) If the livestock are not redeemed before the time fixed for their sale, they shall be sold at public sale to the highest bidder, provided his bid is at or above the minimum amount set by the Superintendent based upon U.S.D.A.'s current Agricultural Statistic's Report for Arizona. If a bid at or above the minimum is not received the livestock may be sold at private sale at or above the minimum amount, reoffered at public sale, condemned and destroyed, or otherwise disposed of. When livestock are sold pursuant to this regulation, the superintendent shall furnish the buyer a bill of sale or other written instrument evidencing the sale.

(h) The proceeds of any sale of impounded livestock shall be applied as follows:

(1) To the payment of all expenses incurred by the United States in gathering, impounding, and feeding or pasturing the livestock;

(2) In payment of any penalties or damages assessed pursuant to § 168.14 of this part which penalties or damages shall be credited to the Hopi tribe as provided in said section;

(3) Any remaining amount shall be paid over to the owner of said livestock upon his submitting proof of ownership.

Any proceeds remaining after payment of the first and second items noted above not claimed with one year from the date of sale, will be credited to the Hopi Tribe.

§ 168.17 Concurrence procedures.

(a) *Definitions.* As used in this section, terms shall have the meaning set forth as follows:

(1) *Concurrence* means agreement by the Area Director and the Hopi Tribe, speaking through the Chairman of the Tribe (or his designee).

(2) *Non-concurrence* means disagreement between the Area Director and the Hopi Tribe, speaking through the Chairman of the Hopi Tribe (or his designee), or a failure of the Hopi Tribe to respond to a proposal by the Area Director in a timely manner.

(3) *Timely manner* means a period of thirty days, unless this period is shortened by the existence of an emergency. Upon request by the Tribal Council, the Area Director may extend the 30 day period. In instances where this period applies to the Area Director, he may extend the period by so notifying the Tribe.

(4) *An emergency* is a condition that the Area Director finds threatens the rights and property of life tenants and persons awaiting relocation or one that the Area Director finds is causing the condition of the range land to deteriorate.

(5) *Conservation practice* is a program consisting of a series of acts in conformance with the Bureau's range management policies and procedures which

maintains or seeks to achieve the grazing potential of range lands on a continuing basis.

(6) *Range restoration activities* is a program consisting of a series of range management acts, including but not limited to procedures which increase range forage production, reduce erosion, improve range usability and reduce stocking by issuing grazing permits to persons residing on Hopi partitioned lands at rates which maximize the carrying capacity of the range lands on a continuing basis.

(7) *Grazing control* is a program consisting of a series of range management acts, including but not limited to procedures by which grazing permits are issued to persons residing on Hopi partitioned lands, which limit the grazing on range lands to its carrying capacity.

(b) The Area Director will seek the participation of the Hopi Tribe in his investigation, formulation and planning of conservation practices for Hopi partitioned lands. The Area Director will submit, in writing, the proposed plan to the Hopi Tribe.

(c) Upon receipt of the Area Director's proposed conservation practices, the Hopi Tribe will deliver, in writing, to the Area Director its concurrence or non-concurrence on all of the proposed conservation practices in a timely manner. The Area Director will continue to seek Hopi Tribal participation during the review process.

(d) Concurrence of the Hopi Tribe will be sought on all conservation practices, range restoration activities, and grazing control programs on the Hopi Partitioned Lands.

(1) If the Area Director and the Hopi Tribe concur on all or part of the proposed conservation practices in writing in a timely manner, those practices concurred upon may be immediately implemented.

(2) If the Hopi Tribe does not concur on all or part of the proposed conservation practices in a timely manner, the Area Director will submit in writing to the Hopi Tribe a declaration of non-concurrence. The Area Director will then notify the Hopi Tribe in writing of a formal hearing to be held not sooner than 15 days from the date of the non-concurrence declaration.

(i) The formal hearing on non-concurrence will permit the submission of written evidence and argument concerning the proposal. Minutes of the hearing will be taken. Following the hearing, the Area Director may amend, alter or otherwise change his proposed conservation practices. Except as provided in § 168.17(d)(1) of this section, if following the hearing, the Area Director altered or amends portions of his proposed plan of action, he will submit those individual altered or amended portions of the plan to the Tribe in a timely manner for their concurrence.

(ii) In the event the Tribe fails or refuses to give its concurrence to the proposal at the hearing, then the implementation of such proposal may only be undertaken in those situations where the Area Director expressly determines in a written order, based upon findings of fact, that the proposed action is necessary to protect the rights and property of life tenants and/or persons awaiting relocation.

§ 168.18 Appeals.

Appeals from decisions issued under this part will be in accordance with procedures in 25 CFR part 2.

§ 168.19 Information collection.

The information collection requirement(s) contained in this regulation have been approved by the Office of Management and Budget under 44 U.S.C. 3501 *et seq.* and assigned clearance number 1076–0027. The information is being collected in order to ascertain eligibility for the issuance of a grazing permit. Response is mandatory in order to obtain a permit.

PART 169—RIGHTS-OF-WAY OVER INDIAN LAND

Subpart A—Purpose, Definitions, General Provisions

Sec.

Subpart B—Service Line Agreements

Subpart C—Obtaining a Right-of-Way

APPLICATION

CONSENT REQUIREMENTS

COMPENSATION REQUIREMENTS

GRANTS OF RIGHTS-OF-WAY

Subpart D—Duration, Renewals, Amendments, Assignments, Mortgages

DURATION & RENEWALS

AUTHORITY: 5 U.S.C. 301; 25 U.S.C. 323–328; 25 U.S.C. 2201 *et seq.*

SOURCE: 80 FR 72534, Nov. 19, 2015, unless otherwise noted.

Subpart A—Purpose, Definitions, General Provisions

§ 169.1 What is the purpose of this part?

(a) This part is intended to streamline the procedures and conditions under which BIA will consider a request to approve (*i.e.*, grant) rights-of-way over and across tribal lands, individually owned Indian lands, and BIA lands, by providing for the use of the broad authority under 25 U.S.C. 323–328, rather than the limited authorities under other statutes. This part is also intended to support tribal self-determination and self-governance by acknowledging and incorporating tribal law and policies in processing a request for a right-of-way across tribal lands and defer to the maximum extent possible to Indian landowner decisions regarding their Indian land.

(b) This part specifies:

(1) Conditions and authorities under which we will consider a request to approve rights-of-way over or across Indian land;

(2) How to obtain a right-of-way;

(3) Terms and conditions required in rights-of-way;

(4) How we administer and enforce rights-of-ways;

(5) How to renew, amend, assign, and mortgage rights-of-way; and

(6) Whether rights-of-way are required for service line agreements.

(c) This part does not cover rights-of-way over or across tribal lands within a reservation for the purpose of Federal

Power Act projects, such as constructing, operating, or maintaining dams, water conduits, reservoirs, powerhouses, transmission lines, or other works which must constitute a part of any project for which a license is required by the Federal Power Act.

(1) The Federal Power Act provides that any license that must be issued to use tribal lands within a reservation must be subject to and contain such conditions as the Secretary deems necessary for the adequate protection and utilization of such lands (16 U.S.C. 797(e)).

(2) In the case of tribal lands belonging to a tribe organized under the Indian Reorganization Act of 1934 (25 U.S.C. 476), the Federal Power Act requires that annual charges for the use of such tribal lands under any license issued by the Federal Energy Regulatory Commission must be subject to the approval of the tribe (16 U.S.C. 803(e)).

(d) This part does not apply to grants of rights-of-way on tribal land under a special act of Congress specifically authorizing rights-of-way on tribal land without our approval.

§ 169.2 What terms do I need to know?

The following terms apply to this part:

Abandonment means the grantee has affirmatively relinquished a right-of-way (as opposed to relinquishing through non-use) either by notifying the BIA of the abandonment or by performing an act indicating an intent to give up and never regain possession of the right-of-way.

Assignment means an agreement between a grantee and an assignee, whereby the assignee acquires all or part of the grantee's rights, and assumes all of the grantee's obligations under a grant.

Avigation hazard easement means the right, acquired by government through purchase or condemnation from the owner of land adjacent to an airport, to the use of the air space above a specific height for the flight of aircraft.

BIA means the Secretary of the Interior or the Bureau of Indian Affairs within the Department of the Interior and any tribe acting on behalf of the Secretary or BIA under § 169.008.

BIA land means any tract, or interest therein, in which the surface estate is owned and administered by the BIA, not including Indian land.

Cancellation means BIA action to end a right-of-way grant.

Compensation means something bargained for that is fair and reasonable under the circumstances of the agreement.

Consent means written authorization by an Indian landowner to a specified action.

Easement means an interest, consisting of the right to use or control, for a specific limited purpose, land owned by another person, or an area above or below it, while title remains vested in the landowner.

Encumbered account means a trust account where some portion of the proceeds are obligated to another party.

Fair market value means the amount of compensation that a right-of-way would most probably command in an open and competitive market.

Fractional interest means an undivided interest in Indian land owned as tenancy in common by individual Indian or tribal landowners and/or fee owners.

Grant means the formal transfer of a right-of-way interest by the Secretary's approval or the document evidencing the formal transfer, including any changes made by a right-of-way document.

Grantee means a person or entity to whom the Secretary grants a right-of-way or to whom the right-of-way has been assigned once the assignment is effective.

Immediate family means, in the absence of a definition under applicable tribal law, a spouse, brother, sister, aunt, uncle, niece, nephew, first cousin, lineal ancestor, lineal descendant, or member of the household.

Indian means:

(1) Any person who is a member of any Indian tribe, is eligible to become a member of any Indian tribe, or is an owner as of October 27, 2004, of a trust or restricted interest in land;

(2) Any person meeting the definition of Indian under the Indian Reorganization Act (25 U.S.C. 479) and the regulations promulgated thereunder; and

(3) With respect to the inheritance and ownership of trust or restricted

land in the State of California under 25 U.S.C. 2206, any person described in paragraph (1) or (2) of this definition or any person who owns a trust or restricted interest in a parcel of such land in that State.

Indian land means individually owned Indian land and/or tribal land.

Indian landowner means a tribe or individual Indian who owns an interest in Indian land.

Indian tribe or *tribe* means an Indian tribe under section 102 of the Federally Recognized Indian Tribe List Act of 1994 (25 U.S.C. 479a).

Individually owned Indian land means any tract in which the surface estate, or an undivided interest in the surface estate, is owned by one or more individual Indians in trust or restricted status.

In-kind compensation means payment is in goods or services rather than money.

Life estate means an interest in property held only for the duration of a designated person(s)' life. A life estate may be created by a conveyance document or by operation of law.

LTRO means the Land Titles and Records Office of BIA.

Map of definite location means a survey plat signed by a professional surveyor or engineer showing the location, size, and extent of the right-of-way and other related parcels, with respect to each affected parcel of individually owned land, tribal land, or BIA land and with reference to the public surveys under 25 U.S.C. 176, 43 U.S.C. 2 and 1764, and showing existing facilities adjacent to the proposed project.

Permanent improvement means pipelines, roads, structures, and other infrastructure attached to the land subject to the right-of-way.

Right-of-way means an easement or a legal right to go over or across tribal land, individually owned Indian land, or BIA land for a specific purpose, including but not limited to building and operating a line or road. This term may also refer to the land subject to the grant of right-of-way; however, in all cases, title to the land remains vested in the landowner. This term does not include service lines.

Right-of-way document means a right-of-way grant, renewal, amendment, assignment, or mortgage of a right-of-way.

Secretary means the Secretary of the Interior or an authorized representative.

Termination means action by Indian landowners to end a right-of-way.

Trespass means any unauthorized occupancy, use of, or action on tribal or individually owned Indian land or BIA land.

Tribal authorization means a duly adopted tribal resolution, tribal ordinance, or other appropriate tribal document authorizing the specified action.

Tribal land means any tract in which the surface estate, or an undivided interest in the surface estate, is owned by one or more tribes in trust or restricted status. The term also includes the surface estate of lands held in trust for a tribe but reserved for BIA administrative purposes and includes the surface estate of lands held in trust for an Indian corporation chartered under section 17 of the Indian Reorganization Act of 1934 (25 U.S.C. 477).

Tribal utility means a utility owned by one or more tribes that is established for the purpose of providing utility service, and that is certified by the tribe to meet the following requirements:

(1) The combined Indian tribe ownership constitutes not less than 51 percent of the utility;

(2) The Indian tribes, together, receive at least a majority of the earnings; and

(3) The management and daily business operations of the utility are controlled by one or more representatives of the tribe.

Trust account means a tribal account or Individual Indian Money (IIM) account for trust funds maintained by the Secretary.

Trust or restricted status means:

(1) That the United States holds title to the tract or interest in trust for the benefit of one or more tribes and/or individual Indians; or

(2) That one or more tribes and/or individual Indians holds title to the tract or interest, but can alienate or encumber it only with the approval of the United States because of limitations in the conveyance instrument under Federal law or limitations in Federal law.

Uniform Standards of Professional Appraisal Practice (USPAP) means the standards promulgated by the Appraisal Standards Board of the Appraisal Foundation to establish requirements and procedures for professional real property appraisal practice.

Us/we/our means the BIA.

Utility cooperative means a cooperative that provides public utilities to its members and either reinvests profits for infrastructure or distributes profits to members of the cooperative.

§ 169.3 To what land does this part apply?

(a) This part applies to Indian land and BIA land.

(b) We will not take any action on a right-of-way across fee land or collect compensation on behalf of fee interest owners. We will not condition our grant of a right-of-way across Indian land or BIA land on the applicant having obtained a right-of-way from the owners of any fee interests. The applicant will be responsible for negotiating directly with and making any payments directly to the owners of any fee interests that may exist in the property on which the right-of-way is granted.

(c) We will not include the fee interests in a tract in calculating the applicable percentage of interests required for consent to a right-of-way.

§ 169.4 When do I need a right-of-way to authorize possession over or across Indian land?

(a) You need an approved right-of-way under this part before crossing Indian land if you meet one of the criteria in the following table:

If you are . . .	then you must obtain a right-of-way under this part . . .
(1) A person or legal entity (including a Federal, State, or local governmental entity) who is not an owner of the Indian land.	from us, with the consent of the owners of the majority interest in the land, and the tribe for tribal land, before crossing the land or any portion thereof.
(2) An individual Indian landowner who owns a fractional interest in the land (even if the individual Indian landowner owns a majority of the fractional interests).	from us, with the consent of the owners of other trust and restricted interests in the land, totaling at least a majority interest in the tract, and with the consent of the tribe for tribal land. You do not need to obtain a right-of-way from us if all of the owners (including the tribe, for tribal land) have given you permission to cross without a right-of-way.
(3) An Indian tribe, agency or instrumentality of the tribe, or an independent legal entity wholly owned and operated by the tribe who owns only a fractional interest in the land (even if the tribe, agency, instrumentality or legal entity owns a majority of the fractional interests).	from us, with the consent of the owners of other trust and restricted interests in the land, totaling at least a majority interest in the tract, unless all of the owners have given you permission to cross without a right-of-way.

(b) You do not need a right-of-way to cross Indian land if:

(1) You are an Indian landowner who owns 100 percent of the trust or restricted interests in the land; or

(2) You are authorized by:

(i) A lease under 25 CFR part 162, 211, 212, or 225 or permit under 25 CFR part 166;

(ii) A tribal land assignment or similar instrument authorizing use of the tribal land without Secretarial approval; or

(iii) Other, tribe-specific authority authorizing use of the tribal land without Secretarial approval; or

(iv) Another land use agreement not subject to this part (e.g., under 25 CFR part 84); or

(3) You meet any of the criteria in the following table:

You do not need a right-of-way if you are . . .	but the following conditions apply . . .
(i) A parent or guardian of a minor child who owns 100 percent of the trust or restricted interests in the land.	We may require you to provide evidence of a direct benefit to the minor child and when the child is no longer a minor, you must obtain a right-of-way to authorize continued possession.
(ii) Authorized by a service line agreement to cross the land.	You must file the agreement with us under § 169.56.

You do not need a right-of-way if you are . . .	but the following conditions apply . . .
(iii) An independent legal entity wholly owned and operated by the tribe that owns 100 percent of the trust or restricted interests in the land.	The tribal governing body must pass a tribal authorization authorizing access without BIA approval and including a legal description, and you must submit both documents to BIA for our records.
(iv) Otherwise authorized by law.	You must comply with the requirements of the applicable law.

§ 169.5 What types of rights-of-way does this part cover?

(a) This part covers rights-of-way over and across Indian or BIA land, for uses including but not limited to the following:

(1) Railroads;

(2) Public roads and highways;

(3) Access roads;

(4) Service roads and trails, even where they are appurtenant to any other right-of-way purpose;

(5) Public and community water lines (including pumping stations and appurtenant facilities);

(6) Public sanitary and storm sewer lines (including sewage disposal and treatment plant lines);

(7) Water control and use projects (including but not limited to, flowage easements, irrigation ditches and canals, and water treatment plant lines);

(8) Oil and gas pipelines (including pump stations, meter stations, and other appurtenant facilities);

(9) Electric transmission and distribution systems (including lines, poles, towers, telecommunication, protection, measurement and data acquisition equipment, other items necessary to operate and maintain the system, and appurtenant facilities);

(10) Telecommunications, broadband, fiber optic lines;

(11) Avigation hazard easements;

(12) Conservation easements not covered by 25 CFR part 84, Encumbrances of Tribal Land—Contract Approvals, or 25 CFR part 162, Leases and Permits; or

(13) Any other new use for which a right-of-way is appropriate but which is unforeseeable as of the effective date of these regulations.

(b) Each of the uses listed above includes the right to access the right-of-way to manage vegetation, inspect, maintain and repair equipment, and conduct other activities that are necessary to maintain the right-of-way use.

§ 169.6 What statutory authority will BIA use to act on requests for rights-of-way under this part?

BIA will act on requests for rights-of-way using the authority in 25 U.S.C. 323–328, and relying on supplementary authority such as 25 U.S.C. 2218, where appropriate.

§ 169.7 Does this part apply to right-of-way grants submitted for approval before December 21, 2015?

(a) If your right-of-way grant is issued on or after April 21, 2016, this part applies.

(b) If we granted your right-of-way before April 21, 2016, the procedural provisions of this part apply except that if the procedural provisions of this part conflict with the explicit provisions of the right-of-way grant or statute authorizing the right-of-way document, then the provisions of the right-of-way grant or authorizing statute apply instead. Non-procedural provisions of this part do not apply.

(c) If you submitted an application for a right-of-way but we did not grant the right-of-way before April 21, 2016, then:

(1) You may choose to withdraw the document and resubmit after April 21, 2016, in which case this part will apply to that document; or

(2) You may choose to proceed without withdrawing, in which case:

(i) We will review the application under the regulations in effect at the time of your submission; and

(ii) Once we grant the right-of-way, the procedural provisions of this part apply except that if the procedural provisions of this part conflict with the explicit provisions of the right-of-way grant or statute authorizing the right-of-way document, then the provisions of the right-of-way grant or authorizing statute apply instead. Non-procedural provisions of this part do not apply.

(d) For any assignments completed before April 21, 2016, the current assignee must, by August 16, 2016, provide BIA with documentation of any past assignments or notify BIA that it needs an extension and explain the reason for the extension.

(e) To the maximum extent possible, BIA will interpret any ambiguous language in the right-of-way document or statute to be consistent with these regulations.

[80 FR 72534, Nov. 19, 2015; 80 FR 79258, Dec. 21, 2015; 81 FR 14976, Mar. 21, 2016]

§ 169.8 May tribes administer this part on BIA's behalf?

A tribe or tribal organization may contract or compact under the Indian Self-Determination and Education Assistance Act (25 U.S.C. 450f *et seq.*) to administer on BIA's behalf any portion of this part that is not a grant, approval, or disapproval of a right-of-way document, waiver of a requirement for right-of-way grant or approval (including but not limited to waivers of fair market value and valuation), cancellation of a right-of-way, or an appeal. Applicants may inquire at either the BIA office or the tribal office to determine whether the tribe has compacted or contracted to administer realty functions.

§ 169.9 What laws apply to rights-of-way approved under this part?

In addition to the regulations in this part, rights-of-way approved under this part:

(a) Are subject to all applicable Federal laws;

(b) Are subject to tribal law; except to the extent that those tribal laws are inconsistent with applicable Federal law; and

(c) Are generally not subject to State law or the law of a political subdivision thereof.

§ 169.10 What is the effect of a right-of-way on a tribe's jurisdiction over the underlying parcel?

A right-of-way is a non-possessory interest in land, and title does not pass to the grantee. The Secretary's grant of a right-of-way will clarify that it does not diminish to any extent:

(a) The Indian tribe's jurisdiction over the land subject to, and any person or activity within, the right-of-way;

(b) The power of the Indian tribe to tax the land, any improvements on the land, or any person or activity within, the right-of-way;

(c) The Indian tribe's authority to enforce tribal law of general or particular application on the land subject to and within the right-of-way, as if there were no grant of right-of-way;

(d) The Indian tribe's inherent sovereign power to exercise civil jurisdiction over non-members on Indian land; or

(e) The character of the land subject to the right-of-way as Indian country under 18 U.S.C. 1151.

§ 169.11 What taxes apply to rights-of-way approved under this part?

(a) Subject only to applicable Federal law:

(1) Permanent improvements in a right-of-way, without regard to ownership of those improvements, are not subject to any fee, tax, assessment, levy, or other charge imposed by any State or political subdivision of a State;

(2) Activities under a right-of-way grant are not subject to any fee, tax, assessment, levy, or other charge (e.g., business use, privilege, public utility, excise, gross revenue taxes) imposed by any State or political subdivision of a State; and

(3) The right-of-way interest is not subject to any fee, tax, assessment, levy, or other charge imposed by any State or political subdivision of a State.

(b) Improvements, activities, and right-of-way interests may be subject to taxation by the Indian tribe with jurisdiction.

§ 169.12 How does BIA provide notice to the parties to a right-of-way?

When this part requires BIA to notify the parties of our intent to grant a right-of-way under § 169.107(b) or our determination to approve or disapprove a right-of-way document, and to provide any right of appeal:

(a) For rights-of-way over or across tribal land, we will notify the applicant and the tribe by first class U.S. mail or, upon request, electronic mail; and

(b) For rights-of-way over or across individually owned Indian land, we will notify the applicant and individual Indian landowners by first class U.S.

mail or, upon request, electronic mail. If the individually owned land is located within a tribe's jurisdiction, we will also notify the tribe by first class U.S. mail or, upon request, electronic mail.

§ 169.13 May decisions under this part be appealed?

(a) Appeals from BIA decisions under this part may be taken under part 2 of this chapter, except our decision to disapprove a right-of-way grant or any other right-of-way document may be appealed only by the applicant or an Indian landowner of the tract over or across which the right-of-way was proposed.

(b) For purposes of appeals from BIA decisions under this part, "interested party" is defined as any person whose land is subject to the right-of-way or located adjacent to or in close proximity to the right-of-way whose own direct economic interest is adversely affected by an action or decision.

§ 169.14 How does the Paperwork Reduction Act affect this part?

The collections of information in this part have been approved by the Office of Management and Budget under 44 U.S.C. 3501 *et seq.* and assigned OMB Control Number 1076–0181. Response is required to obtain a benefit. A Federal agency may not conduct or sponsor, and you are not required to respond to, a collection of information unless it displays a currently valid OMB Control Number.

Subpart B—Service Line Agreements

§ 169.51 Is a right-of-way required for service lines?

Service lines generally branch off from facilities for which a right-of-way must be obtained. A service line is a utility line running from a main line, transmission line, or distribution line that is used only for supplying telephone, water, electricity, gas, internet service, or other utility service to a house, business, or other structure. In the case of a power line, a service line is limited to a voltage of 14.5 kv or less, or a voltage of 34.5 kv or less if serving irrigation pumps and commercial and industrial uses. To obtain access to Indian land for service lines, the right-of-way grantee must file a service line agreement meeting the requirements of this subpart with BIA.

§ 169.52 What is a service line agreement?

Service line agreements are agreements signed by a utility provider and landowners for the purpose of providing limited access to supply the owners (or authorized occupants or users) of one tract of tribal or individually owned Indian land with utilities for use by such owners (or occupants or users) on the premises.

§ 169.53 What should a service line agreement address?

A service line agreement should address what utility services the provider will supply, to whom, and other appropriate details. The service line agreement should also address the mitigation of any damages incurred during construction and the restoration (or reclamation, if agreed to by the owners or authorized occupants or users) of the premises at the termination of the agreement.

§ 169.54 What are the consent requirements for service line agreements?

(a) Before the utility provider may begin any work to construct service lines across tribal land, the utility provider and the tribe (or the legally authorized occupants or users of the tribal land and upon request, the tribe) must execute a service line agreement.

(b) Before the utility provider may begin any work to construct service lines across individually owned land, the utility provider and the owners (or the legally authorized occupants or users) must execute a service line agreement.

§ 169.55 Is a valuation required for service line agreements?

We do not require a valuation for service line agreements.

§ 169.56 Must I file service line agreements with the BIA?

The parties must file an executed copy of service line agreements, together with a plat or diagram, with us within 30 days after the date of execution for recording in the LTRO. The plat or diagram must show the boundary of the ownership parcel and point of connection of the service line with the distribution line. When the plat or diagram is placed on a separate sheet it must include the signatures of the parties.

Subpart C—Obtaining a Right-of-Way

APPLICATION

§ 169.101 How do I obtain a right-of-way across tribal or individually owned Indian land or BIA land?

(a) To obtain a right-of-way across tribal or individually owned Indian land or BIA land, you must submit a complete application to the BIA office with jurisdiction over the land covered by the right-of-way.

(b) If you must obtain access to Indian land to prepare information required by the application (e.g., to survey), you must obtain the consent of the Indian landowners, but our approval to access is not required. Upon written request, we will provide you with the names, addresses, and percentage of ownership of individual Indian landowners, to allow you to obtain the landowners' consent to survey.

(c) If the BIA will be granting the right-of-way across Indian land under § 169.107(b), then the BIA may grant permission to access the land.

§ 169.102 What must an application for a right-of-way include?

(a) An application for a right-of-way must identify:

(1) The applicant;

(2) The tract(s) or parcel(s) affected by the right-of-way;

(3) The general location of the right-of-way;

(4) The purpose of the right-of-way;

(5) The duration of the right-of-way: and

(6) The ownership of permanent improvements associated with the right-of-way and the responsibility for constructing, operating, maintaining, and managing permanent improvements under § 169.105.

(b) The following must be submitted with the application:

(1) An accurate legal description of the right-of-way, its boundaries, and parcels associated with the right-of-way;

(2) A map of definite location of the right-of-way (this requirement does not apply to easements covering the entire tract of land);

(3) Bond(s), insurance, and/or other security meeting the requirements of § 169.103;

(4) Record that notice of the right-of-way was provided to all Indian landowners;

(5) Record of consent for the right-of-way meeting the requirements of § 169.107, or a statement requesting a right-of-way without consent under § 169.107(b);

(6) If applicable, a valuation meeting the requirements of § 169.114;

(7) If the applicant is a corporation, limited liability company, partnership, joint venture, or other legal entity, except a tribal entity, information such as organizational documents, certificates, filing records, and resolutions, demonstrating that:

(i) The representative has authority to execute the application;

(ii) The right-of-way will be enforceable against the applicant; and

(iii) The legal entity is in good standing and authorized to conduct business in the jurisdiction where the land is located;

(8) Environmental and archaeological reports, surveys, and site assessments, as needed to facilitate compliance with applicable Federal and tribal environmental and land use requirements; and

(9) A statement from the appropriate tribal authority that the proposed use is in conformance with applicable tribal law, if required by the tribe.

(c) There is no standard application form.

§ 169.103 What bonds, insurance, or other security must accompany the application?

(a) You must include payment of bonds, insurance, or alternative forms of security with your application for a right-of-way in amounts that cover:

(1) The highest annual rental specified in the grant, unless compensation is a one-time payment;

(2) The estimated damages resulting from the construction of any permanent improvements;

(3) The estimated damages and remediation costs from any potential release of contaminants, explosives, hazardous material or waste;

(4) The operation and maintenance charges for any land located within an irrigation project;

(5) The restoration of the premises to their condition at the start of the right-of-way or reclamation to some other specified condition if agreed to by the landowners.

(b) The bond or other security must be deposited with us and made payable only to us, and may not be modified without our approval, except for tribal land in which case the bond or security may be deposited with and made payable to the tribe, and may not be modified without the approval of the tribe. Any insurance must identify both the Indian landowners and the United States as additional insured parties.

(c) The grant will specify the conditions under which we may adjust the bond, insurance, or security requirements to reflect changing conditions, including consultation with the tribal landowner for tribal land before the adjustment.

(d) We may require that the surety provide any supporting documents needed to show that the bond, insurance, or alternative form of security will be enforceable, and that the surety will be able to perform the guaranteed obligations.

(e) The bond, insurance, or other security instrument must require the surety to provide notice to us, and the tribe for tribal land, at least 60 days before canceling a bond, insurance, or other security. This will allow us to notify the grantee of its obligation to provide a substitute bond, insurance, or other security before the cancellation date. Failure to provide a substitute bond, insurance or security is a violation of the right-of-way.

(f) We may waive the requirement for a bond, insurance, or alternative form of security:

(1) For individually owned Indian land, if the Indian landowners of the majority of the interests request it and we determine, in writing, that a waiver is in the Indian landowners' best interest considering the purpose of and risks associated with the right-of-way, or if the grantee is a utility cooperative and is providing a direct benefit to the Indian land or is a tribal utility.

(2) For tribal land, deferring, to the maximum extent possible, to the tribe's determination that a waiver of a bond, insurance or alternative form of security is in its best interest.

(g) We will accept a bond only in one of the following forms:

(1) Certificates of deposit issued by a federally insured financial institution authorized to do business in the United States;

(2) Irrevocable letters of credit issued by a federally insured financial institution authorized to do business in the United States;

(3) Negotiable Treasury securities; or

(4) Surety bonds issued by a company approved by the U.S. Department of the Treasury.

(h) We may accept an alternative form of security approved by us that provides adequate protection for the Indian landowners and us, including but not limited to an escrow agreement or an assigned savings account.

(i) All forms of bonds or alternative security must, if applicable:

(1) State on their face that BIA approval is required for redemption;

(2) Be accompanied by a statement granting full authority to BIA to make an immediate claim upon or sell them if the grantee violates the terms of the right-of-way grant;

(3) Be irrevocable during the term of the bond or alternative security; and

(4) Be automatically renewable during the term of the right-of-way.

(j) We will not accept cash bonds.

§ 169.104 What is the release process for a bond or alternative form of security?

Upon satisfaction of the requirements for which the bond was security, or upon expiration, termination, or cancellation of the right-of-way, the grantee may ask BIA in writing to release all or part of the bond or alternative form of security and release the grantee from the obligation to maintain insurance. Upon receiving the grantee's request, BIA will:

(a) Confirm with the tribe, for tribal land or, where feasible, with the Indian landowners for individually owned Indian land, that the grantee has complied with all applicable grant obligations; and

(b) Release all or part of the bond or alternative form of security to the grantee, unless we determine that the bond or security must be redeemed to fulfill the contractual obligations.

§ 169.105 What requirements for due diligence must a right-of-way grant include?

(a) If permanent improvements are to be constructed, the right-of-way grant must include due diligence requirements that require the grantee to complete construction of any permanent improvements within the schedule specified in the right-of-way grant or general schedule of construction, and a process for changing the schedule by mutual consent of the parties. If construction does not occur, or is not expected to be completed, within the time period specified in the grant, the grantee must provide the Indian landowners and BIA with an explanation of good cause as to the nature of any delay, the anticipated date of construction of facilities, and evidence of progress toward commencement of construction.

(b) Failure of the grantee to comply with the due diligence requirements of the grant is a violation of the grant and may lead to cancellation of the right-of-way under § 169.405 or § 169.408.

(c) BIA may waive the requirements in this section if we determine, in writing, that a waiver is in the best interest of the Indian landowners.

CONSENT REQUIREMENTS

§ 169.106 How does an applicant identify and contact individual Indian landowners to negotiate a right-of-way?

(a) Applicants may submit a written request to us to obtain the following information. The request must specify that it is for the purpose of negotiating a right-of-way:

(1) Names and addresses of the individual Indian landowners or their representatives;

(2) Information on the location of the parcel; and

(3) The percentage of undivided interest owned by each individual Indian landowner.

(b) We may assist applicants in contacting the individual Indian landowners or their representatives for the purpose of negotiating a right-of-way, upon request.

(c) We will attempt to assist individual Indian landowners in right-of-way negotiations, upon their request.

§ 169.107 Must I obtain tribal or individual Indian landowner consent for a right-of-way across Indian land?

(a) For a right-of-way across tribal land, the applicant must obtain tribal consent, in the form of a tribal authorization and a written agreement with the tribe, if the tribe so requires, to a grant of right-of-way across tribal land. The consent document may impose restrictions or conditions; any restrictions or conditions automatically become conditions and restrictions in the grant.

(b) For a right-of-way across individually owned Indian land, the applicant must notify all individual Indian landowners and, except as provided in paragraph (b)(1) of this section, must obtain written consent from the owners of the majority interest in each tract affected by the grant of right-of-way.

(1) We may issue the grant of right-of-way without the consent of any of the individual Indian owners if all of the following conditions are met:

(i) The owners of interests in the land are so numerous that it would be impracticable to obtain consent as defined in paragraph (c) of this section;

(ii) We determine the grant will cause no substantial injury to the land or any landowner, based on factors including, but not limited to, the reasonableness of the term of the grant, the amount of acreage involved in the grant, the disturbance to land that will result from the grant, the type of activity to be conducted under the grant, the potential for environmental or safety impacts resulting from the grant, and any objections raised by landowners;

(iii) We determine that all of the landowners will be adequately compensated for consideration and any damages that may arise from a grant of right-of-way; and

(iv) We provide notice of our intent to issue the grant of right-of-way to all of the owners at least 60 days prior to the date of the grant using the procedures in § 169.12, and provide landowners with 30 days to object.

(2) For the purposes of this section, the owners of interests in the land are so numerous that it would be impracticable to obtain consent, if there are 50 or more co-owners of undivided trust or restricted interests.

(3) Successors are bound by consent granted by their predecessors-in-interest.

(c) We will determine the number of owners of, and undivided interests in, a fractionated tract of Indian land, for the purposes of calculating the requisite consent based on our records on the date on which the application is submitted to us.

§ 169.108 Who is authorized to consent to a right-of-way?

(a) Indian tribes, adult Indian landowners, and emancipated minors, may consent to a right-of-way over or across their land, including undivided interests in fractionated tracts.

(b) The following individuals or entities may consent on behalf of an individual Indian landowner:

(1) An adult with legal custody acting on behalf of his or her minor children;

(2) A guardian, conservator, or other fiduciary appointed by a court of competent jurisdiction to act on behalf of an individual Indian landowner;

(3) Any person who is authorized to practice before the Department of the Interior under 43 CFR 1.3(b) and has been retained by the Indian landowner for this purpose;

(4) BIA, under the circumstances in paragraph (c) of this section; or

(5) An adult or legal entity who has been given a written power of attorney that:

(i) Meets all of the formal requirements of any applicable law under § 169.9;

(ii) Identifies the attorney-in-fact; and

(iii) Describes the scope of the powers granted, to include granting rights-of-way on land or generally conveying or encumbering interests in Indian land, and any limits on those powers.

(c) BIA may give written consent to a right-of-way on behalf of an individual Indian landowner, as long as we determine that the grant will cause no substantial injury to the land or any landowner, based on factors including, but not limited to, the amount of acreage involved in the grant, the disturbance to land that will result from the grant, the type of activity to be conducted under the grant, the potential for environmental or safety impacts resulting from the grant, and any objections raised by landowners. BIA's consent must be counted in the majority interest under § 169.107, on behalf of:

(1) An individual Indian landowner, if the owner is deceased, and the heirs to, or devisees of, the interest of the deceased owner have not been determined;

(2) An individual Indian landowner whose whereabouts are unknown to us, after we make a reasonable attempt to locate the individual;

(3) An individual Indian landowner who is found to be non compos mentis or determined to be an adult in need of assistance who does not have a guardian duly appointed by a court of competent jurisdiction, or an individual under legal disability as defined in part 115 of this chapter;

(4) An individual Indian landowner who is an orphaned minor and who does not have a guardian duly appointed by a court of competent jurisdiction; and

(5) An individual Indian landowner who has given us a written power of attorney to consent to a right-of-way over or across their land.

§ 169.109 Whose consent do I need for a right-of-way when there is a life estate on the tract?

If there is a life estate on the tract that would be subject to the right-of-way, the applicant must get the consent of both the life tenant and the owners of the majority of the remainder interest known at the time of the application.

COMPENSATION REQUIREMENTS

§ 169.110 How much monetary compensation must be paid for a right-of-way over or across tribal land?

(a) A right-of-way over or across tribal land may allow for any payment amount negotiated by the tribe, and we will defer to the tribe and not require a valuation if the tribe submits a tribal authorization expressly stating that it:

(1) Has agreed upon compensation satisfactory to the tribe;

(2) Waives valuation; and

(3) Has determined that accepting such agreed-upon compensation and waiving valuation is in its best interest.

(b) The tribe may request, in writing, that we determine fair market value, in which case we will use a valuation in accordance with § 169.114. After providing the tribe with the fair market value, we will defer to a tribe's decision to allow for any compensation negotiated by the tribe.

(c) If the conditions in paragraph (a) or (b) of this section are not met, we will require that the grantee pay fair market value based on a valuation in accordance with § 169.114.

§ 169.111 Must a right-of-way grant for tribal land provide for compensation reviews or adjustments?

For a right-of-way grant over or across tribal land, no periodic review of the adequacy of compensation or adjustment is required, unless the tribe negotiates for reviews or adjustments.

§ 169.112 How much monetary compensation must be paid for a right-of-way over or across individually owned Indian land?

(a) A right-of-way over or across individually owned Indian land must require compensation of not less than fair market value, unless paragraph (b) or (c) of this section permit a lesser amount. Compensation may also include additional fees, including but not limited to throughput fees, severance damages, franchise fees, avoidance value, bonuses, or other factors. Compensation may be based on a fixed amount, a percentage of the projected income, or some other method. The grant must establish how the fixed amount, percentage, or combination will be calculated and the frequency at which the payments will be made.

(b) We may approve a right-of-way over or across individually owned Indian land that provides for nominal compensation, or compensation less than a fair market value, if:

(1) The grantee is a utility cooperative and is providing a direct benefit to the Indian land; or

(2) The grantee is a tribal utility; or

(3) The individual Indian landowners execute a written waiver of the right to receive fair market value and we determine it is in the individual Indian landowners' best interest, based on factors including, but not limited to:

(i) The grantee is a member of the immediate family, as defined in § 169.2, of an individual Indian landowner;

(ii) The grantee is a co-owner in the affected tract;

(iii) A special relationship or circumstances exist that we believe warrant approval of the right-of-way; or

(iv) We have waived the requirement for a valuation under paragraph (d) of this section.

(c) We will require a valuation to determine fair market value, unless:

(1) 100 percent of the individual Indian landowners submit to us a written request to waive the valuation requirement; or

(2) We waive the requirement under paragraph (d) of this section.

(d) The grant must provide that the non-consenting individual Indian landowners, and those on whose behalf we have consented under § 169.108(c), or granted the right-of-way without consent under § 169.107(b), receive fair market value, as determined by a valuation, unless:

(1) The grantee is a utility cooperative and is providing a direct benefit to the Indian land; or

(2) The grantee is a tribal utility; or

(3) We waive the requirement because the tribe or grantee will construct infrastructure improvements benefitting the individual Indian landowners, and we determine in writing that the waiver is in the best interest of all the landowners.

§ 169.113 Must a right-of-way grant for individually owned Indian land provide for compensation reviews or adjustments?

(a) For a right-of-way grant of individually owned Indian land, a review of the adequacy of compensation must occur at least every fifth year, in the manner specified in the grant unless:

(1) Payment is a one-time lump sum;

(2) The term of the right-of-way grant is 5 years or less;

(3) The grant provides for automatic adjustments; or

(4) We determine it is in the best interest of the Indian landowners not to require a review or automatic adjustment based on circumstances including, but not limited to, the following:

(i) The right-of-way grant provides for payment of less than fair market value;

(ii) The right-of-way grant provides for most or all of the compensation to be paid during the first 5 years of the grant term or before the date the review would be conducted; or

(iii) The right-of-way grant provides for graduated rent or non-monetary or varying types of compensation.

(b) The grant must specify:

(1) When adjustments take effect;

(2) Who can make adjustments;

(3) What the adjustments are based on; and

(4) How to resolve disputes arising from the adjustments.

(c) When a review results in the need for adjustment of compensation, the Indian landowners must consent to the adjustment in accordance with § 169.107, unless the grant provides otherwise.

§ 169.114 How will BIA determine fair market value for a right-of-way?

(a) We will use a market analysis, appraisal, or other appropriate valuation method to determine the fair market value before we grant a right-of-way over or across individually owned Indian land. We will also use a market analysis, appraisal, or other appropriate valuation method to determine, at the request of the tribe, the fair market value of tribal land.

(b) We will either:

(1) Prepare, or have prepared, a market analysis, appraisal, or other appropriate valuation method; or

(2) Approve use of a market analysis, appraisal, or other appropriate valuation method from the Indian landowners or grantee.

(c) We will use or approve use of a market analysis, appraisal, or other appropriate valuation method only if it:

(1) Has been prepared in accordance with USPAP or a valuation method developed by the Secretary under 25 U.S.C. 2214 and complies with Departmental policies regarding appraisals, including third-party appraisals; or

(2) Has been prepared by another Federal agency.

§ 169.115 When are monetary compensation payments due under a right-of-way?

Compensation for a right-of-way may be a one-time, lump sum payment, or may be paid in increments (for example, annually).

(a) If compensation is a one-time, lump sum payment, the grantee must make the payment by the date we grant the right-of-way, unless stated otherwise in the grant.

(b) If compensation is to be paid in increments, the right-of-way grant must specify the dates on which all payments are due. Payments are due at the time specified in the grant, regardless of whether the grantee receives an advance billing or other notice that a payment is due. Increments may not be more frequent than quarterly if payments are made to us on the Indian landowners' behalf.

§ 169.116 Must a right-of-way specify who receives monetary compensation payments?

(a) A right-of-way grant must specify whether the grantee will make payments directly to the Indian landowners (direct pay) or to us on their behalf.

(b) The grantee may make payments directly to the tribe if the tribe so chooses. The grantee may make payments directly to the Indian landowners if:

(1) The Indian landowners' trust accounts are unencumbered accounts;

(2) There are 10 or fewer beneficial owners; and

(3) One hundred percent of the beneficial owners (including those on whose

behalf we have consented) agree to receive payment directly from the grantee at the start of the right-of-way.

(c) If the right-of-way document provides that the grantee will directly pay the Indian landowners, then:

(1) The right-of-way document must include provisions for proof of payment upon our request.

(2) When we consent on behalf of an Indian landowner, the grantee must make payment to us on behalf of that landowner.

(3) The grantee must send direct payments to the parties and addresses specified in the right-of-way, unless the grantee receives notice of a change of ownership or address.

(4) Unless the right-of-way document provides otherwise, payments may not be made payable directly to anyone other than the Indian landowners.

(5) Direct payments must continue through the duration of the right-of-way, except that:

(i) The grantee must make all Indian landowners' payments to us if 100 percent of the Indian landowners agree to suspend direct pay and provide us with documentation of their agreement; and

(ii) The grantee must make an individual Indian landowner's payment to us if that individual Indian landowner dies, is declared non compos mentis, owes a debt resulting in an encumbered account, or his or her whereabouts become unknown.

§ 169.117 What form of monetary compensation is acceptable under a right-of-way?

(a) If payments are made to us on behalf of the Indian landowners, our preferred method of payment is electronic funds transfer payments. We will also accept:

(1) Money orders;

(2) Personal checks;

(3) Certified checks; or

(4) Cashier's checks.

(b) We will not accept cash or foreign currency.

(c) We will accept third-party checks only from financial institutions or Federal agencies.

(d) The grant of right-of-way will specify the payment method if payments are made by direct pay.

§ 169.118 May the right-of-way provide for non-monetary or varying types of compensation?

(a) A right-of-way grant may provide for alternative forms of compensation and varying types of compensation, subject to the conditions in paragraphs (b) and (c) of this section:

(1) Alternative forms of compensation may include but are not limited to, in-kind consideration and payments based on throughput or percentage of income; or

(2) Varying types of compensation may include but are not limited to different types of payments at specific stages during the life of the right-of-way grant, such as fixed annual payments during construction, payments based on income during an operational period, and bonuses.

(b) For tribal land, we will defer to the tribe's determination that the compensation under paragraph (a) of this section is in its best interest, if the tribe submits a signed certification or tribal authorization stating that it has determined the alternative form of compensation or varying type of compensation to be in its best interest.

(c) For individually owned land, we may grant a right-of-way that provides for an alternative form of compensation or varying type of compensation if we determine that it is in the best interest of the Indian landowners.

§ 169.119 Will BIA notify a grantee when a payment is due for a right-of-way?

Upon request of the Indian landowners, we may issue invoices to a grantee in advance of the dates on which payments are due under the right-of-way. The grantee's obligation to make these payments in a timely manner will not be excused if invoices are not issued, delivered, or received.

§ 169.120 What other types of payments are required for a right-of-way?

(a) The grantee may be required to pay additional fees, taxes, and assessments associated with the application for use of the land or use of the land, as determined by entities having jurisdiction, except as provided in § 169.11. The grantee must pay these amounts to the appropriate office, as applicable.

(b) In addition to, or as part of, the compensation for a right-of-way under §§ 169.110 and 169.112 and the payments provided for in paragraph (a) of this section, the applicant for a right-of-way will be required to pay for all damages to the land, such as those incident to the construction or maintenance of the facility for which the right-of-way is granted.

§ 169.121 How will compensation be distributed among the life tenants and owners of the remainder interests?

If a will created the life estate and specifies how the compensation will be distributed among the life tenants and owners of the remainder interests, those terms will establish the distribution. Otherwise:

(a) The owners of the remainder interests and the life tenant may enter into a right-of-way or other written agreement approved by the Secretary providing for the distribution of rent monies under the right-of-way; or

(b) If the owners of the remainder interests and life tenant did not enter into an agreement for distribution, the life tenant will receive payment in accordance with the distribution and calculation scheme set forth in part 179 of this chapter.

§ 169.122 Who does the grantee pay if there is a life estate on the tract?

The grantee must pay compensation directly to the life tenant under the terms of the right-of-way unless the whereabouts of the life tenant are unknown, in which case we may collect compensation on behalf of the life tenant.

Grants of Rights-of-Way

§ 169.123 What is the process for BIA to grant a right-of-way?

(a) Before we grant a right-of-way, we must determine that the right-of-way is in the best interest of the Indian landowners. In making that determination, we will:

(1) Review the right-of-way application and supporting documents;

(2) Identify potential environmental impacts and adverse impacts, and ensure compliance with all applicable Federal environmental, land use, historic preservation, and cultural resource laws and ordinances; and

(3) Require any modifications or mitigation measures necessary to satisfy any requirements including any other Federal or tribal land use requirements.

(b) Upon receiving a right-of-way application, we will promptly notify the applicant whether the package is complete. A complete package includes all of the information and supporting documents required under this subpart, including but not limited to, an accurate legal description for each affected tract, documentation of landowner consent, NEPA review documentation and valuation documentation, where applicable.

(1) If the right-of-way application package is not complete, our letter will identify the missing information or documents required for a complete package. If we do not respond to the submission of an application package, the parties may take action under § 169.304.

(2) If the right-of-way application package is complete, we will notify the applicant of the date of our receipt of the complete package. Within 60 days of our receipt of a complete package, we will grant or deny the right-of-way, return the package for revision, or inform the applicant in writing that we need additional review time. If we inform the applicant in writing that we need additional time, then:

(i) Our letter informing the applicant that we need additional review time must identify our initial concerns and invite the applicant to respond within 15 days of the date of the letter; and

(ii) We will issue a written determination granting or denying the right-of-way within 30 days from sending the letter informing the applicant that we need additional time.

(c) If we do not meet the deadlines in this section, then the applicant may take appropriate action under § 169.304.

(d) We will provide any right-of-way denial and the basis for the determination, along with notification of any appeal rights under part 2 of this chapter to the parties to the right-of-way. If the right-of-way is granted, we will provide a copy of the right-of-way to the tribal landowner and, upon written request, make copies available to the individual Indian landowners, and provide notice under § 169.12.

§ 169.124 How will BIA determine whether to grant a right-of-way?

Our decision to grant or deny a right-of-way will be in writing.

(a) We will grant a right-of-way unless:

(1) The requirements of this subpart have not been met, such as if the required landowner consent has not been obtained under § 169.107; or

(2) We find a compelling reason to withhold the grant in order to protect the best interests of the Indian landowners.

(b) We will defer, to the maximum extent possible, to the Indian landowners' determination that the right-of-way is in their best interest.

(c) We may not unreasonably withhold our grant of a right-of-way.

(d) We may grant one right-of-way for all of the tracts traversed by the right-of-way, or we may issue separate grants for one or more tracts traversed by the right-of-way.

§ 169.125 What will the grant of right-of-way contain?

(a) The grant will incorporate the conditions or restrictions set out in the Indian landowners' consents.

(b) The grant will address:

(1) The use(s) the grant is authorizing;

(2) Whether assignment of the right-of-way is permitted and, if so, whether additional consent is required for the assignment and whether any additional compensation is owed to the landowners;

(3) Whether mortgaging of the right-of-way is permitted and, if so, whether additional consent is required for the mortgage and whether any additional compensation is owed to the landowners; and

(4) Ownership of permanent improvements under § 169.130.

(c) The grant will state that:

(1) The tribe maintains its existing jurisdiction over the land, activities, and persons within the right-of-way under § 169.10 and reserves the right of the tribe to reasonable access to the lands subject to the grant to determine grantee's compliance with consent conditions or to protect public health and safety;

(2) The grantee has no right to any of the products or resources of the land, including but not limited to, timber, forage, mineral, and animal resources, unless otherwise provided for in the grant;

(3) BIA may treat any provision of a grant that violates Federal law as a violation of the grant; and

(4) If historic properties, archeological resources, human remains, or other cultural items not previously reported are encountered during the course of any activity associated with this grant, all activity in the immediate vicinity of the properties, resources, remains, or items will cease and the grantee will contact BIA and the tribe with jurisdiction over the land to determine how to proceed and appropriate disposition.

(5) The grantee must:

(i) Construct and maintain improvements within the right-of-way in a professional manner consistent with industry standards;

(ii) Pay promptly all damages and compensation, in addition to bond or alternative form of security made pursuant to § 169.103, determined by the BIA to be due the landowners and authorized users and occupants of land as a result of the granting, construction, and maintenance of the right-of-way;

(iii) Restore the land as nearly as may be possible to its original condition, upon the completion of construction, to the extent compatible with the purpose for which the right-of-way was granted, or reclaim the land if agreed to by the landowners;

(iv) Clear and keep clear the land within the right-of-way, to the extent compatible with the purpose of the right-of-way, and dispose of all vegetative and other material cut, uprooted, or otherwise accumulated during the construction and maintenance of the project;

(v) Comply with all applicable laws and obtain all required permits;

(vi) Not commit waste;

(vii) Operate, repair and maintain improvements consistent with the right-of-way grant;

(viii) Build and maintain necessary and suitable crossings for all roads and trails that intersect the improvements constructed, maintained, or operated under the right-of-way;

(ix) Restore the land to its original condition, to the maximum extent reasonably possible, upon cancellation or termination of the right-of-way, or reclaim the land if agreed to by the landowners;

(x) At all times keep the BIA, and the tribe for tribal land, informed of the grantee's address;

(xi) Refrain from interfering with the landowner's use of the land, provided that the landowner's use of the land is not inconsistent with the right-of-way;

(xii) Comply with due diligence requirements under §169.105; and

(xiii) Notify the BIA, and the tribe for tribal land, if it files for bankruptcy or is placed in receivership.

(6) Unless the grantee would be prohibited by law from doing so, the grantee must also:

(i) Hold the United States and the Indian landowners harmless from any loss, liability, or damages resulting from the applicant's use or occupation of the premises; and

(ii) Indemnify the United States and the Indian landowners against all liabilities or costs relating to the use, handling, treatment, removal, storage, transportation, or disposal of hazardous materials, or release or discharge of any hazardous material from the premises that occurs during the term of the grant, regardless of fault, with the exception that the applicant is not required to indemnify the Indian landowners for liability or cost arising from the Indian landowners' negligence or willful misconduct.

(d) The grant must attach or include by reference maps of definite location.

§169.126 May a right-of-way contain a preference consistent with tribal law for employment of tribal members?

A grant of right-of-way over or across Indian land may include a provision, consistent with tribal law, requiring the grantee to give a preference to qualified tribal members, based on their political affiliation with the tribe.

§169.127 Is a new right-of-way grant required for a new use within or overlapping an existing right-of-way?

(a) If you are the grantee, you may use all or a portion of an existing right-of-way for a use not specified in the original grant of the existing right-of-way only if it is within the same scope of the use specified in the original grant of the existing right-of-way.

(1) If you propose to use all or a portion of an existing right-of-way for a use not specified in the original grant of the existing right-of-way and not within the same scope of the use specified in the original grant of the existing right-of-way, and the new use will not require any ground disturbance, you must request an amendment to the existing right-of-way grant.

(2) If you propose to use all or a portion of an existing right-of-way for a use not specified in the original grant of the existing right-of-way and not within the same scope of the use specified in the original grant of the existing right-of-way, and the new use requires ground disturbance, you must request a new right-of-way.

(b) If you are not the grantee:

(1) You may use all or a portion of an existing right-of-way for a use specified in the original grant of the existing right-of-way or a use within the same scope of the use specified in the original grant of the existing right-of-way if the grantee obtains an assignment to authorize the new user; or

(2) You may use all or a portion of an existing right-of-way for a use not specified in the original grant of the existing right-of-way and not within the same scope of use specified in the original grant of the existing right-of-way if you request a new right-of-way within or overlapping the existing right-of-way for the new use.

(c) An example of a use within the same scope is a right-of-way for underground telephone line being used for an underground fiber optic line, and an example of a use that is not within the same scope is a right-of-way for a pipeline being used for a road or railroad.

§ 169.128 When will BIA grant a right-of-way for a new use within or overlapping an existing right-of-way?

We may grant a new right-of-way within or overlapping an existing right-of-way if it meets the following conditions:

(a) The applicant follows the procedures and requirements in this part to obtain a new right-of-way.

(b) The new right-of-way does not interfere with the use or purpose of the existing right-of-way and the applicant has obtained the consent of the existing right-of-way grantee. The existing right-of-way grantee may not unreasonably withhold consent.

§ 169.129 What is required if the location described in the original application and grant differs from the construction location?

(a) If engineering or other complications prevented construction within the location identified in the original application and grant, and required a minor deviation from the location identified in the original application and grant, then we and the tribe, for tribal land, will determine whether the change in location requires one or more of the following:

(1) An amended map of definite location;

(2) Landowner consent;

(3) A valuation or, with landowner consent, a recalculation of compensation;

(4) Additional compensation or security; or

(5) Other actions required to comply with applicable laws.

(b) If BIA and the tribe, for tribal land, determine it is not a minor deviation in location, we may require a new right-of-way grant or amendment to the right-of-way grant.

(c) If we grant a right-of-way for the new route or location, the applicant must execute instruments to extinguish, or amend, as appropriate, the right-of-way at the original location identified in the application.

(d) We will transmit the instruments to extinguish or amend the right-of-way to the LTRO for recording.

§ 169.130 Must a right-of-way grant address ownership of permanent improvements?

(a) A right-of-way grant must specify who will own any permanent improvements the grantee constructs during the grant term and may specify under what conditions, if any, permanent improvements the grantee constructs may be conveyed to the Indian landowners during the grant term. In addition, the grant may indicate whether each specific permanent improvement the grantee constructs will:

(1) Remain on the premises, upon the expiration, cancellation, or termination of the grant, in a condition satisfactory to the Indian landowners, and become the property of the Indian landowners;

(2) Be removed within a time period specified in the grant, at the grantee's expense, with the premises to be restored as closely as possible to their condition before construction of the permanent improvements; or

(3) Be disposed of by other specified means.

(b) A grant that requires the grantee to remove the permanent improvements must also provide the Indian landowners with an option to take possession of and title to the permanent improvements if the improvements are not removed within the specified time period.

Subpart D—Duration, Renewals, Amendments, Assignments, Mortgages

DURATION & RENEWALS

§ 169.201 How long may the duration of a right-of-way grant be?

(a) All rights-of-way granted under this part are limited to the time periods stated in the grant.

(b) For tribal land, we will defer to the tribe's determination that the right-of-way term is reasonable.

(c) For individually owned Indian land, we will review the right-of-way duration to ensure that it is reasonable, given the purpose of the right-of-way. We will generally consider a maximum duration of 20 years to be reasonable for the initial term for rights-of-way for oil and gas purposes and a maximum of 50 years, inclusive of the initial term and any renewals, to be reasonable for rights-of-way for all other purposes. We will consider a duration consistent with use to be reasonable for rights-of-way for conservation easements. We will consider durations different from these guidelines if a different duration would benefit the Indian landowners, is required by another Federal agency, or the tribe has negotiated for a different duration and the right-of-way crosses tribal land.

§ 169.202 Under what circumstances will a grant of right-of-way be renewed?

A renewal is an extension of term of an existing right-of-way without any other change.

(a) The grantee may request a renewal of an existing right-of-way grant and we will renew the grant as long as:

(1) The initial term and renewal terms, together, do not exceed the maximum term determined to be reasonable under § 169.201;

(2) The existing right-of-way grant explicitly allows for automatic renewal or an option to renew and specifies compensation owed to the landowners upon renewal or how compensation will be determined;

(3) The grantee provides us with a signed affidavit that there is no change in size, type, or location, of the right-of-way;

(4) The initial term has not yet ended;

(5) No uncured violation exists regarding the regulations in this part or the grant's conditions or restrictions; and

(6) The grantee provides confirmation that landowner consent has been obtained, or if consent is not required because the original right-of-way grant explicitly allows for renewal without the owners' consent, the grantee provides notice to the landowners of the renewal.

(b) We will record any renewal of a right-of-way grant in the LTRO.

(c) If the proposed renewal involves any change to the original grant or the original grant was silent as to renewals, the grantee must reapply for a new right-of-way, in accordance with § 169.101, and we will handle the application for renewal as an original application for a right-of-way.

§ 169.203 May a right-of-way be renewed multiple times?

There is no prohibition on renewing a right-of-way multiple times, unless the grant expressly prohibits multiple renewals, and subject to the duration limitations for individually owned land in § 169.201. The provisions of § 169.202 apply to each renewal.

AMENDMENTS

§ 169.204 May a grantee amend a right-of-way?

(a) An amendment is required to change any provisions of a right-of-way grant. If the change is a material change to the grant, we may require application for a new right-of-way instead.

(b) A grantee may request that we amend a right-of-way to make an administrative modification (*i.e.*, a modification that is clerical in nature, for example to correct the legal description) without meeting consent requirements, as long as the grantee provides landowners with written notice. For all other amendments, the grantee must meet the consent requirements in § 169.107 and obtain our approval.

§ 169.205 What is the approval process for an amendment of a right-of-way?

(a) When we receive an amendment for our approval, we will notify the grantee of the date we receive it. We have 30 days from receipt of the executed amendment, proof of required consents, and required documentation (including but not limited to a corrected legal description, if any, and NEPA compliance) to approve or disapprove the amendment. Our determination whether to approve the amendment will be in writing and will state the basis for our approval or disapproval.

(b) If we need additional time to review, our letter informing the parties that we need additional time for review must identify our initial concerns and invite the parties to respond within 15 days of the date of the letter. We have 30 days from sending the letter informing the parties that we need additional time to approve or disapprove the amendment.

(c) If we do not meet the deadline in paragraph (a) of this section, or paragraph (b) of this section if applicable, the grantee or Indian landowners may take appropriate action under § 169.304.

§ 169.206 How will BIA decide whether to approve an amendment of a right-of-way?

(a) We may disapprove a request for an amendment of a right-of-way only if at least one of the following is true:

(1) The Indian landowners have not consented to the amendment under § 169.107 and we have not consented on their behalf under § 169.108;

(2) The grantee's sureties for the bonds or alternative securities have not consented;

(3) The grantee is in violation of the right-of-way grant;

(4) The requirements of this subpart have not been met; or

(5) We find a compelling reason to withhold approval in order to protect the best interests of the Indian landowners.

(b) We will defer, to the maximum extent possible, to the Indian landowners' determination that the amendment is in their best interest.

(c) We may not unreasonably withhold approval of an amendment.

ASSIGNMENTS

§ 169.207 May a grantee assign a right-of-way?

(a) A grantee may assign a right-of-way by:

(1) Meeting the consent requirements in § 169.107, unless the grant expressly allows for assignments without further consent; and

(2) Either obtaining our approval, or meeting the conditions in paragraph (b) of this section.

(b) A grantee may assign a right-of-way without BIA approval only if:

(1) The original right-of-way grant expressly allows for assignment without BIA approval; and

(2) The assignee and grantee provide a copy of the assignment and supporting documentation to BIA for recording in the LTRO within 30 days of the assignment.

(c) Assignments that are the result of a corporate merger, acquisition, or transfer by operation of law are excluded from these requirements, except for the requirement to provide a copy of the assignment and supporting documentation to BIA for recording in the LTRO within 30 days and to the tribe for tribal land.

§ 169.208 What is the approval process for an assignment of a right-of-way?

(a) When we receive an assignment for our approval, we will notify the grantee of the date we receive it. If our approval is required, we have 30 days from receipt of the executed assignment, proof of any required consents, and any required documentation to approve or disapprove the assignment. Our determination whether to approve the assignment will be in writing and will state the basis for our approval or disapproval.

(b) If we do not meet the deadline in this section, the grantee or Indian landowners may take appropriate action under § 169.304.

§ 169.209 How will BIA decide whether to approve an assignment of a right-of-way?

(a) We may disapprove an assignment of a right-of-way only if at least one of the following is true:

(1) The Indian landowners have not consented to the assignment under § 169.107 and their consent is required;

(2) Sufficient bonding and/or insurance are not in place;

(3) The grantee is in violation of the right-of-way grant;

(4) The assignee does not agree to be bound by the terms of the right-of-way grant;

(5) The requirements of this subpart have not been met; or

(6) We find a compelling reason to withhold approval in order to protect the best interests of the Indian landowners.

(b) We will defer, to the maximum extent possible, to the Indian landowners' determination that the assignment is in their best interest.

(c) We may not unreasonably withhold approval of an assignment.

MORTGAGES

§ 169.210 May a grantee mortgage a right-of-way?

A grantee may mortgage a right-of-way, if the grant expressly allows mortgaging. The grantee must meet the consent requirements in § 169.107, unless the grant expressly allows for mortgaging without consent, and must obtain our approval for the mortgage.

§ 169.211 What is the approval process for a mortgage of a right-of-way?

(a) When we receive a right-of-way mortgage for our approval, we will notify the grantee of the date we receive it. We have 30 days from receipt of the executed mortgage, proof of required consents, and required documentation to approve or disapprove the mortgage. Our determination whether to approve the mortgage will be in writing and will state the basis for our approval or disapproval.

(b) If we do not meet the deadline in this section, the grantee or Indian landowners may take appropriate action under § 169.304.

§ 169.212 How will BIA decide whether to approve a mortgage of a right-of-way?

(a) We may disapprove a right-of-way mortgage only if at least one of the following is true:

(1) The Indian landowners have not consented;

(2) The grantee's sureties for the bonds have not consented;

(3) The requirements of this subpart have not been met; or

(4) We find a compelling reason to withhold approval in order to protect the best interests of the Indian landowners.

(b) In making the finding required by paragraph (a)(4) of this section, we may consider whether:

(1) The mortgage proceeds would be used for purposes unrelated to the right-of-way purpose; and

(2) The mortgage is limited to the right-of-way.

(c) We will defer, to the maximum extent possible, to the Indian landowners' determination that the mortgage is in their best interest.

(d) We may not unreasonably withhold approval of a right-of-way mortgage.

Subpart E—Effectiveness

§ 169.301 When will a right-of-way document be effective?

(a) A right-of-way document will be effective on the date we approve the right-of-way document, even if an appeal is filed under part 2 of this chapter.

(b) The right-of-way document may specify a date on which the grantee's obligations are triggered. Such date may be before or after the approval date under paragraph (a) of this section.

§ 169.302 Must a right-of-way be recorded?

(a) Any right-of-way document must be recorded in our LTRO with jurisdiction over the affected Indian land.

(1) We will record the right-of-way document immediately following our approval or granting.

(2) In the case of assignments that do not require our approval under § 169.207(b), the parties must provide us with a copy of the assignment and we will record the assignment in the LTRO with jurisdiction over the affected Indian land.

(b) The tribe must record right-of-way documents for the following types of rights-of-way in the LTRO with jurisdiction over the affected Indian lands, even though BIA approval is not required:

(1) Grants on tribal land for a tribal utility under § 169.4;

(2) Grants on tribal land under a special act of Congress authorizing grants without our approval under certain conditions.

§ 169.303 What happens if BIA denies a right-of-way document?

If we deny the right-of-way grant, renewal, amendment, assignment, or mortgage, we will notify the parties immediately and advise the landowners and the applicant of their right to appeal the decision under part 2 of this chapter.

§ 169.304 What happens if BIA does not meet a deadline for issuing a decision on a right-of-way document?

(a) If a Superintendent does not meet a deadline for granting or denying a right-of-way, renewal, amendment, assignment, or mortgage, the parties may file a written notice to compel action with the appropriate Regional Director.

(b) The Regional Director has 15 days from receiving the notice to:

(1) Grant or deny the right-of-way; or

(2) Order the Superintendent to grant or deny the right-of-way within the time set out in the order.

(c) Either party may file a written notice to compel action with the BIA Director if:

(1) The Regional Director does not meet the deadline in paragraph (b) of this section;

(2) The Superintendent does not grant or deny the right-of-way within the time set by the Regional Director under paragraph (b)(2) of this section; or

(3) The initial decision on the right-of-way, renewal, amendment, assignment, or mortgage is with the Regional Director, and he or she does not meet the deadline for such decision.

(d) The BIA Director has 15 days from receiving the notice to:

(1) Grant or deny the right-of-way; or

(2) Order the Regional Director or Superintendent to grant or deny the right-of-way within the time set out in the order.

(e) If the Regional Director or Superintendent does not grant or deny the right-of-way within the time set out in the order under paragraph (d)(2) of this section, then the BIA Director must issue a decision within 15 days from the expiration of the time set out in the order.

(f) The parties may file an appeal from our inaction to the Interior Board of Indian Appeals if the BIA Director does not meet the deadline in paragraph (d) or (e) of this section.

(g) The provisions of 25 CFR 2.8 do not apply to the inaction of BIA officials with respect to a granting or denying a right-of-way, renewal, amendment, assignment, or mortgage under this subpart.

§ 169.305 Will BIA require an appeal bond for an appeal of a decision on a right-of-way document?

(a) If a party appeals our decision on a right-of-way document, then the official to whom the appeal is made may require the appellant to post an appeal bond in accordance with part 2 of this chapter. We will not require an appeal bond if the tribe is a party to the appeal and requests a waiver of the appeal bond.

(b) The appellant may not appeal the appeal bond decision. The appellant may, however, request that the official to whom the appeal is made reconsider the bond decision, based on extraordinary circumstances. Any reconsideration decision is final for the Department.

Subpart F—Compliance and Enforcement

§ 169.401 What is the purpose and scope of this subpart?

This subpart describes the procedures we use to address compliance and enforcement related to rights-of-way on Indian land. Any abandonment, non-use, or violation of the right-of-way grant or right-of-way document, including but not limited to encroachments beyond the defined boundaries, accidental, willful, and/or incidental trespass, unauthorized new construction, changes in use not permitted in the grant, and late or insufficient payment may result in enforcement actions including, but not limited to, cancellation of the grant.

§ 169.402 Who may investigate compliance with a right-of-way?

(a) BIA may investigate compliance with a right-of-way.

(1) If an Indian landowner notifies us that a specific abandonment, non-use, or violation has occurred, we will promptly initiate an appropriate investigation.

(2) We may enter the Indian land subject to a right-of-way at any reasonable time, upon reasonable notice, and consistent with any notice requirements under applicable tribal law and applicable grant documents, to protect the interests of the Indian landowners and to determine if the grantee is in

compliance with the requirements of the right-of-way.

(b) The tribe with jurisdiction may investigate compliance consistent with tribal law.

§ 169.403 May a right-of-way provide for negotiated remedies?

(a) The tribe and the grantee on tribal land may negotiate remedies for a violation, abandonment, or non-use. The negotiated remedies must be stated in the tribe's consent to the right-of-way grant, which BIA will then incorporate into the grant itself. The negotiated remedies may include, but are not limited to, the power to terminate the right-of-way grant. If the negotiated remedies provide one or both parties with the power to terminate the grant:

(1) BIA approval of the termination is not required;

(2) The termination is effective without BIA cancellation; and

(3) The tribe must provide us with written notice of the termination so that we may record it in the LTRO.

(b) The Indian landowners and the grantee to a right-of-way grant on individually owned Indian land may negotiate remedies, so long as the consent also specifies the manner in which those remedies may be exercised by or on behalf of the Indian landowners of the majority interest under § 169.107. If the negotiated remedies provide one or both parties with the power to terminate the grant:

(1) BIA concurrence with the termination is required to ensure that the Indian landowners of the applicable percentage of interests have consented; and

(2) BIA will record the termination in the LTRO.

(c) The parties must notify any surety of any violation that may result in termination and the termination of a right-of-way.

(d) Negotiated remedies may apply in addition to, or instead of, the cancellation remedy available to us, as specified in the right-of-way grant. The landowners may request our assistance in enforcing negotiated remedies.

(e) A right-of-way grant may provide that violations will be addressed by a tribe, and that disputes will be resolved by a tribal court, any other court of competent jurisdiction, or by a tribal governing body in the absence of a tribal court, or through an alternative dispute resolution method. We may not be bound by decisions made in such forums, but we will defer to ongoing actions or proceedings, as appropriate, in deciding whether to exercise any of the remedies available to us.

§ 169.404 What will BIA do about a violation of a right-of-way grant?

(a) In the absence of actions or proceedings described in § 169.403 (negotiated remedies), or if it is not appropriate for us to defer to the actions or proceedings, we will follow the procedures in paragraphs (b) and (c) of this section. We will consult with the tribe for tribal land or, where feasible, communicate with Indian landowners for individually owned Indian land, and determine whether a violation has occurred.

(b) If we determine there has been a violation of the conditions of a grant, other than a violation of payment provisions covered by paragraph (c) of this section, we will promptly send the grantee a written notice of violation.

(1) We will send a copy of the notice of violation to the tribe for tribal land, or provide constructive notice to Indian landowners for individually owned Indian land.

(2) The notice of violation will advise the grantee that, within 10 business days of the receipt of a notice of violation, the grantee must:

(i) Cure the violation and notify us, and the tribe for tribal land, in writing that the violation has been cured;

(ii) Dispute our determination that a violation has occurred; or

(iii) Request additional time to cure the violation.

(3) The notice of violation may order the grantee to cease operations under the right-of-way grant.

(c) A grantee's failure to pay compensation in the time and manner required by a right-of-way grant is a violation, and we will issue a notice of violation in accordance with this paragraph.

(1) We will send the grantees a written notice of violation promptly following the date on which the payment was due.

(2) We will send a copy of the notice of violation to the tribe for tribal land, or provide constructive notice to the Indian landowners for individually owned Indian land.

(3) The notice of violation will require the grantee to provide adequate proof of payment.

(d) The grantee will continue to be responsible for the obligations in the grant until the grant expires, or is terminated or cancelled, as well as any reclamation or other obligations that survive the end of the grant.

§ 169.405 What will BIA do if the grantee does not cure a violation of a right-of-way grant on time?

(a) If the grantee does not cure a violation of a right-of-way grant within the required time period, or provide adequate proof of payment as required in the notice of violation, we will consult with the tribe for tribal land or, where feasible, communicate with Indian landowners for individually owned Indian land, and determine whether:

(1) We should cancel the grant;

(2) The Indian landowners wish to invoke any remedies available to them under the grant;

(3) We should invoke other remedies available under the grant or applicable law, including collection on any available bond or, for failure to pay compensation, referral of the debt to the Department of the Treasury for collection; or

(4) The grantee should be granted additional time in which to cure the violation.

(b) Following consultation with the tribe for tribal land or, where feasible, communication with Indian landowners for individually owned Indian land, we may take action to recover unpaid compensation and any associated late payment charges.

(1) We need not cancel the grant or give any further notice to the grantee before taking action to recover unpaid compensation.

(2) We may take action to recover any unpaid compensation even though we cancel the grant.

(c) If we decide to cancel the grant, we will send the grantee a cancellation letter by certified mail, return receipt requested, within 5 business days of our decision. We will send a copy of the cancellation letter to the tribe for tribal land, and will provide Indian landowners for individually owned Indian land with actual notice of the cancellation. The cancellation letter will:

(1) Explain the grounds for cancellation;

(2) If applicable, notify the grantee of the amount of any unpaid compensation or late payment charges due under the grant;

(3) Notify the grantee of the grantee's right to appeal under part 2 of this chapter, including the possibility that the official to whom the appeal is made may require the grantee to post an appeal bond;

(4) Order the grantee to vacate the property within the timeframe reflected in the termination terms of the grant, or within 31 days of the date of receipt of the cancellation letter, or within such longer period of time in extraordinary circumstances considering the protection of trust resources and the best interest of the Indian landowners, if an appeal is not filed by that time; and

(5) Order the grantee to take any other action BIA deems necessary to protect the Indian land.

(d) We may invoke any other remedies available to us under the grant, including collecting on any available bond, and the Indian landowners may pursue any available remedies under tribal law.

(e) We will issue an appropriate instrument cancelling the right-of-way and transmit it to the LTRO pursuant to 25 CFR part 150 for recording and filing.

§ 169.406 Will late payment charges, penalties, or special fees apply to delinquent payments due under a right-of-way grant?

(a) Late payment charges and penalties will apply as specified in the grant. The failure to pay these amounts will be treated as a violation.

(b) We may assess the following special fees to cover administrative costs incurred by the United States in the collection of the debt, if compensation is not paid in the time and manner required, in addition to the late payment charges that must be paid to the Indian landowners under the grant:

The grantee will pay . . .	For . . .
(1) $50.00	Any dishonored check.
(2) $15.00	Processing of each notice or demand letter.
(3) 18 percent of balance due	Treasury processing following referral for collection of delinquent debt.

§ 169.407 How will payment rights relating to a right-of-way grant be allocated?

The right-of-way grant may allocate rights to payment for any proceeds, trespass damages, condemnation awards, settlement funds, and other payments between the Indian landowners and the grantee. If not specified in the grant, applicable policy, order, award, judgment, or other document, the Indian landowners will be entitled to receive these payments.

§ 169.408 What is the process for cancelling a right-of-way for non-use or abandonment?

(a) We may cancel, in whole or in part, any rights-of-way granted under this part 30 days after mailing written notice to the grantee at its latest address, for a nonuse of the right-of-way for a consecutive 2-year period for the purpose for which it was granted. If the grantee fails to correct the basis for cancellation by the 30th day after we mailed the notice, we will issue an appropriate instrument cancelling the right-of-way and transmit it to the LTRO pursuant to part 150 of this chapter for recording and filing.

(b) We may cancel, in whole or in part, any rights-of-way granted under this part immediately upon abandonment of the right-of-way by the grantee. We will issue an appropriate instrument cancelling the right-of-way and transmit it to the LTRO pursuant to part 150 of this chapter for recording and filing.

(c) The cancellation notice will notify the grantee of the grantee's right to appeal under part 2 of this chapter, including the possibility of that the official to whom the appeal is made will require the grantee to post an appeal bond.

§ 169.409 When will a cancellation of a right-of-way grant be effective?

(a) A cancellation involving a right-of-way grant will not be effective until 31 days after the grantee receives a cancellation letter from us, or 41 days from the date we mailed the letter, whichever is earlier.

(b) The cancellation decision will not be effective if an appeal is filed unless the cancellation is made immediately effective under part 2 of this chapter. When a cancellation decision is not immediately effective, the grantee must continue to pay compensation and comply with the other terms of the grant.

§ 169.410 What will BIA do if a grantee remains in possession after a right-of-way expires or is terminated or cancelled?

If a grantee remains in possession after the expiration, termination, or cancellation of a right-of-way, and is not accessing the land to perform reclamation or other remaining grant obligations, we may treat the unauthorized possession as a trespass under applicable law and will communicate with the Indian landowners in making the determination whether to treat the unauthorized possession as a trespass. Unless the parties have notified us in writing that they are engaged in good faith negotiations to renew or obtain a new right-of-way, we may take action to recover possession on behalf of the Indian landowners, and pursue any additional remedies available under applicable law, such as a forcible entry and detainer action. The holdover time will be charged against the new term.

§ 169.411 Will BIA appeal bond regulations apply to cancellation decisions involving right-of-way grants?

(a) Except as provided in paragraph (b) of this section, the appeal bond provisions in part 2 of this chapter will govern appeals from right-of-way cancellation decisions.

(b) The grantee may not appeal the appeal bond decision. The grantee may, however, request that the official to whom the appeal is made reconsider the appeal bond decision, based on extraordinary circumstances. Any reconsideration decision is final for the Department.

§ 169.412 When will BIA issue a decision on an appeal from a right-of-way decision?

BIA will issue a decision on an appeal from a right-of-way decision within 60 days of receipt of all pleadings.

§ 169.413 What if an individual or entity takes possession of or uses Indian land or BIA land without a right-of-way or other proper authorization?

If an individual or entity takes possession of, or uses, Indian land or BIA land without a right-of-way and a right-of-way is required, the unauthorized possession or use is a trespass. An unauthorized use within an existing right-of-way is also a trespass. We may take action to recover possession, including eviction, on behalf of the Indian landowners and pursue any additional remedies available under applicable law. The Indian landowners may pursue any available remedies under applicable law, including applicable tribal law.

§ 169.414 May BIA take emergency action if Indian land is threatened?

(a) We may take appropriate emergency action if there is a natural disaster or if an individual or entity causes or threatens to cause immediate and significant harm to Indian land or BIA land. Emergency action may include judicial action seeking immediate cessation of the activity resulting in or threatening the harm.

(b) We will make reasonable efforts to notify the individual Indian landowners before and after taking emergency action on Indian land. In all cases, we will notify the Indian landowners after taking emergency action on Indian land. We will provide written notification of our action to the Indian tribe exercising jurisdiction over the Indian land before and after taking emergency action on Indian land.

§ 169.415 How will BIA conduct compliance and enforcement when there is a life estate on the tract?

(a) We may monitor the use of the land, as appropriate, and will enforce the terms of the right-of-way on behalf of the owners of the remainder interests, but will not be responsible for enforcing the right-of-way on behalf of the life tenant.

(b) The life tenant may not cause or allow permanent injury to the land.

PART 170—TRIBAL TRANSPORTATION PROGRAM

Subpart A—Policies, Applicability, and Definitions

Sec.

Subpart B—Tribal Transportation Program Policy and Eligibility

CONSULTATION, COLLABORATION, COORDINATION

Subpart E—Service Delivery for Tribal Transportation Program

Subpart F—Program Oversight and Accountability

Subpart G—Maintenance

Subpart H—Miscellaneous Provisions

AUTHORITY: Pub. L. 112–141, Pub. L. 114–94; 5 U.S.C. 2; 23 U.S.C. 201, 202; 25 U.S.C. 2, 9.

SOURCE: 81 FR 78463, Nov. 7, 2016, unless otherwise noted.

Subpart A—Policies, Applicability, and Definitions

§ 170.1 What does this part do?

This part provides rules and references to the statutory funding formula for the Department of the Interior (DOI), in cooperation with the Department of Transportation (DOT), to implement the Tribal Transportation Program (TTP). Included in this part are references to other title 23 and title 25 transportation programs administered by the Secretary of the Interior (Secretary) and the Secretary of Transportation (together, the "Secretaries") and implemented by Tribes and Consortiums in accordance with the Indian Self-Determination and Education Assistance Act of 1975 (ISDEAA), as amended, FHWA program agreements, and other appropriate agreements.

§ 170.2 What policies govern the TTP?

(a) The Secretaries' policy for the TTP is to:

(1) Provide a uniform and consistent set of rules;

(2) Foster knowledge of the programs by providing information about them and the opportunities that they create;

(3) Facilitate Tribal planning, conduct, and administration of the programs;

(4) Encourage inclusion of these programs under self-determination contracts, self-governance agreements, program agreements, and other appropriate agreements;

(5) Make available all contractible non-inherently Federal administrative functions under self-determination contracts, self-governance agreements, program agreements, and other appropriate agreements; and

(6) Carry out policies, procedures, and practices in consultation with Indian Tribes to ensure the letter, spirit, and goals of Federal transportation programs are fully implemented.

(b) Where this part differs from provisions in the ISDEAA, this part should advance the policy of increasing Tribal autonomy and discretion in program operation.

(c) This part is designed to enable Indian Tribes to participate in all contractible activities of the TTP. The Secretaries will afford Indian Tribes the flexibility, information, and discretion to design transportation programs under self-determination contracts, self-governance agreements, program agreements, and other appropriate agreements to meet the needs of their communities consistent with this part.

(d) Programs, functions, services, and activities, regardless of how they are administered, are an exercise of Indian Tribes' self-determination and self-governance.

(1) The Tribe is responsible for managing the day-to-day operation of its contracted Federal programs, functions, services, and activities.

(2) The Tribe accepts responsibility and accountability to the beneficiaries under self-determination contracts, self-governance agreements, program agreements, and other appropriate agreements for:

(i) Use of the funds; and

(ii) Satisfactory performance of all activities funded under the contract or agreement.

(3) The Secretary will continue to discharge the trust responsibilities to protect and conserve the trust resources of Tribes and the trust resources of individual Indians.

(e) The Secretary should interpret Federal laws and regulations to facilitate including programs covered by this part in the government-to-government agreements authorized under ISDEAA.

(f) The administrative functions referenced in paragraph (a)(5) of this section are contractible without regard to the organizational level within the DOI that carries out these functions. Including TTP administrative functions under self-determination contracts, self- governance agreements, program agreements or other appropriate agreements, does not limit or reduce the funding for any program or service serving any other Tribe.

(g) The Secretaries are not required to reduce funding for a Tribe under these programs to make funds available to another Tribe.

(h) This part must be liberally construed for the benefit of Tribes and to implement the Federal policy of self-determination and self-governance.

(i) Any ambiguities in this part must be construed in favor of the Tribes to facilitate and enable the transfer of programs authorized by 23 U.S.C. 201 and 202 and title 25 of the U.S.C.

§ 170.3 When do other requirements apply to the TTP?

TTP policies, guidance, and directives apply, to the extent permitted by law, only if they are consistent with this part and 25 CFR parts 900 and 1000. See 25 CFR 900.5 for when a Tribe must comply with other unpublished requirements.

§ 170.4 How does this part affect existing Tribal rights?

This part does not:

(a) Affect Tribes' sovereign immunity from suit;

(b) Terminate or reduce the trust responsibility of the United States to Tribes or individual Indians;

(c) Require a Tribe to assume a program relating to the TTP; or

(d) Impede awards by other agencies of the United States or a State to Tribes to administer programs under any other law.

§ 170.5 What definitions apply to this part?

Access road means a public highway or road that provides access to Tribal land and appears on the National Tribal Transportation Facility Inventory (NTTFI).

Agreement means a self-determination contract, self-governance agreement, Program Agreement or other appropriate agreement authorized under 23 U.S.C. 202(a)(2), developed in accordance with 23 U.S.C. 202(b)(6) and(b)(7) as well as 23 U.S.C. 207, to fund and manage the programs, functions, services and activities transferred to a Tribe.

Appeal means a request by a Tribe or consortium for an administrative review of an adverse agency decision.

Asset management as defined in 23 U.S.C. 101(a)(2) means a strategic and systematic process of operating, maintaining, and improving physical assets, with a focus on both engineering and economic analysis based upon quality information, to identify a structured sequence of maintenance, preservation, repair, rehabilitation, and replacement actions that will achieve and sustain a desired state of good repair over the lifecycle of the assets at minimum practicable cost.

BIA Force Account means the performance of work done by BIA employees.

BIA Road System means the Bureau of Indian Affairs Road System under the NTTFI and includes only those existing and proposed facilities for which the BIA has or plans to obtain legal right-of-way.

BIA System Inventory means Bureau of Indian Affairs System Inventory under the NTTFI that includes the BIA Road System, Tribally owned public roads, and facilities not owned by an Indian Tribal government or the BIA in the States of Oklahoma and Alaska that were used to generate road mileage for computation of the funding formula in the Indian Reservation Roads Program prior to October 1, 2004.

Consortium means an organization or association of Tribes that is authorized by those Tribes to negotiate and execute an Agreement to receive funding, manage, and carry out the program functions, services, and activities associated with the Tribal Transportation Program on behalf its member Tribes.

Construction, as defined in 23 U.S.C. 101(a)(4), means the supervising, inspecting, actual building, and incurrence of all costs incidental to the construction or reconstruction of a Tribal transportation facility, as defined in 23 U.S.C. 101(a)(31). The term includes—

(1) Preliminary engineering, engineering, and design-related services directly relating to the construction of a Tribal transportation facility project, including engineering, design, project development and management, construction project management and inspection, surveying, mapping (including the establishment of temporary and permanent geodetic control under specifications of the National Oceanic and Atmospheric Administration), and architectural-related services;

(2) Reconstruction, resurfacing, restoration, rehabilitation, and preservation;

(3) Acquisition of rights-of-way;

(4) Relocation assistance, acquisition of replacement housing sites, and acquisition and rehabilitation, relocation, and construction of replacement housing;

(5) Elimination of hazards of railway-highway grade crossings;

(6) Elimination of roadside hazards;

(7) Improvements that directly facilitate and control traffic flow, such as grade separation of intersections, widening of lanes, channelization of traffic, traffic control systems, and passenger loading and unloading areas; and

(8) Capital improvements that directly facilitate an effective vehicle weight enforcement program, such as scales (fixed and portable), scale pits, scale installation, and scale houses.

Construction contract means a fixed price or cost reimbursement self-determination contract for a construction project or an eligible TTP funded road maintenance project, except that such term does not include any contract—

(1) That is limited to providing planning services and construction management services (or a combination of such services);

(2) For the housing improvement program or roads maintenance program of the BIA administered by the Secretary; or

(3) For the health facility maintenance and improvement program administered by the Secretary of Health and Human Services.

Contract means a self-determination contract as defined in section 4(j) of the ISDEAA or a procurement document issued under Federal or Tribal procurement acquisition regulations.

Days means calendar days, except where the last day of any time period specified in this part falls on a Saturday, Sunday, or a Federal holiday, the period will carry over to the next business day unless otherwise prohibited by law.

Design means services related to preparing drawings, specifications, estimates, and other design submissions specified in a contract or agreement, as well as services during the bidding/negotiating, construction, and operational phases of the project.

Financial constraint or Fiscal constraint means that a plan (metropolitan transportation plan, TTIP, or STIP) includes financial information demonstrating that projects can be implemented using committed, available, or reasonably available revenue sources, with reasonable assurance that the federally supported transportation system is adequately operated and maintained. (*See* 23 U.S.C. 134 and 135.) Documentation must be developed that demonstrates that there is a balance between the expected revenue sources for the transportation investments and the estimated costs of the projects and programs described in the planning documents.

(1) For the TTIP and the STIP, financial constraint/fiscal constraint applies to each program year.

(2) Projects in air quality nonattainment and maintenance areas can be included in the first two years of the TTIP and STIP only if funds are "available" or "committed." See 23 CFR 450.104.

Governmental subdivision of a Tribe means a unit of a Tribe which is authorized to participate in a TTP activity on behalf of the Tribe.

Indian means a person who is a member of a Tribe or as otherwise defined in 25 U.S.C. 450b.

Maintenance means the preservation of the Tribal transportation facilities, including surface, shoulders, roadsides, structures, and such traffic-control devices as are necessary for safe and efficient utilization of the facility (see 23 U.S.C. 101(13)).

National Bridge and Tunnel Inventory (or NBTI) means the database of structural and appraisal data collected to fulfill the requirements of the National Bridge and Tunnel Inspection Standards, as defined in 23 U.S.C. 144. Each State and BIA must maintain an inventory of all bridges and tunnels that are subject to the NBTI standards and provide this data to the FHWA.

National Tribal Transportation Facility Inventory (or NTTFI) means at a minimum, transportation facilities that are eligible for assistance under the Tribal transportation program that an Indian Tribe has requested, including facilities that meet at least one of the following criteria:

(1) Were included in the Bureau of Indian Affairs system inventory prior to October 1, 2004.

(2) Are owned by an Indian Tribal government ("owned" means having the authority to finance, build, operate, or maintain the facility (see 23 U.S.C. 101(a)(20)).

(3) Are owned by the Bureau of Indian Affairs ("owned" means having the authority to finance, build, operate, or maintain the facility (See 23 U.S.C. 101(a)(20)).

(4) Were constructed or reconstructed with funds from the Highway Trust Fund under the Indian reservation roads program since 1983.

(5) Are public roads or bridges within the exterior boundary of Indian reservations, Alaska Native villages, and other recognized Indian communities (including communities in former Indian reservations in the State of Oklahoma) in which the majority of residents are American Indians or Alaska Natives.

(6) Are public roads within or providing access to either:

(i) An Indian reservation or Tribal trust land or restricted Tribal land that is not subject to fee title alienation without the approval of the Federal Government; or

(ii) Indian or Alaska Native villages, groups, or communities whose residents include Indians and Alaska Natives whom the Secretary has determined are eligible for services generally available to Indians under Federal laws applicable to Indians.

(7) Are primary access routes requested by Tribal governments for inclusion in the NTTFI, including roads between villages, roads to landfills, roads to drinking water sources, roads to natural resources identified for economic development, and roads that provide access to intermodal terminals, such as airports, harbors, or boat landings.

NOTE: The Secretaries are not precluded from including additional eligible transportation facilities into the NTTFI if such additional facilities are included in a uniform and consistent manner.

Population adjustment factor means a special portion of the former Indian Reservation Roads (IRR) Program distribution formula that was calculated annually and provided for broader participation in the IRR Program.

Preventive maintenance means the planned strategy of cost effective treatments to an existing roadway system and its appurtenances that preserve the system, impede future deterioration, and maintain or improve the functional condition of the system without increasing structural capacity. Eligible activities should address the aging, oxidation, surface deterioration, and normal wear and tear of the facility caused by day-to-day performance and environmental conditions. In addition, the treatments should extend the service life of the roadway asset or facility to at least achieve the design life of the facility.

Primary access route means a route that is the shortest practicable route connecting two points.

Program means any program, function, service, activity, or portion thereof.

Program agreement means an agreement between the Tribe and Assistant Secretary—Indian Affairs or the Administrator of the Federal Highway Administration, or their respective designees, that transfer all but the inherently Federal program functions, services and activities of the Tribal Transportation Program to the Tribe.

The provisions of 23 U.S.C. 202 (b)(7)(E) apply only to those program agreements entered into by the Administrator of the Federal Highway Administration.

Project planning means project-related activities that precede the design phase of a transportation project. Examples of these activities are: Collecting data on traffic, accidents, or functional, safety or structural deficiencies; corridor studies; conceptual studies, environmental studies; geotechnical studies; archaeological studies; project scoping; public hearings; location analysis; preparing applications for permits and clearances; and meetings with facility owners and transportation officials.

Proposed road or facility means any road or facility, including a primary access route, that will serve public transportation needs, meets the eligibility requirements of the TTP, and does not currently exist.

Public authority as defined in 23 U.S.C. 101(a)(20) means a Federal, State, county, town, or township, Indian Tribe, municipal, or other local government or instrumentality with authority to finance, build, operate, or maintain toll or toll-free facilities.

Public road means any road or street under the jurisdiction of and maintained by a public authority and open to public travel.

Real property means any interest in land together with the improvements, structures, fixtures and appurtenances.

Regionally significant project means a project (other than projects that may be grouped in the STIP/TTIP under 23 CFR 450) that:

(1) Is on a facility which serves regional transportation needs (such as access to and from the area outside of the region, major activity centers in the region, major planned developments such as new retail malls, sports complexes, etc., or transportation terminals as well as most terminals themselves); and

(2) Would normally be included in the modeling of a metropolitan area's transportation network, including, as a minimum, all principal arterial highways and all fixed guideway transit facilities that offer a significant alternative to regional highway travel.

Rehabilitation means the work required to restore the structural integrity of transportation facilities as well as work necessary to correct safety defects.

Relative need distribution factor means a mathematical formula used for distributing construction funds under the former IRR Program.

Relocation means the adjustment of transportation facilities and utilities required by a highway project. It includes removing and reinstalling the facility, including necessary temporary facilities; acquiring necessary right-of-way on the new location; moving, rearranging or changing the type of existing facilities; and taking any necessary safety and protective measures. It also means constructing a replacement facility that is both functionally equivalent to the existing facility and necessary for continuous operation of the utility service, the project economy, or sequence of highway construction.

Relocation services means payment and assistance authorized by the Uniform Relocation and Real Property Acquisitions Policy Act, 42 U.S.C. 4601 *et seq.*, as amended.

Rest area means an area or site established and maintained within or adjacent to the highway right-of-way or under public supervision or control for the convenience of the traveling public.

Seasonal transportation route means a non-recreational transportation route in the NTTFI such as snowmobile trails, ice roads, and overland winter roads that provide access to Indian communities or villages and may not be open for year-round use.

Secretaries means the Secretary of the Interior and the Secretary of Transportation or designees authorized to act on their behalf.

Secretary means the Secretary of the Interior or a designee authorized to act on the Secretary's behalf.

Secretary of Transportation means the Secretary of Transportation or a designee authorized to act on behalf of the Secretary of Transportation.

State Transportation Department as defined in 23 U.S.C. 101 (a)(28) means that department, commission, board, or official of any State charged by its laws with the responsibility for highway construction.

Statewide Transportation Improvement Program or STIP means a financially constrained, multi-year list of projects developed under 23 U.S.C. 134 and 135, and 49 U.S.C. 5303–5305. The Secretary of Transportation reviews and approves the STIP for each State.

Strip map means a graphic representation of a section of road or other transportation facility being added to or modified in the NTTFI. Each strip map clearly: identifies the facility's location with respect to State, county, Tribal, and congressional boundaries; defines the overall dimensions of the facility (including latitude and longitude); includes a north arrow, scale, designation of road sections, traffic counter locations, and other nearby transportation facilities; and includes a table that provides the facility's data information needed for the NTTFI.

Transit means services, equipment, and functions associated with the public movement of people served within a community or network of communities provided by a Tribe or other public authority using Federal funds.

Transportation planning means developing land use, economic development, traffic demand, public safety, health and social strategies to meet transportation current and future needs.

Tribal road system means the Tribally owned roads under the NTTFI. For the purposes of fund distribution as defined in 23 U.S.C. 202(b), the Tribal road system includes only those existing and proposed facilities that are approved and included in the NTTFI as of fiscal year 2012.

Tribal transit program means the planning, administration, acquisition, and operation and maintenance of a system associated with the public movement of people served within a community or network of communities on or near Tribal lands.

Tribal Transportation Program (or TTP) means a program established in Section 1119 of Moving Ahead for Progress in the 21st Century (MAP–21), Pub. L. 112–141 (July 6, 2012), and codified in 23 U.S.C. 201 and 202 to address transportation needs of Tribes. This program was continued under Fixing America's Surface Transportation Act (FAST Act), Pub. L. 114–94 (Dec. 4, 2015).

Tribal transportation facility means a public highway, road, bridge, trail, transit system, or other approved facility that is located on or provides access to Tribal land and appears on the NTTFI described in 23 U.S.C. 202(b)(1).

Tribe or Indian Tribe means any Tribe, nation, band, pueblo, rancheria, colony, or community, including any Alaska Native village or regional or village corporation as defined or established under the Alaska Native Claims Settlement Act, that is federally recognized by the U.S. government for special programs and services provided by the Secretary to Indians because of their status as Indians.

TTIP means Tribal Transportation Improvement Program. It is a multi-year list of proposed transportation projects developed by a Tribe from the Tribal priority list or the long-range transportation plan.

TTP Eligible Transportation Facility means any of the following:

(1) Road systems and related road appurtenances such as signs, traffic signals, pavement striping, trail markers, guardrails, etc;

(2) Highway bridges and drainage structures;

(3) Boardwalks and Board roads;

(4) Adjacent parking areas;

(5) Maintenance yards;

(6) Operations and maintenance of transit programs and facilities;

(7) System public pedestrian walkways, paths, bike and other trails;

(8) Motorized vehicle trails;

(9) Public access roads to heliports and airports;

(10) Seasonal transportation routes;

(11) BIA and Tribal post-secondary school roads and parking lots built with TTP funds;

(12) Public ferry boats and boat ramps; and

(13) Additional facilities as approved by BIA and FHWA.

TTP formula funds means the pool of funds made available to Tribes under 23 U.S.C. 202(b)(3).

TTP funds means the funds authorized under 23 U.S.C. 201 and 202.

TTP planning funds means funds referenced in 23 U.S.C. 202(c)(1).

TTP Program Management and Oversight (PM&O) funds means those funds authorized by 23 U.S.C 202(a)(6) to pay the cost of carrying out inherently Federal program management and oversight, and project-related administrative expenses activities.

TTP System means all of the facilities eligible for inclusion in the NTTFI.

TTPTIP means Tribal Transportation Program Transportation Improvement Program. It is a financially constrained prioritized list of transportation projects and activities eligible for TTP funding covering a period of four years that is developed by BIA and FHWA based on each Tribe's submission of their TTIP or Tribal priority list. It is required for projects and activities to be eligible for funding under title 23 U.S.C. and title 49 U.S.C. chapter 53. The Secretary of Transportation reviews and approves the TTPTIP and distributes copies to each State for inclusion in their respective STIPs without further action.

§ 170.6 Acronyms.

AASHTO—American Association of State Highway and Transportation Officials.
ADR—Alternate dispute resolution
ANCSA—Alaska Native Claims Settlement Act
BIA—Bureau of Indian Affairs, Department of the Interior.
BIADOT—Bureau of Indian Affairs, Indian Services—Division of Transportation—Central Office.
CFR—Code of Federal Regulations.
DOI—Department of the Interior.
DOT—Department of Transportation.
FHWA—Federal Highway Administration, Department of Transportation.
FTA—Federal Transit Administration, Department of Transportation.
ISDEAA—Indian Self-Determination and Education Assistance Act of 1975, Public Law 93–638, as amended.
LRTP—Long-range transportation plan.
MUTCD—Manual of Uniform Traffic Safety Devices
NBTI—National Bridge and Tunnel Inventory.
NEPA—National Environmental Policy Act
NTTFI—National Tribal Transportation Facility Inventory.
PM&O—Program management and oversight.
PS&E—Plans, specifications and estimates
STIP—Statewide Transportation Improvement Program.
TTAC—Tribal Technical Assistance Center
TTIP—Tribal Transportation Improvement Program.
TTP—Tribal Transportation Program.
TTP-S—TTP—Safety
TTPTIP—Tribal Transportation Program Transportation Improvement Program.
U.S.C.—United States Code

§ 170.7 Information collection.

The information collection requirements contained in this part have been approved by the Office of Management and Budget under 44 U.S.C. *et seq.* and assigned control number 1076–0161. A Federal agency may not conduct or sponsor, and you are not required to respond to, a collection of information unless it displays a currently valid OMB control number. Comments and suggestions on the burden estimate or any other aspect of the information collection should be sent to the Information Collection Clearance Officer, Bureau of Indian Affairs, 1849 C Street NW., Washington, DC 20240.

Subpart B—Tribal Transportation Program Policy and Eligibility

CONSULTATION, COLLABORATION, COORDINATION

§ 170.100 What do the terms "consultation," "collaboration," and "coordination" mean?

(a) *Consultation* means government-to-government communication, carried out in accordance with applicable Executive Orders, in a timely manner by all parties about a proposed or contemplated decision. The Departments' Consultation Policies and Plans can be found at *http://www.indianaffairs.gov/WhoWeAre/AS-IA/Consultation/Templates/index.htm* (DOI) or *http://www.fhwa.dot.gov/tribal/news/consultation.htm* (DOT)

(b) *Collaboration* means that all parties involved in carrying out planning and project development work together in a timely manner to achieve a common goal or objective.

(c) *Coordination* means that each party:

(1) Shares and compares in a timely manner its transportation plans, programs, projects, and schedules with the related plans, programs, projects, and schedules of the other parties; and

(2) Adjusts its plans, programs, projects, and schedules to optimize the efficient and consistent delivery of transportation projects and services.

§ 170.101 What is the TTP consultation and coordination policy?

(a) The TTP's government-to-government consultation and coordination policy is to foster and improve communication, cooperation, and coordination among Tribal, Federal, State, and local governments and other transportation organizations when undertaking the following, similar, or related activities:

(1) Identifying data-driven safety needs for improving both vehicle and pedestrian safety;

(2) Developing State, metropolitan, regional, TTP, and TTIPs that impact Tribal lands, communities, and members;

(3) Developing short and long-range transportation plans;

(4) Developing TTP transportation projects;

(5) Developing environmental mitigation measures necessary to protect and/or enhance Tribal lands and the environment, and counteract the impacts of the projects;

(6) Developing plans or projects to carry out the Tribal Transportation Facility Bridge Program identified in 23 U.S.C. 202(d);

(7) Developing plans or projects for disaster and emergency relief response and the repair of eligible damaged TTP transportation facilities;

(8) Assisting in the development of State and Tribal agreements related to the TTP;

(9) Developing and improving transit systems serving Tribal lands and communities;

(10) Assisting in the submission of discretionary grant applications for State and Federal funding for TTP transportation facilities; and

(11) Developing plans and projects for the safety funding identified in 23 U.S.C. 202(e).

(b) Tribal, State and Federal Government agencies may enter into intergovernmental Memoranda of Agreement to streamline and facilitate consultation, collaboration, and coordination.

(c) DOI and DOT operate within a government-to-government relationship with Tribes. As a critical element of this relationship, these agencies assess the impact of Federal transportation policies, plans, projects, and programs on Tribal rights and interests to ensure that these rights and concerns are appropriately considered.

§ 170.102 What goals and principles guide program implementation?

When undertaking transportation activities affecting Tribes, the Secretaries should, to the maximum extent permitted by law:

(a) Establish regular and meaningful consultation and collaboration with affected Tribal governments, including facilitating the direct involvement of Tribal governments in short- and long-range Federal transportation planning efforts;

(b) Promote the rights of Tribal governments to govern their own internal affairs;

(c) Promote the rights of Tribal governments to receive direct transportation services from the Federal Government or to enter into agreements to directly operate any Tribally related transportation programs serving Tribal members;

(d) Ensure the continuation of the trust responsibility of the United States to Tribes and Indian individuals;

(e) Reduce the imposition of unfunded mandates upon Tribal governments;

(f) Encourage flexibility, innovation and implementation of contracting mechanisms used for delivery of the TTP to the greatest extent authorized by Congress by providing the protections afforded by the ISDEAA to Tribes carrying out eligible activities of the TTP;

(g) Reduce, streamline, and eliminate unnecessarily restrictive transportation policies, guidelines, or procedures;

(h) Ensure that Tribal rights and interests are appropriately considered during program development;

(i) Ensure that the TTP is implemented consistent with Tribal sovereignty and the government-to-government relationship; and

(j) Consult with, and solicit the participation of, Tribes in the development of the annual BIA budget proposals.

§ 170.103 Is consultation with Tribal governments required before obligating TTP funds for direct service activities?

Yes. Consultation with Tribal governments is required before obligating TTP funds for direct service activities. Before obligating TTP funds on any project for direct service activities, the Secretary must:

(a) Consult with the affected Tribe to determine Tribal preferences concerning the program, project, or activity; and

(b) Provide information under § 170.600 within 30 days of the notice of availability of funds.

§ 170.104 Are funds available for consultation, collaboration, and coordination activities?

Yes. Funds are available for consultation, collaboration, and coordination activities. To fund consultation, collaboration, and coordination of TTP activities, Tribes may use:

(a) The Tribes' TTP allocations;

(b) Tribal Priority Allocation funds;

(c) Administration for Native Americans funds;

(d) Economic Development Administration funds;

(e) United States Department of Agriculture Rural Development funds;

(f) Community Development Block Grant funds;

(g) Indian Housing Block Grant funds;

(h) Indian Health Service Tribal Management Grant funds;

(i) General funds of the Tribal government; and

(j) Any other funds available for the purpose of consultation, collaboration, and coordination activities.

§ 170.105 When must State governments consult with Tribes?

As identified in 23 U.S.C. 134 and 135, States will develop their STIP in consultation with Tribes in the area where the project is located. This includes providing for a process that coordinates transportation planning efforts carried out by the State with similar efforts carried out by Tribes. Regulations governing STIPs can be found at 23 CFR part 450.

§ 170.106 Should planning organizations and local governments consult with Tribes when planning for transportation projects?

Yes. When planning for transportation projects, planning organizations and local governments should consult with Tribes in the area where the project is located.

§ 170.107 Should Tribes and BIA consult with planning organizations and local governments in developing projects?

Yes. Tribes and BIA should consult with planning organizations and local governments in developing projects.

(a) All regionally significant TTP projects must be:

(1) Developed in cooperation with State and metropolitan planning organizations; and

(2) Included in a FHWA-approved TTPTIP for inclusion in State and metropolitan plans.

(b) BIA and Tribes are encouraged to consult with States, metropolitan and regional planning organizations, and local and municipal governments on transportation matters of common concern.

§ 170.108 How do the Secretaries prevent discrimination or adverse impacts?

The Secretaries ensure that non-discrimination and environmental justice principles are integral TTP program elements. The Secretaries consult with

Tribes early in the program development process to identify potential discrimination and to recommend corrective actions to avoid disproportionately high and adverse effects on Tribes and Indian populations.

§ 170.109 How can State and local governments prevent discrimination or adverse impacts?

(a) Under 23 U.S.C. 134 and 135, and 23 CFR part 450, State and local government officials shall consult and work with Tribes in the development of programs to:

(1) Identify potential discrimination; and

(2) Recommend corrective actions to avoid disproportionately high and adverse effects on Tribes and Indian populations.

(b) Examples of adverse effects include, but are not limited to:

(1) Impeding access to Tribal communities or activities;

(2) Creating excessive access to culturally or religiously sensitive areas;

(3) Negatively affecting natural resources, trust resources, Tribal businesses, religious, and cultural sites;

(4) Harming indigenous plants and animals; and

(5) Impairing the ability of Tribal members to engage in commercial, cultural, and religious activities.

§ 170.110 What if discrimination or adverse impacts occur?

If discrimination or adverse impacts occur, a Tribe should take the following steps in the order listed:

(a) Take reasonable steps to resolve the problem directly with the State or local government involved; and

(b) Contact BIA, FHWA, or the Federal Transit Authority (FTA), as appropriate, to report the problem and seek assistance in resolving the problem.

ELIGIBLE USES OF TTP FUNDS

§ 170.111 What activities may be carried out using TTP funds?

TTP funds will be used to pay the cost of items identified in 23 U.S.C. 202(a)(1). A more detailed list of eligible activities is available in the appendix A to this subpart. Each of the items identified in this appendix must be interpreted in a manner that permits, rather than prohibits, a proposed use of funds.

§ 170.112 What activities are not eligible for TTP funding?

TTP funds cannot be used for any of the following:

(a) Structures and erosion protection unrelated to transportation and roadways;

(b) General or Tribal planning not involving transportation;

(c) Landscaping and irrigation systems not involving transportation programs and projects;

(d) Work or activities that are not listed on an FHWA-approved TTPTIP;

(e) Condemnation of land for recreational trails;

(f) Salaries and/or other incidental costs of any Federal employee or contractor not performing Federal TTP stewardship and oversight, work identified in the appendix to subpart E, or project-related activities identified on an approved TTIP; or

(g) Direct and/or incidental costs associated with the Federal Government's acquisition of goods, services, or construction unrelated to the program.

§ 170.113 How can a Tribe determine whether a new use of funds is allowable?

(a) A Tribe that proposes new uses of TTP funds must ask BIA or FHWA in writing whether the proposed use is eligible under Federal law.

(1) In cases involving eligibility questions that refer to 25 U.S.C., BIA will determine whether the new proposed use of TTP funds is allowable and provide a written response to the requesting Tribe within 45 days of receiving the written inquiry. Tribes may appeal a denial of a proposed use by BIA under 25 CFR part 2. The address is: Department of the Interior, BIA, Division of Transportation, 1849 C Street NW., MS 4513 MIB, Washington, DC 20240.

(2) In cases involving eligibility questions that refer to the TTP or 23 U.S.C., BIA will refer an inquiry to FHWA for decision. FHWA must provide a written response to the requesting Tribe within 45 days of receiving the written inquiry from the Tribe.

Tribes may appeal denials of a proposed use by the FHWA to: FHWA, 1200 New Jersey Ave. SE., Washington, DC 20590.

(b) To the extent practical, the deciding agency must consult with the TTP Coordinating Committee before denying a request.

(c) BIA and FHWA will:

(1) Send copies of all eligibility determinations to the TTP Coordinating Committee and BIA Regional offices;

(2) Coordinate all responses and if the requested agency fails to issue a decision to the requesting Tribe within the required time, the proposed use will be deemed to be allowable for that specific project; and

(3) Promptly make any final determination available on agency Web sites.

USE OF TTP AND CULTURAL SITE OR AREA ENTRY ROADS

§ 170.114 What restrictions apply to the use of a Tribal transportation facility?

(a) All Tribal transportation facilities listed in the approved NTTFI must be open and available for public use as required by 23 U.S.C. 101(a)(31). However, the public authority having jurisdiction over these roads or the Secretary, in consultation with a Tribe and applicable private landowners, may restrict road use or close roads temporarily when:

(1) Required for public health and safety or as provided in § 170.116.

(2) Conducting engineering and traffic analysis to determine maximum speed limits, maximum vehicular size, and weight limits, and identify needed traffic control devices; and

(3) Erecting, maintaining, and enforcing compliance with signs and pavement markings.

(b) Consultation is not required whenever the conditions in paragraph (a) of this section involve immediate safety or life-threatening situations.

(c) A Tribal transportation facility owned by a Tribe or BIA may be permanently closed only when the Tribal government and the Secretary agree. Once this agreement is reached, BIA must remove the facility from the NTTFI and it will be ineligible for expenditure of any TTP funds.

§ 170.115 What is a cultural site or area entry road?

(a) A cultural site or area entry road is a public road that provides access to sites for cultural purposes as defined by Tribal traditions, which may include, for example:

(1) Sacred and medicinal sites;

(2) Gathering medicines or materials such as grasses for basket weaving; and

(3) Other traditional activities, including, but not limited to, subsistence hunting, fishing and gathering.

(b) A Tribal government may unilaterally designate a Tribal road as a cultural site or area entry road. A cultural site or area entry road designation is an entirely voluntary and internal decision made by the Tribe to help it and other public authorities manage, protect, and preserve access to locations that have cultural significance.

(c) In order for a Tribal government to designate a non-tribal road as a cultural site or area entry road, it must enter into an agreement with the public authority having jurisdiction over the road.

(d) Cultural site or area entry roads may be included in the NTTFI if they meet the definition of a TTP facility.

§ 170.116 Can a Tribe close a cultural site or area entry road?

(a) A Tribe with jurisdiction over a cultural site or area entry road can close it. The Tribe can carry this out:

(1) During periods when the Tribe or Tribal members are involved in cultural activities; and

(2) In order to protect the health and safety of the Tribal members or the general public.

(b) Cultural site or area entry roads designated through an agreement with a public authority may only be closed according to the provisions of the agreement. See § 170.115(c).

SEASONAL TRANSPORTATION ROUTES

§ 170.117 Can TTP funds be used on seasonal transportation routes?

Yes. A Tribe may use TTP funds on seasonal transportation routes that are included in the NTTFI.

(a) Information regarding the standards for seasonal transportation routes are found in § 170.454. A Tribe can also develop or adopt standards that are equal to or exceed these standards.

(b) To help ensure the safety of the traveling public, construction of a seasonal transportation route requires a right-of-way, easement, or use permit.

TTP HOUSING SITE OR AREA ENTRY ROADS

§ 170.118 What terms apply to TTP housing site or area entry roads?

(a) *TTP housing site or area entry road* means a public road on the TTP System that provides access to a housing cluster.

(b) *TTP housing street* means a public road on the TTP System that is located within a housing cluster.

(c) *Housing cluster* means three or more existing or proposed housing units.

§ 170.119 Are housing site or area entry roads and housing streets eligible for TTP funding?

Yes. TTP housing site or area entry roads and housing streets on public rights-of-way are eligible for construction, reconstruction, and rehabilitation funding under the TTP. Tribes, following the transportation planning process as required in subpart D, may include housing site or area entry roads and housing street projects on their TTIP.

TOLL, FERRY, AND AIRPORT FACILITIES

§ 170.120 How can Tribes use Federal highway funds for toll and ferry facilities?

(a) A Tribe can use Federal-aid highway funds, including TTP funds, to study, design, construct, and operate toll highways, bridges, and tunnels, as well as ferry boats and ferry terminal facilities. The following table shows how a Tribe can initiate construction of these facilities.

To initiate construction of a . . .	A Tribe must . . .
(1) Toll highway, bridge, or tunnel.	(i) Meet and follow the requirements in 23 U.S.C. 129; and (ii) If TTP funds are used, enter into an Agreement as defined in § 170.5.
(2) Ferry boat or ferry terminal.	Meet and follow the requirements in 23 U.S.C. 129(c).

(b) A Tribe can use TTP funds to fund 100 percent of the conversion or construction of a toll facility.

(c) If a Tribe obtains non-TTP Federal funding for the conversion or construction of a toll facility, the Tribe may use TTP funds to satisfy any matching fund requirements.

§ 170.121 Where is information about designing and operating a toll facility available?

Information on designing and operating a toll highway, bridge or tunnel is available from the International Bridge, Tunnel and Turnpike Association. The Association publishes a variety of reports, statistics, and analyses. The Web site is located at *http://www.ibtta.org*. Information is also available from FHWA.

§ 170.122 When can a Tribe use TTP funds for airport facilities?

(a) A Tribe can use TTP funds for construction of airport and heliport access roads, if the access roads are open to the public.

(b) A Tribe cannot use TTP funds to construct, improve, or maintain airport or heliport facilities.

RECREATION, TOURISM, AND TRAILS

§ 170.123 Can a Tribe use Federal funds for its recreation, tourism, and trails program?

Yes. A Tribe, Consortium, or the BIA may use TTP funds for recreation, tourism, and trails programs if the programs are included in the TTPTIP. Additionally, the following Federal programs may be possible sources of Federal funding for recreation, tourism, and trails projects and activities:

(a) Federal Lands Access Program (23 U.S.C. 204);

(b) National Highway Performance Program (23 U.S.C. 119);

(c) Transportation Alternatives (23 U.S.C. 213);

(d) Surface Transportation Program (23 U.S.C. 133);

(e) Other funding from other Federal departments; and

(f) Other funding that Congress may authorize and appropriate.

a Tribe obtain

..ve funding for programs ... recreation, tourism, and ...goals, a Tribe should:

(1) Identify a program meeting the eligibility guidelines for the funds and have it ready for development; and

(2) Have a viable project ready for improvement or construction, including necessary permits.

(b) Tribes seeking to obtain funding from a State under the programs identified in §170.123(b) through (f) should contact the State directly to determine eligibility, contracting opportunities, funding mechanisms, and project administration requirements. These funds would be made available as provided by §170.627 of this part.

(c) In order to expend any Federal transportation funds, a Tribe must ensure that the eligible project/program is listed on an FHWA-approved TIP or STIP.

§170.125 What types of activities can a recreation, tourism, and trails program include?

(a) The following are examples of activities that Tribes and Consortiums may include in a recreation, tourism, and trails program:

(1) Transportation planning for tourism and recreation travel;

(2) Adjacent public vehicle parking areas;

(3) Development of tourist information and interpretative signs;

(4) Provision for non-motorized trail activities including pedestrians and bicycles;

(5) Provision for motorized trail activities including all-terrain vehicles, motorcycles, snowmobiles, etc.;

(6) Construction improvements that enhance and promote safe travel on trails;

(7) Safety and educational activities;

(8) Maintenance and restoration of existing recreational trails;

(9) Development and rehabilitation of trailside and trailhead facilities and trail linkage for recreational trails;

(10) Purchase and lease of recreational trail construction and maintenance equipment;

(11) Safety considerations for trail intersections;

(12) Landscaping and scenic enhancement (see 23 U.S.C. 319);

(13) Bicycle transportation and pedestrian walkways (see 23 U.S.C. 217); and

(14) Trail access roads.

(b) The items listed in paragraph (a) of this section are not the only activities that are eligible for recreation, tourism, and trails funding. The funding criteria may vary with the specific requirements of the programs.

(c) Tribes may use TTP funds for any activity that is eligible for Federal funding under any provision of title 23 of the U.S.C.

§170.126 Can roads be built in roadless and wild areas?

Under 25 CFR part 265, no roads can be built in an area designated as a roadless and wild area.

TTP SAFETY

§170.127 What are the TTP Safety Funds?

(a) Funds, identified as TTP Safety (TTP–S) funds, are made available for a Tribe's highway safety activities through a TTP set-aside established in 23 U.S.C. 202(e). TTP–S funds are allocated based on identification and analysis of highway safety issues and opportunities on Tribal lands. A TTP–S call for projects will be made annually through a Notice of Funding Opportunity published in the FEDERAL REGISTER.

(b) Tribes may also use their TTP–S funds made available through 23 U.S.C. 202(b) for highway safety activities as well as seek grant and program funding from appropriate State and local agencies and private grant organizations.

(c) A project that uses TTP–S funding or TTP funds made available under 23 U.S.C. 202(b) must be identified on a FHWA-approved TTPTIP before any funds are expended.

§170.128 What activities are eligible for TTP–S funds?

(a) TTP–S funds made available under 23 U.S.C. 202(e) may be used for projects and activities that improve safety in one or more of the following categories:

(1) Safety Plans and Planning activities; and

(2) Other eligible activities as described in 23 U.S.C. 148(a)(4)

(b) Eligible activities for each of the categories listed in paragraph (a) of this section will be included in the annual Notice of Funding Opportunity. An eligibility determination for other proposed activities must be requested from BIA or FHWA under § 170.113.

§ 170.129 How will Tribes receive TTP–S funds?

TTP–S funds made available to Tribes may be included in the Tribe's self-determination contracts, self-governance agreements, program agreements, and other appropriate agreements.

§ 170.130 How can Tribes obtain non-TTP funds for highway safety projects?

FHWA, the National Highway Traffic Safety Administration, BIA, the U.S. Department of Health and Human Services and other Federal agencies may have funding available for Tribes to address safety projects and activities. Please see the respective agency/department Web sites for further information or ask BIA or FHWA for assistance. If funding from these agencies does become available, Tribes may work with BIA or FHWA to include those funds through an ISDEAA contract or agreement, or other appropriate agreement for these projects. If the funding is title 23 funding that is originally made available to a State, the Tribe will need to work with the State to develop an agreement for the funding and work through the process identified in § 170.627 of this part.

Transit Facilities

§ 170.131 How do Tribes identify transit needs?

Tribes identify transit needs during the Tribal transportation planning process (see subpart D of this part). Transit projects using TTP funds must be included in the FHWA-approved TTPTIP.

§ 170.132 What Federal funds are available for a Tribe's transit program?

Title 23 U.S.C. authorizes use of TTP funds for transit facilities as defined in this part. There are many additional sources of Federal funds for Tribal transit programs, including the Federal programs listed in this section. Note that each program has its own terms and conditions of assistance. For further information on these programs and their use for transit, contact the FTA Regional Transit Assistance Program at *www.nationalrtap.org*. Section 170.627 of this part identifies how these funds, if provided to the Tribe from a State or county, can be made available.

(a) *Department of Transportation*. Formula Grants for Public Transportation on Indian Reservations under 49 U.S.C. 5311, Welfare-to-Work, Tribal Transportation Program, transportation and community and systems preservation, Federal transit capital improvement grants, public transportation for non-urbanized areas, capital assistance for elderly and disabilities transportation, education, and Even Start.

(b) *Department of Agriculture*. Community facilities loans; rural development loans; business and industrial loans; rural enterprise grants; commerce, public works and economic development grants; and economic adjustment assistance.

(c) *Department of Housing and Urban Development*. Community development block grants, supportive housing, Tribal housing loan guarantees, resident opportunity and support services.

(d) *Department of Labor*. Indian employment and training, welfare-to-work grants.

(e) *Department of Health and Human Services*. Programs for Indian elders, community service block grants, job opportunities for low-income individuals, Head Start (capital or operating), administration for Indian programs, Medicaid, HIV Care Grants, Healthy Start, and the Indian Health Service.

§ 170.133 May a Tribe or BIA use TTP funds as matching funds?

TTP funds may be used to meet matching or cost participation requirements for any Federal or non-Federal transit grant or program.

§ 170.134 What transit facilities and activities are eligible for TTP funding?

Transit facilities and activities eligible for TTP funding include, but are not limited to:

(a) Acquiring, constructing, operating, supervising or inspecting new, used or refurbished equipment, buildings, facilities, buses, vans, water craft, and other vehicles for use in public transportation;

(b) Transit-related intelligent transportation systems;

(c) Rehabilitating, remanufacturing, and overhauling a transit vehicle;

(d) Preventive maintenance;

(e) Leasing transit vehicles, equipment, buildings, and facilities for use in mass transportation;

(f) Third-party contracts for otherwise eligible transit facilities and activities;

(g) Public transportation improvements that enhance economic and community development, such as bus shelters in shopping centers, parking lots, pedestrian improvements, and support facilities that incorporate other community services;

(h) Passenger shelters, bus stop signs, and similar passenger amenities;

(i) Introduction of new public transportation technology;

(j) Provision of fixed route, demand response services, and non-fixed route paratransit transportation services;

(k) Radio and communication equipment to support Tribal transit programs;

(l) Transit; and

(m) Any additional activities authorized by 49 U.S.C. 5311.

TTP COORDINATING COMMITTEE

§ 170.135 What is the TTP Coordinating Committee?

(a) Under this part, the Secretaries will establish a TTP Coordinating Committee that:

(1) Provides input and recommendations to BIA and FHWA in developing TTP regulations, policies and procedures; and

(2) Supplements government-to-government consultation by coordinating with and obtaining input from Tribes, BIA, and FHWA.

(b) The Committee consists of 24 Tribal regional representatives (two from each BIA Region) and two non-voting Federal representatives (FHWA and BIA).

(c) The Secretary must select the regional Tribal representatives from nominees officially submitted by the region's Tribes.

(1) To the extent possible, the Secretary must make the selection so that there is representation from a broad cross-section of large, medium, and small Tribes.

(2) Tribal nominees must be Tribal governmental officials or Tribal employees with authority to act for their Tribal government.

(d) For purposes of continuity, the Secretary will appoint the Tribal representatives to a three year term. The appointments will be carried out so that only one of a region's two representatives will be appointed in any one year. Should the Tribal appointment or employment of a committee representative terminate during his/her term, the representative must notify the Secretary of this change and his/her membership to the Committee will cease. Upon receipt of the notification, the Secretary will seek nominations from the region's Tribes to replace the representative for the remainder of the term.

(e) Should the need arise, the Secretary will replace representatives.

§ 170.136 What are the TTP Coordinating Committee's responsibilities?

(a) Committee responsibilities are to provide input and recommendations to BIA and FHWA during the development or revision of:

(1) BIA/FHWA TTP Stewardship Plan;

(2) TTP policy and procedures;

(3) TTP eligible activities determination;

(4) TTP transit policy;

(5) TTP regulations;

(6) TTP management systems policy and procedures; and

(7) National Tribal transportation needs.

(b) The Committee may establish work groups to carry out its responsibilities.

(c) The Committee also reviews and provides recommendations on TTP national concerns (including the implementation of this part) brought to its attention.

(d) Committee members are responsible for disseminating TTP Coordinating Committee information and activities to Tribal leadership and transportation officials within their respective BIA Regions.

§ 170.137 How does the TTP Coordinating Committee conduct business?

The Committee holds at least two meetings a year. In order to maximize participation by the Tribal public, the Committee shall submit to the Secretary its proposed meeting dates and locations for each fiscal year no later than October 1st. Subject to approval by the Secretary, additional Committee meetings may be called with the consent of one-third of the Committee members, or by BIA or FHWA. The Committee conducts business at its meetings as follows:

(a) A quorum consists of representation from eight BIA Regions.

(b) The Committee will operate by consensus or majority vote, as determined by the Committee in its protocols.

(c) Any Committee member can submit an agenda item to the Chair.

(d) The Committee will work through a committee-approved annual work plan and budget.

(e) Annually, the Committee must elect from among the Committee membership a Chair, a Vice-Chair, and other officers. These officers will be responsible for preparing for and conducting Committee meetings and summarizing meeting results. These officers will also have other duties that the Committee may prescribe.

(f) The Committee must keep the Secretary and the Tribes informed through an annual accomplishment report provided within 90 days after the end of each fiscal year.

(g) The Committee's budget will be funded through the TTP management and oversight funds, not to exceed $150,000 annually.

Tribal Technical Assistance Centers

§ 170.138 What are Tribal Technical Assistance Centers?

Tribal Technical Assistance Centers (TTAC), which are also referred to as Tribal Technical Assistance Program Centers are authorized under 23 U.S.C. 504(b)(3). The centers assist Tribal governments and other TTP participants in extending their technical capabilities by providing them greater access to transportation technology, training, and research opportunities. Complete information about the centers and the services they offer is available on at *http://ltap.org/about/ttap.php.*

Appendix A to Subpart B—Allowable Uses of TTP funds

TTP funds must be used to pay the cost of those items identified in 23 U.S.C. 202(a)(1), including:

(a) TTP funds can be used for the following planning and design activities:

(1) Planning and design of Tribal Transportation Facilities.

(2) Transportation planning activities, including planning for tourism and recreational travel.

(3) Development, establishment, and implementation of Tribal transportation management systems such as safety, bridge, pavement, and congestion management.

(4) Tribal transportation plans and transportation improvement programs (TIPS).

(5) Coordinated technology implementation program (CTIP) projects.

(6) Traffic engineering and studies.

(7) Identification, implementation, and evaluation of data-driven safety needs.

(8) Tribal transportation standards.

(9) Preliminary engineering studies.

(10) Interagency program/project formulation, coordination and review.

(11) Environmental studies and archeological investigations directly related to transportation programs and projects.

(12) Costs associated with obtaining permits and/or complying with Tribal, Federal, State, and local environmental, archeological and natural resources regulations and standards.

(13) Development of natural habitat and wetland conservation and mitigation plans, including plans authorized under the Water Resources Development Act of 1990, 104 Stat. 4604 (Water Resources Development Act).

(14) Architectural and landscape engineering services related to transportation programs.

(15) Engineering design related to transportation programs, including permitting activities.

(16) Inspection of bridges and structures.

(17) Tribal Transportation Assistance Centers (TTACs).

(18) Safety planning, programming, studies and activities.

(19) Tribal employment rights ordinance (TERO) fees.

(20) Purchase or lease of advanced technological devices used for transportation planning and design activities such as global positioning units, portable weigh-in-motion systems, hand-held data collection units, related hardware and software, etc.

(21) Planning, design and coordination for Innovative Readiness Training projects.

(22) Transportation planning and project development activities associated with border crossings on or affecting Tribal lands.

(23) Public meetings and public involvement activities associated with transportation projects and planning.

(24) Leasing or rental of equipment used in transportation planning or design programs.

(25) Transportation-related technology transfer activities and programs.

(26) Educational activities related to bicycle safety.

(27) Planning and design of mitigation impacts to environmental resources caused by a transportation project, including, but not limited to, wildlife, habitat, ecosystems, historic properties, and wetlands.

(28) Evaluation of community impacts such as land use, mobility, access, social, safety, psychological, displacement, economic, and aesthetic impacts.

(29) Acquisition of land and interests in land required for right-of-way, including control of access thereto from adjoining lands, the cost of appraisals, cost of surveys, cost of examination and abstract of title, the cost of certificate of title, advertising costs, and any fees incidental to such acquisition.

(30) Cost associated with relocation activities including financial assistance for displaced businesses or persons and other activities as authorized by law.

(31) On-the-job education including classroom instruction and pre-apprentice training activities related to transportation planning and design.

(32) Other eligible activities as approved by FHWA.

(33) Any additional activities identified by TTP Coordinating Committee guidance and approved by the appropriate Secretaries (see § 170.137).

(34) Indirect general and administrative costs; and

(35) Other eligible activities described in this part.

(b) TTP funds can be used for the following construction and improvement activities:

(1) Construction, reconstruction, rehabilitation, resurfacing, restoration, and operational improvements for Tribal transportation facilities.

(2) Construction or improvement of Tribal transportation facilities necessary to accommodate other transportation modes.

(3) Construction of toll roads, highway bridges and tunnels, and toll and non-toll ferry boats and terminal facilities, and approaches thereto (except when on the Interstate System) to the extent permitted under 23 U.S.C. 129.

(4) Construction of projects for the elimination of hazards at railway-highway crossings, including the separation or protection of grades at crossings, the reconstruction of existing railroad grade crossing structures, and the relocation of highways to eliminate grade crossings.

(5) Installation of protective devices at railway-highway crossings.

(6) Transit facilities, whether publicly or privately owned, that serve Indian reservations and other communities or that provide access to or are located within an Indian reservation or community (see §§ 170.131 through 170.134 for additional information).

(7) Engineered pavement overlays that add to the structural value and design life or increase the skid resistance of the pavement.

(8) Tribally-owned, post-secondary vocational school transportation facilities.

(9) Road sealing.

(10) The placement of a double bituminous surface and chip seals during the construction of an approved project (as the non-final course) or that form the final surface of low volume roads.

(11) Seismic retrofit, replacement, rehabilitation, and painting of road bridges.

(12) Application of calcium magnesium acetate, sodium acetate/formate, or other environmentally acceptable, minimally corrosive anti-icing and de-icing compositions on road bridges, and approaches thereto and other elevated structures.

(13) Installation of scour countermeasures for road bridges and other elevated structures.

(14) Special pedestrian facilities built in lieu of streets or roads, where standard street or road construction is not feasible.

(15) Standard regulatory, warning, guide, and other official traffic signs, including dual language signs, which comply with the MUTCD that are part of transportation projects. TTP funds may also be used on interpretive signs (signs intended for viewing only by pedestrians, bicyclists, and occupants of vehicles parked out of the flow of traffic) that are culturally relevant (native language, symbols, etc.) that are a part of transportation projects.

(16) Traffic barriers and bridge rails.

(17) Engineered spot safety improvements.

(18) Planning and development of rest areas, recreational trails, parking areas, sanitary facilities, water facilities, and other facilities that accommodate the traveling public.

(19) Public approach roads and interchange ramps that meet the definition of a Tribal Transportation Facility.

(20) Construction of roadway lighting and traffic signals.

(21) Adjustment or relocation of utilities directly related to roadway work, not required to be paid for by local utility companies.

(22) Conduits crossing under the roadway to accommodate utilities that are part of future development plans.

(23) Restoration of borrow and gravel pits created by projects funded from the TTP.

(24) Force account and day labor work, including materials and equipment rental, being performed in accordance with approved plans and specifications.

(25) Experimental features where there is a planned monitoring and evaluation schedule.

(26) Capital and operating costs for traffic monitoring, management, and control facilities and programs.

(27) Safely accommodating the passage of vehicular and pedestrian traffic through construction zones.

(28) Construction engineering including contract/project administration, inspection, and testing.

(29) Construction of temporary and permanent erosion control, including landscaping and seeding of cuts and embankments.

(30) Landscape and roadside development features.

(31) Marine facilities and terminals as intermodal linkages.

(32) Construction of visitor information centers, kiosks, and related items.

(33) Other appropriate public road facilities such as visitor centers as determined by the Secretary of Transportation.

(34) Facilities adjacent to roadways to separate pedestrians and bicyclists from vehicular traffic for operational safety purposes, or special trails on separate rights-of-way.

(35) Construction of pedestrian walkways and bicycle transportation facilities, such as a new or improved lane, path, or shoulder for use by bicyclists and a traffic control device, shelter, or parking facility for bicycles.

(36) Facilities adjacent to roadways to separate modes of traffic for safety purposes.

(37) Acquisition of scenic easements and scenic or historic sites provided they are part of an approved project or projects.

(38) Debt service on bonds or other debt financing instruments issued to finance TTP construction and project support activities.

(39) Any project to encourage the use of carpools and vanpools, including provision of carpooling opportunities to the elderly and individuals with disabilities, systems for locating potential riders and informing them of carpool opportunities, acquiring vehicles for carpool use, designating existing highway lanes as preferential carpool highway lanes, providing related traffic control devices, and designating existing facilities for use for preferential parking for carpools.

(40) Fringe and corridor parking facilities including access roads, buildings, structures, equipment improvements, and interests in land.

(41) Adjacent public parking areas.

(42) Costs associated with obtaining permits and/or complying with Tribal, Federal, State, and local environmental, archeological, and natural resources regulations and standards on TTP projects.

(43) Seasonal transportation routes, including snowmobile trails, ice roads, overland winter roads, and trail markings. (See § 170.117.)

(44) Tribal fees such as employment taxes (TERO), assessments, licensing fees, permits, and other regulatory fees.

(45) On-the-job education including classroom instruction and pre-apprentice training activities related to TTP construction projects such as equipment operations, surveying, construction monitoring, testing, inspection and project management.

(46) Installation of advance technological devices on TTP transportation facilities such as permanent weigh-in-motion systems, informational signs, intelligent transportation system hardware, etc.

(47) Cultural and environmental resource monitoring, management, and mitigation for transportation related activities

(48) Mitigation activities required by Tribal, State, or Federal regulatory agencies and 42 U.S.C. 4321, *et seq.*, the National Environmental Policy Act (NEPA).

(49) Purchasing, leasing or renting of construction or maintenance equipment. All equipment purchase request submittals must be accompanied by written cost analysis and approved by FHWA or BIA. When purchasing construction or maintenance equipment, a Tribe must:

(i) Construction—Develop a lease/purchase cost analysis that identifies the overall benefit of purchasing the piece of equipment versus leasing. This analysis must be submitted to BIA or FHWA for approval per § 170.113. If approved, the funding must be identified on a FHWA-approved TTIP in order to be expended in accordance with 23 U.S.C. 202(b)(4)(B).

(ii) Maintenance—The equipment costs are considered part of the funding identified in 23 U.S.C. 202(a)(8) and must be identified on a FHWA-approved TTIP in accordance with 23 U.S.C. 202(b)(4)(B) in order to be expended.

(50) Coordination and construction materials for innovative readiness training projects operated by entities such as the Department of Defense (DOD), the American Red Cross, the Federal Emergency Management Agency (FEMA), other cooperating Federal agencies, States and their political subdivisions, Tribal governments, or other

appropriate non-governmental organizations.

(51) Emergency repairs on Tribal Transportation Facilities.

(52) Public meetings and public involvement activities.

(53) Construction of roads on dams and levees.

(54) Transportation alternative activities as defined in 23 U.S.C. 101(a).

(55) Modification of public sidewalks adjacent to or within Tribal transportation facilities.

(56) Highway and transit safety infrastructure improvements and hazard eliminations.

(57) Transportation control measures such as employer-based transportation management plans, including incentives, shared-ride services, employer sponsored programs to permit flexible work schedules and other activities, other than clause (xvi) listed in section 108(f)(1)(A) of the Clean Air Act, (42 U.S.C. 7408(f)(1)(A)).

(58) Environmental restoration and pollution abatement activities in order to construct a transportation project or to mitigate impacts caused by a transportation project.

(59) Trail development and related activities as identified in §§ 170.123 through 170.126.

(60) Development of scenic overlooks and information centers.

(61) Natural habitat and wetlands mitigation efforts related to TTP projects, including:

(i) Participation in natural habitat and wetland mitigation banks, including banks authorized under the Water Resources Development Act, and

(ii) Contributions to Tribal, statewide and regional efforts to conserve, restore, enhance, and create natural habitats and wetland, including efforts authorized under the Water Resources Development Act.

(62) Mitigation of damage to wildlife, habitat and ecosystems caused as a result of a transportation project.

(63) Construction of permanent fixed or moveable structures for snow or sand control.

(64) Cultural access roads (see § 170.115).

(65) Other eligible items as approved by the Federal Highway Administration (FHWA).

(66) Any additional activities proposed by a Tribe or the TTP Coordinating Committee and approved by the appropriate Secretaries (see §§ 170.113 and 170.136).

(67) Other eligible activities identified in this part (c) TTP funds can be used for maintenance activities as defined in subpart G of this regulation.

(d) Each of the items identified in this appendix must be interpreted in a manner that permits, rather than prohibits, a proposed use of funds.

Appendix B to Subpart B—Sources of Tribal Transportation Training and Education Opportunities

The following is a list of some of the many governmental sources for Tribal transportation training and education opportunities. There may be other non-governmental, Tribal, or private sources not listed here.

(1) National Highway Institute training courses and fellowships

(2) State and local technical assistance center workshops

(3) Tribal technical assistance centers (TTAC) workshops

(4) FHWA and FTA Research Fellowships

(5) Dwight David Eisenhower Transportation Fellowship (23 U.S.C. 504)

(6) Intergovernmental personnel agreement assignments

(7) BIA transportation cooperative education program

(8) BIA force account operations

(9) Federal Transit Administration workshops

(10) State Departments of Transportation

(11) Federal-aid highway construction and technology training including skill improvement programs under 23 U.S.C. 140(b) and (c)

(12) Other funding sources identified in § 170.150 (Transit)

(13) Department of Labor work force development

(14) Indian Employment, Training, and Related Services Demonstration Act, Public Law 102–477

(15) Garrett Morgan Scholarship (FHWA)

(16) NTRC—National Transit Resource Center

(17) CTER—Council for Tribal Employment Rights

(18) BIA Indian Highway Safety Program

(19) FHWA/STIPDG (Summer Transportation Internship Program for Diverse Groups) and NSTISS (National Summer Transportation Institute for Secondary Students) Student Internship Programs

(20) Environmental Protection Agency (EPA)

(21) Department of Commerce (DOC)

(22) Department of Housing and Urban Development Community Planning and Development

(23) Training program for bridge and tunnel inspectors

(24) Transportation Research Board (TRB)

Subpart C—Tribal Transportation Program Funding

§ 170.200 How do BIA and FHWA determine the TTP funding amount?

23 U.S.C. 202(b)(3)(A) provides the basis for the funding formula and its transition into use. The annual TTP

funding amount available for distribution is determined as follows:

(a) The following set-asides are applied to the Tribal transportation program before the determination of final Tribal shares:

(1) Tribal transportation planning (23 U.S.C. 202(c));

(2) Tribal transportation facility bridges (23 U.S.C. 202(d));

(3) Tribal safety (23 U.S.C 202(e));

(4) Administrative expenses (23 U.S.C 202(a)(6)); and

(5) Tribal supplemental program (23 U.S.C. 202(b)(3)(C)).

(b) After deducting the set asides identified in paragraph (a) of this section, on October 1 of each fiscal year, the Secretaries will distribute the remainder authorized to be appropriated for the TTP among Indian Tribes as follows:

(1) For fiscal year 2016 and thereafter:

(i) For each Indian Tribe, 20 percent of the total relative need distribution factor and population adjustment factor as determined by the Tribal Transportation Allocation Methodology (see 25 CFR 170 dated July 19, 2004)) for the fiscal year 2011 funding amount made available to that Indian Tribe; and

(ii) The remainder using Tribal shares as described in § 170.201 and Tribal supplemental funding as described in § 170.202.

(2) [Reserved]

§ 170.201 What is the statutory distribution formula for Tribal shares?

(a) Tribal shares are determined by using the NTTFI as calculated for fiscal year 2012, and the most recent data on American Indian and Alaska Native population within each Indian Tribe's American Indian/Alaska Native Reservation or Statistical Area, as computed under the Native American Housing Assistance and Self-Determination Act of 1996 (25 U.S.C. 4101 *et seq.*), in the following manner:

(1) 27 percent in the ratio that the total eligible road mileage in each Tribe bears to the total eligible road mileage of all American Indians and Alaskan Natives. For the purposes of this calculation, eligible road mileage will be computed using only facilities included in the inventory described below:

(i) Were included in the BIA System Inventory prior to October 1, 2004;

(ii) Are owned by an Indian Tribal government;

(iii) Are owned by the Bureau of Indian Affairs.

(2) 39 percent in the ratio that the total population in each Tribe bears to the total population of all American Indians and Alaskan Natives; and

(3) 34 percent will be initially divided equally among each BIA Region.

(b) The share of funds will be distributed to each Indian Tribe within the BIA Region in the ratio that the average total relative need distribution factors and population adjustment factors from fiscal years 2005 through 2011 for a Tribe bears to the average total of relative need distribution factors and population adjustment factors for fiscal years 2005 through 2011 in that region.

§ 170.202 How do BIA and FHWA determine and distribute the Tribal supplemental program funds?

(a) The total amount of funding made available for the Tribal supplemental program is determined as follows:

(1) If the amount made available for the TTP is less than or equal to $275,000,000, the Tribal supplemental funding amount will equal 30 percent of such amount.

(2) If the amount made available for the TTP exceeds $275,000,000, the Tribal supplemental funding will equal:

(i) $82,500,000; plus

(ii) 12.5 percent of the amount made available for the Tribal transportation program in excess of $275,000,000.

(b) The Tribal supplemental program funds will be distributed as follows:

(1) Initially, the Tribal supplemental program funding determined in paragraph (a) of this section will be designated among the BIA Regions in proportion to the regional total of Tribal shares based on the cumulative Tribal shares of all Indian Tribes within the region under § 170.201.

(2) After paragraph (b)(1) of this section is completed, the Tribal supplemental program funding designated for each region will be distributed among the Tribes within the region as follows:

(i) The Secretaries will determine which Tribes would be entitled under § 170.200 to receive in a fiscal year less funding than they would receive in fiscal year 2011 pursuant to the relative need distribution factor and population adjustment factor, as described in 25 CFR part 170, subpart C (in effect as of July 5, 2012); and

(ii) The combined amount that such Indian Tribes would be entitled to receive in fiscal year 2011 pursuant to such relative need distribution factor and population adjustment factor in excess of the amount that they would be entitled to receive in the fiscal year under § 170.200.

(c) Subject to paragraph (d) of this section, the Secretaries will distribute a combined amount to each Tribe that meets the criteria described in paragraph (b)(2)(i) of this section a share of funding in proportion to the share of the combined amount determined under paragraph (b)(2)(ii) of this section attributable to such Indian Tribe.

(d) A Tribe may not receive under paragraph (b)(2) of this section and based on its Tribal share under § 170.200 a combined amount that exceeds the amount that such Indian Tribe would be entitled to receive in fiscal year 2011 pursuant to the relative need distribution factor and population adjustment factor, as described in 25 CFR part 170, subpart C.

(e) If the amount made available for a region under paragraph (b)(1) of this section exceeds the amount distributed among Indian Tribes within that region under paragraph (b)(2) of this section, The Secretaries will distribute the remainder of such region's funding under paragraph (b)(1) of this section among all Tribes in that region in proportion to the combined amount that each such Tribe received under § 170.200 and paragraphs (b), (c), and (d) of this section.

§ 170.203 How are Tribal transportation planning funds provided to Tribes?

Tribal transportation planning funds described in § 170.200(a)(1) are calculated pro rata to each Tribe's final percentage as determined under §§ 170.200 through 170.202. Upon request of a Tribal government and approval by the BIA Regional Office or FHWA, these funds are made available to the Tribes under applicable BIA and FHWA contracting procedures.

§ 170.204 What restrictions apply to TTP funds provided to Tribes?

All TTP funds provided to Tribes can be expended only on eligible projects and activities identified in § 170.111 and included in an FHWA-approved TIP per 23 U.S.C. 202(b)(4)(B).

§ 170.205 What is the timeframe for distributing TTP funds?

Not later than 30 days after the date on which funds are made available to the Secretary under this paragraph, the funds shall be distributed to, and made available for immediate use by, eligible Indian Tribes, in accordance with the formula for distribution of funds under the TTP. (See 23 U.S.C. 202(b)(4)(A).)

Formula Data Appeals

§ 170.226 How can a Tribe appeal its share calculation?

(a) In calculating Tribal shares, BIA and FHWA use population data (which may be appealed) and specific prior-year data (which may not be appealed). Share calculations are based upon the requirements of 23 U.S.C. 202(b)(3)(B).

(b) Any appeal of a Tribe's population figure must be directed to Department of Housing and Urban Development, Indian Housing Office of Native American Programs. The population data used is the most recent data on American Indian and Alaska Native population within each Indian Tribe's American Indian/Alaska Native Reservation or Statistical Area. This data is computed under the Native American Housing Assistance and Self-Determination Act of 1996 (25 U.S.C. 4101 *et seq.*).

(c) Appeal processes regarding inventory submissions are found at § 170.444(c), design standards at § 170.457, and new uses of funds at § 170.113.

Flexible Financing

§ 170.227 Can Tribes use flexible financing for TTP projects?

Yes. Tribes may use flexible financing in the same manner as States to finance TTP transportation projects, unless otherwise prohibited by law.

(a) Tribes may issue bonds or enter into other debt-financing instruments under 23 U.S.C. 122 with the expectation of payment of TTP funds to satisfy the instruments.

(b) Under 23 U.S.C. 603, the Secretary of Transportation may enter into an agreement for secured loans or lines of credit for TTP projects meeting the requirements contained in 23 U.S.C. 602. The secured loans or lines of credit must be paid from tolls, user fees, payments owing to the obligor under a public-private partnership or other dedicated revenue sources.

(c) Tribes may use TTP funds as collateral for loans or bonds to finance TTP projects. Upon the request of a Tribe, a BIA region or FHWA will provide necessary documentation to banks and other financial institutions.

§ 170.228 Can a Tribe use TTP funds to leverage other funds or to pay back loans?

(a) A Tribe can use TTP funds to leverage other funds.

(b) A Tribe can use TTP funds to pay back loans or other finance instruments (including those provided through an agreement with another Tribe) that were used for a project that:

(1) The Tribe paid for in advance of the current year using non-TTP funds;

(2) Was included in FHWA-approved TTPTIP; and

(3) Was included in the NTTFI at the time of construction.

§ 170.229 Can a Tribe apply for loans or credit from a State infrastructure bank?

Yes. A Tribe can apply for loans or credit from a State infrastructure bank. Upon the request of a Tribe, BIA region or FHWA will provide necessary documentation to a State infrastructure bank to facilitate obtaining loans and other forms of credit for a TTP project.

§ 170.230 How long must a project financed through flexible financing remain on a TTPTIP?

Tribes must identify each TTP project financed through flexible financing along with the repayment amount on their annual TTPTIP until the flexible financing instrument has been satisfied.

TTP DATA REPORTING

§ 170.240 What TTP project and activity data must be submitted annually to the Secretaries?

(a) In accordance with 23 U.S.C. 201(c)(6)(C), no later than 90 days after the last day of each fiscal year, any entity carrying out a project under the TTP under 23 U.S.C. 202 shall submit to the Secretaries, based on obligations and expenditures under the TTP during the preceding fiscal year, the following data:

(1) The names of projects and activities carried out by the entity under the TTP during the preceding fiscal year.

(2) A description of the projects and activities identified under paragraph (1) of this section;

(3) The current status of the projects and activities identified under paragraph (1) of this section; and

(4) An estimate of the number of jobs created and the number of jobs retained by the projects and activities identified under paragraph (1) of this section.

(b) FHWA and BIA shall provide an electronic portal to assist Tribes in submitting the data needed to fulfill the requirements of 23 U.S.C. 201(c)(6)(C).

Subpart D—Planning, Design, and Construction of Tribal Transportation Program Facilities

TRANSPORTATION PLANNING

§ 170.400 What is the purpose of transportation planning?

The purpose of transportation planning is to address current and future transportation, land use, economic development, traffic demand, public safety, health, and social needs.

§ 170.401 What are BIA's and FHWA's roles in transportation planning?

Except as provided in § 170.402, the functions and activities that BIA and/or FHWA must perform for the TTP transportation planning are:

(a) Reviewing, and approving the TTPTIP as well as providing technical assistance to the Tribes during the development of their TTIP or Priority List:

(b) Oversight of the NTTFI;

(c) Performing quality assurance and validation of NTTFI data updates as needed;

(d) Coordinating with States and their political subdivisions and appropriate planning authorities on regionally significant TTP projects;

(e) Providing technical assistance to Tribal governments;

(f) Developing TTP budgets;

(g) Facilitating public involvement;

(h) Participating in transportation planning and other transportation-related meetings;

(i) Performing quality assurance and validation related to performing traffic studies;

(j) Performing preliminary project planning or project identification studies;

(k) Conducting special transportation studies;

(l) Developing short- and long-range transportation plans;

(m) Mapping;

(n) Developing and maintaining management systems;

(o) Performing transportation planning for operational and maintenance facilities; and

(p) Researching rights-of-way documents for project planning.

§ 170.402 What is the Tribal role in transportation planning?

(a) All Tribes must prepare a TTIP or Tribal priority list.

(b) Tribes operating with a Program Agreement or BIA self-determination contract, TTP agreement, or self-governance agreement may assume any of the following planning functions:

(1) Coordinating with States and their political subdivisions, and appropriate planning authorities on regionally significant TTP projects;

(2) Preparing NTTFI data updates and ensuring that the data is entered into the NTTFI;

(3) Facilitating public involvement;

(4) Performing traffic studies;

(5) Developing short- and long-range transportation plans;

(6) Mapping;

(7) Developing and maintaining Tribal management systems;

(8) Participating in transportation planning and other transportation related meetings;

(9) Performing transportation planning for operational and maintenance facilities;

(10) Developing TTP budgets including transportation planning cost estimates;

(11) Conducting special transportation studies, as appropriate;

(12) Researching rights-of-way documents for project planning; and

(13) Performing preliminary project planning or project identification studies.

§ 170.403 What TTP funds can be used for transportation planning?

Funds as defined in 23 U.S.C. 202(c) are allocated to an Indian Tribal government to carry out transportation planning. Tribes may also identify transportation planning as a priority use for their TTP Tribal share formula funds. In both cases, the fund source and use must be clearly identified on a FHWA-approved TTPTIP.

§ 170.404 Can Tribes use transportation planning funds for other activities?

Yes. After completion of a Tribe's annual planning activities, unexpended planning funds made available under 23 U.S.C. 202(c) may be used on eligible projects or activities provided that they are identified on a FHWA-approved TTPTIP.

§ 170.405 How must Tribes use planning funds?

TTP funds as defined in 23 U.S.C. 202(c) are available to a Tribal government to support Tribal transportation planning and associated activities, including:

(a) Attending transportation planning meetings;

(b) Pursuing other sources of funds; and

(c) Developing the Tribal priority list, TTIP, LRTP, or any of the transportation planning functions and activities listed in § 170.402.

§§ 170.406–170.408 [Reserved]

§ 170.409 What is the purpose of long-range transportation planning?

(a) The purpose of long-range transportation planning is to clearly demonstrate a Tribe's transportation needs and to develop strategies to meet these needs. These strategies should address future land use, economic development, traffic demand, public safety, and health and social needs. The planning process should result in a LRTP.

(b) The time horizon for a LRTP should be 20 years to match State transportation planning horizons.

§ 170.410 How does a long-range transportation plan relate to the NTTFI?

A LRTP is developed using a uniform process that identifies the transportation needs and priorities of a Tribe. The NTTFI (see § 170.442) is derived from transportation facilities identified through an LRTP. It is also a means for identifying projects and activities for the TTP.

§ 170.411 What should a long-range transportation plan include?

A LRTP should include:

(a) An evaluation of a full range of transportation modes and connections between modes such as highway, rail, air, and water, to meet transportation needs;

(b) Trip generation studies, including determination of traffic generators due to land use;

(c) Social and economic development planning to identify transportation improvements or needs to accommodate existing and proposed land use in a safe and economical fashion;

(d) Measures that address health and safety concerns relating to transportation improvements;

(e) A review of the existing and proposed transportation system to identify the relationships between transportation and the environment;

(f) Cultural preservation planning to identify important issues and develop a transportation plan that is sensitive to Tribal cultural preservation;

(g) Scenic byway and tourism plans;

(h) Measures that address energy conservation considerations;

(i) A prioritized list of short- and long-term transportation needs; and

(j) An analysis of funding alternatives to implement plan recommendations.

§ 170.412 How is the Tribal TTP long-range transportation plan developed and approved?

(a) The Tribal TTP long-range transportation plan is developed by either:

(1) A Tribe working through a self-determination contract, self-governance agreement, Program Agreement; and other appropriate agreement; or

(2) BIA or FHWA upon request of, and in consultation with, a Tribe. The Tribe and BIA or FHWA need to agree on the methodology and elements included in development of the TTP long-range transportation plan along with time frames before work begins. The development of a long-range transportation plan on behalf of a Tribe will be funded from the Tribe's share of the TTP funds.

(b) During the development of the TTP long-range transportation plan, the Tribe and BIA or FHWA will jointly conduct a midpoint review.

(c) The public reviews a draft TTP long-range transportation plan as required by § 170.413. The plan is further refined to address any issues identified during the public review process. The Tribe then approves the TTP long-range transportation plan.

§ 170.413 What is the public's role in developing the long-range transportation plan?

BIA, FHWA, or the Tribe must solicit public involvement. If there are no Tribal policies regarding public involvement, a Tribe must use the procedures in this section. Public involvement begins at the same time long-range transportation planning begins and covers the range of users, from stakeholders and private citizens to major public and private entities. Public involvement must include either meetings or notices, or both.

(a) For public meetings, BIA, FHWA or the Tribe must:

(1) Advertise each public meeting in local and Tribal public newspapers at least 15 days before the meeting date.

In the absence of local and Tribal public newspapers, BIA, FHWA, or the Tribe may post notices under locally acceptable practices;

(2) Provide at the meeting copies of the draft LRTP;

(3) Provide information on funding and the planning process; and

(4) Provide the public the opportunity to comment, either orally or in writing.

(b) For public notices, BIA, FHWA, or the Tribe must:

(1) Publish a notice in the local and Tribal public newspapers when the draft LRTP is complete. In the absence of local and Tribal public newspapers, BIA, FHWA, or the Tribe may post notices under locally acceptable practices; and

(2) State in the notice that the LRTP is available for review, where a copy can be obtained, whom to contact for questions, where comments may be submitted, and the deadline for submitting comments (normally 30 days).

§ 170.414 How is the Tribal long-range transportation plan used and updated?

The Tribal government uses its TTP long-range transportation plan to develop transportation projects as documented in a Tribal priority list or TTIP and to identify and justify the Tribe's updates to the NTTFI. To be consistent with State, Metropolitan Planning Organization (MPO) and Regional Planning Organization (RPO) planning practices, the TTP long-range transportation plan must be reviewed annually and updated at least every five years.

§ 170.415 What are pre-project planning and project identification studies?

(a) Pre-project planning and project identification studies are part of overall transportation planning and include the activities conducted before final project approval on the TTPTIP. These processes provide the information necessary to financially constrain and program a project on the four-year TTPTIP but are not the final determination that projects will be designed and built. These activities include:

(1) Preliminary project cost estimates;

(2) Certification of public involvement;

(3) Consultation and coordination with States and/or MPO's for regionally significant projects;

(4) Preliminary needs assessments; and

(5) Preliminary environmental and archeological reviews.

(b) BIA and/or FHWA, upon request of the Tribe, will work cooperatively with Tribal, State, regional, and metropolitan transportation planning organizations concerning the leveraging of funds from non-TTP sources and identification of other funding sources to expedite the planning, design, and construction of projects on the TTPTIP.

§ 170.420 What is the Tribal priority list?

The Tribal priority list is a list of all transportation projects that the Tribe wants funded. The list:

(a) Is not financially constrained; and

(b) Is provided to BIA or FHWA by official Tribal action, unless the Tribal government submits a TTIP.

Tribal Transportation Improvement Programs

§ 170.421 What is the Tribal Transportation Improvement Program (TTIP)?

(a) The TTIP:

(1) Is developed from and must be consistent with the Tribe's Tribal priority list or LRTP;

(2) Is financially constrained for all identified funding sources;

(3) Must identify (year by year) all TTP funded projects and activities that are expected to be carried out over the next four years as well as the projected costs and all other funding sources that are expected to be used on those projects. Although 23 U.S.C. 134(j)(1)(D) indicates a TIP must be updated once every four years, Tribes are encouraged to update the TTIP annually to best represent the plans of the Tribe;

(4) Must identify all projects and activities that are funded through other Federal, State, county, and municipal transportation funds and are carried

out by the Tribe in accordance with 23 U.S.C. 202(a)(9);

(5) Must include public involvement;

(6) Is reviewed and updated as necessary by the Tribal government;

(7) Can be changed only by the Tribal government; and

(8) After approval by the Tribal government, must be forwarded to BIA or FHWA by Tribal resolution or authorized governmental action certifying public involvement has occurred and requesting approval.

(b) A copy of the FHWA-approved TTIP is returned to the Tribe and BIA. Although the FHWA-approved TTIP authorizes the Tribe to expend TTP funds for the projects and/or activities shown, it does not waive or modify other Federal, local, or financial statutory or regulatory requirements associated with the projects or activities.

§ 170.422 How does the public participate in developing the TTIP?

Public involvement is required in the development of the TTIP.

(a) The Tribe must publish a notice in local and/or Tribal newspapers when the draft TTIP is complete. In the absence of local public newspapers, the Tribe or BIA may post notices under locally acceptable practices. The notice must indicate where a copy can be obtained, a contact person for questions, where comments may be submitted, and the deadline for submitting comments. A copy of the notice will be made available to BIA or FHWA upon request.

(b) The Tribe may hold public meetings at which the public may comment orally or in writing.

(c) The Tribe, the State transportation department, or MPO may conduct public involvement activities.

§ 170.423 How are annual updates or amendments to the TTIP conducted?

(a) The TTIP annual update allows:

(1) Changes to schedules and funding amounts for identified projects and activities; and

(2) The addition of transportation projects and activities planned for the next four years.

(b) During the first quarter of a fiscal year, Tribes will be notified of the opportunity to update their TTIP. This notification will contain information on where the Tribes can access their estimated TTP funding amounts for that fiscal year, and will include a copy of their previously approved TTIP, as well as instructions for submitting the annual update.

(c) The Tribe must then review any new transportation planning information and priority lists, update their TTIP using the procedures in § 170.421, and forward the documentation to their respective BIA Regional Office or to FHWA.

(d) If forwarded to:

(1) A BIA Regional Office—The Office will review all submitted information with the Tribe and provide a written response (concurring, denying, or requesting additional information) within 45 days. If the BIA regional office concurs in the TTIP, it is then forwarded to FHWA for final approval.

(2) FHWA–FHWA will review all submitted information with the Tribe and provide a written response (approving, denying, or requesting additional information) within 45 days. Once a proposed TTIP update is approved by FHWA, it will be included in that year's overall TTPTIP.

(e) The Tribe may amend their approved TTIP at any time using the procedures in § 170.421 and paragraph (d) of this section in order to add a new project or activity within the current fiscal year that they intend to expend TTP funds on.

§ 170.424 What is the TTP Transportation Improvement Program (TTPTIP)?

(a) Each year, FHWA will compile the approved TTIPs for all of the Tribes into one document called the TTPTIP. This document will identify all expected projects and activities over a four-year period and will be organized by fiscal year, State, and Tribe.

(b) FHWA and BIA will post the approved TTPTIP on their respective Web sites. A subset of the TTPTIP that identifies only design and construction activities will annually be provided to the pertinent FHWA Division office for further transmittal to each State Transportation Office/Department for inclusion in the STIP without further action per 23 U.S.C. 201(c)(4).

PUBLIC HEARINGS

§ 170.435 When is a public hearing required?

The Tribe, or BIA or FHWA after consultation with the appropriate Tribe and other involved agencies, determines whether or not a public hearing is needed for a TTPTIP, a LRTP, or a project. A public hearing must be held if a project:

(a) Is for the construction of a new route or facility;

(b) Would significantly change the layout or function of connecting or related roads or streets;

(c) Would cause a substantial adverse effect on adjacent property; or

(d) Is controversial or expected to be controversial in nature.

§ 170.436 How are public hearings for TTP planning and projects funded?

Public hearings for a TTIP or a Tribe's LRTP are funded using the Tribe's funds as described in § 170.403.

§ 170.437 If there is no hearing, how must BIA, FHWA, or a Tribe inform the public?

(a) When no public hearing for a TTP project is scheduled, the BIA, FHWA, or a Tribe must give adequate notice to the public before project activities are scheduled to begin. The notice should include:

(1) Project location;

(2) Type of improvement planned;

(3) Dates and schedule for work;

(4) Name and address where more information is available; and

(5) Provisions for requesting a hearing.

(b) If the work is not to be performed by the Tribe, BIA will send a copy of the notice to the affected Tribe.

§ 170.438 How must BIA, FHWA, or a Tribe inform the public of when a hearing is held?

(a) When BIA, FHWA, or a Tribe holds a hearing under this part, it must notify the public of the hearing by publishing a notice with information about the project, how to attend the hearing, and where copies of documents can be obtained or viewed.

(b) BIA or the Tribe must publish the notice by:

(1) Posting the notice and publishing it in a newspaper of general circulation at least 30 days before the public hearing; and,

(2) Sending a courtesy copy of the notice to each affected Tribe and BIA Regional Office.

(c) A second notice for a hearing is optional.

§ 170.439 How is a public hearing conducted?

(a) *Presiding official.* A Tribal (tribal council) or Federal (FHWA or BIA) official will be appointed to preside over the public hearing. The presiding official must encourage a free and open discussion of the issues.

(b) *Record of hearing.* The presiding official is responsible for compiling the official record of the hearing. A record of a hearing is a summary of oral testimony and all written statements submitted at the hearing. Additional written comments made or provided at the hearing, or within five working days of the hearing, will be made a part of the record.

(c) *Hearing process.* (1) The presiding official explains the purpose of the hearing and provides an agenda;

(2) The presiding official solicits public comments from the audience on the merits of TTP projects and activities; and

(3) The presiding official informs the hearing audience of the appropriate procedures for a proposed TTP project or activity that may include, but are not limited to:

(i) Project development activities;

(ii) Rights-of-way acquisition;

(iii) Environmental and archeological clearance;

(iv) Relocation of utilities and relocation services;

(v) Authorized payments under the Uniform Relocation Assistance and Real Property Acquisition Policies Act, 42 U.S.C. 4601 *et seq.*, as amended;

(vi) Draft transportation plan; and

(vii) The scope of the project and its effect on traffic during and after construction.

(d) *Availability of information.* Appropriate maps, plats, project plans, and specifications will be available at the hearing for public review. Appropriate officials must be present to answer questions.

(e) *Opportunity for comment.* Comments are received as follows:

(1) Oral statements at the hearing;

(2) Written statements submitted at the hearing; and

(3) Written statements sent to the address noted in the hearing notice within five working days following the public hearing.

§ 170.440 How can the public learn the results of a public hearing?

Within 20 working days after the public hearing, the presiding official will issue and post at the hearing site a statement that:

(a) Summarizes the results of the hearing;

(b) Explains any needed further action;

(c) Explains how the public may request a copy; and

(d) Outlines appeal procedures.

§ 170.441 Can a decision resulting from a hearing be appealed?

Yes. A decision resulting from the public hearing may be appealed under 25 CFR part 2.

National Tribal Transportation Facility Inventory

§ 170.442 What is the National Tribal Transportation Facility Inventory?

(a) The National Tribal Transportation Facility Inventory (NTTFI), is defined under § 170.5 of this part.

(b) BIA, FHWA, or Tribes can also use the NTTFI to assist in transportation and project planning, justify expenditures, identify transportation needs, maintain existing TTP facilities, and develop management systems.

(c) The Secretaries may include additional transportation facilities in the NTTFI if the additional facilities are included in a uniform and consistent manner nationally.

(d) As required by 23 U.S.C. 144, all bridges in the NTTFI will be inspected and recorded in the national bridge inventory administered by the Secretary of Transportation.

(e) In accordance with 23 U.S.C. 202(b)(1)(A–B) and the principles of program stewardship and oversight, the Secretaries have the authority to maintain the NTTFI and shall ensure the eligibility of the facilities and the accuracy of the data included in the NTTFI.

§ 170.443 What is required to successfully include a proposed transportation facility in the NTTFI?

(a) A proposed transportation facility is any transportation facility, including a highway bridge, that will serve public transportation needs, meets the eligibility requirements of the TTP, and does not currently exist. It must meet the eligibility requirements of the TTP and be open to the public when constructed. In order to have a proposed facility placed on the NTTFI, a Tribe must submit all of the following to the BIADOT/FHWA Quality Assurance Team for consideration:

(1) A Tribal resolution or other official action identifying support for the facility and its placement on the NTTFI.

(2) A copy of the Tribe's LRTP containing:

(i) A description of the current land use and identification of land ownership within the proposed road's corridor (including what public easements may be required);

(ii) A description of need and outcomes for the facility including a description of the project's termini; and

(iii) The sources of funding to be used for construction.

(3) If the landowner is a public authority other than the Tribe or BIA, documentation from the public authority that the proposed road has been identified in their LRTP, STIP approved by FHWA, or other published transportation planning documents.

(4) Documentation clearly identifying that easements or rights-of-way have been acquired or a clear written statement of willingness to provide a right-of-way from each landowner along the route.

(5) Certification that a public involvement process has been carried out for the proposed road.

(6) A synopsis discussing the project's anticipated environmental impacts as well as the engineering and construction challenges.

(7) Documentation that the project can meet financial or fiscal constraint requirements including financial information demonstrating that the project can be implemented using existing or reasonably available funding sources, and that the project route can be adequately maintained after construction. (See 23 U.S.C. 134 and 135.)

(8) Documentation identifying the entity responsible for maintenance of the facility after construction is completed.

(b) For those proposed roads that currently exist in the NTTFI, the requirements identified above as paragraphs (a)(1) through (a)(8) of this section, must be completed and submitted for approval to BIA and FHWA by November 7, 2019, in order to remain on the inventory.

[81 FR 78463, Nov. 7, 2016, as amended at 82 FR 50313, Oct. 31, 2017]

§ 170.444 How is the NTTFI updated?

(a) Submitting data into the NTTFI for a new facility is carried out on an annual basis as follows:

(1) BIA Regional Offices provide each Tribe within its region with a copy of the Tribe's own NTTFI data during the first quarter of each fiscal year.

(2) Tribes review the provided data and are responsible for entering all changes/updates into the database. This work must be completed by March 15. The submissions must include, at a minimum, all required minimum attachments (see § 170.446) and authorizing resolutions or similar official authorizations.

(3) The BIA Regional Office reviews each Tribe's submission. If any errors or omissions are identified, the BIA Regional Office will return the submittals along with a request for corrections to the Tribe no later than May 15. If no errors or omissions are found, the BIA Regional Office validates the data and forwards it to BIADOT for review and approval.

(4) The Tribe must correct any errors or omissions in the data entries or return the corrected submittals back to the BIA Regional Office by June 15.

(5) Each BIA Regional Office must validate its regional data by July 15.

(6) BIADOT approves the current inventory year submissions from BIA Regional Offices by September 30 or returns the submissions to the BIA Regional Office if additional work is required.

(7) New facility data submitted outside of the above referenced dates are not guaranteed for inclusion in the official inventory identified in this subsection.

(b) Updating the data on a facility currently listed in the NTTFI is carried out as follows:

(1) At any time, a Tribe may submit a request to the BIA Region asking for the NTTFI data of an existing facility to be updated. The request must include the Tribe's updated data and background information on how and why the data was obtained. At the request of a Tribe, FHWA may assist BIA and the Tribe in updating the NTTFI data as required under this part.

(2) The BIA Region must review the submitted data and respond to the Tribe within 30 days of its receipt.

(i) If approved, the BIA Region validates the data and forwards it to BIADOT for review and approval.

(ii) If not approved, the BIA Region returns the submittals to the Tribe along with a detailed written explanation and supporting documentation of the reasons for the disapproval. The Tribe must correct the data entries and return the corrected submittals back to the BIA Region.

(3) BIADOT approves the current inventory year submittals from BIA Regional Offices or returns the submittals to the BIA Regional Office if additional work is required.

(c) A Tribe may appeal the rejection of submitted data on a new or existing facility included in the NTTFI by filing a written notice of appeal to the Director, Bureau of Indian Affairs, with a copy to the BIA Regional Director.

(d) To be included in the annual NTTFI update used for administrative and reporting purposes for any given fiscal year, submittals for new facilities and updates for existing facilities must be officially accepted by BIA and FHWA by September 30th of that year.

§ 170.445 [Reserved]

§ 170.446 What minimum attachments are required for an NTTFI submission?

The minimum attachments required for a facility to be added into the NTTFI include the following.

(a) A long-range transportation plan.

(b) A Tribal resolution or official authorization that refers to all route numbers, names, locations, lengths, construction needs, and ownerships.

(c) A Strip map. See § 170.5.

(d) Average Daily Traffic (ADT) documentation.

(e) A typical or representative section photo or bridge profile photo.

(f) Incidental cost verification.

(g) Acknowledgement of Public Authority responsibility.

(h) For proposed roads, see § 170.443 for additional required attachments. Please see the TTP Coding Guide for additional information on the NTTFI minimum attachments.

§ 170.447 How are the allowable lengths of access roads in the NTTFI determined?

The allowable length of an access road in the NTTFI is determined as follows:

(a) If the road section intersects or abuts a federally recognized Tribal boundary, then the length of the access road is the distance from the boundary extending to the intersection of an equal or greater functional classification but no more than 15 miles.

(b) If the road section does not intersect or abut a federally recognized Tribal boundary, the following applies:

(1) If the road section intersects or abuts an Alaska Native Claims Settlement Act (ANCSA) (43 U.S.C. 1601 *et seq.*) village corporation transportation service area, then the length of the access road is the distance from the ANCSA village corporation transportation service area extending to the intersection of an equal or greater functional classification but no more than 15 miles.

(2) If the road section is located outside of an ANCSA village corporation and located within a developed Alaska Native Village with a population more than 50% Alaska Native/American Indian, then the length of the access road is defined as the distance beginning five miles outside of the developed area of the Alaska Native Village extending to the intersection of an equal or greater functional classification but no more than 15 miles.

(3) If the road section intersects or abuts a Tribally owned trust or fee parcel located outside of an incorporated municipal boundary, then the length of the access road is defined as the distance beginning five miles outside of the Tribally owned trust or fee parcel boundary extending to the intersection of an equal or greater functional classification but no more than 15 miles.

(4) If the road section intersects or abuts a Tribally owned trust or fee parcel located inside of an incorporated municipal boundary, then the length of the access road is defined as the distance from the Tribally owned trust or fee parcel boundary extending to the intersection of an equal or greater functional classification but no more than 15 miles.

ENVIRONMENTAL AND ARCHEOLOGICAL REQUIREMENTS

§ 170.450 What archeological and environmental requirements must the TTP meet?

All BIA, FHWA, and Tribal work for the TTP must comply with cultural resource and environmental requirements under applicable Federal laws and regulations. A list of applicable laws and regulations is shown in appendix A to this subpart and is also available in the official Tribal Transportation Program Guide.

§ 170.451 Can TTP funds be used for archeological and environmental compliance?

Yes. For approved TTP projects, TTP funds can be used for environmental and archeological work consistent with § 170.450 and applicable Tribal laws for:

(a) Road and bridge rights-of-way;

(b) Borrow pits and aggregate pits and water sources associated with TTP activities staging areas;

(c) Limited mitigation outside of the construction limits as necessary to address the direct impacts of the construction activity as determined in the environmental analysis and after consultation with all affected Tribes and appropriate Secretaries; and

(d) Construction easements.

§ 170.452 When can TTP funds be used for archeological and environmental activities?

TTP funds can be used on a project's archeological and environmental activities only after the TTP facility is included in the Tribe's LRTP and the NTTFI, and the project identified on an FHWA-approved TTPTIP.

§ 170.453 Do the Categorical Exclusions under the National Environmental Policy Act (NEPA) and the regulations at 23 CFR 771 apply to TTP activities?

Yes. Regardless of whether BIA or FHWA is responsible for the oversight of a Tribe's TTP activities, the Categorical Exclusions under NEPA at 23 CFR 771.117 governing the use of funds made available through title 23 shall apply to all qualifying TTP projects involving the construction or maintenance of roads.

Design

§ 170.454 What design standards are used in the TTP?

(a) Depending on the nature of the project, Tribes must use appropriate design standards approved by FHWA. Appendix B to this subpart as well as the official Tribal Transportation Program Guide list the applicable design standards that can be used.

(b) All other design standards not listed in (a) must receive approval from FHWA.

§ 170.455 What other factors must influence project design?

The appropriate design standards must be applied to each construction project consistent with a minimum 20-year design life for highway projects and 75-year design life for highway bridges. The design of TTP projects must take into consideration:

(a) The existing and planned future use of the facility in a manner that is conducive to safety, durability, and economy of maintenance;

(b) The particular needs of each locality, and the environmental, scenic, historic, aesthetic, community, and other cultural values and mobility needs in a cost effective manner; and

(c) Access and accommodation for other modes of transportation.

§ 170.456 How can a Tribe request an exception from the design standards?

(a) A Tribe can request an exception from the required design standards from FHWA. The engineer of record (the State licensed civil engineer whose name and professional stamp appear on the PS&E or who is responsible for the overall project design) must submit written documentation with appropriate supporting data, sketches, details, and justification based on engineering analysis.

(b) FHWA can approve a project design that does not conform to the minimum criteria only after giving due consideration to all project conditions, such as:

(1) Maximum service and safety benefits for the dollar invested;

(2) Compatibility with adjacent features; and

(3) Probable time before reconstruction of the project due to changed conditions or transportation demands.

(c) FHWA has 30 days from receiving the request to approve or decline the exception.

§ 170.457 Can a Tribe appeal a denial?

Yes. Tribes may appeal the denial of a design exception to: FHWA Office of Federal Lands Highway, 1200 New Jersey Ave. SE., HFL–1, Washington, DC 20590. If FHWA denies a design exception, the Tribe may appeal the decision Office of the FHWA Administrator, 1200 New Jersey Ave. SE., HOA–1, Washington, DC 20590.

Review and Approval of Plans, Specifications and Estimates

§ 170.460 What must a project package include?

The project package must include the following documentation, approved by the appropriate Public Authority, before the start of construction:

(a) Plans, specifications, and estimates;

(b) A Tribal resolution or other authorized document supporting the project;

(c) Certification of compliance with the requirements of 25 CFR part 169, as well as any additional public taking documentation clearances, if applicable.

(d) Required environmental, archeological, and cultural clearances; and

(e) Identification of design exceptions if used in the plans.

§ 170.461 May a Tribe approve plans, specifications, and estimates?

An Indian Tribal government may approve plans, specifications and estimates and commence road and bridge construction with funds made available from the TTP through a self-determination contract, self-governance agreement, Program Agreement or other appropriate agreement, developed in accordance with 23 U.S.C. 202(b)(6) & (b)(7), if the Indian Tribal government:

(a) Provides assurances in the contract or agreement that the construction will meet or exceed applicable health and safety standards;

(b) Obtains advance review of the plans and specifications from a State-licensed civil engineer that has certified that the plans and specifications meet or exceed the applicable health and safety standards;

(c) Provides a copy of the certification under paragraph (a) of this section to the Deputy Assistant Secretary for Tribal Government Affairs, Department of Transportation, or the Assistant Secretary—Indian Affairs, DOI, as appropriate; and

(d) Provides a copy of all project documentation identified in § 170.460 to BIA or FHWA before the start of construction.

§ 170.463 What if a design deficiency is identified?

If the Secretaries identify a design deficiency that may jeopardize public health and safety if the facility is completed, they must:

(a) Immediately notify the Tribe of the design deficiency and request that the Tribe promptly resolve the deficiency under the standards in § 170.454; and

(b) For a BIA-prepared PS&E package, promptly resolve the deficiency under the standards in § 170.454 and notify the Tribe of the required design changes.

CONSTRUCTION AND CONSTRUCTION MONITORING

§ 170.470 Which construction standards must Tribes use?

(a) Tribes must either:

(1) Use the approved standards referred to in § 170.454; or

(2) Request approval for any other road and highway bridge construction standards that are consistent with or exceed the standards referred to in § 170.454.

(b) For designing and building eligible intermodal projects funded by the TTP, Tribes must use either:

(1) Nationally recognized standards for comparable projects; or

(2) Tribally adopted standards that meet or exceed nationally recognized standards for comparable projects.

§ 170.471 How are projects administered?

(a) When a Tribe carries out a TTP project, the project will be administered in accordance with a self-determination contract, self-governance agreement, Program Agreement or other appropriate agreement and this regulation.

(b) If BIA or FHWA discovers a problem during an on-site monitoring visit, BIA or FHWA must promptly notify the Tribe and, if asked, provide technical assistance.

(c) Only the State-licensed professional engineer of record whose name and professional stamp appear on the PS&E or who is responsible for the overall project design may change a TTP project's PS&E during construction.

(1) The original approving agency must review each substantial change. The approving agency is the Federal, Tribal, State, or local entity with PS&E approval authority over the project.

(2) The approving agency must consult with the affected Tribe and the entity having maintenance responsibility.

(3) A change that exceeds the limits of available funding may be made only with the approving agency's consent.

§ 170.472 What construction records must Tribes and BIA keep?

The following table shows which TTP construction records BIA and Tribes must keep and the requirements for access.

Record keeper	Records that must be kept	Access requirements
(a) Tribe	All records required by ISDEAA and 25 CFR 900.130–131 or 25 CFR 1000.243 and 1000.249, as appropriate.	BIA and FHWA are allowed access to Tribal TTP construction and approved project specifications as required under 25 CFR 900.130, 900.131, 25 CFR 1000.243 and 1000.249, or the Program Agreement as appropriate.
(b) BIA	Completed daily reports of construction activities appropriate to the type of construction it is performing.	Upon reasonable advance request by a Tribe, BIA must provide reasonable access to records.

§ 170.473 When is a project complete?

A project is considered substantially complete when all work is completed and accepted (except for minor tasks yet to be completed (punch list)) and the project is open to traffic. The project is completed only after all the requirements of this section are met.

(a) At the end of a construction project, the public authority, agency, or organization responsible for the project must make a final inspection. The inspection determines whether the project has been completed in reasonable conformity with the PS&E.

(1) Appropriate officials from the Tribe, BIA, responsible public authority, and FHWA should participate in the inspection, as well as contractors and maintenance personnel.

(2) All project information must be made available during final inspection and used to develop the TTP construction project closeout report. Some examples of project information are: Daily diaries, weekly progress reports, subcontracts, subcontract expenditures, salaries, equipment expenditures, as-built drawings, etc.

(b) After the final inspection, the facility owner makes final acceptance of the project. At this point, the Tribe or BIA must complete a project closeout and final accounting of all TTP construction project expenditures under § 170.474.

(c) If applicable, all documents required by 25 CFR part 169 must be completed.

§ 170.474 Who conducts the project closeout?

The following table shows who must conduct the TTP construction project closeout and develop the report.

If the project was completed by . . .	then . . .	and the closeout report must . . .
(a) BIA	The region engineer or designee is responsible for closing out the project and preparing the report.	(1) Summarize the construction project records to ensure compliance requirements have been met; (2) Review the bid item quantities and expenditures to ensure reasonable conformance with the PS&E and modifications; (3) Be completed within 120 calendar days of the date of acceptance of the TTP construction project; and (4) Be provided to the affected Tribes and the Secretaries.
(b) A Tribe	Agreements negotiated under ISDEAA, or other appropriate agreements specify who is responsible for closeout and preparing the report.	(1) Meet the requirements of ISDEAA; (2) Comply with 25 CFR 900.130(d) and 131(b)(10) and 25 CFR 1000.249, or the Program Agreement, as applicable; (3) Be completed within 120 calendar days of the date of acceptance of the project; and (4) Be provided to all parties specified in the agreements.

MANAGEMENT SYSTEMS

§ 170.502 Are nationwide management systems required for the TTP?

(a) To the extent appropriate, the Secretaries, in consultation with Tribes, will implement safety, bridge, pavement, and congestion management systems for the Federal and Tribal facilities included in the NTTFI.

(b) A Tribe may develop its own Tribal management system based on the nationwide management system requirements in 23 CFR part 973. The Tribe may use either TTP formula funds or transportation planning funds defined in 23 U.S.C. 202(c) for this purpose. The Tribal system must be consistent with Federal management systems.

TRIBAL TRANSPORTATION FACILITY BRIDGES

§ 170.510 What funds are available for Tribal Transportation Facility Bridge activities?

Funds are made available in 23 U.S.C. 202(d) for improving deficient bridges eligible for the TTP.

§ 170.511 What activities are eligible for Tribal Transportation Facility Bridge funds?

(a) The activities that are eligible for 23 U.S.C. 202(d) funding are:

(1) Carrying out any planning, design, engineering, preconstruction, construction, and inspection of a bridge project to replace, rehabilitate, seismically retrofit, paint, apply calcium magnesium acetate, sodium acetate/formate, or other environmentally acceptable, minimally corrosive anti-icing and deicing composition; or

(2) Implementing any countermeasure for deficient Tribal transportation facility bridges, including multiple-pipe culverts.

(b) Further information regarding the use and availability of these funds can be found at 23 CFR part 661.

§ 170.512 How will Tribal Transportation Facility Bridge funds be made available to the Tribes?

Funds made available to Tribes under 23 U.S.C. 202(d) may be included in the Tribe's self-determination contracts, self-governance agreements, Program Agreements, and other appropriate agreements.

§ 170.513 When and how are bridge inspections performed?

(a) All bridges identified on the NTTFI must be inspected under 23 U.S.C. 144.

(b) Employees performing inspections as required by § 170.513(a) must:

(1) Notify affected Tribes and State and local governments that an inspection will occur;

(2) Offer Tribal and State and local governments the opportunity to accompany the inspectors; and

(3) Otherwise coordinate with Tribal and State and local governments.

(c) The person responsible for the bridge inspection team must meet the qualifications for bridge inspectors as defined in 23 U.S.C. 144.

§ 170.514 Who reviews bridge inspection reports?

The person responsible for the bridge inspection team must send a copy of the inspection report to BIADOT. BIADOT:

(a) Reviews the report for quality assurance and works with FHWA to ensure the requirements of 23 U.S.C. 144 are carried out; and

(b) Furnishes a copy of the report to the BIA Regional Office, which will forward the copy to the affected Tribe.

APPENDIX A TO SUBPART D—CULTURAL RESOURCE AND ENVIRONMENTAL REQUIREMENTS FOR THE TTP

All BIA, FHWA, and Tribal work for the TTP must comply with cultural resource and environmental requirements under applicable Federal laws and regulations, including, but not limited to:

1. 16 U.S.C. 1531, Endangered Species Act.
2. 16 U.S.C. 4601, Land and Water Conservation Fund Act (Section 6(f)).
3. 16 U.S.C. 661–667d, Fish and Wildlife Coordination Act.
4. 23 U.S.C. 138, Preservation of Parklands, commonly referred to as 4(f).
5. 25 U.S.C. 3001–3013, Native American Graves Protection and Repatriation Act.
6. 33 U.S.C. 1251, Federal Water Pollution Control Act and Clean Water Act.
7. 42 U.S.C. 7401, Clean Air Act.
8. 42 U.S.C. 4321, National Environmental Policy Act.
9. 49 U.S.C. 303, Preservation of Parklands.

10. 7 U.S.C. 4201, Farmland Protection Policy Act.
11. 50 CFR part 402, Endangered Species Act regulations.
12. 7 CFR part 658, Farmland Protection Policy Act regulations.
13. 40 CFR part 93, Air Quality Conformity and Priority Procedures for use in Federal-aid Highway and Federally-Funded Transit Programs.
14. 23 CFR part 771, Environmental Impact and Related Procedures.
15. 23 CFR part 772, Procedures for Abatement of Highway Traffic Noises and Construction Noises.
16. 23 CFR part 777, Mitigation of Impacts To Wetlands and Natural Habitat.
17. 36 CFR part 800, Protection of Historic Properties.
18. 40 CFR parts 260–271, Resource Conservation and Recovery Act regulations.
19. Applicable Tribal/State laws.
20. Other applicable Federal laws and regulations.

APPENDIX B TO SUBPART D—DESIGN STANDARDS FOR THE TTP

Depending on the nature of the project, Tribes must use the latest edition of the following design standards, as applicable. Additional standards may also apply. In addition, Tribes may develop design standards that meet or exceed the standards listed in this appendix. To the extent that any provisions of these standards are inconsistent with ISDEAA, these provisions do not apply.
1. AASHTO Policy on Geometric Design of Highways and Streets.
2. AASHTO A Guide for Transportation Landscape and Environmental Design.
3. AASHTO Roadside Design Guide.
4. AASHTO Guide for Selecting, Locating and Designing Traffic Barriers.
5. AASHTO Standard Specifications for Highway Bridges.
6. AASHTO Guidelines of Geometric Design of Very Low-Volume Local Roads (ADT less than or equal to 400).
7. FHWA Federal Lands Highway, Project Development and Design Manual.
8. FHWA Flexibility in Highway Design.
9. FHWA Roadside Improvements for Local Road and Streets.
10. FHWA Improving Guardrail Installations and Local Roads and Streets.
11. 23 CFR part 625, Design Standards for Highways.
12. 23 CFR part 630, Preconstruction Procedures.
13. 23 CFR part 633, Required Contract Provisions.
14. 23 CFR part 635, Construction and Maintenance.
15. 23 CFR part 645, Utilities.
16. 23 CFR part 646, Railroads.
17. 23 U.S.C. 106, PS&E.
18. 23 U.S.C. 109, Standards.
19. DOT Metric Conversion Plan, October 31, 1991.
20. MUTCD Manual of Uniform Traffic Safety Devices.
21. Standard Specifications for Construction of Roads and Bridges on Federal Highway Projects.
22. FHWA-approved State standards.
23. FHWA-approved Tribal design standards.

Subpart E—Service Delivery for Tribal Transportation Program

FUNDING PROCESS

§ 170.600 What must BIA include in the notice of funds availability?

(a) Upon receiving the total or partial fiscal year of TTP funding from FHWA:

(1) BIA will send a notice of funds availability to each BIA Regional Office and FHWA that includes the TTP Tribal share funding available to each Tribe within each region; and

(2) BIA and FHWA will forward the information to the Tribes along with an offer of technical assistance.

(b) BIA and FHWA will distribute Tribal share funds to eligible Tribes upon execution of all required agreements or contracts between BIA/FHWA and the Tribe. This distribution must occur:

(1) Within 30 days after funds are made available to the Secretary under this paragraph; and

(2) Upon execution of all required agreements or contracts between BIA/FHWA and the Tribe.

(c) Funds made available under this section must only be expended on projects and activities identified in an FHWA-approved TTIP. The TTPTIP (see § 170.424) is available on the BIA Transportation and FHWA Web sites.

§ 170.602 If a Tribe incurs unforeseen construction costs, can it get additional funds?

The TTP is a Tribal shares program based upon a statutory funding formula. Therefore, no additional TTP funding beyond each Tribe's share is available for unforeseen construction costs. However, a Tribe may reprogram their TTP Tribal shares from other projects or activities identified on their FHWA-approved TTIP to cover unforeseen costs. In addition, if a Tribe is operating under a self-determination contract, it may request that additional dollars from its TTP Tribal share funds be made available for that project under 25 CFR 900.130(e).

MISCELLANEOUS PROVISIONS

§ 170.605 May BIA or FHWA use force-account methods in the TTP?

When requested by a Tribe, BIA or FHWA may use force-account methods in carrying out the eligible work of the TTP. Applicable Federal acquisition laws and regulations apply to BIA and FHWA when carrying out force-account activities on behalf of a Tribe.

§ 170.606 How do legislation and procurement requirements affect the TTP?

Other legislation and procurement requirements apply to the TTP as shown in the following table:

Legislation, regulation or other requirement	Applies to Tribes under self-determination contracts	Applies to Tribes under self-governance agreements	Applies to Tribes under BIA or FHWA program agreements	Applies to activities performed by the Secretary
Buy Indian Act	No	No	No	Yes.
Buy American Act	No	No	No	Yes.
Federal Acquisition Regulation (FAR)	No(a)	No	No	Yes.
Federal Tort Claims Act	Yes	Yes	Yes	Yes.
Davis-Bacon Act	Yes(b)	Yes(b)	Yes(b)	Yes.

(a) Unless agreed to by the Tribe or Tribal organization under ISDEAA, 25 U.S.C. 450j(a), and 25 CFR 900.115.
(b) Does not apply when Tribe performs work with its own employees.

§ 170.607 Can a Tribe use its allocation of TTP funds for contract support costs?

Yes. Contract support costs are an eligible item out of a Tribe's TTP allocation and must be included in a Tribe's project construction budget.

§ 170.608 Can a Tribe pay contract support costs from DOI or BIA appropriations?

No. Contract support costs for TTP construction projects cannot be paid out of DOI or BIA appropriations.

§ 170.609 Can a Tribe receive additional TTP funds for start-up activities?

No. Additional TTP funding for start-up activities is not available.

CONTRACTS AND AGREEMENTS

§ 170.610 Which TTP functions may a Tribe assume?

A Tribe may assume all TTP functions and activities that are otherwise contractible and non-inherently Federal under self-determination contracts, self-governance agreements, Program Agreements; and other appropriate agreements. The appendix to this subpart contains the list of program functions that cannot be subcontracted. Administrative support functions are an eligible use of TTP funding.

§ 170.611 What special provisions apply to ISDEAA contracts and agreements?

(a) *Multi-year contracts and agreements.* The Secretary can enter into a multi-year TTP self-determination contract and self-governance agreement with a Tribe under sections 105(c)(1)(A) and (2) of ISDEAA. The amount of the contracts or agreements is subject to the availability of appropriations.

(b) *Consortia.* Under title I and title IV of ISDEAA, Tribes and multi-tribal organizations are eligible to assume TTPs under consortium contracts or agreements. For an explanation of self-determination contracts, refer to title I, 25 U.S.C. 450f. For an explanation of self-governance agreements, see title IV, 25 U.S.C. 450b(l) and 458b(b)(2).

(c) *Advance payments.* The Secretary and the Tribe must negotiate a schedule of advance payments as part of the terms of a self-determination contract under 25 CFR 900.132.

(d) *Design and construction contracts.* The Secretary can enter into a design/construct TTP self-determination contract that includes both the design and construction of one or more TTP projects. The Secretary may make advance payments to a Tribe:

(1) Under a self-determination design/construct contract for construction activities based on progress, need, and the payment schedule negotiated under 25 CFR 900.132; and

(2) Under a self-governance agreement in the form of annual or semi-annual installments as indicated in the agreement.

§ 170.612 Can non-contractible functions and activities be included in contracts or agreements?

Non-contractible TTP functions and activities cannot be included in self-determination contracts, self-governance agreements, Program Agreements, or other agreements. The appendix to this subpart contains a list of TTP functions and activities that cannot be contracted.

§ 170.613 What funds are used to pay for non-contractible functions and activities?

(a) The administrative expenses funding identified in 23 U.S.C. 202(a)(6) are used by the BIA and FHWA transportation personnel when performing non-contractible functions and activities, including:

(1) Program management and oversight; and

(2) Project-related administration activities.

(b) If a Tribe enters into a Program Agreement with FHWA under 23 U.S.C. 202(b)(7), the program agreement may include such additional amounts as the Secretary of Transportation determines would equal the amount that would have been withheld for the costs of the Bureau of Indian Affairs for administration of the program or project.

§ 170.614 Can a Tribe receive funds before BIA publishes the final notice of funding availability?

A Tribe can receive funds before BIA publishes the final notice of funding availability required by § 170.600(a) when partial year funding is made available to the TTP through continuing resolutions or other Congressional actions.

§ 170.615 Can a Tribe receive advance payments for non-construction activities under the TTP?

Yes. A Tribe must receive advance payments for non-construction activities under 25 U.S.C. 450*l* for self-determination contracts on a quarterly, semiannual, lump-sum, or other basis proposed by a Tribe and authorized by law.

§ 170.616 How are payments made to Tribes if additional funds are available?

After an Agreement between BIA or FHWA and the Tribe is executed, any additional funds will be made available to Tribes under the terms of the executed Agreement.

§ 170.617 May a Tribe include a contingency in its proposal budget?

(a) A Tribe with a self-determination contract may include a contingency amount in its proposed budget under 25 CFR 900.127(e)(8).

(b) A Tribe with a self-governance agreement may include a project-specific line item for contingencies if the Tribe does not include its full TTP funding allocation in the agreement.

(c) The amounts in both paragraphs (a) and (b) of this section must be within the Tribal share made available or within the negotiated ISDEAA contract or agreement.

§ 170.618 Can a Tribe keep savings resulting from project administration?

All funds made available to a Tribe through the 23 U.S.C. 202(b) are considered "tribal" and are available to the Tribe until expended. However, they must be expended on projects and activities referenced on an FHWA-approved TTPTIP.

§ 170.619 Do Tribal preference and Indian preference apply to TTP funding?

Tribal preference and Indian preference apply to TTP funding as shown in the following table:

If . . .	Then . . .
(a) A contract serves a single Tribe.	Section 7(c) under Title 1 of ISDEAA allows Tribal employment or contract preference laws, including Tribe local preference laws, to govern.
(b) A contract serves more than one Tribe.	Section 7(b) under Title 1 of ISDEAA applies.
(c) A self-governance agreement exists under Title IV of ISDEAA.	25 CFR 1000.406 applies.
(d) A Program Agreement	The language of the Program Agreement applies.

§ 170.620 How do ISDEAA's Indian preference provisions apply?

This section applies when the Secretary or a Tribe enters into a cooperative, reimbursable, or other agreement with a State or local government for a TTP construction project. The Tribe and the parties may choose to incorporate the provisions of section 7(b) of ISDEAA in the agreement.

§ 170.621 What if a Tribe doesn't perform work under a contract or agreement?

If a Tribe fails to substantially perform work under a contract or agreement:

(a) For self-determination contracts, the Secretary must use the monitoring and enforcement procedures in 25 CFR 900.131(a) and (b) and ISDEAA, part 900 subpart L (appeals);

(b) For self-governance agreements, the Secretary must use the monitoring and enforcement procedures in 25 CFR part 1000, subpart K; or

(c) For FHWA or BIA TTP Agreements, the Secretaries will use the procedures identified in the Agreements.

§ 170.622 What TTP functions, services, and activities are subject to the self-governance construction regulations?

All TTP design and construction projects and activities, whether included separately or under a program in the agreement, are subject to the regulations in 25 CFR part 1000, subpart K, including applicable exceptions.

§ 170.623 How are TTP projects and activities included in a self-governance agreement?

To include a TTP project or activity in a self-governance agreement, the following information is required:

(a) All work must be included in the FHWA-approved TTPTIP; and

(b) All other information required under 25 CFR part 1000, subpart K.

§ 170.624 Is technical assistance available?

Yes. Technical assistance is available from BIA, the Office of Self-Governance, and FHWA for Tribes with questions about contracting the TTP or TTP projects.

§ 170.625 What regulations apply to waivers?

The following regulations apply to waivers:

(a) For self-determination contracts, 25 CFR 900.140 through 900.148;

(b) For self-governance agreements, 25 CFR 1000.220 through 1000.232; and

(c) For direct service, 25 CFR 1.2.

§ 170.626 How does a Tribe request a waiver of a Department of Transportation regulation?

A Tribe can request a waiver of a Department of Transportation regulation as shown in the following table:

If the Tribe's contract or agreement is with . . .	and . . .	then the Tribe must . . .
(a) The Secretary	the contract is a self-determination contract.	follow the procedures in ISDEAA, Title I, and 25 CFR 900.140 through 900.148.
(b) The Secretary	the agreement is a Tribal self-governance agreement.	follow the procedures in 25 CFR 1000.220 through 1000.232.
(c) The Secretary of Transportation		make the request to the Secretary of Transportation at: 1200 New Jersey Ave. SE., HFL–1, Washington, DC 20590.

§ 170.627 Can non-TTP funds be provided to a Tribe through an FHWA Program Agreement, BIA TTP Agreement or other appropriate agreement?

In addition to all funds made available under chapter 2 of title 23, the cooperation of States, counties, and other local subdivisions may be accepted in construction and improvement of a Tribal transportation facility. In accordance with 23 U.S.C. 202(a)(9), any funds received from a State, county, or local subdivision may be credited by the Secretaries to appropriations available for the TTP. Subject to an agreement among the Tribe, BIA or FHWA, and the State, county, or local subdivision that addresses the purpose and intent of the funds such funds may be provided to the Tribe through an a self-determination contract, self-governance agreement, Program Agreement or other appropriate agreement developed in accordance with 23 U.S.C. 202(b)(6) & (b)(7).

APPENDIX TO SUBPART E—LIST OF PROGRAM FUNCTIONS THAT CANNOT BE SUBCONTRACTED

Per § 170.612, program functions cannot be included in self-determination contracts, self-governance agreements, Program Agreements, or other agreements. Program functions include all of the following:

(a) TTP project-related pre-contracting activities:

(1) Notifying Tribes of available funding including the right of first refusal; and

(2) Providing technical assistance.

(b) TTP project-related contracting activities:

(1) Providing technical assistance;

(2) Reviewing all scopes of work under 25 CFR 900.122;

(3) Evaluating proposals and making declination decisions, if warranted;

(4) Performing declination activities;

(5) Negotiating and entering into contracts or agreements with State, Tribal, and local governments and other Federal agencies;

(6) Processing progress payments or contract payments;

(7) Approving contract modifications;

(8) Processing claims and disputes with Tribal governments; and

(9) Closing out contracts or agreements.

(c) Planning activities:

(1) Reviewing and approving TTPTIPs developed by Tribes or other contractors; and

(2) Reviewing and approving TTP LRTPs developed by Tribes or other contractors.

(d) Environmental and historical preservation activities:

(1) Reviewing and approving all items required for environmental compliance; and

(2) Reviewing and approving all items required for archaeological compliance.

(e) Processing rights-of-way:

(1) Reviewing rights-of-way applications and certifications;

(2) Approving rights-of-way documents;

(3) Processing grants and acquisition of rights-of-way requests for Tribal trust and allotted lands under 25 CFR part 169;

(4) Responding to information requests;

(5) Reviewing and approving documents attesting that a project was constructed entirely within a right-of-way granted by BIA; and

(6) Performing custodial functions related to storing rights-of-way documents.

(f) Conducting project development and design under 25 CFR 900.131:

(1) Participating in the plan-in-hand reviews on behalf of BIA as facility owner;

(2) Reviewing and/or approving PS&E for health and safety assurance on behalf of BIA as facility owner;

(3) Reviewing PS&E to assure compliance with NEPA as well as all other applicable Federal laws; and

(4) Reviewing PS&E to assure compliance with or exceeding Federal standards for TTP design and construction.

(g) Construction:

(1) Making application for clean air/clean water permits as facility owner;

(2) Ensuring that all required State/tribal/Federal permits are obtained;

(3) Performing quality assurance activities;

(4) Conducting value engineering activities as facility owner;

(5) Negotiating with contractors on behalf of the Federal Government;

(6) Approving contract modifications/change orders;

(7) Conducting periodic site visits;

(8) Performing all Federal Government-required project-related activities contained in the contract documents and required by 25 CFR parts 900 and 1000;

(9) Conducting activities to assure compliance with safety plans as a jurisdictional responsibility hazardous materials, traffic control, OSHA, etc.;

(10) Participating in final inspection and acceptance of project documents or as-built drawings on behalf of BIA as facility owner; and

(11) Reviewing project closeout activities and reports.

(h) Other activities:

(1) Performing other non-contractible required TTP project activities contained in this part, ISDEAA and part 1000; and

(2) Other title 23 non-project-related management activities.

(i) BIADOT program management:

(1) Developing budget on needs for the TTP;

(2) Developing legislative proposals;

(3) Coordinating legislative activities;

(4) Developing and issuing regulations;

(5) Developing and issuing TTP planning, design, and construction standards;

(6) Developing/revising interagency agreements;

(7) Developing and approving TTP stewardship agreements in conjunction with FHWA;

(8) Developing annual TTP obligation and TTP accomplishments reports;

(9) Developing reports on TTP project expenditures and performance measures for the Government Performance and Results Act (GPRA);

(10) Responding to/maintaining data for congressional inquiries;

(11) Developing and maintaining the funding formula and its database;

(12) Allocating TTP and other transportation funding;

(13) Providing technical assistance to Tribes/Consortiums/tribal organizations/agencies/regions;

(14) Providing national program leadership for other Federal transportation related programs including: Transportation Alternatives Program, Tribal Transportation Assistance Program, Recreational Travel and Tourism, Transit Programs, ERFO Program, and Presidential initiatives;

(15) Participating in and supporting Tribal transportation association meetings;

(16) Coordinating with and monitoring Indian Local Technical Assistance Program centers;

(17) Planning, coordinating, and conducting BIA/tribal training;

(18) Developing information management systems to support consistency in data format, use, etc., with the Secretary of Transportation for the TTP;

(19) Participating in special transportation related workgroups, special projects, task forces and meetings as requested by Tribes;

(20) Participating in national, regional, and local transportation organizations;

(21) Participating in and supporting FHWA Coordinated Technology Implementation program;

(22) Participating in national and regional TTP meetings;

(23) Consulting with Tribes on non-project related TTP issues;

(24) Participating in TTP, process, and product reviews;

(25) Developing and approving national indefinite quantity service contracts;

(26) Assisting and supporting the TTP Coordinating Committee;

(27) Processing TTP bridge program projects and other discretionary funding applications or proposals from Tribes;

(28) Coordinating with FHWA;

(29) Performing stewardship of the TTP;

(30) Performing oversight of the TTP and its funded activities;

(31) Performing any other non-contractible TTP activity included in this part; and

(32) Determining eligibility of new uses of TTP funds.

(j) BIADOT Planning:

(1) Maintaining the official TTP inventory;

(2) Reviewing LRTPs;

(3) Reviewing and approving TTPTIPs;

(4) Maintaining nationwide inventory of TTP strip and atlas maps;

(5) Coordinating with Tribal/State/regional/local governments;

(6) Developing and issuing procedures for management systems;

(7) Distributing approved TTPTIPs to BIA regions;

(8) Coordinating with other Federal agencies as applicable;

(9) Coordinating and processing the funding and repair of damaged tribal roads with FHWA;

(10) Calculating and distributing TTP transportation planning funds to BIA regions;

(11) Reprogramming unused TTP transportation planning funds at the end of the fiscal year;

(12) Monitoring the nationwide obligation of TTP transportation planning funds;

(13) Providing technical assistance and training to BIA regions and Tribes;

(14) Approving atlas maps;

(15) Reviewing TTP inventory information for quality assurance; and

(16) Advising BIA regions and Tribes of transportation funding opportunities.

(k) BIADOT engineering:

(1) Participating in the development of design/construction standards with FHWA;

(2) Developing and approving design/construction/maintenance standards;

(3) Conducting TTP/product reviews; and

(4) Developing and issuing technical criteria for management systems.

(l) BIADOT responsibilities for bridges:

(1) Maintaining the National Bridge Inventory information/database for BIA bridges;

(2) Conducting quality assurance of the bridge inspection program;

(3) Reviewing and processing TTP Bridge Program applications;

(4) Participating in second level review of TTP bridge PS&E; and

(5) Developing criteria for bridge management systems.

(m) BIADOT responsibilities to perform other non-contractible required TTP activities contained in this part.

(n) BIA regional offices program management:

(1) Designating TTP System roads;

(2) Notifying Tribes of available funding;

(3) Developing STIPs;

(4) Providing FHWA-approved TTPTIPs to Tribes;

(5) Providing technical assistance to Tribes/Consortiums/tribal organizations/ agencies;

(6) Funding common services as provided as part of the region/agency/BIA Division of Transportation TTP costs;

(7) Processing and investigating non-project related tort claims;

(8) Preparing budgets for BIA regional and agency TTP activities;

(9) Developing/revising interagency agreements;

(10) Developing control schedules/transportation improvement programs;

(11) Developing regional TTP stewardship agreements;

(12) Developing quarterly/annual TTP obligation and program accomplishments reports;

(13) Developing reports on TTP project expenditures and performance measures for Government Performance and Results Act (GPRA);

(14) Responding to/maintaining data for congressional inquiries;

(15) Participating in Indian transportation association meetings;

(16) Participating in Indian Local Technical Assistance Program (LTAP) meetings and workshops;

(17) Participating in BIA/tribal training development highway safety, work zone safety, etc.;

(18) Participating in special workgroups, task forces, and meetings as requested by Tribes and BIA region/agency personnel;

(19) Participating in national, regional, or local transportation organizations meetings and workshops;

(20) Reviewing Coordinated Technology Implementation Program project proposals;

(21) Consulting with Tribal governments on non-project related program issues;

(22) Funding costs for common services as provided as part of BIA TTP region/agency/ contracting support costs;

(23) Reviewing TTP atlas maps;

(24) Processing Freedom of Information Act (FOIA) requests;

(25) Monitoring the obligation and expenditure of all TTP funds allocated to the BIA Region;

(26) Performing activities related to the application for ERFO funds, administration, and oversight of the funds; and

(27) Participating in TTP, process, and product reviews.

(o) BIA regional offices' planning:

(1) Coordinating with Tribal/State/regional/local government;

(2) Coordinating and processing the funding and repair of damaged Tribal Transportation Facility roads with Tribes;

(3) Reviewing and approving TTP inventory data;

(4) Maintaining, reviewing, and approving the management systems databases;

(5) Reviewing and approving STIPs; and

(6) Performing Federal responsibilities identified in the TTP Transportation Planning Procedures and Guidelines manual.

(p) BIA regional offices' engineering:

(1) Approving Tribal standards for TTP use;

(2) Developing and implementing new engineering techniques in the TTP; and

(3) Providing technical assistance.

(q) BIA regional offices' responsibilities for bridges:

(1) Reviewing and processing TTP Bridge Program applications;

(2) Reviewing and processing TTP bridge inspection reports and information; and

(3) Ensuring the safe use of roads and bridges.

(r) BIA regional offices' other responsibilities for performing other non-contractible required TTP activities contained in this part.

Subpart F—Program Oversight and Accountability

§ 170.700 What is the TTP national business plan?

The TTP national business plan delineates the respective roles and responsibilities of BIA and FHWA in the administration of the TTP and the process used for fulfilling those roles and responsibilities.

§ 170.701 May a direct service Tribe and BIA Region sign a Memorandum of Understanding?

Yes. A direct service Tribe and BIA Region may sign a Memorandum of Understanding (MOU). A TTP Tribal/BIA Region MOU is a document that a direct service Tribe and BIA may enter into to help define the roles, responsibilities and consultation process between the BIA regional office and the Indian Tribal government. It describes how the TTP will be carried out by BIA on the Tribe's behalf.

§ 170.702 What activities may the Secretaries review and monitor?

The Secretaries review and monitor the performance of all TTP activities.

§ 170.703 What program reviews do the Secretaries conduct?

(a) In accordance with title 23, the national business plan, 2 CFR part 200, and the Program Agreement or other appropriate agreements, BIADOT and FHWA shall conduct formal program reviews of BIA Regional Offices or Tribes to examine program procedures and identify improvements. For a BIA Regional Office review, the regional Tribes will be notified of these formal program reviews. Tribes may send representatives to these meetings at their own expense.

(b) The review will provide recommendations to improve the program, processes and controls of management, planning, design, construction, financial and administration activities.

(c) After the review, the review team shall:

(1) Make a brief oral report of findings and recommendations to the Tribal leadership or BIA Regional Director; and

(2) Within 60 days, provide a written report of its findings and recommendations to the Tribe, BIA, all participants, and affected Tribal governments and organizations.

§ 170.704 What happens when the review process identifies areas for improvement?

When the review process identifies areas for improvement:

(a) The Tribe or regional office must develop a corrective action plan within 60 days;

(b) BIADOT and FHWA review and approve the plan;

(c) FHWA may provide technical assistance during the development and implementation of the plan; and

(d) The reviewed Tribe or BIA regional office implements the plan and reports either annually or biennially to BIADOT and FHWA on implementation.

Subpart G—Maintenance

§ 170.800 What funds are available for maintenance activities?

(a) Under 23 U.S.C. 202(a)(8), a Tribe can use TTP funding for maintenance, within the following limits, whichever is greater:

(1) 25 percent of its TTP funds; or

(2) $500,000.

(b) These funds can only be used to maintain the public facilities included in the NTTFI.

(c) Road sealing activities are not subject to this limitation.

(d) BIA retains primary responsibility, including annual funding request responsibility, for BIA road maintenance programs on Indian reservations.

(e) The Secretary shall ensure that funding made available under the TTP for maintenance of Tribal transportation facilities for each fiscal year is supplementary to, and not in lieu of, any obligation of funds by the BIA for road maintenance programs on Indian reservations.

§ 170.801 Can TTP funds designated on an FHWA-approved TTIP for maintenance be used to improve TTP transportation facilities?

No. The funds identified for maintenance on a FHWA-approved TTIP cannot be used to improve roads or other TTP transportation facilities to a higher road classification, standard or capacity.

§ 170.802 Can a Tribe perform road maintenance?

Yes. A Tribe may enter into self-determination contracts, self-governance agreements, program agreements, and other appropriate agreements to perform Tribal transportation facility maintenance.

§ 170.803 To what standards must a Tribal transportation facility be maintained?

Subject to availability of funding, Tribal transportation facilities must be maintained under either:

(a) A standard accepted by BIA or FHWA (as identified in the official Tribal Transportation Program guide on either the BIA transportation Web site at *http://www.bia.gov/WhoWeAre/BIA/OIS/Transportation/index.htm* or the Federal Lands Highway—Tribal Transportation Program Web site at *http://flh.fhwa.dot.gov/programs/ttp/guide/*), or

(b) Another Tribal, Federal, State, or local government maintenance standard negotiated in an ISDEAA road maintenance self-determination contract or self-governance agreement.

§ 170.804 Who should be contacted if a Tribal transportation facility is not being maintained to TTP standards due to insufficient funding?

The Tribe may notify BIA or FHWA if the Tribe believes that a facility on the NTTFI is not being adequately maintained to the standards identified in § 170.803. If BIA or FHWA determines that a Tribal transportation facility is not being maintained, it will:

(a) Notify the facility owner;

(b) Provide a draft copy of the report to the affected Tribe for comment before forwarding it to Secretary of Transportation; and

(c) Report these findings to the appropriate office within FHWA.

§ 170.805 What maintenance activities are eligible for TTP funding?

TTP maintenance funding support a wide variety of activities necessary to maintain facilities identified in the NTTFI. A list of eligible activities is shown in the appendix to this part.

APPENDIX TO SUBPART G—LIST OF ELIGIBLE MAINTENANCE ACTIVITIES UNDER THE TRIBAL TRANSPORTATION PROGRAM

The following maintenance activities are eligible for funding under the TTP. The list is not all-inclusive.

1. Cleaning and repairing ditches and culverts.
2. Stabilizing, removing, and controlling slides, drift sand, mud, ice, snow, and other impediments.
3. Adding additional culverts to prevent roadway and adjoining property damage.
4. Repairing, replacing or installing traffic control devices, guardrails and other features necessary to control traffic and protect the road and the traveling public.
5. Removing roadway hazards.
6. Repairing or developing stable road embankments.
7. Repairing parking facilities and appurtenances such as striping, lights, curbs, etc.
8. Repairing transit facilities and appurtenances such as bus shelters, striping, sidewalks, etc.
9. Training maintenance personnel.
10. Administering the BIA transportation facility maintenance program.
11. Performing environmental/archeological mitigation associated with transportation facility maintenance.
12. Leasing, renting, or purchasing of maintenance equipment.
13. Paying utilities cost for roadway lighting and traffic signals.
14. Purchasing maintenance materials.
15. Developing, implementing, and maintaining a BIA Transportation Facility Maintenance Management System (TFMMS).
16. Performing pavement maintenance such as pot hole patching, crack sealing, chip sealing, surface rejuvenation, and thin overlays (less than 1 inch).
17. Performing erosion control.
18. Controlling roadway dust.
19. Re-graveling roads.
20. Controlling vegetation through mowing, noxious weed control, trimming, etc.
21. Making bridge repairs.
22. Paying the cost of closing transportation facilities due to safety or other concerns.
23. Maintaining airport runways, heliport pads, and their public access roads.
24. Maintaining and operating BIA public ferry boats.
25. Making highway alignment changes for safety reasons. These changes require prior notice to the Secretary.
26. Making temporary highway alignment or relocation changes for emergency reasons.
27. Maintaining other TTP intermodal transportation facilities provided that there is a properly executed agreement with the owning public authority within available funding.

Subpart H—Miscellaneous Provisions

REPORTING REQUIREMENTS AND INDIAN PREFERENCE

§ 170.910 What information on the TTP or projects must BIA or FHWA provide?

All available public information regarding the TTP can be found on the BIA transportation Web site at *http://www.bia.gov/WhoWeAre/BIA/OIS/Transportation/index.htm* or the Federal Lands Highway—Tribal Transportation Program Web site at *http://flh.fhwa.dot.gov/programs/ttp/*. If a Tribe would like additional information that is not available on the Web sites, the Tribe should contact FHWA or BIA directly. FHWA and BIA will then provide direction or assistance based upon the Tribe's specific request.

§ 170.911 Are Indians entitled to employment and training preferences?

(a) Federal law gives hiring and training preferences, to the greatest extent feasible, to Indians for all work performed under the TTP.

(b) Under 25 U.S.C. 450e(b), 23 U.S.C. 140(d), 25 U.S.C. 47, and 23 U.S.C. 202(a)(3), Indian organizations and Indian-owned economic enterprises are entitled to a preference, to the greatest extent feasible, in the award of contracts, subcontracts and sub-grants for all work performed under the TTP.

§ 170.912 Does Indian employment preference apply to Federal-aid Highway Projects?

(a) Tribal, State, and local governments may provide an Indian employment preference for Indians living on or near a reservation on projects and contracts that meet the definition of a Tribal transportation facility. (See 23 U.S.C. 101(a)(12) and 140(d), and 23 CFR 635.117(d).)

(b) Tribes may target recruiting efforts toward Indians living on or near Indian reservations, Tribal lands, Alaska Native villages, pueblos, and Indian communities.

(c) Tribes and Tribal employment rights offices should work cooperatively with State and local governments to develop contract provisions promoting employment opportunities for Indians on eligible federally funded transportation projects. Tribal, State, and local representatives should confer to establish Indian employment goals for these projects.

§ 170.913 Do Tribal-specific employment rights and contract preference laws apply?

Yes. When a Tribe or consortium administers a TTP or project intended to benefit that Tribe or a Tribe within the consortium, the benefitting Tribe's employment rights and contracting preference laws apply. (See § 170.619 and 25 U.S.C. 450e(c))

§ 170.914 What is the difference between Tribal preference and Indian preference?

Indian preference is a hiring preference for Indians in general. Tribal preference is a preference adopted by a Tribal government that may or may not include a preference for Indians in general, Indians of a particular Tribe, Indians in a particular region, or any combination thereof.

§ 170.915 May Tribal employment taxes or fees be included in a TTP project budget?

Yes. The cost of Tribal employment taxes or fees may be included in the budget for a TTP project.

§ 170.916 May Tribes impose taxes or fees on those performing TTP services?

Yes. Tribes, as sovereign nations, may impose taxes and fees for TTP activities. When a Tribe administers TTPs or projects under ISDEAA, its Tribal employment and contracting preference laws, including taxes and fees, apply.

§ 170.917 Can Tribes receive direct payment of Tribal employment taxes or fees?

This section applies to non-tribally administered TTP projects. Tribes can request that BIA pay Tribal employment taxes or fees directly to them under a voucher or other written payment instrument, based on a negotiated payment schedule. Tribes may consider requesting direct payment of Tribal employment taxes or fees from other transportation departments in lieu of receiving their payment from the contractor.

§ 170.918 What applies to the Secretaries' collection of data under the TTP?

(a) Under 23 U.S.C. 201(c)(6)(A), the Secretaries will collect and report data necessary to implement the TTP in accordance with ISDEAA, including, but not limited to:

(1) Inventory and condition information on Tribal transportation facilities; and

(2) Bridge inspection and inventory information on any Federal bridge open to the public.

(b) In addition, under 23 U.S.C. 201(c)(6)(C), any entity that carries out a project under the TTP is required to provide the data identified in § 170.240.

TRIBAL TRANSPORTATION DEPARTMENTS

§ 170.930 What is a Tribal transportation department?

A Tribal transportation department is a department, commission, board, or official of any Tribal government charged by its laws with the responsibility for transportation-related responsibilities, including but not limited to, administration, planning, maintenance, and construction activities. Tribal governments, as sovereign nations, have inherent authority to establish their own transportation departments under their own Tribal laws. Tribes may staff and organize transportation departments in any manner that best suits their needs. Tribes can receive technical assistance from TTACs, BIA regional road engineers, FHWA, or AASHTO to establish a Tribal transportation department.

§ 170.931 Can Tribes use TTP funds to pay Tribal transportation department operating costs?

Yes. Tribes can use TTP funds to pay the cost of planning, administration, and performance of approved TTP activities (see § 170.116). Tribes can also use BIA road maintenance funds to pay the cost of planning, administration, and performance of maintenance activities under this part.

§ 170.932 Are there other funding sources for Tribal transportation departments?

There are many sources of funds that may help support a Tribal transportation department. The following are some examples of additional funding sources:

(a) Tribal general funds;

(b) Tribal Priority Allocation;

(c) Tribal permits and license fees;

(d) Tribal fuel tax;

(e) Federal, State, private, and local transportation grants assistance;

(f) Tribal Employment Rights Ordinance fees (TERO); and

(g) Capacity building grants from Administration for Native Americans and other organizations.

§ 170.933 Can Tribes regulate oversize or overweight vehicles?

Yes. Tribal governments can regulate travel on roads under their jurisdiction and establish a permitting process to regulate the travel of oversize or overweight vehicles, under applicable Federal law. BIA may, with the consent of the affected Tribe, establish a permitting process to regulate the travel of oversize or overweight vehicles on the BIA road system.

RESOLVING DISPUTES

§ 170.934 Are alternative dispute resolution procedures available?

(a) Federal agencies should use mediation, conciliation, arbitration, and other techniques to resolve disputes brought by TTP beneficiaries. The goal of these alternative dispute resolution (ADR) procedures is to provide an inexpensive and expeditious forum to resolve disputes. Federal agencies should resolve disputes at the lowest possible staff level and in a consensual manner whenever possible.

(b) Except as required in 25 CFR part 900 and part 1000, Tribes operating under a self-determination contract or self-governance agreement are entitled to use dispute resolution techniques prescribed in:

(1) The ADR Act, 5 U.S.C. 571–583;

(2) The Contract Disputes Act, 41 U.S.C. 601–613; and

(3) The ISDEAA and the implementing regulations (including for non-construction the mediation and alternative dispute resolution options listed in 25 U.S.C. 4501 (model contract section (b)(12)).

(4) Tribes operating under a Program Agreement with FHWA are entitled to use dispute resolution techniques prescribed in 25 CFR 170.934 and Article II, Section 4 of the Agreement.

§ 170.935 How does a direct service Tribe begin the alternative dispute resolution process?

(a) To begin the ADR process, a direct service Tribe must write to the BIA Regional Director, or the Chief of BIA Division of Transportation. The letter must:

(1) Ask to begin one of the ADR procedures in the Administrative Dispute Resolution Act of 1996, 5 U.S.C. 571–583 (ADR Act); and

(2) Explain the factual and legal basis for the dispute.

(b) ADR proceedings will be governed by procedures in the ADR Act and the implementing regulations.

OTHER MISCELLANEOUS PROVISIONS

§ 170.941 May Tribes become involved in transportation research?

Yes. Tribes may:

(a) Participate in Transportation Research Board meetings, committees, and workshops sponsored by the National Science Foundation;

(b) Participate in and coordinate the development of Tribal and TTP transportation research needs;

(c) Submit transportation research proposals to States, FHWA, AASHTO, and FTA;

(d) Prepare and include transportation research proposals in their TTPTIPS;

(e) Access Transportation Research Information System Network (TRISNET) database; and

(f) Participate in transportation research activities under Intergovernmental Personnel Act agreements.

§ 170.942 Can a Tribe use Federal funds for transportation services for quality-of-life programs?

(a) A Tribe can use TTP funds:

(1) To coordinate transportation-related activities to help provide access to jobs and make education, training, childcare, healthcare, and other services more accessible to Tribal members; and

(2) As the matching share for other Federal, State, and local mobility programs.

(b) To the extent authorized by law, additional grants and program funds are available for the purposes in paragraph (a)(1) of this section from other programs administered by the Departments of Transportation, Health and Human Services, and Labor.

(c) Tribes should also apply for Federal and State public transportation and personal mobility program grants and funds.

PART 171—IRRIGATION OPERATION AND MAINTENANCE

Subpart A—General Provisions

Sec.

Subpart B—Irrigation Service

Subpart C—Water Use

Subpart D—Irrigation Facilities

Subpart E—Financial Matters: Assessments, Billing, and Collections

Subpart F—Records, Agreements, and Other Matters

Subpart G—Non-Assessment Status

AUTHORITY: 25 U.S.C. 2; 25 U.S.C. 9; 25 U.S.C. 13; 25 U.S.C. 381; Act of April 4, 1910, 36 Stat. 270, as amended (codified at 25 U.S.C. 385); 25 U.S.C. 386a; Act of June 22, 1936, 49 Stat. 1803 (codified at 25 U.S.C. 389 *et seq.*).

SOURCE: 73 FR 11036, Feb. 29, 2008, unless otherwise noted.

Subpart A—General Provisions

§ 171.100 What are some of the terms I should know for this part?

Annual Assessment Waiver means a mechanism for us to waive your annual operation and maintenance assessment under certain specified circumstances.

Annual operation and maintenance assessment means the charges you must pay us for our costs of administration, operation, maintenance, and rehabilitation of the irrigation facility servicing your farm unit.

Annual operation and maintenance assessment rate means the per acre charge we establish for the irrigation facility servicing your farm unit.

Assessable acres (see *Total assessable acres*).

Authorized use means your use of water delivered by us that supports irrigated agriculture, livestock, Carriage Agreements or other uses defined by laws, regulations, treaty, compact, judicial decree, river regulatory plan, or other authority.

BIA means the Bureau of Indian Affairs within the United States Department of the Interior.

Bill means our statement to you of the assessment charges and/or fees you owe the United States for administration, operation, maintenance, rehabilitation, and/or construction of the irrigation facility servicing your farm unit.

Carriage Agreement means a legally binding contract we enter into:

(1) To convey third-party water through our irrigation facilities; or

(2) To convey our water through third-party facilities.

Construction assessment means the periodic charge we assess you to repay us the funds we used to construct our irrigation facilities serving your farm unit that are determined to be reimbursable under applicable statutes.

Customer means any person or entity to whom we provide irrigation service.

Ditch (see *Farm ditch* or *Service ditch*).

Due date means the date printed on your bill, 30 days after which your bill becomes past due.

Facility (see *Irrigation facility*).

Farm ditch means a ditch or canal that you own, operate, maintain, and rehabilitate.

Farm unit means the smallest parcel of land for which we will establish a delivery point. Farm unit size is defined in the authorizing legislation for each irrigation facility, or in the absence of such legislation, we will define the farm unit size.

I, me, my, you, and *your* means all interested parties, especially persons or entities to which we provide irrigation service and receive use of our irrigation facilities, such as irrigators, landowners, leasees, irrigator organizations, irrigation districts, or other entities affected by this part and our supporting policies, manuals, and handbooks.

Idle lands means lands that are not currently farmed because they have characteristics that limit crop production.

Incentive Agreement means a written agreement between you and us that allows us to waive your annual operation and maintenance assessment, when you agree to improve idle lands and we determine that it is in the best interest of our irrigation facility.

Irrigation bill (see *Bill*).

Irrigation district (see *Representative organization*).

Irrigation facility means all structures and appurtenant works for the delivery, diversion, and storage of irrigation water. These facilities may be referred to as projects, systems, or irrigation areas.

Irrigation service means the full range of services we provide customers, including but not limited to administration, operation, maintenance, and rehabilitation of our irrigation facilities.

Irrigation water or *water* means water we deliver through our facilities for the general purpose of irrigation and other authorized purposes.

Irrigator (see *Customer*).

Landowner means a person or entity that owns fee, tribal trust, and/or individual allotted trust lands.

Leaching Service means our delivery of water to you at your request for the purpose of transporting salts below the root zone of a farm unit.

Lessee means any person or entity that holds a lease approved by us on lands to which we provide irrigation service.

Must means an imperative or mandatory act or requirement.

My land and *your land* mean all or part of your farm unit.

Obstruction means anything permanent or temporary that blocks, hinders, impedes, stops or cuts off our facilities or our ability to perform the services we determine necessary to provide service to our customers.

Organization (see *Representative organization*).

Past due bill means a bill that has not been paid within 30 days of the due date stated on your bill.

Permanently non-assessable acres (PNA) means lands that the Secretary of the Interior has determined to be permanently non-irrigable pursuant to the standards set out in 25 U.S.C. 389b.

Representative organization or *organization* means a legally established organization representing your interests that confers with us on how we provide irrigation service at a particular irrigation facility.

Service(s) (see *Irrigation service*).

Service area means lands designated by us to be served by one of our irrigation facilities.

Service ditch means a ditch or canal which we own, administer, operate, maintain, and rehabilitate that we use to provide irrigation service to your farm unit.

Soil salinity means soils containing high salt content that limit crop production.

Special assessment means a charge to cover the uncontrolled cost arising from an urgency on an irrigation facility.

Structures (see *Irrigation facility*).

Subdivision means a farm unit that has been subdivided into smaller parcels.

Supplemental water means water available for delivery by our irrigation facilities beyond the quantity necessary to provide all project customers requesting water with the per-acre water duty established for that project.

Taxpayer identifying number means either your Social Security Number or your Employer Identification Number.

Temporarily non-assessable acres (TNA) means lands that the Secretary of the

Interior has determined to be temporarily non-irrigable pursuant to the standards set out in 25 U.S.C. 389a.

Total assessable acres means the total acres of land served by one of our irrigation facilities to which we assess operation and maintenance charges. The *Total assessable acres* within the service area of an irrigation facility do not include those acres of land that are designated PNA or TNA, nor those acres of land granted an Annual Assessment Waiver.

Trust or *restricted land* or *land in trust* or restricted status (see definitions in 25 CFR 151.2).

Urgency means a situation that we have determined may adversely impact our irrigation facilities, operation, or other irrigation activities; affect public safety; or damage property or equipment.

Wastewater means surface runoff and subsurface drainage from your farm unit from water delivered by us that exceeds irrigation requirements.

Water (see *Irrigation water*).

Water delivery is an activity that is part of the irrigation service we provide to our customers when water is available.

Water duty means the amount of water, in acre-feet per acre, necessary for full-service irrigation. This value is established by decree, compact, or other legal document, or by specialized engineering studies.

Water user (see *Customer*).

We, us, and *our* means the United States Government, the Secretary of the Interior, BIA, and all who are authorized to represent us in matters covered under this part.

§ 171.105 Does this part apply to me?

This part applies to you if you own or lease land within an irrigation project where we assess fees and collect monies to administer, operate, maintain, and rehabilitate project facilities.

§ 171.110 How does BIA administer its irrigation facilities?

(a) We administer our irrigation facilities by enforcing the applicable statutes, regulations, Executive Orders, directives, Indian Affairs Manual, the Irrigation Handbook, and other written policies, procedures, directives, and practices to ensure the safe, reliable, and efficient administration, operation, maintenance, and rehabilitation of our facilities. Such enforcement can include refusal or termination of irrigation services to you. Copies of the above listed items may be obtained from the irrigation project serving you.

(b) We will cooperate and consult with you, as appropriate, on irrigation activities and policies of the particular irrigation facility serving you.

§ 171.115 Can I and other irrigators establish representative organizations?

Yes. You and other irrigators may establish a representative organization under applicable law to represent your interests for the particular irrigation facilities serving you.

§ 171.120 What are the authorities and responsibilities of a representative organization?

(a) A legally established organization representing you may make rules, policies, and procedures it may find necessary to administer the activities it is authorized to perform.

(b) An organization must not make rules, policies, or procedures that conflict with our regulations or any of our other written policies, procedures, directives, and manuals.

(c) If this organization collects operation and maintenance assessments and construction assessments on your behalf to be paid to us, it must pay us all your past and current operation and maintenance and construction assessment charges before we will provide irrigation service to you.

§ 171.125 Can I appeal BIA decisions?

(a) You may appeal our decisions in accordance with procedures set out in 25 CFR part 2, unless otherwise prohibited by law.

(b) If you appeal an irrigation bill, you must pay the bill in accordance with subpart E before we will provide irrigation service to you. If you prevail on appeal, any overpayment will be refunded to you.

§ 171.130 Who can I contact if I have any questions about these regulations or my irrigation service?

Contact the local irrigation project where you receive service or want to apply for service. If your questions are not addressed to your satisfaction at the local project level, you may contact the appropriate BIA Regional Office.

§ 171.135 Where do I submit written information or requests?

Submit written information to us or make request of us in writing at the irrigation project servicing your farm unit.

§ 171.140 Information collection.

The information collection requirements contained in this part have been approved by the Office of Management and Budget under 44 U.S.C. 3501 *et seq.* and assigned clearance number 1076–0141. This information collection is specifically found in 25 CFR sections 171.200, 171.225, 171.305, 171.310, 171.405, 171.410, 171.530, 171.550, 171.600, 171.605, 171.610, 171.615, 171.710, 171.715. A Federal agency may not conduct or sponsor, and you are not required to respond to, a collection of information unless it displays a currently valid OMB control number.

Subpart B—Irrigation Service

§ 171.200 How do I request irrigation service from the BIA?

(a) You must request service from the irrigation facility servicing your farm unit.

(b) Your request must contain at least the following information:

(1) Your full legal name;

(2) Where you want service;

(3) The time and date you want service to start;

(4) How long you want service;

(5) The rate of water flow you want, if available;

(6) How many acres you want to irrigate; and

(7) Any additional information required by the project office responsible for providing your irrigation service.

(c) You must request supplemental water in accordance with the project guidelines established by the specific project providing your irrigation service.

§ 171.205 How much water will I receive?

The amount of water you receive will be based on your request, your legal entitlement to water, and the available water supply.

§ 171.210 Where will BIA provide my irrigation service?

(a) We will provide service to your farm unit at a single delivery point that we designate.

(b) At our discretion, we may establish additional delivery points when:

(1) We determine it is impractical to deliver water to your farm unit from a single delivery point;

(2) You agree in writing to be responsible for all costs to establish an additional delivery point;

(3) You pay us our costs prior to our establishing an additional delivery point; and

(4) Any work accomplished under this section does not disrupt our service to other customers without their written agreement.

(c) We may establish your delivery point(s) at a well head.

§ 171.215 What if the elevation of my farm unit is too high to receive irrigation water?

(a) We will not change our service ditch level to provide service to you.

(b) You may install, operate, and maintain your own facilities, at your cost, to provide service to your land:

(1) From a delivery point we designate; and

(2) In accordance with specifications we approve.

§ 171.220 What must I do to my farm unit to receive irrigation service?

You must meet the following requirements for us to provide service:

(a) Put water we deliver to authorized uses;

(b) Make sure your farm ditch has sufficient capacity to carry the water we deliver; and

(c) Properly operate, maintain, and rehabilitate your farm ditch.

§ 171.225 What must I do to receive irrigation service to my subdivided farm unit?

In order to receive irrigation service, you must:

(a) Provide us a copy of the recorded plat or map of the subdivision which shows us how the irrigation water will be delivered to the irrigable acres;

(b) Pay for any extensions or alterations to our facilities that we approve to serve the subdivided units;

(c) Construct, at your cost, any facilities within your subdivided farm unit; and

(d) Operate and maintain, at your cost, any facilities within your subdivided farm unit.

§ 171.230 What are my responsibilities for wastewater?

(a) You are responsible for your wastewater.

(b) Wastewater may be returned to our facilities, but only at locations we designate, in a manner we approve, and at your cost.

(c) You must not allow your wastewater to flow or collect on our facilities or roads, except at locations we designate and in a manner we approve.

(d) If you fail to comply with this section, we may withhold services to you.

Subpart C—Water Use

§ 171.300 Does BIA restrict my water use?

(a) You must not interfere with or alter our service to you without our prior written authorization; and

(b) You must only use water we deliver for authorized uses. We may withhold services if you use water for any other purpose.

§ 171.305 Will BIA provide leaching service to me?

(a) We may provide you leaching service if:

(1) You submit a written plan that documents how soil salinity limits your crop production and how leaching service will correct the problem;

(2) We approve your plan in writing; and

(3) Your irrigation bills are not past due.

(b) Leaching service will only be available during the timeframe established by your irrigation facility.

(c) We reserve the right to terminate this service if we determine you are not complying with paragraph (a) of this section.

§ 171.310 Can I use water delivered by BIA for livestock purposes?

Yes, if we determine it will not:

(a) Interfere with the operation, maintenance, or rehabilitation of our facilities;

(b) Be detrimental to or jeopardize our facilities;

(c) Adversely affect the water rights or water supply; or

(d) Cause additional costs to us that we do not agree to in writing.

Subpart D—Irrigation Facilities

§ 171.400 Who is responsible for structures on a BIA irrigation project?

(a) We may build, operate, maintain, rehabilitate or remove structures, including bridges and other crossings, on our irrigation projects.

(b) We may build other structures for your private use during the construction or extension of an irrigation project. We may charge you for structures built for your private use under this section, and we may require you to maintain them.

(c) If we require you to maintain a structure and you do not do so to our satisfaction, we may remove it or perform the necessary maintenance, and we will bill you for our costs.

§ 171.405 Can I build my own structure or take over responsibility of a BIA structure?

You may build a structure on our irrigation facility for your private use or take responsibility of one of our structures, but only under a written agreement between you and us which:

(a) Relieves us from any future liability or responsibility for the structure;

(b) Relieves us from any future costs incurred for maintaining the structure;

(c) Describes what is granted by us and accepted by you; and

(d) Provides that if you do not regularly use a structure for a period of time that we have determined, or you do not properly maintain and rehabilitate the structure, we will notify you in writing that:

(1) You must either remove it or correct any unsafe condition;

(2) If you do not comply with our notice, we may remove the structure and you must reimburse us our costs; and

(3) We may modify, close, or remove your structure without notice due to an urgency we have identified.

§ 171.410 Can I install a fence on a BIA irrigation project?

Yes. Fences are considered structures and may be installed in compliance with § 171.405.

§ 171.415 Can I place an obstruction on a BIA irrigation project?

No. You may not place obstructions on BIA irrigation projects.

(a) If you do so, we will notify you in writing that you must remove it.

(b) If you do not remove your obstruction in compliance with our notice, we will remove it and we will bill you for our costs.

(c) We can remove your obstruction without notice because of an urgency we have identified.

§ 171.420 Can I dispose of sewage, trash, or other refuse on a BIA irrigation project?

No. Sewage, trash, or other refuse are considered obstructions and must be removed in accordance with § 171.415.

Subpart E—Financial Matters: Assessments, Billing, and Collections

§ 171.500 How does BIA determine the annual operation and maintenance assessment rate for the irrigation facility servicing my farm unit?

(a) We calculate the annual operation and maintenance assessment rate by estimating the following annual costs and then dividing by the total assessable acres for your irrigation facility:

(1) Personnel salary and benefits for the facility engineer/manager and employees under their management or control;

(2) Materials and supplies;

(3) Vehicle and equipment repairs;

(4) Equipment costs, including lease fees;

(5) Depreciation;

(6) Acquisition costs;

(7) Maintenance of a reserve fund available for contingencies or emergency costs needed for the reliable operation of the irrigation facility infrastructure;

(8) Maintenance of a vehicle and heavy equipment replacement fund;

(9) Systematic rehabilitation and replacement of project facilities;

(10) Contingencies for unknown costs and omitted budget items; and

(11) Other costs we determine necessary to properly perform the activities and functions characteristic of an irrigation facility.

(b) Annual operation and maintenance assessment rates may be lowered through the exercise of our discretion when items listed in (a) of this section are adjusted pursuant to our authority under 25 U.S.C. 385, 386a and 389.

(c) If you subdivide your farm unit, you may be subject to a higher annual operation and maintenance assessment rate, which we publish annually in the FEDERAL REGISTER.

(d) At projects where supplemental water is available, the calculation of your annual operation and maintenance assessment rate may take into consideration the total estimated annual amount to be collected for supplemental water deliveries.

§ 171.505 How does BIA calculate my annual operation and maintenance assessment?

(a) We calculate your annual operation and maintenance assessment by multiplying the total assessable acres of your land within the service area of our irrigation facility by the annual operation and maintenance assessment rate we establish for that facility.

(b) We will not assess lands that have been re-classified as either permanently non-assessable (PNA) or temporarily non-assessable (TNA) or lands that have been granted an Annual Assessment Waiver.

(c) If your lands are under an approved Incentive Agreement, we may waive your assessment as described in the Incentive Agreement (See § 171.610).

(d) Some irrigation facilities may charge a minimum operation and maintenance assessment. If the irrigation facility serving your farm unit charges a minimum operation and maintenance assessment that is more than your assessment calculated by the method described in subpart (a) of this section, you will be charged the minimum operation and maintenance assessment. We provide public notice of any minimum operation and maintenance assessments annually in the FEDERAL REGISTER (See § 171.565).

§ 171.510 How does BIA calculate my annual operation and maintenance assessment if supplemental water is available on the irrigation facility servicing my farm unit?

(a) For projects where supplemental water is available, and you request and receive supplemental water, your assessment will include two components: a base rate, which is for your per-acre water duty delivered to your farm unit; and a supplemental water rate, which is for water delivered to your farm unit in addition to your per-acre water duty.

(b) We publish base and supplemental water rates annually in the FEDERAL REGISTER. The base and supplemental water rates are established to recover the costs identified in section 171.500(a) of this subpart.

(c) If your project has established a supplemental water rate, and you request and receive supplemental water, we will calculate your total annual operation and maintenance assessment by adding the following two totals:

(1) The total assessable acres of your land within the service area of our irrigation facility multiplied by the annual operation and maintenance assessment rate we establish for that facility; and

(2) The actual quantity of supplemental water you request and we agree to deliver (in acre-feet) times the supplemental water rate established for that facility.

§ 171.515 Who will BIA bill?

(a) We will bill the landowner, unless:

(1) The land is leased under a lease approved by us, in which case we will bill the lessee, or

(2) The landowner(s) is represented by a representative organization that collects annual operation and maintenance assessments on behalf of its members and the representative organization makes a direct payment to us on your behalf.

(b) If you own or lease assessable lands within a BIA irrigation facility, you will be billed for annual operation and maintenance assessments, whether you request water or not, unless otherwise specified in § 171.505(b).

§ 171.520 How will I receive my bill and when do I pay it?

(a) You will receive your bill in the mail at the address of record you provide us.

(b) You should pay your bill no later than the due date stated on your bill.

(c) You will not receive a bill for supplemental water. You must pay us in advance at the supplemental water rate established for you project published annually in the FEDERAL REGISTER.

§ 171.525 How do I pay my bill?

(a) You can pay your bill by:

(1) Personally going to the local office of the irrigation facility authorized to receive your payment during normal business hours;

(2) Depositing your payment in an authorized drop box, if available, at the local office of the irrigation facility; or

(3) Mailing your payment to the address indicated on your bill.

(b) Your payment must be in the form of:

(1) Check or money order in the mail or authorized drop box; or

(2) Cash, check, or money order if you pay in person.

§ 171.530 What information must I provide BIA for billing purposes?

We must obtain certain information from you to ensure we can properly bill, collect, deposit, and account for money you owe the United States. At a minimum, this information is:

(a) Your full legal name;

(b) Your correct mailing address; and

(c) Your taxpayer identifying number.

§ 171.535 Why is BIA collecting this information from me?

(a) As part of doing business with you, we must collect enough information from you to properly bill and service your account.

(b) We are required to collect your taxpayer identifying number under the authority of, and as prescribed in, the Debt Collection Improvement Act of 1996, Public Law 104–134 (110 Stat. 1321–364).

§ 171.540 What can happen if I do not provide this information?

We will not provide you irrigation service.

§ 171.545 What can happen if I don't pay my bill on time?

(a) We will not provide you irrigation service until:

(1) Your bill is paid; or

(2) You make arrangement for payment pursuant to § 171.550 of this part.

(b) If you do not pay your bill prior to the close of business on the 30th day after the due date, we consider your bill past due, send you a notice, and assess you the following:

(1) Interest, as required by 31 U.S.C. 3717. Interest will accrue from the original due date stated on your bill.

(2) An administrative fee, as required by 31 CFR 901.9.

(c) If you do not pay your bill prior to the close of business of the 90th day after the due date, we will assess you a penalty, as required by 31 CFR 901.9(d). Penalties will accrue from the original due date stated on your bill.

(d) We will forward your past due bill to the United States Treasury no later than 180 days after the original due date, as required by 31 CFR 901.1, "Aggressive agency collection activity."

§ 171.550 Can I arrange a Payment Plan if I cannot pay the full amount due?

We may approve a Payment Plan if:

(a) You are a landowner and your land is not leased;

(b) You certify that you are financially unable to make a lump sum payment;

(c) You provide additional information we request, which may include information identified in 31 CFR 901.8, "Collection in installments"; and

(d) You sign our Payment Plan containing terms and conditions we specify.

§ 171.555 What additional costs will I incur if I am granted a Payment Plan?

You will incur the following costs:

(a) An administrative fee to process your Payment Plan, as required by 31 CFR 901.9.

(b) Interest, accrued on your unpaid balance, in accordance with § 171.545.

§ 171.560 What if I fail to make payments as specified in my Payment Plan?

(a) We will discontinue irrigation service until your bill is paid in full;

(b) You will be in default, you will be assessed an administrative fee, and your debt will be immediately forwarded to the United States Treasury in accordance with the Debt Collection Improvement Act of 1996 (Pub. L. 104–134).

(c) You will be ineligible for Payment Plans for the next 6 years.

§ 171.565 How will I know if BIA plans to adjust my annual operation and maintenance assessment rate?

(a) We provide public notice of our proposed rates annually in the FEDERAL REGISTER.

(b) You may contact the irrigation facility servicing your farm unit.

§ 171.570 What is the Federal Register and where can I get it?

(a) The FEDERAL REGISTER is the official daily publication for Rules, Proposed Rules, and Notices of official actions by Federal agencies and organizations, as well as Executive Orders and other Presidential Documents, and is produced by the United States Government Printing Office (GPO).

(b) You can get publications of the FEDERAL REGISTER:

(1) By going on the World Wide Web at *http://www.gpo.gov*;

(2) By writing to the GPO, Superintendent of Documents, P.O. Box 371954, Pittsburgh, Pennsylvania 15250–7954; or

(3) By calling GPO at (202) 512–1530.

§ 171.575 Can BIA charge me a special assessment?

Yes. We will make every reasonable effort to avoid charging special assessments. However, if we determine that we have a significant uncontrolled cost due to an urgency, we may charge you a special assessment. We will only charge special assessments when there are inadequate project funds available, including any emergency reserve funds held by the project.The special assessment rate will be calculated by dividing the total uncontrolled cost, or some portion of that cost, by the total number of assessable acres. Your individual special assessment will be equal to the special assessment rate multiplied by the number of assessable acres in your farm unit.

Subpart F—Records, Agreements, and Other Matters

§ 171.600 What information is collected and retained on the irrigation service I receive?

We will collect and retain at least the following information as part of our record of the irrigation service we have provided you:

(a) Your name;

(b) Delivery point(s) where service was provided;

(c) Beginning date and time of your irrigation service;

(d) Ending date and time of your irrigation service; and

(e) Amount of water we delivered to your farm unit.

§ 171.605 Can I establish a Carriage Agreement with BIA?

(a) We may agree in writing to carry third-party water through our facilities to your lands not served by our facilities if we have determined that our facilities have adequate capacity to do so.

(b) If we determine that carrying water in accordance with paragraph (a) of this section is jeopardizing our ability to provide irrigation service to the lands we are required to serve, we will terminate the Agreement.

(c) We may enter into an agreement with a third party to provide service through their facilities to your isolated assessable lands.

(d) You must pay us all administrative, operating, maintenance, and rehabilitation costs associated with any agreement established under this section before we will convey water.

(e) We will notify you in writing no less than five days before terminating a Carriage Agreement established under this section.

(f) We may terminate a Carriage Agreement without notice due to an urgency we have identified.

§ 171.610 Can I arrange an Incentive Agreement if I want to farm idle lands?

We may approve an Incentive Agreement if:

(a) You request one in writing at least 90 days prior to the beginning of the irrigation season that includes a detailed plan to improve the idle lands, which contains at least the following:

(1) A description of specific improvements you will make, such as clearing, leveling, or other activities that will improve idle lands to a condition that supports authorized use of delivered water;

(2) The estimated cost of the improvements you will make;

(3) The time schedule for your proposed improvements;

(4) Your proposed schedule for water delivery, if necessary; and

(5) Justification for use of irrigation water during the improvement period.

(b) You sign our Incentive Agreement containing terms and conditions we specify.

§ 171.615 Can I request improvements to BIA facilities as part of my Incentive Agreement?

Yes. You may request and we may agree to make improvements as part of your Incentive Agreement that we determine are in the best interest of the irrigation facility servicing your farm unit.

Subpart G—Non-Assessment Status

§ 171.700 When do I not have to pay my annual operation and maintenance assessment?

You do not have to pay your annual operation and maintenance assessment for your land(s) within the service area of your irrigation facility when:

(a) We grant you an Annual Assessment Waiver; or

(b) We grant you an Incentive Agreement which may include waiving your annual operation and maintenance assessment; or

(c) Your land is re-designated as permanently non-assessable or temporarily non-assessable.

§ 171.705 What criteria must be met for my land to be granted an Annual Assessment Waiver?

For your land to be granted an Annual Assessment Waiver, we must determine that our irrigation facilities are not capable of delivering adequate irrigation water to your farm unit. Inadequate water supply due to natural conditions or climate is not justification for us to grant an Annual Assessment Waiver.

§ 171.710 Can I receive irrigation water if I am granted an Annual Assessment Waiver?

No. Water will not be delivered in any quantity to your farm unit if you have been granted an Annual Assessment Waiver.

§ 171.715 How do I obtain an Annual Assessment Waiver?

For your land to be granted an Annual Assessment Waiver, you must:

(a) Send us a request in writing to have your land granted an Annual Assessment Waiver;

(b) Submit your request prior to the bill due date for the year for which you are requesting the Annual Assessment Waiver; and

(c) Receive our approval in writing.

§ 171.720 For what period does an Annual Assessment Waiver apply?

Annual Assessment Waivers are only valid for the year in which they are granted. To obtain an Annual Assessment Waiver for a subsequent year, you must reapply.

PART 172—PUEBLO INDIAN LANDS BENEFITED BY IRRIGATION AND DRAINAGE WORKS OF MIDDLE RIO GRANDE CONSERVANCY DISTRICT, NEW MEXICO

AUTHORITY: 45 Stat. 312.

§ 172.1 Acreage designated.

Pursuant to the provisions of the act of March 13, 1928 (45 Stat. 312) the contract executed between the Middle Rio Grande Conservancy District of New Mexico and the United States under date of December 14, 1928, the official plan approved pursuant thereto, as modified, and the terms of section 24 of a contract between said parties dated September 4, 1936, dealing among other things with the payment of operation and maintenance and betterment assessments by the United States to the District, and section 24 of a similar contract dated April 8, 1938 executed by the representative of the United States, on this date, it is found that a total of 20,242.05 acres of Pueblo Indian lands of the Pueblos of Cochiti, Santo Domingo, San Felipe, Santa Ana, Sandia and Isleta is susceptible of economic irrigation and cultivation and is materially benefited by the works constructed by said District. This acreage is designated as follows:

Lands with recognized water rights not subject to operation and maintenance or betterment charges by the District and designated as "now irrigated"—8,847

Lands classified as "newly reclaimed" lands (exclusive of the purchased area)—11,074.4

Lands classified as newly reclaimed lands (the area recently purchased)—320.65

Total irrigable area materially benefited—20,242.05

[22 FR 10641, Dec. 24, 1957. Redesignated at 47 FR 13327, Mar. 30, 1982]

PART 173—CONCESSIONS, PERMITS AND LEASES ON LANDS WITHDRAWN OR ACQUIRED IN CONNECTION WITH INDIAN IRRIGATION PROJECTS

Sec.

AUTHORITY: 52 Stat. 193; 25 U.S.C. 390.

SOURCE: 22 FR 10642, Dec. 24, 1957, unless otherwise noted. Redesignated at 47 FR 13327, Mar. 30, 1982.

§173.0 Scope.

The regulations in this part are promulgated governing the granting of concessions, business, agricultural and grazing leases or permits on reservoir sites, reserves for canals or flowage areas, and other lands withdrawn or otherwise acquired in connection with the San Carlos, Fort Hall, Flathead and Duck Valley or Western Shoshone irrigation projects.

§173.1 Terms used.

When used in this part "Secretary" refers to the Secretary of the Interior; "project" to the Federal Indian irrigation project on which concession, lease or permit is granted, and "project engineer" to the engineer in charge of said project.

§173.2 Project engineer's authority.

The project engineer is the official charged with the responsibility for the enforcement of this part. He is vested with the authority to issue temporary concession permits to applicants for periods not to exceed 30 days. All except temporary permits shall become effective when approved by the Secretary.

§173.3 Enforcement.

The project engineer shall enforce these and all project regulations now or hereafter promulgated by the Secretary. Willful violation or failure to comply with the provisions of this part and all proper orders of the project engineer shall be cause for revocation of the permit by the Secretary who shall be the judge of what constitutes such violation. The project engineer may suspend any permit for cause. The project engineer shall, immediately after suspending a permit, submit to the Secretary through the Commissioner of Indian Affairs a detailed report of the case, accompanied by his reasons for the action and his recommendations, for final action by the Secretary.

§173.4 Permits subject to existing and future rights-of-way.

Use by the permittee of any land authorized under this part shall be subject to the right of the Secretary to establish trails, roads and other rights-of-way including improvements thereupon or through the premises, and the right to use same by the public. No interference shall be permitted with the continued use of all existing roads, trails and other rights-of-way and improvements thereon.

§173.5 Plans, approval thereof.

No building or other structure shall be erected by permittee except in accordance with plans, specifications and locations approved by the project engineer. All premises and appurtenances shall be kept in a sanitary, safe and sightly condition.

§173.6 Stock grazing.

Permittees may graze upon lands covered by such permits, such stock as may be required in connection with the purposes for which the permit is issued subject to such restrictions and limitations as may be prescribed by the project engineer.

§173.7 Permits, transferable.

Permits may be transferred only with the approval of the Secretary.

§ 173.8 Applications.

All applications for permits must be made on the approved form. The project engineer will furnish copies of this form upon request. All applications must be executed in triplicate.

§ 173.9 Bonds.

Except in cases of temporary concession permits, leases, permits, and traders' licenses granted under parts 166, 162, and 140 of this chapter, which are governed by the requirements of those parts, the applicant shall within 60 days after approval of the application furnish a surety bond for the faithful performance of the terms of the permit in an amount equal to the total sum accruing during the period of the permit. Such bond shall be executed by an approved surety company, or by at least three individual sureties, whose individual unencumbered assets are equal to double the amount of the bond. In the case of temporary concession permits, the permittee shall deposit at the time of receiving the permit, a sum equal to twice the rental, which sum shall, upon the expiration of the permit, be refunded to the permittee, if all the terms and conditions of the permit have been met; otherwise, such sum shall be retained as liquidated damages.

§ 173.10 Payments.

Each permittee shall pay at the time of receiving the permit the first year's charge as fixed therein. When a permit extends over a period of years, the next and succeeding payments shall be due and payable annually in advance. The full amount accruing under a temporary permit shall be paid at the time the application is filed.

§ 173.11 Supervision of permittees' rates.

All rates or charges collected by a permittee for services rendered by the permittee in the operation of the concession granted under a permit, must be submitted through the project engineer to the Secretary for approval. Copies of the approved rate schedule shall be posted in at least two conspicuous places on the premises. Approved rates may not be changed without first obtaining in the same manner a change in the rate schedule. The Secretary shall have the right to readjust rates charged from time to time and to amend or change any permit issued. Failure to comply with the approved rates automatically makes the permit subject to cancellation.

§ 173.12 Services from project.

When the facilities of the project make it possible to supply water for domestic purposes, electricity or any other type of service to the permittee, the cost of connecting the project facilities shall be borne by the permittee and the work must be in accordance with standard practices and accepted by the project engineer, and as provided for in project regulations. All services rendered by the project to the permittee shall be paid for at the existing or modified schedule of rates; or if no schedule has been approved, at a rate to be approved by the Secretary which will reasonably reimburse the project for the cost of such services.

§ 173.13 Permit not a lease.

Any permit issued under this part does not grant any leasehold interest nor cover the sale, barter, merchandising, or renting of any supplies or equipment except as therein specified. Any permittee who engages in trade with the Indians must also apply for and receive a trader's license as provided by part 140 of this chapter.

§ 173.14 Further requirements authorized.

The project engineer is authorized to incorporate into any proposed permit to meet the needs of any particular case, subject to the approval of the Secretary, such further special requirements as may be agreed upon by him and the applicant, such requirements to be consistent with the general purposes of this part.

§ 173.15 Permittee subject to State law.

The holder of any permit issued under this part shall be subject to and abide by the laws and regulations of the United States and State laws if applicable to the conduct of the particular business or activity conducted by the permittee. Violations of this section shall render the permit void but shall not release the permittee from any obligations arising thereunder.

§ 173.16 Reserved area, Coolidge Dam.

No permit for any commercial business or other activity (except boating concessions confined to the Soda Spring Canyon) shall be issued to any applicant to operate within a radius of three-fourths of a mile from the center of the Coolidge Dam, Arizona.

§ 173.17 Agricultural and grazing permits and leases.

(a) Permits or leases may be granted after the lands set forth in § 173.0 have been classified as to use and then only for the purpose for which the land is classified. Permits for grazing lands suitable for division into range units shall be granted in accordance with part 166 of this chapter; and agricultural lands and all other grazing lands shall be leased in accordance with part 166 of this chapter.

(b) Lands for which leases or permits are granted pursuant to the terms and conditions of this part shall not be eligible for benefit payments under the provisions and conditions of the Crop Control and Soil Conservation Act of April 27, 1935 (49 Stat. 163; 16 U.S.C. 590a), as amended by the act of February 29, 1936 (49 Stat. 1148; 16 U.S.C. 590g), and subsequent amendatory acts.

§ 173.18 Term and renewal of permits.

No concession granted under the provisions of this part shall extend for a period in excess of 10 years. An application for the renewal of a lease, permit, or concession permit shall be treated in the same manner as an original application under this part. Should there be an application or applications other than the renewal application for a permit covering the same area, the renewal application may, if the applicant has met all the requirements of the expiring permit and has been a satisfactory permittee, be given preferential consideration for the renewal of the permit should the applicant meet the highest and most satisfactory offer contained in the several applications.

§ 173.19 Improvements.

Title to improvements constructed on the premises by the permittee shall be fixed and determined by the terms of the permit.

§ 173.20 Revocation of permits.

Any permit issued pursuant to this part may be revoked at any time within the discretion of the Secretary. Agricultural and grazing leases dealt with in § 173.17 shall be subject to cancellation as provided for in the respective parts 162 and 166 of this chapter, and the conditions of the instruments executed pursuant thereto.

§ 173.21 Notice to vacate.

A permittee shall within 10 days after notification in writing of the cancellation of his permit by the Secretary, vacate the premises covered by the said permit. Any person occupying lands dealt with in the act of April 4, 1938 (52 Stat. 193) without an approved permit or lease shall be notified in writing by the project engineer of the requirements of this part and that for the failure of such person to comply with these requirements and receive a permit or lease within 60 days after receipt of the written notice shall constitute a willful violation of this part, and the project engineer shall submit promptly to the Commissioner of Indian Affairs a detailed report concerning the case, together with recommendations looking to the taking of appropriate legal action to remove such person from the area and to the collection of such funds to compensate for any use made of the property or damages suffered thereto.

§ 173.22 Disposition of revenue.

Funds derived from concessions or leases under this part except those so derived from Indian tribal property withdrawn for irrigation purposes and for which the tribe has not been compensated, shall be available for expenditure under existing law in the operation and maintenance of the irrigation project on which collected and as provided for in part 161 of this chapter. Funds so derived from Indian tribal property withdrawn for irrigation purposes and for which the tribe has not been compensated, shall be deposited to the credit of the proper tribe.

§ 173.23 Organized tribes.

Concessions and leases on tribal lands withdrawn or reserved for the purposes specified in the act of April 4, 1938 (52 Stat. 193) and dealt with in this part, of any Indian tribe organized under section 16 of the act of June 18, 1934 (48 Stat. 984; 25 U.S.C. 476) for which the tribe has not been compensated shall be made by the organized tribe pursuant to its constitution or charter: *Provided*, No lease or concession so made shall be inconsistent with the primary purpose for which the lands were reserved or withdrawn.

PART 175—ELECTRIC POWER UTILITIES

Subpart A—General Provisions

Sec.

Subpart B—Service Fees, Electric Power Rates, and Revenues

Subpart C—Billing, Payments, and Collections

Subpart D—System Extensions and Upgrades, Rights-of-Way, and Paperwork Reduction Act

AUTHORITY: 5 U.S.C. 301; 25 U.S.C. 13; 25 U.S.C. 385c; 43 Stat. 475–76; 45 Stat. 210–13; 49 Stat. 1039–40; 49 Stat. 1822–23; 54 Stat. 422; 62 Stat. 269–73; 65 Stat. 254; 99 Stat. 319–20.

SOURCE: 83 FR 61119, Nov. 28, 2018, unless otherwise noted.

Subpart A—General Provisions

§ 175.100 What terms I should know for this part?

Agreement means the executed written form between you and the utility providing your service, except for service provided under a Special Agreement.

BIA means the Bureau of Indian Affairs within the United States Department of the Interior or the BIA's authorized representative.

Bill means our written statement notifying you of the charges and/or fees you owe the United States for the administration, operation, maintenance, rehabilitation, and/or construction of the electric power utility servicing you.

CFR means Code of Federal Regulations.

Customer means any person or entity to whom we provide service.

Customer service is the assistance or service provided to customers, except for the actual delivery of electric power or energy. Customer service may include: Line extension, system upgrade, meter testing, connections or disconnection, special meter reading, or other assistance or service as provided in the Operations Manual.

Day(s) means calendar day(s).

Delinquent means an account that has not been paid and settled by the due date.

Due date means the date by which you must pay your bill. The due date is printed on your bill.

Electric energy (see *Electric power*).

Electric power means the energy we deliver to meet customers' electrical needs.

Electric power rate means the charges we establish for delivery of energy to our customers, which includes administration costs and operation and maintenance costs in addition to the cost of purchased power.

Electric power utility means all structures, equipment, components, and human resources necessary for the delivery of electric service.

Electric service means the delivery of electric power by our utility to our customers.

Energy means electric power.

Fee (see *Service fee*).

I, me, my, you, and *your* means all interested parties, especially persons or entities to which we provide service and receive use of our electric power service.

Must means an imperative or mandatory act or requirement.

Operations Manual means the written policies, practices, procedures and requirements of the utility providing your service. The Operations Manual supplements this Part and includes our responsibilities to our customers and our customers' responsibilities to the utility.

Past due bill means a bill that has not been paid by the due date.

Power (see *Energy*).

Public notice is the notice provided by publishing information consistent with the utility's Operations Manual.

Purchased power means the power we must purchase from power marketing providers for resale to our customers to meet changing power demands. Each of our utilities establishes its own power purchasing agreement based on its power demands and firm power availability.

Rate (see *Electric power rate*).

Reserve Funds means funds held in reserve for maintenance, repairs, or unexpected expenses.

Revenue means the monies we collect from our customers through service fees and electric power rates.

Service (see *Electric service*).

Service fee means our charge for providing or performing a specific administrative or customer service.

Special Agreement means a written agreement between you and us for special conditions or circumstances including unmetered services.

Taxpayer identification number means either your Social Security Number or your Employer Identification Number.

Utility(ies) see (*Electric power utility*).

Utility office(s) means our facility used for conducting business with our customers and the general public.

We, us, and *our* means the United States Government, the Secretary of the Interior, the BIA, and all who are authorized to represent us in matters covered under this Part.

§175.105 What is the purpose of this part?

The purpose of this part is to establish the regulations for administering BIA electric power utilities.

§175.110 Does this part apply to me?

This part applies to you if we provide you service or if you request service from us.

§175.115 How does BIA administer its electric power utilities?

We promote efficient administration, operation, maintenance, and construction of our utilities by following and enforcing:

(a) Applicable statutes, regulations, Executive Orders, Indian Affairs manuals, Operations Manuals;

(b) Applicable written policies, procedures, directives, safety codes; and

(c) Utility industry standards.

§175.120 What are Operations Manuals?

(a) We maintain an Operations Manual for each of our utilities. Each utility's Operations Manual is available at the utility.

(b) The Operations Manual sets forth the requirements for the administration, management, policies, and responsibilities of that utility and its customers.

(c) We update our Operations Manual for each utility to reflect changing requirements to administer, operate, or maintain that utility.

(d) When we determine it necessary to revise an Operations Manual, we will:

(1) Provide public notice of the proposed revision;

(2) State the effective date of the proposed revision;

(3) State how and when to submit your comments on our proposed revision;

(4) Provide 30 days from the date of the notice to submit your comments; and

(5) Consider your comments and provide notice of our final decision.

§ 175.125 How do I request and receive service?

(a) If you need electrical service in an area where we provide service, you must contact our utility in that service area.

(b) To receive service, you must enter into an Agreement with that utility after it has determined that you have met its requirements.

§ 175.130 What information must I provide when I request service?

At a minimum, you must provide the utility with the following information when you request service:

(a) Your full legal name or the legal name of the entity needing service;

(b) Your taxpayer identification number;

(c) Your billing address;

(d) Your service address; and

(e) Any additional information required by the utility.

§ 175.135 Why is BIA collecting this information?

We are collecting this information so we can:

(a) Provide you with service;

(b) Bill you for the service we provide; and

(c) Account for monies you pay us, including any deposits as outlined in the Operations Manual.

§ 175.140 What is BIA's authority to collect my tax payer identification number?

We are required to collect your taxpayer identification number under the authority of, and as prescribed in, the Debt Collection Improvement Act of 1996, Public Law 104–134 (110 Stat. 1321–364).

§ 175.145 Can I appeal a BIA decision?

(a) You may appeal a decision in accordance with the procedures set out in 25 CFR part 2, unless otherwise prohibited by law.

(b) If the appeal involves the discontinuation of service, the utility is not required to resume the service during the appeal process unless the customer meets the utility's requirements.

(c) If you appeal your bill, you must pay your bill in accordance with this part to continue to receive service from us.

(1) If the appeal involves the amount of your bill, the bill will be considered paid under protest until the final decision has been rendered on appeal.

(2) If you appeal your bill but do not pay the bill in full, you may not continue to receive service from us. If the final decision rendered in the appeal requires payment of the bill, the bill will be handled as a delinquent account and the amount of the bill may be subject to interest, penalties, and administrative costs pursuant to 31 U.S.C. 3717 and 31 CFR 901.9.

(3) If the appeal involves an electric power rate, the rate will be applied and remain in effect subject to the final decision on the appeal.

Subpart B—Service Fees, Electric Power Rates, and Revenues

§ 175.200 Why does BIA collect revenue from you and the other customers it serves, and how is that revenue used?

(a) The revenue we collect from you and the other customers is authorized by 25 U.S.C. 385c (60 Stat. 895, as amended by 65 Stat. 254).

(b) The revenue we collect may be used to:

(1) Pay for operation and maintenance of the utility;

(2) Maintain Reserve Funds to:

(i) Make repairs and replacements to the utility;

(ii) Defray emergency expenses;

(iii) Ensure the continuous operation of the power system; and

(iv) Pay other allowable expenses and obligations to the extent required or permitted by law.

§ 175.205 When are BIA rates and fees reviewed?

We review our rates and fees at least annually to:

(a) Determine if our financial requirements are being met to ensure the reliable operation of the utility serving you; and

(b) Determine if revenues are sufficient to meet the statutory requirements.

§ 175.210 What is BIA's procedure for adjusting service fees?

If, based on our annual review, we determine our service fees need to be adjusted:

(a) We will notify you at least 30 days prior to the effective date of the adjustment; and

(b) We will publish a schedule of the adjusted service fees in a local newspaper(s) and post them in the local utility office serving you.

§ 175.215 What is BIA's procedure for adjusting electric power rates?

Except for purchased power costs, if we determine electric power rates need to be adjusted, we will:

(a) Hold public meetings and notify you of their respective time, date, and location by newspaper notice and a notice posted in the utility office serving you;

(b) Provide you notice at least 15 days prior to the meeting;

(c) Provide you a description of the proposed rate adjustment;

(d) Provide you information on how, where, and when to submit comments on our proposed rate adjustment;

(e) Make a final determination on the proposed rate adjustment after all comments have been received, reviewed, and evaluated; and

(f) Publish the proposed rate adjustment and the final rate in the FEDERAL REGISTER if we determine the rate adjustment is necessary.

§ 175.220 How long do rate and fee adjustments stay in effect?

These adjustments remain in effect until we conduct a review and determine adjustments are necessary.

§ 175.225 What is the Federal Register, and where can I get it?

The FEDERAL REGISTER is the official daily publication for rules, proposed rules, and notices of official actions by Federal agencies and organizations, as well as Executive Orders and other Presidential Documents and is produced by the Government Printing Office (GPO). You can get FEDERAL REGISTER publications by:

(a) Visiting *www.federalregister.gov* or *www.gpo.gov/fdsys;*

(b) Writing to the GPO at Superintendent of Documents, P.O. Box 371954, Pittsburgh, PA 15250–7954; or

(c) Calling the GPO at (202) 512–1800.

§ 175.230 Why are changes to purchased power costs not included in the procedure for adjusting electric power rates?

Changes to purchased power costs are not included in the procedure for adjusting electric power rates because unforeseen increases in the cost of purchased power are:

(a) Not under our control;

(b) Determined by current market rates; and

(c) Subject to market fluctuations that can occur at an undetermined time and frequency.

§ 175.235 How does BIA include changes in purchased power costs in electric power rates?

When our cost of purchased power changes:

(a) We determine the effect of the change;

(b) We adjust the purchased power component of your bill accordingly;

(c) We add the purchased power adjustment to the existing electric power rate and put it into effect immediately;

(d) The purchased power adjustment remains in effect until we determine future adjustments are necessary;

(e) We must publish in the local newspaper and post at our office a notice of the purchase power adjustment and the basis for the adjustment; and

(f) Our decision to make a purchased power adjustment must be final.

Subpart C—Billing, Payments, and Collections

§ 175.300 How does BIA calculate my electric power bill?

(a) We calculate your electric power bill based on the:

(1) Current rate schedule for your type service; and

(2) Applicable service fees for your type service.

(b) If you have a metered service we must:

(1) Read your meter monthly;

(2) Calculate your bill based on your metered energy consumption; and

(3) Issue your bill monthly, unless otherwise provided in a Special Agreement.

(c) If we are unable to calculate your metered energy consumption, we must make a reasonable estimate based on one of the following reasons:

(1) Your meter has failed;

(2) Your meter has been tampered with; or

(3) Our utility personnel are unable to read your meter.

(d) If you have an unmetered service, we calculate your bill in accordance with your Special Agreement.

§ 175.305 When is my bill due?

The due date is provided on your bill.

§ 175.310 How do I pay my bill?

You may pay your bill by any of the following methods:

(a) In person at our utility office;

(b) Mail your payment to the address stated on your bill; or

(c) As further provided by the electric utility that serves you.

§ 175.315 What will happen if I do not pay my bill?

(a) If you do not pay your bill prior to the close of business on the due date, your bill will be past due.

(b) If your bill is past due we may:

(1) Disconnect your service; and

(2) Not reconnect your service until your bill, including any applicable fees, is paid in full.

(c) Specific regulations regarding non-payment can be found in 25 CFR 143.5(c).

§ 175.320 What will happen if my service is disconnected and my account remains delinquent?

(a) If your service has been disconnected and you still have an outstanding balance, we will assess you interest, penalties, and administrative costs in accordance with 31 CFR 901.9.

(b) We must forward your delinquent balance to the United States Treasury if it is not paid within 180 days after the original due date in accordance with 31 CFR 901.1.

Subpart D—System Extensions and Upgrades, Rights-of-Way, and Paperwork Reduction Act

§ 175.400 Will the utility extend or upgrade its electric system to serve new or increased loads?

The utility may extend or upgrade its electric system to serve new or increased loads. Contact your electric power utility providing service in your area for further information on new or increased loads.

§ 175.500 How does BIA manage rights-of-way?

Contact your electric power utility providing service in your area for further information on rights-of-way.

§ 175.600 How does the Paperwork Reduction Act affect this part?

The collection of information contained in this part have been approved by the Office of Management and Budget under 44 U.S.C. 3501 *et seq.* and assigned OMB Control Number 1076–0021. Response is required to obtain a benefit. A Federal agency may not conduct or sponsor, and you are not required to respond to, a collection of information unless the form or regulation requesting the information displays a currently valid OMB Control Number.

Send comments regarding this collection of information, including suggestions for reducing the burden, to the Information Collection Clearance Officer—Indian Affairs, 1849 C Street NW, Washington, DC 20240.

PART 179—LIFE ESTATES AND FUTURE INTERESTS

Subpart A—General

AUTHORITY: 86 Stat. 530; 86 Stat. 744; 94 Stat. 537; 96 Stat. 2515; 25 U.S.C. 2, 9, 372, 373, 487, 607, and 2201 *et seq.*

SOURCE: 73 FR 67286, Nov. 13, 2008, unless otherwise noted.

Subpart A—General

§179.1 What is the purpose of this part?

This part contains the authorities, policies, and procedures governing the administration of life estates and future interests in trust and restricted property by the Secretary of Interior. This part does not apply to any use rights assigned to tribal members by tribes in the exercise of their jurisdiction over tribal lands.

(a) Subpart A contains general provisions.

(b) Subpart B describes life estates not created under the American Indian Probate Reform Act of 2004 (AIPRA), as described in §179.3(b).

(c) Subpart C describes life estates created under AIPRA, as described in §179.3(a).

§179.2 What definitions do I need to know?

Agency means the Bureau of Indian Affairs (BIA) agency office, or any other designated office in BIA, having jurisdiction over trust or restricted property. This term also means any office of a tribe that has entered into a contract or compact to fulfill applicable BIA functions.

AIPRA means the American Indian Probate Reform Act of 2004, Pub. L. 108–374, as codified at 25 U.S.C. 2201 *et seq.*

BIA means the Bureau of Indian Affairs within the Department of Interior.

Contract bonus means cash consideration paid or agreed to be paid as incentive for execution of a contract.

Income means the rents and profits of real property and the interest on invested principal.

Life estate means an interest in property held for only the duration of a designated person's life. A life estate may be created by a conveyance document or by operation of law.

Life estate without regard to waste means that the holder of the life estate interest in land is entitled to the receipt of all income, including bonuses and royalties, from such land to the exclusion of the remaindermen.

Principal means the corpus and capital of an estate, including any payment received for the sale or diminishment of the corpus, as opposed to the income.

Rents and profits means the income or profit arising from the ownership or possession of property.

Restricted property means real property, the title to which is held by an Indian but which cannot be alienated or encumbered without the Secretary's consent. For the purpose of probate proceedings, restricted property is treated as if it were trust property.

Except as the law may provide otherwise, the term "restricted property" as used in this part does not include the restricted lands of the Five Civilized

Tribes of Oklahoma or the Osage Nation.

Secretary means the Secretary of the Interior or authorized representative.

Trust property means real property, or an interest therein, the title to which is held in trust by the United States for the benefit of an individual Indian or tribe.

§ 179.3 What law applies to life estates?

(a) AIPRA applies to life estates created by operation of law under AIPRA for an individual who died on or after June 20, 2006, owning trust or restricted property.

(b) In the absence of Federal law or federally approved tribal law to the contrary, State law applies to all other life estates.

§ 179.4 When does a life estate terminate?

A life estate terminates upon relinquishment or upon the death of the measuring life.

§ 179.5 What documents will BIA use to record termination of a life estate?

The Agency will file a copy of the relinquishment of the interest or death certificate with the BIA Land Title and Records Office for recording upon receipt of one of the following:

(a) The life estate holder's relinquishment of an interest in trust or restricted property; or

(b) Notice of death of a person who is the measuring life for the life estate in trust or restricted property.

Subpart B—Life Estates Not Created Under AIPRA

§ 179.101 How does the Secretary distribute principal and income to the holder of a life estate?

(a) This section applies to the following cases:

(1) Where the document creating the life estate does not specify a distribution of proceeds;

(2) Where the vested holders of remainder interests and the life tenant have not entered into a written agreement approved by the Secretary providing for the distribution of proceeds; or

(3) Where, by the document or agreement or by the application of State law, the open mine doctrine does not apply.

(b) In all cases listed in paragraph (a) of this section, the Secretary must do the following:

(1) Distribute all rents and profits, as income, to the life tenant;

(2) Distribute any contract bonus one-half each to the life tenant and the remainderman;

(3) In the case of mineral contracts:

(i) Invest the principal, with interest income to be paid to the life tenant during the life estate, except in those instances where the administrative cost of investment is disproportionately high, in which case paragraph (b)(4) of this section applies; and

(ii) Distribute the principal to the remainderman upon termination of the life estate; and

(4) In all other instances:

(i) Distribute the principal immediately according to § 179.102; and

(ii) Invest all proceeds attributable to any contingent remainderman in an account, with disbursement to take place upon determination of the contingent remainderman.

§ 179.102 How does the Secretary calculate the value of a remainder and a life estate?

(a) If income is subject to division, the Secretary will use Actuarial Table S, Valuation of Annuities, found at 26 CFR 20.2031, to determine the value of the interests of the holders of remainder interests and the life tenant.

(b) Actuarial Table S, Valuation of Annuities, specifies the share attributable to the life estate and remainder interests, given the age of the life tenant and an established rate of return published by the Secretary in the FEDERAL REGISTER. We may periodically review and revise the percent rate of return to be used to determine the share attributable to the interests of the life tenant and the holders of remainder interests. The life tenant will receive the balance of the distribution after the shares of the holders of remainder interests have been calculated.

Subpart C—Life Estates Created Under AIPRA

§ 179.201 How does the Secretary distribute principal and income to the holder of a life estate without regard to waste?

The Secretary must distribute all income, including bonuses and royalties, to the life estate holder to the exclusion of any holders of remainder interests.

§ 179.202 May the holder of a life estate without regard to waste deplete the resources?

Yes. The holder of a life estate without regard to waste may cause lawful depletion or benefit from the lawful depletion of the resources. However, a holder of a life estate without regard to waste may not cause or allow damage to the trust property through culpable negligence or an affirmative act of malicious destruction that causes damage to the prejudice of the holders of remainder interests.

PART 181—INDIAN HIGHWAY SAFETY PROGRAM

Sec.

AUTHORITY: 23 U.S.C. 402; 25 U.S.C. 13.

SOURCE: 62 FR 55331, Oct. 24, 1997, unless otherwise noted.

§ 181.1 Purpose.

This part will assist the BIA Indian Highway Safety Program Administrator to disperse funds DOT/NHTSA has made available. The funds assist selected tribes with their proposed Highway Safety Projects. These projects are designed to reduce traffic crashes, reduce impaired driving crashes, increase occupant protection education, provide Emergency Medical Service training, and increase police traffic services.

§ 181.2 Definitions.

Appeal means a written request for review of an action or the inaction of an official of the BIA that is claimed to adversely affect the interested party making the request.

Applicant means an individual or persons on whose behalf an application for assistance and/or services has been made under this part.

Application means the process through which a request is made for assistance or services.

Grant means a written agreement between the BIA and the governing body of an Indian tribe or Indian organization wherein the BIA provides funds to the grantee to plan, conduct, or administer specific programs, services, or activities and where the administrative and programmatic provisions are specifically delineated.

Grantee means the tribal governing body of an Indian tribe or Board of Directors of an Indian organization responsible for grant administration.

Recipient means an individual or persons who have been determined as eligible and are receiving financial assistance or services under this part.

§ 181.3 Am I eligible to receive a program grant?

The Indian Highway Safety Program grant is available to any federally recognized tribe. Because of the limited financial resources available for the program, the Bureau of Indian Affairs (BIA) is unable to award grants to all applicants. Furthermore, some grant recipients may only be awarded a grant to fund certain aspects of their proposed tribal projects.

§ 181.4 How do I obtain an application?

BIA mails grant application packages for a given fiscal year to all federally recognized tribes by the end of February of the preceding fiscal year. Additional application packages are available from the Program Administrator, Indian Highway Safety Program, P.O. Box 2003, Albuquerque, New Mexico 87103. Each application package contains the necessary information concerning the application process, including format, content, and filing requirements.

§ 181.5 How are applications ranked?

BIA ranks each timely filed application by assigning points based upon four factors.

(a) *Factor No. 1—Magnitude of the problem* (Up to 50 points available). In awarding points under this factor, BIA will take into account the following:

(1) Whether a highway safety problem exists.

(2) Whether the problem is significant.

(3) Whether the proposed tribal project will contribute to resolution of the identified highway safety problem.

(4) The number of traffic accidents occurring within the applicant's jurisdiction over the previous 3 years.

(5) The number of alcohol-related traffic accidents occurring within the applicant's jurisdiction over the previous 3 years.

(6) The number of reported traffic fatalities occurring within the applicant's jurisdiction over the previous 3 years.

(7) The number of reported alcohol-related traffic fatalities occurring within the applicant's jurisdiction over the previous 3 years.

(b) *Factor No. 2—Countermeasure selection* (Up to 40 points available). In awarding points under this factor, BIA will take into account the following:

(1) Whether the countermeasures selected are the most effective for the identified highway safety problem.

(2) Whether the countermeasures selected are cost effective.

(3) Whether the applicant's objectives are realistic and attainable.

(4) Whether the applicant's objectives are time framed and, if so, whether the time frames are realistic and attainable.

(c) *Factor No. 3—Tribal Leadership and Community Support* (Up to 10 points available). In awarding points under this factor, BIA will take into account the following:

(1) Whether the applicant proposes using tribal resources in the project.

(2) Whether the appropriate tribal governing body supports the proposal plan, as evidenced by a tribal resolution or otherwise.

(3) Whether the community supports the proposal plan, as evidenced by letters or otherwise.

(d) *Factor No. 4—Past Performance* (+ or −10 points available). In awarding points under this factor, BIA will take into account the following:

(1) Financial and programmatic reporting requirements.

(2) Project accomplishments.

§ 181.6 How are applicants informed of the results?

BIA will send a letter to all applicants notifying them of their selection or non-selection for participation in the Indian Highway Safety Program for the upcoming fiscal year. BIA will explain to each applicant not selected for participation the reason(s) for non-selection.

§ 181.7 Appeals.

You may appeal actions taken by BIA officials under this part by following the procedures in 25 CFR part 2.

PART 183—USE AND DISTRIBUTION OF THE SAN CARLOS APACHE TRIBE DEVELOPMENT TRUST FUND AND SAN CARLOS APACHE TRIBE LEASE FUND

Subpart A—Introduction

Subpart B—Trust Fund Disposition

USE OF PRINCIPAL AND INCOME

CLEARANCE REQUIREMENTS

LIMITATIONS

AUTHORITY: Pub. L. 102–575, 106 Stat. 4740 *et seq.*

SOURCE: 66 FR 21088, Apr. 27, 2001, unless otherwise noted.

Subpart A—Introduction

§ 183.1 What is the purpose of this part?

This part implements section 3707(e) of the San Carlos Apache Tribe Water Settlement Act (the Act), Public Law 102–575, 106 Stat. 4748, that requires regulations to administer the Trust Fund, and the Lease Fund established by the Act.

§ 183.2 What terms do I need to know?

In this part:

Administrative costs means any cost, including indirect costs, incurred by the Tribe reasonably related to an allowed use of funds under the Settlement Act, including indirect costs.

Beneficial use means any use to which the Tribe's water entitlement is put that is authorized by the Settlement Act, the Settlement Agreement, or by the Tribal Council under the Settlement Act, the Settlement Agreement or otherwise permitted by law.

CAP means the Central Arizona Project, a reclamation project authorized under title III of the Colorado River Basin Project Act of 1968 (43 U.S.C. 1521 *et seq.*).

Community development project or purpose means any business, recreational, social, health, education, environment, or general welfare project approved by the Tribal Council for the benefit of any community within the reservation.

Economic development project or purpose means any commercial, industrial, agricultural, or business project approved by the Tribal Council for the purpose of profit to the Tribe.

Income means interest or income earned or accrued on the principal of the Trust Fund or the Lease Fund and is available for distribution to the Tribe in accordance with the Settlement Act and this part. Beginning with calendar year 2001, any income that has been earned or has accrued on the principal of the Trust Fund or the Lease Fund and that has not been requested for distribution by the Tribe by December 31, shall become part of the principal of the Trust Fund or the Lease Fund on January 1 of the next calendar year.

Lease Fund means the San Carlos Apache Tribe Lease Fund established in the Treasury of the United States under section 3711(d)(3)(E)(iv) of the Settlement Act.

Principal means:

(1) The amount of funds in the Trust Fund or the Lease Fund as of January 1, 2002; and

(2) Any income thereon that is not distributed, and has been added to the principal, in accordance with the Settlement Act and this part.

Pro forma budget means a budget, and operating statement, showing the estimated results for operating the economic development project for two years after injection of the principal or income into the operation.

Secretary means the Secretary of the Interior or an authorized representative acting under delegated authority. The term "Secretary':

(1) Includes the Regional Director for the Western Regional Office of the Bureau of Indian Affairs; and

(2) Does not include the Superintendent of the San Carlos Agency of the Bureau of Indian Affairs.

Settlement Act means the San Carlos Apache Tribe Water Settlement Act of 1992, Title XXXVII of Public Law 102–575, 106 Stat. 4740, and any amendments thereto.

Settlement Agreement means the agreement and any amendments executed and approved in accordance with the Settlement Act.

Tribe means the San Carlos Apache Tribe, a Tribe of Apache Indians, under the Apache Treaty, July 1, 1852, 10 Stat. 970, organized under section 16 of the Indian Reorganization Act of June 18, 1934 (48 Stat. 987; 25 U.S.C. 476), and duly recognized by the Secretary of the Interior.

Trust Fund means the San Carlos Apache Tribe Development Trust Fund established in the Treasury of the United States under section 3707(b) of the Settlement Act.

We and *us* mean the Secretary of the Interior as defined in this section.

§ 183.3 Does the American Indian Trust Fund Management Reform Act of 1994 apply to this part?

Yes. We will manage and make distributions from the Trust Fund in accordance with the American Indian Trust Funds Management Act of 1994 (Management Act), except where the Management Act conflicts with the Settlement Act or this part. If there is a conflict, we will follow the provisions of the Settlement Act or this part.

Subpart B—Trust Fund Disposition

USE OF PRINCIPAL AND INCOME

§ 183.4 How can the Tribe use the principal and income from the Trust Fund?

The Tribe may use the principal and income from the Trust Fund in the following ways:

(a) To put to beneficial use the water entitlement provided to the Tribe in the Settlement Act;

(b) To defray the cost to the Tribe of CAP operation, maintenance, and replacement charges;

(c) For economic development purposes; provided, however, that principal may only be used for long-term economic development projects and income may be used for other economic and community development purposes; and

(d) For Administrative Costs reasonably related to the above uses.

CLEARANCE REQUIREMENTS

§ 183.5 What documents must the Tribe submit to request money from the Trust Fund?

To request a distribution of principal or income from the Trust Fund, the Tribe must submit to us all of the following documents.

(a) A certified copy of a duly enacted resolution of the Tribal Council requesting a distribution from the Trust Fund;

(b) A written budget and supporting documentation, approved by the Tribal Council, showing precisely how the tribe will spend the money, including what amounts should come from principal and what amounts should come from income;

(c) A pro forma budget for each identified economic development project, and a program budget for each identified community development project; and

(d) A certification stating that the Tribe will use the funds in accordance with budgets submitted under this section.

§ 183.6 How long will it take to get a decision?

Within 30 days of receiving the information required by § 183.5 we will approve your request if it complies with the Settlement Act and this part. If we disapprove your request we will do so in writing and will provide you with the reasons for disapproval.

§ 183.7 What would cause the Secretary to disapprove a request?

We will only disapprove a request for the distribution of principal or income from the Trust Fund if the request does any of the following:

(a) Fails to provide the documents identified in § 183.5;

(b) Fails to provide reports required under §§ 183.15 and 183.16; or

(c) Includes a use requested or written budget that does not comply with a specific provision of the Settlement Act, or this part.

LIMITATIONS

§ 183.8 How can the Tribe spend funds?

(a) The Tribe must spend principal or income distributed from the Trust Fund only in accordance with a written budget submitted under § 183.5.

(b) The Tribe must not spend the principal or income from the Trust Fund to make per capita payments to members of the Tribe.

Subpart C—Lease Fund Disposition

USE OF PRINCIPAL AND INCOME

§ 183.9 Can the Tribe request the principal of the Lease Fund?

No. We cannot distribute the principal from the Lease Fund to the Tribe.

§ 183.10 How can the Tribe use income from the Lease Fund?

The Tribe may use income from the Lease Fund for the following purposes:

(a) For economic development purposes;

(b) For community development purposes; and

(c) For administrative costs reasonably related to the above.

CLEARANCE REQUIREMENTS

§ 183.11 What documents must the Tribe submit to request money from the Lease Fund?

To request a distribution of income from the Lease Fund, the Tribe must submit to us all of the following documents:

(a) A certified copy of a duly enacted resolution of the Tribal Council requesting a distribution from the Lease Fund;

(b) A pro forma budget for each identified economic development project and a program budget for each identified community development project, approved by the Tribal Council, showing precisely how the Tribe will spend the money;

(c) Supporting documentation for the budgets required by paragraph (b) of this section, and

(d) A certification stating that the Tribe will use the funds in accordance with budgets submitted under this section.

§ 183.12 How long will it take to receive a decision?

Within 30 days of receiving the information required by § 183.11 we will approve your request if it complies with the Settlement Act and this part. If we disapprove your request we will do so in writing and will provide you with the reasons for disapproval.

§ 183.13 What would cause the Secretary to disapprove a request?

We will only disapprove a request for distribution of income from the Lease Fund if the request does any of the following:

(a) Fails to provide the documents identified in § 183.5;

(b) Fails to provide reports required under §§ 183.15 and 183.16; or

(c) Includes a use requested or written budget that does not comply with a specific provision of the Settlement Act or this part.

LIMITATIONS

§ 183.14 What limits are there on how the Tribe can spend funds?

(a) The Tribe must spend income distributed from the Lease Fund only in accordance with a written budget submitted under § 183.5.

(b) The Tribe must not spend the income from the Lease Fund to make per capita payments to members of the Tribe.

Subpart D—Reports

§ 183.15 Must the Tribe submit any reports?

Yes. The Tribe must submit the following reports after receiving funds under this part:

(a) An Annual Report, that must be submitted no later than December 31 of each year; and

(b) A Financial Audit, that must be submitted no later than March 1 of each year.

§ 183.16 What information must be included in the Tribe's annual report?

The Tribe's annual report must contain the following information:

(a) An accounting of the expenditures of funds distributed to the Tribe from the Trust Fund or the Lease Fund for the preceding 12 months;

(b) A description, in detail, of how the Tribe has used the funds distributed from the Trust Fund or the Lease Fund consistently with the requirements in the Settlement Act, this part, and the budget approved by the Tribal Council and the Secretary; and

(c) Sufficient documentation for us to determine that the Tribe has satisfied the requirements of paragraph (b) of this section.

Subpart E—Liability

§ 183.17 If expenditures under this part lead to a claim or cause of action, who is liable?

The Tribe may be liable. The United States must not be liable for any claim or cause of action arising from the Tribe's use or expenditure of monies distributed from the Trust Fund or the Lease Fund.

§ 183.18 Information collection requirements

The information collection requirements contained in this part do not meet the requirements of "ten or more persons" annually; therefore, the Office of Management and Budget does not need to clear the collection. You may direct comments concerning this information collection to the Bureau of Indian Affairs, Information Collection Control Officer, 1849 C Street, NW, Washington, DC 20240.

SUBCHAPTER I—ENERGY AND MINERALS

PART 200—TERMS AND CONDITIONS: COAL LEASES

AUTHORITY: Pub. L. 95-87 (30 U.S.C. 1201 *et seq.*), as amended.

SOURCE: 54 FR 22188, May 22, 1989, unless otherwise noted.

§§ 200.1-200.10 [Reserved]

§ 200.11 Incorporation of coal lease terms and conditions.

(a) All leases of coal on Indian lands, as defined in § 216.101 of this chapter, issued by the Secretary, will include at the time of issuance, renewal, renegotiation, or readjustment, as applicable, the following provision:

The Lessee shall comply with all applicable requirements of the Surface Mining Control and Reclamation Act of 1977, and all regulations promulgated thereunder, including those codified at 30 CFR part 750.

(b) With respect to leases of coal on Indian lands issued by the Secretary after August 3, 1977, the Secretary shall, at the time of issuance, renewal, renegotiation, or readjustment, as applicable, include and enforce in such leases, terms and conditions related to the Surface Mining Control and Reclamation Act of 1977, as requested by the lessor Indian tribe in writing.

§ 200.12 Contract term incorporation.

The requirements of 30 CFR part 750 shall be incorporated in all existing and new contracts entered into for coal mining on Indian lands.

[59 FR 43419, Aug. 23, 1994]

PART 211—LEASING OF TRIBAL LANDS FOR MINERAL DEVELOPMENT

Subpart A—General

Subpart B—How To Acquire Leases

Subpart C—Rents, Royalties, Cancellations and Appeals

AUTHORITY: Sec. 4, Act of May 11, 1938 (52 Stat. 347); Act of August 1, 1956 (70 Stat. 744); 25 U.S.C. 396a–g; 25 U.S.C. 2 and 9; and Sec. 701, Pub. L. 114–74, 129 Stat. 599, unless otherwise noted.

SOURCE: 61 FR 35653, July 8, 1996, unless otherwise noted.

Subpart A—General

§211.1 Purpose and scope.

(a) The regulations in this part govern leases and permits for the development of Indian tribal oil and gas, geothermal, and solid mineral resources except as provided under paragraph (e) of this section. These regulations are applicable to lands or interests in lands the title to which is held in trust by the United States or is subject to a restriction against alienation imposed by the United States. These regulations are intended to ensure that Indian mineral owners desiring to have their resources developed are assured that they will be developed in a manner that maximizes their best economic interests and minimizes any adverse environmental impacts or cultural impacts resulting from such development.

(b) The regulations in this part shall be subject to amendment at any time by the Secretary of the Interior. No regulation that becomes effective after the date of approval of any lease or permit shall operate to affect the duration of the lease or permit, rate of royalty, rental, or acreage unless agreed to by all parties to the lease or permit.

(c) The regulations of the Bureau of Land Management, the Office of Surface Mining Reclamation and Enforcement, and the Minerals Management Service that are referenced in §§211.4, 211.5, and 211.6 are supplemental to the regulations in this part, and apply to parties holding leases or permits for development of Indian mineral resources unless specifically stated otherwise in this part or in such other Federal regulations.

(d) Nothing in the regulations in this part is intended to prevent Indian tribes from exercising their lawful governmental authority to regulate the conduct of persons, businesses, operations or mining within their territorial jurisdiction.

(e) The regulations in this part do not apply to leasing and development governed by regulations in 25 CFR parts 213 (Members of the Five Civilized Tribes of Oklahoma), 226 (Osage), or 227 (Wind River Reservation).

§211.2 Information collection.

The information collection requirements contained in this part do not require a review by the Office of Management and Budget under the Paperwork Reduction Act (44 U.S.C. 3501; *et seq.*).

§211.3 Definitions.

As used in this part, the following words and phrases have the specified meaning except where otherwise indicated:

Applicant means any person seeking a permit, lease, or an assignment from the superintendent or area director.

Approving official means the Bureau of Indians Affairs official with delegated authority to approve a lease or permit.

Area director means the Bureau of Indian Affairs official in charge of an area office.

Authorized officer means any employee of the Bureau of Land Management authorized by law or by lawful delegation of authority to perform the duties described in this part and in 43 CFR parts 3160, 3180, 3260, 3280, 3480 and 3590.

Cooperative agreement means a binding arrangement between two or more parties purporting to the act of agreeing or of coming to a mutual arrangement that is accepted by all parties to a transaction (e.g., communitization and unitization).

Director's representative means the Office of Surface Mining Reclamation and Enforcement director's representative authorized by law or lawful delegation of authority to perform the duties described in 30 CFR part 750.

Gas means any fluid, either combustible or non-combustible, that is produced in a natural state from the earth and that maintains a gaseous or rarefied state at ordinary temperature and pressure conditions.

Geological and geophysical permit means a written authorization to conduct on-site surveys to locate potential deposits of oil and gas, geothermal or solid mineral resources on the lands.

Geothermal resources means:

(1) All products of geothermal processes, including indigenous steam, hot water and hot brines;

(2) Steam and other gases, hot water, and hot brines, resulting from water, gas or other fluids artificially introduced into geothermal formations;

(3) Heat or other associated energy found in geothermal formations; and

(4) Any by-product derived therefrom.

In the best interest of the Indian mineral owner refers to the standards to be applied by the Secretary in considering whether to take an administrative action affecting the interests of an Indian mineral owner. In considering whether it is "in the best interest of the Indian mineral owner" to take a certain action (such as approval of a lease, permit, unitization or communitization agreement), the Secretary shall consider any relevant factor, including, but not limited to: economic considerations, such as date of lease expiration; probable financial effect on the Indian mineral owner; leasability of land concerned; need for change in the terms of the existing lease; marketability; and potential environmental, social, and cultural effects.

Indian lands means any lands owned by any individual Indian or Alaska Native, Indian tribe, band, nation, pueblo, community, rancheria, colony, or other tribal group which owns land or interests in the land, the title to which is held in trust by the United States or is subject to a restriction against alienation imposed by the United States.

Indian mineral owner means an Indian tribe, band, nation, pueblo community, rancheria, colony, or other tribal group which owns mineral interests in oil and gas, geothermal or solid mineral resources, title to which is held in trust by the United States, or is subject to a restriction against alienation imposed by the United States.

Indian surface owner means any individual Indian or Indian tribe whose surface estate is held in trust by the United States, or is subject to restriction against alienation imposed by the United States.

Lease means any contract approved by the United States under the Act of May 11, 1938 (52 Stat. 347) (25 U.S.C. 396a–396g), as amended, that authorizes exploration for, extraction of, or removal of any minerals.

Lessee means a natural person, proprietorship, partnership, corporation, or other entity that has entered into a lease with an Indian mineral owner, or who has been assigned an obligation to make royalty or other payments required by the lease.

Lessor means an Indian mineral owner who is a party to a lease.

Minerals includes both metalliferous and non-metalliferous minerals; all hydrocarbons, including oil and gas, coal and lignite of all ranks; geothermal resources; and includes but is not limited to, sand, gravel, pumice, cinders, granite, building stone, limestone, clay, silt, or any other energy or non-energy mineral.

Minerals Management Service official means any employee of the Minerals Management Service (MMS) authorized by law or by lawful delegation of authority to perform the duties described in 30 CFR chapter II, subchapters A and C.

Mining means the science, technique, and business of mineral development including, but not limited to: opencast work, underground work, and in-situ leaching directed to severance and treatment of minerals; Provided, when sand, gravel, pumice, cinders, granite, building stone, limestone, clay or silt is the subject mineral, an enterprise is considered "mining" only if the extraction of such a mineral exceeds 5,000 cubic yards in any given year.

Oil means all nongaseous hydrocarbon substances other than those substances leasable as coal, oil shale, or gilsonite (including all vein-type solid hydrocarbons). Oil includes liquefiable hydrocarbon substances such as drip gasoline and other natural condensates recovered or recoverable in a liquid state from produced gas without resorting to a manufacturing process.

Permit means any contract issued by the superintendent and/or area director to conduct exploration on; or removal of less than 5,000 cubic yards per year of common varieties of minerals from Indian lands.

Permittee means a person holding or required by this part to hold a permit to conduct exploration operations on; or remove less than 5,000 cubic yards per year of common varieties of minerals from Indian lands.

Secretary means the Secretary of the Interior or an authorized representative.

Solid minerals means all minerals excluding oil, gas and geothermal resources.

Superintendent means the Bureau of Indian Affairs official in charge of the agency office having jurisdiction over the minerals subject to leasing under this part.

§ 211.4 Authority and responsibility of the Bureau of Land Management (BLM).

The functions of the Bureau of Land Management are found in 43 CFR part 3160—Onshore Oil and Gas Operations, 43 CFR part 3180—Onshore Oil and Gas Unit Agreements: Unproven Area, 43 CFR part 3260—Geothermal Resources Operations, 43 CFR part 3280—Geothermal Resources Unit Agreements: Unproven Areas, 43 CFR part 3480—Coal Exploration and Mining Operations, and 43 CFR part 3590—Solid Minerals (other than coal) Exploration and Mining Operations; and currently include, but are not limited to, resource evaluation, approval of drilling permits, mining and reclamation, production plans, mineral appraisals, inspection and enforcement, and production verification. These regulations, apply to leases and permits approved under this part.

§ 211.5 Authority and responsibility of the Office of Surface Mining Reclamation and Enforcement (OSM).

The OSM is the regulatory authority for surface coal mining and reclamation operations on Indian lands pursuant to the Surface Mining Control and Reclamation Act of 1977 (30 U.S.C. 1201 *et seq.*). The relevant regulations for surface coal mining and reclamation operations are found in 30 CFR part 750. Those regulations apply to mining and reclamation on leases approved under this part.

§ 211.6 Authority and responsibility of the Minerals Management Service (MMS).

The functions of the MMS for reporting, accounting, and auditing are found in 30 CFR chapter II, subchapters A and C, which, apply to leases approved under this part. To the extent the parties to a lease or permit are able to provide reasonable provisions satisfactorily addressing the functions governed by MMS regulations, the Secretary may approve alternate provisions in a lease or permit.

§ 211.7 Environmental studies.

(a) The Secretary shall ensure that all environmental studies are prepared as required by the National Environmental Policy Act of 1969 (NEPA) and the regulations promulgated by the Council on Environmental Quality (CEQ), found in 40 CFR parts 1500 through 1508.

(b) The Secretary shall ensure that all necessary surveys are performed and clearances obtained in accordance with 36 CFR parts 60, 63, and 800 and with the requirements of the Archaeological and Historic Preservation Act (16 U.S.C. 469 *et seq.*), the National Historic Preservation Act (16 U.S.C. 470 *et seq.*), The American Indian Religious Freedom Act (42 U.S.C. 1996), and Executive Order 11593, Protection and Enhancement of the Cultural Environment (3 CFR, 1971 through 1975 Comp., p. 559). If these surveys indicate that a mineral development will have an adverse effect on a property listed on or eligible for listing on the National Register of Historic Places, the Secretary shall:

(1) Seek the comments of the Advisory Council on Historic Preservation, in accordance with 36 CFR part 800;

(2) Ensure that the property is avoided, that the adverse effect is mitigated, or;

(3) Ensure that appropriate excavations or other related research is conducted and ensure that complete data describing the historic property is preserved.

§211.8 Government employees cannot acquire leases.

U.S. Government employees are prevented from acquiring leases or interests in leases by the provisions of 25 CFR part 140 and 43 CFR part 20 pertaining to conflicts of interest and ownership of an interest in trust land.

§211.9 Existing permits or leases for minerals issued pursuant to 43 CFR chapter II and acquired for Indian tribes.

(a) Title to the minerals underlying certain Federal lands, which were previously subject to general leasing and mining laws, is now held in trust by the United States for Indian tribes. Existing mineral prospecting permits, exploration and mining leases on these lands, issued prior to these lands being placed in trust status or becoming Indian lands, pursuant to 43 CFR chapter II (and its predecessor regulations), and all actions on the permits and leases shall be administered by the Secretary in accordance with the regulations set forth in 30 CFR chapters II and VII and 43 CFR chapter II, as applicable, provided, that all payment or reports required by a non-producing lease or permit, issued pursuant to 43 CFR chapter II, shall be made to the superintendent having administrative jurisdiction over the land involved, instead of the officer of the Bureau of Land Management designated in 43 CFR unless specifically stated otherwise in the statutes authorizing the United States to hold the land in trust for an Indian tribe. Producing lease payments and reports will be submitted to the Minerals Management Service in accordance with 30 CFR chapter II, subchapters A and C.

(b) Administrative actions regarding an existing lease or permit under this section, may be appealed pursuant to 25 CFR part 2.

Subpart B—How To Acquire Leases

§211.20 Leasing procedures.

(a) Indian mineral owners may, with the approval of the superintendent or area director, lease their land for mining purposes. No oil and gas lease shall be approved unless it has first been offered for bidding at an advertised lease sale in accordance with this section. Leases for minerals other than oil and gas shall be advertised for bids as prescribed in this section unless the Secretary grants the Indian mineral owners written permission to negotiate for lease. Application for leases shall be made to the superintendent having jurisdiction over the lands.

(b) Indian mineral owners may request that the Secretary prepare and advertise or negotiate (if the requirements of this section have been met) mineral leases on their behalf. If requested by an applicant interested in acquiring rights to Indian-owned minerals, the Secretary shall promptly notify the Indian mineral owner, and advise the owner in writing of the alternatives available, including the right to decline to lease. If the Indian mineral owner decides to have the leases advertised, the Secretary shall consult with the Indian mineral owner concerning the appropriate royalty rate and rental. The Secretary may then undertake the responsibility to advertise and lease in accordance with the following procedures:

(1) Leases shall be advertised to receive optimum competition for bonus consideration, under sealed bid, oral auction, or a combination of both. Notice of such advertisement shall be published in at least one local newspaper and in one trade publication at least thirty (30) days in advance of sale. If applicable, such notice must identify the reservation within which the tracts to be leased are found. No specific description of the tracts to be leased need be published. Specific description of such tracts shall be available at the office of the superintendent and/or area director upon request. The complete text of the advertisement, including a specific description, shall be mailed to each person listed on the appropriate agency or area mailing list. Individuals and companies interested in receiving advertisements of lease sales should send their mailing information to the appropriate superintendent or area director for future reference.

(2) The advertisement shall offer the tracts to the responsible bidder offering the highest bonus. The Secretary,

after consultation with the Indian mineral owner, shall establish the rental and royalty rates which shall be stated in the advertisement and shall not be subject to negotiation. The advertisement shall provide that the Secretary reserves the right to reject any or all bids, and that acceptance of the lease bid by the Indian mineral owner is required.

(3) Each sealed bid must be accompanied by a cashier's check, certified check or postal money order, or any combination thereof, payable to the payee designated in the advertisement, in an amount not less than 25 percent of the bonus bid, which shall be returned if that bid is not accepted.

(4) A successful oral auction bidder will be allowed five (5) working days to remit the required 25 percent deposit of the bonus bid.

(5) A successful bidder shall, within thirty (30) days after notification of the bid award, remit to the Secretary the balance of the bonus, the first year's rental, a $75 filing fee, its prorated share of the advertising costs as determined by the Bureau of Indian Affairs, and file with the Secretary all required bonds. The successful bidder shall also file the lease in completed form at that time. However, for good reasons, the Secretary may grant extensions of time in thirty (30) day increments for filing of the lease and all required bonds, provided that additional extension requests are submitted and approved prior to the expiration of the original thirty (30) days or the previously granted extension. Failure on the part of the bidder to take all reasonable actions necessary to comply with the foregoing shall result in forfeiture of the required payment of 25 percent of any bonus bid for the use and benefit of the Indian mineral owner.

(6) If no satisfactory bid is received, or if the accepted bidder fails to complete all requirements necessary for the approval of the lease, or if the Secretary determines that it is not in the best interest of the Indian mineral owner to accept any of the bids the Secretary may re-advertise the lease for sale, or, subject to the consent of the Indian mineral owner, the lease may be let through private negotiations.

(c) The Secretary shall advise the Indian mineral owner of the results of the bidding, and shall not approve the lease until the consent of the Indian mineral owner has been obtained.

(d) The Indian mineral owner may also submit negotiated leases to the Secretary for review and approval.

§211.21 [Reserved]

§211.22 Leases for subsurface storage of oil or gas.

(a) The Secretary, with the consent of the Indian mineral owners, may approve storage leases, or modifications, amendments, or extensions of existing leases, on Indian lands to provide for the subsurface storage of oil or gas, irrespective of the lands from which production is initially obtained. The storage lease, or modification, amendment, or extension to an existing lease, shall provide for the payment of such storage fee or rental on such oil or gas as may be determined adequate in each case, or, in lieu thereof, for a royalty other than that prescribed in the oil and gas lease when such stored oil and gas is produced in conjunction with oil or gas not previously produced.

(b) The Secretary, with consent of the Indian mineral owners, may approve a provision in an oil and gas lease under which storage of oil and gas is authorized, for continuance of the lease at least for the period of such storage use and so long thereafter as oil or gas not previously produced is produced in paying quantities.

(c) Applications for subsurface storage of oil or gas shall be filed in triplicate with the authorized officer and shall disclose the ownership of the lands involved, the parties in interest, the storage fee, rental, or royalty offered to be paid for such storage, and all essential information showing the necessity for such project. Enough copies of the final agreement signed by the Indian mineral owners and other parties in interest shall be submitted for the approval of the Secretary to permit retention of five copies by the Department after approval.

§211.23 Corporate qualifications and requests for information.

(a) The signing in a representative capacity and delivery of bids, geological and geophysical permits, mineral leases, or assignments, bonds, or other instruments required by the regulations in this part constitutes certification that the individual signing (except a surety agent) is authorized to act in such capacity. An agent for a surety shall furnish a power of attorney.

(b) A corporate applicant proposing to acquire an interest in a permit or lease shall have on file with the superintendent or area director a statement showing:

(1) The State(s) in which the corporation is incorporated, and that the corporation is authorized to hold such interests in the State where the land described in the instrument is situated; and

(2) A notarized statement that the corporation has power to conduct all business and operations as described in the lease or permit.

(c) The Secretary may, either before or after the approval of a permit, mineral lease, assignment, or bond, call for any reasonable additional information necessary to carry out the regulations in this part, or other applicable laws and regulations.

§211.24 Bonds.

(a) The lessee, permittee or prospective lessee acquiring a lease, or any interest therein, by assignment shall furnish with each lease, permit or assignment a surety bond or personal bond in an amount sufficient to ensure compliance with all of the terms and conditions of the lease(s), permit(s), or assignment(s) and the statutes and regulations applicable to the lease, permit, or assignment. Surety bonds shall be issued by a qualified company approved by the Department of the Treasury (see Department of the Treasury Circular No. 570).

(b) An operator may file a $75,000 bond for all geothermal, mining, or oil and gas leases, permits, or assignments in any one State, which may also include areas on that part of an Indian reservation extending into any contiguous State. Statewide bonds are subject to approval in the discretion of the Secretary.

(c) An operator may file a $150,000 bond for full nationwide coverage to cover all geothermal or oil and gas leases, permits, or assignments without geographic or acreage limitation to which the operator is or may become a party. Nationwide bonds are subject to approval in the discretion of the Secretary.

(d) Personal bonds shall be accompanied by:

(1) Certificate of deposit issued by a financial institution, the deposits of which are federally insured, explicitly granting the Secretary full authority to demand immediate payment in case of default in the performance of the provisions and conditions of the lease or permit. The certificate shall explicitly indicate on its face that Secretarial approval is required prior to redemption of the certificate of deposit by any party;

(2) Cashier's check;

(3) Certified check;

(4) Negotiable Treasury securities of the United States of a value equal to the amount specified in the bond. Negotiable Treasury securities shall be accompanied by a proper conveyance to the Secretary of full authority to sell such securities in case of default in the performance of the provisions and conditions of a lease or permit; or

(5) Letter of credit issued by a financial institution authorized to do business in the United States and whose deposits are federally insured, and identifying the Secretary as sole payee with full authority to demand immediate payment in the case of default in the performance of the provisions and conditions of a lease or permit.

(i) The letter of credit shall be irrevocable during its term.

(ii) The letter of credit shall be payable to the Bureau of Indian Affairs upon demand, in part or in full, upon receipt from the Secretary of a notice of attachment stating the basis thereof (e.g., default in compliance with the lease or permit provisions and conditions or failure to file a replacement in accordance with paragraph (d)(5)(v) of this section).

(iii) The initial expiration date of the letter of credit shall be at least one (1) year following the date it is filed in the proper Bureau of Indian Affairs office.

(iv) The letter of credit shall contain a provision for automatic renewal for periods of not less than one (1) year in the absence of notice to the proper Bureau of Indian Affairs office at least ninety (90) days prior to the originally stated or any extended expiration date.

(v) A letter of credit used as security for any lease or permit upon which operations have taken place and final approval for abandonment has not been given, or as security for a statewide or nationwide bond, shall be forfeited and shall be collected by the Secretary if not replaced by other suitable bond or letter of credit at least thirty (30) days before its expiration date.

(e) The required amount of bonds may be increased in any particular case at the discretion of the Secretary.

§ 211.25 Acreage limitation.

A lessee may acquire more than one lease but no single lease shall be granted for mineral leasing purposes on Indian tribal or restricted lands in excess of the following acreage except where the rule of approximation applies:

(a) Leases for oil and gas and all other minerals except coal are to be contained within one United States Governmental survey section of land and shall be described by legal subdivisions including lots or tract equivalents not to exceed 640 acres; in instances of irregular surveys, including lands not surveyed under the United States Governmental survey, lands shall be considered in multiples of 40 acres or the nearest aliquot equivalent thereof;

(b) Leases for coal shall ordinarily be limited to 2,560 acres in a reasonably compact form and shall be described by legal subdivisions including lots or tract equivalents. In instances of irregular surveys, including lands not surveyed under the United States Governmental survey, lands shall be considered in multiples of 40 acres or the nearest aliquot equivalent thereof. The Secretary may, upon application and with the consent of the Indian mineral owner, approve the issuance of a single lease for more than 2,560 acres, in a reasonably compact form, upon a finding that the issuance is in the best interest of the lessor.

§ 211.26 [Reserved]

§ 211.27 Duration of leases.

(a) All leases shall be for a term not to exceed a primary term of lease duration of ten (10) years and, absent specific lease provisions to the contrary, shall continue as long thereafter as the minerals specified in the lease are produced in paying quantities. Absent specific lease provisions to the contrary, all provisions in leases governing their duration shall be measured from the date of approval by the Secretary.

(b) An oil and gas or geothermal resource lease which stipulates that it shall continue in full force and effect beyond the expiration of the primary term of lease duration ("commencement clause") if drilling operations have commenced during the primary term, shall be valid and shall hold the lease beyond the primary term of lease duration if the lessee or the lessee's designee has commenced actual drilling by midnight of the last day of the primary term of the lease with a drilling rig designed to reach the total proposed depth, and drilling is continued with reasonable diligence until the well is completed to production or abandoned. However, in no case shall such drilling hold the lease longer than 120 days past the primary term of lease duration without actual production of oil, gas, or geothermal resources. *Provided*, that this extension does not allow a lease to continue past the 10-year statutory limitation. Drilling which meets the requirements of this section and occurs within a unit or communitization agreement to which the lease is committed shall be considered as if it occurs on the leasehold itself. If there is a conflict between the commencement clause and the habendum clause of a lease, the commencement clause will control.

(c) A solid minerals lease which stipulates that it shall continue in full force and effect beyond the expiration of the primary term of lease duration if mining operations have commenced during the primary term (commencement clause), shall be valid and hold the lease beyond the primary term of lease duration if the lessee or the lessee's designee has by midnight of the last day of the primary term of the lease commenced actual removal of mineral materials intended for sale and upon which royalties will be paid. If there is a conflict between the commencement clause and the habendum clause of a lease, the commencement clause will control.

§211.28 Unitization and communitization agreements, and well spacing.

(a) For the purpose of promoting conservation and efficient utilization of minerals, the Secretary may approve a cooperative unit, drilling or other development plan on any leased area upon a determination that approval is advisable and in the best interest of the Indian mineral owner. For the purposes of this section, a cooperative unit, drilling or other development plan means an agreement for the development or operation of a specifically designated area as a single unit without regard to separate ownership of the land included in the agreement. Such cooperative agreements include, but are not limited to, unit agreements, communitization agreements and other types of agreements that allocate costs and benefits.

(b) The consent of the Indian mineral owner to such unit or cooperative agreement shall not be required unless such consent is specifically required in the lease. However, the Secretary shall consult with the Indian mineral owner prior to making a determination concerning a cooperative agreement or well spacing plan.

(c) Requests for approval of cooperative agreements which comply with the requirements of all applicable rules and regulations shall be filed with the superintendent or area director.

(d) All Indian mineral owners of any right, title or interest in the mineral resources to be included in a cooperative agreement must be notified by the lessee at the time the agreement is submitted to the superintendent or area director. An affidavit from the lessee stating that a notice was mailed to each mineral owner of record for whom the superintendent or area director has an address will satisfy this notice requirement.

(e) A request for approval of a proposed cooperative agreement, and all documents incident to such agreement, must be filed with the superintendent or area director at least ninety (90) days prior to the first expiration date of any of the Indian leases in the area proposed to be covered by the cooperative agreement.

(f) Unless otherwise provided in the cooperative agreement, approval of the agreement commits each lease to the unit in the area covered by the agreement on the date approved by the Secretary or the date of first production, whichever is earlier, as long as the agreement is approved before the lease expiration date.

(g) Any lease committed in part to any such cooperative agreement shall be segregated into a separate lease or leases as to the lands committed and lands not committed to the agreement. Segregation shall be effective on the date the agreement is effective.

(h) Wells shall be drilled in conformity with a well spacing program approved by the authorized officer.

§211.29 Exemption of leases and permits made by organized tribes.

The regulations in this part may be superseded by the provisions of any tribal constitution, bylaw or charter issued pursuant to the Indian Reorganization Act of June 18, 1934 (48 Stat. 984; 25 U.S.C. 461–479), the Alaska Act of May 1, 1936 (49 Stat. 1250; 48 U.S.C. 362,258a), or the Oklahoma Indian Welfare Act of June 26, 1936 (49 Stat. 1967; 25 U.S.C., and Sup., 501–509), or by ordinance, resolution, or other action authorized under such constitution, bylaw or charter; Provided, that such tribal law may not supersede the requirements of Federal statutes applicable to Indian mineral leases. The regulations in this part, in so far as they are not so superseded, shall apply to leases and permits made by organized tribes if the validity of the lease or permit depends upon the approval of the Secretary of the Interior.

Subpart C—Rents, Royalties, Cancellations and Appeals

§ 211.40 Manner of payments.

Unless otherwise specifically provided for in a lease, once production has been established, all payments shall be made to the MMS or such other party as may be designated, and shall be made at such time as provided in 30 CFR chapter II, subchapters A and C. Prior to production, all bonus and rental payments, shall be made to the superintendent or area director.

§ 211.41 Rentals and production royalty on oil and gas leases.

(a) A lessee shall pay, in advance, beginning with the effective date of the lease, an annual rental of $2.00 per acre or fraction of an acre or such other greater amount as prescribed in the lease. This rental shall not be credited against production royalty nor shall the rental be prorated or refunded because of surrender or cancellation.

(b) The Secretary shall not approve leases with a royalty rate less than 16–⅔ percent of the amount or value of production produced and sold from the lease unless a lower royalty rate is agreed to by the Indian mineral owner and is found to be in the best interest of the Indian mineral owner. Such approval may only be granted by the area director if the approving official is the superintendent and by the Assistant Secretary for Indian Affairs if the approving official is the area director.

(c) Value of lease production for royalty purposes shall be determined in accordance with applicable lease provisions and regulations in 30 CFR chapter II, subchapters A and C. If the valuation provisions in the lease are inconsistent with the regulations in 30 CFR chapter II, subchapters A and C, the lease provisions shall govern.

(d) If the leased premises produce gas in excess of the lessee's requirements for the development and operation of said premises, then the lessor may use sufficient gas, free of charge, for any desired school or other buildings belonging to the tribe, by making his own connections to a regulator installed, connected to the well and maintained by the lessee, and the lessee shall not be required to pay royalty on gas so used. The use of such gas shall be at the lessor's risk at all times.

§ 211.42 Annual rentals and expenditures for development on leases other than oil and gas, and geothermal resources.

(a) Unless otherwise authorized by the Secretary, a lease for minerals other than oil, gas and geothermal resources shall provide for a yearly development expenditure of not less than $20 per acre. All such leases shall provide for a rental payment of not less than $2.00 for each acre or fraction of an acre payable on or before the first day of each lease year.

(b) Within twenty (20) days after the lease year, an itemized statement, in duplicate, of the expenditure for development under a lease for minerals other than oil and gas shall be filed with the superintendent or area director. The lessee must certify the statement under oath.

§ 211.43 Royalty rates for minerals other than oil and gas.

(a) Except as provided in paragraph (b) of this section, the minimum rates for leases of minerals other than oil and gas shall be as follows:

(1) For substances other than coal, the royalty rate shall be 10 percent of the value of production produced and sold from the lease at the nearest shipping point.

(2) For coal to be strip or open pit mined the royalty rate shall be 12½ percent of the value of production produced and sold from the lease, and for coal removed from an underground mine, the royalty rate shall be 8 percent of the value of production produced and sold from the lease.

(3) For geothermal resources, the royalty rate shall be 10 percent of the amount or value of steam, or any other form of heat or energy derived from production of geothermal resources under the lease and sold or utilized by the lessee. In addition, the royalty rate shall be 5 percent of the value of any byproduct derived from production of geothermal resources under the lease and sold or utilized or reasonably susceptible of sale or utilization by the lessee, except that the royalty for any

mineral byproduct shall be governed by the appropriate paragraph of this section.

(b) A lower royalty rate shall be allowed if it is determined to be in the best interest of the Indian mineral owner. Approval of a lower rate may only be granted by the area director if the approving official is the superintendent or by the Assistant Secretary for Indian Affairs, if the approving official is the area director.

§211.44 Suspension of operations.

(a) After the expiration of the primary term of the lease the Secretary may approve suspension of operations for remedial purposes which are necessary for continued production, to protect the resource, the environment, or for other good reasons. *Provided*, that such remedial operations are conducted in accordance with 43 CFR part 3160, subpart 3165 and under such stipulations and conditions as may be prescribed by the Secretary and are conducted with reasonable diligence. Any suspension shall not relieve the lessee from liability for the payment of rental and other payments as required by lease provisions.

(b) An application for permission to suspend operations or production for economic or marketing reasons on a lease capable of production after the expiration of the primary term of lease duration must be accompanied by the written consent of the Indian mineral owner, an economic analysis, and an executed amendment by the parties to the lease setting forth the provisions pertaining to the suspension of operations and production. Such application shall be treated as a negotiated change to lease provisions, and as such, shall be subject to review and approval by the Secretary.

§211.45 [Reserved]

§211.46 Inspection of premises, books and accounts.

Lessees shall allow the Indian mineral owner, the Indian mineral owner's representatives, or any authorized representative of the Secretary to enter all parts of the leased premises for the purpose of inspection and audit. Lessees shall keep a full and correct account of all operations and submit all related reports required by the lease and applicable regulations. Books and records shall be available for inspection during regular business hours.

§211.47 Diligence, drainage and prevention of waste.

The lessee shall:

(a) Exercise diligence in mining, drilling and operating wells on the leased lands while minerals production can be secured in paying quantities;

(b) Protect the lease from drainage (if oil and gas or geothermal resources are being drained from the lease premises by a well or wells located on lands not included in the lease, the Secretary reserves the right to impose reasonable and equitable terms and conditions to protect the interest of the Indian mineral owner of the lands, such as payment of compensatory royalty for the drainage);

(c) Carry on operations in a good and workmanlike manner in accordance with approved methods and practices;

(d) Have due regard for the prevention of waste of oil or gas or other minerals, the entrance of water through wells drilled by the lessee to other strata, to the destruction or injury of the oil or gas, other mineral deposits, or fresh water aquifers, the preservation and conservation of the property for future productive operations, and the health and safety of workmen and employees;

(e) Securely plug all wells and effectively shut off all water from the oil or gas-bearing strata before abandoning them;

(f) Not construct any well pad location within 200 feet of any structures or improvements without the Indian surface owner's written consent;

(g) Carry out, at the lessee's expense, all reasonable orders and requirements of the authorized officer relative to prevention of waste;

(h) Bury all pipelines crossing tillable lands below plow depth unless other arrangements are made with the Indian surface owner; and

(i) Pay the Indian surface owner all damages, including damages to crops, buildings, and other improvements of the Indian surface owner occasioned by the lessee's operations as determined by the superintendent.

§ 211.48 Permission to start operations.

(a) No exploration, drilling, or mining operations are permitted on any Indian lands before the Secretary has granted written approval of a mineral lease or permit pursuant to the regulations in this part.

(b) After a lease or permit is approved, written permission must be secured from the Secretary before any operations are started on the leased premises, in accordance with applicable rules and regulations in 25 CFR part 216; 30 CFR chapter II, subchapters A and C; 30 CFR part 750 (Requirements for Surface Coal Mining and Reclamation Operations on Indian Lands), 43 CFR parts 3160, 3260, 3480, 3590, and Orders or Notices to Lessees (NTLs) issued thereunder.

§ 211.49 Restrictions on operations.

Leases issued under the provisions of the regulations in this part shall be subject to such restrictions as to time or times for well operations and production from any leased premises as the Secretary judges may be necessary or proper for the protection of the natural resources of the leased land and in the interest of the lessor.

§ 211.50 [Reserved]

§ 211.51 Surrender of leases.

A lessee may, with the approval of the Secretary, surrender a lease or any part of it, on the following conditions:

(a) All royalties and rentals due on the date the request for surrender is received must be paid;

(b) The superintendent, after consultation with the authorized officer, must be satisfied that proper provisions have been made for the conservation and protection of the property, and that all operations on the portion of the lease surrendered have been properly reclaimed, abandoned, or conditioned, as required;

(c) If a lease has been recorded, the lessee must submit a release along with the recording information of the original lease so that, after acceptance of the release, it may be recorded;

(d) If a lessee requests to surrender an entire lease or an entire undivided portion of a lease document, the lessee must deliver to the superintendent or area director the original lease documents; *Provided*, that where the request is made by an assignee to whom no copy of the lease was delivered, the assignee must deliver to the superintendent or area director only its copy of the assignment;

(e) If the lease (or a portion thereof being surrendered) is owned in undivided interests, all lessees owning undivided interests in the lease must join in the request for surrender;

(f) No part of any advance rental shall be refunded to the lessee, nor shall any subsequent surrender or termination of a lease relieve the lessee of the obligation to pay advance rental if advance rental became due prior to the date the request for surrender was received by the superintendent or area director;

(g) If oil, gas, or geothermal resources are being drained from the leased premises by a well or wells located on lands not included in the lease, the Secretary reserves the right, prior to acceptance of the surrender, to impose reasonable and equitable terms and conditions to protect the interests of the Indian mineral owners of the lands surrendered. Such terms and conditions may include payment of compensatory royalty for any drainage; and

(h) Upon expiration or surrender of a solid mineral lease the lessee shall deliver the leased premises in a condition conforming to the approved reclamation plan. Unless otherwise provided in the lease, the machinery necessary to operate the mine is the property of the lessee. However, the machinery may not be removed from the leased premises without the written permission of the Secretary.

§ 211.52 Fees.

Unless otherwise authorized by the Secretary, each permit, lease, sublease, or other contract, or assignment, thereof shall be accompanied by a filing fee of $75.00 at the time of filing.

§211.53 Assignments, overriding royalties, and operating agreements.

(a) Approved leases or any interest therein may be assigned or transferred only with the approval of the Secretary. The Indian mineral owner must also consent if approval of the Indian mineral owner is required in the lease. If consent is not required, then the Secretary shall notify the Indian mineral owner of the proposed assignment. To obtain the approval of the Secretary the assignee must be qualified to hold the lease under existing rules and regulations and shall furnish a satisfactory bond conditioned for the faithful performance of the covenants and conditions of the lease.

(b) No lease or interest therein or the use of such lease shall be assigned, sublet, or transferred, directly or indirectly, by working or drilling contract, or otherwise, without the consent of the Secretary.

(c) Assignments of leases, and stipulations modifying the provisions of existing leases, which stipulations are also subject to the approval of the Secretary, shall be filed with the superintendent within five (5) working days after the date of execution. Upon execution of satisfactory bonds by the assignee the Secretary may permit the release of any bonds executed by the assignor. Upon execution of satisfactory bonds the assignee accepts all the assignor's responsibilities and prior obligations and liabilities of the assignor (including but not limited to any underpaid royalties and rentals) under the lease.

(d) Agreements creating overriding royalties or payments out of production shall not be considered as interests in the leases as such provision is used in this section. Agreements creating overriding royalties or payments out of production, or agreements designating operators are hereby authorized and the approval of the Secretary shall not be required with respect thereto, but such agreements shall be subject to the condition that nothing in such agreements shall be construed as modifying any of the obligations of the lessee, including, but not limited to, obligations imposed by requirements of the MMS for reporting, accounting, and auditing; obligations for diligent development and operation, protection against drainage and mining in trespass, compliance with oil and gas, geothermal, and mining regulations (25 CFR part 216; 43 CFR parts 3160, 3260, 3480, and 3590; and those applicable rules found in 30 CFR chapter II, subchapters A and C) and the requirements for Secretarial approval before abandonment of any oil and gas or geothermal well or mining operation. All such obligations are to remain in full force and effect, the same as if free of any such overriding royalties or payments. The existence of agreements creating overriding royalties or payments out of production, whether or not actually paid, shall not be considered as justification for the approval of abandonment of any oil and gas or geothermal well or mining operation. Nothing in this paragraph revokes the requirement for approval of assignments and other instruments which is required in this section, but any overriding royalties or payments out of production created by the provisions of such assignments or instruments shall be subject to the condition stated in this section. Agreements creating overriding royalties or payments out of production, or agreements designating operators shall be filed with the superintendent unless incorporated in assignments or instruments required to be filed pursuant to this section.

§211.54 Lease or permit cancellation; Bureau of Indian Affairs notice of noncompliance.

(a) If the Secretary determines that a permittee or lessee has failed to comply with the terms of the permit or lease; the regulations in this part; or other applicable laws or regulations; the Secretary may:

(1) Serve a notice of noncompliance specifying in what respect the permittee or lessee has failed to comply with the requirements referenced in this paragraph, and specifying what actions, if any, must be taken to correct the noncompliance; or

(2) Serve a notice of proposed cancellation of the lease or permit. The notice of proposed cancellation shall set forth the reasons why lease or permit cancellation is proposed and shall specify what actions, if any, must be taken to avoid cancellation.

(b) The notice of noncompliance or proposed cancellation shall specify in what respect the permittee or lessee has failed to comply with the requirements referenced in paragraph (a), and shall specify what actions, if any, must be taken to correct the noncompliance.

(c) The notice shall be served upon the permittee or lessee by delivery in person or by certified mail to the permittee or lessee at the permittee's or lessee's last known address. When certified mail is used, the date of service shall be deemed to be when the notice is received or five (5) working days after the date it is mailed, whichever is earlier.

(d) The lessee or permittee shall have thirty (30) days (or such longer time as specified in the notice) from the date that the notice is served to respond, in writing, to the official or the Bureau of Indian Affairs office that issued the notice.

(e) If a permittee or lessee fails to take any action that is prescribed in the notice of proposed cancellation, fails to file a timely written response to the notice, or files a written response that does not, in the discretion of the Secretary, adequately justify the permittee's or lessee's actions, then the Secretary may cancel the lease or permit, specifying the basis for the cancellation.

(f) If a permittee or lessee fails to take corrective action or to file a timely written response adequately justifying the permittee's or lessee's actions pursuant to a notice of noncompliance, the Secretary may issue an order of cessation of operations. If the permittee or lessee fails to comply with the order of cessation, or fails to timely file an appeal of the order of cessation pursuant to paragraph (h), the Secretary may issue an order of lease or permit cancellation.

(g) Cancellation of a lease or permit shall not relieve the lessee or permittee of any continuing obligations under the lease or permit.

(h) Orders of cessation or of lease or permit cancellation issued pursuant to this section may be appealed under 25 CFR part 2.

(i) This section does not limit any other remedies of the Indian mineral owner as set forth in the lease or permit.

(j) Nothing in this section is intended to limit the authority of the authorized officer or the MMS official to take any enforcement action authorized pursuant to statute or regulation.

(k) The authorized officer, MMS official, and the superintendent and/or area director should consult with one another before taking any enforcement actions.

§ 211.55 Penalties.

(a) In addition to or in lieu of cancellation under § 211.54, violations of the terms and conditions of any lease, or the regulations in this part, or failure to comply with a notice of noncompliance or a cessation order issued by the Secretary, or, in the case of solid minerals the authorized officer, may subject a lessee or permittee to a penalty of not more than $1,558 per day for each day that such a violation or noncompliance continues beyond the time limits prescribed for corrective action.

(b) A notice of a proposed penalty shall be served on the lessee or permittee either personally or by certified mail to the lessee or permittee at the lessee's or permittee's last known address. The date of service by certified mail shall be deemed to be the date when received or five (5) working days after the date mailed, whichever is earlier.

(c) The notice shall specify the nature of the violation and the proposed penalty, and shall specifically advise the lessee or permittee of the lessee's or permittee's right to either request a hearing within thirty (30) days from receipt of the notice or pay the proposed penalty. Hearings shall be held before the superintendent and/or area director whose findings shall be conclusive, unless an appeal is taken pursuant to 25 CFR part 2.

(d) If the lessee or permittee served with a notice of proposed penalty requests a hearing, penalties shall accrue each day the violations or noncompliance set forth in the notice continue beyond the time limits prescribed for corrective action. The Secretary may issue a written suspension of the requirement to correct the violations pending completion of the hearings provided by this section only upon a determination, at the discretion of the Secretary, that such a suspension will not be detrimental to the lessor and upon submission and acceptance of a bond deemed adequate to indemnify the lessor from loss or damage. The amount of the bond must be sufficient to cover the cost of correcting the violations set forth in the notice or any disputed amounts plus accrued penalties and interest.

(e) Payment in full of penalties more than ten (10) days after a final decision imposing a penalty shall subject the lessee or permittee to late payment charges. Late payment charges shall be calculated on the basis of a percentage assessment rate of the amount unpaid per month for each month or fraction thereof until payment is received by the Secretary. In the absence of a specific lease provision prescribing a different rate, the interest rate on late payments and underpayments shall be a rate applicable under §6621(a)(2) of the Internal Revenue Code of 1954. Interest shall be charged only on the amount of payment not received and only for the number of days the payment is late.

(f) None of the provisions of this section shall be interpreted as:

(1) Replacing or superseding the independent authority of the authorized officer, the director's representative or the MMS official to impose penalties for violations of applicable regulations pursuant to 43 CFR part 3160, and 43 CFR Groups 3400 and 3500, 30 CFR part 750, or 30 CFR chapter II, subchapters A and C;

(2) Replacing or superseding any penalty provision in the terms and conditions of a lease or permit approved by the Secretary pursuant to this part; or

(3) Authorizing the imposition of a penalty for violations of lease or permit terms for which the authorized officer, director's representative or MMS official, have either statutory or regulatory authority to assess a penalty.

[61 FR 35653, July 8, 1996, as amended at 81 FR 42481, June 30, 2016; 82 FR 7652, Jan. 23, 2017; 83 FR 5195, Feb. 6, 2018]

§211.56 Geological and geophysical permits.

Permits to conduct geological and geophysical operations on Indian lands which do not conflict with any mineral leases entered into pursuant to this part, may be approved by the Secretary with the consent of the Indian mineral owner under the following conditions:

(a) The permit must describe the area to be explored, the duration, and the consideration to be paid the Indian owner;

(b) The permit will not grant the permittee any option or preference rights to a lease or other development contract, or authorize the production of, or removal of oil and gas, geothermal resources, or other minerals, except samples for assay and experimental purposes, unless specifically so stated in the permit; and

(c) Copies of all data collected pursuant to operations conducted under the permit shall be forwarded to the Secretary and the Indian mineral owner, unless otherwise provided in the permit. Data collected under a permit may be held by the Secretary as privileged and proprietary information for the time prescribed in the permit. Where no time period is prescribed in the permit, the Secretary may release such information after six (6) years, with the consent of the Indian mineral owner.

§211.57 Forms.

Leases, bonds, permits, assignments, and other instruments relating to mineral leasing shall be on forms, prescribed by the Secretary, that may be obtained from the superintendent or area director. The provisions of a standard lease or permit may be changed, deleted, or added to by written agreement of all parties with the approval of the Secretary.

§211.58 Appeals.

Appeals from decisions of Bureau of Indian Affairs officers under this part may be taken pursuant to 25 CFR part 2.

PART 212—LEASING OF ALLOTTED LANDS FOR MINERAL DEVELOPMENT

AUTHORITY: Act of March 3, 1909, (35 Stat. 783; 25 U.S.C. 396 (as amended)): Act of May 11, 1938, (Sec. 2, 52 Stat. 347; 25 U.S.C. 396 b-g: Act of August 1, 1956, (70 Stat. 774)); and 25 U.S.C. 2 and 9.

SOURCE: 61 FR 35661, July 8, 1996, unless otherwise noted.

Subpart A—General

§ 212.1 Purpose and scope.

(a) The regulations in this part govern leases for the development of individual Indian oil and gas, geothermal and solid mineral resources. These regulations are applicable to lands or interests in lands the title to which is held, for any individual Indian, in trust by the United States or is subject to restriction against alienation imposed by the United States. These regulations are intended to ensure that Indian mineral owners desiring to have their resources developed are assured that they will be developed in a manner that maximizes their best economic interests and minimizes any adverse environmental impacts or cultural impacts resulting from such development.

(b) The regulations in this part shall be subject to amendment at any time by the Secretary of the Interior. No regulation that becomes effective after the date of approval of any lease or permit shall operate to affect the duration of the lease or permit, rate of royalty, rental, or acreage unless agreed to by all parties to the lease or permit.

(c) Nothing in the regulations in this part is intended to prevent Indian tribes from exercising their lawful governmental authority to regulate the conduct of persons, businesses, operations or mining within their territorial jurisdiction.

(d) The regulations of the Bureau of Land Management, the Office of Surface Mining Reclamation and Enforcement, and the Minerals Management Service that are referenced in §§ 212.4, 212.5, and 212.6 of this part are supplemental to these regulations, and apply to parties holding leases or permits for development of Indian mineral resources unless specifically stated otherwise in this part or in such other Federal regulations.

(e) The regulations in this part do not apply to leasing and development governed by regulations in 25 CFR part 213 (Members of the Five Civilized Tribes of Oklahoma), 226 (Osage), or 227 (Wind River Reservation).

§212.2 Information collection.

The information collection requirements contained in this part do not require a review by the Office of Management and Budget under the Paperwork Reduction Act (44 U.S.C. 3501; *et seq.*).

§212.3 Definitions.

As used in this part, the following words and phrases have the specified meaning except where otherwise indicated:

Applicant means any person seeking a permit, lease, or an assignment from the superintendent or area director.

Approving official means the Bureau of Indian Affairs official with delegated authority to approve a lease or permit.

Area director means the Bureau of Indian Affairs official in charge of an area office.

Authorized officer means any employee of the Bureau of Land Management authorized by law or by lawful delegation of authority to perform the duties described herein and in 43 CFR parts 3160, 3180, 3260, 3280, 3480, and 3590.

Cooperative agreement means a binding arrangement between two or more parties purporting to the act of agreeing or of coming to a mutual arrangement that is accepted by all parties to a transaction (e.g., communitization and unitization).

Director's representative means the Office of Surface Mining Reclamation and Enforcement director's representative authorized by law or lawful delegation of authority to perform the duties described in 30 CFR part 750.

Gas means any fluid, either combustible or non-combustible, that is produced in a natural state from the earth and that maintains a gaseous or rarefied state at ordinary temperature and pressure conditions.

Geological and geophysical permit means a written authorization to conduct on-site surveys to locate potential deposits of oil and gas, geothermal or solid mineral resources on the lands.

Geothermal resources means:

(1) All products of geothermal processes, including indigenous steam, hot water and hot brines;

(2) Steam and other gases, hot water, and hot brines, resulting from water, gas or other fluids artificially introduced into geothermal formations;

(3) Heat or other associated energy found in geothermal formations; and

(4) Any by-product derived therefrom.

In the best interest of the Indian mineral owner refers to the standards to be applied by the Secretary in considering whether to take an administrative action affecting the interests of an Indian mineral owner. In considering whether it is "in the best interest of the Indian mineral owner" to take a certain action (such as approval of a lease, permit, unitization or communitization agreement), the Secretary shall consider any relevant factor, including, but not limited to: economic considerations, such as date of lease expiration; probable financial effect on the Indian mineral owner; leasability of land concerned; need for change in the terms of the existing lease; marketability; and potential environmental, social, and cultural effects.

Indian lands means any lands owned by any individual Indian or Alaska Native, Indian tribe, band, nation, pueblo, community, rancheria, colony, or other tribal group which owns lands or interest in the minerals, the title to which is held in trust by the United States or is subject to restriction against alienation imposed by the United States.

Indian mineral owner means any individual Indian or Alaska Native who owns mineral interests in oil and gas, geothermal, or solid mineral resources, title to which is held in trust by the United States, or is subject to the restriction against alienation imposed by the United States.

Indian surface owner means any individual Indian or Indian tribe whose surface estate is held in trust by the

United States, or is subject to restriction against alienation imposed by the United States.

Lease means any contract, approved by the Secretary of the Interior under the Act of March 3, 1909 (35 Stat. 783)(25 U.S.C. 396), as amended, and the Act of May 11, 1938 (52 Stat. 347) (25 U.S.C. 396a–396g), as amended, that authorize exploration for, extraction of, or removal of any minerals.

Lessee means a natural person, proprietorship, partnership, corporation, or other entity which has entered into a lease with an Indian mineral owner, or who has been assigned an obligation to make royalty or other payments required by the lease.

Lessor means an Indian mineral owner who is a party to a lease.

Minerals includes both metalliferous and non-metalliferous minerals; all hydrocarbons, including oil, gas, coal and lignite of all ranks; geothermal resources; and includes but is not limited to, sand, gravel, pumice, cinders, granite, building stone, limestone, clay, silt, or any other energy or non-energy mineral.

Minerals Management Service official means any employee of the Minerals Management Service (MMS) authorized by law or by lawful delegation of authority to perform the duties described in 30 CFR chapter II, subchapters A and C.

Mining means the science, technique, and business of mineral development including, but not limited to: opencast work, underground work, and in-situ leaching directed to severance and treatment of minerals; *Provided,* when sand, gravel, pumice, cinders, granite, building stone, limestone, clay or silt is the subject mineral, an enterprise is considered "mining" only if the extraction of such a mineral exceeds 5,000 cubic yards in any given year.

Oil means all nongaseous hydrocarbon substances other than those substances leasable as coal, oil shale, or gilsonite (including all vein-type solid hydrocarbons). Oil includes liquefiable hydrocarbon substances such as drip gasoline and other natural condensates recovered or recoverable in a liquid state from produced gas without resorting to a manufacturing process.

Permit means any contract issued by the superintendent and/or area director to conduct exploration on; or removal of less than 5,000 cubic yards per year of common varieties of minerals from Indian lands.

Permittee means a person holding or required by this part to hold a permit to conduct exploration operations on; or remove less than 5,000 cubic yards per year of common varieties of minerals from Indian lands.

Secretary means the Secretary of the Interior or an authorized representative.

Solid minerals means all minerals excluding oil and gas and geothermal resources.

Superintendent means the Bureau of Indian Affairs official in charge of the agency office having jurisdiction over the minerals subject to leasing under this part.

§ 212.4 Authority and responsibility of the Bureau of Land Management (BLM).

The functions of the Bureau of Land Management are found in 43 CFR part 3160—Onshore Oil and Gas Operations, 43 CFR part 3180—Onshore Oil and Gas Unit Agreements: Unproven Area, 43 CFR part 3260—Geothermal Resources Operations, 43 CFR part 3280—Geothermal Resources Unit Agreements: Unproven Areas, 43 CFR part 3480—Coal Exploration and Mining Operations, and 43 CFR part 3590—Solid Minerals (Other Than Coal) Exploration and Mining Operations, and currently include, but are not limited to, resource evaluation, approval of drilling permits, mining and reclamation, production plans, mineral appraisals, inspection and enforcement, and production verification. Those regulations, apply to leases or permits issued under this part.

§ 212.5 Authority and responsibility of the Office of Surface Mining Reclamation and Enforcement (OSM).

The OSM is the regulatory authority for surface coal mining and reclamation operations on Indian lands pursuant to the Surface Mining Control and Reclamation Act of 1977 (30 U.S.C. 1201 *et seq.*). The relevant regulations for surface coal mining and reclamation operations are found in 30 CFR part 750. Those regulations apply to mining and reclamation on leases issued under this part.

§212.6 Authority and responsibility of the Minerals Management Service (MMS).

The functions of the MMS for reporting, accounting, and auditing are found in 30 CFR chapter II, subchapters A and C, which apply to leases approved under this part. To the extent the parties to a lease or permit are able to provide reasonable provisions satisfactorily addressing the functions governed by MMS regulations, the Secretary may approve alternate provisions in a lease or permit.

§212.7 Environmental studies.

The provisions of §211.7 of this subchapter, as amended, are applicable to leases under this part.

§212.8 Government employees cannot acquire leases.

U.S. Government employees are prevented from acquiring leases or interests in leases by the provisions of 25 CFR part 140 and 43 CFR part 20 pertaining to conflicts of interest and ownership of an interest in trust land.

Subpart B—How To Acquire Leases

§212.20 Leasing procedures.

(a) Application for leases shall be made to the superintendent having jurisdiction over the lands.

(b) Indian mineral owners may request the Secretary to prepare, advertise and negotiate mineral leases on their behalf. Leases for minerals shall be advertised for bids as prescribed in this section unless one or more of the Indian mineral owners of a tract sought for lease request the Secretary to negotiate for a lease on their behalf without advertising. Unless the Secretary decides that negotiation of a mineral lease is in the best interests of the Indian mineral owners, he shall use the following procedure for leasing:

(1) Leases shall be advertised to receive optimum competition for bonus consideration, under sealed bid, oral auction, or a combination of both. Notice of such advertisement shall be published in at least one local newspaper and in one trade publication at least thirty (30) days in advance of sale. If applicable, such notice must identify the reservation within which the tracts to be leased are found. No specific description of the tracts to be leased need be published. Specific description of such tracts shall be available at the office of the superintendent and/or area director upon request. The complete text of the advertisement, including a specific description, shall be mailed to each person listed on the appropriate agency or area mailing list. Individuals and companies interested in receiving advertisements on lease sales should send their mailing information to the appropriate agency or area office for future reference.

(2) The advertisement shall offer the tracts to a responsible bidder offering the highest bonus. The Secretary shall establish the rental and royalty rates which shall be stated in the advertisement and will not be subject to negotiation. The advertisement shall provide that the Secretary reserves the right to reject any or all bids, and that acceptance of the lease bid by or on behalf of the Indian mineral owner is required. The requirements under §212.21 are applicable to the acceptance of a lease bid.

(3) Each sealed bid must be accompanied by a cashier's check, certified check or postal money order, or any combination thereof, payable to the payee designated in the advertisement, in an amount not less than 25 percent of the bonus bid, which shall be returned if that bid is not accepted.

(4) A successful oral auction bidder will be allowed five (5) working days to remit the required 25 percent deposit of the bonus bid.

(5) A successful bidder shall, within thirty (30) days after notification of the bid award, remit to the Secretary the balance of the bonus, the first year's rental, a $75 filing fee, its prorated share of the advertising costs as determined by the Bureau of Indian Affairs, and file with the Secretary all required bonds. The successful bidder shall also file the lease in completed form, signed by the Indian mineral owner(s), at that time. However, for

good reasons, the Secretary may grant extensions of time in thirty (30) day increments for filing of the lease and all required bonds, provided that additional extension requests are submitted and approved prior to the expiration of the original thirty (30) days or the previously granted extension. Failure on the part of the bidder to take all reasonable actions necessary to comply with the foregoing shall result in forfeiture of the required payment of 25 percent of any bonus bid for the use and benefit of the Indian mineral owner.

(6) If no satisfactory bid is received, or if the accepted bidder fails to complete all requirements necessary for approval of the lease, or if the Secretary determines that it is not in the best interest of the Indian mineral owner to accept any of the bids the Secretary may re-advertise the tract for sale, or subject to the consent of the Indian mineral owner, a lease may be let through private negotiations.

(c) The Secretary shall advise the Indian mineral owner of the results of the bidding, and shall not approve the lease until the consent of the Indian mineral owner has been obtained. The requirements under § 212.21 are applicable to the approval of a mineral lease.

§ 212.21 Execution of leases.

(a) The Secretary shall not execute a mineral lease on behalf of an Indian mineral owner, except when such owner is deceased and the heirs to or devisee of the estate have not been determined, or if determined, some or all of them cannot be located. Leases involving such interests may be executed by the Secretary, provided that the mineral interest shall have been offered for sale under the provisions of section 212.20(b) (1) through (6).

(b) The Secretary may execute leases on behalf of minors and persons who are incompetent by reason of mental incapacity; *Provided*, that there is no parent, guardian, conservator, or other person who has lawful authority to execute a lease on behalf of the minor or person with mental incapacity.

(c) If an owner is a life tenant, the procedures set forth in 25 CFR part 179 (Life Estates and Future Interests), shall apply.

§ 212.22 Leases for subsurface storage of oil or gas.

The provisions of § 211.22 of this subchapter are applicable to leases under this part.

§ 212.23 Corporate qualifications and requests for information.

The provisions of § 211.23 of this subchapter are applicable to leases under this part.

§ 212.24 Bonds.

The provisions of § 211.24 of this subchapter are applicable to leases under this part.

§ 212.25 Acreage limitation.

The provisions of § 211.25 of this subchapter are applicable to leases under this part.

§ 212.26 [Reserved]

§ 212.27 Duration of leases.

The provisions of § 211.27 of this subchapter are applicable to leases under this part.

§ 212.28 Unitization and communitization agreements, and well spacing.

(a) For the purpose of promoting conservation and efficient utilization of minerals, the Secretary may approve a cooperative unit, drilling or other development plan on any leased area upon a determination that approval is advisable and in the best interest of the Indian mineral owner. For the purposes of this section, a cooperative unit, drilling or other development plan means an agreement for the development or operation of a specifically designated area as a single unit without regard to separate ownership of the land included in the agreement. Such cooperative agreements include, but are not limited to, unit agreements, communitization agreements and other types of agreements that allocate costs and benefits.

(b) The consent of the Indian mineral owner to such unit or cooperative agreement shall not be required unless such consent is specifically required in the lease.

(c) Requests for approval of cooperative agreements which comply with the requirements of all applicable rules and regulations shall be filed with the superintendent or area director.

(d) All Indian mineral owners of any right, title or interest in the mineral resources to be included in a cooperative agreement must be notified by the lessee at the time the agreement is submitted to the superintendent or area director. An affidavit from the lessee stating that a notice was mailed to each mineral owner of record for whom the superintendent or area director has an address will satisfy this notice requirement.

(e) A request for approval of a proposed cooperative agreement, and all documents incident to such agreement, must be filed with the superintendent or area director at least ninety (90) days prior to the first expiration date of any of the Indian leases in the area proposed to be covered by the cooperative agreement.

(f) Unless otherwise provided in the cooperative agreement, approval of the agreement commits each lease to the unit in the area covered by the agreement on the date approved by the Secretary or the date of first production, whichever is earlier, as long as the agreement is approved before the lease expiration date.

(g) Any lease committed in part to any such cooperative agreement shall be segregated into a separate lease or leases as to the lands committed and lands not committed to the agreement. Segregation shall be effective on the date the agreement is effective.

(h) Wells shall be drilled in conformity with a well spacing program approved by the authorized officer.

§ 212.29 [Reserved]

§ 212.30 Removal of restrictions.

(a) Notwithstanding the provisions of any mineral lease to the contrary, the removal of all restrictions against alienation shall operate to divest the Secretary of all supervisory authority and responsibility with respect to the lease. Thereafter, all payments required to be made under the lease shall be made directly to the owner(s).

(b) In the event restrictions are removed from a part of the land included in any lease approved by the Secretary, the entire lease shall continue to be subject to the supervision of the Secretary until such times as the holder of the lease and the unrestricted Indian owner submits to the Secretary satisfactory evidence that adequate arrangements have been made to account for the mineral resources of the restricted land separately from those of the unrestricted. Thereafter, the unrestricted portion shall be relieved from the supervision of the Secretary, the lease, the regulations of this part, and all other applicable laws and regulations.

§§ 212.31–212.32 [Reserved]

§ 212.33 Terms applying after relinquishment.

All leases for individual Indian lands approved by the Secretary under this part shall contain provisions for the relinquishment of supervision and provide for operations of the lease after such relinquishment. These leases shall contain provisions that address the following issues:

(a) *Provisions of relinquishment.* If the Secretary relinquishes supervision at any time during the life of the lease instrument as to all or part of the acreage subject to the lease, the Secretary shall give the Indian mineral owner and the lessee thirty (30) days written notice prior to the termination of supervision. After notice of relinquishment has been given to the lessee, the lease shall be subject to the following conditions:

(1) All rentals and royalties thereafter accruing shall be paid directly to the lessor or the lessor's successors in title, or to a trustee appointed under the provisions of paragraph (b) of this section.

(2) If, at the time supervision is relinquished by the Secretary, the lessee has made all payments then due and has fully performed all obligations on the lessee's part to be performed up to the time of such relinquishment, the bond given to secure the performance of the lease, on file in the appropriate agency or area office, shall be of no further force or effect.

(3) Should relinquishment affect only part of the lease, then the lessee may continue to conduct operations on the

land covered by the lease as an entirety; *Provided*, that the lessee shall pay, in the manner prescribed by the lease and regulations for the benefit of lessor, the same proportion of all rentals and royalties due under the provisions of this part as the acreage retained under the supervision of the Secretary bears to the entire acreage of the lessee, and shall pay the remainder of the rentals and royalties directly to the remaining lessors or successors in title or said trustee as the case may be, as provided in paragraph (a) (1) of this section.

(b) *Division of fee.* If, after the execution of the lease and after the Secretary relinquishes supervision thereof, the fee of the leased land is divided into separate parcels held by different owners, or if the rental or royalty interest is divided in ownership, the obligations of the lessee shall not be modified in any manner except as specifically provided by the provisions of the lease. Notwithstanding such separate ownership, the lessee may continue to conduct operations on said premises as an entirety. Each separate owner shall receive such proportion of all rental and royalties accruing after the vesting of its title as the acreage of the fee, or rental or royalty interest, bears to the entire acreage covered by the lease; or to the entire rental or royalty interest as the case may be. If at any time after departmental supervision of the lease is relinquished, in whole or in part, to rentals and royalties, whether said parties are so entitled by virtue of undivided interest or by virtue of ownership of separate parcels of the land covered, the lessee may elect to withhold the payment of further rentals or royalties (except as the portion due the Indian lessor while under restriction), until all of said parties shall agree upon and designate a trustee in writing and in a recordable instrument to receive all payments due thereunder on behalf of said parties and their respective successors in title. Payments to said trustee shall constitute lawful payments, and the sole risk of an improper or unlawful distribution of said funds by said trustee shall rest upon the parties naming said trustee and their said respective successors in title.

§ 212.34 Individual tribal assignments excluded.

The reference in this part to Indian mineral owners does not include assignments of tribal lands made pursuant to tribal constitutions or ordinances for the use of individual Indians and assignees of such lands.

Subpart C—Rents, Royalties, Cancellations, and Appeals

§ 212.40 Manner of payments.

The provisions of § 211.40 of this subchapter are applicable to leases under this part.

§ 212.41 Rentals and production royalty on oil and gas leases.

(a) A lessee shall pay, in advance, beginning with the effective date of the lease, an annual rental of $2.00 per acre or fraction of an acre or such other greater amount as prescribed in the lease. This rental shall not be credited against production royalty nor shall the rental be prorated or refunded because of surrender or cancellation.

(b) The Secretary shall not approve leases with a royalty rate less than 16–⅔ percent of the amount or value of production produced and sold from the lease unless a lower royalty rate is agreed to by the Indian mineral owner and is found to be in the best interest of the Indian mineral owner. Such approval may only be granted by the area director if the approving official is the superintendent and the Assistant Secretary for Indian Affairs if the approving official is the area director.

(c) Value of lease production for royalty purposes shall be determined in accordance with applicable lease provisions and regulations in 30 CFR chapter II, subchapters A and C. If the valuation provisions in the lease are inconsistent with the regulations in 30 CFR chapter II, subchapters A and C, the lease provisions shall govern.

§ 212.42 Annual rentals and expenditures for development on leases other than oil and gas, and geothermal resources.

The provisions of § 211.42 of this subchapter are applicable to leases under this part.

§212.43 Royalty rates for minerals other than oil and gas.

The provisions of §211.43 of this subchapter are applicable to leases under this part.

§212.44 Suspension of operations.

The provisions of §211.44 of this subchapter are applicable to leases under this part.

§212.45 [Reserved]

§212.46 Inspection of premises, books, and accounts.

The provisions of §211.46 of this subchapter are applicable to leases under this part.

§212.47 Diligence, drainage and prevention of waste.

The provisions of §211.47 of this subchapter are applicable to leases under this part.

§212.48 Permission to start operations.

The provisions of §211.48 of this subchapter are applicable to leases under this part.

§212.49 Restrictions on operations.

The provisions of §211.49 of this subchapter are applicable to leases under this part.

§212.50 [Reserved]

§212.51 Surrender of leases.

The provisions of §211.51 of this subchapter are applicable to leases under this part.

§212.52 Fees.

The provisions of §211.52 of this subchapter are applicable to leases under this part.

§212.53 Assignments, overriding royalties, and operating agreements.

The provisions of §211.53 of this subchapter are applicable to leases under this part.

§212.54 Lease or permit cancellation; Bureau of Indian Affairs notice of noncompliance.

The provisions of §211.54 of this subchapter are applicable to leases under this part.

§212.55 Penalties.

The provisions of §211.55 of this subchapter are applicable to this part.

§212.56 Geological and geophysical permits.

(a) Permits to conduct geological and geophysical operations on Indian lands which do not conflict with any mineral lease entered into pursuant to this part may be approved by the Secretary with the consent of the Indian owner under the following conditions:

(1) The permit must describe the area to be explored, the duration and the consideration to be paid the Indian owner;

(2) The permit may not grant the permittee any option or preference rights to a lease or other development contract, authorize the production of, or removal of oil and gas, or geothermal resources, or other minerals except samples for assay and experimental purposes, unless specifically so stated in the permit; and

(3) Copies of all data collected pursuant to operations conducted under the permit shall be forwarded to the Secretary and made available to the Indian mineral owner, unless otherwise provided in the permit. Data collected under a permit shall be held by the Secretary as privileged and proprietary information for the time prescribed in the permit. Where no time period is prescribed in the permit, the Secretary may, in the discretion of the Secretary, release such information after six (6) years.

(b) A permit may be granted by the Secretary without 100 percent consent of the individual mineral owners if:

(1) The minerals are owned by more than one person, and the owners of a majority of the interest therein consent to the permit;

(2) The whereabouts of one or more owners of the minerals or an interest therein is unknown, and all the remaining owners of the interests consent to the permit;

(3) The heirs or devisee of a deceased owner of the land or an interest therein have not been determined, and the Secretary finds that the permit activity will cause no substantial injury to the land or any owner thereof; or

(4) The owners of interests in the land are so numerous that the Secretary finds it would be impractical to obtain their consent, and also finds that the permit activity will cause no substantial injury to the land or any owner thereof.

(c) A lessee does not need a permit to conduct geological and geophysical operations on Indian lands, if provided for in the lessee's mineral lease, where the Indian mineral owner is also the surface land owner. In instances where the Indian mineral owner is not the surface owner, the lessee must obtain any additional necessary permits or rights of ingress or egress from the surface occupant.

§ 212.57 Forms.

The provisions of § 211.57 of this subchapter are applicable to leases under this part.

§ 212.58 Appeals.

The provisions of § 211.58 of this subchapter are applicable to leases under this part.

PART 213—LEASING OF RESTRICTED LANDS OF MEMBERS OF FIVE CIVILIZED TRIBES, OKLAHOMA, FOR MINING

Authority: Sec. 2, 35 Stat. 312; sec. 18, 41 Stat. 426; sec. 1, 45 Stat. 495; sec. 1, 47 Stat. 777; 25 U.S.C. 356; and Sec. 701, Pub. L. 114–74, 129 Stat. 599. Interpret or apply secs. 3, 11, 35 Stat. 313, 316; sec. 8, 47 Stat. 779, unless otherwise noted.

CROSS REFERENCE: For oil and gas operating regulations of the Geological Survey, see 30 CFR part 221.

SOURCE: 22 FR 10599, Dec. 24, 1957, unless otherwise noted. Redesignated at 47 FR 13327, Mar. 30, 1982.

§213.1 Definitions.

Area Director. The term "Area Director" in this part refers to the officer in charge of the Five Civilized Tribes Indian Agency.

Supervisor. The term "supervisor" in this part refers to a representative of the Secretary of the Interior under direction of the Director of the U.S. Geological Survey, authorized and empowered to supervise and direct operations under oil and gas or other mining leases, to furnish scientific and technical information and advice, to ascertain and record the amount and value of production, and to determine and record rentals and royalties due and paid.

HOW TO ACQUIRE LEASES

§213.2 Applications for leases.

Applications for leases should be made to the Area Director.

§213.3 No Government employee shall acquire leases.

No lease, assignment thereof, or interest therein will be approved to any employee or employees of the U.S. Government, whether connected with the Bureau of Indian Affairs or otherwise, and no employee of the Department of the Interior shall be permitted to acquire any interest in such leases covering restricted Indian lands by ownership of stock in corporations having leases or in any other manner.

(R.S. 2078; 25 U.S.C. 68)

§213.4 Sale of oil and gas leases.

(a) At such times and in such manner as he may deem appropriate, the Area Director shall publish notices at least thirty days prior to the sale, unless a shorter period is authorized by the Commissioner of Indian Affairs, that oil and gas leases on specific tracts, each of which shall be in a reasonably compact body, will be offered to the highest responsible bidder for a bonus consideration, in addition to stipulated rentals and royalties. Each bid must be accompanied by a cashier's check, certified check, or postal money order, payable to the payee designated in the invitation to bid, in an amount not less than 25 percent of the bonus bid. Within 30 days after notification of being the successful bidder, said bidder must remit the balance of the bonus, the first year's rental, and his share of the advertising costs, and shall file with the Area Director the lease in completed form. The Area Director may, for good and sufficient reasons, extend the time for the completion and submission of the lease form, but no extension shall be granted for remitting the balance of monies due. If the successful bidder fails to pay the full consideration within said period, or fails to file the completed lease within said period or extension thereof, or if the lease is disapproved through no fault of the lessor or the Department of the Interior, 25 percent of the bonus bid will be forfeited for the use and benefit of the Indian lessor.

(b) In cases where any part of the bonus bid for a lease is paid directly to the Indian lessor, upon his signing the lease, the lessee must procure and file with the lease an affidavit of the lessor, sworn to before a U.S. Commissioner, Postmaster, Area Director, local representative of the Area Director, county or district judge, Federal judge or clerk of a Federal court, showing the amount of bonus so paid, and the balance thereof must be paid into the office of the Area Director upon filing the lease. Where possible lessees are requested to take the lessor to the nearest United States field clerk who will render all proper assistance in the execution of leases, and before whom the bonus affidavit may be executed in cases where any part of bonus consideration is paid directly to the lessor. Where leases are executed by guardians, under order of court, the affidavit of lessor may be executed before a notary public.

(c) All notices or advertisements of sales of oil and gas leases shall reserve to the Secretary of the Interior the right to reject all bids when in his judgment the interests of the Indians will be best served by so doing, and that if no satisfactory bid is received, or if the accepted bidder fails to complete the lease or if the Secretary of the Interior shall determine that it is unwise in the interests of the Indians to accept the highest bid, the Secretary may readvertise such lease for sale, or if deemed advisable, with the consent of the Indian owners, a lease may be made by private negotiations. The successful bidder or bidders will be required to pay his or their share of the advertising costs. Amounts received from unsuccessful bidders will be returned; but when no bid is accepted on a tract, the costs of advertising will be assessed against the applicant who requested that said tract be advertised.

(Secs. 16, 17, 48 Stat. 987, 988, sec. 9, 49 Stat. 1968, sec. 4, 52 Stat. 348; 25 U.S.C. 396d, 476, 477, 509)

§ 213.5 Term of oil and gas leases.

Oil and gas mining leases which require the approval of the Secretary of the Interior may be made for periods of 10 years from the date of approval of lease by the Secretary of the Interior and as much longer thereafter as oil and/or gas is produced in paying quantities.

§ 213.6 Leases for minerals other than oil and gas.

Uncontested mining leases for minerals other than oil and gas shall be made on forms[1] prescribed by the Department, for a period of 15 years with the right of renewal on such terms as the superintendent may prescribe, and shall be subject only to approval by the Area Director. See provisions of the act of February 14, 1920 (41 Stat. 408). Any persons aggrieved by any decision or order of the Area Director approving, rejecting, or disapproving any such lease may appeal from the same to the Secretary of the Interior within 30 days from the date of such decision or order.

§ 213.7 Fees.

The provisions of § 211.25 of this chapter, or as hereafter amended, are applicable to this part.

[24 FR 7949, Oct. 2, 1959. Redesignated at 47 FR 13327, Mar. 30, 1982]

[1] For further information regarding forms, see § 211.30.

§ 213.8 Filing of lease deemed constructive notice.

The filing of any lease in the office of the Area Director shall be deemed constructive notice of the existence of such lease. See act of March 1, 1907.

(34 Stat. 1026)

§ 213.9 Noncontiguous tracts.

No lease will be approved covering two or more noncontiguous tracts of land, but in such case a lease must be executed on each separate tract.

§ 213.10 Lessor's signature.

Any Indian who cannot write his name will be required to sign all official papers by making a distinct thumbprint which shall be designated as "right" or "left" thumbmark. Such signatures must be witnessed by two persons, one of whom must be a U.S. Government employee (such as field clerk, postmaster, U.S. Commissioner, etc.).

§ 213.11 Minor lessors.

Where the lessor is a minor, certified copies of letters of guardianship and court orders approving leases must be filed.

§ 213.12 Leases executed by guardians of minors.

Leases executed by guardians of minors under order of court for a period extending beyond the minority of the minor will be approved unless it appears that such action would be prejudicial to the interests of the minor: *Provided*, That in the event the minor becomes of age within 1 year from the date of execution of lease the consent of the minor to the execution of the lease should be obtained and submitted with the lease for consideration.

§ 213.13 Inherited lands.

Except to prevent loss or waste, leases on undivided inherited lands will not be approved until the heirship determination has been approved. If the heirs to undivided inherited lands are undetermined or cannot be located, or if the heirs owning less than one-half interest in the lands refuse to sign a lease and it appears necessary to lease the lands to prevent loss or waste, the

Area Director will report the facts to the Commissioner of Indian Affairs and ask for instructions. Minor heirs can lease or joint adult heirs in leasing only through guardians under order of court. Proof of heirship shall be given upon Form F prescribed. If probate or other court proceedings have established the heirship in any case, or the land has been partitioned, certified copy of final order, judgment, or decree of the court will be accepted in lieu of Form F.

§213.14 Corporations and corporate information.

If the applicant for a lease is a corporation, it shall file evidence of authority of its officers to execute papers; and with its first application it shall also file a certified copy of its articles of incorporation, and, if foreign to the State in which the lands are located, evidence showing compliance with the corporation laws thereof. Statements of changes in officers and stockholders shall be furnished by a corporation lessee to the Area Director January 1 of each year, and at such other times as may be requested.

Whenever deemed advisable in any case the Area Director may require a corporation applicant or lessee to file:

(a) List of officers, principal stockholders, and directors, with post office addresses and numbers of shares held by each.

(b) A sworn statement of the proper officer showing:

(1) The total number of shares of the capital stock actually issued and the amount of cash paid into the treasury on each share sold; or, if paid in property, the kind of quantity and value of the same paid per share.

(2) Of the stock sold, how much remains unpaid and subject to assessment.

(3) The amount of cash the company has in its treasury and elsewhere.

(4) The property, exclusive of cash, owned by the company and its value.

(5) The total indebtedness of the company and the nature of its obligations.

(6) Whether the applicant or any person controlling, controlled by or under common control with the applicant has filed any registration statement, application for registration, prospectus or offering sheet with the Securities and Exchange Commission pursuant to the Securities Act of 1933 or the Securities Exchange Act of 1934 or said Commission's rules and regulations under said acts; if so, under what provision of said acts or rules and regulations; and what disposition of any such statement, application, prospectus or offering sheet has been made.

(c) Affidavits of individual stockholders, setting forth in what corporations, or with what persons, firms, or associations such individual stockholders are interested in mining leases on restricted lands within the State, and whether they hold such interest for themselves or in trust.

CROSS REFERENCE: For regulations of the Securities and Exchange Commission, see 17 CFR chapter II.

§213.15 Bonds.

(a) Lessee shall furnish with each mining lease a bond (Form 5–154b), and an assignee of a lease shall furnish with each assignment a bond (Form 5–154m), with an acceptable company authorized to act as sole surety, or with two or more personal sureties and a deposit as collateral security of any public-debt obligations of the United States guaranteed as to principal and interest by the United States, equal to the full amount of such bonds, or other collateral satisfactory to the Secretary of the Interior, or show ownership of unencumbered real estate of the value equal to twice the amount of the bonds. Lessee may file a bond on Form 5–154a without sureties and a deposit as collateral security of Government bonds equal in value to the full amount of the bond. Lease bonds, except as provided in paragraph (c) of this section, shall not be less than the following amounts:

For less than 80 acres	$1,000
For 80 acres and less than 120 acres	1,500
For 120 acres and not more than 160 acres	2,000
For each additional 40 acres, or part thereof, above 160 acres	500

Provided, That for leases for minerals other than oil and gas the Secretary of the Interior or his authorized representative with the consent of the Indian landowner may authorize a bond for a lesser amount if, in his opinion, the circumstances warrant and the interests of the Indian landowners are fully protected: *Provided further*, That a lessee may file a bond (Form 5–154f), in the sum of $15,000 for all leases of minerals up to 10,240 acres under the jurisdiction of the officer in charge of the Five Civilized Tribe Agency.

(b) In lieu of the bonds required under paragraph (a) of this section, a lessee may furnish a bond (Form 5–156) in the sum of $75,000 for full nationwide coverage with an acceptable company authorized to act as sole surety to cover all oil and gas leases and oil and gas prospecting permits without geographic or acreage limitation to which the lessee or permittee is or may become a party.

(c) The right is specifically reserved to increase the amount of bonds and the collateral security prescribed in paragraph (a) of this section in any particular case when the officer in charge deems it proper to do so. The nationwide bond may be increased at any time in the discretion of the Secretary of the Interior.

[22 FR 10599, Dec. 24, 1957, as amended at 26 FR 164, Jan. 10, 1961. Redesignated at 47 FR 13327, Mar. 30, 1982]

§ 213.16 Additional information may be requested by Area Director.

The Area Director, or other Government officer having the matter in charge or under investigation, may, at any time, either before or after approval of a lease, call for any additional information desired to carry out the purpose of the regulations in this part, and such information shall be furnished within the time specified in the request therefor. If the lessee fails to furnish the information requested, the lease will be subject to disapproval or cancellation, whichever is appropriate.

§ 213.17 Government reserves right to purchase minerals produced.

In time of war or other public emergency any of the executive departments of the U.S. Government shall have the option to purchase at the prevailing market price on the date of sale all or any part of the minerals produced under any lease.

RENTS AND ROYALTIES

§ 213.18 Manner of payment of rents and royalties.

(a) Except as provided in paragraph (b) of this section, all rents, royalties and other payments due under leases which have been or may be approved in accordance with this part shall be paid by check or bank draft to the order of the Treasurer of the United States and mailed to the Area Director for deposit to the credit of the various lessors. When lessees and purchasers are instructed, in writing, by the Area Director, which instructions shall be complete as to lessors for each lease, separate remittances for each payment due each lessor shall be mailed to the Area Director. Any payments under this paragraph, covering lands or interests therein from which restrictions have been removed by death or otherwise, may continue to be made in the manner provided by this paragraph until ten days after notice of relinquishment of supervision has been mailed to the lessee.

(b) The Area Director may, in his discretion, whenever it appears to be in the best interest of any lessor, authorize and direct the lessee to pay directly to the lessor, or to the legal guardian of any lessor under guardianship, the rents, royalties and other payments (other than bonuses and advance payments for the first year) due under leases which have been or may be approved in accordance with the regulations in this part. Any such authority for direct payment shall be in writing, addressed to the owner or owners of the lease, and shall expressly provide for its revocation or modification at any time, in writing, by the Area Director. Written authorization for direct payment and written revocations or modifications thereof shall become a part of the lease and shall be distributed as in the case of original leases. All such revocations or modifications shall have a 5-day grace period after date of receipt. Rents, royalties, and other payments paid in accordance therewith shall constitute full compliance with the requirements of the lease pertaining to such payments.

(c) Rents and royalties paid pursuant to paragraphs (a) and (b) of this section on producing leases shall be supported by statements, acceptable to the Secretary or his duly authorized representative, to be transmitted to the Supervisor, in duplicate, covering each lease, identified by contract number and lease number. Such statements shall show the specific items of rents or royalties for which remittances are made, and shall identify each remittance by the remittance number, date, amount, and name of each payee.

(d) Rents paid on nonproducing leases pursuant to paragraphs (a) and (b) of this section shall be supported by a statement, acceptable to the Area Director, to be transmitted to the Area Director covering each lease, identified by contract number and lease number. Each remittance shall be identified by the remittance number, date, amount, name of each payee, and dates of mailing of remittances. Date of mailing, or, if remittance is sent by registered mail, the date of registration receipts covering remittances mailed, shall be considered as date of payment.

(e) For leases other than oil and gas, all advance rentals and royalties for the first year shall be paid to the Area Director at the time of filing the lease, and the advance royalty and 20 percent of the first year's rental so paid shall be and become the property of the lessor, if the lease be disapproved because of the lessee's failure to meet the requirements of the law or of the regulations in this part or because of any other fault or defect chargeable to the lessee.

§ 213.19 Crediting advance annual payments.

In the event of discovery of minerals, all advance rents and advance royalties shall be allowed as credit on stipulated royalties for the year for which such advance payments have been made. No refund of such advance payments made under any lease will be allowed in the event the royalty on production is not sufficient to equal such advance payment; nor will any part of the moneys so paid be refunded to the lessee because of any subsequent surrender or cancellation of the lease.

§ 213.20 [Reserved]

§ 213.21 Rate of rents on leases other than oil and gas.

On all mineral leases of allotted lands other than oil and gas leases, rental shall be paid annually in advance from the date of approval of the lease, as follows: Fifty cents per acre for the first year, 75 cents per acre for the second year, and $1 per acre for the third and each succeeding year of the term of the lease.

§ 213.22 Expenditures under lease other than oil and gas.

(a) On all leases for deposits of minerals other than oil and gas, there shall be expended for each calendar year the lease is in force, and for each fraction of a calendar year greater than 6 months, in actual mining operations, development, or improvements upon the lands leased, or for the benefit thereof, a sum which, with the annual rental, shall amount to not less than $5 per acre.

(b) The expenditures for development required by this section upon application may be waived in writing by the Area Director or other officer in charge of the Five Civilized Tribes Agency either before or after the approval of a lease, such waiver to be subject to termination at any time upon 10 days' written notice to the holder of the lease by the said Area Director or other officer in charge.

(c) Each lessee, except oil and gas lessees, shall file with the Area Director an itemized statement in duplicate, within 20 days after the close of each calendar year, of the amount and character of said expenditures during such years the statement to be certified under oath by the lessee or his agent having personal knowledge of the facts contained therein.

§ 213.23 Royalty rates for minerals other than oil and gas.

Unless otherwise authorized by the Commissioner of Indian Affairs, the minimum rates for minerals other than oil and gas shall be as follows:

(a) For substances other than gold, silver, copper, lead, zinc, tungsten, coal, asphaltum and allied substances, oil, and gas, the lessee shall pay quarterly or as otherwise provided in the lease, a royalty of not less than 10 percent of the value, at the nearest shipping point, of all ores, metals, or minerals marketed.

(b) For gold and silver the lessee shall pay quarterly or as otherwise provided in the lease, a royalty of not less than 10 percent to be computed on the value of bullion as shown by mint returns after deducting forwarding charges to the point of sale; and for copper, lead, zinc, and tungsten, a royalty of not less than 10 percent to be computed on the value of ores and concentrates as shown by reduction returns after deducting freight charges to the point of sale. Duplicate returns shall be filed by the lessee with the Area Director within 10 days after the ending of the quarter or other period specified in the lease within which such returns are made: *Provided, however,* That the lessee shall pay a royalty of not less than 10 percent of the value of the ore or concentrates sold at the mine unless otherwise provided in the lease.

(c) For coal the lessee shall pay quarterly or as otherwise provided in the lease, a royalty of not less than 10 cents per ton of 2,000 pounds of mine run, or coal as taken from the mine, including what is commonly called "slack."

(d) For asphaltum and allied substances the lessee shall pay quarterly or as otherwise provided in the lease, a royalty of not less than 10 cents per ton of 2,000 pounds on crude material or not less than 60 cents per ton on refined substances.

§ 213.24 Rate of rents and royalties on oil and gas leases.

The lessee shall pay, beginning with the date of approval of oil and gas leases by the Secretary of the Interior, a rental of $1.25 per acre per annum in advance during the continuance thereof, together with a royalty of 12½ percent of the value or amount of all oil, gas and/or natural gasoline, and/or all other hydrocarbon substances produced and saved from the land leased, save and except oil and/or gas used by the lessee for development and operation purposes on the lease, which oil or gas shall be royalty free. A higher rate of royalty may be fixed by the Secretary of the Interior or his authorized representative, prior to the advertisement of land for oil and gas leases. During the period of supervision, "value" for the purposes of the lease may, in the discretion of the Secretary of the Interior be calculated on the basis of the highest price paid or offered (whether calculated on the basis of short or actual volume) at the time of production for the major portion of the oil of the same gravity, and gas, and/or natural gasoline, and/or all other hydrocarbon substances produced and sold from the field where the leased lands are situated, and the actual volume of the marketable product less the content of foreign substances as determined by the supervisor. The actual amount realized by the lessee from the sale of said products may, in the discretion of the Secretary of the Interior, be deemed mere evidence of or conclusive evidence of such value. When paid in value, such royalties shall be due and payable monthly at such time as the lease provides; when royalty on oil produced is paid in kind, such royalty oil shall be delivered in tanks provided by the lessee on the premises where produced without cost to the lessor unless otherwise agreed to by the parties thereto, at such time as may be required by the lessor. The lessee shall not be required to hold such royalty oil in storage longer than 30 days after the end of the calendar month in which said oil is produced. The lessee shall be in no manner responsible or held liable for loss or destruction of such oil in storage by causes beyond his control.

§ 213.25 Free use of gas by lessor.

If the leased premises produce gas in excess of the lessee's requirements for the development and operation of said premises, then the lessor may use sufficient gas, free of charge, for all stoves and inside lights in the principal dwelling house on said premises, by making his own connections to a regulator, connected to the well and maintained by the lessee, and the lessee shall not be required to pay royalty on gas so used. The use of such gas shall be at the lessor's risk at all times.

§213.26 Rate of royalty on casing-head gas.

(a) On casing-head gas used or sold for the manufacture of casing-head gasoline the minimum rate of royalty shall be 12½ percent of the value of the casing-head gas, which value shall be determined and computed on the basis and in the manner provided in the applicable operating regulations of the Department.

(b) In cases where gas produced and sold has a value for drip gasoline, casing-head gasoline content, and as dry gas from which the casing-head gasoline has been extracted, then the royalties above provided shall be paid on all such values.

§213.27 Rate of rental for nonutilized gas wells.

If the gas from a gas producing well is not marketed or utilized, other than for operation of the lease, then for each such well the lessee shall pay such rental as may be determined by the supervisor and approved by the Secretary of the Interior, calculated from the date of the completion of the well. Payment of annual gas rentals shall be made within 30 days from the date such payment becomes due.

§213.28 Royalty payments and production reports.

(a) Royalty payments on all oil and gas or other producing leases shall be made at the rates, and at such time, and in the manner prescribed by the terms of the lease.

(b) Quarterly reports shall be made by each lessee on nonproducing leases other than oil and gas within 25 days after December 31, March 31, June 30, and September 30, of each year, upon forms provided, showing manner of operations and total production during such quarter. A lessee may include within one sworn statement all leases upon which there is no production or upon which dry holes have been drilled. Reports of oil and gas leases where royalty accounting is done in the field office of the supervisor will be made as required in the operating regulations.

§213.29 Division orders.

(a) Lessees may make arrangements with the purchasers of oil and gas for the payment of the royalties as provided for in the lease and the regulations but such arrangement, if made, shall not operate to relieve a lessee from responsibility should the purchaser fail or refuse to pay royalties when due. Where lessees avail themselves of this privilege, division orders should be executed by the lessee and forwarded to the supervisor for approval. Purchasers may be authorized by the supervisor to reimburse lessees out of royalties for advance rents and advance royalties. Copies of written instructions, notices, modifications, revocations, and authorizations, as provided for in §213.18 (a) and (b), shall be furnished to purchasers. The right is reserved for the supervisor to cancel a division order at any time or require the purchaser to discontinue to run the oil of any lessee who fails to operate the lease properly or otherwise violates the provisions of the lease, of the regulations in this part, or of the operating regulations.

(b) When oil is taken by authority of a division order, the lessee or his representatives shall be actually present when the oil is gauged and records are made of the temperature, gravity, and impurities. The lessee will be held responsible for the correctness and the correct recording and reporting of all the foregoing measurements, which, except lowest gauge, shall be made at the time the oil is turned into the pipeline. Failure of the lessee to perform properly these duties will subject the division order to revocation.

OPERATIONS

§213.30 Permission to start operations.

No operations will be permitted on any lease before it is approved. Written permission must be secured from the supervisor before any operations are started under any oil and gas lease. Operations must be in accordance with the operating regulations promulgated by the Secretary of the Interior. Copies of these regulations may be secured from either the supervisor or the Area Director and no operations should be attempted without a study of the operating regulations.

§ 213.31 Restrictions on operations.

(a) Oil and gas leases issued under the provisions of this part shall be subject to imposition by the Secretary of the Interior of such restrictions as to time or times for the drilling of wells and as to the production from any well or wells as in his judgment may be necessary or proper for the protection of the natural resources of the leased land and in the interest of the lessor. In the exercise of his judgment the Secretary of the Interior may take into consideration, among other things, the Federal laws, State laws, regulations by competent Federal or State authorities, lawful agreements among operators regulating either drilling or production, or both.

(b) All such leases shall be subject to any cooperative or unit plan of development affecting the leased lands that may be required by the Secretary of the Interior, but no lease shall be included in any cooperative or unit plan without prior approval of the Secretary of the Interior. If said plan effects a change in the lease terms, the consent of the lessor or lessors must be obtained before the plan is effective.

§ 213.32 Wells.

The lessee shall agree (a) to drill and produce all wells necessary to offset or protect the leased land from drainage by wells on adjoining lands not the property of the lessor, or in lieu thereof, compensate the lessor in full each month for the estimated loss of royalty through drainage: *Provided,* That during the period of supervision by the Secretary of the Interior, the necessity for offset wells shall be determined by the supervisor and payment in lieu of drilling and producing shall be with the consent of, and in an amount determined by the Secretary of the Interior; (b) at the election of the lessee to drill and produce other wells: *Provided,* That the right to drill and produce such other wells shall be subject to any system of well spacing or production allotments authorized and approved under applicable law or regulations, approved by the Secretary of the Interior and affecting the field or area in which the leased lands are situated; and (c) if the lessee elects not to drill and produce such other wells for any period the Secretary of the Interior may, within 10 days after due notice in writing, either require the drilling and production of such wells to the number necessary, in his opinion, to insure reasonable diligence in the development and operation of the property, or may in lieu of such additional diligent drilling and production require the payment on and after the first anniversary date of the lease of not to exceed $1 per acre per annum, which sum shall be in addition to any rental or royalty herein specified.

§ 213.33 Diligence and prevention of waste.

The lessee shall exercise diligence in drilling and operating wells for oil and gas on the leased lands while such products can be secured in paying quantities; carry on all operations in a good and workmanlike manner in accordance with approved methods and practice, having due regard for the prevention of waste of oil or gas developed on the land, or the entrance of water through wells drilled by the lessee to the productive sands or oil or gas-bearing strata to the destruction or injury of the oil or gas deposits, the preservation and conservation of the property for future productive operations, and to the health and safety of workmen and employees; plug securely all wells before abandoning the same and to shut off effectually all water from the oil or gas-bearing strata; not drill any well within 200 feet of any house or barn on the premises without the lessor's written consent approved by the Area Director; carry out at his expense all reasonable orders and requirements of the supervisor relative to prevention of waste, and preservation of the property and the health and safety of workmen; bury all pipelines crossing tillable lands below plow depth unless other arrangements therefor are made with the Area Director; pay the lessor all damages to crops, buildings, and other improvements of the lessor occasioned by the lessee's operations: *Provided,* That the lessee shall not be held responsible for delays or casualties occasioned by causes beyond his control.

§213.34 Inspection of premises; books and accounts.

Lessees shall agree to allow the lessors and their agents or any authorized representative of the Interior Department to enter, from time to time, upon and into all parts of the leased premises for the purpose of inspection, and shall further agree to keep a full and correct account of all operations and make reports thereof, as required by the applicable regulations of the Department; and their books and records, showing manner of operations and persons interested, shall be open at all times for examination by such officers of the Department as shall be instructed in writing by the Secretary of the Interior or authorized by regulations to make such examination.

§213.35 Mines to be timbered properly.

In mining operations the lessee shall keep the mine well and sufficiently timbered at all points where necessary, in accordance with good mining practice, and in such manner as may be necessary to the proper preservation of the property leased and safety of workmen.

§213.36 Surrender of leased premises in good condition.

On expiration of the term of a lease, or when a lease is surrendered, the lessee shall deliver to the Government the leased ground, with the mine workings in case of leases other than oil and gas, in good order and condition, and the bondsmen will be held for such delivery in good order and condition, unless relieved by the Secretary of the Interior for cause. It shall, however, be stipulated that the machinery necessary to operate any mine is the property of the lessee, but that it may be removed by him only after the condition of the property has been ascertained by inspection by the Secretary of the Interior or his authorized agents, to be in satisfactory condition.

§213.37 Penalties.

Failure of the lessee to comply with any provisions of the lease, of the operating regulations, of the regulations in this part, orders of the Area Director or his representative, or of the orders of the supervisor or his representative, shall subject the lease to cancellation by the Secretary of the Interior or the lessee to a penalty of not more than $1,296 per day for each day the terms of the lease, the regulations, or such orders are violated, or to both such penalty and cancellation: *Provided*, That the lessee shall be entitled to notice and hearing, within 30 days after such notice, with respect to the terms of the lease, regulations, or orders violated, which hearing shall be held by the supervisor, whose findings shall be conclusive unless an appeal be taken to the Secretary of the Interior within 30 days after notice of the supervisor's decision, and the decision of the Secretary of the Interior upon appeal shall be conclusive.

[22 FR 10599, Dec. 24, 1957, as amended at 81 FR 42481, June 30, 2016; 82 FR 7652, Jan. 23, 2017; 83 FR 5195, Feb. 6, 2018]

§213.38 Assignments and overriding royalties.

(a) Leases or any interest therein, may be assigned or transferred only with the approval of the Secretary of the Interior, and to procure such approval the assignee must be qualified to hold such lease under existing rules and regulations, and shall furnish a satisfactory bond for the faithful performance of the covenants and conditions thereof. No lease or any interest therein, or the use of such lease, shall be assigned, sublet, or transferred, directly or indirectly, by working or drilling contract, or otherwise, without the consent of the Secretary of the Interior. Assignments of leases shall be filed with the Area Director within 20 days after the date of execution.

(b) An agreement creating overriding royalties or payments out of production on oil and gas leases under this part shall be subject to the provisions of §211.26(d) of this subchapter, or as hereafter amended.

[22 FR 10599, Dec. 24, 1957, as amended at 23 FR 9758, Dec. 18, 1958. Redesignated at 47 FR 13327, Mar. 30, 1982]

§213.39 Stipulations.

The lessee under any lease heretofore approved may by stipulation (Form 5–154i) with the consent of the lessor and the approval of the Secretary of the Interior, make such approved lease subject to all the terms, conditions, and provisions contained in the lease form and regulations currently in use. Stipulations shall be filed with the Area Director within 20 days after the date of execution.

§ 213.40 Cancellations.

(a) When, in the opinion of the Secretary of the Interior, the lessee has violated any of the terms and conditions of a lease or of the applicable regulations, or if mining operations are conducted wastefully and without regard to good mining practice, the Secretary of the Interior shall have the right at any time after 30 days' notice to the lessee specifying the terms and conditions violated, and after a hearing, if the lessee shall so request within 30 days after issuance of the notice, to declare such lease null and void, and the lessor shall then be entitled and authorized to take immediate possession of the land.

(b) On the following conditions, the lessee may, on approval of the Secretary of the Interior, surrender a lease or any part of it:

(1) That he make application for cancellation to the Area Director having jurisdiction over the land.

(2) That he pay a surrender fee of $1 at the time the application is made.

(3) That he pay all royalties and rentals due to the date of such application.

(4) That he make a satisfactory showing that full provision has been made for conservation and protection of the property and that all wells, drilled on the portion of the lease surrendered, have been properly abandoned.

(5) If the lease has been recorded, that he file, with his application, a recorded release of the acreage covered by the application.

(6) If the application is for the cancellation of the entire lease or the entire undivided portion, that he surrender the lease: *Provided*, That where the application is made by an assignee to whom no copy of the lease was delivered, he will be required to surrender only his copy of assignment.

(7) If the lease (or portion being surrendered or canceled) is owned in undivided interests by more than one party, then all parties shall join in the application for cancellation.

(8) That all required fees and papers must be in the mail or received on or before the date upon which rents and royalties become due, in order for the lessee and his surety to be relieved from liability for the payment of such royalties and rentals.

(9) If there has been a contest respecting a lease or leases, the approved, the disapproved, or the canceled parts thereof will be held in the office of the Area Director for 5 days after the Department's decision has been promulgated, by mail or delivery, and will not be delivered, if within that period a motion for review and reconsideration be filed, until such motion is passed upon by the Department.

(10) In the event oil or gas is being drained from the leased premises by wells not covered by a lease; the lease, or any part of it, may be surrendered, only on such terms and conditions as the Secretary of the Interior may determine to be reasonable and equitable.

(c) No part of any advance rental shall be refunded to the lessee nor shall he be relieved, by reason of any subsequent surrender or cancellation of the lease, from the obligation to pay said advance rental when it becomes due.

(d) For proper method of terminating departmental leases covering lands from which restrictions have been removed see section 3 of the act of May 27, 1908 (35 Stat. 312).

REMOVAL OF RESTRICTIONS

§ 213.41 Leases executed but not approved before restrictions removed from land.

Leases executed before the removal of restrictions against alienation on land from all of which restrictions against alienation shall be removed after such execution, if such leases contain specific provisions for approval by the Secretary of the Interior, whether now filed with the Department or presented for consideration hereafter, will be considered and acted upon by this Department as heretofore but only for the purpose of approving or disapproving the instrument.

§213.42 Operations after removal of restrictions from leased lands.

(a) Oil and gas leases heretofore approved and leases for other minerals now or hereafter in force on land from all of which restrictions against alienation have been or shall be removed, even if such leases contain provision authorizing supervision by this Department, shall after such removal of restrictions against alienation, be operated entirely free from such supervision, and the authority and power delegated to the Secretary of the Interior in said leases shall cease and all payments required to be made to the Area Director shall thereafter be made to the lessor or the then owner of the land, and changes in regulations thereafter made by the Secretary of the Interior shall not apply to such leased land from which said restrictions are removed.

(b) In the event restrictions are removed from a part of the land included in any lease to which this section applies the entire lease shall continue subject to the supervision of the Secretary of the Interior, and all royalties thereunder shall be paid to the Area Director until such time as the lessor and lessee shall furnish the Secretary of the Interior satisfactory information that adequate arrangements have been made to account for the oil, gas or mineral upon the restricted land separately from that upon the unrestricted. Thereafter the restricted land only shall be subject to the supervision of the Secretary of the Interior: *Provided*, That the unrestricted portion shall be relieved from such supervision as in the lease or regulations provided.

§213.43 Relinquishment of Government supervision.

All oil and gas leases hereafter executed shall contain the following relinquishment of supervision clause and terms operative after such relinquishment, or other provisions similar in substance:

Relinquishment of supervision by the Secretary of the Interior.—Should the Secretary of the Interior, at any time during the life of this instrument, relinquish supervision as to all or part of the acreage covered hereby, such relinquishment shall not bind lessee until said Secretary shall have given 30 days' written notice. Until said requirements are fulfilled, lessee shall continue to make all payments due hereunder as heretofore in section 3(c). After notice of relinquishment has been received by lessee, as herein provided this lease shall be subject to the following further conditions:

(a) All rentals and royalties thereafter accruing shall be paid in the following manner: Rentals and royalties shall be paid to lessor or his successors in title, or to a trustee appointed under the provision of section 9 hereof. Rentals and royalties shall be paid directly to lessor, his successors in title, or to said trustee as the case may be.

(b) If, at the time supervision is relinquished by the Secretary of the Interior, lessee shall have made all payments then due hereunder, and shall have fully performed all obligations on its part to be performed up to the time of such relinquishment, then the bond given to secure the performance hereof, on file in the Indian Office, shall be of no further force or effect.

(c) Should such relinquishment affect only part of the acreage, then lessee may continue to drill and operate the land covered hereby as an entirety: *Provided*, That lessee shall pay in the manner prescribed by section 3(c), for the benefit of lessor such proportion of all rentals and royalties due hereunder as the acreage retained under the supervision of the Secretary of the Interior bears to the entire acreage of the lease, the remainder of such rentals and royalties to be paid directly to lessor or his successors in title or said trustee as the case may be, as provided in subdivision (a) of this section.

Division of fee. It is covenanted and agreed that should the fee of said land be divided into separate parcels, held by different owners, or should the rental or royalty interests hereunder be so divided in ownership, after the execution of this lease and after the Secretary of the Interior relinquishes supervision hereof, the obligations of lessee hereunder shall not be added to or changed in any manner whatsoever save as specifically provided by the terms of this lease. Notwithstanding such separate ownership, lessee may continue to drill and operate said premises as an entirety: *Provided*, That each separate owner shall receive such proportion of all rentals and royalties accruing after the vesting of his title as the acreage of the fee, or rental or royalty interest, bears to the entire acreage covered by the lease; or to the entire rental and royalty interest as the case may be: *Provided further*, That, if, at any time after departmental supervision hereof is relinquished, in whole or in part, there shall be four or more parties entitled to rentals or royalties hereunder, whether said parties are so entitled by virtue of undivided interests or by virtue of ownership of separate parcels of the land covered hereby, lessee at his election may withhold the payment of further rentals or royalties (except as to the portion due the Indian lessor while under restriction), until all of said parties shall agree upon and designate in writing and in a recordable instrument a trustee to receive all payments due hereunder on behalf of said parties and their respective successors in title. Payments to said trustee shall constitute lawful payments hereunder, and the sole risk of an improper or unlawful distribution of said funds by said trustee shall rest upon the parties naming said trustee and their respective successors in title. (The above provisions are copied from oil and gas mining lease Form 5–154h,[1] revised April 24, 1935.)

§ 213.44 Division of royalty to separate fee owners.

Should the removal of restrictions affect only part of the acreage covered by a lease containing provisions to the effect that the royalties accruing under the lease, where the fee is divided into separate parcels, shall be paid to each owner in the proportion which his acreage bears to the entire acreage covered by the lease, the lessee or assignee of such unrestricted portion will be required to make the reports required by the regulations in this part and the operating regulations with respect to the beginning of drilling operations, completion of wells, and production the same as if the restrictions had not been removed. In the event the unrestricted portion of the leased premises is producing, the owner of the lease thereon will be required to pay the portion of the royalties due the Indian lessor at the time and in the manner specified by the regulations in this part.

§ 213.45 Restrictions especially continued as to certain lands.

Restricted lands allotted as either homestead or surplus allotments, designated as tax exempt under section 4 of the act of May 10, 1928, as amended May 24, 1928 (45 Stat. 495, 733), the entire interest in which was acquired by inheritance, gift, devise, or purchase with restricted funds, by persons of one-half or more Indian blood, after the passage of the act of January 27, 1933 (47 Stat. 777), continue to be restricted under the provisions of the last mentioned act and oil and gas leases thereof are subject to the regulations in this part and all such leases to be valid must be approved by the Secretary of the Interior. Lands inherited by or devised to full blood Indians prior to the act of January 27, 1933, are not affected as to restrictions by the provisions of said act and may continue to be leased with the approval of the county court having jurisdiction of the estate of the deceased allottee and without approval of the Secretary of the Interior (54 L.D. 382; 10 F. (2d), 487). Lands acquired prior to the passage of the act of January 27, 1933 by Indians of less than full blood, whether such lands were restricted and tax exempt or restricted and taxable, passed to such persons free of all restrictions. Inherited homesteads restricted prior to April 26, 1931, by section 9,[2] of the act of May 27, 1908 (35 Stat. 312), for the benefit of heirs of one-half or more Indian blood but less than full bloods, born after March 4, 1906, became unrestricted April 26, 1931, or upon the death prior thereto of the heir born subsequent to March 4, 1906, and oil and gas leases thereof are not subject to the regulations in this part nor under the jurisdiction of the Secretary of the Interior.

§ 213.46 Field clerks.

Local representatives known officially as "field clerks" are located in the various districts comprising that part of the State of Oklahoma occupied by the Five Civilized Tribes. Such field clerks shall report to and act under the direction of the Area Director. Any and all counsel and advice desired by allottees concerning deeds, leases, or other instruments or matters relating to lands allotted to them shall be furnished by such field clerks free of charge. Field clerks shall not, during their term of employment, have any personal interest, directly or indirectly, in any transaction concerning leases covering lands of allottees or in the purchase or sale of any such lands regardless of whether the restrictions have or have not been removed. This prohibition, however, shall not apply to lands which such field clerks have

[1] For information relative to obtaining Form 5–154h, see § 211.30.

[2] Repealed restrictions on inherited homesteads, by sec. 2 of the act of May 10, 1928 (45 Stat. 495).

legally acquired before their employment in the Bureau of Indian Affairs. Field clerks shall report to the Area Director at the end of each month the work performed during such period and special reports shall be made immediately of any apparently illegal transaction involving the estates or allotments of allottees.

§213.47 Forms.

The provisions of §211.30 of this chapter, or as hereafter amended, are applicable to this part.

[24 FR 7949, Oct. 2, 1959. Redesignated at 47 FR 13327, Mar. 30, 1982]

§213.48 Effective date.

The regulations in this part shall become effective and in full force from and after the date of approval (Apr. 27, 1938), and shall be subject to change or alteration at any time by the Secretary of the Interior: *Provided,* That no regulations made after the approval of any lease shall operate to affect the term of the lease, rate of royalty, rental, or acreage unless agreed to by both parties to the lease. All former regulations governing the leasing of individually owned lands of the Five Civilized Tribes for mining purposes are superseded by the regulations in this part.

§213.49 Scope of regulations.

The regulations in this part shall apply in so far as practicable to land purchased for Indians under the Oklahoma Indian Welfare Act of June 26, 1936 (49 Stat. 1967; 25 U.S.C. 501-509), as well as to other lands of individual Indians of the Five Civilized Tribes.

PART 214—LEASING OF OSAGE RESERVATION LANDS, OKLAHOMA, FOR MINING, EXCEPT OIL AND GAS

Sec.

AUTHORITY: Sec. 3, 34 Stat. 543.

SOURCE: 22 FR 10605, Dec. 24, 1957, unless otherwise noted. Redesignated at 47 FR 13327, Mar. 30, 1982.

§214.1 Definition.

The term "officer in charge" shall refer to the superintendent of the Osage Indian Agency and school or other representative of the Government who may, for the time, be in charge of the Osage Agency and school, or any person who may be detailed by the Secretary of the Interior or the Commissioner of Indian Affairs to take charge of leasing or mining operations under the regulations in this part.

§214.2 Sale of leases.

Leases of minerals other than oil and gas may be negotiated with the tribal council after permission to do so has been obtained from the officer in charge. Leases with all papers required, shall be filed with the officer in charge within 30 days from the date of execution by the lessee and the principal chief of the Osage Tribe. The lease will be forwarded to the Commissioner of Indian Affairs for consideration by him and the Secretary of the Interior and will become effective only after approval by the Secretary of the Interior. If any lease should be disapproved through no fault of the lessee, all amounts deposited by him will be promptly refunded.

§214.3 Corporate information.

A corporation shall file with its first lease a certified copy of articles of incorporation, and, if a foreign corporation, evidence showing compliance with local corporation laws in duplicate; a list of all stockholders, with their post office addresses, and showing the number of shares of capital stock held by each; together with a sworn statement of its proper officer showing:

(a) The total number of shares of the capital stock actually issued, the number of shares actually sold and the amount of cash paid into the treasury out of the stock sold, or, if paid in property, kind, quantity, and value of the same.

(b) Of the stock sold, how much per share remains unpaid and subject to assessment.

(c) How much cash the company has in its treasury and elsewhere, and from what source it was received.

(d) What property, exclusive of cash, is owned by the company, and its value.

(e) What the total indebtedness of the company is, and the nature of its obligations.

(f) Names of officers and directors.

§214.4 Bonds.

Lessee shall furnish with each lease at the time it is filed with the officer in charge an acceptable bond not less than the following amounts:

For less than 80 acres	$1,000
For 80 acres and less than 120 acres	1,500
For 120 acres and not more than 160 acres	2,000
For each additional 40 acres, or part thereof above 160 acres	500

Provided, That for leases for minerals other than oil and gas the Secretary of the Interior or his authorized representatives with the consent of the Indian landowner may authorize a bond for a lesser amount if, in his opinion, the circumstances warrant and the interests of the Indian landowners are fully protected: *Provided further*, That the lessee shall be allowed to file bond, Form S[1] covering all leases to which he or they are or may become parties instead of a separate bond in each case, such bond to be in the penal sum of $15,000. The right is reserved to change the amount of the bond in any particular case, or to require a new bond in the discretion of the Secretary of the Interior.

[26 FR 164, Jan. 10, 1961. Redesignated at 47 FR 13327, Mar. 30, 1982]

§214.5 Additional information.

The officer in charge may, at any time, either before or after approval of a lease call for any additional information necessary to carry out the purpose and intent of the regulations in this part, and such information shall be furnished within the time specified in the request therefor.

§214.6 Failure of lessee to complete lease.

Should a lessee fail to furnish, within the time specified after his bid is accepted, the papers necessary to put his lease and bond in proper form for consideration, the officer in charge shall recommend that the sale be disapproved and money paid forfeited to the Osage Tribe.

§214.7 Operation not permitted until lease approved; 160 acres maximum for single lease.

No mining or work of any nature will be permitted upon any tract of land until a lease covering such tract shall have been approved by the Secretary of the Interior and delivered to the lessee. All leases shall be made for such period as the title to the minerals remain in the Osage Tribe, which time will expire April 8, 1931, unless otherwise provided by Congress and shall be subject to cancellation or termination as specified in this part. Leases made by corporations shall be accompanied by an affidavit by the secretary or president of the company showing the authority of its officers to execute leases, bonds, and other papers. No lease shall be made covering more than 160 acres.

[1] For further information concerning forms, see §214.24.

§214.8 Acreage limitation.

No person, firm, or corporation shall hold under lease at any one time without special permission from the Secretary of the Interior in excess of the following areas:

(a) For deposits of the nature of lodes, or veins containing ores of gold, silver, copper, or other useful metals, 640 acres.

(b) For beds of placer gold, gypsum, asphaltum, phosphate, iron ores, and other useful minerals, other than coal, lead, and zinc, 960 acres.

(c) For coal, 4,800 acres.

(d) For lead and zinc, 1,280 acres.

§214.9 Advance rental.

(a) Lessees shall pay, in addition to other considerations, annual advance rentals as follows: 15 cents per acre for the first year; 30 cents per acre for the second year; 50 cents per acre for the third year; and $1 per acre per annum for the fourth and each succeeding year during the life of any lease: *Provided*, That all such payments of advance rentals shall be credits on royalties on production during the year for which payment of advance rental is made.

(b) The payment of annual advance rental shall not release the lessee from the obligation to conduct mining operations, as required by the terms of the lease.

§214.10 Royalty rates.

Royalties will be required as follows, subject to the approval of the President, in accordance with the act of June 28, 1906 (34 Stat. 543):

(a) For gold, silver, or copper lessee shall pay quarterly a royalty of 10 percent to be computed on the gross value of the ores as shown by reduction returns after deducting freight and treatment charges. Duplicate reduction returns shall be filed by the lessee with the officer in charge within 20 days after the reduction of the ores.

(b) For coal the lessee shall pay a royalty of 10 cents per ton of 2,000 pounds on mine run or coal as taken from the mines, including what is commonly called "slack."

(c) For asphaltum and allied substances, the lessee shall pay quarterly a royalty of 10 cents per ton of 2,000 pounds on crude material, and 60 cents per ton on refined substances.

(d) For substances other than gold, silver, copper, lead, zinc, coal, and asphaltum the lessee shall pay quarterly a royalty of 10 percent of the value at the nearest shipping point of all ores, metals, or minerals marketed.

(e) The royalties to be paid for lead and zinc shall be computed for each mineral at the same rate that the amount of the concentrates of such mineral bears to the total amount of dirt or rock actually mined, except as stipulated in this section. The royalty so determined shall be increased by adding 1 percent for each increase of $10 in the selling price per ton thereof over and above the following, which shall be the agreed base or standard:

For zinc—$50
For lead—$65

but in no case shall the rate of royalty be less than 5 percent or more than 20 percent. The percentage of recovery shall be computed as nearly as practicable upon the ore included in each sale, but where it is impracticable so to do the officer in charge and the lessee shall agree upon some other method of computation which will produce substantially the same result: *Provided*, That in case of their disagreement the Commissioner of Indian Affairs shall prescribe a rule of computation to be followed in such cases.

NOTE: The royalty would always be determined under this rule by ascertaining the percentage of recovery were it not for two things: (1) the flat rates which are fixed as the minimum and the maximum rates of royalty and (2) variations in the selling price of the ores. Concrete examples coming under the rule are set forth in the following table:

ZINC

[Where the base or standard is $50 per ton]

Percentage of recovery	Selling price	Royalty (percent)
7	$48	7
14	49	14
12	50	12
15	60	16
30	60	20
9	70	11

A similar table might be constructed for royalties on lead, but in so doing it would be necessary to bear in mind that the base or standard selling price for the lead is to be $65 instead of $50.

§ 214.11 Payment of rents and royalties.

All rentals, royalties, damages, or other amounts which may become due under leases approved in accordance with the regulations in this part shall be paid to the disbursing agent at Pawhuska, Okla. The remittances shall be in St. Louis exchange, except that where such exchanges cannot be procured post office or express money orders will be accepted. All royalties or other payments or claims of the Osage Tribe arising under such leases shall be a lien upon the mining plant machinery, and all minerals mined on the property leased or in which the lessee still retains any right, claim, or interest.

§ 214.12 Time of payment of royalties.

Royalties on all minerals produced in any quarter (January-March, April-June, July-September, October-December) shall be paid on or before the 25th day of the month next succeeding, and the remittance shall be accompanied by sworn reports covering all operations, whether there has been production or not. Annual advance rentals shall be paid within 10 days after the beginning of the lease year.

§ 214.13 Diligence; annual expenditures; mining records.

(a) Lessees shall exercise diligence in the conduct of prospecting and mining operations, and on all leases referred to in § 214.8(a) shall expend annually in development work a sum which with the annual rental shall make an amount of not less than $5 per acre. On all leases referred to in § 214.8 (b) and (c) there shall be expended annually in development work a sum which inclusive of the annual rental shall make an amount of not less than $1 for each acre or fraction thereof included in the lease. The lands covered by each lease referred to in § 214.8 (d) shall be prospected for lead and zinc ores by drilling within 1 year test holes aggregating 2,000 feet unless a sufficient ore body is discovered to justify the sinking of a shaft to the ore body and the erecting of a mill when such tract may be released from further prospecting by the written consent of the superintendent: *Provided*, That within 90 days after an ore body of sufficient quantity is discovered, and shown by the logs or records of the drill holes, to justify the expenditure, the sinking of a shaft to the ore body, and the erection of a mill shall be commenced and continued to completion without cessation of work thereon, barring unavoidable accidents or causes beyond the control of the lessee.

(b) Lessee shall keep upon the leased premises accurate records of the drilling, redrilling, or deepening of all holes showing the formations, and upon the completion of such holes, copies of such records shall be transmitted to the superintendent by the lessee after the first completion and of any further drilling thereafter, and a failure to so furnish report within the time prescribed shall be considered a violation of the regulations. Lessee shall, before commencing operations, file with the superintendent a plat and preliminary statement of how the openings are to be made and the property developed.

§ 214.14 Use of surface lands.

(a) Lessees may use so much of the surface of the leased land as shall be reasonably necessary for the prospecting and mining operations and buildings required by the lease, and shall also have the right-of-way over and across such land to any point of prospecting or mining operations, but such use of the surface shall be permissible only under condition of least injury and inconvenience to the allottee or owner of the land. Lessees before commencing and during such operations shall pay all reasonable damages for the use of the surface land and to any growing crops thereon, or to improvements on said land, or any damage that during the life of the lease may be occasioned in any manner whatsoever by the use of the surface, to the allottee or his successor in interest or assignee, or to a lessee of the surface of said land or to an oil and gas lessee, damages to be apportioned among the parties interested in the surface, whether as owner, lessee, or otherwise, as the parties in interest may mutually agree or as their interests may appear. If the parties are unable to agree concerning damages the same shall be determined by arbitration.

(b) All agreements (or authenticated copies thereof) providing for the settlement of damages shall be filed in the Osage Agency if the surface owner is a restricted Indian, and all such amounts which may be due and payable to any such Indian shall be paid to the superintendent and by him immediately remitted to the Indian entitled thereto. All sums due as royalty or damages shall be a lien on all equipment on leased premises.

§214.15 Homesteads.

Lessees and those acting under them shall not conduct prospecting or mining operations within or upon any homestead selection without written consent of the Secretary of the Interior.

§214.16 Settlement of damages.

Any person, other than a lessee or an allottee or the heirs of a deceased allottee, claiming an interest in any leased tract or in damages thereto must furnish to the officer in charge a statment in writing showing his interest, and failure to furnish such statement shall constitute a waiver of notice and estop said person from claiming any part of such damages after the same shall have been disbursed.

§214.17 Use of timber from restricted lands.

Lessees will not be permitted to use any timber from any Osage lands not relieved of restrictions upon alienation except under written agreement with the owner approved by the officer in charge.

§214.18 Assignments.

Approved leases or any interest therein may be transferred or assigned with the consent and approval of the Secretary of the Interior and not otherwise. Transfers or assignments, when so approved, shall be subject to the terms and conditions of the original leases and regulations under which such leases were approved as well as to such additional requirements as the Secretary of the Interior may prescribe. The transferee or assignee shall furnish with his transfer or assignment a satisfactory bond as prescribed in §214.4 in connection with leases. Any attempt to transfer or assign an approved lease or any interest therein without the consent and approval of the Secretary of the Interior shall be absolutely void and shall subject the original lease to cancellation in the discretion of the secretary.

§214.19 Cancellation.

When a lessee makes application for the cancellation of a lease in whole or in part, all royalties or rentals due up to and including the date of the application for cancellation must be paid, and that part of the lease delivered to the lessee shall be surrendered before such application will be considered. In the event a lease is surrendered for cancellation in whole or in part, after a new lease year has been entered upon, the lessee and his surety shall be liable for the advance rentals required to be paid under the lease for that year, and no part of such rentals which may have been paid shall be refunded.

§214.20 Annual reports by corporate lessees.

Lessees and assignees must submit to the officer in charge on January 1, of each year and at such other times as may be required by the Secretary of the Interior, a statement containing the information called for in §214.3(a) and (f) and also showing any changes in officers or changes in or additions to stockholders. At any time individual stockholders may be required to show to the satisfaction of the Secretary of the Interior in what companies or with what persons or firms they are interested in mining leases on the Osage Reservation and whether they hold such stock or interest for themselves or in trust.

§214.21 Inspection of lessees' books and records.

Lessees shall allow the agents and representatives of the lessor, or any authorized representative of the Interior Department, to enter, from time to time, upon and into all parts of the leased premises for the purpose of inspection, and their books and records showing manner of operations and persons interested, shall be open at all times for the examination of such officers of the department as shall be instructed by the Secretary of the Interior to make such examinations.

§ 214.22 Serving of notices.

Wherever notice is provided for in this part it shall be sufficient if notice has been mailed to the last known place of address of the party, and time shall begin to run with the day next ensuing after the mailing or from the date of delivery of personal notice; but where the party is outside the State of Oklahoma the officer in charge may, in his discretion, increase the time allowed.

§ 214.23 Plat of mine location.

Lessees are required, when so requested, to file a plat of their leases showing exact locations of all mines, proposed locations, power houses, etc.

§ 214.24 Forms.

Applications, leases, and other papers must be upon forms prepared by the department, and the superintendent of the Osage Indian school, Pawhuska, Okla., will furnish prospective lessees with such forms at a cost of $1 per set.

Form M. Application for mining lease, including financial showing.
Form N. Lease (except lead and zinc).
Form O. Bond.
Form P. Authority of officers to execute papers.
Form Q. Assignment.
Form R. Lease for lead and zinc.
Form S. Collective bond.

§ 214.25 Forfeiture of lease.

On the failure of any lessee or assignee to comply with any regulation or any obligation in the lease or assignment, the Secretary of the Interior may cancel and annul such lease without resorting to the courts and without any further proceeding: *Provided*, That the party or parties charged with such violation shall be first given not less than 30 days' notice to show cause why such lease should not be canceled and annulled or other order made with reference thereto.

§ 214.26 Fine; notice and hearing.

Violation of any of the terms or conditions of any lease or of the regulations pertaining thereto shall subject the lease to cancellation by the Secretary of the Interior, or the lessee to a fine of not exceeding $500 per day for each and every day the terms of the lease or of the regulations are violated, or the orders of the superintendent in reference thereto are not complied with, or to both such fine and cancellation in the discretion of the Secretary of the Interior: *Provided*, That the lessee shall be entitled to notice and hearing with respect to the terms of the lease or of the regulations violated, which hearing shall be held by the superintendent, whose findings shall be conclusive unless an appeal be taken to the Secretary of the Interior within 30 days after notice of the superintendent's decision, and the decision of the Secretary of the Interior upon appeal shall be conclusive.

§ 214.27 Changes in regulations.

The regulations in this part are subject to change or alteration at any time by the Secretary of the Interior.

§ 214.28 Location of sites for mines and buildings.

In event of disagreement between two or more mineral lessees regarding sites for the location of wells, mines, buildings, plants, etc., the same shall be determined by the superintendent after investigation and after due consideration of prior right of any lessee by reason of date of approval of lease.

§ 214.29 Prospecting; abandonment of mines.

All prospecting or mining operations or the abandonment of a well or mine shall be subject to the approval of the superintendent, and any disagreement between lessees of mineral leases regarding operations likely to result in injury to either lessee shall be determined by the superintendent, whose decision shall be final, unless an appeal is filed with the Secretary of the Interior within 30 days after notice of such decision.

§214.30 Lessees must appoint local representative.

Before actual drilling or development operations are commenced on leased lands, the lessee or assignee shall appoint a local or resident representative within the State, on whom the superintendent or other authorized representative of the department may serve notice or otherwise communicate with in securing compliance with the regulations in this part and shall notify the superintendent of the name and post office address of the representative so appointed.

PART 215—LEAD AND ZINC MINING OPERATIONS AND LEASES, QUAPAW AGENCY

Sec.

AUTHORITY: Sec. 26, 41 Stat. 1248; 50 Stat. 68.

SOURCE: 22 FR 10608, Dec. 24, 1957, unless otherwise noted. Redesignated at 47 FR 13327, Mar. 30, 1982.

§215.0 Definitions.

The following expressions, wherever used in the regulations in this part or leases thereunder, shall have the meaning designated in this section:

(a) *Superintendent.* The term "superintendent" shall mean any person in charge of the Quapaw Indian Agency, or having supervision under the direction of the Secretary of the Interior of the Indian restricted and trust allotted lands thereunder.

(b) *Allottee.* The term "allottee" shall mean any Indian to whom land has been allotted, or any Indian owner of land or interest therein as an heir or devisee.

(c) *Incompetent Indian.* The term "incompetent Indian" or "incompetent" shall mean any Indian who has been declared by the Secretary of the Interior to be incompetent to improve or manage his restricted or trust lands properly or with benefit to himself. The term shall also include any Indian who is a minor and any Indian who is a legal incompetent under the laws of the State. The term shall also apply to any Indian who is in fact incompetent, and the question of whether an Indian is competent or incompetent at the time of making a lease of his restricted or trust Indian lands is one for the Secretary of the Interior to determine.

(d) *Lessee.* The term "lessee," except where otherwise modified or limited in the regulations in this part, shall mean any person, firm, or corporation, their legal representatives, heirs, or assigns, to whom a lead and zinc mining lease has been made by or on behalf of Indians under the provisions of the regulations in this part.

(e) *Lessor.* The term "lessor," except where otherwise modified or limited in the regulations in this part, shall mean any Indian owning or having any interest in restricted or trust allotted any inherited lands under the supervision of the Quapaw Indian Agency, by or for whom a lease has been executed pursuant to the regulations in this part.

(f) *Leased lands.* The terms "leased lands," "leased premises," or "leased tract" shall mean any leased restricted or trust lands within and under jurisdiction of the Quapaw Indian Agency allotted to or inherited by an Indian.

(g) *Mining operations.* The term "mining operation" or "operations," except where otherwise modified or limited in the regulations in this part or in leases thereunder shall mean actual drilling, mining, or construction on the leased lands.

§ 215.1 No operations until lease approved.

No operations under any lease executed under the regulations in this part shall be permitted upon any restricted or trust lands allotted to or inherited by an Indian until such lease covering such tract shall be approved by the Secretary of the Interior.

§ 215.2 Local representative of lessee.

Before actual drilling or development operations are commenced on the leased lands the lessee shall appoint a local or resident representative within Ottawa County, Oklahoma, on whom the superintendent may serve notice or otherwise communicate with in securing compliance with the regulations, and shall notify the superintendent of the name and post office address of the representative so appointed. In the event of the incapacity or absence from the county of Ottawa of such designated local or resident representative, the lessee shall appoint some person to serve in his stead, and in the absence of such representative or of notice of the appointment of a substitute any employee of the lessee upon the leased premises, or the contractor, or other person in charge of mining operations thereon shall be considered the representative of the lessee for the purpose of service of orders or notices as provided in this part, and service upon any employee, contractor, or other person shall be deemed service on the lessee. Wherever a notice is provided for in the regulations in this part or in the lease from it shall be deemed sufficient if notice has been mailed to the last known address of the lessee or his local or resident representatives, and time shall begin to run with the day next ensuing after the mailing, or from date of delivery of personal notice.

§ 215.3 Manner and time of royalty payments.

All royalties belonging to the lessor shall be paid to the superintendent of the Quapaw Agency at Miami, Okla., or such other official as the Secretary of the Interior may designate, for the benefit of the lessor, not later than 15 days from the 1st of each month for ore and concentrates sold during the preceding month.

§ 215.4 Leases to be sold at public auction.

Except as otherwise provided in the regulations in this part, no lead and zinc mining lease under this part of restricted or trust allotted and inherited Indian lands within and under the Quapaw Indian Agency shall be made except to the highest responsible bidder at public auction.

§ 215.5 Royalty rates.

(a) In leases offered for sale at public auction under the regulations in this part the royalty to be paid by the lessee shall be stipulated at a fixed percent of the gross proceeds of all lead and zinc ores and concentrates extracted from the leased premises, the royalty to be computed and based upon each sale of ore or concentrates separately, the rate of royalty to be determined and fixed by the Secretary of the Interior in the case of each lease prior to the offering of such lease for sale. Subject to the right of the Secretary of the Interior to reject any and all bids, leases offered for sale at public auction shall be awarded in each case to the responsible bidder submitting the highest bonus offer.

(b) In leases not offered for sale at public auction but otherwise made and entered into under the provisions of the regulations in this part the royalty stipulated and fixed therein shall be such as may be determined by the Secretary of the Interior or as may be agreed upon in each case, subject to the approval of the Secretary of the Interior.

(c) It shall be further provided, however, that said sale-price basis for the determination of the rates and amount of royalty shall not be less than the highest and best obtainable market price of the lead and zinc ores and concentrates at the usual and customary place of disposing of such ores and concentrates at the time of sale: *Provided, however*, That the right is reserved to the Secretary of the Interior to determine and declare such market price if it is deemed necessary for him to do so for the protection of the interests of the Indian lessor: *And provided further*, That the right is reserved to the Secretary of the Interior on behalf of the Indian lessors to reserve at any time it shall be deemed to be to the best interests of the Indian lessors and upon due notice to the lessee, the royalty share of the gross production of the ore and concentrates and upon such notice that the royalty share of such production shall be stored and not sold, the lessee shall be required to store, free of charge to the Indian lessors in the ore bins of said lessee, said royalty shares of the gross production of ore and concentrates, provided that the lessee may not be required to store ore or concentrates for the lessor in amounts greater than one-third of his bin capacity or for a period longer than 6 months.

§215.6 Applications for leases; consent of Indian owners.

(a) Applications or requests by the Indian owners of restricted or trust land, or by others, that such land be leased or offered for lease for lead and zinc mining purposes should be addressed to the Secretary of the Interior and submitted through the superintendent of the Quapaw Indian Agency. Upon receipt of such applications or requests, the superintendent shall give consideration thereto and forward the same to the Commissioner of Indian Affairs with his report and recommendation.

(b) In no instance will a new lease be executed and delivered (or advertised for sale to the highest bidder) unless the Indian owner thereof, if an adult who has not been specifically found by the Secretary of the Interior to be personally incompetent to transact ordinary business affairs, has agreed to the terms of said lease or the terms under which said lease is advertised for lease, except in cases where the land is owned by several co-tenants, and, in such cases, no such lease shall be given or advertised for sale unless the co-owners or a majority in interest, if adults, and not specifically declared incompetent, have first consented thereto: *Provided*, That in the event the majority in interest is owned by minors, or adults specifically found to be incompetent, then and in that event, the Secretary of the Interior reserves the right to lease the entire tract if, in his opinion, such leasing will inure to the best interest of the restricted Indian owners.

§215.7 Advertisement of sale of leases.

Upon authority being granted by the Secretary of the Interior to the superintendent to offer for sale at public auction a lead and zinc mining lease of any tract or tracts of restricted or trust allotted and inherited Indian lands, the superintendent shall cause a notice to be published once a week for at least 4 weeks in some designated newspaper of general circulation in the county in which the land is located, setting forth that upon a certain day, which shall be not less than 30 days from the first publication of such notice and at a place to be named in the notice, the superintendent or other duly authorized representatives of the Secretary of the Interior will offer for sale at public auction a lead and zinc mining lease of such lands to the highest and best bidder, subject to the rules and regulations prescribed by the Secretary of the Interior, notice to be in such form as may be prescribed by the Secretary of the Interior.

§215.8 Submission of bids.

At the time of public auction bidders may submit their bids in person or by authorized agents, but in the latter case the bids must be accompanied by power of attorney duly executed by the real party or person in interest. Sealed bids may be submitted by mail or otherwise to the superintendent at his office at Miami, Okla., or delivered to him at the place set for the sale at any time prior to the hour fixed for offering the lease for sale. At the time and place of the public auction and before receiving the public bids the officer in charge shall announce the amounts and terms of all sealed bids received by him and the names of the bidders. The persons present, including those, if any, who may have theretofore submitted sealed bids, shall then be allowed to offer public bids. Bids must contain the offer of the stipulated and fixed royalty (see § 215.5 as to royalty) and, in addition thereto, the offer of a bonus payable as follows: 25 percent at time of sale and the balance before or at time of execution of the lease contract. Bidders shall be required to submit with their bids a draft or certified check payable to the order of the superintendent covering the advance rental for the first year on the proposed leasehold and 25 percent of the amount of the bonus offered. The superintendent shall, in each case, determine the highest and best bid, said determination, however, to be subject to the approval of the Secretary of the Interior. Upon approval by the Secretary of the Interior of the award, the successful bidder shall, within 30 days from notice thereof, enter into and execute the lease contract in accordance with said bid and the regulations in this part. The lease so executed shall be subject to the approval of the Secretary of the Interior and may be accepted or rejected by him when submitted for his approval. The right is reserved to the Secretary of the Interior, in the event of the rejection of such lease, to authorize and instruct the superintendent to accept the offer of some competitive bidder or to readvertise the land for lease. The report of the superintendent to the Commissioner of Indian Affairs relative to the auction sale shall contain full information as to all bids received for the lease rights on the land. If any person or party fails or refuses to execute a lease after being declared the highest bidder or after being awarded such lease, the amount tendered with his bid shall be forfeited to the superintendent for the benefit of the owner of the land.

§ 215.9 Execution of leases.

Whenever a lease award to a proposed lessee has been approved by the Secretary of the Interior, as provided in §§ 215.7 and 215.8, the lease contract shall be executed by the Indian owner of the land, if he be an adult and not incompetent as defined in § 215.0(c). Before any lease is entered into by the Indian owners or is approved by the Secretary of the Interior, all the adult and competent owners or co-owners of the tract of land which it is proposed to lease, shall be furnished by the Bureau such geological reports as may be available or that can be secured from the representative of the Geological Survey showing the estimated mineral reserves on said property, the estimated reasonable value of such property for mining purposes, and such other data as might reasonably be necessary to fully advise the owners of said property of the then present status and mining value of their lands. If the Quapaw or other Indian owner of the land is a minor, or is otherwise an incompetent as defined in the regulations in this part, the lease contract shall be executed by the superintendent for and on behalf of such minor or such incompetent. The leases executed, either by the Indian owner of the land or by the superintendent in his behalf, shall be subject to the approval of the Secretary of the Interior and shall be effective only upon such approval.

[22 FR 10608, Dec. 24, 1957. Redesignated at 47 FR 13327, Mar. 30, 1982; 48 FR 13414, Mar. 31, 1983]

§ 215.10 Renewal of leases on developed lands.

(a) In cases where the lands have heretofore been leased, and lead and zinc ores have been discovered hereon, and it shall appear to the Secretary of the Interior to be advisable and to the best interests of the Indian owners of the lands that the terms of the existing lease or leases be extended or that a new lease or leases for an additional period of time, or that a new lease or leases to take effect upon the expiration of present valid leases, should, upon application therefor, be granted to either the present lessees or to parties holding under assignments, subleases, or mining contracts, from such present lessees, or to parties who have expended capital in lead and zinc mining operation and development of the land under such leases, assignments, subleases, or mining contracts, a new lease or leases or contract of extension or existing lease or leases as may be authorized by the Secretary of the Interior may be entered into with the proper party or parties as may be determined by said Secretary of the Interior, and such new lease or leases or contract of extension of existing lease or leases shall be executed subject to the regulations in this part by and between the Indian owner of the land, if an adult and not incompetent as defined in § 215.0 (c), and said proper party or parties. If the Quapaw or other Indian owner of the land is a minor or an otherwise incompetent as defined in § 215.0 (c), the superintendent shall execute the new lease or leases or contract of extension of existing lease or leases for and on behalf of said Indian minor or incompetent. Said new leases or contracts of extension of old leases, whether executed by the Indian owner of the land or by the superintendent for and in his behalf, shall be subject to the approval of the Secretary of the Interior and shall become effective only upon such approval. No offering for sale at public auction or advertisement of sale will be necessary in reference to contracts of extension of leases, or to leases entered into under this section, as above provided, but such lease or contract shall be upon such terms as to bonus and royalty as may be determined and fixed in each case by the Secretary of the Interior under the provisions of § 215.5. The approval by the Secretary of the Interior of new leases or of the contracts of extension of old leases shall be conclusive as to the validity of said leases, or contracts of extension of leases, the manner and method of negotiating the same, and the execution thereof. If, however, in any case where lands have heretofore been leased and lead and zinc ores have been discovered thereon, it shall appear to the Secretary of the Interior that the extension of the existing lease or leases or the granting of new leases to the present lessees, or to the persons or parties holding under said lessees by assignment, sublease, or mining contract, would not be to the best interests of the Indian owners of the land, the Secretary of the Interior may, at the expiration, cancellation, or forfeiture of the existing lease, cause the mining lease rights on said land to be offered for sale at public auction to the highest bidder. If the lead and zinc mining lease on said land be offered for sale at public auction, the same procedure shall be followed as provided in §§ 215.7 through 215.9.

(b) Applications under the provision of this section for a lease or extension of lease or for the approval of such lease or extension of lease will not be received or considered prior to the period of 1 year next preceding the date of the expiration of such valid existing lease or leases as may be on the land covered by such application.

(c) Applications under the provisions of this section for a lease or extension of lease or for the approval of such lease or extension of lease shall be filed with the superintendent of the Quapaw Agency at any time within the period of 1 year next preceding the date of the expiration of such valid existing lease or leases as may be on the land covered by such application, and if the records of or papers in the office of said superintendent or the records of the county court of Ottawa County, Okla., indicate that there are any prior existing leases, subleases, assignments of leases or mining contracts covering any of the land applied for, the superintendent shall notify all persons having or claiming any rights or interest in or under said prior existing leases, subleases, assignments of leases, or mining contract concerning said application for lease or extension of lease, and that they will be allowed 10 days in which to file with the superintendent any objection they may have to the allowance of the application or to the approval of the new lease or extension of existing lease. If objection or protest is made by any owner of the land or by any person claiming rights or interests in or under existing lease, sublease, assignment of lease, or mining contract, a reasonable time, not exceeding 20 days, shall be allowed them in which to file their statement or brief in support of their protest or objection, and a reasonable further time not exceeding 10 days shall be allowed the applicant for new lease or for extension of existing lease to reply in support of the application. In case of contest, hearings may be had if deemed necessary by the Secretary of the Interior or his representative. The application and papers in each case shall be forwarded by the superintendent of the Quapaw Indian Agency to the Commissioner of Indian Affairs with his report and recommendation in regard thereto.

§ 215.11 New leases where prior leases have been forfeited or abandoned.

In cases where the lands have heretofore been leased and lead and zinc ores have been discovered but the mines and mining operations have been abandoned and the leases have been canceled or forfeited or have expired, special arrangements in the matter of the leasing and mining of said lands may be made provided the consent thereto of the Secretary of the Interior be first obtained. Applications containing special offers as to the terms and conditions may be considered by the Secretary of the Interior and the leasing of said lands may be made upon such special terms and conditions as the Secretary of the Interior may in each case deem to be for the best interests of the Indian owners of the land. If, however, in any case, it shall appear to the Secretary of the Interior that the granting of such lease would not be to the best interest of the Indian owners of the land, the Secretary of the Interior may cause the mining lease rights on said land to be offered for sale at public auction to the highest bidder. If the lead and zinc mining lease on said land be offered for sale at public auction, the same procedure shall be followed as provided in §§ 215.7 through 215.9.

§ 215.12 Advertising costs.

All advertising costs, publication fees, expenses incurred for abstracts of lease title, and other expenses incurred in connection with the advertising and sale of leases and in connection with the execution of lease contracts shall be borne by the lessee. In the event a lease of the land is offered to the highest bidder and he fails or refuses to execute such lease when duly notified and as required by or under the regulations in this part, and no other bid is accepted, such costs, fees, and expenses shall be paid from such money as he may have paid with his bid. If no bid is tendered after a tract is advertised, or if all bids are refused, said items of expenses shall be charged to the Indian owner of the land and be paid by him or be paid by the superintendent from any funds held by such superintendent to the credit of such Indian owner of the land.

§ 215.13 Bond.

Every mineral lease made and entered into under the regulations in this part, by an Indian or by the superintendent as his representative or in his behalf, must be accompanied by a surety bond, executed by the lessee and by a responsible surety company or two or more satisfactory sureties, guaranteeing the payment of all deferred installments of bonus and the payment of all specified royalties and rentals and the performance of all covenants and agreements undertaken by the lessee. Such bonds, unless authorized by the Secretary of the Interior or his authorized representative, with the consent of the Indian landowner, shall be not less than the following amounts:

For less than 80 acres—$2,500
For 80 acres and less than 120 acres—3,500
For 120 acres or more—5,000

Provided, however, That the lessee may, in lieu of such surety bond and upon execution of a proper penal bond to the United States in the sum prescribed and a proper power of attorney to the Secretary of the Interior, submit therewith United States bonds or notes in the aggregate sum prescribed as security for the carrying out of the terms, conditions, and provisions of the lease: *Provided further,* That a lessee may file in lieu of such individual lease bonds, one bond in a sum to be fixed by the Secretary of the Interior covering all leases to which he is or may become a party. The right is specifically reserved to the Secretary of the Interior to require an increase of the amount of any bond above the sum named in any particular case where he deems it necessary to require such increased bond.

[26 FR 164, Jan. 10, 1961. Redesignated at 47 FR 13327, Mar. 30, 1982]

§ 215.14 Payments to be made to superintendent.

No bonus, rents, royalties, nor other payments accruing under any mineral lease executed in accordance with or subject to the regulations in this part and approved by the Secretary of the Interior shall be paid direct to the Indian lessor; but all such bonus, rents, royalties, and other payments accruing under any such lease shall be paid to the superintendent for the benefit of the Indian lessors, to be deposited by that officer to the credit of the superintendent in some bank designated for the deposit of individual Indian moneys.

§215.15 Leases to be accompanied by Form D.

Lead and zinc leases should be accompanied, when filed, with application for approval (Form D)[1] made under oath, and said application shall set forth the information therein required.

§215.16 Requirements of corporate lessees.

(a) When the lessee is a corporation, its first application must be accompanied by a sworn statement of its proper officers showing:

(1) The total number of shares of the capital stock actually issued and, specifically, the amount of cash paid into the treasury on each share sold; or, if paid in property, state kind, quantity, and value of the same paid per share.

(2) Of the stock sold how much per share remains unpaid and subject to assessment.

(3) How much cash the company has in its treasury and elsewhere and from what source it was received.

(4) What property, exclusive of cash, is owned by the company and its value.

(5) What the total indebtedness of the company is, and, specifically, the nature of its obligations.

(b) Subsequent applications of the corporation should show briefly the aggregate amounts of assets and liabilities.

§215.17 Additional information required.

Corporations, with their first application, must file one certified copy of articles of incorporation and, if a foreign corporation, evidence showing compliance with local corporation laws; also a list showing officers and stockholders, with post-office addresses and number of shares held by each. Statements of any changes of officers or any changes or additions of stockholders must be furnished to the Indian superintendent on January 1 of each year and at any time when requested. The right is reserved to the Secretary of the Interior to require of individual stockholders affidavits setting forth in what companies or with what persons or firms they are interested in lead and zinc mining leases, or land under the jurisdiction of the Quapaw Indian Agency, and whether they hold such stock for themselves or in trust. Evidence must also be given in a single affidavit (Form I) by the Secretary of the company or by the president of said company, showing authority of the officers of the company to execute the lease, bond, and other papers.

§215.18 Term of leases.

The term of lead and zinc mining leases executed pursuant to acts of Congress and under the regulations in this part shall be for such period of time as may be determined in each case by the Secretary of the Interior, but in no case shall a lease be made to extend beyond the restriction or trust period on the lands covered by such lease.

§215.19 Forms.[2]

Application, leases, and other papers must be upon forms prescribed by the Secretary of the Interior. Except as may be otherwise provided and required by the Secretary of the Interior, the leases and other papers required under the regulations in this part shall be in conformity with the forms designated, respectively, as follows:

Form A. Lease of Quapaw Indian land.
Form B. For lease of Indian land other than Quapaw.
Form C. Application by Indian.
Form D. Application for approval of lease.
Form E. Affidavit of lessor (or of superintendent acting for him) and affidavit of lessee.
Form F. Surety bond.

[1] For further information concerning forms, see §215.19.

[2] Forms may be obtained from the Commissioner of Indian Affairs, Washington, D.C.

Form G. Affidavit of surety on personal bond.

Form H. Certificate as to sufficiency of surety on personal bond.

Form I. Affidavit as to authority of officers of corporation to execute lease and other papers.

Form J. Penal bond (in lieu of surety bond), and accompanying power of attorney.

Form K. Assignment of lead and zinc lease.

§ 215.20 Assignment.

Leases granted or approved under the regulations in this part may be assigned and the leased premises may be subleased or sublet, but only with the consent and authority of the Secretary of the Interior and subject to his approval as to the terms and conditions of such assignments, sublease, and subletting contracts and not otherwise, and provided also that the proposed assignees, sublessee, or sublettee shall be qualified to hold such lease under the regulations in this part and shall furnish such bond as may be required by the Secretary of the Interior, such bond to be with responsible surety to the satisfaction of the Secretary of the Interior and conditioned for the faithful performance of the covenants and conditions of the lease. Upon the filing with the Indian agent of such assignment, financial statement, and bond, the said agent shall at once give notice in writing to all restricted Indian owners of said land, advising them of said proposed assignment, and that if they have any bona fide objections to same, such objections must be filed in writing within 10 days from the date of said notice.

§ 215.21 Payment of gross production tax on lead and zinc.

The superintendent of the Quapaw Indian Agency is hereby authorized and directed to pay at the appropriate times, from the respective individual Indian funds held under his supervision, such gross production tax due the State on production of lead and zinc from restricted lands under his jurisdiction as may be properly assessed under provisions of law against the royalty interests of the respective Indian owners in the mineral produced from their lands.

§ 215.22 Operations.

(a) All shafts shall be securely cribbed to a point at least 8 inches above the immediate surrounding surface and cribbing shall be maintained in good condition during the life of the mining lease: *Provided, however*, That at any time shafts may be permanently sealed by a reinforced concrete slab after first obtaining the written approval of the duly authorized representative of the Department of the Interior. The slab shall be so placed as to prevent caving of the ground around the shaft collar.

(b) All shafts, prior to the expiration, surrender, or upon cancellation of the mining lease or abandonment of the property, shall be permanently sealed so as to prevent the caving of the ground around the shaft collar: *Provided, however*, That this requirement may be waived after first obtaining the written consent of the duly authorized representative of the Department of the Interior.

(c) All shaft entrances not permanently sealed shall be so fenced, boxed, or covered as to prevent persons or animals from falling into the mine when the shaft is not in actual use, and such fencing, boxing, or covering shall be maintained in good condition during the life of the mining lease.

(d) All shafts where hoisting is done shall be boxed or fenced on three sides and the fourth side equipped with a gate which shall be kept closed when access to the shaft is not necessary.

(e) All churn drill holes shall be securely plugged to the surface unless used for ventilation or other mining purposes, in which case they shall be cased or otherwise prevented from caving or becoming a hazard to persons or animals. If cased, the casing shall extend 4 feet above the collar of the hole.

§ 215.23 Cooperation between superintendent and district mining supervisor.

(a) The district mining supervisor of the Miami field office, Geological Survey, directly or through his assistants, shall receive from lessees for the superintendent, all notices, reports, drill logs, maps, and records, and all other information relating to mining operations required by said regulations to be submitted by lessees, and shall maintain a file thereof for the superintendent.

(b) The files of the Geological Survey supervisor relating to lead and zinc leases of Quapaw Indian lands shall be at all times available for inspection and use by authorized employees of the Bureau of Indian Affairs, and the employees of the Geological Survey assigned to work relating to Indian lands shall furnish to authorized employees of the Bureau of Indian Affairs such information and technical advice as may be necessary or appropriate to the most efficient cooperation in the conduct of the work assigned to the two bureaus. Likewise, similar facilities and service shall be provided for the benefit of the authorized employees of the Geological Survey by the Bureau of Indian Affairs.

(c) No orders of any kind will be issued by Geological Survey representatives to any Indian, but such representatives shall have full authority to issue and amend orders to operators relative to production and operations: i.e., the supervision of all operations, including safety and efficiency, health and sanitation, and prevention of material or economic waste, such orders to be prepared with the advice of the local representative of the Bureau of Indian Affairs.

CROSS REFERENCE: For regulations of the Geological Survey, see 30 CFR chapter II.

§ 215.23a Suspension of operations and production on leases for minerals other than oil and gas.

The provisions of § 212.15a of this subchapter are applicable to leases under this part.

[24 FR 9511, Nov. 26, 1959. Redesignated at 47 FR 13327, Mar. 30, 1982]

§ 215.24 Books and accounts.

(a) The lessee shall maintain books in which shall be kept a correct account of all ore and rock mined on the tract, of all ore put through the mill, of all lead and zinc concentrates produced, and of all ore and concentrates sold and to whom sold, the weight, assay value, moisture content, base price, dates, penalties, and price received, and the percentage of lead and zinc recovered. A correct statement of the same for each month shall be furnished the office of the district mining supervisor pursuant to § 215.23 not later than 15 days after the first of each month for the preceding month, together with a certificate from the smelter showing the unit price paid for the mineral purchased and the amount of ore and concentrates purchased during the month from said land.

(b) An audit of the lessee's accounts and books shall be made semiannually, or at such other times as may be directed by the Secretary of the Interior, by certified public accountants, approved by the Secretary, and at the expense of the lessee. The lessee shall furnish free of cost a copy of such semiannual or other audit, through the office of the district mining supervisor pursuant to § 215.23, within 30 days after the completion of each auditing.

§ 215.25 Other minerals and deep-lying lead and zinc minerals.

Except as provided in § 215.6(b), leases on Quapaw Indian lands, for mining minerals other than lead and zinc and for lead and zinc and associated minerals below the horizon of the rock stratum known as the Reed Springs Formation, shall be made pursuant to the provisions of part 212 of this subchapter.

[26 FR 1910, Mar. 4, 1961. Redesignated at 47 FR 13327, Mar. 30, 1982]

PART 216—SURFACE EXPLORATION, MINING, AND RECLAMATION OF LANDS

Subpart A—General Provisions

Sec.

AUTHORITY: 34 Stat. 539, 35 Stat. 312; 25 U.S.C. 355 NT; 35 Stat 781; 25 U.S.C. 396; sec. 1, 49 Stat. 1250; 25 U.S.C. 473a; 49 Stat. 1967, 25 U.S.C. 501, 502; 52 Stat. 347, 25 U.S.C. 396a–f; 5 U.S.C. 301.

Subpart A—General Provisions

SOURCE: 34 FR 813, Jan. 18, 1969, unless otherwise noted. Redesignated at 42 FR 63394, Dec. 16, 1977; and further redesignated at 47 FR 13327, Mar. 30, 1982.

§ 216.1 Purpose.

It is the policy of this Department to encourage the development of the mineral resources underlying Indian lands where mining is authorized. However, interest of the Indian owners and the public at large requires that, with respect to the exploration for, and the surface mining of, such minerals, adequate measures be taken to avoid, minimize, or correct damage to the environment—land, water, and air—and to avoid, minimize, or correct hazards to the public health and safety. The regulations in this part prescribe procedures to that end.

§ 216.2 Scope.

(a) Except as provided in paragraph (b) of this section, the regulations in this part provide for the protection and conservation of nonmineral resources during operations for the discovery, development, surface mining, and onsite processing of minerals under permits or leases issued pursuant to statutes pertaining to Indian lands including but not limited to the following statutes or amendments thereto:

The Act of June 28, 1906 (34 Stat. 539);

The Act of May 27, 1908 (35 Stat. 312);

The Act of March 3, 1909 (35 Stat. 781, 25 U.S.C. 396);

The Act of May 1, 1936 (49 Stat. 1250);

The Act of June 26, 1936 (49 Stat. 1967);

The Act of May 11, 1939 (52 Stat. 347, 25 U.S.C. 396a–f, and 5 U.S.C. 301).

(b) The regulations in this part do not cover the exploration for oil and gas or the issuance of leases, or operations thereunder, nor minerals underlying lands, the surface of which is not owned by the owner of the minerals.

(c) The regulations in this part shall apply only to permits or leases issued subsequent to the date on which these regulations become effective and which are subject to the approval of the Secretary of the Interior or his designated representative.

§ 216.3 Definitions.

As used in the regulations in the part:

(a) *Superintendent* means the superintendent or other officer of the Bureau of Indian Affairs having jurisdiction under delegated authority, over the lands involved.

(b) *Mining supervisor* means the Regional Mining Supervisor, or his authorized representative, of the Geological Survey authorized as provided in 30 CFR 211.3 and 231.2 to supervise operations on the land covered by a permit or lease.

(c) *Overburden* means all the earth and other materials which lie above a natural deposit of minerals and such earth and other materials after removal from their natural state in the process of mining.

(d) *Area of land to be affected* or *area of land affected* means the area of land from which overburden is to be or has been removed and upon which the overburden or waste is to be or has been deposited, and includes all lands affected by the construction of new roads or the improvement or use of existing roads to gain access to an operation and for haulage.

(e) *Operation* means all of the premises, facilities, roads, and equipment used in the process of determining the location, composition or quality of a mineral deposit, or in developing, extracting, or onsite processing of a mineral deposit in a designated area.

(f) *Method of operation* means the method or manner by which a cut or open pit is made, the overburden is placed or handled, water is controlled or affected and other acts performed by the operator in the process of exploring or uncovering and removing or onsite processing of a mineral deposit.

(g) *Holder* or *operator* means the permittee or lessee designated in a permit or lease.

(h) *Reclamation* means measures undertaken to bring about the necessary reconditioning or restoration of land or water that has been affected by exploration or mineral development, mining or onsite processing operations, and waste disposal, in ways which will prevent or control onsite and offsite damage to the environment.

§216.4 Technical examination of prospective surface exploration and mining operations.

(a)(1) In connection with an application for a permit or lease, the superintendent shall make, or cause to be made, a technical examination of the prospective effects of the proposed exploration or surface mining operations upon the environment. The technical examination shall take into consideration the need for the preservation and protection of other resources, including cultural, recreational, scenic, historic, and ecological values; and control of erosion, flooding, and pollution of water; the isolation of toxic materials; the prevention of air pollution; the reclamation by revegetation, replacement of soil or by other means, of lands affected by the exploration or mining operations; the prevention of slides; the protection of fish and wildlife and their habitat; and the prevention of hazards to public health and safety.

(2) A technical examination of an area should be made with the recognition that actual potential mining sites and mining operations vary widely with respect to topography, climate, surrounding land uses, proximity to densely used areas, and other environmental influences and that mining and reclamation requirements should provide sufficient flexibility to permit adjustment to local conditions.

(b) Based upon the technical examination, the superintendent shall formulate the general requirements which the applicant must meet for the protection of nonmineral resources during the conduct of exploration or mining operations and for the reclamation of lands or waters affected by exploration or mining operations. The general requirements shall be made known in writing to the applicant before the issuance of a permit or lease and upon acceptance thereof by the applicant, shall be incorporated in the permit or lease.

(c) In each instance in which an application is made the mining supervisor shall participate in the technical examination and in the formulation of the general requirements.

(d) The superintendent may prohibit or otherwise restrict operations on any part of an area whenever it is determined that such part of the area described in an application for a permit or lease is such that previous experience under similar conditions has shown that operations cannot feasibly be conducted by any known methods or measures to avoid—

(1) Rock or landslides which would be a hazard to human lives or endanger or destroy private or public property; or

(2) Substantial deposition of sediment and silt into streams, lakes, reservoirs; or

(3) A lowering of water quality below standards established by the appropriate State water pollution control agency, or by the Secretary of the Interior, or his authorized representative; or

(4) A lowering of the quality of waters whose quality exceeds that required by the established standards—unless and until it has been affirmatively demonstrated to the Secretary of the Interior, or his authorized representative, that such lowering of quality is necessary to economic and social development and will not preclude any assigned uses made of such waters; or

(5) The destruction of key wildlife habitat or important scenic, historical, or other natural or cultural features.

(e) If, on the basis of a technical examination, the superintendent determines that there is a likelihood that there will be a lowering of water quality as described in paragraphs (d) (3) and (4) of this section caused by the operation, no lease or permit shall be issued until after consultation with the Federal Water Pollution Control Administration and a finding by the Administration that the proposed operation would not be in violation of the Federal Water Pollution Control Act, as amended (33 U.S.C. 466 *et seq.*), or of Executive Order No. 11288 (31 FR 9261). Where a permit or lease is involved the Superintendent's determination shall be made in consultation with the mining supervisor.

§ 216.5 Basis for denial of a permit or lease.

An application for a permit or lease to conduct exploratory or mining operations may be denied any applicant who has forfeited a required bond because of failure to comply with a mining plan. However, a permit or lease may not be denied an applicant because of the forfeiture of a bond if the lands disturbed under his previous permit or lease have subsequently been reclaimed without cost to the lessor or the United States.

§ 216.6 Approval of exploration plan.

(a) Before commencing any surface disturbing operations to explore, test or prospect for minerals, the operator shall file with the mining supervisor a plan for the proposed exploration operations. The mining supervisor shall consult with the superintendent with respect to the surface protection and reclamation aspects before approving said plan.

(b) Depending upon the size and nature of the operation and the requirements established pursuant to § 216.4 the mining supervisor may require that the exploration plan submitted by the operator include any or all of the following:

(1) A description of the area within which exploration is to be conducted;

(2) Two copies of a suitable map or aerial photograph showing topographic, cultural and drainage features;

(3) A statement of proposed exploration methods; i.e., drilling, trenching, etc., and the location of primary support roads and facilities;

(4) A description of measures to be taken to prevent or control fire, soil erosion, pollution of surface and ground water, damage to fish and wildlife or other natural resources, and hazards to public health and safety both during and upon abandonment of exploration activities.

(c) The mining supervisor shall promptly review the exploration plan submitted to him by the operator and shall indicate to the operator any changes, additions, or amendments necessary to meet the requirements formulated pursuant to § 216.4, the provisions of these regulations, and the terms of the permit.

(d) The operator shall comply with the provisions of an approved exploration plan. The mining supervisor may, with respect to such a plan, exercise the authority provided by paragraphs (f) and (g) of § 216.7 respecting a mining plan.

§ 216.7 Approval of mining plan.

(a) Before surface mining operations may commence under any permit or lease, the operator must file a mining plan with the mining supervisor and obtain his approval of the plan. The mining supervisor shall consult with the superintendent with respect to the surface protection and reclamation aspects before approving said plan.

(b) Depending on the size and nature of the operation and the requirements established pursuant to § 216.4 the mining supervisor may require that the mining plan submitted by the operator include any or all of the following:

(1) A description of the location and area to be affected by the operations;

(2) Two copies of a suitable map, or aerial photograph showing the topography, the area covered by the permit or lease, the name and location of major topographic and cultural features, and the drainage plan away from the area affected;

(3) A statement of proposed methods of operating, including a description of proposed roads or vehicular trails; the size and location of structures and facilities to be built;

(4) An estimate of the quantity of water to be used and pollutants that are expected to enter any receiving waters;

(5) A design for the necessary impoundment, treatment or control of all runoff water and drainage from workings so as to reduce soil erosion and sedimentation and to prevent the pollution of receiving waters;

(6) A description of measures to be taken to prevent or control fire, soil erosion, pollution of surface and ground water, damage to fish and wildlife, and hazards to public health and safety; and

(7) A statement of the proposed manner and time of performance of work to

reclaim areas disturbed by the holder's operation.

(c) In those instances in which the permit or lease requires the revegetation of an area of land to be affected, the mining plan shall show:

(1) Proposed methods of preparation and fertilizing the soil prior to replanting;

(2) Types and mixtures of shrubs, trees, or tree seedlings, grasses or legumes to be planted; and

(3) Types and methods of planting, including the amount of grasses or legumes per acre, or the number and spacing of trees, or tree seedlings, or combinations of grasses and trees.

(d) In those instances in which the permit or lease requires regrading and backfilling, the mining plan shall show the proposed methods and the timing of grading and backfilling of areas of land to be affected by the operation.

(e) The mining supervisor shall review the mining plan submitted to him by the operator and shall promptly indicate to the operator any changes, additions, or amendments necessary to meet the requirements formulated pursuant to §216.4, the provisions of these regulations and the terms of the permit or lease. The operator shall comply with the provisions of an approved mining plan.

(f) A mining plan may be changed by mutual consent of the mining supervisor and the operator at any time to adjust to changed conditions or to correct any oversight. To obtain approval of a change or supplemental plan, the operator shall submit a written statement of the proposed changes or supplement and the justification for the changes proposed. The mining supervisor shall promptly notify the operator that he consents to the proposed changes or supplement, or in the event he does not consent, he shall specify the modifications thereto under which the proposed changes or supplement would be acceptable. After mutual acceptance of a change of a plan, the operator shall not depart therefrom without further approval.

(g) If circumstances warrant or if development of a mining plan for the entire operation is dependent upon unknown factors which cannot or will not be determined except during the progress of the operations, a partial plan may be approved and supplemented from time to time. The operator shall not, however, perform any operation except under an approved plan.

§216.8 Performance bond.

(a) Upon approval of an exploration plan or mining plan, the operator shall be required to file a suitable performance bond of not less than $2,000 with satisfactory surety, payable to the Secretary of the Interior, and the bond shall be conditioned upon the faithful compliance with applicable regulations, the terms and conditions of the permit, lease, or contract, and the exploration or mining plan as approved, amended or supplemented. The bond shall be in an amount sufficient to satisfy the reclamation requirements established pursuant to an approved exploration or mining plan, or an approved partial or supplemental plan. In determining the amount of the bond consideration shall be given to the character and nature of the reclamation requirements and the estimated costs of reclamation in the event that the operator forfeits his performance bond. In lieu of a surety bond an operator may elect to deposit cash or negotiable bonds of the U.S. government. The cash deposit or the market value of such securities shall be equal at least to the required sum of the bond.

(b) In a particular instance where the circumstances are such as to warrant an exception, the amount of the bond for a particular operation may be reduced to less than the required minimum of $2,000.

(c) The superintendent shall set the amount of a bond and take the necessary action for an increase or for a complete or partial release of a bond. He shall take action with respect to bonds for leases or permits only after consultation with the mining supervisor.

§216.9 Reports.

(a) Within 30 days after the end of each calendar year, or if operations cease before the end of a calendar year, within 30 days after the cessation of operations, the operator shall submit an operations report to the mining supervisor containing the following information:

(1) An identification of the permit or lease and the location of the operation.

(2) A description of the operations performed during the period of time for which the report is filed.

(3) An identification of the area of land affected by the operations and a description of the manner in which the land has been affected.

(4) A statement as to the number of acres disturbed by the operations and the number of acres which were reclaimed during the period of time.

(5) A description of the method utilized for reclamation and the results thereof.

(6) A statement and description of reclamation work remaining to be done.

(b) Upon completion of such grading and backfilling as may be required by an approved exploration or mining plan, the operator shall make a report thereon to the mining supervisor and request inspection for approval. Whenever it is determined by such inspection that backfilling and grading have been carried out in accordance with the established requirements and approved exploration or mining plan, the superintendent shall issue a release of an appropriate amount of the performance bond for the area graded and backfilled. Appropriate amounts of the bond shall be retained to assure that satisfactory planting, if required, is carried out.

(c)(1) Whenever planting is required by an approved exploration or mining plan, the operator shall file a report with the superintendent whenever such planting is completed. The report shall—

(i) Identify the permit or lease;

(ii) Show the type of planting or seeding, including mixtures and amounts;

(iii) Show the date of planting or seeding;

(iv) Identify or describe the areas of the lands which have been planted;

(v) Contain such other information as may be relevant.

(2) The superintendent, as soon as possible after the completion of the first full growing season, shall make an inspection and evaluation of the vegetative cover and planting to determine if a satisfactory growth has been established.

(3) If it is determined that a satisfactory vegetative cover has been established and is likely to continue to grow, any remaining portion of the surety bond may be released if all requirements have been met by the operator.

(d)(1) Not less than 30 days prior to cessation or abandonment of operations, the operator shall report to the mining supervisor his intention to cease or abandon operations, together with a statement of the exact number of acres of land affected by his operations, the extent of reclamation accomplished and other relevant information.

(2) Upon receipt of such report an inspection shall be made to determine whether operations have been carried out in accordance with the approved exploration or mining plan.

§216.10 Inspection: Notice of noncompliance: Revocation.

(a) The mining supervisor and superintendent shall have the right to enter upon the lands under a permit or lease, at any reasonable time, for the purpose of inspection or investigation to determine whether the terms and conditions of the permit or lease and the requirements of the exploration or mining plan have been complied with.

(b) If the mining supervisor determines that an operator has failed to comply with the terms and conditions of a permit or lease, or with the requirements of an exploration or mining plan, or with the provisions of applicable regulations, the superintendent shall serve a notice of noncompliance upon the operator by delivery in person to him or his agent or by certified or registered mail addressed to the operator at his last known address.

(c) A notice of noncompliance shall specify in what respects the operator has failed to comply with the terms and conditions of a permit or lease or the requirements of an exploration or mining plan, or the provisions of applicable regulations, and shall specify the action which must be taken to correct the noncompliance and the time limits within which such action must be taken.

(d) Failure of the operator to take action in accordance with the notice of noncompliance shall be grounds for suspension by the mining supervisor of operations or for the initiation of action for the cancellation of the permit or lease and for forfeiture of the surety bond required under §216.8.

§216.11 Appeals.

An applicant, permittee, lessee, or lessor aggrieved by a decision or order of a mining supervisor or superintendent may appeal such decision or order. An appeal from a decision or order of a superintendent shall be made pursuant to 25 CFR part 2. An appeal from a decision or order of a mining supervisor shall be made pursuant to 30 CFR parts 211 and 231.

§216.12 Consultation.

A superintendent shall consult with the Indian landowner with respect to actions he proposes to take under §§216.4, 216.6, 216.7, 216.9, and 216.10.

PART 217—MANAGEMENT OF TRIBAL ASSETS OF UTE INDIAN TRIBE, UINTAH AND OURAY RESERVATION, UTAH, BY THE TRIBE AND THE UTE DISTRIBUTION CORP.

AUTHORITY: Secs. 27 and 28 of the Act of August 27, 1954, 68 Stat. 868 (25 U.S.C. 677–677aa); 5 U.S.C. 301; secs. 463, 465 of the Revised Statutes (25 U.S.C. 2 and 9) and 230 DM 1 and 2.

SOURCE: 43 FR 40458, Sept. 12, 1978, unless otherwise noted. Redesignated at 47 FR 13327, Mar. 30, 1982.

§217.1 Definitions.

As used in this part:

Assets means all unadjudicated or unliquidated claims against the United States, all gas, oil, and mineral rights of every kind, and all other assets of the Ute Tribe of Uintah and Ouray Reservation as constituted on August 27, 1954, not distributed in accordance with the terms of the Ute Partition Act.

Business Committee means the Uintah and Ouray Tribal Business Committee, created pursuant to the provisions of the constitution and bylaws of the Ute Indian Tribe of the Uintah and Ouray Reservation.

Board of directors means the board of directors of the Ute Distribution Corp., a corporation organized and existing under the laws of the State of Utah.

Joint manager or *joint managers* means the business committee and the board of directors, or either of them, as is appropriate, within the context where one of those terms is used.

Superintendent means the superintendent of the Uintah and Ouray Agency, Bureau of Indian Affairs.

Secretary means the secretary of the Interior or a subordinate official acting pursuant to authority delegated by said Secretary.

§217.2 Authority and purpose.

In accordance with the Ute Partition Act approved August 27, 1954 (68 Stat. 868; 25 U.S.C. 677–677aa), as amended by the Act of August 2, 1956 (70 Stat. 936), and the Act of September 25, 1962 (76 Stat. 597), assets shall be managed jointly by the business committee and the board of directors. These regulations set out the procedures for exercising such joint management.

§217.3 Referral of questions by superintendent.

The superintendent shall refer all questions and problems related to the management of the assets as they come to his attention, together with his analysis of alternative solutions to each question or problem, to the business committee and to the board of directors for resolution. Such referrals shall be in writing and shall be addressed to the joint managers at such addresses as they furnish to the superintendent and to each other from time to time.

§ 217.4 Referral of questions by the joint managers.

The business committee and the board of directors must refer to each other for resolution any questions or problems related to joint management of the assets which they from time to time determine need to be resolved together with the submitting party's proposal, if any, for solution. Such referrals shall be in writing, addressed to the other joint manager at the address furnished in accordance with § 217.3 of this part. Copies of all such referrals shall also be furnished to the superintendent. Either of the parties may request an analysis of alternative solutions of each question or problem referred pursuant to this section, and the superintendent will furnish such analysis within ten working days, or within such longer period as he may notify the parties is required to prepare such analysis.

§ 217.5 Management decisions.

In arriving at management decisions concerning the assets, the business committee shall be entitled to cast 72.83814 votes and the board of directors shall be entitled to cast 27.16186 votes. Any total number of votes cast exceeding 50 shall be sufficient to determine an issue submitted to the joint managers for resolution. A majority of votes cast will decide an issue.

§ 217.6 Method of casting votes.

Within 30 days after an issue and any analysis provided for in §§ 217.4 and 217.5 have been submitted to the joint managers for resolution, they shall each notify the superintendent in writing of the number of votes cast for and against the proposed or alternative solutions. If either of the joint managers fails or refuses to cast his votes and to notify the superintendent thereof within the time specified, the superintendent may conclude that such joint managers' votes have been cast against the proposed solution or solutions; or, if no solutions have been proposed, for the maintenance of the status quo. At the time they notify the superintendent of the votes cast on an issue, each joint manager shall furnish to the superintendent a certified copy of a resolution of the business committee or the board of directors, as the case may be, authorizing such vote.

§ 217.7 Implementation of decision.

The Secretary shall issue such documents as are necessary or expendient to implement the decisions of the joint managers, insofar as such issuance is authorized by law, and he shall execute and/or approve such documents for and on behalf of the joint managers, or either of them, and on behalf of the United States, as necessary. If it becomes necessary for the Secretary to execute an instrument on behalf of one or both of the joint managers and to approve the same instrument as trustee, two different officials having delegated authority from the Secretary shall serve as executing and approving officers, respectively.

PART 224—TRIBAL ENERGY RESOURCE AGREEMENTS UNDER THE INDIAN TRIBAL ENERGY DEVELOPMENT AND SELF DETERMINATION ACT

Subpart A—General Provisions

Sec.

Subpart B—Procedures for Obtaining Tribal Energy Resource Agreements

PRE-APPLICATION CONSULTATION AND THE FORM OF APPLICATION

PROCESSING APPLICATIONS

APPLICATION CONSULTATION MEETING

TERA REQUIREMENTS

PUBLIC NOTIFICATION AND COMMENT

Subpart C—Approval of Tribal Energy Resource Agreements

Subpart D—Implementation of Tribal Energy Resource Agreements

APPLICABLE AUTHORITIES AND RESPONSIBILITIES

LEASES, BUSINESS AGREEMENTS, AND RIGHTS-OF-WAY UNDER A TERA

VIOLATION OR BREACH

Subpart E—Interested Party Petitions

Subpart F—Periodic Reviews

NONCOMPLIANCE

Subpart G—Reassumption

NOTICE OF INTENT TO REASSUME

Subpart H—Rescission

Subpart I—General Appeal Procedures

AUTHORITY: 25 U.S.C. 2 and 9; 25 U.S.C. 3501–3504; Pub. L. 109–58

SOURCE: 73 FR 12821, Mar. 10, 2008, unless otherwise noted.

Subpart A—General Provisions

§ 224.10 What is the purpose of this part?

This part:

(a) Establishes procedures by which a tribe, at its discretion, may enter into and manage leases, business agreements, and rights-of-way for purposes of energy resource development on tribal land; and

(b) Describes the process for obtaining, implementing, and enforcing a tribal energy resource agreement (TERA) that will allow a tribe to enter into individual leases, business agreements, and rights-of-way without obtaining Secretarial approval.

§ 224.20 How will the Secretary interpret and implement this part and the Act?

(a) The Secretary will interpret and implement this part and the Indian Tribal Energy Development and Self-Determination Act (the Act) in accordance with the self-determination and energy development provisions and policies in the Act.

(b) The Secretary will liberally construe this part and the Act for the benefit of tribes to implement the Federal policy of self-determination. The Secretary will construe any ambiguities in this part or the Act in favor of the tribe to implement a TERA as authorized by this part and the Act.

§ 224.30 What definitions apply to this part?

Act means the Indian Tribal Energy Development and Self-Determination Act of 2005, as promulgated in Title V of the Energy Policy Act of 2005, Public Law 109–58, 25 U.S.C. 3501–3504.

Application means the application submitted for a TERA under subpart B.

Business agreement means:

(1) Any permit, contract, joint venture, option, or other agreement that furthers any activity related to locating, producing, transporting, or marketing energy resources on tribal land;

(2) Any amendment, supplement, or other modification to such an agreement; or

(3) Any other business agreement entered into or subject to administration under a TERA.

Days mean calendar days in computing any period prescribed or allowed by the Act and this part:

(1) Do not include the day of the event from which the period begins to run;

(2) Include the last day of the period, unless it is a Saturday, Sunday, or Federal holiday, in which event the period runs until the end of the next day which is not a Saturday, Sunday, or Federal holiday; and

(3) When the period prescribed or allowed is less than 11 days, exclude intermediate Saturdays, Sundays, and Federal holidays from the computation.

Decision Deadline means the 120-day period within which the Director will make a decision about a petition submitted by an interested party under subpart E. The Director may extend this period for up to 120 days.

Department means the Department of the Interior.

Designated Tribal Official means the official designated in a tribe's pre-application consultation request, application, or agreement to assist in scheduling consultations or to receive communications from the Secretary or the Director to the tribe regarding the status of a TERA or activities under a TERA.

Director means the Director of the Office of Indian Energy and Economic Development or the Secretary's designee, authorized to act on behalf of the Secretary.

Energy Resources means both renewable and nonrenewable energy sources, including, but not limited to, natural gas, oil, uranium, coal, nuclear, wind, solar, geothermal, biomass, and hydrologic resources.

Imminent jeopardy to a physical trust asset means an immediate threat of devaluation, degradation, damage, or loss of a physical trust asset, as determined by the Secretary, caused by the noncompliance of a tribe or third party with a TERA or applicable Federal laws.

Interested party means a person or entity who has filed a petition with the

Secretary under subpart E seeking review of a tribe's compliance with a TERA and who meets the criteria in § 224.101.

Lease means a written agreement, or modification of a written agreement, between a tribe and a tenant or lessee, whereby the tenant or lessee is granted a right to possession of tribal land or energy mineral resources for purposes of energy resource development.

Petitioner means a person or entity who has filed a petition under subpart E with a tribe or the Secretary seeking review of a tribe's compliance under a TERA. A petitioner is not considered to be an interested party unless the petitioner meets the criteria in § 224.101.

Physical trust asset means a physical asset held in trust by the United States for a tribe or individual Indian or by a tribe or individual Indian subject to a restriction against alienation under the laws of the United States. "Physical trust asset" does not include:

(1) Any improvements (for example, wells or structures) to the assets held in trust or restricted status; or

(2) Monetary assets.

Public means one or more natural or legal persons, and their associations, organizations, or groups; or Federal, State, tribal and local government agencies; or private industry and their associations, organizations, or groups.

Right-of-way means an easement, right, or other authorization over tribal lands, granted or subject to administration under a TERA, for a pipeline or electric transmission or distribution line that serves a facility located on tribal land that is related to energy resource development.

Secretary means the Secretary of the Interior or the Secretary's designee.

TERA means tribal energy resource agreement.

Tribal governing body means a tribe's governing entity, such as tribal council or tribal business committee, as established under tribal or Federal law and recognized by the Secretary.

Tribal land means any land or interests in land owned by a tribe or tribes, title to which is held in trust by the United States, or is subject to a restriction against alienation under the laws of the United States. For the purposes of this part, tribal land includes land taken into trust or subject to restrictions on alienation under the laws of the United States after the effective date of the agreement.

Tribe means any Indian tribe, band, nation, or other organized group or community that is recognized as eligible for the special programs and services provided by the United States to Indians because of their status as Indians, except a Native Corporation as defined in the Alaska Native Claims Settlement Act, 43 U.S.C. 1602.

Violation or breach means any breach or other violation by another party of any provision in a lease, business agreement, or right-of-way under a TERA or any activity or occurrence under a lease business agreement or right-of-way that constitutes a violation of Federal or tribal environmental law.

§ 224.40 How does the Act or a TERA affect the Secretary's trust responsibility?

(a) The Act (25 U.S.C. 3504(e)(6)) preserves the Secretary's trust responsibilities relating to mineral and other trust resources and requires the Secretary to act in good faith and in the best interest of Indian tribes.

(b) Neither the Act nor this part absolves the Secretary of responsibilities to Indian tribes under the trust relationship, treaties, statutes, regulations, Executive Orders, agreements or other Federal law.

(c) The Act and this part preserve the Secretary's trust responsibility to ensure that the rights and interests of an Indian tribe are protected if:

(1) Another party to a lease, business agreement, or right-of-way executed under an approved TERA violates any term of the lease, business agreement, or right-of-way, or any applicable Federal law; or

(2) Any provision of a lease, business agreement, or right-of-way violates the TERA under which it was executed.

(d) The United States is not liable for losses to any party (including any tribe) for any negotiated term of, or any loss resulting from, the negotiated terms of a lease, business agreement, or right-of-way the tribe executes under a TERA.

§224.41 When does the Secretary require agreement of more than one tribe to approve a TERA?

When tribal land held for the benefit of more than one tribe is contemplated for inclusion in a TERA, each appropriate tribal governing body must request a pre-application consultation meeting, and submit a resolution or formal act of the tribal governing body approving the submission of any application. Each appropriate tribal governing body must also sign the TERA, if it is approved.

§224.42 How does the Paperwork Reduction Act affect these regulations?

The information collected from the public is cleared and covered by OMB Control Number 1076–0167. The sections of this rule which have information collections are §§224.53, 224.57(d), 224.61, 224.63, 224.64, 224.65, 224.68(d), 224.76, 224.83, 224.87, 224.109, 224.112, 224.120(a), 224.139(b), 224.156, and 224.173. Please note that a Federal Agency may not conduct or sponsor, and you are not required to respond to, a collection of information unless it displays a currently valid OMB control number.

Subpart B—Procedures for Obtaining Tribal Energy Resource Agreements

§224.50 What is the purpose of this subpart?

This subpart establishes procedures for:

(a) Pre-application and application consultations and process;

(b) Requirements for the content of applications;

(c) Submittal of completed applications; and

(d) Secretarial review and processing of applications.

PRE-APPLICATION CONSULTATION AND THE FORM OF APPLICATION

§224.51 What is a pre-application consultation between a tribe and the Director?

(a) A tribe interested in entering into a TERA should request a pre-application consultation by writing to the Director, Office of Indian Energy and Economic Development. The request should include the name and contact information for the Designated Tribal Official who will coordinate scheduling with the Director.

(b) Upon receiving a pre-application consultation request, the Director will contact the Designated Tribal Official to schedule a pre-application consultation meeting. The Director may also initiate pre-application discussions with the tribal governing body.

(c) At the pre-application consultation meeting, the tribe and the Director may discuss any of the matters related to a future application including, but not limited to:

(1) The application process;

(2) The potential scope of the tribe's future application, including any regulatory or administrative activities that the tribe anticipates exercising;

(3) The required content of an application for a TERA;

(4) The energy resource the tribe anticipates developing;

(5) The tribe's capacity to manage and regulate the energy resource development the tribe identifies;

(6) Potential opportunities for funding capacity-building and other activities related to the energy resource the tribe anticipates developing under a TERA; and

(7) Any other matters applicable to this part, the Act, and the tribe.

§224.52 What may a tribe include in a TERA?

A TERA under this part:

(a) May include development of all or part of a tribe's energy resources;

(b) Must specify the type of energy resource included;

(c) May include assumption by the tribe of certain activities normally carried out by the Department, except for inherently Federal functions; and

(d) Must specify the services or resources related to the specific activity related to energy resource development that the tribe proposes to assume from the Department.

§224.53 What must an application for a TERA contain?

(a) An application for a TERA must contain all of the following:

(1) A proposed TERA between the tribe and the Secretary, signed by the authorized representative of the tribe, that contains the provisions required by § 224.63;

(2) A statement that the Secretary recognizes the tribe as an Indian tribe and that the tribe has tribal land;

(3) A brief description of the tribe's form of government;

(4) Copies of relevant portions of tribal documents (see paragraph (b) of this section);

(5) A map, legal description, and general description of the tribal land that the tribe intends to include in the TERA;

(6) A statement that meets the requirements in paragraph (c) of this section;

(7) A statement describing the tribe's experience in negotiating and administering energy-related leases, business agreements, and rights-of-way issued under other Federal laws that includes descriptions of significant leases, business agreements, and rights-of-way the tribe has entered into with third parties or to which it has consented;

(8) A description of the expertise that the tribe will use to administer the TERA and an explanation of how that expertise meets the requirements of paragraph (d) of this section;

(9) A statement of the scope of administrative activities that the tribe intends to conduct and an explanation of how that meets the requirements of paragraph (e) of this section;

(10) A statement that meets the requirements of paragraph (f) of this section describing the capability of the tribe to assume all of the activities the tribe has identified in the application;

(11) A copy of the resolution or formal action of the tribal governing body or bodies under § 224.41 that approves submission of an application for a TERA; and

(12) A designation of, and contact information for, the Designated Tribal Official who will receive notifications from the Secretary or the Director regarding the status of the TERA application.

(b) The documents required by paragraph (a)(4) of this section include documents such as a constitution, code, ordinance, or resolution, that designate the tribal governing body or tribal officials that have authority to enter into leases, business agreements, or rights-of-way on behalf of the tribe.

(c) The statement required by paragraph (a)(6) of this section must:

(1) If applicable, state that the tribe retains the option of entering into energy-related leases or agreements under laws other than the Act for any tribal land that the TERA includes; and

(2) State one of the following:

(i) The tribe intends the TERA to include all tribal land, energy resources, and categories of energy-related leases, business agreements, and rights-of-way; or

(ii) The tribe intends the TERA to include only certain tribal land, energy resources, or categories of energy-related leases, business agreements, or rights-of-way in the TERA. In this case, the statement must specify and describe the tribal land, energy resources, or categories of energy-related leases, business agreements, or rights-of-way that the tribe intends to include in the TERA.

(3) State the tribe's intent to amend or modify leases, business agreements, or rights-of-way that exist when a TERA is approved if those activities are directly related to the activities authorized by the TERA. The tribe's ability to amend or modify such leases, business agreements or rights-of-way requires the agreement of the other parties to the lease, business agreement or rights-of-way, which must be stated in the TERA.

(d) The statement required by paragraph (a)(8) of this section must describe the expertise that the tribe will use in the four areas specified in paragraph (d)(1) of this section. It must also address, at a minimum, the administrative and personnel resources specified in paragraph (d)(2) of this section.

(1) The statement must describe the expertise that the tribe will use to:

(i) Negotiate or review leases, business agreements, or rights-of-way under the TERA;

(ii) Evaluate the environmental effects, including those related to cultural resources, of leases, business agreements, or rights-of-way entered into under a TERA;

(iii) Review proposals for leases, business agreements and rights-of-way under the TERA; and

(iv) Monitor the compliance of a third party with the terms and conditions of any leases, business agreements and rights-of-way covered by the TERA.

(2) The statement must describe the following:

(i) Existing energy resource development related departments or administrative divisions within the tribe;

(ii) Proposed energy resource development related departments or administrative divisions within the tribe;

(iii) Existing energy resource development related expertise possessed by the tribe, including a description of the relevant expertise of designated tribal employees, consultants and/or advisors; and

(iv) Proposed energy resource development related expertise that the tribe may acquire, including a description of the relevant expertise of designated tribal employees, consultants and/or advisors that the tribe intends to hire or retain.

(e) The statement required by paragraph (a)(9) of this section must describe the amount of administrative activities related to the permitting, approval, and monitoring of activities, as applicable, that the tribe proposes to undertake under any lease, business agreement, or right-of-way the tribe executes under an approved TERA.

(1) If the tribe proposes to regulate activities, the tribe must state its intent and describe the scope of the tribe's plan for such administration and management in sufficient detail for the Secretary to determine the tribe's capacity to administer and manage the regulatory activity(ies).

(2) The tribe's intended scope of administrative responsibilities may not include the responsibilities of the Federal Government under the Endangered Species Act or other inherently Federal functions.

(3) If the tribe intends to regulate activities, it should also describe the regulatory activities it desires to assume in the geographical area identified in § 224.53(c)(2) with respect to leases, business agreements, and rights-of-way that exist when a TERA is approved.

(f) The statement required by paragraph (a)(10) of this section must:

(1) Describe the tribe's ability to negotiate and enter into leases, business agreements, and rights-of-way;

(2) Include a discussion of the estimated annual costs to the tribe to assume those activities the tribe has identified in the application and the proposed source of tribal funds to carry out those activities; and

(3) Describe the estimated annual amounts needed to conduct those activities the tribe has identified in the application and identify the Federal program that may provide those funds, if one of the sources of tribal funds includes grants or contract awards from the Department, the Department of Energy, or other Federal agencies.

(4) Include a description of any:

(i) Compacts and contracts between the tribe and the Secretary under the Indian Self-Determination and Education Assistance Act, as amended;

(ii) Environmental programs a tribe has assumed under the Clean Water Act (33 U.S.C. 1251 *et seq.*) or the Clean Air Act (42 U.S.C.A. 7401); or

(iii) Cooperative agreements under the Federal Oil and Gas Royalty Management Act (30 U.S.C. 1701 *et seq.*).

PROCESSING APPLICATIONS

§ 224.54 How must a tribe submit an application?

A tribe must submit an application and all supporting documents in written and electronic form to the Director.

§ 224.55 Is information a tribe submits throughout the TERA process under this part subject to disclosure to third parties?

The requirements of this section implement the requirements of the Freedom of Information Act (5 U.S.C. 552) (FOIA) and 43 CFR part 2:

(a) Information a tribe submits to the Department throughout the TERA process under this part may be subject to disclosure to third parties under FOIA unless a FOIA exemption or exception applies or other provisions of law protect the information.

(b) A tribe may, but is not required to, designate information it submits as confidential commercially or financially sensitive information, as applicable, in any submissions it makes throughout the TERA process, including, but not limited to:

(1) Pre-application information;

(2) Application information

(3) A final proposed TERA;

(4) Any amendments to a TERA; and

(5) Leases, business agreements, and grants of right-of-way executed under an approved TERA.

(c) Upon receipt of a FOIA request for records that contain commercial or financial information a tribe has submitted under the TERA process, as required by 43 CFR part 2 the Department will provide the tribe, as submitter, with written notice of the FOIA request if:

(1) The tribe has designated the information as confidential commercial or financial information; or

(2) The Department has reason to believe that the information requested may be protected under FOIA Exemption 4 (trade secrets and commercial or financial information which is obtained from a person and is privileged or confidential).

(d) The notice to the tribe will:

(1) Include a copy of the FOIA request;

(2) Describe the information requested or include copies of the pertinent records;

(3) Advise the tribe of procedures for objecting to the release of the requested information and specify the time limit for the tribe's response;

(4) Give the tribe no less than ten (10) working days from the Department's notice to object to the release and explain the basis for objection, if any;

(5) Advise the tribe that:

(i) Information contained in the tribe's objections may be subject to disclosure under FOIA if the Department receives a FOIA request for it; and

(ii) If the tribe's objections contain commercial or financial information and a requestor asks for the objections under FOIA, the same notification procedures as above will apply;

(6) Advise the tribe that it is the Department, rather than the tribe, that is responsible for deciding whether the information will be released or withheld;

(7) If the tribe designated the information as commercial or financial information 10 or more years before the FOIA request, the Department will request the tribe's views on whether the tribe still considers the information to be confidential;

(e) If the tribe has any objection to disclosure of the information, the tribe must submit a detailed written statement to the Department including the following:

(1) The justification for withholding any portion of the information under any exemption of FOIA, and if the applicable exemption is Exemption 4, the tribe must submit a specific and detailed discussion of:

(i) Whether the Federal government required the information to be submitted, and, if so, how substantial competitive harm or other business harm would likely result from release of the information; or

(ii) Whether the tribe provided the information voluntarily and, if so, how the information fits into a category of information that the tribe customarily does not release to the public;

(2) A certification that the information is confidential, has not been disclosed to the public by the tribe, and is essentially non-public because it is not routinely available to the public from other sources;

(3) If not already provided, a tribal contact telephone and fax number so that the Department can communicate with the tribe about the FOIA request;

(f) The Department will review and consider all objections to release that are received within the time limits specified in the notice to the tribe, and if the tribe does not respond within the time limits specified in the notice, the Department will presume that the tribe has no objection to release of the information;

(g) If the Department decides to release the information over the objection of the tribe, it will notify the tribe in writing by certified mail, return receipt requested, and will include copies of the records the Department intends to release and the reasons for deciding to release them. The notice will also inform the tribe that it intends to release the records within 10 working days after the tribe's receipt of the notice.

§224.56 What is the effect of the Director's receipt of a tribe's complete application?

The Director's receipt of a tribe's complete application begins a 270-day statutorily mandated period during which the Secretary must approve or disapprove a proposed TERA. With the consent of the tribe, the Secretary may extend the 270-day period for making a decision.

§224.57 What must the Director do upon receipt of an application?

(a) Upon receiving an application for a TERA, the Director must:

(1) Promptly notify the Designated Tribal Official in writing that the Director has received the application and the date it was received;

(2) Within 30 days from the date of receiving the application, determine whether the application is complete; and

(3) Take the following actions:

If the Director determines that . . .	Then the Director must . . .
(i) The application is complete.	(A) Issue a written notice and a request for an application consultation meeting to the Designated Tribal Official; and (B) If appropriate, notify other Departmental bureaus and offices of receiving the application and provide copies.
(ii) The application is not complete.	(A) Issue a written notice to the Designated Tribal Official that the application is not complete; (B) Specify the additional information the tribe is required to submit to make the application complete; and (C) Start the 270-day review period only when the Director receives a complete application.

(b) Unless the Director notifies the Designated Tribal Official during the 30-day review period that the application is not complete, the application is presumed to be complete and the 270-day review period under 25 U.S.C. 3504(e)(2)(A) of the Act will begin as of the date that the application was received.

APPLICATION CONSULTATION MEETING

§224.58 What is an application consultation meeting?

An application consultation meeting is a meeting held at the tribe's headquarters between the Director and the tribal governing body and any other representatives that the tribe may designate to discuss the TERA application. The Secretary will designate representatives of appropriate Departmental offices or bureaus to attend the application consultation meeting, as necessary. The tribe may record the meeting. The meeting will:

(a) Be held at the earliest practicable time after the Director receives a tribe's complete application;

(b) Include a thorough discussion of the tribe's application;

(c) Identify the specific services consistent with the Secretary's ongoing trust responsibility and available resources that the Department would provide to the tribe upon the approval of a TERA;

(d) Include a discussion of the relationship of the tribe to other Federal agencies with responsibilities for implementing or ensuring compliance with the terms and conditions of leases, business agreements, or rights-of-way and applicable Federal laws;

(e) Include a discussion of the relationship of the tribe to its members, to State and local governments, and to non-Indians who may be affected by approval of a TERA or by leases, business agreements, or rights-of-way that the tribe may enter into or grant under an approved TERA;

(f) Include a discussion of the tribal administrative, financial, technical, and managerial capacities needed to carry out the tribe's obligations under a TERA; and

(g) Include a discussion of the form of the TERA and the timing and relative responsibilities of the parties for its preparation.

§224.59 How will the Director use the results of the application consultation meeting?

The Director will use the information gathered during the application consultation meeting in conjunction with information provided through §§224.53

and 224.63 to determine the energy resource development capacity of the tribe as detailed in § 224.72.

§ 224.60 What will the Director provide to the tribe after the application consultation meeting?

Within 30 days following the meeting with the tribe, the Director will provide to the Designated Tribal Official a written report on the application consultation meeting. The report must include the Director's recommendations, if any, for revising the proposed TERA that was submitted as part of the tribe's application.

§ 224.61 What will the tribe provide to the Director after receipt of the Director's report on the application consultation meeting?

If the tribe wishes to proceed with the application, the tribe must submit a final proposed TERA to the Director within 45 days following the date of the Tribe's receipt of the Director's report on the application consultation meeting.

§ 224.62 May a final proposed TERA differ from the original proposed TERA?

The final proposed TERA may or may not contain provisions that differ from the original proposed TERA submitted with the application.

(a) If a final proposed TERA does not differ significantly or materially from the original TERA contained in the complete application, the 270-day review period will begin to run on the date the original complete application was received (under § 224.57(c)) or on the date established by operation of § 224.57(d)).

(b) If a final proposed TERA differs significantly or materially from the original TERA contained in the complete application, the Secretary, with the tribe's consent, may extend the 270-day period for a reasonable time. The Secretary will notify the tribe in writing if an extension of time is necessary.

TERA REQUIREMENTS

§ 224.63 What provisions must a TERA contain?

A TERA must contain all the elements required by this section.

(a) A provision for the Secretary's periodic review and evaluation of the tribe's performance under a TERA.

(b) A provision that recognizes the authority of the Secretary, upon a finding of imminent jeopardy to a physical trust asset, to take actions the Secretary determines to be necessary to protect the asset, including reassumption under subparts F and G of this part.

(c) A provision under which the tribe establishes and ensures compliance with an environmental review process for leases, business agreements, and rights-of-way which, at a minimum:

(1) Identifies and evaluates all significant environmental effects (as compared to a no-action alternative), including effects on cultural resources, arising from a lease, business agreement, or right-of-way;

(2) Identifies proposed mitigation measures, if any, and incorporates appropriate mitigation measures into the lease, business agreement, or right-of-way;

(3) Informs the public and provides opportunity for public comment on the environmental impacts of the approval of the lease, business agreement or right-of-way;

(4) Provides for tribal responses to relevant and substantive public comments before tribal approval of the lease, business agreement or right-of-way;

(5) Provides for sufficient tribal administrative support and technical capability to carry out the environmental review process; and

(6) Develops adequate tribal oversight of energy resource development activities under any lease, business agreement or right-of-way under a TERA that any other party conducts to determine whether the activities comply with the TERA and applicable Federal and tribal environmental laws.

(d) Provisions that require, with respect to any lease, business agreement, or right-of-way approved under a TERA, all of the following:

(1) Mechanisms for obtaining corporate, technical, and financial qualifications of a third party that has applied to enter into a lease, business agreement, or right-of-way;

(2) Express limitations on duration that meet the restrictions of the Act and this Part under § 224.86;

(3) Mechanisms for amendment, transfer, and renewal;

(4) Mechanisms for obtaining, reporting and evaluating the economic return to the tribe;

(5) Mechanisms for securing technical information about activities and ensuring that technical activities are performed in compliance with terms and conditions;

(6) Assurances of the tribe's compliance with all applicable environmental laws;

(7) Requirements that the lessee, operator, or right-of-way grantee will comply with all applicable environmental laws;

(8) Identification of tribal representatives with the authority to approve a lease, business agreement, or right-of-way and the related energy development activities that would occur under a lease, business agreement, or right-of-way;

(9) Public notification that a lease, business agreement, or right-of-way has received final tribal approval;

(10) A process for consultation with affected States regarding off-reservation impacts, if any, identified under paragraph (c) of this section;

(11) A description of remedies for breach;

(12) A statement that any provision that violates an express term or requirement of the TERA is null and void;

(13) A statement that if the Secretary determines that any provision that violates an express term or requirement of the TERA is material, the Secretary may suspend or rescind the lease, business agreement, or right-of-way, or take any action the Secretary determines to be in the best interest of the tribe, including, with the consent of the parties, revising the nonconforming provisions so that they conform to the intent of the applicable portion of the TERA; and

(14) A statement that the lease, business agreement, or right-of-way subject to a TERA, unless otherwise provided, goes into effect when the tribe delivers executed copies of the lease, business agreement, or right-of-way to the Director by first class mail return receipt requested or express delivery. The parties to a lease, business agreement, or right-of-way may agree in writing that any provision of their contract may have retroactive application.

(e) Citations to any applicable tribal laws, regulations, or procedures that:

(1) Provide opportunity for the public to comment on and to participate in public hearings, if any, under paragraph (c)(2) of this section; and

(2) Provide remedies that petitioning parties must exhaust before filing a petition with the Secretary under subpart E of this part.

(f) Provisions that require a tribe to provide the Secretary with citations to any tribal laws, regulations, or procedures the tribe adopts after the effective date of a TERA that establish, amend, or supplement tribal remedies that petitioning parties must exhaust before filing a petition with the Secretary under subpart E of this part.

(g) Provisions that designate a person or entity, together with contact information, authorized by the tribe to maintain and disseminate to requesting members of the public current copies of tribal laws, regulations, or procedures that establish or describe tribal remedies that petitioning parties must exhaust before instituting appeals under subpart E of this part.

(h) Identification of financial assistance, if any, that the Secretary has agreed to provide to the tribe to assist in implementation of the TERA, including the tribe's environmental review of individual energy development activities.

(i) Provisions that require a tribe to notify the Secretary and the Director in writing, as soon as practicable after the tribe receives notice, of a violation or breach as defined in this Part.

(j) Provisions that require the tribe and the tribe's financial experts to adhere to Government auditing standards and to applicable continuing professional education requirements.

(k) Provisions that require the tribe to submit to the Director information and documentation of payments made directly to the tribe, if any. These provisions enable the Secretary to discharge the trust responsibility of the United States to enforce the terms of, and protect the rights of the tribe under, a lease, business agreement, or right-of-way. Required documentation must include documents evidencing proof of payment such as cancelled checks; cash receipt vouchers; copies of money orders or cashiers checks; or verification of electronic payments.

(l) Provisions that ensure the creation, maintenance and preservation of records related to leases, business agreements, or rights-of-way and performance of activities a tribe assumed under a TERA sufficient to facilitate the Secretary's periodic review of the TERA. The Secretary will use these records as part of the periodic review and evaluation process under § 224.132. Approved Departmental records retention procedures under the Federal Records Act (44 U.S.C. Chapters 29, 31, and 33) provide a framework the tribe may use to ensure that its records under a TERA adequately document essential transactions, furnish information necessary to protect its legal and financial rights, and enable the Secretary to discharge the trust responsibility if:

(1) Any other party violates the terms of any lease, business agreement, or right-of-way; or

(2) Any provision of a lease, business agreement or right-of-way violates the TERA.

§ 224.64 How may a tribe assume management of development of different types of energy resources?

In order for a tribe to assume authority for approving leases, business agreements, and rights-of-way for development of another energy resource that is not included in the TERA, a tribe must apply for a new TERA covering the authority for the development of another energy resource it wishes to assume. The Secretary's consideration of a new TERA will include a determination of the tribe's capacity to develop that type of energy resource and will trigger the public notice and opportunity for comment consistent with § 224.67.

§ 224.65 How may a tribe assume additional activities under a TERA?

A tribe may assume additional activities related to the development of the same type of energy resource included in a TERA by negotiating with the Secretary an amendment to the existing TERA to include the additional activities. The Secretary will determine in each case whether the tribe has sufficient capacity to carry out additional activities the tribe may wish to assume under an approved TERA.

§ 224.66 How may a tribe reduce the scope of the TERA?

A tribe may reduce the scope of the TERA by negotiating with the Secretary an amendment to the existing TERA to eliminate an activity assumed under the TERA or a type of energy resource development managed under the TERA. Any such reduction in scope must include the return of all relevant Departmental resources transferred under the TERA and any relevant records and documents.

PUBLIC NOTIFICATION AND COMMENT

§ 224.67 What must the Secretary do upon the Director's receipt of a final proposed TERA?

(a) Within 10 days of the Director's receipt of a final proposed TERA, the Secretary must submit a notice for publication in the FEDERAL REGISTER advising the public:

(1) That the Secretary is considering a final proposed TERA for approval or disapproval: and

(2) Of any National Environmental Policy Act (NEPA) review the Secretary is conducting.

(b) The FEDERAL REGISTER notice will:

(1) Contain information advising the public how to request and receive copies of or participate in any NEPA reviews, as prescribed in subpart C of this part, related to approval of the final proposed TERA; and

(2) Contain information advising the public how to comment on a final proposed TERA.

§ 224.68 How will the Secretary use public comments?

(a) The Secretary will review and consider public comments in deciding to approve or disapprove the final proposed TERA; and

(b) The Secretary will provide copies of the comments to the Designated Tribal Official;

(c) Upon mutual agreement between the tribe and the Secretary, the tribe may make changes in the final proposed TERA based on the comments received; and

(d) If the tribe revises the final proposed TERA based on public comments, the tribal governing body must approve the changes, the authorized representative of the tribe must sign the final proposed TERA as revised, and the tribe must send the revised final proposed TERA to the Director. The Secretary and the tribe will consult on whether an extension of the review period is necessary under §224.62(b).

Subpart C—Approval of Tribal Energy Resource Agreements

§224.70 Will the Secretary review a proposed TERA under the National Environmental Policy Act?

Yes, the Secretary will conduct a review under the National Environmental Policy Act (NEPA) of the potential impacts on the quality of the human environment that might arise from approving a final proposed TERA. The scope of the Secretary's evaluation will be limited to the scope of the TERA. The public comment period, when required, under the NEPA review will occur concurrently with the public comment period for a TERA under §224.67.

§224.71 What standards will the Secretary use to decide to approve a final proposed TERA?

The Secretary will consider the best interests of the tribe and the Federal policy of promoting tribal self-determination in deciding whether to approve a final proposed TERA. The Secretary must approve a final proposed TERA if it contains the provisions required by the Act and this part and the Secretary determines that the tribe has demonstrated sufficient capacity to manage the development of energy resources it proposes to develop.

§224.72 How will the Secretary determine whether a tribe has demonstrated sufficient capacity?

The Secretary will determine whether a tribe has demonstrated sufficient capacity under §224.71 based on the information obtained through the application process. The Secretary will consider:

(a) The specific energy resource development the tribe proposes to regulate;

(b) The scope of the administrative or regulatory activities the tribe seeks to assume;

(c) Materials and information submitted with the application for a TERA, the result of meetings between the tribe and a representative of the Department and the Director's written report;

(d) The history of the tribe's role in energy resource development, including negotiating and approval or disapproval of pre-existing energy-related leases, business agreements, and rights-of-way;

(e) The administrative expertise of the tribe available to regulate energy resource development within the scope of the final proposed TERA or the tribe's plans for establishing that expertise;

(f) The financial capacity of the tribe to maintain or procure the technical expertise needed to evaluate proposals and to monitor anticipated activities in a prudent manner;

(g) The tribe's past performance administering contracts and grants associated with self-determination programs, cooperative agreements with Federal and State agencies, and environmental programs administered by the Environmental Protection Agency;

(h) The tribe's past performance monitoring activities undertaken by third parties under approved leases, business agreements, or rights-of-way; and

(i) Any other factors the Secretary finds to be relevant in light of the scope of the proposed TERA.

§ 224.73 How will the scope of energy resource development affect the Secretary's determination of the tribe's capacity?

The Secretary's review under § 224.72 of the tribe's capacity to manage and regulate energy resource development under the TERA will include a determination as to each type of energy resource development subject to the TERA for which the tribe seeks to regulate, and each type of regulatory activity the tribe proposes to assume. The Secretary's review of a TERA must be limited to activities specified by its provisions.

§ 224.74 When must the Secretary approve or disapprove a final proposed TERA?

The Secretary must approve or disapprove a final proposed TERA or a revised final proposed TERA within 270 days of the Director's receipt of a complete application for a TERA. With the consent of the tribe, or as provided in § 224.62(b), the Secretary may extend the period for a decision.

§ 224.75 What must the Secretary do upon approval or disapproval of a final proposed TERA?

Within 10 days of the Secretary's approval or disapproval of a final proposed TERA, the Secretary must notify the tribal governing body in writing and take the following actions:

If the Secretary's decision is . . .	Then the Secretary will . . .
(a) To approve the final proposed TERA.	(1) Sign the TERA making it effective on the date of signature, and return the signed TERA to the tribal governing body; and (2) Maintain a copy of the TERA and any subsequent amendments or supplements to the TERA.
(b) To disapprove the final proposed TERA.	Send the tribe a notice of disapproval that must include: (1) The basis of the disapproval; (2) The changes or other actions required to address the Secretary's basis for disapproval; and (3) A statement that the decision is a final agency action and is subject to judicial review.

§ 224.76 Upon notification of disapproval, may a tribe re-submit a revised final proposed TERA?

Yes, within 45 days of receiving the notice of disapproval, or a later date as the Secretary and the tribe agree to in writing, the tribe may re-submit a revised final proposed TERA, approved by the tribal governing body and signed by the tribe's authorized representative, to the Director that addresses the Secretary's concerns. Unless the Secretary and the tribe otherwise agree, the Secretary must approve or disapprove the revised final proposed TERA within 60 days of the Director's receipt of the revised final proposed TERA. Within 10 days of the Secretary's approval or disapproval of a revised final proposed TERA, the Secretary must notify the tribal governing body in writing and take the following actions:

If the Secretary's decision is . . .	Then the Secretary will . . .
(a) To approve the revised final proposed TERA.	(1) Sign the TERA making it effective on the date of signature, and return the signed TERA to the tribal governing body; and (2) Maintain a copy of the TERA and any subsequent amendments or supplements to the TERA.
(b) To disapprove the revised final proposed TERA.	Send the tribe a notice of disapproval that must include: (1) The reasons for the disapproval; and (2) A statement that the decision is a final agency action and is subject to judicial review.

§ 224.77 Who may appeal the Secretary's decision on a final proposed TERA or a revised final proposed TERA?

Only a tribe applying for a TERA may appeal the Secretary's decision to disapprove a final proposed TERA or a revised final proposed TERA in accordance with the appeal procedures contained in subpart I of this part. No other person or entity may appeal the Secretary's decision. The Secretary's decision to approve a final proposed TERA or a revised final proposed TERA is a final agency action.

Subpart D—Implementation of Tribal Energy Resource Agreements

APPLICABLE AUTHORITIES AND RESPONSIBILITIES

§ 224.80 Under what authority will a tribe perform activities for energy resource development?

A tribe will perform activities for energy resource development activities undertaken under a TERA under the authorities provided in the approved TERA. Notwithstanding anything in this part or an approved TERA to the contrary, a tribe will retain all sovereign and other powers it otherwise possesses.

§ 224.81 What laws are applicable to activities?

Federal and tribal laws apply to activities under a TERA, unless otherwise specified in the TERA.

§ 224.82 What activities will the Department continue to perform after approval of a TERA?

After approval of a TERA, the Department will provide a tribe:

(a) All activities that the Department performs unless the tribe has assumed such activities under the TERA;

(b) Access to title status information and support services needed by a tribe in the course of evaluating proposals for leases, business agreements, or rights-of-way;

(c) Coordination between the tribe and the Department for ongoing maintenance of accurate real property records;

(d) Access to technical support services within the Department to assist the tribe in evaluating the physical, economic, financial, cultural, social, environmental, and legal consequences of approving proposals for leases, business agreements, or rights-of-way under a TERA; and

(e) Assistance to ensure that third-party violations or breaches of the terms of leases, business agreements, or rights-of-way or applicable provisions of Federal law by third parties are handled appropriately.

LEASES, BUSINESS AGREEMENTS, AND RIGHTS-OF-WAY UNDER A TERA

§ 224.83 What must a tribe do after executing a lease or business agreement, or granting a right-of-way?

Following the execution of a lease, business agreement, or grant of right-of-way under a TERA, a tribe must:

(a) Inform the public of approval of the lease, business agreement, or right-of-way under the authority granted in the TERA; and

(b) Send a copy of the executed lease, business agreement, or right-of-way, or amendments, to the Director within one business day of execution. The copy must be sent by certified mail return receipt requested or by overnight delivery.

§ 224.84 When may a tribe grant a right-of-way?

A tribe may grant a right-of-way under a TERA if the grant of right-of-way is over tribal land for a pipeline or an electric transmission or distribution line if the pipeline or electric transmission or distribution line serves:

(a) An electric generation, transmission, or distribution facility located on tribal land; or

(b) A facility located on tribal land that processes or refines energy resources developed on tribal land.

§ 224.85 When may a tribe enter into a lease or business agreement?

A tribe may enter into a lease or business agreement for the purpose of energy resource development for:

(a) Exploration for, extraction of, or other development of the tribe's energy mineral resources on tribal land including, but not limited to, marketing or distribution;

(b) Construction or operation of an electric generation, transmission, or distribution facility located on tribal land; or

(c) A facility to process or refine energy resources developed on tribal land.

§ 224.86 Are there limits on the duration of leases, business agreements, and rights-of-way?

(a) The duration of leases, business agreements, and rights-of-way entered into under a TERA are limited as follows:

(1) For leases and business agreements, except as provided in paragraph (b) of this section, 30 years;

(2) For leases for production of oil resources and gas resources, or both, 10 years and as long after as oil or gas production continues in paying quantities; and

(3) For rights-of-way, 30 years.

(b) A lease or business agreement a tribe enters into, or a right-of-way a tribe grants may be renewed at the discretion of the tribe as long as the TERA remains in effect and the approved activities have not been rescinded by the tribe or suspended or reassumed by the Department.

VIOLATION OR BREACH

§ 224.87 What are the obligations of a tribe if it discovers a violation or breach?

As soon as practicable after discovering or receiving notice of a violation or breach of a lease, business agreement, or right-of-way of a Federal or tribal environmental law resulting from an activity undertaken by a third party under a lease, business agreement, or right-of-way, the tribe must provide written notice to the Director describing:

(a) The nature of the violation or breach in reasonable detail;

(b) The corrective action taken or planned by the tribe; and

(c) The proposed period for the corrective action to be completed.

§ 224.88 What must the Director do after receiving notice of a violation or breach from the tribe?

After receiving notice of a violation or breach from the tribe, the Director will:

(a) Review the notice and conduct an investigation under § 224.135(b) including, as necessary:

(1) An on-site inspection; and

(2) A review of relevant records, including transactions and reports.

(b) If the Director determines, after the investigation, that a violation or breach is not causing or will not cause imminent jeopardy to a physical trust asset, the Director will review, for concurrence or disapproval, the corrective action to be taken or imposed by the tribe and the proposed period for completion of the corrective action;

(c) If the Director determines, after the investigation, that a violation or breach is causing or will cause imminent jeopardy to a physical trust asset, the Director will proceed under the imminent jeopardy provisions of subpart F of this part.

§ 224.89 What procedures will the Secretary use to enforce leases, business agreements, or rights-of-way?

(a) The Secretary and a tribe will consult with each other regarding enforcement of and Secretarial assistance needed to enforce leases, business agreements, or rights-of-way entered into under a TERA. When appropriate, the Secretary will:

(1) Use the notification and enforcement procedures established in 25 CFR parts 162, 211 and 225 to ensure compliance with leases and business agreements; and

(2) Use the notification and enforcement procedures of 25 CFR part 169 to ensure compliance with rights-of-way.

(b) All enforcement remedies established in 25 CFR parts 162, 211, 225, and 169 are available to the Secretary.

Subpart E—Interested Party Petitions

§ 224.100 May a person or entity ask the Secretary to review a tribe's compliance with a TERA?

In accordance with this subpart, a person or entity that may be an interested party may submit to the Secretary a petition to review a tribe's compliance with a TERA. However, before filing a petition with the Secretary, a person or entity that may be an interested party must first exhaust tribal remedies, if a tribe has provided for such remedies. If a tribe has not provided for tribal remedies, a person or entity that may be an interested party may file a petition directly with the Secretary.

§ 224.101 Who is an interested party?

For the purposes of this part, an interested party is a person or entity that has demonstrated that an interest of the person or entity has sustained, or will sustain, an adverse environmental impact as a result of a tribe's failure to comply with a TERA.

§ 224.102 Must a tribe establish a comment or hearing process for addressing environmental concerns?

Yes. The Act (25 U.S.C. 3504(e)(2)(C)(iii)(I), (II) and 25 U.S.C. 3504(e)(2)(B)(iii)(X)) and subpart B of this part require a tribe to establish an environmental review process under a TERA that:

(a) Ensures that the public is notified about and has an opportunity to comment on the environmental impacts of proposed tribal action to be taken under a TERA;

(b) Requires that the tribe respond to relevant and substantive comments about the environmental impacts of a proposed tribal action before the tribe approves a lease, business agreement, or right-of-way; and

(c) Provides for a process for consultation with any affected States regarding off-reservation environmental impacts, if any, resulting from approval of a lease, business agreement, or right-of-way.

§ 224.103 Must a tribe establish other public participation processes?

No. Except for the environmental review process required by the Act and § 224.63(b)(1), a tribe is not required to establish a process for public participation concerning non-environmental issues in a TERA or leases, business agreements or rights-of-way undertaken under a TERA. However, a tribe may elect to establish procedures that permit the public to participate in public hearings or that expand the scope of matters about which the public may comment.

§ 224.104 Must a tribe enact tribal laws, regulations, or procedures permitting a person or entity to allege that a tribe is not complying with a TERA?

No. A tribe is not required, but may elect, to enact tribal laws, regulations, or procedures permitting a person or entity that may be an interested party to allege that a tribe is not complying with its TERA.

§ 224.105 How may a person or entity obtain copies of tribal laws, regulations, or procedures that would permit an allegation of noncompliance with a TERA?

(a) A person or entity that may be an interested party may obtain copies of tribal laws, regulations, or procedures that establish tribal remedies that permit a person or entity to allege that the tribe is not complying with its TERA by making a request to the tribe in accordance with the TERA and § 224.63(g).

(b) Upon obtaining copies of tribal laws, regulations, or procedures under subsection (a), a person or entity that may be an interested party may file a petition with the tribe under those tribal laws, regulations, or procedures.

(c) If the person or entity that may be an interested party files a petition alleging noncompliance with a TERA, the person or entity becomes a petitioner, and the tribe must respond according to § 224.106.

§ 224.106 If a tribe has enacted tribal laws, regulations, or procedures for challenging tribal action, how must the tribe respond to a petition?

If a tribe has enacted tribal laws, regulations, or procedures under which a petitioner may file a petition alleging noncompliance with a TERA, the tribe must:

(a) Within a reasonable time issue a final written decision under the tribal laws, regulations, or procedures that addresses the claim. The decision may include a determination of whether the petitioner is an interested party;

(b) Provide a copy of its final written decision to the petitioner; and

(c) If the tribe fails, within a reasonable period, to issue a written decision to a petition that a petitioner brings under applicable tribal laws, regulations, or procedures the petitioner may file a petition with the Secretary.

§ 224.107 What must a petitioner do before filing a petition with the Secretary?

Before a petitioner may file a petition with the Secretary under this subpart, the petitioner must have exhausted tribal remedies by participating in any tribal process under

§ 224.106, including any tribal appeal process.

§ 224.108 May tribes offer a resolution of a petitioner's claim?

Yes. In responding to a petition filed under tribal laws, regulations or procedures, a tribe may, with the petitioner's written consent, resolve the petitioner's claims.

§ 224.109 What must a petitioner claim or request in a petition filed with the Secretary?

In a petition filed with the Secretary, a petitioner must:

(a) Claim that the tribe, through its action or inaction has failed to comply with terms or provisions of a TERA, and, as a result, the petitioner's interest has sustained or will sustain an adverse environmental impact.

(b) Request that the Secretary review the claims raised in the petition; and

(c) Request that the Secretary take whatever action is necessary to bring a tribe into compliance with the TERA.

§ 224.110 What must a petition to the Secretary contain?

A petition must contain:

(a) The petitioner's name and contact information;

(b) Specific facts demonstrating that the interested party under § 224.101, including identification of the affected interest;

(c) Specific facts demonstrating that the petitioner exhausted tribal remedies, if tribal laws, regulations, or procedures permitted the petitioner to allege tribal noncompliance with a TERA;

(d) A description of facts supporting the petitioner's allegation of the tribe's noncompliance with a TERA;

(e) A description of the adverse environmental impact that the petitioner's interest has sustained or will sustain because of the tribe's alleged noncompliance with the TERA;

(f) A copy of any written decision the tribe issued responding to the petitioner's claims;

(g) If applicable, a statement that the tribe has issued no written decision within a reasonable time related to a claim a petitioner has filed with the tribe under applicable tribal laws, regulations, or procedures;

(h) If applicable, a statement and supporting documentation that the tribe did not respond to the petitioner's request under § 224.105(a) for copies of any tribal laws, regulations, or procedures allowing the petitioner to allege that the tribe is not complying with a TERA; and

(i) Any other information relevant to the petition.

§ 224.111 When may a petitioner file a petition with the Secretary?

(a) A petitioner may file a petition with the Secretary:

(1) By delivering the petition to the Director within 30 days of receiving the tribe's final written decision addressing the allegation of noncompliance under applicable tribal laws, regulations, or procedures;

(2) Within a reasonable period following the tribe's constructive denial of the petition under § 224.106(c), and the Secretary will determine if the petition is timely in light of the applicable facts and circumstances; or

(3) The tribe did not respond to the petitioner's request for copies of any tribal laws, regulations, or procedures under § 224.105(a).

(b) A petitioner may file a petition directly with the Secretary if the tribe has no tribal laws, regulations or procedures that provide the petitioner an opportunity to allege tribal noncompliance with a TERA.

§ 224.112 What must the Director do upon receipt of a petition?

Within 20 days after receiving a petition, the Director must:

(a) Notify the tribe in writing that the Director has received a petition;

(b) Provide a copy of the complete petition to the tribe;

(c) Initiate a petition consultation with the tribe that will address the petitioner's allegation of a tribe's noncompliance with a TERA and alternatives to resolve any noncompliance; and

(d) Notify the tribe in writing by certified mail, return receipt requested, when the petition consultation is complete.

§224.113 What must the tribe do after it completes petition consultation with the Director?

(a) Within 45 days of receiving the Director's notice that the petition consultation is complete, the tribe must respond to any claim made in the petition by submitting a written response to the Director; and

(b) Within a reasonable time after 45 days following the completion of the petition consultation process, the tribe must cure or otherwise resolve each claim of noncompliance made in the petition.

§224.114 How may the tribe address a petition in its written response?

In addition to responding to the petitioner's claims, the tribe may also:

(a) Include its interpretation of relevant provisions of the TERA and other legal requirements;

(b) Discuss whether the petitioner is an interested party;

(c) State whether the petitioner has exhausted tribal remedies, and if so, how; and

(d) Propose to cure or otherwise resolve the claims within the time frame in §224.113(b).

§224.115 When in the petition process must the Director investigate a tribe's compliance with a TERA?

The Director must investigate the petitioner's claims of the tribe's noncompliance with a TERA only after making a threshold determination that:

(a) The tribe has denied or failed to respond to each claim made in the petition within the period under §224.113(a); or

(b) The tribe has failed, refused, or was unable to cure or otherwise resolve each claim made in the petition within a reasonable period, as determined by the Director, after the expiration of the period in §224.113(b).

§224.116 What is the time period in which the Director must investigate a tribe's compliance with a TERA?

(a) If the Director determines under §224.115 that one of the threshold determinations in §224.114 has been met, then within 120 days of the Director's receipt of a petition, the Director must determine whether or not a tribe is in compliance with the TERA;

(b) The Director may extend the time for determining a tribe's compliance with a TERA up to 120 days in any case in which the Director determines that additional time is necessary to evaluate the claims in the petition and the tribe's written response, if any. If the Director decides to extend the time, the Director must notify the petitioner and the tribe in writing of the extension.

§224.117 Must the Director make a determination of the tribe's compliance with a TERA?

(a) Yes. Upon a finding that one of the threshold determinations in §224.115 has been met, the Director must make a determination of the tribe's compliance with a TERA within the time period in §224.116.

(b) If the Director determines that the tribe is in compliance with the TERA, the Director will notify the tribe and the petitioner in writing;

(c) If the Director determines that the tribe is not in compliance with the TERA, the Director will notify the tribe and the petitioner in writing and, in addition, must provide the tribe:

(1) A written determination that describes the manner in which the TERA has been violated together with a written notice of the violations;

(2) Notice of a reasonable opportunity to comply with the TERA; and

(3) Notice of the tribe's opportunity for a hearing.

§224.118 How must the tribe respond to the Director's notice of the opportunity for a hearing?

The tribe must respond in writing to the Director's notice of the opportunity for a hearing within 20 days of receipt of the notice by requesting a hearing or declining to request a hearing. If the tribe does not respond within the time period, the Director will proceed with making a decision without further input from the tribe.

§224.119 What must the Director do when making a decision on a petition?

(a) The Director must issue a written decision to the tribe and the petitioner stating the basis for the decision about the tribe's compliance or noncompliance with the TERA within 30 days following:

(1) A hearing, if the tribe requested a hearing;

(2) The tribe's declining the opportunity for a hearing; or

(3) The tribe's failure to respond to the opportunity for a hearing within 20 days of the Director's written notice of the opportunity for a hearing.

(b) If the Director decides that the tribe is not in compliance with the TERA, the Director must:

(1) Include findings of fact and conclusions of law with the written decision to the tribe; and

(2) Take action to ensure compliance with the TERA.

§ 224.120 What action may the Director take to ensure compliance with a TERA?

If the Director decides that a tribe is not in compliance with a TERA, the Director may take action to ensure compliance with the TERA including:

(a) Temporarily suspending any activity under a lease, business agreement, or right-of-way until the tribe complies with the TERA; or

(b) Rescinding approval of part of the TERA, or

(c) Rescinding all of the TERA and recommending that the Secretary reassume activities under subpart G of this part.

§ 224.121 How may a tribe or a petitioner appeal the Director's decision about the tribe's compliance with the TERA?

A tribe or a petitioner, or both, may appeal the Director's decision on the petition under § 224.119 to the Principal Deputy Assistant Secretary—Indian Affairs under subpart I of this part.

Subpart F—Periodic Reviews

§ 224.130 What is the purpose of this subpart?

This subpart describes how the Secretary and a tribe will develop and perform the periodic review and evaluation required by the Act and by a TERA.

§ 224.131 What is a periodic review and evaluation?

A periodic review and evaluation is an examination the Director performs to monitor a tribe's performance of activities associated with the development of energy resources and to review compliance with a TERA. During the TERA consultation, a tribe and the Director will develop a periodic review and evaluation process that addresses the tribe's specific circumstances and the terms and conditions of the tribe's TERA. The tribe will include the agreed-upon periodic review and evaluation process in its final proposed TERA.

§ 224.132 How does the Director conduct a periodic review and evaluation?

(a) The Director will conduct a periodic review and evaluation under the TERA, in consultation with the tribe, and in cooperation with other Departmental bureaus and offices whose activities the tribe assumed or that perform activities for the tribe.

(b) The Director will communicate with the Designated Tribal Official throughout the process established by this section.

(c) During the periodic review and evaluation, the Director will:

(1) Review relevant records and documents, including transactions and reports the tribe prepares under the TERA;

(2) Conduct on-site inspections as appropriate; and

(3) Review compliance with statutes and regulations applicable to activities undertaken under the TERA.

(d) Review the effect on physical trust assets resulting from activities undertaken under a TERA.

(e) Upon written request, the tribe should provide the Director with records and documents relevant to the provisions of the TERA. In addition, the tribe should identify any information in these submitted records and documents that is confidential, commercial and financial. Specific exceptions to disclosure under the Freedom of Information Act, or other statutory protections against disclosure, may apply and preclude disclosure of this information to third parties as provided for in § 224.55.

§ 224.133 What must the Director do after a periodic review and evaluation?

After a periodic review and evaluation, the Director must prepare a written report of the results and send the report to the Designated Tribal Official.

§ 224.134 How often must the Director conduct a periodic review and evaluation?

The Director must conduct a periodic review and evaluation annually during the first 3 years of a TERA. After the third annual review and evaluation, the Secretary and the tribe may mutually agree to amend the TERA to conduct periodic reviews and evaluations once every 2 years.

§ 224.135 Under what circumstances may the Director conduct additional reviews and evaluations?

The Director may conduct additional reviews and evaluations:

(a) At a tribe's request;

(b) As part of an investigation undertaken when the tribe notifies the Director of a violation or breach;

(c) As part of an investigation undertaken because of a petition submitted under subpart E of this part;

(d) As follow-up to a determination that harm or the potential for harm to a physical trust asset, previously identified in a periodic review and evaluation, exists; or

(e) As the Secretary determines appropriate to carry out the Secretary's trust responsibilities.

NONCOMPLIANCE

§ 224.136 How will the Director's report address a tribe's noncompliance?

This section applies if the Director conducts a review and evaluation or investigation of a notice of violation of Federal law or the terms of a TERA.

(a) If the Director determines that the tribe has not complied with Federal law or the terms of a TERA, the Director's written report must include a determination of whether the tribe's noncompliance has resulted in harm or the potential for harm to a physical trust asset.

(b) If the Director determines that the tribe's noncompliance may cause harm or has caused harm to a physical trust asset, the Director must also determine whether the noncompliance cause imminent jeopardy to a physical trust asset.

§ 224.137 What must the Director do if a tribe's noncompliance has resulted in harm or the potential for harm to a physical trust asset?

If, because of the tribe's noncompliance with Federal law or the terms of a TERA, the Director determines that there is harm or the potential for harm to a physical trust asset that does not rise to the level of imminent jeopardy to a physical trust asset, the Director must:

(a) Document the issue in the written report of the review and evaluation;

(b) Report the issue in writing to the tribal governing body;

(c) Report the issue in writing to the Assistant Secretary—Indian Affairs; and

(d) Determine what action, if any, the Secretary must take to protect the physical trust asset, which could include temporary suspension of the activity that resulted in non-compliance with the TERA or other applicable Federal laws or rescinding approval of all or part of the TERA.

§ 224.138 What must the Director do if a tribe's noncompliance has caused imminent jeopardy to a physical trust asset?

If the Director finds that a tribe's noncompliance with a Federal law or the terms of a TERA has caused imminent jeopardy to a physical trust asset, the Director must:

(a) Immediately notify the tribe by a telephone call to the Designated Tribal Official followed by a written notice by facsimile to the Designated Tribal Official and the tribal governing body of the imminent jeopardy to a physical trust asset. The notice must contain:

(1) A description of the tribe's noncompliance with Federal law or the terms of the TERA;

(2) A description of the physical trust asset and the nature of the imminent

jeopardy to a physical trust asset resulting from the tribe's noncompliance; and

(3) An order to the tribe to cease specific conduct or take specific action deemed necessary by the Director to correct any condition that caused the imminent jeopardy to a physical trust asset.

(b) Issue a finding that the tribe's noncompliance with the TERA or a Federal law has caused imminent jeopardy to a physical trust asset.

§ 224.139 What must a tribe do after receiving a notice of imminent jeopardy to a physical trust asset?

(a) Upon receipt of a notice of imminent jeopardy to a physical trust asset, the tribe must cease specific conduct outlined in the notice or take specific action the Director orders that is necessary to correct any condition causing the imminent jeopardy; and

(b) Within 5 days of receiving a notice of imminent jeopardy to a physical trust asset, the tribe must submit a written response to the Director that:

(1) Responds to the Director's finding that the tribe has failed to comply with a Federal law or the terms of the TERA;

(2) Responds to the Director's finding of imminent jeopardy to a physical trust asset;

(3) Describes the status of the tribe's cessation of specific conduct or specific action the tribe has taken to correct any condition causing imminent jeopardy to a physical trust asset; and

(4) Describes what further actions, if any, the tribe proposes to take to correct any condition, cited in the notice, causing imminent jeopardy to a physical trust asset.

§ 224.140 What must the Secretary do if the tribe fails to respond to or does not comply with the Director's order?

If the tribe does not respond to or does not comply with the Director's order under § 224.138(a)(3), the Secretary may take any actions the Secretary deems appropriate to protect the physical trust asset, which may include the immediate reassumption of all activities the tribe assumed under the TERA. The procedures in subpart G of this part do not apply to reassumption under this section.

§ 224.141 What must the Secretary do if the tribe responds to the Director's order?

(a) If the tribe responds in a timely manner to the Director's order under § 224.138, the Secretary must:

(1) Evaluate the tribe's response;

(2) Determine whether or not the tribe has complied with the TERA and the Federal law cited in the notice; and

(3) If the Secretary determines, after reviewing the tribe's response, that the tribe has not complied with the TERA or with a Federal law, the Secretary will determine whether the noncompliance caused imminent jeopardy to a physical trust asset.

(b) If the Secretary determines that the tribe's noncompliance has caused imminent jeopardy to a physical trust asset, the Secretary may:

(1) Order the tribe to take any action the Secretary deems necessary to comply with the TERA or Federal law and to protect the physical trust asset; or

(2) Take any action the Secretary deems necessary to protect the physical trust asset, including reassumption under subpart G of this part.

(c) If the Secretary determines, after reviewing the tribe's response, that the tribe has complied with the TERA and with Federal law, the Secretary will withdraw the Director's order.

(d) The Secretary must base a finding of imminent jeopardy to a physical trust asset on the tribe's non-compliance with a TERA or violation of a Federal law.

Subpart G—Reassumption

§ 224.150 What is the purpose of this subpart?

This subpart explains when and how the Secretary may reassume all activities included within a TERA without the consent of the tribe.

§ 224.151 When may the Secretary reassume activities?

Upon issuing a written finding of imminent jeopardy to a physical trust asset, the Secretary may reassume activities under a TERA in accordance with this subpart. The Secretary may also reassume activities approved under a TERA in response to a petition from an interested party under subpart E of this part. Only the Secretary or the Assistant Secretary—Indian Affairs may reassume activities under a TERA.

§ 224.152 Must the Secretary always reassume the activities upon a finding of imminent jeopardy to a physical trust asset?

(a) The Secretary may take whatever actions the Secretary deems necessary to protect the physical trust asset. At the discretion of the Secretary, these actions may include reassumption of the activities a tribe assumed under a TERA.

(b) If the tribe does not respond to or does not comply with the Director's order under § 224.138(a)(3), the Secretary must immediately reassume all activities the tribe assumed under the TERA. The notice procedures in this subpart will not apply to such immediate reassumption.

NOTICE OF INTENT TO REASSUME

§ 224.153 Must the Secretary notify the tribe of an intent to reassume the authority granted?

If the Secretary determines under § 224.152 that reassumption is necessary to protect the physical trust asset, the Secretary will issue a written notice to the tribal governing body of the Secretary's intent to reassume.

§ 224.154 What must a notice of intent to reassume include?

A notice of intent to reassume must include:

(a) A statement of the reasons for the intended reassumption, including, as applicable, a copy of the Secretary's written finding of imminent jeopardy to a physical trust asset;

(b) A description of specific measures that the tribe must take to correct the violation and any condition that caused the imminent jeopardy to a physical trust asset;

(c) The time period within which the tribe must take the measures to correct the violation of the TERA and any condition that caused the imminent jeopardy to a physical trust asset; and

(d) The effective date of the reassumption, if the tribe does not meet the requirements in paragraphs (b) and (c) of this section.

§ 224.155 When must a tribe respond to a notice of intent to reassume?

The tribe must respond to the Director in writing by mail, facsimile, or overnight express within 5 days of receiving the Secretary's notice of intent to reassume. If sent by mail, the tribe must send the response by certified mail, with return receipt requested. The Director will consider the date of the written response as the date it is postmarked.

§ 224.156 What information must the tribe's response to the notice of intent to reassume include?

The tribe's response to the notice of intent to reassume must state that:

(a) The tribe has complied with the Secretary's requirements in the notice of intent to reassume;

(b) The tribe is taking specified measures to comply with the Secretary's requirements, and when the tribe will complete such measures, if the tribe needs more than 5 days to do so; or

(c) The tribe will not comply with the Secretary's requirements.

§ 224.157 How must the Secretary proceed after receiving the tribe's response?

(a) If the Secretary determines that the tribe's proposed or completed actions to comply with the Secretary's requirements are adequate to correct the violation of the TERA or Federal law and any condition that caused the imminent jeopardy, the Secretary will:

(1) Notify the tribe of the adequacy of its response in writing; and

(2) Terminate the reassumption proceedings in writing.

(b) If the Secretary determines that the tribe's proposed or completed actions to comply with the Secretary's requirements are not adequate, then the Secretary will issue a written notice of reassumption.

§ 224.158 What must the Secretary include in a written notice of reassumption?

The written notice of reassumption must include:

(a) A description of the authorities the Secretary is reassuming;

(b) The reasons for the determination under § 224.157(b);

(c) The effective date of the reassumption; and

(d) A statement that the decision is a final agency action and is subject to judicial review.

§ 224.159 How will reassumption affect valid existing rights or lawful actions taken before the effective date of the reassumption?

Reassumption will not affect valid existing rights that vested before the effective date of the reassumption or lawful actions the tribe and the Secretary took before the effective date of the reassumption.

§ 224.160 How will reassumption affect a TERA?

Reassumption of a TERA applies to all of the authority and activities assumed under a TERA. Upon reassumption, the tribe must also return all Departmental resources transferred under the TERA and any relevant records and documents to the Secretary.

§ 224.161 How may reassumption affect the tribe's ability to enter into a new TERA or to modify another TERA to administer additional activities or to assume administration of activities that the Secretary previously reassumed?

Following reassumption, a tribe may submit a request to enter into a new TERA or modify another TERA to administer additional activities, or assume administration of activities that the Secretary previously reassumed. In reviewing a subsequent tribal request, however, the Secretary may consider the fact that activities were reassumed and any change in circumstances supporting the tribe's request.

Subpart H—Rescission

§ 224.170 What is the purpose of this subpart?

This subpart explains the process and requirements under which a tribe may rescind a TERA and therefore return to the Secretary all authority and activities assumed under that TERA.

§ 224.171 Who may rescind a TERA?

Only a tribe may rescind a TERA.

§ 224.172 May a tribe rescind only some of the activities subject to a TERA while retaining a portion of those activities?

No. A tribe may only rescind a TERA in its entirety, including the authority to approve leases, business agreements and grant rights-of-way for specific energy resource development, not some of the authority or activities subject to the TERA.

§ 224.173 How does a tribe rescind a TERA?

To rescind a TERA, a tribe must submit to the Secretary a written tribal resolution or other official action of the tribe's governing body approving the voluntary rescission of the TERA. Upon rescission, the tribe must also return all Departmental resources transferred under the TERA and any relevant records and documents.

§ 224.174 When does a voluntary rescission become effective?

A voluntary rescission becomes effective on the date specified by the Secretary, provided that the date is no more than 90 days after the Secretary receives the tribal resolution or other official action the tribe submits under § 224.173.

§ 224.175 How will rescission affect valid existing rights or lawful actions taken before the rescission?

Rescission does not affect valid existing rights that vested before the effective date of the rescission or lawful actions the tribe and the Secretary took before the effective date of the rescission.

Subpart I—General Appeal Procedures

§ 224.180 What is the purpose of this subpart?

The purpose of this subpart is to explain who may appeal Departmental decisions or inaction under this part and the initial administrative appeal processes, and general administrative appeal processes, including how 25 CFR part 2 and 43 CFR part 4 apply, and the effective dates for appeal decisions.

§ 224.181 Who may appeal Departmental decisions or inaction under this part?

The following persons or entities may appeal Department decisions or inaction under this part:

(a) A tribe that is adversely affected by a decision of or inaction by an official of the Department of the Interior under this part;

(b) A third party who has entered into a lease, right-of-way, or business agreement with a tribe under an approved TERA and is adversely affected by a decision of, or inaction by a Department official under this part; or

(c) An interested party who is adversely affected by a decision of or inaction by the Director under subpart E of this part, provided that the interested party may appeal only those issues raised in its prior participation under subpart E of this part and may not appeal any other decision rendered or inaction under this part.

§ 224.182 What is the Initial Appeal Process?

The initial appeal process is as follows:

(a) Within 30 days of receiving an adverse decision by the Director or within 30 days after the time period within which the Director is required to act under subpart E, a party that may appeal under this subpart may file an appeal to the Principal Deputy Assistant Secretary-Indian Affairs;

(b) Within 60 days of receiving an appeal, the Principal Deputy Assistant Secretary—Indian Affairs will review the record and issue a written decision on the appeal; and

(c) Within 7 days of a decision by the Principal Deputy Assistant Secretary—Indian Affairs, the Secretary will provide a written copy of the decision to the tribe and other participating parties.

§ 224.183 What other administrative appeals processes also apply?

The administrative appeal processes in 25 CFR part 2 and 43 CFR part 4, subject to the limitations in § 224.184, apply to:

(a) An interested party's appeal from an adverse decision or inaction by the Principal Deputy Assistant Secretary—Indian Affairs under § 224.182; and

(b) An appeal by a tribe or a person or entity that has entered into a lease, business agreement, or right-of-way from an adverse decision by or the inaction of a Departmental official taken under this part.

§ 224.184 How do other administrative appeals processes apply?

The administrative appeals process in 25 CFR part 2 and 43 CFR part 4 are modified, only as they apply to appeals under this part, as set forth in this section.

(a) The definition of interested party in 25 CFR part 2 and as incorporated in 43 CFR part 4 does not apply to this part.

(b) The right of persons or entities other than an appealing party to participate in appeals under 25 CFR part 2 and 43 CFR part 4 does not apply to this part, except as permitted under paragraph (c) of this section.

(c) The only persons or entities, other than appealing parties, under § 224.181(a) to (c), who may participate in an appeal under this part are:

(1) The Secretary, if an appeal is taken from a decision of the Director or Principal Deputy Assistant Secretary—Indian Affairs;

(2) A tribe, which may intervene, appear as an amicus curiae, or otherwise appear in any appeal taken under this part by a person or entity who has entered into a lease, business agreement, or right-of-way with the tribe or by an interested party under this part; or

(3) A person or entity that has entered into a lease, business agreement, or right-of-way with a tribe, may intervene, appear as an amicus curiae, or otherwise appear in any appeal taken

under this part by the tribe or by an interested party under this part.

(d) The Secretary does not have an obligation to provide notice and service upon non-appealing persons as provided in 25 CFR part 2 and 43 CFR part 4. The only exception to this principle is that notice and service of all documents must be served consistent with the requirements of 25 CFR part 2 and 43 CFR part 4 on those persons or entities identified in paragraph (c) of this section.

§ 224.185 When are decisions under this part effective?

Decisions under subpart I are effective as follows:

(a) Decisions of the Secretary disapproving a final proposed TERA or a revised final proposed TERA under subpart C of this part, a finding of imminent jeopardy to a physical trust asset under subpart F of this part, and decisions by the Secretary or the Assistant Secretary—Indian Affairs to reassume activities under subpart G of this part are final for the Department. These decisions and findings are effective upon issuance.

(b) Decisions under this part, other than those in paragraph (a) of this section, that adversely affect a tribe and for which an appeal is pending are not final for the Department and are not effective while the appeal is pending, unless:

(1) The tribe had an opportunity for a hearing before the decision was issued;

(2) The tribe had a reasonable amount of time to comply with the TERA after the decision was issued; and

(3) The Interior Board of Indian Appeals (Board), the Secretary, or Assistant Secretary—Indian Affairs issued a written decision that, notwithstanding a reasonable period given the tribe to comply with the TERA, the tribe has failed to take the actions necessary to comply with the TERA.

(c) All other decisions rendered by the Board or the Assistant Secretary—Indian Affairs in an appeal from a Director's decision under subparts E, F, or G of this part are effective when issued.

PART 225—OIL AND GAS, GEOTHERMAL, AND SOLID MINERALS AGREEMENTS

Subpart A—General

Subpart B—Minerals Agreements

AUTHORITY: 25 U.S.C. 2, 9, and 2101–2108; and Sec. 701, Pub. L. 114–74, 129 Stat. 599.

SOURCE: 59 FR 14971, Mar. 30, 1994, unless otherwise noted.

Subpart A—General

§ 225.1 Purpose and scope.

(a) The regulations in this part, administered by the Bureau of Indian Affairs under the direction of the Secretary of the Interior, govern minerals agreements for the development of Indian-owned minerals entered into pursuant to the Indian Mineral Development Act of 1982, 25 U.S.C. 2101–2108

(IMDA). These regulations are applicable to the lands or interests in lands of any Indian tribe, individual Indian or Alaska native the title to which is held in trust by the United States or is subject to a restriction against alienation imposed by the United States. These regulations are intended to ensure that Indian mineral owners are permitted to enter into minerals agreements that will allow the Indian mineral owners to have more responsibility in overseeing and greater flexibility in disposing of their mineral resources, and to allow development in the manner which the Indian mineral owners believe will maximize their best economic interest and minimize any adverse environmental or cultural impact resulting from such development. Pursuant to section 4 of the IMDA (25 U.S.C. 2103(e)), as part of this greater flexibility, where the Secretary has approved a minerals agreement in compliance with the provisions of 25 U.S.C. chap. 23 and any other applicable provision of law, the United States shall not be liable for losses sustained by a tribe or individual Indian under such minerals agreement. However, as further stated in the IMDA, the Secretary continues to have a trust obligation to ensure that the rights of a tribe or individual Indian are protected in the event of a violation of the terms of any minerals agreement, and to uphold the duties of the United States as derived from the trust relationship and from any treaties, executive orders, or agreements between the United States and any Indian tribe.

(b) The regulations in this part shall become effective and in full force on April 29, 1994, and shall be subject to amendment at any time by the Secretary; *Provided*, that no such regulation that becomes effective after the date of approval of any minerals agreement shall operate to affect the duration of the minerals agreement, the rate of royalty or financial consideration, rental, or acreage unless agreed to by all parties to the minerals agreement.

(c) The regulations of the Bureau of Land Management, the Office of Surface Mining Reclamation and Enforcement, and the Minerals Management Service that are referenced in §§225.4, 225.5, and 225.6 are supplemental to these regulations, and apply to minerals agreements for development of Indian mineral resources unless specifically stated otherwise in this part or in other Federal regulations. To the extent the parties to a minerals agreement are able to provide reasonable provisions satisfactorily addressing the issues of valuation, method of payment, accounting, and auditing, governed by the Minerals Management Service regulations, the Secretary may approve alternate provisions in a minerals agreement.

(d) Nothing in these regulations is intended to prevent Indian tribes from exercising their lawful governmental authority to regulate the conduct of persons, businesses, or minerals operations within their territorial jurisdiction.

§225.2 Information collection.

It has been determined by the Office of Management and Budget that the Information Collection Requirements contained in part 225 do not require review under the Paperwork Reduction Act (44 U.S.C. 3501 *et seq.*).

§225.3 Definitions.

As used in this part, the following terms have the specified meaning except where otherwise indicated.

Area Director means the Bureau of Indian Affairs Official in charge of an Area Office.

Assistant Secretary—Indian Affairs means the Assistant Secretary—Indian Affairs of the Department of the Interior, a designee of the Secretary of the Interior who may be specifically authorized by the Secretary to disapprove minerals agreements (25 U.S.C. 2103(d)) and to issue orders of cessation and/or minerals agreement cancellations as final orders of the Department.

Authorized Officer means any employee of the Bureau of Land Management authorized by law or by lawful delegation of authority to perform the duties described herein and in 43 CFR parts 3160, 3180, 3260, 3280, 3480 and 3590.

Director's Representative means the Office of Surface Mining Reclamation and Enforcement Director's Representative authorized by law or by lawful delegation of authority to perform the duties described in 30 CFR part 750 and 25 CFR part 216.

Gas means any fluid, either combustible or noncombustible, that is produced in a natural state from the earth and that maintains a gaseous or rarefied state at ordinary temperature and pressure conditions.

Geothermal resources means: (1) All products of geothermal processes, including indigenous steam, hot water, and hot brines;

(2) Steam and other gases, hot water, and hot brines, resulting from water, gas, or other fluids artificially introduced into geothermal formations;

(3) Heat or other associated energy found in geothermal formations; and

(4) Any by-product derived therefrom.

In the best interest of the Indian mineral owner refers to the standards to be applied by the Secretary in considering whether to take administrative action affecting the interests of an Indian mineral owner. In considering whether it is "in the best interest of the Indian mineral owner" to take a certain action (such as approval of a minerals agreement or a unitization or communitization agreement) the Secretary shall consider any relevant factor, including, but not limited to: economic considerations, such as date of lease or minerals agreement expiration; probable financial effects on the Indian mineral owner; need for change in the terms of the existing minerals agreement; marketability of mineral products; and potential environmental, social and cultural effects.

Indian lands means any lands or interests in lands owned by any individual Indian or Alaska Native, Indian tribe, band, nation, pueblo, community, rancheria, colony, or other group, the title to which is held in trust by the United States or is subject to a restriction against alienation imposed by the United States.

Indian mineral owner means any individual Indian or Alaska Native, or Indian tribe, band, nation, pueblo, community, rancheria, colony, or other group that owns a mineral interest in oil and gas, geothermal resources or solid minerals, title to which is held in trust by the United States or is subject to a restriction against alienation imposed by the United States.

Indian surface owner means any individual Indian or Alaska Native, or Indian tribe, band, nation, pueblo, community, rancheria, colony, or other group that owns the surface estate in land the title to which is held in trust by the United States or is subject to a restriction against alienation imposed by the United States.

Indian tribe means any Indian tribe, band, nation, pueblo, community, rancheria, colony, or other group that owns land or interests in land the title to which is held in trust by the United States or is subject to a restriction against alienation imposed by the United States.

Individual Indian means any individual Indian or Alaska Native who owns land or interests in land the title to which is held in trust by the United States or is subject to a restriction against alienation imposed by the United States.

Minerals includes both metalliferous and non-metalliferous minerals; all hydrocarbons, including oil and gas, coal and lignite of all ranks; geothermal resources; and includes but is not limited to sand, gravel, pumice, cinders, granite, building stone, limestone, clay, silt, or any other energy or non-energy mineral.

Minerals agreement means any joint venture, operating, production sharing, service, managerial, lease (other than a lease entered into pursuant to the Act of May 11, 1938, or the Act of March 3, 1909), contract, or other minerals agreement; or any amendment, supplement or other modification of such minerals agreement, providing for the exploration for, or extraction, processing, or other development of minerals in which an Indian mineral owner owns a beneficial or restricted interest, or providing for the sale or other disposition of the production or products of such minerals.

Minerals Management Service official means any employee of the Minerals Management Service authorized by law or by lawful delegation of authority to perform the duties described in 30 CFR chapter II, subchapters A and C.

Mining means the science, technique, and business of mineral development, including, but not limited to: opencast work, underground work, in-situ leaching, or other methods directed to severance and treatment of minerals; however, when sand, gravel, pumice, cinders, granite, building stone, limestone, clay or silt is the subject mineral, an enterprise is considered "mining" only if the extraction of such a mineral exceeds 5,000 cubic yards in any given year.

Oil means all non-gaseous hydrocarbon substances other than coal, oil shale, or gilsonite (including all vein-type solid hydrocarbons). Oil includes liquefiable hydrocarbon substances such as drip gasoline and other natural condensates recovered or recoverable in a liquid state from produced gas without resorting to a manufacturing process.

Operator means a person, proprietorship, partnership, corporation, or other business entity that has entered into an approved minerals agreement under the authority of the Indian Mineral Development Act of 1982, or who has been assigned an obligation to make royalty or other payments required by the minerals agreement.

Secretary means the Secretary of the Interior or an authorized representative, except that as used in §225.22 (e) and (f) the authorized representative may only be the Assistant Secretary for Indian Affairs (25 U.S.C. 2103(d)).

Solid minerals means all minerals excluding oil, gas, and geothermal resources.

Superintendent means the Bureau of Indian Affairs official in charge of an agency office.

§225.4 Authority and responsibility of the Bureau of Land Management (BLM).

The functions of the Bureau of Land Management are found in 43 CFR part 3160—Onshore Oil and Gas Operations, 43 CFR part 3180—Onshore Oil and Gas Unit Agreements: Unproven Areas, 43 CFR part 3260—Geothermal Resources Operations, 43 CFR part 3280—Geothermal Resources Unit Agreements: Unproven Areas, 43 CFR part 3480—Coal Exploration and Mining Operations, and 43 CFR part 3590—Solid Minerals (Other Than Coal) Exploration and Mining Operations. These functions include, but are not limited to, resource evaluation, approval of drilling permits, approval of mining, reclamation, and production plans, mineral appraisals, inspection and enforcement, and production verification. These regulations, as amended, apply to minerals agreements approved under this part.

§225.5 Authority and responsibility of the Office of Surface Mining Reclamation and Enforcement (OSMRE).

The OSMRE is the regulatory authority for surface coal mining and reclamation operations on Indian lands pursuant to the Surface Mining Control and Reclamation Act of 1977 (30 U.S.C. 1201 *et seq.*). The relevant regulations for surface mining and reclamation operations are found in 30 CFR part 750 and 25 CFR part 216. These regulations, as amended, apply to minerals agreements approved under this part.

§225.6 Authority and responsibility of the Minerals Management Service (MMS).

The functions of the MMS for reporting, accounting, and auditing are found in 30 CFR chapter II, subchapters A and C. These regulations, unless specifically stated otherwise in this part or in other regulations, apply to all minerals agreements approved under this part. To the extent the parties to a minerals agreement are able to provide reasonable provisions satisfactorily addressing the issues or functions governed by the MMS regulations relating to valuation of mineral product, method of payment, accounting procedures, and auditing procedures, the Secretary may approve alternate provisions in a minerals agreement.

Subpart B—Minerals Agreements

§225.20 Authority to contract.

(a) Any Indian tribe, subject to the approval of the Secretary and any limitation or provision contained in its constitution or charter, may enter into a minerals agreement with respect to mineral resources in which the tribe owns a beneficial or restricted interest.

(b) Any individual Indian owning a beneficial or restricted interest in mineral resources may include those resources in a tribal minerals agreement subject to the concurrence of the parties and a finding by the Secretary that inclusion of the resources is in the best interest of the individual Indian mineral owner.

§ 225.21 Negotiation procedures.

(a) An Indian mineral owner that wishes to enter into a minerals agreement may ask the Secretary for advice, assistance, and information during the negotiation process. The Secretary shall provide advice, assistance, and information to the extent allowed by available resources.

(b) No particular form of minerals agreement is prescribed. In preparing the minerals agreement the Indian mineral owner shall, if applicable, address provisions including, but not limited to, the following:

(1) A general statement identifying the parties to the minerals agreement, the legal description of the lands, including, if applicable, rock intervals or thicknesses subject to the minerals agreement, and the purposes of the minerals agreement;

(2) A statement setting forth the duration of the minerals agreement;

(3) A statement providing indemnification to the Indian mineral owner(s) and the United States from all claims, liabilities and causes of action that may be made by persons not a party to the minerals agreement;

(4) Provisions setting forth the obligations of the contracting parties;

(5) Provisions describing the methods of disposition of production;

(6) Provisions outlining the method of payment and amount of compensation to be paid;

(7) Provisions establishing accounting and mineral valuation procedures;

(8) Provisions establishing operating and management procedures;

(9) Provisions establishing any limitations on assignment of interests, including any right of first refusal by the Indian mineral owner in the event of a proposed assignment;

(10) Bond requirements;

(11) Insurance requirements;

(12) Provisions establishing audit procedures;

(13) Provisions for resolving disputes;

(14) A force majeure provision;

(15) Provisions describing the rights of the parties to terminate or suspend the minerals agreement, and the procedures to be followed in the event of termination or suspension;

(16) Provisions describing the nature and schedule of the activities to be conducted by the parties;

(17) Provisions describing the proposed manner and time of performance of future abandonment, reclamation and restoration activities;

(18) Provisions for reporting production and sales;

(19) Provisions for unitizing or communitizing of lands included in a minerals agreement for the purpose of promoting conservation and efficient utilization of natural resources;

(20) Provisions for protection of the minerals agreement lands from drainage and/or unauthorized taking of mineral resources; and

(21) Provisions for record keeping.

(c) In order to avoid delays in obtaining approval, the Indian mineral owner is encouraged to confer with the Secretary prior to formally executing the minerals agreement, and seek advice as to whether the minerals agreement appears to satisfy the requirements of § 225.22, or whether additions or corrections may be required in order to obtain Secretarial approval.

(d) The executed minerals agreement, together with a copy of a tribal resolution authorizing tribal officers to enter into the minerals agreement, shall be forwarded by the tribal representative to the appropriate Superintendent, or in the absence of a Superintendent to the Area Director, for approval.

§ 225.22 Approval of minerals agreements.

(a) A minerals agreement submitted for approval pursuant to § 225.21(d) shall be approved or disapproved within:

(1) One hundred and eighty (180) days after submission, or

(2) Sixty (60) days after compliance, if required, with section 102(2)(C) of the National Environmental Policy Act of 1969 (42 U.S.C. 4332(2)(C)) or any other

requirement of Federal law, whichever is later.

(b) At least thirty (30) days prior to approval or disapproval of any minerals agreement, the affected Indian mineral owners shall be provided with written findings forming the basis of the Secretary's intent to approve or disapprove the minerals agreement.

(1) The written findings shall include an environmental study which meets the requirements of §225.24 and an economic assessment, as described in §225.23.

(2) The Secretary shall include in the written findings any recommendations for changes to the minerals agreement needed to qualify it for approval.

(3) The 30-day period shall commence to run as of the date the written findings are received by the Indian mineral owner.

(4) Notwithstanding any other law, such findings and all projections, studies, data or other information (other than the environmental study required by §225.24) possessed by the Department of the Interior regarding the terms and conditions of the minerals agreement; the financial return to the Indian parties thereto; the extent, nature, value or disposition of the mineral resources; or the production, products or proceeds thereof, shall be held by the Department of the Interior as privileged and proprietary information of the affected Indian mineral owners. The letter containing the written findings should be headed with: PRIVILEGED PROPRIETARY INFORMATION OF THE (names of Indian mineral owners).

(c) A minerals agreement shall be approved if, at the Secretary's discretion, it is determined that the following conditions are met:

(1) The minerals agreement is in the best interest of the Indian mineral owner;

(2) The minerals agreement does not have adverse cultural, social, or environmental impacts sufficient to outweigh its expected benefits to the Indian mineral owners; and,

(3) The minerals agreement complies with the requirements of this part and all other applicable regulations and the provisions of applicable Federal law.

(d) The determinations required by paragraph (c) of this section shall be based on the written findings required by paragraph (b) and paragraphs (b)(1) through (b)(4), inclusive, of this section. The question of "best interest" within the meaning of paragraph (c)(1) of this section shall be determined by the Secretary based on information obtained from the parties, and any other information considered relevant by the Secretary, including, but not limited to, a review of comparable contemporary contractual arrangements or offers for the development of similar mineral resources received by Indian mineral owners, by non-Indian mineral owners, or by the Federal Government, insofar as that information is readily available.

(e) If a Superintendent or Area Director believes that a minerals agreement should not be approved, a written statement of the reasons why the minerals agreement should not be approved shall be prepared and forwarded, together with the minerals agreement, the written findings required by paragraph (b) and subparagraphs (b)(1) through (b)(4), inclusive, of this section, and all other pertinent documents, to the Secretary for a decision with a copy to the affected Indian mineral owner.

(f) The Secretary shall review any minerals agreement referred with a recommendation that it be disapproved, and the Secretary's decision to disapprove a minerals agreement shall be deemed a final Federal agency action (25 U.S.C. 2103(d)).

§225.23 Economic assessments.

The Secretary shall prepare or cause to be prepared an economic assessment that shall address, among other things:

(a) Whether there are assurances in the minerals agreement that operations shall be conducted with appropriate diligence;

(b) Whether the production royalties or other form of return on mineral resources is adequate; and

(c) Whether the minerals agreement is likely to provide the Indian mineral owner with a return on the production comparable to what the owner might otherwise obtain through competitive bidding, when such a comparison can reasonably be made.

§ 225.24 Environmental studies.

(a) The Secretary shall ensure that all environmental studies are prepared as required by the National Environmental Policy Act of 1969 (NEPA) and the regulations promulgated by the Council on Environmental Quality (CEQ) found at 40 CFR parts 1500–1508.

(b) The Secretary shall ensure that all necessary surveys are performed and clearances obtained in accordance with 36 CFR parts 60, 63, and 800 and with the requirements of the Archaeological and Historic Preservation Act (16 U.S.C. 469 *et seq.*), the National Historic Preservation Act (16 U.S.C. 470 *et seq.*), the American Indian Religious Freedom Act (42 U.S.C. 1996), and Executive Order 11593 (3 CFR 1971–1975 Comp., p. 559, May 13, 1971). If these surveys indicate that a mineral development will have an adverse effect on a property listed on or eligible for listing on the National Register of Historic Places, the Secretary shall:

(1) Seek the comments of the Advisory Council on Historic Preservation, in accordance with 36 CFR part 800;

(2) Ensure that the property is avoided, that the adverse effect is mitigated, or that appropriate excavations or other related research is conducted; and

(3) Ensure that complete data describing the historic property is preserved.

§ 225.25 Resolution of disputes.

A minerals agreement shall contain provisions for resolving disputes that may arise between the parties. However, no such provision shall limit the Secretary's authority or ability to ensure that the rights of an Indian mineral owner are protected in the event of a violation of the provisions of the minerals agreement by any other party to the minerals agreement.

§ 225.26 Auditing and accounting.

The Secretary may conduct audits relating to the scope, nature and extent of compliance with the minerals agreement and with applicable regulations and orders to lessees, operators, revenue payors, and other persons with rental, royalty, net profit share and other payment requirements arising from the provisions of a minerals agreement. Procedures and standards used for accounting and auditing of minerals agreements will be in accordance with audit standards established by the Comptroller General of the United States, in "Standards for Auditing of Governmental Organizations, Programs, Activities, and Functions, 1981," and standards established by the American Institute of Certified Public Accountants.

§ 225.27 Forms and reports.

Any forms required to be filed pursuant to a minerals agreement may be obtained from the Superintendent or Area Director. Prescribed forms for filing geothermal production reports required by the BLM (43 CFR part 3260, §§ 3264.1, 3264.2–4 and 3264.2–5) may be obtained from the Superintendent, Area Director, or the Authorized Officer. Applicable reports required by the MMS shall be filed using the forms prescribed in 30 CFR part 210, which are available from MMS. Guidance on how to prepare and submit required information, collection reports, and forms to MMS is available from: Minerals Management Service, Attention: Lessee (or Reporter) Contact Branch, P.O. Box 5760, Denver, Colorado 80217. Additional reporting requirements may be required by the Secretary.

§ 225.28 Approval of amendments to minerals agreements.

An amendment, modification or supplement to a minerals agreement entered into pursuant to the regulations in this part, whether the minerals agreement was approved before or after the effective date of these regulations, must be approved in writing by all parties before being submitted to the Secretary for approval. The provisions of § 225.22 apply to approvals of amendments, modifications, or supplements to minerals agreements entered into under the regulations in this part. However, amendments, modifications, or supplements that do not substantially alter or affect the factors listed in § 225.22(c), may be approved by referencing materials previously submitted for the initial review and approval of the minerals agreement. The Secretary may approve an amendment, modification, or supplement if it is determined that the underlying minerals agreement, as amended, modified, or supplemented meets the criteria for approval set forth in § 225.22(c).

§ 225.29 Corporate qualifications and requests for information.

(a) The signing in a representative capacity of minerals agreements or assignments, bonds, or other instruments required by a minerals agreement or these regulations, constitutes certification that the individual signing (except a surety agent) is authorized to act in such a capacity. An agent for a surety shall furnish a power of attorney.

(b) A prospective corporate operator proposing to acquire an interest in a minerals agreement shall have on file with the Superintendent a statement showing:

(1) The State(s) in which the corporation is incorporated, and a notarized statement that the corporation is authorized to hold such interests in the State where the land described in the minerals agreement is situated; and

(2) A notarized statement that it has power to conduct all business and operations as described in the minerals agreement.

(c) The Secretary may, either before or after the approval of a minerals agreement, assignment, or bond, call for any reasonable additional information necessary to carry out the regulations in this part, or other applicable laws and regulations.

§ 225.30 Bonds.

(a) Bonds required by provisions of a minerals agreement should be in an amount sufficient to ensure compliance with all of the requirements of the minerals agreement and the statutes and regulations applicable to the minerals agreement. Surety bonds shall be issued by a qualified company approved by the Department of the Treasury (see Department of the Treasury Circular No. 570).

(b) An operator may file a $75,000 bond for all geothermal, mining, or oil and gas minerals agreements in any one State, which may also include areas on that part of an Indian reservation extending into any contiguous State. Statewide bonds shall be filed for approval with the Secretary.

(c) An operator may file a $150,000 bond for full nationwide coverage to cover all geothermal or oil and gas minerals agreements without geographic or acreage limitation to which the operator is or may become a party. Nationwide bonds shall be filed for approval with the Secretary.

(d) Personal bonds shall be accompanied by:

(1) Certificate of deposit issued by a financial institution, the deposits of which are Federally insured, explicitly granting the Secretary full authority to demand immediate payment in case of default in the performance of the provisions and conditions of the minerals agreement. The certificate shall explicitly indicate on its face that Secretarial approval is required prior to redemption of the certificate of deposit by any party;

(2) Cashier's check;

(3) Certified check;

(4) Negotiable Treasury securities of the United States of a value equal to the amount specified in the bond. Negotiable Treasury securities shall be accompanied by a proper conveyance to the Secretary of full authority to sell such securities in case of default in the performance of the provisions and conditions of a minerals agreement; or

(5) Letter of credit issued by a financial institution authorized to do business in the United States and whose deposits are Federally insured, and identifying the Secretary as sole payee with full authority to demand immediate payment in the case of default in the performance of the provisions and conditions of a minerals agreement.

(i) The letter of credit shall be irrevocable during its term.

(ii) The letter of credit shall be payable to the Bureau of Indian Affairs on demand, in part or in full, upon receipt from the Secretary of a notice of attachment stating the basis thereof (e.g., default in compliance with the minerals agreement provisions and conditions or failure to file a replacement in accordance with subparagraph (d)(5)(v) of this section).

(iii) The initial expiration date of the letter of credit shall be at least one (1) year following the date it is filed in the proper Bureau of Indian Affairs office.

(iv) The letter of credit shall contain a provision for automatic renewal for periods of not less than one (1) year in the absence of notice to the proper Bureau of Indian Affairs office at least ninety (90) days prior to the originally stated or any extended expiration date.

(v) A letter of credit used as security for any minerals agreement upon which operations have taken place and final approval for abandonment has not been given, or as security for a statewide or nationwide bond, shall be forfeited and shall be collected by the Secretary if not replaced by other suitable bond or letter of credit at least thirty (30) days before its expiration date.

(e) The required amount of a bond may be increased in any particular case at the discretion of the Secretary.

[59 FR 14971, Mar. 30, 1994; 60 FR 10474, Feb. 24, 1995]

§ 225.31 Manner of payments.

Unless specified otherwise in the minerals agreement, after production has been established, all payments due for royalties, bonuses, rentals and other payments under a minerals agreement shall be made to the Secretary or such other party as may be designated, and shall be made at such time as provided in 30 CFR chapter II, subchapters A and C. Prior to production, all bonus and rental payments, shall be made to the Superintendent or Area Director.

§ 225.32 Permission to start operations.

(a) No exploration, drilling, or mining operations are permitted on any Indian lands before the Secretary has granted written approval of the minerals agreement pursuant to the regulations. After a minerals agreement is approved, written permission to start operations must be secured by applying for the permits referred to in paragraph (b) of this section.

(b) Applicable permits in accordance with rules and regulations in 30 CFR part 750, 43 CFR parts 3160, 3260, 3480, 3590, and Orders or Notices to Lessees (NTL) issued thereunder shall be required before actual operations are conducted on the minerals agreement acreage.

§ 225.33 Assignment of minerals agreements.

An assignment of a minerals agreement, or any interest therein, shall not be valid without the approval of the Secretary and, if required in the minerals agreement, the Indian mineral owner. The assignee must be qualified to hold the minerals agreement and shall furnish a satisfactory bond conditioned on the faithful performance of the covenants and conditions thereof as stipulated in the minerals agreement. A fully executed copy of the assignment shall be filed with the Secretary within five (5) working days after execution by all parties. The Secretary may permit the release of any bonds executed by the assignor upon submission of satisfactory bonds to the Bureau of Indian Affairs by the assignee, and a determination that the assignor has satisfied all accrued obligations.

§ 225.34 [Reserved]

§ 225.35 Inspection of premises; books and accounts.

(a) Operators shall allow Indian mineral owners, their authorized representatives, or any authorized representatives of the Secretary to enter all parts of the minerals agreement area for the purpose of inspection. Operators shall keep a full and correct account of all operations and submit all related reports required by the minerals agreement and applicable regulations. Books and records shall be available for inspection during regular business hours.

(b) Operators shall provide records to the Minerals Management Service (MMS) in accordance with MMS regulations and guidelines. All records pertaining to a minerals agreement shall be maintained by an operator in accordance with 30 CFR part 212.

(c) Operators shall provide records to the Authorized Officer in accordance with BLM regulations and guidelines.

(d) Operators shall provide records to the Director's Representative in accordance with OSMRE regulations and guidelines.

§225.36 Minerals agreement cancellation; Bureau of Indian Affairs notice of noncompliance.

(a) If the Secretary determines that an operator has failed to comply with the regulations in this part; other applicable laws or regulations; the terms of the minerals agreement; the requirements of an approved exploration, drilling or mining plan; Secretarial orders; or the orders of the Authorized Officer, the Director's Representative, or the MMS Official, the Secretary may:

(1) Serve a notice of noncompliance; or

(2) Serve a notice of proposed cancellation.

(b) The notice of noncompliance shall specify in what respect the operator has failed to comply with the requirements referenced in paragraph (a), and shall specify what actions, if any, must be taken to correct the noncompliance.

(c) The notice of proposed cancellation shall set forth the reasons why cancellation is proposed.

(d) The notice of proposed cancellation or noncompliance shall be served upon the operator by delivery in person or by certified mail to the operator at the operator's last known address. When certified mail is used, the date of service shall be deemed to be when received or five (5) working days after the date it is mailed, whichever is earlier.

(e) The operator shall have thirty (30) days (or such longer time as specified in the notice) from the date that the Bureau of Indian Affairs notice of proposed cancellation or noncompliance is served to respond, in writing, to the Superintendent or Area Director actually issuing the notice.

(f) If an operator fails to take any action that may be prescribed in the notice of proposed cancellation, fails to file a timely written response to the notice, or files a written response that does not, in the discretion of the Secretary, adequately justify the operator's failure to comply, then the Secretary may cancel the minerals agreement, specifying the basis for the cancellation. Cancellation of a minerals agreement shall not relieve the operator of any continuing obligation under the minerals agreement.

(g) If an operator fails to take corrective action or to file a timely written response adequately justifying the operator's actions pursuant to a notice of noncompliance, the Secretary may issue an order of cessation. If the operator fails to comply with the order of cessation, or fails to timely file an appeal of the order of cessation pursuant to paragraph (k) of this section, the Secretary may issue an order of minerals agreement cancellation.

(h) This section does not limit any other remedies of the Indian mineral owner as set forth in the minerals agreement.

(i) Nothing in this section is intended to limit the authority of the Authorized Officer, the Director's Representative, or the MMS Official to take any enforcement action authorized pursuant to statute or regulation.

(j) The Authorized Officer, the Director's Representative, the MMS Official, and the Superintendent or Area Director should consult with one another before taking any enforcement actions.

(k) If orders of cessation or minerals agreement cancellation issued pursuant to this section are issued by a designee of the Secretary other than the Assistant Secretary for Indian Affairs, the orders may be appealed under 25 CFR part 2. If the orders are issued by the Secretary or the Assistant Secretary for Indian Affairs, and not one of their delegates or subordinates, the orders are the final orders of the Department.

§225.37 Penalties.

(a) In addition to or in lieu of cancellation under §225.36, violations of the terms and conditions of any minerals agreement, the regulations in this part, other applicable laws or regulations, or failure to comply with a notice of noncompliance or a cessation order issued by the Secretary may subject an operator to a penalty of not more than $1,650 per day for each day that such a violation or noncompliance continues beyond the time limits prescribed for corrective action.

(b) A notice of a proposed penalty shall be served on the operator either personally or by certified mail to the operator at the operator's last known address. The date of service by certified mail shall be deemed to be the date received or five (5) working days after the date mailed, whichever is earlier.

(c) The notice shall specify the nature of the violation and the proposed penalty, and shall specifically advise the operator of the operator's right to either request a hearing within thirty (30) days of receipt of the notice or pay the proposed penalty. Hearings shall be held before the Superintendent or Area Director whose findings shall be conclusive, unless an appeal is taken pursuant to 25 CFR part 2. If within thirty (30) days of receipt of the notice of proposed penalty the operator has not requested a hearing or paid the amount of the proposed penalty, a final notice of penalty shall be served.

(d) If the person served with a notice of proposed penalty requests a hearing, penalties shall accrue each day the violations or noncompliance set forth in the notice continue beyond the time limits presented for corrective action. The Secretary may issue a written suspension of the requirement to correct the violations pending completion of the hearings provided by this section only upon a determination, at the discretion of the Secretary, that such a suspension will not be detrimental to the Indian mineral owner and upon submission and acceptance of a bond deemed adequate to indemnify the Indian mineral owner from loss or damage. The amount of the bond must be sufficient to cover the cost of correcting the violations set forth in the notice or any disputed amounts plus accrued penalties and interest.

(e) Payment of penalties in full more than ten (10) days after a final decision imposing a penalty shall subject the operator to late payment charges. Late payment charges shall be calculated on the basis of a percentage assessment rate of the amount unpaid per month for each month or fraction thereof until payment is received by the Secretary. In the absence of a specific minerals agreement provision prescribing a different rate, the interest rate on late payments and underpayments shall be a rate applicable under section 6621(a)(2) of the Internal Revenue Code of 1954. Interest shall be charged only on the amount of payment not received and only for the number of days the payment is late.

(f) None of the provisions of this section shall be interpreted as:

(1) Replacing or superseding the independent authority of the Authorized Officer, the Director's Representative, or the MMS Official to impose penalties under applicable statutory or regulatory authorities;

(2) Replacing, superseding, or replicating any penalty provision in the terms and conditions of a minerals agreement approved by the Secretary pursuant to this part; or

(3) Authorizing the imposition of a penalty for violations of minerals agreement provisions for which the Authorized Officer, Director's Representative, or MMS Official has either statutory or regulatory authority to assess a penalty.

[59 FR 14971, Mar. 30, 1994, as amended at 81 FR 42481, June 30, 2016; 82 FR 7652, Jan. 23, 2017; 83 FR 5195, Feb. 6, 2018]

§ 225.38 Appeals.

Appeals from decisions of Officials of the Bureau of Indian Affairs under this part may be taken pursuant to 25 CFR part 2.

§ 225.39 Fees.

(a) Unless otherwise authorized by the Secretary, each minerals agreement or assignment thereof, shall be accompanied by a filing fee of $75.00 at the time of filing.

(b) An Indian mineral owner shall not be required to pay a filing fee if the Indian mineral owner, pursuant to a provision in the existing minerals agreement, acquires an additional interest in that minerals agreement.

§ 225.40 Government employees cannot acquire minerals agreements.

U.S. Government employees are prevented from acquiring any interest(s) in minerals agreements by the provisions of 25 CFR part 140 and 43 CFR part 20 pertaining to conflicts of interest and ownership of an interest in trust land.

PART 226—LEASING OF OSAGE RESERVATION LANDS FOR OIL AND GAS MINING

AUTHORITY: Sec. 3, 34 Stat. 543; secs. 1, 2, 45 Stat. 1478; sec. 3, 52 Stat. 1034, 1035; sec. 2(a), 92 Stat. 1660; and Sec. 701, Pub. L. 114–74, 129 Stat. 599.

SOURCE: 81 FR 39573, June 17, 2016, unless otherwise noted.

§226.1 Definitions.

As used in this part 226, terms shall have the meanings set forth in this section.

(a) *Secretary* means the Secretary of the Interior or his authorized representative acting under delegated authority.

(b) *Osage Tribal Council* means the duly elected governing body of the Osage Nation or Tribe of Indians of Oklahoma vested with authority to lease or take other actions on oil and gas mining pertaining to the Osage Mineral Estate.

(c) *Superintendent* means the Superintendent of the Osage Agency, Pawhuska, Oklahoma, or his authorized representative acting under delegated authority.

(d) *Oil lessee* means any person, firm, or corporation to whom an oil mining lease is made under the regulations in this part.

(e) *Gas lessee* means any person, firm, or corporation to whom a gas mining lease is made under the regulations in this part.

(f) *Oil and gas lessee* means any person, firm, or corporation to whom an oil and gas mining lease is made under the regulations in this part.

(g) *Primary term* means the basic period of time for which a lease is issued during which the lease contract may be kept in force by payment of rentals.

(h) *Major purchaser* means any one of the minimum number of purchasers taking 95 percent of the oil in Osage County, Oklahoma. Any oil purchased by a purchaser from itself, its subsidiaries, partnerships, associations, or other corporations in which it has a financial or management interest shall be excluded from the determination of a major purchaser.

(i) *Casinghead gas* means gas produced from an oil well as a consequence of oil production from the same formation.

(j) *Natural gas* means any fluid, either combustible or noncombustible, recovered at the surface in the gaseous phase and/or hydrocarbons recovered at the surface as liquids which are the result of condensation caused by reduction of pressure and temperature of hydrocarbons originally existing in a reservoir in the gaseous phase.

(k) *Authorized representative of an oil lessee, gas lessee, or oil and gas lessee* means any person, group, or groups of persons, partnership, association, company, corporation, organization or agent employed by or contracted with a lessee or any subcontractor to conduct oil and gas operations or provide facilities to market oil and gas.

(l) *Oil well* means any well which produces one (1) barrel or more of crude petroleum oil for each 15,000 standard cubic feet of natural gas.

(m) *Gas well* means any well which:

(1) Produces natural gas not associated with crude petroleum oil at the time of production or

(2) Produces more than 15,000 standard cubic feet of natural gas to each barrel of crude petroleum oil from the same producing formation.

Leasing Procedure, Rental and Royalty

§ 226.2 Sale of leases.

(a) Written application, together with any nomination fee, for tracts to be offered for lease shall be filed with the Superintendent.

(b) The Superintendent, with the consent of the Osage Tribal Council, shall publish notices for the sale of oil leases, gas leases, and oil and gas leases to the highest responsible bidder on specific tracts of the unleased Osage Mineral Estate. The Superintendent may require any bidder to submit satisfactory evidence of his good faith and ability to comply with all provisions of the notice of sale. Successful bidders must deposit with the Superintendent on day of sale a check or cash in an amount not less than 25 percent of the cash bonus offered as a guaranty of good faith. Any and all bids shall be subject to the acceptance of the Osage Tribal Council and approval of the Superintendent. Within 20 days after notification of being the successful bidder, and said bidder must submit to the Superintendent the balance of the cash bonus, a $10 filing fee, and the lease in completed form. The Superintendent may extend the time for the completion and submission of the lease form, but no extension shall be granted for remitting the balance of moneys due. If the bidder fails to pay the full cash consideration within said period or fails to file the completed lease within said period or extention thereof, or if the lease is rejected through no fault of the Osage Tribal Council or the Superintendent, 25 percent of the cash bonus bid will be forfeited for the use and benefits of the Osage Tribe. The Superintendent may reject a lease made on an accepted bid, upon evidence satisfactory to him of collusion, fraud, or other irregularity in connection with the notice of sale. The Superintendent may approve oil leases, gas leases, and oil and gas leases made by the Osage Tribal Council in conformity with the notice of sale, regulations in this part, bonds, and other instruments required.

(c) Each oil and/or gas lease and activities and installations associated therewith subject to these regulations shall be assessed and evaluated for its environmental impact prior to its approval by the Superintendent.

(d) Lessee shall accept a lease with the understanding that a mineral not covered by his lease may be leased separately.

(e) No lease, assignment thereof, or interest therein will be approved to any employee or employees of the Government and no such employee shall be permitted to acquire any interest in leases covering the Osage Mineral Estate by ownership of stock in corporations having leases or in any other manner.

(f) The Osage Tribal Council may utilize the following procedures among others, in entering into a mining lease. A contract may be entered into through competitive bidding as outlined in §226.2(b), negotiation, or a combination of both. The Osage Tribal Council may also request the Superintendent to undertake the preparation, advertisement and negotiation. The Superintendent may approve any such contract made by the Osage Tribal Council.

§226.3 Surrender of lease.

Lessee may, with the approval of the Superintendent and payment of a $10 filing fee, surrender all or any portion of any lease, have the lease cancelled as to the portion surrendered and be relieved from all subsequent obligations and liabilities. If the lease, or portion being surrendered, is owned in undivided interests by more than one party, then all parties shall join in the application for cancellation: *Provided*, That if this lease has been recorded, Lessee shall execute a release and record the same in the proper office. Such surrender shall not entitle Lessee to a refund of the unused portion of rental paid in lieu of development, nor shall it relieve Lessee and his sureties of any obligation and liability incurred prior to such surrender: *Provided further*, That when there is a partial surrender of any lease and the acreage to be retained is less than 160 acres or there is a surrender of a separate horizon, such surrender shall become only with the consent of the Osage Tribal Council and approval of the Superintendent.

§226.4 Form of payment.

Sums due under a lease contract and/or the regulations in this part shall be paid by cash or check made payable to the Bureau of Indian Affairs and delivered to the Osage Agency, Pawhuska, Oklahoma 74056. Such sums shall be a prior lien on all equipment and unsold oil on the leased premises.

§226.5 Leases subject to current regulations.

Leases issued pursuant to this part shall be subject to the current regulations of the Secretary, all of which are made a part of such leases: *Provided*, That no amendment or change of such regulations made after the approval of any lease shall operate to affect the term of the lease, rate of royalty, rental, or acreage unless agreed to by both parties and approved by the Superintendent.

§226.6 Bonds.

Lessees shall furnish with each lease a corporate surety bond acceptable to the Superintendent as follows:

(a) A bond on Form D shall be filed with each lease submitted for approval. Such bond shall be in an amount of not less than $5,000 for each quarter section or fractional quarter section covered by said lease: *Provided, however*, That one bond in the penal sum or not less than $50,000 may be filed on Form G covering all oil, gas and combination oil and gas leases not in excess of 10,240 acres to which Lessee is or may become a party.

(b) In lieu of the bonds required under paragraph (a) of this section, a bond in the penal sum of $150,000 may be filed on Form 5–5438 for full nationwide coverage of all leases, without geographic or acreage limitation, to which the Lessee is or may become a party.

(c) A bond on Form H shall be filed in an amount of not less than $5,000 covering a lease acquired through assignment where the assignee does not have a collective bond on form G or nationwide bond, or the corporate surety does not execute its consent to remain bound under the original bond given to secure the faithful performance of the terms and conditions of the lease.

(d) The right is specifically reserved to increase the amount of bonds prescribed in paragraphs (a) and (c) of this section in any particular case when the Superintendent deems it proper. The nationwide bond may be increased at any time in the discretion of the Secretary.

§ 226.7 Provisions of forms made a part of the regulations.

Leases, assignments, and supporting instruments shall be in the form prescribed by the Secretary, and such forms are hereby made a part of the regulations.

§ 226.8 Corporation and corporate information.

(a) If the applicant for a lease is a corporation, it shall file evidence of authority of its officers to execute papers; and with its first application it shall also file a certified copy of its Articles of Incorporation and, if foreign to the State of Oklahoma, evidence showing compliance with the corporation laws thereof.

(b) Whenever deemed advisable the Superintendent may require a corporation to file any additional information necessary to carry out the purpose and intent of the regulations in this part, and such information shall be furnished within a reasonable time.

§ 226.9 Rental and drilling obligations.

(a) Oil leases, gas leases, and combination oil and gas leases. Unless Lessee shall complete and place on production a well producing and selling oil and/or gas in paying quantities on the land embraced within the lease within 12 months from the date of approval of the lease, or as otherwise provided in the lease terms, or 12 months from the date the Superintendent consents to drilling on any restricted homestead selection, the lease shall terminate unless rental at the rate of not less than $1 per acre for an oil or gas lease, or not less than $2.00 per acre for a combination oil and gas lease, shall be paid before the end of the first year of the lease. The lease may also be held for the remainder of its primary term without drilling upon payment of the specified rental annually in advance, commencing with the second lease year. The lease shall terminate as of the due date of the rental unless such rental shall be received by the Superintendent, or shall have been mailed as indicated by postmark on or before said date. The completion of a well producing in paying quantities shall, for so long as such production continues, relieve Lessee from any further payment of rental, except that should such production cease during the primary term the lease may be continued only during the remaining primary term of the lease by payment of advance rental which shall commence on the next anniversary date of the lease. Rental shall be paid on the basis of a full year and no refund will be made of advance rental paid in compliance with the regulations in this part: *Provided,* That the Superintendent in his discretion may order further development of any leased acreage or separate horizon if, in his opinion, a prudent operator would conduct further development. If Lessee refuses to comply, the refusal will be considered a violation of the lease terms and said lease shall be subject to cancellation as to the acreage or horizon the further development of which was ordered: *Provided further,* That the Superintendent may impose restrictions as to time of drilling and rate of production from any well or wells when in his judgment, such action may be necessary or proper for the protection of the natural resources of the leased land and the interests of the Osage Tribe. The superintendent may consider, among other things, Federal and Oklahoma laws regulating either drilling or production. If a lessee holds both an oil lease and a gas lease covering the same acreage, such lessee is subject to the provisions of this section as to both the oil lease and the gas lease.

(b) The Superintendent may, with the consent of and under terms approved by the Osage Tribal Council, grant an extension of the primary term of a lease on which the actual drilling of a well shall have commenced within the term thereof or for the purpose of enabling Lessee to obtain a market for his oil and/or gas production.

§ 226.10 Term of lease.

Leases issued hereunder shall be for a primary term as established by the Osage Tribal Council, approved by the Superintendent, and so stated in the notice of sale of such leases and so long thereafter as the minerals specified are produced in paying quantities.

§ 226.11 Royalty payments.

(a) *Royalty on oil*—(1) *Royalty rate.* Lessee shall pay or cause to be paid to the Superintendent, as royalty, the sum of not less than 162/3 percent of the gross proceeds from sales after deducting the oil used by Lessee for development and operation purposes on the lease: *Provided*, That when the quantity of oil taken from all the producing wells on any quarter-section or fraction thereof, according to the public survey, during any calendar month is sufficient to average one hundred or more barrels per active producing well per day the royalty on such oil shall be not less than 20 percent. The Osage Tribal Council may, upon presentation of justifiable economic evidence by Lessee, agree to a revised royalty rate subject to approval by the Superintendent, applicable to additional oil produced from a lease or leases by enhanced recovery methods, which rate shall not be less than 121/2 percent of the gross proceeds from sale of oil produced by enhanced recovery processes, other than gas injection, after deducting the oil used by Lessee for development and operating purposes on the lease or leases.

(2) Unless the Osage Tribal Council, with approval of the Secretary, shall elect to take the royalty in kind, payment is owing at the time of sale or removal of the oil, except where payments are made on division orders, and settlement shall be based on the actual selling price, but at not less than the highest posted price by a major purchaser (as defined in §226.1(h)) in Osage County, Oklahoma, who purchases production from Osage oil leases.

(3) Royalty in kind. Should Lessor, with approval of the Secretary, elect to take the royalty in kind, Lessee shall furnish free storage for royalty oil for a period not to exceed 60 days from date of production after notice of such election.

(b) *Royalty on gas*—(1) *Oil lease*. All casinghead gas shall belong to the oil Lessee subject to any rights under existing gas leases. All casinghead gas removed from the lease from which it is produced shall be metered unless otherwise approved by the Superintendent and be subject to a royalty of not less than 162/3 percent of the market value of the gas and all products extracted therefrom, less a reasonable allowance for manufacture or processing. If an oil Lessee supplies casinghead gas produced from one lease for operation and/or development of other leases, either his/hers or others, a royalty of not less than 162/3 percent shall be paid on the market value of all casinghead gas so used. All casinghead gas not utilized by the oil Lessee may, with the approval of the Superintendent, be utilized or sold by the gas Lessee, subject to the prescribed royalty of not less than 162/3 percent of the market value.

(2) *Gas lease*. Lessee shall pay a royalty of not less than 162/3 percent of the market value of all natural gas and products extracted therefrom produced and sold from his lease. Natural gas used in the reasonable and prudent operation and development of said lease shall be exempted from royalty payment.

(3) *Combination oil and gas lease*. Lessee shall pay royalty as provided in paragraphs (b)(1) and (2) of this section.

(c) *Minimum royalty*. In no event shall the royalty paid from producing leases during any year be less than an amount equal to the annual rental specified for the lease. Any underpayment of minimum royalty shall be due and payable within 45 days following the end of the lease year. After the primary term, Lessee shall submit with his payment evidence that the lease is producing in paying quantities. The Superintendent is authorized to determine whether the lease is actually producing in paying quantities or has terminated for lack of such production. Payment for any underpayment not made within the time specified shall be subject to a late charge at the rate of not less than 11/2 percent per month for each month or fraction thereof until paid.

§226.12 Government reserves right to purchase oil.

Any of the executive departments of the U.S. Government shall have the option to purchase all or any part of the oil produced from any lease at not less than the highest posted price as defined in §226.11.

§226.13 Time of royalty payments and reports.

(a) Royalty payments due may be paid by either purchaser or Lessee. Unless otherwise provided by the Osage

Tribal Council and approved by the Superintendent, all payments shall be due by the 25th day of each month and shall cover the sales of the preceding month. Failure to make such payments shall subject Lessee or purchaser, whoever is responsible for royalty payment, to a late charge at the rate of not less than 11/2 percent for each month or fraction thereof until paid. The Osage Tribal Council, subject to the approval of the Superintendent, may waive the late charges.

(b) Lessee shall furnish certified monthly reports by the 25th of each following month covering all operations, whether there has been production or not, indicating therein the total amount of oil, natural gas, casinghead gas, and other products subject to royalty payment.

(c) Failure to remit payments or reports shall subject Lessee to further penalties as provided in §§ 226.42 and 226.43 and shall subject the division order to cancellation.

§ 226.14 Contracts and division orders.

(a) Lessee may enter into division orders or contracts with the purchasers of oil, gas, or derivatives therefrom which will provide for the purchaser to make payment of royalty in accordance with his lease: *Provided*, That such division orders or contracts shall not relieve Lessee from responsibility for the payment of the royalty should the purchaser fail to pay. No production shall be removed from the leased premises until a division order and/or contract and its terms are approved by the Superintendent: *Provided further*, That the Superintendent may grant temporary permission to run oil or gas from a lease pending the approval of a division order or contract. Lessee shall file a certified monthly report and pay royalty on the value of all oil and gas used off the premises for development and operating purposes. Lessee shall be responsible for the correct measurement and reporting of all oil and/or gas taken from the leased premises.

(b) Lessee shall require the purchaser of oil and/or gas from his/her lease or leases to furnish the Superintendent, no later than the 25th day of each month, a statement reporting the gross barrels of oil and/or gross Mcf of gas sold during the preceding month. The Superintendent may authorize an extension of time, not to exceed 10 days, for furnishing this statement.

§ 226.15 Unit leases, assignments and related instruments.

(a) *Unitization of leases*. The Osage Tribal Council and Lessee or Lessees, may, with the approval of the Superintendent, unitize or merge, two or more oil or oil and gas leases into a unit or cooperative operating plan to promote the greatest ultimate recovery of oil and gas from a common source of supply or portion thereof embracing the lands covered by such lease or leases. The cooperative or unit agreement shall be subject to the regulations in this part and applicable laws governing the leasing of the Osage Mineral Estate. Any agreement between the parties in interest to terminate a unit or cooperative agreement as to all or any portion of the lands included shall be submitted to the Superintendent for his approval. Upon approval the leases included thereunder shall be restored to their original terms: *Provided*, That for the purpose of preventing waste and to promote the greatest ultimate recovery of oil and gas from a common source of supply or portion thereof, all oil leases, oil and gas leases, and gas leases issued heretofore and hereafter under the provisions of the regulations in this part shall be subject to any unit development plan affecting the leased lands that may be required by the Superintendent with the consent of the Osage Tribal Council, and which plan shall adequately protect the rights of all parties in interest including the Osage Mineral Estate.

(b) *Assignments*. Approved leases or any interest therein may be assigned or transferred only with the approval of the Superintendent. The assignee must be qualified to hold such lease under existing rules and regulations and shall furnish a satisfactory bond conditioned for the faithful performance of the covenants and conditions thereof. Lessee must assign either his entire interest in a lease or legal subdivision thereof, or an undivided interest in the whole lease: *Provided*, That when an assignment covers only a portion of a lease or covers interests in separate horizons such assignment shall be subject to both the consent of the Osage Tribal Council and approval of the Superintendent. If a lease is divided by the assignment of an entire interest in any part, each part shall be considered a separate lease and the assignee shall be bound to comply with all the terms and conditions of the original lease. A fully executed copy of the assignment shall be filed with the Superintendent within 30 days after the date of execution by all parties. If requested within the 30-day period, the Superintendent may grant an extension of 15 days. A filing fee of $10 shall accompany each assignment.

(c) *Overriding royalty.* Agreements creating overriding royalties or payments out of production shall not be considered as an interest in a lease as such term is used in paragraph (b) of this section. Agreements creating overriding royalties or payments out of production are hereby authorized and the approval of the Department of the Interior or any agency thereof shall not be required with respect thereto, but such agreements shall be subject to the condition that nothing in any such agreement shall be construed as modifying any of the obligations of Lessee under his lease and the regulations in this part. All such obligations are to remain in full force and effect, the same as if free of any such royalties or payments. The existence of agreements creating overriding royalties or payments out of production, whether or not actually paid, shall not be considered in justifying the shutdown or abandonment of any well. Agreements creating overriding royalties or payments out of production need not be filed with the Superintendent unless incorporated in assignments or instruments required to be filed pursuant to paragraph (b) of this section. An agreement creating overriding royalties or payment out of production shall be suspended when the working interest income per active producing well is equal to or less than the operational cost of the well, as determined by the Superintendent.

(d) *Drilling contracts.* The Superintendent is authorized to approve drilling contracts with a stipulation that such approval does not in any way bind the Department to approve subsequent assignments that may be provided for in said contracts. Approval merely authorizes entry on the lease for the purpose of development work.

(e) *Combining leases.* The lessee owning both an oil lease and gas lease covering the same acreage is authorized to convert such leases to a combination oil and gas lease.

OPERATIONS

§ 226.16 Commencement of operations.

(a) No operations shall be permitted upon any tract of land until a lease covering such tract shall have been approved by the Superintendent: *Provided,* That the Superintendent may grant authority to any party under such rules, consistent with the regulations in this part that he deems proper, to conduct geophysical and geological exploration work.

(b) Lessee shall submit applications on forms to be furnished by the Superintendent and secure his approval before:

(1) Well drilling, treating, or workover operations are started on the leased premises.

(2) Removing casing from any well.

(c) Lessee shall notify the Superintendent a reasonable time in advance of starting work, of intention to drill, redrill, deepen, plug, or abandon a well.

§ 226.17 How to acquire permission to begin operations on a restricted homestead allotment.

(a) Lessee may conduct operations within or upon a restricted homestead selection only with the written consent of the Superintendent.

(b) If the allottee is unwilling to permit operations on his homestead, the Superintendent will cause an examination of the premises to be made with the allottee and lessee or his representative. Upon finding that the interests of the Osage Tribe require that the tract be developed, the Superintendent will endeavor to have the parties agree upon the terms under which operations on the homestead may be conducted.

(c) In the event the allottee and lessee cannot reach an agreement, the matter shall be presented by all parties before the Osage Tribal Council, and the Council shall make its recommendations. Such recommendations shall be considered as final and binding upon the allottee and lessee. A guardian may represent the allottee. Where no one is authorized or where no person is deemed by the Superintendent to be a proper party to speak for a person of unsound mind or feeble understanding, the Principal Chief of the Osage Tribe shall represent him.

(d) If the allottee or his representative does not appear before the Osage Tribal Council when notified by the Superintendent, or if the Council fails to act within 10 days after the matter is referred to it, the Superintendent may authorize lessee to proceed with operations in conformity with the provisions of his lease and the regulations in this part.

§ 226.18 Information to be given surface owners prior to commencement of drilling operations.

Except for the surveying and staking of a well, no operations of any kind shall commence until the lessee or his/her authorized representative shall meet with the surface owner or his/her representative, if a resident of and present in Osage County, Oklahoma. Unless waived by the Superintendent or otherwise agreed to between the lessee and surface owner, such meeting shall be held at least 10 days prior to the commencement or any operations, except for the surveying and staking of the well. At such meeting lessee or his/her authorized representative shall comply with the following requirements:

(a) Indicate the location of the well or wells to be drilled.

(b) Arrange for route of ingress and egress. Upon failure to agree on route ingress and egress, said route shall be set by the Superintendent.

(c) Impart to said surface owners the name and address of the party or representative upon whom the surface owner shall serve any claim for damages which he may sustain from mineral development or operations, and as to the procedure for settlement thereof as provided in § 226.21.

(d) Where the drilling is to be on restricted land, lessee or his authorized representative in the manner provided above shall meet with the Superintendent.

(e) When the surface owner or his/her representative is not a resident of, or is not physically present in, Osage County, Oklahoma, or cannot be contacted at the last known address, the Superintendent may authorize lessee to proceed with operations.

§ 226.19 Use of surface of land.

(a) Lessee or his/her authorized representative shall have the right to use so much of the surface of the land within the Osage Mineral Estate as may be reasonable for operations and marketing. This includes but is not limited to the right to lay and maintain pipelines, electric lines, pull rods, other appliances necessary for operations and marketing, and the right-of-way for ingress and egress to any point of operations. If Lessee and surface owner are unable to agree as to the routing of pipelines, electric lines, etc., said routing shall be set by the Superintendent. The right to use water for lease operations is established by § 226.24. Lessee shall conduct his/her operations in a workmanlike manner, commit no waste and allow none to be committed upon the land, nor permit any unavoidable nuisance to be maintained on the premises under his/her control.

(b) Before commencing a drilling operation, Lessee shall pay or tender to the surface owner commencement money in the amount of $25 per seismic shot hole and commencement money in the amount of $300 for each well, after which Lessee shall be entitled to immediate possession of the drilling site. Commencement money will not be required for the redrilling of a well which was originally drilled under the currently lease. A drilling site shall be held to the minimum area essential for operations and shall not exceed one and one-half acres in area unless authorized by the Superintendent. Commencement money shall be a credit toward the settlement of the total damages. Acceptance of commencement money by the surface owner does not affect his/her right to compensation for damages as described in § 226.20, occasioned by the drilling and completion of the well for which it was paid. Since actual damage to the surface from operations cannot necessarily be ascertained prior to the completion of a well as a serviceable well or dry hole, a damage settlement covering the drilling operation need not be made until after completion of drilling operations.

(c) Where the surface is restricted land, commencement money shall be paid to the Superintendent for the landowner. All other surface owners shall be paid or tendered such commencement money direct. Where such surface owners are not residents of Osage County nor have a representative located therein, such payment shall be made or tendered to the last known address of the surface owner at least 5 days before commencing drilling operation on any well: *Provided*, That should lessee be unable to reach the owner of the surface of the land for the purpose of tendering the commencement money or if the owner of the surface of the land shall refuse to accept the same, lessee shall deposit such amount with the Superintendent by check payable to the Bureau of Indian Affairs. The superintendent shall thereupon advise the owner of the surface of the land by mail at his last known address that the commencement money is being held for payment to him upon his written request.

(d) Lessee shall also pay fees for tank sites not exceeding 50 feet square at the rate of $100 per tank site or other vessel: *Provided*, That no payment shall be due for a tank temporarily set on a well location site for drilling, completing, or testing. The sum to be paid for a tank occupying more than 50 feet square shall be agreed upon between the surface owner and lessee or, on failure to agree, the same shall be determined by arbitration as provided by § 226.21.

§ 226.20 Settlement of damages claimed.

(a) Lessee or his authorized representative or geophysical permittee shall pay for all damages to growing crops, any improvements on the lands, and all other surface damages as may be occasioned by operations. Commencement money shall be a credit toward the settlement of the total damages occasioned by the drilling and completion of the well for which it was paid. Such damages shall be paid to the owner of the surface and by him apportioned among the parties interested in the surface, whether as owner, surface lessee, or otherwise, as the parties may mutually agree or as their interests may appear. If lessee or his authorized representative and surface owner are unable to agree concerning damages, the same shall be determined by arbitration. Nothing herein contained shall be construed to deny any party the right to file an action in a court of competent jurisdiction if he is dissatisfied with the amount of the award.

(b) Surface owners shall notify their lessees or tenants of the regulations in this part and of the necessary procedure to follow in all cases of alleged damages. If so authorized in writing, surface lessees or tenants may represent the surface owners.

(c) In settlement of damages on restricted land all sums due and payable shall be paid to the Superintendent for credit to the account of the Indian entitled thereto. The Superintendent will make the apportionment between the Indian landowner or owners and surface Lessee of record.

(d) Any person claiming an interest in any leased tract or in damages thereto, must furnish to the Superintendent a statement in writing showing said claimed interest. Failure to furnish such statement shall constitute a waiver of notice and estop said person from claiming any part of such damages after the same shall have been disbursed.

§ 226.21 Procedure for settlement of damages claimed.

Where the surface owner or his lessee suffers damage due to the oil and gas operations and/or marketing of oil or gas by lessee or his authorized representative, the procedure for recovery shall be as follows:

(a) The party or parties aggrieved shall, as soon as possible after the discovery of any damages, serve written notice to Lessee or his authorized representative as provided by § 226.18.

Written notice shall contain the nature and location of the alleged damages, the date of occurrence, the names of the party or parties causing said damages, and the amount of damages. It is not intended by this requirement to limit the time within which action may be brought in the courts to less than the 90-day period allowed by section 2 of the Act of March 2, 1929 (45 Stat. 1478, 1479).

(b) If the alleged damages are not adjusted at the time of such notice, Lessee or his authorized representative shall try to adjust the claim with the party or parties aggrieved within 20 days from receipt of the notice. If the claimant is the owner of restricted property and a settlement results, a copy of the settlement agreement shall be filed with the Superintendent. If the settlement agreement is approved by the Superintendent, payment shall be made to the Superintendent for the benefit of said claimant.

(c) If the parties fail to adjust the claim within the 20 days specified, then within 10 days thereafter each of the interested parties shall appoint an arbitrator who immediately upon their appointment shall agree upon a third arbitrator. If the two arbitrators shall fail to agree upon a third arbitrator within 10 days, they shall immediately notify the parties in interest. If said parties cannot agree upon a third arbitrator within 5 days after receipt of such notice, the Superintendent shall appoint the third arbitrator.

(d) As soon as the third arbitrator is appointed, the arbitrators shall meet; hear the evidence and arguments of the parties; and examine the lands, crops, improvements, or other property alleged to have been injured. Within 10 days they shall render their decision as to the amount of the damage due. The arbitrators shall be disinterested persons. The fees and expenses of the third arbitrator shall be borne equally by the claimant and Lessee or his authorized representative. Each Lessee or his authorized representative and claimant shall pay the fee and expenses for the arbitrator appointed by him.

(e) When an act of an oil or gas lessee or his authorized representative results in injury to both the surface owner and his lessee, the parties aggrieved shall join in the appointment of an arbitrator. Where the injury complained of is chargeable to one or more oil or gas Lessee, or his authorized representative, such lessee or said representative shall join in the appointment of an arbitrator.

(f) Any two of the arbitrators may make a decision as to the amount of damage due. The decision shall be in writing and shall be served forthwith upon the parties in interest. Each party shall have 90 days from the date the decision is served in which to file an action in a court of competent jurisdiction. If no such action is filed within said time and the award is against Lessee or his/her authorized representative, he/she shall pay the same, together with interest at an annual rate established for the Internal Revenue Service from date of award, within 10 days after the expiration of said period for filing an action.

(g) Lessee or his authorized representative shall file with the Superintendent a report on each settlement agreement, setting out the nature and location of the damage, date, and amount of the settlement, and any other pertinent information.

§ 226.22 Prohibition of pollution.

(a) All operators, contractors, drillers, service companies, pipe pulling and salvaging contractors, or other persons, shall at all times conduct their operations and drill, equip, operate, produce, plug and abandon all wells drilled for oil or gas, service wells or exploratory wells (including seismic, core and stratigraphic holes) in a manner that will prevent pollution and the migration of oil, gas, salt water or other substance from one stratum into another, including any fresh water bearing formation.

(b) Pits for drilling mud or deleterious substance used in the drilling, completion, recompletion, or workover of any well shall be constructed and maintained to prevent pollution of surface and subsurface fresh water. These pits shall be enclosed with a fence of at least four strands of barbed wire, or an approved substitute, stretched taut to adequately braced corner posts, unless the surface owner, user, or the Superintendent gives consent to the contrary. Immediately after completion of operations, pits shall be emptied and leveled unless otherwise requested by surface owner or user.

(c) Drilling pits shall be adequate to contain mud and other material extracted from wells and shall have adequate storage to maintain a supply of mud for use in emergencies.

(d) No earthen pit, except those used in the drilling, completion, recompletion or workover of a well, shall be constructed, enlarged, reconstructed or used without approval of the Superintendent. Unlined earthen pits shall not be used for the continued storage of salt water or other deleterious substances.

(e) Deleterious fluids other than fresh water drilling fluids used in drilling or workover operations, which are displaced or produced in well completion or stimulation procedures, including but not limited to fracturing, acidizing, swabbing, and drill stem tests, shall be collected into a pit lined with plastic of at least 30 mil or a metal tank and maintained separately from above-mentioned drilling fluids to allow for separate disposal.

§226.23 Easements for wells off leased premises.

The Superintendent, with the consent of the Osage Tribal Council, may grant commercial and noncommercial easements for wells off the leased premises to be used for purposes associated with oil and gas production. Rental payable to the Osage Tribe for such easements shall be an amount agreed to by Grantee and the Osage Tribal Council subject to the approval of the Superintendent. Grantee shall be responsible for all damages resulting from the use of such wells and settlement therefor shall be made as provided in §226.21.

§226.24 Lessee's use of water.

Lessee or his contractor may, with the approval of the Superintendent, use water from streams and natural water courses to the extent that same does not diminish the supply below the requirements of the surface owner from whose land the water is taken. Similarly, Lessee or his contractor may use water from reservoirs formed by the impoundment of water from such streams and natural water courses, provided such use does not exceed the quantity to which they originally would have been entitled had the reservoirs not been constructed. Lessee or his contractor may install necessary lines and other equipment within the Osage Mineral Estate to obtain such water. Any damage resulting from such installation shall be settled as provided in §226.21.

§226.25 Gas well drilled by oil lessees and vice versa.

Prior to drilling, the oil or gas lessee shall notify the other lessees of his/her intent to drill. When an oil lessee in drilling a well encounters a formation or zone having indications of possible gas production, or the gas lessee in drilling a well encounters a formation or zone having indication of possible oil production, he/she shall immediately notify the other lessee and the Superintendent. Lessee drilling the well shall obtain all information which a prudent operator utilizes to evaluate the productive capability of such formation or zone.

(a) *Gas well to be turned over to gas lessee.* If the oil lessee drills a gas well, he/she shall, without removing from the well any of the casing or other equipment, immediately shut the well in and notify the gas lessee and the Superintendent. If the gas lessee does not, within 45 days after receiving notice and cost of drilling, elect to take over such well and reimburse the oil lessee the cost of drilling, including all damages paid and the cost in-place of casing, tubing, and other equipment, the oil lessee shall immediately confine the gas to the original stratum. The disposition of such well and the production therefrom shall then be subject to the approval of the Superintendent. In the event the oil lessee and gas lessee cannot agree on the cost of the well, such cost shall be apportioned between the oil and gas lessee by the Superintendent. If such apportionment is not accepted, the well shall be plugged by the oil and gas lessee who drilled the well.

(b) Oil well to be turned over to oil lessee. If the gas lessee drills an oil well, he/she must immediately, without removing from the well any of the casing or other equipment, notify the oil lessee and the superintendent.

(1) If the oil lessee does not, within 45 days after receipt of notice and cost of drilling, elect to take over the well, he/she must immediately notify the gas lessee. From that point, the superintendent must approve the disposition of the well, and any gas produced from it.

(2) If the oil lessee chooses to take over the well, he/she must pay to the gas lessee:

(i) The cost of drilling the well, including all damages paid; and

(ii) The cost in place of casing and other equipment.

(3) If the oil lessee and the gas lessee cannot agree on the cost of the well, the superintendent will apportion the cost between the oil and gas lessees. If the lessees do not accept the apportionment, the oil or gas lessee who drilled the well must plug the well.

(c) *Lands not leased.* If the gas lessee shall drill an oil well upon lands not leased for oil purposes or vice versa, the Superintendent may, until such time as said lands are leased, permit the lessee who drilled the well to operate and market the production therefrom. When said lands are leased, the lessee who drilled and completed the well shall be reimbursed by the oil or gas lessee, for the cost of drilling said well, including all damages paid and the cost in-place of casing, tubing, and other equipment. If the lessee does not elect to take over said well as provided above, the disposition of such well and the production therefrom shall be determined by the Superintendent. In the event the oil lessee and gas lessee cannot agree on the cost of the well, such cost shall be apportioned between the oil and gas lessee by the Superintendent. If such apportionment is not accepted, the well shall be plugged by the oil and gas lessee who drilled the well.

§ 226.26 Determining cost of well.

The term "cost of drilling" as applied where one lessee takes over a well drilled by another, shall include all reasonable, usual, necessary, and proper expenditures. A list of expenses mentioned in this section shall be presented to proposed purchasing lessee within 10 days after the completion of the well. In the event of a disagreement between the parties as to the charges assessed against the well that is to be taken over, such charges shall be determined by the Superintendent.

§ 226.27 Gas for operating purposes and tribal use.

(a) *Gas to be furnished oil lessee.* Lessee of a producing gas lease shall furnish the oil lessee sufficient gas for operating purposes at a rate to be agreed upon, or on failure to agree the rate shall be determined by the Superintendent: *Provided,* That the oil lessee shall at his own expense and risk, furnish and install the necessary connections to the gas lessee's well or pipeline. All such connections shall be reported in writing to the Superintendent.

(b) *Use of gas by Osage Tribe.* (1) Gas from any well or wells shall be furnished any Tribal-owned building or enterprise at a rate not to exceed the price less royalty being received or offered by a gas purchaser: *Provided,* That such requirement shall be subject to the determination by the Superintendent that gas in sufficient quantities is available above that needed for lease operation and that no waste would result. In the absence of a gas purchaser the rate to be paid by the Osage Tribe shall be determined by the Superintendent based on prices being paid by purchasers in the Osage Mineral Estate. The Osage Tribe is to furnish all necessary material and labor for such connection with Lessee's gas system. The use of such gas shall be at the risk of the Osage Tribe at all times.

(2) Any member of the Osage Tribe residing in Osage County and outside a corporate city is entitled to the use at his own expense of not to exceed 400,000 cubic feet of gas per calendar year for his principal residence at a rate not to exceed the amount paid by a gas purchaser plus 10 percent: *Provided,* That such requirement shall be subject to the determination by the Superintendent that gas in sufficient quantities is available above that needed for

lease operation and that no waste would result. In the absence of a gas purchaser the amount to be paid by the Tribal member shall be determined by the Superintendent. Gas to Tribal members is not royalty free. The Tribal member is to furnish all necessary material and labor for such connection to Lessee's gas system, and shall maintain his own lines. The use of such gas shall be at the risk of the Tribal member at all times.

(3) Gas furnished by Lessee under paragraphs (b)(1) and (2) of this section may be terminated only with the approval of the Superintendent. Written application for termination must be made to the Superintendent showing justification.

CESSATION OF OPERATIONS

§ 226.28 Shutdown, abandonment, and plugging of wells.

No productive well shall be abandoned until its lack for further profitable production of oil and/or gas has been demonstrated to the satisfaction of the Superintendent. Lessee shall not shut down, abandon, or otherwise discontinue the operation or use of any well for any purpose without the written approval of the Superintendent. All applications for such approval shall be submitted to the Superintendent on forms furnished by him/her.

(a) Application for authority to permanently shut down or discontinue use or operation of a well shall set forth justification, probable duration the means by which the well bore is to be protected, and the contemplated eventual disposition of the well. The method of conditioning such well shall be subject to the approval of the Superintendent.

(b) Prior to permanent abandonment of any well, the oil lessee or the gas lessee, as the case may be, shall offer the well to the other for his recompletion or use under such terms as may be mutually agreed upon but not in conflict with the regulations. Failure of the Lessee receiving the offer to reply within 10 days after receipt thereof shall be deemed as rejection of the offer. If, after indicating acceptance, the two parties cannot agree on the terms of the offer within 30 days, the disposition of such well shall be determined by the Superintendent.

(c) The Superintendent is authorized to shut in a lease when the lessee fails to comply with the terms of the lease, the regulations, and/or orders of the Superintendent.

§ 226.29 Disposition of casings and other improvements.

(a) Upon termination of lease, permanent improvements, unless otherwise provided by written agreement with the surface owner and filed with the Superintendent, shall remain a part of said land and become the property of the surface owner upon termination of the lease, other than by cancellation. Exceptions include personal property not limited to tools, tanks, pipelines, pumping and drilling equipment, derricks, engines, machinery, tubing, and the casings of all wells: Provided, That when any lease terminates, all such personal property shall be removed the word "terminates"; and in the last sentence of the paragraph, within 90 days or such reasonable extension of time as may be granted by the Superintendent. Otherwise, the ownership of all casings shall revert to Lessor and all other personal property and permanent improvements to the surface owner. Nothing herein shall be construed to relieve lessee of responsibility for removing any such personal property or permanent improvements from the premises if required by the Superintendent and restoring the premises as nearly as practicable to the original state.

(b) Upon cancellation of lease. When there has been a cancellation for cause, Lessor shall be entitled and authorized to take immediate possession of the lease premises and all permanent improvements and all other equipment necessary for the operation of the lease.

(c) Wells to be abandoned shall be promptly plugged as prescribed by the Superintendent. Applications to plug shall include a statement affirming compliance with § 226.28(b) and shall set forth reasons for plugging, a detailed statement of the proposed work including kind, location, and length of plugs (by depth), plans for mudding and cementing, testing, parting and removing casing, and any other pertinent information: *Provided*, That the Superintendent may give oral permission and instructions pending receipt of a written application to plug a newly drilled hole. Lessee shall remit a fee of $15 with each written application for authority to plug a well. This fee will be refunded if permission is not granted.

(d) Lessee shall plug and fill all dry or abandoned wells in a manner to confine the fluid in each formation bearing fresh water, oil, gas, salt water, and other minerals, and to protect it against invasion of fluids from other sources. Mud-laden fluid, cement, and other plugs shall be used to fill the hole from bottom to top: *Provided*, That if a satisfactory agreement is reached between Lessee and the surface owner, subject to the approval of the Superintendent, Lessee may condition the well for use as a fresh water well and shall so indicate on the plugging record. The manner in which plugging material shall be introduced and the type of material so used shall be subject to the approval of the Superintendent. Within 10 days after plugging, Lessee shall file with the Superintendent a complete report of the plugging of each well. When any well is plugged and abandoned, Lessee shall, within 90 days, clean up the premises around such well to the satisfaction of the Superintendent.

REQUIREMENTS OF LESSEES

§ 226.30 Lessees subject to Superintendent's orders; books and records open to inspection.

Lessee shall comply with all orders or instructions issued by the Superintendent. The Superintendent or his representative may enter upon the leased premises for the purpose of inspection. Lessee shall keep a full and correct account of all operations, receipts, and disbursements and make reports thereof, as required. Lessee's books and records shall be available to the Superintendent for inspection.

§ 226.31 Lessee's process agents.

(a) Before actual drilling or development operations are commenced on leased lands, Lessee or Assignee, if not a resident of the State of Oklahoma, shall appoint a local or resident representative within the State of Oklahoma on whom the Superintendent may serve notice or otherwise communicate in securing compliance with the regulations in this part, and shall notify the Superintendent of the name and post office address of the representative appointed.

(b) Where several parties own a lease jointly, one representative or agent shall be designated whose duties shall be to act for all parties concerned. Designation of such representative should be made by the party in charge of operations.

(c) In the event of the incapacity or absence from the State of Oklahoma of such designated local or resident representative, Lessee shall appoint a substitute to serve in his stead. In the absence of such representative or appointed substitute, any employee of Lessee upon the leased premises or person in charge of drilling or related operations thereon shall be considered the representative of Lessee for the purpose of service of orders or notices as herein provided.

§ 226.32 Well records and reports.

(a) Lessee shall keep accurate and complete records of the drilling, redrilling, deepening, repairing, treating, plugging, or abandonment of all wells. These records shall show all the formations penetrated, the content and character of oil, gas, or water in each formation, and the kind, weight, size, landed depth and cement record of casing used in drilling each well; the record of drill-stem and other bottom hole pressure or fluid sample surveys, temperature surveys, directional surveys, and the like; the materials and procedure used in the treating or plugging of wells or in preparing them for temporary abandonment; and any other information obtained in the course of well operation.

(b) Lessee shall take such samples and make such tests and surveys as may be required by the Superintendent to determine conditions in the well or producing reservoir and to obtain information concerning formations drilled, and shall furnish reports thereof as required by the Superintendent.

(c) Within 10 days after completion of operations on any well, Lessee shall transmit to the Superintendent the applicable information on forms furnished by the Superintendent; a copy of electrical, mechanical or radioactive log, or other types of survey of the well bore; and core analysis obtained from the well. Lessee shall also submit other reports and records of operations as may be required and in the manner and form prescribed by the Superintendent.

(d) Lessee shall measure production of oil, gas, and water from individual wells at reasonably frequent intervals to the satisfaction of the Superintendent.

(e) Upon request and in the manner and form prescribed by the Superintendent, Lessee shall furnish a plat showing the location, designation, and status of all wells on the leased lands, together with such other pertinent information as the Superintendent may require.

§226.33 Line drilling.

Lessee shall not drill within 300 feet of boundary line of leased lands, nor locate any well or tank within 200 feet of any public highway, any established watering place, or any building used as a dwelling, granary, or barn, except with the written permission of the Superintendent. Failure to obtain advance written permission from the Superintendent shall subject lessee to cancellation of his/her lease and/or plugging of the well.

§226.34 Wells and tank batteries to be marked.

Lessee shall clearly and permanently mark all wells and tank batteries in a conspicuous place with number, legal description, operator, and telephone number, and shall take all necessary precautions to preserve these markings.

§226.35 Formations to be protected.

Lessee shall, to the satisfaction of the Superintendent, take all proper precautions and measures to prevent damage or pollution of oil, gas, fresh water, or other mineral bearing formations.

§226.36 Control devices.

In drilling operations in fields where high pressures, lost circulation, or other conditions exist which could result in blowouts, lessee shall install an approved gate valve or other controlling device which is in proper working condition for use until the well is completed. At all times preventative measures must be taken in all well operations to maintain proper control of subsurface strata.

§226.37 Waste of oil and gas.

Lessee shall conduct all operations in a manner that will prevent waste of oil and gas and shall not wastefully utilize oil or gas. The Superintendent shall have the authority to impose such requirements as he deems necessary to prevent waste of oil and gas and to promote the greatest ultimate recovery of oil and gas. Waste as applied herein includes, but is not limited to, the inefficient excessive or improper use or dissipation of reservoir energy which would reasonably reduce or diminish the quantity of oil or gas that might ultimately be produced, or the unnecessary or excessive surface loss or destruction, without beneficial use, of oil and/or gas.

§226.38 Measuring and storing oil.

All production run from the lease shall be measured according to methods and devices approved by the Superintendent. Facilities suitable for containing and measuring accurately all crude oil produced from the wells shall be provided by Lessee and shall be located on the leasehold unless otherwise approved by the Superintendent. Lessee shall furnish to the Superintendent a copy of 100-percent capacity tank table for each tank. Meters and installations for measuring oil must be approved, and tests of their accuracy shall be made when directed by the Superintendent.

§226.39 Measurement of gas.

All gas, required to be measured, shall be measured by meter (preferably of the orifice meter type) unless otherwise agreed to by the Superintendent. All gas meters must be approved by the

Superintendent and installed at the expense of Lessee or purchaser at such places as may be agreed to by the Superintendent. For computing the volume of all gas produced, sold or subject to royalty, the standard of pressure shall be 14.65 pounds to the square inch, and the standard of temperature shall be 60 degrees F. All measurements of gas shall be adjusted by computation to these standards, regardless of the pressure and temperature at which the gas was actually measured, unless otherwise authorized in writing by the Superintendent.

§ 226.40 Use of gas for lifting oil.

Lessee shall not use natural gas from a distinct or separate stratum for the purpose of flowing or lifting the oil, except where said Lessee has an approved right to both the oil and the gas, and then only with the approval of the Superintendent of such use and of the manner of its use.

§ 226.41 Accidents to be reported.

Lessee shall make a complete report to the Superintendent of all accidents, fires, or acts of theft and vandalism occurring on the leased premises.

PENALTIES

§ 226.42 Penalty for violation of lease terms.

Violation of any of the terms or conditions of any lease or of the regulations in this part shall subject the lease to cancellation by the Superintendent, or Lessee to a fine of not more than $924 per day for each day of such violation or noncompliance with the orders of the Superintendent, or to both such fine and cancellation. Fines not received within 10 days after notice of the decision shall be subject to late charges at the rate of not less than 11/2 percent per month for each month or fraction thereof until paid. The Osage Tribal Council, subject to the approval of the Superintendent, may waive the late charge.

[81 FR 39573, June 17, 2016, as amended at 81 FR 42481, June 30, 2016; 82 FR 7653, Jan. 23, 2017; 83 FR 5195, Feb. 6, 2018]

§ 226.43 Penalties for violation of certain operating regulations.

In lieu of the penalties provided under § 226.42, penalties may be imposed by the Superintendent for violation of certain sections of the regulations of this part as follows:

(a) For failure to obtain permission to start operations required by § 226.16(b), $92 per day until permission is obtained.

(b) For failure to file records required by § 226.32, $92 per day until compliance is met.

(c) For failure to mark wells and tank batteries as required by § 226.34, $92 for each well and tank battery.

(d) For failure to construct and maintain pits as required by § 226.22, $92 for each day after operations are commenced on any well until compliance is met.

(e) For failure to comply with § 226.36 regarding valve or other approved controlling device, $185.

(f) For failure to notify Superintendent before drilling, redrilling, deepening, plugging, or abandoning any well, as required by §§ 226.16(c) and 226.25, $369.

(g) For failure to properly care for and dispose of deleterious fluids as provided in § 226.22, $924 per day until compliance is met.

(h) For failure to file plugging reports as required by § 226.29 and for failure to file reports as required by § 226.13, $92 per day for each violation until compliance is met.

(i) For failure to perform or start an operation within 5 days after ordered by the Superintendent in writing under authority provided in this part, if said operation is thereafter performed by or through the Superintendent, the actual cost of performance thereof, plus 25 percent.

(j) Lessee or his/her authorized representative is hereby notified that criminal procedures are provided by 18 U.S.C. 1001 for knowingly filing fraudulent reports and information.

[81 FR 39573, June 17, 2016, as amended at 81 FR 42481, June 30, 2016; 82 FR 7653, Jan. 23, 2017; 83 FR 5195, Feb. 6, 2018]

APPEALS AND NOTICES

§226.44 Appeals.

Any person, firm or corporation aggrieved by any decision or order issued by or under the authority of the Superintendent, by virtue of the regulations in this part, may appeal pursuant to 25 CFR part 2.

§226.45 Notices.

Notices and orders issued by the Superintendent to the representative and/or operator shall be binding on the lessee. The Superintendent may in his/her discretion increase the time allowed in his/her orders and notices.

§226.46 Information collection.

The Office of Management and Budget has determined that the information collection requirements contained in this part need not be submitted for clearance pursuant to 44 U.S.C. 3501 *et seq.*

PART 227—LEASING OF CERTAIN LANDS IN WIND RIVER INDIAN RESERVATION, WYOMING, FOR OIL AND GAS MINING

Sec.

AUTHORITY: Sec. 1, 39 Stat. 519; and Sec. 701, Pub. L. 114–74, 129 Stat. 599, unless otherwise noted.

SOURCE: 22 FR 10622, Dec. 24, 1957, unless otherwise noted. Redesignated at 47 FR 13327, Mar. 30, 1982.

§227.1 Definitions.

(a) The term "superintendent" in this part refers to the superintendent or other officers of the Bureau of Indian Affairs or of the Government who may have jurisdiction over the Shoshone or Wind River Reservation.

(b) The term "supervisor" in this part refers to a representative of the Secretary of the Interior, under direction of the Director of the U.S. Geological Survey, authorized and empowered to supervise and direct operations under oil and gas mining leases, to furnish scientific and technical information and advice, to ascertain and record the amount and value of production, and to determine and record rentals and royalties due and paid.

CROSS REFERENCE: For rules and regulations of the Geological Survey, see 30 CFR chapter II.

HOW TO ACQUIRE LEASES

§227.2 Applications for leases.

Applications for leases should be made to the superintendent.

§227.3 Leases to citizens of the United States except Government employees.

Leases will be made only to persons who are citizens of the United States or have declared their intention to become so, or corporations which are organized under the laws of the United

States or one of the States or Territories: *Provided*, That no lease, assignment thereof, or interest therein will be approved to any employee or employees of the United States Government, whether connected with the Bureau or otherwise, and no employee of the Interior Department shall be permitted to acquire any interest in such leases by ownership of stock in corporations having leases or in any other manner.

(R.S. 2078; 25 U.S.C. 68)

§ 227.4 Sale of oil and gas leases.

(a) At such times and in such manner as he may deem appropriate, after being authorized by the Joint Business Council of the Shoshone and Arapahoe Tribes or its authorized representative, the superintendent shall publish notices at least thirty days prior to the sale, unless a shorter period is authorized by the Secretary of the Interior or his authorized representative, that oil and gas leases on specific tracts, each of which shall be in a reasonably compact body, will be offered to the highest responsible bidder for a bonus consideration, in addition to stipulated rentals and royalties. Each bid must be accompanied by a cashier's check, certified check, or postal money order, payable to the payee designated in the invitation to bid, in an amount not less than 25 percent of the bonus bid. Within 30 days after notification of being the successful bidder, said bidder must remit the balance of the bonus, the first year's rental, and his share of the advertising costs, and shall file with the superintendent the lease in completed form. The superintendent may for good and sufficient reasons, extend the time for completion and submission of the lease form, but no extension shall be granted for remitting the balance of monies due. If the successful bidder fails to pay the full consideration within said period, or fails to file the completed lease within said period or extension thereof, or if the lease is disapproved through no fault of the lessor or the Department of the Interior, 25 percent of the bonus bid will be forfeited for the use and benefit of the Shoshone and Arapahoe Tribes.

(b) All notices or advertisements of sales of oil and gas leases shall reserve to the Secretary of the Interior the right to reject all bids when in his judgment the interests of the Indians will be best served by so doing, and that if no satisfactory bid is received, or if the accepted bidder fails to complete the lease, or if the Secretary of the Interior shall determine that it is unwise in the interests of the Indians to accept the highest bid, the Secretary may readvertise such lease for sale, or if deemed advisable, with the consent of the tribal council or other governing tribal authorities, a lease may be made by private negotiations. The successful bidder or bidders will be required to pay his or their share of the advertising costs. Amounts received from unsuccessful bidders will be returned; but when no bid is accepted on a tract, the costs of advertising will be assessed against the applicant who requested that said tract be advertised.

[22 FR 10622, Dec. 24, 1957, as amended at 25 FR 7185, July 29, 1960. Redesignated at 47 FR 13327, Mar. 30, 1982]

§ 227.5 Terms of leases, procedure for renewal and execution.

(a) Leases shall be for a period of twenty years with the preferential right in the lessee to renew the same for successive periods of ten years each upon such reasonable terms and conditions as may be prescribed by the Secretary of the Interior or his authorized representative, unless otherwise provided by law at the expiration of any such period. Applications for renewal of leases shall be filed with the superintendent within ninety days prior to the date of expiration of the lease. One copy of the application for renewal shall be filed by the applicant with the Joint Business Council of the Shoshone and Arapahoe Tribes and no lease shall be renewed unless the Joint Business Council or its authorized representative is afforded an opportunity to present the Council's views to the Secretary of the Interior or his authorized representative.

(b) The Secretary of the Interior or his authorized representative may execute oil and gas leases with the consent of the Joint Business Council or its authorized representative, and may execute renewals of leases after consultation with the Joint Business Council or its authorized representative.

[25 FR 7185, July 29, 1960. Redesignated at 47 FR 13327, Mar. 30, 1982]

§227.6 Corporations and corporate information.

(a) If the applicant for a lease is a corporation, it shall file evidence of authority of its officers to execute papers; and with its first application it shall also file a certified copy of its articles of incorporation, and, if foreign to the state in which the lands are located, evidence showing compliance with the corporation laws thereof. Statements of changes in officers and stockholders shall be furnished by a corporation lessee to the superintendent January 1 of each year, and at such other times as may be requested.

(b) Whenever deemed advisable in any case the superintendent may require a corporation applicant or lessee to file:

(1) List of officers, principal stockholders, and directors, with post-office addresses and number of shares held by each.

(2) A sworn statement of the proper officer showing:

(i) The total number of shares of the capital stock actually issued and the amount of cash paid into the treasury on each share sold; or, if paid in property, the kind, quantity, and value of same paid per share.

(ii) Of the stock sold, how much remains unpaid and subject to assessment.

(iii) The amount of cash the company has in its treasury and elsewhere.

(iv) The property, exclusive of cash owned by the company and its value.

(v) The total indebtedness of the company and the nature of its obligations.

(vi) Whether the applicant or any person controlling, controlled by or under common control with the applicant has filed any registration statement, application for registration, prospectus or offering sheet with the Securities and Exchange Commission pursuant to the Securities Act of 1933 or the Securities Exchange Act of 1934 or said Commission's rules and regulations under said acts; if so, under what provision of said acts or rules and regulations; and what disposition of any such statement, application, prospectus or offering sheet has been made.

(c) Affidavits of individual stockholders, setting forth in what corporations, or with what persons, firms, or associations such individual stockholders are interested in mining leases on restricted lands within the state, and whether they hold such interest for themselves or in trust.

CROSS REFERENCE: For rules and regulations of the Securities and Exchange Commission, see 17 CFR chapter II.

§227.7 Additional information from applicant.

The superintendent may, either before or after approval of a lease, call for any additional information desired to carry out the regulations in this part. If a lessee shall fail to furnish the papers necessary to put his lease and bond in proper form for consideration, the superintendent shall forward such lease for disapproval.

§227.8 Bonds.

The provisions of §211.6 of this chapter, or as hereafter amended, are applicable to leases under this part.

§227.9 Acreage limitation: Leases on noncontiguous tracts.

No person, firm, or corporation will be allowed to lease for oil and gas more than 10,240 acres in the aggregate. The land contained in the lease shall be described by legal subdivisions, and leases may be executed to cover only adjoining or contiguous subdivisions. In case a lessee is a successful bidder for two or more tracts of land which are not contiguous, separate leases shall be executed.

§227.10 Minerals other than oil and gas.

Unreserved, unwithdrawn, and unallotted lands which have not been leased for oil and gas under the act of August 21, 1916 (39 Stat. 519) and which are not chiefly valuable therefor, are subject to mineral application or mineral entry, for minerals other than oil and gas, under the supervision of the Bureau of Land Management.

§ 227.11 Bureau of Land Management to be furnished copy of lease.

The Bureau of Land Management shall be furnished with a copy of each lease signed by the Secretary of the Interior.

§ 227.12 Mineral reserves in nonmineral entries.

Where lands have been leased under authority of said act of August 21, 1916 (39 Stat. 519), and nonmineral entry is subsequently lawfully made for such lands with a view to obtaining a restricted patent therefor, all such subsequently allowed nonmineral entries shall be with the mineral reservation prescribed by the act of July 17, 1914 (38 Stat. 509).

§ 227.13 Vested rights to be respected.

All drilling and other oil and natural gas developments and mining operations, work, and improvements, and all other acts and things necessary to be done, in connection with the exploration for mining and production of oil and natural gas from the leased premises, under the terms and conditions of a lease shall be performed with due regard to the rights, statutory and otherwise, of others, if any, who may have or who may acquire a lawful claim or estate to the leased premises, separate and distinct from the oil and gas or other mineral therein contained. See act of July 17, 1914 (38 Stat. 509).

§ 227.14 Government reserves right to purchase oil and gas.

In time of war or other public emergency any of the executive departments of the United States Government shall have the option to purchase at the posted market price on the date of sale all or any part of the minerals produced under any lease.

RENTS AND ROYALTIES

§ 227.15 Manner of payment.

All payments due the lessor shall be made to the superintendent for the benefit of the Shoshone Indian Tribe, in accordance with the act of August 21, 1916 (39 Stat. 519), and no credit will be given any lessee for payments made otherwise. Payments of rentals and royalties except the first year's rental, which shall be paid to the superintendent as prescribed in § 227.4 shall be transmitted to the superintendent through the supervisor. All such payments shall be accompanied by a statement, in triplicate, by the lessee, showing the specific items of royalty or rental that the remittance is intended to cover, and payment of royalties on production shall be made not later than the last day of the calendar month following the production for which such payment is to be made.

§ 227.16 Crediting advance annual payments.

In the event of discovery of minerals in paying quantities all advance rents and advance royalties shall be allowed as credit on stipulated royalties as they accrue for the year for which such advance payments have been made. No refund of any such advance payment made under any lease will be allowed in the event the royalty on production for the year is not sufficient to equal such advance payment; nor will any part of the moneys so paid be refunded to the lessee because of any subsequent surrender or cancellation of the lease.

§ 227.17 Rates of rents and royalties.

(a) The lessee shall pay, beginning with the date of execution of leases by the Secretary of the Interior, a rental of $1.25 per acre per annum in advance during the continuance thereof, together with a royalty of 12½ percent of the value or amount of all oil, gas, and/or natural gasoline, and/or all other hydrocarbon substances produced and saved from the land leased, save and except oil and/or gas used by the lessee for development and operation purposes on the lease, which oil or gas shall be royalty free. A higher rate of royalty may be fixed by the Secretary of the Interior or his authorized representative, prior to the advertisement of land for oil and gas leases. During the period of supervision, "value" for the purposes of the lease may, in the discretion of the Secretary of the Interior, be calculated on the basis of the highest price paid or offered (whether calculated on the basis of short or actual volume) at the time of production for the major portion of the oil of the same gravity, and gas, and/or natural gasoline, and/or all other hydrocarbon substances produced and sold from the field where the leased lands are situated, and the actual volume of the marketable product less the content of foreign substances as determined by the supervisor. The actual amount realized by the lessee from the sale of said products may, in the discretion of the Secretary of the Interior, be deemed mere evidence of or conclusive evidence of such value. When paid in value, such royalties shall be due and payable monthly at such time as the lease provides; when royalty on oil produced is paid in kind, such royalty oil shall be delivered in tanks provided by the lessee on the premises where produced without cost to the lessor unless otherwise agreed to by the parties thereto, at such time as may be required by the lessor. The lessee shall not be required to hold such royalty oil in storage longer than 30 days after the end of the calendar month in which said oil is produced. The lessee shall be in no manner responsible or held liable for loss or destruction of such oil by causes beyond his control.

(b) The proceeds from all leases shall be taken up in the accounts of the superintendent for appropriate deposit for the benefit of the Indians.

§ 227.18 Free use of gas by lessor.

If the leased premises produce gas in excess of the lessee's requirements for the development and operation of said premises, then the lessor may use sufficient gas, free of charge, for any desired school or other buildings belonging to the tribe, by making his own connections to a regulator installed, connected to the well and maintained by the lessee, and the lessee shall not be required to pay royalty on gas so used. The use of such gas shall be at the lessor's risk at all times.

§ 227.19 Division orders.

(a) Lessees may make arrangements with the purchasers of oil for the payment of the royalties on production to the superintendent by such purchasers, but such arrangements, if made, shall not operate to relieve a lessee from responsibility should the purchaser fail or refuse to pay such royalties when due. Where lessees avail themselves of this privilege, division orders permitting the pipeline companies or other purchasers of the oil to withhold the royalty interest shall be executed and forwarded to the supervisor for approval, as pipeline companies are not permitted to accept or run oil from leased Indian lands until after the approval of a division order showing that the lessee has a lease regularly approved and in effect. When the lessee company runs its own oil, it shall execute an intracompany division order and forward it to the supervisor for his consideration. The right is reserved for the supervisor to cancel a division order at any time or require the pipeline company to discontinue to run the oil of any lessee who fails to operate the lease properly or otherwise violates the provisions of the lease, of the regulations in this part, or of the operating regulations.

(b) When oil is taken by authority of a division order, the lessee or his representatives shall be actually present when the oil is gaged and records are made of the temperature, gravity and impurities. The lessee will be held responsible for the correctness and the correct recording and reporting of all the foregoing measurements, which except lowest gage, shall be made at the time the oil is turned into the pipeline. Failure of the lessee to perform properly these duties will subject the division order to revocation.

CROSS REFERENCE: For oil and gas operating regulations of the Geological Survey, see 30 CFR part 221.

OPERATIONS

§ 227.20 Permission to start operations.

(a) No operations will be permitted on any lease before it is executed by the Secretary of the Interior.

(b) Written permission must be secured from the supervisor or his representative before any operations are started on the leased premises. After such permission is secured the operations must be in accordance with the operating regulations promulgated by the Secretary of the Interior. Copies of the regulations in this part may be secured from either the supervisor or the superintendent, and no operations should be attempted without a study of the operating regulations.

§ 227.21 Restrictions on operations.

(a) All leases issued under the provisions of the regulations in this part shall be subject to imposition by the Secretary of the Interior of such restrictions as to time or times for the drilling of wells and as to the production from any well or wells as in his judgment may be necessary or proper for the protection of the natural resources of the leased land and in the interest of the lessor. In the exercise of his judgment the Secretary of the Interior may take into consideration, among other things, the Federal laws, State laws, regulations by competent Federal or State authorities, lawful agreements among operators regulating either drilling or production, or both, and any regulatory action desired by tribal authorities.

(b) All leases issued pursuant to the regulations in this part shall be subject to a co-operative or unit development plan affecting the leased lands if and when required by the Secretary of the Interior, but no lease shall participate in any cooperative or unit plan without prior approval of the Secretary of the Interior.

§ 227.22 Diligence and prevention of waste.

The lessee shall exercise diligence in drilling and operating wells for oil and gas on the leased lands while such products can be secured in paying quantities; carry on all operations in a good and workmanlike manner in accordance with approved methods and practice, having due regard for the prevention of waste of oil or gas developed on the land, or the entrance of water through wells drilled by the lessee to the productive sands or oil or gas-bearing strata to the destruction or injury of the oil or gas deposits, the preservation and conservation of the property for future productive operations, and to the health and safety of workmen and employees; plug securely all wells before abandoning the same and to shut off effectually all water from the oil or gas-bearing strata; not drill any well within 200 feet of any house or barn on the premises without the lessor's written consent; carry out at his expense all reasonable orders and requirements of the supervisor relative to prevention of waste, and preservation of the property and the health and safety of workmen; bury all pipelines crossing tillable lands below plow depth unless other arrangements therefor are made with the superintendent; pay all damages to crops, buildings, and other improvements on the premises occasioned by the lessee's operations: *Provided*, That the lessee shall not be held responsible for delays or casualties occasioned by causes beyond his control.

§ 227.23 Wells.

The lessee shall agree (a) to drill and produce all wells necessary to offset or protect the leased land from drainage by wells on adjoining lands not the property of the lessor, or in lieu thereof, compensate the lessor in full each month for the estimated loss of royalty through drainage: *Provided*, That during the period of supervision by the Secretary of the Interior, the necessity for offset wells shall be determined by the supervisor and payment in lieu of drilling and producing shall be with the consent of, and in an amount determined by the Secretary of the Interior; (b) at the election of the lessee to drill and produce other wells: *Provided*, That the right to drill and produce such other wells shall be subject to any system of well spacing or production allotments authorized and approved under the applicable law or regulations, approved by the Secretary of the Interior and affecting the field or area in which the leased lands are situated; and (c) if the lessee elects not to drill and produce such other wells for any period the Secretary of the Interior may, within 10 days after due notice in writing, either require the drilling and production of such wells to the number necessary, in his opinion, to insure reasonable diligence in the development and operation of the property, or may in lieu of such additional diligent drilling and production require the payment on and after the first anniversary date of the lease of not to exceed $1 per acre per annum, which sum shall be in addition to any rental or royalty herein specified.

§227.24 Penalties.

Failure of the lessee to comply with any provisions of the lease, of the operating regulations, of the regulations in this part, orders of the superintendent or his representative, or of the orders of the supervisor or his representative, shall subject the lessee to a penalty of not more than $1,296 per day for each day the terms of the lease, the regulations, or such orders are violated: *Provided*, That the lessee shall be entitled to notice, and hearing within 30 days after such notice, with respect to the terms of the lease, regulations, or orders violated, which hearing shall be held by the supervisor, whose findings shall be conclusive unless an appeal be taken to the Secretary of the Interior within 30 days after notice of the supervisor's decision, and the decision of the Secretary of the Interior upon appeal shall be conclusive.

[22 FR 10622, Dec. 24, 1957, as amended at 81 FR 42481, June 30, 2016; 82 FR 7653, Jan. 23, 2017; 83 FR 5195, Feb. 6, 2018]

§227.25 Inspection of premises, books and accounts.

Lessee shall agree to allow the lessor and his agents or any authorized representative of the Interior Department to enter, from time to time, upon and into all parts of the leased premises for the purposes of inspection and shall further agree to keep a full and correct account of all operations and make reports thereof, as required by the applicable regulations of the Department; and their books and records, showing manner of operations and persons interested, shall be open at all times for examination of such officers of the Department as shall be instructed in writing by the Secretary of the Interior or authorized by regulations, to make such examination.

§227.26 Assignments and overriding royalties.

(a) Leases, or any interest therein, may be assigned or transferred only with the approval of the Secretary of the Interior, and to procure such approval the assignee must be qualified to hold such lease under existing rules and regulations, and shall furnish a satisfactory bond for the faithful performance of the covenants and conditions thereof. No lease or any interest therein, or the use of such lease, shall be assigned, sublet, or transferred directly or indirectly, by working or drilling contract, or otherwise without the consent of the Secretary of the Interior. Assignments of leases shall be filed with the superintendent within 20 days after the date of execution.

(b) An agreement creating overriding royalties or payments out of production under this part shall be subject to the provisions of §211.26(d) of this chapter, or as hereafter amended.

[22 FR 10622, Dec. 24, 1957, as amended at 23 FR 9759, Dec. 18, 1958. Redesignated at 47 FR 13327, Mar. 30, 1982]

§227.27 Stipulations.

The lessee under any lease heretofore executed may be stipulation (Form 5–154i), with the consent of the lessor, make such lease subject to all the terms, conditions, and provisions contained in the lease form currently in use. Stipulations shall be filed with the superintendent within 20 days after the date of execution.

§227.28 Cancellations.

Leases shall be irrevocable except for breach of the terms and conditions of the same and may be forfeited and cancelled by an appropriate proceeding in the U.S. District Court for the District of Wyoming whenever the lessee fails to comply with their terms and conditions; the lessee may, on approval of the Secretary of the Interior, surrender a lease or any part of it:

(a) That he make application for cancellation to the superintendent having jurisdiction over the land.

(b) That he pay a surrender fee of $1 at the time the application is made.

(c) That he pay all royalties and rentals due to the date of such application.

(d) That he make a satisfactory showing that full provision has been made for conservation and protection of the property and that all wells, drilled on the portion of the lease surrendered, have been properly abandoned.

(e) If the lease has been recorded, that he file, with his application, a recorded release of the acreage covered by the application.

(f) If the application is for the cancellation of the entire lease or the entire undivided portion, that he surrender the lease: *Provided*, That where the application is made by an assignee to whom no copy of the lease was delivered, he will be required to surrender only his copy of the assignment.

(g) If the lease (or portion being surrendered or canceled) is owned in undivided interests by more than one party, then all parties shall join in the application for cancellation.

(h) That all required fees and papers must be in the mail or received on or before the date upon which rents and royalties become due, in order for the lessee and his surety to be relieved from liability for the payment of such royalties and rentals.

(i) In the event oil or gas is being drained from the leased premises by wells not covered by the lease; the lease, or any part of it may be surrendered, only on such terms and conditions as the Secretary of the Interior may determine to be reasonable and equitable.

§ 227.29 Fees.

Unless otherwise authorized by the Secretary of the Interior or his authorized representative, each lease, sublease, or assignment shall be accompanied at the time of filing by a fee of $10.

(Sec. 1, 41 Stat. 415, as amended; 25 U.S.C. 413)

[24 FR 7949, Oct. 2, 1959. Redesignated at 47 FR 13327, Mar. 30, 1982]

§ 227.30 Forms.

The provisions of § 211.30 of this chapter, or as hereafter amended are applicable to this part.

[24 FR 7949, Oct. 2, 1959. Redesignated at 47 FR 13327, Mar. 30, 1982]

SUBCHAPTER J—FISH AND WILDLIFE

PART 241—INDIAN FISHING IN ALASKA

AUTHORITY: 25 U.S.C. 2, 9; 43 U.S.C. 1457; sec. 15, 26 Stat. 1101, 48 U.S.C. 358; Presidential Proclamation, Apr. 28, 1916, 39 Stat. 1777; sec. 2, 49 Stat. 1250, 48 U.S.C. 358a; sec. 4, 72 Stat. 339, as amended 73 Stat. 141.

SOURCE: 28 FR 7183, July 12, 1963, unless otherwise noted. Redesignated at 47 FR 13327, Mar. 30, 1982.

§ 241.1 Purpose.

The purpose of the regulations in this part is to regulate all fishing within the Annette Islands Reserve and to regulate Indian and other native commercial fishing in the Karluk Indian Reservation, but they shall not be construed to limit any rights of Indians or other natives of Alaska not specifically covered hereby.

§ 241.2 Annette Islands Reserve; definition; exclusive fishery; licenses.

(a) *Definition.* The Annette Islands Reserve is defined as the Annette Islands in Alaska, as set apart as a reservation by section 15 of the Act of March 3, 1891 (26 Stat. 1101, 48 U.S.C. sec. 358), and including the area identified in the Presidential Proclamation of April 28, 1916 (39 Stat. 1777), as the waters within three thousand feet from the shore lines at mean low tide of Annette Island, Ham Island, Walker Island, Lewis Island, Spire Island, Hemlock Island, and adjacent rocks and islets, located within the broken line upon the diagram attached to and made a part of said Proclamation; and also the bays of said islands, rocks, and islets.

(b) *Exclusive fishery.* The Annette Islands Reserve is declared to be exclusively reserved for fishing by the members of the Metlakatla Indian Community and such other Alaskan Natives as have joined or may join them in residence on the aforementioned islands, and any other person fishing therein without authority or permission of the Metlakatla Indian Community shall be subject to prosecution under the provisions of section 2 of the Act of July 2, 1960 (74 Stat. 469, 18 U.S.C. sec. 1165).

(c) *Licenses.* Members of the Metlakatla Indian Community, and such other Alaskan Natives as have joined them or may join them in residence on the aforementioned islands, shall not be required to obtain a license or permit from the State of Alaska to engage in fishing in the waters of the Annette Islands Reserve.

§ 241.3 Commercial fishing, Annette Islands Reserve.

(a) *Definition.* Commercial fishing is the taking, fishing for, or possession of fish, shellfish, or other fishery resources with the intent of disposing of such fish, shellfish, or other fishery resources or parts thereof for profit, or by sale, barter, trade, or in commercial channels.

(b) *Trap fishing sites; number and location.* During 1963, and until the Secretary of the Interior or his duly authorized representative determines otherwise, the Metlakatla Indian Community is permitted to operate not more than one trap per site for salmon fishing at any four of the following sites in the Annette Islands Reserve, Alaska:

(1) Annette Island at 55 degrees 15 minutes 09 seconds north latitude, 131 degrees 36 minutes 00 seconds west longitude.

(2) Annette Island at 55 degrees 12 minutes 52 seconds north latitude, 131 degrees 36 minutes 10 seconds west longitude.

(3) Annette Island at 55 degrees 02 minutes 47 seconds north latitude, 131 degrees 38 minutes 53 seconds west longitude.

(4) Annette Island at 55 degrees 05 minutes 41 seconds north latitude, 131 degrees 36 minutes 39 seconds west longitude.

(5) Annette Island at 55 degrees 01 minute 54 seconds north latitude, 131 degrees 38 minutes 36 seconds west longitude.

(6) Annette Island at 55 degrees 00 minutes 45 seconds north latitude, 131 degrees 38 minutes 30 seconds west longitude.

(7) Annette Island at 54 degrees 59 minutes 41 seconds north latitude, 131 degrees 36 minutes 48 seconds west longitude.

(8) Ham Island at 55 degrees 10 minutes 13 seconds north latitude, 131 degrees 19 minutes 31 seconds west longitude.

(c) *Trap fishing season.* Fishing for salmon with traps operated by the Metlakatla Indian Community is permitted only at such times as commercial salmon fishing with purse seines is permitted by order or regulation of the Alaska Board of Fish and Game for Commercial Fishing in any part of the following area: from the point at which meridian 132°17′30″, thence due east along said parallel to longitude 130°49′15″, then due south along said meridian to the point at which it intersects with the United States-Canadian boundary, thence due west along said boundary to the point of beginning, provided, however, that the Secretary or his duly authorized representative may upon request by the Metlakatla Indian Community, authorize fishing for salmon with traps, at such other times as he shall prescribe, which authorization shall be based upon the following criteria:

(1) Number of fish required for spawning escapement and any other requirements reasonable and necessary for conservation;

(2) Fair and equitable sharing of the salmon resource with other user groups fishing in State waters under State law and within the State fisheries management system; and

(3) The federal purpose in the establishment and maintenance of the Metlakatla Indian Reservation.

(d) *Size, construction and closure of fish traps*—(1) *Size.* When any part of a trap is in a greater depth of water than 100 feet, the trap as measured from shore at mean high tide to the outer face of the pot shall not extend beyond 900 feet.

(2) *Construction.* Poles shall be permanently secured to the webbing at each side of the mouth of the pot tunnel and shall extend from the tunnel floor to a height at least four feet above the water. A draw line shall be reeved through the lower end of both poles and the upper end of one.

(3) *Method of closing.* The tunnel walls shall be overlapped as far as possible across the pot gap and the draw line shall be pulled tight and both secured so as to completely close the tunnel. In addition, 25 feet of the webbing of the heart on each side next to the pot shall be lifted or lowered in such manner as to permit the free passage of fish.

(e) *Other forms of commercial fishing.* All commercial fishing, other than with traps, shall be in accordance with the season and gear restrictions established by rule or regulation by the Alaska Board of Fish and Game for Commercial Fishing in any part of the previously defined area; provided, however, that the Secretary or his duly authorized representative may, upon request by the Metlakatla Indian Community authorize such other commercial fishing at such times as he shall prescribe, which authorization shall be based upon the following criteria:

(1) Number of fish required for spawning escapement and any other requirements reasonable and necessary for conservation;

(2) Fair and equitable sharing of the fishery resource with other user groups fishing in State waters under State law and within the State fisheries management system; and

(3) The Federal purpose in the establishment and maintenance of the Metlakatla Indian Reservation.

[28 FR 7183, July 12, 1963; 28 FR 12273, Nov. 20, 1963, as amended at 40 FR 24184, June 5, 1975. Redesignated at 47 FR 13327, Mar. 30, 1982]

§ 241.4 Subsistence and sport fishing, Annette Islands Reserve.

(a) *Definitions.* (1) Subsistence fishing is the taking or attempting to take any species of fish or shellfish for purposes other than sale or barter, except as provided for in paragraph (a)(2) of this section.

(2) Sport fishing is the taking or attempting to take for personal use, and not for sale or barter, any fresh water, marine, or anadromous fish by hook and line or by such means as defined by regulation or statute of the State of Alaska.

(b) *Restrictions.* Subsistence fishing within the Annette Islands Reserve shall be in accordance with the season, gear and bag restrictions established by rule or regulation of the Alaska Board of Fish and Game for Commercial Fishing in Fishing District No. 1. Sport fishing within the Annette Islands Reserve shall be in accordance with the season, gear and bag restrictions established by rule or regulation for Southeastern Alaska by the Alaska Board of Fish and Game. Both subsistence and sport fishing shall also be in accordance with such ordinances as may be adopted by the Council of the Metlakatla Indian Community and approved by the Secretary of the Interior.

§241.5 Commercial fishing, Karluk Indian Reservation.

(a) *Definition.* The Karluk Indian Reservation includes all waters extending 3,000 feet from the shore at mean low tide on Kodiak Island beginning at the end of a point of land on the shore of Shelikof Strait about 1¼ miles east of Rocky Point and in approximate latitude 57 degrees 39 minutes 40 seconds N., longitude 154 degrees 12 minutes 20 seconds W.; thence south approximately 8 miles to latitude 57 degrees 32 minutes 30 seconds N.; thence west approximately 12½ miles to the confluence of the north shore of Sturgeon River with the east shore of Shelikof Strait; thence northeasterly following the easterly shore of Shelikof Strait to the place of beginning, containing approximately 35,200 acres.

(b) *Who may fish; licenses.* The waters of the Karluk Indian Reservation shall be open to commercial fishing by bona fide native inhabitants of the native village of Karluk and vicinity, and to other persons insofar as the fishing activities of the latter do not restrict or interfere with fishing by such natives. Such natives shall not be required to obtain a license to engage in commercial fishing in the waters of the Karluk Indian Reservation.

(c) *Salmon fishing; restrictions.* Commercial fishing for salmon by native inhabitants of the native village of Karluk and vicinity in the waters of the Karluk Indian Reservation shall be in accordance with the seasonal and gear restrictions of the rules and regulations of the Alaska Board of Fish and Game for Commercial Fishing in the fishing district embracing the Karluk Indian Reservation except that:

(1) Beach seines up to 250 fathoms in length may be used northeast of Cape Karluk; and

(2) Prior to July 1, fishing shall be permitted to within 100 yards of the Karluk River where it breaks through the Karluk Spit into Shelikof Strait.

§241.6 Enforcement; violation of regulations; corrective action; penalties; closure of restrictions, Annette Islands Reserve.

(a) *Enforcement.* The regulations in this part shall be enforced by any duly authorized representative of the Secretary of the Interior. Any fish trap, vessel, gear, processing establishment or other operation or equipment subject to the regulations of this part shall be available for inspection at all times by such representative.

(b) *Violation of regulations.* Whenever any duly authorized enforcement representative of the Secretary of the Interior has reasonable cause to believe any violation of the regulations of this part relating to fish traps has occurred, he shall direct immediate closure of the trap involved and shall affix an appropriate seal thereto to prevent further fishing. The matter shall be reported without delay to the Area Director, Bureau of Indian Affairs, who shall thereupon report and recommend to the Secretary of the Interior appropriate corrective action.

(c) *Corrective action.* Any violation of the regulations of this part relating to fish traps shall be ground for the temporary or permanent closure, as the Secretary of the Interior may determine, of any or all traps authorized by §241.3(a), or the withdrawal and rescission of the right to fish for salmon with traps at any or all sites authorized thereby.

(d) *Penalties.* Any person who violates any of the regulations of this part shall be subject to prosecution under section 2 of the Act of July 12, 1960 (74 Stat. 469, 18 U.S.C. sec. 1165), which provides as follows:

Whoever, without lawful authority or permission, willfully and knowingly goes upon any land that belongs to any Indian or Indian tribe, band, or group and either are held by the United States in trust or are subject to a restriction against alienation imposed by the United States, or upon any lands of the United States that are reserved for Indian use, for the purpose of hunting, trapping, or fishing thereon, or for the removal of game, peltries, or fish therefrom, shall be fined not more than $200 or imprisoned not more than ninety days, or both, and all game, fish, and peltries in his possession shall be forfeited.

(e) *Closure or restriction, Annette Islands Reserve.* The Commissioner of Indian Affairs, after consultation with officials of the Metlakatla Indian Community, is authorized and directed, upon a determination of the necessity to promote sound conversation practices, to restrict or close to commercial, subsistence or sport fishing any portion of the Annette Islands Reserve by notice given appropriate local publicity.

[28 FR 7183, July 12, 1963, as amended at 30 FR 5742, Apr. 23, 1965. Redesignated at 47 FR 13327, Mar. 30, 1982]

PART 242—COMMERCIAL FISHING ON RED LAKE INDIAN RESERVATION

Sec.

AUTHORITY: 25 U.S.C. 2; 5 U.S.C. 301.

SOURCE: 25 FR 7784, Aug. 16, 1960, unless otherwise noted. Redesignated at 47 FR 13327, Mar. 30, 1982.

§ 242.1 Definitions.

As used in this part:

(a) "Secretary" means the Secretary of the Interior or his authorized representative.

(b) "Council" means the General Council of the Red Lake Band of the Chippewa Indians as recognized by the Secretary of the Interior.

(c) "Association" means the Red Lake Fisheries Association, incorporated under the laws of the State of Minnesota, and whose articles of incorporation and bylaws and any amendments thereto have been approved by the Council and the Secretary of the Interior.

(d) "Member of Association" means as defined in the Association by-laws.

(e) "Commercial fishing" means the catching of any fish for sale directly or indirectly to others than Indians on the reservations or licensed traders on the reservation for resale to Indians.

§ 242.2 Authority to engage in commercial fishing.

No person shall engage in commercial fishing in the waters of the Red Lakes on the Red Lake Indian Reservation in the State of Minnesota except the Red Lake Fisheries Association, a corporation organized and incorporated under the laws of Minnesota, and its members, and then only in accordance with the regulations in this part. The authority hereby granted to the Association and its members to engage in commercial fishing may, at any time, be canceled and withdrawn and these regulations may be modified and amended.

§ 242.3 Authority to operate.

The association may conduct commercial fishing operations on the reservation under authority of its articles of incorporation and by-laws only in accordance with the regulations in this part.

§ 242.4 Fishing.

(a) Enrolled members of the Red Lake Band of Chippewa Indians may take fish at any time except as prohibited by § 242.6 from waters of the Red Lakes on the Red Lake Indian Reservation for their own use and for sale to:

(1) Other Indians on the reservation and

(2) Licensed traders on the reservation for resale to Indians.

(b) Fish may be taken for commercial purposes only by the Association through members of the Association in residence on the reservation during the fishing season which shall be May 15 to November 15 inclusive. All fish taken for such purposes shall be marketed through the Association.

(c) In connection with commercial fishing, Association members fishermen may be assisted only by Indians who are members of the Red Lake Band.

§ 242.5 Disposition of unmarketable fish.

All unmarketable live fish taken under authority of these regulations must be returned to the water, and all unmarketable dead fish taken must be buried by the person taking the same.

§ 242.6 Spawning season.

Walleye and northern pike (or pickerel) shall not be taken during their spawning season except for propagation purposes.

§ 242.7 Suspension.

All commercial fishing operations may be suspended by order of the Secretary at any time.

§ 242.8 Penalty.

Any Indian violating the provisions of §§ 242.4 and 242.6 shall forfeit his right to take fish for any purpose for a period of three months.

§ 242.9 Quotas.

The Secretary may set such commercial quotas as he may find desirable, based on available biological and other information, on the amount of fish which may be taken under authority of the regulations in this part in any one season. Until otherwise determined by the Secretary, not more than 650,000 pounds of walleyes may be taken in any one fishing season.

§ 242.10 Fishing equipment limitations.

(a) Any variety of fish may be taken by enrolled members of the Band from any waters on the reservation by hook and line, and from Upper and Lower Red Lakes by gill net or entrapment gear for noncommercial use only.

(b) For commercial fishing each member of the Association shall be limited to eight gill nets of 300 feet in length and six feet in depth, of which not to exceed six of such nets may be of nylon and other synthetic material.

(c) Gill nets for taking pike shall have a mesh of not less that 3½ inches extension measure.

(d) Gill nets for taking whitefish shall have a mesh of not less than 5½ inches extension measure.

(e) Entrapment gear may only be used by members of the Association for taking fish of any variety for commercial purposes or propagation, in accordance with such specifications and directions as the manager of the Association may provide.

(f) All nets used in Red Lake Reservation waters must be marked with appropriate tags to be furnished by the Association.

§ 242.11 Royalty.

The Association shall pay five percent of the gross receipts from the sale of fish by the Association to the designated collection officer of the Bureau of Indian Affairs, which shall be deposited to the credit of the Band in the Treasury of the United States.

§ 242.12 Authority to lease.

The Band, with the approval of the Secretary, may execute a lease or permit on its fisheries plant and hatchery at Redby, Minnesota, to the Association.

PART 243—REINDEER IN ALASKA

AUTHORITY: Sec. 12, 50 Stat. 902; 25 U.S.C. 500K; and Sec. 701, Pub. L. 114–74, 129 Stat. 599.

SOURCE: 71 FR 2429, Jan. 13, 2006, unless otherwise noted.

§ 243.1 What is the purpose of this part?

The Department's policy is to encourage and develop the activity and responsibility of Alaska Natives in all branches of the reindeer industry and business in Alaska, and to preserve the Native character of that industry and business. This part contains requirements governing acquisition and transferring reindeer and reindeer products in Alaska.

§ 243.2 What terms do I need to know?

Act means the Reindeer Act of September 1, 1937 (50 Stat. 900; 25 U.S.C. 500 *et seq.*), as amended.

Alaska Native means Eskimos, Indians, and Aleuts inhabiting Alaska at the time of the Treaty of Cession of Alaska to the United States and their descendants currently living in Alaska.

Alaskan reindeer means:

(1) All reindeer descended from those present in Alaska at the time of passage of the Act; and

(2) Any caribou introduced into animal husbandry or that has joined a reindeer herd.

BIA means the Bureau of Indian Affairs within the United States Department of the Interior.

Designee means the person assigned by the Alaska Regional Director to administer the reindeer program.

Imported reindeer means reindeer brought into Alaska from any region outside of Alaska since passage of the Act.

Native reindeer organization means any corporation, association, or other organization, whether incorporated or not, composed solely of Alaska Natives, for the purpose of engaging in or promoting the reindeer industry.

Non-Native means a person who is not an Alaska Native.

Regional Director means the officer in charge of the Alaska Regional Office of the Bureau of Indian Affairs.

Reindeer products mean the meat, hide, antlers, or any other products derived from reindeer.

Transfer means the conveyance of ownership of reindeer or reindeer products, or any interest in them or interest in an Alaska Native reindeer organization, by any method.

We, us and *our* mean the Regional Director or the Director's designee.

§ 243.3 Delegation of authority.

The Secretary of the Interior has delegated authority under the Act through the Assistant Secretary—Indian Affairs to the Alaska Regional Director of the Bureau of Indian Affairs. All claims of ownership of reindeer in Alaska, as required by the Act (section 500b), must be filed with the Regional Director or the Director's designee.

§ 243.4 Who can own or possess Alaskan reindeer?

(a) Only Alaska Natives, organizations of Alaska Natives, or the United States for the benefit of these Natives, can own Alaskan reindeer in Alaska.

(1) Any transfer not allowed by this part is not legal, and does not confer ownership or the right to keep Alaskan reindeer, reindeer products, or any interest in them.

(2) Anyone violating this part will forfeit their reindeer or reindeer products to the Federal Government.

(b) An Alaska Native or a Native reindeer organization may transfer reindeer that they own to other Alaska Natives or Native reindeer organizations without restriction, except as provided in this part.

(c) We may maintain reindeer for research projects, so long as the purpose of the research benefits the Native reindeer industry. We retain title to these reindeer and will determine their eventual disposition.

(d) A non-Native manager of Alaskan reindeer must, by the last day of September each year:

(1) Provide us a copy of the contract with the Native reindeer owner; and

(2) Provide us a written report of all Alaskan reindeer kept, born, died or transferred.

(e) We may permit possession of a limited number of Alaskan reindeer by a non-Native applicant under a Special Use Permit for Public Display.

(1) We can revoke this permit for cause.

(2) The permit will not allow the permit-holder to keep a breeding herd (*i.e.*, a herd that is capable of reproduction).

(3) The permit-holder must report to us in writing by the last day of September each year on all reindeer held under this permit.

§ 243.5 Who can own imported reindeer, and what limitations apply?

(a) Anyone, including non-Natives, may own imported reindeer in Alaska for any legitimate purpose, subject to State and Federal animal health laws and regulations.

(b) Imported reindeer must not be intermingled with, or be bred to, Alaskan reindeer without our written consent. Any offspring resulting from a mating with Alaskan reindeer are considered Alaskan reindeer and a non-Native owner may not maintain these reindeer alive in Alaska.

(c) This paragraph applies if a non-Native owner of imported reindeer in Alaska contracts with a Native reindeer owner to keep and manage the imported reindeer. The non-Native owner must:

(1) Distinguish the imported reindeer from the Alaskan reindeer by applying a distinctly different permanent earmark or tattoo on all imported reindeer; and

(2) Register the earmark or tattoo with the State Division of Agriculture book of livestock brand marks.

§ 243.6 Which sales or transfers of Alaskan reindeer do not require a permit?

The following transfers do not require a permit:

(a) Sale or transfer by Alaska Natives of dead reindeer or reindeer products; and

(b) Sale of transfer of live reindeer between Alaska Natives or Native reindeer organizations.

§ 243.7 How can a non-Native acquire live reindeer?

If you are a non-Native who wants to acquire live Alaskan reindeer, you must apply to us in writing. We will either grant the request and issue a written permit valid for 90 days or reject the request and give our reasons in writing. Any transfer that we authorize is subject to the following conditions:

(a) The transfer must meet the requirements of the Act and this part.

(b) Within 30 days of transfer, you must either butcher the reindeer in Alaska or ship them out of Alaska. If you ship the reindeer out alive:

(1) You must comply with all Federal and State animal health regulations governing transfers and shipments; and

(2) The reindeer and their descendants must never be brought back to Alaska alive.

(c) Within 30 days of the transfer, you must report to us the actual number of reindeer shipped out or slaughtered.

§ 243.8 What penalties apply to violations of this part?

If you are a non-Native transferee of live Alaskan reindeer who violates the provisions of this part, you are subject to the penalties in this section.

(a) Under 25 U.S.C. 500i, you can be fined up to $6,111 if you:

(1) Take possession of reindeer without a permit issued under § 243.7; or

(2) Do not abide by the terms of a permit issued under § 243.7 (including the requirement that you slaughter or export the reindeer within 30 days and not bring them back alive into Alaska).

(b) Under 25 U.S.C. 500b, you are barred from asserting your title to the reindeer if you:

(1) Do not obtain a transfer permit from us and fully comply with its terms; or

(2) Fail to file with us a claim of title to reindeer within 30 days of acquiring them.

[71 FR 2429, Jan. 13, 2006, as amended at 81 FR 42482, June 30, 2016; 82 FR 7653, Jan. 23, 2017; 83 FR 5195, Feb. 6, 2018]

§ 243.9 Who may inherit live Alaskan reindeer and by what means?

(a) Privately-owned live Alaskan reindeer may pass to the deceased owner's Native heirs by descent or devise.

(b) In the event of the death of an owner of Alaskan reindeer, any direct or indirect interest by descent or devise shall be determined by the Department of Interior in a proceeding conducted in accordance with the provisions of 43 CFR part 4, subpart D. During the pendency of such a proceeding, the authority to assume control over the affected Alaskan reindeer pursuant to 43 CFR 4.270 may be exercised by the Alaska Regional Director or his designee.

(c) This paragraph applies if the final probate decree of the Department of the Interior, or the decision of any reviewing Federal court, identifies a non-Native as inheriting Alaskan reindeer. The non-Native may inherit, but must be allowed no more than 30 days from receiving the final determination of heirship to:

(1) Slaughter the reindeer;

(2) Apply for a permit to transfer the reindeer to an out-of-state transferee; or

(3) Transfer ownership of the reindeer to one or more Alaska Native family members or other Alaska Native(s).

§ 243.10 How does the Paperwork Reduction Act affect this rule?

The actions in this rule that are covered by the Paperwork Reduction Act are cleared under OMB Control Number 1076–0047. The parts subject to this control number are 243.4(d), 243.4(e), 243.5(c), 243.7, and 243.9(c). Please note, a Federal agency may not conduct or sponsor, and you are not required to respond to, a collection of information unless it displays a currently valid OMB control number.

§ 243.11 Are transfers of Alaskan reindeer that occurred before issuance of this part valid?

All transfers of live Alaskan reindeer or reindeer products that were completed before the effective date of this part are hereby ratified and confirmed. This ratification does not extend to transfers that:

(a) Were fraudulent;

(b) Were made under duress;

(c) Did not result in payment of fair compensation to the Native transferer; or

(d) Would have been prohibited under §§ 243.6 or 243.8 of this part.

§ 243.12 Are Alaska reindeer trust assets maintained by the U.S. Government for the benefit of Alaska Natives?

Only the titles to Alaskan reindeer retained for research projects, or possessed by non-Natives under Special Use Permits for Public Display, or the titles to any Alaskan reindeer which may be acquired by the Government in the future for purposes of reestablishing a reindeer loan program, are held by the United States in trust for Alaska Natives. Other Alaskan reindeer are the private property of the Alaska Native owners. However, a trust responsibility continues to exist with respect to all Alaskan reindeer, insofar as the Government remains responsible for carrying out the provisions of the Reindeer Act and these regulations, including the provisions requiring approval of transfers to non-Natives, and providing for the determination of inheritance.

§ 243.13 Who may appeal an action under this part?

Any interested party adversely affected by a decision under this part has the right of appeal as provided in 25 CFR part 2 and 43 CFR part 4, subpart D.

PART 247—USE OF COLUMBIA RIVER TREATY FISHING ACCESS SITES

AUTHORITY: 25 U.S.C. 2 and 9; Pub. L. 100–581, Title IV.

SOURCE: 62 FR 50868, Sept. 29, 1997, unless otherwise noted.

§ 247.1 What definitions apply to this part?

Abandoned property means property left at a site while the owner of the property is not actively engaged in fishing or drying or processing fish. Abandoned property may include:

(1) Vehicles;
(2) Mobile trailers;
(3) Campers;
(4) Tents;
(5) Tepees;
(6) Boats, or;
(7) Other personal property.

Archaeological Resource means material remains of prehistoric or historic human life or activities that are of archaeological interest and are at least 50 years of age, and the physical site, location, or context in which they are found.

Area Director means the position responsible for administration of the Portland Area of the Bureau of Indian Affairs.

Campfire means fire, not within any building, motor home or trailer, which is used for cooking, personal warmth, lighting, ceremonial or aesthetic purposes.

Damage means to injure, mutilate, deface, destroy, cut, chop, girdle, dig, excavate, kill or in any way harm or disturb.

Secretary means the Secretary of the Interior or his designee.

Sites means Treaty Fishing Access Sites.

Treaty Fishing Access Sites means all Federal lands acquired by the Secretary of the Army and Transferred to the Secretary of the Interior pursuant to Public Law 100–581, Title IV, November 1, 1988, to be administered to provide access to usual and accustomed fishing areas and ancillary fishing facilities.

Vehicle means any device in, upon, or by which any person or property is or may be transported, and including any motor, frame, chassis, or body of any motor vehicle, or camper shell, except devices used exclusively upon stationary rails or tracks.

§ 247.2 What lands are subject to these regulations?

(a) Any treaty fishing access sites and ancillary fishing facilities.

(b) These sites and facilities are managed for the exclusive use of members of the Nez Perce Tribe, the Confederated Tribes of the Umatilla Reservation, the Confederated Tribes of the Warm Springs Reservation of Oregon, and the Confederated Tribes and Bands of the Yakima Indian Reservation.

(c) The Area Director may suspend or withdraw the privileges of use of any or all of the facilities at the sites for any violation of the regulations in this part or of any rules issued under the regulations in this part.

§ 247.3 Who is eligible to use the sites?

(a) You may use the sites for access to usual and accustomed fishing areas and ancillary fishing facilities if you are a member of the Confederated Tribes and Bands of the Yakima Indian Nation (Yakima), the Confederated Tribes of the Warm Springs Reservation of Oregon (Warm Springs), the Confederated Tribes of the Umatilla Indian Reservation (Umatilla), and the Nez Perce Tribe (Nez Perce).

(b) The general public or people fishing who do not belong to the tribes listed above cannot use these sites.

(c) Families of such Indians may camp on the sites.

(d) You may not deny access to these sites to any eligible user.

§ 247.4 How can eligible users be identified?

(a) In order to use these sites you must posses an identification card issued by your tribe identifying you as a member of that tribe.

(b) You must exhibit the identification upon request of authorized Federal, State, local or tribal officials.

§ 247.5 What laws and regulations apply to the people who use these sites?

You may use access sites only if you obey the following rules:

(a) You may not use any of the sites for any activity that is contrary to the provisions of your tribe or contrary to Federal law or regulation, or in the absence of Federal law or regulation governing health, sanitation, and safety requirements, State or U.S. Public Health Service standards.

(b) The Area Director may suspend or withdraw the privileges of use of any or all of the facilities at the sites for any violation of the regulations in this part or for any violation of any rules issued under the regulations in this part. You cannot dig in, destroy, or remove any portion of a prehistoric or historic archaeological site or artifact.

(c) Nothing contained in the regulations in this part is intended or shall be construed as limiting or affecting any treaty rights of any tribe nor as subjecting any Indian properly exercising tribal treaty rights to State fishing laws or regulations that are not compatible with those rights.

§ 247.6 What will happen if I damage Government-owned property?

If you commit any act of vandalism, depredation, destruction, theft, or misuse of the land, buildings, fences, signs, or other structures that are the property of the United States you will be subject to prosecution under applicable Federal or State law.

§ 247.7 Can I build a structure?

(a) You may not build any structures at the sites except as allowed under paragraph (d) of this section .

(b) You may use the camping facilities that have been constructed at the sites.

(c) In addition to these structures, you may camp in tents, tepees, campers, and mobile trailers. You must remove any tents, tepees, campers, temporary drying sheds, and mobile trailers from the sites at any time you are not actively engaged in fishing, drying fish, or processing fish by other means, and during the time a site is closed for maintenance.

(d) Where the Area Director has designated areas for the construction of temporary drying sheds, you may construct a temporary drying shed where space is available. You must remove any temporary drying shed you build.

(e) If you erect or maintain a structure in violation of this section, the Area Director may order it removed at any time.

(f) The Area Director:

(1) Is not required to notify you before removing the structure; and

(2) Will charge you the cost of disposing of the structure.

§ 247.8 What am I responsible for if I use the facilities?

You are responsible for:

(a) Campsites, drying sheds and other facilities during the time you occupy or use them; and

(b) Any personal property that you erect, place, or maintain on the site during the time you occupy the site, including:

(1) Tents;

(2) Tepees;

(3) Campers;

(4) Mobile trailers;

(5) Temporary drying sheds;

(6) Fishing platforms;

(7) Boats; and

(8) Other fishing equipment.

§ 247.9 What other rules apply while I am using the facilities?

(a) You cannot construct, take possession of, occupy or otherwise use any access site or structure for residential purposes at an access site.

(b) Neither the United States nor any officer or employee thereof warrants, makes any representation, or is responsible for the safety or condition of any personal property.

§ 247.10 What will happen if I abandon property?

If you abandon property at a site, it may be removed without your consent and disposed of at your expense, if the Area Director approves.

§ 247.11 What other restrictions apply to use of the sites?

The Area Director may prescribe and post at the sites regulations covering:

(a) Camping;

(b) Picnicking;

(c) Use of alcoholic beverages;

(d) Setting or use of fires;

(e) Use of the sites for cleaning fish;

(f) Deposit of garbage, paper, cans, bottles, or rubbish of any kind; or

(g) Use of the sites for any commercial activity (including commercial purchase of fish).

§ 247.12 Will I have to pay to use a site?

No. Neither you nor any member of your family will be charged for using a site in accordance with this part.

§ 247.13 Are the facilities available year around?

(a) The Area Director may close facilities at the sites for necessary maintenance during the winter or at other times if necessary. Before closing the facilities, the Area Director will consult with delegated tribal representatives, if possible.

(b) You will still be able to access your treaty fishing rights on the Columbia River through these sites while they are closed.

(c) If any sites are closed or restricted, any affected tribe can contact the Area Director and ask that the sites be opened. The Area Director will work together with the tribes to consider these requests.

§ 247.14 Can I hook up a campsite to on-site or off-site utilities?

(a) You must share access to all on-site facilities.

(b) Because there are a limited number of faucets available, only short-term hose use is allowed to ensure that others have access to water.

(c) You may not tap into electrical lines or outlets, or have electrical power brought in from an outside source for campsite use.

§ 247.15 May I reserve a campsite or drying shed?

No. You may not reserve a campsite, drying shed, or other facility.

(a) You must use campsites, drying sheds, and other facilities on a first-come, first-served basis.

(b) You may not occupy one or more campsites solely for the purpose of reserving a site for another tribal member.

§ 247.16 What fire is permitted?

(a) You may have a fire in designated fire places, and other areas designated for fires.

(b) You may have a fire inside a drying shed in a manner that does not jeopardize the structure.

§ 247.17 What are the restrictions on fires?

(a) You cannot burn timber, trees, slash, brush or grass unless you have a permit issued by the Area Director or his designee.

(b) You cannot build a fire in an unsafe location or leave a fire without completely extinguishing it.

(c) You must control all fire and not allow it to escape.

§ 247.18 What are the sanitation prohibitions?

(a) You cannot deposit in any toilet, toilet vault, or plumbing fixture anything that could damage or interfere with the operation or maintenance of the fixture.

(b) You must dispose of all garbage, including any paper, cans, bottle, sewage, waste water or material, either by removal from the site, or by depositing it into receptacles or at places provided for such purposes.

(c) You may not bring refuse, debris, or toxic or hazardous materials to the sites for disposal.

(d) All toxic or hazardous materials must be properly removed from the sites. You may not dispose of such materials in a sewer line, tank, drain, storm drain, or on the ground.

(e) You must not place in or near the river or other water any substance that pollutes or may pollute the water.

(f) If dumping stations are not available, you must transport sewage off site.

§ 247.19 Can a site be used for commercial enterprises other than fishing enterprises by the tribes?

(a) You may operate commercial activities during commercial fishing seasons, and subsistence activities, incidental to treaty fishing on the site.

(b) You may not construct or operate other types of commercial enterprises, such as firework stands.

§ 247.20 What are the road and trail prohibitions?

(a) You cannot damage or leave in a damaged condition any road, trail, or segment thereof.

(b) You cannot block, restrict, or otherwise interfere with the use of a road, trail, or gate.

§ 247.21 Can I appeal an administrative action?

You may appeal any decision made by the Area Director under this part to the Commissioner of Indian Affairs. You may appeal any decision of the Commissioner of Indian Affairs to the Secretary of the Interior in accordance with part 2 of this chapter.

PART 248—USE OF COLUMBIA RIVER INDIAN IN-LIEU FISHING SITES

Sec.

AUTHORITY: 5 U.S.C. 301; 25 U.S.C. 2, 9.

SOURCE: 32 FR 3945, Mar. 10, 1967, unless otherwise noted. Redesignated at 47 FR 13327, Mar. 30, 1982.

§ 248.1 Fishing sites subject to regulation.

Use of any of the lands acquired by the Secretary of War and transferred to the Secretary of the Interior pursuant to the Act of March 2, 1945 (59 Stat. 22), as amended (hereinafter called "in lieu fishing sites" or "sites") to replace Indian fishing grounds submerged or destroyed as a result of the construction of the Bonneville Dam shall be subject to the following rules and regulations. The Area Director, Portland Area Office, Bureau of Indian Affairs (hereinafter called "Area Director"), may suspend or withdraw the privileges of access to or use of any or all the sites for any violation of the regulations in this part or of any rules issued pursuant to the regulations in this part.

§ 248.2 Persons eligible to use sites.

The in-lieu fishing sites are for the benefit of the Yakima, Umatilla, and Warm Springs Indian Tribes, and such other Columbia River Indians, if any, who had treaty fishing rights at locations inundated or destroyed by Bonneville Dam, to be used is accordance with treaty rights. The use of the sites is restricted to such Indians; however, this shall not preclude the use of camping areas on the sites by the families of such Indians.

§ 248.3 Identification of eligible users.

For the purpose of identification of the persons entitled to use the sites, each eligible Indian shall, when using said sites, have in his possession an identification card issued by his tribe identifying him as a member of that tribe. The Area Director shall issue identification cards to such other Columbia River Indians, if any, as may be eligible to use the sites. Any individual using the sites shall exhibit the identification upon request of authorized Federal, State or local officials.

§ 248.4 Applicability of laws and regulations.

No Indian shall use any of the sites for any activity that is contrary to the provisions of any applicable law or regulation of his tribe or contrary to any applicable State or Federal law or regulation. The Area Director may in his discretion suspend or withdraw privileges for future access to or use of the sites for violation of such laws and regulations: *Provided*, That, nothing contained in the regulations in this part is intended or shall be construed as limiting or affecting any treaty rights of any tribe nor as subjecting any Indian properly exercising tribal treaty rights to State fishing laws or regulations which are not compatible with such rights.

§ 248.5 Damage to Government-owned property.

Anyone committing any act of depredation, destruction, theft, or misuse of the land, buildings, fences, signs, or other structures which are the property of the United States shall be subject to prosecution under applicable Federal or State law.

§ 248.6 Structures.

Dwellings, camping facilities, and other structures such as fish drying facilities and fishing platforms may be erected, placed, or maintained on the sites for use in the conduct of treaty fishing and related activities. Sites must be used in a manner that conforms to the health, sanitation, and safety requirements of the State or local law, or, in the absence of appropriate State or local laws, to the health, sanitation, and safety recommendations of the U.S. Public Health Service. The privileges or right of access to or use of the sites of any individual may be suspended or withdrawn, in the discretion of the Area Director, when such individual having violated such health, sanitation, and safety requirements repeats such violation after having been given notice to cease and desist therefrom.

[59 FR 16757, Apr. 7, 1994]

§ 248.7 Liability for condition and use of structures.

Any private structures including drying sheds, tents, tepees, or fishing platforms erected, placed, or maintained on the sites are the sole responsibility of their owners, and all use of such structures shall be at the user's or owner's sole responsibility and risk. Neither the United States nor any officer or employee thereof warrants, makes any representation, or is responsible for the safety or condition of any such structure.

[34 FR 2248, Feb. 15, 1969. Redesignated at 47 FR 13327, Mar. 30, 1982]

§ 248.8 Abandoned property.

No vehicle, trailer, boat, or other personal property shall be abandoned on the sites. Property abandoned in violation of the regulations in this part may be removed without prior notice to the owner and may be disposed of at the owner's expense as determined by the Area Director.

§ 248.9 Camping and use restrictions.

All camping, picnicking, use of alcoholic beverages, setting or use of fires, use of the sites for cleaning of fish, the deposit of any garbage, paper, cans, bottles, or rubbish of any kind, or use of the sites for any commercial activity (including commercial purchase of fish) shall be subject to such prohibitions, restrictions, or other regulations as the Area Director may prescribe and cause to be posted on the site or sites to which said regulations are applicable; provided that no fee may be charged to any Indian or member of his family for any such use.

§ 248.10 Appeals from administrative actions.

Any decision made by the Area Director under this part 248 shall be subject to appeal to the Commissioner of Indian Affairs, and any decision on the Commissioner of Indian Affairs on such an appeal may be appealed to the Secretary of the Interior in accordance with part 2 of this chapter.

PART 249—OFF-RESERVATION TREATY FISHING

Subpart A—General Provisions

Sec.

AUTHORITY: 25 U.S.C. 2, and 9; 5 U.S.C. 301; and Sec. 701, Pub. L. 114–74, 129 Stat. 599, unless otherwise noted.

SOURCE: 32 FR 10434, July 15, 1967, unless otherwise noted. Redesignated at 47 FR 13327, Mar. 30, 1982.

Subpart A—General Provisions

§ 249.1 Purpose.

(a) The purposes of these regulations (part 249) are:

(1) To assist in protecting the off-reservation nonexclusive fishing rights which are secured to certain Indian tribes by their treaties with the United States;

(2) To promote the proper management, conservation and protection of fisheries resources which are subject to such treaties of the United States;

(3) To provide for determination of restrictions on the manner of exercising nonexclusive fishing privileges under rights secured to Indian tribes by such treaties of the United States necessary for conservation of the fisheries resources;

(4) To assist in the orderly administration of Indian Affairs;

(5) To encourage consultation and cooperation between the states and Indian tribes in the management and improvement of fisheries resources affected by such treaties;

(6) To assist the states in enforcing their laws and regulations for the management and conservation of fisheries resources in a manner compatible with the treaties of the United States which are applicable to such resources.

(b) The conservation regulations of this part 249 are found to be necessary to assure that the nonexclusive rights secured to certain Indian tribes by treaties of the United States to fish at usual and accustomed places outside the boundaries of an Indian reservation shall be protected and preserved for the benefit of present and future members of such tribes in a manner consistent with the nonexclusive character of such rights. Any exercise of an Indian off-reservation treaty fishing right shall be in accordance with this part and any applicable area regulations issued hereunder.

[32 FR 10434, July 15, 1967. Redesignated at 47 FR 13327, Mar. 30, 1982; 48 FR 13414, Mar. 31, 1983]

§ 249.2 Area regulations.

(a) The Secretary of the Interior may upon request of an Indian tribe, request of a State Governor, or upon his own motion, and upon finding that Federal regulation of Indian fishing in any waters in which Indians have a treaty-secured nonexclusive fishing right is necessary to assure the conservation and wise utilization of the fishery resources for the present and future use and enjoyment of the Indians and other persons entitled thereto, promulgate regulations to govern the exercise of such treaty-secured fishing right in such waters for the purpose of preventing, in conjunction with appropriate State conservation laws and regulations governing fishing by persons not fishing under treaty rights, the deterioration of the fishery resources.

(b) In formulating such regulations the Secretary of the Interior may incorporate such State laws or regulations, or such tribal regulations as have been approved by the Commissioner of Indian Affairs, as he finds to be consistent with the Indians' rights under the Treaty and the conservation of the fishery resources.

(c) Before promulgating such regulations the Secretary of the Interior will seek the views of the affected Indian tribes, of the fish or game management agency or agencies of any affected State, and of other interested persons. Except in emergencies where the Secretary finds that the exigencies require the promulgation of regulations to be effective immediately, a notice of proposed rule making will be published in the FEDERAL REGISTER in accordance with 5 U.S.C. 553 to afford an opportunity to submit comments and information, at such times and in such manner as may be specified in the notice. In the event of the emergency promulgation of regulations, interested persons will be afforded, as soon as possible, an opportunity to request amendment or revocation thereof.

(d) Any regulations issued pursuant to this section shall contain provisions for invoking emergency closures or restrictions or the relaxation thereof at the field level when necessary or appropriate to meet conditions not foreseeable at the time the regulations were issued.

(e) Regulations issued pursuant to this § 249.2 may include such requirements for recording and reporting catch statistics as the appropriate state fish and game agencies or the Secretary of the Interior deem necessary for effective fishery management.

§ 249.3 Identification cards.

(a) The Commissioner of Indian Affairs shall arrange for the issuance of an appropriate identification card to any Indian entitled thereto as prima facie evidence that the authorized holder thereof is entitled to exercise the fishing rights secured by the treaty designated thereon. The Commissioner may cause a federal card to be issued for this purpose or may authorize the issuance of cards by proper tribal authorities: *Provided,* That any such tribal cards shall be countersigned by an authorized officer of the Bureau of Indian Affairs certifying that the person named on the card is a member of the tribe issuing such card and that said tribe is recognized by the Bureau of Indian Affairs as having fishing rights under the treaty specified on such card. Copies of the form of any identification card authorized pursuant to this section and a list of the authorized Bureau of Indian Affairs issuing or countersigning officials shall be furnished to the fisheries management and enforcement agencies of any State in which such fishing rights may be exercised.

(b) No such card shall be issued to any Indian who is not on the official membership roll of the tribe which has been approved by the Secretary of the Interior. *Provided,* That until further notice, a temporary card may be issued to any member of a tribe not having an approved current membership roll who submits evidence of his/her entitlement thereto satisfactory to the issuing officer and, in the case of a tribally issued card, to the countersigning officer. Any Indian claiming to have been wrongfully denied a card may appeal the decision in accordance with part 2 of this chapter.

(c) No person shall be issued an identification card on the basis of membership in more than one tribe at any one time.

(d) Each card shall state the name, address, tribal affiliation and enrollment number (if any) of the holder, identify the treaty under which the holder is entitled to fishing rights, contain such additional personal identification data as is required on fishing licenses issued under the law of the State or States within which it is used, and be signed by the issuing officer and by the holder.

(e) No charge or fee of any kind shall be imposed by the Commissioner of Indian Affairs for the issuance of an identification card hereunder: *Provided,* That this shall not prevent any Indian tribe from imposing any fee or tax which it may otherwise be authorized to impose upon the exercise of any tribal fishing right.

(f) All cards issued by the Commissioner of Indian Affairs pursuant to this part 249 shall be and remain the property of the United States and may be retaken by any Federal, State, or tribal enforcement officer from any unauthorized holder. Any card so retaken shall be immediately forwarded to the officer who issued it.

(g) The failure of any person who claims to be entitled to the benefits of a treaty fishing right to have such a card in his immediate personal possession while fishing or engaging in other activity in the claimed exercise of such right to display it upon request to any Federal, State, or tribal enforcement officer shall be prima facie evidence that the person is not entitled to exercise an Indian fishing right under a treaty of the United States.

(h) No person shall allow any use of his identification card by any other person.

(5 U.S.C. 301; R.S. 463 and 465)

[32 FR 10434, July 15, 1967, as amended at 46 FR 4873, Jan. 19, 1981. Redesignated at 47 FR 13327, Mar. 30, 1982, as amended at 48 FR 1052, Jan. 10, 1983]

§ 249.4 Identification of fishing equipment.

All fishing gear or other equipment used in the exercise of any off-reservation treaty fishing right shall be marked in such manner as shall be prescribed in regulations issued pursuant to § 249.2 hereof to disclose the identity of its owner or user. In the absence of proof to the contrary, any fishing gear which is not so marked or labeled shall be presumed not to be used in the exercise of an off-reservation treaty fishing right and shall be subject to control or seizure under State law.

§ 249.5 Use of unauthorized helpers or agents.

No Indian shall, while exercising off-reservations treaty-secured fishing rights, permit any person 12 years of age or older other than the authorized holder of a currently valid identification card issued pursuant to this part 249 to fish for him, assist him in fishing, or use any gear of fishing location identified as his gear or location pursuant to this part 249.

§ 249.6 Enforcement and penalties.

(a) Any Indian tribe with a tribal court may confer jurisdiction upon such court to punish violations by its members of this part 249 or of the area regulations issued pursuant thereto. Jurisdiction is hereby conferred upon each Court of Indian Offenses established pursuant to part 11 of this chapter to punish such violations by members of tribes whose reservations are under the jurisdiction of such court. Courts of Indian Fishing Offenses may be created pursuant to part 11 of this chapter to punish such violations by members of any tribe or group of tribes for which there is otherwise no Court of Indian Offenses or tribal court with jurisdiction to enforce this part 249. The provisions of part 11 of this chapter shall apply to any such court with respect to the exercise of its jurisdiction to enforce this part 249. All jurisdiction conferred by this section shall apply without regard to any territorial limitations otherwise applicable to the jurisdiction of such court.

(b) Acceptance or use of an identification card issued pursuant to this part 249 or use of any fishing gear marked or identified pursuant thereto shall constitute an acknowledgment that the fishing done under such card or with such gear is in the claimed exercise of a tribal fishing right and is subject to the jurisdiction of the tribal court, Court of Indian Offenses, or Court of Indian Fishing Offenses. Except as may be otherwise provided by tribal regulations approved by or on behalf of the Secretary of the Interior, any person claiming to be exercising such tribal right and fishing in violation of the regulations contained in or issued under this part 249 may be punished by a fine of not to exceed $1,296, imprisonment of not to exceed 6 months, or both, and shall have his tribal fishing privileges suspended for not less than 5 days for any violation of this part 249 or of any area regulation issued pursuant thereto. The court shall impound the fishing rights identification card of any person for the period which the fishing privileges are suspended.

[32 FR 10434, July 15, 1967, as amended at 81 FR 42482, June 30, 2016; 82 FR 7653, Jan. 23, 2017; 83 FR 5195, Feb. 6, 2018]

§ 249.7 Savings provisions.

Nothing in this part 249 shall be deemed to:

(a) Prohibit or restrict any persons from engaging in any fishing activity in any manner which is permitted under state law;

(b) Deprive any Indian tribe, band, or group of any right which may be secured it by any treaty or other law of the United States;

(c) Permit any Indian to exercise any tribal fishing right in any manner prohibited by any ordinance or regulation of his tribe;

(d) Enlarge the right, privilege, or immunity of any person to engage in any fishing activity beyond that granted or reserved by treaty with the United States;

(e) Exempt any person or any fishing gear, equipment, boat, vehicle, fish or fish products, or other property from the requirements of any law or regulation pertaining to safety, obstruction of navigable waters, national defense, security of public property, pollution, health and sanitation, or registration of boats or vehicles;

(f) Abrogate or modify the effect of any agreement affecting fishing practices entered into between any Indian tribe and the United States or any State or agency of either.

SUBCHAPTER K—HOUSING

PART 256—HOUSING IMPROVEMENT PROGRAM (HIP)

AUTHORITY: 25 U.S.C. 13, 5 U.S.C. 301, 25 U.S.C. 2 and 9, and 43 U.S.C. 1457.

SOURCE: 80 FR 69596, Nov. 10, 2015, unless otherwise noted.

Subpart A—General Provisions

§ 256.1 Purpose.

The purpose of the part is to define the terms and conditions under which assistance is given to Indians under the Housing Improvement Program (HIP).

§ 256.2 Definitions.

As used in this part:

Agency means the organizational unit of BIA that provides services to or with the governing body or bodies and members of one or more specified Indian tribes.

Appeal means a written request for review of an action or inaction of an official of BIA that is claimed to adversely affect the interested party making the request, as provided in part 2 of this chapter.

Applicant means an individual(s) filing an application for services under the HIP.

BIA means the Bureau of Indian Affairs in the Department of the Interior.

Category A means the HIP funding category for minor repair not to exceed limits in § 256.7 of this part.

Category B means the HIP funding category for renovation not to exceed limits in § 256.7 of this part.

Category C–1 means the HIP funding category to replace a house that cannot be brought up to standard housing condition for $60,000 or less.

Category C–2 means the HIP funding category for building new housing as defined in § 256.13(g)(1)–(5).

Category D means the HIP funding category for assistance as defined in § 256.11(a)–(c).

Certificate of Title or Ownership means a document giving legal right to a house constructed with HIP funds.

Child means a person under the age of 18 or such other age of majority as is established for purposes of parental support by tribal or state law (if any) applicable to the person at his or her residence, except that no person who has been emancipated by marriage can be deemed a child.

Cost effective means the cost of the project is within the cost limits for the category of assistance and adds sufficient years of service to the house to satisfy the recipient's housing needs.

Dilapidated housing means a house which in its present condition endangers the life, health, or safety of the residents.

Disabled means having a physical or intellectual impairment that substantially limits one or more major life activities.

Family means one or more persons living within a household.

Homeless means being without a home.

House means a building for human habitation that serves as living quarters for one or more families.

Household means persons living with the head of household who may be related or unrelated to the head of household and who function as members of a family.

Independent trades person means any person licensed to perform work in a particular vocation pertaining to building construction.

Indian means any person who is a member of any federally recognized Indian tribe.

Indian tribe means an Indian or Alaska Native tribe, band, nation, pueblo, village or community that the Secretary of the Interior acknowledges to exist as an Indian tribe pursuant to Public Law 103–454, 108 Stat. 4791.

Overcrowding means a number of occupants per house that exceeds limits identified in § 256.10(d).

Permanent members of household means adults living in the household who intend to live there continuously and any children who meet the definition of *child* in this part.

Regional Director means the officer in charge of a BIA regional office or his/her authorized delegate.

Secretary means the Secretary of the Interior.

Service area means any of the following within a geographical area designated by the tribe and approved by the Regional Director to which services can be delivered:

(1) Reservations (former reservations in Oklahoma);

(2) Allotments;

(3) Restricted lands; and

(4) Indian-owned lands (including lands owned by corporations established pursuant to the Alaska Native Claims Settlement Act).

Servicing housing office means the tribal housing office or bureau housing office administering the HIP.

Standard housing means a house that meets the definition of *standard housing condition* in this part.

Standard housing condition means meets applicable building codes within that region and meets each of the following conditions:

(1) General construction conforms to applicable tribal, county, State, or national codes and to appropriate building standards for the region.

(2) The heating system has the capacity to maintain a minimum temperature of 70 degrees in the house during the coldest weather in the area and be safe to operate and maintain and deliver a uniform heat distribution.

(3) The plumbing system includes a properly installed system of piping and fixtures certified by a licensed plumbing contractor.

(4) The electrical system includes wiring and equipment properly installed to safely supply electrical energy for lighting and appliance operation certified by a licensed electrician according to the applicable electrical code.

(5) The number of occupants per house does not exceed these limits:

(i) Two-bedroom house: Up to four persons;

(ii) Three-bedroom house: Up to six persons;

(iii) Four-bedroom house: Adequate for all but the largest families.

(6) The first bedroom has up to 120 sq. ft. of floor space and additional bedrooms have up to100 sq. ft. of floor space each.

(7) The house site provides economical access to utilities and is easy to enter and leave.

(8) The house has access to school bus routes, if the household includes children who rely on school buses.

Substandard housing means any house that does not meet the definition of *standard housing condition* in this part.

Superintendent means the BIA official in charge of an agency office.

§256.3 Policy.

(a) The BIA housing policy is that every American Indian and Alaska Native should have the opportunity for a safe and decent home and suitable living conditions, which is consistent with the national housing policy. The HIP will serve the neediest of the needy Indian families who have no other resource for standard housing.

(b) Every American Indian or Alaska Native who meets the basic eligibility criteria defined in §256.6 may participate in the HIP.

(c) The BIA encourages tribal participation in administering the HIP. Tribal involvement is necessary to ensure that the services provided under the program respond to the needs of tribes and program participants.

(d) The BIA encourages partnerships and leveraging with other complementary programs to increase basic benefits derived from the HIP, such as an agreement with:

(1) The Indian Health Service to provide water and sanitation facilities;

(2) The United States Department of Agriculture, Rural Development to leverage down payment assistance for a new unit; or

(3) Any other program and resource.

(e) The servicing housing office will issue a Certificate of Title or Ownership.

§256.4 Information collection.

The information collection requirements contained in this part have been approved by the Office of Management and Budget under 44 U.S.C. 3507 *et seq.* and assigned control number 1076-0184. The information is collected to determine applicant eligibility for services and eligibility to participate in the program. Response is required to obtain a benefit. You may comment to the Bureau at any time with regard to this information collection.

§256.5 What is the Housing Improvement Program?

The HIP is a safety-net program that provides grants for the cost of services to repair, renovate, or replace existing housing and/or provide housing. The program provides grants to the neediest of the needy Indian families who:

(a) Live in substandard housing or are homeless; and

(b) Have no other resource for assistance.

Subpart B—Determining Eligibility

§256.6 Am I eligible for the Housing Improvement Program?

You are eligible for the HIP if you meet all of the following criteria:

(a) You are a member of a federally recognized Indian tribe;

(b) You live in an approved tribal service area;

(c) Your annual income is 150 percent or less of the Department of Health and Human Services poverty income guidelines, which are available from your servicing housing office or the Department of the Interior Web site at *www.bia.gov*;

(d) Your present housing is substandard as defined in §256.2;

(e) You meet the ownership requirements for the assistance needed, as defined in §256.8, §256.9, or §256.10;

(f) You have no other resource for housing assistance;

(g) You have not previously received assistance relating to categories as defined in §§256.9, 256.10, and 256.11; and

(h) You did not acquire your present housing through past participation in a Federal government-sponsored housing program over the previous 20 year period.

§256.7 What housing services are available?

Four categories of assistance are available under the HIP, as outlined in the following table.

Type of assistance	What it provides	Where to find information
Category A	Up to $7,500 in safety or sanitation repairs to the house in which you live, which will remain substandard. Can be provided more than once, but not for more than one house and the total assistance cannot exceed $7,500. (For Alaska, freight cost not to exceed 100 percent of the cost of materials can be added to the cost of the project.).	§ 256.8.
Category B	Up to $60,000 in renovation, which will bring your house to standard housing condition, as defined in § 256.2 of this part. Can only be provided once. (For Alaska, freight cost not to exceed 100 percent of the cost of materials can be added to the cost of the project.).	§ 256.9.
Category C	A modest house that meets the criteria in § 256.10 of this part and the definition of standard housing in § 256.2 of this part and whose costs are determined by and limited to the criteria in § 256.19(b) and (c) of this part. Can only be provided once. (For Alaska, freight cost not to exceed 100 percent of the cost of materials can be added to the cost of the project.).	§ 256.10.
Category D	Assistance towards the purchase of a modest house that meets the definition of standard housing in § 256.2.	§ 256.11.

§ 256.8 When do I qualify for Category A assistance?

You qualify for interim improvement assistance under Category A if it is not cost effective to repair the house in which you live and if either of the following is true:

(a) Other resources to meet your housing needs exist but are not immediately available; or

(b) You qualify for replacement housing under Category C, but there are no HIP funds available to replace your house.

§ 256.9 When do I qualify for Category B assistance?

You qualify for renovation assistance under Category B if you meet all of the following criteria:

(a) Your servicing housing office determines that it is cost effective to renovate the house.

(b) You occupy and own the house.

(c) Your servicing housing office determines that the renovation will bring the house to standard housing condition according to all applicable building codes.

(d) You sign a written agreement stating that, if you sell the house before satisfaction of the Payback Agreement you will be required to repay the tribe, tribal organization that administers the HIP, or BIA the remaining balance according to the terms of the Payback Agreement:

(1) The grant under this part will be voided; and

(2) At the time of settlement of the sale of the house, you will repay the tribe or tribal organization that operates the HIP or BIA the full cost of all renovations made under this part.

§ 256.10 When do I qualify for Category C assistance?

(a) You qualify for replacement housing assistance under Category C if you meet one of the three sets of requirements in the following table.

You qualify for Category C assistance if . . .	And . . .	And . . .
(1) You own the house in which you are living as defined in § 256.13(g)(1)–(5).	The house cannot be brought up to applicable building code standards and to standard housing condition for $60,000 or less. (For Alaska, freight cost not to exceed 100 percent of the cost of materials can be added to the cost of the project).	[No additional requirement].
(2) You do not own a house.	You own land that is suitable for housing	The land has adequate ingress and egress rights and reasonable access to utilities.
(3) You do not own a house.	You have a leasehold or the ability to acquire a leasehold on land that is suitable for housing and the leasehold is undivided and for not less than 25 years at the time you receive assistance.	The land has adequate ingress and egress rights and reasonable access to utilities.

(b) If you qualify for assistance under paragraph (a) of this section, you must sign a written grant agreement stating that, if you sell the house within 10 years of assuming ownership:

(1) The grant under this part will be voided; and

(2) At the time of settlement of the sale of the house, you will repay the tribe or tribal organization that operates the HIP or BIA the full cost of the house.

(c) If you sell the house more than 10 years after you assume ownership, the following conditions apply:

(1) You may retain 10 percent of the original cost of the house per year, beginning with the eleventh year.

(2) If you sell the house after 20 years, you will not have to repay the tribe, tribal organization, or BIA.

(d) A modest house provided with Category C assistance must meet the standards in the following table.

Number of occupants	Number of bedrooms [1]	Total square footage [1] (maximum)
Up to 4 persons	2	1000
Up to six persons	3	1200
7 or more persons	4	1400

[1] Determined by the servicing housing office, based on composition of family. Total living space must comply with applicable American Disabilities Act requirements.

§ 256.11 When do I qualify for Category D assistance?

(a) You qualify for grant assistance under Category D if you apply for financing from tribal, Federal, or other sources of credit and have inadequate income or limited financial resources to meet the lender requirements for home ownership.

(b) The grant must not exceed the amount necessary to secure the loan and may be used for down-payment assistance, closing costs, and pre-home ownership counseling. Participation with other complementary housing programs is encouraged.

(c) The method of awarding the grant must ensure that the funds are used for the purpose intended.

§ 256.12 Who administers the program?

The HIP is administered by a servicing housing office operated by either a tribe (under a Pub. L. 93-638 contract or a self-governance annual funding agreement) or BIA.

Subpart C—Applying for Assistance

§ 256.13 How do I apply for the Housing Improvement Program?

(a) First, obtain an application, BIA Form 6407, from your servicing housing office or the BIA Web site.

(b) Second, complete and sign BIA Form 6407.

(c) Third, submit your completed and signed application to your servicing housing office.

(d) Fourth, furnish to the servicing housing office documentation proving your tribal membership. Examples of acceptable documentation include a copy of your Certificate of Degree of Indian Blood (CDIB) or a copy of your tribal membership card.

(e) Fifth, provide proof of income from all permanent members of your household.

(1) Submit signed copies of current 1040 tax returns from all permanent members of the household, including W-2s and all other attachments. Submit the Social Security number of the applicant only.

(2) Provide proof of all other income from all permanent members of the household. This includes unearned income such as Social Security, general assistance, retirement, and unemployment benefits.

(3) If you or other household members did not file a tax return, submit a signed notarized statement explaining why you did not.

(f) Sixth, furnish a copy of your annual trust income statement for your Individual Indian Money (IIM) account from your home agency. If you do not have an IIM account, furnish a statement from your home agency to that effect.

(g) Seventh, provide proof of ownership of the residence and land or potential leasehold interest:

(1) For fee property, provide a copy of a fully executed deed, which is available at your local county or parish court house;

(2) For trust property, provide certification of ownership from your home agency;

(3) For tribally owned land, provide a copy of a properly executed tribal assignment, certified by the tribe;

(4) For multi-owner property, provide a copy of a properly executed lease;

(5) For a potential lease, provide proof of ability to acquire an undivided leasehold (that is, you will be the only lessee) for a minimum of 25 years from the date of service; or

(6) For down-payment assistance, provide a description and the location of the house to be purchased, verification of your intent to purchase, and the sale price of the house.

(h) Eighth, if you seek down payment assistance, provide a letter from the institution where you have applied for mortgage financing that specifies:

(1) The down payment amount; and

(2) The closing costs required for you to qualify for the loan.

§ 256.14 How is my application processed?

(a) The servicing housing office will review your application. If your application is incomplete, the office will notify you, in writing, of what is needed to complete your application and of the date by which it must be submitted. If you do not return your application by the deadline date, you will not be considered for assistance in that program year.

(b) The servicing housing office will use your completed application to determine if you are eligible for the HIP.

(1) If you are found ineligible for the program, the servicing housing office will advise you in writing within 45 days of receipt of your completed application.

(2) If you are found eligible for the program, the servicing housing office will assess your application for need, according to the factors and numeric values shown in the following table.

Factor	Ranking factor and definition	Ranking description	Point value
1	Annual household income: Must include income of all persons counted in Factors 2, 3, 4. Income includes earned income, royalties, and one-time income. A household with an income 151 percent of more of the Federal poverty guidelines is ineligible for the HIP.	Income as a percentage of the Federal poverty guidelines:	Points:
		0–25	25.
		26–50	20.
		51–75	15.
		76–100	10
		101–125	5.
		126–150	0.
2	Aged person: person age 55 or older and must be living in the house. *Maximum points awarded under this factor is 15, regardless of the number of years over age 55. Thus, 15 points will be added to the score for a resident who is 70 years old or older.*	Years of age: Less than 55 55 and older	Points: 1 point per year over age 54, up to maximum of 15 points.
3	Disabled individual: One or more disabled persons living in the house. Must fit under established definition of "disabled as in § 256.2." *Maximum points awarded under this factor is 10, regardless of the number of disabled residents.*	If a there is a disabled resident.	10.
4	Dependent Children: Must be under the age of 18 or such other age established for purposes of parental support by tribal or state law (if any). Must live in the house and not be married. *Maximum points awarded under this factor is 15.*	Number of dependent children:	Points:
		1	3.
		2	6.
		3	9.
		4	12.
		5 or more	15.
5	Other conditions: • Veteran. • Homeless or Dilapidated house. • Overcrowded conditions. *Maximum points awarded under this factor is 15*	If any of the conditions are present.	5 for each condition that applies.

Factor	Ranking factor and definition	Ranking description	Point value
6	Applicants with an approved financing package	If applicant has approved financing.	25.

(c) The servicing housing office will develop a list of the applications received and considered for the HIP for the current program year. The list will include, at a minimum, all of the following:

(1) The number of applications received and, of those, the number considered.

(2) The rank assigned to applicants in order of need, from highest to lowest, in accordance with tribal approval and knowledge of need, based on the total numeric value assigned using the factors in paragraph (b) of this section. (In case of a tie, the family with the lower income per household member will be listed first.)

(3) The estimated allowable costs of the improvements, renovations, and replacement projects for each applicant and for the entire priority list. This data must identify which applicants will be served based on the amount of available funding, starting with the neediest applicant and continuing until the available funding is depleted.

(4) A list of the applicants not ranked, with an explanation of why they weren't ranked (such as the reason for ineligibility or the reason for incomplete application).

(d) The servicing housing office submits to the regional office an annual fiscal year report that includes all of the following:

(1) Number of eligible applicants;

(2) Number of applicants who received service;

(3) Names of applicants who received service; and

(4) All of the following for each applicant that received service:

(i) Date of construction start;

(ii) Date of construction completion;

(iii) Cost; and

(iv) HIP category.

Subpart D—Receiving Assistance

§256.15 When will I hear if I have received funding?

Your servicing housing office will inform you whether you will receive funds in writing within 45 days after it completes the list required by §256.14(c).

(a) If funding is available, the office will send you complete information on how to obtain HIP services.

(b) If funding is not available, the office will send you instructions on how to update your application for funding for the next available program year.

§256.16 What if I don't receive funding?

If you don't receive funding, your servicing housing office will retain and consider your application for 3 more years. During this 4-year period, you must ensure that the information on your application is still accurate and provide an annual written update if any information has changed.

§256.17 How long will I have to wait for work on my house?

How long it takes to do work on your house depends on:

(a) Your position on the priority list;

(b) Whether funds are available;

(c) The type of work to be done;

(d) The climate and seasonal conditions where your house is located;

(e) The availability of a contractor; and

(f) Other unforeseen factors, such as infrastructure availability.

§256.18 Who decides what work will be done?

The servicing housing office will determine what work is to be done on your house or whether your house will be replaced. The servicing housing office also provides the priority list annually to the Indian Health Service if the Indian Health Service is responsible for verifying availability or feasibility of water and wastewater facilities.

§ 256.19 How are work plans prepared?

(a) First, a trained and qualified representative of your servicing housing office will visit your house to identify what renovation and or replacement will be done under the HIP. The representative will ensure that flood, National Environmental Policy Act (NEPA) and earthquake requirements are met, including the determination that the renovation or replacement is appropriately treated as a categorical exclusion.

(b) Second, based on the list of renovations or replacement to be done, your servicing housing office will estimate the total cost of renovation to your house. Cost estimates will be based on locally available services and product costs, or other regional-based, industry-recognized cost data, such as that provided by the MEANs or Marshall Swift. If the house is located in Alaska, documented, reasonable, substantiated freight costs, in accordance with Federal Property Management Regulations (FPMR 101–40), not to exceed 100 percent of the cost of materials, can be added to the cost of the project.

(c) Third, your servicing housing office will determine which HIP category the improvements to your house meet, based on the estimated cost of renovation or replacement. If the estimated cost to renovate your house is more than $60,000, your servicing housing office will recommend your house for replacement or refer you to another source for housing. The other source does not have to be for a replacement house; it may be for government-subsidized rental units or other sources for standard housing.

(d) Fourth, your servicing housing office will develop a detailed, written report, called a scope of work, that identifies what renovation or construction work on your house will be accomplished and how. The scope of work is used to inform potential bidders of what work is to be done. When the work includes new construction, the scope of work will be supplemented with a set of construction plans and specifications. The construction plans must:

(1) Meet the occupancy and square footage criteria in § 256.10 (d); and

(2) Provide complete and detailed instructions to the builder.

§ 256.20 How will I find out what work is to be done?

The servicing housing office will notify you in writing what work is being scheduled under the HIP. You will be requested to approve the scheduled work by signing a copy of the notice and returning it to the servicing housing office. Work will start after you return the signed copy to the servicing housing office.

§ 256.21 Who does the work?

Your house will be renovated or replaced by either:

(a) A licensed and bonded independent contractor or construction company; or

(b) A tribe that operates the HIP under an Indian Self-Determination and Education Assistance Act agreement.

§ 256.22 How are construction contractors or companies selected and paid?

The servicing housing office must follow Federal procurement or other Bureau-approved tribal procurement policy. Generally, your servicing housing office develops a "bid specification" or statement of work, which identifies the work to be performed. The appropriate contracting office uses the "bid specification" to provide information and invite bids on the project to interested parties. The contracting office selects the winning bidder after technical review of the bids by and written recommendation from the servicing housing office, and after determination that the bidder is qualified and capable of completing the project as advertised.

(a) Partial payments to independent contractors will not exceed 80 percent of the value of the completed and acceptable work.

(b) Recommendation for final payment will be made after final inspection and after all provisions of the contract have been met and all work has been completed.

§ 256.23 Do I have to move out while work is done?

(a) You will be notified by your servicing housing office that you must vacate your house only if:

(1) It is scheduled for major renovations requiring that all occupants vacate the house for safety reasons; or

(2) It is scheduled for replacement, which requires demolition of your current house.

(b) If you are required to vacate the premises during construction, you are responsible for:

(1) Locating other lodging;

(2) Paying all costs associated with vacating and living away from the house; and

(3) Removing all your belongings and furnishings before the scheduled beginning work date.

§ 256.24 How can I be sure that construction work meets minimum standards?

(a) At various stages of construction, a trained and qualified representative of your servicing housing office or a building inspector will review the work to ensure that it meets construction standards and building codes. Upon completion of each stage, further construction can begin only after the inspection occurs and approval is granted.

(b) Inspections of construction and renovation will occur, at a minimum, at the following stages:

(1) Upon completion of inspection footings and foundations;

(2) Upon completion of inspection rough-in, roughwiring, and plumbing; and

(3) At final completion.

§ 256.25 How will I find out that the work is done?

Your servicing housing office will advise you, in writing, that the work has been completed in compliance with the project contract. Also, you will have a final walk-through of the house with a representative of your servicing housing office. You will be requested to verify that you received the notice of completion of the work by signing a copy of the notice and returning it to your servicing housing office.

§ 256.26 Will I need flood insurance?

You will need flood insurance if your house is located in an area identified as having special flood hazards under the Flood Disaster Protection Act of 1973 (Pub. L. 93–234, 87 Stat. 975). Your servicing housing office will advise you.

§ 256.27 Is my Federal government-assisted house eligible for services?

No. The intention of this program is to assist the neediest of the needy, who have never received services from any other Federal entity.

§ 256.28 I have a mobile home; am I eligible for help?

Yes. If you meet the eligibility criteria in § 256.6 and funding is available, you can receive any of the HIP services identified in § 256.7. If you request Category B services and your mobile home has exterior walls less than three inches thick, you must be considered for Category C services.

§ 256.29 Can HIP resources be combined with other available resources?

Yes. HIP resources may be supplemented with other available resources (*e.g.*, in-kind assistance; tribal or housing authority; and any other leveraging mechanism identified in § 256.3(d)) to increase the number of HIP recipients.

§ 256.30 Can I appeal actions taken under this part?

You may appeal action or inaction by a BIA official, in accordance with 25 CFR part 2.

SUBCHAPTER L—HERITAGE PRESERVATION

PART 262—PROTECTION OF ARCHAEOLOGICAL RESOURCES

AUTHORITY: 16 U.S.C. 470aa–11.

CROSS REFERENCE: For uniform regulations issued by the Departments of Agriculture, Defense, and the Interior and the Tennessee Valley Authority pertaining to the protection of archaeological resources, and for supplemental regulations issued by the Department of the Interior pertaining to the same, see 43 CFR part 7, subparts A and B.

SOURCE: 58 FR 65249, Dec. 13, 1993, unless otherwise noted.

§ 262.1 Purpose, scope and information collection.

(a) *Purpose and scope.* The purpose of this part is to implement certain provisions of the Archaeological Resources Protection Act (Act) of 1979 (16 U.S.C. 470aa–11), in accordance with section 10(b) and consistent with uniform regulations promulgated under section 10(a) by the Secretaries of the Interior, Agriculture, and Defense and the Chairman of the Board of the Tennessee Valley Authority (43 CFR part 7, 36 CFR part 296, 32 CFR parts 229 and 1312) on February 6, 1984. This part shall provide guidance to officials of the Bureau of Indian Affairs (BIA) on the implementation of the Act as it pertains to this agency.

(b) *Information collection.* The information collection requirements contained in § 262.5 do not require approval by the Office of Management and Budget under 44 U.S.C. 3501 *et seq.*

§ 262.2 Definitions.

As used for purposes of this part:

(a) *Funerary objects* means objects that, as a part of the death rite or ceremony of a culture, are reasonably believed to have been placed with human remains of Indians either at the time of death or later, or to have been made exclusively for burial purposes or to contain such remains.

(b) *Sacred objects* means specific ceremonial objects that are needed by traditional Indian religious leaders for the practice of traditional Indian religions by their present day adherents.

(c) *Object of cultural patrimony* means an object having ongoing historical, traditional, or cultural importance central to an Indian tribe itself and that shall have been considered inalienable by the tribe at the time the object was separated therefrom.

(d) *Indian individual* means:

(1) Any person who is an enrolled member of a Federally recognized Indian tribe;

(2) Any person who is a descendent of such a member and was, on June 1, 1934, physically residing within the present boundaries of any Indian reservation; or

(3) Any other person of one-half or more Indian blood of tribes indigenous to the United States.

(e) *Lands of Indian tribes* means land or any interest therein:

(1) The title to which is held in trust by the United States for an Indian tribe; or

(2) The title to which is held by an Indian tribe, but which cannot be alienated or encumbered by the owner without the approval of the Secretary because of limitations contained in the conveyance instrument pursuant to Federal law or because of a Federal law directly imposing such restrictions.

(f) *Lands of Indian individuals* means land or any interest therein:

(1) The title to which is held in trust by the United States for the benefit of Indian individuals; or

(2) The title to which is held by Indian individuals, but which cannot be alienated or encumbered by the owner without the approval of the Secretary because of limitations contained in the conveyance instrument pursuant to Federal law or because of a Federal law directly imposing such restrictions.

§262.3 Consultation to determine need for a permit.

(a) Any person, except as provided in the uniform regulations at 43 CFR 7.5(b) through (d), who proposes to excavate or remove archaeological resources on Indian lands or on properties owned or administered by the BIA must first apply for and secure a permit under the Act. Procedures relating thereto are set forth in §262.5 of this part.

(b) No permit under the Act, nor any other Federally issued license or authorization, is required for archaeological investigations that do not involve the excavation or removal of archaeological resources on these lands, except for BIA consent on properties that it owns or administers. Notwithstanding, persons other than those covered under 43 CFR 7.5(b) through (d) shall, before engaging in such investigations:

(1) Write to the head of each tribal government having jurisdiction over the lands where investigations are to be conducted and request that he or she provide, within 30 days, written information on any permit, license or other form of authorization the tribe might require for the work proposed; and

(2) Provide the BIA Area Director with a copy of the tribe's written response (or a copy of the request to the tribe if 30 days have elapsed without any response) plus a brief but clear written description of the proposed work and obtain his or her written determination as to whether or not a permit under the Act is required. Area Directors shall provide determinations within 10 working days after receiving such documentation.

§262.4 Activities by Indian tribes or individuals that require a permit.

(a) No Indian tribe may, without a permit under the Act, excavate or remove archaeological resources on:

(1) Lands of another Indian tribe; or

(2) Lands of Indian individuals, except those on which the law of that tribe regulates such activity.

(b) No individual Indian may, without a permit under the Act, excavate or remove archaeological resources on any Indian lands (including his or her own) other than those on which the law of the tribe of which he or she is a member regulates such activity.

(c) No person, as an employee, consultant, advisor or in any other capacity as an agent for any Indian tribe, shall be exempt from the permit requirements of the Act, except in the cases listed below:

(1) No permit shall be required if a person is a member of the tribe having jurisdiction over the resources in question and the law of that tribe regulates the excavation or removal of archaeological resources on its lands.

(2) Tribal employees need not submit permit applications to the BIA if:

(i) The proposed excavation or removal of archaeological resources is within the normal scope of their duties or otherwise carried out by direction of the tribal government;

(ii) The work is on Indian lands of the tribe or on which the law of that tribe regulates the excavation or removal of archaeological resources;

(iii) The tribe ensures that the provisions for permit issuance in this part and at 43 CFR part 7 have been met by other documented means; and

(iv) Before beginning the work, the tribe notifies the Area Director about the nature and location of the proposed work and allows 10 working days after mailing a notification or 5 working days after an oral notification (provided this is documented) for the Area Director to respond. The Area Director need only respond when action is required under §262.7 of this part, and may do so either in writing or, if documented, orally.

(3) Consultants, advisors, and others serving by contractual agreement as agents for Indian tribes may use the provisions in §262.5(f) of this part to expedite the process of obtaining a permit.

(4) Persons serving as agents for Indian tribes as employees or by contractual agreement may abbreviate the consultation required in §262.3(b) of this part by disregarding the requirement to consult first with the tribe and, provided the communication is documented, by consulting with the Area Director orally. In these cases, the Area Director need only respond when a permit is deemed necessary and

may do so either orally or in writing. If a response is not received within 3 working days after an oral description of the proposed work is made or within 7 working days after a written description is mailed to the Area Director, the work may proceed.

§ 262.5 Application for permits.

(a) Permits from the BIA shall be issued when an applicant meets the requirements set out in 43 CFR 7.8, and may be conditioned, modified, suspended, or revoked by the Area Director. Area Directors may delegate this authority to Agency Superintendents, but only on a permit-by-permit basis and only to those who have adequate professional support available.

(b) Prospective applicants may obtain details on how to apply for a permit by contacting the Area Director, at BIA Area Offices in: Aberdeen, SD; Albuquerque, NM; Anadarko, OK; Arlington, VA; Billings, MT; Gallup, NM; Juneau, AK; Minneapolis, MN; Muskogee, OK; Phoenix, AZ; Portland, OR; or Sacramento, CA; or by writing to the Deputy Commissioner of Indian Affairs, Department of the Interior, Washington, DC 20240.

(c) Permit applications proposing the excavation or removal of archaeological resources on Indian lands shall include the following consent documents:

(1) Written permission from the Indian landowner and from the tribe, if any, having jurisdiction over those lands. This must contain such terms and conditions as the landowner or tribe may request be included in the permit. Where the permission is from a tribe, it should either state that no religious or cultural site will be harmed or destroyed by the proposed work or specify terms and conditions that the permit must include in order to safeguard against such harm or destruction.

(i) For lands of Indian tribes, permission must be granted by the tribe.

(ii) For lands of Indian individuals not under tribal jurisdiction, permission must be granted by the owner(s), except as provided in § 262.6.

(iii) For lands of Indian individuals under tribal jurisdiction, permission must be granted by both the owner(s), except as provided in § 262.6, and the tribe having such jurisdiction. Where an applicant is the owner, consent must still be obtained from the tribe.

(iv) Where the ownership of lands of Indian individuals is multiple, permission must be granted by the owners of a majority of interests, except as provided in § 262.6. The same shall apply where the applicant is one of the owners.

(v) Where the terms and conditions a tribe or landowner requests be included in a permit are in conflict with the provisions of this or any other Act, with Federal regulations, or with each other, the Area Director may negotiate with the requestor to eliminate the conflict. If the conflict remains, the permit may not be issued.

(2) Copies of any permits required by tribal law for archaeological work on lands under tribal jurisdiction. This may serve as written consent from the tribe for the purposes of § 262.5(c)(1).

(3) Written agreement by the Indian landowner(s) to release archaeological resources for curation or study, as specified in § 262.8(b).

(d) Permits issued by the BIA shall include the following or similar condition: "Human remains of Indians, funerary objects, sacred objects, and objects of cultural patrimony may not be excavated or removed unless the permittee has obtained the written consent of the Area Director. In order to obtain consent, the permittee shall present to the Area Director written evidence of prior consultation with the appropriate Indian tribe. If the lands containing the remains or objects are tribal lands, the permittee shall first obtain the written consent of the tribe having jurisdiction over the lands." Determination as to which tribe is the appropriate tribe shall be made in accordance with § 262.8(a). Area Director consent shall be based on the scientific appropriateness of the research objectives and provisions for recovery, recording, and analysis and may, if documented, be oral. This condition may be omitted from the permit when such excavation or removal is proposed, and the requirements of the condition are met, in the permit application.

(e) Information and assistance in contacting Indian tribes and individual

Indian landowners for the purpose of requesting the consent documents listed under paragraph (c) of this section or of seeking the consultation and consent required under paragraph (d) of this section may be obtained from the BIA office to which the permit application is submitted.

(f) Contractual agreements with the BIA or Indian tribes and permits issued by Indian tribes may be accepted as support documents for permit applications. They may also double as permit documents, if they demonstrate that the provisions for permit issuance in this part and at 43 CFR part 7 have been met and they are attached to a Department of the Interior permit form. This form must be signed by the Area Director, but need only contain the following or similar statement: "This permit is issued to the person(s) named, and in accordance with the terms and conditions in the attached (contractual agreement/tribal permit)."

(g) Area Directors shall respond to permit applications within 15 working days of receipt.

§262.6 Landowner consent by the Secretary.

The Secretary of the Interior, or delegate thereof, may, on behalf of the owner(s) of lands of Indian individuals, grant consent for the purposes in §262.5(c)(1) and (3) when the Secretary or his or her delegate finds that such consent will not result in any injury to the land or owner(s) and when one or more of the following conditions exist:

(a) The owner is a minor or a person *non compos mentis;*

(b) The heirs or devisees of a deceased owner have not been determined;

(c) The whereabouts of the owner are unknown;

(d) Multiple owners are so numerous that the Secretary or his or her delegate finds, after documenting his or her efforts to do so, that it would be impractical to obtain their consent, as prescribed in §262.5(c)(1)(iv) and provided the Secretary or his or her delegate also notifies, in writing, the tribe, if any, having jurisdiction over the land and allows 15 working days from the date of mailing date for response; or

(e) The owner has given the Secretary or his or her delegate written authority to grant such consent on his or her behalf.

§262.7 Notice to Indian tribes of possible harm to cultural or religious sites.

When consent by an Indian tribe to proposed excavation or removal of archaeological resources from Indian lands it owns or over which it has jurisdiction contains all of the information written as prescribed and advised in §262.5(c)(1), it may be taken to mean that subject to such terms and conditions as the tribe might specify, issuance of a permit for the proposed work will not result in harm to, or destruction of, any site of religious or cultural importance. No further notification is necessary, unless the Area Director has reason to believe that the proposed work might harm or destroy a site of religious or cultural importance to another tribe or Native American group. He or she shall then follow the notification procedures at 43 CFR 7.7. Those procedures must also be followed when proposed work might affect lands of Indian individuals over which there is no tribal jurisdiction or public lands owned or administered by the BIA.

§262.8 Custody of archaeological resources.

(a) Archaeological resources excavated or removed from Indian lands, except for human remains of Indians, funerary objects, sacred objects and objects of cultural patrimony, remain the property of the Indian tribe or individual(s) having rights of ownership over such lands. Ownership and right of control over the disposition of the excepted items shall be in accordance with the order of priority provided in the Native American Graves Protection and Repatriation Act (Pub. L. 101–601), adapted for the purpose of this rule as follows:

(1) In the case of human remains of Indians and funerary objects, in the lineal descendants of the Indian; or

(2) In any case in which such lineal descendants cannot be ascertained, and in the case of sacred objects and objects of cultural patrimony:

(i) In the Indian tribe on whose tribal lands, or on the individual Indian lands of whose members, such remains or objects are discovered;

(ii) In the Indian tribe recognized as aboriginally occupying the public lands owned or administered by the BIA on which such remains or objects are discovered, if upon notice, that tribe states a claim for those remains or objects; or

(iii) Where it can be so demonstrated by a preponderance of evidence, in the tribe other than that in paragraph (a)(2)(i) or (ii) of this section having the strongest cultural relationship with such remains or objects, if, upon notice, that tribe states a claim for those remains or objects.

(iv) The Area Director shall provide the required notice to any Indian tribe identified under paragraph (a)(2)(ii) or (iii) of this section, in writing, within 5 working days after such identification has been documented and confirmed, and shall at the same time submit a copy of the notice for publication in the FEDERAL REGISTER. This notice shall include a description of the remains or objects; of where, how, and why they were excavated or removed; and of the evidence used to identify the tribe being notified. The remains or objects in question shall be considered the property of the pertinent tribe under paragraph (a)(2)(i) of this section or, in the case of paragraph (a)(2)(ii) of this section, held and administered by the BIA until or unless a claim is stated.

(b) No permit for the excavation or removal of archaeological resources on Indian lands may be issued without the written consent of the Indian landowner(s) either to grant custody of the resources recovered (other than human remains of Indians, funerary objects, sacred objects or objects of cultural patrimony) to a curatorial facility that meets the requirements of 36 CFR part 79 or to allow the permittee a reasonable period of time to hold or have ready access to them at an appropriate location for study. The excepted remains and objects are covered under § 262.5(d) of this part which, in general, permits their excavation or removal only when the research objectives and provisions for recovery, recording, and analysis are scientifically appropriate. Written consent to custody by a curatorial facility may include terms and conditions regarding curation (e.g., cleaning, viewing, loaning, studying, etc.), provided these are consistent with 36 CFR part 79.

(1) On lands of Indian tribes, consent must be obtained from the tribe.

(2) On lands of Indian individuals, consent must be obtained from the owner of the land or the owners of a majority of interests therein, except as provided in § 262.6.

(3) Where consent is by the owners of a majority of interests, it must, if the archaeological resources are to be retained by or returned after study to the interest holders, designate a representative to receive those resources. Whether and how these are subsequently distributed among themselves is a matter for the interest holders to decide.

(c) The Area Director may, after notifying the tribe (if any) having jurisdiction over such lands and allowing 15 working days for response, decline to issue a permit for lands of Indian individuals if he or she has any verifiable reason to believe that archaeological resources retained by the landowner(s) after being studied will be sold or exchanged other than to the tribe having jurisdiction or to a curatorial facility that meets the requirements of 36 CFR part 79. The basis for decline shall be that excavation or removal of resources under such circumstances would not be in the public interest and would thus be contrary to the purposes of the Act.

(d) The landowner(s) alone may grant custody of archaeological resources (except for human remains, funerary objects, sacred objects and objects of cultural patrimony, which are subject to the provisions of paragraph (a) of this section) excavated or removed from lands of Indian individuals that are under tribal jurisdiction to a curatorial facility that meets the requirements of 36 CFR part 79. When, however, such consignment constitutes the ultimate disposition of these resources, the tribe having jurisdiction must also grant its consent. Any subsequent exchange or disposition by the facility must have the consent of both the landowner(s) and the tribe.

PART 265—ESTABLISHMENT OF ROADLESS AND WILD AREAS ON INDIAN RESERVATIONS

CROSS REFERENCE: For general regulations pertaining to the construction of roads, see part 170 of this chapter.

§265.1 Definition of roadless area.

A roadless area has been defined as one which contains no provision for the passage of motorized transportation and which is at least 100,000 acres in extent. Under this definition the Secretary of the Interior ordered (3 FR 609, Mar. 22, 1938) certain roadless areas established on Indian reservations. The following is the only presently existing roadless area:

Name of area—Wind River Reserve.
Reservation—Shoshone.
State—Wyoming.
Approximate acreage—180,387

(a) The boundaries of the Wind River Reserve roadless area are as follows:

WIND RIVER MERIDIAN, WYO.

Starting at the SW corner of sec. 22, T. 2 S., R. 3 W., on the south boundary of the Wind River Indian Reservation, thence north six (6) miles to the NE corner of sec. 28, T. 1 S., R. 3 W., thence west three (3) miles to the SW corner of sec. 19, T. 1 S., R. 3 W., thence north four (4) miles along range line to the Wind River Base Line, thence west one (1) mile along Wind River Base Line to the SW corner of Sec. 36, T. 1 N., R. 4 W., thence north six (6) miles to the NW corner of sec. 1, T. 1 N., R. 4 W., thence west five (5) miles along township line to the NE corner of sec. 1, T. 1 N., R. 5 W., thence north four and one-half (4½) miles along range line to the NE corner of the SE ¼ of sec. 12, T. 2 N., R. 5 W., thence west one and one-half (1½) miles to the center of sec. 11, T. 2 N., R. 5 W., thence on a straight line in a northwesterly direction to the top of Bold Mountain, thence on a straight line to the SE corner of sec. 35, T. 4 N., R. 6 W., thence west one (1) mile along township line to the SW corner of sec. 35, T. 4 N., R. 6 W., thence north two (2) miles to the NW corner of sec. 26, T. 4 N., R. 6 W., thence on a straight line in a northwesterly direction to the point where the north line of sec. 15, T. 4 N., R. 6 W. intersects the west boundary of the reservation, thence south, southeasterly and east along the reservation boundary to point of beginning.

(5 U.S.C. 301)

[30 FR 9813, Aug. 6, 1965. Redesignated at 47 FR 13327, Mar. 30, 1982]

§265.3 Roads prohibited.

(a) Within the boundaries of this officially designated roadless area it will be the policy of the Interior Department to refuse consent to the construction or establishment of any routes passable to motor transportation, including in this restriction highways, roads, truck trails, work roads, and all other types of ways constructed to make possible the passage of motor vehicles either for transportation of people or for the hauling of supplies and equipment, unless the requirements of fire protection, commercial use for the Indians' benefit or actual needs of the Indians clearly demand otherwise.

(b) Foot trails and horse trails are not barred. The Superintendent of the Wind River Reservation on which this roadless area has been established will be held strictly accountable for seeing that the area is maintained in a roadless condition. Elimination of this area or any part thereof from the restriction of this order will be made only upon a written showing of an actual and controlling need.

(5 U.S.C. 301)

[30 FR 9814, Aug. 6, 1965. Redesignated at 47 FR 13327, Mar. 30, 1982]

CROSS REFERENCE: For rights-of-way for highways over Indian lands, see part 169 of this chapter.

SUBCHAPTER M—INDIAN SELF-DETERMINATION AND EDUCATION ASSISTANCE ACT PROGRAM

PART 273—EDUCATION CONTRACTS UNDER JOHNSON-O'MALLEY ACT

AUTHORITY: Secs. 201–203, Pub. L. 93–638, 88 Stat. 2203, 2213–2214 (25 U.S.C. 455–457), unless otherwise noted.

SOURCE: 40 FR 51303, Nov. 4, 1975, unless otherwise noted.

Subpart A—General Provisions

§ 273.1 Purpose and scope.

(a) The purpose of the regulations in this part is to set forth the application and approval process for education contracts under the Johnson-O'Malley Act. Such contracts shall be for the purpose of financially assisting those efforts designed to meet the specialized and unique educational needs of eligible Indian students, including programs supplemental to the regular school program and school operational support, where such support is necessary to maintain established State educational standards.

(b) The application and approval process in this part applies specifically to contracts with a State, school district, or Indian corporation.

(c) Contracts with tribal organizations for supplemental and operational support will be entered into only upon the request of an Indian tribe(s), and shall be subject to the provisions of part 900 of this chapter and 41 CFR part 14H–70, except as provided in § 273.11.

(d) Nothing in these regulations shall be construed as:

(1) Affecting, modifying, diminishing, or otherwise impairing the sovereign immunity from suit enjoyed by an Indian tribe;

(2) Authorizing or requiring the terminiation of any existing trust responsibility of the United States with respect to the Indian people; or,

(3) Permitting significant reduction in services to Indian people as a result of this part.

(e) Nothing in these regulations shall be construed to mandate an Indian tribe to request a contract or contracts. Such requests are strictly voluntary.

[40 FR 51303, Nov. 4, 1975, as amended at 64 FR 13896, Mar. 23, 1999]

§ 273.2 Definitions.

As used in this part:

(a) "Area Director" means the official in charge of a Bureau of Indian Affairs Area Office.

(b) "Bureau" means the Bureau of Indian Affairs.

(c) "Commissioner" means the Commissioner of Indian Affairs, under the direction and supervision of the Assistant Secretary—Indian Affairs, who is responsible for the direction of day-to-day operations of the Bureau of Indian Affairs.

(d) "Days" means calendar days.

(e) "Economic enterprise" means any commercial, industrial, agricultural, or business activity that is at least 51 percent Indian owned, established or organized for the purpose of profit.

(f) "Education plan" means a comprehensive plan for the programmatic and fiscal services of and accountability by a contractor for the education of eligible Indian students under this part.

(g) "Indian tribe" means any Indian tribe, band, nation, rancheria, pueblo, colony or community, including any Alaska Native village or regional or village corporation as defined in or established pursuant to the Alaska Native Claims Settlement Act (85 Stat. 688) which is federally recognized as eligible by the U.S. Government through the Secretary for the special programs and services provided by the Secretary to Indians because of their status as Indians.

(h) "Indian corporation" means a legally established organization of Indians chartered under State or Federal law and which is not included within the definition of "tribal organization" given in paragraph (v) of this section.

(i) "Indian Education Committee" means one of the entities specified by § 273.15.

(j) "Indian" means a person who is a member of an Indian tribe.

(k) "Johnson-O'Malley Act" means the Act of April 16, 1934 (48 Stat. 596), as amended by the Act of June 4, 1936 (49 Stat. 1458, 25 U.S.C. 452–456), and further amended by the Act of January 4, 1975 (88 Stat. 2203).

(l) "Operational support" means those expenditures for school operational costs in order to meet established State educational standards or State-wide requirements.

(m) "Pub. L. 93–638" means the Indian Self-Determination and Education Assistance Act (Pub. L. 93–638; 88 Stat. 2203).

(n) "Previously private school" means a school (other than a Federal school formerly operated by the Bureau) that is operated primarily for Indian students from age 3 years through grades 12; and, which at the time of application is controlled, sanctioned, or chartered by the government body(s) of an Indian tribe(s).

(o) "Reservation" or "Indian reservation" means any Indian tribe's reservation, pueblo, colony, or rancheria, including former reservations in Oklahoma, Alaska Natives regions established pursuant to the Alaska Native Claims Settlement Act (85 Stat. 688), and Indian allotments.

(p) "School district" or "local education agency" means that subdivision of the State which contains the public elementary and secondary educational institutions providing educational services and is controlled by a duly elected board, commission, or similarly constituted assembly.

(q) "Secretary" means the Secretary of the Interior.

(r) "State" means a State of the United States of America or any political subdivision of a State.

(s) "Superintendent" means the official in charge of a Bureau of Indian Affairs Agency Office.

(t) "Supplemental programs" means those programs designed to meet the specialized and unique educational needs of eligible Indian students which may have resulted from socio-economic conditions of the parents, from cultural or language differences or other factors, and as provided by § 273.34(b).

(u) "Tribal government," "tribal governing body" and "tribal Council" means the recognized governing body of an Indian tribe.

(v) "Tribal organization," means the recognized governing body of any Indian tribe or any legally established organization of Indians or tribes which is controlled, sanctioned, or chartered by such governing body or bodies, or which is democratically elected by the adult members of the Indian community to be served by such organization and which includes the maximum participation of Indians in all phases of its activities; *Provided*, That a request for a contract must be made by the Indian tribe that will receive services under the contract; *Provided further*, That in any case where a contract is let to an organization to perform services benefiting more than one Indian tribe, the approval of each such Indian tribe shall be a prerequisite to the letting of such contract.

(w) "Assistant Secretary—Indian Affairs" means the Assistant Secretary—Indian Affairs who discharges the responsibility of the Secretary for activities pertaining to Indians and Indian Affairs.

[40 FR 51303, Nov. 4, 1975, as amended at 41 FR 5098, Feb. 4, 1976; 43 FR 37445, Aug. 23, 1978; 45 FR 13451, Feb. 29, 1980]

§ 273.3 Revision or amendment of regulations.

In order to make any substantive revision or amendments to regulations in this part, the Secretary shall take the following actions:

(a) Consult with Indian tribes and national and regional Indian organizations to the extent practicable about the need for revision or amendment and consider their views in preparing the proposed revision or amendment.

(b) Publish the proposed revisions or amendments in the FEDERAL REGISTER as proposed rulemaking to provide adequate notice to, and receive comments from, all interested parties.

(c) After consideration of all comments received, publish the regulations in the FEDERAL REGISTER in final form not less than 30 days before the date they are made effective.

(d) Annually consult with Indian tribes and national and regional Indian organizations about the need for revision or amendment, and consider their views in preparing the revision or amendment.

(e) Nothing in this section shall preclude Indian tribes or national or regional Indian organizations from initiating request for revisions or amendments subject to paragraphs (a), (b), and (c) of this section.

§ 273.4 Policy of maximum Indian participation.

The meaningful participation in all aspects of educational program development and implementation by those affected by such programs is an essential requisite for success. Such participation not only enhances program responsiveness to the needs of those served, but also provides them with the opportunity to determine and affect the desired level of educational achievement and satisfaction which education can and should provide. Consistent with this concept, maximum Indian participation in the development, approval and implementation of all programs contracted under this part shall be required.

Subpart B—Application Process

§ 273.11 Eligible applicants.

(a) Any State, school district, tribal organization or Indian corporation is eligible to apply for contracts for supplemental or operational support programs. For the purposes of this part, previously private schools as defined in § 273.2(n) are considered tribal organizations.

(b) States, school districts, or Indian corporations shall apply for contracts for supplemental or operational support programs as required in this part.

(c) Tribal organizations must comply with the following requirements to obtain contracts for supplemental programs or operational support:

(1) The application submitted by the tribal organization shall meet the requirements in §273.20 in addition to those in §271.14 of this chapter.

(2) The requirements in §§271.1 through 271.27, 271.41 through 271.52, 271.54, 271.61 through 271.66, and 271.81 through 271.84 shall apply to such contracts with tribal organizations.

(3) The provisions in §§271.71 through 271.77 of this chapter concerning retrocession and reassumption of programs do not apply to a tribal organization retroceding a contract for supplemental programs or operational support as the Bureau does not operate education programs authorized to be contracted under the Johnson-O'Malley Act. However, the tribal organization may retrocede such a contract and the Bureau will then contract with a State, school district, or Indian corporation under this part for the supplemental programs or operational support.

(4) The requirements in §§273.12 through 273.18, 273.20, 273.21, 273.31 through 273.38, 273.41, 273.51 and 273.52 shall apply to such contracts with tribal organizations.

(5) The requirements in 41 CFR part 14H–70 shall apply to such contracts with tribal organizations.

[40 FR 51303, Nov. 4, 1975, as amended at 41 FR 5098, Feb. 4, 1976]

§273.12 Eligible students.

Indian students, from age 3 years through grade(s) 12, except those who are enrolled in Bureau or sectarian operated schools, shall be eligible for benefits provided by a contract pursuant to this part if they are ¼ or more degree Indian blood and recognized by the Secretary as being eligible for Bureau services. Priority shall be given to contracts (a) which would serve Indian students on or near reservations and (b) where a majority of such Indian students will be members of the tribe(s) of such reservations (as defined in §273.2(o)).

§273.13 Proposals eligible for contracts.

(a) Any proposal to contract for funding a program which meets the definition of a supplemental program given in §273.2(t) will be considered an eligible proposal under this part.

(b)(1) To contract for operational support, a public school district shall be required to establish as part of the proposal that:

(i) It cannot meet the applicable minimum State standards or requirements without such funds.

(ii) It has made a reasonable tax effort with a mill levy at least equal to the State average in support of educational programs.

(iii) It has fully utilized all other sources of financial aid, including all forms of State aid and Pub. L. 874 payments. The State aid contribution per pupil must be at least equal to the State average.

(iv) There is at least 70 percent eligible Indian enrollment within the school district.

(v) It shall clearly identify the educational needs of the students intended to benefit from the contract.

(vi) It has made a good faith effort in computing State and local contributions without regard to contract funds pursuant to this part.

(vii) It shall not budget or project a deficit by using contract funds pursuant to this part.

(2) The requirements given in paragraph (b)(1) of this section do not apply to previously private schools.

(c) At his discretion, the Commissioner may consider as eligible a proposal to contract under which a school district will be reimbursed for the full per capita costs of educating Indian students who meet all of the following:

(1) Are members of recognized Indian tribes.

(2) Do not normally reside in the State in which the school district is located.

(3) Are residing in Federal boarding facilities for the purpose of attending public schools within the school district.

§ 273.14 Preparing the education plan.

A prospective contractor in consultation with its Indian Education Committee(s) shall formulate an education plan and submit it to the appropriate Area Director as a part of the application to contract required by § 273.20. Such plan shall become a part of any contract awarded. The education plan shall contain:

(a) The education programs approved by the Indian Education Committee(s) as required in § 273.17.

(b) Other requirements for the education plan given in § 273.18.

§ 273.15 Establishment of Indian Education Committee.

(a) When a school district to be affected by a contract(s) for the education of Indians pursuant to this part has a local school board not composed of a majority of Indians, the tribal governing body(s) of the Indian tribe(s) affected by the contract(s) under this part shall specify one of the following entities to serve as the Indian Education Committee for the purpose of this part:

(1) An Indian Education committee to be elected from among the parents (including persons acting *in loco parentis* except school administrators or officials) of eligible Indian students enrolled in the school(s) affected by a contract(s) under this part; or

(2) A local Indian committee established pursuant to section 305(b)(2)(B)(ii) of the Act of January 23, 1972 (86 Stat. 235) and existing prior to January 4, 1975; or

(3) An Indian advisory school board or Indian Education Committee established pursuant to the Johnson-O'Malley Act and existing prior to January 4, 1975.

(b) When the local school board is not composed of a majority of Indians and the tribal governing body(s) of the Indian tribe(s) affected by a contract(s) under this part determine which of the entities provided for in paragraph (a) of this section is to serve as the Indian Education Committee for the purpose of this part, it shall notify the Area Director of such determination by January 15 preceding the school year for which the contract will be let.

(c) The Indian Education Committee established under paragraph (a) of this section and its members shall establish procedures under which the Committee shall serve. Such procedures shall be set forth in the Committee's organizational documents and by-laws. Each Committee shall file a copy of its organizational documents and by-laws with the appropriate Area Director, together with a list of its officers and members as soon as practicable after the Committee is organized.

(d) The existence of an Indian Education Committee shall not limit the continuing participation of the rest of the Indian community in all aspects of programs contracted under this part.

§ 273.16 Powers and duties of Indian Education Committee.

(a) Consistent with the purpose of the Indian Education Committee, each such Committee shall be vested with the authority to:

(1) Participate fully in the planning, development, implementation, and evaluation of all programs, including both supplemental and operational support, conducted under a contract or contracts pursuant to this part. Such participation shall include further authority to:

(i) Recommend curricula, including texts, materials, and teaching methods to be used in the contracted program or programs.

(ii) Approve budget preparation and execution.

(iii) Recommend criteria for employment in the program.

(iv) Nominate a reasonable number of qualified prospective educational programmatic staff members from which the contractor would be required to select.

(v) Evaluate staff performance and program results and recommend appropriate action to the contractor.

(2) Approve and disapprove all programs to be contracted under this part. All programs contracted pursuant to this part shall require the prior approval of the appropriate Indian Education Committee.

(3) Secure a copy of the negotiated contract(s) which include the program(s) approved by the Indian Education Committee.

(4) Recommend to the Commissioner through the appropriate Bureau contracting officer cancellation or suspension of a contract(s) which contains the program(s) approved by the Indian Education Committee if the contractor fails to permit such Committee to exercise its powers and duties as specified by this section.

(b) The organizational papers and bylaws of the Indian Education Committee may include additional powers and duties which would permit the Committee to:

(1) Participate in negotiations concerning all contracts under this part.

(2) Make an annual assessment of the learning needs of Indian children in the community affected.

(3) Have access to all reports, evaluations, surveys, and other program and budget related documents determined necessary by the Committee to carry out its responsibilities, subject only to the provisions of § 273.49.

(4) Request periodic reports and evaluations regarding the Indian education program.

(5) Hear grievances related to programs in the education plan.

(6) Meet regularly with the professional staff serving Indian children and with the local education agency.

(7) Hold committee meetings on a regular basis which are open to the public.

(8) Have such additional powers as are consistent with these regulations.

§ 273.17 Programs approved by Indian Education Committee.

(a) All programs contracted under this part shall:

(1) Be developed and approved in full compliance with the powers and duties of the Indian Education Committee as set out in § 273.16 and as may be contained in the Committee's organizational documents and by-laws.

(2) Be included as a part of the education plan provided for in § 273.14.

(b) No program contracted pursuant to this part shall be changed from the time of its original approval by the Indian Education Committee to the end of the contract period without the prior approval, in writing, of the Committee.

(c) Programs developed or approved by the Indian Education Committee pursuant to this part may, at the option of such Committee, include funds for the performance of Committee duties, including the following:

(1) Members' attendance at regular and special meetings, workshops and training sessions, as the Committee deems appropriate.

(2) Such other reasonable expenses incurred by the Committee in performing its primary duties, including the planning, development, implementation and evaluation of the program.

§ 273.18 Additional requirements for education plan.

In addition to incorporating the programs approved by the Indian Education Committee(s) as required by § 273.14(a), the education plan prepared by the prospective contractor shall:

(a) Contain educational goals and objectives which adequately address the educational needs of the Indian students to be served by the contract.

(b) Incorporate the program or programs developed and approved by the Indian Education Committee(s). As provided in § 273.17(b), changes in such programs must have prior written approval of the Indian Education Committee(s).

(c) Contain procedures for hearing grievances from Indian students, parents, community members, and tribal representatives relating to the program(s) contracted under this part. Such procedures shall provide for adequate advance notice of the hearing.

(d) Identify established State standards and requirements which shall be maintained in operating programs and services contracted under this part.

(e) Describe how the State standards and requirements will be maintained.

(f) Provide that the contractor shall comply in full with the requirements concerning meaningful participation by the Indian Education Committee as required by § 273.4.

(g) Provide that education facilities receiving funds shall be open to visits and consultations by the Indian Education Committee(s), tribal representatives, Indian parents in the community, and by duly authorized representatives of the Federal and State Governments.

(h) Outline procedures of administrative and fiscal management to be used by the contractor.

(i) Contain justification for requesting funds for operational support. The public school district must establish in its justification that it meets the requirements given in § 273.13(b). The information given should include records of receipt of local, State, and Federal funds.

(j) Include budget estimates and financial information needed to determine program costs to contract for services. This includes, but is not limited to, the following:

(1) State and district average operational cost per pupil.

(2) Other sources of Federal funding the applicant is receiving, the amount received from each, the programs being funded, and the number of eligible Indian students served by such funding.

(3) Administrative costs involved, total number of employees, and total number of Indian employees.

(4) Costs which parents normally are expected to pay for each school.

(5) Supplemental and operational funds outlined in a separate budget, by line item, to facilitate accountability.

(6) Total number of employees for each special program and number of Indian employees for that program.

(k) State the total enrollment of school or district, by age and grade level.

(l) State the eligible Indian enrollment—total and classification by tribal affiliation(s) and by age and grade level.

(m) State the total number of school board members and number of Indian school board members.

(n) List Government equipment needed to carry out the contract.

(o) State the period of contract term requested.

(p) Include the signature of the authorized representative of applicant.

(q) Provide written information regarding:

(1) Program goals and objectives related to the learning needs of potential target students.

(2) Procedures and methods to be used in achieving program objectives, including ways whereby parents, students and communities have been involved in determining needs and priorities.

(3) Overall program implementation including staffing practices, parental and community involvement, evaluation of program results, and dissemination thereof.

(4) Determination of staff and program effectiveness in meeting the stated needs of target students.

§ 273.19 Obtaining application forms.

Application forms, instructions, and related application materials are available from Agency Superintendents, Area Directors and the Commissioner. Use of standard application forms will facilitate processing of applications. However, they are not required if the information required by § 273.20 is given in the application to contract.

§ 273.20 Content of application to contract.

An application for a contract under this part shall be in writing and shall contain the following:

(a) Name, address, and telephone number of the proposed contractor.

(b) Name, address, and telephone number of the tribe(s) to be served by the contract.

(c) Descriptive narrative of the contract proposal.

(d) The education plan required by § 273.14.

(e) A separate budget outlining the Johnson-O'Malley funds for operational support and/or supplemental programs, by line item, to facilitate accountability.

(f) A clear identification of what educational needs the Johnson-O'Malley funds requested for operational support will address.

(g) Documentation of the requirements for operational support in § 273.13(b)(1).

§ 273.21 Tribal request for contract.

(a) An Indian tribal governing body(s) that desires that a contract be entered into with a tribal organization must so notify the Area Director no later than February 1 preceding the school year for which the contract will be let.

(b) If the tribal governing body's notice is not received by the date given in paragraph (a) of this section, the Area Director may contract with the State, school district, or Indian corporation under this part.

§ 273.22 Application approval officials.

(a) Each Area Director is authorized to approve the contract(s) submitted by the State, school district, or Indian corporation under this part which will provide services to Indian children within the jurisdiction of that Area Office.

(b) When a proposed contract(s) will provide services to Indian children within the jurisdiction of more than one Area Office, the contract must be approved by the Commissioner.

§ 273.23 Submitting application to Area Office.

When services under the proposed contract will be provided to Indian children within the jurisdiction of a single Area Office, the completed application shall be submitted to the Area Director of that Area Office.

§ 273.24 Area Office review and decision.

Upon receiving a contract application, the Area Director shall:

(a) Notify the applicant in writing that the application has been received. This notice shall be made within fourteen (14) days after the Area Office receives the application.

(b) Review the application for completeness and request within 20 days any additional information from the applicant which will be needed to reach a decision.

(c) On receiving an application for operational support, make formal written determination and findings supporting the need for such funds. In arriving at such a determination, the Area Director must be assured that each local education agency has made a good faith effort in computing State and local contributions without regard to funds requested pursuant to this part.

(d) Assess the completed application to determine if the contract proposal is feasible and if the proposal and the application comply with the appropriate requirements of the Johnson-O'Malley Act and of the regulations in this part.

(e) Approve or disapprove the application after fully reviewing and assessing the application and any additional information submitted by the applicant.

(f) Promptly notify the applicant in writing of the decision to approve or disapprove the application. If the application is disapproved, the notice will give the reasons for disapproval and the applicant's right to appeal pursuant to part 2 of this chapter.

§ 273.25 Deadline for Area Office action.

(a) The Area Director shall approve or disapprove an application for a contract within sixty (60) days after the Area Office receives the application and any additional information requested in § 273.24(b). The sixty (60) day deadline can be extended after obtaining the written consent of the applicant.

(b) An application under this part cannot be approved before February 1 preceding the school year for which the contract will be let.

§ 273.26 Submitting application to Central Office.

When services under the proposed contract will be provided to Indian children within the jurisdiction of two or more Area Offices, the completed application shall be submitted to the Commissioner through the respective Area Offices.

§ 273.27 Central Office review and decision.

Upon receiving a contract application, the Commissioner shall:

(a) Notify the applicant in writing that the application has been received. This notice shall be made within fourteen (14) days after the Central Office receives the application.

(b) Review the application for completeness and request within 20 days any additional information from the applicant which will be needed to reach a decision.

(c) On receiving an application for operational support, make formal written determination and findings supporting the need for such funds. In arriving at such a determination, the Commissioner must be assured that each local education agency has made a good faith effort in computing State and local contributions without regard to funds requested pursuant to this part.

(d) Assess the completed application to determine if the contract proposal is feasible and if the proposal and the application comply with the appropriate requirements of the Johnson-O'Malley Act and of the regulations in this part.

(e) Approve or disapprove the application after fully reviewing and assessing the application and any additional information submitted by the applicant.

(f) Promptly notify the applicant in writing of the decision to approve or disapprove the application. If the application is disapproved, the notice will give the reasons for disapproval and the applicant's right to appeal pursuant to part 2 of this chapter.

§ 273.28 Deadline for Central Office action.

(a) The Commissioner shall approve or disapprove an application for a contract within sixty (60) days after the Central Office receives the application, and any additional Information requested in § 273.27(b). The sixty (60) day deadline can be extended after obtaining the written consent of the applicant.

(b) An application under this part cannot be approved before February 1 preceding the school year for which the contract will be let.

§ 273.29 Negotiating the contract.

After the proposal for a contract has been approved by the Area Director or Commissioner as provided in § 273.22, the contract will be negotiated by a Bureau contracting officer assisted by Bureau education personnel.

Subpart C—Funding Provisions

§ 273.31 Distribution formula.

(a) Funds shall be distributed to eligible contractors based upon the number of eligible Indian students to be served times twenty-five (25%) percent of the higher of the State or national average per pupil operating cost. Notwithstanding any other provisions of the law, Federal funds appropriated for the purpose shall be allotted pro rata in accordance with the distribution method outlined in this formula.

(b) The Assistant Secretary may make exceptions to the provisions of paragraph (a) of this section based on the special cultural, linguistic, social or educational needs of the communities involved including the actual cost of education in the community only after consultation with all tribes who may be affected by such exceptions.

(25 U.S.C. 452–456; sec. 202, Pub. L. 93–638, 88 Stat. 2203, and Pub. L. 95–561, sec. 1102 (a) and (b))

[45 FR 9241, Feb. 11, 1980]

§ 273.32 Pro rata requirement.

All monies provided by a contract pursuant to this part, shall be expended only for the benefit of eligible Indian students. Where students other than eligible Indian students participate in programs contracted under this part, money expended under such contract shall be prorated to cover the participation of only the eligible Indian students, except where the participation of non-eligible students is so incidental as to be *de minimus*. Such *de minimus* participation must be approved by the Indian Education Committee.

§ 273.33 Use of funds for operational support.

All funds for school operational support shall be used to meet established State educational standards or Statewide requirements.

§ 273.34 Use of other Federal, State and local funds.

(a) Contract funds under this part shall supplement, and not supplant, Federal, State and local funds. Each contract shall require that the use of these contract funds will not result in a decrease in State, local, or Federal funds which would be made available for Indian students if there were no funds under this part.

(b) State, local and other Federal funds must be used to provide comparable services to non-Indian and Indian students prior to the use of contract funds.

(c) Except as hereinafter provided, the school lunch program of the United States Department of Agriculture (USDA) shall constitute the only federally-funded school lunch program for Indian students in public schools. Where Indian students do not qualify to receive free lunches under the National School Lunch Program of USDA because such students are non-needy and do not meet the family size and income guidelines for free USDA lunches, plans prepared pursuant to §273.18 may provide, to the extent of funding available for Johnson-O'Malley programs, for free school lunches for those students who do not qualify for free USDA lunches but who are eligible students under §273.12.

[47 FR 57275, Dec. 23, 1982]

§273.35 Capital outlay or debt retirement.

In no instance shall contract funds provided under this part be used as payment for capital outlay or debt retirement expenses; except that, such costs are allowable if they are considered to be a part of the full per capita cost of educating eligible Indian students who reside in Federal boarding facilities for the purpose of attending public schools.

§273.36 Eligible subcontractors.

No contract funds under the Johnson-O'Malley Act shall be made available by the Bureau directly to other than tribal organizations, States, school districts and Indian corporations. However, tribal organizations, States, school districts, and Indian corporations receiving funds under this part may use the funds to subcontract for necessary services with any appropriate individual, organization or corporation.

§273.37 Use of funds outside of schools.

Nothing in these regulations shall prevent the Commissioner from contracting with Indian corporations who will expend all or part of the funds in places other than the public or private schools in the community affected.

§273.38 Equal quality and standard of education.

Contracts with State education agencies or school districts receiving funds under the provisions of this part shall provide educational opportunities to all Indian children within that school district on the same terms and under the same conditions that apply to all other students provided that it will not affect the rights of eligible Indian children to receive benefits from the supplemental programs as provided for in this part. School districts receiving funds under this part must insure that Indian children receive all aid from the State, and other proper sources other than this contract, which other schools in the district and other school districts similarly situated in the State are entitled to receive. In no instance shall there be discrimination against Indians or schools enrolling such Indians.

Subpart D—General Contract Requirements

§273.41 Special program provisions to be included in contract.

All contracts under this part shall contain the following:

(a) The education plan required by §§273.14 and 273.18 and, as part of the education plan, the education programs approved by the Indian Education Committee(s) under §273.17.

(b) Any formal written determination and findings made by the Area Director or Commissioner supporting the need for operational support as required by §§273.24(c) and 273.27(c).

(c) The provision that State, local, and other Federal Funds shall be used to provide comparable services to non-Indian and Indian students prior to the use of Johnson-O'Malley funds for the provision of supplementary program services to Indian children, as required in §273.34(b).

§ 273.42 Civil Rights Act violations.

In no instance shall there be discrimination against Indians or schools enrolling such Indians. When informed by a complainant or through its own discovery that possible violation of title VI of the Civil Rights Act of 1964 exists within a State school district receiving funds under this part, the Department of the Interior shall, in accordance with Federal requirements, notify the Department of Health, Education, and Welfare of the possible violation of title VI. The Department of Health, Education, and Welfare will conduct an investigation into the matters alleged, pursuant to a Memorandum of Understanding between the Department of the Interior and the Department of Health, Education, and Welfare. If the report of the investigation conducted by the Department of Health, Education, and Welfare discloses a failure or threatened failure to comply with this part, and if the noncompliance cannot be corrected by informal means, compliance with this part may be effected by the suspension or termination of or refusal to contract or to continue financial assistance under the Johnson-O'Malley Act or by any other means authorized by law. As delineated in 43 CFR 17.1, 17.8, and 17.9, such other means may include reference to the Department of Justice with a recommendation that appropriate legal proceedings be brought by the United States to secure compliance or by formal hearing before the Commissioner or, at his discretion, before an administrative law judge designated in accordance with section 11 of the Administrative Procedure Act. The Secretary, may, by agreement with one or more other Federal departments, provide for the conduct of consolidated or joint hearings as prescribed in 43 CFR 17.8(e).

§ 273.43 Advance payments.

Advance payments to States, school districts and Indian corporations will be made in accordance with the applicable provisions of 41 CFR part 1 as supplemented by 41 CFR part 14 and 41 CFR part 14H except 41 CFR part 14H–70.

§ 273.44 Use and transfer of Government property.

(a) The use of Government-owned facilities for school purposes may be authorized when not needed for Government activities. Transfer of title to such facilities (except land) may be arranged under the provisions of the Act of June 4, 1953 (67 Stat. 41) subject to the approval of the tribal government if such property is located on a reservation.

(b) In carrying out a contract made under this part, the Area Director or Commissioner may, with the approval of the tribal government, permit a contractor to use existing buildings, facilities, and related equipment and other personal property owned by the Bureau within his jurisdiction under terms and conditions agreed upon for their use and maintenance. The property at the time of transfer must conform to the minimum standards established by the Occupational Safety and Health Act of 1970 (84 Stat. 1590), as amended (29 U.S.C. 651). Use of Government property is subject to the following conditions:

(1) When nonexpendable Government property is turned over to public school authorities or Indian corporations under a use permit, the permittee shall insure such property against damage by flood, fire, rain windstorm, vandalism, snow, and tornado in amounts and with companies satisfactory to the Federal officer in charge of the property. In case of damage or destruction of the property by flood, fire, rain, windstorm, vandalism, snow or tornado, the insurance money collected shall be expended only for repair or replacement of property. Otherwise, insurance proceeds shall be paid to the Bureau.

(2) If the public school authority is self-insured and can present evidence of that fact to the Area Director or Commissioner, insurance for lost or damaged property will not be required. However, the public school authority will be responsible for replacement of such lost or damaged property at no cost to the Government or for paying the Government enough to replace the property.

(3) The permittee shall maintain the property in a reasonable state of repair

consistent with the intended use and educational purposes.

(c) The contractor may have access to existing Bureau records needed to carry out a contract under this part, as follows:

(1) The Bureau will make the records available subject to the provisions of the Freedom of Information Act (5 U.S.C. 552), as amended by the Act of November 21, 1974 (Pub. L. 93–502, 88 Stat. 1561).

(2) The contractor may have access to needed Bureau records at the appropriate Bureau office for review and making copies of selected records.

(3) If the contractor needs a small volume of identifiable Bureau records, the Bureau will furnish the copies to the contractor.

§ 273.45 Indian preference.

(a) Any contract made by the Bureau with a State, school district or Indian corporation shall provide that the contractor shall, to the greatest extent feasible, give preference in and opportunities for employment and training to Indians.

(b) Any contract made by the Bureau with a State, school district or Indian corporation shall provide that the contractor shall, to the greatest extent feasible, give preference in the award of subcontracts to Indian organizations and Indian-owned economic enterprises.

(c) All subcontractors employed by the contractor shall, to the extent possible, give preference to Indians for employment and training and shall be required to include in their bid submission a plan to achieve maximum use of Indian personnel.

(d) In the performance of contracts under this part 273 and subject to the provisions of part 14H of title 41, a tribal governing body may develop its own Indian preference requirements to the extent that such requirements are not inconsistent with the purpose and intent of paragraphs (a), (b) and (c) of this section.

§ 273.46 Liability and motor vehicle insurance.

(a) States, school districts and Indian corporations shall obtain public liability insurance under contracts entered into with the Bureau under this part. However, where the Bureau contracting officer determines that the risk of death, personal injury or property damage under the contract is small and that the time and cost of procuring the insurance is great in relation to the risk, the contractor may be exempted from this requirement.

(b) Notwithstanding paragraph (a) of this section, any contract which requires or authorizes, either expressly or by implication, the use of motor vehicles must contain a provision requiring the State, school district, or Indian corporation to provide liability insurance, regardless of now small the risk.

(c) If the public school authority is self-insured and can present evidence of that fact to the Area Director or Commissioner, liability and motor vehicle insurance will not be required.

§ 273.47 Recordkeeping.

A contractor will be required to maintain a recordkeeping system which will allow the Bureau to meet its legal records program requirements under the Federal Records Act (44 U.S.C. 3101 *et seq.*). Such a record system shall:

(a) Fully reflect all financial transactions involving the receipt and expenditure of funds provided under the contract in a manner which will provide accurate, current and complete disclosure of finanical status; correlation with budget or allowable cost schedules; and clear audit facilitating data.

(b) Reflect the amounts and sources of funds other than Bureau contract funds which may be included in the operation of the contract.

(c) Provide for the creation, maintenance and safeguarding of records of lasting value, including those involving individual rights, such as permanent records and transcripts.

(d) Provide for the orderly retirement of permanent records in accordance with General Records Schedules and the Bureau Records Control Schedule, when there is no established system set up by the State, school district, or Indian corporation.

§ 273.48 Audit and inspection.

(a) During the term of a contract under this part and for three years after the project or undertaking is completed, the Comptroller General and the Secretary, or any of their duly authorized representatives, shall have access, for audit and examination purposes, to any of the contractor's books, documents, papers, and records which, in their opinion, may be related or pertinent to the contract or any subcontract.

(b) The contractor will be responsible for maintaining all documents such as invoices, purchase orders, canceled checks, balance sheets and all other records relating to financial transactions in a manner which will facilitate auditing. The contractor will be responsible for maintaining files of correspondence and other documents relating to the administration of the contract properly separated from general records or cross-referenced to general files.

(c) The contractor receiving funds under this part shall be responsible for contract compliance.

(d) The records involved in any claim or expenditure that has been questioned shall be further maintained until final determination has been made on the questioned expenditures.

(e) All contracts, non-confidential records concerning all students served by the program, reports, budgets, budget estimates, plans, and other documents pertaining to preceding and current year administration of the contract program shall be made available by the contractor and local school officials to each member of the Indian Education Committee and to members of the public upon request. The contractor or local school official shall provide, free of charge, single copies of such documents upon request.

§ 273.49 Freedom of information.

(a) Unless otherwise required by law, the Bureau shall not place restrictions on contractors which will limit public access to the contractor's records except when records must remain confidential.

(b) A contractor under this part shall make all reports and information concerning the contract available to the Indian people which the contract affects. Reports and information may be withheld from disclosure only when both of the following conditions exist:

(1) The reports and information fall within one of the following exempt categories:

(i) Specifically required by statute or Executive Order to be kept secret.

(ii) Commercial or financial information obtained from a person or firm on a privileged or confidential basis.

(iii) Personnel, medical, social, psychological, academic achievement and similar files where disclosure would be a clearly unwarranted invasion of personal privacy.

(2) Disclosure is prohibited by statute or Executive Order or sound grounds exist for using the exemption given in paragraph (b)(1) of this section.

(c) A request to inspect or copy reports and information shall be in writing and must reasonably describe the reports and information requested. The request may be delivered or mailed to the contractor. Within ten (10) working days after receiving the request, the contractor shall determine whether to grant or deny the request. The requester shall be notified immediately of the determination.

(d) The time limit for making a determination may be extended up to an additional ten (10) working days for good reason. The requester shall be notified in writing of the extension, reasons for the extension, and date on which the determination is expected to be made.

§ 273.50 Annual reporting.

(a) A contractor under this part shall make a detailed annual report to the approving official before September 15 of each year and covering the previous school year. The report shall include, but not be limited to, an accounting of the amounts and purposes for which the contract funds were expended, information on the conduct of the program, a quantitative evaluation of the effectiveness of the contract program in meeting the stated objectives contained in the applicant's educational plans, and a complete accounting of actual receipts at the end of the contract period.

(b) In addition to the yearly reporting requirement given in paragraph (a) of this section, the contractor shall furnish other contracted-related reports when and as required by the Area Director or Commissioner.

(c) A contractor under this part shall send copies of the reports required by paragraphs (a) and (b) of this section to the Indian Education Committee(s) and to the tribe(s) under the contract at the same time as the reports are sent to the Bureau.

§273.51 Penalties.

If any officer, director, agent, or employee of, or connected with, any contractor or subcontractor under this part embezzles, willfully misapplies, steals, or obtains by fraud any of the funds or property connected with the contract or subcontract, he shall be subject to the following penalties:

(a) If the amount involved does not exceed $100, he shall be fined not more than $1,000 or imprisoned not more than one year, or both.

(b) If the amount involved exceeds $100, he shall be fined not more than $10,000 or imprisoned for not more than two years, or both.

§273.52 State school laws.

In those States where Pub. L. 83–280, 18 U.S.C. 1162 and 28 U.S.C. 1360 do not confer civil jurisdiction, State employees may be permitted to enter upon Indian tribal lands, reservations, or allotments if the duly-constituted governing body of the tribe adopts a resolution of consent for the following purposes:

(a) Inspecting school conditions in the public schools located on Indian tribal lands, reservations, or allotments.

(b) Enforcing State compulsory school attendance laws against Indian children, parents or persons standing in *loco parentis*.

§273.53 Applicable procurement regulations.

States, school districts, or Indian corporations wanting to contract with the Bureau under this part must comply with the applicable requirements in the Federal Procurement Regulations (41 CFR part 1), as supplemented by the Interior Procurement Regulations (41 CFR part 14), and the Bureau of Indian Affairs Procurement Regulations (41 CFR part 14H), except 41 CFR part 14H–70.

§273.54 Privacy Act requirements.

(a) When a contractor operates a system of records to accomplish a Bureau function, the contractor shall comply with subpart D of 43 CFR part 2 which implements the Privacy Act (5 U.S.C. 552a). Examples of the contractor's responsibilities are:

(1) To continue maintaining those systems of records declared by the Bureau to be subject to the Privacy Act as published in the FEDERAL REGISTER.

(2) To make such records available to individuals involved.

(3) To disclose an individual's record to third parties only after receiving permission from the individual to whom the record pertains. 43 CFR 2.56 lists exceptions to this procedure.

(4) To establish a procedure to account for access, disclosures, denials, and amendments to records.

(5) To provide safeguards for the protection of the records.

(b) The contractor may not:

(1) Discontinue or alter any established systems of records without prior approval of the appropriate Bureau systems manager.

(2) Deny requests for notification or access of records without prior approval of the appropriate Bureau systems manager.

(3) Approve or deny requests for amendments of records without prior approval of the appropriate Bureau systems manager.

(4) Establish a new system of records without prior approval of the Department of Interior and the Office of Management and Budget.

(5) Collect information about an individual unless it is relevant or necessary to accomplish a purpose of the Bureau as required by statute or Executive Order.

(c) The contractor is subject to the penalties provided in section (i) of 5 U.S.C. 552a.

Subpart E—Contract Revision or Cancellation

§ 273.61 Contract revision or amendment.

Any contract made under this part may be revised or amended as deemed necessary to carry out the purposes of the program being contracted. A contractor may make a written request for a revision or amendment of a contract to the Bureau contracting officer. However, no program approved by the Indian Education Committee shall be altered from the time of its original approval to the end of the contract period without the written approval of the Committee.

§ 273.62 Cancelling a contract for cause.

(a) Any contract entered into under this part may be cancelled for cause when the contractor fails to perform the work called for under the contract or fails to permit an Indian Education Committee to perform its duties pursuant to this part.

(b) Before cancelling the contract, the Bureau will advise the contractor in writing of the following:

(1) The reasons why the Bureau is considering cancelling the contract.

(2) The contractor will be given an opportunity to bring its work up to an acceptable level.

(c) If the contractor does not overcome the deficiencies in its contract performance, the Bureau shall cancel the contract for cause. The Bureau will notify the contractor, in writing, of the cancellation. The notice shall give the reasons for the cancellation and the right of the contractor to appeal under subpart C of 43 CFR part 4.

(d) When a contract is cancelled for cause, the Bureau will attempt to perform the work by another contract.

(e) Any contractor that has a contract cancelled for cause must demonstrate that the cause(s) which led to the cancellation have been remedied before it will be considered for another contract.

Subpart F—Appeals

§ 273.71 Contract appeal.

A contractor may appeal an adverse decision or action of a Bureau contracting officer regarding a contract under this part as provided in subpart C of 43 CFR part 4.

§ 273.72 Appeal from decision to cancel contract for cause.

A contractor may appeal the decision of a Bureau official to cancel a contract under this part for cause. The appeal shall be made as provided in subpart C of 43 CFR part 4.

§ 273.73 Other appeals.

Any decision or action taken by a Bureau official under this part, other than those given in §§ 273.71 and 273.72, may be appealed as provided in part 2 of this chapter.

PART 275—STAFFING

Sec.

AUTHORITY: Sec. 502, Pub. L. 91–648, 84 Stat. 1909, 1925 (42 U.S.C. 4762); Sec. 105, Pub. L. 93–638, 88 Stat. 2203, 2208–2210 (25 U.S.C. 450i); 26 U.S.C. 48.

SOURCE: 40 FR 51316, Nov. 4, 1975, unless otherwise noted.

§ 275.1 Purpose and scope.

The purpose of this part is to outline methods available to tribes for utilizing the services of Bureau employees. These regulations are not intended to prevent an Indian tribe or tribal organization from staffing their programs by other methods they feel appropriate. However, when an Indian tribe or tribal organization decides to provide Bureau employees certain Federal benefits, Civil Service Commission regulations must be adhered to.

§ 275.2 Definitions.

As used in this part:

(a) *Act* means the Indian Self-Determination and Education Assistance Act (Pub. L. 93–638, 88 Stat. 2203).

(b) *Area Director* means the official in charge of a Bureau of Indian Affairs Area Office.

(c) *Bureau* means the Bureau of Indian Affairs.

(d) *Commissioner* means the Commissioner of Indian Affairs, under the direction and supervision of the Assistant Secretary—Indian Affairs, who is responsible for the direction of the day-to-day operations of the Bureau of Indian Affairs.

(e) *Days* means calendar days.

(f) *Indian tribe* means any Indian tribe, band, nation, rancheria, pueblo, colony, or community, including any Alaska Native village or regional or village corporation as defined in or established pursuant to the Alaska Native Claims Settlement Act (85 Stat. 688) which is federally recognized as eligible by the U.S. Government through the Secretary for the special programs and services provided by the Secretary to Indians because of their status as Indians.

(g) *Indian* means a person who is a member of an Indian tribe.

(h) *Superintendent* means the official in charge of a Bureau of Indian Affairs Agency Office.

(i) *Tribal Chairman* means tribal chairman, governor, chief or other person recognized by the tribal government as its chief executive officer.

(j) *Tribal government, tribal governing body,* and *tribal council* means the recognized governing body of any Indian tribe.

(k) *Tribal organization* means the recognized governing body of any Indian tribe; or any legally established organization of Indians or tribes which is controlled, sanctioned, or chartered by such governing body or bodies or which is democratically elected by the adult members of the Indian community to be served by such organization and which includes the maximum participation of Indians in all phases of its activities.

(l) *Assistant Secretary—Indian Affairs* means the Assistant Secretary—Indian Affairs who discharges the authority and responsibility of the Secretary for activities pertaining to Indians and Indian affairs.

[40 FR 51316, Nov. 4, 1975, as amended at 43 FR 37446, Aug. 23, 1978; 45 FR 13452, Feb. 29, 1980]

§ 275.3 Methods for staffing.

(a) An Indian tribal organization may use any of the following three methods to employ or obtain the services of Bureau employees:

(1) Agreement in accordance with the Intergovernmental Personnel Act of 1970 (5 U.S.C. 3371–3376). The agreement may be arranged between the tribal organization, the employee, and the Area Director or Commissioner. Assistance will be provided by the Area Personnel Office in complying with Civil Service instructions (Federal Personnel Manual, chapter 334) for completing an agreement.

(2) Employment of Bureau employees on or before December 31, 1985, when serving under an appointment not limited to one year or less. A mutual agreement will be made between a tribal organization and the employee before leaving Federal employment to retain coverage for any of the following Federal benefits:

(i) Compensation for work injuries.

(ii) Retirement.

(iii) Health insurance.

(iv) Life insurance.

(3) An agreement by an Indian tribe in accordance with the 1834 Act (25 U.S.C. 48) may be made in connection with contracts under section 102 of the Act.

(i) The agreement may provide for the tribal government to direct the day-to-day activities of Bureau employees. Tribal government direction of Bureau employees means the tribal chairman or other tribal official, as designated by the tribal governing body, is responsible for the planning, coordination, and completion of the daily on-the-job assignments of Bureau employees. The daily assignments of each such Bureau employee are limited to those that fall within the general range of duties prescribed in the employee's Bureau position.

(ii) The agreement to direct day-to-day activities of Bureau employees shall include all employees:

(A) Whose positions are in the program or portion of the program to be contracted; or

(B) In a portion of the program to continue under Bureau operation in connection with a contract for other portions of the program.

(iii) The proposed agreement will be worked out between the tribe, the Superintendent, and the Area Director and forwarded to the Commissioner for final approval.

(b) When a contract application under part 900 of this chapter does not include a proposed agreement for direction of Bureau employees, the application must be submitted at least 120 days in advance of the proposed effective date of the contract to allow time for placement of affected employees.

[40 FR 51316, Nov. 4, 1975, as amended at 41 FR 5098, Feb. 4, 1976; 64 FR 13896, Mar. 23, 1999]

§ 275.4 Implementing regulations.

Regulations to implement section 105 of the Act will be issued by the Civil Service Commission. The regulations will cover the situations described in paragraphs (a)(1) and (a)(2) of § 275.3.

PART 276—UNIFORM ADMINISTRATIVE REQUIREMENTS FOR GRANTS

Sec.

AUTHORITY: 34 CFR 256; Sec. 104, Pub. L. 93–638, 88 Stat. 2203, 2207 (25 U.S.C. 450h).

SOURCE: 40 FR 51316, Nov. 4, 1975, unless otherwise noted.

§ 276.1 Purpose and scope.

(a) The purpose of the regulations in this part is to give the uniform administrative requirements for grants awarded by the Bureau of Indian Affairs.

(b) The regulations in this part shall apply to all grants awarded by the Bureau of Indian Affairs unless the part which gives the application process and special requirements for the specific type of grant states otherwise.

§ 276.2 Definitions.

As used in this part:

(a) *Advance by Treasury check* means a payment made by a Treasury check to a grantee upon its request or through the use of predetermined payment schedules before payments are made by the grantee.

(b) *Date of completion* means the date when all work under a grant is completed or the date in the grant award document, or any supplement or amendment thereto, on which Federal assistance ends.

(c) *Disallowed costs* means those charges to a grant which the Bureau or its representative determines to be unallowable.

(d) *Economic enterprise* means any commercial, industrial, agricultural or business activity that is at least 51 percent Indian owned, established or organized for the purpose of profit.

(e) *Excess property* means property under the control of the Bureau which, as determined by the Commissioner, is no longer required for its needs.

(f) *Expendable personal property* means all tangible personal property other than nonexpendable property.

(g) *Grant closeout* means the process by which the Bureau determines that all applicable administrative actions and all required work of the grant have been completed by the grantee and the Bureau.

(h) *Grantee* means the entity which is responsible for administration of the grant.

(i) *Indian tribe* means any Indian tribe, band, nation, rancheria, pueblo, colony or community, including any Alaska Native village or regional or village corporation as defined in or established pursuant to the Alaska Native Claims Settlement Act (85 Stat. 688) which is federally recognized as eligible by the United States Government through the Secretary for the special programs and services provided by the Secretary to Indians because of their status as Indians.

(j) *Letter of credit* means an instrument certified by an authorized official of the Bureau which authorizes a grantee to draw funds when needed from the Treasury, through a Regional Disbursing Office, in accordance with the provisions of Treasury Circular No. 1075 as modified and supplemented by a memorandum of understanding between the Bureau of Government Financial Operation, Department of the Treasury and the Department of the Interior.

(k) *Nonexpendable personal property* means tangible personal property having useful life of more than one year and an acquisition cost of $300 or more per unit. A grantee may use its own definition of nonexpendable personal property provided that such definition would at least include all tangible personal property as defined above.

(l) *Personal property* means property of any kind except real property. It may be tangible—having physical existence, or intangible—having no physical existence, such as patents, inventions, and copyrights.

(m) *Real property* means land, land improvements, structures and appurtenances thereto, excluding removable personal property, machinery and equipment.

(n) *Reimbursement by Treasury check* means a payment made to a grantee with a Treasury check upon request for reimbursement from the grantee.

(o) *Suspension of a grant* means an action by the Bureau which temporarily suspends assistance under the grant pending corrective action by the grantee or pending decision to terminate the grant by the Bureau.

(p) *Termination of a grant* means the cancellation of Federal assistance, in whole or in part, under a grant at any time prior to the date of completion.

(q) *Tribal government, tribal governing body,* and *tribal council* means the recognized governing body of an Indian tribe.

(r) *Tribal organization* means the recognized governing body of any Indian tribe or any legally established organization of Indians which is controlled, sanctioned, or chartered by such governing body or bodies of which is democratically elected by the adult members of the Indian community to be served by such organization and which includes the maximum participation of Indians in all phases of its activities.

§276.3 Cash depositories.

(a) Except for situations described in paragraphs (b) and (c) of this section, the Bureau will not:

(1) Require physical segregation of cash depositories for Bureau grant funds provided to a grantee.

(2) Establish any eligibility requirements for cash depositories in which Bureau grant funds are deposited by grantees or their subgrantees.

(b) A separate bank account shall be used when payments under letter of credit are made on a "check-paid" basis in accordance with agreements entered into by a grantee, the Bureau, and the banking institutions involved. A check-paid basis letter of credit is one under which funds are not drawn from the Treasury until the grantee's checks have been presented to its bank for payment.

(c) Consistent with the national goal of expanding the opportunities for minority business enterprises, grantees are encouraged to use minority banks.

§276.4 Bondings and insurance.

In administering Bureau grants, grantees shall observe their regular requirements and practices with respect to bonding and insurance. The Bureau will not impose additional bonding and insurance requirements, including fidelity bonds, except as provided in paragraphs (a) and (b) of this section.

(a) The recipient of a Bureau grant which requires contracting for construction or facility improvement (including any Bureau grant which provides for alterations or renovations of real property) shall follow its own requirements and practices relating to bid guarantees, performance bonds, and payment bonds except for contracts exceeding $100,000. For contracts exceeding $100,000, the minimum requirements shall be as follows:

(1) A bid guarantee from each bidder equivalent to five percent of the bid price. The bid guarantee shall consist of a firm commitment such as a bid bond, certified check, or other negotiable instrument accompanying a bid as assurance that the bidder will, upon acceptance of his bid, execute such contractual documents as may be required within the time specified.

(2) A performance bond on the part of the contractor for 100 percent of the contract price. A performance bond is one executed in connection with a contract to secure fulfillment of all the contractor's obligations under the contract.

(3) A payment bond on the part of the contractor for 100 per cent of the contract price. A payment bond is one executed in connection with a contract to assure payment as required by law of all persons supplying labor and material in the execution of the work provided for in the contract.

(b) Where, in connection with a Bureau grant, the Bureau also guarantees the payment of money borrowed by the grantee, the Bureau may at its discretion require adequate bonding and insurance if the bonding and insurance requirements of the grantee are not deemed to be sufficient to protect adequately the interests of the Federal Government.

§ 276.5 Recordkeeping.

(a) The Bureau shall not impose record retention requirements over and above those established by the grantee except that financial records, supporting documents, statistical records, and all other records pertinent to a Bureau grant, or to any subgrant (or negotiated contract exceeding $2500) under a grant, shall be retained for a period of three years, with the following qualifications:

(1) The records shall be retained beyond the three-year period if audit findings have not been resolved.

(2) Records for nonexpendable property which was acquired with Bureau grant funds shall be retained for three years after its final disposition.

(3) When grant records are transferred to or maintained by the Bureau, the three-year retention requirement is not applicable to the grantee.

(b) The retention period starts from the date of submission of the final expenditure report or, for grants which are renewed annually, from the date of the submission of the annual expenditure report.

(c) Grantees are authorized, if they desire, to substitute microfilm copies in lieu of original records.

(d) The Bureau shall request transfer of certain records to its custody from grantees when it determines that the records possess long-term retention value. However, in order to avoid duplicate recordkeeping the Bureau may make arrangements with the grantee for the grantee to retain any records which are continuously needed for joint use.

(e) The Secretary of the Interior and the Comptroller General of the United States, or any of their duly authorized representatives shall have access to any books, documents, papers, and records of the grantees and their subgrantees which are pertinent to a specific grant program for the purpose of making audit, examination, excerpts, transcripts and copies at government expense.

(f) Unless otherwise required by law, the Bureau shall not place restrictions on grantees which will limit public access to the grantee's records created as part of the grant except when records must remain confidential. Following are some of the reasons for withholding records:

(1) Prevent a clearly unwarranted invasion of personal privacy;

(2) Specifically required by statute or Executive Order to be kept secret;

(3) Commercial or financial information obtained from a person or firm on a privileged or confidential basis.

§ 276.6 Program income.

(a) No grantee receiving a grant shall be held accountable for interest earned on grant funds, pending their disbursement for program purposes.

(b) Proceeds from the sale of real or personal property, either provided by the Federal Government or purchased in whole or in part with Federal funds, shall be handled in accordance with § 276.11.

(c) Royalties received from copyrights and patents produced under the grant during the grant period shall be retained by the grantee and, in accordance with the grant agreement, be either added to the funds already committed to the program or deducted from total allowable project costs for the purpose of determining the net costs on which the Bureau share of costs will be based. After termination or completion of the grant, the Bureau share of royalties in excess of $200 received annually shall be returned to the Bureau in the absence of other specific agreements between the Bureau and the grantee. The Bureau share of royalties shall be computed on the same ratio basis as the Bureau share of the total project cost.

(d) All other program income earned during the grant period shall be retained by the grantee and, in accordance with the grant agreement, shall be either:

(1) Added to funds committed to the project by the Bureau and the grantee and be used to further eligible program objectives, or

(2) Deducted from the total project costs for the purpose of determining the net costs on which the Bureau share of costs will be based.

(e) Grantees shall record the receipt and expenditures of revenues (such as taxes, special assessments, levies, fines, etc.) as a part of grant project transactions when such revenues are specifically earmarked for a grant project in accordance with grant agreements.

§ 276.7 Standards for grantee financial management systems.

(a) Grantee financial management systems for grants and subgrantee financial management systems for subgrants shall provide for:

(1) Accurate, current, and complete disclosure of the financial results of each grant program in accordance with Federal reporting requirements and for each subgrant in accordance with the grantees' requirements. Except when specifically required by law, the Bureau wll not require financial reporting on the accrual basis from tribal organizations whose records are not maintained on that basis. However, when accrual reporting is required by law, tribal organizations whose records are not maintained on that basis will not be required to convert their accounting systems to the accrual basis; they may develop the accrual information through an analysis of the documentation on hand or on the basis of best estimates.

(2) Records which identify adequately the source and application of funds for grant—or subgrant—supported activities. These records shall contain information pertaining to grant or subgrant awards and authorizations, obligations, unobligated balances, assets, liabilities, outlays, and income.

(3) Effective control over and accountability for all grant or subgrant funds, and real and personal property acquired with grant or subgrant funds. Grantees and subgrantees shall adequately safeguard all such property and shall assure that it is used solely for authorized purposes.

(4) Comparison of actual with budgeted amounts for each grant or subgrant, and, when specifically required by the performance reporting requirements of the grant or subgrant, relation of financial information with performance or productivity data, including the production of unit cost information.

(5) Procedures to minimize the time elapsing between the transfer of funds from the U.S. Treasury and the disbursement by the grantee, whenever funds are advanced by the Federal Government. When advances are made by a letter-of-credit method, the grantees shall make drawdowns from the U.S. Treasury as close as possible to the time of making the disbursements. Subgrantees shall institute similar procedures when funds are advanced by the grantee.

(6) Procedures for determining the allowability and allocability of costs shall be in accordance with the applicable cost principles prescribed in appendix A of this part.

(7) Accounting records which are supported by source documentation.

(8) A systematic method to assure timely and appropriate resolution of audit findings and recommendations.

(b) Grantees shall require subgrantees (recipients of grants which are passed through by the grantee) to adopt all of the standards in paragraph (a) of this section.

§ 276.8 Financial reporting requirements.

Requirements for grantees to report financial information to the Bureau, and to request advances and reimbursment when a letter of credit method is not used, are prescribed in appendix B of this part.

§ 276.9 Monitoring and reporting program performances.

(a) Grantees shall constantly monitor the performance under grant-supported activities to assure that adequate progress is being made toward achieving the goals of the grant. This review shall be made for each program, function, or activity of each grant as set forth in the approved grant application.

(b) Grantees shall submit a performance report for each grant which briefly presents the following for each program, function, or activity involved:

(1) A comparison of actual accomplishments to the goals established for the period. Where the output of grant programs can be readily quantified, such quantitative data should be related to cost data for computation of unit costs.

(2) Reasons for slippage in those cases were established goals were not met.

(3) Other pertinent information including, when appropriate, analysis and explanation of cost overruns or high unit costs.

(c) Grantees shall submit the performance reports to the Bureau with the Financial Status Reports (prescribed in appendix B of this part) in the frequency established by appendix B. The Bureau shall prescribe the frequency with which the performance reports will be submitted with the Request for Advance or Reimbursement (prescribed in appendix B) when that form is used in lieu of the Financial Status Report. In no case shall the performance reports be required more frequently than quarterly or less frequently than annually.

(d) Between the required performance reporting dates, events may occur which have significant impact upon the project or program. In such cases, the grantee shall inform the Bureau as soon as the following types of conditions become known:

(1) Problems, delays, or adverse conditions which will materially affect the ability to attain program objectives, prevent the meeting of time schedules and goals, or preclude the attainment of project work units by established time periods. This disclosure shall be accomplished by a statement of the action taken, or contemplated, and any Bureau assistance needed to resolve the situation.

(2) Favorable developments or events which enable meeting time schedules and goals sooner than anticipated or producing more work units than originally projected.

(e) If any performance review conducted by the grantee discloses the need for change in the budget estimates in accordance with the criteria established in § 276.14, the grantee shall submit a request for budget revision.

(f) The bureau shall make site visits as frequently as practicable to:

(1) Review program accomplishments and management control systems.

(2) Provide such technical assistance as may be required, or requested.

§ 276.10 Grant payment requirements.

(a) Except for construction grants for which the letter-of-credit method is optional, the letter-of-credit funding method shall be used by the Bureau where all of the following conditions exist:

(1) When there is or will be a continuing relationship between a grantee and the Bureau for at least a 12-month period and the total amount of advances to be received within that period from the Bureau is $120,000, or more, as prescribed by Treasury Circular No. 1075.

(2) When the grantee has established or demonstrated to the Bureau the willingness and ability to establish procedures that will minimize the time

elapsing between the transfer of funds and their disbursement by the grantee.

(3) When the grantee's financial management system meets the standards for fund control and accountability prescribed in §276.7.

(b) The method of advancing funds by Treasury check shall be used, in accordance with the provisions of Treasury Circular No. 1075, when the grantee meets all of the requirements specified in paragraphs (a)(2) and (3) of this section.

(c) The reimbursement by Treasury check method shall be the preferred method when the grantee does not meet the requirements specified in either paragraph (a)(2) or (a)(3), or both. This method may also be used when the major portion of the program is accomplished through private market financing or Federal loans, and when the Bureau grant assistance constitutes a minor portion of the program.

(d) Unless otherwise required by law, the Bureau shall not withhold payments for proper charges made by grantees at any time during the grant period unless:

(1) A grantee has failed to comply with the program objectives, grant award conditions, or Bureau reporting requirements; or

(2) The grantee is indebted to the United States and collection of the indebtedness will not impair accomplishment of the objectives of any grant program sponsored by the United States. Under such conditions, the Bureau may, upon reasonable notice, inform the grantee that payments will not be made for obligations incurred after a specified date until the conditions are corrected or the indebtedness to the Federal Government is liquidated.

(e) Appendix B of this part provides the procedures for requesting advances or reimbursements.

[40 FR 51316, Nov. 4, 1975, as amended at 41 FR 5099, Feb. 4, 1976]

§276.11 Property management standards.

(a) Grantees may follow their own property management policies and procedures if they observe the requirements of this section. With respect to property covered by this section, the Bureau may not impose on grantees any requirements (including property reporting requirements)—not authorized by this part unless specifically required by Federal law.

(b) Title to real property to be acquired in whole or in part from a Bureau grant under part 900 of this chapter shall vest in one of the following manners:

(1) Title may be taken by the United States in trust for the Indian tribe upon the request of the tribe and when the real property to be acquired is within the reservation boundaries or adjoins on at least two sides other trust or restricted lands as prescribed in part 900 of this chapter.

(2) Fee title to the acquired real property shall vest in the Indian tribe whenever the acquisition does not meet the criteria in paragraph (b)(1) of this section, unless for other reasons a tribe requests title to be taken in the name of the United States. In the absence of applicable statutory authority governing the disposition of real property acquired by a tribe, the tribe shall use the real property for the authorized purposes and in accordance with any other requirements imposed by the terms and conditions of the original grant. Changes in use compatible to other tribal programs may be authorized by the Bureau. When no longer needed for the authorized purposes, the real property shall be used in accordance with the standards set forth in §276.11(d)(1) for non-expendable personal property. Accordingly, the following priority order for use of such property shall be:

(i) Other grants from the Bureau.

(ii) Grants from other Federal agencies.

(iii) Tribal purposes consistent with those authorized for support by Bureau grants.

(iv) Tribal official activities.

(3) In those instances where the Indian tribe requests, title may be acquired by the United States. Use of these acquired real property interests will be subject to the authorized purposes and in accordance with the provisions of the original grant. Upon a determination that the real property is no longer needed for the authorized purposes, disposition may be made by

declaring it excess under provisions of the Act of January 2, 1975 (88 Stat. 1954) and title transferred to the Secretary to be held by the United States in trust for the tribe. Where real property does not meet the requirements under the Act of January 2, 1975 (88 Stat. 1954), the tribe may elect to acquire title under applicable enabling statutory authorities, or in the absence of statutory authority, request withholding disposition in aid of legislation, or authorize disposal under the General Services Administration procedures.

(c) The provisions of paragraphs (b)(2) and (3) of this section shall also apply when real property is acquired in whole or in part by a Bureau grant other than that provided under part 900 of this chapter. However, when such property is acquired by a grantee other than an Indian tribe, or a tribal governing body, fee simple title to the property shall vest in the grantee upon acquisition. In the absence of applicable statutory provisions governing the use or disposition of such property, it shall be subject to the following requirments, in addition to any other requirements imposed by the terms and conditions of the grant:

(1) The grantee shall use the real property for the authorized purpose of the original grant as long as needed.

(2) The grantee shall obtain approval by the Bureau for the use of the real property in other projects when the grantee determines that the property is no longer needed for the original grant purposes. Use in other projects shall be limited to those under other Federal grant programs, or programs that have purposes consistent with those authorized for support by the grantor.

(3) When the real property is no longer needed as provided in paragraphs (c)(1) and (2) of this section, the grantee shall return all real property furnished or purchased wholly with Bureau grant funds to the control of the Bureau. In the case of property purchased in part with Bureau grant funds, the grantee may be permitted to take title to the Federal interest therein upon compensating the Federal Government for its fair share of the property. The Federal share of the property shall be the amount computed by applying the percentage of the Federal participation in the total cost of the grant program for which the property was acquired to the current fair market value of the property.

(d) Standards and procedures governing ownership, use, and disposition of nonexpendable personal property furnished by the Bureau or acquired with Bureau funds are set forth below:

(1) *Nonexpendable personal property acquired with Bureau funds.* When nonexpendable personal property is acquired by a grantee wholly or in part with Bureau funds, title will not be taken by the Bureau except as provided in paragraph (d)(1)(iv) of this section but shall be vested in the grantee subject to the following restrictions on use and disposition of the property:

(i) The grantee shall retain the property acquired with Bureau funds in the grant program as long as there is a need for the property to accomplish the purpose of the grant program whether or not the program continues to be supported by Bureau funds. When there is no longer a need for the property to accomplish the purpose of the grant program, the grantee shall use the property in connection with the other Federal grants it has received in the following order of priority:

(A) Other grants from the Bureau needing the property.

(B) Grants of other Federal agencies needing the property.

(ii) When the grantee no longer has need for the property in any of its Federal grant programs, or programs that have purposes consistent with those authorized for support by the grantor, the property may be used for its own official activities in accordance with the following standards:

(A) Nonexpendable property with an acquisition cost of less than $500 and used four years or more. The grantee may use the property for its own official activities without reimbursement to the Federal government or sell the property and retain the proceeds.

(B) All other nonexpendable property. The grantee may retain the property for its own use if a fair compensation is made to the Bureau for the latter's share of the property. The amount of compensation shall be computed by applying the percentage of

Bureau participation in the grant program to the current fair market value of the property.

(iii) If the grantee has no need for the property, disposition of the property shall be made as follows:

(A) Nonexpendable property with an acquisition cost of $1,000 or less. Except for that property which meets the criteria of paragraph (d)(1)(ii)(A) of this section, the grantee shall sell the property and reimburse the Bureau an amount which is computed in accordance with paragraph (d)(1)(iii) of this section.

(B) Nonexpendable property with an acquisition cost of over $1,000. The grantee shall request disposition instructions from the Bureau. The Bureau shall determine whether the property can be used to meet the Bureau's requirement. If no requirement exists within the Bureau, the availability of the property shall be reported to the General Services Administration (GSA) by the Bureau to determine whether a requirement for the property exists in other Federal agencies. The Bureau shall issue instructions to the grantee within 120 days and the following procedures shall govern:

(*1*) If the grantee is instructed to ship the property elsewhere, the grantee shall be reimbursed by the benefiting Federal agency with an amount which is computed by applying the percentage of the grantee's participation in the grant program to the current fair market value of the property, plus any shipping or interim storage costs incurred.

(*2*) If the grantee is instructed to otherwise dispose of the property, he shall be reimbursed by the Bureau of such costs incurred in its disposition.

(*3*) If disposition instructions are not issued within 120 days after reporting, the grantee shall sell the property and reimburse the Bureau and amount which is computed by applying the percentage of Bureau participation in the grant program to the sales proceeds. Further, the grantee shall be permitted to retain $100 or 10 percent of the proceeds, whichever is greater, for the grantee's selling and handling expenses.

(iv) Where the Bureau determines that property with an acquisition cost of $1,000 or more and financed solely with Bureau funds is unique, different, or costly to replace, it may reserve title to such property, subject to the following provisions:

(A) The property shall be appropriately identified in the grant agreement or otherwise made known to the grantee.

(B) The Bureau shall issue disposition instructions within 120 days after the completion of the need for the property under the grant for which it was acquired. If the Bureau fails to issue disposition instructions within 120 days, the grantee shall apply the standards of paragraphs (d)(1)(i), (d)(1)(ii)(B), and (d)(1)(iii)(B) of this section.

(2) Federally owned nonexpendable personal property. Unless statutory authority to transfer title has been granted to an agency, title to Federally owned property (property to which the Federal Government retains title including excess property made available by the Bureau to grantees) remains vested by law in the Federal Government. Upon termination of the grant or need for the property, such property shall be reported to the Bureau for further Bureau use or, if appropriate, for reporting to the General Services Administration for other Federal agency use. Appropriate disposition instructions will be issued to the grantee after completion of Bureau review.

(e) The grantee's property management standards for nonexpendable personal property shall also include the following procedural requirements:

(1) Property records shall be maintained accurately and provide for a description of the property; manufacturer's serial number or other identification number; acquisition date and cost; source of the property; percentage of Federal funds used in the purchase of property; location, use, and condition of the property; and ultimate disposition data including sales price or the method used to determine current fair market value if the grantee reimburses the bureau for its share.

(2) A physical inventory of property shall be taken and the results reconciled with the property records at least once every two years to verify the

existence, current use, and continued need for the property.

(3) A control system shall be in effect to insure adequate safeguards to prevent loss, damage, or theft to the property. Any loss, damage, or theft of nonexpendable property shall be investigated and fully documented.

(4) Adequate maintenance procedures shall be implemented to keep the property in good condition.

(5) Proper sales procedures shall be established for unneeded property which would provide for competition to the extent practicable and result in the highest possible return.

(f) When the total inventory value of any unused expendable personal property exceeds $500 at the expiration of need for any grant purposes, the grantee may retain the property or sell the property as long as he compensates the Bureau for its share in the cost. The amount of compensation shall be computed in accordance with paragraph (d)(1)(ii)(B) of this section.

(g) Specific standards for control of intangible property are provided as follows:

(1) If any program produces patentable items, patent rights, processes, or inventions, in the course of work aided by a Bureau grant, such fact shall be promptly and fully reported to the Bureau. Unless there is prior agreement between the grantee and Bureau on disposition of such items, the Bureau shall determine whether protection on such invention or discovery shall be sought and how the rights in the invention or discovery—including rights under any patent issued on it—shall be allocated and administered in order to protect the public interest consistent with "Government Patent Policy" (President's memorandum for heads of executive departments and agencies), dated August 23, 1971, and Statement of Government Patent Policy as printed in 36 FR 16889.

(2) Where the grant results in a book or other copyrightable material, the author or grantee is eligible to copyright the work if it is found that (i) the retention of the copyright is not precluded by statute and (ii) equity or the public interest is best served by doing so, by reason of special circumstances. If it is found that the public interest is best served by limiting the term of any copyright to be obtained, such limits shall be set forth in the grant agreement. "Developmental" copyrights may be requested during the development, testing, or evaluation of copyrightable materials in order to prevent them from prematurely falling into the public domain. The copyright will be in accordance with copyright laws. However, the Government shall receive a royalty-free, nonexclusive and irrevocable license to reproduce, publish, or otherwise use, and to authorize others to use the work for Government purposes. A copy of any copyright obtained by a grantee shall be provided to the Bureau. Program income received as royalties from copyrights on materials produced under grants is retained by the grantee during the grant period and is to be used according to the provisions of § 276.6(c). Specific agreements between the Bureau and the grantee shall be entered into before the grant is awarded to determine the uses of the royalty income after the grant is completed or terminated.

(h) The use of Bureau-owned facilities under the jurisdiction of the Commissioner by a grantee for purposes of carrying out a grant may be authorized when the facilities are not needed for Bureau purposes.

[40 FR 51316, Nov. 4, 1975, as amended at 43 FR 37446, Aug. 23, 1978; 64 FR 13897, Mar. 23, 1999]

§ 276.12 Procurement standards.

(a) The standards contained in this section do not relieve the grantee of the contractual responsibilities arising under its contracts. The grantee is the responsible authority, without recourse to the Bureau regarding the settlement and satisfaction of all contractual and administrative issues arising out of procurements entered into, in support of a grant. This includes but is not limited to: disputes, claims, protests of award, source evaluation or other matters of a contractual nature. Matters concerning violation of law are to be referred to the tribal, Federal or other authority which has proper jurisdiction.

(b) Grantees may use their own procurement regulations provided that procurements made with Bureau grant funds adhere to the standards set forth as follows:

(1) The grantee shall maintain a code or standards of conduct which shall govern the performance of its officers, employees, or agents in contracting with and expending Bureau grant funds. Grantee's officers, employees or agents, shall neither solicit nor accept gratuities, favors, or anything of monetary value from contractors or potential contractors. To the extent permissible by law, rules or regulations, such standards shall provide for penalties, sanctions, or other disciplinary actions to be applied for violations of such standards by either the grantee officers, employees, or agents, or by contractors or their agents.

(2) All procurement transactions regardless of whether negotiated or advertised and without regard to dollar value shall be conducted in a manner so as to provide maximum open and free competition. The grantee should be alert to organizational conflicts of interest or non-competitive practices among contractors which may restrict or eliminate competition or otherwise restrain trade. However, this provision will apply only after the Indian preference requirements prescribed in § 276.13 have been met.

(3) The grantee shall establish procurement procedures which provide for, as a minimum, the following procedural requirements:

(i) Proposed procurement actions shall be reviewed by grantee official to avoid purchasing unnecessary or duplicative items. Where appropriate, an analysis shall be made of lease and purchase alternatives to determine which would be the most economical, practical procurement.

(ii) Invitations for bids or requests for proposals shall be based upon a clear and accurate description of the technical requirements for the material, product, or service to be procured. In competitive procurements, such description shall not contain features which unduly restrict competition. "Brand name or equal" description may be used as a means to define the performance or other salient requirements of a procurement. When so used, the specific features of the named brand which must be met by offerors should be clearly specified.

(iii) Positive efforts shall be made by the grantees to use small business and minority-owned business sources of supplies and services. Such efforts should allow these sources the maximum feasible opportunity to compete for contracts to be performed using Bureau grant funds. However, this provision will apply only after the Indian preference requirements prescribed in § 276.13 have been met.

(iv) The type of procuring instruments used (i.e., fixed price contracts, cost reimbursable contracts, etc.) shall be appropriate for the particular procurement and for promoting the best interest of the grant program involved. The "cost-plus-a-percentage-of-cost" method of contracting shall not be used.

(v) Formal advertising, with adequate purchase description, sealed bids, and public openings shall be the required method of procurement unless negotiation pursuant to paragraph (b)(3)(vi) of this section is necessary to accomplish sound procurement. However, procurement of $10,000 or less need not be so advertised. Where such advertised bids are obtained the awards shall be made to the responsible bidder whose bid is responsive to the invitation and is most advantageous to the grantee, price and other factors considered. (Factors such as discounts, transportation costs, taxes may be considered in determining the lowest bid.) Invitations for bids shall clearly set forth all requirements which the bidder must fulfill in order for his bid to be evaluated by the grantee. Any or all bids may be rejected when it is in the grantee's interest to do so.

(vi) Procurements may be negotiated if it is impractical and unfeasible to use formal advertising. Generally, procurements may be negotiated by the grantee if:

(A) The public exigency will not permit the delay incident to advertising;

(B) The material or service to be procured is available from only one person or firm; (all contemplated sole source procurements where the aggregate expenditure is expected to exceed $5,000 shall be referred to the Bureau for prior approval).

(C) The total amount involved does not exceed $10,000;

(D) The contract is for personal or professional services, or for any service to be rendered by a university, college, or other educational institutions;

(E) No acceptable bids have been received after formal advertising;

(F) The purchases are for highly perishable materials or medical supplies; for material or services where the prices are established by law; for technical items or equipment requiring standardization and interchangeability of parts with existing equipment; for experimental, developmental or research work; for supplies purchased for authorized resale; and for technical or specialized supplies requiring substantial initial investment for manufacture;

(G) Otherwise authorized by law, rules or regulations. Notwithstanding the existence of circumstances justifying negotiation, competition shall be obtained to the maximum extent practicable.

(vii) Contracts shall be made only with responsible contractors who possess the potential ability to perform successfully under the terms and conditions of a proposed procurement. Consideration shall be given to such matters as contractor integrity, record of past performance, financial and technical resources, or accessibility to other necessary resources.

(viii) Procurement records or files for purchases in amounts over $10,000 shall provide at least the following pertinent information: Justification for the use of negotiation in lieu of advertising, contractor selection, and the basis for the cost or price negotiation.

(ix) A system for contract administration shall be maintained to assure contractor conformance with terms, conditions, and specifications of the contract or order, and to assure adequate and timely followup of all purchases.

(c) In addition to provisions to define a sound and complete agreement, the grantee shall include the following provisions in all contracts and subgrants:

(1) Contracts shall contain such contractual provisions or conditions which will allow for administrative, contractual, or legal remedies in instances where contractors violate or breach contract terms, and provide for such sanctions and penalties as may be appropriate.

(2) All contracts, amounts for which are over $10,000 shall contain suitable provisions for termination by the grantee including the manner by which it will be effected and the basis for settlement. In addition, such contracts shall describe conditions where the contract may be terminated for default as well as conditions where the contract may be terminated because of circumstances beyond the control of the contractor.

(3) In all contracts for construction or facility improvement awarded over $100,000, grantees shall observe the bonding requirements provided in § 276.4.

(4) All construction contracts awarded by recipients and their contractors or subgrantees having a value of more than $10,000, shall contain a provision requiring compliance with Executive Order 11246, entitled "Equal Employment Opportunity," as amended by Labor Regulations (41 CFR part 87). However, this Equal Employment Opportunity provision will apply only after the Indian preference requirements prescribed in § 276.13 have been met.

(5) All contracts and subgrants for construction or repair shall include a provision for compliance with the Copeland "Anti-Kick Back" Act (18 U.S.C. 874) as supplemented in Department of Labor regulations (29 CFR part 3). This Act provides that each contractor or subgrantee shall be prohibited from inducing, by any means, any person employed in the construction, completion, or repair of public work, to give up any part of the compensation to which he is otherwise entitled. The grantee shall report all suspected or reported violations to the Bureau.

(6) When required by the Federal grant program legislation, all construction contracts awarded by grantees and subgrantees over $2,000 shall include a provision for compliance with the Davis-Bacon Act (40 U.S.C. 276a to a-7) and as supplemented by Department of Labor regulations (29 CFR part 5). Under this Act, contractors shall be required to pay wages to laborers and

mechanics at a rate not less than the minimum wages specified in a wage determination made by the Secretary of Labor. In addition, contractors shall be required to pay wages not less often than once a week. The grantee shall place a copy of the current prevailing wage determination issued by the Department of Labor in each solicitation and the award of a contract shall be conditioned upon the acceptance of the wage determination. The grantee shall report all suspected or reported violations to the Bureau.

(7) Where applicable, all contracts awarded by grantees and subgrantees over $2,000 for construction contracts and over $2,500 for other contracts which involve the employment of mechanics or laborers shall include a provision for compliance with sections 103 and 107 of the Contract Work Hours and Safety Standards Act (40 U.S.C. 327–330) as supplemented by Department of Labor regulations (29 CFR part 5). Under section 103 of the Act, each contractor shall be required to compute the wages of every mechanic and laborer on the basis of a standard work day of 8 hours and a standard work week of 40 hours. Work in excess of the standard workday or workweek is permissible if the worker is compensated at a rate of not less than 1½ times the basic rate of pay for all hours worked over 8 hours in any calendar day or 40 hours in the work week. Section 107 of the Act applies to construction work and provides that no laborer or mechanic shall be required to work in surroundings or under working conditions which are unsanitary, hazardous, or dangerous to his health and safety as determined under construction, safety, and health standards promulgated by the Secretary of Labor. These requirements do not apply to the purchases of supplies or materials or articles ordinarily available on the open market, or contracts for transportation or transmission of intelligence.

(8) Contracts or agreements, the principal purpose of which is to create, develop, or improve products, processes or methods; or for exploration into fields which directly concern public health, safety, or welfare; or constraints in the field of science or technology in which there has been little significant experience outside of work funded by Federal assistance, shall contain a notice to the effect that matters regarding rights to inventions, and materials generated under the contract or agreement are subject to the regulations issued by the Bureau. The contractor shall be advised as to the source of additional information regarding these matters.

(9) All negotiated contracts (except those of $10,000 or less) awarded by grantees shall include a provision to the effect that the grantee, the Bureau, the Comptroller General of the United States, or any of their duly authorized representatives, shall have access to any books, documents, papers, and records of the contractor which are directly pertinent to a specific grant program for the purpose of making audit, examination, excerpts, and transcriptions.

(10) Contracts and subgrants of amounts over $100,000 shall contain a provision which requires the recipient to agree to comply with all applicable standards, orders, or regulations issued pursuant to the Clean Air Act of 1970 (42 U.S.C. 1251 *et seq.*) as amended. Violations shall be reported to the Bureau and the Regional Office of the Environmental Protection Agency.

§276.13 Indian preference in grant administration.

Any grant or subgrant shall require that to the greatest extent feasible:

(a) Preferences and opportunities for training and employment in connection with the administration of such a grant or subgrant shall be given to Indians.

(b) Preference in the award of a subgrant, contract or subcontract in connection with administration of a grant shall be given to Indian organizations and economic enterprises.

(c) A tribal governing body may develop its own Indian preference requirements to the extent that such requirements are not inconsistent with the purpose and intent of paragraphs (a) and (b) of this section for grants executed under this part.

§ 276.14 Budget revision.

Criteria and procedures to be followed by grantees in reporting deviations from grant budgets and requesting approval for budget revisions are as follows:

(a) For nonconstruction grants, grantees shall request prior approvals promptly from the Bureau for budget revisions whenever:

(1) The revision results from changes in the scope or the objective of the grant-supported program.

(2) The revision indicates the need for additional Bureau funding.

(3) The grant budget is over $100,000 and the cumulative amount of transfers among direct cost object class budget categories exceeds or is expected to exceed $10,000, or five percent of the grant budget, whichever is greater. The same criteria apply to cumulative amount of transfers among programs, functions, and activities when budgeted separately for a grant, except that the Bureau shall permit no transfer which would cause any Federal appropriation, or part thereof, to be used for purposes other than those intended.

(4) The grant budget is $100,000, or less, and the cumulative amount of transfers among direct cost object class budget categories exceeds or is expected to exceed five percent of the grant budget. The same criteria apply to the cumulative amount of transfers among programs, functions, and activities when budgeted separately for a grant, except that the Bureau shall permit no transfer which would cause any Federal appropriation, or part thereof, to be used for purposes other than those intended.

(5) The revisions involve the transfer of amounts budgeted for indirect costs to absorb increases in direct costs.

(6) The revisions pertain to the addition of items requiring approval in accordance with the provisions of appendix A of this part.

(b) All other changes to nonconstruction grant budgets, except for the changes described in paragraph (d) of this section do not require approval. These changes include:

(1) The use of grantee funds in furtherance of program objectives over and above the grantee minimum share included in the approved grant budget and

(2) The transfer of amounts budgeted for direct costs to absorb authorized increases in indirect costs.

(c) For construction grants, grantees shall request prior approval promptly from the Bureau for budget revisions whenever:

(1) The revision results from changes in the scope or the objective of the grant-supported programs.

(2) The revision increases the budgeted amounts of Bureau funds needed to complete the project.

(d) When the Bureau awards a grant which provides support for both construction and nonconstruction work, the Bureau may require, in the grant agreement, the grantee to request prior approval before making any fund or budget transfers between the two types of work supported.

(e) For both construction and nonconstruction grants, the Bureau shall require tribal grantees to notify the Bureau promptly whenever the amount of Bureau authorized funds is expected to exceed the needs of the grantee by more than $5,000 or 5 percent of the Bureau grant, whichever is greater. This notification will not be required when applications for additional funding are submitted for continuing grants.

(f) When requesting approval for budget revisions, grantees shall use the budget forms which were used in the grant application. However, grantees may request by letter the approvals required by the provisions of appendix A of this part.

(g) Within 30 days from the date of receipt of the request for budget revisions, the Bureau shall review the request and notify the grantee whether or not the budget revisions have been approved. If the Bureau does not reach a decision prior to the end of the 30–day period or should the grantee not be notified of the Bureau's decision by the end of the 30-day period the grantee may appeal directly to the Commissioner.

§ 276.15 Grant closeout.

(a) In closing out Bureau grants, the following shall be observed:

(1) Upon request, the Bureau shall make prompt payments to a grantee

for allowable reimbursable costs under the grant being closed out.

(2) The grantee shall immediately refund to the Bureau any unencumbered balance of cash advanced to the grantee.

(3) The Bureau shall obtain from the grantee within 90 days after the date of completion of the grant all financial, peformance, and other reports required as a condition of the grant. The Bureau may grant extensions when requested by the grantee.

(4) The Bureau shall make a settlement for any upward or downward adjustments to the Federal share of costs after these reports are received.

(5) The grantee shall account for any property acquired with grant funds, or received from the Government in accordance with the provisions of § 276.11.

(6) If a final audit has not been performed before the closeout of the grant, the Bureau shall retain the right to recover an appropriate amount after fully considering the recommendations on disallowed costs resulting from the final audit.

(b) *Suspension*. When a grantee has materially failed to comply with the terms and conditions of a grant, the Bureau may after reasonable notice to the grantee, suspend the grant. The notice preceding suspension shall include the effective date of the suspension, the reasons for the suspension, the corrective measures necessary for reinstatement of the grant, and, if there is no immediate threat to safety, a reasonable time frame for corrective action prior to actual suspension. No obligations incurred by the grantee during the period of suspension shall be allowable under the suspended grant, except that the Bureau may at its discretion allow necessary and proper costs which the grantee could not reasonably avoid during the period of suspensions if such costs would otherwise be allowable under the applicable cost principles specified in appendix A of this part. Appropriate adjustments to the payments under the suspended grant will be made, either by withholding the payments or by not allowing the grantee credit for disbursements which he may make in liquidation of unauthorized obligations he incurs during the period of suspension. Suspensions shall remain in effect until the grantee has taken corrective action to the satisfaction of the Bureau or given assurances satisfactory to the Bureau that corrective action will be taken, or until the Bureau cancels the grant.

(c)(1) *Cancellation for cause*. The Bureau may cancel any grant in whole, or in part, at any time before the date of completion, whenever it is determined that the grantee has:

(i) Materially failed to comply with the terms and conditions of the grant;

(ii) Violated the rights or endangered the health, safety, or welfare of any persons;

(iii) Been grossly negligent in or has mismanaged the handling or use of funds provided under the grant.

(2) When it appears that cancellation of a grant shall become necessary, the Bureau shall promptly notify the grantee in writing of this possibility. This written notice shall advise the grantee of the reason for the possible cancellation and the corrective action necessary to avoid cancellation. The Bureau shall also offer, and provide if requested by the grantee, any technical assistance which may be required to effect the corrective action. The grantee shall have 60 days in which to effect this corrective action before the Bureau provides notice of intent to cancel the grant as provided in paragraph (c)(3) of this section.

(3) Upon deciding to cancel for cause, the Bureau shall promptly notify the grantee in writing of that decision, the reasons for the cancellation, and the effective date. The Bureau shall also provide a hearing for the grantee before cancellation, as provided in § 272.51. However, the Bureau may immediately cancel the grant, upon notice to the grantee, if the Bureau determines that continuance of the grant poses an immediate threat to safety. In this event, the Bureau shall provide a hearing for the grantee within ten (10) days of cancellation.

(4) Payments made to grantees or recoveries by the Bureau under grants cancelled for cause shall be in accordance with the legal rights and obligations of the parties.

(d)(1) *Cancellation on other grounds*. Except as provided in paragraph (c) of this section, grants may be cancelled in whole or in part only as follows:

(i) By the Bureau with the consent of the grantee, in which case the two parties shall agree upon the cancellation conditions, including the effective date, and in the case of partial cancellation, the portion to be cancelled; or

(ii) By the grantee, upon written notice to the Bureau, setting forth the reasons for the cancellation, the effective date, and, in the case of partial cancellation, the portion to be cancelled.

(2) When a grant is cancelled in accordance with paragraph (d) of this section, the grantee shall not incur new obligations for the cancelled portion after the effective date, and shall cancel as many outstanding obligations as possible. The Bureau shall allow full credit to the grantee for the Bureau share of the noncancellable obligations properly incurred by the grantee before cancellation.

[40 FR 51316, Nov. 4, 1975, as amended at 45 FR 13452, Feb. 29, 1980]

§ 276.16 Subgrants and subcontracts to non-profit organizations.

The uniform administrative requirements in this part, including the cost principles in appendix A, to this part, are applicable to all subgrants or subcontracts made by a grantee in accordance with the provisions of this chapter. However, these requirements and cost principles are applicable as minimum standards for subgrants or subcontracts made to nonprofit organizations. Accordingly, the grantee may prescribe additional or more stringent requirements with regard to subgrants or subcontracts made to non-profit organizations.

§ 276.17 Printing.

As permitted by paragraph 36–2(c) in the Government Printing and Binding Regulations (October 1974, No. 23), published by the Joint Committee on Printing (JCP), printing required by a grantee in performing work under a grant is considered "incidental printing" (e.g., material which the grantee needs to use to respond to the terms of the grant). Whenever the incidental printing is likely to exceed the exclusions in paragraphs 36–3 and 36–4 of the Joint Committee on Printing (JCP) Printing and Binding Regulations, specific provisions on printing as may be required shall be included in the grant agreement. Grantees shall be given the option of using sources other than the Government Printing Office for incidental printing.

[43 FR 37446, Aug. 23, 1978]

Appendix A to Part 276—Principles for Determining Costs Applicable to Grants

PART I—GENERAL

A. *Purpose and scope.* 1. *Objectives.* This attachment sets forth principles for determining the allowable costs of programs administered by grantees under grants from the Bureau. The principles are for the purpose of cost determination and are not intended to identify the circumstances or dictate the extent of Bureau and tribal participation in the financing of a particular grant. They are designed to provide that Bureau assisted programs bear their fair share of costs recognized under these principles, except where restricted or prohibited by law. No provision for profit or other increment above cost is intended.

2. *Policy guides.* The application of these principles is based on the fundamental premises that:

a. Grantees are responsible for the efficient and effective administration of grant programs through the application of sound management practices.

b. The grantee assumes the responsibility for seeing that Bureau assisted program funds have been expended and accounted for consistent with underlying agreements and program objectives.

c. Each grantee organization, in recognition of its own unique combination of staff facilities and experience, will have the primary responsibility for employing whatever form of organization and management techniques may be necessary to assure proper and efficient administration.

3. *Application.* These principles will be applied by the Bureau in determining costs incurred by grantees under Bureau grants (including subgrants, contracts by grantees and subcontracts).

B. *Definitions.* 1. *Approval or authorization of the Bureau* means documentation evidencing consent prior to incurring specific cost.

2. *Cost allocation plan* means the documentation identifying, accumulating, and distrtibuting allowable costs under grants and contracts together with the allocation methods used.

3. *Cost,* as used herein, means cost as determined on a cash, accrual, or other basis acceptable to the Bureau as a discharge of the grantee's accountability for Bureau funds.

4. *Cost objective* means a pool, center, or area established for the accumulation of cost. Such areas include organizational units, functions, objects or items of expense as well as ultimate cost objectives including specific grants, projects, contracts, and other activities.

5. *Federal agency* means any department, agency, commission, or instrumentality in the executive branch of the Federal Government which makes grants to grantees.

6. *Grant* means an agreement between the Bureau and a grantee whereby the Bureau provides funds or aid in kind to carry out specified programs, services, or activities. The principles and policies stated in this appendix as applicable to grants in general also apply to any Federally sponsored cost reimbursement type of agreement performed by a grantee, including contracts, subcontracts and subgrants.

7. *Grant program* means those activities and operations of the grantee which are necessary to carry out the purposes of the grant, including any portion of the program financed by the grantee.

8. *Grantee* means the entity which is responsible for administration of the grant.

9. *Services,* as used herein, means goods and facilities, as well as services.

10. *Supporting services* means auxiliary functions necessary to sustain the direct effort involved in administering a grant program or an activity providing service to the grant program. These services may be centralized in the grantee department or in some other agency, and include procurement, payroll, personnel functions, maintenance and operation of space, data processing, accounting, budgeting, auditing, mail and messenger service, and the like.

C. *Basic guidelines.* 1. *Factors affecting allowability of costs.* To be allowable under a grant program, costs must meet the following general criteria:

a. Be necessary and reasonable for proper and efficient administration of the grant program, be allocable thereto under these principles, and, except as specifically provided herein, not be a general expense required to carry out the overall responsibilities of a grantee.

b. Be authorized or not prohibited under applicable laws or regulations.

c. Conform to any limitations or exclusions set forth in these principles, Federal laws, or other governing limitations as to types or amounts of cost items.

d. Be consistent with policies, regulations, and procedures that apply uniformly to both Federally assisted and other activities of which the grantee is a part.

e. Be accorded consistent treatment through application of generally accepted accounting principles appropriate to the circumstances.

f. Not be allocable to or included as a cost of any other Federally financed program in either the current or a prior period.

g. Be net of all applicable credits.

2. *Allocable costs.* a. A cost is allocable to a particular cost objective to the extent of benefits received by such objective.

b. Any cost allocable to a particular grant or cost objective under the principles provided for in this appendix may not be shifted to other Federal grant programs to overcome funds deficiencies, avoid restrictions imposed by law or grant agreements, or for other reasons.

c. Where an allocation of joint cost will ultimately result in charges to a grant program, an allocation plan will be required as prescribed in section I.

3. *Applicable credits.* a. Applicable credits refer to those receipts or reduction of expenditure-type transactions which offset or reduce expense items allocable to grants as direct or indirect costs. Examples of such transactions are: purchase discounts; rebates or allowances; recoveries or indemnities on losses; sale of publications, equipment, and scrap; income from personal or incidental services; and adjustments of overpayments or erroneous charges.

b. Applicable credits may also arise when Bureau funds are received or are available from sources other than the grant program involved to finance operations or capital items of the grantee. This includes costs arising from the use of depreciation of items donated or financed by the Bureau to fulfill matching requirements under another grant program. These types of credits should likewise be used to reduce related expenditures in determining the rates or amounts applicable to a given grant.

D. *Composition of cost.* 1. *Total cost.* The total cost of a grant program is comprised of allowable direct cost incident to its performance, plus its allocable portion of allowable indirect costs, less applicable credits.

2. *Classification of costs.* There is no universal rule for classifying certain costs as either direct or indirect under every accounting system. A cost may be direct with respect to some specific service or function, but indirect with respect to the grant or other ultimate cost objective. It is essential, therefore, that each item of cost be treated consistently either as a direct or an indirect cost. Specific guides for determining direct and indirect costs allocable under grant programs are provided in the sections which follow.

E. *Direct costs.* 1. *General.* Direct costs are those that can be identified specifically with a particular cost objective. These costs may be charged directly to grants, contracts, or to other programs against which costs are finally lodged. Direct costs may also be charged to cost objectives used for the other ultimate cost objective.

2. *Application.* Typical direct costs chargeable to grant programs are:

a. Compensation of employees for the time and effort devoted specifically to the execution of grant programs.

b. Cost of materials acquired, consumed, or expended specifically for the purpose of the grant.

c. Equipment and other approved capital expenditures.

d. Other items of expense incurred specifically to carry out the grant agreement.

e. Services furnished specifically for the grant program by other agencies, provided such charges are consistent with criteria outlined in section G of these principles.

F. *Indirect costs.* 1. *General.* Indirect costs are those (a) incurred for a common or joint purpose benefiting more than one cost objective, and (b) not readily assignable to the cost objectives specifically benefited, without effort disproportionate to the results achieved. The term "indirect costs," as used herein, applies to costs of this type originating in the grantee department, as well as those incurred by other departments in supplying goods, services, and facilities, to the grantee department. To facilitate equitable distribution of indirect expenses to the cost objectives served, it may be necessary to establish a number of pools of indirect cost within a grantee department or in other agencies providing services to a grantee department. Indirect cost pools should be distributed to benefiting cost objectives on bases which will produce an equitable result in consideration or relative benefits derived.

2. *Grantee departmental indirect costs.* All grantee departmental indirect costs, including the various levels of supervision, are eligible for allocation to grant programs provided they meet the conditions set forth in this part. In lieu of determining the actual amount of grantee departmental indirect cost allocable to a grant program, the following methods may be used:

a. *Predetermined fixed rates for indirect costs.* A predetermined fixed rate for computing indirect costs applicable to a grant may be negotiated annually in situations where the cost experience and other pertinent facts available are deemed sufficient to enable the contracting parties to reach an informed judgment (1) as to the probable level of indirect costs in the grantee department during the period to be covered by the negotiated rate, and (2) that the amount allowable under the predetermined rate would not exceed actual indirect cost.

b. *Negotiated lump sum for overhead.* A negotiated fixed amount in lieu of indirect costs may be appropriate under circumstances where the benefits derived from a grantee department's indirect services cannot be readily determined as in the case of small, self-contained or isolated activity. When this method is used, a determination should be made that the amount negotiated will be approximately the same as the actual indirect cost that may be incurred. Such amounts negotiated in lieu of indirect costs will be treated as an offset to total indirect expenses of the grantee department before allocation to remaining activities. The base on which such remaining expenses are allocated should be appropriately adjusted.

3. *Limitation on indirect costs.* a. Bureau grants may be subject to laws that limit the amount of indirect costs that may be allowed. In this event, the Bureau will establish procedures which will assure that the amount actually allowed for indirect costs under each such grant does not exceed the maximum allowable under the statutory limitation or the amount otherwise allowable under this appendix, whichever is the smaller.

b. When the amount allowable under a statutory limitation is less than the amount otherwise allocable as indirect costs under this appendix the amount not recoverable as indirect costs under a grant may not be shifted to another Federally sponsored grant program or contract.

G. *Cost incurred by organizations other than the grantee.* 1. *General.* The cost of service provided by other organizations may only include allowable direct costs of the service plus a prorata share of allowable supporting costs and supervision directly required in performing the service, but not supervision of a general nature such as that provided by the head of an organization and his staff assistants not directly involved in operations. However, supervision by the head of an organization whose sole function is providing the service furnished would be an eligible cost. Supporting costs include those furnished by other units of the supplying organizations.

2. *Alternative methods of determining indirect cost.* In lieu of determining actual indirect cost related to a particular service furnished by another organization, either of the following alternative methods may be used provided only one method is used for a specific service during the fiscal year involved.

a. *Standard indirect rate.* An amount equal to ten percent of direct labor cost in providing the service performed by another organization (excluding overtime, shift, or holiday premiums and fringe benefits) may be allowed in lieu of actual allowable indirect cost for that service.

b. *Predetermined fixed rate.* A predetermined fixed rate for indirect cost of the unit or activity providing service may be negotiated as set forth in section F.2.a.

H. *Cost incurred by grantee for others.* 1. *General.* The principles provided in section G will also be used in determining the cost of services provided by the grantee to another agency.

I. *Cost allocation plan.* 1. *General.* A plan for allocation of costs will be required to support the distribution of any joint costs related to the grant program. All costs included in the plan will be supported by formal accounting records which will substantiate the propriety of eventual charges.

2. *Requirements.* The allocation plan of the grantee should cover all joint costs of the grantees as well as costs to be allocated under plans of other agencies or organizational units which are to be included in the costs of federally sponsored programs. The cost allocation plans of all the agencies rendering services to the grantee, to the extent feasible, should be presented in a single document. The allocation plan should contain, but not neessarily be limited to, the following:

a. The nature and extent of services provided and their relevance to the federally sponsored programs.

b. The items of expense to be included.

c. The methods to be used in distributing cost.

3. *Instructions for preparation of cost allocation plans.* The Bureau, in consultation with the other Federal agencies concerned, will be responsible for developing and issuing the instructions for use by grantees in preparation of cost allocation plans.

4. *Submission of indirect cost proposal and negotiation of indirect cost rates.*

a. A grantee should submit its indirect cost proposal to the Federal agency which provides the largest dollar volume of contracts and grants. However, once a Federal agency has handled an indirect cost proposal, that same Federal agency should continue to act upon the proposal even though the preponderance of financial interest may have shifted to another Federal agency, and grantee shall not resubmit its indirect cost proposal to a second Federal agency.

b. Where the grantee submits its proposal to the Department of Interior, the proposal should be sent by the Bureau of Indian Affairs to the cognizant Regional Office of the Department's Office of Audit and Investigation. The Office of Audit and Investigation is responsible for the audit and review of the proposals and negotiation of the indirect cost rates.

c. Grant administrators officers will usually, but are not required to, accept indirect cost rates negotiated by other Federal agencies.

d. The Bureau of Indian Affairs will provide technical assistance in developing indirect cost proposals, if needed.

PART II—STANDARDS FOR SELECTED ITEMS OF COST

A. *Purpose and applicability.* 1. *Objective.* This attachment provides standards for determining the allowability of selected items of cost.

2. *Application.* These standards will apply irrespective of whether a particular item of cost is treated as direct or indirect cost. Failure to mention a particular item of cost in the standards is not intended to imply that it is either allowable or unallowable, rather determination of allowability in each case should be based on the treatment of standards provided for similar or related items of cost. The allowability of the selected items of cost is subject to the general policies and principles stated in part I of this appendix.

B. *Allowable costs.* 1. *Accounting.* The cost of establishing and maintaining accounting and other information systems required for the management of grant programs is allowable. This includes cost incurred by central service agencies for these purposes. The cost of maintaining central accounting records required for overall tribal government purposes, such as appropriation and fund accounts by the Treasurer, Comptroller, or similar officials, is considered to be a general expense of government and is not allowable.

2. *Advertising.* Advertising media includes newspapers, magazines, radio and television programs, direct mail, trade papers, and the like. The advertising costs allowable are those which are solely for:

a. Recruitment of personnel required for the grant program.

b. Solicitation of bids for the procurement of goods and services required.

c. Disposal of scrap or surplus materials acquired in the performance of the grant agreement.

d. Other purposes specifically provided for in the grant agreement.

3. *Advisory councils.* Costs incurred by grantee advisory councils or committees established pursuant to Bureau requirements to carry out grant programs are allowable. The cost of like organizations is allowable when provided for in the grant agreement.

4. *Audit service.* The cost of audits necessary for the administration and management of functions related to grant programs is allowable.

5. *Bonding.* Costs of premiums on bonds covering employees who handle grantee funds are allowable.

6. *Budgeting.* Costs incurred for the development, preparation, presentation, and execution of budgets are allowable. Costs for services of a central budget office are generally not allowable since these are costs of general government. However, where employees of the central budget office activity

participate in the grantee budget process, the cost of identifiable services is allowable.

7. *Building lease management.* The administrative cost for lease management which includes review of lease proposals, maintenance of a list of available property for lease, and related activities is allowable.

8. *Central stores.* The cost of maintaining and operating a central store's organization for supplies, equipment, and materials used either directly or indirectly for grant programs is allowable.

9. *Communications.* Communication costs incurred for telephone calls or service, telegraph, teletype service, wide area telephone service (WATS), centrex, telpak (tie lines), postage, messenger service and similar expenses are allowable.

10. *Compensation for personal services.* a. *General.* Compensation for personal services includes all remuneration, paid currently or accrued, for services rendered during the period of performance under the grant agreement, including but not necessarily limited to wages, salaries, and supplementary compensation and benefits. The costs of such compensation are allowable to the extent that total compensation for individual employees: (1) Is responsible for the services rendered, (2) follows an appointment made in accordance with tribal government ordinances and rules and which meets Federal merit system or other requirements, where applicable; and (3) is determined and supported as provided in b., below. Compensation for employees engaged in federally assisted actvities will be considered reasonable to the extent that it is consistent with that paid for similar work in other activities of the tribal government. In cases where the kinds of employees required for the federally assisted activities are not found in the other activities of the tribal government, compensation will be considered reasonable to the extent that it is comparable to that paid for similar work in the labor market in which the employing government competes for the kind of employees involved. Compensation surveys providing data representative of the labor market involved will be an acceptable basis for evaluating reasonableness.

b. *Payroll and distribution of time.* Amounts charged to grant programs for personal services, regardless of whether treated as direct or indirect costs, will be based on payrolls documented and approved in accordance with generally accepted practice of the tribal government. Payrolls must be supported by time and attendance or equivalent records for individual employees. Salaries and wages of employees chargeable to more than one grant program or other cost objective will be supported by appropriate time distribution records. The method used should produce an equitable distribution of time and effort.

11. *Depreciation and use allowance.* a. Grantees may be compensated for the use of their own buildings, capital improvements, and equipment through use allowances or depreciation. Use allowances are the means of providing compensation in lieu of depreciation or other equivalent costs. However, a combination of the two methods may not be used in connection with a single class of fixed assets.

b. The computation of depreciation or use allowance will be based on acquisition cost. Where actual cost records have not been maintained, a reasonable estimate of the original acquisition cost may be used in the computation. The computation will exclude the cost or any portion of the cost of buildings and equipment donated or borne directly or indirectly by the Federal Government through charges to Federal grant programs or otherwise, irrespective of whether title was originally vested or where it presently resides. In addition, the computation will also exclude the cost of land. Depreciation or a use allowance on idle or excess facilities is not allowable, except when specifically authorized by the grantor Federal agency.

c. Where the depreciation method is followed, adequate property records must be maintained, and any generally accepted method of computing depreciation must be consistently applied for any specific asset or class of assets for all affected Federally sponsored programs and must result in equitable charges considering the extent of the use of the assets for benefit of such programs.

d. In lieu of depreciation, a use allowance for buildings and improvements may be computed at an annual rate not exceeding two percent of acquisition cost. The use allowance for equipment (excluding items properly capitalized as building cost) will be computed at an annual rate not exceeding six and two-thirds percent of acquisition cost of usable equipment.

e. No depreciation or use charge may be allowed on any assets that would be considered as fully depreciated, provided, however, that reasonable use charges may be negotitated for any such assets if warranted after taking into consideration the cost of the facility or item involved, the estimated useful life remaining at time of negotiation, the effect of any increased maintenance charges or decreased efficiency due to age, and any other factors pertinent to utilization of the facility or item for the purpose contemplated.

12. *Disbursing service.* The cost of disbursing grant program funds by the Treasurer or other designated officer is allowable. Disbursing services cover the processing of checks or warrants, from preparation to redemption, including the necessary records of accountability and reconciliation of such records with related cash accounts.

13. *Employee fringe benefits.* Costs identified under a. and b. below are allowable to the extent that total compensation for employees is reasonable as defined in section B.10.

a. Employee benefits in the form of regular compensation paid to employees during periods of authorized absences from the job, such as for annual leave, sick leave, court leave, military leave, and the like, if they are: (1) Provided pursuant to an approved leave system, and (2) the cost thereof is equitably allocated to all related activities, including grant programs.

b. Employee benefits in the form of employers' contribution or expenses for social security, employees' life and health insurance plans, unemployment insurance coverage, workmen's compensation insurance, pension plans, severance pay, and the like, provided such benefits are granted under approved plans and are distributed equitably to grant programs and in other activities.

14. *Employee morale, health and welfare costs.* The costs of health or first-aid clinics and/or infirmaries, recreational facilities, employees' counseling services, employee information publications, and any related expenses incurred, are allowable. Income generated from any of these activities will be offset against expenses.

15. *Exhibits.* Costs of exhibits relating specifically to the grant programs are allowable.

16. *Legal expenses.* The cost of legal expenses required in the administration of grant programs is allowable. Legal services furnished by the chief legal officer of a tribal government or his staff solely for the purpose of discharging his general responsibilities as legal officer are unallowable. Legal expenses for the prosecution of claims against the Federal Government are unallowable.

17. *Maintenance and repair.* Costs incurred for necessary maintenance, repair, or upkeep of property which neither add to the permanent value of the property nor appreciably prolong its intended life, but keep it in an efficient operating condition, are allowable.

18. *Materials and supplies.* The cost of materials and supplies necessary to carry out the grant programs is allowable. Purchases made specifically for the grant program should be charged thereto at their actual prices after deducting all cash discounts, trade discounts, rebates, and allowances received by the grantee. Withdrawals from general stores or stockrooms should be charged at cost under any recognized method of pricing consistently applied. Incoming transportation charges are a proper part of material cost.

19. *Memberships, subscriptions and professional activities.* a. *Memberships.* The cost of membership in civic, business, technical and professional organizations is allowable provided: (1) The benefit from the membership is related to the grant program, (2) the expenditure is for agency membership, (3) the cost of the membership is reasonably related to the value of the services or benefits received, and (4) the expenditure is not for membership in an organization which devotes a substantial part of its activities to influencing legislation.

b. *Reference material.* The cost of books, and subscriptions to civic, business, professional, and technical periodicals is allowable when related to the grant program.

c. *Meetings and conferences.* Costs are allowable when the purpose of the meeting is the dissemination of technical information relating to the grant program and they are consistent with regular practices followed for other activities of the grantee.

20. *Motor pools.* The costs of a service organization which provides automobiles to grantees at a mileage or fixed rate and/or provides vehicle maintenance, inspection and repair services are allowable.

21. *Payroll preparation.* The cost of preparing payrolls and maintaining necessary related wage records is allowable.

22. *Personnel administration.* Costs for the recruitment, examination, certification, classification, training, establishment of pay standards, and related activities for grant programs, are allowable.

23. *Printing and reproduction.* Cost for printing and reproduction services necessary for grant administration, including but not limited to forms, reports, manuals, and informational literature, are allowable. Publication costs of reports or other media relating to grant program accomplishments or results are allowable when provided for in the grant agreement.

24. *Procurement service.* The cost of procurement service, including solicitation of bids, preparation and award of contracts, and all phases of contract administration in providing goods, facilities and services for grant programs, is allowable.

25. *Taxes.* In general, taxes or payments in lieu of taxes which the grantee is legally required to pay are allowable.

26. *Training and education.* The cost of in-service training, customarily provided for employee development which directly or indirectly benefits grant programs is allowable. Out-of-service training involving extended periods of time is allowable only when specifically authorized by the Bureau.

27. *Transportation.* Costs incurred for freight, cartage, express, postage and other transportation costs relating either to goods purchased, delivered, or moved from one location to another are allowable.

28. *Travel.* Travel costs are allowable for expenses for transportation, lodging, subsistence, and related items incurred by employees who are in travel status on official business incident to a grant program. Such costs may be charged on an actual basis, on a per diem or mileage basis in lieu of actual costs

incurred, or on a combination of the two, provided the method used is applied to an entire trip, and results in charges consistent with those normally allowed in like circumstances in non-Federally sponsored activities. The difference in cost between first-class air accommodations and less-than-first-class air accommodations is unallowable except when less-than-first-class air accommodations are not reasonably available.

C. *Costs allowable with approval of the Bureau.* 1. *Automatic data processing.* The cost of data processing services to grant programs is allowable. This cost may include rental of equipment or depreciation on grantee-owned equipment. The acquisition of equipment, whether by outright purchase, rental-purchase agreement or other method of purchase, is allowable only upon specific prior approval of the Bureau as provided under the selected item for capital expenditures. The Bureau must obtain required Departmental clearances before such approval can be given.

2. *Building space and related facilities.* The cost of space in privately or publicly owned buildings used for the benefit of the grant program is allowable subject to the conditions stated below. The total cost of space, whether in a privately or publicly owned building, may not exceed the rental cost of comparable space and facilities in a privately owned building in the same locality. The cost of space procured for grant program usage may not be charged to the program for periods of nonoccupancy, without authorization of the Bureau.

a. *Rental cost.* The rental cost of space in a privately owned building is allowable.

b. *Maintenance and operation.* The cost of utilities, insurance, security, janitorial services, elevator service, upkeep of grounds, normal repairs and alterations and the like, are allowable to the extent they are not otherwise included in rental or other charges for space.

c. *Rearrangements and alterations.* Cost incurred for rearrangement and alteration of facilities required specifically for the grant program or those that materially increase the value or useful life of the facilities (section C.3.) are allowable when specifically approved by the Bureau.

d. *Depreciation and use allowances on publicly owned buildings.* These costs are allowable as provided in section B.11.

e. *Occupancy of space under rental-purchase or a lease with option-to-purchase agreement.* The cost of space procured under such arrangements is allowable when specifically approved by the Bureau.

3. *Capital expenditures.* The cost of facilities, equipment, other capital assets, and repairs which materially increase the value or useful life of capital assets is allowable when such procurement is specifically approved by the Bureau. When assets acquired with Bureau grant funds are (a) sold, (b) no longer available for use in a Federally sponsored program or (c) used for purposes not authorized by the Bureau, the Bureau's equity in the asset will be refunded in the same proportion as Bureau participation in its cost. In case any assets are traded on new items, only the net cost of the newly acquired assets is allowable.

4. *Insurance and indemnification.* a. Costs of insurance required, or approved and maintained pursuant to the grant agreement, is allowable.

b. Costs of other insurance in connection with the general conduct of activities is allowable subject to the following limitations:

(1) Types and extent and cost of coverage will be in accordance with sound business practice.

(2) Costs of insurance or of contributions to any reserve covering the risk of loss of, or damage to, Federal Government property is unallowable except to the extent that the Bureau has specifically required or approved such costs.

c. Contributions to a reserve for a self-insurance program approved by the Bureau are allowable to the extent that the type of coverage, extent of coverage, and the rates and premiums would have been allowed had insurance been purchased to cover the risks.

d. Actual losses which could have been covered by permissible insurance (through an approved self-insurance program or otherwise) are unallowable unless expressly provided for in the grant agreement. However, costs incurred because of losses not covered under nominal deductible insurance coverage provided in keeping with sound management practice, and minor losses not covered by insurance, such as spoilage, breakage and disappearance of small hand tools which occur in the ordinary course of operations, are available.

e. *Indemnification* includes securing the grantee against liabilities to third persons and other losses not compensated by insurance or otherwise. The Bureau is obligated to indemnify the grantee only to the extent expressly provided for in the grant agreement, except as provided in d. above.

5. *Management studies.* The cost of management studies to improve the effectiveness and efficiency of grant management for ongoing programs is allowable except that the cost of studies performed by agencies other than the grantee or outside consultants is allowable only when authorized by the Bureau.

6. *Preagreement costs.* Costs incurred prior to the effective date of the grant, whether or not they would have been allowable thereunder if incurred after such date, are allowable when specifically provided for in the grant agreement.

7. *Professional services.* Cost of professional services rendered by individuals or organizations not a part of the grantee is allowable

subject to such prior authorization as may be required by the Bureau.

8. *Proposal costs.* Costs of preparing proposals on potential Federal Government grant agreements are allowable when specifically provided for in the grant agreement.

9. *Tribal government officer salaries and expenses.* Identifiable salary and expense costs incurred as a direct result of a tribal government officer's service to a grant program provided under this chapter are allowable subject to advance agreement with an approval by the Bureau. A general limitation in this regard is prescribed in section D.6.

D. *Unallowable costs.* 1. *Bad debts.* Any losses arising from uncollectible accounts and other claims, and related costs, are unallowable.

2. *Contingencies.* Contributions to a contingency reserve or any similar provision for unforeseen events are unallowable.

3. *Contributions and donations.* Unallowable.

4. *Entertainments.* Costs of amusements, social activities, and incidental costs relating thereto, such as meals, beverages, lodgings, rentals, transportation, and gratuities, are unallowable.

5. *Fines and penalties.* Costs resulting from violations of, or failure to comply with Federal, State and local laws and regulations are unallowable.

6. *Tribal officer salaries and expenses.* The salaries and expenses of tribal government officers are considered a cost of general tribal government and are unallowable except as prescribed in section C.9.

7. *Interest and other financial costs.* Interest on borrowing (however requested), bond discounts, cost of financing and refinancing operations, and legal and professional fees paid in connection therewith, are unallowable except when authorized by Federal legislation.

8. *Underrecovery of costs under grant agreements.* Any excess of cost over the Federal contribution under one grant agreement is unallowable under other grant agreements.

APPENDIX B TO PART 276—FINANCIAL REPORTING REQUIREMENTS

A. *Purpose and scope.* This appendix prescribes requirements for grantee to report financial information to the Bureau and to request advances and reimbursement when a letter-of-credit method is not used.

B. *Definitions.* 1. *Accrued expenditures.* Accrued expenditures are the charges incurred by the grantee during a given period requiring the provision of funds for: (1) Goods and other tangible property received; (2) services performed by employes, contractors, subgrantees, and other payees; and (3) amounts becoming owed under programs for which no current services or performed are required.

2. *Accrued income.* Accrued income is the earnings during a given period which is a source of funds resulting from: (1) Services performed by the grantee; (2) goods and other tangible property delivered to purchasers; and (3) amounts becoming owed to the grantee for which no current services or performance are required by the grantee.

3. *Disbursements.* Disbursements are payments in cash or by check.

4. *Bureau funds authorized.* Funds authorized represent the total amount of the Bureau funds authorized for obligations and establish the ceilings for obligation of Bureau funds. This amount may include any authorized carryover of unobligated funds from prior fiscal years.

5. *Obligations.* Obligations are the amounts of orders placed, contracts and grants awarded, services received, and similar transactions during a given period, which will require payment during the same or a future period.

6. *Outlays.* Outlays represent charges made to the grant project or program. Outlays can be reported on a cash or accrued expenditure basis.

7. *Program income.* Program income represents earnings by the grantee realized from the grant-supported activities. Such earnings exclude interest income and may include, but will not be limited to, income from service fees, sale of commodities, usage or rental fees, sale of assets purchased with grant funds, and royalties on patents and copy-rights. Program income can be reported on a cash or accrued income basis.

8. *Unobligated balance.* The unobligated balance is the portion of the funds authorized by the Bureau which has not been obligated by the grantee and is determined by deducting the cumulative obligations from the funds authorized.

9. *Unpaid obligations.* Unpaid obligations represent the amout of obligations incurred by the grantee which have not been paid.

C. *Standard forms.* 1. Only the following forms will be authorized for obtaining financial information from grantees for grant programs:

a. *Financial Status Report.* (1) The Bureau shall require grantees to use a standard Financial Status Report to report the status of funds for all nonconstruction grant programs. The Bureau may, however, have the option of not requiring a Federal Status Report when a request for advance or reimbursement (paragraph 2a) is determined to provide adequate information to meet their needs, except that a final Financial Status Report shall be required at the completion of the grant when the Request for Advance or Reimbursement form is used only for advances.

(2) The Bureau shall prescribe whether the report shall be on a cash or accrual basis. If the Bureau requires accrual information and the grantee's accouting records are not normally kept on the accrual basis, the grantee should develop such information through an

analysis of the documentation on hand or on the basis of best estimates.

(3) The grant agreement shall determine the frequency of the Financial Status Report for each grant program considering the size and complexity of the particular program. However, the report shall not be required more frequently than quarterly or less frequently than annually. Also, a final report shall be required at the completion of the grant.

(4) The original and two copies of the Financial Status Report shall be submitted 30 days after the end of each specified reporting period. In addition, final reports shall be submitted 90 days after the end of the grant period or the completion of the project or program. Extensions to reporting due dates may be approved when requested by the grantee.

b. *Report of federal cash transactions.* (1) When funds are advanced to grantees through letters of credit or with Treasury checks, each grantee shall submit a report of Federal Cash Transactions. The Bureau shall use this report to monitor cash advanced to grantees and to obtain disbursement or outlay information for each grant or project from the grantees.

(2) The grant agreement may require forecasts of Federal cash requirement in the Remarks section of the report.

(3) When practical and deemed necessary, the Bureau may require grantees to report in the Remarks section the amount of cash in excess of three days' requirements in the hands of subgrantees or other secondary recipients and to provide short narrative explanations of actions taken by the grantees to reduce the excess balances.

(4) The Bureau shall accept the identical information from the grantees in a machine-usable format in lieu of the Report of Federal Cash Transactions.

(5) Grantees shall submit the original and two copies of the Report of Federal Cash Transactions no later than 15 working days following the end of each quarter. For those grantees receiving annual grants totalling one million dollars or more, the Bureau shall require a monthly report.

(6) The Bureau shall waive the requirement for submission of a Report of Federal Cash Transactions when monthly advances do not exceed $10,000 per grantee provided that such advances are monitored through other forms contained in this appendix or the grantee's accounting controls are adequate to minimize excessive Federal advances.

2. Except as noted below, only the following forms will be authorized for the grantees in requesting advances and reimbursements.

a. *Request for advance or reimbursement.* (1) The "Request for Advance or Reimbursement" form is the standard form for all non-construction grant programs when letters of credit or predetermined automatic advance methods are not used. The Bureau, however, has the option of using this form for construction programs in lieu of an "Outlay Report and Request for Reimbursement for Construction Programs" (paragraph 2b) and shall specify in the grant agreement.

(2) Grantees shall be authorized to submit requests for advances or reimbursement at least monthly when letters of credit are not used. Grantees shall submit the original and two copies of a Request for Advance or Reimbursement.

b. *Outlay Report and Request for Reimbursement for Construction Program.* (1) The "Outlay Report and Request for Reimbursement for Construction Programs" form is the standard format to be used for requesting reimbursement for construction programs. The Bureau may, however, have the option of substituting a "Request for Advance or Reimbursement" form (paragraph 2a) in lieu of this form when the Bureau determines that the former provides adequate information to meet its needs as stated in the grant agreement.

(2) Grantees shall be authorized to submit requests for reimbursement at least monthly when letters of credit are not used. Grantees shall submit the original and two copies of an "Outlay Report and Request for Reimbursement for Construction Programs" form.

3. When the Bureau needs additional information in using these forms, the following shall be observed:

a. When necessary to comply with future legislative requirements, the Bureau shall issue instructions to require grantees to submit such information under the Remarks section of the reports.

b. When necessary to meet specific program needs, the Bureau shall submit the proposed reporting requirements to the General Services Administration for approval under the exception provision of this appendix.

c. The Bureau, in obtaining information as in paragraphs a and b above, must also comply with report clearance requirements of the Office of Management and Budget Circular No. A–40, as revised.

[40 FR 51316, Nov. 4, 1975, as amended at 41 FR 5099, Feb. 4, 1976; 43 FR 37447, Aug. 23, 1978]

SUBCHAPTER N—ECONOMIC ENTERPRISES

PART 286—INDIAN BUSINESS DEVELOPMENT PROGRAM

AUTHORITY: 25 U.S.C. 1524.

SOURCE: 39 FR 44748, Dec. 27, 1974, unless otherwise noted. Redesignated at 47 FR 13328, Mar. 30, 1982.

§ 286.1 Definitions.

As used in this part 286:

Area Director means the Bureau of Indian Affairs official in charge of an area office or his authorized representative.

Assistant Secretary means the Assistant Secretary—Indian Affairs of the United States Department of the Interior or the official in the Bureau of Indian Affairs to whom the Assistant Secretary has delegated authority to act on behalf of the Assistant Secretary.

Cooperative Association means an association of individuals organized pursuant to state, Federal, or tribal law, for the purpose of owning and operating an economic enterprise for profit with profits distributed or allocated to patrons who are members of the organization.

Corporation means an entity organized pursuant to state, Federal, or tribal law, with or without stock, for the purpose of owning and operating an economic enterprise.

Economic enterprise means any Indian-owned, commercial, industrial, agricultural, or business activity established or organized for the purpose of profit, provided that eligible Indian ownership constitutes not less than 51 per centum of the enterprise.

Grantee(s) means the recipient(s) of a nonreimburseable grant under this part.

Indian means a person who is a member of an Indian tribe or a person of Alaska Native descent who is a shareholder in a corporation organized under the Alaska Native Claims Settlement Act (85 Stat. 688), as amended.

Partnership means a form of business organization in which two or more legal persons are associated as co-owners for the purposes of business or professional activities for private pecuniary gain.

Profits means the net income earned after deducting operating expenses from operating revenues.

Reservation means Indian reservation, California rancheria, public domain Indian allotment, former Indian reservation in Oklahoma, and land held by Alaska Native groups incorporated under the provisions of the Alaska Native Claims Settlement Act (85 Stat. 688), as amended.

Secretary means the Secretary of the Interior.

Superintendent means the Bureau official in charge of a Bureau agency office or other local office reporting to an Area Director.

Tribe means any Indian tribe, band, nation, rancheria, pueblo, colony or community, including any Alaska Native village or any regional, village, urban or group corporation as defined in or established pursuant to the Alaska Native Claims Settlement Act (85 Stat. 688) as amended, which is recognized by the Federal Government as eligible for services from the Bureau of Indian Affairs.

[55 FR 36273, Sept. 5, 1990]

§ 286.2 Purpose.

The purpose of this part 286 is to prescribe the regulations and procedures under which non-reimbursable grants may be made to eligible applicants to stimulate and increase Indian entrepreneurship and employment through establishment, acquisition or expansion of profit-making Indian-owned economic enterprises which will contribute to the economy of a reservation.

§ 286.3 Eligible applicants.

Applications for grants may be accepted only from individual Indians, Indian tribes, Indian partnerships, corporations or cooperative associations authorized to do business under State, Federal, or Tribal law. These applicants must have a form of organization acceptable to the Assistant Secretary and unable to meet their total financing needs from their own resources and by loans from other sources such as banks, Farmers Home Administration, Small Business Administration, Production Credit Associations, and Federal Land Banks. Associations, corporations or partnerships shall be at least fifty-one percent owned by eligible Indians or an eligible Indian tribe. This Indian ownership must actively participate in the management and operation of the economic enterprise by representation on the board of directors of a corporation or cooperative association proportionate to the Indian ownership which will enable the Indian owner(s) to control management decisions. The legal organization documents will provide for the number of Indians which are to be on the board of directors, how they along with other directors will be elected or appointed and qualifications required as a condition for becoming a member of the board of directors. The legal organization documents shall provide safeguards which will prevent Indian ownership and control from decreasing below fifty-one percent. Evidence of Indian ownership in a cooperative association or corporation will be evidenced by stock ownership, if stock is or has been issued, or by other evidence satisfactory to the Assistant Secretary. Partnerships will be evidenced by written partnership agreements which show the percentage of Indian ownership, role and authority in making management decisions in controlling the operation of the economic enterprise.

§ 286.4 Eligible economic enterprises.

An economic enterprise as defined in § 286.1(k) is eligible to receive equity capital through non-reimbursable grants if it is or will be self-sustaining and profit-oriented and will create employment for Indians. In the case of Indian-owned cooperative associations, they must distribute or allocate profits for later distribution, to members who are patrons, unless prohibited from doing so by law.

§ 286.5 Information collection.

(a) The collections of information contained in §§ 286.12 and 286.22 have been approved by the Office of Management and Budget under 44 U.S.C. 3501 *et seq.* and assigned clearance number 1076–0093. The information will be used to rate applicants in accordance with the priority criteria listed at 25 CFR 286.8. Response to this request is required to obtain a benefit in accordance with 25 U.S.C. 1521.

(b) Public reporting for this information is estimated to average 45 minutes per response, including the time for reviewing instructions, searching existing data sources, gathering and maintaining the data needed, and completing and reviewing the collection of information. Send comments regarding this burden estimate or any other aspect of this collection of information, including suggestions for reducing the burden, to the Information Collection Clearance Officer, Bureau of Indian Affairs, Mailstop 337–SIB, 18th and C Streets, NW., Washington, DC 20240; and the Office of Management and Budget, Paperwork Reduction Project (1076–0093), Washington, DC 20503.

[55 FR 36273, Sept. 5, 1990]

§ 286.6 [Reserved]

§ 286.7 Location of enterprise.

To be eligible for a grant an economic enterprise must be located on an Indian reservation or located where it makes or will make an economic contribution to a nearby reservation by providing employment to tribal members residing thereon or by expending a portion of its income for materials or services on the reservation. Economic enterprises which are or will be operated on a reservation must comply with the requirements of applicable rules, resolutions or ordinances adopted by the governing body of the tribe, if applicable.

§ 286.8 Priority criteria.

The following priority will be used in selecting economic enterprises for grant funding:

(a) *First priority.* First priority will be given to economic enterprises located on a reservation that will:

(1) Utilize Indian resources, both natural and human.

(2) Create the highest ratio of Indian jobs to the total amount of dollars to be invested, including market value of materials and equipment contributed to the project.

(3) Create the highest ratio of income to a tribe or its members in relation to the total amount of dollars to be invested, including market value of materials or equipment contributed to the project.

(4) Generate the most non-Bureau financing.

(b) *Second priority.* Second priority will be given to projects located in the immediate vicinity of a reservation that will:

(1) Utilize Indian resources, both natural and human.

(2) Create the highest ratio of Indian jobs to the total amount of dollars to be invested, including market value of materials and equipment contributed to the project.

(3) Generate the most non-Bureau financing.

§ 286.9 Environmental and flood disaster protection.

Grant funds will not be advanced until there is assurance of compliance with any applicable provisions of the Flood Disaster Protection Act of 1973 (Pub. L. 93–234), the National Environmental Policy Act (Pub. L. 91–190), 42 U.S.C. 4321 and Executive Order 11514.

§ 286.10 Preservation of historical and archeological data.

The Assistant Secretary before approving a grant where the grant funds and/or the loan funds will be used to finance activities involving excavations, road construction, and land development or involving the disturbance of land on known or reported historical or archeological sites, will take appropriate action to assure compliance with applicable provisions of the Act of June 27, 1960 (74 Stat. 220 (16 U.S.C. 469)), as amended by the Act of May 24, 1974 (Pub. L. 93–291, 88 Stat. 174), relating to the preservation of historical and archeological data.

§ 286.11 Management and technical assistance.

(a) Prior to and concurrent with the making of a grant to finance an Indian economic enterprise, the Assistant Secretary—Indian Affairs will insure that competent management and technical assistance is available to the grantee in the preparation of the application for a grant and/or administration of the funds granted, consistent with the grantee's knowledge and experience and the nature and complexity of the economic enterprise being financed. The competence of the management and technical assistance provided will be determined by the local agency superintendent after consultation with the applicant concerning his business needs.

(b) The lender providing the loan funds under § 286.17(b) to finance an economic enterprise will include with the grantee's application the need for equity capital, the lender's evaluation of the applicant's need for management and technical assistance, specific areas of need and whether the lender will provide such assistance to the applicant.

[39 FR 44748, Dec. 27, 1974. Redesignated at 47 FR 13328, Mar. 30, 1982, as amended at 55 FR 36274, Sept. 5, 1990]

§ 286.12 Content of application.

Applications shall be on a form prescribed by the Assistant Secretary which shall at the minimum include:

(a) Total capital requirement, including operating capital required until such time as the cash generated from operations will be sufficient to make the enterprise self-sustaining.

(b) Amount of total financing required as well as what is obtainable from other sources, including the applicant's personal resources, and a statement of terms and conditions under which any borrowed portion is obtainable.

(c) Capital deficiency, which will be the basis for the amount of grant requested.

(d) Pro forma balance sheets and operating statements showing estimated expenses, income and net profit from operations for three years following receipt of the requested grant.

(e) Annual operating statements and balance sheets, audited if available, for the prior two years or applicable years for enterprises already in operation.

(f) Current financial statements, consisting of a balance sheet and operating statement.

(g) A plan of operation which shall be acceptable to the lender making the loan and the Assistant Secretary.

§§ 286.13–286.14 [Reserved]

§ 286.15 Application procedures.

Applications are to be submitted to the Superintendent having administrative jurisdiction over the reservation on which an enterprise will be or is located. If the enterprise site is near two or more reservations, application is to be made to the Superintendent having administrative jurisdiction over the reservation nearest to the location of the enterprise which the enterprise will benefit economically.

§ 286.16 Grant approval authority.

Applications for grants require approval by the Assistant Secretary.

§ 286.17 Grant limitations and requirements.

(a) Grants will be made to assist in establishing new economic enterprises, or in purchasing or expanding established ones. However, a grant may be made only when in the opinion of the Assistant Secretary the applicant is unable to obtain adequate financing from other sources. Prior to making any grant, the Assistant Secretary shall assure that, to the extent practical, the applicant's own resources have been invested in the proposed project. The applicant shall not be required to invest own resources to the extent that they are already committed to endeavors deemed by the Assistant Secretary to be essential to the welfare of the applicant. If the information in an application, which must include personal financial statements, indicates that it may be possible for the applicant to obtain financing without a grant, the Assistant Secretary will require the applicant to furnish letters from two customary lenders in the area, if available, who are making loans for similar purpose, showing whether or not they will make a loan to the applicant for the total financing needed without a grant.

(b) A grant may be made only to an applicant who is able to obtain at least 75 percent of the necessary financing from other sources.

(c) No grant in excess of $250,000 may be made to an Indian tribe or in excess of $100,000 to an Indian individual, partnership, corporation, or cooperative association.

(d) Revolving loan funds as prescribed in title I of the Indian Financing Act of 1974 and guaranteed or insured loans as prescribed in title II of said Act may not be used as the sources of the loan portion of the total financing requirement if financing from other governmental or institutional lenders is available on reasonable terms and conditions. If a loan is not available from other sources, guaranteed or insured loans under the provisions of title II of said Act may then be considered. If a guaranteed or insured loan is not available loans under the provisions of title I of said Act may then be considered. Applicants for a loan from either source must meet the eligibility requirements for such loans.

(e) A grant will not be approved unless there is assurance the applicant can and will be provided with needed competent technical and management assistance commensurate with the nature of the enterprise to be funded and the knowledge and management skills of the applicant.

(f) Grant funds may not be used for refinancing or debt consolidation unless approval is justified and required due to the applicant's financial position and is clearly to the advantage of the grant applicant.

(g) Ordinarily, not more than one grant will be made for a project. Nevertheless, in certain circumstances a second grant may be made to applicants for a new project or expansion of the original project. An additional grant will not be approved for an economic enterprise previously funded under the provisions of title IV of the Indian Financing Act of 1974 except for expanding a successful enterprise, provided the total of grants made shall not exceed $250,000 to an Indian tribe and $100,000 to an Indian individual, partnership, corporation, or cooperative association.

(h) An application for a second grant will not be approved if the applicant:

(1) Has not complied with the reporting requirements in connection with the first grant, or

(2) Has not followed the plan of operation, if any, developed for the management and operation of the economic enterprise, or

(3) Did not follow and use the management and technical assistance furnished, or

(4) Is in violation of one or more provisions of the loan agreement entered into between the applicant and the lender who furnished the loan portion of the financing in connection with the first grant.

(i) An applicant for an expansion grant must meet the same eligibility requirements as an original applicant.

(j) A grantee will be required to return all or a portion of the grant if the business or enterprise for which the grant was utilized is sold within three years of the date on which the grant was disbursed to the grantee, unless the proceeds from the sale are re-invested in a new business or business expansion which will benefit the Indian reservation economy. Such sale and re-investment must have the prior approval of the local agency superintendent. The grantee shall refund the lessor of the grant amount or a pro rata portion of sales proceeds. The pro rata portion of sales proceeds shall be based on the ratio of grant amount to its corresponding matching financing. The new business or business expansion utilizing such sale proceeds must meet the same criteria for eligibility as an original grant.

[39 FR 44748, Dec. 27, 1974. Redesignated at 47 FR 13328, Mar. 30, 1982, as amended at 55 FR 36274, Sept. 5, 1990; 56 FR 12436, Mar. 25, 1991]

§ 286.18 Written notice.

The applicant for a grant which is disapproved will be notified by letter, stating the reasons for disapproval and the right of appeal pursuant to 25 CFR 2. A copy of the letter will be sent to the prospective lender.

[39 FR 44748, Dec. 27, 1974. Redesignated at 47 FR 13328, Mar. 30, 1982; 48 FR 13414, Mar. 31, 1983]

§ 286.19 [Reserved]

§ 286.20 Disbursement of grant funds.

Unless otherwise provided by an agreement between a lender and the grantee, the Assistant Secretary may in his discretion advance grant funds directly to a grantee. He may require the funds to be deposited in a special account at the appropriate Agency headquarters office or deposited in a joint account in a bank and disbursed as needed by the grantee. The terms of a lender's loan agreement may require the lender's approval before disbursement of the funds. Grant funds will not be disbursed to a grantee until the Assistant Secretary has been informed by the lender that a loan has been approved for the grantee in the amount of the loan financing needed.

§ 286.21 Return of unused funds.

Grantees will be required to return unused grant funds to the Assistant Secretary if the economic enterprise for which the grant was approved is not initiated, i.e., lease obtained, if needed, construction started, equipment purchased or other, within the time stated in the grant agreement. The Assistant Secretary may, if warranted by circumstances beyond the control of the grantee, extend the time to allow for initiation of the enterprise, provided there is assurance the enterprise will be initiated forthwith within the extended time period. The Assistant Secretary will notify the lender in writing of a proposed action to require the return of grant funds or of a proposal to extend the time.

§ 286.22 Reports.

(a) Grantees are required to furnish the Assistant Secretary comparative balance sheets and profit and loss statements semi-annually for the first two years of operation following receipt of the grant, and annually thereafter for the succeeding three years. These may be copied of financial statements required by and furnished to the lender which provided the loan portion of the total financing required. If the lender does not require financial statements, the grantee must prepare and furnish copies of comparative balance sheets and profit and loss statements to the Assistant Secretary.

(b) The Assistant Secretary will establish accounting and reporting systems which will appropriately show the status of the Indian Business Development Program at all times.

PART 290—TRIBAL REVENUE ALLOCATION PLANS

Sec.

AUTHORITY: 5 U.S.C. 301; 25 U.S.C. 2, 9, and 2710.

SOURCE: 65 FR 14467, Mar. 17, 2000, unless otherwise noted.

§ 290.1 Purpose.

This part contains procedures for submitting, reviewing, and approving tribal revenue allocation plans for distributing net gaming revenues from tribal gaming activities. It applies to review of tribal revenue allocation plans adopted under IGRA.

§ 290.2 Definitions.

Appropriate Bureau official (ABO) means the Bureau official with delegated authority to approve tribal revenue allocation plans.

IGRA means the Indian Gaming Regulatory Act of 1988 (Public Law 100–497) 102 Stat. 2467 dated October 17, 1988, (Codified at 25 U.S.C. 2701–2721(1988)) and any amendments.

Indian Tribe means any Indian tribe, band, nation, or other organized group or community of Indians that the Secretary recognizes as:

(1) Eligible for the speci al programs and services provided by the United States to Indians because of their status as Indians; and

(2) Having powers of self-government.

Legal incompetent means an individual who is eligible to participate in a per capita payment and who has been declared to be under a legal disability, other than being a minor, by a court of competent jurisdiction, including tribal justice systems or as established by the tribe.

Member of an Indian tribe means an individual who meets the requirements established by applicable tribal law for enrollment in the tribe and—

(1) Is listed on the tribal rolls of that tribe if such rolls are kept or

(2) Is recognized as a member by the tribal governing body if tribal rolls are not kept.

Minor means an individual who is eligible to participate in a per capita payment and who has not reached the age of 18 years.

Per capita payment means the distribution of money or other thing of value to all members of the tribe, or to identified groups of members, which is paid directly from the net revenues of any tribal gaming activity. This definition does not apply to payments which have been set aside by the tribe for special purposes or programs, such as payments made for social welfare, medical assistance, education, housing or other similar, specifically identified needs.

Resolution means the formal document in which the tribal governing body expresses its legislative will in accordance with applicable tribal law.

Secretary means the Secretary of the Interior or his/her authorized representative.

Superintendent means the official or other designated representative of the BIA in charge of the field office which has immediate administrative responsibility for the affairs of the tribe for which a tribal revenue allocation plan is prepared.

Tribal governing body means the governing body of an Indian tribe recognized by the Secretary.

Tribal revenue allocation plan or *allocation plan* means the document submitted by an Indian tribe that provides for distributing net gaming revenues.

You or your means the Indian tribe.

§290.3 Information collection.

The information collection requirements contained in §§290.12, 290.17, 290.24 and 290.26 have been approved by the OMB under the Paperwork Reduction Act of 1995, 44 U.S.C. 3507(d), and assigned clearance number 1076–0152.

§290.4 What is a tribal revenue allocation plan?

It is the document you must submit that describes how you will allocate net gaming revenues.

§290.5 Who approves tribal revenue allocation plans?

The ABO will review and approve tribal revenue allocation plans for compliance with IGRA.

§290.6 Who must submit a tribal revenue allocation plan?

Any Indian tribe that intends to make a per capita payment from net gaming revenues must submit one.

§290.7 Must an Indian tribe have a tribal revenue allocation plan if it is not making per capita payments?

No, if you do not make per capita payments, you do not need to submit a tribal revenue allocation plan.

§290.8 Do Indian tribes have to make per capita payments from net gaming revenues to tribal members?

No. You do not have to make per capita payments.

§290.9 How may an Indian tribe use net gaming revenues if it does not have an approved tribal revenue allocation plan?

Without an approved tribal revenue allocation plan, you may use net gaming revenues to fund tribal government operations or programs; to provide for the general welfare of your tribe and its members; to promote tribal economic development; to donate to charitable organizations; or to help fund operations of local government agencies.

§ 290.10 Is an Indian tribe in violation of IGRA if it makes per capita payments to its members from net gaming revenues without an approved tribal revenue allocation plan?

Yes, you are in violation of IGRA if you make per capita payments to your tribal members from net gaming revenues without an approved tribal revenue allocation plan. If you refuse to comply, the DOJ or NIGC may enforce the per capita requirements of IGRA.

§ 290.11 May an Indian tribe distribute per capita payments from net gaming revenues derived from either Class II or Class III gaming without a tribal revenue allocation plan?

No, IGRA requires that you have an approved tribal revenue allocation plan.

§ 290.12 What information must the tribal revenue allocation plan contain?

(a) You must prepare a tribal revenue allocation plan that includes a percentage breakdown of the uses for which you will allocate net gaming revenues. The percentage breakdown must total 100 percent.

(b) The tribal revenue allocation plan must meet the following criteria:

(1) It must reserve an adequate portion of net gaming revenues from the tribal gaming activity for one or more of the following purposes:

(i) To fund tribal government operations or programs;

(ii) To provide for the general welfare of the tribe or its members;

(iii) To promote tribal economic development;

(iv) To donate to charitable organizations; or

(v) To help fund operations of local government.

(2) It must contain detailed information to allow the ABO to determine that it complies with this section and IGRA particularly regarding funding for tribal governmental operations or programs and for promoting tribal economic development.

(3) It must protect and preserve the interests of minors and other legally incompetent persons who are entitled to receive per capita payments by:

(i) Ensuring that tribes make per capita payments for eligible minors or incompetents to the parents or legal guardians of these minors or incompetents at times and in such amounts as necessary for the health, education, or welfare of the minor or incompetent;

(ii) Establishing criteria for withdrawal of the funds, acceptable proof and/or receipts for accountability of the expenditure of the funds and the circumstances for denial of the withdrawal of the minors' and legal incompetents' per capita payments by the parent or legal guardian; and

(iii) Establishing a process, system, or forum for dispute resolution.

(4) It must describe how you will notify members of the tax liability for per capita payments and how you will withhold taxes for all recipients in accordance with IRS regulations in 26 CFR part 31.

(5) It must authorize the distribution of per capita payments to members according to specific eligibility requirements and must utilize or establish a tribal court system, forum or administrative process for resolution of disputes concerning the allocation of net gaming revenues and the distribution of per capita payments.

§ 290.13 Under what conditions may an Indian tribe distribute per capita payments?

You may make per capita payments only after the ABO approves your tribal revenue allocation plan.

§ 290.14 Who can share in a per capita payment?

(a) You must establish your own criteria for determining whether all members or identified groups of members are eligible for per capita payments.

(b) If the tribal revenue allocation plan calls for distributing per capita payments to an identified group of members rather than to all members, you must justify limiting this payment to the identified group of members. You must make sure that:

(1) The distinction between members eligible to receive payments and members ineligible to receive payments is reasonable and not arbitrary;

(2) The distinction does not discriminate or otherwise violate the Indian Civil Rights Act; and

(3) The justification complies with applicable tribal law.

§290.15 Must the Indian tribe establish trust accounts with financial institutions for minors and legal incompetents?

No. The tribe may establish trust accounts with financial institutions but should explore investment options to structure the accounts to the benefit of their members while ensuring compliance with IGRA and this part.

§290.16 Can the per capita payments of minors and legal incompetents be deposited into accounts held by BIA or OTFM?

No. The Secretary will not accept any deposits of payments or funds derived from net gaming revenues to any account held by BIA or OTFM.

§290.17 What documents must the Indian tribe include with the tribal revenue allocation plan?

You must include:

(a) A written request for approval of the tribal revenue allocation plan; and

(b) A tribal resolution or other document, including the date and place of adoption and the result of any vote taken, that certifies you have adopted the tribal revenue allocation plan in accordance with applicable tribal law.

§290.18 Where should the Indian tribe submit the tribal revenue allocation plan?

You must submit your tribal revenue allocation plan to your respective Superintendent. The Superintendent will review the tribal revenue allocation plan to make sure it has been properly adopted in accordance with applicable tribal law. The Superintendent will then transmit the tribal revenue allocation plan promptly to the ABO.

§290.19 How long will the ABO take to review and approve the tribal revenue allocation plan?

The ABO must review and act on your tribal revenue allocation plan within 60 days of receiving it. A tribal revenue allocation plan is not effective without the ABO's written approval.

(a) If the tribal revenue allocation plan conforms with this part and the IGRA, the ABO must approve it.

(b) If the tribal revenue allocation plan does not conform with this part and the IGRA, the ABO will send you a written notice that:

(1) Explains why the plan doesn't conform to this part of the IGRA; and

(2) Tells you how to bring the plan into conformance.

(c) If the ABO doesn't act within 60 days, you can appeal the inaction under 25 CFR part 2. A tribal revenue allocation plan is not effective without the express written approval of the ABO.

§290.20 When will the ABO disapprove a tribal revenue allocation plan?

The ABO will not approve any tribal revenue allocation plan for distribution of net gaming revenues from a tribal gaming activity if:

(a) The tribal revenue allocation plan is inadequate, particularly with respect to the requirements in §290.12 and IGRA, and you fail to bring it into compliance;

(b) The tribal revenue allocation plan is not adopted in accordance with applicable tribal law;

(c) The tribal revenue allocation plan does not include a reasonable justification for limiting per capita payments to certain groups of members; or

(d) The tribal revenue allocation plan violates the Indian Civil Rights Act of 1968, any other provision of Federal law, or the United States' trust obligations.

§290.21 May an Indian tribe appeal the ABO's decision?

Yes, you may appeal the ABO's decision in accordance with the regulations at 25 CFR part 2.

§290.22 How does the Indian tribe ensure compliance with its tribal revenue allocation plan?

You must utilize or establish a tribal court system, forum or administrative process in the tribal revenue allocation plan for reviewing expenditures of net gaming revenues and explain how you will correct deficiencies.

§ 290.23 How does the Indian tribe resolve disputes arising from per capita payments to individual members or identified groups of members?

You must utilize or establish a tribal court system, forum or administrative process for resolving disputes arising from the allocation of net gaming revenue and the distribution of per capita payments.

§ 290.24 Do revisions/amendments to a tribal revenue allocation plan require approval?

Yes, revisions/amendments to a tribal revenue allocation plan must be submitted to the ABO for approval to ensure that they comply with § 290.12 and IGRA.

§ 290.25 What is the liability of the United States under this part?

The United States is not liable for the manner in which a tribe distributes funds from net gaming revenues.

§ 290.26 Are previously approved tribal revenue allocation plans, revisions, or amendments subject to review in accordance with this part?

No. This part applies only to tribal revenue allocation plans, revisions, or amendments submitted for approval after April 17, 2000.

(a) If the ABO approved your tribal revenue allocation plan, revisions, or amendments before April 17, 2000, you need not resubmit it for approval.

(b) If you are amending or revising a previously approved allocation plan, you must submit the amended or revised plan to the ABO for review and approval under this part.

PART 291—CLASS III GAMING PROCEDURES

Sec.

AUTHORITY: 5 U.S.C. 301; 25 U.S.C. sections 2,9 and 2710.

SOURCE: 64 FR 17543, Apr. 12, 1999, unless otherwise noted.

§ 291.1 Purpose and scope.

The regulations in this part establish procedures that the Secretary will use to promulgate rules for the conduct of Class III Indian gaming when:

(a) A State and an Indian tribe are unable to voluntarily agree to a compact and;

(b) The State has asserted its immunity from suit brought by an Indian tribe under 25 U.S.C. 2710(d)(7)(B).

§ 291.2 Definitions

(a) All terms have the same meaning as set forth in the definitional section of IGRA, 25 U.S.C. section 2703(1)–(10).

(b) The term "compact" includes renewal of an existing compact.

§ 291.3 When may an Indian tribe ask the Secretary to issue Class III gaming procedures?

An Indian tribe may ask the Secretary to issue Class III gaming procedures when the following steps have taken place:

(a) The Indian tribe submitted a written request to the State to enter into negotiations to establish a Tribal-State compact governing the conduct of Class III gaming activities;

(b) The State and the Indian tribe failed to negotiate a compact 180 days after the State received the Indian tribe's request;

(c) The Indian tribe initiated a cause of action in Federal district court against the State alleging that the State did not respond, or did not respond in good faith, to the request of the Indian tribe to negotiate such a compact;

(d) The State raised an Eleventh Amendment defense to the tribal action; and

(e) The Federal district court dismissed the action due to the State's sovereign immunity under the Eleventh Amendment.

§ 291.4 What must a proposal requesting Class III gaming procedures contain?

A proposal requesting Class III gaming procedures must include the following information:

(a) The full name, address, and telephone number of the Indian tribe submitting the proposal;

(b) A copy of the authorizing resolution from the Indian tribe submitting the proposal;

(c) A copy of the Indian tribe's gaming ordinance or resolution approved by the NIGC in accordance with 25 U.S.C. 2710, if any;

(d) A copy of the Indian tribe's organic documents, if any;

(e) A copy of the Indian tribe's written request to the State to enter into compact negotiations, along with the Indian tribe's proposed compact, if any;

(f) A copy of the State's response to the tribal request and/or proposed compact, if any;

(g) A copy of the tribe's Complaint (with attached exhibits, if any); the State's Motion to Dismiss; any Response by the tribe to the State's Motion to Dismiss; any Opinion or other written documents from the court regarding the State's Motion to Dismiss; and the Court's Order of dismissal;

(h) The Indian tribe's factual and legal authority for the scope of gaming specified in paragraph (j)(13) of this section;

(i) Regulatory scheme for the State's oversight role, if any, in monitoring and enforcing compliance; and

(j) Proposed procedures under which the Indian tribe will conduct Class III gaming activities, including:

(1) A certification that the tribe's accounting procedures are maintained in accordance with American Institute of Certified Public Accountants Standards for Audits of Casinos, including maintenance of books and records in accordance with Generally Accepted Accounting Principles and applicable NIGC regulations;

(2) A reporting system for the payment of taxes and fees in a timely manner and in compliance with Internal Revenue Code and Bank Secrecy Act requirements;

(3) Preparation of financial statements covering all financial activities of the Indian tribe's gaming operations;

(4) Internal control standards designed to ensure fiscal integrity of gaming operations as set forth in 25 CFR Part 542;

(5) Provisions for records retention, maintenance, and accessibility;

(6) Conduct of games, including patron requirements, posting of game rules, and hours of operation;

(7) Procedures to protect the integrity of the rules for playing games;

(8) Rules governing employees of the gaming operation, including code of conduct, age requirements, conflict of interest provisions, licensing requirements, and such background investigations of all management officials and key employees as are required by IGRA, NIGC regulations, and applicable tribal gaming laws;

(9) Policies and procedures that protect the health and safety of patrons and employees and that address insurance and liability issues, as well as safety systems for fire and emergency services at all gaming locations;

(10) Surveillance procedures and security personnel and systems capable of monitoring movement of cash and chips, entrances and exits of gaming facilities, and other critical areas of any gaming facility;

(11) An administrative and/or tribal judicial process to resolve disputes between gaming establishment, employees and patrons, including a process to protect the rights of individuals injured on gaming premises by reason of

negligence in the operation of the facility;

(12) Hearing procedures for licensing purposes;

(13) A list of gaming activities proposed to be offered by the Indian tribe at its gaming facilities;

(14) A description of the location of proposed gaming facilities;

(15) A copy of the Indian tribe's liquor ordinance approved by the Secretary if intoxicants, as used in 18 U.S.C. 1154, will be served in the gaming facility;

(16) Provisions for a tribal regulatory gaming entity, independent of gaming management;

(17) Provisions for tribal enforcement and investigatory mechanisms, including the imposition of sanctions, monetary penalties, closure, and an administrative appeal process relating to enforcement and investigatory actions;

(18) The length of time the procedures will remain in effect; and

(19) Any other provisions deemed necessary by the Indian tribe.

§ 291.5 Where must the proposal requesting Class III gaming procedures be filed?

Any proposal requesting Class III gaming procedures must be filed with the Director, Indian Gaming Management Staff, Bureau of Indian Affairs, U.S. Department of the Interior, MS 2070-MIB, 1849 C Street NW, Washington, DC 20240.

§ 291.6 What must the Secretary do upon receiving a proposal?

Upon receipt of a proposal requesting Class III gaming procedures, the Secretary must:

(a) Within 15 days, notify the Indian tribe in writing that the proposal has been received, and whether any information required under § 291.4 is missing;

(b) Within 30 days of receiving a complete proposal, notify the Indian tribe in writing whether the Indian tribe meets the eligibility requirements in § 291.3. The Secretary's eligibility determination is final for the Department.

§ 291.7 What must the Secretary do if it has been determined that the Indian tribe is eligible to request Class III gaming procedures?

(a) If the Secretary determines that the Indian tribe is eligible to request Class III gaming procedures and that the Indian tribe's proposal is complete, the Secretary must submit the Indian tribe's proposal to the Governor and the Attorney General of the State where the gaming is proposed.

(b) The Governor and Attorney General will have 60 days to comment on:

(1) Whether the State is in agreement with the Indian tribe's proposal;

(2) Whether the proposal is consistent with relevant provisions of the laws of the State;

(3) Whether contemplated gaming activities are permitted in the State for any purposes, by any person, organization, or entity.

(c) The Secretary will also invite the State's Governor and Attorney General to submit an alternative proposal to the Indian tribe's proposed Class III gaming procedures.

§ 291.8 What must the Secretary do at the expiration of the 60-day comment period if the State has not submitted an alternative proposal?

(a) Upon expiration of the 60-day comment period specified in § 291.7, if the State has not submitted an alternative proposal, the Secretary must review the Indian tribe's proposal to determine:

(1) Whether all requirements of § 291.4 are adequately addressed;

(2) Whether Class III gaming activities will be conducted on Indian lands over which the Indian tribe has jurisdiction;

(3) Whether contemplated gaming activities are permitted in the State for any purposes by any person, organization, or entity;

(4) Whether the proposal is consistent with relevant provisions of the laws of the State;

(5) Whether the proposal is consistent with the trust obligations of the United States to the Indian tribe;

(6) Whether the proposal is consistent with all applicable provisions of IGRA; and

(7) Whether the proposal is consistent with provisions of other applicable Federal laws.

(b) Within 60 days of the expiration of the 60-day comment period in §291.7, the Secretary must notify the Indian tribe, the Governor, and the Attorney General of the State in writing that he/she has:

(1) Approved the proposal if the Secretary determines that there are no objections to the Indian tribe's proposal; or

(2) Identified unresolved issues and areas of disagreements in the proposal, and invite the Indian tribe, the Governor and the Attorney General to participate in an informal conference, within 30 days of notification unless the parties agree otherwise, to resolve identified unresolved issues and areas of disagreement.

(c) Within 30 days of the informal conference, the Secretary must prepare and mail to the Indian tribe, the Governor and the Attorney General:

(1) A written report that summarizes the results of the informal conference; and

(2) A final decision either setting forth the Secretary's proposed Class III gaming procedures for the Indian tribe, or disapproving the proposal for any of the reasons in paragraph (a) of this section.

§291.9 What must the Secretary do at the end of the 60-day comment period if the State offers an alternative proposal for Class III gaming procedures?

Within 30 days of receiving the State's alternative proposal, the Secretary must appoint a mediator who:

(a) Has no official, financial, or personal conflict of interest with respect to the issues in controversy; and

(b) Must convene a process to resolve differences between the two proposals.

§291.10 What is the role of the mediator appointed by the Secretary?

(a) The mediator must ask the Indian tribe and the State to submit their last best proposal for Class III gaming procedures.

(b) After giving the Indian tribe and the State an opportunity to be heard and present information supporting their respective positions, the mediator must select from the two proposals the one that best comports with the terms of IGRA and any other applicable Federal law. The mediator must submit the proposal selected to the Indian tribe, the State, and the Secretary.

§291.11 What must the Secretary do upon receiving the proposal selected by the mediator?

Within 60 days of receiving the proposal selected by the mediator, the Secretary must do one of the following:

(a) Notify the Indian tribe, the Governor and the Attorney General in writing of his/her decision to approve the proposal for Class III gaming procedures selected by the mediator; or

(b) Notify the Indian tribe, the Governor and the Attorney General in writing of his/her decision to disapprove the proposal selected by the mediator for any of the following reasons:

(1) The requirements of §291.4 are not adequately addressed;

(2) Gaming activities would not be conducted on Indian lands over which the Indian tribe has jurisdiction;

(3) Contemplated gaming activities are not permitted in the State for any purpose by any person, organization, or entity;

(4) The proposal is not consistent with relevant provisions of the laws of the State;

(5) The proposal is not consistent with the trust obligations of the United States to the Indian tribe;

(6) The proposal is not consistent with applicable provisions of IGRA; or

(7) The proposal is not consistent with provisions of other applicable Federal laws.

(c) If the Secretary rejects the mediator's proposal under paragraph (b) of this section, he/she must prescribe appropriate procedures within 60 days under which Class III gaming may take place that comport with the mediator's selected proposal as much as possible, the provisions of IGRA, and the relevant provisions of the laws of the State.

§ 291.12 Who will monitor and enforce tribal compliance with the Class III gaming procedures?

The Indian tribe and the State may have an agreement regarding monitoring and enforcement of tribal compliance with the Indian tribe's Class III gaming procedures. In addition, under existing law, the NIGC will monitor and enforce tribal compliance with the Indian tribe's Class III gaming procedures.

§ 291.13 When do Class III gaming procedures for an Indian tribe become effective?

Upon approval of Class III gaming procedures for the Indian tribe under either § 291.8(b), § 291.8(c), or § 291.11(a), the Indian tribe shall have 90 days in which to approve and execute the Secretarial procedures and forward its approval and execution to the Secretary, who shall publish notice of their approval in the FEDERAL REGISTER. The procedures take effect upon their publication in the FEDERAL REGISTER.

§ 291.14 How can Class III gaming procedures approved by the Secretary be amended?

An Indian tribe may ask the Secretary to amend approved Class III gaming procedures by submitting an amendment proposal to the Secretary. The Secretary must review the proposal by following the approval process for initial tribal proposals, except that the requirements of § 291.3 are not applicable and he/she may waive the requirements of § 291.4 to the extent they do not apply to the amendment request.

§ 291.15 How long do Class III gaming procedures remain in effect?

Class III gaming procedures remain in effect for the duration specified in the procedures or until amended pursuant to § 291.14.

PART 292—GAMING ON TRUST LANDS ACQUIRED AFTER OCTOBER 17, 1988

Subpart A—General Provisions

Sec.

Subpart B—Exceptions to Prohibition on Gaming on Newly Acquired Lands

SETTLEMENT OF A LAND CLAIM" EXCEPTION

"INITIAL RESERVATION" EXCEPTION

RESTORED LANDS" EXCEPTION

Subpart C—Secretarial Determination and Governor's Concurrence

APPLICATION CONTENTS

CONSULTATION

AUTHORITY: 5 U.S.C. 301, 25 U.S.C. 2, 9, 2719, 43 U.S.C. 1457.

SOURCE: 73 FR 29375, May 20, 2008, unless otherwise noted.

Subpart A—General Provisions

§ 292.1 What is the purpose of this part?

The Indian Gaming Regulatory Act of 1988 (IGRA) contains several exceptions under which class II or class III gaming may occur on lands acquired by the United States in trust for an Indian tribe after October 17, 1988, if other applicable requirements of IGRA are met. This part contains procedures that the Department of the Interior will use to determine whether these exceptions apply.

§ 292.2 How are key terms defined in this part?

For purposes of this part, all terms have the same meaning as set forth in the definitional section of IGRA, 25 U.S.C. 2703. In addition, the following terms have the meanings given in this section.

Appropriate State and local officials means the Governor of the State and local government officials within a 25-mile radius of the proposed gaming establishment.

BIA means Bureau of Indian Affairs.

Contiguous means two parcels of land having a common boundary notwithstanding the existence of non-navigable waters or a public road or right-of-way and includes parcels that touch at a point.

Former reservation means lands in Oklahoma that are within the exterior boundaries of the last reservation that was established by treaty, Executive Order, or Secretarial Order for an Oklahoma tribe.

IGRA means the Indian Gaming Regulatory Act of 1988, as amended and codified at 25 U.S.C. 2701–2721.

Indian tribe or tribe means any Indian tribe, band, nation, or other organized group or community of Indians that is recognized by the Secretary as having a government-to-government relationship with the United States and is eligible for the special programs and services provided by the United States to Indians because of their status as Indians, as evidenced by inclusion of the tribe on the list of recognized tribes published by the Secretary under 25 U.S.C. 479a–1.

Land claim means any claim by a tribe concerning the impairment of title or other real property interest or loss of possession that:

(1) Arises under the United States Constitution, Federal common law, Federal statute or treaty;

(2) Is in conflict with the right, or title or other real property interest claimed by an individual or entity (private, public, or governmental); and

(3) Either accrued on or before October 17, 1988, or involves lands held in trust or restricted fee for the tribe prior to October 17, 1988.

Legislative termination means Federal legislation that specifically terminates or prohibits the government-to-government relationship with an Indian tribe or that otherwise specifically denies the tribe, or its members, access to or eligibility for government services.

Nearby Indian tribe means an Indian tribe with tribal Indian lands located within a 25-mile radius of the location of the proposed gaming establishment, or, if the tribe has no trust lands, within a 25-mile radius of its government headquarters.

Newly acquired lands means land that has been taken, or will be taken, in trust for the benefit of an Indian tribe by the United States after October 17, 1988.

Office of Indian Gaming means the office within the Office of the Assistant Secretary-Indian Affairs, within the Department of the Interior.

Regional Director means the official in charge of the BIA Regional Office responsible for BIA activities within the geographical area where the proposed gaming establishment is to be located.

Reservation means:

(1) Land set aside by the United States by final ratified treaty, agreement, Executive Order, Proclamation, Secretarial Order or Federal statute for the tribe, notwithstanding the issuance of any patent;

(2) Land of Indian colonies and rancherias (including rancherias restored by judicial action) set aside by the United States for the permanent settlement of the Indians as its homeland;

(3) Land acquired by the United States to reorganize adult Indians pursuant to statute; or

(4) Land acquired by a tribe through a grant from a sovereign, including pueblo lands, which is subject to a Federal restriction against alienation.

Secretarial Determination means a two-part determination that a gaming establishment on newly acquired lands:

(1) Would be in the best interest of the Indian tribe and its members; and

(2) Would not be detrimental to the surrounding community.

Secretary means the Secretary of the Interior or authorized representative.

Significant historical connection means the land is located within the boundaries of the tribe's last reservation under a ratified or unratified treaty, or a tribe can demonstrate by historical documentation the existence of the tribe's villages, burial grounds, occupancy or subsistence use in the vicinity of the land.

Surrounding community means local governments and nearby Indian tribes located within a 25-mile radius of the site of the proposed gaming establishment. A local government or nearby Indian tribe located beyond the 25-mile radius may petition for consultation if it can establish that its governmental functions, infrastructure or services will be directly, immediately and significantly impacted by the proposed gaming establishment.

Subpart B—Exceptions to Prohibitions on Gaming on Newly Acquired Lands

§ 292.3 How does a tribe seek an opinion on whether its newly acquired lands meet, or will meet, one of the exceptions in this subpart?

(a) If the newly acquired lands are already in trust and the request does not concern whether a specific area of land is a "reservation," the tribe may submit a request for an opinion to either the National Indian Gaming Commission or the Office of Indian Gaming.

(b) If the tribe seeks to game on newly acquired lands that require a land-into-trust application or the request concerns whether a specific area of land is a "reservation," the tribe must submit a request for an opinion to the Office of Indian Gaming.

§ 292.4 What criteria must newly acquired lands meet under the exceptions regarding tribes with and without a reservation?

For gaming to be allowed on newly acquired lands under the exceptions in 25 U.S.C. 2719(a) of IGRA, the land must meet the location requirements in either paragraph (a) or paragraph (b) of this section.

(a) If the tribe had a reservation on October 17, 1988, the lands must be located within or contiguous to the boundaries of the reservation.

(b) If the tribe had no reservation on October 17, 1988, the lands must be either:

(1) Located in Oklahoma and within the boundaries of the tribe's former reservation or contiguous to other land held in trust or restricted status for the tribe in Oklahoma; or

(2) Located in a State other than Oklahoma and within the tribe's last recognized reservation within the State or States within which the tribe is presently located, as evidenced by the tribe's governmental presence and tribal population.

SETTLEMENT OF A LAND CLAIM'' EXCEPTION

§ 292.5 When can gaming occur on newly acquired lands under a settlement of a land claim?

This section contains criteria for meeting the requirements of 25 U.S.C. 2719(b)(1)(B)(i), known as the ''settlement of a land claim'' exception. Gaming may occur on newly acquired lands if the land at issue is either:

(a) Acquired under a settlement of a land claim that resolves or extinguishes with finality the tribe's land claim in whole or in part, thereby resulting in the alienation or loss of possession of some or all of the lands claimed by the tribe, in legislation enacted by Congress; or

(b) Acquired under a settlement of a land claim that:

(1) Is executed by the parties, which includes the United States, returns to the tribe all or part of the land claimed by the tribe, and resolves or extinguishes with finality the claims regarding the returned land; or

(2) Is not executed by the United States, but is entered as a final order by a court of competent jurisdiction or is an enforceable agreement that in either case predates October 17, 1988 and resolves or extinguishes with finality the land claim at issue.

INITIAL RESERVATION'' EXCEPTION

§ 292.6 What must be demonstrated to meet the "initial reservation" exception?

This section contains criteria for meeting the requirements of 25 U.S.C. 2719(b)(1)(B)(ii), known as the ''initial reservation'' exception. Gaming may occur on newly acquired lands under this exception only when all of the following conditions in this section are met:

(a) The tribe has been acknowledged (federally recognized) through the administrative process under part 83 of this chapter.

(b) The tribe has no gaming facility on newly acquired lands under the restored land exception of these regulations.

(c) The land has been proclaimed to be a reservation under 25 U.S.C. 467 and is the first proclaimed reservation of the tribe following acknowledgment.

(d) If a tribe does not have a proclaimed reservation on the effective date of these regulations, to be proclaimed an initial reservation under this exception, the tribe must demonstrate the land is located within the State or States where the Indian tribe is now located, as evidenced by the tribe's governmental presence and tribal population, and within an area where the tribe has significant historical connections and one or more of the following modern connections to the land:

(1) The land is near where a significant number of tribal members reside; or

(2) The land is within a 25-mile radius of the tribe's headquarters or other tribal governmental facilities that have existed at that location for at least 2 years at the time of the application for land-into-trust; or

(3) The tribe can demonstrate other factors that establish the tribe's current connection to the land.

RESTORED LANDS'' EXCEPTION

§ 292.7 What must be demonstrated to meet the "restored lands" exception?

This section contains criteria for meeting the requirements of 25 U.S.C. 2719(b)(1)(B)(iii), known as the ''restored lands'' exception. Gaming may occur on newly acquired lands under this exception only when all of the following conditions in this section are met:

(a) The tribe at one time was federally recognized, as evidenced by its meeting the criteria in § 292.8;

(b) The tribe at some later time lost its government-to-government relationship by one of the means specified in § 292.9;

(c) At a time after the tribe lost its government-to-government relationship, the tribe was restored to Federal recognition by one of the means specified in § 292.10; and

(d) The newly acquired lands meet the criteria of ''restored lands'' in § 292.11.

§ 292.8 How does a tribe qualify as having been federally recognized?

For a tribe to qualify as having been at one time federally recognized for purposes of § 292.7, one of the following must be true:

(a) The United States at one time entered into treaty negotiations with the tribe;

(b) The Department determined that the tribe could organize under the Indian Reorganization Act or the Oklahoma Indian Welfare Act;

(c) Congress enacted legislation specific to, or naming, the tribe indicating that a government-to-government relationship existed;

(d) The United States at one time acquired land for the tribe's benefit; or

(e) Some other evidence demonstrates the existence of a government-to-government relationship between the tribe and the United States.

§ 292.9 How does a tribe show that it lost its government-to-government relationship?

For a tribe to qualify as having lost its government-to-government relationship for purposes of § 292.7, it must show that its government-to-government relationship was terminated by one of the following means:

(a) Legislative termination;

(b) Consistent historical written documentation from the Federal Government effectively stating that it no longer recognized a government-to-government relationship with the tribe or its members or taking action to end the government-to-government relationship; or

(c) Congressional restoration legislation that recognizes the existence of the previous government-to-government relationship.

§ 292.10 How does a tribe qualify as having been restored to Federal recognition?

For a tribe to qualify as having been restored to Federal recognition for purposes of § 292.7, the tribe must show at least one of the following:

(a) Congressional enactment of legislation recognizing, acknowledging, affirming, reaffirming, or restoring the government-to-government relationship between the United States and the tribe (required for tribes terminated by Congressional action);

(b) Recognition through the administrative Federal Acknowledgment Process under § 83.8 of this chapter; or

(c) A Federal court determination in which the United States is a party or court-approved settlement agreement entered into by the United States.

§ 292.11 What are "restored lands"?

For newly acquired lands to qualify as "restored lands" for purposes of § 292.7, the tribe acquiring the lands must meet the requirements of paragraph (a), (b), or (c) of this section.

(a) If the tribe was restored by a Congressional enactment of legislation recognizing, acknowledging, affirming, reaffirming, or restoring the government-to-government relationship between the United States and the tribe, the tribe must show that either:

(1) The legislation requires or authorizes the Secretary to take land into trust for the benefit of the tribe within a specific geographic area and the lands are within the specific geographic area; or

(2) If the legislation does not provide a specific geographic area for the restoration of lands, the tribe must meet the requirements of § 292.12.

(b) If the tribe is acknowledged under § 83.8 of this chapter, it must show that it:

(1) Meets the requirements of § 292.12; and

(2) Does not already have an initial reservation proclaimed after October 17, 1988.

(c) If the tribe was restored by a Federal court determination in which the United States is a party or by a court-approved settlement agreement entered into by the United States, it must meet the requirements of § 292.12.

§ 292.12 How does a tribe establish connections to newly acquired lands for the purposes of the "restored lands" exception?

To establish a connection to the newly acquired lands for purposes of § 292.11, the tribe must meet the criteria in this section.

(a) The newly acquired lands must be located within the State or States where the tribe is now located, as evidenced by the tribe's governmental presence and tribal population, and the tribe must demonstrate one or more of the following modern connections to the land:

(1) The land is within reasonable commuting distance of the tribe's existing reservation;

(2) If the tribe has no reservation, the land is near where a significant number of tribal members reside;

(3) The land is within a 25-mile radius of the tribe's headquarters or other tribal governmental facilities that have existed at that location for at least 2 years at the time of the application for land-into-trust; or

(4) Other factors demonstrate the tribe's current connection to the land.

(b) The tribe must demonstrate a significant historical connection to the land.

(c) The tribe must demonstrate a temporal connection between the date of the acquisition of the land and the date of the tribe's restoration. To demonstrate this connection, the tribe must be able to show that either:

(1) The land is included in the tribe's first request for newly acquired lands since the tribe was restored to Federal recognition; or

(2) The tribe submitted an application to take the land into trust within 25 years after the tribe was restored to Federal recognition and the tribe is not gaming on other lands.

Subpart C—Secretarial Determination and Governor's Concurrence

§292.13 When can a tribe conduct gaming activities on newly acquired lands that do not qualify under one of the exceptions in subpart B of this part?

A tribe may conduct gaming on newly acquired lands that do not meet the criteria in subpart B of this part only after all of the following occur:

(a) The tribe asks the Secretary in writing to make a Secretarial Determination that a gaming establishment on land subject to this part is in the best interest of the tribe and its members and not detrimental to the surrounding community;

(b) The Secretary consults with the tribe and appropriate State and local officials, including officials of other nearby Indian tribes;

(c) The Secretary makes a determination that a gaming establishment on newly acquired lands would be in the best interest of the tribe and its members and would not be detrimental to the surrounding community; and

(d) The Governor of the State in which the gaming establishment is located concurs in the Secretary's Determination (25 U.S.C. 2719(b)(1)(A)).

§292.14 Where must a tribe file an application for a Secretarial Determination?

A tribe must file its application for a Secretarial Determination with the Regional Director of the BIA Regional Office having responsibility over the land where the gaming establishment is to be located.

§292.15 May a tribe apply for a Secretarial Determination for lands not yet held in trust?

Yes. A tribe can apply for a Secretarial Determination under §292.13 for land not yet held in trust at the same time that it applies under part 151 of this chapter to have the land taken into trust.

APPLICATION CONTENTS

§292.16 What must an application for a Secretarial Determination contain?

A tribe's application requesting a Secretarial Determination under §292.13 must include the following information:

(a) The full name, address, and telephone number of the tribe submitting the application;

(b) A description of the location of the land, including a legal description supported by a survey or other document;

(c) Proof of identity of present ownership and title status of the land;

(d) Distance of the land from the tribe's reservation or trust lands, if any, and tribal government headquarters;

(e) Information required by §292.17 to assist the Secretary in determining whether the proposed gaming establishment will be in the best interest of the tribe and its members;

(f) Information required by § 292.18 to assist the Secretary in determining whether the proposed gaming establishment will not be detrimental to the surrounding community;

(g) The authorizing resolution from the tribe submitting the application;

(h) The tribe's gaming ordinance or resolution approved by the National Indian Gaming Commission in accordance with 25 U.S.C. 2710, if any;

(i) The tribe's organic documents, if any;

(j) The tribe's class III gaming compact with the State where the gaming establishment is to be located, if one has been negotiated;

(k) If the tribe has not negotiated a class III gaming compact with the State where the gaming establishment is to be located, the tribe's proposed scope of gaming, including the size of the proposed gaming establishment; and

(l) A copy of the existing or proposed management contract required to be approved by the National Indian Gaming Commission under 25 U.S.C. 2711 and part 533 of this title, if any.

§ 292.17 How must an application describe the benefits and impacts of the proposed gaming establishment to the tribe and its members?

To satisfy the requirements of § 292.16(e), an application must contain:

(a) Projections of class II and class III gaming income statements, balance sheets, fixed assets accounting, and cash flow statements for the gaming entity and the tribe;

(b) Projected tribal employment, job training, and career development;

(c) Projected benefits to the tribe and its members from tourism;

(d) Projected benefits to the tribe and its members from the proposed uses of the increased tribal income;

(e) Projected benefits to the relationship between the tribe and non-Indian communities;

(f) Possible adverse impacts on the tribe and its members and plans for addressing those impacts;

(g) Distance of the land from the location where the tribe maintains core governmental functions;

(h) Evidence that the tribe owns the land in fee or holds an option to acquire the land at the sole discretion of the tribe, or holds other contractual rights to cause the lands to be transferred from a third party to the tribe or directly to the United States;

(i) Evidence of significant historical connections, if any, to the land; and

(j) Any other information that may provide a basis for a Secretarial Determination that the gaming establishment would be in the best interest of the tribe and its members, including copies of any:

(1) Consulting agreements relating to the proposed gaming establishment;

(2) Financial and loan agreements relating to the proposed gaming establishment; and

(3) Other agreements relative to the purchase, acquisition, construction, or financing of the proposed gaming establishment, or the acquisition of the land where the gaming establishment will be located.

§ 292.18 What information must an application contain on detrimental impacts to the surrounding community?

To satisfy the requirements of § 292.16(f), an application must contain the following information on detrimental impacts of the proposed gaming establishment:

(a) Information regarding environmental impacts and plans for mitigating adverse impacts, including an Environmental Assessment (EA), an Environmental Impact Statement (EIS), or other information required by the National Environmental Policy Act (NEPA);

(b) Anticipated impacts on the social structure, infrastructure, services, housing, community character, and land use patterns of the surrounding community;

(c) Anticipated impacts on the economic development, income, and employment of the surrounding community;

(d) Anticipated costs of impacts to the surrounding community and identification of sources of revenue to mitigate them;

(e) Anticipated cost, if any, to the surrounding community of treatment programs for compulsive gambling attributable to the proposed gaming establishment;

(f) If a nearby Indian tribe has a significant historical connection to the land, then the impact on that tribe's traditional cultural connection to the land; and

(g) Any other information that may provide a basis for a Secretarial Determination whether the proposed gaming establishment would or would not be detrimental to the surrounding community, including memoranda of understanding and inter-governmental agreements with affected local governments.

CONSULTATION

§ 292.19 How will the Regional Director conduct the consultation process?

(a) The Regional Director will send a letter that meets the requirements in § 292.20 and that solicits comments within a 60-day period from:

(1) Appropriate State and local officials; and

(2) Officials of nearby Indian tribes.

(b) Upon written request, the Regional Director may extend the 60-day comment period for an additional 30 days.

(c) After the close of the consultation period, the Regional Director must:

(1) Provide a copy of all comments received during the consultation process to the applicant tribe; and

(2) Allow the tribe to address or resolve any issues raised in the comments.

(d) The applicant tribe must submit written responses, if any, to the Regional Director within 60 days of receipt of the consultation comments.

(e) On written request from the applicant tribe, the Regional Director may extend the 60-day comment period in paragraph (d) of this section for an additional 30 days.

§ 292.20 What information must the consultation letter include?

(a) The consultation letter required by § 292.19(a) must:

(1) Describe or show the location of the proposed gaming establishment;

(2) Provide information on the proposed scope of gaming; and

(3) Include other information that may be relevant to a specific proposal, such as the size of the proposed gaming establishment, if known.

(b) The consultation letter must include a request to the recipients to submit comments, if any, on the following areas within 60 days of receiving the letter:

(1) Information regarding environmental impacts on the surrounding community and plans for mitigating adverse impacts;

(2) Anticipated impacts on the social structure, infrastructure, services, housing, community character, and land use patterns of the surrounding community;

(3) Anticipated impact on the economic development, income, and employment of the surrounding community;

(4) Anticipated costs of impacts to the surrounding community and identification of sources of revenue to mitigate them;

(5) Anticipated costs, if any, to the surrounding community of treatment programs for compulsive gambling attributable to the proposed gaming establishment; and

(6) Any other information that may assist the Secretary in determining whether the proposed gaming establishment would or would not be detrimental to the surrounding community.

EVALUATION AND CONCURRENCE

§ 292.21 How will the Secretary evaluate a proposed gaming establishment?

(a) The Secretary will consider all the information submitted under §§ 292.16–292.19 in evaluating whether the proposed gaming establishment is in the best interest of the tribe and its members and whether it would or would not be detrimental to the surrounding community.

(b) If the Secretary makes an unfavorable Secretarial Determination, the Secretary will inform the tribe that its application has been disapproved, and set forth the reasons for the disapproval.

(c) If the Secretary makes a favorable Secretarial Determination, the Secretary will proceed under § 292.22.

§ 292.22 How does the Secretary request the Governor's concurrence?

If the Secretary makes a favorable Secretarial Determination, the Secretary will send to the Governor of the State:

(a) A written notification of the Secretarial Determination and Findings of Fact supporting the determination;

(b) A copy of the entire application record; and

(c) A request for the Governor's concurrence in the Secretarial Determination.

§ 292.23 What happens if the Governor does not affirmatively concur with the Secretarial Determination?

(a) If the Governor provides a written non-concurrence with the Secretarial Determination:

(1) The applicant tribe may use the newly acquired lands only for non-gaming purposes; and

(2) If a notice of intent to take the land into trust has been issued, then the Secretary will withdraw that notice pending a revised application for a non-gaming purpose.

(b) If the Governor does not affirmatively concur in the Secretarial Determination within one year of the date of the request, the Secretary may, at the request of the applicant tribe or the Governor, grant an extension of up to 180 days.

(c) If no extension is granted or if the Governor does not respond during the extension period, the Secretarial Determination will no longer be valid.

§ 292.24 Can the public review the Secretarial Determination?

Subject to restrictions on disclosure required by the Freedom of Information Act (5 U.S.C. 552), the Privacy Act (5 U.S.C. 552a), and the Trade Secrets Act (18 U.S.C. 1905), the Secretarial Determination and the supporting documents will be available for review at the local BIA agency or Regional Office having administrative jurisdiction over the land.

INFORMATION COLLECTION

§ 292.25 Do information collections in this part have Office of Management and Budget approval?

The information collection requirements in §§ 292.16, 292.17, and 292.18 have been approved by the Office of Management and Budget (OMB). The information collection control number is 1076–0158. A Federal agency may not collect or sponsor and a person is not required to respond to, a collection of information unless it displays a currently valid OMB control.

Subpart D—Effect of Regulations

§ 292.26 What effect do these regulations have on pending applications, final agency decisions, and opinions already issued?

These regulations apply to all requests pursuant to 25 U.S.C. 2719, except:

(a) These regulations do not alter final agency decisions made pursuant to 25 U.S.C. 2719 before the date of enactment of these regulations.

(b) These regulations apply to final agency action taken after the effective date of these regulations except that these regulations shall not apply to applicable agency actions when, before the effective date of these regulations, the Department or the National Indian Gaming Commission (NIGC) issued a written opinion regarding the applicability of 25 U.S.C. 2719 for land to be used for a particular gaming establishment, provided that the Department or the NIGC retains full discretion to qualify, withdraw or modify such opinions.

PART 293—CLASS III TRIBAL STATE GAMING COMPACT PROCESS

Sec.

AUTHORITY: 5 U.S.C. 301; 25 U.S.C. 2, 9, 2710.

SOURCE: 73 FR 74009, Dec. 5, 2008, unless otherwise noted.

§ 293.1 What is the purpose of this part?

This part contains procedures that:

(a) Indian tribes and States must use when submitting Tribal-State compacts and compact amendments to the Department of the Interior; and

(b) The Secretary will use for reviewing such Tribal-State compacts or compact amendments.

§ 293.2 How are key terms defined in this part?

(a) For purposes of this part, all terms have the same meaning as set forth in the definitional section of the Indian Gaming Regulatory Act of 1988, 25 U.S.C. 2703 and any amendments thereto.

(b) As used in this part:

(1) *Amendment* means an amendment to a class III Tribal-State gaming compact.

(2) *Compact* or *Tribal-State Gaming Compact* means an intergovernmental agreement executed between Tribal and State governments under the Indian Gaming Regulatory Act that establishes between the parties the terms and conditions for the operation and regulation of the tribe's Class III gaming activities.

(3) *Extensions* means changes to the timeframe of the compacts or amendments.

§ 293.3 What authority does the Secretary have to approve or disapprove compacts and amendments?

The Secretary has the authority to approve compacts or amendments "entered into" by an Indian tribe and a State, as evidenced by the appropriate signature of both parties. See § 293.14 for the Secretary's authority to disapprove compacts or amendments.

§ 293.4 Are compacts and amendments subject to review and approval?

(a) Compacts are subject to review and approval by the Secretary.

(b) All amendments, regardless of whether they are substantive amendments or technical amendments, are subject to review and approval by the Secretary.

§ 293.5 Are extensions to compacts subject to review and approval?

No. Approval of an extension is not required if the extension of the compact does not include any amendment to the terms of the compact. However, the tribe must submit the extension executed by both the tribe and the State along with the documents required under paragraphs (b) and (c) of § 293.8.

§ 293.6 Who can submit a compact or amendment?

Either party (Indian tribe or State) to a compact or amendment can submit the compact or amendment to the Secretary for review and approval.

§ 293.7 When should the Indian Tribe or State submit a compact or amendment for review and approval?

The Indian tribe or State should submit the compact or amendment after it has been legally entered into by both parties.

§ 293.8 What documents must be submitted with a compact or amendment?

Documentation submitted with a compact or amendment must include:

(a) At least one original compact or amendment executed by both the tribe and the State;

(b) A tribal resolution or other document, including the date and place of adoption and the result of any vote taken, that certifies that the tribe has approved the compact or amendment in accordance with applicable tribal law;

(c) Certification from the Governor or other representative of the State that he or she is authorized under State law to enter into the compact or amendment;

(d) Any other documentation requested by the Secretary that is necessary to determine whether to approve or disapprove the compact or amendment.

§ 293.9 Where should a compact or amendment be submitted for review and approval?

Submit compacts and amendments to the Director, Office of Indian Gaming, U.S. Department of the Interior, 1849 C Street, NW., Mail Stop 3657, Main Interior Building, Washington, DC 20240. If this address changes, a notice with the new address will be published in the FEDERAL REGISTER within 5 business days.

§ 293.10 How long will the Secretary take to review a compact or amendment?

(a) The Secretary must approve or disapprove a compact or amendment within 45 calendar days after receiving the compact or amendment.

(b) The Secretary will notify the Indian tribe and the State in writing of the decision to approve or disapprove a compact or amendment.

§ 293.11 When will the 45-day timeline begin?

The 45-day timeline will begin when a compact or amendment is received and date stamped in the Office of Indian Gaming at the address listed in § 293.9.

§ 293.12 What happens if the Secretary does not act on the compact or amendment within the 45-day review period?

If the Secretary neither affirmatively approves nor disapproves a compact or amendment within the 45-day review period, the compact or amendment is considered to have been approved, but only to the extent it complies with the provisions of the Indian Gaming Regulatory Act.

§ 293.13 Who can withdraw a compact or amendment after it has been received by the Secretary?

To withdraw a compact or amendment after it has been received by the Secretary, the Indian tribe and State must submit a written request to the Director, Office of Indian Gaming at the address listed in § 293.9.

§ 293.14 When may the Secretary disapprove a compact or amendment?

The Secretary may disapprove a compact or amendment only if it violates:

(a) Any provision of the Indian Gaming Regulatory Act;

(b) Any other provision of Federal law that does not relate to jurisdiction over gaming on Indian lands; or

(c) The trust obligations of the United States to Indians.

§ 293.15 When does an approved or considered-to-have-been-approved compact or amendment take effect?

(a) An approved or considered-to-have-been-approved compact or amendment takes effect on the date that notice of its approval is published in the FEDERAL REGISTER.

(b) The notice of approval must be published in the FEDERAL REGISTER within 90 days from the date the compact or amendment is received by the Office of Indian Gaming.

§ 293.16 How does the Paperwork Reduction Act affect this part?

The information collection requirements contained in this part have been approved by the OMB under the Paperwork Reduction Act of 1995, 44 U.S.C. 3507(d), and assigned control number 1076–0172. A Federal agency may not conduct or sponsor, and you are not required to respond to, a collection of information unless it displays a currently valid OMB control number.

PARTS 294–299 [RESERVED]

SUBCHAPTER O—MISCELLANEOUS [RESERVED]

APPENDIX TO CHAPTER I—EXTENSION OF THE TRUST OR RESTRICTED STATUS OF CERTAIN INDIAN LANDS

This appendix contains citations of Executive orders and acts of Congress continuing the trust or restricted period of Indian land, which would have expired otherwise, within the several Indian reservations in the States named. The asterisk to the left of the name of a reservation indicates that the reservation is subject to the benefits of the Indian Reorganization Act of June 18, 1934 (48 Stat. 984; 25 U.S.C. 461-479), as amended, and as therein provided the trust or restricted period of the land is extended indefinitely. Where the name of a reservation is not preceded by an asterisk, such reservation is not subject to the Reorganization Act and is not subject to the benefits of such indefinite trust or restricted period extension, but such reservation is dependent upon acts of Congress or Executive orders for extension of the trust or restricted period of the land.

For the purpose of insuring the continuation of the trust or restricted status of Indian allotments within Indian reservations not subject to the Reorganization Act, Congress by the act of June 15, 1935 (49 Stat. 378) reimposed such restrictions as may have been expired between the dates of June 18, 1934, and December 31, 1936.

State	Reservation	E. O. No.	Date	Period of extension
Arizona	*Papago	2066	Oct. 27, 1914	10 years.
Do	......do	4464	June 28, 1926	Do.
California	Agua Caliente	3446	Apr. 30, 1921	Do.
Do	......do	5580	Mar. 16, 1931	Do.
Do	Cabazon and Twenty-nine Palms	3302	July 7, 1920	5 years.
Do	......do	4159	Feb. 19, 1925	10 years.
Do	*Capitan Grande	3048	Feb. 27, 1919	5 years.
Do	......do		Act of Feb. 8, 1927 (44 Stat. 1061)	10 years.
Do	Hoopa Valley (Klamath River)	2943	Aug. 23, 1918	1 year.
Do	......do		Sept. 23, 1919	Do.
Do	......do	3304	July 10, 1920	10 years.
Do	......do	3980	Mar. 26, 1924	15 years.
Do	......do	5416	Aug. 4, 1930	10 years.
	Mission Bands:.			
Do	Augustine	2795	Jan. 26, 1918	Do.
Do	Campo	2795	......do	Do.
Do	*Cuyapipe	2795	......do	Do.
Do	Inaja	2795	......do	Do.
Do	*Laguna	2795	......do	Do.
Do	*La Posta	2795	......do	Do.
Do	*Manzanita	2795	......do	Do.
Do	Mesa Grande	2795	......do	Do.
Do	Pala	2795	......do	Do.
Do	Ramona	2795	......do	Do.
Do	Santa Ysabel	2795	......do	Do.
Do	Sycuan	2795	......do	Do.
Do	......do	3383	Jan. 7, 1921	25 years.
Do	San Manuel	2795	Jan. 26, 1918	10 years.
Do	Temecula	2795	...........do	Do.
Do	All of above Mission Bands	4765	Nov. 23, 1927	Do.
Do	Morongo	6341	Oct. 17, 1933	Do.
Do	Pala	3383	Jan. 7, 1921	25 years.
Do	......do		Act of Feb. 11, 1936 (49 Stat. 1106)	10 years.
Do	Potrero and Rincon	2684	Aug. 16, 1917	Do.
Do	......do	4687	July 11, 1927	Do.
Do	*Round Valley	3223	Feb. 5, 1920	3 years.
Do	......do	3805	Mar. 5, 1923	10 years.
Do	......do	3995	Apr. 19, 1924	Do.
Do	......do	5953	Nov. 23, 1932	Do.
Do	Temecula	3699	June 27, 1922	Do.
Do	......do	5768	Dec. 30, 1931	Do.
Do	Torres-Martinez	7009	Apr. 10, 1935	Do.
Idaho	Nez Perce	3250	Mar. 24, 1920	Do.
Idaho	Nez Perce	4694	July 22, 1927	10 years.
Do	......do	5305	Mar. 18, 1930	Do.
Kansas and Nebraska	*Iowa	2966	Sept. 23, 1918	Do.
Do	......do	5023	Jan. 10, 1929	Do.
Do	*Sac and Fox	2607	May 4, 1917	Do.
Do	......do	4571	Jan. 24, 1927	Do.
Do	......do	5768	Dec. 30, 1931	Do.

State	Reservation	E. O. No.	Date	Period of extension
Do	Kickapoo	3301	July 3, 1920	1 year.
Do	.....do	3447	May 2, 1921	10 years.
Do	.....do	5415	Aug. 4, 1930	Do.
Do	.....do	5626	May 18, 1931	Do.
Do	*Potawatomi	2747	Nov. 2, 1917	Do.
Do	.....do	2927	July 30, 1918	Do.
Do	.....do	3312	July 21, 1920	Do.
Do	.....do	4688	July 11, 1927	Do.
Do	.....do	4858	Apr. 16, 1928	Do.
Do	.....do	5299	Mar. 10, 1930	Do.
Do	.....do	5356	May 28, 1930	Do.
Do	.....do	5556	Feb. 11, 1931	Do.
Minnesota	*Fond du Lac	3445	Apr. 30, 1921	Do.
Do	.....do	5575	Mar. 12, 1931	Do.
Do	*Grand Portage	3613	Jan. 12, 1922	Do.
Do	.....do	5768	Dec. 30, 1931	Do.
Do	*Winnibigoshish	3614	Jan. 12, 1922	Do.
Do	.....do	5466	Oct. 22, 1930	Do.
Do	.....do	5768	Dec. 30, 1931	Do.
Do	*Deer Creek	4154	Feb. 10, 1925	Do.
Do	*Bois Fort	4233	May 26, 1925	Do.
Do	*Leech Lake, Cass Lake, and White Oak Point.	4298	Aug. 29, 1925	Do.
Do	.....do	5466	Oct. 22, 1930	Do.
Do	*White Earth	4642	May 5, 1927	Do.
Do	.....do	5768	Dec. 30, 1931	Do.
Do	.....do	5953	Nov. 23, 1932	Do.
Do	*Red Lake	5383	June 26, 1930	Do.
Montana	Crow	5301	Mar. 12, 1930	Do.
Do	.....do	5768	Dec. 30, 1931	Do.
Do	.....do	7001	Apr. 5, 1935	Do.
Do	.....do		Act of April 1940 (54 Stat. 106)	To May 23, 1940.
Do	*Flathead	5953	Nov. 23, 1932	Do.
Nebraska	*Omaha		July 3, 1909	Do.
Do	.....do	3111	July 10, 1919	Do.
Do	.....do	4145	Jan. 28, 1925	Do.
Do	.....do	4548	Dec. 4, 1926	Do.
Do	.....do	5148	July 3, 1929	Do.
Do	.....do	5253	Dec. 31, 1929	Do.
Do	*Ponca	2374	Apr. 29, 1916	Do.
Do	.....do	4407	Mar. 30, 1926	Do.
Do	*Santee		Dec. 12, 1910	Do.
Do	.....do	3348	Nov. 5, 1920	Do.
Do	.....do	3722	Aug. 12, 1922	Do.
Do	*Santee Sarah Jones allotment	4075	Sept. 17, 1924	Do.
Do	*Santee	5474	Oct. 31, 1930	Do.
Do	.....do	5768	Dec. 30, 1931	Do.
Do	.....do	5953	Nov. 23, 1932	Do.
Do	*Winnebago	2965	Sept. 20, 1918	Do.
Do	.....do	4548	Dec. 4, 1926	Do.
Do	.....do	4979	Oct. 16, 1928	Do.
Do	.....do	4994	Nov. 14, 1928	Do.
Do	*Sac and Fox, William Banks allotment.	3878	July 27, 1923	1 year.
Nevada	*Walker River	5730	Oct. 8, 1931	10 years.
North Dakota	Devils Lake	2804	Feb. 11, 1918	Do.
Do	.....do	3853	May 23, 1923	Do.
Do	.....do	4775	Nov. 30, 1927	Do.
Do	.....do	5303	Mar. 12, 1930	Do.
Do	.....do	5768	Dec. 30, 1931	Do.
Do	.....do	5953	Nov. 23, 1932	Do.
Do	*Fort Berthold	4293	Aug. 25, 1925	Do.
Do	*Standing Rock	5768	Dec. 30, 1931	Do.
Do	.....do	5953	Nov. 23, 1932	Do.
Oklahoma	Absentee Shawnee and Citizen Potawatomi.	2494	Nov. 24, 1916	Do.
Do	.....do	2512	Jan. 15, 1917	Do.
Do	.....do	4557	Dec. 23, 1926	Do.
Do	Cheyenne and Arapaho	2580	Apr. 4, 1917	Do.
Do	.....do	4587	Feb. 17, 1927	Do.
Do	Eastern Shawnee	2317	Feb. 15, 1916	Do.
Do	.....do	4384	Feb. 20, 1926	Do.
Do	.....do	5768	Dec. 30, 1931	Do.

State	Reservation	E. O. No.	Date	Period of extension
Do	Mexican Kickapoo	3047	Feb. 27, 1919	5 years.
Do	......do	4029	June 19, 1924	10 years.
Do	......do		Act of Feb. 17, 1933 (47 Stat. 819)	Do.
Do	Modoc	2453	Sept. 14, 1916	Do.
Do	......do	4470	July 1, 1926	Do.
Do	Ottawa, Seneca and Wyandotte	2591	Apr. 11, 1917	Do.
Do	......do	4588	Feb. 17, 1927	Do.
Do	Pawnee	2816	Mar. 2, 1918	Do.
Do	......do	4898	May 29, 1928	Do.
Do	Ponca	3327	Sept. 19, 1920	1 year.
Do	......do	3363	Dec. 1, 1920	25 years.
Do	......do	5539	Jan. 23, 1931	10 years.
Do	Sac and Fox, and Iowa		Mar. 27, 1896	Do.
Do	......do		July 23, 1906	Do.
Do	......do		Aug. 28, 1906	Do.
Do	......do	2432	Aug. 1, 1916	Do.
Do	......do	4435	Apr. 29, 1926	Do.
Do	Tonkawa	2866	May 25, 1918	Do.
Do	Tonkawa (Oakland)	4816	Feb. 25, 1928	Do.
Do	Kaw		Act of March 1923 (42 Stat. 1561)	25 years.
Do	......do		Act of May 27, 1924 (43 Stat. 176)	20 years.
Do	Otoe and Missouri	4281	Aug. 11, 1925	10 years.
Do	......do	5728	Sept. 29, 1931	Do.
Do	......do	5768	Dec. 30, 1931	Do.
Do	Kiowa, Comanche, Apache, and Wichita.	4398	Mar. 18, 1926	Do.
Do	......do	5953	Nov. 23, 1932	Do.
Do	......do	5955	Nov. 30, 1932 (Gertrude Lamb)	Do.
Do	Seneca	5306	Mar. 18, 1930	Do.
Do	Quapaw		Act of Mar. 3, 1921 (41 Stat. 1248) as amended Nov. 18, 1921 (42 Stat. 1570).	25 years.
Do	......do		As supplemented or amended by the act of July 27, 1939 (53 Stat. 1127).	Do.
Oregon	*Grande Ronde	2376	Apr. 29, 1916	10 years.
Do	......do	4408	Mar. 30, 1926	Do.
Do	Siletz	3110	July 10, 1919	Do.
Do	Siletz (cont.)	5087	Apr. 1, 1929	Do.
Do	*Warm Springs	3586	Dec. 7, 1921	Do.
Do	......do	5734	Oct. 17, 1931	Do.
Do	Umatilla	4024	June 10, 1924	Do.
Do	......do	5516	Dec. 17, 1930	Do.
Do	Klamath	6961	Feb. 4, 1935	Do.
Do	......do		Act of Dec. 24, 1942 (56 Stat. 1081)	25 years.
South Dakota	Crow Creek	3362	Nov. 30, 1920	Do.
Do	......do	5768	Dec. 30, 1931	10 years.
Do	......do	6968	Feb. 9, 1935	Do.
Do	*Rosebud	4417	Apr. 14, 1926	Do.
Do	......do	5028	Jan. 16, 1929	Do.
Do	......do	5302	Mar. 12, 1930	Do.
Do	......do	5768	Dec. 30, 1931	Do.
Do	Sisseton and Wahpeton	1916	Apr. 16, 1914	Do.
Do	......do	3994	Apr. 19, 1924	15 years.
Do	*Yankton Sioux	2363	Apr. 20, 1916	10 years.
Do	......do	4406	Mar. 30, 1926	Do.
South Dakota	Crow Creek	5173	Aug. 9, 1929	10 years.
Do	*Lower Brule	4981	Oct. 20, 1923	Do.
Do	*Pine Ridge	5557	Feb. 13, 1931	Do.
Do	......do	5768	Dec. 30, 1931	Do.
Do	......do	5953	Nov. 23, 1932	Do.
Do	*Cheyenne River	5546	Jan. 31, 1931	Do.
Do	......do	5768	Dec. 30, 1931	Do.
Utah	*Uncompahgre, Uintah and White River Bands of Utes.	5357	May 29, 1930	Do.
Washington	Chief Moses Band	2109	Dec. 23, 1914	Do.
Do	......do	4382	Feb. 10, 1926	10 years from Mar. 8, 1926.
Do	Colville	4157	Feb. 17, 1925	10 years.
Do	......do	6962	Feb. 4, 1935	Do.
Do	*Quinaielt	5768	Dec. 30, 1931	Do.
Do	Spokane	6939	Jan. 7, 1935	10 years.
Do	Yakima	3630	Feb. 3, 1922	Do.

State	Reservation	E. O. No.	Date	Period of extension
Do	......do	4168	Mar. 11, 1925	Do.
Do	......do	5746	Nov. 10, 1931	Do.
Do	......do	7036	May 8, 1935	Do.
Do	......do		Act of May 27, 1937 (50 Stat. 210)	To July 9, 1942.
Wisconsin	*Oneida	2623	May 19, 1917	1 year.
Do	......do	2856	May 4, 1918	9 years.
Do	......do	4600	Mar. 1, 1927	10 years.
Wyoming	Wind River	5768	Dec. 30, 1931	Do.
Do	......do	5953	Nov. 23, 1932	Do.

Pursuant to act of June 21, 1906 (34 Stat. 325) extending trust or other period of restriction contained in patents issued to Indians for land on the public domain, the following orders have been promulgated:

E. O. No.	Date	Period of extension
2133	Feb. 3, 1915	1 year.
2326	Feb. 23, 1916	Do.
2505	Jan. 3, 1917	Do.
2778	Dec. 31, 1917	Do.
3024	Jan. 11, 1919	Do.
3204	Dec. 23, 1919	Do.
3365	Dec. 7, 1920	25 years.

No further separate orders covering extension of trust periods on public domain allotments were issued subsequent to Executive Order 3365 of December 7, 1920. The trust or other periods of restriction contained in patents issued to Indians for land on the public domain have thereafter been extended by the terms of the general Executive orders.

General Orders

E. O. No.	Date	Period of extension
6498	Dec. 15, 1933	10 years.
6926	Dec. 20, 1934 (Oklahoma only)	Do.
7206	Oct. 14, 1935 (Oklahoma only)	Do.
7464	Sept. 30, 1936	25 years.
7716	Sept. 29, 1937	Do.
7984	Oct. 7, 1938	25 years.
8276	Oct. 28, 1939	Do.
8580	Oct. 29, 1940	Do.
8965	Dec. 10, 1941	Do.
9272	Nov. 17, 1942	Do.
9398	Nov. 25, 1943	Do.
9500	Nov. 14, 1944	Do.
9659	Nov. 21, 1945	Do.
9811	Dec. 17, 1946	Do.
9920	Jan. 8, 1948, effective Jan. 1, 1948	Do.
10027	Jan. 6, 1949	Do.
10091	Dec. 11, 1949	Do.
10191	Dec. 13, 1950	Do.

Beginning with Executive Order 6498, issued December 15, 1933, regardless of the location of the allotments, all trust or restrictive periods on allotments expiring on a given date have been extended by one general Executive order issued annually.

General Orders

Order	Date	Per. of exten.	FR citation
Sec. Int.	Dec. 29, 1951	1 year	17 FR 799.
Do	Dec. 29, 1952	...do	18 FR 106.
Do	Dec. 28, 1953	...do	18 FR 8897.
Do	Dec. 17, 1954	...do	19 FR 8658.
Do	Nov. 17, 1955	...do	20 FR 8519.
Do	Dec. 6, 1956	...do	21 FR 9644.
Do	Jan. 7, 1958	...do	23 FR 112.
Do	Jan. 7, 1959	5 yrs	24 FR 127.
Do	Dec. 8, 1959	...do	24 FR 9847.
Do	Dec. 24, 1960	...do	25 FR 13688.
Do	Dec. 28, 1961	...do	26 FR 12569.
Sec. Int.	Jan. 4, 1963	...do	28 FR 122.
Do	Oct. 31, 1963	...do	28 FR 11630.
Do	Oct. 9, 1968	...do	33 FR 15067.
Dep. Ass	Dec. 14, 1973	...do	38 FR 33463.
Sec. Int	Dec. 14, 1978	...do	43 FR 58369.
Do	July 27, 1983	...do	48 FR 34026
Sec. Int	Aug. 15, 1988	5 yrs.	53 FR 30674.

NOTE: Executive orders and orders of the Secretary of the Interior (17 FR 799, Jan. 26, 1952; 18 FR 106, Jan. 6, 1953; 18 FR 8897, Dec. 31, 1953; 19 FR 8658, Dec. 17, 1954; 20 FR 8519, Nov. 11, 1955; 21 FR 9644, Dec. 6, 1956; 23 FR 112, Jan. 7, 1958; 24 FR 127, Jan. 7, 1959; 24 FR 9847, Dec. 8, 1959; 25 FR 13688, Dec. 24, 1960; 26 FR 12569, Dec. 28, 1961; 28 FR 122, Jan. 4, 1963; 28 FR 11630, Oct. 31, 1963; 33 FR 15067, Oct. 9, 1968; 38 FR 34463, Dec. 14, 1973; 43 FR 58369, Dec. 14, 1978; 48 FR 34026, July 27, 1983); 53 FR 30674, Aug. 15, 1988, extended the trust periods on Indian lands expiring during the calendar years of 1949, 1950, 1951, 1952, 1953, 1954, 1955, 1956, 1957, 1958, 1959, 1960, 1961, 1962, 1963, 1964–1968, 1969–1973, 1974–1978, 1979–1983, 1984–1988, 1989–1993 respectively.

FINDING AIDS

A list of CFR titles, subtitles, chapters, subchapters and parts and an alphabetical list of agencies publishing in the CFR are included in the CFR Index and Finding Aids volume to the Code of Federal Regulations which is published separately and revised annually.

Table of CFR Titles and Chapters

(Revised as of April 1, 2019)

Title 1—General Provisions

Title 2—Grants and Agreements

Title 2—Grants and Agreements—Continued

Chap.	
XXVII	Small Business Administration (Parts 2700—2799)
XXVIII	Department of Justice (Parts 2800—2899)
XXIX	Department of Labor (Parts 2900—2999)
XXX	Department of Homeland Security (Parts 3000—3099)
XXXI	Institute of Museum and Library Services (Parts 3100—3199)
XXXII	National Endowment for the Arts (Parts 3200—3299)
XXXIII	National Endowment for the Humanities (Parts 3300—3399)
XXXIV	Department of Education (Parts 3400—3499)
XXXV	Export-Import Bank of the United States (Parts 3500—3599)
XXXVI	Office of National Drug Control Policy, Executive Office of the President (Parts 3600—3699)
XXXVII	Peace Corps (Parts 3700—3799)
LVIII	Election Assistance Commission (Parts 5800—5899)
LIX	Gulf Coast Ecosystem Restoration Council (Parts 5900—5999)

Title 3—The President

I	Executive Office of the President (Parts 100—199)

Title 4—Accounts

I	Government Accountability Office (Parts 1—199)

Title 5—Administrative Personnel

I	Office of Personnel Management (Parts 1—1199)
II	Merit Systems Protection Board (Parts 1200—1299)
III	Office of Management and Budget (Parts 1300—1399)
IV	Office of Personnel Management and Office of the Director of National Intelligence (Parts 1400—1499)
V	The International Organizations Employees Loyalty Board (Parts 1500—1599)
VI	Federal Retirement Thrift Investment Board (Parts 1600—1699)
VIII	Office of Special Counsel (Parts 1800—1899)
IX	Appalachian Regional Commission (Parts 1900—1999)
XI	Armed Forces Retirement Home (Parts 2100—2199)
XIV	Federal Labor Relations Authority, General Counsel of the Federal Labor Relations Authority and Federal Service Impasses Panel (Parts 2400—2499)
XVI	Office of Government Ethics (Parts 2600—2699)
XXI	Department of the Treasury (Parts 3100—3199)
XXII	Federal Deposit Insurance Corporation (Parts 3200—3299)
XXIII	Department of Energy (Parts 3300—3399)
XXIV	Federal Energy Regulatory Commission (Parts 3400—3499)
XXV	Department of the Interior (Parts 3500—3599)
XXVI	Department of Defense (Parts 3600—3699)

Title 5—Administrative Personnel—Continued

Chap.	
LXXIV	Federal Mine Safety and Health Review Commission (Parts 8400—8499)
LXXVI	Federal Retirement Thrift Investment Board (Parts 8600—8699)
LXXVII	Office of Management and Budget (Parts 8700—8799)
LXXX	Federal Housing Finance Agency (Parts 9000—9099)
LXXXIII	Special Inspector General for Afghanistan Reconstruction (Parts 9300—9399)
LXXXIV	Bureau of Consumer Financial Protection (Parts 9400—9499)
LXXXVI	National Credit Union Administration (Parts 9600—9699)
XCVII	Department of Homeland Security Human Resources Management System (Department of Homeland Security—Office of Personnel Management) (Parts 9700—9799)
XCVIII	Council of the Inspectors General on Integrity and Efficiency (Parts 9800—9899)
XCIX	Military Compensation and Retirement Modernization Commission (Parts 9900—9999)
C	National Council on Disability (Parts 10000—10049)
CI	National Mediation Board (Part 10101)

Title 6—Domestic Security

I	Department of Homeland Security, Office of the Secretary (Parts 1—199)
X	Privacy and Civil Liberties Oversight Board (Parts 1000—1099)

Title 7—Agriculture

	SUBTITLE A—OFFICE OF THE SECRETARY OF AGRICULTURE (PARTS 0—26)
	SUBTITLE B—REGULATIONS OF THE DEPARTMENT OF AGRICULTURE
I	Agricultural Marketing Service (Standards, Inspections, Marketing Practices), Department of Agriculture (Parts 27—209)
II	Food and Nutrition Service, Department of Agriculture (Parts 210—299)
III	Animal and Plant Health Inspection Service, Department of Agriculture (Parts 300—399)
IV	Federal Crop Insurance Corporation, Department of Agriculture (Parts 400—499)
V	Agricultural Research Service, Department of Agriculture (Parts 500—599)
VI	Natural Resources Conservation Service, Department of Agriculture (Parts 600—699)
VII	Farm Service Agency, Department of Agriculture (Parts 700—799)
VIII	Grain Inspection, Packers and Stockyards Administration (Federal Grain Inspection Service), Department of Agriculture (Parts 800—899)

Title 8—Aliens and Nationality

Chap.

I Department of Homeland Security (Immigration and Naturalization) (Parts 1—499)

V Executive Office for Immigration Review, Department of Justice (Parts 1000—1399)

Title 9—Animals and Animal Products

I Animal and Plant Health Inspection Service, Department of Agriculture (Parts 1—199)

II Grain Inspection, Packers and Stockyards Administration (Packers and Stockyards Programs), Department of Agriculture (Parts 200—299)

III Food Safety and Inspection Service, Department of Agriculture (Parts 300—599)

Title 10—Energy

I Nuclear Regulatory Commission (Parts 0—199)

II Department of Energy (Parts 200—699)

III Department of Energy (Parts 700—999)

X Department of Energy (General Provisions) (Parts 1000—1099)

XIII Nuclear Waste Technical Review Board (Parts 1300—1399)

XVII Defense Nuclear Facilities Safety Board (Parts 1700—1799)

XVIII Northeast Interstate Low-Level Radioactive Waste Commission (Parts 1800—1899)

Title 11—Federal Elections

I Federal Election Commission (Parts 1—9099)

II Election Assistance Commission (Parts 9400—9499)

Title 12—Banks and Banking

I Comptroller of the Currency, Department of the Treasury (Parts 1—199)

II Federal Reserve System (Parts 200—299)

III Federal Deposit Insurance Corporation (Parts 300—399)

IV Export-Import Bank of the United States (Parts 400—499)

V (Parts 500—599) [Reserved]

VI Farm Credit Administration (Parts 600—699)

VII National Credit Union Administration (Parts 700—799)

VIII Federal Financing Bank (Parts 800—899)

IX Federal Housing Finance Board (Parts 900—999)

X Bureau of Consumer Financial Protection (Parts 1000—1099)

XI Federal Financial Institutions Examination Council (Parts 1100—1199)

XII Federal Housing Finance Agency (Parts 1200—1299)

XIII Financial Stability Oversight Council (Parts 1300—1399)

Title 12—Banks and Banking—Continued

Title 13—Business Credit and Assistance

Title 14—Aeronautics and Space

Title 15—Commerce and Foreign Trade

Title 16—Commercial Practices

Title 17—Commodity and Securities Exchanges

Title 18—Conservation of Power and Water Resources

Title 19—Customs Duties

Title 20—Employees' Benefits

Title 20—Employees' Benefits—Continued

Chap.

Chap.	
IV	Employees' Compensation Appeals Board, Department of Labor (Parts 500—599)
V	Employment and Training Administration, Department of Labor (Parts 600—699)
VI	Office of Workers' Compensation Programs, Department of Labor (Parts 700—799)
VII	Benefits Review Board, Department of Labor (Parts 800—899)
VIII	Joint Board for the Enrollment of Actuaries (Parts 900—999)
IX	Office of the Assistant Secretary for Veterans' Employment and Training Service, Department of Labor (Parts 1000—1099)

Title 21—Food and Drugs

I	Food and Drug Administration, Department of Health and Human Services (Parts 1—1299)
II	Drug Enforcement Administration, Department of Justice (Parts 1300—1399)
III	Office of National Drug Control Policy (Parts 1400—1499)

Title 22—Foreign Relations

I	Department of State (Parts 1—199)
II	Agency for International Development (Parts 200—299)
III	Peace Corps (Parts 300—399)
IV	International Joint Commission, United States and Canada (Parts 400—499)
V	Broadcasting Board of Governors (Parts 500—599)
VII	Overseas Private Investment Corporation (Parts 700—799)
IX	Foreign Service Grievance Board (Parts 900—999)
X	Inter-American Foundation (Parts 1000—1099)
XI	International Boundary and Water Commission, United States and Mexico, United States Section (Parts 1100—1199)
XII	United States International Development Cooperation Agency (Parts 1200—1299)
XIII	Millennium Challenge Corporation (Parts 1300—1399)
XIV	Foreign Service Labor Relations Board; Federal Labor Relations Authority; General Counsel of the Federal Labor Relations Authority; and the Foreign Service Impasse Disputes Panel (Parts 1400—1499)
XV	African Development Foundation (Parts 1500—1599)
XVI	Japan-United States Friendship Commission (Parts 1600—1699)
XVII	United States Institute of Peace (Parts 1700—1799)

Title 23—Highways

I	Federal Highway Administration, Department of Transportation (Parts 1—999)

Title 23—Highways—Continued

Chap.

II National Highway Traffic Safety Administration and Federal Highway Administration, Department of Transportation (Parts 1200—1299)

III National Highway Traffic Safety Administration, Department of Transportation (Parts 1300—1399)

Title 24—Housing and Urban Development

SUBTITLE A—OFFICE OF THE SECRETARY, DEPARTMENT OF HOUSING AND URBAN DEVELOPMENT (PARTS 0—99)

SUBTITLE B—REGULATIONS RELATING TO HOUSING AND URBAN DEVELOPMENT

I Office of Assistant Secretary for Equal Opportunity, Department of Housing and Urban Development (Parts 100—199)

II Office of Assistant Secretary for Housing-Federal Housing Commissioner, Department of Housing and Urban Development (Parts 200—299)

III Government National Mortgage Association, Department of Housing and Urban Development (Parts 300—399)

IV Office of Housing and Office of Multifamily Housing Assistance Restructuring, Department of Housing and Urban Development (Parts 400—499)

V Office of Assistant Secretary for Community Planning and Development, Department of Housing and Urban Development (Parts 500—599)

VI Office of Assistant Secretary for Community Planning and Development, Department of Housing and Urban Development (Parts 600—699) [Reserved]

VII Office of the Secretary, Department of Housing and Urban Development (Housing Assistance Programs and Public and Indian Housing Programs) (Parts 700—799)

VIII Office of the Assistant Secretary for Housing—Federal Housing Commissioner, Department of Housing and Urban Development (Section 8 Housing Assistance Programs, Section 202 Direct Loan Program, Section 202 Supportive Housing for the Elderly Program and Section 811 Supportive Housing for Persons With Disabilities Program) (Parts 800—899)

IX Office of Assistant Secretary for Public and Indian Housing, Department of Housing and Urban Development (Parts 900—1699)

XII Office of Inspector General, Department of Housing and Urban Development (Parts 2000—2099)

XV Emergency Mortgage Insurance and Loan Programs, Department of Housing and Urban Development (Parts 2700—2799) [Reserved]

XX Office of Assistant Secretary for Housing—Federal Housing Commissioner, Department of Housing and Urban Development (Parts 3200—3899)

XXIV Board of Directors of the HOPE for Homeowners Program (Parts 4000—4099) [Reserved]

XXV Neighborhood Reinvestment Corporation (Parts 4100—4199)

Title 25—Indians

Chap.

I Bureau of Indian Affairs, Department of the Interior (Parts 1—299)

II Indian Arts and Crafts Board, Department of the Interior (Parts 300—399)

III National Indian Gaming Commission, Department of the Interior (Parts 500—599)

IV Office of Navajo and Hopi Indian Relocation (Parts 700—899)

V Bureau of Indian Affairs, Department of the Interior, and Indian Health Service, Department of Health and Human Services (Part 900—999)

VI Office of the Assistant Secretary, Indian Affairs, Department of the Interior (Parts 1000—1199)

VII Office of the Special Trustee for American Indians, Department of the Interior (Parts 1200—1299)

Title 26—Internal Revenue

I Internal Revenue Service, Department of the Treasury (Parts 1—End)

Title 27—Alcohol, Tobacco Products and Firearms

I Alcohol and Tobacco Tax and Trade Bureau, Department of the Treasury (Parts 1—399)

II Bureau of Alcohol, Tobacco, Firearms, and Explosives, Department of Justice (Parts 400—699)

Title 28—Judicial Administration

I Department of Justice (Parts 0—299)

III Federal Prison Industries, Inc., Department of Justice (Parts 300—399)

V Bureau of Prisons, Department of Justice (Parts 500—599)

VI Offices of Independent Counsel, Department of Justice (Parts 600—699)

VII Office of Independent Counsel (Parts 700—799)

VIII Court Services and Offender Supervision Agency for the District of Columbia (Parts 800—899)

IX National Crime Prevention and Privacy Compact Council (Parts 900—999)

XI Department of Justice and Department of State (Parts 1100—1199)

Title 29—Labor

SUBTITLE A—OFFICE OF THE SECRETARY OF LABOR (PARTS 0—99)

SUBTITLE B—REGULATIONS RELATING TO LABOR

I National Labor Relations Board (Parts 100—199)

Title 29—Labor—Continued

Title 30—Mineral Resources

Title 31—Money and Finance: Treasury

Title 31—Money and Finance: Treasury—Continued

Chap.

VIII Office of Investment Security, Department of the Treasury (Parts 800—899)

IX Federal Claims Collection Standards (Department of the Treasury—Department of Justice) (Parts 900—999)

X Financial Crimes Enforcement Network, Department of the Treasury (Parts 1000—1099)

Title 32—National Defense

SUBTITLE A—DEPARTMENT OF DEFENSE

I Office of the Secretary of Defense (Parts 1—399)

V Department of the Army (Parts 400—699)

VI Department of the Navy (Parts 700—799)

VII Department of the Air Force (Parts 800—1099)

SUBTITLE B—OTHER REGULATIONS RELATING TO NATIONAL DEFENSE

XII Defense Logistics Agency (Parts 1200—1299)

XVI Selective Service System (Parts 1600—1699)

XVII Office of the Director of National Intelligence (Parts 1700—1799)

XVIII National Counterintelligence Center (Parts 1800—1899)

XIX Central Intelligence Agency (Parts 1900—1999)

XX Information Security Oversight Office, National Archives and Records Administration (Parts 2000—2099)

XXI National Security Council (Parts 2100—2199)

XXIV Office of Science and Technology Policy (Parts 2400—2499)

XXVII Office for Micronesian Status Negotiations (Parts 2700—2799)

XXVIII Office of the Vice President of the United States (Parts 2800—2899)

Title 33—Navigation and Navigable Waters

I Coast Guard, Department of Homeland Security (Parts 1—199)

II Corps of Engineers, Department of the Army, Department of Defense (Parts 200—399)

IV Saint Lawrence Seaway Development Corporation, Department of Transportation (Parts 400—499)

Title 34—Education

SUBTITLE A—OFFICE OF THE SECRETARY, DEPARTMENT OF EDUCATION (PARTS 1—99)

SUBTITLE B—REGULATIONS OF THE OFFICES OF THE DEPARTMENT OF EDUCATION

I Office for Civil Rights, Department of Education (Parts 100—199)

II Office of Elementary and Secondary Education, Department of Education (Parts 200—299)

III Office of Special Education and Rehabilitative Services, Department of Education (Parts 300—399)

Title 34—Education—Continued

Chap.

IV Office of Career, Technical and Adult Education, Department of Education (Parts 400—499)

V Office of Bilingual Education and Minority Languages Affairs, Department of Education (Parts 500—599) [Reserved]

VI Office of Postsecondary Education, Department of Education (Parts 600—699)

VII Office of Educational Research and Improvement, Department of Education (Parts 700—799) [Reserved]

SUBTITLE C—REGULATIONS RELATING TO EDUCATION

XI (Parts 1100—1199) [Reserved]

XII National Council on Disability (Parts 1200—1299)

Title 35 [Reserved]

Title 36—Parks, Forests, and Public Property

I National Park Service, Department of the Interior (Parts 1—199)

II Forest Service, Department of Agriculture (Parts 200—299)

III Corps of Engineers, Department of the Army (Parts 300—399)

IV American Battle Monuments Commission (Parts 400—499)

V Smithsonian Institution (Parts 500—599)

VI [Reserved]

VII Library of Congress (Parts 700—799)

VIII Advisory Council on Historic Preservation (Parts 800—899)

IX Pennsylvania Avenue Development Corporation (Parts 900—999)

X Presidio Trust (Parts 1000—1099)

XI Architectural and Transportation Barriers Compliance Board (Parts 1100—1199)

XII National Archives and Records Administration (Parts 1200—1299)

XV Oklahoma City National Memorial Trust (Parts 1500—1599)

XVI Morris K. Udall Scholarship and Excellence in National Environmental Policy Foundation (Parts 1600—1699)

Title 37—Patents, Trademarks, and Copyrights

I United States Patent and Trademark Office, Department of Commerce (Parts 1—199)

II U.S. Copyright Office, Library of Congress (Parts 200—299)

III Copyright Royalty Board, Library of Congress (Parts 300—399)

IV National Institute of Standards and Technology, Department of Commerce (Parts 400—599)

Title 38—Pensions, Bonuses, and Veterans' Relief

I Department of Veterans Affairs (Parts 0—199)

II Armed Forces Retirement Home (Parts 200—299)

Title 39—Postal Service

Chap.	
I	United States Postal Service (Parts 1—999)
III	Postal Regulatory Commission (Parts 3000—3099)

Title 40—Protection of Environment

I	Environmental Protection Agency (Parts 1—1099)
IV	Environmental Protection Agency and Department of Justice (Parts 1400—1499)
V	Council on Environmental Quality (Parts 1500—1599)
VI	Chemical Safety and Hazard Investigation Board (Parts 1600—1699)
VII	Environmental Protection Agency and Department of Defense; Uniform National Discharge Standards for Vessels of the Armed Forces (Parts 1700—1799)
VIII	Gulf Coast Ecosystem Restoration Council (Parts 1800—1899)

Title 41—Public Contracts and Property Management

	SUBTITLE A—FEDERAL PROCUREMENT REGULATIONS SYSTEM [NOTE]
	SUBTITLE B—OTHER PROVISIONS RELATING TO PUBLIC CONTRACTS
50	Public Contracts, Department of Labor (Parts 50-1—50-999)
51	Committee for Purchase From People Who Are Blind or Severely Disabled (Parts 51-1—51-99)
60	Office of Federal Contract Compliance Programs, Equal Employment Opportunity, Department of Labor (Parts 60-1—60-999)
61	Office of the Assistant Secretary for Veterans' Employment and Training Service, Department of Labor (Parts 61-1—61-999)
62—100	[Reserved]
	SUBTITLE C—FEDERAL PROPERTY MANAGEMENT REGULATIONS SYSTEM
101	Federal Property Management Regulations (Parts 101-1—101-99)
102	Federal Management Regulation (Parts 102-1—102-299)
103—104	[Reserved]
105	General Services Administration (Parts 105-1—105-999)
109	Department of Energy Property Management Regulations (Parts 109-1—109-99)
114	Department of the Interior (Parts 114-1—114-99)
115	Environmental Protection Agency (Parts 115-1—115-99)
128	Department of Justice (Parts 128-1—128-99)
129—200	[Reserved]
	SUBTITLE D—OTHER PROVISIONS RELATING TO PROPERTY MANAGEMENT [RESERVED]
	SUBTITLE E—FEDERAL INFORMATION RESOURCES MANAGEMENT REGULATIONS SYSTEM [RESERVED]
	SUBTITLE F—FEDERAL TRAVEL REGULATION SYSTEM
300	General (Parts 300-1—300-99)
301	Temporary Duty (TDY) Travel Allowances (Parts 301-1—301-99)

Title 41—Public Contracts and Property Management—Continued

Chap.

302 Relocation Allowances (Parts 302-1—302-99)

303 Payment of Expenses Connected with the Death of Certain Employees (Part 303-1—303-99)

304 Payment of Travel Expenses from a Non-Federal Source (Parts 304-1—304-99)

Title 42—Public Health

I Public Health Service, Department of Health and Human Services (Parts 1—199)

II—III [Reserved]

IV Centers for Medicare & Medicaid Services, Department of Health and Human Services (Parts 400—699)

V Office of Inspector General-Health Care, Department of Health and Human Services (Parts 1000—1099)

Title 43—Public Lands: Interior

SUBTITLE A—OFFICE OF THE SECRETARY OF THE INTERIOR (PARTS 1—199)

SUBTITLE B—REGULATIONS RELATING TO PUBLIC LANDS

I Bureau of Reclamation, Department of the Interior (Parts 400—999)

II Bureau of Land Management, Department of the Interior (Parts 1000—9999)

III Utah Reclamation Mitigation and Conservation Commission (Parts 10000—10099)

Title 44—Emergency Management and Assistance

I Federal Emergency Management Agency, Department of Homeland Security (Parts 0—399)

IV Department of Commerce and Department of Transportation (Parts 400—499)

Title 45—Public Welfare

SUBTITLE A—DEPARTMENT OF HEALTH AND HUMAN SERVICES (PARTS 1—199)

SUBTITLE B—REGULATIONS RELATING TO PUBLIC WELFARE

II Office of Family Assistance (Assistance Programs), Administration for Children and Families, Department of Health and Human Services (Parts 200—299)

III Office of Child Support Enforcement (Child Support Enforcement Program), Administration for Children and Families, Department of Health and Human Services (Parts 300—399)

IV Office of Refugee Resettlement, Administration for Children and Families, Department of Health and Human Services (Parts 400—499)

Chap.

Chap.	
V	Foreign Claims Settlement Commission of the United States, Department of Justice (Parts 500—599)
VI	National Science Foundation (Parts 600—699)
VII	Commission on Civil Rights (Parts 700—799)
VIII	Office of Personnel Management (Parts 800—899)
IX	Denali Commission (Parts 900—999)
X	Office of Community Services, Administration for Children and Families, Department of Health and Human Services (Parts 1000—1099)
XI	National Foundation on the Arts and the Humanities (Parts 1100—1199)
XII	Corporation for National and Community Service (Parts 1200—1299)
XIII	Administration for Children and Families, Department of Health and Human Services (Parts 1300—1399)
XVI	Legal Services Corporation (Parts 1600—1699)
XVII	National Commission on Libraries and Information Science (Parts 1700—1799)
XVIII	Harry S. Truman Scholarship Foundation (Parts 1800—1899)
XXI	Commission of Fine Arts (Parts 2100—2199)
XXIII	Arctic Research Commission (Parts 2300—2399)
XXIV	James Madison Memorial Fellowship Foundation (Parts 2400—2499)
XXV	Corporation for National and Community Service (Parts 2500—2599)

Title 46—Shipping

I	Coast Guard, Department of Homeland Security (Parts 1—199)
II	Maritime Administration, Department of Transportation (Parts 200—399)
III	Coast Guard (Great Lakes Pilotage), Department of Homeland Security (Parts 400—499)
IV	Federal Maritime Commission (Parts 500—599)

Title 47—Telecommunication

I	Federal Communications Commission (Parts 0—199)
II	Office of Science and Technology Policy and National Security Council (Parts 200—299)
III	National Telecommunications and Information Administration, Department of Commerce (Parts 300—399)
IV	National Telecommunications and Information Administration, Department of Commerce, and National Highway Traffic Safety Administration, Department of Transportation (Parts 400—499)
V	The First Responder Network Authority (Parts 500—599)

Title 48—Federal Acquisition Regulations System

Chap.

1 Federal Acquisition Regulation (Parts 1—99)

2 Defense Acquisition Regulations System, Department of Defense (Parts 200—299)

3 Department of Health and Human Services (Parts 300—399)

4 Department of Agriculture (Parts 400—499)

5 General Services Administration (Parts 500—599)

6 Department of State (Parts 600—699)

7 Agency for International Development (Parts 700—799)

8 Department of Veterans Affairs (Parts 800—899)

9 Department of Energy (Parts 900—999)

10 Department of the Treasury (Parts 1000—1099)

12 Department of Transportation (Parts 1200—1299)

13 Department of Commerce (Parts 1300—1399)

14 Department of the Interior (Parts 1400—1499)

15 Environmental Protection Agency (Parts 1500—1599)

16 Office of Personnel Management, Federal Employees Health Benefits Acquisition Regulation (Parts 1600—1699)

17 Office of Personnel Management (Parts 1700—1799)

18 National Aeronautics and Space Administration (Parts 1800—1899)

19 Broadcasting Board of Governors (Parts 1900—1999)

20 Nuclear Regulatory Commission (Parts 2000—2099)

21 Office of Personnel Management, Federal Employees Group Life Insurance Federal Acquisition Regulation (Parts 2100—2199)

23 Social Security Administration (Parts 2300—2399)

24 Department of Housing and Urban Development (Parts 2400—2499)

25 National Science Foundation (Parts 2500—2599)

28 Department of Justice (Parts 2800—2899)

29 Department of Labor (Parts 2900—2999)

30 Department of Homeland Security, Homeland Security Acquisition Regulation (HSAR) (Parts 3000—3099)

34 Department of Education Acquisition Regulation (Parts 3400—3499)

51 Department of the Army Acquisition Regulations (Parts 5100—5199)

52 Department of the Navy Acquisition Regulations (Parts 5200—5299)

53 Department of the Air Force Federal Acquisition Regulation Supplement (Parts 5300—5399) [Reserved]

54 Defense Logistics Agency, Department of Defense (Parts 5400—5499)

57 African Development Foundation (Parts 5700—5799)

61 Civilian Board of Contract Appeals, General Services Administration (Parts 6100—6199)

99 Cost Accounting Standards Board, Office of Federal Procurement Policy, Office of Management and Budget (Parts 9900—9999)

Title 49—Transportation

Chap.

SUBTITLE A—OFFICE OF THE SECRETARY OF TRANSPORTATION (PARTS 1—99)

SUBTITLE B—OTHER REGULATIONS RELATING TO TRANSPORTATION

I Pipeline and Hazardous Materials Safety Administration, Department of Transportation (Parts 100—199)

II Federal Railroad Administration, Department of Transportation (Parts 200—299)

III Federal Motor Carrier Safety Administration, Department of Transportation (Parts 300—399)

IV Coast Guard, Department of Homeland Security (Parts 400—499)

V National Highway Traffic Safety Administration, Department of Transportation (Parts 500—599)

VI Federal Transit Administration, Department of Transportation (Parts 600—699)

VII National Railroad Passenger Corporation (AMTRAK) (Parts 700—799)

VIII National Transportation Safety Board (Parts 800—999)

X Surface Transportation Board (Parts 1000—1399)

XI Research and Innovative Technology Administration, Department of Transportation (Parts 1400—1499) [Reserved]

XII Transportation Security Administration, Department of Homeland Security (Parts 1500—1699)

Title 50—Wildlife and Fisheries

I United States Fish and Wildlife Service, Department of the Interior (Parts 1—199)

II National Marine Fisheries Service, National Oceanic and Atmospheric Administration, Department of Commerce (Parts 200—299)

III International Fishing and Related Activities (Parts 300—399)

IV Joint Regulations (United States Fish and Wildlife Service, Department of the Interior and National Marine Fisheries Service, National Oceanic and Atmospheric Administration, Department of Commerce); Endangered Species Committee Regulations (Parts 400—499)

V Marine Mammal Commission (Parts 500—599)

VI Fishery Conservation and Management, National Oceanic and Atmospheric Administration, Department of Commerce (Parts 600—699)

Alphabetical List of Agencies Appearing in the CFR

(Revised as of April 1, 2019)

Agency	CFR Title, Subtitle or Chapter
Administrative Conference of the United States	1, III
Advisory Council on Historic Preservation	36, VIII
Advocacy and Outreach, Office of	7, XXV
Afghanistan Reconstruction, Special Inspector General for	5, LXXXIII
African Development Foundation	22, XV
Federal Acquisition Regulation	48, 57
Agency for International Development	2, VII; 22, II
Federal Acquisition Regulation	48, 7
Agricultural Marketing Service	7, I, IX, X, XI
Agricultural Research Service	7, V
Agriculture, Department of	2, IV; 5, LXXIII
Advocacy and Outreach, Office of	7, XXV
Agricultural Marketing Service	7, I, IX, X, XI
Agricultural Research Service	7, V
Animal and Plant Health Inspection Service	7, III; 9, I
Chief Financial Officer, Office of	7, XXX
Commodity Credit Corporation	7, XIV
Economic Research Service	7, XXXVII
Energy Policy and New Uses, Office of	2, IX; 7, XXIX
Environmental Quality, Office of	7, XXXI
Farm Service Agency	7, VII, XVIII
Federal Acquisition Regulation	48, 4
Federal Crop Insurance Corporation	7, IV
Food and Nutrition Service	7, II
Food Safety and Inspection Service	9, III
Foreign Agricultural Service	7, XV
Forest Service	36, II
Grain Inspection, Packers and Stockyards Administration	7, VIII; 9, II
Information Resources Management, Office of	7, XXVII
Inspector General, Office of	7, XXVI
National Agricultural Library	7, XLI
National Agricultural Statistics Service	7, XXXVI
National Institute of Food and Agriculture	7, XXXIV
Natural Resources Conservation Service	7, VI
Operations, Office of	7, XXVIII
Procurement and Property Management, Office of	7, XXXII
Rural Business-Cooperative Service	7, XVIII, XLII
Rural Development Administration	7, XLII
Rural Housing Service	7, XVIII, XXXV
Rural Telephone Bank	7, XVI
Rural Utilities Service	7, XVII, XVIII, XLII
Secretary of Agriculture, Office of	7, Subtitle A
Transportation, Office of	7, XXXIII
World Agricultural Outlook Board	7, XXXVIII
Air Force, Department of	32, VII
Federal Acquisition Regulation Supplement	48, 53
Air Transportation Stabilization Board	14, VI
Alcohol and Tobacco Tax and Trade Bureau	27, I
Alcohol, Tobacco, Firearms, and Explosives, Bureau of	27, II
AMTRAK	49, VII
American Battle Monuments Commission	36, IV
American Indians, Office of the Special Trustee	25, VII
Animal and Plant Health Inspection Service	7, III; 9, I

Agency	CFR Title, Subtitle or Chapter
Appalachian Regional Commission	5, IX
Architectural and Transportation Barriers Compliance Board	36, XI
Arctic Research Commission	45, XXIII
Armed Forces Retirement Home	5, XI
Army, Department of	32, V
Engineers, Corps of	33, II; 36, III
Federal Acquisition Regulation	48, 51
Bilingual Education and Minority Languages Affairs, Office of	34, V
Blind or Severely Disabled, Committee for Purchase from People Who Are	41, 51
Broadcasting Board of Governors	22, V
Federal Acquisition Regulation	48, 19
Career, Technical, and Adult Education, Office of	34, IV
Census Bureau	15, I
Centers for Medicare & Medicaid Services	42, IV
Central Intelligence Agency	32, XIX
Chemical Safety and Hazardous Investigation Board	40, VI
Chief Financial Officer, Office of	7, XXX
Child Support Enforcement, Office of	45, III
Children and Families, Administration for	45, II, III, IV, X, XIII
Civil Rights, Commission on	5, LXVIII; 45, VII
Civil Rights, Office for	34, I
Council of the Inspectors General on Integrity and Efficiency	5, XCVIII
Court Services and Offender Supervision Agency for the District of Columbia	5, LXX
Coast Guard	33, I; 46, I; 49, IV
Coast Guard (Great Lakes Pilotage)	46, III
Commerce, Department of	2, XIII; 44, IV; 50, VI
Census Bureau	15, I
Economic Analysis, Bureau of	15, VIII
Economic Development Administration	13, III
Emergency Management and Assistance	44, IV
Federal Acquisition Regulation	48, 13
Foreign-Trade Zones Board	15, IV
Industry and Security, Bureau of	15, VII
International Trade Administration	15, III; 19, III
National Institute of Standards and Technology	15, II; 37, IV
National Marine Fisheries Service	50, II, IV
National Oceanic and Atmospheric Administration	15, IX; 50, II, III, IV, VI
National Technical Information Service	15, XI
National Telecommunications and Information Administration	15, XXIII; 47, III, IV
National Weather Service	15, IX
Patent and Trademark Office, United States	37, I
Secretary of Commerce, Office of	15, Subtitle A
Commercial Space Transportation	14, III
Commodity Credit Corporation	7, XIV
Commodity Futures Trading Commission	5, XLI; 17, I
Community Planning and Development, Office of Assistant Secretary for	24, V, VI
Community Services, Office of	45, X
Comptroller of the Currency	12, I
Construction Industry Collective Bargaining Commission	29, IX
Consumer Financial Protection Bureau	5, LXXXIV; 12, X
Consumer Product Safety Commission	5, LXXI; 16, II
Copyright Royalty Board	37, III
Corporation for National and Community Service	2, XXII; 45, XII, XXV
Cost Accounting Standards Board	48, 99
Council on Environmental Quality	40, V
Court Services and Offender Supervision Agency for the District of Columbia	5, LXX; 28, VIII
Customs and Border Protection	19, I
Defense Contract Audit Agency	32, I
Defense, Department of	2, XI; 5, XXVI; 32, Subtitle A; 40, VII
Advanced Research Projects Agency	32, I
Air Force Department	32, VII

Agency	CFR Title, Subtitle or Chapter
Presidential Documents	3
Science and Technology Policy, Office of	32, XXIV; 47, II
Trade Representative, Office of the United States	15, XX
Export-Import Bank of the United States	2, XXXV; 5, LII; 12, IV
Family Assistance, Office of	45, II
Farm Credit Administration	5, XXXI; 12, VI
Farm Credit System Insurance Corporation	5, XXX; 12, XIV
Farm Service Agency	7, VII, XVIII
Federal Acquisition Regulation	48, 1
Federal Aviation Administration	14, I
Commercial Space Transportation	14, III
Federal Claims Collection Standards	31, IX
Federal Communications Commission	5, XXIX; 47, I
Federal Contract Compliance Programs, Office of	41, 60
Federal Crop Insurance Corporation	7, IV
Federal Deposit Insurance Corporation	5, XXII; 12, III
Federal Election Commission	5, XXXVII; 11, I
Federal Emergency Management Agency	44, I
Federal Employees Group Life Insurance Federal Acquisition Regulation	48, 21
Federal Employees Health Benefits Acquisition Regulation	48, 16
Federal Energy Regulatory Commission	5, XXIV; 18, I
Federal Financial Institutions Examination Council	12, XI
Federal Financing Bank	12, VIII
Federal Highway Administration	23, I, II
Federal Home Loan Mortgage Corporation	1, IV
Federal Housing Enterprise Oversight Office	12, XVII
Federal Housing Finance Agency	5, LXXX; 12, XII
Federal Housing Finance Board	12, IX
Federal Labor Relations Authority	5, XIV, XLIX; 22, XIV
Federal Law Enforcement Training Center	31, VII
Federal Management Regulation	41, 102
Federal Maritime Commission	46, IV
Federal Mediation and Conciliation Service	29, XII
Federal Mine Safety and Health Review Commission	5, LXXIV; 29, XXVII
Federal Motor Carrier Safety Administration	49, III
Federal Prison Industries, Inc.	28, III
Federal Procurement Policy Office	48, 99
Federal Property Management Regulations	41, 101
Federal Railroad Administration	49, II
Federal Register, Administrative Committee of	1, I
Federal Register, Office of	1, II
Federal Reserve System	12, II
Board of Governors	5, LVIII
Federal Retirement Thrift Investment Board	5, VI, LXXVI
Federal Service Impasses Panel	5, XIV
Federal Trade Commission	5, XLVII; 16, I
Federal Transit Administration	49, VI
Federal Travel Regulation System	41, Subtitle F
Financial Crimes Enforcement Network	31, X
Financial Research Office	12, XVI
Financial Stability Oversight Council	12, XIII
Fine Arts, Commission of	45, XXI
Fiscal Service	31, II
Fish and Wildlife Service, United States	50, I, IV
Food and Drug Administration	21, I
Food and Nutrition Service	7, II
Food Safety and Inspection Service	9, III
Foreign Agricultural Service	7, XV
Foreign Assets Control, Office of	31, V
Foreign Claims Settlement Commission of the United States	45, V
Foreign Service Grievance Board	22, IX
Foreign Service Impasse Disputes Panel	22, XIV
Foreign Service Labor Relations Board	22, XIV
Foreign-Trade Zones Board	15, IV
Forest Service	36, II
General Services Administration	5, LVII; 41, 105

Agency	CFR Title, Subtitle or Chapter
Contract Appeals, Board of	48, 61
Federal Acquisition Regulation	48, 5
Federal Management Regulation	41, 102
Federal Property Management Regulations	41, 101
Federal Travel Regulation System	41, Subtitle F
General	41, 300
Payment From a Non-Federal Source for Travel Expenses	41, 304
Payment of Expenses Connected With the Death of Certain Employees	41, 303
Relocation Allowances	41, 302
Temporary Duty (TDY) Travel Allowances	41, 301
Geological Survey	30, IV
Government Accountability Office	4, I
Government Ethics, Office of	5, XVI
Government National Mortgage Association	24, III
Grain Inspection, Packers and Stockyards Administration	7, VIII; 9, II
Gulf Coast Ecosystem Restoration Council	2, LIX; 40, VIII
Harry S. Truman Scholarship Foundation	45, XVIII
Health and Human Services, Department of	2, III; 5, XLV; 45, Subtitle A
Centers for Medicare & Medicaid Services	42, IV
Child Support Enforcement, Office of	45, III
Children and Families, Administration for	45, II, III, IV, X, XIII
Community Services, Office of	45, X
Family Assistance, Office of	45, II
Federal Acquisition Regulation	48, 3
Food and Drug Administration	21, I
Indian Health Service	25, V
Inspector General (Health Care), Office of	42, V
Public Health Service	42, I
Refugee Resettlement, Office of	45, IV
Homeland Security, Department of	2, XXX; 5, XXXVI; 6, I; 8, I
Coast Guard	33, I; 46, I; 49, IV
Coast Guard (Great Lakes Pilotage)	46, III
Customs and Border Protection	19, I
Federal Emergency Management Agency	44, I
Human Resources Management and Labor Relations Systems	5, XCVII
Immigration and Customs Enforcement Bureau	19, IV
Transportation Security Administration	49, XII
HOPE for Homeowners Program, Board of Directors of	24, XXIV
Housing and Urban Development, Department of	2, XXIV; 5, LXV; 24, Subtitle B
Community Planning and Development, Office of Assistant Secretary for	24, V, VI
Equal Opportunity, Office of Assistant Secretary for	24, I
Federal Acquisition Regulation	48, 24
Federal Housing Enterprise Oversight, Office of	12, XVII
Government National Mortgage Association	24, III
Housing—Federal Housing Commissioner, Office of Assistant Secretary for	24, II, VIII, X, XX
Housing, Office of, and Multifamily Housing Assistance Restructuring, Office of	24, IV
Inspector General, Office of	24, XII
Public and Indian Housing, Office of Assistant Secretary for	24, IX
Secretary, Office of	24, Subtitle A, VII
Housing—Federal Housing Commissioner, Office of Assistant Secretary for	24, II, VIII, X, XX
Housing, Office of, and Multifamily Housing Assistance Restructuring, Office of	24, IV
Immigration and Customs Enforcement Bureau	19, IV
Immigration Review, Executive Office for	8, V
Independent Counsel, Office of	28, VII
Independent Counsel, Offices of	28, VI
Indian Affairs, Bureau of	25, I, V
Indian Affairs, Office of the Assistant Secretary	25, VI

Agency	CFR Title, Subtitle or Chapter
Indian Arts and Crafts Board	25, II
Indian Health Service	25, V
Industry and Security, Bureau of	15, VII
Information Resources Management, Office of	7, XXVII
Information Security Oversight Office, National Archives and Records Administration	32, XX
Inspector General	
Agriculture Department	7, XXVI
Health and Human Services Department	42, V
Housing and Urban Development Department	24, XII, XV
Institute of Peace, United States	22, XVII
Inter-American Foundation	5, LXIII; 22, X
Interior, Department of	2, XIV
American Indians, Office of the Special Trustee	25, VII
Endangered Species Committee	50, IV
Federal Acquisition Regulation	48, 14
Federal Property Management Regulations System	41, 114
Fish and Wildlife Service, United States	50, I, IV
Geological Survey	30, IV
Indian Affairs, Bureau of	25, I, V
Indian Affairs, Office of the Assistant Secretary	25, VI
Indian Arts and Crafts Board	25, II
Land Management, Bureau of	43, II
National Indian Gaming Commission	25, III
National Park Service	36, I
Natural Resource Revenue, Office of	30, XII
Ocean Energy Management, Bureau of	30, V
Reclamation, Bureau of	43, I
Safety and Enforcement Bureau, Bureau of	30, II
Secretary of the Interior, Office of	2, XIV; 43, Subtitle A
Surface Mining Reclamation and Enforcement, Office of	30, VII
Internal Revenue Service	26, I
International Boundary and Water Commission, United States and Mexico, United States Section	22, XI
International Development, United States Agency for	22, II
Federal Acquisition Regulation	48, 7
International Development Cooperation Agency, United States	22, XII
International Joint Commission, United States and Canada	22, IV
International Organizations Employees Loyalty Board	5, V
International Trade Administration	15, III; 19, III
International Trade Commission, United States	19, II
Interstate Commerce Commission	5, XL
Investment Security, Office of	31, VIII
James Madison Memorial Fellowship Foundation	45, XXIV
Japan–United States Friendship Commission	22, XVI
Joint Board for the Enrollment of Actuaries	20, VIII
Justice, Department of	2, XXVIII; 5, XXVIII; 28, I, XI; 40, IV
Alcohol, Tobacco, Firearms, and Explosives, Bureau of	27, II
Drug Enforcement Administration	21, II
Federal Acquisition Regulation	48, 28
Federal Claims Collection Standards	31, IX
Federal Prison Industries, Inc.	28, III
Foreign Claims Settlement Commission of the United States	45, V
Immigration Review, Executive Office for	8, V
Independent Counsel, Offices of	28, VI
Prisons, Bureau of	28, V
Property Management Regulations	41, 128
Labor, Department of	2, XXIX; 5, XLII
Employee Benefits Security Administration	29, XXV
Employees' Compensation Appeals Board	20, IV
Employment and Training Administration	20, V
Employment Standards Administration	20, VI
Federal Acquisition Regulation	48, 29
Federal Contract Compliance Programs, Office of	41, 60

Agency	CFR Title, Subtitle or Chapter
Federal Procurement Regulations System	41, 50
Labor-Management Standards, Office of	29, II, IV
Mine Safety and Health Administration	30, I
Occupational Safety and Health Administration	29, XVII
Public Contracts	41, 50
Secretary of Labor, Office of	29, Subtitle A
Veterans' Employment and Training Service, Office of the Assistant Secretary for	41, 61; 20, IX
Wage and Hour Division	29, V
Workers' Compensation Programs, Office of	20, I, VII
Labor-Management Standards, Office of	29, II, IV
Land Management, Bureau of	43, II
Legal Services Corporation	45, XVI
Libraries and Information Science, National Commission on	45, XVII
Library of Congress	36, VII
Copyright Royalty Board	37, III
U.S. Copyright Office	37, II
Local Television Loan Guarantee Board	7, XX
Management and Budget, Office of	5, III, LXXVII; 14, VI; 48, 99
Marine Mammal Commission	50, V
Maritime Administration	46, II
Merit Systems Protection Board	5, II, LXIV
Micronesian Status Negotiations, Office for	32, XXVII
Military Compensation and Retirement Modernization Commission	5, XCIX
Millennium Challenge Corporation	22, XIII
Mine Safety and Health Administration	30, I
Minority Business Development Agency	15, XIV
Miscellaneous Agencies	1, IV
Monetary Offices	31, I
Morris K. Udall Scholarship and Excellence in National Environmental Policy Foundation	36, XVI
Museum and Library Services, Institute of	2, XXXI
National Aeronautics and Space Administration	2, XVIII; 5, LIX; 14, V
Federal Acquisition Regulation	48, 18
National Agricultural Library	7, XLI
National Agricultural Statistics Service	7, XXXVI
National and Community Service, Corporation for	2, XXII; 45, XII, XXV
National Archives and Records Administration	2, XXVI; 5, LXVI; 36, XII
Information Security Oversight Office	32, XX
National Capital Planning Commission	1, IV, VI
National Counterintelligence Center	32, XVIII
National Credit Union Administration	5, LXXXVI; 12, VII
National Crime Prevention and Privacy Compact Council	28, IX
National Drug Control Policy, Office of	2, XXXVI; 21, III
National Endowment for the Arts	2, XXXII
National Endowment for the Humanities	2, XXXIII
National Foundation on the Arts and the Humanities	45, XI
National Geospatial-Intelligence Agency	32, I
National Highway Traffic Safety Administration	23, II, III; 47, VI; 49, V
National Imagery and Mapping Agency	32, I
National Indian Gaming Commission	25, III
National Institute of Food and Agriculture	7, XXXIV
National Institute of Standards and Technology	15, II; 37, IV
National Intelligence, Office of Director of	5, IV; 32, XVII
National Labor Relations Board	5, LXI; 29, I
National Marine Fisheries Service	50, II, IV
National Mediation Board	5, CI; 29, X
National Oceanic and Atmospheric Administration	15, IX; 50, II, III, IV, VI
National Park Service	36, I
National Railroad Adjustment Board	29, III
National Railroad Passenger Corporation (AMTRAK)	49, VII
National Science Foundation	2, XXV; 5, XLIII; 45, VI
Federal Acquisition Regulation	48, 25
National Security Council	32, XXI

Agency	CFR Title, Subtitle or Chapter
National Security Council and Office of Science and Technology Policy	47, II
National Technical Information Service	15, XI
National Telecommunications and Information Administration	15, XXIII; 47, III, IV, V
National Transportation Safety Board	49, VIII
Natural Resources Conservation Service	7, VI
Natural Resource Revenue, Office of	30, XII
Navajo and Hopi Indian Relocation, Office of	25, IV
Navy, Department of	32, VI
Federal Acquisition Regulation	48, 52
Neighborhood Reinvestment Corporation	24, XXV
Northeast Interstate Low-Level Radioactive Waste Commission	10, XVIII
Nuclear Regulatory Commission	2, XX; 5, XLVIII; 10, I
Federal Acquisition Regulation	48, 20
Occupational Safety and Health Administration	29, XVII
Occupational Safety and Health Review Commission	29, XX
Ocean Energy Management, Bureau of	30, V
Oklahoma City National Memorial Trust	36, XV
Operations Office	7, XXVIII
Overseas Private Investment Corporation	5, XXXIII; 22, VII
Patent and Trademark Office, United States	37, I
Payment From a Non-Federal Source for Travel Expenses	41, 304
Payment of Expenses Connected With the Death of Certain Employees	41, 303
Peace Corps	2, XXXVII; 22, III
Pennsylvania Avenue Development Corporation	36, IX
Pension Benefit Guaranty Corporation	29, XL
Personnel Management, Office of	5, I, XXXV; 5, IV; 45, VIII
Human Resources Management and Labor Relations Systems, Department of Homeland Security	5, XCVII
Federal Acquisition Regulation	48, 17
Federal Employees Group Life Insurance Federal Acquisition Regulation	48, 21
Federal Employees Health Benefits Acquisition Regulation	48, 16
Pipeline and Hazardous Materials Safety Administration	49, I
Postal Regulatory Commission	5, XLVI; 39, III
Postal Service, United States	5, LX; 39, I
Postsecondary Education, Office of	34, VI
President's Commission on White House Fellowships	1, IV
Presidential Documents	3
Presidio Trust	36, X
Prisons, Bureau of	28, V
Privacy and Civil Liberties Oversight Board	6, X
Procurement and Property Management, Office of	7, XXXII
Public Contracts, Department of Labor	41, 50
Public and Indian Housing, Office of Assistant Secretary for	24, IX
Public Health Service	42, I
Railroad Retirement Board	20, II
Reclamation, Bureau of	43, I
Refugee Resettlement, Office of	45, IV
Relocation Allowances	41, 302
Research and Innovative Technology Administration	49, XI
Rural Business-Cooperative Service	7, XVIII, XLII
Rural Development Administration	7, XLII
Rural Housing Service	7, XVIII, XXXV
Rural Telephone Bank	7, XVI
Rural Utilities Service	7, XVII, XVIII, XLII
Safety and Environmental Enforcement, Bureau of	30, II
Saint Lawrence Seaway Development Corporation	33, IV
Science and Technology Policy, Office of	32, XXIV
Science and Technology Policy, Office of, and National Security Council	47, II
Secret Service	31, IV
Securities and Exchange Commission	5, XXXIV; 17, II

Agency	CFR Title, Subtitle or Chapter
Selective Service System	32, XVI
Small Business Administration	2, XXVII; 13, I
Smithsonian Institution	36, V
Social Security Administration	2, XXIII; 20, III; 48, 23
Soldiers' and Airmen's Home, United States	5, XI
Special Counsel, Office of	5, VIII
Special Education and Rehabilitative Services, Office of	34, III
State, Department of	2, VI; 22, I; 28, XI
Federal Acquisition Regulation	48, 6
Surface Mining Reclamation and Enforcement, Office of	30, VII
Surface Transportation Board	49, X
Susquehanna River Basin Commission	18, VIII
Tennessee Valley Authority	5, LXIX; 18, XIII
Trade Representative, United States, Office of	15, XX
Transportation, Department of	2, XII; 5, L
Commercial Space Transportation	14, III
Emergency Management and Assistance	44, IV
Federal Acquisition Regulation	48, 12
Federal Aviation Administration	14, I
Federal Highway Administration	23, I, II
Federal Motor Carrier Safety Administration	49, III
Federal Railroad Administration	49, II
Federal Transit Administration	49, VI
Maritime Administration	46, II
National Highway Traffic Safety Administration	23, II, III; 47, IV; 49, V
Pipeline and Hazardous Materials Safety Administration	49, I
Saint Lawrence Seaway Development Corporation	33, IV
Secretary of Transportation, Office of	14, II; 49, Subtitle A
Transportation Statistics Bureau	49, XI
Transportation, Office of	7, XXXIII
Transportation Security Administration	49, XII
Transportation Statistics Bureau	49, XI
Travel Allowances, Temporary Duty (TDY)	41, 301
Treasury, Department of the	2, X;5, XXI; 12, XV; 17, IV; 31, IX
Alcohol and Tobacco Tax and Trade Bureau	27, I
Community Development Financial Institutions Fund	12, XVIII
Comptroller of the Currency	12, I
Customs and Border Protection	19, I
Engraving and Printing, Bureau of	31, VI
Federal Acquisition Regulation	48, 10
Federal Claims Collection Standards	31, IX
Federal Law Enforcement Training Center	31, VII
Financial Crimes Enforcement Network	31, X
Fiscal Service	31, II
Foreign Assets Control, Office of	31, V
Internal Revenue Service	26, I
Investment Security, Office of	31, VIII
Monetary Offices	31, I
Secret Service	31, IV
Secretary of the Treasury, Office of	31, Subtitle A
Truman, Harry S. Scholarship Foundation	45, XVIII
United States and Canada, International Joint Commission	22, IV
United States and Mexico, International Boundary and Water Commission, United States Section	22, XI
U.S. Copyright Office	37, II
Utah Reclamation Mitigation and Conservation Commission	43, III
Veterans Affairs, Department of	2, VIII; 38, I
Federal Acquisition Regulation	48, 8
Veterans' Employment and Training Service, Office of the Assistant Secretary for	41, 61; 20, IX
Vice President of the United States, Office of	32, XXVIII
Wage and Hour Division	29, V
Water Resources Council	18, VI
Workers' Compensation Programs, Office of	20, I, VII
World Agricultural Outlook Board	7, XXXVIII

List of CFR Sections Affected

All changes in this volume of the Code of Federal Regulations (CFR) that were made by documents published in the FEDERAL REGISTER since January 1, 2014 are enumerated in the following list. Entries indicate the nature of the changes effected. Page numbers refer to FEDERAL REGISTER pages. The user should consult the entries for chapters, parts and subparts as well as sections for revisions.

For changes to this volume of the CFR prior to this listing, consult the annual edition of the monthly List of CFR Sections Affected (LSA). The LSA is available at *www.govinfo.gov*. For changes to this volume of the CFR prior to 2001, see the "List of CFR Sections Affected, 1949–1963, 1964–1972, 1973–1985, and 1986–2000" published in 11 separate volumes. The "List of CFR Sections Affected 1986–2000" is available at *www.govinfo.gov*.

2014

25 CFR

79 FR Page

Chapter I

23 Nomenclature changes 27190
23.11 (c)(1) revised 27190
151.1 Revised 76897

2015

25 CFR

80 FR Page

Chapter I

81 Revised 63106
82 Removed 63115
83 Policy statement 37538
Revised; eff. 7-31-15 37887
169 Revised 72534
Regulation at 80 FR 72534 eff. date extended to 3-21-16 79258
169.7 Amended 79258
226 Revised 27018
256 Revised 69596

2016

25 CFR

81 FR Page

Chapter I

11.100 (d) added; interim 74677
20.325 (a) revised; interim; eff. 4-15-16 10477
Regulation at 81 FR 10477 confirmed 26692
23 Training sessions 47288

25 CFR—Continued

81 FR Page

Chapter I—Continued

23.2 Amended 38864
23.11 Revised 38866
23.71 Revised 38867
23.101—23.144 (Subpart I) Added 38867
41 Revised 38587
140 Authority citation revised 42481
Regulation at 81 FR 42481 confirmed 86953
140.3 Amended; interim 42481
Regulation at 81 FR 42481 confirmed 86953
141 Authority citation revised 42481
Regulation at 81 FR 42481 confirmed 86953
141.50 Amended; interim 42481
Regulation at 81 FR 42481 confirmed 86953
151.13 Revised; interim; eff. 4-15-16 10479
Regulation at 81 FR 19468 eff. date delayed 22183
Regulation at 81 FR 10479 confirmed; revised 30177
169 Policy statement 19877
169.7 Amended 14976
170 Revised 78463
211 Authority citation revised 42481
Regulation at 81 FR 42481 confirmed 86953
211.55 (a) amended; interim 42481

25 CFR—Continued

81 FR Page

Chapter I—Continued
Regulation at 81 FR 42481 confirmed....86953
213 Authority citation revised....42481
Regulation at 81 FR 42481 confirmed....86953
213.37 Amended; interim....42481
Regulation at 81 FR 42481 confirmed....86953
225 Authority citation revised....42481
Regulation at 81 FR 42481 confirmed....86953
225.37 (a) amended; interim....42481
Regulation at 81 FR 42481 confirmed....86953
226 Revised....39573
Authority citation revised....42481
Regulation at 81 FR 42481 confirmed....86953
226.42 Amended; interim....42481
Regulation at 81 FR 42481 confirmed....86953
226.43 Amended; (e), (f) and (g) amended; interim....42481
Regulation at 81 FR 42481 confirmed....86953
227 Authority citation revised....42481
Regulation at 81 FR 42481 confirmed....86953
227.24 Amended; interim....42481
Regulation at 81 FR 42481 confirmed....86953
243 Authority citation revised....42481
Regulation at 81 FR 42481 confirmed....86953
243.8 (a) amended; interim....42482
Regulation at 81 FR 42482 confirmed....86953
249 Authority citation revised....42482
Regulation at 81 FR 42482 confirmed....86953
249.6 (b) amended; interim....42482
Regulation at 81 FR 42482 confirmed....86953

2017

25 CFR

82 FR Page

Chapter I
Policy statement....50532
11 Policy statement....61450
11.100 Regulation at 81 FR 74677 confirmed....61450

25 CFR—Continued

82 FR Page

Chapter I—Continued
140 Authority citation revised....7652
140.3 Amended....7652
141 Authority citation revised....7652
141.50 Amended....7652
211 Authority citation revised....7652
211.55 (a) amended....7652
213 Authority citation revised....7652
213.37 Amended....7652
225 Authority citation revised....7652
225.37 (a) amended....7652
226 Authority citation revised....7653
226.42 Amended....7653
226.43 Amended; (e), (f) and (g) amended....7653
227 Authority citation revised....7653
227.24 Amended....7653
243 Authority citation revised....7653
243.8 (a) introductory text amended....7653
249 Authority citation revised....7653
249.6 (b) amended....7653

2018

25 CFR

83 FR Page

Chapter I
23.11 (b)(2) and (7) revised....55268
23.140 (a) introductory text revised....55269
83.20 Revised....33826
140.3 Amended....5195
141.50 Amended....5195
170.443 Regulation at 82 FR 50313 confirmed....8610
175 Revised....61119
211.55 (a) amended....5195
213.37 Amended....5195
225.37 (a) amended....5195
226.42 Amended....5195
226.43 (e), (f), (g) and section amended....5195
227.24 Amended....5195
243.8 (a) introductory text amended....5195
249.6 (b) amended....5195

2019

(No regulations published from January 1, 2019, through April 1, 2019)

○

www.ingramcontent.com/pod-product-compliance
Lightning Source LLC
Chambersburg PA
CBHW052055230326
41599CB00054B/1703